MW01014077

THE ACTS OF THE APOSTLES

The Acts
of the Apostles

A Socio-Rhetorical Commentary

Ben Witherington, III

WILLIAM B. EERDMANS PUBLISHING COMPANY
GRAND RAPIDS, MICHIGAN / CAMBRIDGE, U.K.

THE PATERNOSTER PRESS
CARLISLE

© 1998 Wm. B. Eerdmans Publishing Co.
255 Jefferson Ave. S.E., Grand Rapids, Michigan 49503 /
P.O. Box 163, Cambridge CB3 9PU U.K.

First published 1998 jointly
in the United States by
Wm. B. Eerdmans Publishing Company
and in the U.K. by
The Paternoster Press
P.O. Box 300, Carlisle, Cumbria CA3 0Q5

All rights reserved

Printed in the United States of America

10 09 08 07 06 05 04   9 8 7 6 5 4 3

Library of Congress Cataloging-in-Publication Data

Witherington, Ben, 1951-
    The Acts of the Apostles: a socio-rhetorical commentary / Ben
    Witherington III
        p.   cm.
    Includes bibliographical references and index.
    ISBN 0-8028-4501-0 (pbk.: alk. paper)
    1. Bible. N.T. Acts — Criticism, interpretation, etc.   2. Bible.
    N.T. Acts — Socio-rhetorical criticism.   I. Title.
    BS2625.2.W58   1998
    226.6'07 — dc21   97-25597
                                                    CIP

Except as noted, all photographs are by the author.

Contents

Foreword

Safely tucked away at Yale, in New Haven, Connecticut, out of the sight of all but the most inquiring eyes and minds, is an ancient papyrus with a portion of the book of Acts on it — P Yale 3, otherwise known as P 50. On this papyrus we find not just Greek characters but also accents, punctuation, and breathing marks, which make clear that this document was meant from early times to be read publicly in a persuasive and appealing manner, with due attention to pronunciation, pauses, and the general aural effect of the text.

It is my belief that this was probably the case with Acts from the beginning. It was a document written to be read aloud, and the author attended to his writing so that what he had written could be rhetorically effective when read and heard by the first listener or listeners. The rhetorical dimension of Acts has not been much explored in recent commentaries on the book, in part because of the waning influence of classical studies on biblical studies in this century. Nor for that matter has sufficient attention been paid in commentaries to how similar Acts is to other ancient Hellenistic historiographic works. It is perhaps the main overall goal of this commentary to try to reintroduce the reader to those neglected dimensions of the text which immersing oneself in ancient historiography and ancient rhetoric can bring to light. I believe that when this larger context is brought to bear on Acts, one discovers a carefully crafted document that those familiar not just with the Greek OT but also with Polybius or Thucydides or Ephorus, or to a lesser degree Josephus, would have found impressive and persuasive.

Abbreviations of Periodicals
and Other Reference Works

ABD	*Anchor Bible Dictionary*
ABR	*Australian Biblical Review*
AIIFC	The Book of Acts in Its First Century Setting
AJA	*American Journal of Archaeology*
ANRW	*Aufstieg und Niedergang der römischen Welt*
AUSS	*Andrews University Seminary Studies*
BA	*Biblical Archaeologist*
BAG	W. Bauer, W. F. Arndt, and F. W. Gingrich, *A Greek-English Lexicon of the New Testament*
BAR	*Biblical Archeology Review*
Bib	*Biblica*
BJRL	*Bulletin of the John Rylands Library*
BR	*Biblical Research*
BS	*Bibliotheca Sacra*
BT	*Bible Translator*
BZ	*Biblische Zeitschrift*
CBQ	*Catholic Biblical Quarterly*
CJ	*Classical Journal*
CP	*Classical Philology*
CQ	*Classical Quarterly*
CR	*Critical Review of Books in Religion*
CTM	*Concordia Theological Monthly*
ET	*Expository Times*
ETL	*Etudes théologiques et religieuses*

EvQ	*Evangelical Quarterly*
EvT	*Evangelische Theologie*
HTR	*Harvard Theological Review*
HUCA	*Hebrew Union College Annual*
IBS	*Irish Biblical Studies*
IEJ	*Israel Exploration Journal*
Interp	*Interpretation*
JAAR	*Journal of the American Academy of Religion*
JAC	Jahrbuch für Antike und Christentum
JBL	*Journal of Biblical Literature*
JHS	*Journal of Hellenic Studies*
JQR	*Jewish Quarterly Review*
JRH	*Journal of Religious History*
JRS	*Journal of Roman Studies*
JSNT	*Journal for the Study of the New Testament*
JTC	*Journal for Theology and the Church*
JTS	*Journal of Theological Studies*
NovT	*Novum Testamentum*
NRT	*La nouvelle revue théologie*
NTS	*New Testament Studies*
RB	*Revue Biblique*
ResQ	*Restoration Quarterly*
RevThom	*Revue Thomiste*
RPPR	*Revue d'histoire et de philosophie religieuses*
RSCR	*Revue des sciences religieuses*
SBLMS	Society of Biblical Literature Monograph Series
SBT	Studies in Biblical Theology
SEÅ	*Svensk exegetisk årsbok*
SJT	*Scottish Journal of Theology*
ST	*Studia Theologica*
Str-B	H. Strack and P. Billerbeck, *Kommentar zum Neuen Testament*
TAPA	*Translations of the American Philological Association*
TBT	*The Bible Today*
TDNT	*Theological Dictionary of the New Testament*
TGl	*Theologie und Glaube*
TS	*Texts and Studies*
TSK	*Theologische Studien und Kritiken*
TynB	*Tyndale Bulletin*
TZ	*Theologische Zeitschrift*
ZNW	*Zeitschrift für die neutestamentliche Wissenschaft*
ZTK	*Zeitschrift für Theologie und Kirche*

Bibliography

This bibliography is by no means intended to be exhaustive; it simply represents the works in English, French, and German that I found useful in the preparation of this commentary. Quite naturally the bibliography focuses on works that help illuminate the historical, rhetorical, and social dimensions of Acts. In the case of collections of articles on or related to Acts, I have found it more useful to list individual articles which specify the subject matter rather than the collections themselves. The full titles of various of the collections of essays on Acts appear with one entry from each of these collections. In other entries the title is abbreviated. The primary exception to this rule is the important recent series on The Book of Acts in Its First Century Setting, which I have abbreviated throughout the book as AIIFCS. I have listed the two volumes in this series done by individuals as monographs, but for the volumes that are essays by various scholars, I have referred to the articles individually. The standard abbreviations for biblical, classical, and historical journals have been followed, but a few other necessary abbreviations that crop up frequently in the book are listed below:

ABD — *The Anchor Bible Dictionary,* ed. D. N. Freedman, 6 vols. (New York: Doubleday, 1992).
AIIFCS — the five-volume series published by Eerdmans on The Book of Acts in Its First Century Setting: vol. 1: *Literary Setting,* ed. B. W. Winter and A. Clarke (1993); vol. 2: *Graeco-Roman Setting,* ed. D. W. J. Gill and C. Gempf (1994); vol. 3: *Paul in Roman Custody,* B. Rapske (1994); vol. 4: *Palestinian Setting,* ed. R. Bauckham (1995); vol. 5: *Diaspora Setting,* I. Levinskaya (1996).
ANRW — the multivolume series of essays published in Berlin by W. de Gruy-

ter with the general title *Aufstieg und Niedergang der römischen Welt;* the volumes of concern to this study were edited by W. Haase and range from vol. 16.1 (1978) to 27.1 (1993).

Beginnings — the six-volume set of essays and commentary on Acts edited by J. Foakes-Jackson and K. Lake under the title *The Beginnings of Christianity* (London: Macmillan, 1920-33).

New Docs — the seven-volume series of articles and commentary on recent inscriptional data edited by G. H. R. Horsley (except the sixth volume, which was edited by S. R. Llewelyn) entitled *New Documents Illustrating Early Christianity* (North Ryde: Macquarrie University), vol. 1 (1981), vol. 2 (1982), vol. 3 (1983), vol. 4 (1987), vol. 5 (1989), vol. 6 (1992), and vol. 7 (1996).

For a brief guide to the study of Acts with interaction with recent study and bibliography see I. H. Marshall, *The Acts of the Apostles* (Sheffield: JSOT Press, 1992). Two useful surveys of the questions Acts raises are W. C. van Unnik, "Luke-Acts, A Storm Center in Contemporary Scholarship," in *Sparsa Collecta I* (Leiden: Brill, 1973), pp. 92-110; and J. Jervell, "Retrospect and Prospect in Luke-Acts Interpretation," in *SBL 1991 Seminar Papers,* ed. E. H. Lovering (Atlanta: Scholars Press, 1991), pp. 383-404. On the history of the interpretation of Acts see W. W. Gasque, *A History of the Interpretation of the Acts of the Apostles* (Peabody, Mass.: Hendrickson, 1989). This is essentially the same as the 1975 edition except for an appendix in which Gasque discusses more recent literarure up to 1988. There is now available a very full annotated bibliography dealing with the various aspects of the hypothesis that Luke's work should be seen as some sort of history writing. See J. B. Green and M. C. McKeever, *Luke-Acts and New Testament Historiography* (Grand Rapids: Baker, 1994), though unfortunately the treatment is almost exclusively of works in English.

Articles

Aberbach, M. "The Conflicting Accounts of Josephus and Tacitus concerning Cumanus' and Felix' Terms of Office." *JQR* 40 (1949-50): 1-14.

Achtemeier, P. J. *"Omne verbum sonat:* The New Testament and the Oral Environment of Late Western Antiquity." *JBL* 109 (1990): 3-27.

Acworth, A. "Where Was St. Paul Shipwrecked?" *JTS* 24 (1973): 190-93.

Alexander, L. C. A. "Acts and Ancient Intellectual Biography." In AIIFCS, 1:31-63.

———. "Chronology of Paul." In *Dictionary of Paul and His Letters,* pp. 115-23. Downers Grove: InterVarsity, 1993.

———. "Luke's Preface in the Context of Greek Preface-Writing." *NovT* 28, no. 1 (1986): 48-74.

———. "The Preface of Acts and the Historians." In *History, Literature, and Society in the Book of Acts,* edited by B. Witherington III, pp. 73-103. Cambridge: Cambridge University Press, 1996.

Arichea, D. C. "Some Notes on Acts 2.17-21." *BT* 35 (1984): 442-43.

Arnold, B. T. "Luke's Characterizing Use of the Old Testament in the Book of Acts." In *History, Literature, and Society in the Book of Acts,* edited by B. Witherington III, pp. 300-323. Cambridge: Cambridge University Press, 1996.

Ascough, R. S. "The Formation and Propagation of Greco-Roman Associations." Paper delivered at the 1995 SBL meeting in Philadelphia and abstracted in *AAR/SBL Abstracts 1995,* pp. 159-60.

Aune, D. E. "Magic in Early Christianity." *ANRW II,* 23.2, pp. 1507-57. Berlin: de Gruyter, 1980.

Balch, D. L. "The Areopagus Speech: An Appeal to the Stoic Historian Posidonus against Later Stoics and the Epicureans." In *Greeks, Romans, and Christians,* edited by D. L. Balch et al., pp. 52-79. Minneapolis: Fortress, 1990.

Bammel, E. "Der Text von Apostelgeschichte 15." In *Les Actes des Apôtres. Traditions, rédaction, théologie,* edited by J. Kremer, pp. 439-46. Leuven: Leuven University Press, 1979.

Barnes, T. D. "An Apostle on Trial." *JTS* 22 (1969): 407-19.

Barnett, P. W. "The Jewish Sign Prophets, A.D. 40-70 — Their Intentions and Origins." *NTS* 27 (1980-81): 679-97.

Barrett, C. K. "Apollos and the Twelve Disciples of Ephesus." In *The New Testament Age,* vol. 1, pp. 29-39. Macon: Mercer, 1984.

———. "How History Should Be Written." In *History, Literature, and Society in the Book of Acts,* edited by B. Witherington III, pp. 33-57. Cambridge: Cambridge University Press, 1996.

———. "Light on the Holy Spirit from Simon Magus (Acts 8,4-25)." In *Les Actes des Apôtres. Traditions, rédaction, théologie,* edited by J. Kremer, pp. 281-95. Leuven: Leuven University Press, 1979.

———. "Luke/Acts." In *It Is Written: Scripture Citing Scripture,* edited by D. A. Carson and H. G. M. Williamson, pp. 231-44. Cambridge: Cambridge University Press, 1988.

———. "Paul's Address to the Ephesian Elders." In *God's Christ and His People: Studies in Honour of Nils Alstrup Dahl,* edited by J. Jervell and W. A. Meeks, pp. 107-21. Oslo: Universitetforlaget, 1977.

———. "Paul Shipwrecked." In *Scripture: Meaning and Method,* edited by B. P. Thompson, pp. 51-63. Hull: Hull University Press, 1987.

———. "Paul's Speech on the Areopagus." In *New Testament Christianity for Africa and the World: Essays in Honour of Harry Sawyer,* edited by M. E. Glasswell and E. W. Fashole-Luke, pp. 69-77. London: SPCK, 1974.

————. "Stephen and the Son of Man." In *Apophoreta: Festschrift für Ernst Haenchen*, pp. 32-38. Berlin: de Gruyter, 1964.

————. "Things Sacrificed to Idols." In *Essays on Paul*, pp. 40-59. Philadelphia: Westminster, 1982.

————. "The Third Gospel as a Preface to Acts? Some Reflections." In *The Four Gospels 1992. Festschrift Frans Neirynck*, edited by F. Van Segbroeck et al., pp. 1451-66. Leuven: Leuven University Press, 1992.

Bartsch, H. W. "Traditions-geschichtliches zur 'goldenen Regel' und zum Aposteldekret." *ZNW* 75 (1984): 128-32.

Bauckham R. "The *Acts of Paul* as a Sequel to Acts." In AIIFCS, 1:105-52.

————. "James and the Gentiles (Acts 15.13-21)." In *History, Literature, and Society in the Book of Acts*, edited by B. Witherington III, pp. 154-84. Cambridge: Cambridge University Press, 1996.

————. "James and the Jerusalem Church." In AIIFCS, 4:415-80.

Bayer, H. F. "Christ-Centered Eschatology in Acts 3.17-26." In *Jesus of Nazareth: Lord and Christ*, edited by J. B. Green, pp. 236-50. Grand Rapids: Eerdmans, 1994.

Best, E. "Acts 13.1-3." *JTS* 11 (1960): 344-48.

Bickerman, E. J. "The Name of Christians." *HTR* 42 (1949): 109-24.

Black, C. C. II. "The Rhetorical Form of the Hellenistic Jewish and Early Christian Sermon: A Response to Lawrence Wills." *HTR* 81 (1988): 1-18.

Blaiklock, E. M. "Lystra." In *The New International Dictionary of Biblical Archaeology*, edited by E. M. Blaiklock and R. K. Harrison, p. 294. Grand Rapids: Zondervan, 1983.

Blass, F. W. "Priscilla und Aquila." *TSK* 74 (1901): 124-26.

Boman, T. "Das Textkritsche Problem des Sogennanten Aposteldekrets." *NovT* 7 (1964): 26-36.

Bovon, F. "Le Saint-Esprit, L'Église et les relations humaine selon Actes 20,36–21,16." In *Les Actes des Apôtres. Traditions, rédaction, théologie*, edited by J. Kremer, pp. 341-58. Leuven: Leuven University Press, 1979.

————. " 'Schön hat der heilige Geist durchen den Propheten Jesaja zu euren Vatern gesprochen.' " *ZNW* 75 (1984): 226-32.

————. "Tradition et redaction en Actes 10,1–11,18." *TZ* 26 (1970): 22-45.

Bower, E. W. "*Ephodos* and *Insinuatio* in Greek and Latin Rhetoric." *CQ* 8 (1958): 224-30.

Bowker, J. W. "Speeches in Acts: A Study in Proem and Yelamedenu Form." *NTS* 14 (1967-68): 96-111.

Brändle, R., and E. W. Stegemann. "Die Entstehung der ersten 'christlichen Gemeinde' Roms im Kontext der jüdischen Gemeinden." *NTS* 42 (1996): 1-11.

Bratcher, R. "Αχουω in Acts 9.7 and 22.9." *ET* 71 (1959-60): 243-45.

Brawley, R. "Paul in Acts: Lucan Apology and Conciliation." In *Luke-Acts: New*

Perspectives from the SBL Seminar, edited by C. H. Talbert, pp. 129-47. New York: Crossroad, 1984.

Breytenbach, C. "Zeus und der lebendige Gott: Anmerkungen zu Apostelgeschichte 14.11-17." *NTS* 39 (1993): 396-413.

Brock, S. "Barnabas, *huios parakleseos.*" *JTS* 25 (1974): 93-98.

Brodie, T. L. "Toward Unraveling the Rhetorical Imitation of Sources in Acts: 2 Kngs 5 as One Component of Acts 8,9-40." *Bib* 67 (1986): 41-67.

Broneer, O. "Athens 'City of Idol Worship.' " *BA* 21 (1958): 2-28.

Brosend, W. "The Means of Absent Ends." In *History, Literature, and Society in the Book of Acts,* edited by B. Witherington III, pp. 348-62. Cambridge: Cambridge University Press, 1996.

Broughton, T. R. S. "The Roman Army." In *Beginnings,* 5:441-43.

Bruce, F. F. "Christianity under Claudius." *BJRL* 44 (1962): 309-26.

————. "Chronological Questions in the Acts of the Apostles." *BJRL* 68 (1986): 273-95.

————. "The Church of Jerusalem in the Acts of the Apostles." *BJRL* 67 (1984-85): 641-61.

————. "Eschatology in Acts." In *Eschatology and the New Testament: Essays in Honor of George Beasley-Murray,* edited by W. H. Gloer, pp. 51-63. Peabody: Hendrickson, 1988.

————. "The Full Name of the Procurator Felix." *JSNT* 1 (1978): 33-36.

————. "Paul in Acts and Letters." In *Dictionary of Paul and His Letters,* pp. 679-92. Downers Grove: InterVarsity, 1993.

————. "Stephen's Apologia." In *Scripture: Meaning and Method,* edited by B. P. Thompson, pp. 37-50. Hull: Hull University Press, 1987.

Brunt, P. A. "Charges of Provincial Maladministration under the Early Principate." *Historia* 10 (1961): 189-227.

————. "Cicero and Historiography." In *Miscellanea di studi classici in onore di Eugenio Manni,* pp. 311-40. Rome, 1979.

Bryan, C. "A Further Look at Acts 16.1-3." *JBL* 107 (1988): 292-94.

Burchard, C. "A Note on 'PHMA in JosAs 17:1; Luke 2:15, 17; Acts 10:37." *NovT* 27, no. 4 (1985): 281-95.

Burrell, B., K. Gleason, and E. Netzer. "Uncovering Herod's Seaside Palace." *BAR* 19 (1993): 50-57, 76.

Burton, G. P. "Proconsuls, Assizes, and the Administration of Justice under the Empire." *JRS* 65 (1975): 92-106.

Cadbury, H. J. "Four Features of Lukan Style." In *Studies in Luke-Acts,* edited by L. E. Keck and J. L. Martyn, pp. 87-102. London: SPCK, 1968.

————. "The Hellenists." In *Beginnings,* 5:59-74.

————. "Lexical Notes on Luke-Acts: Luke's Interest in Lodging." *JBL* 45 (1926): 305-22.

————. "Names for Christians and Christianity in Acts." In *Beginnings,* 5:383-86.

————. "Roman Law and the Trial of Paul." In *Beginnings*, 5:297-338.

————. "The Summaries in Acts." In *Beginnings*, 5:392-402.

————. "The Tradition." In *Beginnings*, 2:279.

————. " 'We' and 'I' Passages in Luke-Acts." *NTS* 3 (1957): 128-32.

Calder, W. M. "A Cult of the Homonades." *CR* 24 (1910): 76-81.

Callan, T. "The Background of the Apostolic Decree (Acts 15.20, 29; 21.25)." *CBQ* 55 (1993): 284-97.

————. "The Preface of Luke-Acts and Historiography." *NTS* 31 (1985): 576-81.

Campbell, T. H. "Paul's Missionary Journeys as Reflected in His Letters." *JBL* 74 (1955): 80-87.

Capper, B. "The Palestinian Cultural Context of the Earliest Christian Community of Goods." In AIIFCS, 4:323ff.

Carroll, J. T. "Literary and Social Dimensions of Luke's Apology for Paul." In *SBL 1988 Seminar Papers*, edited by D. J. Lull, pp. 106-18. Atlanta: Scholars Press, 1988.

Casey, R. P. "Simon Magus." In *Beginnings*, 5:151-63.

Catchpole, D. R. "Paul, James, and the Apostolic Decree." *NTS* 23 (1976-77): 428-43.

Ciraolo, L. J. "The Warmth and Breath of Life: Animating Physical Object πάρεδροι in the Greek Magical Papyri." In *SBL 1992 Seminar Papers*, pp. 240-54.

Clarke, A. D. "Rome and Italy." In AIIFCS, 2:455-81.

Clarke W. K. L. "The Use of the Septuagint in Acts." In *Beginnings*, 1:66-105.

Coggins, R. J. "The Samaritans and Acts." *NTS* 28 (1982): 423-34.

Cohen, S. J. D. "Was Timothy Jewish? Patristic Exegesis, Rabbinic Law, and Matrilineal Descent." *JBL* 105 (1986): 251-68.

Collins, J. J. "A Symbol of Otherness: Circumcision and Salvation in the First Century." In *To See Ourselves as Others See Us*, edited by J. Neusner and E. S. Frerichs, pp. 163-86. Chico: Scholars Press, 1985.

Conzelmann, H. "The Address of Paul on the Areopagus." In *Studies in Luke-Acts*, edited by L. E. Keck and J. L. Martyn, pp. 217-30. London: SPCK, 1968.

Cosgrove, C. "The Divine Δεῖ in Luke-Acts." *NovT* 26 (1984): 168-90.

Crocker, P. T. "Ephesus: Its Silversmiths, Its Tradesmen and Its Riots." *Buried History* 23 (1987): 76-78.

Cullmann, O. "Courants multiples dans la communauté primitive: à propos du martyre de Jacques fils de Zebedee." *RSCR* 60 (1972): 55-68.

Dahl, N. A. "A People for His Name (Acts 15.14)." *NTS* 4 (1957-58): 319-27.

————. "The Story of Abraham in Luke-Acts." In *Studies in Luke-Acts*, edited by L. E. Keck and J. L. Martyn, pp. 139-58. London: SPCK, 1968.

Danker, F. W. "Reciprocity in the Ancient World and in Acts 15.23-29." In

Political Issues in Luke-Acts, edited by R. J. Cassidy and P. J. Sharper, pp. 49-58. Maryknoll: Orbis, 1983.

Daube, D. "On Acts 23: Sadducees and Angels." *JBL* 109 (1990): 493-97.

Davies, P. "The Ending of Acts." *ET* 94 (1983): 334-35.

Davies, S. "Women in the Third Gospel and the New Testament Apocrypha." In *"Women Like These": New Perspectives on Jewish Women in the Greco-Roman World,* edited by A.-J. Levine, pp. 185-97. Atlanta: Scholars Press, 1991.

De Lacey, D. R. "Paul in Jerusalem." *NTS* 20 (1973): 82-86.

Delebecque, E. "La dernière étape du troisième voyage missionairie de saint Paul selon les deux versions des Actes des Apôtres (21,16-17)." *Revue théologique de Louvain* 14 (1983): 446-55.

———. "Les Deux Versions du voyage de saint Paul de Corinthe à Troas (Ac 20,3-6)." *Bib* 64 (1983): 556-64.

———. "Paul entre les Juifs et Romains selon les deux Versions de Act. xxiii." *RevThom* 84 (1984): 83-91.

———. "Silas, Paul et Barnabe a Antioche selon le text 'Occidental' d'Actes 15,34 et 38." *RHPR* 64 (1984): 47-52.

Derrett, J. D. M. "Ananias, Sapphira, and the Right of Property." In *Studies in the New Testament Volume One,* pp. 193-201. Leiden: Brill, 1977.

———. "Simon Magus (Acts 8,9-24)." *ZNW* 73 (1982): 52-68.

DeVine, C. F. "The 'Blood of God' in Acts 20.28." *CBQ* 9 (1947): 381-408.

de Vos, C. S. "The Significance of the Change from οικος to οικια in Luke's Account of the Philippian Gaoler (Acts 16.30-34)." *NTS* 41 (1995): 292-96.

Dibelius, M. "Paul in Athens." In Dibelius, *Studies in the Acts of the Apostles,* pp. 78-83. London: SCM, 1956.

———. "Paul on the Areopagus." In Dibelius, *Studies in the Acts of the Apostles,* pp. 26-77. London: SCM, 1956.

Dillistone, F. W. "προσπεινος (Acts x.10)." *ET* 46 (1934-35): 380.

Dockx, S. "Luc, a-t-il ete le compagnon d'apostolat de Paul?" *NRT* 103 (1981): 385-400.

———. "Silas a-t-il ete le compagnon de voyage de Paul d'Antioche à Corinthe." *NRT* 104 (1982): 749-53.

Donfried, K. P. "The Cults of Thessalonica and the Thessalonian Correspondence." *NTS* 31 (1985): 336-56.

Downing, F. G. "Common Ground with Paganism in Luke and Josephus." *NTS* 28 (1982): 546-59.

Drews, R. "Ephorus and History Written *kata genos.*" *American Journal of Philology* 84 (1963): 44-55.

———. "Ephorus' *kata genos* History Revisited." *Hermes* 104 (1976): 497-98.

Dupont, J. "La conclusion des Actes et son rapport a l'ensemble de l'ouvrage de Luc." In *Les Actes des Apôtres. Traditions, rédaction, théologie,* edited by J. Kremer, pp. 359-404. Leuven: Leuven University Press, 1979.

————. "La destinée de Judas prophétisee par David (Actes 1,16-20)." In *Études sur les Actes des Apôtres,* pp. 309-20. Paris: Cerf, 1967.

————. "La Mission de Paul à Jerusalem (Actes 12,25)." *NovT* 1 (1956): 275-303.

————. "Pierre délivre de prison." In *Nouvelle etudes sur les Actes des Apostles,* pp. 329-42. Paris: Cerf, 1984.

————. "La structure oratoire du discours d'Étienne (Actes 7)." *Bib* 66 (1985): 153-67.

Earl, D. "Prologue-Form in Ancient Historiography." In *ANRW,* vol. 1.2, pp. 842-56. Berlin: de Gruyter, 1972.

Elliott, J. H. "Temple vs. Household in Luke-Acts: A Contrast in Social Institutions." In *The Social World of Luke-Acts,* edited by J. H. Neyrey, pp. 211-40. Peabody: Hendrickson, 1991.

Ellis, E. E. "The Role of the Christian Prophet in Acts." In *Apostolic History and the Gospel: Essays Presented to F. F. Bruce,* edited by W. W. Gasque and R. P. Martin, pp. 55-67. Grand Rapids: Eerdmans, 1970.

Ellis, I. M. "Codex Bezae at Acts 15." *IBS* 2 (1980): 134-40.

Epp, E. J. "The 'Ignorance Motif' in Acts and Anti-Judaic Tendencies in Codex Bezae." *HTR* 55 (1962): 51-62.

Fears, J. R. "Rome: The Ideology of Imperial Power." *Thought* 55 (1980): 98-109.

Fiensy, D. A. "The Composition of the Jerusalem Church." AIIFCS, 4:213-36.

Filson, F. V. "Ephesus and the New Testament." *BA* 8 (1945): 73-80.

Finn, T. M. "The God-Fearers Reconsidered." *CBQ* 47 (1985): 75-84.

Fitzmyer, J. A. "The Ascension of Christ and Pentecost." *TS* 45 (1984): 434-36.

————. "David, Being Therefore a Prophet . . ." *CBQ* 34 (1972): 332-39.

————. "Jewish Christianity in Acts in Light of the Qumran Scrolls." In *Studies in Luke-Acts,* edited by L. E. Keck and J. L. Martyn, pp. 233-57. London: SPCK, 1968.

————. "The Pauline Letters and the Lucan Account of Paul's Missionary Journeys." In *SBL 1988 Seminar Papers,* edited by D. J. Lull, pp. 82-89. Atlanta: Scholars Press, 1988.

————. "The Use of the Old Testament in Luke-Acts." In *SBL 1992 Seminar Papers,* pp. 524-38.

Foerster, G. "The Ancient Synagogues of Galilee." In *The Galilee in Late Antiquity,* edited by L. I. Levine. New York: Jewish Theological Seminary, 1992, pp. 289-319.

Fohrer G. "σωζω/σωτηρια." *TDNT,* vol. 7 (1971), pp. 965-1024.

Fowl, S. "The Simeons of Acts 15.14: A Comparison between Reader and Author Oriented Criticisms." *AAR/SBL Abstracts 1995,* pp. 124-25.

Frey, J. B. "Le judaisme a Rom aux premiers temps de l'Eglise." *Bib* 12 (1931): 129-56.

Funk, R. W. "The Enigma of the Famine Visit." *JBL* 75 (1956): 130-36.

Fusco, V. "Le sezione-noi degli Atti nella discussione recente." *Biblia e Oriente* 25 (1983): 73-86.

Gabba, E. "True History and False History in Classical Antiquity." *JRS* 71 (1981): 50-62.

Gapp, K. S. "Notes: The Universal Famine under Claudius." *HTR* 28 (1935): 258-65.

Garnsey, P. "The *Lex Iulia* and Appeal under the Empire." *JRS* 56 (1966): 167-89.

————. "Mass Diet and Nutrition in the City of Rome." In *Nourir la plebe*, edited by A. Giovanni, pp. 67-101. Basel: Herder, 1991.

Garrett, S. "Exodus from Bondage: Luke 9.31 and Acts 12.1-24." *CBQ* 52 (1990): 656-80.

Gärtner, B. "Paulus und Barnabas in Lystra: Zu Apg. 14,8-15." *SEÅ* 27 (1962): 83-88.

Gaventa, B. R. "The Overthrown Enemy: Luke's Portrait of Paul." In *SBL 1985 Seminar Papers*, pp. 439-49.

————. "To Speak the Word with All Boldness, Acts 4.23-31." *Faith and Mission* 3 (1986): 76-82.

Geagan, D. J. "Ordo Areopagitarum Atheniensium." In *Phoros: Tribute to Benjamin Dean Meritt*, edited by D. W. Bradeen and M. F. McGregor, pp. 51-56. New York, 1974.

Gempf, C. H. "The God-Fearers." In C. Hemer, *The Book of Acts in the Setting of Hellenistic History*, app. 2, pp. 444-47. Winona Lake: Eisenbrauns, 1990.

————. "Public Speaking and Published Accounts." In AIIFCS, 1:259-303.

Gerhardsson, B. "Einige Bemerkungen zu Apg. 4,32." *ST* 24 (1970): 142-49.

Giles, K. N. "Luke's Use of the Term ΕΚΚΛΗΣΙΑ with Special Reference to Acts 20.28 and 9.31." *NTS* 31 (1985): 135-42.

Gill, D. W. J. "Achaia." In AIIFCS, 2:433-53.

————. "Behind the Classical Facade: Local Religions of the Roman Empire." In *One God, One Lord: Christianity in a World of Religious Pluralism*, edited by A. D. Clarke and B. W. Winter, pp. 85-100. Grand Rapids: Baker, 1992.

————. "Macedonia." In AIIFCS, 2:397-431.

————. "Paul's Travels through Cyprus (Acts 13.4-12)." *TynB* 46 (1995): 219-28.

Gill, D. W. J., and B. W. Winter. "Acts and Roman Religion." In AIIFCS, 2:79-103.

Glombitza, O. "Akta XIII,15-41. Analyse einer Lukanischen Predigt vor Juden." *NTS* 5 (1958-59): 306-17.

Goodspeed, E. J. "Gaius Titius Justus." *JBL* 69 (1950): 382-83.

Graf, D. F. "Aretas." In *ABD*, 1:373-76.

Green, J. B. "Internal Repetition in Luke-Acts: Contemporary Narratology and Lukan Historiography." In *History, Literature, and Society in the Book of Acts*, edited by B. Witherington III, pp. 283-99. Cambridge: Cambridge University Press, 1996.

Haacker, K. "Das Bekenntnis des Paulus zur Hoffnung Israels nach der Apostelgeschichte des Lukas." *NTS* 31 (1985): 437-51.

———. "Einige Fälle von 'Erlebter Rede' im Neuen Testament." *NovT* 12 (1970): 70-77.

———. "Die Gallio-Episode und die paulinische Chronologie." *BZ* 16 (1972): 252-55.

Haenchen, E. "Acts 27." In *Zeit und Geschichte*, pp. 235-64. Tübingen: Mohr, 1964.

Hall, D. R. "Acts 3.1-10: The Healing of the Temple Beggar in Lucan Theology." *Bib* 67 (1986): 305-19.

———. "St. Paul and Famine Relief: A Study in Gal. 2.10." *ET* 82 (1970-71): 309-11.

———. "'We' in Acts and the Itinerary." *JTC* 1 (1965): 65-99.

Hansen, G. W. "Galatia." In AIIFCS, 2:377-95.

Hanson, R. P. C. "The Journey of Paul and the Journey of Nikias." In *Studies in Christian Antiquity*, pp. 22-26. Edinburgh: T & T Clark, 1985.

Harding, M. "On the Historicity of Acts: Comparing Acts 9.23-5 with 2 Corinthians 11.32-33." *NTS* 39 (1993): 518-38.

Hardon, J. A. "The Miracle Narratives in the Acts of the Apostles." *CBQ* 16 (1954): 303-19.

Hardy, E. G. "The Speech of Claudius on the Adlection of Gallic Senators." *Cambridge Journal of Philology* 32 (1913): 79-95.

Hare, D. R. A. "The Rejection of the Jews in the Synoptic Gospels and Acts." In *Antisemitism and the Foundations of Christianity*, edited by A. Davies, pp. 27-47. New York: Paulist, 1979.

Harle, P. "Un 'private-joke' de Paul dans le livre des Actes (xxvi.28-29)." *NTS* 24 (1978): 527-32.

Head, P. "Acts and the Problem of Its Texts." In AIIFCS, 1:415-44.

Hedrick, C. W. "Paul's Conversion/Call: A Comparative Analysis of the Three Reports in Acts." *JBL* 100 (1981): 415-32.

Hemer, C. J. "Acts and Galatians Reconsidered." *Themelios* 2 (1977): 81-88.

———. "The Adjective Phrygia." *JTS* 27 (1976): 122-26.

———. "Alexandria Troas." *TynB* 26 (1975): 79-112.

———. "Euraquilo and Melita." *JTS* 26 (1975): 1010.

———. "First Person Narrative in Acts 27–28." *TynB* 36 (1985): 79-109.

———. "The Name of Felix Again." *JSNT* 31 (1987): 45-49.

———. "The Name of Paul." *TynB* 36 (1986): 179-83.

———. "Paul at Athens: A Topographical Note." *NTS* 20 (1974): 341-50.

———. "Phrygia: A Further Note." *JTS* 28 (1977): 99-101.

———. "The Speeches of Acts I: The Ephesian Elders at Miletus." *TynB* 40 (1989): 77-85.

———. "The Speeches of Acts II: The Areopagus Address." *TynB* 40 (1989): 239-59.

Hengel, M. "The Geography of Palestine in Acts." In AIIFCS, 4:27-78.

———. "Jakobus der Herrenbruder — der erste Papst?" In *Glaube und Eschatologie,* edited by E. Grässer and O. Merk, pp. 71-104. Tübingen: Mohr, 1985.

Hilton, A. "Baffling Boldness: Illiterate Παρρησια in Acts 4 and the Early Empire." Paper delivered at the 1995 SBL meeting in Philadelphia and abstracted in *AAR/SBL Abstracts 1995,* pp. 18-19.

Hock, R. F. "Paul's Tent-Making and the Problem of His Social Class." *JBL* 97 (1978): 555-64.

Horsley, G. H. R. "The Inscriptions of Ephesos and the New Testament." *NovT* 34 (1992): 105-68.

———. "Politarchs." In *ABD,* 5:384-89.

———. "The Politarchs." In AIIFCS, 2:419-31.

———. "Speeches and Dialogue in Acts." *NTS* 32 (1986): 609-14.

House, C. "Defilement by Association: Some Insights from the Use of *Koinos/Koinoo* in Acts 10–11." *AUSS* 21 (1983): 143-53.

Hubbard, B. J. "The Role of Commissioning Accounts in Acts." In *Perspectives on Luke-Acts,* edited by C. H. Talbert, pp. 187-98. Danville: Association of Baptist Professors of Religion, 1978.

Hunkin, J. W. "The Prohibitions of the Council at Jerusalem (Acts xv.28-29)." *JTS* 27 (1925-26): 272-83.

Irvin, D. "The Ministry of Women in the Early Church: The Archaeological Evidence." *Duke Divinity Review* 45 (1980): 76-86.

Jacobson, G. R. "Paul in Luke-Acts: The Savior Who Is Present." In *SBL 1983 Seminar Papers,* edited by K. H. Richards, pp. 131-43. Chico: Scholars Press, 1983.

Jeremias, J. "Paarweise Sendung im NT." In *New Testament Essays: Studies in Memory of T. W. Manson,* pp. 136-43. Manchester: University of Manchester Press, 1959.

———. "Untersuchungen der Quellenproblem der Apostelgeschichte." *ZNW* 36 (1937): 208-13.

Jervell, J. "The Future of the Past: Luke's Vision of Salvation History and Its Bearing on His Writing of History." In *History, Literature, and Society in the Book of Acts,* edited by B. Witherington III, pp. 104-26. Cambridge: Cambridge University Press, 1996.

————. "Paul in the Acts of the Apostles: Tradition, History, Theology." In Jervell, *The Unknown Paul*, pp. 68-76. Minneapolis: Augsburg, 1984.

Jones, A. H. M. "Imperial and Senatorial Jurisdiction in the Early Principate." *Historia* 3 (1955): 464-88.

Jones, D. "The Title 'Servant' in Luke-Acts." In *Luke-Acts: New Perspectives from the SBL Seminar*, edited by C. H. Talbert, pp. 148-65. New York: Crossroad, 1984.

Judge, E. A. "Cultural Conformity and Innovation in Paul." *TynB* 35 (1984): 3-24.

————. "The Decrees of Caesar at Thessalonica." *Reformed Theological Review* 30 (1971): 1-7.

————. "Paul's Boasting in Relation to Contemporary Professional Practice." *ABR* 16 (1968): 37-50.

————. "St. Paul and Classical Society." *JAC* 15 (1972): 19-36.

————. "St. Paul as a Radical Social Critic of Society." *Interchange* 16 (1974): 191-203.

————. "The Social Identity of the First Christians." *JRH* 11 (1980): 201-17.

Käsemann, E. "The Disciples of John the Baptist in Ephesus." In *Essays on New Testament Themes*, pp. 136-48. London: SCM, 1964.

Kaye, B. N. "Acts' Portrait of Silas." *NovT* 21 (1979): 13-26.

Kearsley, R. A. "The Asiarchs." In AIIFCS, 2:363-76.

Kee, H. C. "The Changing Meaning of Synagogue: A Response to Richard Oster." *NTS* 40 (1992): 281-83.

————. "Early Christianity in the Galilee." In *The Galilee*, pp. 3-22.

————. "The Transformation of the Synagogue after 70 c.e.: Its Import for Early Christianity." *NTS* 36 (1990): 1-24.

Keinath, H. O. A. "The Contacts of the Book of Acts with Roman Political Institutions." *CTM* 1 (1930): 117-23, 191-99.

Kelly, S. "The First Lukan Convert: The Ethiopian Eunuch or Cornelius?" Paper delivered at the 1995 SBL meeting in Philadelphia (see *AAR/SBL Abstracts 1995*, p. 176).

Keyes, C. W. "The Greek Letter of Introduction." *American Journal of Philology* 56 (1935): 28-44.

Kilgallen, J. J. "Acts 13,38-39: Culmination of Paul's Speech in Psidia." *Bib* 69 (1988): 480-506.

————. "Did Peter Actually Fail to Get a Word In?" *Bib* 71 (1990): 405-10.

————. "The Function of Stephen's Speech (Acts 7.3-53)." *Bib* 70 (1989): 173-93.

————. "Paul before Agrippa (Acts 26,2-23): Some Considerations." *Bib* 69 (1988): 170-95.

Kilpatrick, G. D. "Acts xxiii,23. δεξιολαβοι." *JTS* 14 (1963): 393-94.

————. "Acts xix.27 απελεγμον." *JTS*, n.s. 10 (1959): 327.

Klijn, A. F. J. "Stephen's Speech — Acts vii.2-53." *NTS* 4 (1957): 25-31.

Knibbe, D. "Via Sacra Ephesiaca: New Aspects of the Cult of Artemis Ephesia." In *Ephesos: Metropolis of Asia*, edited by H. Koester, pp. 141-54. Valley Forge: Trinity, 1995.

Kodell, J. " 'The Word of God Grew' — The Ecclesial Tendency of *Logos* in Acts 6.7; 12.24; 19.20." *Bib* 55 (1974): 505-19.

Koester, H. "Ephesos in Early Christian Literature." In *Ephesos: Metropolis of Asia*, edited by H. Koester, pp. 119-40. Valley Forge: Trinity, 1995.

Krabel, A. T. "The Disappearance of the 'God-Fearers.'" *Numen* 28, no. 2 (1981): 113-23.

Kraemer, R. S. "Women in the Religions of the Greco-Roman World." *Religious Studies Review* 9, no. 2 (1983): 127-39.

Kurz, W. S. "Acts 3.19-26 as a Test of the Role of Eschatology in Lukan Christology." In *SBL 1977 Seminar Papers*, pp. 309-23. Missoula: Scholars Press, 1977.

———. "Hellenistic Rhetoric in the Christological Proof of Luke-Acts." *CBQ* 42 (1980): 171-95.

———. "Narrative Models for Imitation in Luke-Acts." In *Greeks, Romans, and Christians*, edited by D. L. Balch et al., pp. 171-89. Minneapolis: Fortress, 1990.

Ladouceur, D. "Hellenistic Preconceptions of Shipwreck and Pollution as a Context for Acts 27–28." *HTR* 73 (1980): 435-49.

Lake, K. "The Apostolic Council." In *Beginnings*, 5:195-212.

———. "Proselytes and God-Fearers." In *Beginnings*, 5:74-96.

———. "The Unknown God." In *Beginnings*, 5:240-46.

Lambrecht, J. "Paul's Farewell Address at Miletus (Acts 20,17-38)." In *Les Actes des Apôtres. Traditions, rédaction, théologie*, edited by J. Kremer, pp. 307-37. Leuven: Leuven University Press, 1979.

Lampe, G. W. H. "Miracles in the Acts of the Apostles." In *Miracles: Cambridge Studies in Their Philosophy and History*, edited by C. F. D. Moule, pp. 165-78. London: Mowbray, 1965.

Leary, T. J. "Paul's Improper Name." *NTS* 38 (1992): 467-69.

Legasse, S. "Paul's Pre-Christian Career according to Acts." In AIIFCS, 4:365-90.

Lerle, E. "Die Predigt in Lystra." *NTS* 7 (1960): 46-55.

Levine, L. I. "The Second Temple Synagogue: The Formative Years." In *The Synagogue in Late Antiquity*, edited by L. I. Levine, pp. 7-31. Philadelphia: American Schools of Oriental Research, 1987.

Lichtenberger, H. "Taufergemeinden und frühchristliche Tauferpolemik im letzen Drittel des I. Jahrhunderts," *ZTK* 84 (1987): 36-57.

LiDonnici, L. R. "The Image of Artemis Ephesia and Greco-Roman Worship: A Reconsideration." *HTR* 85 (1992): 389-415.

Lincoln, A. T. "Theology and History in the Interpretation of Luke's Pentecost."
    ET 96 (1985): 204-29.
Long, W. R. "The Paulusbild in the Trial of Paul in Acts." In *SBL 1983 Seminar
    Papers,* edited by K. H. Richards, pp. 87-105. Chico: Scholars Press, 1983.
Löning, K. "Die Kornelius-tradition." *BZ* 18 (1974): 1-19.
Lösch, S. "Die Dankesrede de Tertullus: Apg. 24.1-4." *Theologische Quar-
    talschrift* 12 (1931): 295-319.
Lövestam, E. "Paul's Address at Miletus." *ST* 41 (1987): 1-10.
Luce, T. J. "Ancient Views of the Cause of Bias in Historical Writing." *Classical
    Philology* 84 (1989): 16-31.
Lührmann, D. "Paul and the Pharisaic Tradition." *JSNT* 36 (1989): 75-94.
MacDonald, A. H. "Herodotus on the Miraculous." In *Miracles: Cambridge
    Studies in Their Philosophy and History,* edited by C. F. D. Moule, pp.
    83-91. London: Mowbray, 1965.
MacKay, B. S. "Plutarch and the Miraculous." In *Miracles: Cambridge Studies
    in Their Philosophy and History,* edited by C. F. D. Moule, pp. 95-111.
    London: Mowbray, 1965.
MacMullen, R. "Women in Public in the Roman Empire." *Historia* 29, no. 2
    (1980): 208-18.
Malherbe, A. " 'Not in a Corner': Early Christian Apologetic in Acts 26.26." In
    Paul and the Popular Philosophers, pp. 147-63. Minneapolis: Fortress,
    1989.
Malina, B. J., and J. H. Neyrey. "Honor and Shame in Luke-Acts: Pivotal Values
    of the Mediterranean World." In *The Social World of Luke-Acts,* edited
    by J. H. Neyrey, pp. 25-65. Peabody: Hendrickson, 1991.
Marshall, A. J. "Roman Women and the Provinces." *Ancient Society* 6 (1975):
    108-27.
Marshall, I. H. "Acts and the 'Former Treatise.' " In *The Book of Acts,* vol. 1, pp.
    163-82.
————. "Church and Temple in the New Testament" *TynB* 40 (1989): 203-22.
————. "The Significance of Pentecost." *SJT* 30 (1977): 347-69.
Martin, C. J. "A Chamberlain's Journey and the Challenge of Interpretation
    for Liberation." *Semeia* 47 (1989): 105-35.
Martin, L. H. "Gods or Ambassadors of God? Barnabas and Paul in Lystra."
    NTS 41 (1995): 152-56.
Martin, T. W. "Hellenists." *ABD,* 3:135-36.
Mason, S. "Chief Priests, Sadducees, Pharisees, and Sanhedrin in Acts." In
    AIIFCS, 4:115-77.
Mastin, B. A. "A Note on Acts 19.14." *Bib* 59 (1978): 97-99.
————. "Scaeva the Chief Priest." *JTS,* n.s. 27 (1976): 405-12.
Matera, F. J. "Responsibility for the Death of Jesus in Acts." *JSNT* 39 (1990):
    77-93.

Matthew, C. R. "Philip and Simon, Luke and Peter: A Lukan Sequel and Its Intertextual Sources." In *SBL 1992 Seminar Papers*, pp. 133-53.

Mattill, A. J. "The Purpose of Acts: Schneckenberger Reconsidered." In *Apostolic History and the Gospel: Essays Presented to F. F. Bruce*, edited by W. W. Gasque and R. P. Martin, pp. 108-22. Grand Rapids: Eerdmans, 1970.

————. "The Value of Acts as a Source for the Study of Paul." In *Perspectives on Luke-Acts*, edited by C. H. Talbert, pp. 76-98. Edinburgh: T & T Clark, 1978.

Mattingly, H. B. "The Origin of the Name Christiani." *JTS* 9 (1958): 26-37.

McCoy, W. J. "In the Shadow of Thucydides." In *History, Literature, and Society in the Book of Acts*, edited by B. Witherington III, pp. 3-33. Cambridge: Cambridge University Press, 1996.

McDonald, W. A. "Archaeology and St. Paul's Journeys in Greek Lands." *BA* 3 (1940): 18-24.

Mealand, D. "Acts 28.30-31 and Its Hellenistic Greek Vocabulary." *NTS* 36 (1990): 583-97.

————. "Hellenistic Historians and the Style of Acts." *ZNW* 82 (1991): 42-66.

————. "The Phrase 'Many Proofs' in Acts 1,3 and in Hellenistic Writers." *ZNW* 80 (1989): 134-35.

Meir, C. "Historical Answers to Historical Questions: The Origins of History in Ancient Greece." *Arethusa* 20 (1987): 41-57.

Menoud, Ph.-H. "L'Mort d' Ananias et de Sapphira (Actes 5.1-11)." In *Aux Sources de la Tradition Chrétienne: Mélanges Maurice Goguel*, edited by O. Cullmann and P. Menoud, pp. 146-54. Neuchatel: Delachaux et Niestle, 1950.

Merrins, E. M. "The Death of Antiochus IV, Herod the Great, and Herod Agrippa I." *BS* 61 (1904): 561-66.

Metzger, B. M. "Ancient Astrological Geography and Acts 2.9-11." In *Apostolic History and the Gospel: Essays Presented to F. F. Bruce*, edited by W. W. Gasque and R. P. Martin, pp. 123-33. Grand Rapids: Eerdmans, 1970.

————. "The Christianization of Nubia and the Old Nubian Version of the New Testament." In Metzger, *Historical and Literary Studies*, pp. 111-22. Leiden: Brill, 1968.

————. "St. Paul and the Magicians." *Princeton Seminary Bulletin* 38 (1944): 27-30.

Meyshan, J. "The Coinage of Agrippa the First." *IEJ* 4 (1954): 186-200.

Miles, G. B., and G. Trompf. "Luke and Antiphon: The Theology of Acts 27–28 in the Light of Pagan Beliefs about Divine Retribution, Pollution, Shipwreck." *HTR* 69 (1976): 259-67.

Mitchell, A. C. "The Social Function of Friendship in Acts 2.44-47 and 4.32-37." *JBL* 111 (1992): 262-64.

Mitchell, S. "Iconium and Ninica: Two Double Communities in Roman Asia Minor." *Historia* 28 (1979): 435-78.

―――. "Population and the Land in Roman Galatia." In *ANRW II*, vol. 7.2 (1980), p. 1073.

Mitford, T. B. "Religious Documents from Roman Cyprus." *JHS* 66 (1946): 36-42.

Moessner, D. P. " 'The Christ Must Suffer': New Light on the Jesus, Peter, Stephen, Paul Parallels in Luke-Acts." *NovT* 28 (1986): 220-56.

―――. "The Meaning of *KATHESES* in the Lukan Prologue as the Key to the Distinctive Contribution of Luke's Narration among the 'Many.' " In *The Four Gospels 1992. Festschrift Frans Neirynck,* edited by F. Van Segbroeck et al., pp. 1513-28. Leuven: Leuven University Press, 1992.

―――. "Paul in Acts: Preacher of Eschatological Repentance to Israel." *NTS* 34 (1988): 96-104.

―――. "Re-Reading Talbert's Luke: The *Bios* of 'Balance' or the 'Bias' of History?" In *Cadbury, Knox, and Talbert: American Contributions to the Study of the Acts,* edited by M. C. Parsons and J. B. Tyson, pp. 203-28. Atlanta: Scholars Press, 1992.

―――. "The Script of the Scriptures in Acts: Suffering as God's Plan (βουλη) for the World for the Release of Sins." In *History, Literature, and Society in the Book of Acts,* edited by B. Witherington III, pp. 218-50. Cambridge: Cambridge University Press, 1996.

Momigliano, A. "Tradition and the Classical Historian." *History and Theory* 11 (1972): 279-93.

Mommsen, T. "Die Rechtverhältnisse des Apostels Paulus." *ZNW* 2 (1901): 81-96.

Montague, G. T. "Paul and Athens." *TBT* 49 (1970): 14-23.

Morgenstern, J. "The Channukah Festival and the Calendar of Ancient Israel." *HUCA* 20 (1947): 1-136.

Morris, L. *"Kai hapax kai Dis,"* *NovT* 1 (1956): 205-8.

Mosley, A. W. "Historical Reporting in the Ancient World." *NTS* 12 (1965-66): 8-25.

Moule, C. F. D. "The Christology of Acts." In *Studies in Luke-Acts,* edited by L. E. Keck and J. L. Martyn, pp. 159-85. London: SPCK, 1968.

―――. "Once More, Who Were the Hellenists?" *ET* 70 (1958-59): 100-103.

Munck, J. "Discours d'adieu dans le Nouveau Testament et dans la litterature biblique." In *Aux Sources de la Tradition Chrétienne: Mélanges Maurice Goguel,* edited by O. Cullmann and P. Menoud, pp. 155-70. Neuchatel: Delachaux et Niestle, 1950.

Murphy, J. J. "Early Christianity as a Persuasive Campaign." In *Rhetoric and the New Testament: Essays from the 1992 Heidelberg Conference,* edited by S. E. Porter and Thomas H. Ohlbricht, pp. 90-99. Sheffield: JSOT Press, 1993.

Murphy-O'Connor, J. "The Cenacle and Community: The Background of Acts 2.44-45." In *Scripture and Other Artifacts: Essays on the Bible and Archaeology in Honor of Philip J. King,* edited by M. D. Coogan et al., pp. 296-310. Louisville: Westminster/J. Knox, 1994.

―――. "On the Road and on the Sea with St. Paul." *BR* 1, no. 2 (1985): 38-47.

―――. "Paul in Arabia." *CBQ* 55 (1993): 732-37.

Nadel, G. H. "Philosophy of History before Historicism." *History and Theory* 3 (1964): 291-315.

Nauck, W. "Die Tradition und Komposition der Areopagrede." *ZNW* 53 (1956): 11-52.

Neirynck, F. "Acts 10,36a τον λογον ον." *ETL* 60 (1984): 118-23.

Neyrey, J. H. "Acts 17, Epicureans, and Theodicy." In *Greeks, Romans, and Christians,* edited by D. L. Balch et al., pp. 118-34. Minneapolis: Fortress, 1990.

―――. "The Forensic Defense Speech and Paul's Trial Speeches in Acts 22-26: Form and Function." In *Luke-Acts: New Perspectives from the SBL Seminar,* edited by C. H. Talbert, pp. 210-24. New York: Crossroad, 1984.

―――. "Luke's Social Location of Paul: Cultural Anthropology and the Status of Paul in Acts." In *History, Literature, and Society in the Book of Acts,* edited by B. Witherington III, pp. 251-79. Cambridge: Cambridge University Press, 1996.

Nobbs, A. "Cyprus." In AIIFCS, 2:279-89.

Nock, A. D. "Paul and the Magus." In *Beginnings,* 5:164-88.

Nolland, J. "A Fresh Look at Acts 15.10." *TS* 27 (1980): 105-15.

North, H. F. "Rhetoric and Historiography." *Quarterly Journal of Speech* 42 (1956): 234-42.

Ogg, G. "Derbe." *NTS* 9 (1962-63): 367-70.

Oliver, J. H. "The Epistle of Claudius Which Mentions the Proconsul Junius Gallio." *Hesperia* 40 (1971): 239-40.

Oster, R. E. "Acts 19.23-41 and an Ephesian Inscription." *HTR* 77 (1984): 233-37.

―――. "The Ephesian Artemis as an Opponent of Early Christianity." *JAC* 19 (1976): 24-44.

―――. "Ephesus." *ABD,* 2:542-49.

―――. "Ephesus as a Religious Center under the Principate, I. Paganism before Constantine." In *ANRW II,* vol. 18.3 (1990), pp. 1661-1728.

―――. "Supposed Anachronism in Luke-Acts' Use of *sunagoge:* A Rejoinder to H. C. Kee." *NTS* 39 (1993): 178-208.

O'Toole, R. F. "Philip and Ethiopian Eunuch (Acts 8,25-40)." *JSNT* 17 (1983): 25-34.

Overman, J. A. "The God-Fearers: Some Neglected Features." *JSNT* 32 (1988): 17-26.

Palmer, D. W. "Acts and Ancient Historical Monograph." In AIIFCS, 1:1-30.
———. "The Literary Background of Acts 1.1-4." *NTS* 33 (1987): 427-38.
Parratt, R. K. "The Rebaptism of the Ephesian Disciples." *ET* 79 (1967-68): 182-83.
Pathrapankal, J. "Christianity as a 'Way' according to the Acts of the Apostles." In *Les Actes des Apôtres. Traditions, rédaction, théologie,* edited by J. Kremer, pp. 533-39. Leuven: Leuven University Press, 1979.
Patsch, H. "Die Prophetie des Agabus." *TZ* 28 (1972): 228-32.
Penna, R. "Les Juifs à Rome au Temps de l-Apôtre Paul." *NTS* 28 (1982): 321-47.
Peterson, D. "The Motif of Fulfilment and the Purpose of Luke-Acts." In AIIFCS, 1:83-104.
Phillips, C. R. "On Ritual and Theodicy in Roman Paganism." Paper delivered at the 1995 SBL Meeting in Philadelphia and abstracted in *AAR/SBL Abstracts 1995,* pp. 160-61.
Pilch, J. J. "Sickness and Healing in Luke-Acts." In *The Social World of Luke-Acts,* edited by J. H. Neyrey, pp. 181-209. Peabody, Mass.: Hendrickson, 1991.
Plümacher, E. "Wirklichkeitserfahrung und Geschichtsschreibung bei Lukas: Erwägungen zu den Wir-Stücken der Apostelgeschichte." *ZNW* 68 (1977): 2-22.
Plunkett, M. A. "Ethnocentricity and Salvation History in the Cornelius Episode (Acts 10.1–11.18)." In *SBL 1985 Seminar Papers,* pp. 465-79.
Pokorny, P. "Die Romfahrt des Paulus und der antike Roman." *ZNW* 64 (1973): 233-44.
Porter, S. "Thucydides 1.22.1 and Speeches in Acts: Is There a Thucydidean View?" *NovT* 2 (1990): 121-42.
———. "The 'We' Passages." In AIIFCS, 2:545-74.
Potter, D. S. "Lystra." *ABD,* 4:426-27.
Praeder, S. M. "Acts 27.1–28.16: Sea Voyages in Ancient Literature and the Theology of Luke-Acts." *CBQ* 46 (1984): 683-706.
———. "Jesus-Paul, Peter-Paul, and Jesus-Peter Parallelisms in Luke-Acts: A History of Reader Response." In *SBL 1984 Seminar Papers,* edited by K. H. Richards, pp. 23-39. Chico: Scholars Press, 1984.
———. "Miracle Worker and Missionary: Paul in the Acts of the Apostles." In *SBL 1983 Seminar Papers,* edited by K. H. Richards, pp. 107-29. Chico: Scholars Press, 1983.
———. "The Problem of First Person Narration in Acts." *NovT* 29 (1987): 193-218.
Radl, W. "Befreiung aus dem Gefängnis: Die Darstellung eines biblischen Grundthemas in Apg. 12." *BZ* 27 (1983): 81-96.
Rajak, T. "Josephus and the 'Archaeology' of the Jews." *Journal of Jewish Studies* 33 (1982): 465-77.

————. "Was There a Roman Charter for the Jews?" *JRS* 74 (1984): 107-23.

Rapske, B. "Acts, Travel, and Shipwreck." In AIIFCS, 2:1-47.

Redalie, Y. "Conversion ou liberation? Notes sur Actes 16,11-40." *Bulletin du Centre Protestant d'Etudes* 26, no. 7 (1974): 7-17.

Reeder, E. D. "The Mother of the Gods and the Hellenistic Bronze Matrix." *AJA* 91 (1987): 423-40.

Richards, E. "Pentecost as a Recurrent Theme in Luke-Acts." In *New Views on Luke-Acts,* pp. 133-49. Collegeville: Liturgical Press, 1990.

Riddle, D. W. "Early Christian Hospitality: A Factor in the Gospel Transmission." *JBL* 57 (1938): 141-54.

Riesenfeld, H. "The Text of Acts 10.36." In *Text and Interpretation: Studies in the New Testament Presented to Matthew Black,* edited by E. Best and R. McL. Wilson, pp. 191-94. Cambridge: Cambridge University Press, 1979.

Riesner, R. "James' Speech (Acts 15.13-21), Simeon's Hymn (Luke 2.29-32), and Luke's Sources." In *Jesus of Nazareth: Lord and Christ,* edited by J. B. Green, pp. 263-78. Grand Rapids: Eerdmans, 1994.

————. "Synagogues in Jerusalem." In AIIFCS, 4:179-210.

Robbins, V. K. "By Land and by Sea: The We-Passages and Ancient Sea Voyages." In *Perspectives on Luke-Acts,* edited by C. H. Talbert, pp. 215-42. Edinburgh: T & T Clark, 1978.

————. "Prefaces in Greco-Roman Biography and Luke-Acts." *Perspectives in Religious Studies* 6 (1979): 94-108.

————. "The Social Location of the Implied Author of Luke-Acts." In *The Social World of Luke-Acts,* edited by J. H. Neyrey, pp. 305-32. Peabody: Hendrickson, 1991.

————. "The We-Passages in Acts and Ancient Sea Voyages." *BR* 20 (1975): 5-18.

Ropes, J. H. "An Observation on the Style of S. Luke." *Harvard Studies in Classical Philology* 12 (1901): 299-305.

————. "St. Luke's Preface: ασφαλεια and παρακολοθειν." *JTS* 25 (1923-24): 67-71.

Rosner, B. "Acts and Biblical History." In AIIFCS, 1:65-82.

Ross, R. C. "*Superstitio.*" *CJ* 64 (1968-69): 356-57.

Sacks, K. S. "The Lesser Prooemia of Diodorus Siculus." *Hermes* 110 (1982): 434-43.

————. "Rhetorical Approaches to Greek History Writing." In *SBL 1984 Seminar Papers,* edited by K. H. Richards, pp. 123-33. Chico: Scholars Press, 1984.

Sanders, H. A. "The Birth Certificate of a Roman Citizen." *CP* 22 (1927): 409-13.

Sanders, J. T. "The Salvation of the Jews in Luke-Acts." In *Luke-Acts: New Perspectives from the SBL Seminar,* edited by C. H. Talbert, pp. 104-28. New York: Crossroad, 1984.

Satterthwaite, P. E. "Acts against the Background of Classical Rhetoric." In
    AIIFCS, 1:337-79.
Scarupa, H. J. "Blacks in the Classical World." *American Visions* (October
    1987), pp. 20-25.
Schaps, D. "The Women Least Mentioned: Etiquette and Women's Names."
    CQ 27 (1977): 323-30.
Schmidt, D. D. "Syntactical Style in the 'We'-Sections of Acts: How Lukan Is
    It?" In *SBL 1989 Seminar Papers,* pp. 300-308.
Schnackeburg, R. "Ephesus: Entwickling einer Gemeinde von Paulus zu Jo-
    hannes." *BZ* 35 (1991): 41-64.
Schneider, J., and C. Brown. "Redemption." In *Dictionary of New Testament
    Theology,* vol. 3, pp. 205-23. Grand Rapids: Zondervan, 1978.
Schubert, P. "The Final Cycle of Speeches in the Book of Acts." *JBL* 87 (1968):
    1-16.
————. "The Place of the Areopagus Speech in the Composition of Acts." In
    Transitions in Biblical Scholarship, edited by J. Coert Rylaarsdam, pp.
    235-61. Chicago: University of Chicago Press, 1968.
Schulz, F. "Roman Registers of Birth and Birth Certificates." Part 1 in *JRS* 32
    (1942): 78-91; and part 2 in *JRS* 33 (1943): 55-64.
Schumacher, R. "Aquila und Priscilla." *TGl* 12 (1920): 86-99.
Schwartz, D. R. "Non-Joining Sympathizers (Acts 5,13-14)." *Bib* 64 (1983):
    550-55.
Schweizer, E. "Die Bekehrung des Apollos, Apg. 18.24-26." *EvT* 6 (1955): 247-54.
————. "The Concept of the Davidic 'Son of God' in Acts and Its Old Testa-
    ment Background." In *Studies in Luke-Acts,* edited by L. E. Keck and J. L.
    Martyn, pp. 186-93. London: SPCK, 1968.
Scroggs, R. "The Sociological Interpretation of the New Testament: The Present
    State of Research." *NTS* 26 (1980): 164-79.
Segal, A. F. "The Cost of Proselytism and Conversions." In *SBL 1988 Seminar
    Papers,* edited by D. J. Lull, pp. 336-69. Atlanta: Scholars Press, 1988.
Sharp, D. S. "The Meaning of μεν ουν in Acts xiv,3." *ET* 44 (1932-33): 528.
Shaw, B. D. "The Bandit." In *The Romans,* edited by A. Giardina, pp. 300-341.
    Chicago: University of Chicago Press, 1993.
Shields, B. E. "The Areopagus Sermon and Romans 1.18ff: A Study in Creation
    Theology." *ResQ* 20 (1977): 23-40.
Simon, M. "The Apostolic Decree and Its Setting in the Ancient Church." *BJRL*
    52 (1970): 437-60.
Silva, D. De. "The Meaning and Function of Acts 7.46-50." *JBL* 106 (1987):
    261-75.
Siotis, M. A. "From Greek Hairesis to Christian Heresy." *Theologique Historique*
    53 (1979): 101-16.
————. "Luke the Evangelist as St. Paul's Collaborator." In *Neues Testament*

und Geschichte, edited by H. Baltensweiler and B. Reicke, pp. 105-11. Tübingen: Mohr, 1972.

Smalley, S. S. "The Christology of Acts." *ET* 73 (1961-62): 358-62.

————. "The Christology of Acts Again." In *Christ and Spirit in the New Testament,* edited by B. Lindars and S. S. Smalley, pp. 79-93. Cambridge: Cambridge University Press, 1973.

Smallwood, E. M. "The Alleged Jewish Tendencies of Poppaea Sabina." *JTS,* n.s. 10 (1959): 329-35.

Smith, A. " 'Put Outside for a While': Luke's Ironic Portrait of Gamaliel (Acts 5.27-42)." Paper delivered at the 1995 meeting of the SBL in Philadelphia and abstracted in *AAR/SBL Abstracts 1995,* pp. 66-67.

Soards, M. L. "Review of Pervo's *Profit with Delight.*" *JAAR* 58 (1990): 307-10.

————. "The Speeches in Acts in Relation to Other Pertinent Ancient Literature." *ETL* 70 (1994): 65-90.

Sokolowski, F. "A New Testimony on the Cult of Artemis of Ephesus." *HTR* 58 (1965): 427-31.

Stanley, D. M. "Paul's Conversion in Acts: Why the Three Accounts." *CBQ* 15 (1953): 315-38.

Stark, R. "The Class Basis of Early Christianity: Inferences from a Sociological Model." *Sociological Analysis* 47 (1986): 216-25.

Starr, R. J. "The Circulation of Literary Texts in the Roman World." *CQ* 37 (1987): 213-23.

Stegmann, W. "War der Apostel Paulus ein römanischer Bürger?" *ZNW* 87 (1987): 200-209.

Sterling, G. " 'Athletes of Virtue': An Analysis of the Summaries in Acts (2.41-47; 4.32-35; 5.12-16)." *JBL* 113 (1994): 679-96.

Stoops, R. F. "Riot and Assembly: The Social Context of Acts 19.23-41." *JBL* 108 (1989): 73-91.

Stowers, S. "Social Status, Public Speaking and Private Teaching: The Circumstances of Paul's Preaching Activity." *NovT* 26 (1984): 59-82.

Strange, W. A. "The Sons of Sceva and the Text of Acts 19.14." *JTS,* n.s. 38 (1987): 97-107.

Strobel, A. "Passa-Symbolic und passa-Wunder in Apg. 12.3ff." *NTS* 4 (1958): 210-15.

Talbert, C. H. "The Acts of the Apostle: Monograph or 'Bios'?" In *History, Literature, and Society in the Book of Acts,* edited by B. Witherington III, pp. 58-72. Cambridge: Cambridge University Press, 1996.

————. "Again: Paul's Visits to Jerusalem." *NovT* 9 (1967): 26-40.

————. "Martyrdom and the Lukan Social Ethic." In *Political Issues in Luke-Acts,* edited by R. J. Cassidy and P. J. Scharper, pp. 99-110. Maryknoll: Orbis, 1983.

————. "Once Again: Gospel Genre." *Semeia* 43 (1988): 53-74.

Talbert, C. H., and J. H. Hayes, "A Theology of Sea Storms in Luke-Acts." In *SBL 1995 Seminar Papers,* edited by E. H. Lovering, pp. 321-36. Atlanta: Scholars Press, 1995.

Tannehill, R. "The Narrator's Strategy in the Scenes of Paul's Defense: Acts 21.27–26.32." *Foundations and Facets Forum* 8, nos. 3-4 (September-December 1992): 245-69.

———. "Rejection by Jews and Turning to Gentiles: The Pattern of Paul's Mission in Acts." In *SBL 1986 Seminar Papers,* pp. 130-41.

Thomas, C. "At Home in the City of Artemis." In *Ephesos: Metropolis of Asia,* edited by H. Koester, pp. 81-117. Valley Forge: Trinity, 1995.

Thornton, T. C. G. "To the End of the Earth: Acts 1.8." *ET* 89 (1977-78): 374-75.

Tissot, Y. "Les Prescriptions des Presbytres (Actes xv,41,d)." *RB* 77 (1970): 321-46.

Torrance, T. F. "St. Paul at Philippi: Three Startling Conversions. Acts 16.6-40," *EvQ* 13 (1941): 62-74.

Townsend, J. T. "Acts 9.1-29 and Early Church Tradition." In *SBL 1988 Seminar Papers,* edited by D. J. Lull, pp. 119-31. Atlanta: Scholars Press, 1988.

Tracy, R. "Syria." In AIIFCS, 2:223-78.

Trebilco, P. "Asia." In AIIFCS, 2:291-362.

———. "Paul and Silas — 'Servants of the Most High God.'" *JSNT* 36 (1989): 51-73.

Trites, A. A. "The Importance of Legal Scenes in the Book of Acts." *NovT* 15 (1974): 278-84.

Trompf, G. W. "On Why Luke Declined to Recount the Death of Paul: Acts 27–28 and Beyond." In *Luke-Acts: New Perspectives from the SBL Seminar,* edited by C. H. Talbert, pp. 225-39. New York: Crossroad, 1984.

Trumbower, J. A. "The Historical Jesus and the Speech of Gamaliel (Acts 5.35-39)." *NTS* 39 (1993): 500-517.

Tyson, J. B. "The Gentile Mission and the Authority of Scripture." *NTS* 33 (1987): 619-31.

———. "The Problem of Jewish Rejection in Acts." In *Luke-Acts and the Jewish People: Eight Critical Perspectives,* edited by J. B. Tyson, pp. 124-37. Minneapolis: Augsburg, 1988.

Ullman, B. L. "History and Tragedy." *TAPA* 73 (1942): 25-53.

Unnik, W. C. van. "The 'Book of Acts' the Confirmation of the Gospel." *NovT* 4 (1960): 26-59.

———. "Luke's Second Book and the Rules of Hellenistic Historiography." In *Les Actes des Apôtres. Traditions, rédaction, théologie,* edited by J. Kremer, pp. 37-60. Leuven: Leuven University Press, 1979.

van der Horst, P. "The Altar of the 'Unknown God' in Athens (Acts 17.23) and the Cults of 'Unknown Gods' in the Graeco-Roman World." In van der

Horst, *Hellenism-Judaism-Christianity,* pp. 165-202. Kampen: Kok Pharos Pub., 1994.

———. "Hellenistic Parallels to Acts (Chapters 3 and 4)." *JSNT* 35 (1989): 37-46.

———. "Hellenistic Parallels to the Acts of the Apostles." *JSNT* 25 (1985): 49-60.

———. "A New Altar of a Godfearer?" In van der Horst, *Hellenism-Judaism-Christianity,* pp. 65-72. Kampen: Kok Pharos Pub., 1994.

———. "Peter's Shadow: The Religio-Historical Background of Acts V.15." *NTS* 23 (1976-77): 204-12.

Van Elderen, B. "Some Archaeological Observations on Paul's First Missionary Journey." In *Apostolic History and the Gospel: Essays Presented to F. F. Bruce,* edited by W. W. Gasque and R. P. Martin, pp. 151-61. Grand Rapids: Eerdmans, 1970.

Veltman, F. "The Defense Speeches of St. Paul." In *Perspectives on Luke-Acts,* edited by C. H. Talbert, pp. 243-56. Edinburgh: T & T Clark, 1978.

Vielhauer, P. "On the 'Paulinism' of Acts." In *Studies in Luke-Acts,* edited by L. E. Keck and J. L. Martyn, pp. 33-50. London: SPCK, 1968.

Vermeule, C. C. "Greek, Etruscan, and Roman Bronzes Acquired by the Museum of Fine Arts, Boston." *CJ* 60 (1960): 199-200.

Völkel, M. "Exegetische Erwägungen zum Verständnis des Begriff *kathezes* im Lukanischen Prolog." *NTS* 20 (1973-74): 289-99.

Wall, R. W. "Successors to the 'Twelve' according to Acts 12.1-17." *CBQ* 53 (1991): 628-43.

Walsh, P. G. "Livy's Preface and the Distortion of History." *American Journal of Philology* 76 (1955): 369-83.

Wanke, J. "Ἑλληνιστής." In *Exegetical Dictionary of the NT,* vol. 1 (1990), pp. 436-37. Grand Rapids: Eerdmans, 1990.

Warfield, B. B. "The Reading Ἕλληνας and Ελληνιστας." *JBL* 3 (1883): 113-27.

Watson, D. F. "Paul's Speech to the Ephesian Elders (Acts 20.17-38): Epideictic Rhetoric of Farewell." In *Persuasive Artistry: Studies in Honor of George A. Kennedy,* edited by D. F. Watson, pp. 184-208. Sheffield: Sheffield Academic Press, 1991.

Wellesley, K. "Can You Trust Tacitus?" *Greece and Rome* 1 (1951): 13-37.

Wenham, D. "Acts and the Pauline Corpus: II. The Evidence of the Parallels." In AIIFCS, 1:215-58.

Wenham, G. "The Theology of Unclean Food." *EvQ* 53 (1981): 6-15.

Wenham, J. "Did Peter Go to Rome in A.D. 42?" *TB* 23 (1972): 94-102.

White, L. M. "The Delos Synagogue Revisited: Recent Fieldwork in the Graeco-Roman Diaspora." *HTR* 80, no. 2 (1987): 133-60.

———. "Social Authority in the House Church Setting and Ephesians 4.1-16." *ResQ* 29 (1987): 209-18.

————. "Urban Development and Social Change." In *Ephesos: Metropolis of Asia*, edited by H. Koester, pp. 27-79. Valley Forge: Trinity, 1995.

Wikgren, A. "The Problem of Acts 16.12." In *New Testament Textual Criticism, Its Significance for Exegesis: Essays in Honour of Bruce M. Metzger*, edited by E. J. Epp and G. D. Fee, pp. 171-78. Oxford: Oxford University Press, 1981.

Wilcox, M. "The 'God-Fearers' in Acts — A Reconsideration." *JSNT* 13 (1981): 102-22.

————. "Luke and the Bezan Text of Acts." In *Les Actes des Apôtres. Traditions, rédaction, théologie*, edited by J. Kremer, pp. 447-55. Leuven: Leuven University Press, 1979.

Williams, M. H. "Θεοσεβὴς γαρ ην — The Jewish Tendencies of Poppaea Sabina." *JTS*, n.s. 39 (1988): 97-111.

Wilson, J. "What Does Thucydides Claim for His Speeches." *Phoenix* 36 (1982): 95-103.

Winter, B. W. "Acts and Food Shortages." In AIIFCS, 1:59-78.

————. "The Importance of the *Captatio Benevolentiae* in the Speeches of Tertullus and Paul in Acts 24.1-21." *JTS*, n.s. 42 (1991): 505-31.

————. "Official Proceedings and the Forensic Speeches in Acts 24–26." In AIIFCS, 1:305-36.

————. "On Introducing Gods to Athens: An Alternative Reading of Acts 17.18-20." *TynB* 47, no. 1 (1996): 71-90.

Wiseman, J. "A Distinguished Macedonian Family of the Roman Imperial Period." *AJA* 88 (1984): 567-82.

Witherington, B. III. "The Anti-Feminist Tendencies of the Western Text in Acts." *JBL* 103 (1984): 82-84.

————. "Editing the Good News: Some Synoptic Lessons for the Study of Acts." In *History, Literature, and Society in the Book of Acts*, edited by B. Witherington III, pp. 324-47. Cambridge: Cambridge University Press, 1996.

————. "Not So Idle Thoughts about EIDOLOTHUTON." *TynB* 44, no. 2 (1993): 237-54.

Workman, W. P. "A New Date-Indication in Acts." *ET* 11 (1899-1900): 316-19.

Wycherley, R. E. "St. Paul in Athens." *JTS* 19 (1968): 619-21.

Yamauchi, E. "Magic or Miracle? Disease, Demons, and Exorcisms." In *Gospel Perspectives*. Vol. 6, *The Miracles of Jesus*, edited by D. Wenham and C. Blomberg, pp. 89-183. Sheffield: JSOT, 1986.

Zakovitch, Y. "Miracle OT," and H. E. Remus, "Miracle, NT." In *ABD*, 4:845-69.

Ziesler, J. A. "The Name of Jesus in the Acts of the Apostles." *JSNT* 4 (1979): 28-41.

Zeitlin, S. "A History of Jewish Historiography: From the Biblical Books to the *Sefer Ha-Kabbalah* with Special Emphasis on Josephus." *JQR* 59 (1968-69): 171-214.

Zweck, D. "The *Exordium* of the Areopagus Speech, Acts 17.22, 23." *NTS* 35 (1989): 94-103.

Monographs

Achtemeier, P. *The Quest for Unity in the New Testament Church.* Philadelphia: Fortress, 1987.

Aejamelaeus, L. *Die Rezeption der Paulusbriefe in der Miletrede, Apg. 20,18-35.* Helsinki, 1987.

Alexander, L. C. A. *The Preface to Luke's Gospel: Literary Convention and Social Context in Luke 1.1-4 and Acts 1.1.* Cambridge: Cambridge University Press, 1993.

Alon, G. *Jews, Judaism, and the Classical World: Studies in Jewish History in the Times of the Second Temple and Talmud.* Jerusalem: Magnes Press, 1977.

Arnold, C. E. *Ephesians: Power and Magic.* Cambridge: Cambridge University Press, 1989.

Aune, D. *The New Testament in Its Literary Environment.* Philadelphia: Westminster, 1987.

Balsdon, J. P. V. D. *Romans and Aliens.* Chapel Hill: University of North Carolina Press, 1979.

Barrett, A. A. *Caligula: The Corruption of Power.* New Haven: Yale University Press, 1989.

Barrett, C. K. *Essays on Paul.* Philadelphia: Westminster, 1982.

————. *Freedom and Obligation.* Philadelphia: Westminster, 1985.

————. *Luke the Historian in Recent Study.* Philadelphia: Fortress, 1970.

————. *New Testament Essays.* London: SPCK, 1972.

————. *Paul: An Introduction to His Thought.* Louisville: Westminster/J. Knox, 1994.

Benko, S. *Pagan Rome and the Early Christians.* Bloomington: Indiana University Press, 1984.

Betz, H. D., ed. *The Greek Magical Papyri in Translation.* Chicago: University of Chicago Press, 1986.

Boismard, M. E., and A. Lamouille. *Les Actes des Deux Apôtres.* Paris: Gabalda, 1990.

Bowersock, G. W. *Roman Arabia.* Cambridge: Harvard University Press, 1983.

Bradley, K. R. *Discovering the Roman Family: Studies in Social History.* Oxford: Oxford University Press, 1991.

Brawley, R. L. *Luke-Acts and the Jews.* Philadelphia: Westminster, 1987.

Brooten, B. J. *Women Leaders in the Ancient Synagogues.* Atlanta: Scholars Press, 1982.

Brown, R. E. *The Death of the Messiah*. 2 vols. New York: Doubleday, 1994.

Brown, R. E., and J. P. Meier. *Antioch and Rome: New Testament Cradles of Catholic Christianity*. New York: Paulist, 1983.

Bruce, F. F. *The Speeches in the Acts of the Apostles*. London: Tyndale, 1942.

Burkett, W. *Ancient Mystery Cults*. Cambridge: Harvard University Press, 1987.

Burridge, R. A. *What Are the Gospels? A Comparison with Graeco-Roman Biography*. Cambridge: Cambridge University Press, 1992.

Buss, M. F.-J. *Die Missionspredigt des Apostels Paulus im Psidian Antiochen. Analysis von Apg 13,16-41 im Hinblick auf die literarische und thematische Einheit der Paulusrede*. Stuttgart: Verlag Katholisches Bibelwerk, 1980.

Cadbury, H. J. *The Book of Acts in History*. London: A & C Black, 1955.

———. *The Making of Luke-Acts*. London: SPCK, 1958.

———. *Style and Literary Method of Luke*. Part 1. Cambridge: Harvard University Press, 1920.

Cadbury, H. J., and K. Lake. *The Beginnings of Christianity*. Vols. 1-5. London: Macmillan, 1933.

Cantarella, E. *Pandora's Daughters*. Baltimore: Johns Hopkins University Press, 1987.

Carroll, J. T. *Response to the End of History: Eschatology and Situation in Luke-Acts*. Atlanta: Scholars Press, 1988.

Cassidy, R. *Society and Politics in the Acts of the Apostles*. Maryknoll: Orbis, 1987.

Casson, L. *Ships and Seamanship in the Ancient World*. Princeton: Princeton University Press, 1971.

———. *Travel in the Ancient World*. London: Allen and Unwin, 1974.

Clark, D. *Rhetoric in Greco-Roman Education*. New York: Columbia University Press, 1957.

Cohen, S. J. D. *Josephus in Galilee and Rome: His Vita and Development as a Historian*. Leiden: Brill, 1979.

Coles, R. A. *Reports of Proceedings in Papyri*. Brussels, 1966.

Conzelmann, H. *The Theology of St. Luke*. New York: Harper and Row, 1960.

Crown, A. D., ed. *The Samaritans*. Tübingen: Mohr, 1989.

Deissmann, A. *Light from the Ancient Near East*. Grand Rapids: Baker, 1978.

———. *Paul: A Study in Social and Religious History*. Gloucester: Peter Smith, 1972.

Dibelius, M. *Studies in the Acts of the Apostles*. London: SCM, 1956.

Dodd, C. H. *According to the Scriptures*. New York: Scribners, 1953.

———. *The Apostolic Preaching and Its Development*. London: Hodder, 1944.

Dodds, E. R. *Pagan and Christian in an Age of Anxiety*. Cambridge: Cambridge University Press, 1965.

Downey, G. *A History of Antioch in Syria from Seleucus to the Arab Conquest*.

Princeton: Princeton University Press, 1961. Abridged in Downey, *Ancient Antioch* (Princeton, 1963).

Duff, A. M. *Freedmen in the Early Roman Empire.* 2d ed. Oxford: Oxford University Press, 1957.

Dumais, M. *Le Langage de L'Evangelisation. L'announce missionaire en milieu juif (Actes 13,16-41).* Montreal: Bellarmin, 1976.

Dunn, J. D. G. *Baptism in the Holy Spirit.* London: SCM, 1975.

———. *Jesus and the Spirit.* London: SCM, 1975.

———. *Unity and Diversity in the New Testament.* Philadelphia: Westminster, 1977.

Dupont, J. *Le discours de Milet. Testament pastoral de Saint Paul (Actes 20,18-36).* Paris: Cerf, 1962.

———. *The Sources of Acts: The Present Position.* London: Darton, Longman, 1964.

Ehrhardt, A. *The Acts of the Apostles.* Manchester: Manchester University Press, 1969.

Ekschmitt, W. *Die Seben Weltwunder.* Mainz, 1984.

Elliger, W. *Ephesos: Geschichte einer antiken Weltstadt.* Stuttgart: Kohlhammer, 1985.

Epp, E. J. *The Theological Tendency of Codex Bezae Cantabrigiensis in Acts.* Cambridge: Cambridge University Press, 1966.

Esler, P. F. *Community and Gospel in Luke-Acts: The Social and Political Motivations of Lucan Theology.* Cambridge: Cambridge University Press, 1987.

Evans, C. A., and J. A. Sanders. *Luke and Scripture.* Minneapolis: Fortress, 1993.

Ferguson, E. *Backgrounds of Early Christianity.* 2d ed. Grand Rapids: Eerdmans, 1993.

Fiorenza, E. Schüssler. *In Memory of Her.* New York: Crossroad, 1983.

Fitzmyer, J. A. *Luke the Theologian: Aspects of His Teaching.* Mahwah: Paulist, 1989.

Flender, H. *St. Luke — Theologian of Redemptive History.* London: SPCK, 1967.

Fontenrose, J. *The Delphic Oracle.* Berkeley: University of California Press, 1978.

Fornara, C. W. *The Nature of History in Ancient Greece and Rome.* Berkeley: University of California Press, 1983.

Fossum, J. E. *The Name of God and the Angel of the Lord: Samaritan and Jewish Concepts of Intermediation and the Origin of Gnosticism.* Tübingen: Mohr, 1985.

Fox, R. L. *Pagans and Christians.* New York: Knopf, 1989.

Friesen, S. *Twice Neokoros: Ephesus, Asia, and the Cult of Flavian Imperial Family.* Leiden: Brill, 1993.

Gamble, H. Y. *Books and Readers in the Early Church: A History of Early Christian Texts.* New Haven: Yale University Press, 1995.

Garnsey, P. *Famine and Food Supply in the Graeco-Roman World.* Cambridge: Cambridge University Press, 1988.

———. *Social Status and Legal Privilege in the Roman Empire.* Oxford: Oxford University Press, 1970.

Garnsey, P., and R. Saller. *The Roman Empire: Economy, Society, Culture.* Berkeley: University of California Press, 1987.

Gärtner, B. *The Areopagus Speech and Natural Revelation.* Lund: C. W. K. Gleerup, 1955.

Gaventa, B. R. *From Darkness to Light: Aspects of Conversion in the New Testament.* Philadelphia: Fortress, 1986.

Goodman, M. *The Ruling Class of Judaea.* Cambridge: Cambridge University Press, 1987.

Grant, M. *The Ancient Historians.* New York: Scribners, 1970.

———. *Saint Peter.* New York: Scribners, 1994.

Griffin, M. T. *Nero: The End of a Dynasty.* New Haven: Yale University Press, 1985.

Grudem, W. *The Gift of Prophecy in 1 Corinthians.* Washington: University Press, 1982.

Hägg, T. *Narrative Technique in Ancient Greek Romances.* Stockholm: Almquist and Wiksell, 1971.

Hands, A. R. *Charities and Social Aid in Greece and Rome.* Ithaca: Cornell University Press, 1968.

Harnack, A. Von. *Luke the Physician.* London: Williams and Norgate, 1907.

Hauser, H. J. *Strukturen der Abschlusserzählung der Apostelgeschichte (Apg. 28,16-31).* Rome: Pontifical Institute Press, 1979.

Hawkins, J. H. *Horae Synopticae.* Oxford: Clarendon Press, 1909.

Hemer, C. *The Book of Acts in the Setting of Hellenistic History.* Winona Lake: Eisenbrauns, 1990.

Hengel, M. *Acts and the History of Earliest Christianity.* London: SCM, 1979.

———. *Between Jesus and Paul.* Philadelphia: Fortress, 1983.

———. *The Hellenization of Judaea in the First Century after Christ.* Philadelphia: Trinity, 1989.

———. *The Pre-Christian Paul.* Philadelphia: Trinity, 1991.

Hengel, M., and A. M. Schwemer. *Paul between Damascus and Antioch.* Louisville: Westminster/J. Knox, 1997.

Hill, C. C. *Hellenists and Hebrews: Reappraising Division within the Earliest Church.* Minneapolis: Fortress, 1992.

Hobart, W. K. *The Medical Language of St. Luke.* London: Longmans Green, 1882.

Hock, R. F. *The Social Context of Paul's Ministry.* Philadelphia: Fortress, 1980.

Hodges, Z. C., and A. W Farstad. *The Greek New Testament according to the Majority Text.* Nashville: Broadman, 1982.

Hooker, M. D. *Jesus and the Servant: The Influence of the Servant Concept of Deutero-Isaiah in the New Testament.* London: SPCK, 1959.

Horsley, G. A. R. *New Documents Illustrating Early Christianity,* vols. 1-7. North Ryde: Macquarrie University, 1981-96.

Hull, J. M. *Hellenistic Magic and the Synoptic Tradition.* Naperville: Allenson, 1974.

Janson, T. *Latin Prose Prefaces.* Stockholm: Almquist and Wiksell, 1964.

Jeremias, J. *Jerusalem in the Times of Jesus.* Philadelphia: Fortress, 1989.

―――. *Unknown Sayings of Jesus.* London: SCM, 1957.

Jervell, J. *Luke and the People of God.* Minneapolis: Augsburg, 1972.

―――. *The Unknown Paul.* Minneapolis: Augsburg, 1984.

Jewett, R. *A Chronology of Paul's Life.* Philadelphia: Fortress, 1979.

Johnson, S. E. *Paul the Apostle and His Cities.* Wilmington: Glazier, 1987.

Jones, A. H. M. *The Criminal Courts of the Roman Republic and Empire.* Oxford: Oxford University Press, 1972.

―――. *Documents Illustrating the Reigns of Augustus and Tiberius.* Oxford: Clarendon Press, 1949.

―――. *Studies in Roman Government and Law.* Oxford: Basil Blackwell, 1960.

Judge, E. A. *Rank and Status in the World of the Caesars and St. Paul.* Christchurch: University of Canterbury, 1982.

―――. *The Social Pattern of Christian Groups in the First Century.* London: Tyndale, 1960.

Kee, H. C. *Good News to the Ends of the Earth.* Philadelphia: Trinity, 1990.

―――. *Miracle in the Early Christian World.* New Haven: Yale University Press, 1983.

Keener, C. *Bible Background Commentary.* Downers Grove: InterVarsity, 1993.

Kemmler, D. W. *Faith and Human Reason: A Study of Paul's Method of Preaching as Illustrated by 1-2 Thessalonians and Acts 17,2-4.* Leiden: Brill, 1975.

Kennedy, G. A. *New Testament Interpretation through Rhetorical Criticism.* Chapel Hill: University of North Carolina Press, 1984.

Kenyon, F. G. *Books and Readers in Ancient Greece and Rome.* Oxford: Clarendon Press, 1951.

Kilgallen, J. *The Stephen Speech: A Literary and Redactional Study of Acts 7,2-53.* Rome: Pontifical Biblical Institute Press, 1976.

Kim, S. *The Origin of Paul's Gospel.* Grand Rapids: Eerdmans, 1981.

Krantz, E. S. *Des Schiffes Weg mitten im Meer: Beiträge zur Erforschung der nautischen Terminologie des Alten Testament.* Lund: Gleerup, 1982.

Kratz, R. *Rettungswunder.* Frankfurt: Peter Lang, 1979.

Kümmel, W. G. *Introduction to the New Testament.* 2d ed. Nashville: Abingdon, 1975.

Lake, K. *The Earliest Epistles of Paul*. London: Hodder, 1930.

Lampe, P. *Die stadrömischen Christen in den ersten beiden Jahrhunderten*. Tübingen: Mohr, 1987.

Lentz, J. C. *Luke's Portrait of Paul*. Cambridge: Cambridge University Press, 1993.

Levick, B. *Claudius*. New Haven: Yale University Press, 1990.

———. *Roman Colonies in Southern Asia Minor*. Oxford: Clarendon Press, 1967.

Levinskaya, I. *The Book of Acts in Its Diaspora Setting*. Vol. 5 of AIIFCS. Grand Rapids: Eerdmans, 1996.

Litfin, D. F. *St. Paul's Theology of Proclamation*. Cambridge: Cambridge University Press, 1994.

Loening, K. *Die Saulustradition in der Apostelgeschichte*. Münster: Aschendorff, 1973.

Long, W. R. "The Trial of Paul in the Book of Acts: History, Literary, and Theological Considerations." Ph.D. diss., Brown University, 1982.

Lövestam, E. *Son and Saviour: A Study of Acts 13,32-37. With an Appendix: 'Son of God' in the Synoptic Gospels*. Lund: Gleerup, 1961.

Lüdemann, G. *Early Christianity according to the Traditions in Acts*. Minneapolis: Fortress, 1989.

———. *Paul, Apostle to the Gentiles: Studies in Chronology*. Philadelphia: Fortress, 1984.

Lyons, G. *Pauline Autobiography: Toward a New Understanding*. Atlanta: Scholars Press, 1985.

MacMullen, R. *Enemies of the Roman Order: Treason, Unrest, and Alienation in the Empire*. Cambridge: Harvard University Press, 1966.

———. *Paganism in the Roman Empire*. New Haven: Yale University Press, 1981.

———. *Roman Social Relations, 50 B.C. to A.D. 284*. New Haven: Yale University Press 1974.

Maddox, R. *The Purpose of Luke-Acts*. Edinburgh: T & T Clark, 1982.

Magie, D. *Roman Rule in Asia Minor to the End of the Third Century after Christ*. 2 vols. Princeton: Princeton University Press, 1950.

Malherbe, A. *Paul and the Popular Philosophers*. Minneapolis: Fortress, 1989.

Martin, D. B. *The Corinthian Body*. New Haven: Yale University Press, 1995.

Mason, S. *Josephus and the New Testament*. Peabody: Hendrickson, 1992.

Mattill, A. J. *Luke and the Last Things: A Perspective for the Understanding of Lukan Thought*. Dillsboro: Western N.C. Press, 1979.

McKnight, S. *A Light among the Gentiles: Jewish Missionary Activity in the Second Temple Period*. Minneapolis: Fortress, 1991.

Meeks, W. A. *The First Urban Christians: The Social World of the Apostle Paul*. New Haven: Yale University Press, 1983.

Meeks, W. A., and R. L. Wilken. *Jews and Christians in Antioch in the First Four Centuries.* Missoula: Scholars Press, 1978.

Meier, J. *A Marginal Jew: Rethinking the Historical Jesus.* Vols. 1 and 2. New York: Doubleday, 1991, 1994.

Mellor, R. *Tacitus.* London: Routledge, 1993.

Metzger, B. M. *A Textual Commentary on the Greek New Testament.* London: United Bible Society, 1971.

Meyer, B. F. *The Early Christians: Their World Mission and Self Discovery.* Wilmington: Glazier, 1986.

Millar, F. *The Roman Near East, 31* B.C.–A.D. *337.* Cambridge: Harvard University Press, 1993.

Mitchell, M. M. *Paul and the Rhetoric of Reconciliation.* Tübingen: Mohr, 1991.

Mitchell, S. *Anatolia: Land, Men, and Gods in Asia Minor.* Vol. 1, *The Celts in Anatolia and the Impact of Roman Rule.* Oxford: Clarendon Press, 1993.

Momigliano, A. *The Development of Greek Biography.* Cambridge: Harvard University Press, 1971.

Morgenthaler, R. *Lukas und Quintilian. Rhetorik als Erzählkunst.* Zürich: Gotthelf Verlag, 1993.

Murphy-O'Connor, J. *Paul: A Critical Life.* Oxford: Oxford University Press, 1996.

Murray, G. *Five Stages of Greek Religion.* Garden City: Doubleday, 1955.

Newman, B. M., and E. A. Nida. *A Translator's Handbook on the Acts of the Apostles.* London: UBS, 1972.

Nock, A. D. *Conversion: The Old and New in Religion from Alexander the Great to Augustine of Hippo.* Reprint, Oxford: Oxford University Press, 1961.

———. *Essays on Religion and the Ancient World I and II.* Harvard: Harvard University Press, 1972.

———. *St. Paul.* London: Butterworth, 1938.

Nolland, J. L. "Luke's Readers: A Study of Luke 4.22-28; Acts 13.46; 18.6; 28.28 and Luke 21.5-36." D.Phil. diss., Cambridge University, 1977.

Ogg, G. *The Odyssey of Paul.* Old Tappan: Fleming Revell, 1968.

Oglivie, R. M. *The Romans and Their Gods in the Age of Augustus.* New York: Norton, 1969.

Ollrog, W.-H. *Paulus und die seine Mitarbeiter.* Neukirchen: Neukirchen Verlag, 1978.

Oster, R. E. *A Bibliography of Ancient Ephesus.* Metuchen: Scarecrow Press, 1987.

O'Toole, R. *The Christological Climax of Paul's Defense.* Rome: Biblical Institute Press, 1978.

Parker, D. C. *Codex Bezae, An Early Christian Manuscript and Its Text.* Cambridge: Cambridge University Press, 1992.

Parks, E. P. *The Roman Rhetorical Schools as a Preparation for the Courts under the Early Empire.* Baltimore: Johns Hopkins University Press, 1945.

Parsons, M., and R. Pervo. *Rethinking the Unity of Luke and Acts.* Minneapolis: Fortress, 1990.

Pereira, F. *Ephesus: Climax of Universalism in Luke-Acts — A Redaction Critical Study of Paul's Ephesian Ministry.* Amand, India: Gujarat Sahitya Prakash, 1983.

Perry, B. E. *The Ancient Romances.* Berkeley: University of California, 1967.

Pervo, R. I. *Profit with Delight: The Literary Genre of the Acts of the Apostles.* Philadelphia: Fortress, 1987.

Peterman, G. W. "Giving and Receiving in Paul's Epistles." D.Phil. thesis, King's College, London, 1992.

Plümacher, E. *Lukas als hellenistischer Schriftsteller: Studien zur Apostel-geschichte.* Göttingen: Vandenhoeck and Ruprecht, 1972.

Preisendanz, K. *Papyri graecae magicae: Die griechischen Zauberpapyri.* 2 vols. Leipzig and Berlin: Teubner, 1928, 1931.

Pummer, R. *The Samaritans.* Leiden: Brill, 1987.

Radl, W. *Paulus und Jesus im lukanischen Doppelwerk: Untersuchungen zu Par-allelmotiven im Lukasevangelium und in der Apostelgeschichte.* Frankfurt: P. Lang, 1975.

Ramsay, W. M. *The Bearing of Recent Discovery on the Trustworthiness of the New Testament.* London: Hodder, 1920.

————. *Cities of Paul.* Reprint, Minneapolis: James Family Christian Pub., n.d.

————. *St. Paul the Traveller and the Roman Citzen.* London: Hodder and Stoughton, 1895.

Rapske, B. *Paul in Roman Custody.* Vol. 3 of AIIFCS. Grand Rapids: Eerdmans, 1994.

Rawson, B., ed. *The Family in Ancient Rome: New Perspectives.* London: Croom Helm, 1986.

Reardon, B. P. *The Form of the Greek Romance.* Princeton: Princeton University Press, 1991.

Reimer, I. Richter. *Women in the Acts of the Apostles.* Minneapolis: Fortress, 1996.

Reinach, S. *Jewish Coins.* Chicago: Argonaut, 1966.

Reynolds, J., and R. Tannebaum. *Jews and Godfearers at Aphrodisias.* Cambridge: Cambridge University Press, 1987.

Richards, E. *Acts 6.1–8.4: The Author's Method of Composition.* Missoula: Scholars Press, 1978.

Riesner, R. *Die Frühzeit des Apostels Paulus.* Tübingen: Mohr, 1994.

Saldarini, A. J. *Pharisees, Scribes, and Sadducees.* Wilmington: M. Glazier, 1988.

Saller, R. P. *Personal Patronage under the Empire.* Cambridge: Cambridge University Press, 1982.

Sanders, E. P. *Judaism: Practice and Belief, 63 B.C.E.–66 C.E.* Philadelphia: Trinity, 1992.

Sanders, J. T. *The Jews in Luke-Acts.* London: SCM, 1987.

Scharlemann, M. *Stephen: A Singular Saint.* Rome: Pontifical Biblical Institute Press, 1968.

Schürer, E. *The History of the Jewish People in the Age of Jesus Christ (175 B.C.–A.D. 135).* Vols. 1–3.2. Revised and edited by G. Vermes et al. Edinburgh: T & T Clark, 1973-87.

Scobie, C. H. J. *John the Baptist.* Philadelphia: Fortress, 1964.

Scott, K. *The Imperial Cult under the Flavians.* Stuttgart-Berlin, 1936.

Seesemann, H. *Der Begriff Koinonia im Neuen Testament.* Giessen: Töpelmann, 1933.

Segal, A. *Paul the Convert: The Apostolate and Apostasy of Saul the Pharisee.* New Haven: Yale University Press, 1990.

Seim, T. K. *The Double Message: Patterns of Gender in Luke and Acts.* Nashville: Abingdon, 1994.

Seters, J. Van. *In Search of History: Historiography in the Ancient World and the Origins of Biblical History.* New Haven: Yale University Press, 1983.

Shanks, H. *In the Temple of Solomon and the Tomb of Caiaphas.* Washington: BAS, 1993.

Sheely, S. M. *Narrative Asides in Luke-Acts.* Sheffield: JSOT, 1992.

Sherk, R. K. *The Roman Empire: Augustus to Hadrian.* Cambridge: Cambridge University Press, 1988.

Sherwin-White, A. N. *The Roman Citizenship.* Oxford: Oxford University Press, 1939.

―――. *Roman Law and Roman Society.* Reprint, Grand Rapids: Baker, 1992.

Smallwood, E. M. *Documents Illustrating the Principates of Gaius, Claudius, and Nero.* Cambridge: Cambridge University Press, 1967.

―――. *The Jews under Roman Rule: From Pompey to Diocletian.* Leiden: Brill, 1976.

Smith, J. *The Voyage and Shipwreck of St. Paul.* 4th ed. Reprint, Grand Rapids: Baker, 1978.

Snowden, F. M. *Before Color Prejudice: The Ancient View of Blacks.* Cambridge: Harvard University Press, 1983.

―――. *Blacks in Antiquity: Ethiopians in the Graeco-Roman Experience.* Cambridge: Harvard University Press, 1970.

Soards, M. *The Speeches in Acts: Their Content, Context, and Concerns.* Louisville: Westminster/J. Knox, 1994.

Söder, R. *Die apokryphen Apostelgeschichten und die romanhafte Literatur der Antike.* Stüttgart: Kohlhammer, 1932.

Soren, D., and J. James. *Kourion: The Search for a Lost Roman City.* New York: Doubleday, 1988.

Spencer, F. Scott. *The Portrait of Philip in Acts: A Study of Roles and Relations.* Sheffield: JSOT Press, 1992.

Squires, J. T. *The Plan of God in Luke-Acts.* Cambridge: Cambridge University Press, 1993.

Stanton, G. N. *Jesus of Nazareth in New Testament Preaching.* Cambridge: Cambridge University Press, 1974.

Stark, R. *The Rise of Christianity.* Princeton: Princeton University Press, 1996.

Steck, O. H. *Israel und das gewaltsame Geschick der Propheten.* Neukirchen-Vluyn: Neukirchener, 1967.

Sterling, G. E. *Historiography and Self-Definition: Josephos, Luke-Acts, and Apologetic Historiography.* Leiden: Brill, 1992.

Stonehouse, N. B. *Paul before the Areopagus and Other New Testament Studies.* Grand Rapids: Eerdmans, 1957.

Strange, W. A. *The Problem of the Text of Acts.* Cambridge: Cambridge University Press, 1992.

Tajara, H. W. *The Martyrdom of St. Paul.* Tübingen: Mohr, 1994.

———. *The Trial of Paul.* Tübingen: Mohr, 1989.

Talbert, C. H. *Literary Patterns, Theological Themes, and the Genre of Luke-Acts.* SBLMS 20. Missoula: Scholars Press, 1974.

———. *What Is a Gospel? The Genre of the Canonical Gospels.* Philadelphia: Fortress, 1977.

Tannehill, R. *The Narrative Unity of Luke-Acts: A Literary Interpretation.* Vols. 1 and 2. Minneapolis: Fortress, 1986, 1990.

Tarn, W. W., and G. W. Griffith. *Hellenistic Civilisation.* 3d ed. London: Arnold, 1952.

Theissen, G. *The Miracle Stories of the Early Christian Tradition.* Philadelphia: Fortress, 1983.

Thornton, C. J. *Der Zeuge des Zeugen, Lukas als Historiker der Paulusreisen.* Tübingen: Mohr, 1991.

Trebilco, P. *Jewish Communities in Asia Minor.* Cambridge: Cambridge University Press, 1991.

Trocme, E. *Le 'Livre des Acts' et L'Histoire.* Paris: University of France Press, 1957.

Trompf, G. W. *The Idea of Historical Recurrence in Western Thought.* Berkeley: University of California Press, 1979.

Tyson, J. B. *Images of Judaism in Luke-Acts.* Columbia: University of South Carolina Press, 1992.

Unnik, W. C. van. *Tarsus or Jerusalem: The City of Paul's Youth.* Translated by G. Ogg. London: Epworth Press, 1962.

Usher, S. *The Historians of Greece and Rome.* London: Duckworth, 1985.

Vermes, G. *Jesus the Jew.* Philadelphia: Fortress, 1973.

Walaskay, P. W. *"And So We Came to Rome": The Political Perspective of St. Luke.* Cambridge: Cambridge University Press, 1983.

Wallace-Hadrill, D. S. *Christian Antioch: A Study of Christian Thought in the East.* Cambridge: Cambridge University Press, 1982.

Walters, E. J. *Attic Grave Reliefs That Represent Women in the Dress of Isis. Hesperia.* Supplement 22. Princeton: American School of Classical Studies, 1988.

Wankel, H., et al. *Die Inschriften von Ephesos; Inschriften griechischen Städte aus Kleinasien 11.1–17.4.* Bonn: R. Habelt, 1979-84.

Weatherly, J. A. *Jewish Responsibility for the Death of Jesus in Luke-Acts.* Sheffield: Sheffield Academic Press, 1994.

Wehnert, J. *Der Wir-Passagen der Apostelgeschichte: Ein lukanisches Stilmittel aus jüdischen Tradition.* Göttingen: Vandenhoeck and Ruprecht, 1989.

White, L. M. *Building God's House in the Roman World.* Baltimore: Johns Hopkins University Press, 1990.

Wilson, A. N. *Paul: The Mind of the Apostle.* New York: Norton, 1997.

Wilson, B. R. *Magic and Millennium: A Sociological Study of Religious Movements.* New York: Harper and Row, 1973.

Wilson, S. G. *The Gentiles and the Gentile Mission in Luke-Acts.* Cambridge: Cambridge University Press, 1973.

———. *Luke and the Law.* Cambridge: Cambridge University Press, 1983.

———. *Luke and the Pastoral Epistles.* London: SPCK, 1979.

Winter, B. W. *Seek the Welfare of the City: Christians as Benefactors and Citizens.* Grand Rapids: Eerdmans, 1994.

Witherington, B. III. *The Christology of Jesus.* Philadelphia: Fortress, 1990.

———. *Jesus, Paul, and the End of the World.* Downers Grove: InterVarsity, 1992.

———. *JesusQuest: The Third Search for the Historical Jesus.* Downers Grove: InterVarsity, 1995.

———. *Jesus the Sage: The Pilgrimage of Wisdom.* Minneapolis: Fortress, 1994.

———. *Paul's Narrative Thought World: The Tapestry of Tragedy and Triumph.* Louisville: Westminster/J. Knox, 1994.

———. *Women in the Earliest Churches.* Cambridge: Cambridge University Press, 1988.

———. *Women in the Ministry of Jesus.* Cambridge: Cambridge University Press, 1984.

Witherup, R. D. *Conversion in the New Testament.* Collegeville: Liturgical Press, 1994.

Woodman, A. J. *Rhetoric in Classical Historiography.* London: Croom Helm, 1988.

Zehnle, R. F. *Peter's Pentecost Discourse.* Nashville: Abingdon, 1971.

Commentaries

Barrett, C. K. *A Critical and Exegetical Commentary on the Acts of the Apostles.* Vol. 1. Edinburgh: T & T Clark, 1994.

Boismard, M. E., and A. Lamouille, *Les Actes des deux Apôtres.* New York: Norton, 1990.

Bruce, F. F. *The Acts of the Apostles.* 3d ed. Grand Rapids: Eerdmans, 1990.

————. *The Book of Acts.* Grand Rapids: Eerdmans, 1988.

Conzelmann, H. *Acts of the Apostles.* Philadelphia: Fortress, 1987.

Dunn, J. D. G. *The Acts of the Apostles.* Valley Forge: Trinity Press, 1996.

Fitzmyer, J. A. *The Gospel according to Luke I–IX.* Garden City: Doubleday, 1981.

Foakes-Jackson, F. J. *The Acts of the Apostles.* London: Hodder, 1931.

Haenchen, E. *The Acts of the Apostles.* Philadelphia: Westminster, 1971.

Hanson, R. P. C. *The Acts of the Apostles.* Oxford: Oxford University Press, 1967.

Johnson, L. T. *The Acts of the Apostles.* Collegeville: Glazier, 1992.

————. *The Gospel of Luke.* Collegeville: Liturgical Press, 1991.

Larkin, W. J. *Acts.* Downers Grove: InterVarsity, 1995.

Longenecker, R. N. *The Acts of the Apostles.* In *The Expositor's Bible Commentary,* vol. 9, general editor F. E. Gabelein, pp. 207-573. Grand Rapids: Zondervan, 1981.

Marshall, I. H. *The Acts of the Apostles.* Grand Rapids: Eerdmans, 1980.

————. *The Gospel of Luke.* Exeter: Paternoster Press, 1978.

Munck, J. *The Acts of the Apostles.* Revised by W. F. Albright and C. S. Mann. New York: Doubleday, 1967.

Nolland, J. *Luke 1–9:20.* Waco: Word, 1989.

Pesch, R. *Die Apostelgeschichte (1–12).* Zurich: Benziger, 1986.

————. *Die Apostelgeschichte (Apg. 13–28).* Zurich: Benziger, 1986.

Polhill, J. P. *The Acts of the Apostles.* Nashville: Broadman, 1992.

Roloff, J. *Die Apostelgeschichte.* Göttingen: Vandenhoeck, 1981.

Schneider, G. *Die Apostelgeschichte I.* Freiburg: Herder, 1980.

————. *Die Apostelgeschichte II.* Freiburg: Herder, 1982.

Williams, D. J. *Acts.* San Francisco: Harper, 1985.

Witherington, B. *Conflict and Community in Corinth.* Grand Rapids: Eerdmans, 1995.

————. *Friendship and Finances in Philippi.* Valley Forge: Trinity Press, 1994.

————. *Grace in Galatia.* Edinburgh: T & T Clark, 1997.

The Acts of the Apostles: An Introduction

Acts is one of the most interesting and puzzling books in the New Testament.[1] On the one hand it seems to be a simple chronological account of what happened to the church between Jesus' ascension and Paul's arrival in Rome, that is, roughly between A.D. 30 and A.D. 60. It is the only document in the NT that appears to be attempting a historical record of the time after Jesus' life, but it does not even carry us up to the end of Paul's life (probably in Rome in 64-68) or up to the destruction of Jerusalem in 70. We have no similar historical record at all about the last third of the first century when the church moved on beyond the lifetime of the eyewitnesses. Acts then, from our later perspective, seems to be about the *beginnings* of the Christian movement as it spread from Jerusalem to other parts of the Roman Empire, and it may not be intended to be more than the open-ended document Acts 28 suggests it is (see below). If you go to Acts to answer all of the later questions about infant baptism, church order, or apostles after the first generation, you will be frustrated because of a lack of complete, and sometimes any, answers. Luke's agenda was not ours.

In modern scholarship Luke has been a battlefield or "storm center" because of the difficult questions it raises.[2] What shall we make of the fact that a fourth or more of Acts (at least some 365 verses) is made up of speeches most of which the author apparently was not present to hear?[3] Why are so many things

---

1. For a brief bibliographic guide to the study of Acts, see Marshall, *Acts.*

2. Two useful surveys of the questions Acts raises are van Unnik, "Luke-Acts, A Storm Center," and Jervell, "Retrospect and Prospect." On the history of the interpretation of Acts see Gasque, *History of the Interpretation.*

3. The definitive study in English of all the speech material in Acts is now Soards, *The Speeches in Acts.*

repeated in Acts in what obviously is a brief and selective account (e.g., Paul's conversion and the Cornelius episode are both repeated in varying forms)? If Luke's purpose is history in this document, why do we have so few chronological points of reference? Why is it that Peter fades out of the picture after Acts 15? Why is it that after Acts 9 we largely get the story of the expansion of the church by Paul, so that some have even wrongly dubbed this book the Acts of Paul?

Certainly the author isn't attempting to provide a record of the acts of *all* the apostles, and thus its traditional title is a misnomer. Indeed, Acts's latter half is preoccupied with the events and mission work and trials of a person who is only in *one* narrative even *called* an apostle (Acts 14:4, 14), and even that reference is debated.

Why is it that so many things important in Paul's letters, such as the Judaizers and the collection, are apparently omitted here? Why is it that one-fourth of this book is devoted to Paul's trial when we are not even told the outcome? Why is it that the Paul of Acts has so often struck scholars as a different Paul from the Paul of the letters? To say Acts raises as many questions as it answers is putting it mildly.

I have no delusions about being able to answer all the difficult questions about Acts in this commentary, but I do hope to bring to bear some of the fresh light that has been shed on this complex work by recent studies by scholars of ancient history, rhetoric, the classics, social developments, and other related matters, as well as dealing with various of the traditional exegetical matters. I believe a reasonably coherent picture of the nature and meaning of Acts emerges from these recent endeavors which helps us to understand much not only about the time of the author of Acts but also the times that on the face of it he chronicles. We must begin this study by dealing immediately with some of the thorny background and foreground issues the Acts of the Apostles raises, perhaps the thorniest of which is the issue of the genre and character of Luke's work.

I. Acts and the Question of Genre

The discussion of the genre of the Acts of the Apostles has taken many turns in the twentieth century. Are we dealing with some sort of Hellenistic historical monograph, or should Acts, especially the concluding sea travel adventures of Paul, be evaluated in light of ancient romances?[4] Could Acts be seen as some

---

4. On the latter cf. Pervo, *Profit with Delight,* and see the helpful critique by Soards in *JAAR,* and also by Brosend, "The Means of Absent Ends," in *History, Literature, and Society,* ed. B. Witherington, pp. 348-62.

sort of biographical narrative, or perhaps as a scientific treatise? All these suggestions have in common the basic assumption that Acts must be evaluated in light of ancient literary conventions, rather than modern ones. This assumption is surely correct, especially in light of the prefaces we find at Luke 1:1-4 and Acts 1:1-2, which sound so much like the prefaces in various other ancient works (see below). Accordingly, we will begin our genre discussion by examining these prefaces closely.

It should be said from the outset, however, that whatever Luke may *claim* in these prefaces, these claims must be evaluated in light of the character of the data that follow them. It often happened in antiquity that writers like Josephus would insist in their prefaces that their accounts were true and unembellished (cf. *Jewish Wars* 1.1-2), but on closer inspection we discover that Josephus's account, while containing much valuable historical data, must be evaluated critically because it is intended as a propaganda piece, attempting to rehabilitate the image of at least some Jews in the eyes of non-Jews in the Roman Empire, as well as attempting to reconcile Jews to the notion that God had destined the Romans to rule over them at this juncture in history.[5]

Whenever twentieth-century persons use the word "history," they normally think of either the events of the *past*, often the distant past, or the record of those events. It is also often taken for granted that a certain distance in time or space from one's subject is required if one is to present an "objective" account. This definition, however, is far too narrow if the subject is the study of ancient historiography where monographs on contemporary events or events of only the previous generation were common and the word ιστορια referred to "investigation," often of happenings that were still having immediate effects or were in the process of being completed.

Thus, history writing in antiquity, at least in the monograph as opposed to the universal history form, was often more like a newspaper chronicling current or recent events than a modern history book. According to Luke 1:1-4, the author does not propose to chronicle the events of hoary antiquity but rather the "events that have been fulfilled among us," but this would not distinguish him from ancient historians.

---

5. See Zeitlin, "A History of Jewish Historiography," on Josephus's tendentiousness and his free invention of speeches. Nevertheless, Zeitlin stresses that on the basic *facts* about the Jewish War, Josephus is historically trustworthy (p. 205), while his interpretations are frequently misleading, sometimes deliberately so since this is a propaganda piece (see the continuation of the above article in *JQR* 60 [1969-70]: 37-68, here p. 66, where it is made clear that in his *Life* Josephus corrects various deliberately false impressions left in his earliest work). All of this must be borne in mind when we begin to evaluate Acts at places where it refers to the same persons or facts as Josephus does (e.g., the Theudas affair). Cf. the discussion of Luke and Josephus, pp. 235-39 below.

A. The Prefaces in Acts 1:1-2 and Luke 1:1-4

1. A Two-Volume Work or Two Works?

Almost every word of these prefaces has been closely scrutinized and debated at length, but before we may proceed along the path of exegesis we must first ask — Does Luke 1:1-4 have anything whatsoever to do with Acts, or are these verses only about the Gospel of Luke? To put it another way, are Luke and Acts two separate works that should be evaluated differently, or are they two volumes of one work that deserves to be called Luke-Acts or at least spoken of in the same breath as Luke and Acts?

It is evident from texts like Heb. 2:3b-4 that it was possible for early Christians to conceive of their own era as a continuation of what happened during the ministry of Jesus, for the author of that document states about the good news of salvation: "It was declared at first through the Lord, and it was attested to us by those who heard him, while God added his testimony by signs and wonders and various miracles, and by gifts of the Holy Spirit, distributed according to his will."[6] But did Luke undertake the project of providing a continuous narrative of what has been called "salvation history" from the coming of Jesus through the early years of the Christian movement?[7]

Admittedly the Gospel of Luke *can* be read as an independent narrative, one Gospel among several attempts at Gospel writing, which reaches an appropriate closure in Luke 24 with the blessing of the disciples, the ascension of Jesus, and the return of the disciples to Jerusalem and the temple where they give thanks to God for what God has done through Jesus. In some respects this closure resembles that in the Gospel of Matthew, though the settings are obviously different.[8] Because the Gospel of Luke *can* stand on its own as a complete narrative, it surely cannot be evaluated as a *mere* preface to the Acts of the Apostles.[9] This, however, does not settle the question of whether Acts can and should be seen as a proper *sequel* to the Gospel of Luke, and so the second volume of a two-volume work that has considerable continuity of themes, structure, style, and perspective throughout the work.[10] The issue here is not whether Luke's Gospel can be seen as a distinguishable volume from

6. The implications of this text for the study of Acts were first noted by van Unnik, "The 'Book of Acts.'"

7. On Luke's presentation of salvation history see now the helpful updated survey in Jervell, "The Future of the Past."

8. Some of the parallels would include: (1) an appearance of Jesus to the disciples that brings closure to their earthly relationships; (2) the reference to worship; (3) a commissioning, either given or implied.

9. Cf. Barrett, "The Third Gospel."

10. See the helpful detailed discussion in Talbert, *Literary Patterns*.

Acts which can stand on its own, because in fact it can. Luke 24 does bring a sort of closure to the Gospel, though it is also, like the ending of Acts, in some respects open-ended, implying the story continued.[11] The question is whether Acts was meant to be read with the "first book" in mind, and whether Luke wrote his first volume already having Acts in mind.[12]

We must be careful when we use the terminology *Luke-Acts* to make clear what sort of *unity* we have in mind by this term. Does the term *Luke-Acts* refer to authorial or compositional or narrative or generic or theological or thematic unity, or several of these sorts of unity all at once?[13]

The view that Luke and Acts were written by two different persons is not much discussed today by scholars because of the considerable linguistic, grammatical, thematic, and theological evidence that these volumes both come from the same hand. Most scholars in fact would argue for the theological and thematic similarity and unity of the two volumes.[14] R. Tannehill has argued at length for the narrative unity of these two volumes, in the sense that they are bound together by a consistent and continuous story pursuing a particular trajectory and sharing common themes and ideas.[15] There are in addition a variety of similar literary patterns in the two volumes, for example in the way the trial of Jesus and Paul is presented.[16] These similarities have created a presumption in the mind of many that there is also some sort of generic unity shared by Luke and Acts. In regard to the possibility of the compositional unity of Luke-Acts, it must be remembered that writing in antiquity had certain

11. Very few scholars would hold that Luke-Acts was originally only one volume, arbitrarily separated at a later time by the canonizing process, with an ending being tacked on to the Gospel and a beginning to Acts by some later ecclesiastical redactor.

12. Here I quite agree with Parsons and Pervo, *Rethinking the Unity*, p. 59. A distinguishable volume, however, does not need to suggest a fundamental generic or narrative or theological difference between the two volumes in terms of approach and character. Obviously the two works differ considerably in historical content.

13. See the way Parsons helpfully puts the matter in Parsons and Pervo, *Rethinking the Unity*, p. 7. One thing that is not clear from this study is that while Parsons and Pervo are willing to talk about Acts being a sequel to the Gospel of Luke, they do not make fully clear what this means if the two works do not share substantial unity at least in the narrative and theological dimensions of the work, and perhaps in the genre dimension as well.

14. Detailed arguments for the unity of Luke-Acts can be found in Trocme, *Le 'Livre des Acts' et L'Histoire;* see his conclusions in regard to Acts and historical matters, pp. 215ff.

15. Tannehill, *Narrative Unity of Luke-Acts,* vols. 1 and 2.

16. This is not to say that Luke is a slave to issues of symmetry. There are certainly considerable differences in content between Luke and Acts. For example, the Gospel has a good many parables, while Acts does not; instead, it has various set speeches. At the level of Greek style as well there are some differences, for example, in the use of τε as a connective in Acts in addition to καὶ and δε. See Parsons and Pervo, *Rethinking the Unity,* pp. 45ff. None of this negates the impressive amount of similarity between the two works both in form and in content.

constraints we do not face today. For one thing, literary texts did not circulate in the same fashion as they do today. They tended first to be sent to patrons or friends, who might have copies made of them for others. In other words, unless a manuscript was deliberately placed in one of the few great city libraries in antiquity, it normally had private circulation only. Occasionally an author would take a manuscript to a bookshop in a large city like Rome, which would make and sell copies, but we must not think in terms of modern publication methods.[17] The connection between Luke and Theophilus may be important in this regard, especially if Theophilus was Luke's patron (see below).

Another constraint faced by ancient writers like Luke was the length of composition one could get on a papyrus roll. The content of the Acts of the Apostles represents about the maximum one could include on one normal papyrus role writing in a medium-sized Greek script, following the normal procedure of leaving no gaps between words or sentences.[18] Papyrus rolls came in stock sizes with a normal maximum length of about forty feet. A thirty-foot roll could contain about one hundred columns of writing with thirty to forty lines per column and twenty characters per line. Luke's Gospel (19,404 words) would have fit on a thirty-five-foot roll and Acts (18,374 words) on a thirty-two-foot roll if he wrote in a normal hand and with normal spacing.[19]

The sheer length of his Gospel required Luke to round off the narrative *close to* the point where he did, though he could have included a few brief additional narratives of about the same length as the material in Luke 24.[20] What is clear enough is that Luke could never have included all of Luke and Acts on *one* papyrus roll, nor is it likely it was ever included in one codex,

17. Cf. Starr, "Circulation of Literary Texts," and Gamble, *Books and Readers,* pp. 1-81.

18. See Kenyon, *Books and Readers,* p. 64: "a roll of about 32-35 feet would hold, in a medium-sized hand, *one* of the longer books of the New Testament (Matthew, Luke, or Acts) . . . but no more." Kenyon, pp. 90ff., also shows that papyrus rolls were, even at the close of the first century A.D., the overwhelmingly dominant medium on which books were written. The suggestion that either Luke or Acts was produced first in codex form is unlikely, because the codex was only just coming into use and would have been expensive to procure.

19. See Aune, *New Testament,* p. 117.

20. There *would* surely have been room on the roll with this Gospel for a "succession list" if Luke had really been interested in writing a philosophical biography of Jesus and then following it with a brief mention of his successors, on analogy with the biography of Aristotle which concludes with such a succession list, or Diogenes Laertius's life of Zeno, which is followed by a brief narrative about his successors. The fact that Luke does not do this with his Gospel must tell against the suggestion of C. H. Talbert that Acts should be seen as the biography of Jesus' successors, in particular Peter and Paul (see his most recent effort at arguing this case, "The Acts of the Apostle"). For further arguments against Talbert's view cf. below, pp. 20ff. For other problems with seeing Luke-Acts as biographical in the tradition of the lives of the philosophers and their successors, cf. Alexander, "Acts and Ancient Intellectual Biography."

apart from other early Christian literature. Luke and Acts are respectively the longest and second longest compositions in the New Testament.

It is worth noting that the very dimensions of the two volumes suggest that Luke is following ancient Greek historiographical conventions. "Greco-Roman authors often tried to keep the size of books roughly symmetrical (Diodorus 1.29.6; 1.41.10; Josephus *Against Apion* 1.320)."[21] Furthermore, it is surely no accident that the first volume covers roughly the same amount of time (from about 4 B.C. to A.D. 30) as the second volume does (from about A.D. 30 to 60, or to 62 if one counts the reference to "two whole years" in Acts 28). There is also a certain symmetry in the fact that the last 23 percent of Luke's Gospel (19:28–24:53) presents the events leading to and including Jesus' trial(s), death, resurrection, and ascension while the last 24 percent of Acts (21:27–28:31) deals with Paul's arrest, trials, and arrival in Rome.[22] The question then becomes: Are there intimations in the Third Gospel, *apart* from the preface itself, that suggest Luke intended a sequel?

C. K. Barrett has assembled the evidence, and the overall impression it leaves suggests a positive answer to the question.[23] In particular, the promise of light for the Gentiles, indeed "all flesh," in Luke 2:32 and 3:6, and of help for various non-Jewish peoples implied in the paradigmatic speech of Jesus in Luke 4:24-27, is not truly brought to fulfillment before the book of Acts. Nor for that matter is the fulfillment of the promise in Luke 24 of "power from on high" for the disciples recorded in the Gospel; in view of how important the empowerment of the Holy Spirit is in the Lukan schema of things, it is hard to doubt he intended at some point to record this promise's fulfillment. There was space enough at the end of the roll to include at least some of the material in Acts 1–2 in his Gospel had Luke chosen to do so.[24] Another key foreshadowing comes at Luke 22:33 where Peter says he is prepared to go with Christ *to prison* and to death. The parallels in Matthew and Mark do not include the reference to prison, and "it is hard to resist the impression that this rendering of his words has been formulated with the incidents in Acts 4, 5 and especially 12 in mind."[25]

Furthermore, the Lukan form of the telling of the parable of the great dinner in Luke 14:15-24 likely alludes to the gathering in of Gentiles to the eschatological banquet. Then, too, we may point to the Lukan form of the prophecy in Luke 21:12-13, which speaks about the witness the disciples would

21. Aune, *New Testament,* p. 118.

22. Ibid., p. 119.

23. In his "The Third Gospel," pp. 1453ff.

24. Especially since some of the material in Luke 24 and Acts 1 about Jesus' ascension overlaps.

25. Marshall, *Acts,* p. 26.

bear, which should be compared to 24:48 where the disciples are informed they will be witnesses, a key theme which then is picked up in Acts 1:8. The fulfillment of Luke 21:12-13 is then portrayed in places like Acts 4:3; 5:18-25; 8:3; 12:1, 3-6; and 16:23.[26]

Equally telling is the omission of the material in Mark 7 about clean and unclean in the parallel passage in Luke's Gospel, only to see it come to light in Acts 10 with Peter. One could also point to the omission in the Lukan Passion narrative of the charge about Jesus attacking the temple found in Mark 14:58, a charge which nevertheless surfaces in Acts 6:14 in the accusations against Stephen.[27] Luke is a good and careful editor of his sources and does not wish to tread the same path twice if it can be avoided, unless there is some special point of emphasis he is pressing as with the three tellings of Saul's conversion.[28]

There are other telltale points in the Gospel that are picked up and further developed in Acts, such as the favorable attitude toward the Samaritans (cf. Luke 9:52-56; 17:11-19 to Acts 8), the idea that Judaism deserves a second chance (cf. Luke 13:6-9 to Paul's repeated returns to the synagogue in Acts), the role of women in the Jesus movement (cf. Luke 8:1-3 to Acts 16; 18; and passim),[29] and the clarification that John the Baptist was not the Messiah (cf. Luke 3:15 to Acts 13:25; 19:5).

A great deal more could be said along these lines, but this is sufficient to show that Luke planted some seeds in his Gospel that he did not intend to fully cultivate and bring to harvest before his second volume. In short, the first volume was likely written with at least one eye already on the sequel. In other words, there is indeed some sort of compositional unity to Luke-Acts, and this raises the question about the generic unity of the two volumes. This brings us back to the issue of the prefaces in Luke 1:1-4 and Acts 1:1-2.

2. The Meaning of the Acts Preface

Since our task in this commentary is to focus on Acts, we will begin with the preface to it. This preface would have been seen as a "secondary" preface in terms of both its form and its content. It conforms to the "table of contents" sort of prefaces used by Diodorus Siculus in his histories (cf. the beginnings of books 2 and 3).[30] What is interesting is that it refers *back* to the contents

---

26. See the helpful discussion in Soards, *The Speeches in Acts,* pp. 194-96.

27. See Sterling, *Historiography and Self-Definition,* pp. 335-36.

28. This is also shown by the fact that Luke avoids Markan doublets, leaving out the second round of feeding the masses (cf. Mark 8 to Luke 9).

29. On this whole matter cf. my *Women in the Ministry of Jesus* and my *Women in the Earliest Churches.*

30. See Sacks, "Lesser Prooemia of Diodorus Siculus."

of the previous volume or roll. The word πρωτος, meaning first, indicates there was only one prior document in this series, and that the author now proposes to give a second one.[31] This way of expressing the matter probably also suggests that Luke did not intend a third volume.[32]

Acts 1:1-2 is not a full-fledged preface but is rather resumptive, indicating a continuation.[33] It is rather like what one finds in Philo's *Quod Omn. Prob. Lib.* 1, where one reads in part ο μεν πρωτερος λογος ην, ο Θεοδοτε, περι του. . . . Luke's silence about predecessors at the beginning of the second volume may be significant, as it would seem to suggest that Luke knew of no previous attempts to do what he was going to do in his second volume.[34] This, however, does not suggest that Luke did not have a variety of sources both written and oral to draw on and edit in his second volume, as G. Lüdemann's careful work has shown.[35] Luke says in Acts 1:1-2 with typical rhetorical hyperbole that he covered in the first roll "everything" (περι παντων) which Jesus "did and taught."[36] This claim, however, is more than just a rhetorical flourish because, as D. P. Moessner points out, it suggests that Luke sees his first volume as aiming at comprehensiveness and completeness, qualities that were characteristic of the claims made about ancient historiography, in contrast to ancient biography which deliberately had a more limited scope and focus (cf. Lucian, *Historia* 55; Diodorus Siculus, *Library of History* 16.1).[37]

The verb ηρξατο, "began," may also suggest an ongoing concern with historical eras and their sequence. Even if this is overpressing this verb, it is surely no accident that the synchronisms in Luke's two volumes which connect John, Jesus, and/or their followers with important persons and events on the larger stage of political history (cf., e.g., Luke 2:1-2; Acts 4:5-6, 27) occur near the *beginning* of each volume, signaling the historiographical intent of the author to the audience. As D. Aune stresses, "Luke introduces the careers of

---

31. Bruce, *The Acts of the Apostles,* p. 97. Bruce also notes that λογος is used here for a division of a work that has more than one papyrus roll.

32. In other words, πρωτος indicates the first in a sequence of two. See Polhill, *Acts,* p. 79.

33. See Sterling, *Historiography and Self-Definition,* p. 331: "The reference back to the 'former book' and summary of its contents are the clear signs of a secondary preface . . . which presupposes an earlier prooemium." This practice of writing a secondary preface for a continuation of a work was common (cf. Diodorus Siculus 2.1.1-3; 3.1.1-3; 4.1.1-7).

34. So Barrett, *Luke the Historian,* p. 21. I would depart from Barrett's judgment (p. 27), however, that Luke was compelled to proceed along different lines in Acts due to a lack of formulated tradition. Cf. the following note, and also my article "Editing the Good News."

35. Cf. G. Lüdemann, *Early Christianity,* and below, pp. 105ff.

36. On the rhetorical device of overstatement *(amplificatio)* for the sake of effect used even by Thucydides, cf. Thucydides, *History* 2.65.2 and 9.

37. Cf. Moessner, "Re-Reading Talbert's Luke," p. 216 n. 29.

both John and Jesus with similar devices because his intentions are historical rather than biographical."[38]

It has often been suggested that the word ηρξατο intimates that Luke's second volume will be about what Jesus "continued" to do and teach through the apostles and by means of the Holy Spirit. On first blush this claim seems plausible, but the phrase in question probably should be taken simply to mean "what Jesus did and said."[39] For example, in Luke 4:21 we read, "But he began (ηρξατο) to say, 'Today this Scripture is fulfilled in your hearing.'" Does Luke really mean to say that Jesus started to say this but was interrupted, or more likely that he simply said it? The latter seems more plausible. I would suggest, then, that it is probably overpressing the verb ηρξατο to suggest that it means more than "he did and said" in Acts 1, or to suggest it implies continuation of the exact same subject in Acts.

In any case, in Acts 1:1-2 the stress is on the words and deeds as the things which changed and continued to change the course of history.[40] This stress would seem to signal the historiographic intent of the author of Luke-Acts. As Aristotle had put it long before the time of Luke, the task of history is to be concerned with human deeds or πραξεις (*Rhet.* 1.1360A.35). This was also the judgment of Luke's contemporary Quintilian, who says history is "the narration of deeds" (*gestae rei expositio; Inst. Or.* 2.4.2). Quintilian also clearly contrasted the historical narrative with tragedy and poetry, which he says are not only not true but also hardly resemble the truth. He also contrasts *historia* with comedies, which, though false, nonetheless have a certain verisimilitude (*vero simile*).[41]

The theory of Quintilian actually draws on a long tradition of Greek

---

38. Aune, *New Testament,* p. 133.

39. Furthermore, as Cadbury and Lake long ago noted in *The Beginnings of Christianity,* 4:3, the phrase may mean no more than εποιησε or εποιησαμην. The first volume was about what Jesus did and taught.

40. Earl, "Prologue-Form in Ancient Historiography," stresses that it was historical prologues that indicated the content of what followed in the first sentence. ". . . if a historian began his work with a formal prologue, then it was obligatory to set out his subject in the very first sentence" (p. 843). Notice that Luke in Acts 1:1 is referring back to the content of the first volume, which tells us something about how he viewed the first volume, as well as the second.

41. Nevertheless, this did not mean that history was not to be connected with rhetoric. The rhetor should look first to history for examples based in actual facts (cf. below). Sextus Empiricus (*Adv. gramm.* 266-68) is very clear that it is the duty of the rhetorician to articulate the principles of history writing. Cicero stresses that history more than any other genre is rhetoric's very own because it affords the opportunity for stylistic expression in both speeches and the account of deeds, and the rhetorical amplification of the subject matter so as to impress on the audience the significance and often the *pathos* of the subject matter (*opus unum hoc oratorium maxime,* cf. *De legibus* 1.1.1-2). See the discussion in Fornara, *History in Ancient Greece and Rome,* pp. 135-39.

historiography, and in particular on Polybius, who argued that the task of the historian was to teach and persuade the lover of knowledge by means of true deeds and speeches (2.56.11), which was the opposite of the tragedian, who was to frighten and charm by means of persuasive speech. As we shall see, Luke's preface in Luke 1:1-4 suggests he is far closer to Polybius than to various other ancient historians in his understanding that his job is to instruct and reassure Theophilus about the nature and meaning of the events (both words and deeds) that had happened "among us."

Lucian tells us that in a rhetorical speech or a work heavily influenced by rhetorical conventions (like encomiastic biographies) it was de rigueur to appeal for a favorable hearing and play to the audience, but in a historical work's preface one must attract the attention of one's audience by making clear that one's *subject matter* was historically important, essential, personally relevant, or useful to the hearer (53).[42]

If one takes both Acts 1:1 and Luke 1:1-4 at face value, they sound a good deal more like prefaces to a historical work than to some sort of encomium or biography.[43] W. C. van Unnik some time ago pointed out, "I wish to emphasize . . . Luke's use of the words διηγησιν περι των . . . πραγματων, because these are more or less technical terms in historiography, πραγματα being the facts about which the historian makes an orderly narrative whereas διηγησις expresses the activity of the historian that came after the collection of the material and by which he brought that material into the shape of a real history."[44] Luke does not suggest in either Luke 1:1-4 or Acts 1:1-2 that he sees it as his essential task to give pleasure, to entertain, to edify, or even in the main to encourage certain virtues, but rather he will recount important things that are of great relevance both to himself and to Theophilus, for they involve the fulfillment of divine promises.[45]

---

42. Earl, "Prologue-Form in Ancient Historiography," p. 856: "There were good practical reasons why rigid rules were observed as to the form of opening sentences in written works. The technique of ancient book production, the physical nature of the *volumen,* did not allow the reader easily to scan the body of the work to ascertain its subject. The first sentence and the first paragraph performed much of the function of the title page and list of contents in a modern codex. Hence, *the obligation to make quite clear in your first sentence at least what type of literature you were writing. . . .*" On the basis of Luke 1:1-4 alone, even attentive listeners would never guess that a biography might be following, but the term *pragmata* would certainly alert them that a record of deeds and events was forthcoming.

43. But on the latter see the unpersuasive arguments of Robbins, "Prefaces."

44. Van Unnik, "Luke's Second Book," p. 42.

45. See rightly Aune, *New Testament,* p. 121: "In fact, the phrase 'the *events* completed among us,' the subject of Luke's composition, indicates a *historical* rather than biographical focus, even though (following Hellenistic practice) prominent personalities dominate both books. Prefaces had long been conventional features of Greco-Roman historiography with

As A. Momigliano reminds us, the main emphasis of ancient historians during the Empire was on "the destruction of the past, on the emergence
of new institutions, habits, vices. Tacitus' historical books are entirely per-
vaded by this sense of change and by resignation to it."[46] Luke's second
volume, like his first, is *also* about social change, but unlike Tacitus, he
believes he is witnessing a change for the better, something to be reported
as good news. He does not look back with anger and longing, as do Tacitus
and other Roman historians who wrote during the Empire. The primary
provenance of a historian was to write about events that changed the world,
for better or for worse. It is not accidental that Luke's characteristic way of
speaking about Jesus' purpose in life is that he came "to preach the kingdom"
(Luke 4:43). What is striking about this Lukan way of putting the matter is
that it makes clear that the focus of Jesus' message was on events that
changed things, in particular on God's divine saving activity among human
beings (Luke 4:18). Luke, like Jesus, must focus on speaking about such
events.[47]

While Momigliano can find no Greek or Roman historian who positively
recommended social change, he has obviously overlooked Luke, whose chronicling of the effects of proclaiming the good news is precisely a chronicling of
change. Luke is not interested, like Tacitus, in informing his audience how they
can be reconciled to or live with inevitable or already extant change, but rather
he is providing historical perspective for Theophilus so he will see what it
means to be a part of such a religious change. Change is not seen as a problem
to be managed, but as a positive possibility to be embraced and understood
in its proper historical framework. All this must be kept steadily in view when
we examine Luke 1:1-4 in detail, and to this task we now turn.

3. The Meaning of Luke 1:1-4

The first and perhaps most striking thing to notice about Luke 1:1-4 is that
nowhere is Jesus, or Jesus' life (βιος), mentioned in these verses. Rather, Luke
1:1-4, like Acts 1:1-2, mentions a narration of deeds (and words). This is
especially important because in ancient prefaces the main subject that was to
be discoursed on was supposed to be indicated to the hearer in the opening
remarks. Ancient historical writing in Luke's age was influenced by rhetorical

---

a distinct constellation of traditional *topoi* or motifs (Lucian, *History* 23, 52-55). The *topoi*
which Luke uses include the dedication to Theophilus, the exaggerated mention of 'many'
predecessors . . . mention of eyewitness sources, emphasis on proper historical method and
accuracy, and concern with usefulness."

46. Momigliano, "Tradition and the Classical Historian," p. 283.
47. See Maddox, *The Purpose of Luke-Acts,* p. 133.

conventions, and these conventions indicate that the main subject to be treated should be announced at the outset.

On the showing of Luke 1:1-4 the hearer would expect a narrative (διηγησις) about the *things* (πραγματον) which have been accomplished or fulfilled (cf. below) "among us." "The use of 'things' in the plural is an odd way of referring simply to the life-story of one person. And the word 'fulfil' may also suggest more than simply the life of Jesus, the more especially since Jesus himself spoke of things that were yet to be fulfilled in the activity of his followers (Lk. 24.47-9).''[48] In other words, this is going to be a historical narrative about certain events and speech acts that others have written about previously.

As the original meaning of the term ιστορια suggests, a historical narrative is one that should be written after a careful "investigation." History is "the investigations (ιστοριαι) of those who write about *the deeds*" (Aristotle, *Rhetoric* 1.1360A.35). Luke's claims about investigation in Luke 1:1-4 suggest a historical narrative is to follow, and by describing and *explaining* a sequential development in Luke and Acts, not merely reporting it, he met the most essential requirement of Greek historiography already set forth in Herodotus's seminal work.[49]

Another obvious factor that closely links Luke 1:1-4 to the preface in Acts 1:1-2 is the mention of Theophilus. This was a common personal name in that era, used by both Jews and Gentiles.[50] Both these volumes are written *to him* (σοι).[51] He is characterized by the term χρατιστε, "most excellent," a term which likely indicates his social importance. Josephus uses it of his patron Epaphroditus in a preface (*Ap.* 1.1, cf. 2.1), and this adequately explains the usage in Luke 1:1 as well. Unconvincing is the argument that because Luke elsewhere uses χρατιστε when a Roman procurator is addressed (cf. Acts 23:26; 24:3; 26:25), Theophilus was also a Roman official. As the Josephus reference

48. Marshall, "Acts and the 'Former Treatise,' " p. 173.

49. See the discussion in Fornara, *History in Ancient Greece and Rome*, p. 16. Luke is like Herodotus in another essential regard as well — he chose to write what may be called theological historiography, something that was not characteristic of Thucydides and for the most part Polybius, who give scant attention to the divine and do not see it as an essential cause of the actions in the narrative. Cf. Fornara, p. 78 n. 36. It must also be kept steadily in view that in the middle of the first century A.D., Thucydides was rediscovered and set alongside the widely admired Polybius. This meant that there were at least two prominent influential Greek models for careful historiography by the time Luke was writing his work in the 70s or 80s (see Fornara, p. 138).

50. For the Jewish use, see Aristeas, *Ep. ad Philocraten* 49.

51. The way Luke 1:3 reads (σοι γραψαι) suggests a good deal more than that Luke is merely dedicating these volumes to Theophilus, pace Fitzmyer, *Luke I–IX*, p. 299. On patrons and their underwriting the cost of publication of volumes dedicated to them, cf. Cadbury, *The Making of Luke-Acts*, pp. 202-3.

shows, κράτιστε is not a technical term used only of such Roman officials; it is a status term indicating social importance, and Roman officials were not the only important persons in antiquity.[52] The book of Acts is surely *not* a brief for Paul written to a Roman official, for there is too much material in the first half of Acts which has little or nothing to do directly with Paul and his case.

We have noticed thus far the stress both in Acts 1:1-2 and in Luke 1:1-4 on actions, both words and deeds, which have had some significant effect. They are not just any sort of historically important actions but πεπληροφορη-μένων (Luke 1:1). Semantically there is a bit of difficulty in the use of this term, for strictly speaking we can understand what it would mean to say that Scriptures have been fulfilled, but events are not predictions or promises to be fulfilled; rather, they are accomplished or completed.[53] Accordingly, some commentators have preferred the translation "accomplished" here.[54] Yet in 2 Tim. 4:5 it can be said that a ministerial service is "fulfilled," and perhaps Luke is thinking of the ministers of the word fulfilling their duties of proclamation since he refers to them in v. 2. Furthermore, Luke elsewhere uses the synonym πληροῦν (Acts 19:21) in a closely similar fashion to speak of deeds. Luke 24:44 speaks of all *things* written in Scripture needing to be fulfilled (πληπωθῆναι). I thus conclude that Luke is using a form of shorthand here to speak of the salvation events, promised in Scripture, which have been fulfilled or accomplished during the era beginning with the coming of John the Baptist. This comports with the references in both volumes to the fulfillment of Scripture and other divine promises (cf., e.g., Luke 1:45; 4:21; Acts 2:16, 31). Luke will write the story about the crucial events which began the messianic age in which the Scriptures would be fulfilled.

4. A Scientific Treatise?

In a recent study, L. Alexander has compared the preface in Luke 1:1-4 to the prefaces of a variety of types of ancient documents and has concluded that Luke's preface(s) are closest to those found in scientific treatises.[55] The

---

52. Cf. Marshall, *Luke,* pp. 41-42.

53. There is, however, a certain parallel to the preface of Sallust in *Cat.* 4.2-3, where he says he will write about the accomplishments of the Roman people, but first dwells on the Cataline conspiracy which could hardly be called an accomplishment or something included under the heading of *res gestae.* See Palmer, "Acts and Ancient Historical Monograph," p. 9.

54. Cf., e.g., A. Plummer, *The Gospel according to St. Luke* (Edinburgh: T & T Clark, 1975), p. 3.

55. Cf. Alexander, "Luke's Preface," and her dissertation now published as *The Preface to Luke's Gospel.*

points she makes are sufficient to show that a certain similarity of style, vocabulary, and form is shared by Luke 1:1-4 and some scientific prefaces, for example ones by Galen or Hero of Alexandria. She then claims that the preface in Luke 1:1-4 is of a "detachable" sort, which allows her to avoid relating it in any depth to the content or style of the book that follows it. As G. E. Sterling remarks, this will not do, for this preface not only does but must relate to what follows it. The preface in Acts 1:1-2, which refers *back* to the content of the first volume, intimates that there must be some relationship between the preface and the content and form of what follows Luke 1:1-4.

At most, the evidence Alexander presents may lead to the conclusion that Luke knew some scientific treatises and was influenced by the style and form of their prefaces. This could provide one argument for the contention that the tradition in Col. 4:14 has some historical substance, namely, that Luke was a physician. What this evidence can *not* do is help us to characterize either Luke or Acts in regard to the matter of genre, purpose, or overall style, for clearly neither are scientific treatises, the subjects of which included things like the study of medicinal plants, diseases, and the like, and the form of which is not historical narrative by and large. Even in the broader sense of "scientific," meaning a technical monograph on some precise and analytical subject, Acts would not seem to qualify.[56] Finally, even if Luke 1:1-4 has some resemblances to scientific prefaces, this does not rule out Luke's use of rhetoric either here or elsewhere in his two volumes, because it may be argued with equal force that Luke's prefaces also bear some striking resemblances to prefaces by Polybius, Josephus, Philo, and other nonscientific writers.

5. Luke's Gospel as Biography?

We need at this point to ask whether the Gospel of Luke, *in spite of* the indications in the preface in Luke 1:1-4, ought to be seen as some sort of ancient biography, rather than a historical monograph.[57] A strong case, much stronger than the case for Acts, has been made by C. H. Talbert, and now more recently by R. A. Burridge, that Luke's Gospel would have been viewed as an ancient biography.[58]

---

56. It is furthermore doubtful that broadening the term "scientific" this much really helps Alexander's case, because it then would seem to cover a very wide range of materials, including historiographical works.

57. We will deal with the other exegetical questions about this preface and the one in Acts 1:1-4 in the commentary itself. See pp. 105ff. below.

58. Cf. Talbert, *What Is a Gospel?* to Burridge, *What Are the Gospels?*.

Burridge argues against making rigid genre distinctions between biography and other sorts of ancient historical writing. The "borders between the genres of historiography, monograph, and biography are blurred and flexible. . . . They are only differentiated by internal features such as subject or focus."[59] This judgment can and should be questioned. As Fornara stresses, these two genres were directed to "mutually exclusive ends . . . history, the record of man's memorable deeds, was irrelevant to biography except when deeds illuminate character. Conversely, subjects for illustration suitable to biography — for example, a sense of humor indicated by characterizing anecdotes — were unsuitable to history."[60]

Plutarch, like Nepos before him, makes quite clear the distinction between the two genres. One is concerned with virtues and characterization for ethical ends, the other with deeds or actions that caused historical change and their significance. Plutarch says, "We are not writing history but lives. Revelation of virtue and vice is not always manifest in the most famous actions. A small thing, a word or a jest, frequently has made a greater indication of character than casualty-filled battles" (*Alexander* 1.2). Having stressed this distinction, we must also add that history writing in the first century A.D. did often have *some* biographical elements or passages, but this is quite beside the point. The issue is in what sort of framework and to what sort of ends were these elements put.[61]

The focus of ancient biography was on character and characterization of a particular person, usually for some didactic purpose, as is the case with Plutarch's *Lives,* and events and speeches were related insofar as they served to reveal the person's character. Furthermore, most ancient biographies indicate initially in their prefaces that they are accounts of the life (βιος) of someone (cf., e.g., Philo, *Life of Moses* 1.1: "I intend to write the life of Moses").[62] Ancient biographers tended to focus on the adult person, and seem for the most part to have believed in the idea that human character was a rather fixed thing, which was progressively revealed over the course of a person's lifetime. Only occasionally do we hear of a person whose character is said to change, perhaps through some crisis experience. Biography could

---

59. Burridge, *What Are the Gospels?* p. 245.

60. Fornara, *History in Ancient Greece and Rome,* pp. 184-85.

61. Parsons and Pervo, *Rethinking the Unity,* p. 26, say: "Insofar as they focused upon the public life of a famous figure, monographs could resemble biographies." Resemblance in some respects, however, does not equal identity.

62. Cf. Plutarch, *Demosthenes* 3.1; *Theseus* 1.1; *Dion* 1.1; *Aratus* 1.3; *Agis and Cleomenes* 1.1; Tacitus, *Agricola* 1.4; Eunapius, *Lives of the Philosophers and Sophists* 454. Some works have no real prefaces; cf. Xenophon's *Memorabilia* and Plutarch's *Lycurgus.* Cf. Callan, "The Preface of Luke-Acts."

include rather trivial events which nonetheless revealed the character of the person in question.[63]

Ancient historiography by comparison focused on events *more* than on persons or personalities, and was concerned not only to record significant happenings but to probe and if possible explain the causes of these happenings. It is very hard to escape Luke's concern about causation in both Luke and Acts, as both the theme of God's βουλη (plan or counsel) and the stress on the fulfillment of Scripture are used again and again to explain why things turned out as they did, including such surprising things as Jesus' death and the failure of the majority of Jews to recognize Jesus as Messiah.[64]

Of course some ancient historians, like Thucydides and Polybius, were better and more objective in such analysis than others, but all seem to have understood their task as dealing with the broader canvas of events that had significant effects on large numbers of people. This was true not only of the Greek historians, such as those mentioned above, but also of Roman historians such as Tacitus.[65]

What has in part engendered the genre debate about both Luke and Acts is that there is ample evidence that a biography could include a good deal more than just a discussion of events of personal significance for the main subject (cf. Tacitus's *Agricola*, which spends a good deal of time speaking about British geography, among other subjects); on the other hand, both universal histories and historical monographs could include significant amounts of biographical material, *if it was thought that a particular person was largely responsible for changing the course of history* (like Alexander the Great, or Jesus of Nazareth). For instance, Polybius shows considerable biographical interest in Hannibal, not only chronicling his mighty deeds and demise but also showing interest in his strength of character that allowed him to do such things (cf. Fragment 58, 8.7, 10.47). Or again, Xenophon gives significant attention to the deeds of Jason of Pherae in his historical work (*Hell.* 6.1.19). Even more strikingly, Tacitus, writing shortly after the time of Luke, announces that his study of Agricola, which most would see as a biography, is a first installment of his *Histories* (cf. *Agr.* 3).[66]

---

63. On all this see Momigliano, *The Development of Greek Biography*. On p. 63 he rightly stresses: "History went on being concerned with political events, even when they were guided and dominated by one man; biographical experiments turned on the personal life of the individual." Notice that Luke is little interested in the personal life of Jesus, only his public face, and those events in which he interacted with the larger world. This is even true in Luke 2:41-52.

64. See Squires, *Plan of God in Luke-Acts*.

65. On the ancient historians one should consult Usher, *Historians of Greece and Rome*; Grant, *The Ancient Historians*.

66. See the discussion in Grant, *The Ancient Historians*, pp. 278-79.

A. Momigliano stresses how difficult it is to distinguish between a historical monograph that focuses primarily on one person's accomplishments and words and a biography of such a person.[67] I concede, then, that it is conceivable that Luke might have written a two-volume historical work of *mixed* genre — the first volume being largely biography, while the second is some sort of historical monograph.[68] This, however, does not seem to me to be the best explanation of the data.

I would suggest that the reason for the confusion about the genre of Luke's Gospel is twofold: (1) because it is a historical monograph that focuses *primarily* on the words and deeds of one person, Jesus of Nazareth, which were thought to be so important because they were believed to have literally changed the course of the history of God's people, or, better said, brought it to its intended ends; and (2) because Luke was grouped together by later Christians with other "Gospels," some of which at least *do* appear to be biographical in genre.[69] Especially the latter fact seems to be the main reason some scholars have been misled about Luke's Gospel, and this factor has nothing necessarily to do with the text itself, but rather with its later, early Christian collection and use during the period when the church was gradually sorting out its NT canon.

I thus grant that it is *possible* to analyze Luke's Gospel as an ancient biography, for clearly enough the spotlight in this work shines on Jesus again and again, and other characters are brought in as they have bearing on Jesus' life or ministry. Yet it is not only possible but *more plausible* to analyze Luke's Gospel as a historical monograph focusing on Jesus' words and deeds, and as the first volume of a two-volume monographic historical work.[70]

Consider, for example, the fact that there are notable differences between Luke and one of his sources, Mark. Mark shows no interest in synchronisms, nor is he fond of recording long speeches, with the notable exception of Jesus' final one in Mark 13. In Mark, Jesus is the subject of the verbs over 24 percent of the time, while in Luke he is the subject just over 17 percent of the time.[71]

---

67. Momigliano, *The Development of Greek Biography,* p. 83: "Surely it is impossible to try and enforce a rigid separation of biography from the monograph centred on one man."

68. Fornara, *History in Ancient Greece and Rome,* p. 35, stresses how after Alexander a deep interest in individuals arose in historiographical works and that "the numerous histories of the Hellenistic kings who succeeded to portions of Alexander's great empire, spawned a type of history strictly coterminous with the deeds of a single individual."

69. Mark, and probably John, for example. It is interesting and telling that Luke is not much given to the use of the term "good news" in his first volume, and avoids following Mark's precedent in prefacing his work with a reference to the term.

70. See the helpful discussion in Palmer, "Acts and Ancient Historical Monograph," in regard to Acts.

71. See the charts in Burridge, *What Are the Gospels?* pp. 271-73.

While this statistic alone does not reveal all, when one couples it with the fact that a variety of *others* are the subjects of verbs in Luke's Gospel over 20 percent of the time, it should tell us something. Notice also that in Luke the subject of verbs with Jesus' *teaching* (including parables) amounts to another 36 percent of the subjects, compared to only 20 percent in Mark. What this suggests is that Luke is more interested in what Jesus *said* than Mark is, bearing in mind that speeches or discourses were stock items in ancient historiographical works but do not feature as prominently in ancient biographies.[72] Anecdotes or pithy replies characterize ancient biographies, as Momigliano has shown,[73] and Mark has these sprinkled throughout his account, *without* also adding lengthy speeches.[74]

Luke *is* the only writer who shows any real interest in saying something about Jesus' character development before adulthood (Luke 2:41-52); *however,* the interest in the development of character was not characteristic of ancient biographical writing as it is in modern biographies; rather, it reflects what *was* typical of ancient historians — an interest in causes and effects, historical developments, and what happens to a person or persons over a period of time. Talbert himself admits that ancient biographies show "virtually no interest in tracing development" because the "essence of a person was not examined in its chronological development but only as a fixed constituent in a 'life.'"[75] In other words, the very passage of Luke's Gospel which most resembles what moderns might take as evidence of a biographical interest in Jesus reflects largely historical interests instead![76]

The crucial question is whether the sustained focus and subject of the Gospel is Jesus' character and characterization, as portrayed largely indirectly through his words and deeds, or whether the sustained focus and subject is the words and deeds of Jesus as part of some *larger* historical enterprise (e.g., the proclaiming and bringing in of God's eschatological saving activity), an

---

72. Unlike the pronouncement stories of Mark, which end with a pithy saying of Jesus, Luke has arranged things so that there are several concentrated sections of speech material by Jesus, though occasionally there are interjected questions or comments. Cf. Luke 4:21-27; 6:20-49; 7:22-35; 8:5-18; 9:22-27; 10:2-24; 10:29-37; 11:2-13; 11:17-28, 29-35; 11:39-52; 12:1–13:9; 13:23-35; 14:7-24; 14:25-35; 15:3–17:10; 17:20-37; 18:2-14; 19:12-27; 19:41-44; 20:9-19; 20:34-47; 21:7-38; 23:28-31; 24:36-49. More could be added to this list, but the above is sufficient to show that Jesus' speech material is spaced throughout the narrative of the ministry, leaving the overwhelming impression of Jesus as a great teacher, "mighty in word." When this material is coupled with the actions of Jesus, he appears in this Gospel as much more than a teacher, for he is mighty in deed also. Note that speeches also take up almost a third of Acts.

73. Momigliano, *The Development of Greek Biography,* pp. 76ff.

74. The one exception being Mark 13.

75. Talbert, "Once Again: Gospel Genre," p. 56.

76. See Moessner, "Re-Reading Talbert's Luke," p. 212.

enterprise which is continued by Jesus' followers after his ascension as chronicled in Acts.[77]

6. Acts as Biography?

Because of the apparent narrative unity or sequentiality of Luke and Acts, it
has been necessary to spend considerable time in this introduction talking
about the genre of Luke's Gospel, but what then is to be said about Acts? I
would stress that Acts is not *by and large* a study of the character *or* early
Christian characterization of the apostles such as Peter and James, or even of
Paul.[78] As the extended speech material and narrative about deeds *without* any
accompanying attempt to discuss the birth, death, appearance, remarkable
character traits, and the like of these early Christian leaders show, Luke is not
mainly interested in writing biographical sketches about these figures. Even in
the case of Paul, who is so prominent in the second half of Acts, Luke is
unconcerned to relate the close of his life, which in ancient biographical
literature was so often assumed to be crucial because of what it suggested
about the person's life and character. What is of *first* importance in Acts is
what was said and done, and the personalities or virtues of the Christians who
did these things is of lesser concern, when it comes up at all. The summary
judgment of R. Maddox deserves to be quoted at this juncture:

> Paul in Acts has no very distinct character: in his style of thinking and acting
> he is not noticeably different from Peter or Barnabas, Stephen or Philip, and
> he can even agree with James. His distinction lies simply in the fact that he
> is the greatest of the early Christian leaders and missionaries. . . . This
> should warn us against taking Luke's concentration on Paul as necessarily
> implying a strictly personal interest in him: and all the more so, because he
> avoids reporting Paul's death, which he could hardly have done if his interest
> was really in the person of Paul as such. . . . He is more important for what
> he represents than for his own sake.[79]

---

77. These followers are not, for the most part, treated biographically in the second
volume, for we hear little or nothing about the birth, death, appearance, apparel, virtues,
and the like of a variety of these figures, including Peter, James, Philip, John, John Mark,
and others. They appear and disappear as they play significant roles in the larger drama of
salvation history. The interest does not for the most part lie in their character or characterization. Only when someone like Paul is under attack because of his actions does the
issue of character, origins, and pedigree surface.

78. Though of course one may indirectly discern something about the character of
these Christians from their words and deeds, the point is that that is not the main purpose
of Luke's narration. See Soards, *The Speeches in Acts*, p. 142, on the issue of characterization.

79. Maddox, *The Purpose of Luke-Acts*, p. 70.

Finally, the only really viable model thus far offered that might suggest Acts should be seen as biography is the model of the narrative about a great philosopher followed by a narrative about or list of his successors. Unfortunately, as G. Schneider rightly points out, the document which really has been seen as providing the pattern or key to the analysis of Luke followed by Acts, namely, Diogenes Laertius's *Lives of Eminent Philosophers,* was written far too late to have influenced the composition of Luke or Acts.[80] As interesting as this comparison is, Diogenes Laertius's work cannot be dated earlier than the end of the second century A.D.[81]

7. Conclusions

We may sum up this section of the discussion by stating and partially reiterating some of the factors that lead me to insist that Luke and Acts together must be seen as some sort of two-volume historiographical work.[82] Luke in his second volume is writing a continuous narrative about the growth and development of a remarkable historical phenomenon, early Christianity, which he believed was the result of divinely initiated social change; he is not presenting a loosely related collection of anecdotes or stories meant to reveal the character of certain key human beings. The manner in which Luke writes this narrative is from a theological point of view, for Luke believes that it is God, and God's salvation plan, that is the engine that drives and connects the various facets of his account. If there is any dominant actor in the book of Acts, it is God in the person of the Holy Spirit who guides and directs the words and deeds especially of the main protagonists in the narrative (cf., e.g., Acts 15:7, 28; 16:6).[83]

In fact, the focus of *both* Luke and Acts is primarily theocentric and, as a subset of that fact, also christocentric. We are talking about the mighty deeds of God performed on the stage of history by and through Jesus and his followers. Jesus is seen as divine in both these works (Luke calls him "the Lord" throughout). But Jesus does not exhaust the Godhead; rather, he is portrayed as the One sent by God as part of a larger salvation plan.[84] For example, the

---

80. Schneider, *Die Apostelgeschichte I*, p. 76.

81. It is of course also to the point to remind ourselves again that Acts is no mere succession list of those who followed Jesus, and so Luke-Acts does not fit the pattern: narrative about the founder plus succession list.

82. For what it is worth, the earliest Christian readers of Acts seem to have seen it as simple history. Clement, *Strom.* 5.12; Jerome, *Epistle* 53.8, in fact calls it unadorned history *(nuda historia).*

83. See now Green, "Internal Repetition in Luke-Acts."

84. It is of course also true that Jesus is portrayed as a great human being, a prophet, a sage, and a messianic person, but Luke does not see these categories as circumscribing all that Jesus was.

angel Gabriel is sent *by God* to announce to Mary her part in this larger drama (Luke 1:26), indicating it is not Jesus who is setting in motion this sequence of events. The actor behind the scenes throughout the two volumes is God, and this sometimes means God in Christ,[85] but it also sometimes has another or broader meaning as in Luke 1:26.

Secondly, the most natural way to read the preface in Luke 1:1-4 is that it is the preface for *both* volumes of Luke's work, perhaps written after he completed both. The "among us" in Luke 1:1 points in this direction. Luke is connecting his own generation of Christians with the first generation of Jesus' followers, who were eyewitnesses, all being part of the same drama. Also pointing in this direction is the fact that various of the things fulfilled are not recorded until the book of Acts (cf. above), and perhaps equally telling, the reference to eyewitnesses and servants of the word is close to the way Paul describes himself in Acts 26:16.[86]

Thirdly, Luke claims he has received the crucial tradition and has closely investigated "everything" from the beginning until the time when the narrative closes at the end of Acts with Paul proclaiming the word in Rome. In other words, in the fashion of some careful ancient historians like Thucydides or Polybius he proposes to write not a universal history going back to the dawn of the human race, as Josephus attempts in his *Antiquities*[87] or Livy attempts in going back to the foundations of Rome, but about recent events of the last two generations covering from about 4 B.C. to A.D. 62 that are in Luke's mind of universal significance and are still open to critical inquiry without relying purely on documents and official records.

Fourthly, the "us" in the preface in due course helps the listener make sense of the limited claims made toward the end of the two volumes in the famous "we" passages, beginning in Acts 16 and continuing off and on until the end of the second volume in Acts 28. Luke appears to be claiming to fulfill the requirements imposed by Thucydides, Polybius, and other writers of historical monographs about recent events that one not merely investigate sources both oral and written, or consult eyewitnesses, but that one must be a participant in at least some of the recounted historic events.[88] Of course claims are

---

85. See Luke 24:49, where it is Jesus sending the Spirit upon them which God has promised his people in the Scriptures, clearly an act only a divine person can do.

86. So Marshall, "Acts and the 'Former Treatise,'" p. 173. That the same person can be called both of these things in Acts militates against the conclusion that in Luke 1:1-4 Luke means two different groups of persons, with Luke himself only being in contact with ministers of the word, not also with eyewitnesses.

87. See Rajak, "Josephus."

88. Cf. Meir, "Historical Answers to Historical Questions." Van Seters, *In Search of History*, on the nature of *historia* requiring *historie* (investigation), p. 12: "It was the very nature of this method to scrutinize and correct previous views as well as to gather new information firsthand." This is surely what Luke is *claiming* to do.

one thing and reality often another, and so we shall have to investigate the sticky problem of the "we" passages when we reach them, but no one has yet produced telling evidence from ancient historical documents that such "we" passages in *these* sorts of historiographical works ever were added purely for verisimilitude or as a veiled claim to be using a source written by another.[89]

Fifthly, the synchronisms (already referred to above) are a powerful hint that Luke intends that this work be evaluated as some sort of history writing. Notice that they are prominent at the beginning of Luke, occurring at the very beginning of the Gospel narrative (1:5), at the beginning of the narrative about Jesus' birth (2:1-2), and again at the beginning of the story about the period of Jesus' ministry (3:1-2). Luke is alerting the careful auditor from the outset that he should evaluate this story in light of the larger historical setting in which it occurred. This is a tale meant to inform the listener about important historical developments. There is also a considerable concern with historical synchronicity in Acts when one considers the historical references in Gamaliel's speech (Acts 5), the famine under Claudius (Acts 11), the reign of Herod Agrippa (Acts 12), the expulsion of Jews from Rome and Paul's encounter with Gallio (Acts 18), or the reigns of Felix and Festus (Acts 21–26).[90]

Sixthly, the Gospel of Luke does *not* begin the narration with the introduction of Jesus, or the tale of his birth, but with a substantial account of the antecedents of John the Baptist's birth, something no other Gospel includes. Similarly, it is equally striking that the recital of the kerygma in various of the speeches in Acts also does not begin with the story of Jesus but rather with the story of Israel and at various points includes the Baptist as the immediate prelude to the story of Jesus (cf. Acts 10:37; 13:24-25). In short, the story of Jesus is set in a wider historical framework. If Theophilus had been an outsider he might be forgiven for thinking he was about to hear a story focusing on John the Baptist after listening to Luke 1, if, that is, he had not picked up the historiographical hints in the preface that what was to follow was about πραγματα, words and deeds of various people fulfilling divine promises.

Seventhly, in the two passages where one would expect a singular focus on Jesus' character and identity if Luke's Gospel was intended to be a biography — namely, Peter's great confession about Jesus' identity and following the Lukan transfiguration narrative — Luke does not give the prominence to the identity issue one would expect. The Lukan confession narrative receives only three scant verses in Luke 9:18-20 (contrast Matt. 16:13-20), and is sandwiched between the commissioning of the Twelve in Luke 9 and the commissioning of the Seventy in Luke 10. Nowhere is it made more apparent than in this sequence that Jesus is the initiator of a series of events and proclamations that

---

89. See below, pp. 480ff.
90. As L. Johnston has stressed to me in correspondence.

his disciples undertake during and then after his time. The focus is not just on Jesus but on the historical Jesus movement of which he was the catalyst and focal point. Note also in the ensuing narration of the transfiguration in 9:30-31 that it is Luke alone who tells us what was happening in the transfiguration — Jesus, Moses, and Elijah were discussing Jesus' "exodus" which he was about to "accomplish" or fulfill (πληρουν) in Jerusalem. The affirmation of Jesus' identity comes after the focus on his upcoming *deeds* in Jerusalem, and seems to serve as a sort of rebuke to the befuddled disciples to pay attention to what Jesus tells them. What Jesus next teaches the disciples (in 9:43-45) is about his upcoming deeds or "exodus" in Jerusalem.

Similarly, in Acts 4 the hearer is alerted to pay attention in Acts to what people like Peter and John say and do and *not* to their traits, such as the fact that they were uneducated and ordinary persons (4:13).[91] Such traits do not tell the tale, for it is not their personality or character that determines their words and deeds, but rather the fact that they are vehicles through whom God the Holy Spirit speaks and acts.

This should suffice to show that Luke in his Gospel is portraying the story of Jesus as part of a larger historical process, and thus he both deals with the crucial historical antecedents to the coming of Jesus in some depth and also spends considerable time foreshadowing the subsequent developments by giving twofold attention to the mission work of the disciples, which points us nicely forward to the plot of the second volume. Hence, Luke's Gospel must be evaluated in light of its sequel, but more importantly for our purposes Acts must be evaluated in light of its literary predecessor. None of the above answers the second order question of what species of ancient history writing we find in Luke-Acts, a question to which we now turn.

B. Luke among the Ancient Historians[92]

1. Greek and Roman Historiography

a. The Varieties

To conclude that Luke in his two-volume work intended to write history as it was written in antiquity tells modern readers very little about the document itself for two reasons: (1) ancient historiography was both different from

---

91. Notice that it is the opponents or outsiders, not Luke or his protagonists, who are interested in the curricula vitae of these two early Christian leaders.

92. See the annotated bibliography in Green and McKeever, *Luke-Acts and New Testament Historiography*.

modern historiography in some respects and similar to it in other respects; (2) Luke may have intended to write in a particular manner and failed to do so. The bottom line is whether Luke achieved the sort of standards he professed to set for himself in Luke 1:1-4. We can only address the latter issue in the commentary itself, but we must take some pains at this point to sketch the character of ancient historiography.

First, let it be said that we may dismiss the old argument that the ancients were unable to distinguish fact from fiction. No one who has read Thucydides or Polybius or Tacitus carefully could think that critical scrutiny of historical processes was impossible in antiquity or that no one was interested in such critical distinctions.[93] Thucydides, for one, was quite clear about distinguishing myths from historical facts.

Even Lucian, while never attempting to write history in the manner in which he discussed it, nevertheless knew very well the sort of high standards a true historian should set for his narrative. He says plainly in his treatise on "How History Ought to Be Written": "History cannot admit a lie, even a tiny one . . ." (9). He stresses that a good historian must go out and investigate and not simply rely on documents or what others tell him (38). "The historian's sole task is to tell the tale as it happened . . ." (42). "As to the facts themselves, he should not assemble them at random, but only after much laborious and painstaking investigation. He should . . . be an eyewitness, but, if not, listen to those who tell the more impartial story, those whom one would suppose least likely to subtract from the facts or add to them out of favor or malice . . ." (50). Lucian also adds that history should be useful, not merely entertaining or pandering to the audience's desires. In saying this, Lucian is not arguing against the applying of any rhetorical conventions to ancient history writing but against a particular kind of rhetorical approach to history writing that treats it like an exercise in declamation or epideictic rhetoric where the facts are neglected or distorted for the sake of praising or blaming one or another historical figure (8-9).[94]

Cicero, too, though no historian himself but rather a great orator, knew well what the conventions and standards of history writing were. History was not intended to be encomiastic (*Att.* 1.19.10). Rather,

> who does not know history's first law to be that an author must not dare to tell anything but the truth? And its second that he must make bold to

93. See Mosley, "Historical Reporting." For a sensitive and balanced evaluation of Luke among the ancient historians, cf. Hemer, *Book of Acts*, pp. 63-100.

94. Lucian's treatise is entitled "How History Should Be Written." See the discussion in Barrett, "How History Should Be Written." In fact, Lucian in this essay is discussing history writing in light of the various rhetorical conventions and concerns of his day, and is far from simply dismissing these concerns.

tell the whole truth? That there must be no suggestion of partiality anywhere in his writings? Nor of malice? This groundwork of course is familiar to everyone; the completed structure however rests upon the story and the diction. The nature of the subject needs chronological arrangement and geographical representation. (*De Or.* 2.62-63)[95]

We will say more about various of these matters shortly, but here it is sufficient to point out that Luke goes out of his way to provide both chronological arrangement *and* geographical representation in *both* Luke and Acts.

It must be acknowledged that such standards were not observed a good deal of the time in antiquity. Thucydides and Polybius *were* in various regards exceptional,[96] but it is also true that it was not impossible for a well-educated and apparently well-traveled person like Luke, who claims to have taken time and pains to investigate matters closely, to follow in the footsteps of other exceptional historians. Nor would his use of rhetoric have necessarily led to distortion of the facts. As P. A. Brunt says, rhetoric "could be the handmaiden of truth or falsehood. In principle Cicero thought it should be the handmaiden of truth."[97] While the use of rhetoric could lead to distortion, it could also be used to induce the hearer to pay attention to the facts being narrated and make that narration convincing.[98]

Perhaps one of the most important distinctions that has a bearing on our evaluation of Luke-Acts is that between historiography in the Greek tradition of Thucydides and Polybius and the tradition of history writing largely by Roman authors or those heavily influenced by them that developed during the rise and growth of the Roman Empire.[99] As Fornara has shown, there was

95. The arguments of Woodman, *Rhetoric in Classical Historiography,* p. 82, in regard to the famous letter by Cicero to Lucceius are not persuasive. Cicero is not arguing that history written in his era inherently allowed for the bending of the truth in view of rhetorical conventions. Rather, as Fornara, *History in Ancient Greece and Rome,* pp. 101ff., had already shown, "Cicero clearly had not asserted that the laws of the monograph abet distortion or magnification; on the contrary, he would like the laws of history *bent* in a monograph about himself" (emphasis mine). In short he was urging Lucceius to go *against* the well-known conventions of such history writing. On the need for a reliable account in a historical work, cf. Tacitus, *Annals* 1.1; Arrian, *Anabasis of Alexander* preface; Dio Cassius, *Roman History* 1.2; Herodian, *History of the Empire* 1.3. These texts reflect the fact that it was widely known that reliability was one of the major goals in historical works.

96. See the discussion by Gabba, "True History and False History."

97. Brunt, "Cicero and Historiography," p. 340.

98. Ibid.

99. In the latter category I would include such diverse writers as Dionysius of Halicarnassus, who mirrors what happened when history became subsumed under the heading of epideictic rhetoric with the rise of the Second Sophistic in the late first and early second century A.D. (on which see my *Conflict and Community in Corinth,* pp. 10ff.), and also Josephus in his *Antiquities,* who writes an ethnographic work in the tradition of the

a difference between the approach to history writing of the Greek historians writing prior to the first century A.D. and that of the Roman historians who began to come to the fore starting with Fabius Pictor, and then the series of annalists leading up to and including Tacitus.

Roman historians, almost without exception, focused on the history of one city, Rome, and its people. They coupled the chronicling of the deeds of great human beings with what has been called horography — the chronicling of a city's life on a year-by-year basis, including records of priests, crop harvests, and notable meteorological events. On this front, Luke's work stands much closer to Greek historiography than to the Roman sort,[100] whereas Josephus, by limiting himself to the chronicling of the developments among one people (the Jews rather than the Romans) and attempting a "universal history" of this one people, much more closely approximates some of his Roman predecessors and contemporaries.

For the Greek historian the hallmark of true ιστορια was personal observation *(autopsia)* and participation in events, travel, inquiry, the consultation of eyewitnesses. The Roman historians, especially those who like Livy wrote universal histories, were often satisfied to stay at home and consult documents and records. In this matter as well, Luke seems much nearer to Greek history writing.[101] Partly, this practice by the Roman historians was caused by the fact that while Greek historians took the writing of history as a task meant for one's best years, when one was able-bodied, could travel, and had sharpness of mind, the Romans saw history as the provenance of retired statesmen and military figures. In either case, "these conditions excluded all but members of the highest levels of society. Wealth and social contacts were essential to the craft."[102]

While Luke may not have been wealthy by some standards, very likely he was either a retainer of a wealthy patron or a person of independent means who had the wherewithal to travel, and the education to write the sort of account he did. His social status must have been relatively high, at least compared to that of many early Christians. "If style is the man, then the man with whom we have to do is for his time and station a gentleman of ability and breadth of interest, whatever his past reading and training may have been."[103] This opinion of

---

universal histories at the end of the first century A.D. The arguments that Luke is indebted to him or vice versa either in method or matter are weak and have been set in the right framework by Sterling, *Historiography and Self-Definition*, pp. 100ff., though I would differ with a variety of his conclusions.

100. See Fornara, *History in Ancient Greece and Rome*, pp. 25ff.

101. See ibid., p. 49.

102. Ibid. It is not incidental or accidental that Josephus wrote his *Antiquities* at the close of his life, following the Roman model.

103. Cadbury, *The Making of Luke-Acts*, p. 220.

Cadbury's has recently been seconded by Mealand, who concludes after a detailed study of Lukan style that Luke "is a skilful literary artist who can use varieties of style for effect."[104]

It is noteworthy that the Greek historians as a whole did not tend to be politicians or statesmen, though many were involved in the affairs they recorded and some, like Thucydides and Xenophon, were involved militarily in the events they recorded. Luke only claims involvement, like Thucydides, at certain limited junctures. The authority of the Greek historian lay not in his social status, which, as in the case of Thucydides, he never mentioned or made an issue of, but in his interest and involvement in his subject matter. This stands in contrast to most Roman historians whose narrative had *auctoritas* mainly because of who wrote it.[105]

An account without formal mention of an author but with a statement of the author's participation in some of the events, which is what we have in Luke-Acts, certainly stands in the Greek rather than in the Roman tradition of historiography. Notably, "The concept of research finds no place in the Latin prefaces."[106]

The ethnographical and geographical scope of Greek historiography was usually more universal than its Roman counterpart. "The Romans wrote the history of their city and only incidentally of the world," whereas "the Greeks wished to record the memorable deeds of both Greeks and barbarians, and thus purposefully tried to avoid ethnography and its more narrow scope."[107] Luke makes clear at the outset of his narrative that his will be a narrative about and of import for both Jew and Gentile alike, for he seeks to convey the story of a universal salvation (Luke 2:32).

Though the Greek historians were patriotic enough in their own way, they strove for a certain objectivity and even neutrality in their narrative and did not hesitate to criticize their own kind in a manner and to a degree not usually characteristic of Roman historiography. In Greek historiography "in-

---

104. Mealand, "Hellenistic Historians," p. 59.

105. Again note how much weight Josephus places on being an *important* and leading participant in the contemporary events which he chronicles, both as a military figure (cf. *The Jewish Wars*) and as a statesman and advocate of sorts on behalf of the Jews. The author of Luke-Acts makes considerably less grandiose claims; in fact, he is prepared to be formally anonymous, which comports with Greek not Roman notions about historians.

106. Fornara, *History in Ancient Greece and Rome*, p. 56. Cf. Janson, *Latin Prose Prefaces*.

107. Fornara, *History in Ancient Greece and Rome*, p. 53. It is worth stressing that, unlike Luke, Josephus in his *Antiquities* is indeed doing ethnography, the history of its people, including its origins. I stress this because "the conventions of ethnography vitally differed from those of history. The laws of evidence and obedience to truth were at least in theory mandatory in history. Ethnography permitted the publication of the unconfirmed report of even the improbable" (Fornara, p. 15).

dividuals were not necessarily good or bad because of the side they represented or because they were Greeks or barbarians. Even in a work intended for the winning side, there was no room for caricature of an opponent simply because he was an opponent."[108] In this regard it is notable how Luke records the story of an Ananias and Sapphira (Acts 5) or of an Apollos who needed more instruction (Acts 18) or of the falling-out between Paul and Barnabas over Mark (Acts 15), or on the other side of the ledger how Luke presents various non-Christians, even those who were potential opponents such as Gamaliel, in a positive light.

Also striking to me is the *lack* of broadscale polemics against either Jews or Romans, though both are portrayed as persecuting or causing problems for Christians at various points in the narrative.[109] Rather, Luke provides both positive and negative portrayals of those who were not Christians. He refuses to stereotype people simply because they are not yet followers of "the Way." Were Luke-Acts a Roman apologetic work, we might expect a quiet omission or even in some cases a glossing over of stories that portray Christians or Romans in a negative light and others in a positive one. This conclusion is of some importance when we come to evaluate whether Luke has seriously distorted the outcome and terms of the Jerusalem council recorded in Acts 15. It appears to me that Luke wrote in the Greek tradition, not like Livy or for that matter like Dionysius of Halicarnassus, both of whom would have history subsumed under a large rhetorical umbrella, leading to considerable distortion.[110]

In terms of subject matter, ancient historiographical works could include a great deal of things not common in modern histories — lengthy genealogical accounts, discussions of myths, geographical and travel chronicles, biographical sketches, wonders, legendary stories about the foundations of races or cities.[111] Most of these elements usually occurred not in historical works about recent events, like that written by Thucydides or Luke, but in the so-called universal histories where the historian was at the mercy of all sorts of traditions

---

108. Ibid., p. 62. On the issue of rhetoric and bias, cf. pp. 49ff. below.

109. See rightly van Unnik, "Luke's Second Book," p. 51: "Luke cannot be called partial, not even toward the Jews. Texts like 7.54 (the Jews were enraged) and those of persecutions by the Jews are more a sign of vivid description than of partiality." Cf. pp. 20ff. above.

110. The great fault in an otherwise helpful study by Plümacher is that he chooses to compare Luke to two historians with whom he had little in common and certainly was not likely influenced by — Livy and Dionysius of Halicarnassus. But cf. his *Lukas als hellenistischer Schriftsteller.*

111. Even Tacitus, who shows no great interest or belief in pagan religion, never mind other sorts, nevertheless quite readily includes discussions of religious beliefs and practices in his historical works because historians of all stripes had done so for centuries. See the discussion in Mellor, *Tacitus,* pp. 14ff., and see *Histories* 4.83-84 on Isis and Serapis.

and sources since the events were too remote to investigate and no eyewitnesses were still living. When Livy discusses the founding of the city of Rome, it is clear enough that objective historiography suffers, because the dead could not rise up to help him write his narrative and he was not all that careful an investigator or critical scrutinizer of his sources in any case.[112] Careful historians often eschewed the writing of universal histories precisely because of the lack of control and corroboration of data from eyewitnesses. Sextus Empiricus said true history could be distinguished from false history in that the latter was constructed out of myths and genealogies, dwelling on things that were largely immune to historical scrutiny because they dealt with hoary antiquity (*Adv. Math.* 1.253-61).

Another sort of history writing has been called local history. It deals with the sacred traditions, kept by priests in local temples, and with the history of a particular town or shrine or ethnic group in a particular geographical region. The breadth of the material in Luke-Acts shows Luke is not trying to write this sort of history. Nor is his narrative simply an expanded exercise in ethnography, the chronicling of the history of one particular ethnic group, as can be said about Josephus's *Antiquities.*

While the outsider who heard or read Luke's work might recognize a certain similarity in the account to Greek or even Roman *religious* history writing, on the whole the account would appear different from such accounts. This latter sort of history writing

> was always tied to cults and places of the cult. Transmission of knowledge in such cases was ensured by priests and temple attendants. . . . Temple traditions in Egypt are related to statues, monuments, inscriptions, cult places in general, ritual. Historical information as such tends to be anecdotal and often scandalous, particularly if it refers to the private life of kings. Priests, who give the appearance of being learned, in fact retail fables, oddities and portents. Sacerdotal tradition in fact is really popularizing, and its market is popular.[113]

Even a cursory reading of Acts will show that this is not what Luke is about. Once the story gets beyond Jerusalem, where Christians have some contact with the temple, it becomes apparent that he is telling about a social movement that did not have priests, temples, or sacrifices, and so was not recounting *local* traditions about such places and forms of religion. Luke's account is much more cosmopolitan than that and its focus is elsewhere. Furthermore, the purveyors of the Christian traditions were a wide variety of

---

112. See Walsh, "Livy's Preface."
113. Gabba, "True History and False History," p. 60.

people ranging from the unlettered to the more well educated like Luke himself, and involving people with a wide range of professions.

It must also be candidly admitted that the author of Luke-Acts is in at least two important respects unlike Thucydides and Polybius. He is not in the main concerned about the political or military history of the larger culture, but about the social and religious history of a particular group or subculture within the Empire. Luke believes it is a group which can and should continue to have a growing and ever broader impact, for they proclaim a universal savior and salvation. Also, had Thucydides lived in Luke's era and read Luke's account he would have not been pleased with the amount of attention Luke gives to prophecies, portents, signs, miracles, wonders, and the like. This latter trait, however, would not distinguish Luke from other historians, for instance Herodotus himself, the so-called father of Greek historiography, who wrote what can rightly be called a form of theological historiography where the divine is a major player in the drama recorded.[114] As E. Gabba points out, various of the ancients would "assign to true history not only human actions located in time and space, but also the biographies of gods and heroes alongside those of famous men. In other words, divine history was accepted as a narrative of events."[115] This of course distinguishes ancient history from the way most modern historians would view and write history.[116] Yet it would also be clear

---

114. Ephorus objects to the use of the marvelous simply to give the audience a thrill, but not if it is used properly to furnish examples of morality and justice. See the discussion in Ullman, "History and Tragedy," pp. 30-31. Ullman is right to note how history writing was influenced by other genres such as the epic and tragedy. Luke clearly shows he has a sense of drama in various of his episodes (cf., e.g., the Miletus story in Acts 20:17ff.). He is not above playing to the emotions of empathy or even fear (cf. Acts 5:1-11), as did the ancient tragedians. It would be wrong, however, to rank Luke among the tragic historians, if by that one means he was primarily interested in the dramatic potential of a given story rather than its historical substance, as if the desire to move his audience explains why Luke includes what he does in Luke-Acts. Luke's primary intent is to inform Theophilus and assure him both about the facts and the meaning of "the things fulfilled among us." Ullman is also right to stress that from the time of at least Isocrates on, the writing of history was influenced by rhetoric and its conventions (pp. 33ff.).

115. Gabba, "True History and False History," p. 54.

116. Cf., e.g., Grant, *The Ancient Historians,* p. 357, who criticizes Eusebius's church history by saying that his "whole subject encourages departure from cold secular truth, and invites a deliberate neglect of plausible worldly causes and connexions." It is not just that Grant is claiming that in some cases a belief in the miraculous or supernatural *can* lead to gullibility in the evaluation of dramatic claims and accounts, but like many post-Enlightenment historians he takes it as beyond cavil that anyone who believes in and makes claims about the supernatural is not using critical historical scrutiny in the evaluation of the historian's data, and therefore is unable to deal with what he sees as the cold, hard, secular truth. This may in part explain why in an otherwise helpful and comprehensive survey of ancient historians including Eusebius and Josephus, he does not deal with Luke's work at all.

enough to the careful hearer or reader that Luke was not attempting, as various ancients did, to write about the amazing or supernatural in such a manner that his subject was immune to historical scrutiny, unlike some of the literature about the "fabulous" in antiquity. For example, it was a popular venture even as early as the third century B.C. to write about utopian societies in remote places such as faraway countries or isolated islands. When Euhemerus, Iamblichus, and others wrote about such places, often making claims about prodigies and miracles, they did so with certainty that their claims about these societies could not be investigated by their audiences and probably would not be taken as unadulterated historical fact in any case. The major function of such narratives was either to set forward certain ideals or to entertain or both. Luke's tale by contrast is set all over the Mediterranean crescent, especially in its major cities, and though some of his summaries do depict early Christianity as a somewhat ideal society (cf., e.g., Acts 2:43-47), he is careful to reveal some of the problems and troublemakers that were part of early Christian life as well (cf. Acts 5; 15). He insists throughout that even public officials like King Agrippa will have heard about the events "that have been fulfilled among us," and that such officials had contact with various of the people involved because "none of these things has escaped [their] notice, *for this was not done in a corner*" (Acts 26:26, emphasis added).

Luke is not writing either about remote utopian societies, secret religious sects and rites, or words and deeds that he feels are immune to historical scrutiny. His claim is that the Jesus movement and the rise of Christianity are real historical phenomena that at least from time to time touch on the larger historical events and processes of the Empire (hence the synchronisms), and so are subject to careful historical scrutiny in an ancient mode, which is to say, with some openness to claims about the supernatural.

b. Luke, Polybius, and Ephorus

Of all the historians writing in Greek, Luke's work seems to me to be most like the Greek historiography of someone like Polybius, and, to lesser degree, Thucydides. Indeed, a reasonable case can be made that in terms of method, style, and type of historiography Luke is following this particular Greek tradition of history writing, with some signs of influence by Ephorus as well (cf. below).

For example, consider the words of Polybius in his famous preface (1.1-4). Polybius speaks of "a phenomenon unprecedented in the annals of humankind" (1.1), as does Luke, though the former refers to the rise to prominence and dominance of the Roman Empire, while Luke refers to the appearance of the eschatological dominion of God spreading across the Mediterranean crescent. Polybius says: "The unity of events imposes upon the historian a similar unity of composition in depicting for his readers *the operations of the laws of Fortuna* (fortune) upon the grand scale, and this has been my principal inducement and stimulus in the work which I have undertaken." He speaks of not "passing over without remark one of the most admirable and instructive performances of Fortune. That mighty revolutionary, whose pawns are human lives, has never before achieved such an astonishing *tour de force* as she has staged for the benefit of our generation; yet the monographs of the historical specialists give no inkling of the whole picture" (1.3-4). In 9.1-2 he goes on to speak of the fact that he writes more for the sake of instruction of the serious student than entertainment of the general reader.

Luke also writes for a serious student who needs instruction about the remarkable things that have happened "among us" recently. He shares Polybius's view that something unique in the annals of history had transpired which could not simply be explained either piecemeal or on the basis of certain historical precedents or analogies. Luke, like Polybius, clearly has a sense of the magnitude of the historical moment and believes that it is somehow divinely guided, that the unity of events leading to particular ends reflects and reveals the singular hand of a larger guiding force or Being. By comparison to these two writers, Josephus seems much more defensive and resigned, like the tone of the work of Tacitus, placing blame on human social forces, especially for what transpired leading up to A.D. 70.

Polybius is quite clear about the conventions of handling speeches, and the function they should have in a historical narrative. The "whole *genus* of orations . . . may be regarded as summaries of events and *as the unifying element in historical writing*" (12.25a-b; cf. 36.1). He then goes on to castigate another writer who had the pretensions to write history, Timaeus, for inventing speeches when "it is the function of history in the first place to ascertain the exact words spoken, whatever they may be, and in the second place to inquire into the cause which crowned the action taken or the words spoken with success or failure. . . . A historian . . . who suppresses both the words spoken and their cause and replaces them by fictitious expositions and verbosities, destroys, in so doing, the characteristic quality of history" (12.25a-b). As Fornara has stressed, there was no *convention* of inventing speeches for Greek historical works, though some bad historians did so. The portion of Polybius underscored above is especially striking because of the recent work of M. Soards, which makes very plain that perhaps the major function of the speeches in Acts is to unify the narrative through a repetition of the major themes of the good news proclamation.[117] It appears that Luke is carefully following the methodology enunciated by Polybius in his handling of speeches (cf. below on Thucydides).

117. Soards, *The Speeches in Acts,* pp. 199ff.

It is also Polybius who tells the listener well into his narrative (36.12), "The fact that I am deeply involved in a personal sense in the πραξεις which I have to narrate *from this point onwards* makes it essential for me to vary my references to myself." Part of the point of this is to explain why the first person suddenly appears so late in his histories, not unlike the case in Acts, and partly to explain why he varies the references to himself. Here again the practice has an echo in Acts and suggests Luke's participation in some of the events.[118] J. Jervell has recently stressed the

> rule of ancient historiography, the *autopsia,* is followed as Luke indicates that he personally had taken part in some of the reported events. He announces himself as an eyewitness, co-worker, and companion of Paul in using "we" (16.10-17; 20.5-15; 21.1-8; 27.1–28.16). There is a wealth of details in these sections compared to other parts of Paul, even details with no significance for his account. . . . We can safely assume that Luke took notes when events happened and used his notes years later. On this point he met the standards of historiography, at least formally.[119]

It is also important to note that both Luke and Acts bear some striking resemblance to the Greek κατα γενος style of arranging one's history, whereby the work proceeds along geographical as well as chronological lines. This sort of approach is seen in the work of Ephorus, whose basic principle of arrangement of material seems to be that in a given book or section he will only deal with matters in a particular geographical or major cultural region, usually proceeding with it in chronological order.[120] "Polybius and Diodorus also kept separate the histories of the various regions, although they integrated their material more closely than did Ephorus."[121] For good or ill, Ephorus's approach became standard for Greek historians after him, and I would submit that Luke follows this method.[122]

For example, it has been widely remarked on how Luke's Gospel basically follows not only a chronological arrangement of material but also a geographical arrangement whereby after the preliminary material in Luke 1–2 we find Jesus first in Galilee, then in Samaria, and finally in Jerusalem and its surrounding villages. In other words, Luke's Gospel has a "going up to Jerusalem" trajectory, whereas Acts basically moves from one region to another, starting in Jerusalem and branching out in various directions, eventually ending in the

---

118. See rightly Aune, *New Testament,* p. 124.
119. Jervell, "The Future of the Past," p. 117.
120. See the discussion in Drews, "Ephorus and History Written *kata genos,*" and the further evidence he gives in "Ephorus' *kata genos* History Revisited."
121. Ibid., p. 53.
122. See on this Fornara, *History in Ancient Greece and Rome,* pp. 43-45.

Empire's capital, Rome. It was Ephorus who was apparently first to divide up his historical subjects into separate rolls on the basis of geographical considerations.[123] This might in part explain why the two volumes of Luke-Acts are divided as they are. The first volume will deal with the geographical theater in which Jesus' ministry took place, while the book of Acts will deal with the geographical regions where the early Christian movement and its ministry spread the good news, largely using the missionary travels of Peter, Philip, and especially Paul from Acts 13 on to structure the development of the narrative.

2. Jewish Historiography

Various scholars, including recently B. Rosner and Jervell, have argued that if there is an ancient historical niche into which Luke's work seems more nearly to fit it is as a continuation of the sort of history writing one finds in the Hebrew Scriptures, perhaps especially in its Greek translation in the LXX. A closely allied view is that Luke is pursuing the sort of writing one finds in the late Hellenized Jewish apologetic historians.[124] For the latter sort of writing G. E. Sterling helpfully offers the following definition: "Apologetic historiography is the story of a subgroup of people in an extended prose narrative written by a member of the group who follows the group's own traditions but Hellenizes them in an effort to establish the identity of the group within the setting of the larger world."[125]

Yet Acts has some *major* differences from Hellenized Jewish writers such as Artapanos, Demetrios, Pseudo-Eupolemos, and Josephus.[126] These historians fall into the category of ethnographers of a sort, recounting the history of a particular people, while Luke very candidly makes clear that the Christian movement, while growing out of Judaism, involved people from a wide variety of ethnic groups, from various sorts of both Semites and Gentiles. Indeed, one of the major functions of Luke's work seems to be explaining why Christianity, at least by his day, is *not* predominantly Jewish. Despite the approaching of Jews in synagogues all over the Empire with the message about Jesus, only a minority of Jews have responded positively to the appeal. On the other hand, he recounts repeatedly in detail how Gentiles like Cornelius and others have responded enthusiastically to the good news. In other words, Luke is trying to explain why his form of religion is one that *crosses* ethnic boundaries, indeed is a universal religion, inclusive of all ethnic groups.

---

123. See especially Drews, p. 53.
124. See, e.g., Rosner, "Acts and Biblical History"; Jervell, "The Future of the Past," pp. 104ff.
125. Sterling, *Historiography and Self-Definition*, p. 17.
126. Cf. ibid., pp. 220ff.

M. Soards has helpfully noted that there is very little to compare between the speeches in Acts and what we find in 1 and 2 Maccabees or Josephus.[127] While in the case of at least 2 Maccabees and Josephus we have works that are dedicated to presenting and defending Judaism in a favorable light in the wider context of the Hellenized Greco-Roman world, and this may be something like what Luke seeks to do for Christianity, it must be said that the results are very different.[128] Second Maccabees is a work that much better suits Pervo's description of the ancient romance than Acts does.[129] Here indeed the main goal is profit with delight, or in this case delight with some profit. Here the author's rhetoric is a matter of style and sensationalistic storytelling by piling up adjectives and descriptive phrases, and interjecting regular value judgments. It can be said to be an exercise in epideictic rhetoric, the rhetoric of praise and blame, which in this case involves the praising of Judas Maccabeus and other loyal Jews like him and the blaming of villains like Antiochus Epiphanes, all with a hortatory aim in sight (namely, character formation).[130] Clearly 2 Maccabees suffers by comparison with Acts, *if one evaluates 2 Maccabees as serious historiography.* I would submit, however, that this was not the intent of the author, as his preface and epilogue and the way he handles his data show.[131] As an exercise in moralizing rhetoric using some historical events as a source of illustration the author is successful. The upshot of all this is that in both content and intent, both in method and style, 2 Maccabees has more differences from than similarities to Acts.

The longer one listens to the account in the Acts, the clearer it becomes that while the offer of salvation continues to be made to the Jew first even in Rome at the close of Acts, for they are the original people of God, it is also

127. Soards, *The Speeches in Acts,* pp. 159ff.
128. Gärtner, *Areopagus Speech and Natural Revelation,* pp. 20ff., rightly in my view shows that Josephus and Luke differ considerably in methods, aims, and understandings of history.
129. See his *Profit with Delight.*
130. Notice how the author places the mention of his hero Judas Maccabeus at the beginning of his preface in chapter 2. When the conventions and interests of epideictic rhetoric are applied to historical material, in the end this produces material much more like the moralistic biographical works of Plutarch in his parallel lives than like serious ancient historiography.
131. Since there is overlap between 1 Maccabees and 2 Maccabees, it is useful to compare and contrast the handling of the common material. For one thing 2 Maccabees resorts to rhetorical hyperbole, depicting the armies and deaths as considerably larger in number than the accounts in 1 Maccabees. For another thing 2 Maccabees differs in the accounts of Judas's conflicts with other nations, in particular in the chronological correlation of these events with the death of Antiochus Epiphanes (cf. 1 Macc. 6:1-16; 2 Macc. 1:12-16 and chap. 9). On this see H. C. Kee's introduction in *The Cambridge Annotated Study Apocrypha* (Cambridge: Cambridge University Press, 1994), pp. xxvi-xxvii.

for everyone. It is not a defense of a particular ethnic group. Luke's account is in part a defense of, or at least a sympathetic explanation of, a cross-cultural social movement, not just of an ethnic group and its history. Unlike the aforementioned Hellenistic Jewish histories, Luke-Acts is not written *ad maioram Iudaeorum gloriam*, though equally clearly it should not be seen as a super-secessionist polemic *against* early Judaism either.[132]

In fact, if one allows that Luke is writing for a Christian audience of some sort, it is in order to point out, as P. F. Esler rightly does, that the term "apologetic" is perhaps not very apt to describe Luke's purposes, as he is not defending the faith to outsiders. Rather, he is trying to legitimate it for insiders who may have had various questions and doubts about their new religion. This view explains Luke's concern to demonstrate the claims of Christianity as the legitimate development of Judaism as well as the theory that Luke is doing apologetics.[133]

In regard to the case made by Jervell and others that Luke is writing a continuation of biblical history, perhaps especially as it is found in the LXX, the following should be said. M. Soards has rightly noted the similarities between Neh. 9:6-38 and portions of Acts 4:24-30; 7:2-53; 13:16-41, 46-47. There is no arguing with the fact that the author is deeply indebted to the Scriptures, especially their prophetic portions. It is evident in the way he views the *content* of his narrative and its significance. Furthermore, Luke shares some important things with both biblical and other Jewish historians that he does not share with Greek ones, for instance his vision of the God of the Bible, the concept of a chosen people, and the idea of a people guided by a holy book. Greek historians say nothing about the latter. One can also point to the way Acts ends in a fashion not unlike what we find at the end of 2 Kings.[134]

What is not noted by those who wish to see Acts as a continuation of OT or at least LXX history writing is that the *sort* of history Luke chooses to write about is different in crucial respects from the sort found in the OT, or in the Maccabean literature, or in the Hellenistic Jewish historians. OT and early Jewish historiography is, like ancient Greek historiography, about battles, political intrigue, and the like, though of course God is a or even *the* major player in such dramas. By contrast, Luke is writing about *salvation* history, God's saving eschatological acts, and fulfillment of scriptural promises and prophecies that does not by and large come to pass by means of political or military means, but rather by preaching. Political figures and historical synchronisms play a much less central role.

---

132. See the discussion in Tannehill, *Narrative Unity of Luke-Acts*, 2:2ff. and works cited there.

133. See Esler, *Community and Gospel*, pp. 16ff. and pp. 68-69. Legitimation "is a process which is carried out after a social institution has originated in the first place."

134. See pp. 60ff. below.

One is also struck by the fact that Luke's sense of the time or age in which he lives differs markedly from both the earlier Jewish writers in the Bible and his contemporary Josephus. Luke envisions a radical social change initiated by God, not a critical historical *development* with normal historical antecedents. Acts does not read like the *Jewish Wars* in this regard.

It is not adequate to see Luke-Acts as simply a *continuation* of earlier Jewish historiographic works, if by that one means an organic further development of them. Luke is not writing a mere *sequel* to the OT: he does not focus on political and military events but rather on the story of the beginning of the fulfillment of all OT hopes, dreams, promises, and prophecies by means of the dramatic and surprising intervention of God in Jesus. This is about theological intrusion, not mere historical development. Or put another way, it is about the fulfillment of the ends of sacred history caused by divine intrusion in human lives and situations.[135]

More to the point, Luke's view of the people of God is much more inclusive and universal than one finds in the LXX or in early Hellenistic Jewish historiography. Out of an ethnographic womb has come forth a rather different historical child. It is not accidental that each volume of Luke-Acts begins with a strong Semitic flavor and then becomes more cosmopolitan, even to the extent of an Areopagus address such as we find in Acts 17. It is also not accidental that Jesus' genealogy goes back to Adam, not merely to Abraham (Luke 3:23-38). The Gentiles will be included within the people of God, and not on narrowly Jewish terms that would require the adopting of a particular cultural and ethnic identity (cf. the commentary on Acts 15). Indeed, God's plan (βουλη) involves the incorporation of Gentiles into the people of God by planned missionary work, Law-free and on the basis of grace and faith. Even Peter himself is made to realize this through a vision, and he announces it at the critical council in Acts 15, sounding much like Paul (Acts 15:6-11)! Instead of Gentiles streaming to Zion, Luke envisions Paul going to Rome and explaining even to Jews this new twist in the tale of salvation history.

There were then some *partial* Jewish antecedents for the general sort of historiographic writing Luke was undertaking, since both sorts of works were indebted in some content and theological and ethical concepts to biblical historiography and later Jewish works such as the accounts of the Maccabean revolt, but Luke-Acts does not fit this mold entirely and should be evaluated on its own terms as a two-volume historical work about a particular religious and social movement.

---

135. Cf. C. E. B. Cranfield, *The First Epistle of Peter* (London: SCM, 1950), p. 92: "The new order is not part of the historical process, it does not evolve from the present order; on the contrary, it is the breaking in of that which is outside and beyond history, the replacing, not the self-fulfillment of this order." This can, however, be discussed as the fulfillment of the divine plan and purpose.

3. Conclusions

Our conclusion in this subsection of our discussion is that Luke-Acts bears some strong resemblances to earlier Greek historiographic works in form and method and general arrangement of material, as well as some similarities to Hellenized Jewish historiography in content and general apologetic aims. Furthermore, the echoes and quotes of the OT in Luke-Acts as well as the stress on fulfillment reveal a vital link to the biblical promises and prophecies of the past. Luke's work follows no one model, but clearly enough it would not have been seen as a work like Roman historiography, Greek biography, or Greek scientific treatises. It would surely, however, have been seen as some sort of Hellenistic historiography, especially by a Gentile audience.[136]

This does not mean that there are not some similarities to other traditions; for instance, Tacitus's attempt to write moral history that looks for moral causes of human behavior and events finds some analogy in Luke's work. Or again Tacitus's shunning of sordid gossip and his seriousness of purpose are like what we find in Luke-Acts. Then, too, Tacitus's belief that personal participation and, failing that, personal research were essential to writing about recent events seems also to have been Luke's belief.[137]

II. Luke-Acts and Rhetoric

A. Rhetoric, History, and Style

At this juncture we must deal with a subject that sets much of ancient historiography apart from modern history writing — the influence of rhetoric and

---

136. It should be noted, however, that even some good Roman historians, like Tacitus, while sometimes composing speeches, also often relied on speeches they found in the records of the Roman Senate. Cf. Mellor, *Tacitus,* p. 19.

137. See the discussion in ibid., pp. 30ff. I suspect however if Tacitus had read Acts it would have had entirely too much of a Greek and Eastern flavor to it to suit him. In particular, its ready use of prophecies, portents, miracles, visions, and the like, which was much more characteristic of non-Roman than Roman historiography, would have probably disgusted the sober and often cynical Tacitus, even though he was not averse to reporting a prophecy, suspending his usual disbelief, if it added to the power of his story. Cf. *Histories* 2.78-79; 4.81; 5.13; cf. also ibid., p. 49. I also suspect he would have been very skeptical of all the stories in Luke-Acts about people going through character transformation by conversion, for "Tacitus, like most Roman writers, usually regarded moral character as fixed at birth and the human personality as essentially static" (ibid., p. 54). Nor does Luke show the snobbish disdain for slaves, freedmen and freedwomen, and the lower classes so typical of Romans of higher status such as Tacitus.

rhetorical conventions.[138] Various historians and classics scholars have canvassed this latter subject, and the verdict seems clear enough.[139] Early Greek history writing as embodied in Herodotus and Thucydides was affected by the earlier genres of Greek drama and epic poetry. From the time of Aristotle on there was an increasing influence of other literary traditions as well, especially rhetorical conventions, on the writing of history. By the time we arrive at the first century A.D. some works that claimed to be ιστορια often owed more to declamation and Greco-Roman rhetoric than to careful historical study of sources and consulting of witnesses.

For example, Livy, who saw the transition from the Roman Republic to the Empire, was steeped "in Ciceronian rhetorical theory, and profoundly influenced by that orator's style." He "probably spent more time upon the literary composition of his history, which included many full-length speeches, than upon the study and comparison of his source material."[140] Even a more sober, cynical, and cautious historian like Tacitus can be shown to have taken considerable rhetorical liberties in the presentation of a famous speech by Claudius for which we have an independent record.[141] Some ancients even considered history and history writing a subset or part of the science of rhetoric.[142]

Yet interestingly, even a Livy, whose use of sources can be checked when he draws on a speech from Polybius, does not seem to have engaged in the free invention of speeches; rather, "he substantially reproduced the source-content of the speeches he inherited from others."[143] If one cannot assume with a highly rhetorical writer like Livy that the free composition of speeches was engaged in, it would be even less warranted to do so with someone like Luke, especially since there was no *convention* that ancient historians were free to create speeches.[144]

---

138. For a general introduction to rhetoric in Luke-Acts, see Kurz, "Hellenistic Rhetoric." Kurz shows that Luke's *manner* of arguing follows the form of the enthymeme, arguing from premise to conclusion as Aristotle advised (*Rhetoric* 1.1.11), rather than a Jewish form of argumentation such as proof from prophecy. Further, even in speeches by people like Peter who are "unlettered" we find stock rhetorical items such as the Hellenistic address form ανδρες αδελφοι, the stress on speaking with παρρησια (free speech), and the use of the oath as evidence (Acts 2:30).

139. This is stressed by both the historians and the classics scholars; see Usher, *Historians of Greece and Rome,* pp. 100ff.; North, "Rhetoric and Historiography"; and especially Woodman, *Rhetoric in Classical Historiography.*

140. Usher, *Historians of Greece and Rome,* pp. 180-81.

141. See the discussion in Hardy, "The Speech of Claudius," and Wellesley, "Can You Trust Tacitus?"

142. See Sacks, "Greek History Writing."

143. Fornara, *History in Ancient Greece and Rome,* p. 161.

144. I have spoken to this matter at some length in *History, Literature, and Society in the Book of Acts,* ed. B. Witherington III (Cambridge: Cambridge University Press, 1996), pp. 23-32.

Even well before the Empire there was an internal debate among historians about how much concession should be given to rhetorical concerns in the writing of history, with continuators of Thucydides like Cratippus disapproving of the inclusion of speeches in history *at all* since it gave too much freedom for rhetorical invention, while on the other end of the scale Theopompus was so obsessed with the literary qualities of his history writing that it may be said that he never saw a rhetorical device that he did not like and use.[145]

It was not, however, a matter of the nonrhetorical historians versus the rhetorical ones. The debate was over whether distortion or free invention was allowable in a historical work in the service of higher rhetorical aims. No one was seriously arguing that composers of written history should eschew all literary considerations. As H. F. North says, "there were two essential elements in the ancient concept of history: fidelity to truth and perfection of style — *narratio* and *exornatio*."[146]

We must speak of a sliding scale of those historians like Livy who are more dominated by rhetorical considerations and those like Cratippus who are less so.[147] Even so serious a historian as Tacitus gave full attention to rhetorical considerations, especially in his speech material and vivid descriptions of battles and other events told in ways meant to evoke *pathos*. As Mellor says, Tacitus "regarded rhetorical training not merely as a bag of oratorical tricks but as the acquisition of a profound literary culture."[148] I would suggest the same seems to have been true of Luke as well.

Ancient historical works were meant to be *heard* primarily and read only secondarily, and this meant that considerable attention had to be given to the aural impression a work would leave on the audience. Furthermore, the audience for such works was well-educated people of some social standing in

---

145. See Usher, *Historians of Greece and Rome*, pp. 100-101.

146. See North, "Rhetoric and Historiography," p. 242. On the subject of whether the influence of rhetoric on history writing was a bane or a blessing, she rightly concludes that much depends on the period and on the person. How much freedom did the writer have to tell the truth during the period in which he wrote and about the subject he addressed? Secondly, how much personal and moral commitment did the person have to telling the truth, even if the work suffered somewhat from an aesthetic point of view? In view of the rough spots, even in some of the speeches in Acts, it seems clear that Luke's concern for style was subordinated to his concern for conveying truthful and accurate substance. Relating the good news required a considerable standard of fidelity to the truth about one's sources. Luke also does not seem to be laboring with any imposed external constraints in the telling of his tale. Sometimes he records things that were embarrassing to early Christianity (e.g., the Ananias and Sapphira episode, the squabbling over the dole for the widows, etc.).

147. Those like Cratippus insisted that *veritas* replace *verisimilitudo*. See ibid., p. 239.

148. Mellor, *Tacitus*, p. 7. People often forget that Tacitus was a very gifted rhetor and lawyer long before he became a historian.

the overwhelming majority of cases. In other words, they were first-century people who, with rare exceptions, will have had some rhetorical education at both the secondary and tertiary levels of schooling. Furthermore, in "the normal Graeco-Roman curriculum, which varied but little from the Hellenistic Age to that of the Second Sophistic [in the second century A.D.], history had a firm place in the schools, but it was never studied for its own sake — always for what it could bring to oratory."[149]

This brings us back to Theophilus, probably Luke's patron, and more certainly of some social standing and thus likely having considerable education. If Luke wished for Theophilus to give *ear* to the case he was making, he would almost certainly have had to give attention to the rhetorical properties and potentialities of his composition. It may come as some surprise to us, but it was often thought in antiquity that the person most suited to write a work of history was a great orator, like a Cicero.[150] A work of history could be seen as an exercise in producing an extended *narratio* — the statement of the facts that provide the points of reference for a rhetorical speech.

Dionysius of Halicarnassus strongly criticized Thucydides for failing to adequately pay attention to the rhetorical conventions in regard to invention, arrangement, and style. Others during the Roman Empire criticized Thucydides' choice of subject as inappropriate for ιστορια, which many thought should be a sort of encomium or epideictic exercise in praising great men, great deeds, great cities, great nations.

Roughly speaking we may divide the influences of rhetoric into two schools of approach. There were those who thought that the more scientific approach to history writing was in order, and felt Aristotle's advice about rhetoric and history writing should be followed. Polybius, for example, felt that while it was the task of the poet to move or to charm, it was the task of the historian to teach and persuade, but to do so by a selection of events and speeches that record what really happened or really was said, however commonplace (cf. 2.56.1-13).

In other words, the art of persuasion, otherwise known as rhetoric, *was* essential in history writing, *but* serious historians would follow the conventions of deliberative rhetoric which had to do with giving advice and counsel about the future, and perhaps also forensic rhetoric which had to do with defending the past, but would stay largely away from epideictic rhetoric, the rhetoric of free invention, and mere display and declamation. C. Gempf is right to stress that one should not oversimplify the picture as if there was one clear developing trend in the use of rhetoric or in historiographic methodology in the first century A.D.[151] My point is that there was a variety of views in regard to the use of rhetoric

---

149. North, "Rhetoric and Historiography," p. 235.
150. See ibid., p. 234.
151. Gempf, "Public Speaking and Published Accounts."

in writing history in Luke's day and that Luke's use of the art of persuasion is more like that of the more serious earlier Greek historians such as Polybius than it is of a Livy or a Dionysius of Halicarnassus.[152]

As Fornara has pointed out, style is a function of genre, or, to put it differently, different sorts of documents were supposed to be written in different kinds of Greek style.[153] Form and content were expected to coinhere, cooperate, and offer confirmation to one another. This being the case, something can be said about Luke's purposes and intent by evaluating the style and rhetoric of Luke-Acts.

Not incidentally, it has now been demonstrated, after extensive use of the TLG and computer-aided comparisons, that Luke's Greek style is in various important ways like that of the serious Hellenistic historians, Polybius in particular.[154] Luke is basically no Atticist in his style, nor does he indulge in the florid rhetorical exuberance of a Theopompus.[155] This is important because style was an important indicator of how a work should be evaluated in antiquity. Luke's style suggests that he wishes to be heard as a serious Hellenistic historian would be heard, like a Polybius.

Furthermore, in his ability to vary his style from more to less Semitic, depending on the subject matter (more when in Jerusalem, less the closer he gets to Greece and Rome), he is following the advice of the rhetoricians about

152. On the development of rhetoric before and during the Empire, cf. Litfin, *St. Paul's Theology of Proclamation*, pp. 1-134.

153. Fornara, *History in Ancient Greece and Rome*, p. 19. As we read in *Ad Herrennium* 4.42.54: "We shall not repeat the same thing precisely — for that, to be sure, would weary the hearer and not refine the idea, but with changes . . . in the words, in the delivery, and in the treatment."

154. See Mealand, "Hellenistic Historians," pp. 42-65.

155. The only real concessions of Luke to Atticizing tendencies in the writings of historians in the late first century A.D. may be said to be his use of the optative mood, which was very rare in Hellenistic vernacular (cf. Acts 8:31; 17:18, 26, 29, and Bruce, *The Acts of the Apostles*, p. 67), as well as the Areopagus address in Acts 17:22-31, where Paul is addressing an audience which might have appreciated such efforts. This is not to say that he does not sometimes archaize, perhaps especially in the first few chapters of Acts, to give it a Semitic flavor, as is also the case in Luke 1–2. The contrast between the Hellenistic Greek of the preface and the rest of Luke 1–2 has often been noted (cf. Cadbury, *The Making of Luke-Acts*, p. 223). More importantly for our concerns, Acts becomes progressively more Hellenistic or secular and less Semitic in its style, climaxing in the speech in Acts 17, and in the travel narrative that closes the book (cf. Cadbury, *The Making of Luke-Acts*, p. 224). The ability to vary style, including at points to write in the style of the LXX and other early Jewish documents, shows Luke's considerable skills. If we may take the eyewitness portions toward the close of Acts as a reflection of Luke's normal style (notice how the OT is quoted infrequently in the last eight or so chapters of Acts) when not relying on written sources but simply engaging in free composition, then it must be said that he is Semitizing the early portions of his Gospel and Acts, or else relying on Semitic sources which he does not fully transform.

the necessity of varying one's style if one wants to appeal to a literate audience.[156] Luke is also attentive to the rhetorical canons of style in regard to the differences that should exist between narrative and reported speeches. Aristides in his *Ars rhetorica* (1.13.4) sums up the matter neatly: "While the flowing and loose structure is appropriate for narrative and emotional passages, the periodic structure is appropriate for declamations and *prooemia* and arguments." It is no accident that Luke's rhetorical skills are more in evidence in the preface and speeches than elsewhere in Luke-Acts.

In his freedom to use Semitisms and the like, especially in Luke 1–2 and Acts 1–12 where it was appropriate, Luke would have been courting a listener who knew and appreciated the cadences and substance of the LXX.[157] This latter Semitizing or Setuagintalizing move was in fact not without precedent in a general way in Greek historiography during the Empire, for it was a form of deliberate archaizing not unlike that of those who attempted to Atticize their historical narrative in the latter part of the first century A.D.[158] This simply shows that our author has been influenced by a variety of traditions and is trying to write in a fashion that will allow him to show that the gospel is for a broad audience including both Gentile and Jew. Archaizing also served the function of stressing a certain kind of link with the past, which is indeed one of Luke's purposes in Luke-Acts. Christianity is not to be seen as a purely new religion, but rather the fulfillment in a more universal mode of a very old one, bringing to fruition ancient prophecies to God's people.[159]

Other historical writers in Luke's era, who seem to have been in the majority during the Empire, preferred to heed the example and successors of Isocrates with the emphasis placed on: (1) the moral purpose of history writing (to provide *exempli* to follow or shun); (2) following an encomiastic and epideictic method characterizing and praising great persons, a method that had more in common with ancient biographical writing than with serious history written by a Polybius or Thucydides; (3) making excessive use of declamation, moralizing digressions, the display of rhetorical virtuosity for stylistic effect, and the introduction of wonders into the narrative for the sake of entertainment.[160]

---

156. That Luke is style conscious is shown by the very fact that in Luke 1–2 and the first few chapters of Acts we find more Semitisms. Luke tries to suit the style of his narrative and speeches to the Jewish subject matter, just as in Acts 17:16ff. we find a much more Hellenized style, suiting the occasion of a speech before the Areopagus. See below, pp. 63ff.

157. See Ropes, "Style of S. Luke." Luke pays especial attention to the rhetorical canons about variation when one is repeating an idea, motif, or portion of one's narrative as a means to ornament a narrative and avoid monotony.

158. See Aune, *New Testament*, p. 117.

159. For more on Luke's style, cf. pp. 63ff. below. On the issue of Christianity as a *religio licita*, see the excursus pp. 539ff. below.

160. See North, "Rhetoric and Historiography," p. 236.

It must be said that one finds precious few moralizing asides or other sorts of intrusions or digressions in Acts (though see Acts 17:21). Furthermore, most of the narrative, apart perhaps from a few aspects of the final travel narrative, could not be said to be intended for entertainment.[161] The tone and purpose of the account seem far too serious for that. Nor do we find much rhetorical virtuosity displayed *for its own sake.*

This is not to say that there is not considerable evidence that suggests Luke has certain rhetorical skills and aims. For example, the prologue or *exordium* in Luke 1:1-4 reflects Luke's rhetorical interests. This sentence has rightly been called the best Greek period in the NT. Not only does Luke use a variety of words not found elsewhere in Luke-Acts or the NT (e.g., Επειδηπερ, διηγησις, αναταξασθαι, πληροφορημενος, αυτοπτας), showing his concern to immediately impress upon Theophilus by the style of his composition that this was an important subject worthy of careful listening,[162] but he writes in a clear and direct manner in this sentence as Quintilian required in an *exordium* (*Inst. Or.* 4.1.34).[163]

We may also point to a variety of the speeches in Acts that reflect the clear use of forensic and deliberative rhetoric.[164] One may consider, for example, the forensic rhetoric of the defense speeches in Acts 22–26.[165] Or again one may note the careful rhetorical argument in Paul's synagogue speech in Acts 13:16b-41.[166] P. E. Satterthwaite has shown that Luke's choice and arrangement of material in Acts show familiarity with rhetorical conventions in regard to invention, arrangement, and style of a piece if it was to be persuasive.[167] "At point after point Acts can be shown to operate according to con-

161. The travel narrative that concludes Acts hardly fits the romance mold, not least because it involves no romance, nor any happy romantic conclusion. We will say more about this later in the commentary, pp. 376ff. below.

162. An elevated subject deserves an elevated or stately style. That what follows does not measure up to this same high standard is in part because Luke goes immediately into a Semitic mode, and in part because the opening of any book on a papyrus roll had to be impressive to get the reader or listener to pay attention to the rest. First impressions were crucial if one did not want one's composition to be quickly discarded as not fit for a literate audience's attentions.

163. Morgenthaler, *Lukas und Quintilian,* pp. 393-95. As in his other works Morgenthaler overpresses what one can learn from statistical analysis, but this does not invalidate many of his observations about Luke's use of rhetoric. The style of writing in Luke 1:1-4 is clear but not without rhetorical embellishment. Besides the use of unique words, one may point to the elegant use of hyperbaton in the phrase αυτοπται και υπηρεται, as well as the reference to have investigated "*everything* carefully."

164. See now Soards, *The Speeches in Acts,* pp. 18ff.

165. Cf. Neyrey, "Forensic Defense Speech," and Winter, "Importance of the *Captatio Benevolentiae.*"

166. Cf. Black, "The Rhetorical Form," pp. 8ff.

167. Satterthwaite, "Background of Classic Rhetoric."

ventions similar to those outlined in classical rhetorical treatises. There are some aspects which it is hard to explain other than by concluding that Luke was aware of rhetorical conventions: the preface; the layout of the speeches; the presentation of the legal proceedings in Acts 24–26."[168] More will be said on this matter in the commentary itself. In general, the places where Luke's use of rhetoric becomes most apparent are in the prologues, in the speech material, in his summaries, and in his own travelogue at the end of Acts, as we shall see.

B. Rhetoric, Speeches, and Thucydides' Approach

At this juncture it may be appropriate to raise the question of whether these rhetorical speeches reflect Luke's skills, or those of the sources he cites, or perhaps some of both. In view of the fact that M. Soards has now demonstrated at length that whatever sources Luke may have used for these speeches, he has made them his own in terms of style, vocabulary, syntax, and the like, it is safe to say that they *at least* reflect Luke's rhetorical skill, since what we have in almost every case is a précis or edited summary of a speech, and not an entire speech.[169]

If, as we have suggested, Luke intends to be seen as a serious historian of contemporary events, like a Polybius or a Thucydides, it is appropriate to ask at this juncture about the troublesome matter of Thucydides' theory about speeches in historical narratives, especially in light of what we have just said about rhetoric and Luke's speeches. Note that though there is a great deal of speech material in Acts, Luke's speeches are considerably *shorter* than some found in Hellenistic historical works. Nor in general do Luke's speeches function to present a variety of viewpoints, though the speeches in Acts 15 may be said to represent something of an exception.[170] Furthermore, Luke gives more space and obviously more importance to the narrative settings of his speeches in Acts than does Thucydides.[171] Also the speeches function somewhat differently in the work of Thucydides as compared to that of Luke: "In Thucydides speeches function as a commentary on events. In Luke-Acts, speeches are an essential feature of the action itself, which is the spread of the word of God."[172]

---

168. Ibid., p. 378. On rhetoric, the legal proceedings, and Acts 24–26, cf. Winter, "Official Proceedings."

169. On Paul's rhetorical skills see my *Conflict and Community in Corinth*, pp. 40ff., and my commentary on Philippians, *Friendship and Finances in Philippi* (Valley Forge, Pa.: Trinity, 1994).

170. See Soards, *The Speeches in Acts*, p. 141.

171. See Aune, *New Testament*, p. 125.

172. Ibid., p. 125.

Bearing these things in mind, let us turn to the crucial Thucydidean text in 1.22.1-2, which has been analyzed endlessly by classics scholars, ancient historians, and biblical scholars.[173] If one takes this passage in its larger context, it seems clear enough that Thucydides is trying to say that he has been as accurate as he can be (cf. 1.22.3-4, where he disclaims interest in romance or myth). Much of the debate has centered around whether Thucydides was contradicting himself in this passage by on the one hand claiming to adhere as closely as possible to what was actually said, and on the other claiming to make his speakers say what in his view they *ought* to have said. Though this view of the matter has been both popular and has led to much puzzlement, it is probably incorrect.

The εδοκουν in our quote should be compared to the use of εδοκει in 22.2, where it means "seemed likely." It follows from this that Thucydides was claiming that he presented his speech-makers as saying what it seemed likely that they *did* say (not what they ought to have said), adhering as closely as he could to what he knew of what they actually spoke.[174]

The second semantic conundrum centers around the word ξυμπασα. There are various examples in Thucydides where this word is used with an accompanying noun to mean the complete amount of something or something taken altogether (6.43.1). When coupled with the word γνωμη it surely can*not* mean "the main thesis." Far more likely it means something like taking into account all the ideas, thoughts, points behind or expressed in the speech. "What Thucydides claims here is not to *give* us all the γνωμη: he claims that what he gives is consonant with, indeed partly the result of, his keeping all the γνωμη in mind and sticking to it as closely as possible. . . . Such a procedure is very different from the attempt to summarise a 'main thesis', though in brief reportage it may amount to the same thing."[175] This of course does not mean that Thucydides claimed to offer a speech verbatim.

J. Wilson concludes (after evaluating Thucydides' claims in light of what we can know of his actual practice, his limits or rules of literary license in dealing with speeches) that he offered: (1) reportage in his own style, not that of the speaker; (2) a selection from a number of speeches actually made; (3) a selection, but not all, of the ideas or thoughts (γνωμη) expressed in the speech; (4) a reporting which contains nothing that does not count as γνωμη; (5) the adding of words to make the γνωμη clearer; (6) an abbreviating or expanding so long as the γνωμη is clear; (7) a casting of the γνωμη in terms which might

---

173. See, e.g., Woodman, *Rhetoric in Classical Historiography,* pp. 10ff. and his bibliography; Grant, *The Ancient Historians,* pp. 88ff.; Wilson, "What Does Thucydides Claim"; Porter, "Thucydides 1.22.1."

174. See Wilson, "What Does Thucydides Claim," p. 97.

175. Ibid., p. 99.

serve his particular purposes (e.g., the pairing of remarks in two different speeches [e.g., 1.69 and 144] or the arrangement into a formal dialogue [5.84-133]).[176] In other words, Thucydides does not handle speeches in a radically different fashion than he handles the reporting of events. Both are subject to close scrutiny, analysis, and then a presentation in Thucydides' own style and way, with some concern for literary and rhetorical considerations.[177]

The very reason someone like Dionysius of Halicarnassus so severely criticizes Thucydides in his famous *Letter to Pompey* 3 is precisely that he does *not* treat history as an exercise in epideictic rhetoric, the writing of encomiums for great persons and about great events. Thucydides does not see it as an occasion for free invention of speeches and for saying whatever is likely to best please one's audience. Hermogenes recognized that this did not mean that Thucydides did not use rhetoric, but rather "he is as much forensic and deliberative as panegyrical" (*De Ideis* 422.10). I suspect that the limitations listed above for Thucydides in handling speeches come close to the practice of Luke, who means to write accurately on a serious subject without neglecting certain concerns for style and rhetorical conventions. This conclusion is supported by the closeness of Luke at various points to Polybius, in view of what Polybius *also* says about speeches (cf. above).

One must not underestimate the influence of Thucydides and Polybius in establishing the conventions in regard to the use of speeches in historiographical works. Leaving aside the Declaimers during the Empire who ignored traditional conventions and cannot be ranked among serious historians, we should bear in mind the warnings of Fornara:

> conventions set the parameters of conduct; we are not entitled to proceed on the assumption that the historians considered themselves at liberty to write up speeches out of their own heads. That some or many or most actually did so is perhaps hypothetically conceivable. We must recognize, however, that such a procedure would have been contrary to convention and *not, as all too many moderns seem to suppose, a convention in its own right.*[178]

Diodorus Siculus in the first century B.C. warned against some writers who "by excessive use of rhetorical passages have made their entire historical work into an appendage of oratory" (20.1-2.2), because there was both the less rhetorical and the more rhetorical approach to history writing already

---

176. Ibid., p. 103. This view is much more convincing than that of Woodman, *Rhetoric in Classical Historiography,* pp. 40ff., who follows the "main gist" theory of G. E. M. De Ste. Croix.
177. See now the important essay by McCoy, "In the Shadow of Thucydides."
178. Fornara, *History in Ancient Greece and Rome,* pp. 154-55, emphasis mine.

extant in his day, and he is arguing for the more traditional, Thucydidean approach. "The principle was established that speeches were to be recorded accurately, though in the words of the historian, and always with the reservation that the historian could 'clarify.' . . ."[179]

C. The Question of Bias

Another important consideration in evaluating Luke-Acts in the context of ancient historiography is the discussion of the matter of bias. Various ancient historians, including especially the more serious ones like Tacitus, frequently would make protestations that they were writing *sine ira et studio* (*Annals* 1.1.3), without malice, preconception, showing favoritism, or what we would call bias. This issue was usually raised in the context of the discussion of a person's skill in rhetoric, or the lack thereof. Lucian in his famous essay insists that the historian is "in his books a stranger and a man without a country, independent, subject to no sovereign, not reckoning what this or that man will think, but stating the facts" (41.1). Polybius insists that concentration must be placed on educating one's audience about the truth of the history one is writing, and not on merely pleasing or entertaining the audience. History without truth is but a body without eyes (12.12.1-3).[180]

The claim to be free from partiality or hatred is one repeatedly made by historians of recent or contemporary events, but it is never or almost never made by those writing about the distant past. In other words, it was a claim characteristic of those who wrote historical monographs on current subject matter but not of those who wrote universal histories.[181] The reason for such a disclaimer was in part because of the nature of the patronage system to which most writers in antiquity were beholden. The remark was meant to indicate that one had not been unduly influenced by one's patron or other socially and politically important figures that were alive and figured in the narrative. The praise or blame rendered in the narrative was thought more likely to be true when spoken of dead persons than of live ones, for in the case of the latter one might be trying to flatter or invoke enmity conventions against them.

The claim of Tacitus and others was meant to fend off the suspicion that the judgments rendered in the historical work might be calculated to aid the writer in advancing his status or position as a receiver of patronage, honor, or fame. Luke in his claim to have investigated everything carefully from the

---

179. Ibid., p. 145.
180. See the discussion in Nadel, "Philosophy of History before Historicism."
181. See the important discussion by Luce, "Ancient Views."

beginning (of salvation history proper), and to have written an orderly account
conveying things accurately or securely (ασφαλειαν — Luke 1:4), is sensitive
to the issue of bias and makes his own disclaimer in this regard.[182]

What the claim of lack of bias did *not* mean is that the author was
claiming to be a *neutral* observer of the historical process. Indeed, "according
to the ancient view, then, a historian could be biased for personal reasons, the
favors and injuries that he himself may have received from the men who
populate his work."[183] In particular, a writer was not expected to be neutral
about his own family, friends, or country. Dionysius of Halicarnassus strongly
censures Thucydides for his lack of patriotism toward his own region and
people in his histories (*Let. to Pompeius* 3). Above all, it must be kept in mind
that "the ancients did not regard an ideological belief as bias."[184]

Evaluating what is said in Luke 1:1-4 in light of all the above data, we
may draw the following further conclusions: (1) Luke professes to be one of
many who have written about the matters of his work, and apparently his
decision to attempt this work is based on the fact that there was precedent for
writing this sort of work. (2) Luke's concern is with a community's history; it
is microhistory, not macrohistory, for it is about what has happened "among
us," though it has universal significance and implications as it potentially
includes all kinds and races of people. (3) Theophilus has already been at least
partially instructed about these matters, but Luke wants to make sure he knows
the truth about what he had learned. This *may* suggest that other attempts
were seen as biased in some unacceptable way or at least as inadequate from
Luke's view and for Theophilus's purposes.[185] (4) Luke promises an orderly
account, and here while καθεξης could refer to chronological or even geographical order in part, in view of its use in Acts 11:4 it would seem to primarily
have the sense of an account written in such a fashion and order that one can
make sense of or discern the truth in the maze of events.[186] (5) Luke's reference
to a careful investigation of "everything" from the beginning, coupled with his
reliance on the sacred tradition passed down by those who were both eyewit-

182. As Aune, *New Testament*, p. 136, translates it, he wants to provide "exact information."

183. Luce, "Ancient Views," p. 21.

184. Mellor, *Tacitus*, p. 36.

185. But on this see my discussion of Acts 1:1-2 in the commentary, pp. 105ff. below.

186. As Moessner, "The Meaning of *KATHESES*," shows. Moessner demonstrates by
comparing Acts 10 and 11 that the "order" followed in Acts 11 is not exactly the same as
the order of events recorded in Acts 10. The point is that order in Acts 11 as in Luke 1
means some kind of logical or narratological order that helps the hearer understand the
truth and significance of these events. See also Völkel, "Exegetische Erwägungen zum
Verständnis des Begriff *kathezes* im Lukanischen Prolog," who argues it means the continuity
of items within a logical whole.

nesses and ministers of the word,[187] amounts to his profession to being a serious religious historian.[188]

It would appear that Theophilus was a socially significant recent convert who has been informed or more likely instructed about the Christian faith but still had some confusion and questions. He had been inadequately socialized in Luke's view. Luke does not profess to be an outsider who is neutral and will come in and set the record straight, but rather a reliable insider without the wrong sort of bias and malice that would cause him to skew or distort his narrative about "us" and the sacred tradition that was handed down "to us." He is prepared to guide Theophilus to understand the truth and historical logic of what has happened "among us."[189]

III. Acts: Authorship, Date, and Audience

A. *The Authorship of Acts*

The book of Acts, like the Gospel of Luke, is formally anonymous, in that nowhere in the text is the author's name mentioned. It is not likely an attempt on the part of the author to disguise his identity, in view of the fact that this document has a formal addressee, Theophilus, who surely must have known who had written these volumes to him, especially if, as seems likely, Theophilus was the patron of the writer. In order to discern who likely wrote this work we must consider first the internal hints in Luke-Acts, which is the primary

187. The grammar here, with the two nouns sharing one article, surely makes clear that we are not dealing with two groups but rather one who has first seen and then proclaimed. This in turn means Luke is not implying that a generation of proclaimers existed as an intermediary between him and the eyewitnesses. Rather, he is claiming to have contact with at least some of the eyewitnesses who were commissioned to be ministers of the word. Cf. Marshall, *Luke*, p. 42.

188. Wilson, *Paul*, p. 15, accuses Luke of bias (indeed, he calls him "a hard-fisted historian who attempts to put a shape on recalitrant material," p. 67) because he sees Jesus as the starter of a new movement which eventually led to the church. Yet there were many early starters of movements (cf., e.g., John the Baptist), movements which developed in unexpected ways, after the death of the founder. I would caution that while Luke was certainly capable of distorting the facts, he is less likely to have done so than we at 2,000 years remove.

189. There would have been considerable difficulty explaining the concept of grace to someone like Theophilus, who was used to the system of patronage and reciprocity set up in the Roman Empire. Tacitus once remarked, "For assistance is welcome as long as a reciprocal reward seems possible, but once it goes beyond that point it produces hatred instead of gratitude" (*Annals* 4.18).

data, and then second the external attestation about authorship from hints in the NT and then from later extracanonical sources.

First, the preface in Luke 1:1-4 indicates that the author was not an eyewitness of the ministry of Jesus, but had contact with some who were. The argument that we should distinguish the eyewitnesses from the ministers of the word and suppose the author only had contact with the latter is grammatically very doubtful (cf. below). The author then claims to be a second-generation Christian.

Secondly, the preface, and indeed the Greek in the two volumes in general, suggests someone whose native tongue is Greek. It is clearly the best Hellenistic Greek in the NT. Furthermore, there are clear signs that he had had considerable education, for he knows the conventions of Greco-Roman rhetoric (cf. above). His knowledge of rhetoric indicates that he had progressed to the higher levels of Greco-Roman education.[190] It is equally clear that our author knew a good deal about ancient historiography and its conventions. Various hints alluded to earlier in this discussion suggest he may have read other Greek historians such as Polybius or Thucydides or Ephorus. His stress on the relation of history to the plan or providential counsel of God may also suggest his familiarity with the work of his predecessor Diodorus Siculus.[191]

When we couple this with the fact that the author does not appear to know either Hebrew or Aramaic, as is shown by his failure to take over various Aramaic phrases from Mark, except the word *amen*, which was surely common in Christian and Jewish assemblies throughout the Empire, this conclusion is further reinforced. This strongly suggests that our author was not a Palestinian Jew. His lack of attention to Jesus' controversies with the Pharisees also points in this direction.[192] The apparent knowledge he has of Athenians (Acts 17:21) and of Asia Minor also points away from Palestine.

On the face of things, the "we" passages which show up in the second half of Acts suggest that our author was a sometime companion of Paul. It does not follow from this that he either had read any letters Paul may have written prior to their meeting (in Troas? — 16:10) on Paul's second missionary

---

190. On the early rhetorical schools see Parks, *The Roman Rhetorical Schools*, pp. 62-97. As Parks says (p. 65), the rhetorical school focused on both prose composition and elocution, and this in turn led to a concern about the *aural* dimensions of one's prose. We will note Luke's attention to various aural literary devices as the commentary proceeds. It is also important to point out that the student in a rhetorical school was first trained to use deliberative rhetoric, the art of persuading in regard to a future course of action. Forensic rhetoric, the rhetoric of attack and defense, was taught after the student had become adept at deliberative rhetoric (Parks, pp. 85-86). We will find both sorts of speeches in Acts, but very little epideictic rhetoric.

191. See the discussion in Squires, *Plan of God in Luke-Acts*, pp. 15ff.

192. See Fitzmyer, *Luke I–IX*, p. 41.

journey in the early 50s A.D., or for that matter that he read the letters Paul wrote during the portions of the second and third missionary journeys during which the author does *not* claim to have been with Paul.[193] If, as Acts 20–28 suggest, the author was with Paul during his travels to Jerusalem, his time in Caesarea Maritima, and then his trip to Rome, he may have known about or have read letters Paul wrote during this period of time. The "we" passages also support the suggestion that our author lived somewhere outside the Holy Land, perhaps in Asia Minor or Philippi, but this may only have been true at the time when Paul first came in contact with him.

The argument that Luke is quoting or heavily reliant on someone else's diary or journal in the "we" passages is weak for the very good reason that the style, grammar, and vocabulary of the "we" passages are very much the same as that found elsewhere in Luke-Acts. In other words, apart from the mere use of "we" itself, the theory of a non-Lukan source here has little concrete linguistic evidence to support it. The detailed documentation of this linguistic correspondence by J. C. Hawkins has never been seriously challenged. For example, there are some twenty-one words found in the NT only in the "we" passages and in the rest of Acts, some seventeen other words and phrases found only in the "we" passages and in Luke (and in some cases in Acts as well), and a further twenty-eight found in the "we" passages and almost always in Luke-Acts in the rest of the NT.[194] Hawkins's conclusion deserves to be quoted: "there is an immense balance of internal and external linguistic evidence in favor of the view that the original writer of these sections was the same person as the main author of the Acts and of the Third Gospel."[195] The point to be stressed is that if Luke was going to rewrite a source that completely, why leave the "we" in, thereby misleading various generations of readers, including the earliest ones in the second century, who knew Greek writing conventions much better than moderns do? The argument that falsely claiming participation in some events was an ancient "convention" that Luke chose to follow, fails to come to grips with what was and was not "conventional" in ancient Greek historiographical and biographical works. There was no such "convention" for

193. There may be something to the suggestion of Siotis, "Luke the Evangelist," that we should take seriously the clue in 2 Cor. 2:12 that Paul did some evangelistic work in Troas, which may in turn explain the appearance of Luke in the Acts narrative at this juncture. Luke, then, may have been one of Paul's first converts there, or perhaps in Philippi (cf. Acts 16:9).

194. See Hawkins, *Horae Synopticae*, pp. 185-89. Notice, for example, the use of litotes using ου with an adjective or adverb, which is found four times in the "we" passages, twelve times in the rest of Acts, twice in Luke, and very rarely in the rest of the NT.

195. Ibid., p. 188. See the detailed charts on pp. 182-88. It is also very interesting that Hawkins is able to show that in many regards Acts (in particular the first half) is quite close to the style and vocabulary of Luke 1–2.

the sort of literature Luke was trying to write and would likely have been perceived as trying to write.

The older arguments of W. Hobart that the author could be shown to be a physician from his use of ancient Greek medical terminology[196] were dealt a serious blow by H. J. Cadbury, who showed that these same terms could be found in nonmedical writers like Plutarch, Lucian, and others.[197] Nevertheless, this evidence would support and be consistent with the view that the author was a doctor, if one could provide other evidence for this view. More recent evidence, presented by L. Alexander in regard to the prefaces of Luke and Acts, seems to suggest the author was familiar with some scientific writings and the conventions in regard to writing prefaces for such works.[198]

Another factor which must be considered is the author's clear knowledge not only of Christian traditions, but also of the LXX. This could be attributed to a Diaspora Jew, or perhaps a non-Jew who had been a synagogue adherent before becoming a Christian, but it seems unlikely that the author could have been converted to Christianity from a purely pagan background. The author's obvious interest in and knowledge about Judaism and Diaspora synagogues comport with either of the two aforementioned possibilities. There is little else to be said about the internal hints from Luke and Acts, except on the basis of an analysis of the social location of the implied author, to which we now turn.[199]

Though a distinction can often be made between the implied and real author of a document, especially when one is dealing with fiction of some sort, whether ancient or modern, in view of the genre of Luke-Acts it is unlikely that such a distinction can be sustained with the material presently under scrutiny in this work. Accordingly, what the text suggests about the social location of the implied author is likely also information about the real author. For instance, there is no disputing the author's interest in the biblical heritage and in early Judaism, as well as his familiarity with urban locales in the eastern half of the Mediterranean crescent. What is notable by its absence is any reference to countries west of Italy, north of the Euxine Sea, or east of Israel beyond those countries immediately bordering the Holy Land. This suggests the author is well traveled at least in the countries bordering the sea in the eastern portion of the Empire, and is especially familiar with the Jewish sub-culture (noting the repeated references to the synagogue and Jerusalem).

A further point of considerable importance is the fact that our author has the leisure to write a two-volume work such as Luke-Acts, and to do so

196. Hobart, *Medical Language of St. Luke.*
197. Cadbury, *Style and Literary Method*, part 1.
198. See Alexander, *The Preface to Luke's Gospel.*
199. Here we are drawing on the very helpful insights of Robbins, "Social Location."

with some skill and grace. This suggests either a person of independent means, or more likely a retainer of a well-to-do person, here identified as Theophilus. "It surely is informative that the inscribed author of Luke-Acts has used the same address in the prologues that subordinates use of their Roman superiors in the stories of Acts [cf. Acts 23:26; 24:2; 24:24]. These data suggest that our inscribed author addresses Theophilus in a mode associated with a person who is willingly or unwillingly in a subordinate position to a person of rank in Roman society."[200]

One must also ask what it means about the social location of our author that his presentation not only of people of the official strata of society but also of those of the artisan strata is favorable and familiar. Furthermore, in regard to officials "the narrator depicts a majority of these people as holding a favorable attitude toward Christianity."[201] The favorable attitude toward artisans in Luke-Acts was not a typical attitude of many in the upper strata of society, but it was typical of how artisans and retainers viewed themselves, and how Jews in general viewed work so long as it was not ritually defiling.[202] A further question arises in regard to the fact that the author can turn on and off a Septuagintal style apparently at will, and that the central character Paul can quote Greek writers.

If we put all these clues together they suggest: (1) an author who is not among the elite of society but is certainly in contact with them; (2) an author with considerable education, bicultural in orientation, at home in the Greco-Roman world but very familiar with its Jewish subculture; (3) an author who does not look down on artisans but freely associates with them; (4) a person who is deeply concerned that Christianity be accepted by the social elite and especially the official elite of society, not least because repeatedly in Luke-Acts Christ and Christians are portrayed as being in a precarious position in regard to the law, often finding themselves on trial or in prison, or even in the case of Jesus being executed in a way reserved for the dregs of society; (5) a person who senses not only a distance between Christianity and Roman officials but also between Christianity and those whom he calls Jews, especially in regard to matters such as ritual purity.

The author goes out of his way to suggest that Christianity is a more inclusive religion, not requiring the observance of certain purity and dietary rules of its members (see below on Acts 15). The line is drawn at behavior

---

200. Ibid., pp. 321-22. As Fitzmyer, *Luke I–IX,* p. 300, points out, κρατιστε is the equivalent of the Latin *optimus,* and is attested in a first-century document as the proper form of address for any official. It was, however, also used in general of social superiors (cf. above).

201. Robbins, "Social Location," p. 328.

202. See my discussion in *Conflict and Community in Corinth,* pp. 208-12.

that connotes moral not ritual impurity; otherwise all persons and foods are clean. Yet our author feels a strong kinship with Jews and does not have a strongly negative view of Roman officials in general. The above data support the suggestion that our author is a well-traveled retainer of the social elite, well educated, deeply concerned about religious matters, knowledgeable about Judaism, but no prisoner of any subculture in the Empire. Rather, he is a cosmopolitan person with a more universalistic vision of the potential scope of impact of his faith, both up and down the social ladder, and also across geographical, ethnic, and other social boundaries.

The external evidence is considerably more straightforward and specific. The earliest extant manuscript, p75, of the first volume of Luke-Acts has at its end the ancient title Ευαγγελιον κατα Λουκαν. This papyrus codex dates somewhere between A.D. 175 and 225. Possibly even a little earlier (A.D. 170-80?) than this is the old canon list known as the Muratorian Canon, which refers to "Luke the physician and companion of Paul" as the author of a Gospel and Acts. At the end of the second century we have the testimony of Irenaeus in his *Against Heresies* 3.1.1 and 3.14.1, which stresses that Luke was an inseparable companion of Paul, a conclusion also supported by various other patristic witnesses, at least in regard to Luke being a companion of Paul.[203] There is also an ancient prologue to Luke's Gospel (*SQE*, 533) from perhaps the end of the second century A.D. which says that Luke was a Syrian of Antioch, a physician, a disciple of the apostles, and later a companion of Paul.[204] It may be of some significance that the Western text of Acts 11:28 has a "we," which would place the author in Antioch at the start of Paul's missionary career. Though it is likely this is not an original reading, it may reflect an authentic tradition about the author. Certainly, the book of Acts suggests the author knew a good deal about the Christian community in Syrian Antioch.

In fact, the testimony about Luke-Acts from both the manuscript evidence and the church fathers is basically unanimous. There seems to have been no dispute in the early church about the authorship of these documents, which in itself is remarkable considering the fact that no one was contending that Luke was either an apostle or an eyewitness of much of what he records. Indeed, the tone of various of the early church traditions about Luke as author of the two works that make up about 27 percent of the NT is often defensive (e.g., in Irenaeus), which strongly suggests that no one would have invented the idea that a nonapostle, noneyewitness (of much of his subject matter) about whom so little seems to have been known was the author of these

203. For example, Clement of Alexandria, *Miscellanies* 5.12; Eusebius, *Church History* 3.4; Jerome, *Commentary on Isaiah* 3.6; *Epistle* 53.9; *Lives of Illustrious Men* 7.
204. See the discussion in Fitzmyer, *Luke I–IX*, pp. 38-39, and more recently his reflections in *Luke the Theologian*, pp. 1-26.

documents. But having identified the author as Luke, the question may be properly asked — which Luke of those mentioned in the NT are we discussing?

The name Λουκας is a shortened Greek form of a Latin name — either Lucanus, Lucianus, Lucius, or Lucillus. A. Deissmann long ago presented evidence that the Greek name Λουκας could also be written as Λουκιος, and there is clear evidence that the latter is the equivalent of the Latin Lucius, so this may have been Luke's Latin name.[205] This name does not give us any further clear clues about the author's identity, as it could have been used by a Diaspora Jew as well as by a Gentile, but if it was the former it would suggest that he was a Jewish freedman, which *may* not comport with the education level reflected by the literary ability of our author.

In the NT there are three candidates to be considered. There is first of all the Lucius mentioned in Rom. 16:21 as a kinsman of Paul, and thus a Jewish Christian. Origen (*Comm. in Ep. ad Rom.* 10.39) knew of various persons who thought this identification was correct. The problem with this conclusion is that elsewhere in Paul the person in question is identified as Λουκας (Col. 4:14; 2 Tim. 4:11), not as Λουκιος as in Romans. Less plausible is the identification of our author with Lucius (Λουκιος) of Cyrene mentioned in Acts 13:1 as one of the prophets and teachers in Antioch at the time when Barnabas and Saul were commissioned there. Though this would comport with the church tradition that links Luke to Antioch, elsewhere our author only identifies himself in the *first* person, not in the third, and this brief, passing third-person reference in Acts 13:1 would be a very oblique and confusing way to introduce himself into the narrative, if he was also going to use "I" and "we" elsewhere (cf. Acts 1:1; 16:10). This leaves us with the three references in Paul not yet discussed.

The only reference in the undisputed Paulines is found at Philem. 24, where Λουκας is said to be one of Paul's coworkers along with Mark, Aristarchus, and Demas. Though the matter is disputed, most scholars, including myself, still believe that Philemon, like Philippians, was written from a Roman setting while Paul was under some sort of house arrest.[206] This comports with the ending of Acts, which finds the author in Rome with Paul.[207] In regard to the important term συνεργος, in the Pauline Epistles it refers to someone who has some sort of Christian leadership role, perhaps as an assistant to Paul in his missionary tasks.[208]

---

205. Cf. Deissmann, *Ancient Near East*, pp. 435-38. See the discussion in Fitzmyer, *Luke I–IX*, pp. 42ff.

206. I have dealt with this issue in *Friendship and Finances in Philippi*, pp. 1ff.

207. If one is going to compare the Paul of Acts with the Paul of the letters, one would do well to look at these two undisputed Pauline letters as well as Colossians, not at the earlier Thessalonian, Galatian, Corinthian, or Roman letters. See pp. 430ff. below.

208. See my *Women in the Earliest Churches*, pp. 111-12.

The second text is found in Col. 4:14 and is in some ways even more important. Most scholars still believe that Paul wrote Colossians, but even if not, there is no reason why Col. 4:14 could not reflect authentic Pauline tradition about Luke as a companion of Paul. There is no apparent reason why this passing reference would have been concocted by a later Paulinist as it adds nothing to the substance or message of the letter, for it is simply a greeting. Luke is again grouped here with Demas. More importantly here is the only reference to Luke as "the beloved physician."[209]

I have reviewed elsewhere the evidence that Paul had an ongoing physical malady, a "thorn in the flesh," that may have required periodic treatment.[210] There is some reason to think that he may have had an eye disease that made him appear to have a weak ethos to those who were rhetorically adept (cf. Gal. 4:13-15; 2 Cor. 10:10; 12:7-8). The term *beloved* suggests Paul's high opinion and affection for Luke, but it also suggests that he was well known and loved in Asia Minor.

It has also been argued on the basis of Col. 4:11 when it is compared to 4:14 that this text makes clear that Luke was *not* among the circumcision, that is, that he was not a Jew. In addition, it is contended that since in the intervening verses reference is made to Epaphras, who is apparently one with his audience in being a convert from paganism, the drift of the text would suggest that Luke is also a Gentile.[211] This argument has some weight and perhaps tips the scales just slightly in the direction of Luke being a Gentile. The other possibility would be that Luke is a non-Jewish (hence noncircumcised) Semite, perhaps from Syrian Antioch. The third text is 2 Tim. 4:11, but besides the fact that most scholars feel this letter is deutero-Pauline, it really adds nothing to what we have learned in Colossians and Philemon, namely, that Luke was with Paul during his period(s) of imprisonment.

We may now sum up the evidence about authorship. Both the internal and external evidence strongly points to Luke being the author of Acts. The evidence does not, however, suggest that Luke was always a companion of Paul.[212] Indeed, the ostensible evidence of the "we" passages suggests otherwise. It has been contended by many scholars that despite all the above evidence the Luke who wrote Acts could not have known or been a companion of Paul because of the way he misrepresents Paul's preaching and teaching as well as the arrangement hammered out at the Jerusalem council in Acts 15.

---

209. There is interesting evidence of husband-and-wife doctor teams, and some of these doctors itinerated. See *New Docs,* 2 (1982), no. 2, pp. 20-23.

210. See my *Conflict and Community in Corinth,* pp. 459-64.

211. See the careful analysis by Fitzmyer, *Luke I–IX,* pp. 43-44.

212. See the discussion in ibid., pp. 38-39; and also his more recent reflections in *Luke the Theologian,* pp. 1-26. See now Dunn, *Acts,* p. x; Hengel and Schwemer, *Paul,* p. 7.

We will deal with this argument in detail in the commentary itself. We may say at this juncture, however, that *even if* this claim about misrepresentation were to prove true, it would still not rule out Luke from being a sometime companion of Paul. It would simply mean he had not clearly or at least adequately understood Paul's message, and in this Luke would not have been alone (cf. 2 Pet. 3:15-16).

Long ago, in reviewing M. Dibelius's important work on Acts, A. D. Nock, who knew the Greco-Roman world and literature perhaps better than any of those of his era who *also* had some expertise in the NT, drew the following conclusions about Acts: (1) It was about the acts of God rather than the acts of the apostles. (2) Because of (1) Luke "gave no . . . personal characterizations of the leading speakers." In other words, he was not writing biography in this work. (3) The author was setting himself apart from his (Christian) predecessors rather than following in their footsteps, for "the Gospel had a preface and a dating (3.1-2) in correct style and claimed to be an orderly presentation (i.3), i.e. something different from earlier treatments of the same theme." (4) Nock's own search for possible parallels to the use of "we" in the closing chapters of Acts led him to the conclusion that with one possible exception there were no such parallels except in literature that was obviously fiction. Thus, he concluded, "Personally, I regard this as an authentic transcript of the recollections of an eyewitness, with the confusion and coloring which so easily attach themselves to recollections." (5) "Further we read in Lk. 1.3, which is the foreword to the two volumes, that the writer had followed from far back the whole course of 'the things which have been accomplished among us'; this is an explicit assertion of contact with the Christian movement in its early days; it goes beyond the assertion implicit in 'we'. Since on stylistic grounds the hypothesis of a redactor is excluded, I think we must take these statement at their face value."[213] (6) It may have been that Luke was not long intimate with Paul when he wrote this work. If Luke failed to fully grasp Paul's theology, he was not alone in that. It is worth repeating the caution of the ancient historian R. Mellor as we move on to the next section: "Neither Tacitus, nor any other ancient historian, thought of his work as a series of facts (or judgments) to be quoted out of context. His historical judgments and ideas derive their value precisely from the narrative, and a hunt for minor discrepancies misses the value of ancient historiography."[214]

Nock's evaluation, originally written in 1953 by someone who could by no means be accused of attempting to provide an *apologia* or conservative defense of Luke as a historian, seems to me very near the mark. The truth of

213. The quotes may be found in Nock, *Essays on Religion,* pp. 822, 823, and 828 respectively. The whole review should be consulted, pp. 821-32.
214. Mellor, *Tacitus,* p. 70.

this evaluation is borne out by careful investigation of Acts, an investigation to which we will turn after examining the other traditional background issues.

B. The Dating of Acts

The dating of Acts in part depends on how one dates Luke's Gospel. The argument that Acts was written *before* the Gospel is not persuasive in view of the fact that the preface in Acts 1:1 indicates that what follows will be the second volume. Thus, we must evaluate the date of Acts in light of the date of Luke's Gospel as its sequel.

This leads us to make some comments on the proto-Luke hypothesis, the idea that there was more than one edition of Luke's Gospel, and that perhaps only in the second edition had Luke added such material as that which he derived from Mark's Gospel. As W. G. Kümmel has pointed out, the proto-Luke hypothesis is not convincing for at least the following reasons. (1) This argument is usually suggested in tandem with an argument for the early date of Luke's Gospel and Acts, but Luke himself says that *many* (Luke 1:1) had undertaken to write an account of the material he would record beginning in Luke 1:5. There is simply no evidence that already in the 50s or early 60s there had been many attempts to compose a Gospel. (2) Though Luke does alternate Markan and non-Markan material in his Gospel, if one subtracts all the Markan material one really does not have a complete Gospel. The Markan material does not appear to be a mere supplement to an already composed account. (3) The *way* the Markan material is divided up in Luke's Gospel suggests strongly that Luke had Mark as well as other material before him when he began to compose his Gospel and used Mark to provide a basic outline of the Galilean ministry. For example, Luke separates the Markan Passion predictions (Mark 8:31; 9:31; 10:32) in such a way that the first two appear in close succession in Luke 9:22 and 43ff. but the last one occurs *after* the large, uniquely Lukan travel narrative (9:51–18:14) in Luke 18:31ff., yet the three occur in the same order in Mark and Luke. Or again, the way Luke inserts the genealogy *between* the account of the baptism and the temptation suggests that Luke knew the Markan account where these two items were found together. These examples suggest that when Luke begins to recount the ministry of Jesus, Mark provides his basic outline and inserts other material into it.[215] This evidence means that the dating of Luke-Acts depends in part on the dating of Mark.

Most scholars rightly suggest that Mark's is the earliest Gospel, and internal evidence, particularly in Mark 13, suggests it was written no earlier

---

215. Cf. Kümmel, *Introduction to the New Testament*, pp. 134-35.

than the late 60s when Christians in Rome were under persecution and were concerned about the contemporary events then happening in Jerusalem (see Mark 13:14). This in turn means that the Gospel of Luke must have been written sometime after Mark's account. I am among those who think that the *way* the fall of Jerusalem is portrayed in Luke 21:20ff., and its difference from the account in Mark 13:14-23, suggests that Luke was likely writing *after* A.D. 70 with the benefit of hindsight. It is noteworthy that F. F. Bruce, in the last edition of his Acts commentary, changed his mind about the date of Acts precisely because of this material in Luke 21 and its relationship to both Mark 13 and the actual destruction of Jerusalem.[216] At the very earliest Acts may have been composed in the 70s, but perhaps the early 80s is more likely.

It is not convincing to argue that the ending of Acts indicates that Acts was composed around A.D. 61-62. Acts is not a biographical work, and its intent is not to portray the life of Paul, but rather the progress of the gospel and salvation history, finishing in the capital of the Empire. Furthermore, Acts 28:30 suggests that the author is writing with the benefit of considerable hindsight and knows of the termination of Paul's house arrest after two years. He knows, for example, that at some point Paul went on to testify before the emperor. He is not likely writing while these final events recorded in Acts are still in process. I would tentatively suggest that Luke wrote Acts after one or more stays in Rome, during at least one of which he obtained a copy of Mark, which served as at least one stimulus for the composition of his Gospel. The way Acts begins, reprising some of the events recorded in Luke 24 with certain differences in the two accounts, would seem to suggest that Acts may have been composed and sent to Theophilus sometime after the Gospel was composed, though obviously in close enough succession that Luke did not have to remind his hearers of more than a little bit about the ending of the first volume.

It by no means follows from what I have just said that Luke looks at the time he records in Acts as a bygone golden age. Too many things count against Luke's having been writing at the very *end* of the first century or the beginning of the second: (1) his primitive Christology and lack of a developed theology of the cross; (2) even more telling, his primitive ecclesiology, which bears no resemblance to what we find in Ignatius or other Christian writers of the later era; (3) his failure to address even indirectly some of the major third- and fourth-generation problems such as Gnosticism, Montanism, and the like; (4) his apparent ignorance of many of the elements of Pauline theology that we find in such capital Pauline letters as Romans, 1 and 2 Corinthians, or Galatians. How could this have happened if Acts was written at a time when Paul's letters were already at least partially collected and circulating as a revered

216. See Bruce, *The Acts of the Apostles*, pp. 12-18.

corpus of early Christian writings (2 Pet. 3:15-16)? (5) When one couples the "we" passages which lead us up to the conclusion of Acts with the open-ended conclusion itself, the suggestion is ready to hand that Luke sees his own time as a continuation of the time when the story concludes. His own time is the further development of the events recorded in Acts 1–28.[217] One must also pay close attention to the apparent allusion to Acts in Justin Martyr's *First Apology* 39.3, 50.12 and *Second Apology* 10 from the middle of the second century suggesting a first-century date for the book. A portion of this evidence deserves to be quoted at this point. *First Apology* 50.12 states:

> afterwards, when He had risen from the dead and appeared to them, and had taught them to read the prophecies in which all these things were foretold as coming to pass, and when they had seen Him ascending into heaven, and had believed, and had received power sent there by Him upon them, and went to every race of human beings, they taught these things, and were called apostles.

All in all, the late 70s or early 80s seems most likely for the date when Acts was composed.[218]

The above leads me to offer a conjecture based on what we know about the intellectual climate during the reigns of the Flavian emperors (A.D. 69-96, including Vespasian, Titus, and Domitian). Tacitus is a very good gauge of what was and was not safe to write in the era when the Flavians ruled, as often he tells us explicitly what was going on then. In particular he reminds us that the acts of publishing eulogies of the victims of Nero and the Flavians "were capital crimes, and cruel punishment fell not only on the authors but even on their books. The public executioners had the task of burning in the Forum those tributes to our noblest philosophers" (*Agricola* 2).[219] This was likely to be all the more the case if the book in question acclaimed some human being *other* than the emperor as Lord, God, or the like.

Is it possible that one of the copies, perhaps made by Theophilus for

---

217. See Marshall, *Acts*, p. 54.

218. See, rightly, Johnson, *Luke*, p. 2: "attempts to place Luke-Acts as late as the second century are clearly excessive. In fact nothing in the writing prohibits composition by a companion of Paul who was eyewitness of some of the events he narrates. If a thirty-year-old man joined Paul's circle around the year 50, he would still be only sixty in the year 80, young enough to do vigorous research, yet old enough and at sufficient distance to describe the time of beginnings with a certain nostalgia. The fact that Luke does not use Paul's letters or even mention that Paul wrote letters obviously argues for an earlier rather than a later date. It is far more likely for Paul's letters to be ignored before their collection and canonization than after."

219. This is apparently Tacitus's earliest work, published about A.D. 98. Cf. Mellor, *Tacitus*, p. 10.

literate friends, fell into the wrong hands and led to a collecting and burning of whatever copies could be found of Luke's work, at least in Rome? Wouldn't these documents have been seen as exalting Jesus in a way only befitting the emperor, or eulogizing someone like Jesus or Peter or Paul who were executed by the Romans, the latter two probably during Nero's reign? Might this explain why Acts especially has such a twisted and complex textual history; namely, that the manuscript had to be kept secret for a considerable period of time once Christians began to be executed regularly in various parts of the Empire, and its contents were passed along sometimes orally, sometimes in written form, but always carefully and privately? Finally, might it not explain a lot about why Luke is so cautious in his presentation of the Roman authorities in both of his volumes; namely, because he wrote in a dark era, when he knew of the dangers which the quote of Tacitus above recounts?

C. The Audience of Acts

Luke tells us quite clearly who his audience is — namely, Theophilus. This was a perfectly normal Greek name, used by both Jews and Gentiles alike, and without any concrete evidence to the contrary there is no good reason to doubt that a particular person is meant.[220] The question then becomes — What sort of person would have needed, and could have understood and appreciated, this two-volume work?

On the one hand, a pagan Gentile audience would neither have clearly understood nor necessarily appreciated the numerous references to the scriptures and their fulfillment in this work, and, on the other, a non-Christian Jewish audience could not have been called one of "us" in the phrase "among us" in the preface in Luke 1:1-4. D. Peterson has put it aptly when he says, "Luke's appeal is to 'insiders,' using the categories provided by 'outsiders.'"[221] This means that while there is an apologetic quality to this work, especially in the speech and trial material in Luke-Acts, Luke is making a defense for one who already has at least a neophyte's knowledge of and belief in the good news. This is not a defense for a pure outsider's ears where nothing in common could be presumed or presupposed. Rather, it is a reassurance or confirmation for someone who may have had doubts or was insufficiently socialized into "the Way" at the time of Acts's composition.

---

220. I am more than a little doubtful about the attempts to try to reconstruct some sort of "Lukan community" the author is supposed to be addressing. There is no reason here, anymore than in the case of various Pauline letters addressed to individuals, to suppose this work was *not* written to a particular person.

221. Peterson, "The Motif of Fulfilment," p. 103.

What may we ferret out of the document itself about Theophilus? As we have said, κρατιστε strongly suggests his social status. It was precisely persons of high status who had to make the most sacrifices to be part of the Christian community. We may conceive of Theophilus as a fairly recent convert who had not yet been thoroughly socialized, either in regard to knowing and grasping all the basic story of Jesus and his followers or to understanding all its theological, ethical, and social consequences.

J. Nolland has indeed made a strong case for Theophilus having come out of a synagogue setting, and thus requiring an explanation of: (1) why so many Jews had rejected Christ, and so many Gentiles accepted him; and (2) why "the Way" should be seen as the true expression of God's people, involving as it did Jew and Gentile united in Christ.[222] This background of Theophilus would also explain why Luke is able to assume a shared knowledge of and appreciation for the Hebrew Scriptures. Whether he had been a full proselyte to Judaism, or more likely in view of his higher status as a synagogue adherent, Luke's continual reference to the gospel going to the Jew and the synagogue first would likely have struck a responsive chord with Theophilus, who may well have first heard the good news in such a setting.[223] Luke's emphasis on a continual return to the synagogue and to Jews with this message right to the end of Acts, despite significant resistance and rejection, not only shows the universal way in which Luke envisioned the gospel and the salvation it brought, but also would have encouraged Theophilus not to sever all social ties he may have had with Jews and the Diaspora synagogue in the past. Theophilus may well have identified with a Cornelius in Acts, and have taken heart from the repeated efforts of Paul, Apollos, Aquila, Priscilla, and others to announce the message of salvation history in the synagogue.

Luke was no anti-Semite, nor is it probable that Theophilus was either. Luke had to defend the course God had chosen to take precisely because both the author and the audience to whom he wrote had great love for Jews and

---

222. Nolland, "Luke's Readers."

223. See Schneider, *Die Apostelgeschichte I*, p. 146: "Man wird sich den Widmung-sempfänger nicht als 'Gottesfürchtigen' auf der Schwelle zum Christentum vorzustellen haben, sondern als einen Christen, der ehedem zu jenen 'Gottesfürchtigen' gehörte, die aus Heidentum kamen und der jüdischen Synagogue nahestanden." Is it really plausible, though, that a mere pagan Jewish sympathizer who had only listened to what "God-fearers" said would have appreciated the rich allusions to Torah in Luke-Acts or the Septuagintal style of various parts of the work? This seems unlikely, and so it would be better to see Theophilus as a Gentile convert who had previously been a synagogue adherent. He would have to have been someone who already saw the LXX as a sacred text and was familiar with its tone and style. Otherwise, the Septuagintal style, in an age of style consciousness (including Atticizing tendencies), would have been seen as offensive and not consistent with Greek history writing at its best.

many of the traditions of Judaism, especially the Scriptures. The "ignorance" motif in Acts betokens an author who feels constrained to explain, without totally exonerating them, why many Jews had rejected the Jewish messiah Jesus.

Finally, Luke's decision to use the methods and rhetoric of Greek historiography, even though his message is in so many ways an essentially Jewish one with many resonances with the OT, suggests an audience with a Hellenistic education in at least some rhetoric and Greek history prior to coming to Christian faith, and surely prior to becoming a synagogue adherent as well. To appreciate Luke-Acts's style and historical method, such a background would have been not merely helpful but in various regards necessary. One must be able to compare Luke's work not merely to and with the Hebrew Scriptures but also to the likes of Polybius and Ephorus, if not also Thucydides, as well as to writers on Greek rhetoric such as Aristotle and Isocrates. If Theophilus was Luke's patron, going to such lengths to make the document listenable and pleasing in both form and content is all the more understandable.

IV. The Text of Acts

Perhaps more than any other book in the NT, the text of the Acts of the Apostles has been under debate for the last 150 years. This debate is not just over one or another manuscript but over so-called text types, of which there are three major sorts: (1) the Alexandrian text represented chiefly by codex ℵ and B; (2) the Byzantine text represented by the uncials H, L, P, and S; (3) and the so-called Western text chiefly witnessed by Codex Bezae, called D, and the Harclean Syriac.

The vast majority of scholars are in agreement that the Byzantine text, though its text type is represented in the vast majority of manuscripts from the fifth century on (hence its common name, "the Majority Text"), is a *later* text type which combines many of the distinctive features and readings of earlier textual traditions. This conclusion has been vigorously disputed by advocates of the first printed Greek text of the NT (1516, 1633 2d ed.),[224] the so-called Textus Receptus. The Textus Receptus is based on the Byzantine text type with minor deviations, and in turn was the Greek basis for the NT portion of the translation called the Authorized or King James Version in 1611, as well

---

224. For a good edition of the Byzantine text, not incidentally edited and published by two scholars who are strong advocates for the "Majority Text," cf. Hodges and Farstad, *Greek New Testament.*

as other famous versions such as Luther's German NT (1522) and, later, Tyndale's English translation (1522, 1534 2d ed.).[225]

The reasons the Byzantine text type is unlikely to reflect the original text of Acts may be summed up as follows: (1) This text type has no manuscript evidence prior to the fourth century A.D. (2) It is, at various points, a stylistic and grammatical improvement on either or both of the other two major text types, and in general scribes did not *introduce* grammatical errors and infelicities into the text. (3) This text type has many agreements with the Western text but also some with the old uncials. It is believable that this would be the case if the originator of this textual tradition had before him examples of both the other two textual types and selectively followed each, but to argue the other way around is far more difficult.[226] (4) Manuscripts must be weighed, not merely counted. The fact that the Byzantine tradition has produced "the Majority Text" shows its popularity from about the fifth century A.D. on, not its originality. It may be worth adding that if the translators of the AV/KJV had in 1611 the manuscript evidence we have now about the text of the NT in general and Acts in particular, they would likely have produced a very different translation.

The real debate among most scholars is whether the Western text type or the Alexandrian one more nearly represents what Luke actually wrote. Some scholars, most recently W. A. Strange, have sought to have it both ways by suggesting either that Luke produced two editions of Acts, or that the distinctive Western readings go back to marginal annotations of Luke, or, as Strange personally advocates, that both Western and non-Western readings represent versions of a text left unedited by Luke.[227] This both/and approach has notable weaknesses, as was recently pointed out by P. Head.[228] For one thing Acts, like the Gospel of Luke, has an addressee, Theophilus, which, while not suggesting publication in the modern sense (cf. above), nonetheless suggests a finished manuscript sent to Theophilus. Are we really to believe that the Gospel was sent and Acts was not, and if Acts was not sent how did the manuscript of Acts ever come to light? The argument that the ending of Acts suggests an unfinished manuscript will be dealt with in the commentary itself.

Head points out that: (1) Strange's argument requires us to believe that no version of Acts was publicly available before the middle of the second century A.D. I would add that this is especially unlikely in view of the existence of Acts in the Muratorian canon list (cf. above), the mention of Acts in the

---

225. See Bruce, *The Acts of the Apostles,* p. 70 and n. 2. Strictly speaking, the term *Textus Receptus* applied to the second edition of this first printed Greek NT.

226. See J. H. Ropes, *The Beginnings of Christianity,* vol. 3, *The Text of Acts* (London: Macmillan, 1926), pp. cclxxviiiff.

227. See Strange, *Problem of the Text,* pp. 184ff.

228. Head, "Problem of Its Texts."

anti-Marcionite prologue, the apparent allusion to Acts in Justin Martyr's *First Apology* 39.3, 50.12 and *Second Apology* 10 from the middle of the second century,[229] and perhaps also the existence of p91, which possibly dates to the second century A.D. (2) As Head says, Strange's hypothesis requires us to believe that two forms of Luke's notes or rough draft were kept for over eighty years but never used or published. (3) Furthermore, Acts 1:1-2 connects Acts with the Gospel and suggests that they were sent in succession within the span of no more than a few years.[230]

That some of the Western readings bear a resemblance to Luke's style is hardly surprising if the copyist and expander who first produced the Western text had Acts before him and was editing it and adding to it while under the influence of the vocabulary and style of the original document. Furthermore, the idea that the Western text as an alternate version ultimately goes back to Luke himself, in view of the Western text's antifeminist tendency, is antithetical to the spirit and views of the original author of the document.[231] There is also the matter that Luke reflects a clear historical consciousness in the way he uses certain key terms. For example, he uses the term "the Lord" or the phrase "the Lord Jesus Christ" of Jesus in the Gospel *only* in the narrative portions of the text, and the term is not found on the lips of the disciples until after the resurrection and when speaking to other Christians. "The Western Text neglects this nicety, as, for example, at Acts 13.33, 14.10, 16.4, 18.8."[232]

One may also add that it hardly seems likely that if Acts 8 had originally had the eunuch making a Christian confession a *later editor* would have left it out in view of the growing importance of confession in the early church, or that if the Western reading of the decree of James in Acts 15 had been original, it would have been changed to the more difficult text we find in the Alexandrian text.

The most one can say about the Western text is that it may occasionally provide some historically plausible data (e.g., in Acts 28:16 it adds that the centurion delivered the prisoners to the stratopedarch), but this does not prove

---

229. See Polhill, *Acts*, p. 21.

230. See Head, "Problem of Its Texts," pp. 427-28.

231. I have dealt with this matter in "Anti-Feminist Tendencies." On Luke's interest in women, including in women having ministerial roles in the early church, see my *Women in the Earliest Churches*, pp. 128ff., especially pp. 143ff. One would have to posit a total volte-face in Luke's views to conclude that he produced both the Alexandrian and Western text types, and for such a change we have no evidence. One may add that in view of the increasingly strict views about women's roles in the church from the second century on (see my *Women in the Earliest Churches*, pp. 183ff.), it is much more plausible to see the Western text's creator as a later tendentious Christian scribe caught up in the social struggles of his era.

232. Rightly Cadbury, *The Making of Luke-Acts*, p. 229.

that such data go back to Luke. Knowledge of geography or of Roman practices or even Roman military offices could be gained over the long period of time while the Empire existed and does not necessarily suggest that such data go back to Luke.[233] I must thus conclude that the Alexandrian text type, represented by the two great uncials ℵ and B, is much more likely to be closer to the original text of Acts than the Western text is, though certain interesting Western variants will be dealt with on a case-by-case basis in the commentary at the appropriate spots in the text.

Finally, I would like to offer a conjecture in regard to why it was that two distinct text types of Acts developed as early as the second century A.D. I think we must take into account the relative neglect of Acts by the early church in general before the time John Chrysostom wrote his homilies on Acts around the year A.D. 400.[234] In fact, he is the first to comment on or use the book in a significant way. This suggests that the book was *not* the subject of great attention, much less furor, something Chrysostom himself confirms at the beginning of his first homily on Acts when he says, "To many persons this Book is so little known, both it and its author, that they are not even aware there is such a book in existence," a complaint he had already made when speaking about Acts as early as A.D. 387.

Had this book been the subject of much controversy in the early church we might expect a closer supervision of the way the manuscript was passed on and also the making of many more copies. Precisely because this was not the case with Acts, two different versions arose quietly and were never carefully compared to or corrected by the other before the time of the Byzantine text.

V. The Structure, Theology, and Purposes of Luke-Acts

When Luke took up his pen to write his two-volume work, he knew that at least in regard to the Gospel various others had tried their hand at writing such an account. There is some debate as to whether we should read Luke 1:1-4 to suggest that Luke proposes to set the record straight, which in turn would imply a somewhat negative evaluation of one or more of Luke's predecessors and perhaps even some of his source material (Mark? Q?), or not. It

---

233. See the careful evaluation of the Western variants by Hemer, *Book of Acts*, pp. 193-201. His conclusion that not one of the variants clearly suggests that the Western text is the earlier version is significant. Cf. Metzger, *Textual Commentary*, p. 272: "some of the information incorporated in certain Western expansions may well be factually accurate, though not deriving from the original author of Acts."

234. Chrysostom gave these homilies in Constantinople where he was archbishop, but he had already given some at Antioch on Acts in 387.

seems clear enough from Luke 1:4 that Theophilus, not just Luke, had heard various things about the "things that have been fulfilled among us," and that Luke is seeking to offer the proper interpretation of these things. As J. B. Green has recently stressed, the issue would seem to be not validation but *signification* — How has the past been represented, what is its significance?[235] In other words, Luke does not primarily intend to defend the record of the "things which have been fulfilled among us" so as to explain it in an orderly fashion that will help Theophilus understand its sense and meaning. "Luke's purpose is hermeneutical. He is not hoping to prove *that* something happened, but rather to communicate *what these events signify*."[236] By referring to fulfillment Luke is suggesting that one can only understand and properly exegete these things in the larger historical and biblical framework he intends to provide. That he has chosen to do this, much as Ephorus suggested, κατα γενος,[237] shows that he is sensitive not only to biblical historiographical precedents but to Greek ones as well.

There is an overall structure to Luke-Acts which may be stated as follows. The Gospel of Luke chronicles, using a broad and general chronological framework, the spread of the good news up and down the social scale from the least to the greatest in Israelite society, and in the course of doing that it maintains a "from Galilee through Samaria to Jerusalem" orientation. Jesus must in the end go up *to* Jerusalem, and in the end the disciples must wait in Jerusalem until they receive power from on high. This stands in contrast to the "*from* Jerusalem to Rome" (and to other places in the Diaspora) orientation of the book of Acts. Luke in short is interested in the universal spread of the good news not only up and down the social scale but geographically outward to the world. This theme of the universal scope of this gospel is announced in Luke 2:30-32:

> for my eyes have seen your salvation,
>> which you have prepared in the presence of all peoples,
> a light for revelation to the Gentiles
>> and for glory to your people Israel.

The spread of this good news even to the least, last, and lost is made clear in the paradigmatic speech in Luke 4:18-21 where Jesus quotes Isaiah 61.

One can say then that the Gospel focuses on the vertical (up and down the social scale) universalization of the gospel, while Acts focuses on its horizontal universalization (to all peoples throughout the Empire). This means that one must take the material in Acts 2:1-21 as setting the agenda in Acts in

---

235. Green, "Internal Repetition in Luke-Acts," pp. 283-99.
236. Ibid., p. 288.
237. See p. 34 above and pp. 72ff. below on the structure.

the same way Luke 4:18-21 does in the Gospel. In Acts 2 various Jews from many nations hear the good news in their own tongue, which suggests this news is for peoples of all tongues and nations, but to the Jew first.

What lies behind this agenda is that Luke believes that Jesus is the *one* savior for *all* peoples and this is why he must be proclaimed *to* all peoples. There is stress upon both continuity of the Jesus movement with Israel and her Scriptures in some ways and discontinuity with Israel in others throughout the two volumes. It is hard to doubt that what determines the discontinuity is the universalistic agenda — those facets of Judaism that make difficult or impossible the welcoming of other ethnic groups into the people of God purely on the basis of faith must be critiqued or be seen as obsolescent.

Even the geographical orientation of the Gospel of Luke is in part caused by the concern about salvation. Jesus must go up to Jerusalem, for it is the center from which Jews looked for salvation (Luke 9:51; 13:22, 33, 35; 17:11; 18:31; 19:11, 28). Jesus must accomplish or finish his earthly work there so that salvation and its message may go forth from Jerusalem to the world, as the Hebrew Scriptures had always suggested.

The belief that salvation comes from the Jews engenders the "to Jerusalem" orientation of Luke's Gospel, which in turn explains why Luke relates the story of Jesus going up to the temple as a boy (Luke 2:22ff.), why the prophecies of Simeon and Anna about Jesus as the world's savior come from the temple (2:25-38), why Luke wishes to show that Jesus is in the line of the OT prophets (13:33), and finally why Jesus' life and teaching are all presented as a fulfillment of the prophecies of the OT (4:18-21; 16:31; 18:31; 24:27, 45). The disciples must remain in Jerusalem until they receive power from on high, for not only is Jerusalem the place from which salvation comes but the place from which empowerment to preach it comes as well (Luke 24:47, 53; Acts 1:4). Thus Luke 24:47, rounding out the Gospel, foreshadows the fact that Acts will deal with the horizontal spread of the gospel "beginning from Jerusalem" unto all the nations.

The medium by which the message is conveyed is the Holy Spirit, and Luke more than all other Gospel writers stresses the role of the Spirit in both his books. Thus, for instance, in the Gospel it is by the Spirit that Mary is impregnated (1:35), the Spirit fills the mouths of the prophets (1:41, 67; 2:25), Jesus will baptize with that Spirit (3:16; 11:13; 24:49), but the Spirit had already empowered Jesus (3:22) and leads him (4:1), and teaches the disciples what they are to say when they go out and witness (12:12). The Holy Spirit, then, is the means, the person who empowers the disciples as well as Jesus for preaching, teaching, and healing. He leads and guides the disciples in Acts as he did Jesus in the Gospel (cf. Acts 1:2, 16; 2:4, 13; 4:13; 10:44; 16:6; passim). We cannot tarry here to demonstrate to what lengths Luke goes in his Gospel to show Jesus' concern for the least, last, and lost, including women and the poor.[238] Suffice it to say that when we turn to Acts we find relatively the same agenda.

For instance, Luke reveals the same interest in Acts in how the good news comes to the poor, the oppressed, possessed, imprisoned, with the Holy Spirit empowering those within the community as the church tries to minister to their needs. We also see reiterated in Acts another Lukan stress found in the Gospel — the intensification of demands ("take up [your] cross *daily*," Luke 9:23; never look back, Luke 9:62; give up everything, Luke 14:26; 18:18-30). These themes are of course interlocking, and the Holy Spirit is the key that makes proclamation, salvation, liberation, and strenuous discipleship possible. Briefly we would like at this point to give examples of how Luke's major themes of universalization of the gospel to both the up-and-in and down-and-out, but with special concern for the poor, diseased, imprisoned, oppressed, and possessed, is evidenced. In addition, we will note the evidence of intensification of demands.

> On the poor, cf. Acts 6; 9:36ff.
> On the diseased, cf. Acts 5:12-16; 9:32ff.
> On women, cf. Acts 9:36-42; 12:12-17; 16:12-15, 40; 18:24ff.; 21:8-9.
> On the possessed, cf. Acts 8:4-8; 16:16ff.
> On intensification of demands, cf. Acts 4:32–5:11.

The references to the Holy Spirit in Acts are too numerous to list.

It is interesting that Luke was not content to show that the universalization of the gospel involved the oppressed (Luke 4:18c). Rather, in truly universalistic fashion he shows how Christ's gospel was likewise for the oppressor, usually the upper echelon of the social ladder. They, too, were captives who needed to be set free, whether from money, power, or pious religiosity. Thus we see Jesus eating with Levi and many other tax collectors (Luke 5:29), or with Simon the Pharisee (7:36). Jesus redeems Zacchaeus, a tax collector and a rich man who begins immediately to right his wrongs of overtaxing (19:1ff.). Luke points out that it is a Roman centurion, a representative of the emperor Caesar, in whom Jesus finds more faith than in all of God's chosen people Israel (7:1-10). Luke even records Jesus calling a *rich* young ruler to give up all his money and follow him (cf. 5:11 and 18:18). These agendas in the Gospel simply prepare for similar treatments in Acts of people like the Ethiopian eunuch, Cornelius, and others of some social status. One suspects that Theophilus would have seen himself in the telling of the story at various points and would have understood the degree to which the story was for him as well as for others.

---

238. See my *Women in the Earliest Churches*, pp. 128-57.

The universalization of the gospel will embrace not only all ethnic diversity in the Empire but also people up and down the social scale, including both the oppressed and the oppressor. Furthermore, a concern will be shown in both Luke and Acts for the physical as well as the spiritual welfare of humankind so that the gospel's liberation is not merely to come to all people but is to affect every aspect of their lives. Such a total salvation requires a total response of discipleship. One must be prepared to leave *everything* and follow (Luke 5:11), renounce all (14:33), take up one's cross *daily* (9:23), and put one's hand to the plow and not look back (9:62) — agendas reiterated in Acts 3–6 and elsewhere. The whole gospel must be proclaimed to the whole person in the whole world, for there is one, all-sufficient Savior for all, and therefore all must be for this one.

There is a sense in which if the major figure in Luke was Jesus, in Acts it is not any human being, but the Holy Spirit, so that some have called this document the Acts of the Holy Spirit. Yet the focus is actually on events, not on persons or personalities, even of God. Clearly Luke intends us to see movement in this story from Jerusalem to Rome, and it is possible that we should see Jerusalem as the center of Jewish Christianity and Rome as the center of Gentile Christianity. The book then develops as the church did, away from Jewish Christianity to Gentile Christianity and in a sense away from Peter to Paul. Yet Peter and Paul are simply vehicles of God, who speaks and acts in the same way through both men. Consider the Peter–Paul parallels noted by Dunn:

Peter	Paul
2:22-29	13:26-41
3:1-10	14:8-11
4:8	13:9
5:15	19:12
8:17	19:6
8:18-24	13:6-11
9:36-41	20:9-12
12:6-11	16:25-41[239]

J. Jervell is indeed right that throughout the book of Acts, as in Luke's Gospel, the point is made over and over again, "to the Jew first and then to the Gentiles."[240] This motif is evident even in the Gentile mission section of Acts from Acts 13 on, for Paul always goes to the synagogue first to fulfill this mandate, though once the church had separated from the synagogue this has

---

239. Dunn, *Acts,* p. xiv.
240. See his *Luke and the People of God.*

less and less success. Paul's last speech in Rome speaks of an unhindered gospel, but note also that he quotes Scripture. The rejection by the Jews is seen as a fulfillment of Scripture, and Luke's purpose throughout Acts, as in Luke, is to show that all this was part of God's plan.[241] This is likewise emphasized by Peter at Pentecost as he quotes Joel, and Stephen as he shows the history of Jewish apostasy.

It seems, then, that Luke is not trying merely to chronicle the unstoppable word, nor is he trying to say that the church is taking the place of God's first chosen people. Rather, we must see that Paul is also conferring with the synagogue even in Rome, and some are converted. Luke is then trying to show that Jew and Gentile united in Christ is the true Israel, not the new Israel. Some Jews do accept the gospel — this thread runs throughout the book of Acts right to Rome. Nor should we overemphasize the last word of Paul about turning to the Gentiles, because Paul has said the same thing before in Acts 13 and intimated it elsewhere, though he nowhere stops the mission to the synagogue. Even Paul's trials first in Jerusalem and then in Rome betoken this pattern of first to the Jew then to the Gentile.

The problem with Jervell's view is that he does not recognize that the Gentile mission is a crucial if not *the* crucial event for Luke in Acts, hence the repeating of the Cornelius narrative three times and the conversion of *the* missionary to the Gentiles three times. But there is one other event that Luke records three times — Paul's trial. Why? Because Luke also has a concern to show that the Roman Empire was not basically antagonistic toward, nor should it oppose, the Christian church, just because it had become a separate entity from synagogue-based Judaism. Notice how the very trials of Paul advance the movement and spread of the gospel to Rome, and that recording them also helps reveal how the word arrived in Rome. Perhaps Luke was also writing at a time when the church faced some opposition from (local?) Roman authorities as well as Jewish ones.

Paul, like Jesus, is said to be guilty of no crime, over and over. The state, then, should not be concerned that these Gentiles will not sacrifice to the emperor. They are good citizens, as indeed especially Paul shows on his voyage when he helps the centurion, and earlier when he refuses to escape from jail when he could. The missionary to the Gentiles is a Roman citizen, and he makes good use of this, as does God, for as Luke wishes to show, God is using even the Roman state to spread his gospel. Therefore it should not oppose it as Herod did. Acts, then, is not just a defense of Paul — too much does not deal with this in its first fifteen chapters — but there is an apologetic element in Acts as well as in the Gospel.

Finally, perhaps the *occasion* for Luke's writing Luke-Acts is that

241. See Squires, *Plan of God in Luke-Acts*, pp. 23ff.

Theophilus, himself perhaps a former synagogue adherent like Cornelius, had raised the question: How can the Christian church be the true Israel of God when it is rejected by Jews and there are so few Jewish converts to it?[242] Also, how can it be legitimate if the Roman state likewise opposes and persecutes it (see Acts 18)? The crucial theme of God's plan and Scripture fulfillment had to be emphasized to show that "the Way" was no innovation, but all along was intended by God. God's real plan of spreading the good news about Jesus from Jerusalem (1:1–6:7), to Judea and Samaria (6:7–9:31), to the Gentiles (9:32–12:24), then to Asia (12:24–16:5), Europe (16:5–19:20), and Rome (19:20-28) is the overall schema that manifests this purpose.

There are several key junctures that indicate growth, movement, and development as repeated themes in the narrative in Acts (cf. 6:7; 9:31; 12:24; 16:5; 19:20). Notice the development:

1. 6:7 — Word of God increased, Jerusalem disciples multiplied;
2. 9:31 — Church throughout Galilee and Judea built up and multiplied in (by) Holy Spirit;
3. 12:24 — Word of God grew and multiplied, involving Paul and Barnabas (cf. v. 25);
4. 16:5 — Churches strengthened in faith and increased in numbers — Paul and Timothy going through Asia (Minor);
5. 19:20 — Paul in Asia (Minor) and Ephesus in particular — all the residents of Asia hear (v. 10); word of God prevailed mightily.

These summary statements provide reasonable clues to the development and subsectioning by Luke of his material as follows:

Section 1 — 1:1–6:7 — primitive church in Jerusalem
Section 2 — 6:8–9:31 — Judea and Samaria
Section 3 — 9:32–12:24 — the gospel to the Gentiles (ethnic, nongeographical)
Section 4 — 12:25–16:5 — Asia and shift to Gentile missions
Section 5 — 16:6–19:20 — Europe (but with a return to Ephesus)
Section 6 — 19:21–28:31 — to Rome[243]

G. Schneider opts for a rather simple threefold structure after the introductory material in 1:1-26: (1) the witness to Christ of the apostles in Jerusalem (2:1–5:42); (2) the witness to Christ going forth from Jerusalem

---

242. See Nolland, *Luke,* pp. 33ff.
243. Here I follow a proposal of my former mentor G. D. Fee, which is similar to various other suggestions by scholars about the "panels" of Acts. Cf. Polhill, *Acts,* pp. 72ff.

and the taking of his way to the Gentiles (6:1–15:35); and (3) the Christian witness on the way to the ends of the earth (15:36–28:31).[244] This analysis properly stresses the theme of witnessing in Acts and avoids a stress on the apostles, which is not in fact a major issue in Acts, especially after the first few chapters. This analysis, however, does not take into account the numerous secondary breaks in the account, and a more complex analysis proves to be more helpful.

Another possible analysis of the structure of Acts has been offered by R. Pesch as follows:

1. The exposition of the second book — 1:1-11
2. The time of waiting on the Holy Spirit — 1:12-26
3. The witness of the apostles in Jerusalem — 2:1–6:7

4. The extension of the church beyond the environs of Jerusalem — 6:8–9:31
5. The beginning of the Gentile mission — 9:32–12:25

7. The mission of Paul in Europe and Asia — 15:35–19:20
8. The journey of Paul to Jerusalem — 19:21–21:14
9. The captivity of Paul in Jerusalem and Caesarea — 21:15–26:32
10. The journey of Paul to Rome — 27:1–28:16

11. The witness of Paul to the Jews in Rome — 28:17-28
12. The two years of unhindered preaching by Paul in Rome — 28:29-31

In this outline (1) and (2) are seen as prologue and (11) and (12) as epilogue. This outline has much to commend it although it does not convey the importance of Peter in the first half of Acts.[245]

A. Smith has recently shown that in the smaller units in Acts 1–8 there is a rhetorical structure and attempt to build to some sort of climax. He offers the following analysis:

First rhetorical unit (1:12–4:31)
1:12-26 — An internal problem: apostasy
2:1–4:31 — Validation through signs, wonders, and initial conflict
    (1) 2:1–3:26 — Miraculous signs and wonders
    (2) 4:1-4 — Arrest and imprisonment (and church growth)
    (3) 4:5-31 — Trial episodes, ending with release and vindication

244. Schneider, *Die Apostelgeschichte I*, p. 68.
245. Pesch, *Die Apostelgeschichte (1–12)*, p. 41.

Second rhetorical unit (4:32–5:42)
    4:32–5:11 — An internal problem: deception
    5:12-42 — Validation through signs, wonders, and a second conflict
       (1) 5:12-16 — Miraculous signs and wonders
       (2) 5:17-26 — Arrest and imprisonment (and escape)
       (3) 5:40-42 — Whipping, release, and vindication

He goes on to point out that each of the three missionary excursions builds to a climactic conclusion, with either death or narrow escapes from death recorded.[246] What is illuminating about Smith's analysis is that it reveals how Luke follows the rhetorical canons about using a crescendo effect as well as variation when one is going to repeat a pattern. My own more detailed structural analysis can be found in the table of contents.

On any showing, Luke's accomplishments in writing the Acts of the Apostles are numerous. In a single stroke he provided early Christianity with a sense of definition, identity, and legitimization, things Theophilus presumably needed reassurance or more certainty about. As D. Aune so aptly puts it:

> Christianity needed *definition* because during the first generation of its existence, it exhibited a broad spectrum of beliefs and practices, sometimes manifest in splinter groups making exclusive claims. . . . Christianity needed *identity* because unlike other ancient Mediterranean religions, it had ceased to remain tied to a particular ethnic group (i.e. it had increasingly looser relations to Judaism). . . . Christianity needed *legitimation* because no religious movement or philosophical sect could be credible unless it was rooted in antiquity. Luke provided legitimation by demonstrating the Jewish origins of Christianity and by emphasizing the divine providence which was reflected in every aspect of the development and expansion of the early church.[247]

The above neatly sums up the *social* aims of Luke in writing Acts, though he has other aims as well, as the earlier brief survey of major themes shows. Much more can and will be said along these lines in the commentary itself, but now we must turn to the discussion of complex chronological matters.

---

246. Smith, " 'Put Outside for a While' "; the outline was distributed by Prof. Smith before the paper was given.
247. Aune, *New Testament,* p. 137.

VI. Acts Chronology[248]

Luke tells us in Luke 1:1-4 that he intends to give his audience some sort of orderly account.[249] It must be kept in mind that Luke is for the most part editing source material, since he does not claim to be an eyewitness of most of the events he recounts. He is only a sometime companion of Paul, starting during the middle of the second missionary journey and continuing off and on until the end of the events recorded in Acts. To put it another way, if the "we" passages are any clue,[250] Luke could only personally account for the events of the last ten years or so of his narrative, or roughly A.D. 50-60, and even during that time span he was not present for all that he records, especially during the latter part of the second missionary journey of Paul. Therefore, Luke is only going to be as accurate and orderly as his sources allow him to be, especially when he recounts the material found in Acts 1:1–16:11 and 17:1–20:7.

We have some clues as to how Luke handled his sources by evaluating the way he handled Mark and Q in his Gospel.[251] What a survey of this material shows is that Luke is on the whole a rather conservative editor of his sources, Hellenizing them and deeschatologizing them to a certain extent. We also learn that Luke, unlike Matthew, tended to use his sources in blocks. It is possible that the block of material on Philip found in Acts 8:4-40, or the block of material on Peter in 9:32–11:18 and 12:1-19, while in basic chronological order in themselves, causes displacement of other blocks of material.

For example, notice that Acts 11:27-30 is picked up again in 12:25 by way of a summary remark. The summary remarks in 11:30 and 12:24-25 are in fact about famine relief, something which happened *after* the release of Peter from prison and after the death of Herod Agrippa I. It thus appears that the Peter material was originally connected to the Herod material because Herod was responsible for Peter's incarceration, making the Peter block begin at 9:32 and continue through 12:23. Luke has interrupted this block of material with an Antioch block found in 11:19-30, especially in order to report the prediction of the famine made by Agabus in Antioch. Thus 11:30 is a foreshadowing of an event, famine relief, which is properly reported in 12:25 as having actually transpired *after* the death of Herod, in other words after A.D. 44 (see below). Displacement, due to block editing, must be borne in mind as a tendency of Luke when we are evaluating chronological matters in the first half of Acts.[252]

---

248. On what follows one should compare Bruce, "Chronological Questions."
249. See pp. 12ff. above in the introduction on the meaning and significance of this prologue.
250. On which see the excursus, pp. 480ff. below.
251. See my essay "Editing the Good News."
252. On Luke's sources for Acts see the excursus, pp. 165ff. below.

Unfortunately, the discussion of chronological matters in Acts involves only a few certain reference points on which to base one's conclusions.[253] The starting point must be Jesus' death during the Passover in Jerusalem under the reign of Pontius Pilate. The possibilities can be narrowed down rather quickly to either A.D. 30 or 33, as the recent thorough discussion of J. P. Meier shows.[254] The problem with arguing for a date of 33 for Jesus' death is that it suggests a ministry much longer than either the Synoptics or John suggests. The only years during the relevant period (A.D. 29-33) when Nisan 14 fell on a Friday are April 7, A.D. 30, and April 3, A.D. 33, and on the whole the former date is to be preferred, as most NT scholars agree. This gives us a starting point for Acts 1.

We must now turn to the other end of the spectrum, the dating of the events recorded in Acts 28. This hinges on at least two major factors: (1) the date when Festus replaced Felix as the governor of Judea; and (2) the length of time it took for Paul to travel from Caesarea by sea and land to Rome, making allowance for the mishaps along the way. It seems reasonably clear that Felix took office about A.D. 52, before the demise of Claudius. How long he stayed in office is unclear. Some would suggest he lasted until 59; others make his tenure shorter. The relevant data in Suetonius and especially in Josephus strongly suggest that Felix was in Caesarea until at least 59 and possibly until 60 (Josephus, *Ant.* 20.7.1; 20.8.9; *War* 2.12.8; 2.14.1; Suetonius, *Claud.* 28).[255] Since we are told that Paul did not leave Caesarea before Festus took over (see Acts 26), this means he did not leave before 59. The seasonal data included in Acts suggest that Paul probably arrived in Rome no earlier than 60. A secondary possible confirmation of the above reasoning may come from the fact that we are told that Paul gave his testimony before Ananias the high priest (Acts 23:2; 24:1), and Josephus links the transfer of high-priestly power from Ananias to Ishmael with the time of the transfer of power from Felix to Festus. In other words, Paul must have testified before the high priest *before* 59-60, since Ananias's reign seems to have lasted from about 47 to 59, perhaps with an interruption in 52 (see Josephus, *Ant.* 20.6.2-3).

We are told by Luke that Paul spent two years in Rome under what amounted to house arrest (28:30). Thus, the narrative carries us up to no later than 62. This was before the really bad years under Nero — well before the fire in Rome in 64, before the Neronian persecution of Christians as scapegoats,

---

253. On the German discussion and for a chart of various opinions on these reference points, see Schneider, *Die Apostelgeschichte I*, pp. 129-33.

254. Meier, *A Marginal Jew*, 1:401-6 and the notes.

255. See Ferguson, *Backgrounds of Early Christianity*, p. 395. The change in provincial coinage in A.D. 58-59 points to this year as the time Felix left office. See J. Murphy-O'Connor, *Paul*, p. 23.

and eight years before the fall and destruction of Jerusalem in 70. The tone of the close of the narrative is positive and does not suggest the later ominous turn of events.

Broadly speaking, then, Acts recounts for us in episodic fashion some of the events of importance for early Christianity that transpired between 30 and 60. Though Luke mentions at the very end of his work Paul's two-year stay in Rome, the narrative in Acts 28 seems to discuss only the beginning of the Roman house-arrest period in 60.

Are there any fixed landmarks to help us along the way in regard to other events recounted in the text? A few can be mentioned that we can calculate with varying degrees of certainty. Certainly, the least questionable of these is the dates during which Gallio was the Roman authority for Corinth. Ancient historians, classics scholars, and biblical scholars alike are in general agreement that the relevant Claudian rescript found in Delphi places Gallio in Corinth during the twenty-sixth acclamation of Claudius as emperor, which means he was governor in Corinth between the summers of 51 and 52.[256] This, in turn, means that Paul must have arrived in Corinth in about 50 (possibly late in 50) or early 51. This gives us a reasonably clear date for this portion of Paul's second missionary journey. It also means, if Luke is to be believed, that the council recorded in Acts 15 transpired before 51. Probably, it was at least as early as 50 if allowance for Paul's travel time and missionary work in Corinth is to be allowed, and more likely it should be pushed a little further back to the latter part of 49.[257]

Working backward, we also have a reasonable degree of certainty that the expulsion of Jews from Rome mentioned in Acts 18:2 transpired in 49,[258] and led to Paul's meeting of Priscilla and Aquila in Corinth in about 50.

One step further back brings us to news of the famine reported in Acts 11:27-30 as transpiring, broadly speaking, during the reign of Claudius (A.D. 41-54). Again we must rely on some partial evidence from Josephus if we wish to be more specific. *Ant.* 20.51-53 and 20.101 suggest that the famine took place during the time when Tiberius Alexander was governor in Judea, namely, sometime during 46-48. This comports nicely with the suggestion we have made[259] that the famine visit of Paul and Barnabas took place in 48. It would have taken some time for Paul and Barnabas to gather funds before going up, and furthermore it seems likely the situation would have been aggravated in Judea by the fact that 47-48 seems to have been a sabbatical year (cf. *m. Soṭa*

256. See Alexander, "Chronology of Paul," on all these matters, here p. 120; cf. Jewett, *A Chronology of Paul's Life*, pp. 38-40; Murphy-O'Connor, *Paul*, pp. 15-22.

257. As Alexander has rightly stressed to me in a letter dated July 1994.

258. See the excursus on Claudius and his decrees below, pp. 539ff.

259. See the Pauline chronology, pp. 86-97.

7:8).[260] It must also be kept in mind, as Barrett reminds us, that it "is mistaken to claim that Luke dates the famine wrongly because 11.27-30 precedes the death of Herod Agrippa I (12.12); what happens in 11.27 is not the famine but a prophecy that there will be a famine."[261] The prophecy must necessarily have preceded the event if it was genuine predictive prophecy of the OT sort, as the text suggests. In this case it was apparently several years before the event.

We may be able to be more specific in view of the work of K. S. Gapp, who has evaluated the records from Egypt, the breadbasket of the Empire, in regard to grain prices, and he confirms that a famine must have taken place beginning in 45 or 46 due to a deficient or excessive seasonal tide of the Nile and continuing into the following spring of 46 or possibly 47.[262] The famine probably really began to affect Jerusalem and Judea in 46, and its effects were exacerbated in Judea by the sabbatical year 47-48. Queen Helena of Adiabene is said to have come to Jerusalem during this time, seen people dying, and sent to Cyprus for figs and to Egypt for grain to alleviate the problem (*Ant.* 3.320f.; 20.51-53, 101).[263]

We must now consider the date of Herod Agrippa's death. Josephus suggests that his death took place in early March, A.D. 44 (*Ant.* 19.8.2). If we read Acts 12:3-23 carefully, then Peter was imprisoned in 43 or very early in 44.

The restriction of Jews in Rome by Claudius in 41 and the Claudian edict about Alexandrian Jews in the same year[264] do not really help us date anything in particular in Acts. Equally frustrating is the lack of clearly datable material about Sergius Paulus and his rule on Cyprus (cf. Acts 13:7), but nothing in our present state of knowledge prevents Paul from encountering him on Cyprus in the late 40s.[265]

The Aretas incident is an important one as it provides a synchronism between Acts and Paul (cf. Acts 9:25 to 2 Cor. 11:32). Aretas IV is by far the most notable of the Nabatean rulers, not least because his reign stretched to almost half a century (9-8 B.C. to A.D. 40-41). His capital was at the justly

---

260. See the discussion in Barrett, *Acts*, vol. 1, p. 563.

261. Ibid., pp. 563-64, correcting Lake, "Chronology," in *Beginnings*, 5:468.

262. Gapp, "Universal Famine under Claudius."

263. On all of this see Winter, "Acts and Food Shortages," especially pp. 63-64.

264. On both of which see pp. 539ff.

265. See the discussion in Hemer, *Book of Acts*, p. 109 and n. 20, and in Barrett, *Acts*, vol. 1, pp. 614ff. The inscription in *CIL* 6.4, 2 (no. 31545) does mention L. Sergius Paulus as a curator of the Tiber during the reign of Claudius. To fit our data, Sergius would have had to go to Cyprus sometime in the 40s in the reign of Claudius after being a curator, unless he retained the latter office while assuming another one abroad, which is not impossible. All that we can say for sure is that nothing in the present state of the data about Sergius causes any problems for our dating of Paul's encounter with him during the first missionary journey in A.D. 48 (cf. pp. 390ff.).

famous city carved out of rock appropriately called Petra. There is considerable debate among scholars as to whether Aretas could have had control of Damascus at some point, or whether the mention by Paul of the ethnarch of Aretas guarding the city in order to capture Paul suggests a significant commercial colony or even a community of Nabateans in Damascus of whom the ethnarch was in charge.[266] Obviously, this incident must have transpired before A.D. 40-41, and if, as some suggest, Aretas actually died between 38 and 40, we must push the date back even further.

Perhaps crucial to this discussion is the fact that when Caligula ascended the throne in A.D. 37, this led to a new Roman policy in regard to client kings. Thus, some have suggested that Caligula may have granted Aretas the city in 37, and in any case Aretas's control of the city is unlikely before the reign of Caligula.[267] But neither Acts 9 nor 2 Corinthians 11 requires that Aretas be in control of the city, and thus the dating of the incident to 37 is very plausible, but not certain.[268]

There is very little else of consequence to help us in clearly dating the material in Acts. The following summary gives us the basic outline that results from the above data, which must be compared to the more detailed outline that follows, which we have drawn up in regard to Paul and his letters.

Basic Acts Timeline

A.D. 30 — Jesus is crucified under Pontius Pilate. Resurrection appearances, Pentecost, initial growth of the church in and around Jerusalem.

A.D. 31-33 — The events of Acts 3–7 transpire with mounting concern on the part of Jews and especially the Jewish authorities in Jerusalem. The rising tension results in vigilante action taken against Stephen, and then an authorized effort under Saul to disrupt and even destroy this new messianic sect, involving persecution and even the death of some Christians (cf. Acts 8:1-3 to Gal. 1:13). The persecution led various Christians such as Philip to go elsewhere, such as Samaria, and bear witness (Acts 8:4-40). THE FIRST EIGHT CHAPTERS OF ACTS COVER ONLY THE PERIOD FROM ABOUT 30 TO 33.[269]

A.D. 33 or 34 — Saul is converted on the road to Damascus during his period of persecuting the church (Acts 9; Galatians 1).

266. Cf. Bowersock, *Roman Arabia*, p. 68, to Graf, "Aretas," p. 375.
267. See the brief discussion in Barrett, *Caligula*, p. 183 and notes. Cf. Jewett, *A Chronology of Paul's Life*, pp. 30-33.
268. Rightly Hemer, *Book of Acts*, pp. 163-64.
269. Rightly stressed by Lake, "Chronology," pp. 445f.

A.D. 34-37 or 38 — Saul is in Damascus and Arabia; he returns to Jerusalem for the first time as a Christian in 37.

A.D. 37-46 — Saul sent off to Tarsus and home region. In the meantime, Peter has a notable ministry up and down the Mediterranean coast between Lydda, Joppa, and Caesarea, involving at least one notable Gentile and his family. This, in turn, leads to a report to the Jerusalem church (Acts 11). The precise timing is unknown.

A.D. 43 — James (brother of John) is killed, and Peter is imprisoned.

A.D. 44 — Agabus's prophecy in Antioch; Herod Agrippa dies.

NOTE THAT LUKE'S DATA FOR THE PERIOD A.D. 37-46 ARE CLEARLY SKETCHY. HE IS BETTER INFORMED ABOUT THE PERIOD AFTER THE JERUSALEM COUNCIL (49), IN PARTICULAR ABOUT THE PAULINE PART OF THE STORY.

A.D. 46-48 — famine in Judea.

A.D. 48 — Second visit by Paul to Jerusalem (with Barnabas, cf. Galatians 2) for famine relief to Jerusalem (Acts 11:29-30).

A.D. 49 — Claudius expels Jews from Rome; Priscilla and Aquila go to Corinth; Jerusalem council (Acts 15).

A.D. 50-52 — Paul's second missionary journey (Acts 15:36–18:23).

A.D. 51 or 52 — The Gallio incident in Corinth (Acts 18).

A.D. 53-57 — Paul's third missionary journey (Acts 18:23–21:26).

A.D. 57-59 — Paul in custody under Felix, and then briefly under Festus.

A.D. 59-60 — Paul goes to Rome (for a fuller discussion of the Pauline material for the period from 48 to 50, see below).

A.D. 60-62 — Paul under house arrest in Rome.

Chronology of Paul's Life and Letters[270]

Phase One — Pre-Christian Saul

A.D. 5-10 — Saul is born in Tarsus in Cilicia of orthodox Pharisaic Jews who are Roman citizens.

A.D. 10 + — Saul's family moves to Jerusalem while he is still quite young (Acts 26:4).

A.D. 15-20 — Saul begins his studies in Jerusalem with Rabbi Gamaliel, grandson of Rabbi Gamaliel the elder.

A.D. 30 (or 33) — Jesus is crucified by Pontius Pilate.

A.D. 31?-34 — Saul persecutes the church in Jerusalem/Judea, Samaria); Stephen is stoned (Acts 6–7, ca. 32-33).

---

270. On all of what follows one should compare the somewhat different conclusions in Jewett, *A Chronology of Paul's Life.*

Phase Two — Conversion and "Hidden Years"

A.D. 33 (or 34) — Saul is converted on the Damascus road and then travels on to Damascus (Ananias episode).

A.D. 34-37 — Saul in Arabia, the Nabatean region of Syria east of Damascus and in the Transjordan (cf. Gal. 1.17). Saul returns to Damascus and narrowly escapes the authorities under King Aretas IV, who may have controlled the city beginning in 37 once Gaius Caligula became Emperor (cf. 2 Cor. 11:32/Acts 9:23-25).

A.D. 37 — Saul's first visit to Jerusalem, a private meeting with Peter and James (Gal. 1:18-20). Saul preaches to the Hellenists, and escapes to his home region of Syria and Cilicia by way of boat from Caesarea Maritima (Acts 9:29-30).

A.D. 37-46 — Saul preaches in home region; results unknown or inconsequential (possible great persecutions, cf. 2 Cor. 11:23-29).

A.D. 41-42 — Saul has a visionary experience; receives "thorn in the flesh" (2 Cor. 12:1-10), a physical malady possibly involving his eyes (Gal. 4:13-16).

A.D. 47 — Saul is found by Barnabas in Tarsus and brought to Antioch; preaches there for a year (Acts 11:25-26).

A.D. 48 — Second visit to Jerusalem (the famine visit) with Barnabas and Titus (Acts 11:27-30/Gal. 2:1-10). Private agreement between Saul and the church leaders that he and Barnabas would go to Gentiles, Peter and others to Jews, and circumcision not be imposed. Issues of food and fellowship between Jewish and Gentile Christians unresolved (cf. Gal. 2:11-14).

Phase Three — Paul Begins His Endorsed Missionary Travels and Efforts

A.D. 48 — First missionary journey with Barnabas and Mark; commissioned by Antioch church after basic endorsement from Jerusalem (Acts 13–14). Saul uses his Greco-Roman name Paul (Paulos).

A.D. 48 — Return to Antioch.[271] Antioch incident with Peter and Barnabas withdrawing from fellowship meals with Gentiles due to pressure from Judaizers from Jerusalem (Pharisaic Jewish Christians, Gal. 2:11-14).

A.D. 49 (early) — Paul discovers the Judaizers had moved on to Asia Minor and were upsetting some of his converts made during the first missionary journey in south Galatia (Pisidian Antioch, Iconium, etc.). He writes his letter to the Galatians shortly before going up to Jerusalem for the third time.

A.D. 49 (later) — Apostolic council in Jerusalem. Public agreement that Gentiles not be required to become Jews in order to become Christians. Apostolic decree mandates that Gentiles must forsake idolatry and im-

---

271. Lake, *Beginnings,* 5:469, stresses that a thirty-two-week minimum was required for this journey; in other words, the portion of one year that was good for travel.

morality, in particular, dining in pagan temples where such things transpire (i.e., no eating of meat offered to and partaken of in the presence of idols, Acts 15).

A.D. 50-52 — Second missionary journey of Paul with Silas (Silvanus) instead of Barnabas and Mark. This is important, for Silas is the apostolic delegate who was to explain the decree to the churches, and he had independent authority from Jerusalem, not from Paul (Acts 15:22). Paul travels to Philippi and Thessalonica, and eventually he stays a considerable time in Corinth before going to Ephesus and then Jerusalem, returning afterward to Antioch (Acts 15:40–18:23). On this journey he picks up Timothy in Lystra (Acts 16:1) and Luke in Troas (16:10ff.).

A.D. 51-52 — During his stay in Corinth, Paul writes 1 and 2 Thessalonians, with the help of Silvanus.

A.D. 51 or 52 — The Gallio incident (Acts 18:12-18) and increasing troubles from Jews in Corinth eventually precipitate Paul leaving Corinth after staying between eighteen and twenty-four months.

A.D. 52 — Second missionary period concludes apparently with a report to the Jerusalem church (Acts 18:22), and a return to Antioch.

Later Pauline Chronology

A.D. 53-57(58) — Third missionary journey. After an eighteen-month stay in Corinth (Acts 18:11), Paul sails for Syria, probably in the spring of 52, stopping briefly in the port of Ephesus and leaving Aquila and Priscilla to lay the groundwork for future missionary work (cf. below). After preaching once in the synagogue and promising to return (18:19), he goes to Caesarea Maritima, visits briefly in Jerusalem, and returns to Syrian Antioch. After a stay there, Paul sets out on his last major missionary period as a free man, passing through the Galatian region and strengthening the congregation there, but pressing on to Ephesus where he stays for at least two and perhaps three years.

A.D. 54 (55) — Paul writes 1 Corinthians from Ephesus. Not the first letter he had written them, but the first one still extant (cf. 1 Cor. 5:9-10). This letter addresses the many questions and problems raised by the Corinthians both orally and in writing in their communication with Paul since he had left there. First Corinthians failed to solve the problems in Corinth, however, as 2 Corinthians makes evident. News, perhaps from Timothy, comes to Paul of real trouble in Corinth after writing 1 Corinthians.

A.D. 55 — The painful visit to Corinth (2 Cor. 2:1, not mentioned in Acts). This visit is a disaster, as opposition comes to a head. Paul's authority is questioned and he leaves, feeling humiliated. As a result, Paul writes a stinging, forceful letter (the so-called severe letter), a fragment of which may be found in 2 Corinthians 10–13. Titus is the bearer of this severe letter. Paul begins to regret this letter, and after some missionary work in Troas he crosses over into Macedonia anxious to hear Titus's report on the results of the severe letter (this journey corresponds to the journey from Troas to Macedonia found in Acts 20:1-16).

Fall A.D. 55 or 56 — After hearing some good news from Titus, Paul writes 2 Corinthians (at least chaps. 1–9) with some relief, though he realizes there are still problems to be overcome. Shortly after, he journeys to Corinth, where he stays for three months, then returns to Philippi in Macedonia at Passover.

Late A.D. 56 or early 57 — Paul writes Romans from Corinth (cf. Rom. 16:1), shortly before setting out for Jerusalem for the last time (Rom. 15:25).

A.D. 57 — Paul travels by way of boat from Philippi to Troas (where the famous Eutychus incident happens, Acts 20:7-12), and then to Miletus, where he makes his famous farewell speech (Acts 20:18ff.), and finally hastens on to be in Jerusalem in time for Pentecost in May 57. Landing at Tyre, he strengthens Christians there and is warned not to go to Jerusalem, but he continues southward, stopping at Caesarea Maritima to visit with Philip the evangelist and his prophesying daughters (Acts 21:8-9). Here he encounters Agabus, who prophesies his being taken captive and handed over to the Gentiles (NOTE THAT LUKE WAS WITH PAUL ON THIS JOURNEY AND LATER CHRONICLED THESE EVENTS).

A.D. 57-59 — After an incident in the temple courts which leads to Paul being taken into custody by a Roman tribune, Paul asks to speak to his people and recount his conversion and mission (Acts 22, in Aramaic). A near riot breaks out, and Paul is taken to the Roman ruler's Palestinian head-quarters in Caesarea Maritima so that Governor Felix can deal with Paul. He is allowed to languish in some kind of prison or house arrest situation for two years until Festus becomes governor (probably in 59 or at the latest, 60). Some scholars believe Paul wrote the Captivity Epistles (Philemon, Philippians, Colossians, and Ephesians) from Caesarea before departure for Rome by boat.

A.D. 59-60 — Seasonal data suggest the journey to Rome took place in late 59, during the risky time for sea travel, and that Paul probably arrived in Rome at least by February of 60 (cf. Acts 27–28).

A.D. 60-62 — Paul is under house arrest in Rome, during which time he is traditionally thought to have written the Captivity Epistles, with Philippians probably being the last of these (in 62, shortly before the resolution of Paul's trial).

NOTE THAT ALL DATA BEYOND THIS POINT IS LARGELY INFERENTIAL AND CONJECTURAL SINCE ACTS ENDS WITH PAUL IN ROME, AND SINCE EVEN IF THE PASTORAL EPISTLES ARE BY PAUL, THEY DO NOT TELL US A GREAT DEAL ABOUT PAUL'S MOVEMENTS.

A.D. 62 — The conclusion of Acts shows that Luke knows that Paul was under house arrest for only two years, and it is to be pointed out that at no point in his many interviews or trials is Paul ever found guilty of any crime at the hands of the Romans (cf. especially Acts 24–26). Furthermore, if Paul's case was resolved in 62, this was before the time of the fire in Rome (July 64), which also means it was before the time Nero descended into tyranny and was looking for scapegoats, and before Christianity really had come under close imperial scrutiny. Note, too, that the Pastorals do not suggest a situation of house arrest but rather imprisonment by Roman authorities; in other words, a situation that Paul was not in during the period from 60 to 62, so far as we know. The following scenario is possible if Paul was released in 62.

A.D. 62-64 or later — Paul travels back east in response to problems. This includes a possible summer in Asia Minor (Ephesus?) and a summer and winter in Crete and Greece.

Sometime after July 64, Paul is arrested in Asia Minor and taken overland to Rome.

A.D. 64 (late) to 68 — The years of the Neronian tyranny and paranoia. If the Pastorals are by Paul, then they were likely written during this time when Paul appears to have been in Mamertine prison, or a similar facility in Rome. Under such circumstances, it is likely that Paul would have had to rely heavily on a trusted amanuensis (secretary) to write the Pastoral Epistles for him. The most likely conjecture is that Luke provided this service, which explains why these letters often reflect Lukan style, diction, and even some ideas.

A.D. 65-68. Paul is executed as a Roman citizen by beheading.

VII. Pauline Chronology: The Galatian Data

A. Preliminary Matters

There has been a trend, at least since the publication of R. Jewett's important work, to stress that the Pauline data must be treated as primary data and the Acts data as secondary, which leads then to the further argument that Acts chronology should be fitted into the Pauline framework, if possible, or rejected where it does not fit.[272]

---

272. See Jewett, *A Chronology of Paul's Life*, and Lüdemann, *Early Christianity*, but cf. G. Ogg, *The Odyssey of Paul*, who is heavily indebted to the much earlier work by D. Plooij, *De chronologie van het leven van Paulus* (1918).

There are at least three major problems with this whole approach: (1) The rhetorical character of Paul's letters, including Galatians, makes it quite impossible to read them as nontendentious documents. When, on rare occasion, Paul does make remarks that have clear bearing on matters of chronology, he does not do so in the manner of a disinterested historian. Rather, his comments are ad hoc, occasional, selective, and often highly rhetorical, intended as part of an act of persuasion. This is clearly the case in Galatians 1–2. (2) The fact that Paul is frequently an eyewitness to the events he mentions or alludes to has to be balanced against the fact that Paul's remarks on these subjects are often indirect or in passing. (3) Paul does not mention *enough* historical events, persons, or locations, even in passing, to come up with anything like a broad chronological framework of his life, either purely on the basis of Paul's letters or through an attempt at synchronisms with the rare external data that can be brought into the discussion (such as, e.g., when Gallio was in Corinth or when Aretas was alive and could be connected with events in Damascus). Regardless of one's view of the degree of historically authentic data in Acts, eventually Acts must and always is brought into the equation, and rightly so. The question is whether Acts can or should be considered an equal dialogue partner with the Pauline letters in discussions of matters of chronology and history.[273]

I would like to suggest several reasons why the material in Acts must be taken very seriously in these sorts of discussions. (1) First, we have already shown how it is probable that Luke intends us to see this document as a piece of historical narrative, not as a romance, a scientific treatise, or even a biography.[274] As such it needs to be compared especially to the work of other Hellenistic historiographers such as Thucydides, Polybius, Ephorus, to a lesser degree with Josephus and the Jewish historians, and to an even lesser degree with the Roman historians such as Livy, Sallust, and Tacitus. In particular Luke claims to stand in the tradition of the great Hellenistic historians who wrote monographs on contemporary or recent events, traveled, did research, were eyewitnesses of at least some of the events they recounted, and consulted such eyewitnesses when they were not present. This modus operandi was unlike that of various Roman armchair historians, who relied to a much greater degree on available records and documents in Rome, often only wrote after retiring from their life's work, and often composed not only speeches but some sections of their works almost entirely out of their fertile imaginations or on the basis of gossip or pure hearsay. In short, the *genre* of Acts at the very least demands that we treat it with the same

273. See on all this Hemer, *Book of Acts*, pp. 14ff.
274. Dunn, *Acts*, p. xvi: ". . . the reader can justifiably be confident of the historical basis of most of his narratives."

respect we would give to other ancient historical sources, including Josephus's efforts at apologetic historiography.[275] (2) The material in Acts, being historical narrative, is *direct* evidence about events, speeches, locations, and persons in a way that is not true of Paul's letters. Luke *intends* to discuss the very subjects one needs to discuss if one is going to compose a chronology of Paul's life or of early Christianity or both, though of course Luke is selective, limited by his evidence, and has his own aims, purposes, and editorial tendencies. (3) As we shall later argue, the most plausible view of the "we passages" (including both the "we" and the actual data included in these sections) suggests our author was an eyewitness of a good deal of the material in the last eight chapters of Acts and was a companion of Paul, who could have been consulted about a good deal of the material found in the earlier chapters in Acts.[276] Furthermore, both Acts and various references in the Pauline corpus (cf. Col. 4:14; 2 Tim. 4:11) encourage us to consider the evidence in Paul's letters and Acts together. At the least, Acts may be indebted to Paul if not to some of his letters. (4) In the places where Acts can be checked against extracanonical data, Luke appears to be generally reliable in his historical reporting, though there are undeniable problems in some of the speech material (cf., e.g., Acts 5:36-37).

I thus must conclude this brief preliminary discussion by suggesting that Paul's letters and Acts should be taken together and both must be critically sifted if one wishes to draw up a chronology of the life of Paul or of the events in early Christianity. I see no good reason to give Paul's letters much greater weight than Acts in these matters, not least because Paul does not by and large give us much *direct* evidence. Rather, I would suggest that the Pauline evidence deserves only a slight preference over the Acts data where they both mention the same subject.

B. *The Galatian Chronological Data*

Without a doubt, the material found in Galatians 1–2 is crucial to any discussion of either Pauline chronology or Acts chronology or the relationship of the two to each other. It is thus necessary at this point to deal with a few of the crucial matters that have a bearing on our discussions.

As is well known, the issue of whether Paul is referring to a fourteen-year period or a seventeen-year period between his conversion and his second trip to Jerusalem has long been debated, and there is probably no knockdown argument that can completely rule out one view or the other.

---

275. See pp. 35ff. above.
276. See the mature conclusions of Cadbury, " 'We' and 'I' Passages."

Rather, it is a matter of weighing probabilities and grammatical tendencies. It should be noted that critical scholars have come down on both sides of this issue.[277]

First, it must be accepted that the threefold επειτα in Gal. 1:18, 21 and 2:1 sets up a chronological sequence of some sort involving a trip to Jerusalem, a trip into the regions of Syria and Cilicia, and finally a second trip to Jerusalem. Paul uses this same term elsewhere to set up a clear chronological sequence (cf. 1 Cor. 15:5, 6, 7, 23, and 46; 1 Thess. 4:17). Secondly, the crucial phrase in 2:1, δια δεκατεσσαρων ετων, differs somewhat from the phrase in 1:18 (μετα ετη τρια). The first phrase above in all likelihood means "after fourteen years," while the latter may be translated either "in the third year" (cf. Mark 8:31; 10:34 to the parallels in Luke 9:22 and 18:33) or "after three years." The emphasis in this whole passage is on the time Paul was *not* in Jerusalem, and on the *few* times he met with the "pillars," and the use of the time markers suggests an attempt at completeness. Paul's argument would have been vitiated if he had omitted any other visits to Jerusalem that occurred during this period.[278] On the whole, then, the most natural way to read Gal. 2:1, especially in light of the reference to going up to Jerusalem *again*,[279] is that Paul is calculating the timing of his second visit in relationship to the timing of his first visit, *not* in relationship to his conversion.

Must we then think that Paul is necessarily referring to seventeen entire years, as Jewett and others insist?[280] This conclusion is by no means necessary for two very good reasons: (1) in the Greco-Roman world, of which Galatia was certainly a part, it was a regular practice to count parts of years as wholes at the beginning and/or ending of a sequence of time. Thus, fourteen years could in fact mean fourteen calendar years had passed. If the period referred to began late in the first calendar year of reckoning and ended early in the last year of the period, we could be talking about a period of twelve and a half years or thereabouts. Ancients were far less concerned about chronological precision than moderns, and thus our modern concern for precision should

---

277. Cf., e.g., D. Lührmann, *Galatians* (Minneapolis: Fortress, 1992), p. 38, who argues that the fourteen years *includes* the three years mentioned in 1:18 as being the period between the conversion and the first visit by Paul to Jerusalem, while so conservative a commentator as J. B. Lightfoot concluded that Gal. 2:1 must refer to fourteen years in addition to the three years already mentioned (cf. his *Saint Paul's Epistle to the Galatians* [London: Macmillan, 1896], p. 102).

278. See rightly F. F. Bruce, *Commentary on Galatians* (Grand Rapids: Eerdmans, 1982), p. 106.

279. Παλιν is in the vast majority of the earliest and best manuscripts and is in all likelihood original.

280. See Jewett, *A Chronology of Paul's Life*, pp. 52-53 and passim.

not be imposed on ancients; (2) the phrase in 1:18 can certainly mean "in the third year" after the conversion/call, in which case it could refer to as little as a year and a half or even a bit less. This means that Paul's two time references in 1:18 and 2:1 could refer to as few as fourteen complete years or to as many as seventeen. Especially in view of 1:18 I would urge that Paul likely means less than seventeen years.

To sum up, I would suggest that we reckon about a year and a half, give or take a month or two, between Paul's conversion in A.D. 34 and his first visit to Jerusalem in early 37, and then another twelve and a bit years or slightly more before his second visit to Jerusalem in 48 for a total of slightly more than fourteen years between his conversion (34) and his second visit to Jerusalem (48). Alternately, one could follow Lührmann and others and use inclusive reckoning (three plus eleven years), which would mean that fourteen total years are meant by Gal. 1:18 and 2:1, in which case one still comes up with the same result. In either scenario one begins the period between Paul's conversion and second visit to Jerusalem with A.D. 34 and ends it in 48. Nothing compels us to assume a full seventeen years elapsed between Paul's conversion and his second visit to Jerusalem.

C. The Galatian and Acts Historical Data

It is scarcely an exaggeration to say that one of the most difficult problems in NT studies is assessing the relationship, if any, between Galatians 2 and Acts 11:30; 12:25; and 15. Probably a majority of scholars still think that Paul's second visit mentioned in Galatians 2 should be seen as referring to the same meeting as that mentioned in Acts 15, though of course each author discusses the matter from his own perspective. A significant and vocal minority have on the other hand suggested that Acts 11–12 mentions in passing the meeting Paul refers to in Galatians 2. On all accounts there is little dispute that the visit to Jerusalem recounted in Gal. 1:18-20 corresponds to the one mentioned in Acts 9:26-29, a visit which we suggest happened in A.D. 37, not long after the escape from Damascus in a basket.

Bound up with all this are questions about the date when Paul wrote Galatians, clearly one of Paul's most polemical letters. On the one hand, if Galatians was written after the meeting referred to in Acts 15, then Galatians 2 lets us know that there were still serious ongoing tensions, disputes, and problems between Paul and other early Christians over circumcision, food, and keeping the Mosaic Law in general. The so-called apostolic council of Acts 15 settled little or nothing on this showing. Furthermore, if Galatians was written after the event described in Acts 15 transpired, then either Paul has conveniently failed to mention one of his trips to Jerusalem (which is unlikely since he is defending himself in Galatians and making clear how many times he went to Jerusalem), or else Luke has made a mistake in referring to three visits to Jerusalem by the time of the Acts 15 council. It has also been suggested that Luke has divided up one occasion (referred to in Galatians 2) into two parts (Acts 11:30 and Acts 15), thus muddying the historical waters.

At this juncture it will be helpful to list the usual reasons given for identifying the Acts 15 visit and the one mentioned in Galatians 2:

1. Both texts refer to an event that happened in Jerusalem.
2. Both texts have the same major players involved (Paul, Barnabas, Peter, James, and Judaizing Christians).
3. Both texts on the surface *seem* to be dealing with the same issue, namely, the basis of acceptance of Gentiles into the Christian fold — must they be circumcised and keep the food laws or not?
4. It fits one possible chronology mentioned above; namely, the Acts 15 meeting takes place seventeen years after Paul's conversion in A.D. 50, and rightly comes before Paul goes to Corinth in 50-51.
5. Both texts mention that circumcision was not required of Gentiles.
6. The problems discussed in both texts are "in-house" problems and do not involve the relationship of Christians with non-Christian Jews.

There are, however, several serious problems with the reasoning presented above:

1. There remains the problem of two visits mentioned by Paul but three mentioned by Luke, a problem which is exacerbated if Luke was at any point a companion of Paul or even if he knew Galatians but not Paul. This problem can be overcome if, as I would suggest, Galatians is the earliest letter we have from Paul's hand, written in A.D. 49 shortly *before* the meeting mentioned in Acts 15. Usually this problem is solved, however, by suggesting that Luke simply made a mistake.
2. In Acts Paul is sent up to the meeting in Jerusalem as a representative of the Antioch church, while in Galatians Paul says he went up by revelation.
3. In Galatians the issue appears to be raised after Paul arrives in Jerusalem, while in Acts it is clear that the issue and its discussion is going on before then.
4. Paul says in Galatians 2 that he met privately with the pillar apostles, whereas Acts 15 is clearly depicted as a larger and more public meeting.
5. Paul calls the Judaizers false brethren, while Luke simply mentions the

objections of Pharisaic Christians, without casting any aspersions on
their faith.

6. Paul does not mention the decree of James *at all* in Galatians, which he
   surely could and should have done if he wanted to stop the Judaizers
   from trying to force circumcision on Galatian Gentile Christians, by
   means of citing an authority the Judaizers would respect!

7. In Galatians 2 Paul plays a significant role in the discussion, but in Acts
   15 he is clearly overshadowed by Peter and James and simply reports.
   Indeed, Luke gives his "hero" only one verse in Acts 15, a very surprising
   move, especially if he knew he played a more prominent role in the
   discussion and resolution of the matter.

Not all of the items listed above are of equal weight, but I would place
especial stress on numbers 3-7. It seems most unlikely, if the decree by James
had already been given in any form and involved food and circumcision, that
the events recorded in Galatians 2 would have transpired as Paul records
them happening. We can understand Judaizers claiming James's support and
claiming Paul's ministry and message were illegitimate *before* the council and
decree, but it is much more difficult to imagine this happening in the way
Paul records it after the Acts 15 meeting. Then, too, Peter's and Barnabas's
vacillation as recorded in Galatians 2 is more easily understood if they
occurred before the Acts 15 meeting. Some of these problems can be resolved
if Galatians is indeed a letter written before the Acts 15 council occurred,
but not all of them.

Various factors point to an identification of the meeting mentioned in
passing in Acts 11:30 and 12:25 with that recorded in Galatians 2.

1. Barnabas and Paul are salient figures in *both* Acts 11 and 15. Thus their
   mention in Galatians 2 gives no greater support to one view or the other.
   The same can be said for the mention of Jerusalem in Acts 11–12; 15;
   and Galatians 2. It favors neither view or it favors both.

2. More telling is the fact that Paul in Galatians 2 says he went up the
   second time to Jerusalem in response to a *revelation*, and he does *not*
   say it was a revelation given to him directly from God. This dovetails
   nicely with Acts 11:27-29, which says Agabus came to Antioch and
   revealed that there would be a severe famine and hence the need for
   famine relief, especially for the poor and marginalized Christians in
   Jerusalem and Judea who would most feel its effects.

3. Gal. 2:10 clearly mentions that Paul and Barnabas were asked to remember the poor. This is quite natural if the famine was ongoing and what
   Paul and Barnabas had brought (cf. Acts 11:30) was only a start toward
   solving the problem. Notice that Gal. 2:10 says literally that "this very

thing I *had been eager* to do." The aorist verb εσπουδασα clearly suggests that Paul had *already* been concerned about this matter before this request came, which comports nicely with the report in Acts 11:30 that Paul brought famine relief with him to this second meeting in Jerusalem. Furthermore, the verb μνημονευωμεν is in the subjunctive and means "we were to continue to bear in mind the poor," also implying an ongoing activity.[281]

4. Notice that the discussion in Galatians 2 is about events that transpired in Antioch and in places visited on Paul's first missionary journey and then were further discussed in Jerusalem — events involving Peter, Barnabas, Paul, and Judaizers. For what it is worth, the main discussion of the Antioch church comes in Acts 11, not in Acts 15, and Peter is a prominent player in Acts 10–12, while Acts 13–14 records the first missionary journey, which also transpires before the Acts 15 council. Then, too, Peter is not portrayed as a major figure *after* Acts 15. The Judaizers appear in Acts 15:1 and 5. The point I am making is that the configuration of prominent figures and events mentioned in both Galatians 2 and Acts all occur in portions of Acts that precede the decree in Acts 15 — indeed, all occur in the material that immediately precedes the Jerusalem conference.

5. Notice that the incident in Antioch according to Paul in Galatians 2 is in fact over table fellowship, *not* circumcision. This comports with the earlier discussions recorded in Acts 10–11, but less well with the later discussions in Acts 15 where the circumcision issue is settled and a different kind of food and fellowship is discussed, namely, food and fellowship in pagan temples.[282]

6. Paul in Galatians is clearly on the defensive, not merely because of the Judaizers but also because of the behavior of Peter, Barnabas, and perhaps even James. He contemplates the possibility of people preaching other gospels (Galatians 1), and his position seems more vulnerable here than in any of his other letters. Notice that in 1 Corinthians Paul is able to speak of Peter in more positive tones as a fellow apostle whose be-

---

281. On this see H. D. Betz, *Galatians* (Philadelphia: Fortress, 1979), pp. 54-56.

282. Cf. the discussion on Acts 15, and on ειδωλοθυτον see my article "Not So Idle Thoughts." As Hill, *Hellenists and Hebrews,* p. 109, says, "But the incident at Antioch did not have to do with the conditions surrounding Gentile admission; it had instead to do with the conditions surrounding mixed fellowship, which is to say, laws governing food or purity. In other words the issue in Antioch, unlike that at the Jerusalem Conference, was not Gentile but *Jewish* obedience." *Notice* that Paul in Galatians 2 does not tell us the outcome after he rebuked Peter. I would suggest this is because the issue was not settled then and there, but later, after Galatians was written, at the Jerusalem conference, or because Paul lost this battle.

havior could be emulated by Paul if he chose to do so (1 Cor. 9:5 and 3:22).[283] This sense of alienation, even from his fellow apostles that Galatians seems to exude, is much more understandable if this letter reflects a period before some sort of agreement had been hammered out at a conference in Jerusalem on these matters.

7. It is understandable how Judaizers might be able to come to Antioch and then go on to the churches of Galatia presenting themselves as representatives of the Jerusalem church and of its views, before a public resolution of the circumcision matter had happened. This sort of influence with any sort of Jerusalem backing is much less understandable after the Jerusalem council.

Why then has Luke not told us in Acts 11–12 that the second trip to Jerusalem involved Paul in significant discussions with the pillar apostles? I would suggest two reasons: (1) Paul says his meeting with James and the pillars was a private one. Apparently the Galatians will not have heard of it before this Pauline letter was written. Luke by and large is recording the significant events of early Christianity that were of a broader and more public character. (2) Whatever may have been privately agreed upon on the occasion of Paul's second visit to Jerusalem, it is clear that it did not settle the crucial issues about food and circumcision for the church as a whole, nor did the church as a whole know that Paul's Gentile mission had been basically approved by the pillars. In short, this private meeting may have settled things for Paul and in his mind, but it settled nothing for the church as a whole. A further public conclave was required.

I must conclude that there are no views that are without problems, but the one which creates the most problems is the suggestion that Luke's account has little or no historical value and involves major distortion. The other two views, outlined above, both have their pluses and minuses, but on the whole the view which creates the least difficulties and solves the most problems is that the visit mentioned in Galatians 2 is equivalent to the one mentioned briefly in Acts 11 and 12.

It is not at all improbable that while Paul had privately gotten endorsement for his mission to the Gentiles from the pillar apostles on his second visit, there were many who opposed such a mission if it was pursued on the basis of a law-free gospel preached to the Gentiles. Until there was a public

---

283. Note that there is no evidence that the opponents dealt with in 1 Corinthians 10–13 have anything to do with Peter, James, or the Jerusalem church leadership. In fact there is not even clear evidence that they are Judaizers, since circumcision is not an issue in these chapters, or even earlier in 2 Corinthians. On these matters see now my *Conflict and Community in Corinth*, ad loc.

pronouncement the Judaizing controversy could and would go on, and could claim implicit endorsement from the Jerusalem church and perhaps even from James.

Notice that in Acts 11:2 Peter is criticized by the circumcised believers because of the Cornelius episode. I suspect that it is this occasion and the later one when the same sort of Christians came and criticized Peter in Antioch for the same thing (cf. "Why did you go to uncircumcised men and eat with them?" Acts 11:3 to Gal. 2:12), combined with the visit from "the men who came from James," that cumulatively caused Peter to withdraw from fellowshiping with Gentiles in Antioch.

I also suspect that we are meant to think that it is representatives of this same group of very conservative Jewish Christians who are referred to again in Acts 15:1, 5 as having gone to Antioch and argued that circumcision was necessary for salvation. This comports well with what we read in Gal. 2:4, 12, where they are clearly called the circumcision faction.[284]

The Galatians material suggests that before the council mentioned in Acts 15, James may have been sympathetic to the cause of the circumcision faction and their concerns, and actually had sent some of them to investigate what was happening in Antioch. Perhaps he had not yet decided what to do about the matter, especially since the Cornelius episode could be viewed as an isolated exception, but a Gentile mission with many Gentile converts could not be viewed in such a light. What we know about James from other sources including especially Josephus strongly suggests that James was especially careful to maintain his Jewish piety after he became a follower of Jesus, and it is understandable why he would be sympathetic to the circumcision party's concerns and views.[285]

Luke of course, ever the apologete and diplomat, does not convey the magnitude of trouble and tension created between the Judaizers and people like Paul in the early church, much less the tensions between Peter and Paul, or Paul and James. Nor does he suggest, as Gal. 2:12 may (but see below), that James may at least initially have been in broad agreement with the circumcision party's views. Yet, as Paul says, by the second visit (in 48) it is clear that James is not vocal about imposing circumcision on the likes of a Titus. Thus I think we must suppose that if the "men who came from James" are the same as the "false brothers," they came authorized to investigate by James but went beyond

---

284. Notice that the mention of the visit of the Judaizers in Acts 15:1 precedes the Acts 15 council. If we follow the order of events in Galatians, the *last events* mentioned in Galatians 2 are: (1) the Judaizers come to Antioch, and (2) the fallout between Peter and Paul. The meeting described in Gal. 2:1-10 would surely have appeared to the recipients of this letter to have happened before the Antioch incident.

285. See further below, pp. 439ff., on Acts 15 where this material is recapitulated and expanded upon in the context of the exegesis of Acts 15.

their writ when they urged circumcision. The alternative is to suppose that
the group mentioned in Gal. 2:4 are the Judaizers, while those mentioned in
2:12 are those who came from James to do damage control and manage the
problem, by means of suggesting a withdrawal from eating with Gentiles by
Peter and Barnabas. If there are indeed two groups, as I am inclined to believe,
Paul opposes both the one (whom he calls false brothers) and the other (whom
he sees as appeasers who compromise the basic principles of a law-free gospel
to the Gentiles).

Luke in Acts writes retrospectively knowing that these issues were eventually resolved, in part by the fact of who came to adhere to the gospel message
in large numbers in the middle decades of the first century. But to his credit,
Luke makes clear in Acts 15:1 and 5 that there *was* a circumcision party in the
Judean church, while at the same time carefully avoiding identifying this group
with James or the whole Jerusalem church. In Luke's presentation, the Judaizers
are a faction and an important factor within the Jerusalem church, but they
don't speak for that church as James does. If James had at some earlier point
identified with the Judaizers, the decree in Acts 15 suggests he distinguishes
himself from them in important ways.

What James decided was to be required of Gentiles was avoiding pagan
idolatry and immorality, in particular by avoiding pagan temple banquets.
This is what is meant by avoiding "things polluted by idols" (Acts 15:20).
Avoiding idolatry and immorality was the heart of the Mosaic Law, as the Ten
Commandments make clear, and surely it was the Ten Commandments along
with the Shema that one could most regularly expect to hear read in synagogues within range of the listening ears of Gentile proselytes and synagogue
adherents (Acts 15:21). James is most concerned with Gentile Christians al-
ienating Jews from being or becoming followers of Christ by continuing to
behave like Gentiles in regard to matters of idolatry and immorality. This is
also what Paul is concerned about in 1 Corinthians 8–10, and in that text, in
one of the first letters we have from Paul's hand written *after* the Jerusalem
conference, we see how Paul attempted to implement the ruling of James about
the behavior of Gentile Christians.

In the end Luke was right *not* to portray James and Peter and Paul as
always at odds with one another. Though there was much initial tension and
many ongoing problems, at least at the level of early Christian apostolic
leadership there was, by and large, a meeting of the minds as a result of the
Jerusalem conference about what would and wouldn't be required of Gentiles
as they became followers of Jesus. The old Baur hypothesis, as C. Hill has
shown, should be laid to rest once and for all.[286] Paul sums up well the essence
of the matter in 1 Thessalonians, the first letter he wrote after the Jerusalem

---

286. See especially Hill, *Hellenists and Hebrews*, pp. 103-47.

council (about A.D. 51), when he boasts that in the whole region people know how the Thessalonians "turned to God from idols, to serve a living and true God" (1 Thess. 1:9). This is what Moses demanded, James required, Paul preached, and the Thessalonians came to practice. It was also what Paul in good faith tried to make the Corinthians practice as a way of honoring the decree. Luke has not deceived us about the meetings mentioned in Acts 11 and Acts 15 and their impact. The former set the collection in motion, the latter provided the official basis of a law-free gospel that paradoxically was true to the heart of what Moses and God required of all believers. We will discuss these matters further in the commentary on Acts 15 itself.

VIII. Acts and Hermeneutics[287]

Since this work is intended to be read not only by scholars and seminary students but also by pastors and educated laypersons, it is in order to ask how the church can best use the material found in Acts. The fundamental assumption I am making by engaging in this discussion is that Luke's historical purposes did not exclude his having other purposes as well. It is hard to doubt, for instance, that Luke's interest in the actual character and content of the stories he includes goes beyond mere antiquarian curiosity. Luke writes as a believing Christian. He states rather clearly that he is writing so Theophilus may have a sure understanding and knowledge of the things about which he had already been instructed (Luke 1:4). This means that he is striving to be a reliable and careful narrator of the material he is conveying, not only because he is a good historian but also because he believes that this material can and should be used for instruction in his own day.

Luke's mentioning that Theophilus had already been instructed about these things *points* to the ongoing hortatory and pedagogical use of the historical traditions. As a reliable narrator, then, Luke will seek to properly characterize various persons and actions that he describes. He gives us no reason not to trust him when he portrays Simon Magus or Ananias and Sapphira or the magician Elymas as those whose examples he would not want his audience to follow. Nor do we need to doubt that his portrayal of Peter or Paul is in essence on the mark, even if there is something of the hero's halo added to each character at various points.

There are in fact two levels on which the hermeneutical discussion can

---

287. What follows here should be seen as only preliminary remarks. The real hermeneutical task cannot be undertaken without first having a detailed engagement with the text itself, resulting in sound exegesis.

be broached: (1) at the level of what Luke intended his audience to learn and do as a result of hearing or reading Acts, and (2) at the canonical level at which point it became the judgment of the church that Luke's work was Holy Writ. The issue of norms and normativity can be raised in both cases.

What was *normal* for the earliest church might not be seen by Luke as a *norm* for his own or other churches. Take, for instance, the example of the earliest Jerusalem Christians sharing all things in common. This fact is mentioned more than once in the narrative (Acts 2:45; 4:32). Once we get beyond Jerusalem, however, nothing is said of this pattern being replicated, for instance, in Antioch or Corinth or Philippi. What do we make of this?

Much depends on how idealized Luke's portrait of the early church is, and also how ideal he saw the earliest Christians' lives, faith, worship, and behavior as being. Luke *may* be suggesting that the earliest church in Jerusalem is the model for the church in later generations, but then again in certain instances his purposes may be more strictly historical — describing what *was,* not necessarily what *ought* to be. If the Jerusalem church is seen as a model, the question becomes in what ways and to what degree?

No doubt Luke would not want his church to repeat the blunders of Ananias and Sapphira. Their behavior was far from exemplary, unless of course we take them as an example meant to teach how to "go and do otherwise." On the other hand, it is hard to doubt that faithful witnesses like Peter and Paul are being seen as exemplary in a positive sense, as patterns to be followed by Theophilus and others.

It is also hard to doubt that Luke believed that God continued to act in his own day in similar fashion to the way God in the person of the Holy Spirit is portrayed as acting in Acts. There is no hint, for instance, that Luke takes the so-called apostolic age as somehow totally unique and unrepeatable, and so to be radically distinguished from the time in which he wrote insofar as either belief or behavior or even the miraculous activity of God is concerned.[288] There is, furthermore, nothing in the church's decision to accept Acts into the canon that should signal to us an attempt to suggest that the issues raised in that book had already been brought to a closure.[289] To the

---

288. One suspects that Luke's strong insistence on distinguishing between magic and miracles at various points in Acts reflects his attempts to help his audience sort out the difference, in which case these sorts of matters were still live issues when he wrote.

289. So far as I can see, the older argument that the apostolic age was viewed, even in Acts, as unrepeatable halcyon days does not adequately deal with Luke's own attitude. His emphasis in Acts is not on apostolicity, but on witness, not merely on someone like Peter but also on someone like a Philip or an Apollos or an Aquila or Priscilla. That is, he emphasizes the continuity between his own time and the earliest period of church history. In both times there was ongoing witness to Christ by a variety of people, and in both times the Holy Spirit was still active, inspiring witness and works of various sorts.

contrary, canonization reflected a belief in the abiding worth, importance, and relevance of the substance of the book for ongoing church life.[290]

When we examine Acts from a hermeneutical point of view, we are confronted with all the problems and promise that narrative raises, and in this regard the hermeneutics of Acts will be much the same as the hermeneutics of other biblical narratives, for example, the Gospels. Then, too, the speech material in Acts should probably be evaluated much the same as speech material elsewhere in narrative contexts in the NT. The latter is of course easier to handle than narrative because in speeches we have direct exhortations about what to believe, do, say, or experience, whereas narrative operates in a more subtle and indirect fashion.

At this juncture it will be useful simply to list several hermeneutical principles that may help us to learn how to use Acts in church settings today. Though characterization is not a *major* concern of Luke, it is fair to say that he intends his own Christian audience to follow in the footsteps of people like Peter, or James, or Philip, or Barnabas, or Apollos, or Mary, or the mother of John Mark, or Tabitha, or Lydia, or Priscilla and Aquila in terms of their words and deeds.[291] In other words, the vast majority of the behavior of the *Christian* characters in the story are probably meant to be seen as exemplary. This is not always the case of course, as the example of Mark's abandoning of the missionary journey or of Ananias and Sapphira shows. Thus, even the Christian characters in the narrative have to be scrutinized on the basis of Christian standards or ideals listed in the text.

By standards or ideals, I mean the sort of material we find in the summary passages in Acts 2:43-47 or 4:32-37. It is widely recognized that these are Lukan redactional summaries meant to boil down into a few phrases some of the essential positive characteristics of the Jerusalem church. These standards can be used to evaluate, for example, Ananias and Sapphira, or the uneven distribution of food to the widows in Acts 6, in a negative way. There are then internal clues as to what Luke sees as a norm for Christian behavior.

There are also plenty of clues as to what Luke sees as the norm in Christian belief as well. Particular attention should be paid to the repeated themes in the speeches of Peter and Paul, who in Luke's eyes speak for early Christianity more clearly and more frequently than anyone else.[292] When

290. In other words, canonization should not be seen as primarily an attempt to create an archive about how things *used* to be, but no longer were.

291. That is, in terms of their public face, for Luke as a historian is not interested in their private lives or in telling anecdotes that reveal something of what they are like as individuals or private persons.

292. The other speeches in Acts, such as the speech of Stephen or the speech of James in Acts 15, are more situation specific, as are the defense speeches found in Acts 21ff. The latter, however, are probably meant to help prepare Christians being prosecuted or persecuted to see how they should respond in such a situation.

analysis is given to the Petrine and Pauline speeches that we find in Acts 2–20, it becomes clear that for Luke the heart of the faith has to do with the narrative of Jesus' life, death, and resurrection (especially the latter two) and the sending of the Spirit. To this may be added the belief that God is a God of all peoples and individuals, and that God shows no partiality. We also see reflected the belief in an all-powerful creator God who made everything, and in a future judgment and resurrection. The theme of God's overarching plan of salvation and the breaking in of the kingdom through the ministry of Jesus and his followers helps to tie these major emphases together. In short, Luke sees a certain christological and eschatological message as central to the preaching. Much less is said in the speeches about ecclesiological matters, but a good deal is implied by the attempt to witness to all persons, Jew and Greek alike. This witness to all suggests all are lost and in need of the salvation that is to be found in Christ. True Israel for Luke is made up of all those who respond positively to the gospel, both Jew and Gentile.

Distinguishing what Luke sees as norms and what he sees as merely historically interesting is difficult, but I would suggest that using the following approaches produces some fruit:[293] (1) look for positive repeated patterns in the text, or (2) look for when there is only one pattern, or (3) look for when there is clear divine approval or disapproval in the text for some belief or behavior or experience or religious practice. Several examples will illustrate what I mean.

If we look at the summary passages again in Acts 2:43-47 and 4:32-37, we discover that things like miracles, prayer, praising God, eating together, and sharing possessions are mentioned more than once as characterizing the life of the early church (see also 5:12-16). By contrast we find only one example in which a leader in the early church is said to be chosen by casting lots (1:24-25), and this was before the Holy Spirit had come upon the followers of Jesus in any case. This suggests that Luke sees the repeated examples cited in these summary passages as normal for the early church, and perhaps normative for the church in later times as well. By contrast it would be difficult to argue that casting of lots is mandated as a normal or normative Christian practice since it is mentioned only once, and, more to the point, later examples of the appointing of leaders or missionaries follow other procedures (see 6:3-6; 13:2-3).[294]

Let us take a second and more controversial example. What is Luke saying

---

293. These principles were first suggested to me by my mentor G. D. Fee.

294. Notice especially in the second example how the Spirit's guidance is seen as primary. It would be equally dubious to argue that because Luke records that Paul undertook a Nazaritic vow at one point during his Christian life, Luke's audience ought to feel obligated to do so as well.

to us about the chronological and/or theological relationship of the reception of the Spirit and water baptism? In some texts we see that water precedes the reception of the Spirit (e.g., Acts 8:4-25). In other texts we see that the Spirit is received prior to water baptism (e.g., Acts 9:17-18; 10:44-48). In still other texts water and Spirit seem to be received virtually simultaneously, though the two are never simply identified in Acts (see Acts 8:26-40). In still other texts we have persons full of the Spirit who know little or nothing about Christian water baptism (Apollos — Acts 18:24-28). Luke in this matter has rightly suggested that history is messy and things do not always happen in the order one might expect or desire. In other words, there is no *one* pattern being suggested in Acts, though receiving the Spirit then water seems to be the most common order of things. *Are you kidding?!*

In this case, one could argue either that Luke is *not* trying to suggest a particular order of events, and/or that Luke means to tell us that God can send the Spirit at whatever point God wants to do so. What one clearly cannot do is take one example from Acts and *assume* it is normative while other texts are speaking about exceptional situations. One would have to argue for such a conclusion. Whatever else one may want to say, it seems clear enough from Acts 10:44-48 that it was believed that *withholding* water baptism once one had received the Spirit was not appropriate. One could also deduce from Acts 19 that Luke's view is that a person without knowledge and experience of the Holy Spirit is not a Christian at all and needs to go through the full conversion-initiation process.[295]

Another good example of a text that needs some careful handling is Acts 2, especially when compared to Acts 10. The story of Pentecost is indeed a story about the reception of the Spirit, who miraculously inspires speech in a variety of human languages. The focus of the story in Acts 2 is empowerment and enablement for witness. The story of Cornelius and those with him in Acts 10 is a story of conversion which is made possible by the gift of the Holy Spirit and made evident by speaking in tongues. Nothing is said in the latter text about foreign languages or witnessing to foreigners through pneumatically inspired speech. In other words, these two texts have some similarities (it was the same Spirit that caused both of these experiences and that filled both Jewish and Gentile Christians), but they also have notable differences. Specifically, two different sorts of Spirit-inspired speech utterances are involved.

In other words, Luke does not intend to portray Acts 10 as a simple duplication of what happened in Acts 2, with the only difference being that the audience was Gentile. Acts 10 is not really the Gentile Pentecost. Other than the fact that the Spirit was received in both cases, these two stories are quite different, and only the latter is really about the conversion of a person

295. See the discussion in the commentary on Acts 19.

who has not previously heard the gospel.[296] Nevertheless these texts also suggest that Luke does believe that a person is not a full-fledged Christian if he or she has not yet received the Spirit.

If we ask what would be an example of finding only one positive pattern in Acts, this would of course be the fact that the book suggests that everyone must repent and believe the gospel, regardless of background or previous religious affiliation (cf., e.g., 2:37-42 to 19:1-7). This same gospel message calling for change on the part of everyone is found throughout the book of Acts, though it is expressed in various ways.

As an example of clear divine disapproval we may take the repeated tellings of the story of Saul's conversion in Acts 9; 22; and 26. They all share in common the fact that God stopped Saul dead in his tracks when on Damascus road, preventing him from persecuting Christians. We may gather from this that Luke is telling us that God never approves such actions.

Hopefully this brief discussion will show that careful reflection must be given to how a narrative text or even speech material in Acts may be used by the church today, for the hermeneutics of Acts is a complex matter. Luke does not encourage us simply to play first-century "Bible land" and assume that all the early church did and said should be replicated today. This means that the text must be sifted and narratives must be weighed before they are used or applied. It is both sounder and safer to look for positive repeated patterns in the text of beliefs, behavior, and experiences that are endorsed and replicated in the lives of various of the persons who seem to be seen as examples in Acts. In this way the reader will find a surer guide for preaching and teaching the book of Acts.

---

296. I am here referring to a comparison between those who initially received the Spirit and spoke on Pentecost and Cornelius, not between those who were in fact converted on Pentecost (2:37-42) and Cornelius. Nothing is said directly about the spiritual experience or Spirit-inspired speaking of the group of converts mentioned in 2:37-42.

THE COMMENTARY

I. Prologue and Recapitulation
(Acts 1:1-14)[1]

The prologue in Acts follows various historiographical and rhetorical conventions of the day.[2] It is in some ways closest to the one we find in Philo, *Quod Omnis* 1 (ο μεν προτερος λογος ην ω Θεοδοτε. περι του . . .), and is resumptive in character. It is a "secondary" prologue typically used to introduce new volumes of a multivolume work (cf., e.g., some of the disputed prologues to Xenophon's *Anabasis* and Herodian's *History of the Empire*).[3] As such, it looks backward

---

1. As Barrett, *Acts*, vol. 1, p. 61, points out, the vast majority of the material in vv. 1-14 is mentioned in some form in Luke 24 or earlier in Luke (on the list of apostles' names, cf. Acts 1:13 to Luke 6:14-16), and thus it is best to see this whole section as recapitulation, with some expansion, before breaking new ground with Peter's first speech in 1:15ff.

2. Alexander's survey "The Preface of Acts" needs to be consulted. She shows that while the traits of the preface in Acts are not exclusively the sort found in historical works (such traits are also seen in scientific, and even in some cases biographical works), what we find in Acts is suitable for the beginning of a historical work, in this case a historical monograph. Her own attempts (see the discussion, pp. 14ff. above) to see the two Lukan prefaces as being more nearly akin to the scientific prefaces is not convincing, for neither Luke nor Acts is a scientific treatise like Galen's study of plants. The most this sort of argument shows is that Luke may have been familiar with scientific prefaces, a sort of indirect piece of evidence possibly supporting the notion that he was a doctor. Her further attempt to relate the Pauline material in Acts to the biographical traditions about Socrates (cf. her "Acts and Intellectual Biography") relies on too little data. Acts 17 should not be overpressed. Her argument especially fails to convince since Paul's death is not related in Acts.

3. See Polhill, *Acts*, p. 78.

before the text moves on to new material, mentioning the scope of the previous volume.[4] This in itself is not unusual in a multivolume historical work and strongly suggests the connection between Luke and Acts in the author's mind.[5]

Unlike Luke 1:1-4, the transition between prologue and narrative is very smooth in Acts 1:1-2, and Luke does not think it necessary to state again his purpose for writing. The book begins with the "I" style of a prologue (1:1), then gives way to reported speech, and finally in v. 4 to direct speech.[6] Luke simply reminds Theophilus of the *content* of the previous volume and then recapitulates and expands the close of the previous volume. We are thus informed by the reference to Theophilus that the second volume is addressed to the very same audience as the first one.[7]

Some scholars have complained that Luke breaks with convention by not giving a preview of what is to come in the following volume, but this is not quite accurate, for in fact Jesus' speech serves in this capacity, especially v. 8.[8] The Acts prologue shows Luke's penchant for stressing the importance of something by resorting to rhetorical hyperbole *(amplificatio)*, for of course Luke's Gospel does not include even "all" Luke knows about what Jesus said and did.[9] The proper translation here is likely "all that Jesus did and taught," not "all that Jesus began to do and teach,"[10] and this makes quite clear that Luke's focus in the first volume was on activities or deeds, which is only appropriate in a historical work. The

4. The phrase πρωτον λογον here indicates it was the first volume in the series. Cf. Bruce, *The Acts of the Apostles*, p. 97.

5. Palmer, however, has suggested that this prologue is like the sort which is both retrospective and prospective. See his "Literary Background of Acts 1.1-4." Against this conclusion the postresurrection appearances, preaching or teaching, promise, and commissioning by Jesus are all mentioned in Luke 24. It is possible that v. 2b is slightly alluding to v. 7, and v. 3 to vv. 6-7, but the basic character of the prologue is retrospective — it reminds the listener that volume one recorded what happened *until* (αχρι) the day Jesus was taken up, not what happened on that day. Since vv. 1-4 must be taken as prologue and transitional, looking primarily backward, volume two deals with what happened from the day of the ascension onward.

6. See ibid., p. 428. This transition does lead to the historically prospective comment about being baptized by the Spirit, but of course from a narrative point of view this subject of the coming of the Spirit on the disciples was already broached in Luke 24.

7. I agree with Barrett's suggestion (*Acts*, vol. 1, p. 66) that Theophilus was an inquirer or catechumen, surely a Christian seeking further or perhaps clearer information about the origins of his faith and the early history of the church. On the indications that Theophilus was likely a person of some social status but not a Roman official, see p. 42 above and *New Docs*, 3:11.

8. See rightly Tannehill, *Narrative Unity of Luke-Acts*, 2:9.

9. See, e.g., Acts 20:35, where an otherwise unknown saying of Jesus is quoted. On Luke's penchant for using "all" words, see Luke 1:3 and the discussion in Cadbury, *The Making of Luke-Acts*, pp. 213ff.

10. See the discussion above, pp. 9ff.

first volume was about what Jesus did and taught from the beginning until his ascension. The second volume will begin just prior to the ascension and continue from there. In this way Theophilus's memory is refreshed.[11]

V. 2 is interesting on several accounts. First, it suggests that Jesus instructed the disciples "through the Holy Spirit." The matter is perhaps put this way because hereafter the Spirit is also the means of instruction in the church — designated spokesmen and spokeswomen will speak through the Holy Spirit.[12] Secondly, we are told that the instructions are given "to the apostles whom he had chosen." This is a clear link back to the Gospel, where the term αποστολοι refers to the Twelve whom Jesus chose and commissioned (cf. Luke 6:13; 9:10; 11:49; and cf. 17:5; 22:14: 24:10). Acts 1:21-22 will make clear that the term is used of those who had witnessed the ministry of Jesus up to and including the resurrection appearances. Unless Acts 14:4, 14 are exceptions,[13] it appears that Luke confines the apostles to the Twelve. It is possible, however, that the term αποστολος is not a technical term anywhere in Luke-Acts, but simply means a missionary, a sent agent of Jesus, in which case Luke does not distinguish the Twelve from Paul and Barnabas in this regard. There can be little doubt, however, that the Twelve are the important transitional group in Luke's mind, binding the historical Jesus to the early church. He also affirms that they will play a role at the eschaton when the kingdom fully comes on earth, judging the twelve tribes of Israel (Luke 22:30).

Scholars have long debated the variations in the report in Luke 24 and Acts 1, usually without taking into account three important factors: (1) the narrative function that Luke intends each telling of the ascension and final instructions of Jesus to have; and (2) Luke's following of the rhetorical conventions about variation in style when one is retelling something. (3) The *recapitulative* character of Acts 1:1-11 is important to bear in mind if the reader is not to be distracted unnecessarily by questions concerning multiple and conflicting accounts of the ascension. Lucian advises the historian: "the first and second topics must not merely be neighbors but have common matter and overlap" (*How to Write History* 55).

In Luke 24 the account serves as a means of closing the first volume, but in Acts 1 the story of the ascension and final instructions serves to initiate what follows. In Luke 24 Luke has telescoped his accounts, so that the impression implicitly given is that all took place on one day (cf. 24:1, 13, 28, 36, 50),[14]

---

11. Which suggests the previous volume had reached him sometime prior to the second one.

12. It is also possible that the phrase "through the Holy Spirit" modifies "whom he had chosen."

13. See below, pp. 450ff.

14. It must be admitted, however, that the chronological connection of Luke 24:50 to what precedes it is vague.

whereas in Acts Luke speaks of a "forty"-day period when Jesus appeared to the disciples and thus "presented himself alive to them by many convincing proofs."[15] Forty is of course a conventional biblical number, but the point is that it refers to a considerable period of time, not just one day. This latter impression of an extended period of appearances is also what the close of Matthew, John, and 1 Corinthians 15 suggest.

The reference to many convincing τεχμηριοις in v. 3 is important, for this is a technical term for a "necessary proof" (see Aristotle, *Rhetor.* 1.2.16f.). Quintilian (*Inst. Or.* 5.9.3) puts it more strongly: τεχμηρια are things which involve a conclusion, "those which cannot be otherwise are called τεχμηρια by the Greeks, because they are indications from which there is no getting away." In other words, Luke believes the resurrection appearances of Jesus are strong, irrefutable proofs that Jesus is alive, providing a basis for all that follows, including the sending of the Spirit, the creation of the church, the success of the Christian mission. That Luke stresses that Jesus gave such proofs that he was alive indicates already that he is engaged in volume two, as he was in volume one, in the art of persuasion, in apologetics, in order to strengthen or confirm Theophilus in his faith.[16] Equally important is the evidence D. L. Mealand has generated using the *TLG*, showing that the phrase "many proofs" is very rare in Greek literature *except* in Greek historiographical works (cf. Josephus, *Ant.* 3.317-18; Diodorus Siculus 3.66.4.4; Dionysius of Halicarnassus, *Ant. Rom.* 1.90.2.2).[17] Here is probably another small hint that Luke is indebted to and writing in a Hellenistic historiographical mode.

It may be worthwhile to consider what function the ascension has in Luke's narrative, since he is the only Evangelist who really mentions such an idea, and does so in both of his volumes. It may not be accidental that his audience is Gentile, for Gentiles were well familiar with the idea of gods or semidivine figures materializing on earth in disguise and then being transported back into the heavens,[18] but were much less familiar with the idea of

15. Thus already we see the effort by Luke at apologetics, to help confirm his listener in his newfound faith.

16. See Johnson, *Acts,* p. 25: "Luke's concern for 'evidence' accords with his overall intention of providing 'assurance' to his reader (Luke 1.4). . . . Such 'evidences,' we imagine, would figure in the rhetorical disputations carried out by the apostles (Acts 9.29; 17.1-3; 18.4; 19; 19.8; 28.23)."

17. Mealand, "The Phrase 'Many Proofs.'"

18. Cf. Dionysius of Halicarnassus, *Ant. Rom.* 1.64.4 (Aeneas); 1.77.2 (a god); 2.56.2 (Romulus); cf. Livy 1.16.1f.; Philostratus, *Vit. Apoll.* 8.30. The account of the assumption of Herakles in Apollodorus 2.7.7 speaks of a cloud standing under Herakles which, with a thunderclap, conveyed him to heaven. For what it is worth, among these texts Luke's account seems the most like the account about the god in Dionysius, but its theophanic qualities are equally reminiscent of contemporary accounts of ascensions indebted to the biblical tradition, such as that of Moses or Elijah; cf. Josephus, *Ant.* 4.326 (Moses); Philo, *Quaest. Gen.* 1.86

resurrection, unless they had had some contact with Judaism. Thus it is resurrection that Luke must be convincing about, and it must be *distinguished* from pagan notions of various sorts. Nevertheless, the christological implications of this narrative for a Gentile audience familiar with the deification accounts of figures like Herakles should not be overlooked. Jesus is being portrayed here as a human yet divine figure worthy of a place in heaven alongside the Creator of the universe.

Luke stresses that the resurrected Jesus was no mere spirit but was tangible and could eat and drink with the disciples (cf. Luke 24:30, 37-39, 41-43). That is, in Luke's view the resurrection appearances were not merely visions from heaven, but happenings on earth. Thus, the ascension serves the function of making clear to the disciples (and in this case to Theophilus) that Jesus' life on earth had a definite closure, *after the resurrection appearances.* The disciples will not be called upon to be witnesses to any transcendent events, but only to things they saw and heard while Jesus was on earth — in particular, the resurrection appearances.[19]

The subject of Jesus' messages after the resurrection is stated in *v. 3* to be the dominion of God, which binds the content of Jesus' earthly teaching to that about which the disciples will instruct others to the very end of Acts (cf. 8:12; 14:22; 19:8; 20:25; 28:23, 31). Luke is concerned with various continuities throughout Acts. The continuity between the ministry of Jesus and that of his followers (including both the message and the empowering presence of the Spirit), the continuity between Judaism and Christianity, the continuity between OT prophecy and the events that transpired among Jesus' followers both before and after Easter (and Pentecost). This concern is understandable in the first century, because the one thing bound to offend many pagans in the Empire was a religion that was too new, a religion which could not claim a lengthy pedigree going back into hoary antiquity.[20]

Jesus identifies the Holy Spirit as "the promise of the Father," thus connecting it with OT prophecy, which prepares us for what follows in Acts 2:16-22. In view of the parallelism of *vv. 3-4* it seems likely that in Luke's mind the coming of the kingdom or dominion of God is synonymous with, or at least closely associated with, the coming of the Holy Spirit in power (cf. Luke 11:13, 20).[21] This last conclusion is confirmed by what follows in *vv. 4b-5,*

(Enoch and Elijah). On Hellenistic parallels to this whole section, cf. P. W. van der Horst, "Hellenistic Parallels to the Acts of the Apostles: 1.1-26," *ZNW* 74 (1983): 17-26, here pp. 21-22.

19. Notice there is no mention of the ascension as the subject of witness in Acts 1:22.

20. See the excursus about Claudius and the idea of a *religio licita*, pp. 539ff. below.

21. At least the latter is seen as the first clear manifestation of the dominion of God in the midst of humankind.

where we are told that what Jesus taught during his ministry was about being baptized by or with the Holy Spirit in contradistinction to John's baptism, which was merely by or with water.

The promise of baptism with the Holy Spirit in *v. 5* also carries with it a time limit — "not many days" from now. It is possible that Luke arrived at the forty-day-appearance period by calculating back from the date of Pentecost, which of course was fifty days after Passover,[22] and then allowing for a few extra days after the ascension. The issue of timing here is brought up in more than one connection.

The promise of the Spirit in "not many days" prompts the question, "Is this the time when you will restore the kingdom to Israel?" *(v. 6).*[23] It is a natural question not only in view of the connection in Luke's thought between the pouring out of the Spirit and the coming of the kingdom, but also because of the speculations in early Judaism about the restoration of the land (cf. Sir. 48:10, the LXX of Mal. 3:23). In terms of Lukan theology, what this verse shows is that while Luke does believe that the coming of the Spirit inaugurates the kingdom, he does not believe that that is all there is to be said about the kingdom. This verse suggests that God will one day fulfill his promises to Israel, in fact that God has already set that time and determined the interval before it by his own authority, but that human speculation about the timing of such an event is unfruitful, since only God knows that timing and he is not revealing it to mortals.[24] What this also shows is that Luke believes, not surprisingly, that many early followers of Jesus believed in the restoration of the control of the land to Israel (cf. Luke 24:21).

What *vv. 6-8,* which should be read closely together, indicate is not merely the delay in the restoration of Israel but also that in the interim there are important things to be accomplished. *V. 8* should be seen as briefly announcing the tasks that need to be completed before "the restoration," namely, witnessing in Jerusalem, in all of Judea and Samaria, "and to the ends of the earth." This last phrase has often been thought to refer to Rome (*Pss. Sol.* 8:15). In other words, as H. Conzelmann pointed out, v. 8 is seen as to a certain extent programmatic for Acts.[25] Yet it is possible to see this verse as programmatic without identifying Rome with the ends of the earth, since Acts 28

22. See Wilson, *Gentiles and the Gentile Mission,* pp. 100-103.

23. This verse shows that χρονος, which usually means a span of time, is sometimes indistinguishable from καιρος, for here χρονος means a moment in time.

24. This is an important point, not least because it shows that those who claim Luke is anti-Semitic are wrong. What Luke is opposed to is Judaism that rejects Jesus as Messiah, not all forms of Judaism.

25. See Conzelmann, *Acts,* p. 7. Contrast Pesch, *Die Apostelgeschichte (1–12),* p. 70, who probably rightly stresses that Rome is not meant but rather that the text should be read in light of Luke 24:47 — the gospel must go to all peoples.

is an intentionally open-ended conclusion.[26] It is programmatic in the sense that it alludes to a worldwide mission, and probably also to a mission to both Jew and Gentile in the Diaspora, not that it alludes to Rome.[27]

This verse also announces one of, if not the major, theme(s) of Acts. Witnesses, empowered by the Holy Spirit, are sent out from Jerusalem in various directions. This statement is in some ways as significant for what it does not say as for what it mentions. Notice that no clear mention is made of witnessing to Gentiles. Luke also does not mention witnessing in Galilee here, even though of course he knows that both Jesus and the first disciples were Galileans (cf. Luke 24:6; Acts 2:7), and he knows that in due course there were Christian disciples in Galilee (Acts 9:31). I would suggest this is because Luke does not know the details about the evangelization of Galilee.[28]

In general we may look for Luke to be the same sort of careful editor of his source material in the second volume as he was in his Gospel. He is limited by the sources he has, and he continues to edit them according to various formal and material agendas he has; for example: (1) rhetorical concerns about variation when using the same phrase or material more than once; (2) concerns to make the narrative more "Hellenized" so that a Gentile could grasp it, which affects the editing in regard to both form and content; (3) concerns about salvation history and the present, which lead him to deemphasize, though not dismiss, future eschatological material in favor of focusing on the present work of the Spirit, the present task of witnessing, and the like; (4) concerns about the more universal and inclusive potential of the gospel which comports with his emphasis on Gentile inclusion among the people of God, and his rejection of too-sectarian an approach to Christianity.

---

26. On the ends of the earth, see on Acts 8 at pp. 290ff. below, and see Acts 28 on the ending of the book, pp. 783ff.

27. See the discussion in Schneider, *Die Apostelgeschichte I*, pp. 225-27. A special focus on Gentiles might be in view if Schneider is right that Isa. 49:6 lies in the background here, which seems probable.

28. His primary sources for this early period in the Holy Land are Paul, perhaps Philip the evangelist and/or his family, other disciples in Caesarea Maritima, and some Jerusalem disciples such as the family of John Mark. That he had met Peter, or at least had discussed Galilee with him, seems unlikely, for Luke was not in the Holy Land prior to A.D. 57 or so at the end of the third missionary journey. On Luke's sources, cf. pp. 165ff. below and my article "Editing the Good News." I do not deny that Luke had a Petrine source, for he has a variety of early Petrine traditions, but this may have been John Mark or his family. In the main Luke's sources in Acts seem to have been *oral*, though a few of the early Jerusalem stories were probably written down by the late 50s, perhaps especially the Pentecost and Acts council (Acts 15) stories and in general some of the traditions involving Peter and James (and John?). I do not think the elaborate source theories of various scholars are either provable or necessary *if* Luke proves to be a second-generation Christian who was a sometime companion of Paul, but cf. Dupont, *The Sources of Acts,* and Lüdemann, *Early Christianity.*

Vv. 9-11 narrate the event of the ascension. The emphasis on the cloud which envelops Jesus and seems to transport him away is perhaps caused by Luke's desire to parallel the way Jesus leaves with the way early Christian tradition based on Daniel believed he would return again — on the clouds (cf. Dan. 7:13; Mark 14:62; Luke 21:27). Yet one is also struck by certain parallels with the account in 2 Kings 2 about the ascension of Elijah and the giving of the double portion of his spirit to his successor Elisha, who would assume his mantle (cf. also the assumption of Enoch).[29] In other words, this account is about the passing on of the power and authority to Jesus' witnesses so that they might continue the kingdom work he had begun.[30] The two figures who appear to bring to a close the disciples' gazing into the sky are likely meant to be seen as interpreting angels (cf. Luke 24:4; Acts 10:30).[31] Their question is apparently meant as a reproach, but they also reassure the disciples that Jesus will return in the same fashion in which he left *(v. 11).*[32]

Inevitably the comparison of this account both with OT literature and with pagan assumption stories raises the question of whether Luke invented this ascension story, especially since it is apparently absent in the other Gospels. It should be noted, however, that the concept of the ascension is not found in Mark because the last authentic verse we have is 16:8, which leaves us at the point before the resurrection appearances. Neither Matthew nor John records the event, but it would have transpired *after* the last event recorded in their respective Gospels. The Johannine language, however, about Jesus returning to the Father (see John 14–17) seems to presuppose a knowledge of the idea. Finally, Justin Martyr (*Apol.* 1.50) gives a firm place to the ascension in his creedal remarks apparently as something the church had passed on to him as an early tradition, but he may simply be dependent on Acts itself.[33] When one puts these facts together, they suggest that Luke did not invent the idea of the ascension; rather, he drew on early Christian tradition about the event. In fact, as Schneider rightly points out, the ascension is presupposed in the discussion of Jesus' parousia.[34] It is not unimportant, then, that we find the concept of

29. See Palmer, "Literary Background of Acts 1.1-4," pp. 431-32.
30. The receiving power from on high has chiefly to do with witnessing. Luke does not really comment on its soteriological significance, nor is he all that interested in its ecclesiological significance, if by that one is referring to church offices. For example, the reception of the Spirit by the Samaritans or Cornelius did not make them apostles, but it did make them witnesses, and this book is about witnesses, whether apostles or not.
31. Johnson, *Acts*, p. 31, suggests that we have here an imaginative allusion to Moses and Elijah (cf. Luke 9:31). This seems unlikely, not least because it is improbable that Theophilus could have understood such a vague and unspecified allusion.
32. See Marshall, *Acts*, p. 61.
33. See rightly, Pesch, *Die Apostelgeschichte (1–12)*, p. 75.
34. See the critical discussion in Schneider, *Die Apostelgeschichte I*, pp. 208-10.

the parousia in even the earliest Pauline letters (cf. 1 Thess. 4:16-18; 2 Thes. 2:8-9). For our purposes we must stress that the interpreting angel juxtaposes the ascension and the parousia in 1:11 as similar processes moving in opposite directions.[35]

Though *vv. 12-14* could be taken as a separate unit, in fact this passage is part of the recapitulation and expansion of the information already given at the close of Luke 24. The return of the disciples to Jerusalem involves a return to an upstairs room where they were staying. It is often assumed, but the text does not clearly state, that this is the same location where the Spirit first fell upon the disciples (see 2:1). The reference to a sabbath's day journey (about ¾ of a mile) in *v. 12* is intriguing and at the very least suggests that our author was familiar with Jewish ways of putting things, or even had been a God-fearer or proselyte and became used to speaking in Jewish ways.[36]

The list of the eleven in *v. 13* differs little from the list in Luke 6:14-16 with two notable exceptions. John is placed in the second spot, presumably because Luke knew some traditions about John (cf. Acts 3–5)[37] but not about Andrew and so wanted to place him at the forefront at this point, and of course Judas is left out of this list. *V. 14* is intriguing as it gives a brief glimpse of the inner life of the early Christian community. The word ομοθυμαδον ("united") is found only in Luke's writings in the NT and appears to be one of his favorite terms to describe the spiritual unity of believers (cf. 2:46; 4:24, 5:12; 8:6; 15:25) but also their opponents (7:57; 12:20; 18:12; 19:29).[38] The phrase συν γυναιξιν is taken in Codex D to refer to the wives of the apostles, and so it adds "and children." Since, however, the wives of the apostles have played no role up to this point in Luke-Acts, and since Mary is also mentioned, who is certainly no wife of an apostle, it is much more natural to assume that Luke means the same women he had mentioned at the end of his first volume — the female disciples (cf. Luke 23:55; 24:1, 9, 22), which is surely how Theophilus would have understood this reference.[39] The early church involved both the family of faith and the physical family of Jesus, the latter of whom had joined Jesus' followers, presumably as a result of the Passion and Easter events. Perhaps in particular the resurrection appearance to James prompted this move by Jesus' family (cf. 1 Cor. 15:7). Mary is present only here in Acts, as she was present

35. See also Pesch, *Die Apostelgeschichte (1–12)*, pp. 76-77.

36. Compare, for example, the reckoning of time by the Jewish feasts in Acts 20:5 in a "we" passage — "but we sailed from Philippi after the days of Unleavened Bread."

37. So Lüdemann, *Early Christianity*, p. 29.

38. Johnson, *Acts*, p. 34.

39. The reading of D at this point in all probability should be seen as another example of the antifeminist readings of the Western texts of Acts, particularly Acts 17–18, which seek to sublimate, eliminate, or change the roles women played in the early church. Cf. my article "Anti-Feminist Tendencies."

at the beginning of the Gospel, and in both cases she is associated with a special work of the Holy Spirit. Just as she was overshadowed by the Spirit, so shall, in a different sense, all Jesus' faithful followers be.[40] In any case, the early church is depicted in this earliest of portraits as both united and pious, remaining constantly (προσκαρτεροῦντες) in prayer, being the church expectant, especially prior to Pentecost (cf. Luke 24:52-53).

V. 14 concludes the material involved in the recapitulation, and with v. 15 Luke will break new ground by discussing the replacement of Judas among the Twelve. He has accomplished much in these first fourteen verses. Barrett rightly points out at least seven aims that are accomplished by this section. (1) It points the reader or listener both backward and forward and so indicates the continuity between the two volumes. (2) It stresses the work of the Holy Spirit as an essential feature of the new volume, but one which was announced near the beginning of the first volume (cf. Luke 3:16). In short, Luke has been carefully preparing for the Pentecost story all along as he wrote. (3) This section stresses the idea of the apostles as witnesses, a major theme in Acts. (4) It points out that the church's witness is to extend to the ends of the earth. (5) It indicates that details about the eschatological future, while known to and planned by God, are not known by mortals, even apostles. (6) Nevertheless this opening section shows that Luke conceives of the story of the church within an eschatological framework — between the ascension and the parousia, with Jesus going and coming again in similar manner. (7) At the heart of the fellowship of Jesus' earliest followers are the Eleven and members of Jesus' physical family (the latter integrated into the former), to which I would add the female disciples.[41]

---

40. See Johnson, *Acts*, p. 34.
41. See Barrett, *Acts*, vol. 1, p. 63.

II. The Rhetoric of Replacement (Acts 1:15-26)

In what follows in Acts 1:15ff. we begin to see how the art of persuasion worked within the context of the early church. As George Kennedy points out, what we have in the first speech of Peter is a brief example of deliberative rhetoric — an act of persuasion meant to produce a certain course of action in the near future.[1] The exigence or problem that needs to be solved and overcome by this speech is the need to fill a vacancy in the Twelve. What is interesting about this speech from a rhetorical point of view is that Luke's inserted remarks in vv. 18-19 (cf. below), which are not actually part of the speech, nonetheless serve the rhetorical function of providing the proof that action needs to be taken, which would be a regular part of a rhetorical piece. In other words, it is Luke who has shaped this source material into a form that a Gentile audience would recognize as rhetorically persuasive.[2]

---

1. See Kennedy, *New Testament Interpretation,* p. 116.

2. If indeed 1 Peter goes ultimately back to Peter, there is little in that letter to suggest that Peter was rhetorically adept, something we would not expect from a Galilean fisherman who, unlike Paul, had not studied at higher levels and had no occasion to gain rhetorical skills. It must be kept steadily in mind that Luke characterizes Peter and John as ordinary and "unlettered" men (4:13 — ἀγράμματοι). Whatever else this means, it surely means they did not have higher education or training in the art of eloquence. Thus Luke may be suggesting that Peter's eloquence is Spirit-inspired, not "learned." It must also be considered highly likely in view of the audience (non-Diaspora Jews) that this brief speech was originally given in Aramaic, *not* Greek. To convey the Spirit-inspired eloquence of Peter and other early Christians to his Gentile audience, Luke has shaped these speech summaries in accord with the conventions of Greco-Roman rhetoric. Not until we get to the speeches of Paul (and those of others, like Tertullus) is there consid-

The phrase "in those days" in *v. 15,* and elsewhere in Luke's writings, indicates a transition to a new section (Acts 6:1; 11:27; cf. Luke 2:1). As J. Dupont has noted, this section has a carefully crafted overall structure: (1) introductory verse (v. 15); (2) the subject of the death of and vacancy left by Judas is treated (vv. 16-19); (3) linking Scripture citation in v. 20 with two proofs, the first relating to the prior section (Judas's death), the latter relating to what follows; (4) discussion of Judas's replacement (vv. 21-26).[3]

What one notices immediately about this section is the leadership role that Peter assumes, a role that is to continue in the next few chapters in Acts. This is especially striking in view of Peter's denial of Christ, which is the last major episode prior to this in Luke-Acts in which he was a prominent figure (cf. Luke 22:54-62). This role among the disciples is presumably to be accounted for by the fact that Jesus appeared to Peter personally and restored him (1 Cor. 15:5),[4] a tradition Luke knows *about* (cf. Luke 24:34) but either does not have sufficient data to relate or does not choose to tell the story, probably the former.

It is important to note that Luke shows very little interest in trying to establish exactly what the structure of the early church was, and precisely what roles various prominent figures played. This story is the only one in Acts 1–4 where Peter is singled out when the subject is the *internal* affairs of the community of Christ.[5] In fact, at this point Luke is concerned to speak about the restoration to full strength of a group whose primary role is seen to be in relationship to Israel, *not* to the church, as we shall see in a moment. Apart from the brief parting words of Jesus in Acts 1:7-8, we have in 1:16-22 the first real speech in Acts, and so some general comments on the speeches in Acts are in order at this juncture.

A Closer Look — The Speeches in Acts ──────────────

Undoubtedly, the greatest problem for those who want to maintain that Luke was a good historian is explaining the copious speech material in Acts, at least most of which Luke was surely not present to hear. The speech material in Acts makes up some 365

---

erable possibility that the original speech source material already reflected the conventions of Greco-Roman rhetoric.

3. Dupont, "La destinee de Judas prophetisee par David (Actes 1,16-20)"; cf. Polhill, *Acts,* p. 90.

4. See Bruce, *The Acts of the Apostles,* p. 108. Peter may have been the first apostle to whom Jesus appeared, if the list in 1 Corinthians 15 is in fact in some sort of chronological order.

5. So rightly Tannehill, *Narrative Unity of Luke-Acts,* 2:21.

verses out of a total of approximately one thousand, or about one-third. Two hundred ninety-five of these verses are found in twenty-four speeches usually referred to by scholars.[6]

We have already had occasion to discuss in some detail the use of speeches in ancient historiographical works,[7] and several important conclusions emerged. First, we noted that, as various ancient historians and classics scholars have pointed out, there was no *convention* of creating speeches in antiquity, though certainly various writers did this, in lieu of evidence of what was actually said or because they were not following the more Greek and Hellenistic approach to historiography which involved research and consultation of eyewitnesses. Luke claims in Luke 1:1-4 to be following the Greek tradition. Secondly, we noted that what can be gathered from Thucydides and Polybius and those who followed their lead is that unless there was documentary evidence, writers could seldom produce *verbatim* a speech which had been heard.[8] Rather, they offered up summaries which conveyed various of the major points of what was spoken, not just *the* gist or main point.[9] Thirdly, as careful study of the relevant material shows, it was the custom of Thucydides and his kin to render speeches in their own words and style, a custom Luke clearly follows.[10] Thus, while it can*not* be assumed that Luke created the speeches in Acts,[11] the evidence suggests that he has made his source material his own, such that the ferreting out of his sources for this material is difficult if not impossible.

If Luke was, as I think, a careful historian in the mold of Thucydides and Polybius, we may expect from him adequate and accurate (so far as his sources allowed) summaries of what was said on one or another occasion, especially because he had opportunity to consult with various of the ear-witnesses who heard these speeches, or in some cases with early Christians and ministers of the word to whom the first listeners

6. Soards, *The Speeches in Acts*, p. 1, is right that if one wants to be complete, there are: (1) twenty-seven or twenty-eight speeches, (2) seven partial speeches, and (3) at least three dialogues to be taken into account. On the entire subject and the literature see Schneider, *Die Apostelgeschichte I*, pp. 95-103.

7. See the introduction, pp. 39ff.

8. On the occasional possibility of Luke using a rescript or documentary evidence from court proceedings, see pp. 642ff. below and Winter, "Official Proceedings." Shorthand of a sort was known in antiquity, particularly in the Greco-Roman world where attempts were made to copy down the orations of famous rhetoricians while they spoke, but it must be remembered that Luke was not present to hear the speeches we find in the first two-thirds of Acts, and so whatever skills in note taking he may have had do not come into play. He was relying on sources for this material, which he then put into his own words.

9. In other words we are talking about a skeletal outline, plus perhaps some memorable phrases and stylistic features.

10. See Soards, *The Speeches in Acts*. The great virtue of this work is that it deals with all the speech material in Acts, not just the major speeches, and shows that certain Lukan stylistic traits and themes crop up regularly.

11. The persistent misreading of historical conventions in regard to speeches in ancient historiographical works by scholars today can in part be attributed to the enormous influence of the work of M. Dibelius. See especially his "The Speeches in Acts and Ancient Historiography," in *Studies in the Acts of the Apostles* (London: SCM, 1956), pp. 138-85.

had conveyed a brief summary of what was said. In all probability, with the possible exception of some of the longer speeches (Peter in Acts 2? Stephen?) and some of the court proceedings (Acts 24–26), we must not *assume* that we have *more* than just summaries of speeches. This is especially the case because some of these summaries take only a minute or two to recite out loud, which surely cannot be the entirety of what was said.

Something needs to be said at this juncture about why Luke has proportionally so much *more* speech material in his history than Herodotus, Tacitus, Josephus, Polybius, or Thucydides, for example.[12] This is because Luke is chronicling a historical movement that was carried forward in the main by evangelistic preaching.[13] This distinguishes his work from that of these other historians who are more interested in the macrohistorical events involving wars, political maneuvering, and the like. In fact, if we compare the length of individual speeches, the speeches in the Greek and Latin historiographical works tend to be longer than the speeches in Acts, indeed in some cases much longer, but they take up less of the overall work than do Luke's speeches.[14]

The following schematic shows the distribution of the major speeches, and their reputed sources in Acts:

A. Eight speeches by Peter — Acts 1; 2; 3; 4; 5; 10; 11; 13
B. Two speeches by James — Acts 15; 21
C. One speech by Stephen — Acts 7
D. Nine speeches by Paul — Acts 13; 14; 17; 20; 22; 23; 24; 26; 28
E. Four longish speeches by non-Christians — Acts 5:35-39 (Gamaliel); Acts 19:35-40 (town clerk in Ephesus); 24:2-8 (Tertullus); Acts 25:14-21, 24-27 (recapitulation by Festus)

The speeches in category E are not the sort of speeches that early Christians would likely take notes on or memorize in any case, though the two lattermost may have been available through records of court proceedings. Furthermore, apart from

---

12. Horsley, "Speeches and Dialogue in Acts," estimates that the density of speeches in Acts is twice that in Tacitus's *Annals* or Herodotus's *Histories,* four times that in Josephus's *Wars,* eight times that in Thucydides' *History,* and sixteen times that in Polybius's *Histories.* As Soards, *The Speeches in Acts,* p. 183 n. 3, notes, however, Horsley deals only with the major Acts speeches, so if anything he has underestimated things.

13. This is all the more reason why Luke needed to be careful to record a good variety of speech summaries to show what it was that precipitated the remarkable growth and spread of the Christian movement. I suspect, since early Christianity, like the ministry of Jesus before it, was a movement that relied on the word spoken and received, that Luke was likely as careful with his handling of the speech material of the early Christians as he was with the Jesus material (cf. my "Editing the Good News," pp. 324ff.). I suspect this in part because the early Christian speech material originated more closely in time to his own era and he had *more* direct access to eyewitnesses and oral testimony than was the case with the Jesus tradition. For the latter he certainly had to rely more on written sources.

14. See Soards, "Speeches in Acts in Relation," pp. 71-72.

the Miletus speech in Acts 20 and the defense speeches beginning in Acts 23, Luke was not present to hear these speeches.[15]

Then, too, various of the so-called missionary speeches by Peter or Paul do sound similar at certain points (cf. Peter in Acts 2; 3; 10 and Paul in Acts 13), and also on occasion include the use of similar proof texts in similar settings. This last may at least in part be explained by the use of the basic kerygma and *testimonia*, not just by Peter and Paul but by various early Christian preachers.[16] After all, what sort of early Christian evangelistic preaching would it be if it did not include some remarks on Jesus and his death and resurrection?[17]

That few of the speeches of Peter and Paul sound much like the canonical letters of these two early Christians is in part to be explained by the fact that they are not addressed to the same sorts of audiences. The letters are all addressed to those already Christian, most of the speeches are *not,* and when there is a rare exception to this as in the Miletus speech in Acts 20, we do indeed find some of the familiar Pauline themes also found in the letters.

If we analyze the speeches closely we notice that basically Peter is portrayed as carrying the load of the preaching of the good news in the first half of Acts, and that Paul picks up where Peter leaves off. We also note that James's speeches come at, and just after, the crucial juncture in the narrative of Acts, and help set the church off in a new direction. Indeed, it can be said that the speeches in Acts usually come at crucial junctures and in some cases precipitate, and in some cases are part of, the action, and in general help bind together the narrative into a whole.[18]

That neither the Miletus speech nor the Stephen speech sounds very Lukan in various ways suggests the use of source material, as does the fact that starting even with the very first speech in Acts 1:16ff. there are small repetitions and rough edges in these speeches, which suggests a writer accommodating to his source material rather than freely composing speeches.

We must conclude this brief discussion by admitting that we do not know how Luke could have gotten some of his information. For example the *private* discussion between Festus and Agrippa in Acts 25:13ff. is not the sort of material Luke would likely have had access to, and so here, when there was no source, Luke may be following the advice of his predecessors in making the speakers say what was appropriate to the

15. I have argued, pp. 51ff. above and cf. pp. 480ff. below, that the "we" passages are most naturally taken as a record indicating the presence of the author during these events.

16. Cf. Dodd, *Apostolic Preaching and Its Development;* on the use of *testimonia* and the speeches in general, cf. Bruce, *The Book of Acts,* pp. 34-40.

17. Notice that even in the Areopagus speech, this subject matter is being broached at the end (17:31) before Paul is dismissed.

18. See Soards, *The Speeches in Acts,* pp. 182ff. That the speeches occur at critical junctures in the narrative and in some cases in important places — in Jerusalem, in Athens — shows that Luke has selected representative material to show how the gospel was proclaimed in different sorts of settings. This is probably just good editorial technique, not an indication of free composition. One must remember that when Peter spoke on Pentecost or Paul in Athens, or Paul in a Diaspora Jewish setting, these were indeed important occasions where there was a critical need for something to be said.

occasion. By and large, however, there is good reason to think that Luke is using sources for his speeches, but presenting summaries of the speeches, editing them according to his own agendas, and sometimes rendering portions in his own words for stylistic purposes. He also reflects the influence not only of the Greek historians in the handling of speeches but also of the handling of speeches in the LXX.[19] None of these facts rules out that the speech material likely has considerable historical substance. A brief quote from F. J. Foakes-Jackson will be apposite as we close this discussion: "Whatever these speeches may be, it cannot be disputed that they are wonderfully varied as to their character, and as a rule admirably suited to the occasion on which they were delivered. Luke seems to have been able to give us an extraordinarily accurate picture of the undeveloped theology of the earliest Christians, and enables us to determine the character of the most primitive presentation of the Gospel. However produced, the speeches in Acts are masterpieces, and deserve the most careful attention."[20]

On the whole, Luke is not a very intrusive author, by which I mean he is not given to including a lot of his own comments, by way of parenthetical aside, in the text of Acts. There are two exceptions to this in our present text, the first of which occurs in *v. 15*, where we hear that when Peter stood up among the brothers and sisters,[21] there were about 120 of them.[22] Much has been made of this number, as though Luke was indicating that this was the proper number for an early Jewish assembly which needed twelve leaders (one for each quorum or ten).[23] The problem with this view is that women are included in Luke's "about one hundred twenty," which would probably not have been the case with the figuring of a Jewish quorum for a proper assembly, at least in Palestine.[24] More probable is the suggestion that Luke merely intends to indicate that there were about ten times as many believers as apostles at this juncture.[25]

19. See rightly Soards, "Speeches in Acts in Relation," pp. 76-85.

20. Foakes-Jackson, *Acts*, p. xvi.

21. The term αδελφοι is used in the Greek text here in a gender-inclusive fashion. It is interesting that Luke can even use the term ανδρες in a gender-inclusive manner; cf. 1:16 to 17:34, where Damaris appears to be included among those called ανδρες. For our purposes what is crucial to note is that the language of family is used here and elsewhere (cf. 6:3) to refer to Christian believers, a practice which may have been derived from early Judaism (cf. the very same address, ανδρες αδελφοι, in 4 Macc. 8:19, and on Jews as "brothers" cf. Acts 2:29, 37) but in any case characterized early Christians.

22. Luke frequently offers round numbers and approximations, as is indicated by the use of terms like ωσει, "about," found here (cf., e.g., Luke 3:23).

23. Cf. 1QS 6:3f.; CD 13:1f.

24. See Barrett, *Acts*, vol. 1, p. 96.

25. Notice the term "disciple" does not occur in the first five chapters of Acts, perhaps because Luke understands that the distinctive entity later called Christianity only gradually evolved out of Judaism, and thus at this stage these messianic Jews are not yet to be distinguished as χριστιανοι or followers of "the Way."

The second aside, which most certainly goes back to Luke addressing Theophilus, and does not involve Peter addressing his own audience, is found in *vv. 18-19*. This is clear from the fact that the original followers of Jesus did not need to be informed of the fate of Judas — they already knew about it — from the reference to "*their* dialect"[26] (i.e., Aramaic), and from the explanation that the Aramaic term *hakeldama* means field of blood. Peter's audience needed none of this material, but Luke's apparently did.

That Luke is using source material in these asides is hard to doubt, and it has been pointed out repeatedly that Luke's version of the death of Judas differs considerably from that found in Matt. 27:3-10. The two accounts agree that Judas met with a violent end and that there was some connection between him and a field which came to be called the Field of Blood. In Matthew's version the field is called this because blood money was used by the priests to buy the field, in Luke's because Judas himself had bought the field with his betrayal money and then died due to a violent fall there which caused his internal organs to come out.

Both of these stories could be *etiological* legends based on the fact that it was known that Judas was somehow connected to this field. Such etiological stories were not uncommon in ancient writings, including in historiographical works. On the other hand, Luke's version may find some support from the fact that there were some independent traditions which suggested that Judas was a greedy fellow, the sort that might take money and use it for his own benefit (cf. John 12:4-6), though the telling of our narrative may be in part modeled on the story of Amasa's end in 2 Sam. 20:10 (cf. *b. Ḥul.* 56b). In addition, there are later church traditions known to Papias which more nearly resemble Luke's account of things than Matthew's.[27]

When we omit the asides, Peter's brief speech is not about Judas's death but about the need to replace him. One of the major themes that resurfaces throughout Acts is enunciated in the very first words Peter utters in *v. 16*: "The scripture had to be fulfilled. . . ." The idea of divine necessity is a common one in ancient historiography, especially in Hellenistic historiography,[28] but Luke's interest is in a more comprehensive and detailed idea than just the Greco-Roman idea of fate. His interest also goes beyond the notion of divine providence, though that, too, is involved at various points in Luke-Acts. At this juncture what Peter is referring to is the plan of God set forth in the Holy Scriptures, which must be fulfilled. Luke is not talking about some hidden, inscrutable design of a deity, but rather about the revealed will of God. J. T. Squires helpfully sums things up as follows:

---

26. Thus probably distinguishing both Luke and Theophilus from Aramaic-speaking Christians.

27. Cf. Lake, *Beginnings*, 5:22-30.

28. See now Squires, *Plan of God in Luke-Acts*, pp. 15ff.

The theme of the plan of God plays an important role in Luke-Acts. The author refers to God's guidance of events from the very beginning of the Gospel through to the end of Acts. At key points in the narrative, such divine control is emphasized; however, Luke intends throughout to convey the message that God's guidance is comprehensive in scope and consistent in nature, underlying all the reported events. . . . Two particular events are emphasized as occurring within the plan of God: the crucifixion and the mission to the Gentiles. Both events may be construed as involving a change of course in that original divine plan: thus Luke carefully presents each event as integral to God's purposes. . . . This theme functions apologetically to defend Christian beliefs and attack other views. . . . [The latter is] displayed most clearly in the speeches in which Stephen and Paul attack idolatry by using themes of divine providence which were commonly part of rhetorical techniques to attack idolatry in the Hellenistic world.[29]

For our purposes what is crucial to note is that Peter is using Scripture apologetically to explain the surprising outcome of Judas's life and the divine justification for his replacement. Of course the betrayal of the Messiah by one of his followers, leading to his death, required such an explanation, since this was no part of early Jewish messianic expectation. Judas is said not merely to have been the one who guided the arresters of Jesus *(v. 16b)*, but also one "numbered among us . . . allotted his [lot] in this ministry." Judas was not only *not* an outsider, he was one of the chosen Twelve who had shared in the ministry of Jesus and his followers.

The term κληρον used in *v. 17* literally means a "lot,"[30] and its connection here to a ministerial service (διακονια) is probably drawing on the notion of the "lot" apportioned to the Levites whose task for Israel was performing ministerial service (cf. Num. 18:21-26).[31] This foreshadows what follows about the casting of lots for a new twelfth apostle in v. 26. It also may be connected to what is said in vv. 18-19 and v. 25 about Judas' buying a lot or portion of land with "the reward of his wickedness" and then his "turn[ing] aside to go to his own place" (i.e., going to the place allotted to such a betrayer — hell). What the story of Judas shows is that though he was someone chosen by Jesus and though he ministered as one of the Twelve apostles, this in no way guaranteed his eternal salvation.

V. 16 also indicates that the Holy Spirit through David foretold these outcomes. Here we come in contact not only with the belief that all the OT could be seen as prophetic in character, including the psalms which are quoted here, but also the belief that David is the author of the psalms. The psalm

29. Ibid., pp. 76-77.
30. It is the source of the English term "cleric."
31. See Johnson, *Acts*, p. 35.

cited first is Ps. 68:26, followed by a citation of Ps. 108:8. Both of these citations are closer to the LXX than the Hebrew, and more importantly in the case of the second citation the argument of Peter only works with the LXX. The Hebrew of Ps. 108:8 has "may another seize his goods," while the LXX has "may another take over his επισκοπην [office, position of overseer]." This brings us to the very complicated matter of the use of the OT in Luke-Acts.

A Closer Look — Luke's Use of the OT

Various scholars have carefully canvassed the way Luke uses the OT in Luke-Acts.[32] It is fair to say that Fitzmyer's conclusion represents a rather broad consensus when he says, "in [the] forty-five examples of OT quotations introduced explicitly by formulas . . . in *no case* is there a citation that follows the Hebrew MT rather than the Greek, when the latter differs from the Hebrew. . . . Luke quotes the OT almost always in a form either corresponding to the LXX or close to it, and not according to the Hebrew MT."[33]

A listing of the textual basis for the Acts portion of this conclusion is in order:

I. Instances where the LXX is cited verbatim

Acts 2:25-28 citing Ps. 16:8-11ab
Acts 2:34-35 citing Ps. 110:1
Acts 4:25-26 citing Ps. 2:1-2
Acts 7:49-50 citing Isa. 66:1-2 (with change in word order)
Acts 13:33 citing Ps. 2:7
Acts 13:35 citing Ps. 16:10
Acts 28:26-27 citing Isa. 6:9-10 (except for the introductory phrase)

II. Instances where Luke cites the OT in a manner close to but not exactly corresponding with the LXX

Acts 1:20a citing Ps. 69:26
Acts 1:20b citing Ps. 109:8
Acts 2:17-21 citing Joel 3:1-5a
Acts 3:22 (and 7:27) citing Deut. 18:15
Acts 3:23 citing Lev. 23:39 conflated with Deut. 18:19
Acts 3:25 citing Gen. 22:18
Acts 7:6-7a citing Gen. 15:13-14
Acts 7:42-43 citing Amos 5:25-27
Acts 13:34 citing Isa. 55:3

---

32. See notably Clarke, "Septuagint in Acts"; Fitzmyer, "Old Testament in Luke-Acts"; and Barrett, "Luke/Acts," for introductions to this subject and the literature they cite. Cf. also Arnold, "Luke's Characterizing Use."
33. Fitzmyer, "Old Testament in Luke-Acts," pp. 534-35.

Acts 13:41 citing Hab. 1:5
Acts 13:47 citing Isa. 49:6 and separately citing Amos 9:11-12
Acts 23:5 citing Exod. 22:27

III. Instances where the citation is not close to the LXX and it is difficult to tell whether Luke is quoting from memory, conflating, or citing a different Greek version of the OT
Acts 4:11 citing Ps. 118:22
Acts 7:7 citing Exod. 3:12[34]

What the above shows is that there is no real case to be made that Luke knew or used the Hebrew OT (or for that matter Aramaic targums) while there is a strong reason for concluding that he likely relied almost solely if not solely on the LXX, though occasionally he offered his own version, perhaps from memory, or some other Greek version of the OT.

This material also shows the wide scope of the Scripture citations used by Luke and/or his sources to make christological and other sorts of points. This arises out of the profound conviction that the early Christians were living in the age when God was fulfilling the OT promises, and filling out the larger meaning or significance of various portions of the OT that did not specifically speak prophetically about the future.

The further conclusion drawn by Fitzmyer and others, that Luke's use of the OT indicates that Luke saw himself as writing biblical history, is somewhat more questionable if by that is meant he thought he was simply writing a continuation of the same sort of history as we find in the OT (and the Maccabean literature). The problem with this conclusion is that Luke sees a disjunction between the time before John the Baptist (cf. Luke 16:16) and the time of John and Jesus. Luke's concern is with salvation history, the story of the age inaugurated by the coming of the Messiah on the stage of human history, especially beginning with his baptism (cf. on Acts 1:22 below), a history which reaches a further stage of development after the death, resurrection, and ascension of Jesus because the Spirit which brings about salvation is only sent after Jesus leaves the earth.

It would be better, then, to speak of a continuation of and new development in the people of God, but not simply a continuation of biblical history, for Luke believes that since the coming of Jesus, and even more since Pentecost, God's people are living in the eschatological age when God's word will spread across the earth, and many different peoples will respond to it. There is perhaps more to be said for the view of J. Jervell that Luke saw himself as writing Scripture, modeling his work to some extent on the style and tenor of the LXX, but if so it is a new sort of Scripture, a Scripture that focuses on fulfillment and the completion of God's providential salvation plan.[35] It is not simply more of the same of what is found in the LXX. In any case, all of the above reminds us that Luke's use of the OT, like his use of speech material, is a complex matter not easily deciphered or explained with simplistic formulae.

34. I have here extracted the Acts material and rearranged the data cited in ibid., pp. 533-34.
35. See Jervell, "The Future of the Past."

We must emphasize here that, quite apart from the Scripture citations, Luke's own narrative style reflects the influence of the LXX again and again, and he seems to be able to write in a deliberate LXX and Semitic style at will.[36] Thus it is quite believable that he would cite the version of the OT throughout Luke-Acts which he himself and his Gentile audience were familiar with and could read.[37] The matter is complicated by texts just such as this one, for Acts 1:20 appears to have Peter depending on the LXX to make his point about Judas. While it is common among scholars to assume that Luke has simply created this argument out of the LXX (and if so, it does not reflect Peter's original argument), it is also possible that Peter cited the Greek OT, following the version that fit the argument he wished to make, which was not an uncommon practice in early Jewish exegesis. Marshall, however, argues that it is possible that Peter could have made the same basic argument that we find here based on the Hebrew OT.[38] Thus, we must not too quickly assume that Luke has simply created these discussions based on the LXX.

The upshot of the loss of Judas is that Peter says in *vv. 21-22* that one of those who have accompanied Jesus and the Twelve, beginning from the baptism, must become "a witness with us of the resurrection." This last phrase, using μαρτυς, is wonderfully ambiguous and can be taken to mean not just that the person chosen must have seen the risen Lord, but also that he must bear witness about it. This was the most defining requirement for being an apostle (as Acts 4:33 shows), and it may be that because this was the most essential part, Luke saw Paul and Barnabas as functioning as apostles in this most crucial matter, and so used the term αποστολοι of them briefly in Acts 14 to indicate this. What becomes clearer as Acts proceeds is that Luke is primarily interested in the broader subject of early Christian witnesses including the apostles, not just in the witness of those deemed apostles.

According to *v. 23* the gathering of believers proposed two candidates to fill the slot of the twelfth apostle — Joseph called Barsabbas (also known by the Roman name Justus) and Matthias. The procedure followed of casting lots should not be seen as an example of congregational election, for the choice is left up to God, as is shown both by the prayer and by the casting of the lots. This process for determining God's will was traditional in Judaism (cf. Lev. 16:8; Num. 26:55; Jon. 1:7-8; 1QS 5:3, 6:16), and there is probably no implied criticism of it by Luke, though scholars have often contrasted this story with those which follow Pentecost where the guidance of the Spirit is relied upon. Clearly, Luke thinks the choice here (and so presumably the method) valid for

---

36. See Fitzmyer, *Luke I–IX*, pp. 107-25, and N. Turner, *A Grammar of the New Testament Greek: Vol. IV* (Edinburgh: T & T Clark, 1976), pp. 56-57.

37. See especially Fitzmyer, "Old Testament in Luke-Acts," p. 525.

38. Marshall, *Acts*, p. 65.

its day — the disciples could not be criticized for not relying on a source of power and discernment they had not yet received. The process was likely the same as we see in 1 Chron. 26:13-14 — stones in some way marked to distinguish them were placed in a container or jar and shaken until one came out, in this case the one that represented Matthias.[39]

The larger issue here is the filling up of the Twelve. What was the point of this action, especially since when James the son of Zebedee died it was apparently not felt necessary to repeat it (see Acts 12:2)? The answer to this question seems to be that Luke anticipates the Twelve having a role, not in relationship to the church or its later mission to Gentiles, but rather in relationship to Israel, in particular Jews who live in the Holy Land (and points east?).[40] Nothing is said here about the Twelve being the foundation of the church,[41] nor is the idea of apostolic succession either broached or made plausible since apostles had to be eyewitnesses of the risen Lord, nor is the idea that they are the true Israel made clear, though the latter idea may be intimated.

The role of the Twelve is as witnesses about the risen Jesus to Israel, and at the eschaton as Israel's judges. The former role is demonstrated in Acts 2, where Peter with the Eleven (2:14) witnesses to the whole house of Israel and Jews from every nation gathered in Jerusalem for the festival (cf. 2:5, 36; 4:10). "Thus the next scene of Acts presents the twelve apostles performing their role of witnesses to Israel, to *all* Israel."[42] The later witness to the Gentiles should not be read into this text. Especially because of their eschatological role, the Twelve had to be filled up with faithful apostles, so that in the resurrection there would be twelve to sit on the thrones and judge. These two clearly circumscribed roles (to Israel, judging at the eschaton), it seems to me, are likely the reasons why the Twelve play in some cases so little a part (with the partial exception of Peter and John) and in some cases no role at all in the rest of Acts.

To put the matter a little differently, the Twelve's field of mission was to Jews, and particularly Jews who happened to be in Judea, Samaria, and Galilee. Luke knows almost nothing about the mission in Galilee (cf. 9:31), and what he knows about the former two he records in the first eight chapters of Acts. Even so, he makes clear that in Samaria it was Philip, and not one of the Twelve, who led the way.

39. As Barrett, *Acts*, vol. 1, p. 103, notes, it is striking that James, Jesus' brother, is not a candidate to join the Twelve, presumably because he was not a believer before Easter (see John 7:5).
40. See Tannehill, *Narrative Unity of Luke-Acts*, 2:21: "Reconstituting the twelve is an important step in preparation for the witness to Israel."
41. Pace Polhill, *Acts*, p. 93.
42. Tannehill, *Narrative Unity of Luke-Acts*, 2:22.

Luke wishes to chronicle the successful growth of the church from Jerusalem to Rome, and the Twelve, apart from Peter in particular, seem to have played little or no role in this process. In other words, he wishes to show how it developed away from being a purely Jewish sect to being a world religion, with a growing majority of Gentiles as members by Luke's time. Whatever successes the Twelve may have had in Israel or points east, the former were apparently short-lived due to the Jewish war which began in the 60s, and the latter were unknown to Luke, if such "eastern" missionary work ever transpired. Obviously Luke could not chronicle the eschatological work in advance (cf. Luke 22:30). In regard to the Gentile mission, the growth area for the church the further one gets into the first century, Luke chooses to focus on Paul as the one, humanly speaking, most responsible for the fulfillment of the directive "to the ends of the earth." Thus Acts is also a chronicle of a movement away from Jerusalem and James, and even from Peter, who disappears after the Acts 15 council, and a movement toward Paul and his churches.[43]

This is the story Luke knows to tell, and he tells it with consummate narrative art and skill. The fact that he chronicles only part of the story of the development of early Christianity should not prevent us from appreciating his accomplishments. As a historian who may not even have made it to Israel before about A.D. 57-58, he was limited by the sources of information he had about what transpired in Israel. It should also not be said that he simply glosses over the problems of the early church that he knows about. The narrative chronicling the need for a new twelfth apostle, the narrative about Ananias and Sapphira, the narrative about Simon Magus, the narratives about Cornelius and the Acts council, the narrative about a Christian preacher who knew only of John's baptism (Acts 18), and more all show that he is well enough aware that all was not a bed of roses, or neat and tidy during the course of the history of the earliest period. He felt it necessary to tell Theophilus about some of these struggles and difficulties. Luke does not gild the lily, or simply present an idealistic picture of the halcyon days of yore. His positive summary statements (cf. Acts 2:43-47; 4:32-37; 9:31) must not be taken in isolation from the narratives they connect. These things must be kept in mind as we proceed through Acts.

---

43. See the discussion of the Twelve and their historical role in Schneider, *Die Apostelgeschichte I*, pp. 221-32 and the literature cited there.

III. Pentecost: The Medium, the Message, and the Manifestations (Acts 2:1-47)

No text in Acts has received closer scrutiny than Acts 2. Whole theologies and denominations have been built up around the Acts 2 accounts. We must therefore analyze the text carefully. As we have pointed out already, the Pentecost episode immediately follows the story of the filling up of the Twelve. The reason seems to be that the Twelve had a special mission to Israel both in the present as witnesses to Israel and at the eschaton, sitting on the twelve thrones, judging the twelve tribes. Inasmuch as the gospel had to come first to the Jews and then to the Gentiles, the initial or essential task of the Twelve, the first witnesses, was the preaching of the gospel to the Jews. To a large extent this is exactly what Acts 2 is about, as we shall see.

In terms of structure, Acts 2 can be divided into three main parts: (1) the empowering event and the first witnessing (vv. 1-13); (2) the sermon of Peter and the response to it (vv. 14-41); and (3) the first summary passage in Acts characterizing the early community of Christ (vv. 42-47). Perhaps equally important is the fact that Luke has intentionally structured this material so that parallels would be noticed with some of the inaugural events in Luke's Gospel, in particular the introductory proclamation of the Baptist, "He will baptize you with the Holy Spirit and fire" (Luke 3:16), followed by the baptism and reception of the Spirit by Jesus (Luke 3:21-22), followed by his programmatic sermon in Nazareth indicating that the time of the fulfillment of God's promises and prophecy had come (Luke 4:16-30), and then finally by his witness to Jews and occasionally others in Galilee, Samaria, and Judea (Luke 4:31ff.). The same pattern recurs here.[1]

This sort of setting up of parallelism is not uncommon in both ancient historical and in biographical works (e.g., Plutarch's *Parallel Lives*). For our purposes it is important to notice four things: (1) these and other parallels between Luke and Acts strongly suggest that Acts was composed after the Gospel and on the basis of it; (2) they also suggest that Luke is a master of his source material, and is treating the subject matter in each volume in similar fashion using the same literary and rhetorical approaches;[2] (3) in view of (2), this also strongly suggests that Luke sees these two volumes as being of one generic sort;[3] (4) finally, it suggests that quite beyond ordinary ancient ideas of historical recurrence,[4] Luke believes that God is faithful to his plan and promised purposes and that one can see certain patterns in history that indicate the regularity of God's workings and especially a pattern in his divine saving activity among human beings.

A. Power at Pentecost (2:1-13)

Only the book of Acts records this story that we find in Acts 2, and this has seemed historically problematic to some scholars, even though Acts is the only Christian historical narrative we have from this period.[5] For Luke, it is clearly

---

1. See especially in general Talbert, *Literary Patterns*, p. 16, although Talbert does not say enough about the parallels we have just mentioned.

2. On this see my "Editing the Good News," pp. 324ff.

3. A point Talbert also makes, though we disagree about which one genre both works reflect.

4. On which see Trompf, *Idea of Historical Recurrence*, especially p. 121. His essential conclusions I believe are correct and worth repeating (p. 129): "Luke was not interested in arranging his material as orderly *midrashim* or *pesherim* (commentary or interpretations) upon long sequences found in the scriptures, nor was prophecy fulfillment for him only a way of authenticating Jesus or showing the ancient oracles to be right. Luke was fundamentally interested in more direct historical connections, as a historian of the Hellenistic period. He wrote as though established historical events, which for him were divinely guided, had their own inner relatedness, connections between events amounting to the virtual reenactment of special happenings . . . the main point is that he emerges as an historian comparable to Polybius (who, after all, managed to infuse a theological significance into his work), rather than as someone concerned to make a series of evangelistic and theological assertions in the form of a narrative."

5. See, e.g., the discussion by Marshall, "The Significance of Pentecost"; Dunn, *Jesus and the Spirit*, pp. 135-56; Lincoln, "Theology and History"; and on Luke's sources here

*The oldest map of Jerusalem, a sixth-century-*A.D. *mosaic from Medeba. The Damascus Gate is on the left.*

a critical event which sets in motion all that follows. Without the coming of the Spirit there would be no prophecy, no preaching, no mission, no conversions, and no worldwide Christian movement. Luke, then, encourages us to examine this material very carefully.

The feast of Pentecost was in NT times the name for the celebration of

Lüdemann, *Early Christianity*, pp. 38-43. It is not convincing to argue that Luke invented the notion of the coming of the Spirit at Pentecost. For one thing we have independent testimony that Jesus had indeed promised to send the Spirit, *after* he had departed from the disciples (cf. John 14:15ff.). For another, the idea that Luke has artificially distinguished resurrection appearances from the sending of power from on high does not work. In the earliest listings of resurrection appearances in 1 Corinthians 15, written up in the 50s but from an earlier period, there is no mention of the Spirit at all. Paul is able to distinguish quite clearly at various points in his letters the exalted Lord and the Spirit, and 2 Corinthians 3 provides no example to the contrary (cf. my *End of the World*, pp. 109ff.). Thirdly, nothing suggests that the story in Acts 2 was once a Christophany. Fourthly, the disjunctions and hints in the story (how and when the story moves from a house to the temple is not explained; the list of nations is, to say the least, odd; the variety of Jews and visitors present points to a festival) point to Luke's editing of source material about an event at Pentecost, not to free-form composition (contra Haenchen, *Acts*, pp. 173-75). Some of the particular difficulties will be addressed in the text of the commentary below.

the Feast of Weeks because it occurred on the fiftieth day after Passover. It was a one-day festival in which special sacrifices were offered, and originally it was a harvest (firstfruits) festival (Exod. 23:16; 34:22; Lev. 23:15-21; Num. 28:26; Deut. 16:9-12). It is possible, but not certain, that as early as this time this festival was associated with the giving of the Law on Sinai. There is an interesting tradition, of a later period, that the Law had been initially promulgated in the seventy languages of the nations that made up the whole world (*b. Shab.* 88b). Even more intriguing is what Philo, writing well before the time of Luke, says about the giving of the Law: "Then from the midst of the fire that streamed from heaven there sounded forth to their utter amazement a voice, for the flame became the articulate speech in the language familiar to the audience" (*Decal.* 46). If Luke knew such traditions his portrayal of these Pentecost events could be taken to suggest not only that Christianity will have a worldwide impact, but that the giving of the Spirit is parallel to (and supersedes?) the giving of the Law. In favor of this connection is the fact that Luke uses the Moses typology consistently as he tells the story of Jesus, and of course in Luke's view it is Jesus who is sending the Spirit.[6] More broadly this feast was associated with the renewal of the covenant with Noah, before and during the first century A.D. (cf. *Jub.* 6:17, 18). There is no hard evidence that Luke intended Theophilus to think of Pentecost as the Tower of Babel in reverse, not least because the Spirit does not eliminate the difference in languages, but rather allows each to hear in those different languages.

This event on Pentecost[7] begins in a house where the disciples were "all together" (*v. 1*).[8] It is not made clear whether this is the same location as the "upper room" where the Last Supper was eaten, or where the disciples were staying (cf. 1:13). There is some interesting evidence of the validity of the tradition that the place on Mount Zion now known as the Cenacle was the location where the earliest Christians met and that it quickly became a holy

---

6. See the discussion by Johnson, *Acts*, p. 46.

7. Luke uses an odd phrase to introduce this event, literally "in the fulfillment of the day of Pentecost," but clearly from what follows the day is yet young (cf. 2:15), so he cannot mean as the Day of Pentecost drew to a close. Presumably he either means "as the period of Pentecost drew to a close" (cf. Barrett, *Acts*, vol. 1, p. 110 [but why then use the term "day"?]), or more likely Luke has in mind the fulfillment of the intended purpose of the feast of Pentecost — namely, God gives the real firstfruits of the eschatological or harvest time: the Holy Spirit (cf. Rom. 8:23). The time is fulfilled and the promise of the Father is at hand (cf. Luke 24:49; Acts 1:4). For our purposes it is important to point out that εν plus the infinitive is a favorite construction of Luke (thirty-two times in Luke-Acts), and that it was a characteristic construction in historical works from the second century B.C. to the first century A.D. (See Bruce, *The Acts of the Apostles*, p. 113 and sources cited there.) On the use of the key verb here see *New Docs*, 2:98.

8. Probably another rhetorical use of the term "all" (see pp. 106ff. above), for it is unlikely that Luke is thinking of a Christian house holding 120 people.

site, a place for ongoing Christian worship.[9] Somewhere along the line the event migrates to the temple precincts, the only place such a crowd could or would likely be congregated, but Luke does not explain the sequence, only the events.

In these first few verses of Acts 2 Luke uses the principle of analogy, as Marshall points out.[10] The sound from heaven in *v. 2* was *like* a violent wind, but was not one.[11] The tongues were *like* fire but were not fire. In *v. 3* Luke is reserved in his description. He says there seemed to be tongues like fire that came to rest on each believer. In any case, the sound of this event is said to fill or echo throughout the whole house where the disciples were sitting.[12]

Divided tongues like fire appeared and rested upon each one there present (cf. Luke 3:22). There is no indication that this phenomenon was only experienced by the Twelve, as some sort of empowerment for leadership. To the contrary, what follows in Peter's speech suggests the Spirit empowers the witness of all God's people, including those of lowest social status. All in the room were filled with the Spirit and began to speak in "other tongues" as the Spirit gave them utterance.

Luke's focus in this passage is on one event that happened to the early followers of Jesus as a corporate gathering, but then affected many others because of their witness. Luke is not trying here to give us a detailed description or chronology of individual Christian experience. It is quite clear that in crucial ways this event is unique. It is the beginning of the creation of God's eschatological people, properly speaking. It is the empowering of them to do their job — to witness to Christ. While it is certainly true that every individual Christian must have his or her own filling by the Spirit in order to be Christian, his or her own "Pentecost" so to speak, that is not what this text is about.

It is interesting to note the parallels to various OT theophanies where God comes down and there is fire on the mountain and Moses or someone is given a word to speak for the Lord (Exod. 19:18; 2 Sam. 22:16; Ezek. 13:13). In those events as well, we are talking about the experiences of a group of God's people when together.

---

9. For the evidence of a second-century church on this site and a careful discussion of this matter, cf. now Murphy-O'Connor, "The Cenacle and Community."

10. Marshall, *Acts*, p. 68.

11. The word πνοής is used here in v. 2, not the word πνευμα (which of course can mean either breath, spirit, or wind). Thus we are to think of this as a theophanic phenomenon that accompanied the coming of the Spirit, but was not the Spirit. The Spirit in Luke's theology is not just a force or power or a wind (this is surely why he uses two different words for wind and for the Spirit), but the living presence of a powerful God. See Kee, *Good News*, pp. 28ff.

12. It was customary in synagogue worship for the worshipers to sit, unlike those in temple worship. See Barrett, *Acts*, vol. 1, p. 114.

The verb "filled" (επλησθησαν) in *v. 4* is an important one. Elsewhere in Luke-Acts it describes an initial endowment of someone by the Spirit for service (Luke 1:15; Acts 9:17) or when they are inspired to speak God's word (Acts 4:8, 31; 13:9), as is certainly the case here (cf. 2:5ff.). Related forms of this verb can be used to describe the repeated filling or continuous process of filling of Christians (Acts 13:52; Eph. 5:18).

References such as Acts 6:3, 5; 7:55; 11:24; and Luke 4:1 all indicate that a person who already has been filled with the Spirit can receive a fresh filling for some specific task or proclamation. A great deal of this usage is Old Testamental, as when the Spirit filled the prophets to speak, or enabled them to do a mighty deed (cf. Samson). Elsewhere what is here called a "filling" is called a baptizing (Acts 1:5; 11:16) or a pouring out (2:17f.; 10:45), or a receiving (10:47). In other words these terms can be and are used by Luke interchangeably, and cannot be treated as technical terms or be neatly parceled out to line up a chronology of different spiritual experiences. As Marshall states: "The basic act of receiving the Spirit can be described as being baptized or filled, but the verb 'baptize' is *not* used for subsequent experiences. . . . The noun-phrase 'baptism with the Spirit' does not occur in the New Testament."[13] Marshall also conjectures that the term "filled" is used because the disciples are inspired to speak in ετεραις γλωσσαις. We must examine this last crucial phrase at this point.

First, there is no doubt that the phrase ετεραις γλωσσαις can refer to speaking in other human languages, and would normally be understood to mean just that.[14] When someone says "other languages," we must ask, "other" than what? What is the point of comparison — other than human or other than their native tongue? Clearly what follows in Acts 2:5ff. suggests that the audience is hearing these people speaking in other than their native tongues (cf. vv. 7-8). These people are Galileans, and yet they speak not in Aramaic but in all the various languages or dialects of their audience.[15] As has been pointed out by various scholars, if simple ecstatic speech was in view here, Luke ought simply to have used the term γλωσσαις, not ετεραις γλωσσαις. It is no argument against this conclusion that when these disciples were heard in the temple courts they were accused of drunkenness. If they were, as Luke tells us, exuberantly praising and speaking and perhaps even singing of the mighty acts of God (v. 11b) at an early hour in the morning, this could have

---

13. Marshall, *Acts,* p. 69.

14. For example, in line 22 of the Greek Prologue to Sirach we find the words, "For what was originally expressed in Hebrew does not have exactly the same sense when translated *into another language*" (εις ετεραν γλωσσαν).

15. On the distinctives of Galilean speech patterns, including the loss of aspirates that would have enabled those who knew Aramaic to single out these persons' places of origin, cf. Bruce, *The Acts of the Apostles,* p. 116 and sources cited there.

easily prompted the accusation of drunkenness.[16] In short, other things than ecstatic speech could have prompted such a suggestion.

A Closer Look — Multiple Pentecosts?

Acts 2 is frequently compared to Acts 10:46 and the Cornelius episode, which is sometimes called the Gentile Pentecost. At 10:46 it is simply said that they spoke γλωσσαις and praised God, and there is no mention of any foreigners or foreign languages being involved. Nonetheless, many have seen in Acts 10 a parallel to Acts 2, only with a different ethnic group involved. What prompts this suggestion is that Acts 10:46-47 does say, "for they heard them speaking in tongues and extolling God . . . these people who have received the Holy Spirit just as we have." This spiritual phenomenon is proof to Peter and these Jewish Christians that God has filled them with the Spirit and accepted the Gentiles just as he did the Jews.

Nonetheless, Peter only indicates that the filling and the fact that speech and praise were prompted parallel the earlier Pentecost experience. The text does not indicate that the character of the speech is exactly the same, only that both were prompted by the same Spirit. It is thus very possible, perhaps even probable, that Acts 10 is about ecstatic speech while Acts 2 is not because Acts 10 is not about breaking the human communication barrier caused by foreign languages.

Another suggestion is that Acts 2 could be about ecstatic speech (a sign of the Spirit and a miracle in itself) which was also miraculously heard in various languages.[17] In short, there was a double miracle.[18] The Greek syntax, however, surely dictates that the phrase "in his own language" must go with the word "speaking," not "hearing," in

16. *Testament of Job* 48–52 is often pointed to because it includes a clear reference to speaking in the language of angels (48:2) and uses the phrase "the mighty acts of God" of such speech (51:3). This is true enough, but it certainly does not determine how Luke uses this phrase. Luke's Gentile audience was perhaps likely to think of divinely inspired intelligible speech, for this in the end was what was called prophecy at Delphi and elsewhere. See my discussion of prophecy in the Greco-Roman world in *Conflict and Community in Corinth*, pp. 276ff. It is of course also true that there was sometimes an association of drunkenness and ecstasy in pagan religion (especially in connection with Bacchic rites), but the subject matter here is prophecy, and in particular prophecy in the biblical tradition about which Joel spoke, as Peter's speech makes clear. Seeing visions and dreaming dreams and speaking prophecy in the biblical tradition involve intelligible communications, not just ecstasy. But cf. van der Horst, "Hellenistic Parallels to the Acts of the Apostles," on all this and other parallels as well.

17. See Lake, in *Beginnings*, 5:111-21.

18. As Polhill, *Acts,* p. 100, says, the "hearing miracle" view would seem to require that the *crowd*, or most of them, had already received the Spirit, but this is surely not indicated this early in the story. What would be the point of spending so much time on the reception of the Spirit by the disciples, if in fact at least the primary miracle at Pentecost happened to others?

v. 6.[19] They heard them *speaking* in their own languages.[20] This, then, would rule out simple ecstatic speech or angelic speech at Pentecost, and must also count against the double miracle view.

Numerous questions arise at this point. Perhaps the most important of these is: How does this miraculous spiritual gift of speaking in foreign languages compare to what Paul talks about in 1 Corinthians 12–14? Note first that in Acts 2, unlike in 1 Corinthians 14, while there is need for an explanation of what is happening and why the disciples are saying what they say, there is no need for *translation by an interpreter*. In 1 Corinthians 14 Paul is quite explicit that speaking in (angelic) tongues (cf. 1 Cor. 13:1) does not produce *intelligible sounds* unless there is an interpreter. But intelligible sounds is precisely what is remarked about in Acts 2:6 — they spoke words recognizable in various languages! It appears, then, that we are dealing with a different phenomenon in Acts 2 and 1 Corinthians 14.[21] It is, however, perhaps probable that Acts 10 and 1 Corinthians 14 do describe the same sort of spiritual event.

We are unsure where Luke gets his list of countries, but in all of them there were apparently some Diaspora Jews. He wishes to indicate that they represented every nation under heaven, though of course the list is of countries around the Mediterranean and the then known world. The major point of all this is that the Spirit overcomes all barriers, even of languages, to witness to the various parts of the known world, even to "the ends of the earth."

In *v. 5* the verb κατοικουντες normally means "residing" or "dwelling," in which case we would probably not in the main be talking about pilgrims come to Jerusalem from the Diaspora for the feast, but rather Diaspora Jews who had come to live or retire in Jerusalem, and no doubt would have attended some of the synagogues founded in Jerusalem by Diaspora Jews (cf. Acts 6:9).[22] There is clear archaeological evidence from Jerusalem tomb inscriptions of such immigrants who lived out their latter days in the Holy City, wishing to conclude life and be buried there.[23] These Jews are called "pious men" in v. 5b. Ευλαβεις is a term used only by Luke in the NT to refer to devout Jews, not proselytes or God-fearers (cf. Luke 2:25; Acts 8:2; 22:12).[24] Luke, with typical

19. So rightly Barrett, *Acts,* vol. 1, p. 124: It is not merely that "we hear each one in his own language," but "we hear them speaking in our tongues."

20. Luke does not distinguish here between the term "language" (γλωσσα) and "dialect" (διαλεκτος), as we moderns would. These terms are synonyms in this text.

21. See, rightly, Polhill, *Acts,* p. 99. As he points out, while the term γλωσσα could have several possible meanings, the term διαλεκτος in v. 6 can only refer to a known human dialect or language.

22. On this see Hengel, *Between Jesus and Paul,* pp. 2ff.

23. See the evidence in Schneider, *Die Apostelgeschichte I,* p. 251.

24. On which see pp. 341ff. below. See Hengel, *Paul,* pp. 27ff.

rhetorical hyperbole, says these devout Jews were from *every* nation under heaven. The point is to emphasize the scope of the audience.

If there is any allusion in this story to the events that transpired at the Tower of Babel (Genesis 11), it is perhaps to be found here in *v. 6*, for we are told that the sound of hearing these Galilean Jews speaking in their own native tongues *confused them* (συνεχύθη), or in other words we see here Babel reversed. There the unintelligibility factor caused by many tongues caused the confusion; here the intelligibility factor does so![25]

Vv. 7-8 place especial stress on the fact that it is Galileans the crowd hears speaking in their native languages, and there may be here reflected something of the snobbery or stereotyping of Galileans as "unlettered" that did from time to time happen in Judea and Jerusalem (cf. Acts 4:13; Mark 14:70).[26]

The list of nations in *vv. 9-11* is difficult in various respects.[27] For one thing scholars have found the reference to "Jews" in v. 10 a bit odd in a list that refers to Jews anyway, and the reference to Judea in v. 9 very odd indeed.[28] For another thing, there does not appear to be a clear trajectory or direction being pursued by listing the nations in this order. The arguments that Luke is following an astrological list (of later provenance in any case) are not very strong since there are only five names that both lists have in common in some form.[29]

Perhaps, however, there is a certain method to Luke's list. The point is not to provide a tour of the known world but to mention nations that had known extensive Jewish populations, which of course would include Judea.[30] More to the point, Luke's arrangement involves first listing the major inhabited nations or regions, then those from the islands (Cretans), then finally those from desert regions (Arabs).[31]

In *v. 10b* the reference to "Ρωμαιοι [both Jews and proselytes]" at the end of the listing of major inhabited lands is especially apt, for they presage

25. On the allusion see Barrett, *Acts,* vol. 1, p. 119.

26. For popular opinions about Galileans, cf. Vermes, *Jesus the Jew,* pp. 42-57.

27. While as it stands the list appears to be part of the speech of the crowd, likely we should see it as a parenthetical insertion of Luke, enumerating the nations present. See, rightly, Polhill, *Acts,* p. 102.

28. There are a number of textual variants for "Judea" in v. 9, which shows the difficulty was felt early on, but the great majority of the witnesses support the reading, and leaving it in is certainly more difficult than omitting it, for the reference to Judea comes quite unexpectedly between Mesopotamia and Cappadocia.

29. See the clear arguments of Metzger, "Ancient Astrological Geography."

30. On the evidence for this in these countries see Williams, *Acts,* pp. 28-29.

31. Perhaps this last term is a reference to the desert kingdom of Arabia belonging to the Nabateans, the capital of which was at Petra. Paul obviously had dealings with them (cf. below, pp. 313ff., on Acts 9:23-25 and 2 Cor. 11:30-33, and Gal. 1:17, where Syrian Arabia is in view). In general see Bowersock, *Roman Arabia,* pp. 68ff.

where the word will finally go by the end of Acts.[32] The contrast here might be between all these residents of Jerusalem (cf. above) and those who are simply visitors from Rome. On the other hand, elsewhere in Acts this term means not visitors from Rome, but rather Roman citizens (cf. 16:21, 37, 38; 22:25, 26),[33] and so is probably meant here as well.[34] It is quite certain that Luke is very interested in the fact that Christianity attracted a certain number of converts of rather high social status,[35] which may have been a point of no little importance for Theophilus.

V. 12 indicates that the crowd, while recognizing what was said, does not understand what they heard. It requires interpretation in a Jewish framework. *V. 13* says some jeered or mocked and thought the disciples were drunk with new wine. The term γλευκος means new, hence sweet, wine and thus a ready cause of drunkenness since more of it would be drunk because of its sweet taste.[36] It is sometimes pointed out that Pentecost occurs before there could be new wine available, but this is not quite true, for even in antiquity there were means of storing and preserving new wine over considerable periods of time without it losing its flavor and freshness.[37] V. 13 provides a transition to the next section of this passage, for it brings to light the crowd which hears what the disciples are saying.

B. Preaching at Pentecost (2:14-42)

It was a common practice of Hellenistic historians in their speech material to imitate the style of the speeches of the earlier Greek historians such as Thucydides.[38] Luke is well aware of this sort of practice of archaizing, but of course

32. They may also be meant to provide a hint of how there came to be a Christian community in Rome prior to the arrival of Paul or Peter or other major missionaries.

33. See Barrett, *Acts*, vol. 1, p. 123.

34. Could this be an allusion to Paul and other Jews in Jerusalem who were from the Diaspora and were Roman citizens?

35. On which see the discussion below, pp. 210ff.

36. See Johnson, *Acts*, p. 44.

37. See, for example, Columella 1.87; 2.65; and Cato, *De Re Rustica* 120, for methods. Fitzmyer, "Ascension of Christ and Pentecost," points to the fact that Qumran apparently observed three Pentecosts, each separated by fifty days, with the second one being after the grape harvest and being a "wine" (as opposed to a wheat or oil) Pentecost celebration one hundred days after Passover. The problems with this view are: (1) there is no good evidence Luke knew about such Qumran practices. He seems to speak of only one Pentecost and Pentecost season, which was now coming to a close on the fiftieth day; (2) there is certainly no evidence that ordinary Jews in Jerusalem followed such a threefold practice of Pentecost.

38. See Plümacher, *Lukas als hellenistischer Schriftsteller*, pp. 38-72.

he must work with a Jewish speaker speaking on Jewish subject matter quoting the Hebrew Scriptures. Thus, here and in several similar speeches (cf. below on Acts 3; 13) Luke follows this sort of archaizing practice by Septuagintalizing his source material. In doing this Luke shows himself concerned with the matter of suitability (προσωποποιια). Because he is presenting a Greek summary of a Jewish speech, perhaps even a speech originally in Aramaic spoken with a Galilean accent, he will nonetheless suit his presentation to the speaker and occasion by Septuagintalizing the summary, especially in the handling of the OT quotation (cf. below).[39]

At the same time, in order to persuade his Gentile audience, Luke follows, with some flexibility, some of the forms of Greco-Roman rhetorical oratory in various elements of these speeches. Thus, for example, we have here an example of forensic rhetoric, the rhetoric of defense and attack using Jewish subject matter: (1) vv. 14-21 refute the charge of drunkenness; (2) vv. 22-36 turn to the attack, indicting certain Jews for killing Jesus. Thus the innocence of the first group (of drunkenness) is shown, and the guilt of the second group (in killing) is demonstrated. This first speech largely succeeds in its aims with the result that many in the crowd are heart-stricken and ask what they must do now (v. 37).[40] (3) This in turn prompts what amounts to a *second* brief speech by Peter that is an example of deliberative rhetoric telling the audience the proper course of action to take in the near future (vv. 38-40). This speech, too, prompts the appropriate response (vv. 41-42). It is also noteworthy that Peter is said to stand and lift up his voice in *v. 14*, which is the typical stance of the orator in antiquity, in particular the Greek orator or rhetor.[41]

Concerns of ethos or character are of major import if a speech is to persuade an audience, and Luke makes clear in subtle ways that Peter has established the necessary rapport with his audience to convince many. For

39. On the matter of "appropriateness," cf. Lucian, *How to Write History* 58: "let his language suit his person and his subject, [but at the same time] you can play the orator and show your eloquence." Luke has reduced more extensive subject matter into a masterful Greek summary suitable to the original speaker, occasion, and audience, but is also on target with the expectations of his own current audience in terms of form and style so as to be persuasive. See Johnson, *Acts*, p. 53.

40. See Johnson, *Acts*, p. 54: "By no means is the speech a casual collection of assertions. It is a rhetorically sophisticated argument, involving refutation of common opinion (that the disciples could be drunk [2.15] or that David was speaking of himself in the psalms [2.29-30]); an appeal to eyewitness testimony (of the apostles [2.32]); and an appeal to scriptural prophecy concerning this event (2.17-21) and its cause (2.25-35)." On the judicial and deliberative elements in 2:14-40, cf. also Black, "The Rhetorical Form," p. 5. As Black points out, a full *exordium* was not necessary in a speech when it was not necessary to spend extended time lulling the audience into a favorable disposition to hear the arguments that followed (p. 7). See Quintilian, *Inst. Or.* 3.8.7; 4.1.5-6.

41. See Haenchen, *Acts*, p. 178.

instance, notice the progression in the way Peter addresses his audience. Both "men Jews (or Judeans)" (v. 14) and "men Israelites" (v. 22) are formal, but in v. 29 we have "men brothers," to which the audience responds in kind with the same intimate address in v. 37. "The successive salutations show Peter progressively winning over his audience with the result of the mass conversion of 2.41."[42]

Luke tells Theophilus in this first lengthy example of speech material that he is deliberately summarizing his material (in a form his audience would recognize and appreciate) — "and he testified with many other arguments" (v. 40a).[43] Luke does not include all the πιστοι or proofs/arguments, but instead proceeds directly to the *peroratio,* the final exhortation and emotional appeal involving *pathos*[44] — "save yourselves from this wicked generation."[45] "Paraphrase was a well-known exercise of rhetorical training,"[46] and we see this art at work in the speeches of Acts.

The two parts of the speech material in vv. 14-40 have a certain unity and coherence: (1) "to call upon the name of the Lord" (v. 21) is another way of speaking about the event that involves being baptized "in the name of Jesus Christ" (v. 38); (2) the promise in vv. 17-18 prepares for the promise of receiving the Spirit (v. 38); (3) the *peroratio* or final exhortation in v. 40b reiterates the conclusion of the Joel quote in v. 21.[47] It is not for nothing that this first major speech summary has been called a rhetorical masterpiece.[48]

We are told at the outset in *v. 14* that the Eleven are also standing there, thus making clear that Peter speaks as the representative of the group, as was true in Acts 1, and before that in the Gospel. He is the interpreter of what has happened. In this initial paradigmatic speech we find a fullness of expression about what conversion entails that is not usually the case in the speeches that follow. Three examples will suffice to demonstrate this point: (1) while the call to repentance is not infrequent in these "missionary" speeches (cf. Acts 17:30; 26:20), the direct appeal using μετανοησατε (v. 38) is found only at 2:38 and 3:19, in the first two major speeches; (2) only in Acts 2 is there an

---

42. Zehnle, *Peter's Pentecost Discourse,* p. 21. He also rightly notices that the same device to establish rapport is found in Paul's first real speech in Acts 13:16, 26, 38.

43. This, as various scholars have noted, is a technical rhetorical device meant to convey the idea the speaker had much more to say. As Zehnle, *Peter's Pentecost Discourse,* p. 36, says, it "leaves the author free to allow the speaker to say only what lies in his plan at this point."

44. The audience needs to be alert and personally concerned about saving themselves from a wicked world.

45. On all this see Kennedy, *New Testament Interpretation,* pp. 116-18.

46. Cadbury, "Four Features of Lukan Style," p. 92.

47. Schneider, *Die Apostelgeschichte I,* p. 264.

48. By Zehnle, *Peter's Pentecost Discourse,* p. 37, following J. A. T. Robinson.

explicit demand that the hearers be baptized, especially significant since the audience is Jewish; (3) only at 2:38 is there a promise in the discourse that reception of the Spirit results from conversion.[49]

Throughout Acts, the presence of the Spirit is seen as the distinguishing mark of Christianity — it is what makes a person a Christian. Acts 2:21 indicates that the giving of the Spirit is not just for ecstatic speech or gifts, because it enables one to confess the Lord's name from the heart and be saved in the first place. The Spirit, then, is the *sine qua non* for being a Christian, not merely a means by which one gets a spiritual booster shot subsequent to conversion.[50] Paul likewise indicates that it is in or by the Spirit that believers are baptized into the body of Christ (cf. 1 Cor. 12:13). For him spiritual baptism has to do with entering Christ's body, not attaining a higher spiritual plane in one's faith. There is, then, a certain similarity in theological outlook on the part of Luke and Paul on these matters.

As is clear from Peter's speech and the quoting from Joel 2:28-32 at Acts 2:17ff., the working of the Spirit is seen as the sign that the eschatological age has begun, and that the promises of the OT era are being fulfilled in the lives of those who follow Jesus. In general the point of the Joel passage is that not just some but all of God's people from the least to the greatest will have the Spirit and be equipped for witness or service with various gifts in the eschatological age ushered in by Jesus. For Luke, as Acts 2:16ff. indicates, there had been no general dispensation of the Spirit to believers before this time.[51]

It cannot be stressed too strongly that the event recorded in Acts 2 is not really about the inauguration of the worldwide Gentile mission. In Acts 2:14 Peter addresses his fellow (local?) Jews,[52] but also all others who κατοικουντες ("*and* those who were dwelling") in Jerusalem. Peter's preaching, then, in vv. 14ff.

---

49. See ibid., pp. 35-36.

50. One suspects that, if asked, Luke would have said that there are of course plenty of opportunities to have numerous spiritual experiences *after* conversion, for example when a Christian prophet is filled by the Spirit in a moment of inspiration and speaks or performs a prophetic act (cf. Acts 11:28; 21:10-11). These experiences may be called blessings or fillings, but these do not make one a Christian.

51. Whether this conflicts with what one finds in John 20 may be debated. In terms of the Fourth Evangelist's *own* theology, it is possible to see John 20:22 as a prophetic promise, not an actual bestowal of the Spirit, especially in view of the fact that the rest of John 20 does not suggest the disciples have received any such empowerment or peace yet as that which Jesus promised when he first appeared in the upper room. See my *John's Wisdom: A Commentary on the Fourth Gospel* (Louisville: Westminster/J. Knox, 1995), ad loc. Alternatively, John 20 could be the Johannine version of the Pentecost narrative found in Acts 2:1-4. The problem with this last suggestion is of course that in John we have a Christophany and no real indication of empowerment by the Spirit of the disciples, while in Acts we have the reverse of this.

52. Whether the use of the phrase ανδρες 'Ιουδαιοι in v. 14 is meant to refer to males only can be doubted. See pp. 120ff. above.

must be seen as essentially a message to the Jews of the world, not to the whole world. This, then, is about the beginning of the spread of the gospel to Jews both within and outside of Judea. It would signal the worldwide mission of the church even to the Gentiles, but that is not the focus here. Such an idea is perhaps barely hinted at by the use of πας in v. 21 and v. 39b ("and all who are far off"), though even the latter could be a reference to Jews in faraway places.

Peter's speech is not just an attempt to defend the experience of his fellow disciples, but a call to Jewish repentance, especially of course to those Jews most directly responsible for Jesus' death. As C. A. Evans says, this call to Jews for repentance for the forgiveness of sins is an important repeated theme in Acts (cf. 3:19; 10:43; 11:18; 17:30; 26:18, 20).[53] That its function is *not* to seal Jews under condemnation and so provide a rationale for the Gentile mission is shown not only by the fact that Peter, Paul, and others keep approaching Jews throughout Acts, even long *after* the Gentile mission had begun, but also by the fact that almost everywhere the Christian missionaries go they begin at the synagogue and there are almost always at least some Jewish converts, as is even the case at the very end of Acts (28:17-25).[54]

The *scale* of the Jewish rejection, that it involves most Jews everywhere, does, however, cause the missionaries to turn to evangelizing Gentiles in more earnest, but one must remember that the outreach to Gentiles in Luke's view begins with direct divine guidance from God to Peter that they are to be approached *also*, since they are not to be seen as unclean (Acts 10).[55] In sum, it appears that Luke, like Paul, believes that the gospel and its salvation is for the Jew first, but *also* for the Gentile (cf. Rom. 1:16). This of course implies that both Jews and Gentiles *need* to repent, believe, and be saved through faith in Jesus. This is where the rub comes, for, in Luke's view and historically as well, many Jews did not see themselves as having such a need. Both the promise and the call to repentance in Acts 2 focus on the Jews and have a christological reference point. We are meant to see here the fulfillment of Israel's hope for the permanent giving of God's presence and power to God's people.[56] There

53. See Evans and Sanders, *Luke and Scripture,* pp. 188ff.

54. This account of things, as ibid., pp. 188ff., points out, cannot be called anti-Semitic, but rather is a reflection of a heated debate between Jewish Christians and non-Christian Jews. This is a fraternal and largely in-house debate.

55. See below, pp. 339ff.

56. The charge of anti-Semitism against Luke is ill founded. Cf. now Weatherly, *Jewish Responsibility,* correcting the earlier, flawed analyses of Sanders, *The Jews in Luke-Acts,* and Hare, "Rejection of the Jews," among others. The critique of Israel in Luke-Acts falls along the lines of earlier Jewish prophetic critiques by Jeremiah, Amos, and others. Luke's view must not be confused with that of the later second-century editor of the Western text of Acts (see pp. 65ff., above), nor with later Christian anti-Semitic *use* of Acts, taking certain texts out of their original historical and literary contexts.

is evidence of the use of this same Joel quotation in other early Jewish discussions about the Messiah, but they all postdate our text (see Seder Eliyyahu Rabbah 4[19]).[57] It is right to say that "the central conflict of the plot [in Acts], repeatedly emphasized and still present in the last major scene of Acts, is a conflict *within Judaism* provoked by Jewish Christian preachers (including Paul). Acts 2.1–8.3 traces the development of this conflict in Jerusalem."[58] Thus "the function of the Pentecost speech is to disclose to the Jerusalem Jews that they have blindly rejected their own Messiah and must repent. . . . Peter begins, 'Let this be known to you,' and concludes, 'Therefore let the whole house of Israel know assuredly . . . ,' forming an inclusion (21.4, 36)."[59]

The Septuagintalizing of Luke's source is shown not only in the Scripture citation but also in the narrative of the speech. For instance, in *v. 14b* the phrase "let it be put in your ears," found only here in the NT, is frequent in the LXX (cf. Gen. 4:23; Exod. 15:26; Job 32:11; Ps. 5:1; Joel 1:2). Luke modifies the LXX citation only slightly, which begins in *v. 17,* changing "after these things" to the more eschatologically specific "in the last days." This Pentecost must be seen as an end-time event. Notice also the addition of "my" to the LXX text in *v. 18,* which turns "servants" into "my servants," making them servants of God, not merely persons of low social status.[60]

Visions and dreams are an important part of Luke's narrative, not least because the main protagonists are portrayed as prophets in Acts, and are guided like earlier prophets by such means of revelation (cf. Acts 7:31, 55-56; 9:3-10, 12; 10:3, 17, 19; 11:5; 16:9-10; 18:9; 27:23).[61] The significance of dreams and visions would not have been lost on an educated Gentile like Theophilus, for whether he was a God-fearer or simply a pagan before his conversion, in the Greco-Roman world dreams and visions were widely recognized as a means of divine guidance.[62]

Vv. 19-20 refer to "signs and wonders," and the debate has been as to whether we are meant to think that Luke believed these sorts of things happened on that Pentecost. Notice the additions to the LXX form of these verses of the words "above" and "below." Perhaps we are meant to think of the signs

---

57. See Evans and Sanders, *Luke and Scripture*, p. 187.

58. Tannehill, *Narrative Unity of Luke-Acts*, 2:34, emphasis mine.

59. Ibid., p. 35.

60. It appears also that the phrase "and they will prophesy" is an original Lukan addition in v. 18 to the LXX text; cf. Metzger, *Textual Commentary*, p. 297. The omission of this phrase in the Western text may be explained by the fact that the phrase's closest antecedent is "my women servants" and the antifeminist tendencies of the Western text are clear elsewhere in Acts; cf. pp. 65ff. above.

61. This point is made forcefully by Johnson, *Acts*, pp. 49ff. and passim, who shows how both Jesus and his early followers are portrayed as prophetic figures.

62. See van der Horst, "Hellenistic Parallels to the Acts of the Apostles," pp. 56ff.

"below" (blood, fire, thick smoke) as relating to the death of Jesus and the fire of the Spirit coming down on the disciples,[63] but that still leaves v. 20 unaccounted for. More likely we should simply see vv. 19-20 as references to the final eschatological events before the end, and thus we are being told that the coming of the Spirit is an eschatological event, indeed the inauguration of those end times, with more events to follow.

Because the end has been set in motion already, there is urgency in *v. 21* and v. 38 — people need to repent, believe, and be saved. V. 21 reassures that all who call on the Lord's name will indeed be saved. Here it will be in order to say something about Luke's understand of salvation.

A Closer Look — Salvation in Luke-Acts

Elsewhere in this book I have dealt in detail with the subject of Luke's conception of salvation.[64] At this point I would like to stress that Luke's concept has social, physical, and spiritual dimensions. For example, in the paradigmatic speech of Jesus in Luke 4 salvation is equated with the preaching of good news to the poor, release to the captives, recovery of sight to the blind, and freeing of those oppressed. The social dimension is seen in the concern for the poor and the release of the captives, the latter of which includes release from demonic possession but is not confined to that realm. We see this social dimension in the parable of the prodigal son (Luke 15), where family reconciliation is in view; in the story of Zacchaeus in Luke 19, who is being set free from social prejudice against tax collectors; and in the story of the sinner woman of Luke 7 who is freed from social stigma and being an outcast from society. Healing and exorcism are also seen as means or forms of salvation (cf. Luke 8:48, where the text reads literally "your faith has *saved* [i.e., healed] you"): they are ways to "save life" (Luke 6:9). Both in these social and physical dimensions Luke's concept of salvation in the Gospel differs little from the usual concepts of salvation in the Greco-Roman world, which involve rescue, help, healing, exorcism, social restoration, and the like. The point I wish to make is that these same notions of salvation carry over into the book of Acts, but it must be stressed that they do not exhaust Luke's concept of salvation.

For example, already in the Gospel we hear of salvation in the form of forgiveness of sins, a very Jewish way of viewing salvation (cf. Luke 5:20, though even there the physical and spiritual concepts are interrelated if not intertwined). This latter, more "spiritual" (and also social) view of salvation becomes much more prominent in the book of Acts than it was in the Gospel. Doubtless this reflects Luke's keen sense of historical development and process, for he is careful not simply to equate what happened during Jesus' ministry with what began to happen after Pentecost. Luke believes

63. See Arichea, "Some Notes on Acts 2.17-21."
64. See Appendix 2, "Salvation and Health in Christian Antiquity," pp. 821ff. below.

that with the sending of the eschatological Spirit the eschatological blessings of God's divine saving activity, including release from sins, begin to manifest themselves more fully and repeatedly.

This is why, for example, in the paradigmatic speech in Acts 2, as a comparison of v. 21 and v. 38 will show, the emphasis is placed on salvation involving the forgiveness of sins.[65] Yet the integral connection between healing and salvation continues to be clear in Acts, as a careful reading of Acts 3–4 will show. In Acts 4:9-10 the healing of the crippled beggar is clearly spoken of as something that happened in Jesus' name, and then Peter proceeds to conclude, "There is salvation in no one else, for there is no other name under heaven given among mortals by which we must be saved." The reference to the name in 4:12 echoes 3:6 — "in the name of Jesus Christ of Nazareth, stand up and walk." Healings and exorcisms (see Acts 19:11ff.) as well as punitive miracles (e.g., Ananias and Sapphira) are the "signs and wonders" which attract many to Christianity and at least in their positive form are part of the work of salvation (cf. Acts 5:12). Luke can even use the language of salvation to refer to physical rescue from danger (in the sense of "being kept safe"), but only rarely (cf. Acts 27:31). In sum, what accounts for a focus on the more spiritual dimensions of salvation in Acts is the coming of the dispenser of final salvation, the Spirit, in plenitude. The development in this direction from Luke to Acts shows Luke's keen awareness of historical progression and developments.

V. 22 introduces the subject of Jesus, and it is here that Peter begins to go on the offensive. There is no attempt to hide that Jesus is from Nazareth, undoubtedly a controversial point that would have ruled out his being Messiah in some minds. Yet human opinion is not really important because Jesus was accredited by God in several ways: (1) by deeds of power (δυναμεις) and wonders and signs God did through Jesus, and (2) by God's raising him up from the dead, the ultimate divine validation. Notice, as Marshall points out, that the resurrection of Jesus is not argued for, it is simply proclaimed.[66] Of course many early Jews (including Jesus), and in particular Pharisaic Jews, believed in the idea of resurrection of the dead (cf. Acts 23:6-8; John 5:29).

As v. 22b suggests, even some of the audience could themselves attest to Jesus' mighty deeds, a fact not contested even later in the Talmud, but rather ascribed to Jesus' reliance on the powers of darkness (cf. Mark 3:20-30: b. Hul. 2.22-23). In v. 23 we see the juxtaposition, common in various parts of the NT, of God's divine plan with human actions for which humans are held responsible. One and the same event, Jesus' being handed over to be killed,

---

65. Notice that even in a speech to a purely, or almost purely, Gentile audience in Acts 17:16-31, Paul is working his way around to the concept of final judgment and human accountability for human behavior. On the whole subject of Luke's theology of the cross and of forgiveness, cf. now Moessner, "The Script of the Scriptures."

66. Marshall, Acts, p. 75.

can be said to be "according to God's definite plan and foreknowledge" and at the same time is seen as a blameworthy sin on the part of some of Jesus' fellow Jews. Luke certainly knows who it was who actually crucified Jesus (cf. Luke 23:25, 47), for he speaks in 23b of Jesus being "killed by the hands of those outside the law," clearly non-Jews. Yet at the same time the culpability of Jews, in particular some Jews of Jerusalem who are being especially addressed in this speech, is asserted by the words "having affixed him to a cross, you killed. . . ."[67] This was only possible because God "gave him up" (εκδοτον).

V. 24 seems to involve another intriguing example of Luke's use of the LXX, for the phrase "the (birth) pangs of death" occurs only in the LXX of 2 Sam. 22:6 (and Ps. 17:5, 6), but the Hebrew has "cords of death."[68] The point is that God was not going to allow Jesus' ministry and work to end in this fashion. Indeed, v. 24b suggests that Jesus was such a righteous and powerful person that death had no permanent power over him and his body. This leads to yet another citation from the Scriptures in vv. 25-28.

The citation in vv. 25-28 is exact from the LXX of Ps. 15:8-11. As was customary, since David's name was appended to the psalm it is read as a comment by David, and Peter says David was commenting about Jesus' experience.[69] In this citation, then, Jesus is said never to lose sight of God even in death. Rather, Jesus' flesh lived in hope, for God would not abandon his Holy One to the land of the dead or allow him to see corruption.

As is true elsewhere in Luke-Acts, *hades* here refers not to hell but to the OT notion of *sheol*, the land of the dead, similar to the Greco-Roman concept of hades (cf. Luke 10:15; 16:23). It was an early Jewish belief that the spirit of a person stayed with the body for three days and on the fourth day departed, at which point corruption of the flesh well and truly set in (cf. John 11:17, 39). According to the Gospel story, Jesus' body was not in the tomb for that amount of time, rather only for a day and a half (Friday evening to early Sunday morning) at most. V. 28 speaks metaphorically of Jesus' resurrection as involving God revealing to him the paths back to life, and his being filled with gladness. This same Psalm 15 (LXX) text is also cited by Paul in Acts 13:34-35 (in conjunction with a citing of Isaiah 55). It appears likely that there were early Christian collections of key OT texts or *testimonia* which various

---

67. This is not a redundancy, for, as Luke knew, not all crucified persons died. Some not under close observation by guards were rescued from their crosses.

68. It would appear the LXX translator reads *hebel* with a pointing which leads to the translation "pang," while a different pointing of the same Hebrew radical leads to the translation "cord." See Johnson, *Acts*, p. 51.

69. On the Jewish evidence (of later provenance) that this text was understood to refer to resurrection, cf. *Midr. Ps.* 16.10-11 and *b. B. Bat.* 17a and the discussion by Evans and Sanders, *Luke and Scripture*, p. 189.

early Christian preachers used along with the basic kerygma about Jesus' death and resurrection especially when speaking with Jews about Jesus. It was especially Jesus' death by crucifixion that required scriptural validation if Jews were to accept Jesus, since there is thus far no hard evidence early Jews before or during Jesus' day were actually looking for a crucified messiah.[70] In any event, the function of this Scripture citation is meant to show that what happened to Jesus was part of a preordained plan, as revealed in Scripture. The emphasis here is not on demonstrating that Jesus fulfilled Scripture.[71]

Peter's interpretation and application of the Psalms text are found in *vv. 29-36*, an effort that involves the further citation of one of the truly key texts from the Psalms for early Christians — Ps. 110:1 (cited in vv. 34b-35). Peter's essential argument is that despite what many Jews might think, David in Psalm 16 could not have been speaking of his own (future) experience because he died and was buried a long time before the era of Jesus, and "his tomb is with us to this day." The tomb of David is mentioned in the postexilic text Neh. 3:16, and we are told by Josephus that this tomb was opened and robbed by John Hyrcanus during the siege of Jerusalem (135 B.C.). In addition, Herod the Great apparently attempted the same sort of sacrilege, but tradition says he was stopped by divine intervention, and made amends by building a white marble monument at the tomb entrance (cf. *Ant.* 7.393; 13.249; 16.179-83; *Wars* 1.61). The location of David's tomb according to ancient tradition is thought to have been near the old city of David, which is south of the present city, thus near the pool of Siloam.

Peter's point is that David's tomb was still in plain view for any Jew to see and there was no evidence of David having vacated the premises. Thus, it follows he must be referring in the psalm to another. The application is made clearly in v. 31, where David himself is seen as a prophet foreseeing the future and speaking in advance about the experience of the Messiah. It was not uncommon in early Judaism to stress that David was a prophetic figure on the basis of the Psalms (cf. 11QPsa 27:11).[72]

V. 30 involves an allusion to Ps. 132:11ff. (131 LXX), where we find the reference to God swearing to place one of David's descendants on the throne (cf. 2 Sam. 7:12-16). This psalm was clearly used at Qumran in a messianic way (see 4QFlor 1:7-13), and thus what is distinctive about Peter's use is that it is applied to a specific, known historical figure of the recent past — Jesus of Nazareth.

---

70. There has been some report that there may be such new evidence from Qumran, but thus far those scholars best in a position to say this is positively the case have not done so. In short, the fragmentary evidence is debatable and can be read in other ways.

71. See Evans and Sanders, *Luke and Scripture,* p. 189.

72. See Fitzmyer, "David, Being Therefore a Prophet. . . ."

V. 32 brings in the motif of witness. Peter does not merely proclaim the resurrection, he claims with the Eleven to have been a witness of the resurrection appearances. Thus Peter himself is in a double sense a witness — one who has seen and one who reports or bears witness. But this is not all, for Peter is also a witness of and about the coming of the Spirit, and so he explains in *v. 33* that it was the ascended Jesus who was given the promise of the Spirit (cf. on Acts 1:4 above), and sent it now on Pentecost. This last fact the audience themselves could attest to on the basis of what they had just seen and especially what they had heard. David did not ascend to send such a gift to God's people. The citation of Ps. 110:1 in *v. 34* is not followed by exposition, but especially important in the citation is the reference to two Lords, something made much of elsewhere in the early Jesus tradition (cf. Mark 12:35-36 and par.).[73]

V. 36 has been seen as a classic exposition of the very primitive "adoptionist" Christology of early Jewish Christianity, for the text suggests that God made Jesus these things (both Lord and Messiah) *after* he died, and perhaps on the basis of the crucifixion. In other words, Lord and Messiah describe roles that Jesus only fully assumed after his death. While I would quite agree that the theology here likely reflects the earliest stage of Christian thinking about Jesus, the problem with the term "adoptionist" lies in the fact that Luke's Christology is affected by the fact that he is writing in the main as a historian, not primarily as a theologian, which means he is viewing these matters in terms of historical progression on the one hand and in terms of the story of Jesus (its narrative development, including its posthistorical portions) on the other. It will be useful to reflect in more detail on Luke's Christology at this point.

A Closer Look — Luke's Christology[74]

The term κυριος is the most frequently used christological title in all of Luke-Acts, used almost twice as frequently as the term "Christ." Of 717 occurrences of κυριος in the NT the vast majority are to be found either in Luke-Acts (210) or in the Pauline letters (275). This emphasis in Luke-Acts comports with Luke's basic stress on God's sovereignty over and in history as it is expressed in the form of God's plan of salvation for the world which comes to fruition through Jesus.[75] Jesus is the one who expresses

73. See my discussion of this important text, and Jesus' possible use of it, as well as the discussion of the early Jewish use of the text in *The Christology of Jesus,* pp. 189-91.

74. Some of the following material on Jesus as Lord and Christ will appear in a somewhat different form in the forthcoming Inter-Varsity dictionary companion to their Jesus and Paul dictionaries which covers the rest of the canon.

75. See Squires, *Plan of God in Luke-Acts,* passim.

and executes this salvation plan, both by his acts in space and time and by his acts as the exalted Lord sending the Holy Spirit to work on earth in his behalf and place. It becomes clear that the basic connotation for Luke of the term κυριος is of one who exercises dominion over the world and in particular over human lives and events. In other words, the term is always used relationally because one cannot be a Lord over someone or something unless there are others or other things to fulfill the subordinate role in the relationship.

The term κυριος appears 104 times in Acts, some 18 of which definitely refer to God; 47 definitely to Jesus; 4 to secular masters, owners, or rulers; and the remainder either to Jesus or God, though in these instances it is not clear which is meant.[76] Luke is familiar with the use of the term (even with the article) to refer to a secular ruler (Acts 25:26, of Nero) or of an owner or master of a slave (cf. 16:16, 19), but clearly his interest lies elsewhere. Κυριος clearly refers to Jesus in some texts, because the term is combined either with the name Jesus (cf. 1:21; 4:33; 8:16; 15:11; 16:31; 19:5, 13, 17; 20:24, 35; 21:13) or with the combined referent Jesus Christ (11:17; 15:26; 28:31). Elsewhere the context makes evident that it is Jesus who is meant (cf., e.g., 9:5, 10, 11). There are also some instances, primarily in quotations of the OT, where we have the combination of κυριος with θεος, in which it is evident that God and not Jesus is meant (cf. 2:39; 3:22). Some of the confusion could be resolved if we could know for certain that Luke does not draw on the concept of the preexistent Son of God, but texts like Acts 2:25 may suggest he knows of such an idea.

The quotation from Ps. 110:1 in Acts 2:34 where both God and Jesus are referred to as κυριος shows how flexible Luke was prepared to be in his use of the term κυριος. It would be wrong to conclude from such a text that Luke saw Jesus as merely the *believer's* Lord, for in Acts 10:36 he is called the Lord of all (παντων κυριος).

It seems wise to conclude that when an OT phrase or concept such as the Day of the Lord (2:20), the angel of the Lord (5:19; 12:11, 23), the fear of the Lord (9:31), or the hand of the Lord (13:11) appears in the text, Lord likely means God in such texts. On the other hand, the phrase "the word of the Lord," especially if one takes it as an objective genitive (the word about the Lord), would appear to refer to Jesus (cf. 8:25; 13:44, 49; 15:35, 36; 19:20), as is likely the case with the phrase "the Way of the Lord" (18:25). Further, the phrase "the name of the Lord" in 9:28 seems to refer to Jesus, especially in view of clearer texts such as 19:5, 13, and 17.

One of the keys to understanding Luke's use of κυριος in Acts is to recognize the narrative framework (which includes a historical component) in which he views all christological matters. Not merely must the κυριος material in Acts be compared and contrasted to the material in Luke's Gospel, but in general what Luke says about Jesus depends on what point in the trajectory of his career Luke is at the moment discussing. One must ask whether Luke is referring to Jesus during his historical ministry, or to what Luke believes to be true about Jesus after the resurrection and ascension.

For example, Luke uses the term κυριος in the narrative framework and in the editorial comments in his Gospel in a way other Synoptic writers basically do not,

---

76. See Kee, *Good News,* p. 19.

while at the same time no character in the Gospel narrative calls Jesus κυριος unless it is under inspiration (Luke 1:43, 76), or involves an angel (2:11) or Jesus obliquely alluding to himself (19:31, 34). As soon as the narrative gets beyond Easter, however, various human beings can and do use κυριος of Jesus (cf. Luke 24:34; Acts 10:36-38).[77] This may in part be explained as an example of Luke's desire to avoid historical anachronisms, but it also shows that he does not wish to violate the internal logic of the narrative and so have characters get ahead of what they ought to be saying at a particular juncture in the story.

The assertion that Luke is adoptionist in his christological thinking is based on texts like Acts 2:36 — "God has made this Jesus whom you crucified both κυριος and Christ." The problem with this conclusion is that here, as elsewhere in Acts, Luke is using his christological language in a way that suits his narrative. From Luke's point of view, Jesus did not in any full sense assume the roles of Lord and Messiah over all until after the resurrection and ascension. It was not that Jesus became *someone* different from who he was before, but that he entered a new stage in his career, or assumed new roles after the ascension. Only as an exalted one could Jesus take on the tasks of Lord over all and universal Messiah.[78]

Luke's basic interest is in the story of Jesus from his birth until he assumes and begins to exercise the role of Lord from heaven, though a text like Acts 2:25 may imply that Luke knew of the concept of the preexistent Lord (cf. Acts 2:24). It is the narrative about Jesus and its progress which affects how the terminology is used, not a concern to settle a later debate about functional over against ontological Christology. Then, too, nice distinctions between being and doing would probably have seemed inappropriate to Luke. The Lord Jesus is able to do what he does because he is who he is. The roles he assumes are roles that are appropriate, in Luke's mind, for the exalted Jesus to assume. Jesus' lordship is not viewed as a mere honorary title, but a description of his *status* and *activity* since at least the resurrection.

It is important not to underestimate the significance of the transfer of the term κυριος from Yahweh to Christ at various points in Acts. As J. Fitzmyer says: "In using κυριος of both Yahweh and Jesus in his writings Luke continues the sense of the title already being used in the early Christian community, which in some sense regarded Jesus as on a level with Yahweh."[79]

Acts indicates, as the Pauline Epistles also suggest, that the basic confession of the early church was the acknowledgment that Jesus is the (risen) Lord (cf. Acts 10:40-42; 11:16; 16:31; 20:21). It is Jesus the risen and exalted Lord whom people are called upon to turn to and believe in (Acts 5:14; 9:35; 11:17). It is this risen Lord who confronts Saul on the Damascus road (9:10-17; 18:9), and to whom believers must remain faithful (20:19). It is the Lord Jesus whom the original disciples traveled with (Acts 1:21), whose teaching Paul can quote (20:35), and who commissions people for ministry (20:24). In these texts, the name Jesus seems to be appended to κυριος to

---

77. See Moule, "The Christology of Acts."

78. See Schneider's excursus on Christology in *Die Apostelgeschichte I*, pp. 331-35, here p. 335.

79. Fitzmyer, *Luke I–IX*, p. 203.

make clear the identity of this Lord. The continuity of the Lord's identity before and after Easter makes it possible for Luke to refer to Jesus' earthly activity and teaching using the term κυριος, even though he knows that Jesus does not fully or truly assume the roles of exalted Lord until after Easter.

In other texts where it is the Lord God and not Jesus that is meant by κυριος (Acts 2:39; 3:19, 22; 4:26; 7:31; 10:4, 33), it is striking that these references are found either in the first few chapters of Acts or on the lips of Jews or apparent proselytes to Judaism, whereas the further one gets into Acts and the more Christians speak for themselves, it is almost always Jesus who is referred to as the Lord. Notably, after the crucial Apostolic Council and decree in Acts 15 there is only one text where κυριος seems *clearly* to refer to God and not Jesus — in the apologetic speech of Paul before the Areopagus (cf. 17:24). That is, in almost half of Acts where Luke himself may have drawn on his own knowledge and travel accounts beginning in Acts 16, references to God as κυριος are strikingly lacking.

In some passages one could debate whether Jesus or God is the referent. For example, in Acts 2:47 "the Lord" is probably God (cf. v. 34), but in a text like 21:14 it could refer to either Jesus or God (cf. v. 13). In Acts 12:11, 17 (cf. v. 5) the "Lord" seems to refer to God, as is more clearly the case in 12:23. But in 7:60; 13:2; and 16:14-15 it appears that it is Jesus who is prayed to, worshiped, and believed in.[80] This sort of ambiguity does not trouble Luke because in his view the terminology is equally appropriate when used of either God or Jesus, not least because he viewed Jesus as a proper object of worship and petitionary prayer.

Of the some twenty-six references to Χριστος in Acts, not surprisingly all of them are used to refer to Jesus. The term occurs only rarely in conjunction with an OT citation, no doubt because the term is rather rare in the Greek OT. Nevertheless Acts 4:26 does contain a citation of some form of Ps. 2:2, where God as Lord is distinguished from "his anointed one" (in Acts, του Χριστου αυτου). Texts such as this one and others where the qualifier "his" occurs (cf. Acts 3:18) make clear that the author knows the root meaning of the word Χριστος, and understands its relational character. If one is "the Christ," one must be anointed by someone else, in this case the Father. Jesus is God's Christ, God's anointed one, but he is the believer's Lord. Hence when we find the phrase "our Lord, Jesus Christ" in Acts (cf. Acts 15:26; 20:21), we see at least by implication the two relationships that are implied — Jesus is the anointed one of God, and the believer's Lord.

Luke makes explicit that essential to being a Christian is confessing Jesus to be "the Christ" (ο Χριστος — 9:22; 17:3). Not surprisingly, it is in the witness to Jews in the synagogue that this issue is pressed. This is precisely the point which had to be demonstrated from the Scriptures if Jews were to be followers of Jesus. If one is to generalize, it appears in Acts that "Christ" mainly functions as a name when the audience is Gentile, but can serve as a functional description or title when the audience is Jewish. The phrase "in/by the name of Jesus Christ" or a variant thereof, which occurs at 2:38; 4:10; 8:12; 10:48; 15:26; 16:18, shows, however, not only that Christ could be used as part of a name even in a Jewish context (cf. 4:18, noting the Jewish

---

80. See Kee, *Good News,* p. 20.

authorities leave out the "Christ" portion of the phrase), but that it was believed that confessing, invoking, proclaiming, praying, or even exorcising in this name produced miraculous events, including conversions and healings. Baptism "in the name of Jesus Christ" is seen as the characteristic entrance rite into the Christian community for both Jews and Gentiles (cf. Acts 2:38; 10:48).

Luke places much stress on the necessity of Jesus' sufferings and resurrection (cf. Luke 24:26-27), and in this context it is worth noting that he asserts that it was God's plan revealed in Scripture for "the Christ" to suffer (Acts 17:2-3) and to be raised (2:31, citing Ps. 16:10).[81] The fulfillment of Scripture in these matters is stressed in the context of the synagogue or where the audience is Jewish. It is no accident that usually when the audience is solely or almost solely Gentiles who are not synagogue adherents or connected with Jews, the term "Christ" as a title or description does not arise, and in fact in various cases it does not even arise as a name in such contexts (cf. Paul's speech to the Lystrans in Acts 14:15-17 and to the Athenians in Acts 17:22-31). What was critical for a Jewish audience to confess was that Jesus was the Christ (9:22; 17:3), while for a Gentile audience what was paramount was confessing that the person called Jesus Christ was Lord (cf. 15:23-26). The community of Christian Jews and Gentiles shared the confession of Jesus as "our Lord" (cf. 15:26; 20:21). One was to have faith in him (20:21; 24:24). One should probably not make too much out of Acts 2:36, for while this text does speak of God "making" Jesus the Messiah (presumably after his crucifixion), elsewhere in this same work he speaks of him suffering as Messiah (17:3). In other words, at most 2:36 suggested to the author that Jesus entered a new stage of his messianic roles and duties after his death. What we find notably lacking in Acts is the Pauline idea of being "in Christ" or being participants in his body or the notion of Christ's preexistence. His Christology has sometimes been dubbed "absentee Christology" since Luke stresses that Christ ascended and rules from heaven (see Acts 3:11-26).[82] This terminology is not very apt, not least because in Luke's view Jesus continues to act in, through, and for the church by means of the Holy Spirit, and so his power and presence are not seen as totally absent.

A good example of continuity as well as discontinuity between Luke and Acts created because of historical perspective and the development of the narrative would be the fact that only in Acts, outside the Gospels, do we find Jesus being called Son of Man in a text not quoting Daniel. Whereas in the Gospel we only find the term *Son of Man* on the lips of Jesus (or on rare occasion possibly the editor), at Acts 7:56 we find Stephen referring to Jesus with this phrase. There are, however, as Moule points out, significant differences between the way the term is used here and in Luke's Gospel. In the Gospel Son of Man and glory are talked about purely in terms of the future tense, unlike the case in Acts 7:56. Secondly, the Son of Man is here standing at attention, not merely seated at the right hand. The Christology is being expressed very carefully with full knowledge of the time frame — that is, that Jesus had already ascended and was at the right hand of God, and thus that the church was in the

81. Cf. Moessner, "The Script of the Scriptures," pp. 218-50.
82. Cf. Moule, "The Christology of Acts," p. 159 and his discussion of Robinson's earlier proposal.

postresurrection era. This image would have been out of place in the Gospel. In general Luke's use of christological titles shows this sort of clear historical perspective recognizing the differences between the pre- and postresurrection situation. In Luke's thought the death and resurrection have decisively changed history, and thus changed the way one must look not only at the people of God, but also how one must view God's Messiah.

It is an indication of Luke's exaltation Christology that both in his Gospel and in Acts the idea of the ascension is given significant space, which makes evident Christ's absence, including the absence of his body. A variety of texts stress that Jesus is in heaven, even if by means of vision he appears to some on earth, such as Stephen or Paul (cf. 2:33; 3:21; 9:3; 22:6; 26:13). This is why the sending of the Spirit is so crucial in Acts.[83] If Jesus is absent, the church must have some source of power and direction, and this they receive from the Spirit. God now acts by means of the Spirit or an angel on earth (cf. 8:26, 29, 39; 11:28; 12:7; 13:4; 15:28; 16:6; 20:23; 21:11; 27:23). Nor is there any sort of "Immanuel" theology predicated of Christ in Acts, as we find at the beginning and end of Matthew's Gospel. The ascension, however, should probably not be seen as a Lukan theologoumena, not least because the christological hymns reflect this notion when they refer to the exaltation of Christ to the right hand (cf. Phil. 2:9-11; Heb. 1:3-4).

Luke's primary concern is with presenting a narrative Christology that tells the story of Jesus from his birth until his present exaltation to heaven and his reign from there as Lord over all. This is not to say that Luke does not also refer to Jesus as a coming judge (Acts 10:42; 17:31), but this is not his central concern. Because Luke is concerned with historical matters, he tells the tale of how Christ related to God's people during his earthly life and to the church on earth in the present. In the paradigmatic speech in Acts 2 we are told of the whole compass or scope of this work and ministry of Jesus from his birth (2:22) to his exaltation and coronation (2:33-36). The humanness of Jesus, and thus his fitness to act in a historical drama, is stressed in Acts by the repeated reference to the fact that he is from Nazareth (3:6; 4:10 et al.; notice it is often in conjunction with the name Jesus Christ, not just the name Jesus).

E. Schweizer has amply shown[84] that Luke is also concerned to reveal Jesus as the Davidic Messiah and Son of God, a connection made by way of Ps. 2:7, among other texts. Acts 2:30 and 13:33 bring to the fore "a Messianic figure, God's Son of Davidic descent who rules over Israel in the latter days."[85] Somewhat related to this development is the fact that we have in Acts 3–4, and only there, a theology of Jesus as servant drawing on the Isaianic material (cf. 4:27-30; 3:13). S. Smalley has argued, plausibly, that there may well be a Petrine source behind this usage (cf. 1 Peter), not least because it only really occurs in Petrine speeches in Acts.[86]

In his use of the term *Son* in the Gospel and then in Acts we see once again Luke's historical sensitivity. He is called the Son only by other than human voices in

---

83. On which see the discussion, pp. 129ff. above.
84. See his "Davidic 'Son of God.'"
85. Ibid., p. 191.
86. See Smalley, "The Christology of Acts Again"; cf. his "The Christology of Acts."

the Gospel (1:32, 35; 3:22; 4:3, 9, 41; 8:28), but in Acts both at 9:20 and 13:33 Paul clearly calls him this openly. Luke was well aware of the decisive difference the resurrection made both in terms of who Jesus was and how his followers confessed him. Then, too, words about Jesus as Savior or as one saving are found only on superhuman lips in the Gospel (2:11; 2:30; 3:6), but after the resurrection we find such talk as an essential part of the church's confession (cf. Acts 4:12; 5:31; 13:23).[87]

Acts purports to be a record of christological thinking at a time prior to when Luke wrote, but during and after the beginning of the Christian community. The very variety of Christologies that appear and disappear in Acts give no aid to those who assume that Luke is simply inserting his own ideas about Christ throughout Acts. The primitive titles such as Christ as αρχηγος (5:13; 13:23) point to Luke's access to early Jewish Christian thinking about the more than merely human roles of the Christ (cf., e.g., Heb. 12:2).[88] Rather, he is trying to present the variety of Christologies which he found in his sources. He is not interested in ironing out the divergences and differences between his sources in these matters, but rather in faithfully presenting a representative sampling of the ideas, some of which are quite primitive and some of which rightly fade into the background once the gospel leaves Palestinian soil. Luke acts as a historian in his handling of these matters, but not one without theological interests.

V. 37 tells us that Peter was indeed very persuasive — the audience was "cut to the heart."[89] This is to be expected, for if Peter's words were really believed, then his audience would realize they had been party to a truly horrible act. They had done something no Jew would ever want to be credited with — acting in such a way as to lead to the death of the Jewish Messiah, the one who was to deliver Israel. The audience wishes to know what they must do in view of such a calamity. This response of the crowd is directed not just to Peter but to the other apostles as well, the Eleven. Luke stresses this to indicate further that already the Twelve were fulfilling their role in relationship to their fellow Jews that they were intended to play (2:14).

Vv. 38-39, as we have already noted, provide the fullest summary of what was required (and what the benefits would be) if one wished to become a follower of Jesus. That Peter is calling for Jews to repent and be baptized is of course not unprecedented, for this is precisely what John the Baptist had done as well (cf. Luke 3). It is thus not surprising that the response of the audience here is seen to exactly parallel that of John's audience in Luke 3:10 (τι ποιη-

---

87. On Luke's understanding of salvation, see pp. 821ff. below.

88. See Schneider, *Die Apostelgeschichte I*, p. 333.

89. The verb κατενυγησαν with "the heart" as its object refers to strong emotion, and occurs only here in the NT. In the LXX its meaning ranges from "remorseful" (Gen. 27:38) to "anger" (Gen. 34:7) to "stung" (Sir. 12:12) to "humbled" (Ps. 108:16) to "struck silent" (Lev. 10:3). Here the meaning is something like remorseful, or, as the RSV and NRSV have it, "cut to the heart."

σωμεν — v. 37).[90] Yet Peter's further words to the crowd differ considerably from those of John, and here we begin to see what would be distinctive about Christian baptism. Not the connection between repentance and baptism but the additional connection of baptism with the name of Jesus and the reception of the Holy Spirit sets Christian baptism apart. Baptism is to be done "in the name of Jesus," which probably means that Jesus was named as the baptizing was being done, though it could mean with the authority of Jesus. Nothing is said here to suggest that only apostles could or would baptize. Even more interesting is the connection of baptism with the promise that one would receive the Holy Spirit.

Any careful analysis of Acts will show that Luke (and probably the earliest Christians before him as well) was not interested in nice distinctions about the chronology of events in a particular person's life. By this I mean we have some texts in Acts where water baptism *precedes* the reception of the Spirit (cf. Acts 8:4-25), some texts where water baptism *follows* the reception of the Spirit (cf. Acts 10:44-48), and others, as here in Acts 2 and Acts 8:38-39,[91] where the two seem to happen almost simultaneously. One can only conclude from this that Luke was not trying to teach his audience some sort of normative order to be followed in later church practice. God can do it however God wants to do it. Acts seems rather innocent of such later ecclesiological concerns about church polity and practice in general.[92] Without neglecting or disparaging Luke's theological acumen one must say that his interests lie primarily in the realm of history, albeit a theological sort of history — salvation history.

What one can say is that Luke intends his audience to know that repentance, faith, baptism, the name of Jesus, and reception of the Spirit were all important elements when the matter of "what must we do" or how people enter the community of Christ comes up. One can also say that Luke wishes his audience to know that John's "baptism of repentance" and believing in it and John (19:4) are not simply equivalent to Christian baptism and Christian faith, even though there is some overlap in associating baptism with repentance. John's baptism is not seen as sufficient for one becoming a Christian (cf. 18:24-26; 19:4-5).

It is thus quite correct to stress that in Acts 2 we see repentance (and

---

90. Οὖν is added in the Gospel text, but otherwise the response is identical.

91. Note the reference to joy as a sign of the reception of the Spirit.

92. This is an important point in the reckoning of the date when Acts would likely have been written. Both the primitive Christology and the primitive ecclesiology must count strongly against a second-century dating, at which time we have evidence of things like monarchical bishops, as in the letters of Ignatius of Antioch, or grave concerns about postbaptismal sin. Luke knows about early Christian elders (cf. Acts 20:17) but not bishops, and surely the usual Lukan limiting of the apostles to the Twelve points us to an earlier not a later stage of thinking about such matters.

faith) leading to baptism, the forgiveness of sins, and the reception of the Holy Spirit.[93] This was apparently normally the case. Acts then provides us with a record of "missionary" baptisms, stories about the conversion of those on the outside who are then brought into the family of Christian faith. What Acts does not seem to do is ask or answer the second- and third-generation question of what was appropriate practice in regard to the children of believers, those raised *within* the church.[94]

Notice in *v. 38* that Peter stresses that every one of his audience needed to repent and be baptized. The practice of a onetime baptism of proselytes to Judaism was probably known as early as the A.D. 30s,[95] and more to the point the Baptist went around baptizing those who were already Jews, not just proselytes. The point here is that Peter (and Luke) believes that without change, his Jewish audience faced God's judgment for their sins. They stand in danger of being part of a generation lost because of their corruption *(v. 40)*. Not just outsiders or Gentiles need to be saved, but insiders as well, especially those involved in Jesus' death. Nevertheless, the text stresses that the situation is not irremediable. The promises of God are still "for you, and your children, and those who are far off," meaning the Jewish audience (v. 39), and these promises can bear fruit in their lives if they will repent and believe the gospel about Jesus.

There has been considerable debate about *v. 39*. Who are "those who are far off"? Are they: (1) future generations of Jews; (2) Jews in distant lands; (3) Gentiles? On the one hand, Acts 13:32-33 would seem to suggest that the meaning is Jewish offspring, in this case those not yet born. On the other hand, it is possible that Isa. 57:19 (LXX) is in view where proximity in space is the issue,

93. See, e.g., Polhill, *Acts,* p. 117; Bruce, *The Book of Acts,* pp. 69-71.

94. This is probably another telltale sign of the relative primitiveness of Acts and its composition before the 90s. It is improbable that one can extract a theology of "household" baptisms from a text like Acts 10, if by household one means including infants and very small children. We are not just told that Cornelius gathered his relatives and friends for Peter's coming (v. 24). We are also told that the Holy Spirit fell upon those who *heard the word* (v. 44) and then received baptism (vv. 47-48). A case has also sometimes been made on the basis of the baptism of Lydia's (or the Lydian's) household (16:15) or the reference to the household of the Philippian jailor (16:31-34). The problem with the former text is that it is an argument from silence, since infants and small children are not specifically mentioned, and the problem with using the latter text that way is that 16:32 says Paul spoke the word to *all* the jailor's household and that after they were baptized the *entire* household rejoiced (v. 34). This does not sound like it included infants. A better question would be whether Luke believed that the *faith* of the head of the household provided some sort of inclusion of the rest of the household as well within the fold (cf. 16:31, 34). In any case, the focus in Acts 16 is clearly on the faith of the heads of these households — Lydia and the jailor.

95. See Segal, "Cost of Proselytism and Conversions." For evidence of first-century Jewish proselytes in Jerusalem and possible evidence that some may have become Christians, see the ossuary inscription cited in *New Docs,* 4:268. See now Hengel, *Paul,* pp. 43ff.

and in that text Jews seem surely in view (cf. 57:14, "my people"; Sir. 24:32).[96] Yet in Eph. 2:13, 17 the reference is clearly to Gentiles when the phrase "those who are far off" is used. I would suggest that in view of Luke's geographical approach to history writing and the telling of the story of the early church, probably (2) is what is meant, with (1) as the second most likely possibility. The connection with the Ephesians passage is more remote, as is any connection with later rabbinic use of Isa. 5:19. In any case, it is said that the promise is for everyone, which by implication could include Gentiles — anyone who calls on the name of the Lord, and at the same time anyone whom the Lord calls (v. 39b).

V. 40, as we have pointed out above, is a technical device used in the reporting of rhetorical speeches, in particular in historical works (cf. Polybius 3.111.11; Xenophon, *Hellenica* 2.4.42). Whether Luke actually knew more of this speech, or whether, more likely, his source simply informed him there was a good deal more along the same lines, is not made clear.

V. 41 brings this section of the discussion to a close and provides a certain transition to the summary passage which follows in vv. 42-47. Probably too much has been made over the claim of 3,000 converts. On the one hand, it could just mean that Luke is indicating a surprisingly large number of the crowd responded positively to Peter's call for repentance, faith, and baptism. On the other hand, the number itself is not out of the realm of possibility.

In the first place, the population of Jerusalem at feast time was quite large, perhaps even as high as 180,000 to 200,000, and interestingly enough careful estimates have shown that the temple precincts could even accommodate such a huge crowd.[97] In the second place if there was even close to such numbers in the temple area, 3,000 would have been a distinct minority of the crowd. In the third place, there was ample water supply in Jerusalem, especially at the pools (Bethesda, Siloam), for a large number of baptisms. It is wise not to dismiss such claims when hard evidence to the contrary does not exist. The text, then, suggests that the number of Christian believers swelled from 120 to 3,120 at this time. This no doubt would have drawn the attention of the Jewish authorities rather rapidly, as Acts 3 shows.

C. The People of Pentecost (2:42-47)

Vv. 42-47 provide us with our first summary glimpse at the interior life of the early church. These summaries paint a strongly positive portrait of the early church, and no doubt they were intended to have a certain propaganda value

---

96. See Haenchen, *Acts,* p. 184.
97. See Polhill, *Acts,* p. 118 and n. 135; Jeremias, *Jerusalem,* p. 83.

as Luke intends to convince Theophilus about the true character of the early church when it was at its best, despite its detractors and despisers, both cultured and otherwise. These summary passages are of course retrospective from a historical point of view, and also serve as links or bridging passages from a narrative point of view. As Cadbury points out, they also serve to separate the various episodes in Acts.[98]

It must be stressed, however, that the material that the summaries link together is not unreservedly positive. There are stories about the likes of Ananias and Sapphira or Simon Magus which show that Luke is not trying simply to gild the lily. The Acts of the Apostles is not simply a wistful reverie about the good old days, though clearly its dominant tone is positive. Luke of course writes as a convinced Christian and wishes on the whole to put the church's best foot forward in his account. The point is that he does not entirely neglect the darker side of the early church with its problems, and thus it is wrong to take these summary passages *in isolation* from the source material they link together. Studying the summaries alone leads to distortion and false impressions. The summaries are Lukan creations, but grounded in the best things Luke could find to in good conscience about the early church.[99]

A Closer Look — The Summaries in Acts

It is important to look at the summaries from various angles and ask about their function as a whole in Acts, not just as individual linking passages. It is also useful to distinguish between summary *statements* and summary *passages*. For example, 2:41 is in a sense a summary statement concluding the previous narrative, and 2:42 is probably most naturally taken with what follows as part of a summary passage. Our concern

98. Cadbury, "The Summaries in Acts." As with many ancient historians who used sources extensively, Luke's style of narration is episodic, and this in turn requires certain linking material. See Plümacher, *Lukas als hellenistischer Schriftsteller,* passim.

99. See Hengel, *Paul,* pp. 10ff. The most one could accuse Luke of is that he may have left out too much of the trouble and difficulties the early church experienced. That he did leave a good deal out is shown by any careful reading of Paul's letters. Yet Luke writes knowing the eventual outcome of things like the debate over circumcision (see below, pp. 450ff., on Acts 15), and so he may have felt as a historian that it was pointless to dwell on difficulties and squabbles that eventually were resolved one way or another, or went away and no longer characterized the church in his day. See the balanced assessment of Barrett, *Acts,* vol. 1, p. 166: "In this verse Luke gives an idealized picture of the earliest church — idealized but not for that reason necessarily misleading. . . . The idealizing is in the participle προσκαρτερουντες, and that Luke did not intend it to be understood as unmarked by exceptions is shown by his story of Ananias and Sapphira (5.1-11). There is no ground for doubting the outline of Luke's account; if he had not given it we should doubtless have conjectured something of the kind."

here is primarily with the latter, of which there are a goodly number early on in Acts. In general one may say that summary *statements* are used to link together the narrative panels of Acts (6:7; 9:31; 12:24; 16:5; 19:20), and so the function of summary *passages* must be something else. The *statements,* like the panels they link, are meant to chronicle the spread of the word through the Mediterranean crescent, and as such they function much like similar statements about the spread of the word in Luke's Gospel (cf. Luke 4:37; 7:17; and 4:14).

Cadbury's general observations about the summary statements bear repeating: (1) they are Lukan creations, and are later than the intervening panels they link; (2) they are derived from generalization, probably from some of the specific adjacent material;[100] (3) these summaries are liable to freer treatment than the material they link together and are liable to combination;[101] (4) when the summaries are similar to one another in subject matter (as all the summary *statements* are), this may be due to Luke's well-known tendency to repeat things with certain variations when he is dealing with the same theme on more than one occasion.[102] Cadbury's final remarks deserve to be stressed: "they are undoubtedly pieces of editorial workmanship, devised by the author or his predecessor for the creation of a narrative out of the raw materials. They serve a double purpose — to divide and connect. They give continuity and historical perspective, but they are also of later vintage than the single episodes. . . . They indicate the material is *typical,* that the action was *continued,* that the effect was *general.* They fill in the lacunae . . . they suggest that there was plenty more material of the same kind. . . . Certain items are mentioned with a definiteness and brevity that imply that his knowledge or sources were more complete. In that case the summaries may rest on more information than we ourselves now have access to."[103] This last remark is crucial, for it suggests, as Hengel has elsewhere stressed, that in the case of Luke we are dealing with someone who is basically a condenser of a larger array of source material than he presents in Acts, rather than a creator of stories and statements based on too few, or in some cases no, sources at all.[104]

---

100. This is more evident in some cases than in others, and it seems likely that sometimes the summaries are based on generalizations that Luke received from his sources which are not included in larger form in Acts, and not simply generalizations based on the narratives he includes.

101. This is no doubt because in their present form these summaries are Lukan creations to begin with, unlike a good deal of Luke's material.

102. Cadbury, "The Summaries in Acts," p. 396. Repetition is a key clue to Luke's overall purposes. As Barrett, *Acts,* vol. 1, p. 160, rightly stresses: "the summaries confirm his central theme of the triumph, the irresistible progress of the word of God. The Gospel is accepted by more and more people and the quality of Christian life is maintained and developed in depth and intensity." The last part of this quote applies to the summary passages, the former to the summary statements which do not really deal with the interior life of the early Christian community.

103. Cadbury, "The Summaries in Acts," pp. 401-2. The emphasis is mine. Cadbury is in part quoting himself here from *The Making of Luke-Acts,* pp. 58ff.

104. Cf. Hengel, *History of Earliest Christianity,* pp. 3-34. Luke 1:1-4 certainly suggests a goodly number of predecessors which Luke knew about, and this presumably implies a goodly number of sources for his own work as well.

It will be noted that the summary *passages,* unlike various summary statements, occur in the earlier part of Acts, suggesting perhaps that Luke has fewer and less extensive sources for the earlier period than for what he recounts later in the narrative. His sources only summarized much of these earliest days for him. In particular these summaries have to do with earliest Christian life in *Jerusalem* (2:42-47; 4:32-37; 5:12-16; 8:1b-4). We do not find these sorts of summary paragraphs about the interior life of the early church later in Acts.[105]

Summing up, it is important to distinguish between summary statements and summary passages. The latter occur in the first eight chapters of Acts, the former in various places throughout. A further distinction can be made between summary remarks that link the so-called panels of Acts[106] and remarks which conclude and summarize a particular episode in Acts, such as we find in 2:41. The panel-linking summaries have a very similar theme and vocabulary dealing with the spread of God's word. The other sorts of summary remarks vary considerably. The summary paragraphs tend to share a common theme about the nature of the interior life of the early church, seen at its best. Finally, it should be pointed out that the use of such summary material, including linking summary remarks, is rather typical of ancient historiographical works that were based on research and the use of sources, which were by nature episodic in character.[107]

What I would like to stress about the summary statements between the panels and summary passages which occur only in the first eight chapters of Acts beginning at 2:42 is that the former point out the cause of the existence

---

105. Unless one counts 11:27-30 about Antioch, but this is not so much a generalizing summary as a brief account of a particular incident — Agabus's prophecy prompts a collection for famine relief for the Judean church sent up to Jerusalem by the elders of Antioch by means of Paul and Barnabas.

106. On which see pp. 74ff. above in the introduction.

107. See Fornara, *History in Ancient Greece and Rome,* pp. 47ff. It should be noted that Luke, like Ephorus and Polybius before him, divides the world into geographical regions and proceeds to discuss what is happening in each, one at a time. This inevitably leads to some chronological overlap as well as a necessarily episodic way of dealing with events, hence the need for summaries as connective tissue. "For good or ill, Ephorus's system of topical organization within narrow chronological limits became the norm for Greek writers thereafter. Polybius himself . . . divided the world into distinct theatres and proceeded to discuss each locality" (Fornara, p. 45). Luke is also very much like Herodotus in his belief that the supernatural has a crucial role to play in human history and that it is guided by a divine hand. "As we read Herodotus the conviction grows within us of history unfolding at the silent direction of invisible powers who will interpose themselves on the rare occasion when their will is likely to be thwarted" (Fornara, p. 78). This last sentence could just as easily have been written about Luke's two volumes. Notice how it is at crucial junctures that God directly intervenes beyond familiar miracles or providential happenings (e.g., at the conversion of Paul, or at a crucial turning point in the missionary work — 16:7-9).

and growth of the Christian community, while the latter deal with the interior life of the community.[108] They serve different but related functions and purposes.

That *v. 42* is transitional is shown by the fact that some of its content seems to be repeated in *v. 44*, the bit about sharing in common.[109] The converts are said to devote themselves to four things: (1) the teaching of the apostles, (2) κοινωνια, (3) the breaking of bread, and (4) prayer. R. Pesch has suggested, perhaps rightly, that in fact only two things are really mentioned here, teaching and κοινωνια, with the latter further defined as involving the breaking of bread and prayer.[110] I tend to think this suggestion is correct.

The term κοινωνια is found only here in all of Luke-Acts, though the idea is common. The term itself means a participation or sharing in common of something with someone else, in this case eating and praying.[111] Thus, fellowship is not a very helpful translation, for fellowship is the result of κοινωνια, of sharing in common; it is not the κοινωνια itself. Κοινωνια is an activity which can result in fellowship of some sort, and it can entail things like sharing not just spiritual activities such as prayer but also physical food or other goods in common (v. 45, cf. 4:32-37).[112]

The phrase "the breaking of bread" could refer to an ordinary meal, especially in view of the fact that this was the act which opened a Jewish meal, though the phrase was not a technical term in Judaism for such a meal.[113] On the other hand, Theophilus will already have heard about the Last Supper meal in the first volume, and perhaps more importantly about the recognition of Jesus at the breaking of the bread in the (for Luke) crucial Emmaus road resurrection appearance story (Luke 24:35), which suggests Luke emphasizes the connection between Jesus' presence and such meals (cf. Luke 24:41-42; Acts 1:4; 10:41).[114] Furthermore, texts like Acts 2:42, 46 and 20:7, 11 all suggest that this sort of breaking of bread was part of an act of worship that involved

108. There are of course summaries at the ends of particular narratives as well, such as we find in 2:41, and they function rather diferently than the summaries between the panels. The former narrative summaries are more particular, the latter more general in character, but sometimes both deal with growth, as is the case with 2:41. Cadbury, "The Summaries in Luke-Acts," p. 400, notes this difference.

109. This may suggest that v. 42 is the end of the source, and triggered Luke's creating of the summary that follows on the basis of general reports he had about the early church fellowship in Jerusalem.

110. See Pesch, *Die Apostelgeschichte (1–12)*, p. 130.

111. On the meaning of κοινωνια see my discussion in *Conflict and Community in Corinth*, pp. 224-25, and the fundamental study by Seesemann, *Der Begriff Koinonia im Neuen Testament*.

112. For various sorts of uses of the term, cf. 1 Cor. 10:16 and 2 Cor. 9:13.

113. See Marshall, *Acts*, p. 83, and Barrett *Acts*, vol. 1, p. 165.

114. See Johnson, *Acts*, p. 58.

eating, praying, teaching, and singing in homes, to mention but a few elements of the service. On the whole, then, the phrase "the breaking of bread" seems to be a primitive way of alluding to the Lord's Supper, though it cannot be ruled out that the reference is to an ordinary meal.[115] The disciples are then said to be devoted both to teaching and sharing meals and prayers (plural here) in common in v. 42.

Vv. 43-47 suggest in general that in the earliest days of the Christian community, the Jewish followers of Jesus did not in any full way separate themselves from their Jewish context and heritage, but rather participated in it, going regularly (day by day) to the temple (5:12 says they met in Solomon's portico). At the same time, they were generally highly esteemed by many of their fellow Jews (cf. 2:46; 5:13), in part apparently due to the performance of signs and wonders — in short, miracles. No doubt they were recognized by other pious Jews as having zeal for their faith. Teaching, preaching, miracles, meals, sharing of goods, and worship are said in general to characterize the early church, and no doubt this is an accurate historical summation, but one that needs a little more unpacking.

In *v. 43* and elsewhere (cf. Luke 1:12, 65; 7:16; Acts 5:5, 11; 19:17) the term φοβος is used to refer to religious awe, which is said, because of the signs and wonders (cf. 4:30; 5:12), to come upon παση ψυχη, which presumably refers not just to the disciples but to both them and their audience ("everyone," cf. v. 47).[116] Luke clearly believes in the evidential value and effect of miracles in attesting to the authenticity of God's work in the lives of Jesus' followers.

Vv. 44-45 should be taken together. The phrase επι το αυτο is an important one, and it appears both here and in v. 47 (as well as elsewhere in the first four chapters of Acts, cf. 1:15; 2:1; 4:26). The intent of using the phrase is to say something about the unity or togetherness of the early Christians, even if its precise translation may be debated. Usually it seems to mean something like "together," or in v. 47 "in the community," or "with one accord" or "in assembly."[117] It refers to a gathered group in harmony with one another.

---

115. The social significance of this portrait needs to be stressed. The early Christians met in homes and treated each other as family, sharing meals and possessions as well as more spiritual and verbal fare. Theophilus would likely have thought of the Greco-Roman banquet or συμποσιον, which would have involved teaching and discussion after the meal. Jews had already adopted such Greek customs, even before the time of the early church (cf., e.g., Luke 7:36-50, "he reclined at table" — or is Luke Hellenizing this narrative?). For a more detailed discussion of Greco-Roman meal customs, cf. my *Conflict and Community in Corinth,* pp. 191ff., 241ff., and on evidence outside of Acts that meals were a significant part of early Christian worship and sharing, cf. 1 Cor. 11:17-26. Note that in this last text Paul begins by discussing a meal which is to include the Lord's Supper, and ends by discussing the details of the tradition about the latter.

116. Yet another example of an "all" word; cf. pp. 106ff. above.

117. Much the same as εν εκκλησια; cf. 1 Cor. 11:18 *and* 20.

Interestingly, the Hebrew equivalent *(hayahad)* is something of a technical term for the community at Qumran (cf. 1QS 1:1; 3:7).

V. 44 also tells us that this group of Christians were not just in accord, but also shared all things in common. This is explained more fully in v. 45 to mean that they would sell their possessions and real estate and distribute the proceeds to any who had need. The imperfect verb tense here suggests this was not a onetime occurrence but rather a recurrent past practice, presumably undertaken whenever need arose.[118] The practice is described more fully in another summary passage at 4:32-35, and we will deal with the early church's sharing of goods more fully there.[119] Here it is sufficient to point out that taken together, vv. 44-45 do not at all suggest what we would call communism, or some sort of system where there was no such thing as private property. Rather, what is described here is that no one was claiming any exclusive right to whatever property he or she had, and when need arose the early Christians readily liquidated what assets they had to take care of fellow believers' needs. That this is the right interpretation of what Luke is saying here becomes clearer in Acts 4:32–5:11, especially when Ananias and Sapphira are upbraided *not* because they did not give all (Peter says it was still theirs to give or not to give) but because they lied about the amount they gave.

The description here of the early Christians is much like the proverbial Hellenistic commonplace that friends share all things in common (cf. Plato, *Republic* 449C; Aristotle, *Nic. Ethics* 1168B; Philo, *Abr.* 235). What is interesting about this for our purposes is that while this idea was commonly associated with utopian societies in the Greco-Roman world,[120] it was an idea already being actually practiced in some form at Qumran (cf. 1QS 5:1-3; CD 9:1-15), but there the motivation was the demands of ritual purity (and avoiding sin and temptation), not an ideal of friendship (see 1QS 9:3-11).[121] Theophilus, if he was at all literate, would likely have known about the Greco-Roman thoughts about such ideal communities, and this feature of early Christianity he may have found attractive, especially if it meant that he, like a Barnabas, might become a benefactor to the community to help the less fortunate.[122] In

---

118. *BDF* para. 367 — αν with the imperfect indicates habitual past action. The imperfect tense thus suggests that in Luke's day such practices were no longer followed, or were very rare. See Barrett, *Acts,* vol. 1, p. 169.

119. See pp. 204ff. below.

120. See van der Horst, "Hellenistic Parallels to the Acts of the Apostles," p. 59.

121. Here I am following Johnson, *Acts,* p. 59. Above all it must be kept in mind both in the case of the Qumran community and of the earliest Christian community in Jerusalem we are talking about a rather small, tightly knit group, in other words a group in which such total sharing was actually possible in many ways, not merely an ideal.

122. See the helpful discussion of the notions of benefaction in early Christianity in Winter, *Seek the Welfare.*

any case, a "Hellenistic reader would recognize in Luke's description the sort of 'foundation story' that was rather widespread in Hellenistic literature."[123]

Vv. 46-47 indicate that Christians were meeting daily together, sharing food "from house to house," which might suggest they rotated where they ate, or more likely that since there were a goodly number they did this sharing in various homes.[124] But they also had a public face, spending much time together in the temple. Luke does not say clearly here that this was at least in part for witnessing, though that is surely implied by the earlier portion of Acts 2 and v. 47 as well perhaps. These early Christians were characterized by having glad and sincere hearts that prompted praise of God, and goodwill among the local Jews in general. The result was that daily God added those who were being saved to this community. Its presence and witness were infectious. This summary description may also mean the early Christians had not yet fully worked out the implications of Christ's death, if their time in the temple also involved offering sacrifices of something other than praise. Clearly at this stage the followers of Jesus are being portrayed by Luke as true, messianic Jews, attempting to rescue other Jews so they might be part of a righteous remnant of Israel, the eschatological people of God.

123. Johnson, *Acts,* p. 62; cf. especially Plato, *Critias* 110C-D, who speaks of a time when "none of its members possessed any private property, but they regarded all they had as the common property of all."

124. As Barrett, *Acts,* vol. 1, p. 170, notes, the reference to daily meals means we are not talking about some sort of weekly celebration of the Lord's Supper. Furthermore, we are probably not referring to just one meeting with everyone present, which would surely have been impossible even if there were only a few hundred Christians at this point, for even larger homes would not accommodate them.

IV. The Mighty Work, the Mighty Word, the Mighty Ones (Acts 3:1–4:22)

The material in Acts 3:1–8:3 has to do with the life of the early church in Jerusalem, and the simultaneous growing opposition to it on the part of Jewish officials and popular support for it that continued to increase. The first major subunit of this material deals with the subject of a healing which prompts preaching, both of which lead to the preachers being brought before Jewish authorities. That we are at an end of the first subunit is shown by the final reference to the healed man in 4:22. In general, Luke goes back and forth between relating, on the one hand, the public life and controversies of the early Christians with outsiders and, on the other, telling of the interior life and difficulties within the community itself. As with Acts 2, we have in Acts 3–4 a drama in essentially three parts.

A. The Mighty Work (3:1-10)

The summary in 2:42-47 can now be seen to be clearly prospective in character, for we find in Acts 3:1-10 two key elements mentioned there: (1) attendance at temple worship by Christians; (2) the mighty works of the apostles. To this one might also add Peter's denial of any personal funds in 3:6, which could be seen as an example of the kind of thing referred to in 2:43, and also the mention of many believing (cf. 2:41, 47 to 4:4).[1] In general, the major actions

---

1. So Tannehill, *Narrative Unity of Luke-Acts*, 2:48.

164

in the book of Acts are precipitated by what Christian leaders either say or do, with the words of the apostles actually seen as a form of action. Something should be said at this point about Luke's use of sources in Acts, for it is widely agreed that it seems especially apparent in Acts 3 that he is using them.[2]

A Closer Look — Luke's Use of Sources in Acts

Most scholars are still willing to recognize that Luke must have used sources in Acts, as he clearly did in his Gospel, even if the sources in Acts are much more difficult to delineate since we have no similar written Christian source from this period with which to compare Acts.[3] I have argued elsewhere that there is no good reason to suspect that Luke's historical methodology or the way he treated his sources in Acts was radically different from the way he handled his Gospel material. Indeed, the various parallels between the two volumes, including the *tendency* in both volumes to deal with blocks of material as a whole without dividing them up (e.g., in Acts a Peter block, or a Philip block), point us in this direction.[4] Furthermore, since at least some of the events Luke records in Acts probably overlap with his own lifetime, it may be suspected that his sources for Acts may have been even fresher, more firsthand than the material he conveys in his Gospel (see below).

Though a good deal has been made through the years of Luke's interest in hospitality and lodging, not enough has been said or done to suggest a connection

---

2. See the discussion in Zehnle, *Peter's Pentecost Discourse,* pp. 71ff.; Lüdemann, *Early Christianity,* pp. 49-55; and Barrett, *Acts,* vol. 1, pp. 187ff., on this particular passage. Some of the things usually pointed to as indicating the use of a source in Acts 3 are: (1) the grammatical awkwardness of several verses (e.g., 16 and 20); (2) some of the particulars in the text (e.g., the reference to the Beautiful Gate); (3) some of the christological terms used (Jesus as the Righteous One, or as the Author of Life); (4) some of the eschatological language, especially in v. 20; (5) the reference to John (what would be the point of Luke introducing him into the narrative since he plays no active role in Acts 3–4?). I agree with Johnson, *Acts,* p. 73, that the awkwardnesses in Acts 3 suggest the *compression* of source material, not its expansion, for if Luke was simply creating material we would not expect these sorts of infelicities, for he is capable of very good Greek. I also agree with Barrett, *Acts,* vol. 1, pp. 175ff., that the grammatical difficulties suggest that we are dealing (in the Alexandrian family of manuscripts) with an unrevised version of Acts, while the Western text does its best to smooth out various infelicities and explain numerous obscurities, and these tendencies point to its later provenance. We must reckon with the possibility that while Luke's Gospel was indeed revised and sent (it has far fewer grammatical, syntactical, and textual difficulties), Acts may have been completed but either never sent, or perhaps more likely it never underwent a final revision before it was sent.

3. See, for example, the discussion of sources in Acts in the last generation by Dupont, *The Sources of Acts,* and more recently by Lüdemann, *Early Christianity,* and M. E. Boismard and A. Lamouille, *Les Actes des deux Apôtres.* This later work is far too atomistic in approach.

4. See my "Editing the Good News."

between this interest and Luke's sources. It will be in order to show briefly the interest in lodgings of Christians in Acts. The first Christian prayer meeting takes place somewhere in Jerusalem in an upstairs room where some of the apostles were staying (1:13). One of the first mentions of what appears to be clearly a church meeting after Pentecost is said to take place "in the house of Mary" (mother of John Mark — 12:12). What is said to epitomize the early church is that Christians break bread from house to house (κατ' οικον, 2:46). On many occasions Luke mentions a person's name solely because he was a host to Peter or Paul or some other Christian missionary (cf. 9:43, Simon the tanner; 17:5-9, Jason; 21:8-9, Philip and his daughters, where the main concern is that Paul stayed with them; 21:16, Mnason; 28:7, Publius). On two occasions we are given complete addresses of where Peter or Paul stayed (9:11 — Judas, Strait Street, Damascus; 10:5-6 — Simon the tanner's, House-by-the-Sea, Joppa). There are also other occasions when Luke's main concern is not with lodging or hospitality but these things are mentioned in passing, for instance: (1) Paul's lodgings in Rome (28:16, 23, 30); (2) Paul's lodging in Corinth with Priscilla and Aquila (18:2-3, cf. v. 7); and Paul's hosts in Philippi (16:14-15, Lydia; 16:34, jailor's house). Luke also mentions various places where Peter and Paul teach or heal but do not stay: (1) upper room in Lydda (9:37-40); (2) upper room in Troas (20:7-8; the purpose of the meeting is "breaking bread"); (3) the lecture hall of Tyrannus in Ephesus (19:9). Finally, we may mention Luke's often debated use of the verb συναλιζομαι, which may mean "to eat with" (1:4).

While much more could be made of Luke's interest in what could be called the mundane social settings and actions of Christians,[5] it is in order to ask here: *Why* is Luke so interested in such matters as lodging, eating, and hospitality in general? A long time ago D. W. Riddle suggested that these people and places are mentioned not in order to "historicize" an otherwise generic and nondescriptive group of narratives or to provide them with an air of verisimilitude, but to recognize those who helped in the early days in the transmission of the gospel and other early church traditions.[6] Luke's second volume is about the spread of the word and those who made it possible.[7] Thus these people (and their places of lodging), who are not significant actors in the story itself (sometimes *only* their name is mentioned), are referred to as vital supports to the movement. Lodging is important not just because it provided a place where missionaries could rest but also because it provided a venue where Christians could meet, eat, pray, preach, and relate stories about the movement. In short, these residences may well have become places where oral and written Christian traditions were not just passed on but also collected. As various missionaries would pass through, more news would be passed on, not only about the life of Jesus but also about current events

---

5. See especially Elliott, "Temple vs. Household in Luke-Acts." Elliott definitely overdoes the contrast element, since the earliest Christians in Jerusalem (in Acts 1–8) are not seen as at odds with the temple. Rather, they worship and preach and heal there as well as elsewhere. In Luke's view, the problem for early Christians comes from Jewish authorities in the Sanhedrin (including Saul) and from some other Jerusalem Jews. The temple is not seen as problematic in itself.

6. Riddle, "Early Christian Hospitality."

7. See pp. 157ff. above about the summary statements between the so-called panels in Acts.

involving Christians, and, when prophets spoke, about future events as well. We can see this very process at work in Acts 11:27-30. Thus we may see hospitality not only as the physical support that kept the message going but also as the medium in which the message took hold and was preserved.

All of this has some bearing on evaluating Luke's use of sources, especially if, as we have already argued, he was following in the tradition of the better Hellenistic historians who believed in research, consulting eyewitnesses, gathering up information, and in general the use of sources (cf. Luke 1:1-4).[8] Luke was necessarily limited by the sources he had, which goes some way to explaining the lopsidedness of Acts, with its heavy concentration on Petrine and Pauline material. Clearly enough there was not time enough to ask everyone about everything, but as he traveled around and benefited from Christian hospitality in various places, what could be more natural than that he asked his hosts or hostesses while breaking bread with them what and whom they had known?

We will not have occasion to give a full argument about the "we" passages in Acts until later in this commentary,[9] but it must be said that once one takes seriously the idea that Luke was writing as a Hellenistic historian, one who did research and especially valued any opportunity to participate in the events about which he would write, it becomes highly probable, as classics scholars and ancient historians such as A. D. Nock have pointed out, that the "we" passages represent an eyewitness source.[10] That Luke, a companion of Paul, is giving his own personal reminiscences in these "we" passages is also the conclusion of an important recent detailed monograph by C. J. Thornton.[11] Polybius himself says he varied the personal references in his histories at points when he was involved in what was happening, but clearly he felt obliged to let his reader know when he was present (36.12).[12] I would suggest that in the "we" passages we are dealing with Luke's expansion of his own notes taken while traveling with Paul.[13]

Let us then suppose that the familiar and still common hypothesis is correct that Luke was a sometime companion of Paul during parts of the second and third Pauline missionary journeys recorded in Acts. We note that the "we" shows up for the first time in Troas (16:11).[14] Notice that it is said in Acts 20:6-7 that this is where Paul

8. On all this see pp. 24ff. in the introduction.

9. See pp. 480ff. below. We have already partially addressed this matter, pp. 51ff. above.

10. See pp. 59ff. above.

11. See Thornton, *Der Zeuge des Zeugen. Lukas als Historiker der Paulusreisen.*

12. See pp. 28ff. above. Thucydides is also fastidious about indicating in his narrative the points when he was present.

13. See rightly, Jervell, "The Future of the Past," p. 117: "The rule of ancient historiography, the *autopsia*, is followed as Luke indicates that he personally had taken part in some of the reported events. . . . There is a wealth of details in these sections compared to other parts of Acts, even details with no significance for his account. . . . We can safely assume that Luke took notes when events happened and used his notes years later. On this point he met the standards of historiography, at least formally."

14. I am discounting the reference in the Western text of Acts 11:28, as most scholars do. It is suspicious, in view of the later traditions that Luke was from Antioch and that the Western text has a singular "we" reference here. See Metzger, *Textual Commentary,* p. 391. On the supposed connection of Luke with Antioch, see pp. 51ff. in the Introduction and Hengel, *Paul,* p. 19.

stayed for a week on his third missionary journey. Notice next that in the first sequence of "we" passages after leaving Troas Paul and his companions went to Philippi. The "we" has its last mention in Philippi at 16:16 before Paul and Silas are incarcerated. That is, Luke is not claiming to have been with Paul when he went on to Thessalonica, Beroea, Athens, Corinth, and then finally back to Antioch. There is nothing in this material to associate Luke with Antioch, but much to associate him with Troas or Philippi or both.[15] It is surely not a pure accident that the "we" recurs again precisely at Philippi (20:5-6), and then involves a week's stay in Troas. I would suggest that this intimates that either Philippi, or less probably Troas, was at one time the home of the author of Luke-Acts, and if it was Troas, Paul may have stayed with Luke there. There is clear evidence from Greek epitaphs of peripatetic doctors who traveled around the Mediterranean practicing their trade, and Luke may well have been one of them.[16] After the occasion recorded in Acts 20:7-12, Luke is then a traveling companion with Paul for the balance of the events recorded in Acts.

If indeed the "we" passages reflect the author's own experience, what could Luke have known and what sort of information could he have gathered during his travels with Paul? First, he would have had personal experience of what Paul and others said and did in Troas and Philippi. Secondly, he would have had personal experience of most of what is recorded from Acts 20:7 on, and where he was not directly present he could have gotten most of the remaining information from Paul.[17] Equally importantly, in his travels with Paul the author is said to have stopped in the following places — Miletus, Tyre, Ptolemais, Caesarea Maritima, Jerusalem, Myra in Lycia, Fair Havens on Crete, Malta, Syracuse, Rhegium, and then Puteoli and Rome in Italy itself.

Some of the above locations (e.g., Malta) are of little or no help in reconstructing what sources Luke may have drawn on, but some are enormously suggestive. At Miletus Luke was in touch with the Ephesian church officials, who presumably were in a position to tell Luke about Apollos's visit to Ephesus when Paul was not present there (Acts 18:24-28). At Tyre, where he is said to have stayed for seven days, it is not impossible that he learned things about the church up the coast in Antioch, things which he may not have been able to learn from Paul (e.g., cf. Acts 11:19-24), who was certainly there periodically (Gal. 2:11-14). Much more crucial is the lengthy stay in the Holy Land, lasting about two years and involving visits to both Jerusalem and Caesarea. During this particular period of time Luke could have learned about many (if not all?) of the things recorded in Acts 1–8.

15. For conjectures about the true "yokefellow" of Phil. 4:3 being Luke, see my *Friendship and Finances in Philippi* (Valley Forge, Pa.: Trinity, 1994), pp. 106ff.

16. See *New Docs*, 2:10-21, especially pp. 19-21. As Horsley suggests, if Paul practiced his trade while traveling on his journeys, it is reasonable to expect that his companions did so as well. One wonders if Luke became Paul's more regular companion after the second missionary journey due to the apostle's health needs (cf., e.g., Gal. 4:13; 2 Corinthians 11).

17. There may of course be exceptions to this rule. For example, it is hard to see how either Luke or Paul could have known what Festus said to Agrippa because neither seems to have been present on that occasion (Acts 25:13-22). This may well be an example of the composition of speech material on the basis of conjecture about what they *must* have or were likely to have discussed.

For example, we are told quite explicitly that Paul, Luke, and others stayed with Philip for several days, during which time the material in Acts 8 could easily have been gathered. The time in Jerusalem and Caesarea could have given Luke personal contact with the mother church in Jerusalem and possibly with a variety of key figures (James, Mary the mother of John Mark, Mary Magdalene, Joanna [from whom he could have gotten stories about the Herods], and possibly even the mother of Jesus herself). Even if Luke was not able to consult such major figures, he could at least have talked to other eyewitnesses and those who knew these named early Christian figures. In short, one way or another most of the information found in Acts 1–8 could have resulted from such time in Jerusalem in contact with eyewitnesses or those who had known them.

It is also very possible that during his time in the area of Caesarea Luke gathered together certain other Petrine traditions the Jerusalem church may not have known about (at least not in full). For example, Luke could have gathered the Cornelius material while in Caesarea, and he could with very little travel have gone to Joppa and Lydda while waiting for Paul's case to be resolved.[18] Indeed, he could even have traveled on to Damascus and Antioch during this time, but nothing in the "we" passages really suggests such a trip. Of course, all this is conjecture, but at least it is conjecture that has a starting point in the text of Acts itself.

There are telltale signs in the way Luke handles his information that Luke was not in the business of making up the story of the early church as he went along, but rather was limited to and by his sources. For example, we see the same sort of block quotation of source material that we find in the Gospels: (1) in Acts 1:12–5:42 we have a block of material which has as its overwhelmingly dominant character Peter; (2) in Acts 6–7 we have the prologue to and then the story of Stephen; (3) in Acts 8:4-40 we have a block about Philip; (4) in Acts 9:32–12:23 we have a Petrine block (though here the focus is not Jerusalem), with only the interruption in 11:19-30 of an Antioch block of material; (5) in Acts 13–14 we have a block of Paul and Barnabas material. All of this bespeaks a person wrestling with and trying to integrate sources, not composing them from scratch.

Notice, then, what Luke has done. After the introductory material found in Acts 1:1-11, which involves a new prologue and a recapitulation of material found in Luke 24 in a new form, Luke has interspersed some summary passages (2:43-47; 4:32-37)[19] into the above blocks of material, but basically left the blocks intact with rare interruptions. Doubtless he has edited the whole material and has made efforts in the handling of all the sources to put them into his own words, and into a form suitable for his audience. Since Luke knew the most about Paul, having more Pauline traditions than anything else, and since he intends to focus his narrative in due course on this person whom he sees, humanly speaking, as a pivotal figure, it is not surprising that

---

18. It must be remembered that Luke would not have arrived in Jerusalem until the late 50s, and some eyewitnesses were likely by then off the scene, such as Peter, and some (such as James son of Zebedee, Acts 12:1-2) will have died. It is not, however, convincing to argue that all the eyewitnesses were dead or gone by the late 50s. On the chronological issues, cf. pp. 77ff. above and pp. 817ff. below.

19. On which see pp. 157ff. above.

Pauline material is briefly introduced at 8:1-4, in preparation for 9:1-31 and for all that follows from Acts 13 on in the book. As Tannehill has shown, Luke is very concerned with the flow of his narrative, and his transitions do not tend to be abrupt. He will introduce a subject one way or another (for example, in summary passages, or by brief reference; cf. Acts 6:5 to 8:5) before he intends to treat it more fully.[20]

If we analyze the above carefully, it is not hard to see that Luke does not seem to have had or to have needed a vast amount of sources to compose Acts as we have it. Primarily, he needed to consult Paul extensively, and make good use of his time in Jerusalem and Caesarea, and perhaps in Miletus. Almost everything in Acts 1–28 can be accounted for on this basis. Even the fact that Luke apparently did not have occasion to go to Antioch during the third missionary journey could be compensated for either by what he may have learned while in Tyre or more probably what he could have learned from someone like Nicolaus, a proselyte of Antioch who is mentioned as being in Jerusalem at Acts 6:5.[21] My point is simply this: *the "we" passages in Acts ostensibly bring the author into enough contact with primary persons and locations to account for all that we have in this book.* This fact should not be lightly dismissed. Had Luke been inventing as he went along, we might have expected a book which was more nearly "the Acts of the Apostles" than this one is. Even the two major figures, Peter and Paul, come in for short shrift when it comes to explaining what happened to them in the end.

There is one more factor that needs to be brought into play.[22] As most scholars agree, not only does Acts say nothing about Paul as a letter writer, it seems to reflect little if any knowledge of Paul's letters, with the possible exception of some of the Captivity Epistles, which I would argue were written from Rome. If one studies the Pauline chronology I have outlined above[23] and compares it to the "we" passages in Acts, Luke was not in a position to be present when Paul wrote *any* of the earlier so-called capital Pauline letters, nor was he in places where he could have read them. We have no evidence he was in Galatia, Thessalonica, or Corinth. When he got to Rome, he could perhaps have found or heard about a copy of Romans, but Acts shows little evidence of it.[24] Acts ends in Rome, and very little is said about the church there, hence there was little opportunity to show a knowledge of Romans. If, however, Luke was with Paul while he was in Rome (cf. Col. 4:14), he could have been present when the Captivity Epistles were written.[25]

---

20. See Tannehill, *Narrative Unity of Luke-Acts,* vol. 2 passim.

21. Acts 8:1 of course suggests that all but the apostles (or leadership?) were scattered from Jerusalem by Saul the persecutor, but they are not said to have gone far — Judea and Samaria! The "all" is probably yet another Lukan example of rhetorical cliche or hyperbole. Cf. pp. 105ff. above.

22. See Hemer, *Book of Acts,* pp. 244ff.

23. See pp. 77ff. above.

24. I do not say none, for there are verses like Acts 3:26 that, when compared to Rom. 1:16, may suggest that he had heard Romans.

25. Prof. Dunn has recently suggested to a colleague of mine that Luke may have written even Colossians at Paul's request, in view of certain parallels of grammar, syntax, vocabulary, and thought. I consider this a distinct possibility.

Finally, if Luke was, as some scholars think, a third- or fourth-generation Christian who wrote in the very late 80s, 90s, or even later, and if he was someone who revered Paul, it is hard for me to doubt that he would have sought out and used at least some of the capital Paulines. As H. Y. Gamble has recently stressed, there is good reason to think there was a collection of many of Paul's letters already at the end of the first century A.D., a collection which had circulated through a considerable portion of the areas where Paul founded churches. For example, Clement of Rome, Ignatius of Antioch, and Polycarp of Smyrna all reflect knowledge of several Pauline letters, in the late first or early second century, and 2 Pet. 3:15-16 already suggests an early collection of these letters, as does the canon list of Marcion, which mentions ten Pauline letters.[26] Yet Luke shows little or no sign of knowing or using the sort of valuable source material found in the capital Paulines, even in the Pauline speech material, with the possible exception of the Miletus speech. Of course, since the Miletus speech is the only Pauline speech really addressed to Christians in Acts, it is not surprising that it is the one that sounds something like the Paul of the letters. Yet even in the case of this speech, if Luke was present to hear it as the "we" passages suggest, even this speech need not suggest Luke knew some of the capital Pauline letters.

The upshot of all that I have said in this excursus is that on the basis of the evidence of Acts itself, while no view is without difficulties, it is surely easier to believe in a Luke who is a sometime companion of Paul but does not know Paul's early letters than it is to believe in a third-generation Luke who sees Paul as his hero, uses sources extensively, *but can't find any of Paul's main letters to use.* At the same time it is right to stress that Acts reflects a certain distance from the events it records, which makes a dating of this work in the 60s quite unlikely. Luke, with the benefit of hindsight, leaves out many of the indications of major fights and tensions in the early church that Paul's early letters reflect. He also barely mentions the collection and does not make Paul's apostleship a real issue. This is believable if Luke wrote at least a couple of decades after the events spoken of in Paul's earlier letters transpired, that is, in the 70s after the fall of Jerusalem or in the 80s, but much less believable if he wrote in the 60s.

It is interesting to me that in the very letters Luke might have been in a place to know something about, those written from captivity in Rome (e.g., Philippians, Philemon, Colossians, and Ephesians if it is by Paul), and possibly also Romans, we do not find Paul's apostleship and authority, the Judaizers, or the collection as major issues. Notably in Philippians Paul introduces himself as a servant in the prescript, while in Philemon he calls himself a prisoner (or one in chains). In these other documents Paul's apostleship is mentioned but not made a point of debate or controversy. In short, the attention Luke gives to the matter of Paul's apostleship (cf. Acts 14) is not much less than we find in these letters.

One must balance the obvious distance from the early events recorded in Acts with the more detailed and extensive knowledge of the events of the period A.D. 57ff. that involved Paul especially.[27] Also, one must account for the lack of knowledge of

---

26. See the helpful discussion in Gamble, *Books and Readers,* pp. 58-59, 98-101.
27. See especially Hemer, *Book of Acts,* pp. 101-220.

Paul's earlier letters. What best comports with all this is positing a second-generation Christian who was a sometime companion of Paul and wrote in the 70s or early 80s. If he had been in his thirties when he first traveled with Paul in the 50s, then he would only have been in his 60s by about A.D. 80.

This somewhat lengthy discussion of Luke's use of sources and the implications they have for a variety of issues must be brought to a close by discussing briefly Luke's actual means of composing Acts. It was a standard procedure for ancient historians to compose a υπομνημα, a detailed outline or series of notes arranged in chronological order which would then be filled out when it was time to compose the document itself.[28] It is not hard to imagine Luke composing such a υπομνημα during his travels with Paul, especially during the third missionary journey with its long lag times in Caesarea and then in Rome.[29]

Probably Luke composed his two-part work in chronological sequence on two papyrus rolls,[30] with Acts being written at some distance in time after the first volume had already been sent to Theophilus.[31] I would suggest that, as with many ancient volumes, we must not think of modern publication methods, but rather of a somewhat narrow circulation for a considerable period of time, perhaps in Rome alone among Theophilus's friends and the Christian community.

We must be able to account for two puzzling facts about the reception of Acts in the later church: (1) Why it is that Acts appears largely unknown in the second century and, in the case of some Christian writers of the period, entirely unknown. In fact, before Chrysostom in the fourth century wrote his famous homilies few seem to cite or know about Acts. At the least it does not seem to have been an influential document. (2) Why we have two very different major textual traditions of Acts. I would suggest these two facts are related to each other. Acts was relatively little known or used in the second and into the third century A.D. and was not the subject of controversies in the way various other NT documents came to be, partly due to its narrow

28. See Cohen, *Josephus in Galilee and Rome,* pp. 22-23, 235.

29. See rightly Jervell, "The Future of the Past." It is much less likely that Luke was composing while traveling, for he needed to sift and integrate his sources, rewriting them in his own style. The preface in Luke 1:1-4 suggests a period of writing after others have written *and* after having carefully reflected on "the events that have been fulfilled among us." Nevertheless, the parallels L. C. A. Alexander, "The Pauline Itinerary and the Archives of Theophanes" (SNTS Lecture, Strassburg, 1996), has produced for the keeping of a travel diary (with notation of stopping points and expenditures) as a tool for later fuller composition is important.

30. See pp. 51ff. above.

31. This was also the view of Hawkins, *Horae Synopticae,* pp. 177-82, on the grounds of some of the differences in vocabulary and style in Luke and Acts. He was not referring to differences caused by subject matter (such as the more Semitic material in Luke 1–2), but rather he asked, "Would it be at all likely that an author . . . would so alter his style in two nearly contemporaneous books as e.g. to drop ειπεν δε, εν τω with the infinitive, and και αυτος, to take to μεν ουν, τε κελευειν, and συνερχομαι, and to substitute the infinitive for the finite verb after εγενετο, to an extent that has now appeared? We thus have some internal evidence in favor of placing Luke at a considerably earlier date than Acts."

circulation.[32] This relative obscurity allowed a major second-century revision of Acts, namely, the Western text, to develop unchecked and without correction. Only at the time of Irenaeus and Chrysostom does Acts emerge from its obscurity and begin to be more widely used by Christians, but by then the two major textual traditions had had a long time to develop and become established (Irenaeus, for example, knows the Western text), with claims to antiquity and authenticity.

It is important to note that the miracle referred to in 3:1-10 has notable parallels with Jesus' healing of the paralytic in Luke 5:17-26. Jesus' healing follows his calling of his first disciples (5:1-11), while the first Acts miracle follows the first account of converts to the Christian movement in Acts 2. It is equally important to note the parallels between this story and that of Paul's healing of the man lame from birth in Acts 14:8-18. The essential difference between the healing by Peter and that by Jesus is that Peter performs the act "in the name of Jesus," whereas Jesus neither invokes nor needs such a formula. The miracles the apostles perform are not different in kind from those Jesus performed.

We are told in *3:1* that Peter and John were going up to the temple. Though there are theoretically at least two Johns this could refer to (John, son of Zebedee, or John Mark), one must take into account that the only John thus far mentioned in Acts as a disciple is John the apostle, who in 1:13 is closely associated with Peter and James (Zebedee). More importantly, Theophilus or any hearer of the first volume would surely assume that the reference was to the John associated with Peter in the first volume (cf. Luke 5:8-10; 6:14; 9:28; 22:8; and Acts 3:11; 4:13; 8:14). They went to the temple at the hour of prayer which accompanied the evening sacrifice, about 3 P.M.[33] Here again is clear evidence that the earliest Christians continued to live as observant Jews, probably still offering sacrifices in the temple.[34] The implications of Jesus' death in regard to such Jewish practices was not understood in these earliest days.

V. 2 refers to a man who was "lame from the womb," that is, from birth, which meant he could not fully participate in temple worship (cf. Lev. 21:17-20;

32. On the whole, the apocryphal Acts do not appear to be imitations of our Acts, but rather examples of the biographical and hagiographical genres. See Bauckham, "The *Acts of Paul*," who is right to distinguish the genre of these later Acts from the canonical Acts. I am less persuaded than Bauckham of any real influence of the canonical Acts on these later biographical works.

33. Note that Josephus confirms that the ninth hour was the time of these events (cf. *Ant.* 14.65). This sacrifice was called the *Tamid*; cf. Num. 28:4.

34. And Luke stresses this fact. He is concerned to establish that early Christianity grew out of early Judaism and so had a right to claim that the promises in the Hebrew Scriptures were indeed fulfilled in Jesus and were being fulfilled in their movement.

2 Sam. 5:8; *m. Shab.* 6:8). It also means his instant healing is all the more miraculous. The timing and location of the placement of this man show the intent was to maximize his possible opportunity to receive alms.[35] Unfortunately, we are uncertain which gate Luke means by calling it the Beautiful Gate. On the one hand, the descriptive term used to characterize this gate makes one think the reference is to the famous Nicanor Gate, which is said in the Mishnah to lead from the outer court into the Court of the Women (cf. *m. Mid.* 2:3), but the evidence in Josephus suggests it was between the Court of the Women and the Court of the Gentiles (*War* 2.411; 6.293). This gate was made of Corinthian bronze, which distinguished it from other gates which had silver and/or gold overlay (cf. Josephus, *War* 5.201, 204).[36] A case can also be made for the Shushan Gate, which provided immediate access to Solomon's colonnade, where Peter later speaks (v. 11). The access to this gate, however, was up a steep path from the east which would not have been a good place for begging since it was not one of the gates most frequently used by those in Jerusalem.[37] Much depends on what one makes of the term ιερον used in 3:1. Is Luke referring to the temple complex in general or the inner sanctuary of it? It is certainly possible it is the latter.[38] While it is not possible to be certain, on the whole the Nicanor Gate with a location within the temple precincts seems the most likely location, and it is probably to be identified as the Beautiful Gate.[39]

According to v. 3 the lame man saw Peter and John going into the (inner) temple precincts for worship and asked them for alms. Peter's response involves looking intently at the man and demanding he reciprocate by giving Peter his undivided attention. The man does this, undoubtedly expecting to

35. Of course almsgiving was one of the pillars of early Judaism. For this very reason some early Jews opposed the sharing of all things in common (unlike the Christians in Jerusalem) because it made almsgiving impossible and perhaps even unnecessary in some places (at Qumran?).

36. Whether one should make anything of the fact that this gate was associated with miracles even when these gates were being delivered to Jerusalem from Alexandria is not clear. Probably the tradition in Tosephta, *Yoma* 2.4, is from a later period.

37. See Cadbury and Lake, *The Beginnings of Christianity,* 4:32; Hall, "Acts 3.1-10." See the judicious discussion in Polhill, *Acts,* p. 126.

38. All the more so if Luke himself was a Gentile not allowed to enter into the inner sanctum of the temple in Jerusalem but only into the outer Court of the Gentiles. See the helpful discussion in Hengel, *Between Jesus and Paul,* pp. 102-5 and the notes.

39. This is one of those cases where we cannot be certain about the degree of Luke's accuracy and the extent of his knowledge of Jerusalem on the basis of comparison with the secondary literature alone, since the latter involves complex and often conflicting testimony. See Hemer, *Book of Acts,* pp. 223-24. I am inclined to go with the testimony of Josephus, who was an eyewitness of the temple. Certainly there is nothing here in Acts 3 which warrants the conclusion that Luke did not have such precise knowledge of Jerusalem, and if, as I have argued, he had occasion to visit Jerusalem during the end of Paul's third missionary journey, then he himself was an eyewitness or earwitness of these things.

receive some sort of gracious gift. Peter, however, says in *v. 6* that he has no silver or gold to dispense. This perhaps points to the fact that the apostles were not keepers of the Christian community's funds.[40] Instead Peter had something to dispense which money could not buy — healthy limbs.

Peter directly commands the lame man in *v. 6b*, "in the name of Jesus Christ of Nazareth, stand up and walk." The meaning of the use of Jesus' name has been debated. Some scholars have thought that we see a form of early Christian magic here in which the pronunciation of the powerful name is believed to result in powerful effects. There is no disputing that many of the ancients believed in the power of certain sacred, secret, and divine names.[41] Luke, however, is in fact interested in distinguishing Christian actions from ancient magical practices (cf. Acts 8:9-11, 19; 19:18-19). Furthermore, J. A. Ziesler has shown that Luke uses "the name" in a variety of ways, none of which really comports with magical practices.[42] Here the phrase in question may mean either "by the authority and power of Jesus" or "on behalf of Jesus [I say]," probably the former. Luke is probably not suggesting that the name is a full periphrasis for the personal presence of Jesus, though that is not impossible.[43]

V. 7 says he aids the man by taking him by the right hand and raising him up, at which point his feet and ankles are immediately made strong, showing the great power at work.[44] In *v. 8* we have the result. The man not

40. As Barrett, *Acts*, vol. 1, p. 182, says, Luke portrays the apostles as poor men (cf. 2:44-45; 4:32-35).

41. See, e.g., van der Horst, "Hellenistic Parallels to Acts (Chapters 3 and 4)," pp. 38-39.

42. See Ziesler, "The Name of Jesus."

43. See Barrett's (*Acts*, vol. 1, pp. 182-83) careful assessment: "the evidence does not support the view that the *name* is used in Acts as a magical formula . . . [in] 19.13ff. . . . mere invocation of the name has an effect very different from that which its user hopes for, [which] shows a belief that Jesus is exalted above all magical compulsion. In fact both Acts 3 and 19 are among Luke's great anti-magical passages. . . . in Acts 3 and 4, as well as elsewhere, he does his best to combat it." In terms of Luke's theology it must be remembered that Luke believes that Jesus is personally absent, being in heaven and not on earth (cf. Acts 7:56), and he has sent the Holy Spirit as the promise of the Father to act on earth, bringing to fruition God's divine plan for humankind (cf. Acts 16:7 — "the Spirit of Jesus prevented," which surely means the Spirit Jesus personally sent as his agent).

44. The terms βασεις and σφυδρα in v. 7 are anatomically correct and precise, indicating the body parts usually responsible for lameness. Though these terms are not technical medical terms (or at least they are also found in sources other than just in the medical literature of the age), it is, however, true they were terms *often* used by doctors. Especially σφυδρα points to someone with a desire to be precise, for it refers to the ankle bones. These terms may then be taken as one small piece of evidence consistent with and supporting the notion that Luke was a doctor, though by no means proving it. Cf. Barrett, *Acts*, vol. 1, p. 184, and *Beginnings*, 4:34.

only jumps up and walks, but leaps and praises God as well. This description owes something to the LXX text of Isa. 35:6, for there we find the same rare verb for jumping (εξαλλομαι) in the phrase "Then will the lame leap like a deer," referring to the blessings of the eschatological age.[45] This miracle, then, is not seen as an isolated incident but as part of the grand scheme of God to bring to fulfillment the promises of the Hebrew Scriptures in and through Jesus and his followers.

As is typical of miracle narratives of the Synoptic Evangelists, the story ends with the reaction of the crowd. V. 9 tells us that "all the people" saw the lame man and recognized him as one who regularly begged at the Beautiful Gate (cf. John 9:8-12, 20), and so they were filled with amazement and wonder in regard to what happened to him, which does not mean they instantly became Christians. Being impressed by a miracle, as Luke illustrates elsewhere, is not the same as being converted (see Acts 14:10ff.).[46] Nevertheless, the reference to the emotional response is important in a work like this that is rhetorically sensitive. Rhetoricians stress that for a communication to be persuasive it must not only appeal to the intellect but tug at the heartstrings as well, including an appeal to the deeper and more powerful emotions, and Luke knows how to accomplish this rhetorical aim.[47]

B. The Mighty Word (3:11-26)

In regard to both technique and rhetorical strategy the speech material in this section varies little from the speech found in Acts 2. We begin with a forensic or judicial speech that involves defense and attack (vv. 12-18), and this material serves as the proem and narration that prepares for the deliberative speech which follows. Vv. 19-21 offer the basic proposition the speaker wishes to emphasize followed by a proof based on prophecy (vv. 22-25), and there is a brief epilogue in conclusion (v. 26). Once again the results of the speech are seen as very successful, but here for the first time there is significant opposition involving the Jewish authorities in Jerusalem (priests and Sadducees). Here we can begin to see why there is indeed an apologetic character to Acts, why Luke must endeavor to set the record straight or at least make his audience certain of the proper interpretation of the foun-

---

45. See Johnson, *Acts*, p. 66.

46. Once again the use of "all" is an example of rhetorical hyperbole intended to convey the idea that many saw and were impacted by this event. On Luke's view of miracles see the excursus, pp. 220ff. below.

47. See my *Conflict and Community in Corinth*, pp. 43ff.

dational events:[48] "Hostility to the gospel supplies Acts throughout with a dramatic plot, which here moves toward a climax in the death of Stephen and then in the second half . . . rises to a second climax in the trial of Paul. Dissension among Christians on the observance of the law provides a subplot for the first half of Acts, represented as happily resolved by the compromise of James."[49]

Despite the similarities between the speeches in Acts 2 and 3 it should be seen that they are by no means identical, nor do they function in exactly the same way. Acts 2 is more of a keynote speech, while the speech in Acts 3 moves the argument further along, especially in the discussion of Christology, eschatology, and the responsibility of Jews for Jesus' death (the ignorance motif is introduced). There is also oddly enough no appeal to have faith in Jesus' name (though cf. v. 16) or to be baptized in Acts 3.

> The Pentecost speech emphasizes Jesus' resurrection and exaltation but the temple speech recalls details of Jesus' trial. The Pentecost speech briefly refers to Jesus' earthly ministry, but the temple speech anticipates the Parousia. The Pentecost speech emphasizes God's oath to David; the temple speech recalls God's promises to Abraham and refers to the Mosaic prophet. The Pentecost speech focuses on the titles "Messiah" and "Lord"; the Temple speech introduces other titles — "servant" (παις), "holy and just one," "leader of life." The Pentecost speech cites a prophetic book and the Psalms, but the temple speech cites the Pentateuch. . . . Both speeches emphasize repentance and release of sins, but the wording is mostly different. Both speeches refer to the future participation of others in salvation (2.39; 3.26); again the wording is different. Thus the two speeches are complementary, probably deliberately so, even though they address the same type of audience about the same situation. A much broader and richer understanding of Christian preaching to Jews emerges from hearing two speeches rather than one.[50]

The differences between the two speeches have led various scholars to suggest that we have some very primitive source material in (and behind) the speech in Acts 3.[51] This speech stands as an example of the early attempts to make the gospel understandable and acceptable to a Jewish (and especially Jerusalemite?) audience.[52] One must also note how a wide variety of themes

---

48. See above, pp. 4ff., on the meaning of Luke 1:1-4.

49. Kennedy, *New Testament Interpretation,* pp. 118-19. In all the above I am basically following Kennedy's suggestions. Cf. also Soards, *The Speeches in Acts,* pp. 38-39.

50. Tannehill, *Narrative Unity of Luke-Acts,* 2:58.

51. See Zehnle, *Peter's Pentecost Discourse,* pp. 71-94. On the possible Aramaic "Vorlage," cf. Bruce, *The Speeches in the Acts of the Apostles,* pp. 8-11.

52. See Zehnle, *Peter's Pentecost Discourse,* pp. 134-35.

Solomon's Portico in its possible location along the south side of the Temple court, as it is represented in the Holy Land Hotel's scale model of Herodian Jerusalem.

and motifs introduced in this speech crop up again in Stephen's speech in Acts 7 (e.g., the same texts are used, the Jesus-as-prophet-like-Moses is prominent only in these two speeches), and so the listener is partially prepared for that later speech here. The speech reflects the same masterful movement from formal address to the crowd at the outset ("men Israelites"),[53] to the more familial "brothers" when the transition to the deliberative part of the speech is being made, in order to persuade the audience to be disposed to act as Peter will suggest in vv. 19ff.

V. 11 refers to the fact that Peter and John went to Solomon's portico or colonnade, an interesting point in view of the fact that in the Gospel tradition this is the spot where Jesus is said to have taught as well (cf. John 10:23). This portico lay along the eastern wall of the temple precincts across the Court of the Gentiles, and so some way from the sanctuary entrance.[54] That Acts 5:12 also mentions this location as a gathering spot for Christians suggests it was the regular meeting (and teaching) place for them, following the precedent of

53. Again ανδρες is possibly used in a generic sense to include both men and women, but this is not certain.
54. See Josephus, *War* 5.12.

Jesus.[55] The man who was healed clung to Peter and John as they moved to Solomon's portico, and it may be that we are meant to see this move as an attempt to avoid too much attention being focused on the miracle. However, "all the people ran together . . . utterly astonished."[56]

According to *v. 12* it is only when Peter sees the reaction of the crowd that he decides to speak to them. He had not initially come to this place to draw a crowd and speak; he is reacting to circumstances beyond his control. Once more Peter must be the interpreter of what has happened and what it means.

The speech begins in *v. 12b* by remarking about the crowd's amazement and suggesting that it is misguided if it is based on the assumption that Peter and John had accomplished this healing by their own power and piety. Here we have the only NT use of the term ευσεβεια outside the Pastorals and 2 Peter. The term was of course frequently used in pagan religious contexts and even in deeds to indicate that the person was of good character.[57] It is a term with which Theophilus would surely have been familiar, and it may suggest Luke wants to make clear from the outset that Peter and the other apostles are not to be seen as "divine men," even though miracles occur through them.[58]

The awe of the crowd is to be redirected toward God, the God of Abraham, Isaac, and Jacob, "our [Jewish] ancestors." The drift of the conversation here is meant to suggest that what the apostles do they do through the power of the one true God. They are not magicians or pagan holy men or healers. But Peter is not satisfied just to refer to God; he must also connect this event with what God has done for and in Christ.

The ancestral God had "glorified" his servant (or child) Jesus, whom the Jerusalem Jews had rejected and handed over to Pilate, but Pilate decided to release him. The term παιδα in *v. 13* can be rendered either child or servant. There is much debate over which rendering is warranted here, and whether if one translates the term "servant" the theology of the Servant Songs of Isaiah stands in the background. It is hard to doubt that Isa. 52:13-14 (LXX) lies in the background of this text, for it says, "my servant . . . shall be exalted and lifted up, and shall be very high. Just as there were many who

---

55. Notice how once again the Western text here attempts to solve dilemmas in the earlier textual tradition. The Alexandrian text does not mention any leaving of the sanctuary by Peter and the others, and so the Western text adds εκπορευομενου to v. 11 to make this clear.

56. Another classic example of rhetorical hyperbole meant to convey the idea of a large response or action. See pp. 105ff.

57. See, e.g., *New Docs*, 1:78-79.

58. By contrast with familiar figures like Simon Magus, of whom it is said, "This man is the power of God that is called Great" (8:10), or with the later figure of Apollonius of Tyana, cf. Philostratus, *Life of Apollonius* 3.18; 8.5, 7. Notice that Paul also tries to make clear he is not a "divine man" (14:15).

were astonished at him." Not only do we have the motif of exaltation, but also the note of astonishment follows it, which is the opening subject of Peter's speech (and what prompts it) in the first place. "In other words, prophecy was now being fulfilled, for Peter was claiming that what happened to Jesus was the divine glorification of God's servant."[59] In this same context we may point to various possible allusions to the Servant Songs, including the reference to Jesus' death (v. 15) and suffering (v. 18), to Jesus being the Righteous One (v. 14), and to the "blotting out" of sins (v. 19).[60] Explicit servant Christology involving the use of the term "servant" of Jesus is something distinctive to Acts (3:26; 4:27, 30; cf. 8:32-33), but it is probably implied in various other places in the NT (cf. Mark 10:45; 14:24; Luke 22:37; John 12:38; 1 Pet. 2:22-25).[61]

It quickly becomes apparent that this speech will stress the involvement of Jerusalem Jews in the death of Jesus as the problem, but also that at the end it will emphasize the promise and opportunity given to them to repent and be blessed. Especially telling is the repeated use of the emphatic nominative pronoun "you" (pl., υμεις) found in vv. 13 and 14,[62] and then again at the end of the speech in vv. 25 and 26 where the promises are mentioned and offered.[63]

The reference to Pilate's decision to release Jesus alludes to Luke 23:4, 16 and could be seen as part of Luke's attempt not to place too much blame on the Romans (but cf. 2:23). *V. 14* further amplifies what has already been said in v. 13. The Jerusalem Jews compounded their guilt not only by rejecting the Holy and Righteous One and insisting on his murder but by instead

---

59. Marshall, *Acts* (1980), p. 91.

60. In view of 3:19 it is doubtful that one can conclude, as Hooker does (*Jesus and the Servant*, p. 110), that only the delivering-up and exaltation motifs are possibly drawn from the Servant Songs. Isaiah 52–53 are too full of atonement language and Luke is too familiar with these texts and the notions of release from or the blotting out of sins not to suspect a fuller connection. For a corrective to the continued undervaluing of the Lukan theology of the cross, cf. Moessner, "The Script of the Scriptures."

61. It is my view that 1 Peter may still be attributed to Peter himself, though perhaps he was using an amanuensis. I therefore doubt that it is an accident that Peter is presented here, as in 1 Peter 2, as the first, and perhaps only truly major, Christian expositor of a servant Christology. This Christology was in any case primitive and does not appear to have become a major way of viewing Jesus, at least in the Pauline communities. I find the arguments of Jones, "The Title 'Servant' in Luke-Acts," and others unconvincing that Luke uses the term more broadly simply to refer to someone who was a servant of God (not the suffering servant). Nor am I convinced that the term is simply used interchangeably with Christ or Son of God. Were the latter true we might expect the term to be used far more frequently than it in fact is in Luke-Acts.

62. In contrast to the "we" who are witnesses in v. 15b.

63. The latter example is a dative pronoun in the emphatic position. See Tannehill, *Narrative Unity in Luke-Acts,* 2:54.

requesting that a murderer be released![64] This is clearly strong and polemical language, and it is necessary to ask how it functions here. The purpose of this language is to bring God's people to the point of repentance by a "shock of recognition" technique and then to open them up to the reception of the restoration and blessings long ago promised to them and available through Christ. In other words, this language is meant to make the audience see what is at stake and to persuade them, using the strongest language possible, to make a positive decision about Jesus. Thus even the polemical language is intended to have a positive function. That the author does not have an anti-Semitic motive is made quite clear from the "ignorance" motif (cf. below).[65]

The title "Holy and Righteous One" in *v. 14* seems to be a combination of the OT title of God ("Holy One"; cf. Lev. 11:44-45 and the LXX of Pss. 77:41; 98:5; 102:1) and the prophetic term "the righteous one," which refers to a human being (cf. Hab. 2:4; Rom. 1:17; Gal. 3:11; Heb. 10:38). Even more germane is Isa. 53:11, which refers to the Righteous Servant in overtones that are messianic, unlike the case in Hab. 2:4. Then, too, the "Righteous One" seems to be a messianic designation in intertestamental Jewish sources (cf. *1 Enoch* 38:2; 46:3; 53:6 and *Pss. Sol.* 17:35). Notice that already in Luke 1:35 Jesus is already called holy (cf. 2:23), and that in Luke 4:34 he is addressed as "the Holy One of God" by the demon. Also in Luke 23:47 Jesus is said to be a righteous man.

If it was paradoxical to have Jesus murdered in order to free a murderer, it is equally paradoxical to speak in *v. 15* of killing the Author/Originator/Cause of Life! The phrase αρχηγον της ζωης is difficult to render because of the various possible meanings of αρχηγος and because we find it in combination with the term *Savior* in Acts 5:31 (cf. Heb. 2:10). I agree with Johnson that the intended contrast is between the one who gives life and those who take it away.[66] Going one step further with the paradox, we are told that God raised the Author of Life from the dead, that is, gave him a more permanent

---

64. Cf. 7:35, where it is said in similar language that they had rejected the earlier prophet Moses.

65. See Matera, "Death of Jesus in Acts," p. 93: "The accusations of killing Jesus are not, in themselves, anti-Jewish, and Luke did not employ these texts to denigrate the Jews. Luke has framed the majority of these texts as contrast formulas and set most of them within missionary discourses *where their primary function is to summon people to repentance. The inhabitants of Jerusalem receive a second chance*" (emphasis mine). Cf. also Weatherly, *Jewish Responsibility,* pp. 225-42.

66. Johnson, *Acts,* p. 68. As Bruce, *The Acts of the Apostles,* p. 141, points out, the phrase "the author/originator of life" in Aramaic would be identical to "the author/originator of salvation" found in Heb. 2:10 since the Aramaic ℵ is equivalent to both life and salvation. Here the sense of the text requires some such translation of this key phrase as we suggested above in the text, but in Acts 5 the meaning of the noun may well be leader (see below).

form of life![67] Peter stresses that he (and John) and others are witnesses that
God raised him from the dead; they saw the results of that event, a risen Jesus.
Again, witness here probably has the double sense of one who has seen and
one who relates what she or he has seen.[68] It is an important theme for Luke
also because he is presenting an account in the tradition of the Hellenistic
historiographers who put a premium on eyewitness testimony.[69]

The grammar and syntax of *v. 16* are very clumsy, and here we have
another verse which suggests a lack of final revision of the text.[70] The verse is
awkward in part because it is transitional to the deliberative part of the speech
(or second speech?). The basic meaning of the verse seems clear enough. There
is both an objective and a subjective element in the man's healing — Christ's
name, standing for Christ on the one hand and faith on the other.[71] It is not
clear whose faith is referred to in the latter part of the verse — Peter's or the
lame man's? In view of the fact that nothing was said earlier about the man
exercising faith, while the issue of Peter's faith in and reliance on Jesus and his
power is implicitly raised (vv. 12-13), probably we are meant to think of Peter's
(and John's) faith and trust in the trustworthy name of Jesus.[72]

The term ολοκληριαν, found only here in the NT, is used in the LXX
to refer to the unblemished animal that could be offered in sacrifice (cf. Isa.
1:6; Zech. 11:16). The use of the term here is telling because formerly the lame
man was "blemished" and could not enter the sanctuary. Now he was whole
and seen to be made whole by his Jewish peers, who could testify of his former
condition and the change wrought.[73]

V. 17 is one of the more important verses in Acts for understanding
Luke's view of Jews, including especially those who had a hand in Jesus' death,
and also for understanding his view of salvation history. It is Luke's under-

---

67. It is not impossible that αρχηγος refers to the fact that Jesus is the firstborn from
the dead in view of v. 15b. The translation then would be something like "the leader (or
pioneer) of life," which might mean leader to a (new) life. See Barrett, *Acts,* vol. 1, p. 198.

68. See pp. 115ff. above on μαρτυς. To judge from comparing this text to 1:8 and other
texts, sometimes the bearing witness is more to the fore, and sometimes the seeing is.

69. See the introduction, pp. 13ff.

70. See rightly Barrett, *Acts,* vol. 1, p. 199.

71. Perhaps it would be possible to render the verse as follows: "and because of the
trustworthiness of his name, his name healed (him) whom you see and know, and the faith,
that which is through him, has given him this wholeness in the presence of all of you." On
πιστις Χριστου, meaning the faithfulness, trustworthiness of Christ, see my *Paul's Narrative
Thought World,* pp. 268-69.

72. See Newman and Nida, *A Translator's Handbook,* pp. 79-80.

73. Again the term is not a technical medical term (cf. Barrett, *Acts,* vol. 1, p. 200),
but it is the sort of term a doctor might frequently use to speak of someone who was
completely cured, healed, or whose body was made whole, having been previously crippled.
On the use of this term in connection with healing, see Plato, *Timaeus* 44C.

standing that now that Christ, the Spirit, and the renewed people of God have come on the stage of human history, the times of ignorance and excuse because of ignorance are gone. This thinking is applied not only to Jews here (cf. 13:27-28) but also to Gentiles in 17:30. This latter verse could just as well be part of this speech, for it says: "While God has overlooked the times of human ignorance, now he commands all people everywhere to repent." The same appeal is being made in both places, only here it is being directed more narrowly to Jews, and in particular to Jerusalem Jews who have some culpability for Jesus' death, just as one would expect on the basis of Luke 13:33-34.[74]

Remarkably v. 17 says that both these Jerusalem Jews *and* their rulers acted in ignorance.[75] In the OT law there was atonement for such unwitting sins, sins committed in ignorance (cf. Num. 15:27-31), but not for sins committed "with a high hand," deliberate sins.[76] They had not committed some unforgivable sin. There is another mitigating factor as well: God's divine plan was at work in Jesus' death. The call for Jews to repent and/or turn back to God is familiar in the prophetic literature. The background to the appeal here goes back to the prophetic call, in particular the recent call of the Baptist and then of Jesus. It is interesting that in later Jewish sources we hear things like "If the Israelites repent, they will be redeemed, but if not they will not be redeemed" (*b. Sanh.* 97b, R. Eliezer ben Hyrcanus, A.D. 90), or even "If the Israelites would repent for a day, the son of David (messiah) would come immediately" (*p. Ta'an.* 1:1 [64a]).[77]

V. 18 offers what could be seen as a mild contrast to v. 17, or perhaps in view of the use of ουτως we should say a coordination of efforts. What these humans intended for evil, God intended and used for good. Through the very acts of these Jews, in this surprising manner (ουτως) God fulfilled what the Scriptures had said about a suffering Messiah. With typical rhetorical hyperbole we hear that "*all* the prophets foretold the suffering of God's Messiah." It seems likely that Luke (and Peter) have in mind primarily Isa. 52:13–53:12, but there are other texts that could be alluded to as well (cf. Jer. 11:19; Zech. 12:10; 13:7; Pss. 22; 31; 34; 69).

---

74. This latter text is crucial because it shows that Luke views certain particular Jews as responsible for the death of prophetic figures such as Jesus. See Polhill, *Acts*, p. 133.

75. The Western text (in this case D, E it[h, p] cop [G67]) again reveals its anti-Semitic tendencies (cf. Epp, *Theological Tendency*, pp. 41ff.). This is seen in two changes: (1) the adding of μεν in v. 17 to make the contrast between the Jews' action and God's purpose stronger and clearer; (2) the adding of πονηρον after επραξατε. As Metzger, *Textual Commentary*, p. 314, says, this leads to the rendering "*We* know that *you*, on the one hand, did a *wicked thing* in ignorance . . . but on the other hand God. . . ."

76. Notice Acts 13:39, where Paul speaks of release from sins in Jesus that one could not be absolved of under Mosaic Law.

77. This last text, however, dates well into the Christian era, about A.D. 320. On these and other such texts, cf. Zehnle, *Peter's Pentecost Discourse*, pp. 71-73.

V. 19 brings us to the crucial juncture in the speech — the call for a turnaround, an about-face on the part of the audience. It is not just a matter of turning from sin (repentance-μετανοια), but of turning to God. This turning involves moving from rejecting to accepting Jesus. It also brings with it many blessings, as v. 20 makes clear.

Vv. 20-21 must be taken together and compared closely with v. 26. These verses begin to reveal something of Luke's understanding of eschatology, which is a complex matter calling for more detailed comment.[78]

A Closer Look — Lukan Eschatology

Since at least the time of H. Conzelmann's landmark study *The Theology of St. Luke*,[79] there has been an enormous amount of debate about Luke's eschatology or lack thereof. Is his work really a reaction to the delay of the parousia? Can his eschatology be said to be simply "realized" in character? What is the relationship of Luke's Christology to his eschatology? Whatever conclusions one draws on these and related questions, one must certainly take into account both Luke's Gospel and Acts, not just one or the other.[80]

On the one hand, it can be said with some assurance from a careful evaluation of Luke's editing of Mark and the Q material that Luke is Hellenizing his material, and a part of this agenda involves a certain amount of editing out or transforming of the highly Jewish and sometimes apocalyptic future eschatological material in the Gospels. Several examples will have to suffice. At the outset of the record of Jesus' ministry Mark has "Repent, for the dominion of God is at hand" (1:15), but Luke omits this and replaces it with a simple statement about Jesus' teaching in synagogues. Furthermore, the teaching offered in the paradigmatic sermon in Luke 4 amounts to saying that the Scriptures about the eschatological realities are not merely going to be fulfilled soon, but are even fulfilled "today" in the hearing of the audience then present.[81] One may also compare Mark 9:1 to Luke 9:27, where Luke has eliminated the reference to the (future) *coming* of God's dominion. Luke's introduction to the Q parable of the pounds is equally telling. People thought that the kingdom was to appear immediately (19:11; cf. Matt. 25:13), and so Jesus tells this parable as a corrective. In the L material as well we hear that "the kingdom of God is among you" (17:20-21). Perhaps most telling is comparing in detail Mark 13 to the equivalent material in Luke 21. Luke omits the apocalyptic image of the abomination which makes desolate (Mark 13:14)

---

78. Note Fitzmyer's conclusion in *Luke I–IX*, p. 231: "This is the most difficult and most controverted aspect of Lucan theology today."

79. *The Theology of St. Luke* (New York: Harper and Row, 1960).

80. See Mattill, *Luke and the Last Things*.

81. See Fitzmyer, *Luke I–IX*, p. 232. In this paragraph I am basically following Fitzmyer's analysis with some amplification.

and replaces it with the more mundane idea of the enemy armies surrounding Jerusalem as a sign that the city's desolation is near (21:20). In other words, Luke uses familiar language about the sacking of a city, perhaps even in some part based on his knowledge of what happened to Jerusalem in A.D. 70, instead of the apocalyptic language of Dan. 9:27 and 12:11.

Though one must not underplay any of the above, none of this should be taken to mean that Luke has some sort of consistent realized eschatology that totally dismisses, ignores, or neglects future eschatology. Both in the Gospel and in Acts we hear about the Son of Man's future coming (Luke 21:27; indeed, he will come as he went Acts 1:11), and occasionally there is a note about vindication of the saints εν ταχει (Luke 18:7-8).[82] What one can say is that the emphasis in Luke-Acts lies on what has already and is now happening, what has already been fulfilled and is now being fulfilled. As Fitzmyer suggests, the shift is from focusing primarily on the eschaton to emphasizing what has happened and is happening "today" (cf. the use of σημερον in Luke 4:21; 5:26; 19:5, 9; 23:43, or of καθ' ημεραν ["daily"] in Luke 9:23; 11:3; 16:19; 19:47).[83] Part of this emphasis on the past and present is only what we would expect since Luke intends to present a two-volume work of historiography, not primarily a collection of prophecies about the future.

The historian's business is with what has happened, and sometimes with its implications for what is and will yet happen. Luke is especially concerned with salvation history, a sort of mixture of history with eschatological events which have broken into ordinary history before the actual conclusion of all history.[84] Despite Conzelmann's arguments, Luke does not radically distinguish between the time of Jesus and the time of the church. In fact, he does not radically distinguish the time of Israel from the time of Jesus or the church because in his view the community of Jesus' disciples is the logical development of Israel according to God's plan. Jew and Gentile united in Christ are the beginning of Israel restored. Contra Conzelmann, what is distinctive about Luke's work is his attempt to connect the life and times of Jesus *with* the ongoing life of the church by adding an Acts to his Gospel, the former developing out of the latter. The age of the fulfillment of prophecies and promises is inaugurated by Jesus and continues after the ascension, and even well after Pentecost.

Another factor which must clearly be taken into consideration in evaluating Luke's eschatology is how his Christology affects it.[85] The coming of Christ and equally importantly his death and resurrection have modified the conception of eschatology. Jesus' resurrection has already happened as an eschatological event which triggers other eschatological events such as the sending of the Spirit, but it will take a further coming

---

82. Even here, though, the note of imminence is not certain. Do we take εν ταχει as adverbial, telling us *how* the Son of Man will come (suddenly, swiftly, with dispatch; cf. Deut. 11:17; Ps. 2:12; Sir. 27:3), or do we take it as temporal, telling us when (soon)? Cf. my *Women in the Ministry of Jesus*, pp. 35-38 and the notes. If we compare the use of the phrase in Acts 12:7; 22:18; and 25:4, the translation "soon" seems likely.

83. Fitzmyer, *Luke I–IX*, p. 234.

84. On this see Jervell, "The Future of the Past."

85. See now Bayer, "Christ-Centered Eschatology"; Kurz, "Acts 3.19-26 as a Test"; and in general Mattill, *Luke and the Last Things*.

of Jesus to trigger the final eschatological events, for example the general resurrection (cf. Luke 20:27-40; Acts 24:15) and the final judgment of the world by Jesus (Acts 17:31). In short, Christ's coming in the past has divided up the eschatological events into already and not yet, which suggests that Luke views the present as some sort of eschatological age in which some "final" things have already happened and others are looked for.

Three things seem clear: (1) as Acts 2, 3, 17, and other texts with speeches make clear, it is an age in which one must make up one's mind about Jesus — in short, it is an age of decision; (2) it is an age when ignorance can no longer be overlooked, not least because times of refreshing and restoration can and are already happening because the Spirit has already been sent (cf. below); (3) it is an age in which knowing the present *times,* that is, knowing (1) and (2), is important, but knowing matters of *timing* about the future ("times and seasons" when the concluding eschatological events affecting Israel and others will happen, cf. Acts 1:7) is *not.* Matters of timing are in God's hands and plans, but they are not for the disciples to know. In short, Luke rules out speculation, or eschatological forecasting of such matters. This means, I think, that J. T. Carroll is right to say that the "baseline, as Luke sees it, is the unpredictability of the parousia. No one knows — or can know — the timing of the End. Chronology remains a matter of the freedom and prerogative of God. . . . Yet ignorance of the 'when' is countered by certainty of the 'that.'"[86] But if we accept this conclusion, then it is improper to speak about Luke believing in a "delay" of the parousia, for the concept of delay implies that the event is late, that it did not occur at the expected and predicted time.[87] Agnosticism about *timing* means one cannot speak in such terms.[88]

In conclusion, Kurz may be right that one key to understanding Luke's eschatology is to recognize the distinction between discussions about "the day," whether the day of judgment or the day of the return of the Son of Man is meant, and discussions about eschatological times or days (plural) that involve the present and the future in Luke's view. The former refers to a particular eschatological event which is definitely in the future, the latter to a series or sequence of eschatological events already inaugurated (but cf. Acts 1:7).[89] In any event, while Luke does not neglect future eschatology, his emphasis lies quite naturally on what has already and is now happening that amounts to fulfillment, climax, conclusion of God's plans and dealings with Jews and others. This is only to be expected from a historian.

86. Carroll, *End of History,* p. 165.

87. Against Schneider, *Die Apostelgeschichte I,* pp. 336-37, Acts 3:20-21 implies nothing about the length of the time before the parousia or universal restoration will happen. See pp. 187ff. below.

88. In a more nuanced approach, one could argue that Luke is reacting to those who think, feel, or teach that the parousia is delayed (as exemplified by the disciples in Acts 1:6-8 or by the remark in Luke 18:7-8), though he himself does not agree. This is where Carroll's study falls short, for he simply agrees with Conzelmann that Luke incorporates delay into his eschatological scenario and goes so far as to say (*End of History,* p. 166): "as Conzelmann rightly observed, delay is a dominant theme in Luke's handling of traditions concerning the end-time."

89. Kurz, "Acts 3.19-26 as a Test," p. 309.

Clearly the phrases in *vv. 20-21* and *v. 26* refer to a variety of events which span Luke's and (Peter's) past, present, and future. For example, in v. 20 and 21 we hear about the future sending of Jesus and the fact that he must remain in heaven until "the restoration of all." In v. 26 we hear about the past resurrection of Jesus. The cause and effect relationship between what is mentioned in v. 19 (repentance) and what is said in v. 20 (times of refreshing) should be compared to v. 26, which speaks of "blessing you in the turning of each from your wickedness." The "you" in each case is Jews, who, as Acts 1:6 has already said, are looking for the restoration of the kingdom to Israel. In v. 20 the "Lord" seems to mean God who will send Christ again, and Christ's second coming is seen as in some sense dependent on Israel's repentance (cf. Rom. 11:12, 15, 26).[90]

Probably Kurz is right that the emphasis in *v. 21* should be placed on the word πας (all). Christ will not come back until the restoration of "all."[91] In view of the use the cognate term in 1:6 it is hard not to see in this a reference to the restoration of all Israel, not some sort of generic universal restoration of "everything" or all persons.[92] Alternatively, it is possible but less probable that the meaning is that Christ will return after the "establishment" or "fulfillment" of all (the Scriptures spoke of).[93] The context is against this last translation, for the focus here is on the appeal to repent, which shows that the restoration in mind is likely of Jewish persons to their proper relationship to God through Christ.[94] Finally, it is important to note that the word *first* (v. 26) suggests the wider mission to Gentiles which will be chronicled later in Acts and so may be a Lukan addition to his source. God sent Jesus his servant to his own people first to bless them by turning them from their sins and back to a right relationship with God.[95]

Vv. 22-25 provide a scriptural argument to support and illuminate what is said elsewhere in the speech. The coming of the prophet like Moses is a

90. On these latter texts see my *End of the World*, pp. 113ff.

91. This would seem to mean all Israel, on which cf. Rom. 11:26.

92. Contrast the translation in the NRSV, "universal restoration." The NRSV translation requires that one distinguish what is referred to in v. 20 and v. 21. Cf. Johnson, *Acts*, p. 69. The translation "all persons" requires taking παντων as masculine, which is less likely, but cf. Barrett, *Acts*, vol. 1, p. 206. Barrett is right, however, that it does not make sense to talk about the restoration of all the things of which God spoke.

93. See, e.g., Marshall, *Acts*, p. 94. In favor of this view is the phrase "all the things written/spoken," which occurs throughout Luke-Acts (cf. Luke 18:31; 21:22; 22:37; 24:44; Acts 13:29; 24:14). Cf. Polhill, *Acts*, p. 135 and n. 22.

94. See the discussion in Bruce, "Eschatology in Acts."

95. A careful reading of this speech suggests certain connections with Paul's basic argument about Israel and her restoration in Romans 9–11, and with Rom. 1:16, which speaks of salvation (restoration) for Jews first. This is not surprising if in fact Luke was a sometime companion of Paul and they discussed such things.

subject discussed at Qumran on the basis of the implications of the same text used here (Deut. 18:15-16, 19; cf. 1QS 9:11; 4QTestim. 1:5-8; cf. 1 Macc. 14:41).[96] Josephus also speaks of figures in the first century, like Theudas (ca. A.D. 45), who attempted to play the part of this latter-day Moses by commanding the Jordan to part (*Ant.* 20.5.1). The function of the first quote, which concludes with a warning about being rooted out of the people of God, is not to condemn Israel but to warn her to repent lest dire consequences follow.[97]

V. 24 is a general verse referring to the fact that from Samuel on, "all" the prophets also predicted "these days," the times of fulfillment set in motion by Jesus and especially by his death, resurrection, ascension, and sending of the Spirit.[98] The early Christians, like the Qumranites, saw their own present experiences as something spoken of in advance in the Scriptures.[99]

V. 25 reminds the audience that they are descendants of the prophets and that God had given their ancestors the covenant, in particular to Abraham. V. 25b alludes to Gen. 12:3 (cf. 22:18; 28:14; cf. 17:4, 5; 18:18; 26:4). What is interesting is that while Christian exegesis of this Genesis material speaks favorably of "the families of the earth" being blessed in Abraham's descendants, some (later) Jewish exegesis said things such as the nations would be blessed for Israel's sake (*b. Yebam.* 63a) or even that Israel in the days of the Messiah would destroy the nations (*Num. Rab.* 2:13).[100] Here and in v. 26 the blessing of the Gentiles is clearly alluded to, but only in connection with Jews or after the Jews. Luke is masterfully preparing for later developments in his narrative.[101]

C. The Mighty Ones (4:1-22)

One of the regular features of the way Luke handles his speech material is that speeches tend to be concluded by way of interruption, or at least they appear to be unfinished (cf. 7:54; 10:44; 17:32; 22:22; 26:24). Doubtless such speeches were sometimes interrupted since the message of early Jewish Christians was seen as inflammatory by various early non-Christian Jews. It is fair to say,

---

96. See the discussion in Evans and Sanders, *Luke and Scripture*, p. 190.

97. See rightly ibid., p. 192: "He wishes to attract Jews, not drive them away (see . . . Acts 13.41)." The language about rooting out, of course, supposes that these Jews are "in" until excluded by their failure to repent and accept what God has done in Jesus.

98. Clearly a reference to what had already happened in Jesus' life, and what was then happening in the early church.

99. See Marshall, *Acts*, p. 95.

100. See Evans and Sanders, *Luke and Scripture*, p. 192.

101. The connection of the Abrahamic covenant and what was happening in and through Christ also strikes a familiar Pauline note; see pp. 51ff. above.

however, that Luke also believes that these speeches (which are especially plentiful in the first half of Acts and make up about a third of the book if all instances of direct speech are taken into account) are both part of the action and also prompt action, and this accounts for some of what we find. "Thus the author of Acts displays an interest in direct speech that is not readily paralleled in other ancient literature. The reason for this preoccupation is not difficult to understand, however: the progress of the good news is the very subject of the book of Acts, and preaching of that word (and the words spoken in opposition to it) is therefore the heart of the matter, not mere illustrative material as it might be to authors who write about the history of nations or the cause and effects of war."[102] Early Christianity is about the movement and progress of the word and of the Spirit.

Chapter 4 begins with the arrival of Jewish authorities "while Peter and John were speaking." V. *1* tells us that these authorities were the priests, the captain of the temple, and the Sadducees.[103] Their presence signals to the listener that the issue of power and authority is about to be raised. In short, we see here the beginnings of a power struggle for the hearts of the Jewish people. All three of these mentioned authority groups had close connections with the temple and had a vested interest in what went on in its precincts. In that regard this confrontation is historically quite believable. The captain of the temple is in all likelihood the *sagan ha-kohanim* whose job was the oversight of the whole body of priests and the activities that transpired in the temple area. He was also the chief of the policing forces for the temple. Both Luke and Josephus use the term στρατηγός to refer to this person (cf. *Ant.* 20.131, where Ananus the son of the high priest Ananias fills this role, and *War* 6.294).[104] The Sadducees were, in general, the landed lay aristocracy who lived in and around Jerusalem and who probably dominated the Jewish power structure in the Holy City at this time. As Barrett says, they were related to the leading priestly families in any case, and we must assume that these priests held views very close to if not identical with the Sadducees on a host of subjects, including apparently the problematic nature of early Jewish Christian actions and preaching.[105]

---

102. Hemer, *Book of Acts*, p. 418.

103. Since the term αρχιερεις, "high priests," occurs much more frequently in the NT than the term "priests," it is surely more likely than not that the reading of the former in manuscripts B and C is a later modification. Cf. Metzger, *Textual Commentary*, p. 316.

104. It is right to point out, as Johnson, *Acts*, p. 76, does, that Luke uses the plural στρατηγοι elsewhere (Luke 22:4, 52) to refer to temple officers or police.

105. This is not the place for a lengthy discussion of the Sadducees, who may have ultimately derived their name from Zadok, the high priest in Solomon's day. The Sadducees, however, were certainly not Zadokites in the later sense of the term, for the last Zadokite priest fled to Egypt in the second century b.c., and by NT times all the high priests were non-Zadokites. Cf. Polhill, *Acts*, p. 139.

V. 2 tells us these authorities are annoyed because Peter was teaching the people and proclaiming "in Jesus the resurrection from the (realm of) the dead (ones)."[106] The word νεκρος refers to dead persons, unlike νεκρωσις, which refers to the state or event of "death." What was being proclaimed, then, was an isolated resurrection of Jesus from out of the realm of dead persons, not merely resurrection from death. It is possible that what Luke means here is that Jesus foreshadows or triggers the general resurrection, or even that the general resurrection transpired in what happened to Jesus. Probably, Barrett is right that we should see the key clause as instrumental — "they were proclaiming the resurrection from the dead *by means of Jesus*."[107]

Such a proclamation was bound to irritate the Sadducees, who seem to have not believed in the concept of resurrection at all and certainly would not have entertained the notion of a resurrected Messiah (cf. Acts 23:8). The verb διαπονουμενοι expresses the idea of complete exasperation, and so it is not surprising that we are told in *v. 3* that Peter and John, without further ado, are simply arrested for what they are doing. It needs to be borne in mind that incarceration in antiquity was often not a means of punishment, but rather a means of holding a suspect until a trial could be had or a judgment rendered. In fact, in a first-century Jewish setting custody seems never to have been seen as a means of punishment.[108] It was apparently too late to deal with the apostles on this day, it being already evening, and so they were held.

Here and elsewhere Luke will emphasize that measures, including the use of force, taken against the followers of Jesus are not effective; indeed, they often backfire and lead to further growth of the Christian group. Thus, in *v. 4* we hear that in spite of what was said in the previous verse many heard and believed the word of Peter, and we are told they numbered about five thousand.[109] *V. 5* tells us that the next day rulers, elders, and scribes assembled together with the high priest and other members of the priestly family. Luke in *v. 6* calls *Annas* the high priest, even though he was only high priest from A.D. 6-15. It is thus possible that Luke has made a simple mistake here. Luke 3:2, however, may lead one to think otherwise, for there he speaks of the high priesthood of *both* Annas and Caiaphas, the latter of whom was Annas's son-in-law (John 18:13). He assumed the high priesthood in A.D. 18 and

---

106. The phrase here is peculiar in several regards, especially because of the "in Jesus" clause.

107. Barrett, *Acts,* vol. 1, p. 220.

108. See Rapske, *Paul in Custody,* pp. 9-35. We are talking here about Jewish custody, and the evidence seems clear that Jews did not punish by custody. The Greek εις τηρησιν could mean either "in detention" or "in the keep" (in jail); cf. Polhill, *Acts,* p. 140 n. 35.

109. The term ανδρων may mean just men here, since elsewhere it is coupled with the word γυναικες (women) (cf. 5:14; 8:3, 12; 9:2; 17:12; 22:4, and Barrett, *Acts,* vol. 1, p. 222, but cf. pp. 120-21 above).

continued in it until A.D. 36.[110] Caiaphas is mentioned here as well immediately after Annas. It needs to be kept in view that high priests during this period seem to have kept their titles and membership in the Sanhedrin after they were deposed.[111]

It may be that Luke is suggesting that Annas was the real power behind this action against the apostles, and perhaps the one who manipulated his son-in-law.[112] That he was still in control at the time of Jesus' death in A.D. 30 is strongly suggested by John 18:13, which tells us that Jesus was *first* taken to the house of Annas to be examined and presumably have his future determined.[113] Of the two others mentioned by name, John and Alexander, we know nothing, unless the John in question is in fact Jonathan, as the Western text reads.[114] This sort of inconsequential detail, the mentioning of names that do not really play a role in the narrative, is characteristic of Luke and suggests his use of sources.

The term "Sanhedrin" is not mentioned in the course of the discussion until v. 15, but Luke clearly intends to depict a meeting of the council of which the high priest was the head. There has been a tremendous amount of debate among scholars of late in regard to not only the nature but even the existence of the Sanhedrin during the period being written about in this text.

E. P. Sanders has in various places challenged the idea that there was a legislative and judicial body called *the Sanhedrin* in Jerusalem that carried out trials in the time of Jesus or shortly thereafter. It is his view, as I understand it, that Caiaphas and other high priests may have had an advisory council which counseled the rulers who came to be called the Sanhedrin, but that only the rulers actually had power and ruled. He sees the idea of the Sanhedrin as some sort of democratically elected parliament or even a court in the NT time as a myth. He believes that both the NT and the later Jewish sources such as

---

110. Which means he lasted until the end of Pontius Pilate's tenure and must therefore have had a good working relationship with the prefect.

111. See Jeremias, *Jerusalem*, p. 157.

112. This is not mere conjecture since we know that five of Annas's sons, one grandson, and one son-in-law all became high priests during his lifetime. There is considerable evidence that Annas had vast economic resources as a part of his power. Cf. P. Gaechter, "The Hatred of the House of Annas," *TS* 8 (1947): 3-34. In addition, we now can examine the beautiful and elaborate ossuary of Caiaphas which shows the family's wealth and power. Cf. Shanks, *Temple of Solomon*, pp. 34-44.

113. Notice, too, how Caiaphas in John 18:13 is ironically said to be high priest "that year," suggesting the tenuousness of his power. On this text see my *John's Wisdom: A Sapiential Commentary of the Fourth Gospel* (Louisville: Westminster, 1995), ad loc.

114. This looks like a later clarification, for as Josephus (*Ant.* 18.4.3) indicates, Jonathan became high priest after Caiaphas in A.D. 36. See Metzger, *Textual Commentary*, p. 317.

the Mishnah have idealized the situation in the earlier period.[115] The following needs to be said about these views: (1) Sanders is in all likelihood right that we should not think of a fully independent representative parliament, much less an elected one; (2) on the other hand, there is evidence in both Josephus and the NT, including Luke-Acts, that cannot be explained away; (3) this evidence is sufficient to warrant the conclusion that the chief priests, as the highest Jewish authorities,

> typically ruled by means of a council or senate headed by the serving High Priest, which had a designated meeting place in or near the Temple precinct. . . . [B]oth [Luke and Josephus] assume conciliar aristocratic rule as the norm. . . . [B]oth assume that it was a regular body with an executive function. The chief priests had security or police force at their disposal, tried capital cases . . . [but] [i]n spite of their visible authority, however, the chief priests always had to be concerned about popular sentiment, often mediated by the Pharisees, which frequently hampered their own programme.[116]

In general Sanders seems to be too eager to exonerate various early Jewish groups, especially the Pharisees but also the priestly aristocracy, at the expense of both NT writers and Josephus. This is understandable in view of the deplorable history of anti-Semitism in the church, but the point is that he is overreacting and overcompensating. Some actions of early Jewish authority figures in this period clearly ought not to be defended, for instance in the case of Jesus' and James's death.[117]

V. 7, when read together with v. 5, suggests that the Sanhedrin sat in a semicircle, in the middle of which the apostles were made to stand. The question raised was, "By what power or in what name did you do this?" The question is, what is the antecedent of τουτο? Is this a question about the

115. He recently reiterated these views in his oral review of Brown's *The Death of the Messiah* at the November 1994 SBL meeting in Chicago. See his earlier treatment of the subject in *Judaism*, especially pp. 472ff. Cf. similarly Goodman, *The Ruling Class of Judaea*, pp. 113-18.

116. Mason, "Chief Priests," pp. 175-76. The one place where I would strongly disagree with the assessment of Mason is in his view that this body had the power of capital punishment. This is by no means clear, especially in view of the case of Jesus, who was certainly executed by the Romans. The case of Stephen we will consider later; see pp. 251ff. below. Nevertheless, see Mason's helpful study. Mason's assessment is important since he has expertise in both Josephus and the NT.

117. See below, pp. 376ff., on Acts 12:2. Wilson, *Paul*, p. 54, makes the novel suggestion that Paul was in the employ of the high priest as one of the temple police, possibly as early as Jesus' arrest. Acts, however, says nothing of Paul being one of the temple police. That he goes to the high priest and asks for letters (Acts 9) rather than being sent or commanded by the high priest suggests that Wilson is wrong. The temple police in any case were not Sanhedrin members (see Acts 26:10).

miraculous healing or about the preaching in the temple precincts, or perhaps both? It must be remembered that Luke has just told us that a very large number of people had believed the preaching, which these authorities might well believe could not happen without some sort of power out of the ordinary. In short, the question may be about both the preaching and the healing.[118]

V. 8 indicates that Peter began to speak once he was inspired by the Spirit. Here Luke is surely using the phrase "filled with the Holy Spirit" not to discourse about Peter's sanctification level or spiritual experiences but to indicate that, like the prophets of old, Peter was going to speak God's word, prompted and guided in what he would say by the Spirit.[119] This is the way Luke uses the phrase elsewhere, indicating the prophetic character of the speaker (cf. Luke 1:15, 41, 67; 4:1; Acts 2:4; 4:31; 6:3, 5; 7:55; 9:17; 11:24; 13:9).[120]

Peter's brief speech in vv. 8b-12 is basically a reiteration of the major elements of the sermon summaries already presented in Acts 2 and 3. This particular speech, like these others, is primarily judicial in character, an exercise in defense, only here the setting is even more apropos than the earlier settings. It is clear that the issue here is one of authority and power; this is the exigence or problem which prompts the speech and dictates its character.

The speech begins in a respectful fashion with an address that suggests a recognition of the authority of the questioners — "rulers of the people and elders." While there may be some irony in this form of address, overall the speech is not highly polemical in character though it is adamant about defending a point of view — v. 12 could hardly be more emphatic. The address then recognizes the social status of the questioners and serves as a *captatio benevolentiae,* meant to make the audience more receptive to what follows.[121]

The speech does not use a lot of proofs but relies chiefly on ethos and the direct statement of the facts as Peter sees them. At issue in part is the *quality* of Peter's action — was it a good deed?[122] *V. 9* indicates that Peter assumes that the main thing at issue is the performance of the miracle. *V. 10*

118. As Marshall, *Acts,* pp. 99-100, says, the two events hang together, not least because the healing is used as evidence that Jesus is at work, and so the word about "his name" should be heard and heeded.

119. It is right to see here a fulfillment of Jesus' promise that the disciples would be guided in what they said by the Spirit when they faced trials and authority figures. Cf. Luke 12:12 and 21:15 and the discussion in Barrett, *Acts,* vol. 1, p. 226.

120. See Johnson, *Acts,* p. 77.

121. See Soards, *The Speeches in Acts,* p. 45, who is probably right that we should see vv. 19-20 as a sort of epilogue to the speech still in a judicial vein, appealing to the judges to judge their own request.

122. On all this see Kennedy, *New Testament Interpretation,* p. 119, who stresses that the *stasis* is one of quality.

relates that Peter is not just playing to this particular audience. What he says to the authorities he likewise declares to all Israel, that the healed man[123] standing before them is in that condition "by the name of Jesus Christ of Nazareth, whom you crucified, [but] whom God raised from the dead." The opening "let it be known" is important because the authorities are now living in the age when ignorance is no longer an excuse, and now that they have been told the source of this miracle, they are responsible for what they know. The reference to the name again[124] is simply a shorthand way of saying that the power of Jesus, invoked by name, is the source of this miracle. The charge that the audience is responsible for the crucifixion takes on especial force in view of who the audience here is.

V. 11 further makes clear the character of Jesus. Though Jesus was rejected by the human authorities, he was selected by the ultimate divine authority for great things. Luke here is using Ps. 117:22, previously used in Luke 20:17 at the end of the parable of the vineyard. As always Luke's (or Peter's) modifications are noteworthy. A stone cannot be "scorned" but a person can, and Luke has changed the verb in v. 11 to "scorned" (ἐξουθενηθείς) to indicate the attitude of the authorities standing before Peter. He also adds "by you" before "builders" to make clear the allusion is directly perceived by the immediate audience. Alluding to these authority figures as builders is particularly appropriate in view of their concern with and roles in the temple, then still in process of being built.[125] This "scorned stone" has become "the head of the corner." The translation "corner-stone" is probably not apt here, for a stone that was at the top of a wall or an arch seems to be in view. Either a capstone/keystone or a stone that bound together from the top two parts of a wall at the angle where they met, is meant, probably the latter (cf. *Test. Sol.* 22:7ff.).[126]

V. 12 concludes this brief address with an emphatic statement: "There is not salvation in any other, for no other name under heaven is given among human beings by which we must be saved." Peter (and/or Luke) is no advocate of modern notions of religious pluralism. In terms of soteriology all need to be saved (hence δει), and there is no other means, no other name to appeal to, than Jesus'. Salvation here as elsewhere has spiritual, physical, and social dimensions, as the very presence of the healed man in this Sanhedrin session demonstrates.[127] "The primary meaning of salvation is detachment from the

---

123. "Saved" in v. 9 clearly means healed. See pp. 821ff. below, Appendix 2, on Luke's salvation language.

124. See pp. 156ff. above.

125. The passages that refer to rabbinic scholars as builders in StrB 1, p. 876, are too late and probably not relevant here.

126. Barrett, *Acts*, vol. 1, p. 230, is probably right that there is not a clear allusion to the building of the church here, but that is not impossible.

127. See Johnson, *Acts*, p. 78.

world of the unbelieving and disobedient and attachment to the true people of God of the last days, the εκκλησια, the community which is constituted on the one hand by its loyalty to Jesus, and on the other by his gift of the Spirit, which makes possible a new life conformed to the new loyalty and in other ways too."[128]

The reaction of the authorities in *v. 13* is one of amazement. The term παρρησια and its cognates play an important part in Acts (cf. 2:29; 4:13, 29, 31; 28:31 for the noun form; 9:27, 28; 13:46; 14:3; 18:26; 19:28, 26:26 for the verb), and it is used almost always to describe the way the gospel was preached to the Jews. If Acts was addressed to an educated Gentile, it is in order to point out that this is the quality remarked on over and over again about certain Greek philosophers, especially the Cynics.[129]

The boldness or freedom of speech of Peter (and John) was undeniable, and it was shocking because they were αγραμματοι and ιδιωται. Peter appears like a mighty rhetor in a public assembly. The root meaning of αγραμματοι is "without letters" or illiterate (one who could not write or read), a meaning regularly attested in the papyri and Greek literature.[130] In view of texts such as John 7:15 and the religious context here it probably has a more limited meaning here, namely, one not trained in the Law, the opposite of a γραμματευς or Torah scribe.[131] The second term means a private person, hence an ordinary person, not a public figure or an expert. In a religious context such as this we might call him a layperson. One cannot help noting, however, in view of Peter's response in v. 19, that Luke is probably suggesting that Peter spoke with Spirit-inspired rhetoric and eloquence, something he did not obtain by studying Torah or the rudiments of the art of persuasion in Jerusalem. Under the inspiration of the Spirit he can even sound like one of the greatest of Greek philosophers and teachers — Socrates (cf. below on v. 19). This, I think, is how Theophilus, with his probable Greco-Roman education, would

128. Barrett, *Acts,* vol. 1, p. 231.
129. See the discussion in my *Jesus the Sage,* pp. 123ff. Mason, "Chief Priests," p. 133, is right to note that the philosophical overtones in Acts are striking: (1) Christianity is seen as a αιρεσεως, a term used of philosophical schools; (2) as in the cases of the Pythagoreans and Essenes, a community of goods is practiced; (3) the apostles, in particular Peter and Paul, speak like philosophers with boldness and are persuasive (cf. Acts 2 and 3 to Acts 13, 14, and 17); (4) Christians like Stephen face death without fear, as Socrates did.
130. See Xenophon, *Mem.* 4.2.20; Plutarch, *Apophth. Reg.* 186A; and van der Horst, "Hellenistic Parallels to Acts (Chapters 3 and 4)," p. 42. See now the discussion by Hilton, "Baffling Boldness." Hilton shows the regular connection of education and boldness of speech in antiquity, but here the issue is not just education but eloquence in speech, and how to account for both eloquence and boldness, given the lack of "letters" or formal training in rhetoric and public speaking of the apostles.
131. See Barrett, *Acts,* vol. 1, p. 234.

have heard this account.[132] The point of *v. 13b* is that the authorities recognized not only that these men were companions of Jesus, but that in terms of their amazing speech, and lack of training, they were cut from the same cloth.[133]

The council has nothing to say immediately in response, not least because, as *v. 14* tells us, the healed man is standing right in front of them, so they would have great difficulty denying the power and good work of the apostles. It becomes clear in v. 22 that Luke sees this healing as a sign (σημειον) of larger things, namely, a witness to the validity of the claims made about Jesus in the preaching.[134] Thus the healed man himself is testimony to the validity of Peter's claims.

V. 15 says the apostles, and presumably the healed man, are ordered to leave the council[135] so they can discuss matters in private. One may rightly wonder how Luke could have known the substance of the private deliberations of the Sanhedrin that follow. One possible answer, though it is only a conjecture, is that Saul/Paul was involved in this meeting (cf. Acts 22:4-5; 26:9-10). Alternatively, this may be a case where Luke, like other ancient historians, writes up a scene suggesting what must have been discussed in view of the known outcome of the meeting.

The debate of the council in *vv. 16-17* centers around the fact that the apostles have performed an undeniable sign, one that is obvious to "all who live in Jerusalem."[136] Thus *v. 17* suggests that the council decides to resort to damage control to prevent faith in Jesus from spreading. They would warn the apostles to "speak no more to anyone in this name." In short, what they wish to do, according to *v. 18,* is stop the speaking and teaching about Jesus altogether;[137] nothing is said about stopping them from doing good. It is the linking of such deeds with a particular theological outlook and the historical person of Jesus that concerns the council. This command provides the basis for the future prosecution of the apostles when they choose to disregard and

132. We will reserve what v. 13 tells us about the social level of the earliest Christians for the discussion of 4:32-37 below, pp. 210ff.

133. As is typical of its amplification of the darker side of Jewish faults, the Western text in vv. 13-16 magnifies the perplexity and lack of spiritual perceptivity of the council, while at the same time reducing the criticism of the apostles (D drops και ιδιωται in v. 13). See Metzger, *Textual Commentary,* p. 319.

134. Possibly the healed man had been called in to be interrogated in hopes of making him a witness against the apostles (cf. John 9), but if so Luke does not tell us about this attempt.

135. Συνεδριον probably means the gathering of the assembly here rather than a building where they met, but it could mean council chamber.

136. This is another example of rhetorical hyperbole meant to suggest that it was very widely known and recognized as a good deed.

137. Notice that the text means they are to give up speaking and teaching, an action they had already begun.

disobey it and are brought before the assembly again. It needs to be recognized here that the assembly appears to be operating according to usual Jewish judicial procedure in such cases, whereby one sternly warns the accused the first time, and only prosecutes them if the action recurs.[138] If this is correct, then it is in order to point out that the similar material in Acts 5:17ff. should not be seen as a literary doublet, a second version of the same story.[139]

The response of Peter and John in *v. 19* and even more in 5:29 should be compared to Socrates' words when he was on trial before the Athenian judges and was ordered to stop teaching his philosophy: "I shall obey God rather than you, and while I have life and strength I shall never cease from the practice and teaching of philosophy" (Plato, *Apolog.* 29D). The trial of Socrates was of course famous throughout the Greco-Roman world, and the story of it influenced the way various similar tales were told.[140] I would suggest something along these lines is happening here.

Luke is suggesting that Christianity is an equally noble philosophy and that the truth about it must come out. It must be borne in mind that when Luke was writing, the early Christians had no temples, no priests, and no animal sacrifices. Rather, they met in homes. To a person like Theophilus, Christianity would have appeared not as a formal public religion but as some sort of religious philosophy, something which could be discussed over a Greco-Roman meal. Under these circumstances it was apt to portray early Christians as like the most noble Greek philosopher and martyr of all, especially since some would give their lives for their beliefs, as Socrates did. Interestingly, here in *v. 19* Peter's response leaves judgment in the hands of the authorities. Even they would have to agree that one must obey God rather than human judges if the two are in conflict.

V. 20 says bluntly that the apostles can't keep from being witnesses, relating what they had seen and heard. This is the fundamental task of an apostle, but also of all disciples (cf. Acts 1:8, 22). After offering further threats the authorities let the apostles go. After all, they had not yet violated anything the council commanded them to do, for there was no ban on such preaching before this meeting.

V. 21 implies that the apostles are released because the authorities are afraid of the reaction of *the people*, of whom it is said, "*all of them* praised God for what happened."[141] The term λαος recurs frequently in Acts, and Luke

---

138. See my discussion of this procedure in *Women in the Ministry of Jesus*, pp. 21ff. and the notes.

139. See Marshall, *Acts*, pp. 97ff.

140. See, e.g., the way Josephus, *Ant.* 17.158-59, recounts the story of the Maccabees.

141. Again rhetorical hyperbole, but it indicates that the response had been large enough that the authorities were afraid to take strong action.

uses it to distinguish which Jews are the real opponents of Christianity, namely, the Jerusalem authorities, and not even all of them (cf. 5:34). Later in Acts some of the people as well as various of the Jewish leaders turn against the followers of Jesus, but even then Luke wants to indicate that the Jewish leadership was not totally opposed to the Jesus movement (cf. Acts 6:7, where a great many priests become Christians). It is this state of the division of the house of Israel over Jesus and his followers that Luke wishes to record. He is not interested in presenting some sort of lopsided anti-Semitic propaganda which tars all Jews with the same negative brush. "Jewish repentance and salvation remain options through to the very end of Acts; Acts 28 claims that some of the Roman Jews were 'persuaded' by Paul (Acts 28.24)."[142]

V. 22 concludes this section of the narration with a final reference to the healed man, whose healing prompts the people's praise. This miracle was an outstanding one, not just because it was done before many eyes, but because the recipient had been lame for so long.[143] He was a full generation old, in fact more than forty years of age, when he was healed. This bears witness to the power available to the apostles, a power that no council could stop or stifle.

---

142. Rightly Mason, "Chief Priests," p. 122. Here he is following the helpful study of Brawley, *Luke-Acts and the Jews*, p. 141, whose views are basically summed up in the sentence quoted above.

143. It is of course characteristic of such miracle tales to stress the duration or magnitude of the problem, which only magnifies the cure. Cf., e.g., Luke 8:43; John 9:1.

V. Prayer, Possessions, Persecution, and Proclamation (Acts 4:23–8:3)

The material found in Acts 4:23–8:3 focuses on several major themes oscillating back and forth between the internal life of the community of Jesus, its external activities, especially preaching and healing, and the public response to these activities. There is a crescendo of persecution in this section which becomes so severe that a great deal of the church is scattered to nearby regions, something which paradoxically aids the mission and spread of the very thing the persecutors sought to snuff out. In fact, throughout this somewhat lengthy section Luke brings up at various points how what human beings intended for evil, God had already planned for good. Luke's literary skills are evident throughout, especially in the way he deftly introduces a major character or theme briefly in advance of giving this character or theme full treatment. Though a variety of subdivisions of this major section of the book are possible, especially since it involves two of the so-called panels of Acts which are linked at 6:7, the following divisions seem the most natural in my view: (a) prayer and power, 4:23-31; (b) the community of goods, 4:32-37; (c) Ananias and Sapphira, 5:1-11; (d) the sum of the matter, 5:12-16; (e) portents and persecutions, 5:17-42; (f) the seven servants, 6:1-7; (g) the trial, testimony, and termination of Stephen, 6:8–8:1a; (h) a summary of severity, 8:1b-3. It will be seen from the above that at the heart of this section is the story, including the stoning, of Stephen, for which the previous persecutions and trials prepare us.

A. Prayer and Power (4:23-31)

The response of the apostles to persecution is prayer, not for relief or deliverance from persecution but for boldness and power to continue to proclaim the word even in the midst of such adversity. This section has sometimes been thought to be constructed either out of an early Christian exegesis of Psalm 2 or as a sort of doublet of the Pentecost story. Neither explanation is cogent, as B. Gaventa has shown, because this "incident marks the beginning of the church's response to persecution. Because the petitions of the prayer are granted, the church is enabled to continue to respond to persecution with forthright proclamation accompanied by acts from God's hand."[1] Other views do not take the essential character of this passage into account. There was no persecution of the church leading up to Pentecost, and there is no witness in foreign languages here.

A discerning reading of the *pesher* or contemporizing interpretation of Psalm 2 in this text will show that it is often taken to refer to events in the life of Jesus, *but the narrative here is about events in the life of the church.* That Luke sees an analogy between the two events (persecution of Jesus and the apostles) because the source and object of the persecution is true enough, but clearly Luke has not simply created his story out of this early Christian exegesis of the psalm.

Furthermore, as Lüdemann points out, the application of Psalm 2 to Herod and Pilate sits somewhat uneasily with Luke's presentation of them in his Gospel as *not* responsible, finally, for Christ's death.[2] At the heart of this section is once again speech material, this time a prayer in the form of: (1) invocation, (2) quotation, (3) explanation/narration, and (4) petition. Though this prayer in vv. 29-30 has been said to have a deliberative conclusion,[3] on the whole this is not an example of speech in rhetorical form.

For our purposes it is important to point out that the elements of prayer, predestination, and portents in this section are all characteristic of Hellenistic historiography.[4] Luke tends to emphasize especially God's predestination and

---

1. Gaventa, "To Speak the Word," p. 80.

2. See Lüdemann, *Early Christianity*, p. 58; Marshall, *Acts*, p. 104. This must count against the whole theory of Haenchen, *Acts*, pp. 226-29, that we have some sort of free composition by Luke here. Also against such a theory is v. 25, which is in very rough Greek and suggests an unrevised source. V. 25 is but one more clue that we seem to have Acts in some sort of rough draft form, which may partially explain why later Western revisers felt free to add and subtract as they did from the text. See pp. 65ff. above.

3. See Kennedy, *New Testament Interpretation*, p. 120. Soards, *The Speeches in Acts*, p. 47, suggests there is an epideictic proem at the beginning here, but the invocation involves a simple statement of fact or belief — praise is not mentioned.

4. See Squires, *Plan of God in Luke-Acts*, pp. 98ff.

plan when he is talking about controversial matters, especially the death and resurrection of Jesus, but also the persecution and powerful witness of his followers. This is very similar to the way earlier Greek historians treat the theme of the fated protagonist.[5] In short, Luke is doing apologetics here on behalf of Christ and the early Christians.

V. 23 informs us that, once released, the apostles went to "their own" (τους ιδιους). This phrase would normally refer to one's own family or people (cf. Acts 24:23; John 1:11; 13:1), but here the family of faith is in view,[6] with its leaders especially referred to in vv. 29-30.[7] Perhaps we should see this scene as being rather like that found later in 12:12ff., where Peter again comes to the community after having been held, finds them in prayer, and gives his report. The report here involves relating what the priests and elders said, though of course Peter and John have no intention of obeying their orders.[8]

The report does not produce consternation but rather concentration in prayer. *V. 24* suggests a corporate and audible prayer, though it is possible this prayer was spoken only by one or more of the leaders. Luke intends to emphasize the unanimity of the early church at this point by using the term ομοθυμαδον (together), in similar fashion to 1:14. This term, along with the use of πας and the phrase επι το αυτο, indicates the corporate character and κοινωνια of the early church (cf. 1:14; 2:46; 4:12; 15:25).[9]

God is addressed in *v. 24* as δεσποτα (from which we get the English word *despot*). It is a term found elsewhere in Luke-Acts at Luke 2:29 (cf. Rev. 6:10; 3 Macc. 2:2), and it connotes one with great power and control of circumstances, something those being persecuted naturally need to know about and affirm. The point of the citation that follows is to make that control very clear. The God who made all things has human history well in hand, for human beings are only one sort of God's creatures.[10]

---

5. Cf. Plümacher, *Lukas als hellenistischer Schriftsteller,* pp. 111ff.

6. Probably not the apostles in particular, pace Johnson, *Acts,* pp. 83ff. The picture here is too similar to what follows in 4:32ff. (and 2:43ff.) for "their own" to mean something more narrow than their own community. Cf. Barrett, *Acts,* vol. 1, p. 243. For the possible meaning of the phrase in the papyri being one's true friends, see *New Docs,* 3:148.

7. This prayer is about the witnesses, and note that they are not limited to the apostles, as the extended narratives about Stephen in Acts 7 and Philip in Acts 8 show. See Polhill, *Acts,* p. 148.

8. It may be significant that the scribes are not mentioned here as threatening the apostles but rather the priests and the lay aristocracy. In other words, the opposition in Jerusalem to the apostles, much as was the case with Jesus, is largely non-Pharisaic in character. See Polhill, *Acts,* p. 148 n. 60.

9. See Gaventa, "To Speak the Word," p. 77.

10. This standard way of addressing God as the creator of all is repeated nearly verbatim in Acts 14:15 and 17:24 and goes back to such texts as Gen. 14:19; Exod. 20:11; Isa. 37:16. See Johnson, *Acts,* p. 81.

Though the general drift of *v. 25* is clear enough, the grammar is very awkward.[11] Here alone in Acts do we have the idea that God speaks by means (διὰ) of the Holy Spirit (cf. 1:2) as well as through human mouthpieces, in this case through the mouth of David "your servant."[12] The reference to David as "our father" reminds us once again not only of the Jewish character of this material but also of the fact that the early Christians saw themselves as the true Israel, true messianic Jews, and the heirs of the OT promises.

The quotation of Ps. 2:1-2 in *vv. 25-26* is verbatim from the LXX, which again suggests that this is Luke's own rendering of his source material, since it may be doubted that a group of early Aramaic-speaking Jewish Christians would normally or naturally cite the OT in the Greek, especially in their prayer language (cf. the use of *abba* in Gal. 4:6; Rom. 8:15; cf. 1 Cor. 16:22 for an early Aramaic prayer).[13] There is a clear parallel structure to this psalm material, and Luke naturally takes εθνη (nations) to refer to Gentiles and λαοι (peoples) to refer to Jews, while the kings of the earth are seen as represented by Herod and the rulers by Pilate.[14] In the original peoples likely referred to Gentiles, not Jews. The plural λαοι, though in a citation, is still striking here when applied to Israel, and suggests Jews being in opposition to their own Messiah. All of these people are said to be against God and God's Christ. This is then explained in v. 27 to refer to Jesus God's servant whom God anointed (εχρισας). It is a notable fact that the speech material in Acts shows a clearer knowledge of the etymological significance of Χριστος than other parts of the NT, including Paul's letters, which in turn suggests the primitiveness of this material.[15]

Vv. 27-28 indicate that while Herod, Pilate, the Jews, and the Gentiles all intended ill, God had other intentions. These human actors were only doing what God's hand and plan had destined in advance to transpire. The particular verb used here, προ-οριζειν, occurs only here in Acts, but various related Greek words that begin with the prefix *pro*, indicating foreknowledge (2:23; 26:5) or

11. See the attempted emendations in various manuscripts in Metzger, *Textual Commentary*, pp. 321-23.

12. On παις as servant rather than child, see pp. 147ff. above. Here the reference to God as Sovereign Lord coupled with the reference to Jesus as Servant and the disciples as slaves/servants (δουλοι) in v. 29 all suggest the translation "servant" of David. Jesus is the ultimate Son of David and, like him, is God's servant.

13. This portion of Psalm 2 seems to have been little used in early Christianity, though there is some evidence that the text was used at Qumran in an eschatological manner. Cf. 4QFlor 1:18-19 and see the discussion by Evans and Sanders, *Luke and Scripture*, p. 193.

14. Another plausible view is that both Herod and Pilate are represented by the term "kings," and the term "rulers" refers to the Jewish authorities with whom the Christians would soon collide.

15. On Χριστος see pp. 147ff. above.

foretelling/proclaiming in advance (cf. 1:14; 3:18; 7:52; 13:24), are used elsewhere by Luke in reference to God's working out of his salvation plan for humankind in the life of Jesus and in events Luke records in Acts.[16]

The prayer thus far has served as a sort of preamble to the petition found in *vv. 29-30.* It is appropriate at this juncture to compare what we have here with other prayer material in the Bible. In particular, Hezekiah's prayer in Isa. 37:16-20 has been seen as a model for the prayer in Acts because it includes: (1) an address to God as Creator and Lord; (2) a reference to the threat of Israel's enemies; and (3) a concluding petition. It is precisely in this last part that we find the most salient differences. Hezekiah prays for deliverance or rescue, while Peter and the Christians pray for courage and boldness. Also in the prayer in Acts, the reference to enemies is part of a scriptural citation which is actually understood to refer to the experience of Jesus. The point of this citation is made clear by Gaventa: "For Luke, the persecution of the apostles *corresponds* to the persecution of Jesus. The threats against Peter and John by the Jewish leaders are the equivalent of the threats against Jesus. Later on in Acts, a similar connection occurs between those who persecute the prophets and Paul's persecution of the church (7.52-53; 8.3)."[17]

The transition to the petition is made with the formula καὶ τὰ νῦν in *v. 29.* τὰ νῦν is unique to Acts in the NT (4:29; 5:38; 17:30; 20:32; 27:22, cf. 24:25). This expression is common in the larger corpus of Greek literature, and we find the similar καὶ νῦν introducing a request in the LXX (including a prayer request in Isa. 37:20 and 2 Chron. 20:10, 11). For our purposes it is important to point out that this expression and references to παρρησία are especially common in rhetorical historiography (e.g., in Dionysius of Halicarnassus).[18]

The prayer here is that God will "grant to your servants to speak your word with all boldness, while you stretch out your hand to heal. . . ." Once again we find the word παρρησία, and the subject is boldness or powerfulness of speech; in short, the prayer is for Spirit-inspired rhetoric that will persuade.[19] Notice here that while the "servants" see themselves as responsible for the proclamation, they see God as the one who spreads out his hand and performs miracles.[20] This comports with what we have seen earlier in 3:12-15, where Peter disavows having power in himself but affirms power in Jesus'

---

16. See Gaventa, "To Speak the Word," pp. 78-79 and notes.

17. Ibid., p. 79.

18. See Conzelmann, *Acts,* p. 35.

19. On παρρησία and rhetoric see pp. 39ff. above.

20. Notice the connection between David, Jesus, and the early Christians as God's servants. Continuity of relationship with God and continuity of forms of service are assumed. It is these sorts of connections that allowed the early Christians to see the OT as referring not just to Jesus' experiences but their own. See Marshall, *Acts,* pp. 105ff.

name. Miracles, then, are seen as God's confirmation of the word which the apostles proclaimed, a familiar view in ancient historical literature of the relationship of prophecy and portents, the latter verifying the former. Miracles, then, are seen to have an apologetic function in Acts.

In *v. 31* we are told that the divine response to the prayer is immediate in the form of the shaking of the room where they were gathered together. This form of divine activity, in which the Deity indicates assent or advent, is often remarked on in ancient Greek literature, including of course the LXX (cf. Ps. 17:7-8 LXX; *T. Levi* 3:9; Josephus, *Ant.* 7.76-77; Plutarch, *Vita Publica* 9.6; Lucian, *Menip.* 9-10).[21] The second half of the verse indicates that the disciples' prayers were answered not just by a portent but by an empowerment — they were all filled with the Holy Spirit and spoke God's word with boldness. This is once again Luke's way of talking about prophetic inspiration and power in speaking and should not be taken as indicating something about the level of sanctification of those involved. The issue here is empowerment for witnessing, not personal spiritual formation or growth.[22] The point is empowerment for speech in the face of persecution, not a gift of foreign languages, and so this text is not about a repetition of the Pentecost experience.[23]

B. The Community of Goods (4:32-37)

The second major summary passage occurs at this juncture, linking what has come before with what follows. There is room for debate as to whether vv. 36-37 should be seen as part of this summary, but in view of the summary character of these two verses which introduce Barnabas, and in view of the fact that in the next summary passage we have a particular remark about Peter (cf. 5:15), we can say at least that vv. 36-37 are transitional, providing a segue to the narrative in Acts 5. Barnabas on the one hand and Ananias and Sapphira on the other represent positive and negative examples of how money and

21. See the texts and discussion by van der Horst, "Hellenistic Parallels to Acts (Chapters 3 and 4)," pp. 44-45.

22. In other words, this text tells us nothing about the idea of blessings or spiritual experiences subsequent to conversion in a way that would allow us to discern a schematized order of Christian experience of the Holy Spirit. Luke is here indebted to the OT stories about inspiration and empowerment, even including such stories as that of Samson. A moment's reflection on this latter story will remind us that God can use very flawed and unsanctified vessels to speak the divine word or perform a miraculous work. That one is a channel for divine power does not necessarily indicate one's purity.

23. *Pace* Richards, "Pentecost as a Recurrent Theme," pp. 135-36.

goods should and should not be handled in the church. The summary in 4:32-35 provides a general introduction to this subject.

There is still considerable debate as to whether summary passages like we find in 4:32ff. should be seen simply as Lukan creations, based on the narratives that surround them, or whether they are based, as I think, on some sort of extra source material. Since we have already addressed this issue,[24] it is in order to point out here that Luke is trying to present both a descriptive and perhaps a prescriptive portrait — a picture of what he believed Christianity was once like, and ought to be again. The use of the iterative imperfect verbs ("they used to sell . . . ," etc.) suggests historical distance from a practice that was repeated or ongoing for a period of time.[25]

It is also in order to stress that Luke presents the early Jerusalem church as being like other early Jewish groups, such as the Essenes who practiced a community of goods,[26] but he also uses language that a Theophilus would recognize as reflecting the Greek ideals about how true friends should act. Aristotle said that true friends held everything in common (απαντα κοινα) and were of one mind (ψυχη μια — *Nic. Eth.* 9.8.2), much the same as is said here. What is interesting about the Christian use of such conventions is that while friendship in the Greco-Roman mold often involved reciprocity between those who were basically social equals, what Luke seems to be inculcating here is conventions whereby Christians with goods will provide funds to the community for those who are needy *without thought of return,* and thus he is suggesting something more akin to family duties.

The language of friendship was of course also used for patronage or benefaction situations in the Greco-Roman world, and as the example of Barnabas will show, this is more nearly what Luke has in mind here.[27] One may suspect that Barnabas is being held up as an example for Theophilus himself as a person of some social status to follow.[28] In any case this summary, which reflects both Jewish and Hellenistic characteristics, is apologetic in character, though "an example of an indirect rather than a direct apology, that is, the text addresses insiders [Theophilus] who will have to deal with the outside world. The summaries help them formulate an understanding of

24. See pp. 157ff. above.

25. See Polhill, *Acts,* p. 153.

26. See pp. 156ff. above and Capper, "Palestinian Cultural Context." Especially important is Capper's discussion of the evidence that the Essene movement was broader than just what has been found at Qumran, and could have been an influence in Jerusalem itself, which is said to have an Essene presence during this time period.

27. See my discussion of friendship conventions in *Friendship and Finances in Philippi* (Valley Forge, Pa.: Trinity, 1994), pp. 118-21.

28. On Christians as benefactors see Winter, *Seek the Welfare,* passim.

themselves as Christians. The question it addresses is whether Christians are at all comparable to other people. The answer is yes: Christianity has also its αθλεται αρετης."[29]

The term πληθους in v. 32, which means something like "whole assembly,"[30] is significant on several grounds. First, it is a Lukan term (eight times in the Gospel and sixteen in Acts, out of a total of thirty-one in the NT). Secondly, the term refers to the whole community of Christians here and as such mirrors Jewish usage of the term (cf. *CIJ* 2.804 — "peace and mercy upon παν το πληθους"). Luke further defines the group by calling them "those who had become believers" (πιστευσαντων).[31] Faith is seen as the essential characteristic of the early Christians.

These believers are said to be of one heart and mind (or being), a description which only in the second half (μια ψυχη) conjures up Greco-Roman friendship ideas (cf. above). In fact, the phrase "heart and mind" is an OT expression which is *not* found in pagan Greek literature, and one may suspect that texts like Deut. 6:5 (LXX) may stand behind this expression.[32] The last major thought in v. 32 indicates that "no one called private/personal anything that belonged to him. Everything was (shared) in common."[33] What this suggests is a picture of no one claiming owner's rights, no one exhibiting selfishness or possessiveness. It is a picture of sharing without thought of reciprocity, something which would be very surprising in a world where almost all relationships involving property were assumed to operate on the basis of some sort of reciprocity.[34] As Lüdemann says, "the idea of sharing with those not of equal rank is more Jewish than Greek."[35] The theme of

---

29. Sterling, " 'Athletes of Virtue,' " p. 696. One must be careful in applying the friendship material to the situations described in Acts, for the earliest Christians saw themselves as family, not just as friends, and thus couched their obligations in terms of familial language and duties, but cf. Mitchell, "Social Function of Friendship."

30. Not "multitude" since we are talking about a purposeful gathering — in other words, a synonym for εκκλησια. See the use of the term to translate *qahal* in the LXX of Exod. 12:6; 2 Chron. 31:18; cf. Luke 8:37; 23:1; Acts 6:2; 14:4, and Johnson, *Acts*, p. 86.

31. An aorist inceptive participle.

32. Cf. Gerhardsson, "Einige Bemerkungen zu Apg. 4, 32." Gerhardsson plausibly suggests that the first half of v. 32 describes loving God with one's whole being, and the second half about sharing property describes loving neighbor as self.

33. On κοινα and κοινωνια, cf. pp. 157ff. above on 2:44. The important point is that the term κοινα/κοινωνια conveys the idea of a sharing in common or participation with others in something. See my *Conflict and Community in Corinth*, pp. 224-25. It is an active term about sharing, and probably should not be translated "held in common," as if there were a communal storehouse.

34. Cf. Polhill, *Acts*, p. 151: "The Greek literally reads 'everything was in common with them.' Taken by itself, this could refer to shared ownership but in conjunction with the first expression, it also refers to a practice of freely sharing one's goods with another."

35. Lüdemann, *Early Christianity*, p. 61.

what was done with property by the early Christians will be revisited in
v. 34.[36]

V. 33 has been seen as something of an insertion into a summary about
property, but as Johnson rightly points out, Luke's intent is to place the
apostles into the middle of the community's life to begin to indicate the
relationship of authority to property (cf. Acts 6:1-6), and it prepares us for
the remark in vv. 35-36 about laying funds at the apostles' feet.[37] V. 33 opens
with a remark about the great power given to the witnesses, in particular
the apostles whose task it was to testify about the resurrection of the Lord
Jesus (cf. 1:22). It closes with a remark about the great grace/favor that rests
upon all of them. This last could be taken to refer to the regard of the Jewish
people who still viewed the early Christians favorably, but in view of the
first half of the verse it likely refers to God's grace resting on the whole
congregation.[38]

Vv. 34-35 go together and speak of how the early church dealt with
members who were needy (ενδεης). Though the literal rendering of the text
is "there was not anyone needy among them," this must not be read apart
from the last half of the verse, which speaks of people selling property to take
care of the needy. What Luke means is that those Christians who were in need
were soon provided for. This was a social obligation early Christians apparently
felt keenly, probably in part because of the earlier teaching of Jesus (cf., e.g.,
Matt. 25:35-40), but also the OT was clear about God providing: "There will,
however, be no one in need among you, because the LORD is sure to bless you
in the land" (Deut. 15:4).[39]

The phrase κτητορες χωριων refers to owners of land, which is followed
by a reference to houses. "They would sell (them) and would bring the
proceeds of what they sold and would place it at the apostles' feet." It is perfectly
possible to take this sentence to mean that various of the more well-to-do
Christians sold *some* of the properties they possessed and brought *all* of the
proceeds of that sale to the apostles.[40] Nothing is said here about a transfer

---

36. As is often the case, the Western text amplifies and clarifies what is said in v. 32
by adding "and there was no quarrel among them at all," or in E, "and there was not any
division among them." These are surely later hagiographic expansions meant to emphasize
even more than Luke already does the unity of the primitive church. See Metzger, *Textual
Commentary*, p. 325.

37. See Johnson, *Acts*, p. 86.

38. Thus this verse stands in contrast to 2:47, where the χαρις or favor/regard of the
people is clearly in view. The background here lies in texts in the LXX such as Exod. 3:21;
11:3; 12:36; and 33:12-13.

39. It would appear that the Jerusalem Church regularly had to deal with im-
poverished members, not just after A.D. 46. See Hengel, *Paul*, pp. 240ff.

40. See Barrett, *Acts*, vol. 1, p. 255; Polhill, *Acts*, pp. 152-53.

of ownership of property or any requirement to surrender it, unlike the case at Qumran; rather, the discussion is about the liquidation of some assets.[41] Nor is there any evidence of control of ownership of all property by the community; rather, there is control and distribution of the funds given to the community. Notice that Luke calls those who give in this text "owners," which comports with what he will say in Acts 5. The overall impression left by both this summary and the following examples of Barnabas as well as Ananias and Sapphira is that the giving was voluntary, not required. As a result, Barnabas's act is seen as meritorious while the couple's act is seen as wicked, not because of what they held back but because of their attempt to deceive, to appear more virtuous than they were.[42] It is on target to add that these "actions do not reflect an ascetic ideal, as in some Greek and Jewish sects, but instead the practice of radically valuing people over possessions. Such behavior reportedly continued among Christians well into the second century, and it was long ridiculed by pagans."[43]

The phrase "lay at the feet of the apostles" (cf. 4:37; 5:2; 7:58) is Semitic and conveys the idea of submission to apostolic authority and request. The distribution of the funds was undertaken by the apostles, something that at some point would become burdensome (cf. below on Acts 6), and the basis of the distribution was not some ethic that all should have exactly the same amount of goods or money but that no believer should be in need. The funds were given out as anyone had need, which suggests on an ad hoc basis, not as a regular weekly or monthly distribution. This perhaps explains how need could continue to arise as a problem.

Whether we see *vv. 36-37* as the conclusion of this summary, as I have suggested, providing a concrete positive example of what Luke has in mind, or whether it is taken together with what follows in Acts 5,[44] this material is important for several reasons. First, it introduces us to someone who will prove to be a very important bridge figure between the Jerusalem church and Paul, and in general between the Jerusalem church and the mission work outside

41. See pp. 157ff. above.

42. It is not convincing to argue that this summary is at odds with the discussion of Barnabas and the material in Acts 5 on the matter of property, not least because the style of both sets of material is Lukan, reflecting Lukan remodeling of sources. Had Luke seen any incongruity between the summary and what follows, he could easily have edited it out. See Lüdemann, *Early Christianity*, pp. 61ff.

43. Keener, *Bible Background Commentary*, p. 330.

44. Which raises the question why the two examples are not more similar in length if they were meant to be taken together and were seen as a contrasting pair. It makes better sense to see vv. 36-37 as transitional, and basically as a conclusion of the summary. The repetition of the phrase "laid at the feet of the apostles" in vv. 35 and 37 suggests that vv. 36-37 should be seen as going with what precedes, illustrating it. Lukan summaries are by nature positive in character whether they involve generalities or specific examples.

the Holy Land. Secondly, it reveals that Luke does not have to deal in mere generalities with the earliest Christian community — he has specific examples to draw upon. In this case he could have learned about Barnabas from Paul, who is attested to have crossed paths with Barnabas not only in Acts but also in the Pauline corpus (cf. Gal. 2:1-14).[45]

The person in question's proper name was Joseph, but he was called by the apostles, as a nickname, Barnabas. Luke in an aside explains that this Jewish name means "son of exhortation/ encouragement."[46] This aside, like the one in 1:19, strongly suggests that Theophilus did not know Aramaic, and probably also that he was not familiar with some of the stories and key figures involved at the beginning of the church.[47]

The term παρακλησεως refers to some sort of speech activity, and to judge from Luke's use elsewhere (cf. Luke 5:34; 10:6; 16:8; 20:34, 36 and, especially of Barnabas, Acts 11:23) the translation "encouragement" can be argued to have the edge. In terms of derivation, however, while clearly enough *bar* means "son" in Aramaic, as Barrett shows, the most probable origin of *nabas* is some form of the term *nabi* — prophet/preacher.[48] Since Luke does indeed have a concern to portray Barnabas not just as an encourager but perhaps even more as a preacher and missionary, on the whole the translation "son of exhortation" (= preacher) seems preferable.[49]

Barnabas is identified as a Levite. Though in the earliest periods of Israel's history Levites were said to hold no land (cf. Josh. 21:1-41), by NT times it is clear that they did have property.[50] He is also identified as a Cypriot, one who was, or whose family was, from Cyprus. There is certainly evidence for a large

45. Notice that Barnabas is involved with Paul not only in Antioch but also in Jerusalem, as Acts also attests.

46. On Luke's use of asides, which are not that frequent, cf. Sheely, *Narrative Asides in Luke-Acts.* Sheely suggests that Luke's usage is like that found in romances (e.g., *The Golden Ass*), more than it is like that used in histories (though he sees similarities with 1 Maccabees). His conclusion is: "Generally, the distribution of narrative asides in Luke-Acts shows a better correlation with romances and histories than with biographies" (p. 180). This is so because in Luke-Acts the asides are normally used to explain, whereas in biography they are part of self-conscious narration. This conclusion comports with some of our remarks in the introduction explaining why Acts should not be seen as an example of biography. See pp. 4ff. above.

47. Later asides, such as the one in 17:21, suggest that Theophilus had not traveled to at least some of the places about which Luke writes.

48. See the discussion in Barrett, *Acts,* vol. 1, pp. 258-59.

49. The meaning "comfort" for παρακλησεως must be said to be doubtful. On the whole question of the derivation of the name Barnabas, see Brock, "Barnabas, *huios parakleseos.*" Hengel, *Paul,* pp. 213-14.

50. Cf. Josephus, *Life* 68-83. In an even later period there were Levites said to be noted for their wealth. See Jeremias, *Jerusalem,* p. 105. Even before NT times, Jeremiah, a priest, is said to own land (Jer. 32:6-15).

Jewish community on Cyprus,[51] and this reference may be meant to connect Barnabas to the missionaries from there who go and evangelize places like Antioch (cf. 11:19-20; 21:16). What is not clear is whether Barnabas's land was in Cyprus or Judea. In any case his selling of it and giving the proceeds to the community (v. 37) can be said to be the antithesis of the behavior of Judas, who betrays Jesus and with the blood money buys land (1:18-19). One thing becomes clear from reading the summaries in the early portion of Acts — Luke wishes to stress the positive side of things about the early church, as is to be expected in an apologetic work. This in part explains why Luke does not spend as much time on the problems and tensions of the early church, though, as Acts 5 shows, he does not neglect such difficulties altogether. What this amounts to is not so much painting a portrait of life as it never was, but emphasizing one aspect of the truth over another. Perhaps Luke felt that airing all the earliest church's dirty linen in the 70s or 80s could serve no good purpose, especially since many of the problems had since disappeared or been resolved. Luke is not just a historian but an advocate for the faith once given. The entire above discussion leads to a more detailed examination of the social level and status of the earliest Christians.

A Closer Look — The Social Status and Level of the Earliest Christians

Discussion of the social level and status of the earliest Christians has been considerable in recent years.[52] When the discussion has centered on Acts it has tended to focus on the person of Paul and the way he is portrayed in Acts.[53] We will have a good deal to say on this last subject later in the commentary.[54] Our interest here is to address the broader question of the portrayal of the social level of the earliest Christians in Jerusalem, and to make some introductory comments about Christians elsewhere. It is fair to say that Luke only really presents us with sufficient detail in the descriptions of the church at Jerusalem and perhaps the one at Antioch to get any kind of clear picture of how things were in the earliest period.[55] One must also keep in mind that Luke appears to be writing to someone of relatively high social status, and so it should not surprise us that from time to time he emphasizes that people like Theophilus were either converts or sympathetic to Christianity (cf., e.g., Acts 10:1ff.; 13:7-12; 16:14;

---

51. See Josephus, *Ant.* 13.285-88.
52. See my *Conflict and Community in Corinth*, pp. 19ff.; and Stark, *Rise of Christianity.*
53. See Lentz, *Luke's Portrait of Paul*, and Neyrey, "Luke's Social Location of Paul."
54. See below, pp. 430ff.
55. See Sterling, " 'Athletes of Virtue,' " pp. 679ff.

17:34; etc.). It is also well to keep steadily in view that modern notions and terminology about classes, especially middle classes, do not really apply very well to the ancient world, and modern assumptions about the character of cities, and how and where people lived, should not be imported into the discussion of Acts.[56]

It must be remembered that there are several sorts of clues to the social level and status of the earliest Christians. One of these of course is education, and we have already learned that Peter and John were regarded as lacking in higher education (4:13), and that their rhetoric or powers of persuasion were primarily Spirit-inspired rather than learned. We learn nothing in Acts 1–8 to contradict this assessment of at least the Galilean male leadership of the early Christians. There is, however, some evidence that there may have been a few female followers of Jesus, such as Joanna the wife of Chuza, who may have been of higher education and social status (Luke 8:3), and Luke locates them in Jerusalem during the Easter events (cf. Luke 23:55; 24:10) and probably afterward as well (Acts 1:14). One may also rightly point to Mary, the mother of John Mark, as a person of higher status who had a large enough home to allow various early Christians to meet in her abode, and at least one domestic servant but probably more (Acts 12:12-13). If the Gospel of Mark goes back to this same John Mark, as many scholars still hold, then it is in order to point out that he has some ability to compose a document in Greek which reflects a more than rudimentary education in and knowledge of Greek.

A second major factor to be considered is the whole issue of housing and hospitality. As we have already discussed, the early church was dependent on the hospitality and the houses of the members, presumably the more well-to-do believers, in order to provide a venue for meeting and a social medium for the message to be retained and passed on.[57] The detailed study of B. Blue confirms this conclusion and reveals the size of some of the more well-to-do homes in Jerusalem; namely, that most of them could not likely hold more than about 50 persons for a meeting, though if there was a peristyle or courtyard it is conceivable that up to 120 or so could be accommodated.[58] The evidence suggests, however, that the disciples met in an "upper room," which was apparently not an unusual location for early Jews to gather to dine and study Torah (cf. Acts 1:13; *m. Shab.* 1:4). The upshot of the fact that Christians met in homes in Jerusalem is to suggest, especially in view of the growing number of converts, that at least several Christians had large enough homes to accommodate a goodly number in a church meeting, but that no one locale was sufficient to house them all, even very shortly after Pentecost (cf. Acts 2:46; 12:17). This in turn suggests that at least a few early Jewish Christians were of some social status.

The third factor to take into account is what is actually said about money and finances in Acts 1–8. We have already seen various hints that at least some early Christians had land and houses which they could sell and give the proceeds to the

---

56. See rightly the cautionary words of R. L. Rohrbaugh, "The Pre-Industrial City in Luke-Acts: Urban Social Relations," in *The Social World of Luke-Acts,* ed. J. H. Neyrey (Peabody, Mass.: Hendrickson, 1991), pp. 125-49.

57. See pp. 157ff. above.

58. See B. Blue, "Acts and the House Church," in AIIFCS, 2:119-222. This estimate holds for villas and homes elsewhere in the Mediterranean as well. See especially p. 131 n. 44.

community (cf. Acts 2:45; 4:36-37). Even allowing for hyperbole, if in this earliest period few were in need or want because Christians shared with one another, this presupposes that various of them had something they could share, some goods they could part with in order to make sure others had at least food, shelter, and clothing. Such texts also suggest that some early Christians were quite poor and could easily be made indigent. This conclusion is confirmed not only by texts like Acts 6, but also by the evidence from the Pauline corpus, which suggests there was a considerable quotient of the poor in the Jerusalem and Judean churches that needed to be taken care of, especially during times of famine (cf. Gal. 2:10; 2 Cor. 9:12; Rom. 15:25-26).

A fourth bit of evidence to be taken into account is the mention of names, titles, or functions, which may suggest a person of some social status. This comes up with a figure like Barnabas who is said to be a Levite; or with the priests who are said to have become followers of Jesus (Acts 6:7); or perhaps with figures like Joseph of Arimathea or Nicodemus who seem to have been part of the Sanhedrin, the former of whom is said to have been a disciple of Jesus in the Fourth Gospel (cf. John 19:38-39; Luke 23:50 at least suggests he was a sympathizer).[59] The tomb of Joseph used to bury Jesus suggests to most that Joseph was a reasonably well-to-do person. This evidence, however, is not univocal, not least because various of the priests and Levites could be rather poor, and apart from their religious status not really be better off than various merchants, craftsmen, and unskilled laborers.[60] Sometimes Levites could supplement their income by being scribes.[61]

In a recent detailed study, D. A. Fiensy has suggested that the church was a microcosm of the city of Jerusalem itself. Neither the wealthy nor the poor were excluded, and it is remarkable how seldom social or economic status is even mentioned in Acts.[62] The location where the first disciples met (apparently on Mount Zion near the temple)[63] suggests that at least some early Christians were of a relatively high social status, for the upper class lived in the Upper City including especially on Mount Zion. "The farther one was from the centre socially and economically, the farther one lived also from the centre geographically."[64] Thus there were some who were reasonably well off, though probably not among the wealthiest elites.

---

59. The credence one gives to the Johannine testimony depends on whom one thinks wrote the Fourth Gospel. It is my view, and that of various other scholars, that this Gospel contains the testimony of a Judean disciple who knew Jerusalem well, even knew members of the priestly hierarchy, and came to be called the Beloved Disciple in the Johannine community. I would also suggest that the Last Supper probably transpired in his home, since the portrayal of him reclining at the head of the table with Jesus in John 13 suggests he may have been the host (John 13:23); cf. my *John's Wisdom: A Sapiential Commentary of the Fourth Gospel* (Louisville: Westminster, 1995), pp. 1ff. If indeed John Mark was a relative of Barnabas (cf. Col. 4:10), he may have been a Levite as well.

60. The poorer priests could end up working in trades such as stonecutting or the sale of olive oil; cf. *b. Yoma* 1.6; *Beṣa* 3.8, Diodorus Siculus 40.3.7.

61. See Jeremias, *Jerusalem*, p. 234.

62. See Fiensy, "Composition of the Jerusalem Church."

63. See Murphy-O'Connor, "The Cenacle and Community," pp. 303-18.

64. Fiensy, "Composition of the Jerusalem Church," p. 224.

On the whole the evidence suggests the following conclusions: (1) the earliest Christians ranged from reasonably high to quite low social status, with the level of the majority being moderate to lower status; (2) nevertheless the number of reasonably well-to-do converts in Jerusalem was significant enough to make available some reasonably large houses as meeting places, even on Mount Zion; (3) earliest Christianity in Judea, to judge from Acts 1–8, was no proletarian movement; it appealed to a broad range of people up and down the social ladder;[65] (4) the sharing of property and of food suggests an attempt to remove the extreme inequities that existed in ancient societies in the context of the Christian fellowship without reconstructing the external society per se. Early Christian meetings and meals seem to have moved things in a more equitable and egalitarian direction by means of sharing, and perhaps also by the avoidance of pecking orders and differences in food among the participants (unlike the case in Corinth, cf. 1 Corinthians 11).[66] We will discuss the portrait of Antioch at the appropriate point in the commentary, but it is in order to point out here that the evidence there does not suggest a different conclusion about social level than what we have drawn about the Jerusalem church, except that the Jerusalem church seems to have had more needy Christians.[67]

C. Ananias and Sapphira (5:1-11)

The story of Ananias is singular in many regards. It reflects the first example in Luke-Acts (cf. 13:11) of what has been called a punitive or rule (violation) miracle.[68] As such it has caused no little controversy and has been seen as contrary to the spirit of Jesus, who when he did miracles performed acts of compassion. This of course overlooks the withering of the fig tree story in Mark 11, which Luke does not record. It also ignores not only the considerable number of examples of oracles of judgment or woe sayings (cf., e.g., Luke 21:23) found on Jesus' lips in the Synoptic tradition, not to mention examples of this sort of story found in both OT and pagan literature.[69] It seems probable that the story of Achan in Joshua 7 has in some regards shaped how Luke tells this story. There, however, the issue is the violation of

---

65. See the discussion in *New Docs*, 5:110-11, rejecting the older hypothesis of A. Deissmann about the social level of the early Christians.

66. See my discussion in *Conflict and Community in Corinth*, pp. 241ff.

67. For a rather similar conclusion arrived at by using a modern sociological model, see Stark, "Class Basis of Early Christianity." Cf. also Judge, *Social Pattern of Christian Groups;* Meeks, *The First Urban Christians;* Scroggs, "Sociological Interpretation."

68. See the discussion in Theissen, *Miracle Stories*, pp. 109-10.

69. In the pagan stories there are examples where a vow to God, which is violated, is involved, and this leads to divine punishment; cf. *New Docs*, 3:27-28. In these inscriptions as in Acts, and unlike what we find in Joshua 7, the punishment comes from the deity directly.

the *harem* or ban by taking gold and other assets which did not belong to Achan, and the punishment is stoning by the community.[70] Perhaps even more of an influence is the telling of what happened to those who misguidedly offered unholy fire before God in Lev. 10:1-5 and who "died before the LORD" and were carried out in the clothes they had on, not being allowed any of the usual customs of respect performed for the deceased in Jewish culture. Luke's view is that the God of the Hebrew Scriptures is the same God Jesus and the disciples served, and so one should expect continuity of character and action.[71]

The structure of the Acts narrative has two parts which are deliberately parallel, for the fate of these two marital partners is the same. Consequently, each half of the story closes with the same refrain (cf. vv. 5b and 11). We see in this story a very good example of Luke's technique of repetition with variation, following the canons of historiography that had some rhetorical concerns about style.[72] There is no reason to see the second half of the story simply as a doublet, since Peter's words differ and the situation is not identical (cf. below).

This narrative is joined to the previous one by δε, probably an adversative "but," contrasting what has gone immediately before with what follows. We are immediately introduced to a couple, Ananias and his wife Sapphira. The former name is the Greek rendering of the Hebrew name Hananiah, while the wife's name probably is the Greek form of the Aramaic adjective for beautiful (Sappīrā). An ossuary has been found in Jerusalem with both the Aramaic and Greek form of this latter name, and there are inscriptions with the name from this period and place as well, though positive correlation of any of this material with the Sapphira in this story is not possible.[73]

We are told at the very outset *(v. 1)* that this couple sold a piece of land. With his wife's knowledge, Ananias kept back some of the money gained from

70. See the balanced assessment of Johnson, *Acts,* p. 92.

71. As for the source of this tradition in Acts 5:1-11, which is quite specific, one may suspect that Luke obtained this from the Jerusalem church when he was in the Holy Land in the late 50s (cf. Lüdemann, *Early Christianity,* p. 66), though I would not rule out the possibility that Luke met Peter in Rome in the 60s and heard the story firsthand from him.

72. See Cadbury, "Four Features of Lukan Style," p. 93: "The following unusual expressions occur twice each: νοσφιζομαι (each time with απο της τιμης), and εκψυχω, τι οτι, and each half of the incident ends with the refrain [which] is verbatim in part. . . . On the other hand, the property is called both κτημα and χωριον; for 'sell' the verbs επωλησεν, πραθεν, απεδοσθε are used; the young men are first οι νεωτεροι, then οι νεανισκοι; the Holy Spirit is both το πνευμα το αγιον and το πνευμα του κυριου; ψευδομαι is construed in one sentence with the accusative, in another with the dative; collusion is expressed alternately by συνειδυιης and by συνεφωνηθη. . . ."

73. See Barrett, *Acts ,* vol. 1, p. 264.

the sale of the property.[74] J. D. M. Derrett has made the novel suggestion that the woman's *ketubah* is involved, but there is nothing in the story to suggest this conclusion.[75] In Luke's view this couple is guilty of secrecy, collusion, and attempting to lie to the Holy Spirit. What is at stake here is the κοινωνια of the community which the Spirit indwelt. One act of secrecy and selfishness violates the character of openness and honesty which characterized the earliest community of Jesus' followers.

V. 2 informs us that Ananias came and laid the part of the money he resolved to give at the feet of the apostles. This gesture suggests several things. First, it suggests submission to the authority of Peter and the other authorities. Secondly, it may be significant that the text does not say he placed the money into the hands of the apostles but at their feet "in order that the apostles should acquire it not as a personal gift but as trustees by way of a dedication."[76]

Peter is portrayed in *v. 3* as a person of prophetic insight, one who can, by the inspiration of the Spirit, see into the hearts of others and can know that Ananias has given only part of the money he got from the sale of the property.[77] Peter says that Satan has filled Ananias's heart, and the result is that he lies, not just to Peter, or the community, but to the Spirit which dwells in the community.[78] Ananias then is described in terms that Luke has previously reserved for Judas Iscariot (cf. Luke 22:3). Clearly, this is seen as a very grave violation of the integrity and κοινωνια of the community. Luke sees this story not just as being about human greed and duplicitous actions but about an invasion of the community of the Spirit by the powers of darkness, by means of Ananias.

It must be said that despite the arguments of various scholars Acts *5:4*

---

74. The verb ενοσφισατο always has a negative connotation, and means something like "embezzled," referring to a secret theft of a part of a larger amount, sometimes of something placed in trust. See Cadbury and Lake, *The Beginnings of Christianity,* 4:50. It is an obscure word, and the fact that it is also found in Josh. 7:1 suggests Luke saw a link between the two stories. Capper, "Palestinian Cultural Context," pp. 337ff., has suggested on the basis of Acts 2:44 and this story that the early Christians operated with the same sort of system as one finds at Qumran of placing funds in trust for a period of time while one was a novice in the community, until one decided to become a full member. During the trial period the money or property was still in the hand of the original owner. The problem with this conclusion is: (1) Acts does not suggest that the exact same sort of rigid property rules applied to early Christians as applied at Qumran (one might expect the looser sort of arrangements one may have found in the Essene community in Jerusalem); (2) it is not at all clear Acts 2:44 involves a *terminus technicus;* (3) Acts 5 does not suggest that Ananias or his wife were catechumens or novices.

75. See his "Ananias, Sapphira."

76. Ibid., p. 195. Acts 3:6 may be of relevance here. Peter has, or at least carries, no money, and of the church's money he is but a trustee (cf. below on Acts 6:1-2).

77. This is one of the trademarks of a prophetic person in Luke's view, cf. Luke 5:22; 7:39; 9:47; 24:38, and cf. Johnson, *Acts,* p. 88.

78. See Polhill, *Acts,* p. 157.

and 4:34 do not necessarily contradict each other.[79] Acts 4:34 states that Christians sold property and brought the proceeds to the apostles, laying it at their feet. It does not say they sold *all* their property, but it does probably imply that they gave *all* the proceeds of what they *did* sell. Acts 5:4 tells us not only that the property belonged to Ananias before he sold it, but that even after he sold it the proceeds were at his disposal. In other words, the giving was strictly voluntary, not mandatory. This is precisely why giving is portrayed as meritorious and gracious in the case of Barnabas. Peter then accuses Ananias of duplicity. He is not guilty of a mere accidental oversight, for Peter says that Ananias planned to do things this way, as v. 1 indicates as well. He is guilty of lying not merely to human beings but to God in the person of the Spirit.[80]

The reaction of Ananias to being unmasked and having his heart laid bare by Peter is, according to *v. 5*, that he fell down and died. The verb εξεψυξεν is often found in medical contexts,[81] but in Acts it is found only here and at 12:23 of Herod (cf. Judg. 4:21 LXX). Literally it means the person exhaled or breathed out his life force, and so expired.[82] Notice that it is not said that Peter either killed Ananias or uttered a curse that killed him. In other words, it is possible that we do not have a punitive miracle here at all, unlike the cursing of the fig tree. For all we know, Ananias may have died of a heart attack caused by shock, as sometimes happens to those who are suddenly found out, especially if they have at least somewhat sensitive consciences.[83]

79. Contra Barrett, *Acts,* vol. 1, p. 267.

80. It is worth noting that the Spirit here is treated as a person, one who can be lied to, not merely a power. Furthermore, the Spirit is equated with God, as a comparison of vv. 3 and 4 shows.

81. See, e.g., Hippocrates, *De Morbis* 1.5. Since this word is also found in nonmedical contexts and literature (cf. Ezek. 21:12), it certainly does not prove the author is a doctor, but it is consistent with such a view.

82. Menoud, "L'Mort d' Ananias et de Sapphira (Actes 5.1-11)," argues that we are dealing with a legend about the first deaths in the Christian community, the actual cause of which was forgotten or unknown. On this view, Ananias and Sapphira died when it was still expected that all believers would live until Christ returned. The deaths were seen as inexplicable and so the story arose that they must have been guilty of some horrible sin. Luke then took up and expanded the legend into a story useful to his interests. One must ask of this theory why Luke, in an apologetic document keen on evangelism, would expand or report the expanded story in this way. Surely, this story would scare more off than it would attract! It is much more likely that he had hard evidence that this story had a strong basis in fact, and he felt he must include at least some traditions that showed that the earliest church was not perfect.

83. The suggestion that Ananias was an inherently wicked person does not meet the facts of the story. The story suggests that he succumbed to the influences of the powers of darkness at one particular point and in regard to a particular activity — what he would do with his money from the land sale which he apparently had promised to give all of to the community. There is no reason to doubt he had been a member in good standing in the community prior to this occasion.

We are told that the reaction of others is also dramatic — great fear or dread seized all who heard about this incident. Φοβος here, while it could be translated "awe," probably should be translated "fear," especially in view of the fact that this is said to be the reaction of "all those hearing about it."

V. 6 indicates that young men of the community wrapped up Ananias's body and carried him off and buried him. Here, Derrett's suggestions seem more fruitful, and the material in Lev. 10:1-5 may be helpful. Honorable burial was a very great concern and a family matter in the ancient Near East. The idea of non–family members burying Ananias without even notifying his wife strongly suggests that we are dealing with an unusual situation. On the basis of such texts as Lev. 10:1-5 and Joshua 7, Derrett suggests that

> when a man had been struck down by the hand of Heaven (as Joshua specifically says was the case with Achan: Josh. 7.25) his corpse must surely be consigned rapidly and silently to the grave. No one should mourn him. The suicide, the rebel against society, the excommunicate, the apostate, and the criminal condemned to death by the Jewish court would be buried . . . in haste and without ceremonial, and no one might (or need) observe the usual lengthy and troublesome rituals of mourning for him.[84]

The great sacrilege that Ananias had committed is expressed strongly in the Greek "you belied/falsified the Holy Spirit" (v. 3). His action was a falsification of what the Spirit was doing and was prompting the community to do and to be.[85] The parallel between Ananias and Judas includes not only the entering of the heart by Satan, but also money is involved as a stumbling block in both cases, as is land, and finally neither seems to have had an honorable burial and mourning period (cf. Acts 1).

After about three hours Sapphira appears, not knowing what has transpired.[86] It must be noticed that Sapphira is treated somewhat differently by Peter. She is, in effect, given an opportunity to corroborate or falsify her husband's assertions about the price the land brought when it was sold. Perhaps this is because it was assumed that Ananias was mainly responsible for the actual selling of the land itself, even though Sapphira was in on the plan from the outset.

That in *v. 8* Sapphira confirms to Peter that the sale was for a certain amount[87] indicates to him that this couple had agreed in advance on what they

---

84. Derrett, "Ananias, Sapphira," p. 198.

85. See Polhill, *Acts,* p. 157.

86. Luke regularly uses ως or the like with such references to indicate a rough estimate of the length of time.

87. The text does not mention an actual figure; the Greek should be rendered "for so much" (τοσουτος).

would say, had agreed in advance to try to deceive. As it turns out, as Peter in *v. 9* makes clear, what Ananias and Sapphira had actually agreed upon together was not merely a deceptive plan or a price that would attempt to fool humans, but rather they had agreed to put the Spirit of God to the test. This is something the temptation narrative suggests the devil is apt to try to lead one to do, and something the OT says one must never do (cf. Luke 4:12; Deut. 6:16). Peter's response comes in the form of a question: "Why is it that you agreed together to test the Spirit of the Lord?"[88] As such, this does not seem to be a curse formula, but rather a response of anguish and anger to so serious a sin.

Ananias and Sapphira were together in this deed (συνεφωνήθη; cf. συν in v. 1), but it was the wrong sort of togetherness. It was a togetherness that violated the togetherness of the Christian community. It should be noted that Sapphira, in the way that Peter has confronted her and asked her about the price, was given an opportunity to repent and confess, but she did not avail herself of it.

The second half of v. 9 reads, "Behold, the feet of the buriers of your husband are at the door, and they will carry you out." This also is not a curse formula, but rather a prophetic word. Just as Peter knew the hearts of this couple, so also by the Spirit of God he knew their ends as well. He even knew who was at the door of the house in which the church was meeting.[89] Even in this case it is not impossible that we are talking about death by heart attack brought on by a double shock — not only the shock of being caught colluding in a deception of the church but the equal shock of learning that one's spouse was already dead and buried! "Peter's role was to confront — not to judge. The judgment came from God."[90] Luke certainly does not play up the miraculous element in these deaths, if these are examples of punitive miracles.[91]

Though we may perhaps speak of a punitive miracle here, is it an example of a rule miracle, a punishment engendered by the violation of a sacred rule, law, or taboo?[92] That there are examples of such a punishment both within and outside of Scripture is no proof this is such a case.[93] At issue is whether

88. Codex Bezae seems to attempt to soften the blow by having Peter ask more politely, "I will ask if you indeed sold the land for so much," which conveys a tone of suspicion that a discerning person would have recognized. See Metzger, *Textual Commentary*, p. 328. CopG67 is more blunt.

89. Haenchen, *Acts*, p. 239, far exceeds the meaning of the text when he asserts: "Peter does not merely prophesy Sapphira's death but . . . wants to kill — and succeeds."

90. Polhill, *Acts*, p. 159.

91. For example, he says nothing about the hand of the Lord striking them down, or the like (contrast 4:30).

92. Cf. Theissen, *Miracle Stories*, p. 110: "in the Jewish rule miracles the issue is almost always one of life or death. Breaches of law lead to death; observance of the law preserves from death. The law does not chastise; it kills. . . . The Greek punishment miracles are more humane, more educative, and that is certainly no accident."

93. See ibid., pp. 109-11.

there was a rule in the Jerusalem community that everyone had to give everything to the community, that all property was "corban" or dedicated to God by rule. But v. 4 of this very story makes clear that there was no such rule. The sin of Ananias and Sapphira was the attempted deception of the community and the putting of the Spirit which dwelt in the community to the test by deliberate lying words and actions. They were under no obligation to give all their property to the community. Their sin is heinous especially because they had free choice about what to do with both the property and the proceeds from the sale of it.[94]

The reaction of Sapphira to Peter's words is no less dramatic than in the case of her husband — *v. 10* says that she fell at Peter's feet and expired (εξεψυξεν again). There is probably some deliberate irony here. Those who had laid money at the feet of the apostles were now themselves in that same posture. Sapphira then was carried off and buried by the same young men who had buried the husband.[95]

V. 11 indicates that the very same reaction, one of great fear or dread, overtook the whole εκκλησια and all others who heard about this remarkable incident.[96] This is the first occurrence of the term εκκλησια in Acts, which is used fifteen times altogether for the Christian community in Acts 1–15, and four times thereafter.[97] This word is not inherently a technical term for the church, as 7:38; 19:32, 39, and 40 (41) show, and so should probably not be translated "church."[98] A more apt translation would be the assembly or congregation, with the usual reference being to the assembly of God's people (except in Acts 19). As such it is the Greek rendering of the Hebrew *qāhāl* (cf.,

94. The point is that in view of v. 4, which Luke could have omitted or rephrased if he so chose, Luke's presentation of the story does not support the view that a violation of a sacred community rule about property is at issue here.

95. It is possible, if this was a couple of some wealth as seems likely, that the burial simply amounted to laying the body in a rock or cave tomb without any ceremonial attention or wrapping spices in the winding sheet. If so, a period of under three hours to complete the whole task including coming and going is quite believable. Of course it is possible the couple was not buried in their own tomb in this case, but rather taken somewhere outside the city and laid to rest in a pauper's grave. Luke does not editorialize about the couple's eternal destiny. Derrett, "Ananias, Sapphira," p. 199, suggests that the Jewish view of misfortune as an atonement for sin is assumed, but Luke says nothing of this.

96. This reaction as a response to the holy is not uncommon in Luke-Acts; cf. Luke 1:12, 65; 2:9; 7:16, 8:37; Acts 2:43; 19:17.

97. I am not counting the example which appears only in the text of D at 2:47. Notice in 7:58 it is used of the Jewish congregation of God's people in OT times. This is the way the term is frequently used in the LXX.

98. In Acts 19 the reference is to a secular assembly in Ephesus, in Acts 7 to the OT congregation.

e.g., Josh. 8:35 LXX).[99] The significance of introducing the term here is perhaps that Luke is stressing that by this point the followers of Jesus had a sense of being a corporate entity — the people of God. Thus, an egregious violation of the sense of corporate identity and the holiness of the community simply reinforced in the minds of the people who and whose they were — they were the community in which dwelled the Spirit of God.[100]

D. The Sum of the Matter (5:12-16)

That *v. 12* follows hard on the heels of the Ananias and Sapphira story suggests that Luke does indeed see the previous story as involving one or two punitive miracles enacted against the deceptive couple. This raises the whole issue of how Luke deals with miracles in Acts, and what he considers a sign, a wonder, or a mighty work. We will now give some detailed attention to this subject.

A Closer Look — Miracles in Acts

In Acts we find all the varieties of miracles seen in Luke's Gospel, plus some additional sorts such as the punitive miracles we seem to have in Acts 5:1-11, and more clearly in Acts 9; 12:20-23; 13:11, and possibly 19:16. The following is a basic list: (1) healing of the lame man at Beautiful Gate (3:1-10); (2) miraculous knowledge (Acts 5, but also Acts 2; 27:10, 31, 34); (3) a healing shadow (5:15); (4) blinding and restoration of sight (9:8, 18; 13:11-12); (5) healing of the paralytic Aeneas (9:33-35); (6) raising of the dead, Tabitha (9:36-42), and possibly Eutychus (20:8-12); (7) healing of the cripple (14:8-10); (8) casting out of demons (16:16-18); (9) healing handkerchiefs and aprons (19:12); (10) healing of Publius's father (28:8); (11) miraculous release from prison (5:19-21; 12:7-10; 16:25-26 [by earthquake]); (12) miraculous protection from snakebite (28:3-6) and miraculous speech of various sorts including glossolalia (2:4; 10:46; 19:6).[101]

99. See my discussion of this term in *Conflict and Community in Corinth*, pp. 90-93. The fact that εκκλησια is introduced for the first time here may reflect the general tendency of Luke to move gradually in Acts from more to less Semitic language as the narrative progresses from more to less Semitic cultural settings.

100. See Marshall, *Acts*, p. 114. Polhill, *Acts*, p. 161, rightly remarks: "Luke depicts it as a unique period, the new people of God in Christ, filled with the Spirit, growing by leaps and bounds. There was no room for distrust, for duplicity, for any breach in fellowship. The same Spirit that gave the community its growth also maintained its purity."

101. See Hemer, *Book of Acts*, pp. 435-36.

Perhaps the first thing to be said about this list is that Luke does not make the modern distinction between supernatural and natural events or actions. His distinction appears to be between the ordinary providence and plan of God, which entails a wider scope of happenings than mere signs and wonders (see 2:23 on Jesus' death), and specific exceptional events that can be categorized as signs, wonders, or mighty works, such as those listed above. It is also true, as Theissen points out, that one must see Luke's discussion of miracles in the context of his view of salvation history, especially since various miracles are seen as confirmations of the truth of the saving word or even part of the acts of salvation.[102] Luke believes that in the church age, and even before during the ministry of Jesus, the age of salvation has dawned, and thus not surprisingly the age of numerous stupendous miracles has also come. "For Luke, miracle functions, not only to heighten the drama of the narrative, but also to show that at every significant point in the transitions of Christianity from its Jewish origins in Jerusalem to its Gentile outreaching to Rome itself, the hand of God is evident in the form of public miraculous confirmation. A corollary of this is the implicit claim that God also has shown his hand in wielding swift judgment on those who oppose the movement or seek to exploit its extraordinary power for personal gain. And finally, miracle is always effected for human benefit, not for the accomplishment of political ends."[103]

It will be noticed from a close scrutiny of the list above that the miracles are basically presented as involving Luke's two main human protagonists, Peter and Paul. There is some attempt to parallel their accomplishments in this regard, so, for example, we have both healing people, both raising the dead, both exhibiting supernatural knowledge, both being miraculously released from prison, both performing punitive miracles (Paul is even the victim of one!), and the like. This does not happen by accident, for Luke wishes to present Paul and Peter as being on a rather equal plane in terms of authority and power, and thus in terms of witness and success in mission. One may suspect that this amounts to an attempt to elevate Paul to the same stature as Peter was already thought to have.[104]

Sometimes because of the miracle stories, modern scholars have berated Luke, along with other early Christians, for their gullibility, or lack of critical consciousness. This is in part because Luke does not qualify his miracle tales with such conventional rationalizing phrases as "it is said" (λεγεται) or "the story is told that" (μυθολο-γουσαι)[105] or "however, on these matters everyone is welcome to his own opinion." The latter phrase is found with some frequency in Josephus (cf. *Ant.* 1.108; 3.81; 4.158; 19.108). This judgment has also come about in part because some of the more ratio-

---

102. See Theissen, *Miracles Stories,* pp. 259ff.: "Primitive Christian miracle stories have a social intention and there is no better description of that intention than the doctrinal formula 'your faith has saved you.' The miracle stories promise rescue, salvation, redemption." That this is not always the case is of course shown in the punitive miracles. On Luke's views on salvation see the excursus above, pp. 143ff.

103. Kee, *Miracle,* p. 220.

104. See the discussion in Hardon, "Miracle Narratives."

105. On the use of these phrases by Plutarch, cf. the helpful essay by MacKay, "Plutarch and the Miraculous," here p. 99.

nalizing ancient historians, such as Thucydides, Polybius, and Tacitus, were generally, though not totally, skeptical about claims about the miraculous. Plutarch, a contemporary of Luke, for example believes in critically sifting such tales and claims, but he does not dismiss all claims about portents, dreams, healings, and the like.[106] Our modern tendency is to focus on the more skeptical like Thucydides, but one must not overlook that many ancient historians, including especially Herodotus, the "father" of Greek historiography, believed in divine intervention in human affairs and included miraculous tales in their accounts that they thought credible.[107]

Luke then cannot be strongly distinguished from most other ancient historians on the basis of his reporting of the miraculous. Furthermore, it does not follow from his doing so that he did not exercise some critical judgment in scrutinizing the miraculous stories he heard about the early church. Since Luke is something of an apologete and rhetor seeking to persuade his audience, it appears that he has simply left out tales he felt were lacking in credibility and historical substance.[108] Nevertheless, something of a critical consciousness can be discerned not merely in Luke's claims in the prologue in Luke 1:1-4, but perhaps also in the way he tends to handle non-Christian claims about power or magic. For example, in Acts 8 he reports the people claim that Simon "is the power of God called Great" (v. 10), but in the next verse he calls it a matter of magic (μαγειαις), and in the end Simon is said to attempt to buy power from the apostles (8:18-19). One can also see this sort of critique in Acts 19:11-20, where the sons of Sceva attempt exorcisms but are overcome by the evil spirit and those who relied on magic books are portrayed as people without supernatural power. On the other hand, Luke clearly believes that not all non-Christians who claim supernatural power or abilities are simply charlatans. The story in Acts 16:16-18 shows that Luke believes that in some cases evil spirits do give some people certain extraordinary powers or abilities.[109]

It is also instructive to compare the account of Herod Agrippa's death in 12:20-23 to Josephus's account of the same event (*Ant.* 19.8.2). "For both Luke and Josephus, this story is an indication of God's control over history rather than an instance of magic (no technique is hinted at) or of a miraculous action on the part of any human being."[110] In short, though Josephus, Luke's contemporary, shows reservations about

---

106. See ibid., p. 108ff. "There are certain miraculous events in the New Testament that Plutarch would have accepted without question" (p. 108), among which MacKay lists dreams and visions, voices from heaven, epiphanies like the transfiguration, exorcisms such as that found in Acts 16, and healing miracles with the exception of things like giving of sight to the blind or raising the dead.

107. On Herodotus and the supernatural, cf. MacDonald, "Herodotus on the Miraculous," and Fornara, *History in Ancient Greece and Rome*, pp. 78ff. Like Herodotus, Luke believes that history is developing under the guidance of an invisible divine hand and plan.

108. Perhaps something can be discerned from the way he handles Mark and Q. For instance, did he have doubts about the cursing of the fig tree incident, which he certainly would have found in his Markan source?

109. See the excursus, pp. 577ff. below, on magic and its relationship to miracle.

110. Kee, *Miracle*, p. 216.

various miracle stories and often uses rationalizing formulas or offers nonsupernatural explanations of some apparent miracles, he is perfectly ready to give credence to others, and in this he is probably no different in his approach than Luke. Neither one should be dismissed as a credible historian on many matters simply because of this fact. The "ancient debate over miracle and magic was in the main not a conflict between believers and rationalists, but between two sorts of believers."[111]

If we were to evaluate the way Luke tells his miracle stories in Acts, on the whole his manner of dealing with them differs little from the Synoptic approach to such acts or events, and all such accounts seem primarily indebted to the OT in the way a miracle and its significance is conceived. Even the phrase "signs and wonders" (5:12) or the mention of the hand of God in Acts likely draws on the accounts in Deuteronomy (LXX) about God's deliverance of the Israelites from Egyptian bondage by means of miracles and other similar acts of rescue or salvation (cf. Deut. 7:19; 11:3; 26:8; 29:2; 34:11). "Just remember . . . the signs and wonders, the mighty hand and the outstretched arm by which the LORD your God brought you out" (Deut. 7:18-19).[112] This is not to say that there are not miracles in Acts that seem to border on magic and seem nearer to the Hellenistic wonders (e.g., Peter's healing shadow in 5:15, or the healing aprons in 19:12), but interestingly Luke mentions these sorts of happenings only in passing.[113] On the whole his account of miracles seems much more like those found in the OT, especially the material in the Pentateuch and the Elijah-Elisha cycles, than like Hellenistic wonder accounts.

G. W. H. Lampe is right to stress that we must not overlook the way miracles fit into the larger schema of Luke's history writing. "Miracles are, therefore, in Luke's understanding of the matter, part and parcel of the entire mission of witness. The whole is miraculous, in so far as it is a continuous mighty work of God. By the divine power the gospel is preached, converts are made, the Church is established in unity and brotherhood, the opposing powers, whether human or demonic are conquered. . . . The whole mission . . . [is] . . . effected by supernatural power, whether in the guidance given to the missionaries, in their dramatic release from prison or deliverance from enemies or shipwreck, or in the signs of healing and raising from the dead. . . . It is consequently difficult to pick out the miraculous from the non-miraculous in Luke's story."[114] This is not surprising since in Luke's view, as the Pentecost narrative in Acts 2 makes quite plain, Luke understands himself to be living in the age when the promises and prophecies of the OT are being fulfilled, and miracles are one sign and means of that fulfillment.[115]

These stories will no doubt continue to create problems for some moderns who rule out in advance the supernatural, including supernatural events such as miracles,

---

111. Ibid., p. 217.

112. See the discussion of miracle in both OT and NT by Y. Zakovitch ("Miracle OT") and H. E. Remus ("Miracle, NT") in the *ABD*, 4:845-69.

113. Such healings are based on the belief that there is a potency the healer has which can be conveyed to articles of clothing or things he touches, or even that the power can unknowingly radiate from the person (cf., e.g., Luke 8:44).

114. Lampe, "Miracles," p. 171.

115. See ibid., p. 173.

and dismiss all history writing that includes such tales as precritical and naive in character.[116] I would suggest that such an a priori approach to miracles is equally uncritical and naive, not least because science has hardly begun to plumb the depths of what is and is not possible in our universe, and especially because we are regularly being warned by scientists (particularly physicists) that assumptions about natural laws and a closed mechanistic universe and the like do not cover all the known data. One must also take into account that in every age of human history there have been numerous claims about the miraculous, many of which were made by highly intelligent and rational persons not readily given to superstition. Luke seems to have been one such person, for as we have seen there is some reason to think he critically sifted his data.

The use of the phrase σημεια και τερατα (or vice versa) found in *v. 12* is by no means uncommon in Acts (cf. 2:43; 4:16, 22, 30; 5:12; 6:8; 8:6, 13; 14:3; 15:12). The phrase is common in the LXX (cf., e.g., Pss. 77:43; 104:27; 134:9, and the excursus above), and Johnson is right to note that it frequently occurs in association with the portrayal of Moses as a prophetic figure (cf. Deut. 34:10-12).[117] Here it introduces the third summary passage, indicating the kind of activities the apostles did. Luke is careful to make clear that the power came through the apostles rather than from them by saying that these things happened "*through* (δια) the hands of the apostles."

While the first two summary passages in Acts 2 and 4 mainly focused on the interior life of the early Christian community (their worship, their meals, and their handling of property), this third one has more to do with the relationship of the apostles to outsiders. This is appropriate because, as we have seen, Luke tends to alternate narratives about the interior life of the early Christians with narratives about their external witness and work, their dealings with outsiders. The signs and wonders are not done within the confines of the house church but among the "people" (λαος), which here must surely mean the Jewish people who are not yet converts. Perhaps the most natural way to take the second half of v. 12 is to read it as a statement that at least focuses on the apostles being all together,[118] in the portico or colonnade of Solomon in the temple precincts, where, as we learned in 3:1ff., the community gathered for teaching and near which Peter had healed the lame man. In other words, v. 12b can be seen as retrospective, as by and large this entire summary in vv. 12-16 seems to be.

116. Classicists and ancient historians often tend to avoid the NT altogether, though they sometimes give due attention and recognition to Josephus. Cf., e.g., Grant, *The Ancient Historians*, who treats both Josephus and Eusebius, but not Luke!
117. Johnson, *Acts*, pp. 49-50.
118. On ομοθυμαδον see pp. 157ff. above.

There are difficulties in construing the meaning of *vv. 13-15*, and, coupled with the grammatical complications, the suggestion is ready to hand that Luke is combining some particular traditions about Peter with his own general summary of things, resulting in a less than smooth-flowing passage.[119] The first question about *v. 13* is — Who are "the rest"? The resolution of this question in part turns on what we make of the verb κολλασθαι. If it is taken as some sort of technical term for conversion or joining the Christian community, then v. 13 would seem to flatly contradict v. 14, which speaks of believers being added to the community's number more than ever!

Clearly enough the verb κολλασθαι does not need to be seen as a technical term, for its meaning can range from physical proximity to adherence of some sort. In Luke-Acts it has a variety of meanings: (1) in Luke 10:11 it refers to the clinging or adhering of dust to one's feet; (2) in Luke 15:15 it refers to a person attaching himself to a citizen in the sense of hiring himself out; (3) in Acts 8:29 it refers to Philip catching up with or coming alongside the chariot of the eunuch; (4) in Acts 10:28 it refers to one person associating with or visiting another (in this case a Jew with a Gentile); (5) in Acts 17:4 it may imply conversion since the text says some were persuaded and joined Paul and Silas, but this second verb could mean decided to travel with or accompany them, having been persuaded. Acts 9:26 speaks of the attempt of Saul to join the disciples, but here we are talking about an event which transpires *after* Saul's Damascus road experience and thus after his conversion. In short, there is no compelling evidence of this verb being used as technical language for conversion in Luke-Acts. It is thus possible that v. 13 looks back to the story of Ananias and Sapphira, and the meaning would be that various people were afraid to get near Peter and the apostles due to the possible adverse effect of doing so. While making sense of the syntax, this does not fully convince in view of what follows, namely, the mention of admiration of the (non-Christian) people and the conversion of some to the faith.

Thus a second alternative is to take the phrase "the rest" to refer to the rest of the Christians who were afraid to join the apostles in the temple in view of what happened the first time — namely, the arousal of the anger of the Jewish authorities and the trial of the Christian leaders. On this scenario the apostles are courageous and willing to speak the word and heal boldly in the temple precincts, even though it may produce judicial action, which in fact Acts 5:17ff. says did transpire.[120] It is not convincing to argue that "the rest" is a technical phrase for non-Christians anymore than it was convincing

119. Cf. Barrett, *Acts*, vol. 1, p. 273; Marshall, *Acts*, p. 114.

120. I see no good reason to put a full stop in the Greek text between the first and second half of v. 12 (i.e., after λαω) as is regularly done, if those who are altogether in the temple are the apostles in this case.

to argue that the verb κολλαομαι was a technical term.[121] This means that the summary we have in Acts 5 is not simply a glowing report but indicates something of the tension the community was under.[122] Yet the Jewish people (to be distinguished from their leaders) continued to admire the apostles and their work greatly.[123]

V. 14 tells us that some went beyond admiration to conversion, with more believers than ever being added to the Lord, both men and women. This gender-inclusive nature of the Christian community is emphasized at various points. We have already seen this in Acts 1:14, and of course Acts 5:1-11 also suggests this, though the tone of the story is negative.[124] Despite adversity both within and outside the community, Luke stresses that it continued to grow.

V. 15 begins with ωστε (so that) connecting the conversions to the signs and wonders the apostles performed. This is not surprising since Luke believed healing was a part of the redemptive work Jesus and his followers came to do, but also because he believed in the evidential value of miracles as acts that could lead people to be open and to have faith in Jesus. There seems to be some kind of relationship between this verse and the summary description found in Mark 6:55-56, a summary Luke does not include in his Gospel.[125] Luke obviously sees the apostles performing the same sort of works as Jesus, and in effect carrying on his ministry in his name.[126] Clearly enough, Luke portrays the people of Jerusalem and the surrounding area as having a belief

121. Λοιποις is a common, colorless Greek term, and if one notices how vv. 12 and 13 begin similarly — "but through the hands of the apostles . . . but none of the rest . . ." — it is natural to take the two verses together speaking of the leaders of the group, followed by a reference to the rest of the same group. As Schwartz, "Non-Joining Sympathizers (Acts 5,13-14)," has shown, in all of the ten other cases in which λοιποι is used in Luke-Acts it appears *after* the referent with which it is contrasted. The grammatical structure of vv. 12-13 favors a contrast with the apostles, not with Christian disciples in general.

122. One must keep steadily in view Acts 5:1-11 as well, where we are told twice that the powerful actions of the apostle Peter produced great fear, even in the community of Christians.

123. The αλλα denotes a contrast between the "people" in the latter half of v. 13 and "the rest" in the first half, and should be translated "but."

124. We will have more to say about this inclusiveness later; see pp. 334ff. below. For now it is well to recognize it as part of Luke's emphasis on the universal scope of the gospel's adherents. As Kee, *Miracle*, p. 198, says: "The . . . community is seen to be inclusive economically [cf. Acts 6:1-6], ethnically [cf. Acts 8; 10], sexually [cf. Acts 13:50], ritually [cf. Acts 11:19-25], and socially [cf. Acts 9:43]."

125. See Lüdemann, *Early Christianity*, p. 67.

126. What this echo also suggests, as does an aspect of Stephen's speech (cf. below), is that Luke composed Acts after his Gospel, and both works are composed with a clear knowledge of Mark's Gospel. It further suggests that when he composed his Gospel, Luke was already thinking ahead to what he would include in his second volume, and so held certain phrases, ideas, motifs back until he composed Acts.

in the potency of Peter's shadow because he was a holy man,[127] apparently a not uncommon idea in antiquity,[128] so much so that they laid people in the main streets so that when Peter passed by his shadow might fall on them, even if he didn't have to touch them (or vice versa). It is not clear whether Luke also holds this belief, but v. 16b probably suggests he did (cf. Acts 19:12). In any event, this verse was intended to impress upon Luke's audience the great power that worked through Peter for healing.[129]

V. 16 suggests that the news of the miracles traveled fast and people from outlying communities came to Jerusalem to have their sick cured and their possessed freed from unclean or evil spirits. These efforts were not for nought, for Luke tells us "they were *all cured*."[130] The word πολεων (cities) is used by Luke of both villages and cities, and so this verse should not be taken to indicate Luke's ignorance of the fact that Jerusalem was the only real city in the area.[131] The recent detailed and meticulous work of Martin Hengel has shown that Luke appears to have a good knowledge of Jerusalem and its immediate environs, Caesarea, and the road up the coastal plains to Caesarea, but that he shows no detailed knowledge of the geography of Samaria or Galilee. This is only what we would expect if he had exposure to the Holy Land only during the time he was Paul's companion on the third missionary journey, as the "we" passages suggest.[132]

127. The Western text makes explicit that Peter's shadow did actually have a healing effect. See Metzger, *Textual Commentary*, p. 330, on both E's and Codex Bezae's additions, along with several other manuscripts. This is part of the overall tendency of the Western text to enhance the image of Peter.

128. As has been shown by van der Horst, "Peter's Shadow." Especially apt is the citation of a passage from the Roman dramatist Ennius in Cicero's *Tusc. Disp.* 3.12.26, where we hear of a shadow harming those who draw near. A related notion can be found in the historian Polybius's work (16.12.7), where we read of a worry that if one enters the Temple of Zeus in Arcadia one will lose one's shadow and so die. The shadow was seen as an extension of the person or personality, perhaps even in some contexts a manifestation of the soul or spiritual life force of a person. As van der Horst suggests, this may have some bearing on how one should read Luke 1:35, where Mary is overshadowed by the most potent of all life forces — God in the person of the Holy Spirit.

129. See Polhill, *Acts*, p. 164.

130. Probably another example of rhetorical hyperbole for dramatic effect, indicating a very great number of cures.

131. See Bruce, *The Acts of the Apostles*, p. 168.

132. See Hengel, "Geography of Palestine in Acts," especially pp. 75ff. What this suggests is that he has few or no sources for happenings in Galilee during the time of the early church, and his sources for the period of the ministry of Jesus in this region are principally Mark and Q, and perhaps the occasional bit of unique information from someone like Joanna of Chuza, or perhaps a member of Jesus' family. In short, Luke is limited by the sources he has, and he does not seek to speculate beyond them.

E. Portents and Persecutions (5:17-42)

The first obligation of every good ancient historian who had rhetorical concerns, concerns about persuading an audience, was to choose a noble subject
and tell the story in a way that was edifying or uplifting, showing the characters'
(and the author's) true humanity.[133] Luke admirably meets this criterion as
well as other rhetorical concerns for clarity, vividness, boldness of speech, and
the like in this portion of his work.[134] His subject is nothing less than salvation,
a salvation available to all, even to the persecutors of those who offer this
salvation. The apostles are shown to have the largeness of soul to offer it even
to those who had a large responsibility for Jesus' trial and death. Peter and the
apostles are the leaders of a "persuasive campaign" and are now attempting
to reach those at the very heart of Judaism, the priests and other religious
authorities.[135] Thus in this section we find a brief forensic or judicial summary
by Peter (and the apostles) summing up the core of the kerygma as part of a
defense in a trial, followed by the deliberative speech of a surprising ally
(Gamaliel the Pharisee) who persuades the authorities not to take drastic
action at this point against the apostles.[136] Unlike other sections in the early
chapters of Acts, this portion has about equal proportions of narrative and
speech material.

In a helpful discussion, Tannehill has shown how the material in Acts
4–7 must be read as a whole, for it builds to a climax or crisis, leading to the
death of Stephen and the scattering of the witnesses.[137] It is a drama in three
basic parts, involving a preliminary hearing, a trial, and finally an act of passion
by a mob, as the bold preaching of the gospel and performance of mighty
works precipitate this crisis of authority and allegiance at the heart of Judaism.
This narrative is furthermore full of echoes of the Lukan Passion narrative.
The treatment of Jesus and his faithful followers are closely linked, but besides
these parallels the disciples also experience what Jesus said would happen to
them — Spirit-inspired witness, persecution, joy in suffering.[138]

Thus, the material in Acts 5:17-42 must not be seen as a simple doublet
of the previous judicial proceedings in Acts 4. Rather, it represents a further
development of the story. In particular, as J. Jeremias has shown, we are now

---

133. See the discussion in van Unnik, "Luke's Second Book," pp. 48ff.
134. As we have pointed out in the introduction, pp. 58ff. above, he also admirably
meets the Greek criteria of collection of sources, eyewitness participation where possible,
and arrangement of sources in a broadly chronological and geographical fashion.
135. See Murphy, "Early Christianity."
136. On the form of these speeches, cf. Kennedy, *New Testament Interpretation,* pp.
120-21; and Soards, *The Speeches in Acts,* pp. 50-55.
137. Tannehill, *Narrative Unity of Luke-Acts,* 2:64-79.
138. See ibid., pp. 68ff.

finally at a real trial, for the apostles had been warned about preaching (see Acts 4). They were now in violation of a direct order of the high priests and the Sanhedrin.[139] The following notable differences from the material in Acts 4 must be stressed: (1) this proceeding involves all the apostles, not just Peter and John. The net of prosecution is spread more widely; (2) here the issue is the teaching of the apostles, not miracles; (3) the servant language (παις) does not come up here; (4) we have here for the first time a miraculous rescue by means of angelic intervention; (5) the apostles are actually punished (beaten — v. 40); and (6) a surprising figure intervenes, Gamaliel.[140]

Luke's rhetorical abilities are shown as he brings out the irony of the story, as he did in his Passion narrative. It is not just that the authorities' impotence is shown, for they think they have the apostles well under lock and key when in fact the apostles are back in the temple precincts preaching, exercising their authority. There is the even larger irony that God and his faithful followers in the end win by losing, "by letting their opponents win and then transforming the expected result."[141] The suffering and even death of disciples, like that of their Master, doesn't lead to the squelching of the Jesus movement, it leads to its success and expansion.

V. 17 tells of the high priest, and those with him (presumably the inner circle of his advisers in the Sanhedrin), taking action. The inner circle is identified by Luke in an aside as the αιρεσις of the Sadducees. This term here and elsewhere in Acts does not have its later technical sense of "heresy," but rather refers to a sect, party, or religious school of thought and can be used of the Sadducees as here, the Pharisees (15:5; 26:5), and even the followers of the Nazarene (24:5, 14, 22). Josephus uses this term as part of an attempt to categorize the Pharisees, Sadducees, and Essenes as the Jews' three philosophical schools (see *Ant.* 18.9-11). Probably, Theophilus would have understood the term in this way as well. It must be remembered that early Christianity, which had no priests, temples, or sacrifices, would likely have been seen by most Greco-Romans as some sort of religious philosophy.

We are told that these authorities are filled with ζηλος, which could mean "religious zeal" but more probably means envy or jealousy here (cf. NRSV), because of the admiration and popularity of the apostles. It may be that Luke is following the Hellenistic *topos* which regularly connects envy with the urge to kill (cf. Plutarch, *Moral.* 487F; Plato, *Laws* 869E-870A; Wis. 2:24; Philo, *Joseph* 12; cf. Acts 7:9; 17:5).[142]

V. 18 informs us that the authorities readily laid hands on the apostles

139. See Jeremias, "Untersuchungen der Quellenproblem der Apostelgeschichte."
140. Here I am following Barrett, *Acts,* vol. 1, p. 281.
141. Tannehill, *Narrative Unity of Luke-Acts,* 2:73.
142. See Johnson, *Acts,* p. 96.

and placed them in public custody, or perhaps the Greek should be read in "custody publicly."[143] The latter reading would suggest their making a public display of their actions, which sets them up for public humiliation when the apostles easily escape.

Divine intervention for the apostles came in the form of the "angel of the Lord." This being is mentioned regularly in the OT (the *malak Yahweh;* see, e.g., Gen. 16:7), and he plays a significant role in the account in Luke-Acts (cf. Luke 1:11, 26; 2:9, 13; 22:43; 24:23; Acts 8:26; 10:3, 7, 22; 11:13; 12:7-15, 23; 27:23). In Luke's view this angel is certainly not to be identified with Christ, for Luke does not see Christ as an angel, and Christ's main agent on earth is seen to be the Holy Spirit. Here this angel not merely sets the apostles free but functions as angels regularly do in the Bible, conveying a divine message. There are more elaborate escapes from prison by Peter (cf. 12:6-11) and Paul (16:26-31) later in the narrative of Acts. Luke's intent is not to focus on the miracle here; it is but a means to an end, mentioned briefly. Stories of the miraculous freeing from prison of persecuted religious people were not uncommon in antiquity (see Euripides, *Bacchae* 346-640).

Once the angel had opened the door of the prison, in *v. 20* he gives the command to "Go, stand in the temple, and tell all the people the message about this life." *Life* was of course a synonym for salvation, including acts of rescue such as this one.[144] Accordingly, in *v. 21* we are told that the apostles entered the temple at daybreak and carried on with their teaching.[145]

These activities transpired without the knowledge of the religious authorities. According to *v. 21b* the high priest and those with him called a meeting of the Sanhedrin, that is, all the council of the sons of Israel, and then ordered to have the apostles brought before them.[146]

Vv. 22-23 provide us with the action and report of the temple police (υπηρεται — literally, "attendants"). They go to the prison and find it locked but nobody inside the jail, and so they return and report to the authorities.

143. See Barrett, *Acts,* vol. 1, pp. 283-84; Polhill, *Acts,* p. 166 and notes.

144. Notice how in the Fourth Gospel the author prefers the more Old Testamental language of life, rather than the more Hellenistic language of salvation which predominates in Acts. Compare the similar phrase in John 6:68.

145. The temple was closed at night, but opened at dawn for the dawn sacrifice; cf. *m. Sheqal.* 5:1; Josephus, *Apion* 2.119; Exod. 29:39; Num. 28:4.

146. Probably the και is explanatory — the Sanhedrin — that is, the whole γερουσια. The latter term Luke uses only here (but cf. the synonym πρεσβυτεριον in Luke 22:66; Acts 22:50). The former term Luke uses often (Luke 22:66; Acts 4:15; 6:12, 15; 22:30; 23:1, 6, 15, 20, 28; 24:20). Luke is only interested in this body insofar as it intersects with the activities of Jesus and his followers, which explains why the term appears where it does in the narrative. On the existence of the Sanhedrin as a council and court, see pp. 188ff. above.

At *v. 24* the στρατηγος, or head of the temple police,[147] along with the high priests, is mentioned as being perplexed. This is hardly surprising since he was in charge of security in the temple precincts, and presumably there was some sort of jail or holding cell very near the precincts that he used if he had to incarcerate someone. A breach of security was obviously his domain, and he figures doubly into the story because next in *v. 25* a report came saying that the apostles were back in the temple standing and teaching again. *V. 26* indicates the captain and his police acted with dispatch, retrieving the apostles and bringing them to the authorities. The phrase "not with Βιας" means without force, and the reason is given: "for they feared the people that perhaps they might have been stoned [by them]."[148]

The additional clause "that perhaps they might have been stoned"[149] is instructive, for it points to the danger of the people taking "justice" or at least stones into their own hands to resolve a matter. This foreshadows what actually does happen in Acts 7 to Stephen. Notice that in this case, however, it is the representatives of the authorities that fear the wrath of the people. The theme of the Jewish authorities being afraid of the people and the potential for mob action can be found already in Luke 20:19 and 22:2.

There is some question whether in *v. 28* we are dealing with a declarative statement or a question (in the latter case, "Did we not command you a command . . . ?"), but probably the ου is a later addition.[150] The high priest, then, is stating the facts about the previous hearing — the apostles were ordered not to teach in the name of Jesus (4:18). They had blatantly violated this order, a fact Peter and the apostles don't deny. *V. 28b* further elucidates the charge. Not only had the apostles filled Jerusalem with their teaching, "but you are determined to bring this man's blood on us."[151] This last phrase means to lay the blame for someone's death (cf. Gen. 4:10-11; 2 Sam. 1:16; Hos. 12:14; Ezek. 18:13; 33:2-4). This is a very serious charge. The authorities are being accused of the murdering of Jesus, even if in ignorance of who he really was. The high priest is not mistaken in these words, for Acts 4:10-11 does indeed place the blame for Jesus' death ultimately on the Jewish leaders (rather than

---

147. On his role see pp. 187ff. above. He is the one Jews called the *sagan.*

148. It is instructive to compare this use of εφοβουντο γαρ to that in Mark 16:8. It shows how the verb would normally be expected to take an object (here "the people") after the γαρ, making it unlikely that Mark would end a paragraph, never mind a whole book, in this fashion.

149. An aorist subjunctive passive verb with μη probably meaning "that perhaps" here (cf. Luke 11:35).

150. See Metzger, *Textual Commentary,* p. 288.

151. It has often been noted how in the early discourse material in Acts the speakers, whether Christians or other Jews, speak in "Biblese," sounding like the LXX. See Johnson, *Acts,* pp. 97ff.

the Jewish people).[152] Suddenly, it is the high priest rather than the apostles who seems to be on trial.

In *v. 29* Peter simply reiterates what he had said before at the earlier hearing, only this time his words are even closer to those of Socrates.[153] God rather than human beings must be obeyed if their commands come into conflict with one another. Then in *vv. 30-32* Peter simply summarizes the kerygma he had been preaching (see Acts 2–4).[154] It was precisely the God of the Jews, "the God of our fathers," who raised up Jesus.[155] This same Jesus the Jewish authorities had killed by "hanging him on a tree" (cf. Acts 10:39). This last phrase echoes Deut. 21:23, and there it likely refers to the display of a corpse after execution (presumably as a deterrent and an exercise in public shaming, cf. 1 Sam. 31:10). Josephus indicates that such a public hanging of the body followed stoning and was the punishment for the crime of blasphemy (*Ant.* 4.202).[156] God not only raised Jesus but exalted him to his right hand as leader[157] and savior.

The term σωτήρ is infrequent in the Greek OT (cf. Judg. 3:9) and not all that frequent as a noun in Luke-Acts (cf. Luke 1:47; 2:11; Acts 13:23), though the verbal form is common. This is the first occurrence of the noun in Acts.[158] The second half of v. 31 should be stressed — Jesus died so he might give repentance and forgiveness of sins to Israel, including the very Jewish leaders involved in the events that led to his execution. The focus on the salvation of Israel is clear in Acts 1–8 (cf. 1:6; 2:36; 4:10, 27; 5:21). "The sermons with their persistent themes demonstrate the persistence of the apostles, who neither crumble before powerful opponents nor despair of the possibility of repentance."[159]

V. 32 mentions two kinds of witnesses to these things — the apostles but also the Holy Spirit, "whom God has given to those who obey him." The implication may be that the Spirit and the insight the Spirit brings into Jesus and the Scriptures has not been given to the religious authorities. This would

---

152. Cf. ibid., p. 98.

153. See pp. 176ff. above.

154. This is perhaps the most compact summary of it.

155. While this could refer to God's bringing Jesus onto the human scene, in view of what follows it probably refers to his resurrection by God.

156. The idea of one suffering such a fate being cursed by God is not mentioned by Luke, but it is well developed by Paul; cf. Gal. 3:13.

157. Here αρχηγός probably means leader rather than author.

158. That it is more common in the later Paulines (Eph. 5:23; Phil. 3:20; ten times in the Pastorals) has been one piece of evidence suggesting that Luke wrote in a period later than that of the capital Paulines, and has even furthered the suggestion that Luke might have written the Pastorals. Cf. Wilson, *Luke and the Pastoral Epistles.* I suspect all this kind of evidence really tells us is that Luke is a Gentile, using language familiar to his Gentile audience. But cf. pp. 430ff. on Luke's relationship to the Pauline Epistles.

159. Tannehill, *Narrative Unity of Luke-Acts,* 2:66.

explain the strong response in *v. 33* — "upon hearing this the authorities were enraged and wanted to kill them."[160]

Apparently recognizing a dangerous situation when he saw one, involving charges and countercharges, a Pharisee named Gamaliel intervened at this point, according to *v. 34*. The Jewish sources do not tell us a great deal about Gamaliel I, not least because he seems to be frequently confused with his grandson who lived at the end of the first century. It appears this Gamaliel was a leading figure in Pharisaism from about A.D. 25 on for some time. He may have been the grandson of the famous Hillel, although the evidence for this seems weak.[161] The Mishnah recognizes him as a very great teacher of the Law — "When Rabban Gamaliel the Elder died, the glory of the Law ceased and purity and abstinence died" (*Soṭa* 9.15). Here he is portrayed as giving advice that may have been proverbial: "R. Johann the Sandal-Maker (a pupil of Akiba) says: Any assembling together for the sake of heaven shall in the end be established, but any that is not for the sake of Heaven shall not in the end be established" (*m. 'Abot* 4:11).

Despite the remarks of Johnson,[162] it seems rather clear that Luke is portraying Gamaliel in a positive light here, especially since he voices the very view Luke would have authorities adopt about early Christianity (that it is of God and should be left alone). Furthermore, the presentation of Pharisees as a whole in Acts is certainly more favorable than the presentation of the Sadducees or priests, and this is all the more remarkable if Luke was intending to tailor his remarks to suit his own situation, since only the Pharisees were left standing after the disasters of the Jewish War and the demise of the temple in A.D. 70. More likely Luke is simply trying to be a good historian here, not to rewrite his sources in some heavily tendentious manner so that the data are skewed. The Pharisees, who believed in the Messiah, resurrection, the afterlife, angels, and demons, were much more likely to be sympathetic to Christian views than the Sadducees or priests, and on the whole this seems to be the way things were. Tannehill rightly says: "In Acts Pharisees are consistently

---

160. The verb translated "enraged" (διαπρίω) suggests very strong emotion and actually means "sawn in two." Used metaphorically here, it should be translated idiomatically — "torn up inside."

161. See the discussion in Lüdemann, *Early Christianity*, pp. 72-73.

162. Johnson, *Acts*, pp. 98ff. See also Smith, " 'Put Outside for a While.' " This paper is very suggestive. On the one hand Luke seems to be critiquing Gamaliel's historical allusions (see below), and on the other hand he agrees with Gamaliel's counsel of nonviolence. Gamaliel here gives this counsel on the basis of human reasoning, and so there is irony here because he seems not to draw these conclusions for the right reason — namely, that it actually is God's plan that is at work here. Gamaliel allows for this possibility without advocating it. Smith also argues that the controlled power of the apostles is contrasted with the abusive use of power by the Sanhedrin, something that reflects a major Lukan agenda.

presented as either open in attitude toward Christians or as having actually accepted the Christian message (cf. 15.5; 23.6-9; 26.5). This is a different picture than that presented in Luke."[163]

The difference was presumably caused by the newfound insistence after Easter about resurrection by the followers of Jesus, including the future resurrection of at least the righteous, and in general a spiritual worldview that included angels and demons, as well as a strong belief in God's sovereignty though without denying human ability to make choices. Then, too, the Christian proclamation of the Messiah comes after Easter as well. In short, theologically the Christian Jews had a lot more in common with the Pharisees than they did with the Sadducees.[164]

Gamaliel is said to be a teacher of the Law who was respected by all the people. His clout is quite clear, for v. 34 tells us he arose and ordered that the apostles be put out of the room so a closed session of the Sanhedrin could be held. This may be one of those occasions when Luke has composed a speech on the basis of what one could conjecture the speaker likely did say,[165] but on the other hand it is possible that Gamaliel's pupil Saul was either present on this occasion or heard a detailed report from Gamaliel about it later. Luke, then, could have gotten the information from Paul.

Gamaliel's basic counsel is that the Sanhedrin carefully consider what they are about to do, and not act rashly. He cites two historical examples to support his concluding contention that if a movement is of God it will prosper, and if it is not, it won't. Vv. 36-37 speak of a Theudas who some time ago rose up claiming to be somebody and was joined by about four hundred people and then was killed, with his followers dispersing; and then the more famous figure of Judas the Galilean is mentioned, who urged resistance to the census of Quirinius in A.D. 6-7, gathered a following but also perished, and his followers likewise were scattered.

This leads to the advice in vv. 38-39 — keep away from these men. If their work is merely human in character it will fail; if it is of God not only will the Sanhedrin be unable to put a damper on it, but they will discover they themselves are opposing God![166] The grammar of v. 39 is rather suggestive,

---

163. Tannehill, *Narrative Unity of Luke-Acts*, 2:67.

164. On the historical character and views of these various Jewish groups after a careful critical sifting of the data, see Saldarini, *Pharisees, Scribes, and Sadducees*. There are also some glimmerings even in Luke of a more open view of Jesus by some Pharisees; cf. Luke 7:36; 11:37; 14:1, and in none of the Gospels are they directly connected with Jesus' death.

165. See pp. 116ff. above on speech conventions.

166. Trumbower, "The Historical Jesus," rightly suggests that one of Luke's aims in this narrative is to distinguish Jesus from the likes of Theudas and Judas. This is because Luke does not view, nor does he present, Jesus as merely another sign prophet or messianic pretender or zealot. See the excursus, pp. 147ff. above, on Luke's Christology.

involving in the first case εαν with the present subjunctive, indicating a less probable condition ("if it might be of human beings . . ."), and then ει with the present indicative ("if it is of God . . ."), indicating a much more probable condition.[167] Luke may be suggesting Gamaliel inclines to the latter view, which is of course the author's own view. Unfortunately, the two historical examples cited have caused no end of controversy about the historical value of Acts and the relationship of Luke's work to that of Josephus, and so a more detailed discussion is in order at this juncture.

A Closer Look — Luke, Josephus, and Historical Reliability ————

It comes as no surprise, since the works of Josephus and those of Luke sometimes tread the same ground, that they have often been compared. This is only to be expected, since they both wrote in the last third of the first century A.D. and both are writing apologetic history works that involve first-century Jews as well as others. In particular, Josephus and Luke refer to some of the same figures of their own era or of the recent past, for example: Quirinius, who took a census around the turn of the era; Judas the Galilean, possibly Theudas, and the Egyptian prophet; Agrippa I, in particular knowledge about Agrippa's death; Felix and Drusilla; and Agrippa II and Bernice. Since Luke and Josephus do not always agree on matters to which they both refer, the question becomes which of these two historians, if either, should be trusted on such matters.

A prima facie case can be made to give Josephus the nod over Luke, in particular because of his personal experience in Judea and Galilee, and Luke's assumed lack of knowledge, geographical and otherwise, of these realms.[168] Furthermore, on the theory that Luke-Acts is a very late document, possibly even from the second century A.D., it is sometimes even argued that Luke knew Josephus's work. For example, in a recent study S. Mason, while not ruling out that Luke may have had independent information, suggests that Luke may have at least heard portions of Josephus's histories read at some point before he wrote. He argues that "we cannot prove beyond doubt that Luke knew the writings of Josephus. If he did not, however, we have a nearly incredible series of coincidences, which require that Luke knew something that closely approximated Josephus' narrative in several distinct ways. This source (or these sources) spoke of: Agrippa's death after his robes shone; the extramarital affairs of both Felix and Agrippa II; the harshness of the Sadducees toward Christianity; the census under Quirinius as a watershed event in Palestine; Judas the Galilean as an arch-rebel at the time of the census; Judas, Theudas, and the Egyptian as three rebels in the Jerusalem area worthy of special mention among a host of others; Theudas and Judas in the same piece of narrative; the Egyptian, the desert, and the *sicarii* in close proximity; Judaism

167. See Bruce, *The Acts of the Apostles*, p. 178.
168. But in fact Luke does know the geography of some of the Holy Land rather well. See Hengel, "Geography of Palestine in Acts," pp. 27ff.

as a philosophical system; the Pharisees and Sadducees as philosophical schools; and the Pharisees as the most precise of the schools. We know of no other work that even remotely approximates Josephus' presentation on such a wide range of issues. I find it easier to believe that Luke knew something of Josephus' work than that he independently arrived at these points of agreement."[169]

Throughout, Mason reflects a predisposition to use Josephus as a measuring rod to evaluate Luke's work at various points, and there is also a certain tendency again and again to give Josephus the benefit of the doubt on historical matters. Yet it is worth asking whether or not Josephus was always or even usually a very careful historian himself.

In the first place, it has often been noted that Josephus was writing at a time when the Second Sophistic was on the rise, and equally importantly writing in a place (Rome) where the rhetorical concerns of the more sophistical historians were strongly affecting the writing of history to the point of distorting the truth in various ways. Josephus operated in a milieu where Dionysius of Halicarnassus, who wrote in the late first century B.C., was seen as something of a mentor for Hellenistic historians.[170] Like Dionysius, Josephus recognized the necessity of "charm of exposition" (*Ant.* 14.2-3). It is more than a coincidence that Josephus's *Jewish Antiquities* covers twenty books, the exact number Dionysius's *Roman Antiquities* does.

Josephus remolds the OT narrative to suit a Hellenized audience and Hellenistic stylistic ideals even to the point of giving Joseph and others long speeches that do not fit their narrative context and are not found in the Hebrew Scriptures. If Josephus did such things to his sacred traditions, it is hardly surprising when he is writing about later Jewish history (in this case about Herod, compare *War* 1.373ff. to *Ant.* 15.127ff.), that Josephus records the same speech by the same person on the same occasion in two different works and yet the two versions are very different. But it is by no means just the speech material that Josephus treats so freely.

As Shaye Cohen has shown, when one compares the major works of Josephus to each other there are frequent contradictions in names, numbers, and in the order in which events are reported. For example, when one compares Josephus's *Vita* to his *War,* there are differences in the order of six important episodes.[171] Furthermore, when Josephus finds a difficulty in the Bible, he is willing to rearrange, edit, or delete material as needed (cf. *Ant.* 1.113-20 to 1.122-47). We are not encouraged when Cohen concludes that Josephus paraphrases his sources' language while *usually* preserving its content but then adds that "even that [content] can be sacrificed if necessary."[172] Cohen illustrates his conclusions over and over, and it is not necessary to repeat his work here. It is useful to consider his overall final conclusions after he compared and analyzed all the major works of Josephus.

"Josephus normally revises the language of his source. . . . the result is Josephan Greek, not a mechanical crib of the source. . . . With revision of language some revision

169. Mason, *Josephus and the New Testament,* pp. 224-25.
170. See, rightly, Gärtner, *Areopagus Speech and Natural Revelation,* p. 24.
171. Cohen, *Josephus in Galilee and Rome,* pp. 6-7.
172. Ibid., p. 32.

of content is inevitable. Details are added, omitted, or changed, not always with reason. Although his fondness for the dramatic, pathetic, erotic, and the exaggerated is evident throughout, as a rule Josephus remains fairly close to his original. Even when he modifies the source to suit a certain aim he still reproduces the essence of the story. Most importantly he does not engage in the free invention of episodes. . . . When analyzing Josephan chronology we must always keep in mind the possibility that Josephus deliberately departed from the historical sequence for [a] literary reason. . . . We have [also] emphasized another aspect of Josephus' work: his inveterate sloppiness. Texts suitable for tendentious revision as well as passages which contradict his motives are sometimes left untouched. The narrative is frequently confused, obscure, and contradictory."[173] To the above one must add that Josephus does indeed invent speeches, though perhaps not narrative episodes, as Cohen says.

What we should conclude from the above is that Josephus must be read critically, giving his work very close scrutiny, just as Luke's work is to be read critically. Josephus is no *canon* or measuring rod by which Luke's historical work, too often assumed to be inferior and derivative, can automatically be shown to be wanting in historical veracity.

If we return for a moment to the list Mason gives of important correspondences in major figures and events between Josephus and Luke, it will be immediately seen that in each case we are talking about *major* political figures whose lives and exploits were widely known among Jews, especially among Jews in the Holy Land. It is far from unlikely that Luke could have had independent information of these figures and their lives from sources other than Josephus. Indeed, it is perfectly plausible that he had such information from his own investigations during his time in Caesarea and Jerusalem.[174] It is even possible, if indeed Luke wrote in the 70s or 80s for a patron such as Theophilus in Rome, that Josephus had access to Luke's work, though on the whole I think they both drew independently on traditions and stories about these major figures.

It remains here for us to consider the material that for Mason seems to clinch the matter that Luke is probably indebted to Josephus — the Theudas, Judas, Egyptian references found in Acts 5:36-37; 21:38 and in *Ant.* 20.102, 97, 171 as well as some reference in *War* 2.259-64. Let us first point out that the reference to the Egyptian is historically perfectly plausible in Acts 21 and comports with what Josephus suggests in regard to *some* of the substance and the date — the Egyptian was a figure who appeared and caused trouble during the rule of Felix (A.D. 52-59), the end of which period is also the time when Paul is taken into custody in Jerusalem. Yet Luke and Josephus also *disagree* on important facts — Acts 21 suggests the Egyptian led a band of "daggermen" *(sicarii)*. Josephus suggests he was not associated with such people, but rather was a prophetic figure. Acts suggests he led about four thousand into the desert, Josephus that he led his followers (thirty thousand!) to the Mount of Olives to prepare to seize the city. Mason admits these differences, but he attributes them to Luke's poor memory of what Josephus said. Poor memory might lead to a jumbling

173. Ibid., pp. 232, 33.
174. See pp. 165ff. above.

up of some facts, but it hardly accounts for the difference in the numbers of followers — are we to think Luke picked a number at random, not remembering at all what Josephus said? Is it not more plausible to conclude that Luke and Josephus had independent traditions about the Egyptian that differed on some important matters?[175]

There is one further factor Mason does not take into account — Luke is reporting here the off-the-cuff remarks of a Roman tribune under duress, who himself could have jumbled up the facts. Were these the remarks of one of Luke's main positive characters, one could more plausibly assume that the views expressed reflected Luke's own understanding. This is less certain in a case like this one, especially since we will see in Lysias's letter to the procurator his ability to bend the truth.[176]

We turn now to the more difficult matter of what to make of the references to Theudas and Judas, in that order. Mason points to the same order in Josephus's discussion of these two figures in *Ant.* 20.97-99, 100-102.[177] He suggests that Luke remembered the order of Josephus's discussion but forgot that Josephus had indicated that Judas was a much earlier figure. In short, his memory was selective and what he remembered was not the actual substance of Josephus's account but the order. It must be admitted that this seems strange, especially when one is talking about an ancient historian like Luke who was far more likely to concentrate on matters of substance than matters of chronological order. As Bruce says, "only a very superficial and cursory glance at Josephus could give a reader the impression that Judas himself came after Theudas."[178] There is also the conundrum pointed out by Johnson that if Luke was simply following Josephus in regard to Theudas, rather than drawing on independent testimony, why would he have left out the fact that Theudas saw himself as the prophet mentioned by Moses, since Theudas as false prophet could have served as a perfect foil to Luke's portrayal of Jesus as the true Mosaic prophet?[179] If there is a more plausible explanation, it should be given preference to this theory of selective bad and good memory. Let us consider the other options.

First, Josephus could have been right about the existence of a troublemaker named Theudas but wrong about his causing trouble during the governorship of Fadus (A.D. 44-46; cf. *Ant.* 20.5.1.97-98). I do not think that we should automatically give Josephus the benefit of the doubt in light of Cohen's study, especially in view of Josephus's track record on rearranging episodes and on various chronological matters.

Secondly, Luke could have made a mistake in his dating of Theudas. This must be frankly admitted.[180] Since he was not present to hear Gamaliel, perhaps he had

175. In view of Josephus's track record with numbers, it is easier to believe he exaggerated, turning four thousand into many more, than that Luke, who had no obvious reason to change the figures, did the opposite.

176. See pp. 679ff. below. The issue of characterization (i.e., to what degree is Lysias meant to be seen as a reliable, truthful character in the narrative) is not taken into account by Mason.

177. Mason, *Josephus and the New Testament*, p. 211.

178. Bruce, *The Acts of the Apostles*, p. 176.

179. Johnson, *Acts*, pp. 99-100.

180. See Barrett, *Acts*, vol. 1, p. 296.

been told that the Jewish sage referred to various troublemakers in Judea. Luke then inserted those he knew about and the little information he knew about them.[181] This is not impossible if Luke was following Thucydides' advice about making the speaker say approximately the kind of thing he *did* say, lacking more specific data.

A more cynical, and I think more implausible, hypothesis would be to suggest that Luke deliberately made Gamaliel misspeak, since he was a Jew. This last suggestion especially doesn't work since Luke portrays Gamaliel as a helpful figure.

Fourthly, there is the possibility, which should not be leaped to but not dismissed either, that there was an earlier Theudas who caused difficulties before 6 A.D. when the Judas matter arose.[182] As the inscriptional evidence lets us know, Theudas was a common enough name (*CIG* 2684, 3563, 3920, 5698), and as anyone who has carefully read Josephus knows, the latter mentions four Simons within forty years and three Judases within ten years as instigators of rebellion! Add to this that the testimony of Codex Bezae tells us that the Theudas mentioned in Acts committed suicide, while Josephus tells us he was captured alive and beheaded (*Ant.* 20.5.1) and one can understand why some text critics think that Luke and Josephus are referring to two different Theudases.[183] In view of these facts, the suggestion of two troublemakers named Theudas seems a modest proposal.[184]

On the whole I incline to the fourth or the first of these alternatives to Mason's proposal, but I certainly would not rule out the second one. I incline to the fourth because I think Luke was Paul's sometime companion and could have gotten accurate information from the apostle about this matter, either because Paul was present on the occasion or heard about it shortly thereafter. In any case I agree with Bruce that Luke should be seen as at least as trustworthy an ancient historian as Josephus, and indeed more so in various matters. Both his data and Josephus's must be critically sifted. Josephus should in all probability not be seen as a measuring rod or as a source for Luke, especially in matters of chronology.[185]

According to *v. 39b* Gamaliel's deliberative rhetoric was convincing, and the Sanhedrin was persuaded. *V. 40* indicates that the apostles were brought back in, admonished not to speak in Jesus' name, and flogged. This was no light punishment if it involved the prescribed forty lashes (minus one) for

181. It is not implausible that Saul was present on this occasion, in which case he could have reported to Luke what was said. See Barrett, *Acts,* vol. 1, p. 296.

182. See the discussion in Hemer, *Book of Acts,* pp. 162-63.

183. See Metzger, *Textual Commentary,* p. 334.

184. And is the view of Bruce, *The Book of Acts,* p. 176.

185. Notice Rajak's ("Josephus") pertinent observation (p. 469) that in the *Antiquities* "external attestations for the chronological claims are not felt to be necessary; nor are explicit and detailed synchronizations with other events in world history." This is all the more reason not to make unwarranted assumptions about the accuracy of Josephus's chronological ordering of events like the Theudas and Judas affairs. We have no external way of checking him in most cases, unless Luke provides such a check.

offenses against the Jewish law (cf. Deut. 25:3; Acts 22:19; 2 Cor. 11:24; Mark 13:9; *m. Mak.* 3:10-14). Some had even died from this punishment.[186]

Vv. 41-42 serve as a summary conclusion to the previous episode. Paradoxically, the apostles rejoiced in their suffering, because it was received as a result of their bold witness to Jesus. Though from a human point of view being flogged amounted to being shamed or dishonored, from the disciples' viewpoint, which involved a transvaluation of normal ancient values, it was considered an honor.[187] The apostles were in no manner hindered or inhibited in their teaching because of this experience. Rather they continued to teach every day in the temple and from house(church) to house(church), proclaiming Jesus to be the Jewish Messiah.[188]

F. The Seven Servants (6:1-7)

The material in 6:1–8:3 is some of the most complex and controverted in the whole book of Acts, and calls for careful discussion and detailed analysis. Not only is this material difficult in itself, but matters become even more complex when some of this material is compared to similar data in the Pauline corpus.

A Closer Look — The Hellenists

Luke introduces us at Acts 6:1 to a mysterious group of people called "Hellenists." This terminology is found again at 9:29, and possibly also at 11:20 (but see below). Since the term Ἑλληνιστής is not found in any literature prior to Acts, one must rely primarily on the context and the etymological roots of the term to help us understand what Luke means by the term.[189] As M. Hengel has pointed out, the word Ἑλληνιστής is in all likelihood derived from the verbal form ἑλληνίζειν and likely means "one who speaks Greek." This is how the earliest Christian exegete of this material, John Chrysostom, understood the term (*Hom.* 14 col. 113; *Hom.* 21). The question is whether it also connotes something more, such as a person who "Hellenizes" or follows Greek ways, or even, as H. Cadbury argued, a Gentile.[190]

186. Marshall, *Acts*, p. 124.
187. See the discussion of this whole matter by Malina and Neyrey, "Honor and Shame in Luke-Acts."
188. V. 42 seems to follow the rhetorical pattern of a chiasm (A, B, B, A) with preaching being associated with the temple and teaching with what happened in the houses. See Polhill, *Acts*, p. 174.
189. Cf. Wanke, "'Ἑλληνιστής'"; Martin, "Hellenists."
190. Cf. Cadbury, "The Hellenists."

As most commentators have recognized, this last view of Cadbury's has very serious problems. He begins with the difficult text of 11:20 and tries to interpret the other two texts in its light. But the suggestion that Luke thought there were Gentiles already in the earliest church in Jerusalem, besides crediting Luke with gross anachronism, makes little sense of the Lukan narrative itself. As C. K. Barrett has put it, "If from 6.1 (or from the day of Pentecost . . .) there had been Jewish and Gentile elements in the Jerusalem church, or if Luke had believed that it was so, could he have made so much of Peter's preaching to Cornelius, of the founding of the mixed church in Antioch, of Paul's break with the synagogue at Pisidian Antioch and of the Council of Ch. 15?"[191] The answer to these questions is surely no, and thus Cadbury's views must be rejected, at the very least in regard to Acts 6:1 and 9:29.[192]

Other suggestions in regard to what Ἑλληνιστης connotes in Acts 6:1 and 9:29 have included: (1) it refers to Jewish proselytes, but if this is the case it is next to impossible to explain why only Nicolaus among the "Seven" is singled out as a proselyte in 6:5; (2) it refers to a syncretistic Jewish fringe group (such as Samaritans or Essenes). This fails to make sense of either 6:9 or 9:2, where those who oppose Stephen and then Paul appear to be very traditional, archconservative Jews interested in protecting things like existing temple worship in Jerusalem.

On the other hand, the Lukan linguistic data can take us a bit further in the right direction. As Johnson has pointed out, when Luke wants to make an *ethnic* distinction between Jews and Greeks he uses the term Ἑλλην (cf. 14:1; 16:1; 19:17; 21:18 where the ethnic distinction is explicit; 17:4 and 19:10 where it is implicit), *not* Ἑλληνιστης. Furthermore, while only here does Luke use the noun form Ἑβραιος, when he uses the adjectival equivalent (Ἑβραις) he always means by it "the Hebrew (or Aramaic) dialect" (cf., e.g., Acts 26:14).[193] In other words, Lukan usage suggests that the term "Hellenist" has as at least its primary meaning "one who speaks Greek." This leads to the suggestion that only the context can determine whether the person in question is thought of as a Jew or a Gentile.[194]

This more narrow "linguistic" definition of the term in question allows us to make sense of both 6:1 and 9:29. In the former text, the term refers to Greek-speaking Jewish Christians, as opposed to those Jewish Christians whose everyday spoken language was Aramaic (or less likely Hebrew).[195] In the latter text the reference is to

191. Barrett, *Acts,* vol. 1, p. 309.

192. See Johnson, *Acts,* p. 105: "the suggestion that Luke meant by Ἑλληνιστες 'Greek Gentiles' in the present passage has little to recommend it, particularly since Luke takes such pains to show the gradual development of the Gentile mission *after* the close of the Jerusalem narrative."

193. Johnson, *Acts,* p. 105.

194. See rightly Metzger, *Textual Commentary,* p. 388: "whether the person be a Jew or a Roman or any other non-Greek must be gathered from the context."

195. Moule's qualification (in "Once More") is that the "Hebrews" meant those who in addition to Greek spoke Aramaic, while the Hellenists spoke only Greek. I would refine this a bit by agreeing to the last half of the statement (the Hellenists did *not* speak Aramaic or Hebrew), but I would stress that the chief spoken language of the Hebrews was Aramaic and this was reflected in their discussions and their worship (cf., e.g., 1 Cor. 16:22), though

Greek-speaking Jews who are not Christians, but rather are hostile to the Christian message Paul preaches.

This takes us to the difficult text in 11:20. If, as Bruce, Moule, and many others have argued, Ἕλλην is the proper reading, then our discussion is at an end, and this text has no bearing on figuring out who the "Hellenists" were. On this reading Acts 11:20 refers to an ethnic distinction between Jews and "Greeks" (which presumably here would mean Hellenizing Gentiles, not immigrants from Greece). The textual evidence, however, slightly favors the reading Ἑλληνιστής,[196] and this is surely the more difficult reading in terms of making sense of the text. What would 11:20 mean on this showing? Vv. 19-20 must be taken together. The former verse speaks of those scattered by the persecution who traveled as far as Phoenicia, Cyprus, and Antioch and spoke the word "to no one except Jews" (ει μη μονον ᾽Ιουδαιοις), while v. 20 appears to offer a qualification of this remark — "But (δε) some from among these men, Cyprians and Cyrenians, coming to Antioch spoke also (και) to the Hellenists. . . ." If we take the two verses together as we ought, the term "Hellenist" can quite readily mean Greek-speaking persons in Antioch who were not Jews.[197] The latter fact is made clear by the context, not by the term itself.[198]

Thus we conclude that the term Ἑλληνιστής in all three texts means a Greek-speaking person, with the context defining more precisely what sort of Greek-speaking person Luke has in mind, ranging from Jewish Christians, to Jews, to pagans. This in turn means that Luke does not use "Hellenist" as some sort of technical term for a specific kind of Christian. Nevertheless, it is clear that the disagreements between Aramaic- and Greek-speaking Jewish Christians referred to in Acts 6:1ff. is important as a clue to the varied character of even the earliest Christian fellowship in Jerusalem.

If one takes all the clues that Luke gives us in Acts 6–11, it appears that in Acts 6 and 9 Luke uses the term "Hellenist" to refer to Diaspora Jews living in or around Jerusalem (or their descendants) for whom Greek is their spoken language, and who attended synagogues where Greek was the language of worship (e.g., the synagogue of the Freedmen — 6:9). Some of these people, such as Stephen, have become Christians. Without minimizing the differences that Acts 6 indicates existed between the "Hebrews" and "Hellenists" in regard to the care of the widows, which was essentially a practical matter, it must be said that there is nothing in Acts 6 that suggests a significant "doctrinal" rift between these two groups of Christians unless it is thought that Stephen's speech suggests such a rift.[199]

---

some of them (such as Peter) also were at least competent in Greek. This explains why it is that some real difficulties arose, at least in part engendered by the significant language differences between a Semitic tongue and Greek.

196. See the discussion in Warfield, "The Reading Ἕλληνας and Ἑλληνιστας," and Metzger, *Textual Commentary*, pp. 386-89.

197. See rightly Barrett, *Acts*, vol. 1, pp. 550-51.

198. Cf. Metzger, *Textual Commentary*, p. 388-89; Martin, "Hellenists," p. 136: "If the majority reading is original it may still attest to the meaning 'speaking Greek,' but with variable racial connotation *which must be taken from the context*" (emphasis mine).

199. This view is still exceedingly common, especially among German scholars. See Schneider, *Die Apostelgeschichte I*, pp. 406-16; Pesch, *Die Apostelgeschichte (1–12)*, pp. 258-59.

Several things in the text of Acts suggest that it is high time to dismiss the old radical dichotomy of F. C. Baur between the "Hebrews" and the "Hellenists," with the former representing very conservative Jewish Christians who continued to be observant of the Torah and attended the temple while the latter were more Hellenizing Christians who had more liberal views of the Torah, the necessity of temple worship, and the like. C. C. Hill's detailed study of this matter calls this whole approach into question.[200]

In the first place, notice that the people who oppose Paul in Acts 9 are "Hellenists." In this text, they do not appear to be more broad-minded Jews at all, but rather conservative Greek-speaking Jews who are scandalized by Paul's more "liberal" message about Jesus as the Jewish Messiah. In other words, this text provides no basis for associating a liberal ideology with the term "Hellenist." If we look at Acts 6 again, we must ask — Who is it that is said to first oppose Stephen, and on what grounds? The answer to this question is, Diaspora Jews who belong to the synagogue of the Freedmen and do not like what Stephen says about Moses (the Law), God, and the holy place (6:8-13). In short, these people match rather nicely the probable profile of "Hellenists" in Acts 9:29 if the question is matters of ideology. But it must then be doubtful that even in Acts 6 the term "Hellenist" is meant to tell us something distinctive about the *ideology* of a particular group of Christians, since Stephen, a Greek-speaking Jew, is being opposed by other Greek-speaking Jews who sound very conservative indeed and both are in the sense argued above "Hellenists"! In other words, "Hellenists" should be dropped from the discussion of Acts 6 and 9 as a technical term if it means something ideological, something more than a Greek-speaking person (in this case Jews).

One of the more amazing parts of the argument of Baur and others who have followed him is that they insist that the *false witnesses* referred to in Acts 6:11-14 are in fact telling the truth about what Stephen's views are! Yet Luke quite clearly brands these witnesses as false ones in 6:13. This leads one to ask: Does Luke really think that Stephen was speaking against Torah and temple per se? Is it really the case that Stephen should be seen as a Pauline prototype of some sort, and that this is what got him killed? Does Acts 6 really warrant the suggestion of a deep division in early Christianity that Luke has somewhat papered over between "liberal" and "conservative" Jewish Christians in the Jerusalem church (and elsewhere)? Is there any justification at all for suggesting that only the Greek-speaking Christians were persecuted by non-Christian Jews, and only they were scattered as a result of this persecution to various places outside Jerusalem? We must explore some of these matters in a little more detail now.

Let us consider the last question first. Acts 8:1-3, which is widely recognized as a redactional summary of Luke's, reflects his penchant for using words that indicate magnitude or breadth of scope in part for rhetorical effect (in this case he uses "severe" and "all"). Even allowing for a certain amount of dramatic hyperbole, what this summary tells us is that Luke thought the persecution that hit the early church in Jerusalem affected all the various groups, with the exception of the "apostles," a term

---

200. *Hellenists and Hebrews.*

which surely here means the Twelve, the inner leadership in Jerusalem (cf. 6:2).[201] In other words, the Greek-speaking Jewish Christians or "Hellenists" are *not* said to have been singled out for special attention, and nothing suggests they were persecuted because they had certain ideological commitments that other early Christians in Jerusalem did not have. That they are affected by the persecution is surely indicated by what follows in 8:4ff. and in 11:19ff. What *is* also suggested by a close reading of Acts 8–11 is that while various of the "Hebrews" seem to have returned to Jerusalem after the persecution had run its course (cf. 9:26, 31; 11:1), many, perhaps even most, of the Greek-speaking Jewish Christians, who had likely come from the Diaspora (or descended from those who did), kept going not only into Judea and Samaria but into the Diaspora proper, including Syrian Antioch, as 11:19ff. suggests.[202]

In general the above reconstruction of events comports nicely with what Paul says in Galatians 1–2 and 1 Thessalonians. First, we note that in a very early letter Paul refers to the persecution of the churches in Judea by Jews, a persecution that "drove us out" (1 Thess. 2:14-15). Notice he says nothing about a special persecution of one group within or among these churches. This passage presumably refers to the events recounted in Acts 8–9, which in the case of Paul involved him first as a persecutor (Acts 8:1-4) and then as one persecuted (9:28-29). Similarly, in Gal. 1:13 we hear of Paul persecuting "the church of God," not a particular group in it, which comports with Acts 8:1-3.

Gal. 1:18-23 speaks of Paul's first visit to Jerusalem after his conversion. Paul says he saw only Peter and James among the apostles and then went away into the region of Syria and Cilicia. Acts 9:26-29 is more general in character, but again it suggests a face-to-face visit with apostles, a personal testimony, and then a departure with the aid of fellow believers from Caesarea to Paul's home region.[203] What Acts 9 *adds* is that what precipitated Paul's leaving Jerusalem was that his life was in danger, which was caused by his arguing with various Greek-speaking Jews ("Hellenists") in Jerusalem.

The one major sticking point is Gal. 1:22 — "I was still unknown *by sight* to the churches of Judaea, they had only *heard* 'The one who formerly was persecuting us is

201. Here Moule's suggestion ("Once More," p. 101) that perhaps the Twelve, having come from Galilee, had never joined a Jerusalem synagogue and thus escaped this synagogue-based purge, seems possible. There is also another possibility; namely, that because the celebrated Jewish leader Gamaliel had given quite specific advice *not* to persecute Peter and the other apostles (cf. 5:18, 40: "the apostles"; 5:38: "I tell you, keep away from these men and let them alone"), this advice was still heeded when the later persecution broke out and so it was differently directed than the earlier one (cf. and contrast Acts 5:17ff. to 8:1ff.). It will be noted that while Stephen is a leader (one of the Seven), he is never said to be one of the Twelve or the apostles, and so he is no exception to this rule.

202. In other words, those who had never had any other ancestral home than Palestine returned to it, but those from the Diaspora had more than one place they could call home and so had more viable options when persecuted than did the "Hebrews."

203. One further point of comparison is that Acts 9:27 says Barnabas introduced Paul to the apostles, and Gal. 2:1 may at least imply the same thing — "I went up again to Jerusalem with Barnabas. . . ."

now proclaiming. . . .'" It should be noted that the problem here is not merely trying to reconcile Galatians to Acts, but to reconcile Paul to himself! In Gal. 1:13 Paul says he violently persecuted the church of God, but in v. 22 he is unknown by sight to the churches of Judea! Leaving Acts out of the equation for the moment, surely the most natural way to read this is that Paul persecuted the church in Jerusalem, and was known by sight to them, but that he had not branched out to the churches of Judea, and so was not known by sight to them. The members of these outlying Judean churches had only *heard* (presumably from the Jerusalem church members) about Paul as persecutor and then as convert.[204]

When we turn back to Acts 8–9, what does it tell us? First, it says explicitly that Saul persecuted the church in Jerusalem, going house to house (8:1, 3). It says nothing about his going to the churches in Judea. The next thing mentioned is that he requested permission to go to the synagogues in Damascus (9:1-2).[205] Again nothing is said of Judean churches being attacked by Paul personally. Finally, after his conversion, 9:26 says that he returned to *Jerusalem* and tried to join the Christians there, but they were afraid of him. His witnessing is also said to be confined to Jerusalem (v. 28). Paul is whisked off the stage quickly at 9:30 *before* Luke says, "Meanwhile the churches throughout Judaea, Galilee, and Samaria had peace and were built up . . ." (v. 31).

Because there is no contrast between churches in Jerusalem and Judea in 1 Thess. 2:14-15, unlike what seems to be implied in Galatians, it is likely that in the broader Thessalonian text Paul is *including* the Jerusalem churches under the heading "churches of God that are in Judaea."[206] In short, none of these texts is inexplicable, and Acts is very specific about Saul's activities in Judea being limited to Jerusalem.

How does this help us to understand "the Hellenists"? First, nothing that *either* Acts or Paul's letters say suggests that Greek-speaking Jewish Christians were especially singled out for persecution, much less that they were singled out because of their theological views. Furthermore, there is nothing in Acts or Paul that suggests that the Greek-speaking Christians were persecuted by one group while the "Hebrew" Christians were persecuted by another.[207] To the contrary, even in the case of Stephen, while the action is first taken up by "Hellenists" against him (6:9), we are told quite specifically that he was taken at some point to the high priest (7:1), the very same authority before whom the apostles had been dragged in 5:17, and notice that in 4:1-22 these same Jewish leaders are involved with the apostles earlier (cf. 4:5).[208] Thus we must conclude

---

204. Hengel, *Paul*, p. 36, argues that Paul is using the Roman provincial designation, which included Samaria and Galilee. This may well be correct.

205. It may be noted that this suggests that Saul's was an urban campaign. The approach he took to stifle Christianity is the same as he later took to spread it — strike at the major urban centers from which satellite churches in the outlying areas eventually come.

206. Paul was surely not on a one-man campaign against the church of God, and this makes it quite believable that other equally incensed Jews were attacking the churches outside of Jerusalem, at least at some point. Luke has simply focused on the activity of Paul for obvious reasons.

207. Hengel, *Between Jesus and Paul*, pp. 1ff., argues in this fashion.

208. Hill, *Hellenists and Hebrews*, pp. 34-35, is right to object that the mention of

that if "the persecution *was not* selective, then it would serve to unite, rather than to distinguish between, the Hellenists and the Hebrews."[209]

There is also the important matter of Stephen's speech, which is assumed to involve a radical critique of the Law and the temple, a critique later taken up by Paul, which in turn leads to the supposition that the "Hellenists" provide the bridge between Jesus and the Twelve on the one hand and Paul and the Pauline Gentile mission on the other. We will examine the speech in some detail in the text itself. Here it is sufficient to point out the following: (1) It is doubtful that we should simply assume the false witnesses are thought by Luke to tell the truth about Stephen's views (6:13-14). (2) Stephen is giving a review of what may be called salvation history, drawing on the LXX (or some Greek OT) version of the stories, a not surprising approach by a Greek-speaking Jewish Christian. (3) Stephen is not in general repudiating this Jewish story of election and selection, but striving to show what God's overall intent and plan was all along and how he used major figures like Abraham, Moses, and Joseph. (4) Stephen seeks to show the long history of unfaithfulness to God's purposes on the part of God's people, beginning at least as early as at Sinai (6:39). They are seen as a people who repeatedly fail to *keep the Law* (v. 53), which is not seen as a virtue by Stephen but rather as a fault! (5) It is possible that there is some sort of criticism of the temple as opposed to the tent of meeting in vv. 44-50, but if so it is no different from the sort of prophetic critiques one finds in an Amos or a Jeremiah or in Isa. 66:1-2, or for that matter in some of the Samuel material. Stephen seems to be mainly critical of the idea that God *dwells* in earthly temples made by human hands, when in fact heaven is God's proper dwelling place. (6) Stephen identifies Jesus (and himself) with the OT prophetic tradition (cf. 7:37, 52), and the reaction of the people to Jesus and himself with the reaction of early Jews to the prophets. In other words, he is identifying with one important stream of Jewish tradition. (7) To judge from the point of the outburst, the crowd reacts to Stephen apparently because of his criticism of God's people and their unfaithfulness, *not because of some criticism of the Law or temple. His views on the latter are rather conventional in a prophetic vein.*[210] In short, there is nothing in the speech of Stephen, unless one overplays the material in vv. 44-50, that warrants the conclusion that here we find "radical" "Hellenist" theology about Law and temple. In Luke's view, it is not Stephen but *Peter* and then *Paul* who pave the way for a different approach to the Law.

---

elders and scribes in 6:12 does not necessarily suggest any Pharisees (as opposed to temple officials), since this very same phrase is used in 4:5 (its only other use in Acts) to refer to members of the Sanhedrin who were involved in the flogging of Peter and John!

209. Ibid., p. 40. I disagree with Hill that Luke has invented the idea of a severe persecution, especially in view of the references in 1 Thessalonians and Galatians, but I would allow that a certain amount of dramatic hyperbole is regularly used by Luke to indicate the significance of the event. The hyperbole comes perhaps in regard to the scope of those driven out, but when people lose their lives in religious struggles the word "severe" is warranted.

210. See ibid., pp. 41ff. Proof that old views die hard is shown by the importance of the Baur "Hellenist" argument to Hengel's overall reconstruction of pre-Pauline early Christianity. See Hengel, *Paul,* pp. 33ff., 208ff.

This is not to deny that Greek-speaking Jewish Christians from Jerusalem played an important role in spreading the gospel in the Diaspora (cf. 11:19-20), and in particular took the lead in spreading the message to other Greek-speaking people (both Jew and Gentile). Nor is it to dispute that Antioch seems to be the key church where the issue of a Law-free gospel for Gentiles really came to the fore (cf. Galatians 2 to Acts 11:19ff.). There is nothing, however, in either Acts or Paul that justifies Baur's hypothesis of a deep division between Hebrews and Hellenists either in Jerusalem or elsewhere. In all likelihood there was a wide range of views on the subject of how Jews and Gentiles could have fellowship in Christ, and whether Gentiles needed to keep the Law to be Christians. I would suggest that it is a mistake to identify the views of the Judaizers (Pharisaic Jewish Christians) with the views of James and the early apostles such as Peter. The Judaizers were influential in the Jerusalem church (cf. 11:2; 15:5), and to judge from Galatians they sought to be influential in Antioch and Galatia as well, but at the end of the day, even James disagreed with their views.[211]

A much more plausible model of early Christianity would be that it involved converts who ranged from extreme Judaizers to rather antinomian teachers, but that Peter, James, John, Philip, and even Paul held views somewhere in between these two radical extremes. James would be in various ways closer to the Judaizers' views on some issues, including some forms of zeal for the Law (see Acts 21:17-26), while Paul would be closer to some Gentile Christians and perhaps also some Greek-speaking Jewish ones on such matters. What Acts 15 suggests, however, is that on the most basic matter of the basis of salvation in Christ especially for Gentiles, there was no major disagreement between a James and a Paul, something that Paul himself also suggests in Gal. 2:7-9.

Acts 6:1-7 seems to be based on several sources of information, including a traditional list of the Seven.[212] Luke seems to know very little about these seven men, except for Stephen and Philip (cf. 8:5; 21:8ff.), the latter of whom is not to be confused with the Philip who was one of the Twelve. In fact, Luke seems to be making a point of distinguishing the Seven from the Twelve, for this is the only text where he uses the phrase "the Twelve" (v. 2). This story about the interior life of the early church once again suggests that material goods were a source of both blessing and friction in the earliest Christian community. As Tannehill points out, it is not correct to say that Luke has simply idealized the inner life of the community. In fact, in addition to Acts 5 and the present text, one could also point to 8:18-24; 9:26-28; 11:1-18; 15:1-35; and 21:20-36 as providing clear evidence that Luke has not glossed over the problems in the early

211. See below on Acts 15, pp. 439ff.
212. See Lüdemann, *Early Christianity,* pp. 77-78. That the Seven is a formal designation is probably shown by Acts 21:8; cf. Haenchen, *Acts,* p. 263.

Christian communities.[213] He does not, however, dwell on these problems, but narrates briefly how they were resolved. He is apparently more interested in the external sources of problems and possibilities.

The solution the apostles arrive at here is a rather novel one for antiquity. One commentator has called it the first example of affirmative action — "Those with political power generally repressed complaining minorities; here the apostles hand the whole system over to the offended minority."[214] The discussion here and the resolution of the problem should probably be seen in the light of the OT and early Jewish provisions for widows and other marginalized people in a highly patriarchal society (cf. Exod. 22:22; Deut. 10:18; 14:29; Ps. 146:9).[213] In such a society, widows were often put in positions where they were entitled not to an inheritance but merely to maintenance by their larger family, and even when they did have the possibility of inheriting, the males in the family had first claim on the inheritance.[216]

In our particular narrative there may have been a special set of circumstances. If the "Hellenist" widows were indeed the widows of Greek-speaking Jews, some or many of whom may have immigrated to Jerusalem in order to die in the Holy City, they may have been left without support when their husbands died because their family (and that of their husbands as well) may have been far away in the Diaspora, or perhaps the Greek-speaking Jewish Christians were just fewer in number and so the widows of this group had less of a natural constituency to rely on.[217]

---

213. Tannehill, *Narrative Unity of Luke-Acts,* 2:80-81. He is right that Luke is not mainly concerned with this inner life, but rather with the outer witness and its effects. This may explain why he tends to spend less time explaining how the internal tensions and problems were resolved than in dealing with the external sources of problems and persecutions.

214. Keener, *Bible Background Commentary,* p. 338.

215. It is not clear whether the Mishnaic material reflects the practice of pre-A.D. 70 in regard to the treatment of the widows, but if it does it may be of relevance here. The *tamhuy* was the daily distribution for the wandering or traveling poor and consisted of food (bread, beans, fruit, wine), while the *quppah* was a weekly dole for the poor of the city consisting of food and clothing (cf. *m. Ketub.* 13:1-2; *m. Pesah.* 10:1; *m. Sheqal.* 5:6; *m. Pe'a* 8:7). The Christian problem and practice are different from both of these in some measure. It may be, however, that by this point in time the Christian widows had been excluded from any dole offered in the city (by the Jewish authorities?), and that the more substantial Semitic-speaking community had taken care of their own widows, but the Hellenistic widows were not being given the same support, perhaps because the Greek-speaking Jewish Christian group was considerably smaller.

216. See my discussion in *Women in the Ministry of Jesus,* pp. 5ff.

217. See Keener, *Bible Background Commentary,* p. 338. There is interesting evidence in the papyri from Egypt of the ongoing nature of this kind of problem for the church. For example, *P.Oxy* 16 (1924) 1954-56 provides us with orders to a wine seller to provide wine for widows of the church. See the discussion in *New Docs,* 2:192-93.

Clearly enough *v. 1* indicates, however, that the problem of the lack of support for the Hellenistic widows was in the main created by a growth problem, and the verse suggests that there was a general daily distribution of food in the community for the needy. This neglect or oversight[218] led to murmuring by the Hellenists among the disciples.[219]

We must think here of Jewish ideas about charity and the poor governing the earliest Christians' considerations of these matters, not the views of the larger Greco-Roman world. As A. R. Hands remarks, in "contrast with what is found in many Jewish texts, where the poor tend to be equated with the pious and deserving who are destined for happiness in the next world, if not in this, at Rome the poor are described as *leves, inquinati, improbi, scelerati,* etc., terms implying dishonesty." As Hands goes on to point out, the modern notion of charity goes back to Judeo-Christian concepts of giving without thought of return, of being "gracious," concepts that are just the opposite of Greek and Roman notions of "giving and receiving," in which a gift sets off a chain of reciprocity and in general one only gives to achieve personal honor or gain and only to those one thinks can in some way reciprocate (at least with votes or vocal support, if not monetarily).[220]

In response to the murmuring and the problem, the Twelve called together a meeting of the whole community of disciples to settle the matter. Until this point, the summaries in Acts 2 and 4, and the narrative in Acts 5:1ff., have suggested that the apostles seem to have administered the material concerns of the community, at least in regard to property and money. Now they seem to have been faced with the additional prospect of administering the distribution of food, which may have been done in piecemeal fashion up to this point. They could not afford to neglect the ministry of the word in order to "wait on tables," which is what διαϰονια surely must mean here.[221]

Peter in *v. 3* thus exhorts the community to select seven men of good standing in the community, men full of wisdom and the Spirit, whom the apostles could appoint for the task. The procedure here seems quite similar to what we find in Acts 1:23 insofar as it is the community and not the apostles who propose the candidates. The number seven may be of some significance since Josephus tells us he appointed seven judges in each city in Galilee during his days as authority figure there (cf. *War* 2.571; *b. Meg.* 26a, and the reference to the Roman Septemviri in Tacitus, *Ann.* 3.64).

---

218. Johnson, *Acts*, p. 105, suggests that we translate παραθεωρεω "slighted" here.

219. Μαθητης occurs for the first time here in Acts, but it is frequent hereafter (cf. 6:7; 9:1; 10:19, 25; 11:26, 29; 13:52, etc.). This may reflect Luke's care about style, as he gradually makes the narrative less Semitic in language and character.

220. See Hands, *Charities and Social Aid*, pp. 64ff.

221. The term διαϰονια refers to an activity here, and nothing is said of an office of deacons or deaconesses, though this text was appealed to in later church history as a precedent.

These men must be given a good report by the community. Notice that here as in the discussion of overseers and deacons in 1 Timothy 3 the main issue is character, not special talents or abilities, and on their being full of the Spirit (cf. 2:4; 4:8, 31). The reference to σοφια (cf. 6:10) here refers to the ability to discern the right thing to do when choices must be made, and it may be that Luke is referring to Spirit-inspired wisdom (cf. 18:24-25).[222]

If the Seven are assigned the task of waiting on tables, then the Twelve according to v. 4 will be able to devote themselves completely to prayer and the serving (διαχονια) of the word. Both ministries are seen as forms of public religious service, or as they would be called in the Greek world, λειτουργοι (liturgies). Nothing in this entire text suggests that the division of labor, or the difficulties that led to this division of labor, reflects some sort of significant theological differences between Hebrews and Hellenists. As we shall see, neither does the speech of Stephen. There were some language and thus some cultural differences between the Hebrews and Hellenists, but nothing suggests the differences amounted to conservative versus liberal views on either theological or ethical and practical matters. The major proponents of a more universal theology or a greater openness to Gentiles in Acts (and elsewhere) turn out to be not Stephen or the Hellenists but a former Galilean fisherman named Simon Peter and a former Pharisaic Jew born in the Diaspora but raised and educated in conservative Judaism in Jerusalem named Saul/Paul.[223]

V. 5 indicates that the community as a whole was well pleased with the suggestion of the apostles. The list of seven in v. 5 includes only men with Greek names, which is surely no accident. This seems to suggest that the community as a whole, in order to avoid even the appearance of favoritism, named mostly if not exclusively Greek-speaking Jewish Christians to administer the food distribution. The first two mentioned, Stephen (said to be a man full of faith and the Holy Spirit) and Philip, Luke knows a good deal more about, but apparently he knows little or nothing about the rest — Prochorus, Nicanor, Timon, Parmenas, and Nicolaus, who is said to be a proselyte from Antioch. This last distinction suggests that all the rest were born Jews, Nicolaus being the only convert to Judaism.[224]

---

222. See chap. 1 of my *Jesus the Sage.*

223. For an attempt to argue for significant theological distinctions between the Hebrews and Hellenists on the basis of very little in Acts, cf. Meyer, *The Early Christians,* pp. 53ff.

224. Irenaus (*Adv. Haer.* 1.26.3) and Eusebius, *H.E.* 3.29.1-3, both suggest that the Gnostic sect of the Nicolaitans was founded by this Nicolaus, but Clement of Alexandria minimizes the possible connection (*Strom.* 2.220.118). This conclusion probably has no basis in history but is the result of wrongly associating the group called the Nicolaitans in Rev. 2:6, 15 with this Nicolaus. The Nicolaitans, however, are associated with Ephesus and Pergamum, which is far from Syrian Antioch.

The Seven came forward, and the Twelve prayed and then laid hands on them. This should probably be seen as an act of commissioning for the task and so a conveying of authority, not a formal rite of ordination, which came later in church history (cf. 13:1-3). There are echoes of the stories about the choice of Joshua as Moses' successor by laying on of hands (cf. Num. 27:15-23), which is quite appropriate since in Acts 7–8 we will see the first two of these figures taking up the mantle of leadership, *not by waiting on tables or administering food* (an internal matter for the community) but by preaching and teaching just as the Twelve have done heretofore. In other words, Luke is going to portray them as the bridge figures leading to the next stage of mission and witness, in this case outside of Jerusalem but still in the Holy Land.[225]

V. 7 is another of the summary sentences in Acts,[226] but this one does not seem to join two "panels" together, for the narrative continues on in 6:8ff., building on the list in 6:5. Luke tells us that the word of God[227] continued to grow.[228] This probably alludes to the Lukan telling of the parable of the sower (cf. Luke 8:4ff.), in which the seed is understood to be the word (v. 11).[229] This of course means that the number of disciples increased and included many priests who became "obedient to the faith." There were apparently literally thousands of priests in and around the Jerusalem area, many of them having to support themselves and having little in common with the leading priests. Thus, we need not think Luke is suggesting the conversion of the leading and more well-to-do priests in Jerusalem.[230]

G. The Trial, Testimony, and Termination of Stephen (6:8–8:3)

The introduction of Stephen in the list in 6:5 leads to a somewhat lengthy presentation of the events that led to the end of his life. The very length of Stephen's speech in Acts 7, the longest in a book full of speeches, probably indicates something of the importance Luke assigned to this episode in the

---

225. Once again we see Luke's artistry as he quietly introduces two major figures (Stephen and Philip) that will soon figure in a large way in the story just as he had earlier done with Barnabas, and would soon do with Saul/Paul.

226. See the excursus above, pp. 157ff.

227. This is the better reading here, especially in view of v. 2, rather than word of the Lord. See Metzger, *Textual Commentary*, p. 338.

228. Not "spread" as NRSV has it.

229. See Kodell, " 'The Word of God Grew.' " Possibly Exod. 1:7 LXX stands in the background here. Cf. Tannehill, *Narrative Unity of Luke-Acts*, 2:82.

230. See Jeremias, *Jerusalem*, p. 204.

history of earliest Christianity.[231] This story ends a series of three trials before the Sanhedrin chronicled in Acts 4–7, with escalating results (warning, flogging, and in this case death).[232] There can be little doubt that Luke sees the death of Stephen as engendering a crisis for the earliest Christians and a turning point.[233] For one thing, for the first time "the people" and not just the authorities become antagonistic toward the followers of Jesus. For another, the death of Stephen causes various of his fellow Christians to flee Jerusalem and persecution, which in turn leads to the evangelizing of other places.[234] This in turn causes the focus of the story to begin to shift away from Jerusalem after Acts 8:1. Luke is concerned to show why the church developed and moved in the east-to-west direction that it did.

V. 8 begins by informing us again of the personal characteristics and also the actions of Stephen — he was full of χαρις and power, and he performed great wonders and signs among the people.[235] This description tells us that he was involved not only in the internal life of the Christian community (the administering of food distribution), but also in its external life and witness. The two depictions of Stephen's roles in Acts 6 are not contradictory, but speak to tasks in two different spheres of action.[236] As Barrett suggests, these men probably originally began "with the charitable work of the Jerusalem church but developed their Christian action beyond this so as to become a group of leaders not necessarily in opposition to but at least distinct from the Twelve."[237]

One of the overarching impressions of the material in Acts 6:8–8:3 is that Luke is deliberately writing this story to indicate how Stephen's last days and end parallel those of his master, Jesus. Not only so, but Stephen is depicted

---

231. The conservative estimate by Haenchen (*Acts*, p. 104 n. 1) of 295 verses out of about 1,000 in Acts given over to speeches apparently only takes into account the traditional portions called and evaluated as speeches. If one takes into account all the discourse material, the count of Soards, *The Speeches in Acts*, p. 1, is nearer the mark — 365 verses out of about 1,000, or over one-third of the book.

232. See Polhill, *Acts*, p. 183. The issue of the sources used in Acts 6–7 is a very complicated one, but most scholars are convinced that at least in Acts 6 Luke is using source material, perhaps even a written source. Cf. Lüdemann, *Early Christianity*, pp. 79ff. We will say more about the speech, which is widely regarded as a Lukan composition, below.

233. See Pesch, *Die Apostelgeschichte (1–12)*, pp. 266-67.

234. In other words, it is Luke's testimony that at least a part of the church took up the cause of missions elsewhere not due to planned efforts engendered by the Jerusalem church or the apostles, but due to persecution.

235. The term χαρις here could simply mean charm (cf. Luke 4:22; Acts 4:33), but probably carries the religious overtone of "grace" since it is coupled with power. See Bruce, *The Acts of the Apostles*, p. 185.

236. Nevertheless, the differences between 6:1-6 and 6:8 suggest Luke was using a traditional list in the earlier passage, perhaps derived from the Jerusalem church.

237. Barrett, *Acts*, vol. 1, p. 319. On their possible connection with the founding of a mixed Jewish and Gentile church in Syrian Antioch see below, pp. 366ff.

as standing in an even longer line of holy figures including not only the later prophets but also especially Moses and even before him, Joseph. Like Joseph, Moses, and Jesus Stephen is full of grace and power and inspired words, and is depicted as someone of great character and stature — appropriate for the church's first martyr. The parallels between the passion of Jesus and of Stephen need to be enumerated:

1. Trial before high priest/Sanhedrin (Mark 14:53 and par./Acts 6:12; 7:1)
2. False witnesses (Mark 14:56-57; Matt. 26:60-61; *not in Luke*/Acts 6:13)
3. Testimony concerning the destruction of the temple (Mark 14:58; Matt. 26:61; *not in Luke*/Acts 6:14)
4. Temple "made with hands" (Mark 14:58; *not in Luke*/Acts 7:48)
5. Son of Man saying (Mark 14:62 and par./Acts 7:56)
6. Charge of blasphemy (Mark 14:64, Matt. 26:65; *not in Luke*/Acts 6:11)
7. High priest's question (Mark 14:61; Matt. 26:63; *not in Luke* [cf. 22:67, "they"]/Acts 7:1)
8. Committal of spirit (*only in Luke 23:46*/Acts 7:59)
9. Cry out with a loud voice (Mark 15:34 = Matt. 27:46; Mark 15:37 and par./Acts 7:60)
10. Intercession for enemies forgiveness (*only in Luke 23:34*/Acts 7:60)[238]

Two striking things need to be noted about this list of parallels. Two of the ten items are found only in Luke and Acts and nowhere else (nos. 8 and 10). Five of the ten items are found in Acts and in the other Synoptic accounts of Jesus' death, but *not* in Luke's Gospel. Here is compelling evidence that Luke had Acts in mind while writing his Gospel, and edited certain items out of his Markan source about Jesus' Passion, but wrote up the Stephen story using language reminiscent of the Markan Passion account! The end result in any case is to highlight the close parallels between Stephen's end and that of Jesus.

V. 9 is grammatically difficult. Does it refer to one, two, or even five synagogues? The least problematic approach seems to be to recognize that only one synagogue is in mind, the synagogue of the Freedmen, and that those who participated in it were from a variety of Diaspora locations — Cyrenians and Alexandrians from Africa, and those from Cilicia and Asia.[239] Freedmen were those who had been set free from slavery by their masters, though the term could also refer to sons of such persons (see Suetonius, *Claudius* 24.1).[240]

238. Here I am simply following the excellent analysis of Hill, *Hellenists and Hebrews,* p. 59; cf. also Richard, *Acts 6.1–8.4,* p. 281.
239. See the discussion in Barrett, *Acts,* vol. 1, pp. 323-25.
240. On this whole process cf. Duff, *Freedmen.* There is no solid textual basis for emending Λιβερτινων to "Libyans." See Metzger, *Textual Commentary,* pp. 339-40.

The synagogue assembly room at Masada.

It has been suggested that this synagogue may in fact be the one mentioned in the famous Theodotus synagogue inscription found in Jerusalem (cf. *CIJ* 2, no. 1404). The inscription tells us that the synagogue was founded by one Theodotus, son of Vettenus, and refers to its members as "those who came from abroad." The name Vettenus suggests the *gens Vettena,* "and the suggestion is ready to hand that the father, or possibly an earlier ancestor, of Theodotus had been a slave of and received his freedom from one of the Vetteni."[241] I find the above suggestion plausible, but not provable beyond the shadow of a doubt. If it is correct, it may suggest that this synagogue of the Freedmen was the place of worship for one Saul of Tarsus (in Cilicia), which helps explain his sudden mention in 7:58ff. As we shall see, Saul is proof, if any were needed, that Diaspora Jews, *as a group,* should never be categorized as necessarily more liberal or broad in their views of things like the temple and Torah. In view of recent scholarly debates something needs to be said at this juncture about the existence of synagogue buildings prior to A.D. 70.

---

241. Barrett, *Acts,* vol. 1, p. 324. It may be this same synagogue that is referred to in rabbinic literature in some cases as the synagogue of the Alexandrians (*t. Meg.* 3:6 [224]; *y. Meg.* 3:1, 73d.35) and in another as that of the Tarsians (from Cilicia — cf. *y. Meg.* 26a).

A Closer Look — Synagogues?

There is an enormous amount of debate among scholars as to when the institution of synagogues as specifically religious buildings began, and this debate is especially heated in regard to the situation in the Holy Land.[242] Was it merely in homes, or was it in homes or multipurpose buildings used as synagogues on occasion, or was it in buildings which had a specifically religious function? It is easy enough to prove that in rabbinic literature there are references to second-century-A.D. Jewish teachers speaking of places specifically called synagogues. For example, Abba Benjamin remarked: "One's prayer is heard only in the synagogue" (*b. Ber.* 6a), and R. Judah I and R. Yohanan are mentioned as having studied in front of the large synagogue in Sepphoris (*y. Ber.* 5.1.9a). The problem with this evidence is of course that it appears in sources that were not compiled until much later than the second century A.D.; thus it can be argued that the terminology used in these sayings is anachronistic, perhaps deliberately so. The lintel from the Diaspora synagogue in Corinth, which reads "synagogue of the Hebrews" and seems securely dated to at least as early as the second century A.D., seems better evidence, but this still doesn't give us clear first-century evidence.[243]

We may then work our way back to the evidence in Josephus, who had spent considerable time in Galilee and elsewhere in the Mediterranean crescent and was in a position to know whether or not there were synagogue buildings in these places. In *War* 2.285-91 Josephus refers to a συναγωγην adjoined to a plot of ground owned by a Greek person in Caesarea Maritima. This must be taken as a reference to a place, not an assembly of people. The same may be said about the reference in *War* 7.43-44 which speaks of a synagogue in Syrian Antioch. Since Josephus's *War* in even its Greek form was probably available by A.D. 80, and the Aramaic version came forth earlier than this, here is first-century evidence that speaks of a place called a συναγωγη. Philo as well at least once can use συναγωγη for a synagogue building (*Quod omnis* 81). Even earlier, and perhaps more impressive, is the Jewish inscription from the African city of Berenice dated A.D. 56 which speaks of the repair of the synagogue, clearly not a reference to the repairing of a group or assembly of people (*SEG* 17, no. 16)![244]

The chief archaeological evidence for first-century synagogues in the Holy Land come from Masada, the Herodium, and Gamala.[245] Especially the last of these has

---

242. See Kee, "Transformation of the Synagogue"; Oster, "Supposed Anachronism"; and Kee, "The Changing Meaning of Synagogue." On the Diaspora synagogue see now White, "The Delos Synagogue Revisited." My discussion here appears in another form in my *JesusQuest*, chap. 1.

243. See my *Conflict and Community in Corinth*, ad loc.

244. It should be noted that in the majority of the inscriptional evidence from the Diaspora, including the Bosphoran material surveyed by I. Levinskaya, when there is use of Greek, the usual term is not "synagogue" but προσευχη. See Levinskaya's AIIFCS volume, *Acts in Its Diaspora Setting*.

245. The following argument is not meant to deny that many, if not most, of the pre-70 synagogues in the Holy Land may have been slightly modified rooms in public

features suggestive of a building specifically constructed for religious purposes, including: (1) a ritual bath adjacent to it; (2) the presence of second temple Jewish iconography on a lintel found with the synagogue (a rosette); (3) the size and design of the building, the main hall of which is twenty-by-sixteen meters, not the dimensions of a household room. One may also point to the thoroughgoing Jewishness of the city throughout its brief history.[246] The conclusion of L. I. Levine is warranted that in Gamala we have a first-century synagogue specifically set up for religious purposes, whatever else it may also have been used for.[247]

More importantly in terms of our discussions of Acts, the arguments by Kee either that the famous Theodotus synagogue inscription in Jerusalem dates to much later than the first century[248] or that Luke's use of the term *synagogue* for a place where Jews met weekly for religious services is anachronistic are not convincing, especially in light of the recent careful arguments of R. Riesner.[249] The paleographic evidence, as well as the archaeological evidence (showing no building activity in the whole area where the inscription was found during the Byzantine period), argues for a pre–second century date for this inscription and the building to which it refers.[250] Especially telling was the finding of five Herodian period oil lamps and *nothing later than the Herodian period* in the areas adjacent to where the inscription was found.[251] There is in fact no evidence this particular area was inhabited at all after A.D. 70, at least for a century or more. Finally, the inscription was found with stones deposited in an orderly fashion, as if stored, and some of these stones were decorated with rosettes and geometrical designs (cf. above), which are typical of second temple design.

Luke-Acts, like other portions of the NT, provides good first-century evidence for the existence of synagogues as places and not just as gatherings of people, in a variety of locations in the Mediterranean crescent, and also for the use of the term

---

buildings or private homes, which would explain why so few remains of synagogues from this earlier period have been found. For this sort of argument, cf. White, *Building God's House*, pp. 60-101. My point, and that of Riesner, is that this sort of conclusion does not apply to *all* the germane evidence. The argument of White, however, is suggestive. Perhaps the earliest Jewish Christian house church was simply a continuation of the already existing practice of Jews meeting in homes in certain places, in lieu of purpose-built buildings.

246. On all this see Oster, "Supposed Anachronism," p. 195.

247. Levine, "The Second Temple Synagogue."

248. This inscription refers to a leader and builder of a synagogue and was found in Jerusalem in the bottom of a cistern. It is generally dated to the first century because of the sort of script it has, but see Kee, "Early Christianity in the Galilee," pp. 4-6.

249. Riesner, "Synagogues in Jerusalem."

250. One must bear in mind that after the destruction of the temple and its environs in A.D. 70 no Jewish buildings of any consequence seem to have been built for a considerable period of time, and certainly no religious buildings built by immigrant Diaspora Jews, most of whom seem to have fled before the destruction. This means that one must either date the Theodotus inscription pre-70, or much later, perhaps not before the end of the second century A.D.

251. See Riesner, "Synagogues in Jerusalem," p. 196.

συναγωγη/συναγωγης of these places.[252] That the term προσευχη was perhaps more frequently used in the early first century for such a building or meeting need not be disputed. All that this latter sort of evidence is likely to prove is that Luke, writing in the 70s or 80s, used the term that had become or was becoming more dominant toward the end of the first century.[253]

V. 9b indicates that these Diaspora Jews stood up and debated with Stephen about whatever it was he was teaching. We are not told at this juncture what this teaching involved. What we are told in *v. 10* is that his debating partners couldn't withstand the "wisdom and Spirit" with which he spoke. This in all likelihood means the wisdom which the Spirit provided and inspired in him. We are meant to hear an echo of Jesus' promise found in Luke 21:15 — "for I will give you a mouth and wisdom that none of your opponents will be able to withstand or contradict." Stephen's life not merely parallels Jesus', but we see in him the fulfillment of what Jesus promised his disciples he would equip them with for their witness.

The portrayal of some of the members of the synagogue of the Freedmen in *vv. 11-14* is far from flattering. First it is said that they suborned[254] some men to say "We have heard him speak blasphemous things against Moses and God." Secondly it is said that this same group of synagogue participants stirred up the Jewish people as well as the elders and scribes and, suddenly confronting Stephen, seized him and carted him off to appear before the Council or Sanhedrin. Finally, this same group is said to set up *false witnesses* (μαρτυρας ψευδεις) who say to the Council essentially the same thing as was said before, "This man never stops saying things against this holy place and the law," to which is added the new charge: "*because* (γαρ) we have heard him say that this Jesus of Nazareth will destroy this place and change the customs that Moses handed on to us."

This is quite a litany, and at every step along the way Luke makes

---

252. More debatable, however, is when the term συναγωγη became almost a technical term for a religious meeting place, and here it is right to point out that in Philo and elsewhere in the first century the term can be used to refer to something other than a Jewish place of worship. It can, for instance, refer to the people who have assembled for that purpose. See the evidence in Kee, "The Changing Meaning of Synagogue," pp. 281-82. On Galilean synagogues, including the earliest ones which go back to the first century A.D., see Foerster, "The Ancient Synagogues of Galilee."

253. Some of the earliest evidence of synagogues as buildings (called προσευχην) comes from Egypt. See *New Docs,* 4, no. 94, p. 121, citing an example from the time of Ptolemy III Eugeretes which can be dated about 246-221 B.C.

254. The verb υπεβαλον is a strong one and carries the idea of putting up something or someone in an underhanded or fraudulent manner. See Appian's use of it in *Bell. Civ.* 1.74.

abundantly clear that the witnesses and the testimony are false and those synagogue members who are putting people up to saying these sorts of things are guilty of fraudulent and underhanded activities. Luke has in essence here used repetition as a rhetorical device, and probably J. Kilgallen is correct in saying that the accusations in vv. 13-14 are meant to be seen as successive intensifications and clarifications of the charges made in v. 11.[255] In other words, there are essentially two charges: (1) that Stephen is saying blasphemous things against the Law of Moses involving something to do with changing the customs that Moses passed on, and (2) that he is speaking against the temple, in particular that Jesus will destroy it.

Nothing is said here about the replacement of the temple, and it will be seen that the speech of Stephen in the following chapter does not seem to address or answer these charges, or if it does it only speaks briefly and tangentially to the second charge. There is a good reason for this. These are in essence false charges, and Stephen intends to present his own true witness, not answer someone else's trumped-up charges. We have here a battle of witnesses — the false ones versus the true one, whose integrity and witness are maintained and demonstrated even at the price of his life. As Hill puts it, his is not a plea of innocence but a plea for *veritas*.[256]

Now it is quite amazing in the face of the whole way that Luke presents the material in 6:11-14 that many scholars have concluded that though Luke tells us that the witnesses were false and the whole process rigged, an example of vigilante justice at its worst, nonetheless we should *believe these charges*. We are asked to believe that Stephen really was a *radical* critic of the Law and of the temple, even though his speech in Acts 7 doesn't really support such a notion. One scholar even says that the charges in 6:11-14 were indeed false, "but not in the sense of being contrary to fact"!![257]

If this were not enough, we are also asked to believe that Stephen was a *representative* radical critic, that his theology characterized that of the "Hellenists," even though nothing in Acts 6–7 even remotely suggests such an idea.[258] On the basis of this amazing analysis a whole theory about early Christianity has been created, a theory that is still influential in many quarters today. It goes back to F. C. Baur and pits the conservative Aramaic-speaking native Jewish Christians versus the more liberal Greek-speaking Diaspora Jewish Christians also originally based in Jerusalem. It must be said that if the

---

255. See J. Kilgallen, *The Stephen Speech*, pp. 31-32.

256. Hill, *Hellenists and Hebrews*, p. 53, though Hill has doubts about this conclusion.

257. Scharlemann, *Stephen*, p. 102.

258. It should be noted that nothing in Acts 11:19-20 is said about Jewish Christians speaking *as* "Hellenists." They are, however, in this text said to speak *to* Hellenists. See the excursus above, pp. 240ff. and below pp. 366ff.

theory of a radical Hellenistic Christian theology that goes ultimately back to Stephen is not a total myth, it is surely a significant distortion by overmagnification of what little evidence there is that Stephen was Law and temple critical, as we shall shortly see.[259]

Luke concludes the narrative portion of the material in *v. 15* by making very clear who reflects the character of the divine in this whole scene. It is Stephen, whom we are told the Council stared at intently and saw that his face was like that of an angel. This unusual expression is nonetheless not unprecedented as the apocryphal version (cf. LXX) of Esth. 15:13 shows, where the king's face is said to be like that of an angel (cf. Dan. 3:92 LXX).[260] The point of this expression is to convey the idea of a person reflecting some of God's glory and character as a result of being close to God and in God's very presence. One is of course reminded of Moses and the account in Exod. 34:29ff., and the point here is of divine endorsement, inspiration, and ultimately vindication[261] of Stephen of these scurrilous charges.[262] Stephen has been endowed or imbued with the divine presence, and he is now prepared to speak the authoritative word to God's people, whether they are spiritually prepared to receive it or not.

The modern discussion of Acts *7:1–8:1a* has to a large extent been affected by the work of Dibelius in which he argued that most of this speech is irrelevant, since it is assumed it should be seen as a response to the charges against Stephen.[263] A second major assumption about this longest of all speeches in Acts is based on the where-there's-smoke-there's-fire theory (i.e., if the witnesses against Stephen claim he said something against Law and temple, he must have done so). In the discussion that follows, it will be seen that I think both of these assumptions (that much of the speech is irrelevant and that Stephen is Law and temple critical) are basically wrong. This speech is not an apologetic one in which Stephen is defending himself against false charges,[264] nor is it in essence either Law or temple critical. Rather, it is critical of those Jews who down through the ages have rejected God's prophets and messengers and their messages, and critical of some of these Jews' assumptions, including assumptions about God dwelling in the temple.

---

259. It is interesting to see how this view of Stephen being temple critical is perpetuated even by so conservative a critic as F. F. Bruce, and even though he recognizes that Luke himself is not temple critical. See his "Stephen's Apologia."

260. One may also compare the account in the second-century *Acts of Paul and Thecla* 3, where we find a similar description of Paul.

261. This sort of description appears to have become standard for Christians about to become martyrs in later Christian writings. See *Martyrdom of Polycarp* 9:1ff.

262. See Marshall, *Acts*, p. 131.

263. See his *Studies in the Acts*, pp. 167-69.

264. Pace Bruce, *The Speeches in Acts*, pp. 21ff.

The author of this oratory is going on the offensive, not being defensive. Furthermore, this speech fits nicely into its narrative context, drawing on what has gone before and bringing to a climax the witness in Jerusalem to Jews.[265] It also provides the catalyst for what is to come, for the reaction to this speech leads to the scattering of witnesses into Judea and Samaria.

I am convinced that a major reason why this speech has been misunderstood and not been seen as a coherent whole is because of the failure to notice the rhetorical form of this forensic piece of oratory, and the failure to recognize how the different parts of a speech function rhetorically. While Kennedy and Soards are quite right in seeing this speech as an example of judicial or forensic rhetoric, and Kennedy rightly adds that we have (counter)accusation here, neither provides as full and satisfactory a rhetorical analysis as is needed.[266]

The first thing that needs to be noticed is that the audience for this speech is clearly portrayed as hostile, not neutral, and as such the orator, if he is going to be heard, must follow the indirect route of *insinuatio*. This speech is a long one because such a procedure was followed. In such a speech a long *narratio* is often necessary, and it is critical that it be not merely neutral but positive in content, establishing common ground with the audience in the attempt to persuade. Stephen will demonstrate that he shares a common history with his auditors, and that they both are part of a tragic history of partial acceptance and partial rejection of God's message and the messengers sent to God's people. In the end Stephen will himself provide, by the giving of his life, the most recent proof that his analysis of God's people and their uncircumcised hearts is correct.

The most persuasive analysis of the crucial Stephen speech is offered by J. Dupont, who divides the speech up according to its rhetorical parts as follows: (1) *exordium* (v. 2a — very brief); (2) *narratio* (vv. 2b-34); (3) transition/*propositio* (v. 35);[267] (4) *argumentatio* (vv. 36-50); (5) *peroratio* (vv. 51-

---

265. See the very helpful discussion in Tannehill, *Narrative Unity of Luke-Acts*, 2:84-101.

266. See Kennedy, *New Testament Interpretation*, pp. 121-22; Soards, *The Speeches in Acts*, pp. 57-70. Bruce, "Stephen's Apologia," p. 39, recognizes the rhetorical nature of the speech and its forensic context, but oddly pronounces it not a forensic speech, even though he calls it an apologia. But speeches that attack, as well as speeches that defend, are forensic in character.

267. V. 35 can be seen as a *propositio* even though it is indirect, for here is the first statement of the real theme or point the speech is driving at — that God has continually sent messengers, but they have been continually rejected by many of God's people, who instead of hearing and heeding them ask hostile questions such as, "Who made you a ruler and a judge?" The theme, then, is "what humans have rejected, God had selected," and as such echoes the speech of Peter in 4:5ff. given to the selfsame audience (cf. especially vv. 10, 11).

53).[268] As is true of all proper rhetorical pieces, the first part of the speech must be more positive to establish *ethos* or rapport with the audience. The *narratio* must prepare for but not really anticipate the actual arguments.[269] This is followed by the *logos* section of the speech where the major arguments are laid out. The narration only prepares for the arguments, it does not really offer them in advance. Finally, the peroration offers the emotional appeal, the *pathos*. The mystery of why the early part of the speech is neutral or positive and the latter part is more polemical is solved when the speech is broken down into its normal rhetorical parts. One must ask what function each part of the speech is supposed to have in order to understand why it takes the form it does.

In view of the extensive use of the LXX in the speech (even if we just mention the quotes or allusions that are formally introduced as Scripture, we have ten of these),[270] it seems clear that this speech originated in Greek. It is not impossible that it goes back to Stephen, for indeed he seems to have been a Jew whose only real spoken language was Greek, and whose Bible was the LXX. Nevertheless, what we have here is doubtless Luke's précis of the speech (derived perhaps from Saul/Paul), and one suspects that he is the one who has structured and edited it to fit a rhetorical outline.[271] It suits well his perspectives on salvation history.

Two more preliminary issues need to be addressed before turning to the detailed exegesis of the speech itself: (1) is it Law critical, and (2) is it temple critical? In regard to the first issue there is frankly very little evidence to suggest what Stephen's view of the Law is, and what little evidence there is suggests it was positive. For example, in 7:38 Stephen calls the Law "living oracles" divine in character, and clearly enough he sees Moses as a positive paradigm of a righteous prophetic figure. The history of Israel's rejection of God's word including disobedience to the Law is brought up at the end of the speech as causing guilt, which suggests a positive view of the Law as well. Finally, Stephen cites portions of the Pentateuch positively and alludes to others as he builds his case that much of Israel has a long history of rejecting God's messengers and message. In fact Stephen builds his case *mainly* by citing Scriptures from the Pentateuch some ten times (especially Genesis and Exodus, cf. below).[272] Notice, too, that Stephen's

---

268. Dupont, "La structure oratoire du discours d'Etienne (Actes 7)." On the procedure of *insinuatio* used in the *narratio*, see p. 157 n. 10.

269. See ibid., p. 157.

270. See Soards, *The Speeches in Acts*, p. 60 n. 139.

271. I would not rule out that Stephen was rhetorically adept, especially since there is evidence of the teaching of Greek rhetoric in Jerusalem during this era. Cf. my *Conflict and Community in Corinth*, pp. 2ff.

272. See Tannehill, *Narrative Unity of Luke-Acts*, 2:85-86.

final and most telling indictment of his audience is that they do not keep the Law (v. 53).

It can even be argued that Stephen is following a Deuteronomistic view of Israel's history, following this pattern: (1) repeatedly disobedient Israelites (2) are admonished by God's prophets, (3) whose words are rejected, (4) bringing judgment on the disobedient Israelites. This pattern is seen in 2 Kings 17:7-20; Neh. 9:26 (the prophets were killed); and 2 Chron. 36:14-16.[273]

The second major debated issue is whether Stephen's speech can be called temple critical or not. If it is, it would seem to go against the general portrayal of the temple elsewhere in Luke-Acts. For example, in Luke 1–2 the temple is portrayed in a positive light as the proper place for teaching, cleansing rituals, and sacrifice. Though Jesus is said to predict the dismantling of the Herodian temple (Luke 21:6), this does not constitute criticism of the temple cultus per se, as a glance at the Qumran literature will show.[274] This is all the more the case since Jesus is described shortly after this passage as one who taught day after day in the temple (Luke 22:53). Worshiping in the temple is seen as a positive trait that was characteristic of the early church in the Lukan summary in Acts 2:46, and the early teaching and healing of the apostles is seen as appropriately done there as well (cf. Acts 3–4). In short, if Stephen's speech is a Lukan-edited summary of a source, and even more if it is a Lukan creation, there is nothing in the earlier portions of Luke-Acts to prepare Theophilus for this speech to be radically temple critical.

The suggestion that the speech is temple critical is largely based on an assumed contrast between things made with human hands and things made by God, and secondarily on a perceived contrast between the tent of witness and the temple as a "house" built by Solomon for God.[275] In other words, it is based on material that does not begin to appear in the speech before v. 40, even though the more polemical portion of the speech begins in v. 35 and is clearly directed against the rejection of their leaders by God's people. It is often overlooked that the perceived contrast between things made with human

---

273. See Steck, *Israel und das gewaltsame Geschick der Propheten*, pp. 66-68, 74-77.

274. Notice that Luke *omits* the word about the Abomination of Desolation being set up in the temple found in Mark (cf. Mark 13:14 to Luke 21:20) and substitutes a word about the desolation of the city in general. Luke also omits the story about the withering of the fig tree which is related to the Herodian temple and its downfall in Mark and Matthew.

275. The contrast between what is said in Luke 13:32 and Luke 19:46 about the "house" is instructive. In the latter text the "house" (i.e., temple) is clearly said to be God's, but in 13:32 it is said to be "your house." This reference to "your house" is not due to the fact that it was built by human hands, but because God had abandoned the place, for Jerusalem had rejected Jesus. In short, Luke 13:32 is not a criticism of the idea that God's presence could be found in the temple (when God chose to manifest the divine presence there). It is a criticism of God's people and their rejection of their Messiah, which in turn causes them to be abandoned by the presence of God in the city.

hands and things made by God does not parallel the supposed contrast between tent and house, not least because the tent of witness was also made with human hands.[276] Furthermore, the terms σκηνη (tent) and οικος (house) are not used consistently in the speech to set up a good/bad contrast. For example, in 7:43 there is a reference to the bad "tent" of Moloch, and in vv. 46-47 there is at the least a nonpolemical reference to God's dwelling place or house.

It is highly doubtful that the δε in v. 47 should be seen as adversative, setting up a contrast between the dwelling place of God and the "house." The contrast comes rather at v. 48 with the αλλα ("yet").[277] This means that the issue is not "tent" versus "house" but rather true and false thinking about God's presence. As D. De Silva has persuasively shown, what the Stephen speech is arguing for is that God transcends human structures, not that God's presence can't be found in temples.[278] God does not *dwell* in, by which is meant God is not confined by or to, structures made with human hands.[279] This point comports nicely with Luke's theology of a universal salvation that can be conveyed anytime and anywhere by the presence of God in the person of the Holy Spirit. We have already seen the Holy Spirit at work in the temple precincts in Acts 2–6, and Luke is not suggesting anything different by passing along the Stephen speech. Tannehill's final conclusions on this matter bear repeating:

> The promise in 7.7 anticipates a specific place of worship within the land, and that place will be the temple. This observation implies that Stephen's statement in 7.47-50 is neither a rejection of the temple nor a criticism of Solomon for building it. The "place" of worship is an important part of the promise to Abraham. The fulfillment of this promise through building the temple was appropriate. Nevertheless, there is a distinct note of warning in 7.48-50. . . . Stephen warns against any implied restriction of God to the temple. With the assistance of Isa. 66.1-2 he proclaims the transcendence of God. God is not dependent on works of human hands, nor do temples of human construction define God's location or "place of rest." God is the maker of all things; humans do not make things for God, as if God were in need of anything. This view will later be argued before a pagan audience by a reliable spokesman for the implied author, suggesting that it is a funda-

276. See Hill, *Hellenists and Hebrews*, p. 79.
277. Here I am following ibid., pp. 71ff.
278. De Silva, "Meaning and Function of Acts 7.46-50." As Hill, *Hellenists and Hebrews*, p. 69 n. 144, stresses, the fact that Luke believes the temple was destroyed because of Jewish (particularly Jerusalem's) rejection of Jesus, that is, because of unbelief, does not constitute temple criticism but rather is a criticism of unbelief.
279. There may be something to the suggestion that calling the temple an οικος has overtones of seeing it as a place where God's presence is confined or dwells on earth. Cf. Kilgallen, "Function of Stephen's Speech (Acts 7.3-53)," pp. 177ff.

mental theological axiom (17.24-25). This declaration of God's independence of the Jerusalem temple is also a declaration of God's availability to
all with or without the temple.[280]

The speech of Stephen is in various ways like similar speeches that are
recorded in ancient historiographical works and said to have been given in
crises. In particular, as L. Johnson has pointed out, the reciting of ancestral
traditions is quite frequent in these sorts of speeches.[281] For example, already
in Herodotus both sides in a fierce battle give defense speeches justifying
their claims by reciting various ancestral traditions (see *Persian Wars* 9.26-
27). Thucydides also records even lengthy speeches given in crisis that include
considerable recounting of historical matters and precedents (*Pelop. War* 1,
3, 68-70; 2, 6, 35-47). Even closer in kinship in some respects is the speech
presented by Josephus in *War* 5.376-419 where he relates various precedents
from the Bible for the current dilemma the residents of Jerusalem find
themselves in, being surrounded by the Roman army. In other words, this
lengthy speech fits nicely within the usual limits and character for these sorts
of crucial speeches in historiographical works. Such speeches are usually
depicted as changing the course of events, and Stephen's is no different. It is
the straw that breaks the camel's back, causing escalated persecution of the
Jerusalem church and the scattering of many of its members, which in turn
causes the narrative of salvation history to turn its focus to a variety of other
places than Jerusalem.

Chapter 7 begins with the high priest (presumably Caiaphas) asking
Stephen directly if the charges laid against him by the (false) witnesses are
true. It is clear that we are dealing with a trial scene complete with formal
witnesses and testimony. Equally clearly from what follows in 7:2-53, Stephen
does not answer the charges, or at least does not do so directly.

The speech of Stephen is framed with glory, beginning with a reference
to the glory of God appearing to Abraham *(v. 2)* and concluding with a
glorious apocalyptic vision of the Son of Man in heaven *(v. 56),* which places
Stephen in the line of these other devout Jews who had dynamic encounters
with God and whom God chose as leaders along the way, including Abraham,
Joseph, Moses, the prophets, Jesus, Peter, and now Stephen. This sense of
continuity, namely, that the early Jewish Christians are the logical heirs and
successors of the stream of earlier faithful and righteous Jews, is an important
part of what this speech asserts.

The initial address in *v. 2,* "men, brothers and fathers," indicates the
proper rhetorical approach of trying to establish rapport and contact with

---

280. Tannehill, *Narrative Unity of Luke-Acts,* 2:93.
281. See Johnson, *Acts,* p. 120.

one's audience (cf. above). Stephen will not distinguish himself from his audience until after the speech becomes overtly polemical.

In general it must be noted that this speech, in regard to form and style, is not noticeably Lukan in character, with the possible exception of vv. 37 (a quote of Deut. 18:15, cf. Acts 3:22) and 52.[282] Most scholars therefore rightly recognize Luke drawing on some sort of source here. The theory that it was a Samaritan source because Stephen at points cites the OT in a way like the Samaritan Pentateuch has not convinced most scholars, not least because the content of the speech does not contain any real elements of what could be called distinctive Samaritan belief.[283] The sermon is also not specifically Christian, at least before vv. 52ff., but this need not suggest a combination of sources. To judge from the speech in Acts 17:16ff., which has certain affinities with Stephen's speech, it was simply good early Christian rhetorical technique to leave the possibly most objectionable part of one's speech until the end (namely, the mention of Jesus or the resurrection or other distinctive beliefs), hoping that the speaker's ethos would be established by then.

It has also been argued that this speech represents Hellenistic (and Diaspora) Jewish thought, but the speech's affinities with the earlier critical speeches of Peter in Acts 3–4 make this suggestion doubtful. Frankly, there does not seem to be anything in this speech that Peter could not have said, including the criticism of some Jews' attitudes about the temple as a place where God *dwelled* (see below). In short, it is doubtful that we should see this speech as a sample of some sort of Hellenist diatribe that distinguished the Hellenists from the Hebrews among the early Christians.[284] My tentative suggestion is that this speech was one heard by Saul of Tarsus, whether in an earlier form in the synagogue of the Freedmen and Cilicians, or in the Council, and deemed by Saul/Paul to have caused a critical turning point in the relationships between Christian and non-Christian Jews in Jerusalem. It was in some fashion related to Luke by Saul/Paul because of its critical nature when Luke was inquiring about the early history of the Jerusalem Christian community.

The use of the OT in this speech is basically by way of allusion and the occasional quote of the LXX, and in many instances it is not clear whether Stephen is following some sort of unknown version of the OT or simply paraphrasing and adding things from early Jewish tradition along the way, probably the latter, as the reference to angels mediating the Law suggests (cf. vv. 38, 53 to Gal. 3:19; Heb. 2:2; *Jub.* 1:29; *T. Dan.* 6:2; Josephus, *Ant.* 15.136 and the LXX of Deut. 33:2).[285]

282. See Barrett, *Acts*, vol. 1, p. 338.
283. Cf. Dupont, *The Sources of Acts*, pp. 55ff.
284. See pp. 240ff. above.
285. See the discussion in Evans and Sanders, *Luke and Scripture*, pp. 194-99.

Stephen starts by suggesting that God appeared in glory to Abraham "our ancestor" when he was in Mesopotamia before he lived in Haran. While the LXX of Gen. 12:7 does refer to God appearing to Abraham, neither the biblical account nor early Jewish tradition refers to a theophany, but only to an oracle Abraham received (cf. Philo, *On Abraham* 62). Like most early Jews, Stephen sees the story of Abraham as the proper beginning of the story of God's people, and for Luke Abraham is important as father of the Jews (cf. Luke 3:8; 16:24). According to Gen. 12:1 the call comes to Abraham *in Haran*, but it is clear from Gen. 15:7 and Neh. 9:7 that God called Abraham out of Ur, so we should probably assume there was an earlier call in Ur as well (so Philo, *On Abr.* 66-67). What is more critical for our purposes is to notice that the speech begins, and continues, with references to God appearing and speaking to his chosen ones *outside the context of the temple in Jerusalem*. In short, much of this lengthy speech prepares us for the argument that God transcends the temple.

V. 3 records the command to leave "your country" and go to a land that God will show Abraham in due course. This verse is basically a citation from the LXX version of Gen. 12:1 (cf. Heb. 11:8; *Jub.* 12:22-23). *V. 4* indicates that Abraham was obedient to the command, leaving the "country of the Chaldeans" and going as far as Haran, but not going farther until his father Terah died (cf. Gen. 11:33).[286] God then had Abraham move to "this country in which you are now living." Thus *v. 5* says God showed Abraham the Promised Land but did not give him even a foot's length of it as a personal inheritance at the time (cf. Gen. 15:7). Nevertheless it was promised to him and to his progeny, even though he had none at the time.

Vv. 6-7 serve as a foreshadowing of the discussion of Moses and the exodus, speaking about the Israelites becoming resident aliens in a foreign land where they would be enslaved and mistreated for four hundred years (cf. Gen. 15:13). The first part of *v. 7* cites Genesis 15, but the second half comes from Exod. 3:12. What is interesting is that the Exodus text actually refers to worship on "this mountain" (i.e., Sinai) after the exodus, while Stephen uses the language of this verse to speak of worship in Canaan ("this place").

V. 8 refers to the covenant of circumcision (cf. Gen. 17:10) that God made with Abraham, by which is meant the covenant of which circumcision is the sign, or ratification symbol. Circumcision would hereafter be seen as the sign that a person was one of God's chosen, and so Stephen's accusation in v. 51 that his audience is uncircumcised in heart is tantamount to saying

286. On the problem of calculating when Terah died, whether before or after Abraham left Haran, and at what age and the various discrepancies between various versions of the account (the Samaritan Pentateuch and Philo agree that Terah died at 145 and then Abraham left), see Marshall, *Acts*, p. 135.

that they are spiritually outside God's people. *V. 8b* speaks of Abraham becoming the father of Isaac, whom he circumcised on the eighth day, who in turn became the father of Jacob, and he in turn of the twelve patriarchs. The term πατριαρχας used of Jacob's sons doesn't occur anywhere in earlier extant Greek literature and so the occurrence here may be the earliest example.[287] In some ways what Stephen does not say about Abraham is as significant as what he does say. There is nothing said about Abraham's faith, or his faith being reckoned in the stead of righteousness. "We may safely assume that the divine word about the history of Abraham's posterity has been placed intentionally in the foreground."[288] The point is to focus on God's promise of land and progeny, a promise which God fulfilled.

Stephen skips over most of the story of Isaac and Jacob and focuses in *v. 9* on the jealousy of Joseph's brothers. This Joseph section in vv. 9-16 marks the second major topic and section of the speech.[289] Despite the jealousy of the brothers and Joseph's being sold into slavery in Egypt (cf. Gen. 37:28; 45:4), God was with Joseph, regularly rescuing him from his afflictions. He is a clear example that opposition to something or someone that is favored by God will not succeed; indeed, it may backfire. Though Stephen does not make the overtones of the discussion clear, a Christian listener to Luke's narrative would likely see in Joseph's life a foreshadowing of Jesus' experience, who was likewise opposed and even sold by one of a different twelve, but was vindicated by God.[290]

For our purposes what is crucial at this point is that Stephen has introduced the theme of opposition within the people of God to one favored and chosen by God as a leader, a theme he will continue to develop further as the speech goes on, so that in the end Stephen's own audience, or at least much of it, will be portrayed as the latest in a long line of stiff-necked and spiritually insensitive persons among the chosen people. Notice, too, how Stephen has already been portrayed as manifesting the same positive traits as the main positive characters in this speech — Abraham, Joseph, Moses, and of course Jesus (cf. Acts 6:5, 8).

According to *v. 10* Joseph even won favor and showed wisdom (presumably in the interpretation of dreams) in the Egyptian court (cf. the same traits in the young Moses and Jesus — Acts 7:22; Luke 2:52). So great was the estimate of Joseph by Pharaoh that he was appointed governor over the land and all Pharaoh's household, an amazing reversal for one who started in Egypt as a slave. *V. 11* refers to the great famine in Egypt and Canaan. The land of

---

287. See Cadbury and Lake, *The Beginnings of Christianity,* 4:72.
288. Dahl, "The Story of Abraham," p. 143.
289. See Marshall, *Acts,* p. 137.
290. See Johnson, *Acts,* p. 121.

Egypt was the breadbasket for much of the region; thus when famine hit Egypt it rapidly affected nearby regions as well. Stephen says that "our ancestors" could find no food. Notice that he still at this point is emphasizing that he shares this ancestry in common with his audience. So it was that Jacob sent his sons to obtain grain in Egypt.

The emphasis on there being two visits in *vv. 13-14* should not be overlooked. Luke's own theological outlook is that frequently in salvation history God will favor or visit his people, but they will not recognize it. When God "visits" or blesses them a second time however, in the person of a Joseph, or a Moses who makes two visits to Egypt, or a Jesus, they can no longer claim ignorance. This theme leads in fact to the conclusion of the speech. Jesus came once and was killed in ignorance through the machinations of the Jewish leaders. Now he is visiting them again through figures like Peter and Stephen, and there can be no excusing a negative response this time around — hence the speech's concluding condemnation.[291] According to the Genesis narrative, this time after the recognition of Joseph there was a happy conclusion to the story, with the family being reunited in Egypt, seventy-five in all.[292]

Vv. 15-16 involve a telescoping of several stories about the burials of the patriarchs, which took place in Hebron and Shechem (cf. Genesis 23, 49–50; Josh. 24:32). Stephen's account differs from the OT account in locating the tomb which Abraham bought at Shechem rather than Hebron, and he adds that Joseph's brothers were buried in Shechem as well.[293] One wonders if we are meant to see here a Lukan preparation for the material about the evangelization of Samaria in the next chapter of Acts.[294] In any case, the locating of the burial spot as being exclusively at Shechem was not likely to warm the hearts of the Judean Jews Stephen had for an audience, in view of the first-century antipathies between Jews and Samaritans.[295]

V. 17 suggests that the promise to Abraham of the land was fulfilled when the land first became fully occupied by the Israelites after the wilderness wandering.[296] Again Stephen refers to "our people" — still trying to establish shared identity with his audience. The problems began when, as *v. 18* puts it, another pharaoh came to the throne in Egypt who did not know Joseph had once ruled the land, and had no sympathy for resident alien Jews. This

291. See ibid., p. 118.
292. The LXX of Gen. 46:27 and Exod. 1:5 has seventy-five, while the Hebrew text has seventy. The difference may be because the larger total is deduced by omitting Jacob and Joseph and including the remaining seven sons of Joseph.
293. See Bruce, *The Acts of the Apostles*, p. 196.
294. See Marshall, *Acts*, p. 139.
295. See, e.g., John 4:9, and my discussion of that text in *John's Wisdom*, ad loc.
296. In general this is how Luke views prophecy — as something to be fulfilled during the course of salvation history, not usually at the end of time (cf. Luke 1:53, 73).

pharaoh, according to *v. 19*, is said to have dealt craftily with "our race," forcing them to expose and abandon their infants so they would not survive.[297]

V. 20 indicates that at this very time of crisis, Moses was born and was beautiful in God's eyes (cf. Jon. 3:3).[298] The story of Moses is told in this speech by dividing it up basically into three forty-year periods. Luke also follows a well-known Greek threefold pattern of speaking of his birth, early upbringing, and then education, a pattern he also uses to describe Paul (cf. 22:3; and Plato, *Crito* 50E, 51C; Philo, *Against Flaccus* 158). The OT does not record it, but Stephen, like Philo, speaks of Moses' education in Egyptian ways and wisdom (cf. Philo, *Life of Moses* 1.21-24). Moses then was brought up by Pharaoh's daughter as her own son and, having learned Egyptian wisdom, became powerful in word and deed (cf. 6:8 of Stephen, and 2:22 of Jesus).

The second forty years of Moses' life is discussed in *vv. 23-29*. In this period Moses is portrayed as a ruler and a judge of God's people (v. 27) who even strikes down an Egyptian who attacks Moses' fellow Jew (v. 24). He is also portrayed as one who tries to reconcile one Jew to another, and is rejected by the Jew who is trying to wrong his neighbor.

V. 25 is especially crucial as it is not found in the Exodus account. It is rather an editorial comment reflecting the views of the speaker (and author). Moses assumed that his kinfolk would understand what he was trying to do on their behalf, indeed understand that "God through him was rescuing them," but they did not understand. This misunderstanding is paradoxically understandable in Luke's view because this is only the first period of interaction between Moses and God's people, and their ignorance of who Moses really was is not surprising, as is also later the case with Jesus (Acts 3:17). By portraying Moses as a reconciler Luke is indicating that Moses should be seen as an exemplary sage, just as Joseph was, and, later, Jesus and Stephen (cf. Dio, *Or.* 22, 38; Lucian, *Demonax* 9; Philostratus, *Apollonius* 1.15).[299] Thus it comes about that some of Moses' own people reject him and reveal that he has murdered an Egyptian, which causes him to flee and become a resident alien in Midian, becoming the father of two sons.

It is difficult to determine where the third section of the Moses discussion ends (v. 44?), though clearly it begins in *v. 30*. We are told immediately that

---

297. Βρεφος here refers to a newborn infant. Cf. Luke 2:12, 16 and *New Docs,* 2 (1979), sec. 12, p. 40.

298. The term αστειος comes from Exod. 2:2 LXX and could have meanings ranging from witty to pretty. Barrett, *Acts,* vol. 1, p. 355, suggests it means without physical or mental defect. With the addition of the phrase "before (or in the eyes of) God," this is a Semitic idiom. Cf. the similar expression in Luke 1:6, 15. The expression conveys more than just the idea of how God views someone. It speaks of a character trait which is deemed good and approved by God.

299. See the discussion in Johnson, *Acts,* p. 127.

an angel appeared to Moses in the wilderness of Sinai in the burning bush (cf. Exod. 3:2 LXX). Here we have another example where, with the location specifically stated, God manifests the divine presence *outside* the temple, and indeed outside the Promised Land. As Johnson says, the point seems to be that "Holy . . . is where the presence of God is."[300] The sight is said to amaze Moses *(v. 31),* and when he draws near to examine the bush the voice of God speaks, indicating "I am the God of your ancestors." Moses begins to tremble and seeks to avert his eyes. He is portrayed as a pious man who knows the tradition that no one can look on God and live. Moses is told to take off his shoes, for he is on holy ground. The report is given to Moses of mistreatment of the Israelites in Egypt and that God has "come down to rescue them." Moses is to be the messenger and agent of this rescue, now dispatched to Egypt. The "story being told emphasizes God's initiative, which produces revelation to Moses, direction to Moses, and deliverance through Moses."[301]

Beginning at v. 35 the discourse becomes more pointed, giving way finally to direct address and clear-cut polemics. More specifically we have a series of declarative statements about Moses in *vv. 35-39,* and the sentences hinge on the repeating, five times, of the demonstrative pronoun "this," each time with reference to Moses (*"this* Moses").[302] We are probably meant to hear an echo of Acts 3:13-15, where essentially the same thing is said about the rejection and vindication of Jesus by certain Jews.

It is perhaps important to stress at this juncture that Stephen is pointing out a repeated pattern of behavior both on the part of God (sending leaders to Israel) and of God's people (rejecting the leaders sent), but it would be a mistake to assume that Luke sees in Jesus nothing more than just another prophetic figure in the mold of Moses. For Luke, as the speeches in Acts 2–4 make abundantly clear, Jesus is in many respects a unique figure. His is the only name under heaven by which people can now be saved. He is not merely another redeemer in the long development of salvation history, not merely another holy man or prophet like Moses, but rather the climax and culminator of the whole process of God's plan for the salvation of humankind. After Jesus, there can only be figures like Peter or Stephen who speak or act on behalf of Jesus, or model Christlike qualities but *do not supersede or succeed* Jesus.[303]

---

300. Ibid., p. 128.

301. Soards, *The Speeches in Acts,* p. 65.

302. See Johnson, *Acts,* p. 129.

303. See the helpful discussion of Moessner, " 'The Christ Must Suffer,' " critiquing the efforts of Johnson and others. "Jesus' . . . death for the sinful nation and raising up from the dead ushers in the *final* salvation, promised by the prophets for the eschatological remnant of Israel. In this fulfillment, Jesus as the prophet like Moses stands unique. None of the apostolic suffering or martyrdom in Acts accomplishes the decisive saving act as the suffering and death of the Lord's messiah. Once Acts begins, Israel is offered, a second time, through the prophet-

It was this same Moses, who heard the voice of God in the burning bush, whom *v. 35* says God sent as a ruler and liberator of God's people in Egypt. This Moses led them out from Egypt, having performed signs and wonders to accomplish this end, and he continued to lead and perform such acts during forty years in the wilderness, *v. 36* tells us. At *v. 37* we have the first overt reminder of where this discourse is leading — this Moses prophesied that God would raise up a prophet from among Israel "for you."[304] This verse draws on Deut. 18:15, applying it to Jesus just as is done in Acts 3:22 by Peter. Stephen's speech is not unique in the way it views Jesus.

It is probably not accidental that in *v. 38* we hear about the εκκλησια in the wilderness, the assembly or congregation of God's OT people. "[I]t could be that Christians would see a certain parallelism between the presence of Jesus with the new people of God on their earthly pilgrimage," and that of Moses in the midst of God's OT wilderness wandering people.[305] The motif of God's people being a people on pilgrimage will be continued with the discussion of the tent of meeting.[306] Moses received living oracles, the very word of God to convey to the congregation of God's people. Moses is thus presented as the founder of true religion, where God's word is proclaimed in the midst of the congregation and in the presence of God, whose presence makes any place hallowed ground.[307]

Unfortunately, *v. 39* tells us quite bluntly that "our ancestors" pushed Moses aside, were unwilling to obey him, and worse still in their hearts longed for Egypt. In fact, *vv. 40-41* speak of the horror of God's people turning to idolatry, making with their own hands a calf and offering sacrifice to this idol. The issue here is not whether this object was handmade or not, but that it was a deity of human devising and therefore an idol as opposed to the true God (see below). It becomes clear at this point that one of the things this speech is driving at is the distinction between true and false worship. The result of this false worship was that, according to *v. 42*, God turned these Israelites over to worship false gods, even the hosts of heaven. As in what we find in Rom. 1:24-28, Stephen suggests that sometimes God "allowed the people to become captive to the consequences of their own evil choices."[308] When the Israelites

---

apostles, the final redemption through the prophet like Moses" (p. 226). The view of Talbert that Acts could be seen as a biographical sketch of Jesus' first successors founders on the fact that Luke thinks Jesus has no successors, only followers who can call on his name for aid.

304. There is a certain amount of irony here since the "you" in question is the very Jewish leaders who worked to have Jesus killed.

305. Marshall, *Acts*, p. 143.

306. The parallels between this speech and the book of Hebrews have often been noted. See especially Heb. 12:18-24.

307. So Bruce, *The Acts of the Apostles*, p. 202.

308. Johnson, *Acts*, p. 131.

fashioned an idol with their own hands, God handed them over to such false lusts and their consequences.

In *vv. 42b-43* we have a quotation of Amos 5:25-27 (LXX), except that there is inserted the additional phrase "to worship them" in v. 43, indicating the point that is being made by the speaker, and Babylon rather than Damascus is said to be the region beyond which one will go into exile. The original prophecy was directed to the northern tribes who went into Assyrian exile beyond Damascus, but here it has been modified to suit a Judean audience for whom the Babylonian exile was a remembered experience. In addition, the expected answer to the first question in v. 42b is no since the question begins with the Greek word μη. Notice that whatever the question in its original context meant to suggest (perhaps that there were no sacrifices in the wilderness?), here v. 43 makes clear that sacrifices were offered in the wilderness all right, but to the wrong deity.[309]

V. 44 says that in effect there was no need for the tent of Moloch, since "our ancestors" had the tent of meeting in the wilderness, made according to the pattern God had passed along to Moses on the mountain (cf. Exod. 25:8 and 40 LXX). This tent of meeting was brought into the land *(v. 45)* when Joshua and God's people entered it, with God driving out their adversaries. Throughout this entire speech the major actor is God, as is particularly clear in vv. 44-45. According to v. 45b the tent of testimony was still in the land in the time of David. Stephen is not interested in arguing about or dwelling on the royal line of Jewish kings; his concern is about worship and places of worship. Thus David and Solomon are mentioned only in passing insofar as they have something to do with these matters.

V. 46a reminds us that David, like Moses and Joseph before him, found favor with God and requested that he might find a dwelling place — but for what? Here we have a significant textual problem. The basic question is whether the text reads οικω or θεω. Is David finding a dwelling place for the house of Jacob, or for the God of Jacob? "House" has stronger external testimony (p74, א*, B, D, and others), and it is certainly the more difficult reading.[310]

The real issue here is whether one can make sense of the reading "house of Jacob." There are two possible ways in which one can make sense of this reading. (1) The temple was thought to be a place where God's people could come and be with God, and so in a real sense it was a dwelling place for the house of Jacob. After all, the psalmist frequently spoke of dwelling in the house

309. The references to Moloch and Rephan are drawn from the LXX, for the Hebrew text speaks of Sakkuth and Kaiwan. The LXX version thus refers to the Canaanite-Phoenician sun god Moloch, and possibly to the Egyptian term for the God Saturn, Repa.

310. See Metzger, *Textual Commentary,* pp. 351-53.

of the Lord forever (or repeatedly, cf. Pss. 23:6; 24:6; 27:4; 52:8), and it is notable how often in the psalms involving the temple God is called the God of Jacob; so it would be natural to speak of the house of Jacob in such a context (cf. Pss. 24:6; 46:11; 47:4; 76:6; 81:4). That a Jew would want to dwell in the house of God was a sign of deep piety. (2) Less likely but possible is the idea that Stephen is alluding to a "house" (in this case meaning the community of Jewish Christians) within the house of Israel as being a substitute for the temple.[311] Thus the more difficult reading should stand. There is a slight possibility that Stephen is even engaging in a bit of polemic here. The audience thinks of the temple as the house where God dwells, but it is really just a house built for the house of Jacob.

This last suggestion is probably incorrect, since *v. 47* follows immediately, and no criticism is placed on David for asking that he might find God a dwelling place (cf. Ps. 132:5, which is drawn on here), or on Solomon for building God a temple. After all, Solomon in 1 Kings 8:27 is said to express the same theology as the passage cited from Isaiah. The contrast comes not between vv. 46 and 47, but between *v. 48* and what precedes it. Αλλα at the beginning of v. 48 should be translated "yet," and vv. 48-50, including the quotation of Isa. 66:1-2, must be taken together. The point of all three of these verses is not that God's presence can't be found in the temple (clearly Acts 2–4 shows it can), but that God's presence can't be confined there, nor can God be controlled or manipulated by the building of a temple and by the rituals of the temple cultus or the power moves of the temple hierarchy. What is being opposed is a God-in-the-box theology that has magical overtones, suggesting that if God can be located and confined, God can be magically manipulated and used to human ends. Such an approach is idolatry — the attempt to fashion or control God with human hands and according to human devices.

In contrast to such a view Stephen stresses that God does not *dwell* or reside in the Jerusalem temple, God dwells in heaven, and furthermore not only is God and God's true dwelling not handmade, instead all the world and all that is in it is God-made.[312] "Nothing is wrong with the temple nor with building it, but it is wrong to believe that it (and perhaps it alone) is the habitation of God. Moreover, allegiance to a temple built with human hands

311. See Klijn, "Stephen's Speech — Acts vii.2-53." As Klijn points out, a parallel to this last suggestion, of a community being the true temple of God, can be found in the Qumran material in the Manual of Discipline. On the idea of the church as God's temple see Marshall, "Church and Temple." I agree with Marshall that Stephen is probably not suggesting this in this speech.

312. As Hill, *Hellenists and Hebrews*, p. 74, points out, in some respects Stephen's polemic is the familiar and standard sort of fare Jews used against pagan temples and the theology of God's residence that was entailed in pagan thought (cf. Acts 17:16ff.).

could place Israel in danger of repeating its earlier wilderness sin, for the golden calf had also been made by 'their hands' (v. 41)."[313]

The quotation from Isa. 66:1-2 shows that Stephen stands in the line of the prophetic critique of a temple theology that neglects or negates the transcendence of God, and in fact he does not go beyond it. It is to be stressed that the crowd does not burst in at this point. The reaction comes when Stephen directly attacks the character of his audience in v. 51. This shows that what is truly offensive about Stephen's speech is the criticism of God's people, including the audience who do indeed act like the jealous brothers, or the Jew in Egypt who questioned Moses' authority, or the wilderness wandering generation. It is thus not surprising that all of this has been leading up to v. 51 — the indictment of the present audience as being like previous examples of God's disobedient and spiritually obtuse people.

The indictment in the *peroratio* involves the charges that the audience is: (1) stiff-necked (i.e., stubborn, unwilling to bend or rethink things); (2) uncircumcised in heart and ears (spiritually dead and unwilling to listen to the truth);[314] and thus in general (3) always opposing the Holy Spirit. The implication is that Stephen is speaking at the direction of the Spirit and to oppose his words is like opposing the words of Moses or others in previous generations. They are acting just like *"your ancestors used to do."* The turn to direct address in v. 51 is notable, for now Stephen distinguishes himself from his audience.

V. 52 speaks of the persecution and killing of the prophets. The former is clearly enough in evidence in the OT, as is the latter, though only in later Jewish and Christian tradition do we hear specifics about Isaiah being sawed in two and the like (cf. 1 Kings 19:10, 14; Neh. 9:26; Jer. 26:20-24; *Mart. Isa.* 5:1-14).[315] The ancestors killed the ones who foretold the coming of the Righteous One, "and now *you* have become his betrayers and murderers." The title "Righteous One" is appropriate in a forensic speech, indicating Jesus' innocence (cf. Acts 3:14) and the guilt of Stephen's audience. Instead of dealing with Stephen's "crimes" or guilt, the speech becomes an indictment of the crimes and guilt of the audience.

V. 53 should be emphasized — the audience received the Law as or-

---

313. Evans and Sanders, *Luke and Scripture,* p. 198. In short the issue is who is in control and gets to define the terms, nature, and location of God's presence — God or the people, in particular the temple hierarchy?

314. These charges come right out of the Pentateuch, where they were used of the recalcitrant wilderness-wandering Jews (cf. Exod. 33:3, 5; 34:9; Deut. 9:6, 13 on stiff-necked, and Lev. 26:41; Jer. 4:4; 6:10; 9:26; Ezek. 44:7, 9 on uncircumcised in heart and ears).

315. See Cadbury and Lake, *The Beginnings of Christianity,* 4:82; Bruce, *The Acts of the Apostles,* p. 208.

dained by angels, *and yet they have not kept it.* Clearly enough Stephen believes the Law and indeed all of Scripture to be God's word, and so the ultimate indictment is that God's people have failed to keep it, including the prophetic portions which foretold the Righteous One. Stephen's speech is *not* Law or temple critical, it is people critical on the basis of the Law and the Prophets, and of a proper theology of God's presence and transcendence and so a proper theology of God's dwelling place.

V. 54 shows that there was an immediate response to the direct criticism of the audience, involving a very strong reaction. Διαπριεσθαι (literally, "their hearts were torn in two") occurs only here and at Acts 5:33, and the text follows this by saying they ground or gnashed their teeth at Stephen (cf. Luke 13:28; Ps. 35:16), another sign of extreme anger.

By contrast we have Stephen who is serene and according to *vv. 55-56* has an apocalyptic vision — he saw the glory of God, just as Abraham had (7:2), and Jesus standing at the right hand of God. There has been much debate about the meaning of Jesus standing (standing to receive Stephen at his death?[316] standing in approbation of Stephen's witness?), but more probably we should think of the words found in Luke 12:8 which suggest a legal role of Jesus in heaven — witnessing before God about the one who had witnessed for him on earth.[317] Jesus has stood to give the ultimate witness to the first μαρτυς — the one who witnessed even unto death.

As C. H. Talbert has pointed out, like other ancients Luke assumes that martyrdom legitimates or places the ultimate seal on one's witness. While martyrdom is not something to be sought, it is also not to be avoided as it is an honor to suffer on behalf of Christ. Like Jesus before him, Stephen does not practice violent resistance to Jewish leaders and the corrupt temple hierarchy, but he does offer a bold prophetic witness against it, thus offering a form of nonviolent resistance to sin and corruption in high places.[318]

V. 56 provides us with the only example of the phrase "the Son of Man" outside the Gospels as a semitechnical title for Jesus.[319] It was as Son of Man that Jesus suffered and was vindicated by God (Luke 9:22), for only as a human being could he experience death. The title envisions Jesus fulfilling the roles

---

316. See, e.g., Barrett, "Stephen," who suggests that Luke is thinking of a personal coming or parousia of Christ for the dying Christian.

317. See Bruce, *The Acts of the Apostles*, p. 210; Tannehill, *Narrative Unity of Luke-Acts*, 2:99.

318. See Talbert, "Martyrdom."

319. It is my view that Mark 2:10 provides us with an editorial use of the phrase by Mark, but otherwise this phrase only appears on the lips of Jesus or in this one instance of Stephen. This indicates Stephen is part of the earliest community of believers, for as the Pauline letters show, this title was not used of Jesus later. Cf. my *The Christology of Jesus*, pp. 233f.

described in Daniel 7 and predicated of "one like a Son of Man" who comes into the presence of the Almighty.

V. 57 suggests that the audience believes they have heard blasphemy, for the idea that a human being could be at the right hand of God in heaven, especially a crucified manual worker from Galilee, was unthinkable. Thus they cover their ears, but then also spontaneously rush forward against Stephen and drag him out of the city and stone him. The stoning makes clear that they thought Stephen was blaspheming. It should be noted that nothing is said about the high priest offering a verdict, no formal sentence is announced, and nothing here suggests anything other than a lynching, an act of violent passion. This means that debates about whether the Sanhedrin had the legal authority to execute are moot, for we are not talking about a legal action here.[320] It seems clear the audience thought they had the moral authority and perhaps a duty to perform this act.[321] Standing by, and clearly approving of this action (so *8:1*), is a young man named Saul, whom Luke introduces us to at *v. 58*.[322]

The utterances of Stephen at death deliberately echo the words of Jesus at the same juncture. As Jesus had, Stephen in *v. 59* prays that his spirit may be received (cf. Luke 23:46), only Stephen prays to Jesus to do so while Jesus prayed to the Father.[323] Also probably like Jesus, in *v. 60* Stephen prays that this gross miscarriage of justice not be held against the perpetrators (cf. Luke 23:34).[324] Stephen speaks his final words in a posture of prayer and supplication, kneeling down and crying out like Jesus in a loud voice.[325] *V. 60b* indicates that after saying this Stephen "fell asleep," a Jewish euphemism for death, and one that was particularly appropriate for a person like Luke who believed in

320. Speculation about this taking place during the interregnum in A.D. 36-37 is also moot and in any case unlikely because Paul's conversion surely happened before A.D. 36, and thus Stephen's death transpired even earlier. As Bruce, *The Acts of the Apostles,* p. 212, points out, there was actually no interregnum in A.D. 36-37 for Jewish authorities to take advantage of. Vitellius, the legate in Syria, saw to this in advance (see Josephus, *Ant.* 18.89).

321. Equally moot are discussions about whether they followed correctly the later rabbinic legal procedures for a stoning, but cf. *m. Sanh.* 6:1-6. Had they done so we might have expected not just the dragging outside the city, but the sort of stones involved in the stoning that would have killed instantly. But this is not the case here. The crowd simply picked up whatever was ready to hand.

322. Luke regularly uses this deft technique of briefly mentioning a figure who will later become important in narrative. See pp. 240ff. above. The term νεανιου does not in itself indicate how young, but it could on occasion imply an unmarried younger male.

323. See Tannehill, *Narrative Unity of Luke-Acts,* 2:99.

324. Luke 23:34 is absent from some important early manuscripts, including p75, B, D*, W, and others, and may not be original to the Gospel. See Metzger, *Textual Commentary,* p. 180. The text in Acts, however, is not in doubt.

325. Cf. Mark 15:37, which is absent from the Lukan Gospel, but this verse in Acts probably shows he knew the text.

resurrection, namely, that one would arise from such a state, renewed and refreshed.[326]

As Luke's narrative of the birth and growth of the Jerusalem church has now been brought to a climax through the recounting of the crisis precipitated by Stephen and his speech, it is worth pausing and summing up. Dahl helpfully sums up the thrust of what Stephen's speech meant and implied as follows:

> Stephen confronts the Jews of Jerusalem with their own sacred history, showing that God has kept his promises. But the history has also another aspect, that of constant disobedience and opposition to God and his messengers. The Bible itself provided materials for this point of view, but Stephen sharpens it, contending that by their betrayal and murder of Jesus the Jews of Jerusalem have created a solidarity between themselves and the contemporaries of Moses and the persecutors of the prophets. Over against this continuous resistance to the prophetic Holy Spirit stands the succession of righteous sufferers Joseph, Moses, the prophets, Jesus, and Stephen himself. The conclusion to be drawn is, evidently, that along this line the divine promises are brought to fulfillment, while those who reject Jesus and his witnesses disinherit themselves from God's promises to the offspring of Abraham. . . . The account of Stephen's speech and martyrdom is given as the last preaching of the early apostles and evangelists in Jerusalem. Stephen's own history is the continuation of that history which began by God's revelation to Abraham; it leads to the preaching in Samaria and beyond.[327]

8:1b-3 provides a Lukan transitional passage that in v. 2 sums up the preceding account, and in vv. 1 and 3 prepares for what is to follow. The reason for this structuring rather than having v. 2 first seems to be that Luke wishes to emphasize that it is the stoning and death of Stephen which initiates the persecutions which scatter the Jerusalem church, except for the apostles. We are told at v. 2 that ευλαβεις, that is, devout Jews, gave Stephen proper burial and mourning.[328] Since we are not told they are Christians, one suspects Luke is indicating that despite the mob reaction some Jews at least had respect for Stephen and his views and saw him as a noble and righteous man.[329]

---

326. Cf., e.g., Mark 5:39; John 11:11-15; 1 Cor. 15:51.

327. Dahl, "The Story of Abraham," pp. 147-48.

328. This term is used throughout Acts for devout Jews (cf. 2:5; 22:12; cf. Luke 2:25). Since *m. Sanh.* 6:6 forbids public lamentation for one publicly executed after a trial, it may be in order to conclude that these Jews did not believe Stephen was publicly and legally executed, or less likely that they were protesting his execution by mourning, in violation of law and custom.

329. See Tannehill, *Narrative Unity of Luke-Acts,* 2:100-101. This means that Luke's narrative is more nuanced than those who see him as anti-Semitic think.

V. 1b says that very day a severe persecution began against the church in Jerusalem. Nothing is said about it being particularly directed against the Hellenists, though no doubt they were included, perhaps even targeted first since Stephen had been part of their synagogue. The only group said to be exempted are the apostles, but this is not unexpected since Acts 1–6 has stressed the great respect for these early Jewish Christian leaders among the populace of Jerusalem and the fear of them by the authorities.[330]

It is plausible to conjecture, since Saul from Cilicia was the ringleader of this persecution, even going from house(church) to house(church) and dragging both men and women off to prison, that he had been a part of the synagogue that Stephen had been a member of (cf. 6:9) and had been one of those disputing with him there (cf. 6:10-14), eventually prompting the trial of Stephen. It is thus plausible that Saul and other Zionistic conservative Jews from the Diaspora led this persecution. But as Hill points out, it is not possible to paint this persecution as a purely inter-Hellenist struggle, either at the persecutor or the persecuted end. First, one "is left to imagine a state of affairs in which Hellenist synagogue officials or Hellenist mobs could continue (that is, beyond the death of Stephen) to do as they pleased across Jerusalem; in which the high priests and elders themselves took no interest in the resultant commotion, although it was reputed to concern both temple and law; and further, in which no appeal to higher authority was ever made, either by Hellenist or by Hebrew Christians."[331] This is frankly not believable, especially in view of texts like Acts 22:4-5 where Paul says he acted with the knowledge and consent of the high priest (and his council).

Secondly, the text does not say that the persecution was limited to Hellenists on either end, though Acts 8 will make clear that figures like Philip were certainly among the persecuted. Thirdly, nothing in Stephen's speech really suggests that his theology significantly differed from that of Peter or other early Jewish Christians. Like Peter, Stephen is portrayed as full of the Spirit and standing in the line of the prophetic critique of Israel's sin beginning with Moses and continuing through the OT. Finally, the portrait of Paul as a persecutor of early Christians in Jerusalem is consistent with what we know from his letters (cf. 1 Cor. 15:9; Gal. 1:13, 23; Phil. 3:6; 1 Tim. 1:13).[332]

---

330. It is understandable that moderns might expect the leaders to be the first or primary ones to be persecuted, on the theory that if one cuts off the head the body will die. The problem with this theory is that it does not square with the awe and respect and even superstition ancients had for holy persons of power, especially for healers. It was one thing to attack an ordinary person, another to attack a person possessing divine power of some sort. It is perhaps telling that neither Paul himself in his letters nor Luke suggests that James or Peter or John had ever been the object of Paul's persecuting activity. He had persecuted the church, and had gone after ordinary Christians in various places. The "pillars" he had not touched.

331. Hill, *Hellenists and Hebrews*, pp. 33-34.

332. On the tensions in the Galatian material, cf. pp. 302ff. below.

VI. Philip on the Fringes of Judaism (Acts 8:4-40)

The material in Acts 8:4-40 chronicles the missionary work of Philip the evangelist, one of the Seven (cf. Acts 6:5). That it is one of the Seven and not one of the Twelve who undertakes these pioneering missionary activities comes as something of a surprise given the emphasis on the apostles in Acts 1–6 and the fact that Philip was simply introduced in 6:5 as one chosen to help serve the needs of the widows. Strangely enough, this intriguing material has produced very few monographs that deal with Philip himself.[1]

A. Surprise in Samaria (8:4-25)

It is important to recognize from the outset that Luke intends the reader to see these episodes in Acts 8 as part of the fulfillment of Jesus' words that his witnesses will carry out their work not only in Jerusalem, but also "in all Judea and Samaria and unto the ends of the earth" (Acts 1:8).[2] The coupling of the two regions of Judea and Samaria when distinguished from both Jerusalem and "the ends of the earth" provides a clue that Luke quite properly sees

---

1. The one notable exception is the recent University of Durham doctoral thesis of F. Scott Spencer, now published as *The Portrait of Philip in Acts: A Study of Roles and Relations* (Sheffield: JSOT Press, 1992). Cf. the review of this work by C. R. Matthews in *JBL* 113 (1994): 160-62. A great deal of interest has been shown in the last half-century in Simon Magus and in the Samaritans, but strangely not in Philip.

2. See Matthew, "Philip and Simon," p. 141.

Samaria as part of the Holy Land, and at least most of its residents as some sort of Jews, though they are Jews on the fringes of Judaism. It is thus not surprising that this story is coupled with the story of the Ethiopian eunuch, who is portrayed as another example of those on the fringes of Judaism, whether a proselyte or more likely a God-fearer (cf. vv. 27, 30).[3] In both cases we are dealing with people who generally stand under the broad umbrella of early Judaism or at least on its edges, not with pure pagans.[4] Even if the Samaritans were seen as lost sheep of the Israelite fold, the point is that it is from Judaism that they had wandered.

Luke clearly does not see Samaritans as just like Judean or Galilean Jews. He is well aware that most Galilean and Judean Jews viewed Samaritans as at best half-breeds and at worst foreigners (cf. Luke 17:18 — αλλογενης, "of another race/kind"). They are viewed as ethnically strange and religiously rather heterodox, but not simply as pagans or Gentiles (cf., e.g., Josephus, *Ant.* 11.340-41). The antipathy between Samaritans and Jews is reflected in uniquely Lukan stories such as those found in Luke 9:51-56 and 10:25-27, but Luke also sees Samaritans as ultimately worshiping the same God as Jews (cf. Luke 17:11-19, especially vv. 14, 18). It is thus premature to talk about the beginnings of the Gentile mission being recorded in Acts 8,[5] and not quite accurate to see it as the connecting link to such a mission.[6] The Samaritan mission does not *lead* to the Gentile mission. We are at that intermediate stage between the period of the mission only to ordinary Jews and the mission to Gentiles, probably sometime in the mid to late 30s.

Almost all scholars are in agreement that Luke is using a source or sources in this chapter.[7] The most recent and detailed monograph on Philip accepts the view that the author of Acts was among Paul's traveling companions alluded to in the "we" passages, including during the time when Paul visited Philip (see Acts 21:8-10). If, as I think, this is correct,[8] it is then unnecessary to posit either written sources other than Luke's own υπομνημα or notes, or to posit long histories of

3. On these two groups see the excursus, pp. 341ff. below.

4. See rightly Jervell, *Luke and the People,* pp. 123ff. In point of fact we don't really appear to reach the stage of a real "Gentile" mission, if by that one means a mission to those who have no relationship to early Judaism before Acts 11:19ff. and the missionary work in Antioch. It is not an accident that only here we first hear of the term χριστιανος.

5. See, e.g., Johnson, *Acts,* p. 150.

6. Against Hengel, *Between Jesus and Paul,* pp. 121ff.

7. See, e.g., Dupont, *The Sources of Acts,* pp. 55ff., and Lüdemann, *Early Christianity,* pp. 98ff. This is somewhat surprising coming from those who think the author was not a companion of Paul and so not a direct participant in any of the events recorded in Acts, for the two stories reflect Lukan style and themes to such a high degree. This is not a problem for the viewpoint suggested in this commentary, since I believe Luke had direct access to Philip and/or his daughters over the course of a few days in Caesarea and took his own notes.

8. See my discussion of Luke's sources above, pp. 165ff.

The Herodian assembly hall or basilica at Sebaste/Samaria.

transmission and editing of this material. In fact, this material at various points appears not to have received the benefit of much, if any, editing, and certainly not of a final literary polishing (see below on vv. 6-7).

Though there are rough edges to the pericopes in Acts 8, they do have a general shape. This first passage falls into two parts, the first focusing on Philip and his work in Samaria (vv. 4-13) and the second on Peter and his confirmation and supplementation of Philip's work and confrontation with Simon (vv. 14-25).[9] The two portions are bound together by the presence of Samaritans and Simon in each part, and the former part prepares for the latter part.[10]

9. See Tannehill, *Narrative Unity of Luke-Acts,* 2:104, for the suggestion that a cooperative effort of Philip and Peter is involved. That Luke is not trying to suggest that Peter comes to rein in some sort of unauthorized mission work is shown by the story which follows in Acts 8, where no one comes to supplement or supplant after Philip has encountered the eunuch.

10. By this I mean that what happens to the Samaritans and Simon in the first portion of the passage serves as a necessary preparation for what happens when Peter and John show up. The former is in part about Simon's entering the Christian community, the latter about his wishing to assume a role of authority and ministry dispensing the Holy Spirit. The latter part presupposes and depends on the former. This means that the part about Peter and Simon probably never stood alone as an independent narrative. See, however, Barrett, *Acts,* vol. 1, pp. 395ff.

V. 4 indicates that the scattering of the Jerusalem disciples (except for the apostles) led to the spreading of the word. The μεν ουν (roughly "now," or we might say "so then") at the beginning of v. 4 is Luke's characteristic way of indicating a new turn or stage in the narrative (cf. 1:6, 18; 5:41; 8:25; 9:31; 11:19; 12:5; 13:4; 14:3; 15:3, 30; 16:5; 17:12, 17, 30; 19:32, 38; 23:18, 22, 31; 25:4, 11; 26:4, 9; 28:5). V. 5 tells us that Philip went to "a/the city of Samaria." There is a textual problem here. The external evidence tends to favor the inclusion of the definite article (p74, ℵ, A, B, 69 et al.), but internal considerations call this conclusion into question (e.g., v. 8 refers indefinitely to "that city," and see similarly Luke 1:39).[11] In any case, Samaria refers to a region, and it is unlikely that Luke had in mind the mostly Gentile city of Sebaste which Herod had constructed at the site of the old capital called Samaria.[12] Other conjectures, such as that Luke had Shechem in mind (cf. Acts 7:16, but it had been basically destroyed in 128 B.C. along with the temple on Mount Gerizim) or even Gitta, the hometown of Simon Magus, can neither be proved nor refuted. Apparently, for Luke it was not important to specify the city; the issue was the encounter with the Samaritans as a people.[13]

We are told that Philip went and proclaimed the Messiah to the Samaritans, which in v. 12 is further specified as involving proclaiming the good news of the kingdom of God. Philip is accordingly being portrayed as carrying on the Christian evangelistic task with much the same message and results (though see below) already seen with the preaching of Peter. The Samaritans had a rather distinctive understanding of the Coming One or Messiah, because they accepted only the Pentateuch as their Holy Scriptures. In sum, they spoke of a *Taheb* who would be a prophet like Moses (or even Moses come back again), fulfilling the promise of Deut. 18:15 and restoring true worship on Mount Gerizim.[14] Josephus tells us that messianic expectation in Samaria was considerable during this general period, such that it was even possible during the reign of Pilate for a messianic pretender to lead Samaritans up Mount Gerizim with a promise to disclose where the hidden sacred temple vessels were (cf. *Ant.* 18.85-87).[15] Josephus also tells us that the Samaritans sometimes

---

11. See Metzger, *Textual Commentary,* pp. 355-56.

12. See the discussion in Hengel, *Between Jesus and Paul,* pp. 123ff.

13. This becomes especially clear in v. 9 where Luke refers to the εθνος of Samaria. In short, the Samaritans can be distinguished as a people or nation who are not entirely Jews in the usual or most familiar sense, but neither are they Gentiles.

14. In general see the discussions in Coggins, "The Samaritans and Acts," and R. Pummer, *The Samaritans,* and Crown, *The Samaritans.* The major problem is that our sources for Samaritan beliefs postdate the NT, and so it is not certain how much they reflect the first-century situation.

15. See my discussion of the Samaritans in *Women in the Ministry of Jesus,* pp. 57-63 and the notes.

claimed to be kin to the Jews when Jews were prospering, but when they were not they claimed to be aliens of another race (*Ant.* 9.29). This expresses the ambivalent and in-between state of their condition admirably.

It is thus not surprising that we hear in *v.* 6 that the crowds listened to Philip "with one accord" (ομοθυμαδον, cf. 1:14). His message is described as involving proclaiming "the messiah," or the kingdom of God and Jesus' name (v. 12). They also saw Philip's performance of miracles, including exorcisms and healings of the paralyzed and lame. Luke calls these works signs, for he sees them as pointing beyond themselves as confirmation of the message, which is more critical.[16] Philip is being portrayed as the same sort of positive evangelizing figure as Peter — one who is powerful in word and deed, as Jesus himself had been (cf. 1:22). The reaction to these words and deeds was joy in that city.[17]

Having introduced the protagonist in the story, Luke now turns to the antagonist — a certain man named Simon. Luke does not use the term μαγος of him, but he does refer to his practicing magic (μαγευω) and performing magical acts (μαγεια, v. 11). It is also said that Simon claimed he was someone great (μεγαν). It is important from the outset to recognize that Luke does not portray Simon as an early broker of Gnostic wisdom, but rather as a magician hungry for power (and money). In other words, his portrayal differs in important respects from the later second- and third-century Christian portraits of the man, and the latter should probably not be read back into the text of Acts.[18] Barrett's conclusion should be emphasized: "There is nothing in Luke's

---

16. See pp. 280ff. above.

17. Though joy sometimes can be a sign in Acts of a conversion having just taken place (cf. 8:39), it is unlikely this is the case here, for Luke has yet to relate the conversion of Samaritans. Here, then, we see the reaction of a city that had messianic hopes and was thankful for the healing of their relatives and friends. See Barrett, *Acts,* vol. 1, p. 404.

18. Justin Martyr, who is the earliest of the extrabiblical commentators on Simon and might be thought to have been in a position to know something since he was from Samaria, says Simon was worshiped by "almost all" of the Samaritans of his day as "the first god." Justin also says Simon arose during the reign of Claudius, and journeyed to Rome where he was worshiped as a god and had a statue erected to him with the inscription "to the holy God Simon." He also speaks of Simon being accompanied by a former prostitute named Helen, whom Simon's followers claimed was "the first idea generated by him." See *I Apol.* 26.3. There are various problems with this analysis, not the least of which is that the probable statue in question was dredged up out of the Tiber in the sixteenth century and its inscription reads *"Semoni deo sancto"* — to the holy god Semon, a Sabbine divinity (on the inscription, cf. *CIL* 6.657). In the second place, while Simon may well have still been around during the reign of Claudius, and even in Rome, Luke indicates he is already active in the 30s in Samaria (cf. Lüdemann, *Early Christianity,* p. 100). It should be pointed out that there is nothing necessarily Gnostic about Justin's report, unless the statement about Helen being the first idea points in that direction. It certainly does not require a Gnostic conclusion. The material in *Acts of Peter 4,* of uncertain date, adds little

text to suggest the initiator of a gnostic doctrine."[19] Nor is there anything to suggest that Simon was really a gnostic but that Luke has polemically downgraded him into a mere magician.[20]

Luke has no problem polemicizing against what he deems to be false teachings or bad theology when he thinks it is warranted (cf. Acts 17:21). The only point that may be of interest to us from the later material of Justin Martyr on Simon is his association with Rome. This may well be an important reason why Luke takes the time to tell this tale, for Theophilus, even if he did not live in Rome, may well have known of Simon through his connection with or reputation in Rome.

We are told in *v. 10* that the Samaritans also listened to Simon eagerly when he spoke prior to the coming of Philip. They even said of him, "This man is the Power of God, the one called Great." This designation seems close to the inscriptional evidence about a god who is less than the supreme god but nonetheless very powerful (cf. *PGM* 4.1225-29) and called "the Great Power."[21] Though it is of a later date, there is evidence from the Samaritan targums and from *Memar Marqah* that the Samaritans rendered the Hebrew name for God as "the Power" or "the Powerful One," which may indeed be of relevance to our passage.[22]

---

to the NT or Justin's reports except to confirm that Simon claimed to be the Great Power of God.

The late second-century material in Irenaeus, *Against Heresies* 1.23.1-3, comes from a period when the church is clearly combating Gnosticism. More clearly here Helen is said to become Ennoia, or wisdom, an emanation from the godhead (the text of Acts says nothing about "Ennoia," but rather refers to επινοια, the intent of Simon's heart in v. 22). In short, Irenaeus reflects the later Gnostic controversy, as do the even later sources of Simon material in Hippolytus, Epiphanius, and the (pseudo)-Clementines. None of this late material should be read back into the NT account, and only the material in Justin may be somewhat helpful in understanding something about the historical Simon. The suggestion is ready to hand that Simon, a well-known first-century figure, who was thought even by some in his own day to be a "divine man," was co-opted and claimed by later Gnostics and used for their own purposes. Later church figures like Irenaeus reacted to such use of Simon and apparently accepted some of the later Gnostic characterization of Simon uncritically, just as some twentieth-century scholars have done. On this whole matter, cf. the still helpful article by Casey, "Simon Magus"; also Derrett, "Simon Magus (Acts 8,9-24)." See the conclusions of Spencer, *The Portrait of Philip*, pp. 90-91.

19. Barrett, *Acts*, vol. 1, p. 406.

20. Such suggestions are made by Lüdemann, *Early Christianity*, pp. 98ff., and his "The Acts of the Apostles and the Beginnings of Simonian Gnosis," *NTS* 33 (1987): 420-26, and Haenchen, *Acts*, pp. 301ff., in part on the basis of a later dating, possibly even a second-century dating, of Acts. But Acts manifests and presupposes neither early (second-century) Gnosticism nor early Catholicism (on which see pp. 56ff.).

21. See the discussion in *New Docs*, 1:107, and also *New Docs*, 3:32.

22. See the discussion in Spencer, *The Portrait of Philip*, pp. 92-93. Cf. Fossum, *The Name of God*, pp. 171-72: "The divine name of Great Power, which appears in the oldest account of Simon [Acts 8], is . . . a Samaritan name of YHWH."

V. 11 tells us that the reason the Samaritans listened eagerly to Simon was that he had long amazed them with magical acts. This must be compared to what is said in v. 6 about the crowds and Philip. The upshot is that Luke is paralleling the two responses, even while setting up a contrast between the two major figures in the drama that prompt the response. Philip and Simon are in a sort of competition for the same audience, and Simon had a head start.[23] What is important about this is that once one parallels v. 6 and vv. 10-11, one is less inclined to see v. 6 as a response that amounts to faith or conversion. The verb προσεῖχον is used in both texts and refers to paying attention in a favorable way, or in a way that prompts a favorable response.[24]

The contrast in response (introduced by an adversative δε) only comes at *v. 12,* where we hear that the crowd believed Philip, who was preaching about the kingdom and the name of Jesus. Thereafter, baptism followed of both men and women (cf. 8:3). At *v. 13* even (καὶ) Simon is said to believe and be baptized,[25] and then follows Philip around like a fan of a rock star, amazed at the signs and great miracles Philip performed. It should be noted at this point that while there is some indication of *what* the Samaritans believed from v. 12, v. 13 is more succinct — Simon is simply said to believe and be baptized without our being told the content of his faith. Furthermore, the description of Simon in v. 13b seems to place him at the same point where the Samaritans were *initially* when they heard Philip (cf. vv. 6-7), amazed and believing that Philip could and was performing great miracles. It is the miracles which evidently led Simon to stay constantly with Philip and watch his every action. This brings act one of this minidrama to a close.

Act 2 of the drama opens with the word that the apostles at Jerusalem heard that "Samaria" (i.e., a large number of Samaritans) had accepted the word of God. Peter and John are sent down by the group of apostles, presumably to check the report received. *V. 14* (cf. v. 25) provides us with our last real mention of John's activities in Acts (cf. 12:2, where he is named), and as we have already seen, he is always mentioned as being in the company with Peter. Luke seems to know very little about him and his activities other than that he accompanied Peter during the early days in Jerusalem and then in Samaria (cf. Gal. 2:9).[26] It is, however, apposite to notice that Luke 9:54 says

---

23. See Spencer, *The Portrait of Philip*, pp. 88ff.

24. Cf. Johnson, *Acts*, pp. 145-46; Bruce, *The Acts of the Apostles*, p. 217.

25. This way of putting it suggests that Luke thinks the audience may be surprised by this response of Simon's. Possibly this is put this way for its apologetic value — Christianity must be a powerful religion if even notable and powerful figures of other religious orientations seek to be baptized into the Christian community.

26. The treatment of John by Luke suggests that Luke did not try to go beyond what his sources told him. There was ample occasion for him to embellish or elaborate on the deeds of John the apostle in these early chapters in the fashion of ancient romances if he

he and his brother James once wished to call down fire on a Samaritan village for failing to offer Jesus hospitality, and so Luke may wish us to assume that he would not be automatically convinced by reports of Samaritan conversions without further evidence.

Vv. 15-17 indicate that Peter and John did not attempt to start over from scratch with the Samaritans, which would have suggested that the work of Philip was invalid or defective. They are not said to preach or to baptize or to perform miracles for the audience Philip had previously approached. Rather, they prayed that they might receive the Holy Spirit, then laid hands on them, and finally the Holy Spirit was received. *V. 16* is another example of a narrative aside. It suggests that Theophilus would need an explanation to the effect that the Holy Spirit had not yet fallen on any of the Samaritans, but rather they previously had only received water baptism in Jesus' name. Theophilus might have assumed from the accounts in Acts 2–3 that water and Spirit would in the normal course of affairs come more closely together.

Vv. 18-19 return us to the subject of Simon, whom we are told saw that the Spirit was given through the laying on of apostolic hands, and so he offered Peter and John money, *not* so that he might have the Holy Spirit, but so that he might have the power to dispense it to "anyone on whom I lay my hands." Simon must have thought, here "is a technique worth purchasing, a way of gaining a 'share' in the leadership of this movement."[27] Thus once again "the use of possessions symbolizes the disposition of the heart."[28]

Peter's response in *vv. 20-23* is immediate and stern — "May your silver and you go to destruction (or hell), because you thought you could obtain God's gift with money!" Here, as is frequently the case in Luke-Acts, greed; the attempt to hoard money; the acquisitive, self-centered instinct; and especially the attempt to buy or control the power or blessing of God are sharply condemned. V. 21 refers to the fact that Simon will have no part/lot (κλῆρος) in this ministry,[29] because his heart is not right with God. *V. 22* calls Simon to repent of this wickedness and pray in the hope that perhaps the intent of

---

had wanted to write such a fictitious account. That he does not do so must count against the "romantic" view of the genre of Acts. Cf. pp. 376ff. below on the work of R. Pervo. It is also apposite to point out that Luke seems to know a good deal about the Pauline mission in Ephesus, but nothing of this John, the companion of Peter, ever being there. This comports with my suggestion that the Beloved Disciple referred to in the Fourth Gospel was someone other than John the son of Zebedee, about whom Luke knows only his connections with the Holy Land. See my *John's Wisdom: A Sapiential Commentary of the Fourth Gospel* (Louisville: Westminster, 1995), pp. 1-75.

27. Johnson, *Acts*, p. 152.
28. Ibid.
29. The term κλῆρος is used in the discussion of ministerial roles already in Acts 1:25-26.

his heart be forgiven, *if possible*.[30] *V. 23* once again indicates Peter's prophetic insight into human character (cf., e.g., 5:3). Simon is said to be filled with "the gall of bitterness and the chains of wickedness." The section concludes with the request in *v. 24* by Simon for Peter to pray on Simon's behalf that none of what Peter said would happen to him. *V. 25* serves as a postlude, indicating that Peter and John do indeed endorse, support, and are willing to take up themselves a ministry in the villages of Samaria. They did not just return to Jerusalem, they returned proclaiming the good news along the way.

There are many surprising aspects to this story, and one of the keys to understanding it is that Luke intends for us to see the evangelist Philip and the apostles working cooperatively in the Samaritan mission.[31] They are not to be seen as in competition, nor are the apostles coming in late and trying to undo or redo what Philip had done. Tannehill suggests that Luke is intending to convey the notion of one party being the initiator and the other being the verifier or confirmer of the work in Samaria.[32] There is, however, more to it than that, as Spencer has recognized. It is closer to the mark to see Philip as the author or initiator (under God) and the apostles as the finishers of the work of salvation in Samaria. Spencer notes certain parallels between what we find here and the way Luke describes the relationship of the ministry of John the Baptist as forerunner and baptizer and the later ministry of Jesus as Spirit dispenser, a pattern also somewhat in evidence in the case of Apollos and Paul in Acts 18–19.[33] There may be something to this suggestion. In any case, nothing derogatory is being suggested about Philip and his work. It was good as far as it went.

This text raises a multitude of questions about Luke's views on the relationship of water baptism, reception of the Spirit, and the laying on of hands — or to put it another way, on the relationship of initiation and conversion. Barrett is quite right that whatever other conclusions one should draw from a careful study of Luke's views on such matters, it "is quite mistaken to regard Acts 8 as a specimen of Lucan *Frühkatholizismus,* as if Luke were concerned to emphasize the sacramental indispensability of the apostles, or to argue for the distribution of different kinds of competence."[34] Luke's fundamental conviction is "that the Spirit does not respond to certain stimuli,

---

30. Ει αρα αφεθησεται is a conditional statement mixed with a final construction (in order that). The use of ει plus the future subjunctive indicates a possible, but far from certain condition. The use of αρα strengthens the measure of doubt the speaker is indicating about such an outcome. Moule, *IB,* p. 158, suggests it be translated "in the hope that perhaps . . . ."

31. So rightly Barrett, *Acts,* vol. 1, p. 412.

32. See Tannehill, *Narrative Unity of Luke-Acts,* 2:102-3.

33. See Spencer, *The Portrait of Philip,* pp. 188ff.

34. Barrett, "Light on the Holy Spirit," p. 293.

such as laying on of hands, more or less in the manner of Pavlov's dog. . . . It is God, not magicians or even apostles, who gives his own Spirit."[35] The Spirit comes sometimes with apostles present, sometimes without (cf. 9:17); sometimes with the laying on of hands, sometimes without (cf. 2:38); sometimes very close to the time of water baptism, sometimes not; sometimes before water baptism, sometimes after (as here).[36] The point is that God's gift is in God's control. The book of Acts suggests God's sovereignty over the whole matter, not that the matter is in the control of clerics, not even apostles.

Something more, however, deserves to be said on the relationship of initiation and conversion as it is portrayed in Acts, especially as we try to understand the portrayal of Simon. There are several ways of looking at the matter: (1) The Samaritans were really converted, as was Simon, but only the Samaritans later received the Spirit. (2) The Samaritans were really converted by Philip (and Peter?), but Simon was not. On this view salvation is seen as more of a process involving at least two events, and not simply *an* event. (3) The Samaritans were not really or fully Christians until they received the Spirit, and Simon never was.[37]

There are at least several hints in the text that regardless of what one may conclude about the Samaritans, Simon was never converted at all. These hints include: (1) the way Simon is introduced in the narrative in pejorative terms (vv. 9-11); (2) the fact that while it is said that Simon believed, we are not told *what* he believed, unlike the case with the Samaritans (see vv. 12-13). Apparently Luke means that Simon affirmed the reality of the miracles and the power that accomplished them and sought to have such power himself; (3) the καί in v. 13 and his separate treatment suggest a distinction between Simon and the Samaritans; (4) vv. 18-19 suggest one who wishes to buy the power of bestowing the Holy Spirit and then dispense it himself. As vv. 20ff. make clear, Simon's heart is not right before God, and he is in danger of going to destruction or hell. This is why Peter's message to him is that he must repent; (5) v. 23 is as telling a description of an unregenerate person as one could want — trapped in the chains of wickedness; (6) at the end Simon is not said to pray or be remorseful, he is only frightened of the negative consequences forewarned by Peter.[38] In short, Luke portrays Simon as not con-

35. Ibid.

36. See Barrett, *Acts*, vol. 1, p. 398: "Luke appears to have no hard and fast views on the relation between baptism and the Holy Spirit . . . and on the proper form and basis of missionary work."

37. On this entire matter, cf. Dunn, *Baptism in the Holy Spirit*, pp. 55-68.

38. It is interesting that the Bezan text adds that Simon "did not stop weeping copiously," suggesting remorse and repentance. See Metzger, *Textual Commentary*, pp. 358-59. In the Clementine literature Simon weeps but his tears are tears of rage and disappointment (cf. *Clem. Hom.* 20.21; *Recog.* 10.63).

verted, only strongly impressed with the apparent miracle-working power of Philip and Peter.

What then of the Samaritans? Dunn concludes that they were not in any full sense Christians until they received the Spirit.[39] V. 16 is about as explicit as one could wish that none of them had received the Spirit *at all* prior to Peter and John's coming. It is thus unlikely that one could argue that the Samaritans had received the Spirit quietly but only later received the visible manifestations of the indwelling Spirit, such as tongues or prophecy. This is clearly *not* what v. 16 suggests. Even with the conclusion that the Samaritans did not receive the Spirit before the apostles came, this does not, however, mean that what they had believed or said or done in response to Philip's evangelistic work *before* receiving the Spirit was inaccurate or defective. They were simply not fully equipped yet to be full-fledged Christians.

Perhaps, as some have suggested, the right question to ask about this text is why Luke would think that in this particular and perhaps unique situation the Spirit had been *withheld* until the apostles came down from Jerusalem to see the genuineness of the work in Samaria.[40] The answer to this question would seem to be because of the long-standing antipathy and hostilities between Jews and Samaritans (cf., e.g., John 4:9). Confirmation of true conversions would be needed by the mother church if Judean and Galilean Jews were to believe in the salvation of Samaritans. That confirmation comes in the form of the Samaritans receiving the Holy Spirit when the apostles laid hands on them, the same sort of infallible confirmation that Peter later remarks on as proof that God also accepts Gentiles among his people (cf. 11:15-17).

In all of this it is clear that Luke believes one can tell (or at least with prophetic insight into character such as Peter had one could tell) whether someone had the Holy Spirit in his or her life or not. By the end of this narrative the Samaritans did, and so could be recognized as true and full-fledged Christians, while Simon did not and could not be so recognized.

Whatever conclusions one draws on the above matter, it must be recognized that here water baptism is administered prior to the Spirit "falling" on the Samaritans, whereas in Acts 10:44 belief and Spirit precede the administering of water baptism, and in the case of the Ethiopian eunuch later in Acts 8 Spirit and water may have been received virtually simultaneously. In short, Luke portrays a *variety* of patterns of initiation and conversion and does not try to insist that any one was normative or always characterized the early church. Had Luke really been the advocate of "early Catholicism" some have

39. Dunn, *Baptism in the Holy Spirit*, pp. 55ff.
40. See Marshall, *Acts*, p. 157.

thought he was, we would expect more clarity and uniformity in the portrayal of these matters.[41]

B. Philip and a Unique Eunuch (8:26-40)

We have pointed out in the introduction to this commentary that Luke, like Ephorus and other ancient Hellenistic historians, seems to have followed a procedure of arranging his data κατα γενος, by which is meant both by geographical region and therefore also by ethnic group.[42] Acts 8 is a perfect example of Luke following this sort of arrangement, indicating the historical tradition out of which he writes.

It is perhaps crucial at this point to note that in ancient Greek historiographical works there was considerable interest in Ethiopia and Ethiopians precisely because of their ethnic and racially distinctive features. This was true not only in Luke's own time, but also even as far back as Herodotus.[43] Furthermore, in the mythological geography of the ancient Greek historians and other writers as well, Ethiopia was quite frequently identified with the ends of the earth (cf. Herodotus, *Hist.* 3.25.114; Strabo, *Geog.* 1.1.6; 1.2.24; Philostratus, *Vita Apoll.* 6.1)[44] in a way that Rome most definitely was not.[45] We are entitled, then, to suspect that Luke the historian has decided to portray in miniature a foreshadowing of the fulfillment of the rest of Jesus' mandate (Acts 1:8) in Acts 8, for here we find stories both about a mission in Samaria and (with the eunuch) in Judea, but also in the case of the eunuch a mission that potentially would reach the ends of the earth, as the eunuch went on his way back to Ethiopia. The goal of reaching the earth's limits with the message of salvation of course goes back not just to the commission or promise in Acts 1:8, but long before that to the author

---

41. This untidiness on such institutional and sacramental matters surely favors the view that Luke wrote a fair bit of time before the end of the first century when things began to be more uniform and institutionalized.

42. See pp. 32ff. above.

43. See the definitive study by Snowden, *Blacks in Antiquity,* and the review article by Scarupa, "Blacks in the Classical World."

44. See the discussion in Thornton, "To the End."

45. To the contrary Rome was at the heart of the Empire, and it was well known that if one wanted to talk about the limits of the west one had to go on further to Spain (cf. Paul's intent in Rom. 15:24, 28). Thornton, "To the End," p. 374, is quite right that "There is no evidence that any Jew, Greek, or Roman around the first century A.D. ever conceived of Rome as being at the end of the earth." This is the opposite of the case of what was thought about Ethiopia and Ethiopians. As Homer put it, the Ethiopians are "the most distant of people" (*Odyssey* 1.23).

of the Isaianic Servant Songs, who spoke specifically in these terms (cf., e.g., Isa. 49:6; 62:11).

Scholars have long noted the echoes in Acts 8:26-40 of certain OT stories, in particular the stories about Elijah and Elisha such as are found in 1 Kings 18 and 2 Kings 2 and 5.[46] The question to be raised about this is whether Luke is simply modeling various aspects of his own narrative and its characters on these earlier biblical stories, but these biblical stories don't serve as the *main source* for the material in Acts 8, or whether, as T. L. Brodie suggests, we are dealing with what he calls the rhetorical imitation of sources, which largely involves the creating of fictitious stories using biblical models and modifying them somewhat.

It must be said that there are some serious problems with Brodie's views, which may be enumerated briefly: (1) Ancient rhetorical handbooks, including Quintilian, when they are discussing the sort of imitation Brodie has in mind, are generally discussing the copying of rhetorical *speeches,* not narratives as we have in Acts 8. (2) There is a major difference between the use of historical examples as models to be imitated or expounded upon in rhetorical speeches and "the rhetorical imitation of sources," as Brodie puts it.[47] About the former Quintilian says that the rhetorician "should begin with the historical narrative (. . . which is an exposition of actual fact . . .) whose force is in proportion to its truth" (*Inst. Or.* 2.4.20). Only afterward should one turn to fictitious or realistic narratives for models or examples. About the sort of *imitatio* Brodie has in mind, Quintilian says nothing in his discussion of narratives.[48] If Luke's goal as a rhetorically adept historian was persuasion in regard to the truth about a historical movement involving Jesus and his followers, it is quite likely he would have followed the advice of Quintilian and others when dealing with narratives to rely on historical accounts first and foremost and only to create such accounts as were well

46. See Brodie, "Rhetorical Imitation of Sources."

47. The use of historical examples or models in ancient sources that are rhetorically adept in hopes the audience will follow them is a very different matter from "the rhetorical imitation of sources." On the former cf. Kurz, "Narrative Models for Imitation."

48. It is telling that in his article "Greco-Roman Imitation of Texts as a Partial Guide to Luke's Use of Sources," in *Luke-Acts,* pp. 17-46, Brodie relies primarily on examples of textual imitation from poetry and drama (cf. pp. 22-23) and not from historiography, and then when he does give examples from historiographical sources he does not do justice to the differences between Thucydides and his heirs on the one hand, and the more Sophistic and highly rhetorical approaches to writing history on the other (cf. pp. 30-31). Isocrates and Polybius do not approach rhetorical matters and the use of sources in the same way. Cf. Litfin, *St. Paul's Theology of Proclamation,* pp. 21-134, for a carefully nuanced approach to the two basic approaches to the use of rhetoric by historiographers and others.

grounded in history, for a historical narrative's "force is in proportion to its truth." (3) As Brodie himself recognizes, in many essentials the story in 2 Kings 5 differs from both of the stories in Acts 8.[49] For example, in neither story in Acts 8 are we dealing with the healing and cleansing of a leper. In fact, in many ways Acts 8 is closer to 1 Kings 18 (cf., e.g., the figure of Obadiah who was in charge of Ahab's palace). It is accordingly better to conclude that Luke has written up his own source material so that it has the sound and the "echoes" of certain aspects of the narratives of the LXX (more a matter of style than substance), in this case the Elijah-Elisha cycle, but not to argue that Luke is simply creating his own stories with only the OT as his source-book. His access to Philip as a companion of Paul also points us to this latter conclusion.

Perhaps more compelling are the arguments that our narrative has deliberate echoes of the Emmaus road story in Luke 24. Consider the following: (1) Jesus joins two travelers leaving Jerusalem, presumably on their way home, who do not know him, and similarly Philip joins another traveler on the way home who does not know Philip; (2) Jesus and Philip both engage their fellow traveler by means of a pointed question (cf. Luke 24:17; Acts 8:30); (3) Jesus' death and resurrection becomes the subject of conversation in each case by means of messianic interpretation of the OT; (4) both narratives conclude with what could be called sacred or even sacramental acts — breaking of bread and baptism; (5) Jesus and Philip both abruptly vanish from the scene and then reappear in another place (cf. Luke 24:31, 36-43; Acts 8:39-40); (6) the travelers are deeply affected emotionally by the encounter (Luke 24:32; Acts 8:39).[50]

There is evidence that Luke has very carefully structured his narrative in the form of a chiasm. Vv. 32-35, the citation of Isa. 53:7-8, are at the heart of the passage and serve as its hinge.[51] Though it is probable that the eunuch was a Gentile, Luke makes nothing of this, and this story has no consequences for the issue of Gentile admission into the church, unlike the narrative which follows it.[52] The fact is that Luke has carefully presented this story so that the

---

49. See the critique by Spencer, *The Portrait of Philip*, pp. 136-40.

50. Here I am following ibid., pp. 141-42. Spencer has to make too much out of Luke 4:26-27 and the parallels between Naaman and the eunuch however to insist that Philip is being presented as the inaugurator of the Gentile mission for the church. The closer parallels are with Luke 24, and that narrative is not about a mission to Gentiles.

51. See ibid., p. 132. For this chiasm to work completely, however, one must include v. 25, which is more of a concluding verse for the previous pericope, or at most only transitional to the eunuch story.

52. Cf. Tannehill, *Narrative Unity of Luke-Acts*, 2:108: "The scene is important for what it anticipates and symbolizes rather than for its consequences. It is prophetic of the gospel's reach" to the ends of the earth.

eunuch is portrayed as someone on the fringes of Judaism, as the eunuch's reading of Isaiah shows.[53]

One of the major themes throughout Luke-Acts is the universalization of the gospel — that it is for all people from the last, least, and lost to the first, most, and found.[54] This is a theme Luke found in his favorite prophetic book, Isaiah, and it is highlighted both early and often in Luke-Acts (cf., e.g., Luke 3:6, "all flesh shall see the salvation of God," to Isa. 52:10). The story of the Ethiopian eunuch may be said to be exhibit A of this promise being fulfilled, not least because the actual text of Isa. 52:10 says all the ends of the earth shall see God's salvation, and that is precisely where the Ethiopian comes from as things were viewed in Luke's day.

It is easy to forget that the ancient world was not simply divided into Jews and Greeks and Romans and the various peoples who were their clients or relatives or were subjected within the immediate bounds of the Empire. There were also those who lived at or beyond the fringes of the Roman Empire, those whom Greco-Romans would have seen as living at the ends of the earth, including some of those whom the Greeks called βαρβαροι, by which was meant non-Greek-speaking peoples (cf. Acts 28:2).[55] A reasonable case can be made for seeing this narrative as being about the reaching of those from the parts of Africa that were at or beyond the borders of the Empire, those that were at the ends of the earth. Indeed, this story is about the reaching of these sorts of people of color apparently before the gospel comes to what we would call Europe today.[56]

An especial stress is placed throughout this narrative on God's engineering of this conversion, and thus that it is part of God's plan. It is the angel of the Lord that tells Philip to go where he would encounter the eunuch (v. 26), then it is God's Spirit that specifically tells Philip to go over and join the eunuch in his chariot (v. 29), and then providentially Philip overhears the eunuch reading the precise portion of the Servant Songs most apt for the discussion of matters messianic — Isaiah 53. Then, not accidentally Philip and the

53. See the discussion in Wilson, *Gentiles and the Gentile Mission*, pp. 171-72. He is not portrayed as the first pure pagan convert, and Luke places no major stress on his Gentile character. In fact he could have been an Ethiopian Jew, but Luke does not make this matter clear. For the view that he was the first Gentile convert see now Kelly, "The First Lukan Convert."

54. See the discussion in the introduction, pp. 68ff. above.

55. Of course as Acts 28:2 shows, non-Greek-speaking persons, or persons without Greco-Roman culture, could exist within the bounds of the Empire. The formula in Col. 3:11 shows that Paul, as well as others, knew that the world involved more than Jews and Greeks. It included those on the fringes of the Empire.

56. See the discussion in P. De Meester, " 'Philippe et l'eunuque éthiopien' ou 'Le baptême d'un pèlerin de Nubie'?" *La nouvelle revue théologique* 103 (1981): 360-74.

eunuch happen upon water at the point when the eunuch is prepared to become a follower of Jesus (v. 36). Finally, the eunuch goes on his way with joy, and Philip is snatched away by God's Spirit to another location up the coast (v. 39). Thus, Luke aptly illustrates two of his major themes in one story — God's sovereignty and God's salvation plan that was meant to include all sorts of people. Bearing these things in mind, the detailed exegesis becomes easier.

It is not clear from *v. 26* whether, in view of v. 25, we are meant to think that Philip had returned to Jerusalem briefly and then took the main road from Jerusalem to Gaza, or whether he made his way to Gaza in a more roundabout fashion from Samaria, perhaps going over to Caesarea and down the coastal road. The former view seems more likely (cf. v. 26b). The one who directs Philip at this point is said to be an angel of the Lord (cf. Acts 5:19; 10:3, 7, 22; 11:13; 12:7-11, 23; 27:23), who is probably not to be identified with the Holy Spirit though they act in concert in this story.[57] The term μεσημβριαν can be used either to indicate a time of day (noon, cf. Gen. 18:1; 43:16) or a direction (south — the position of the sun at midday, cf. Dan. 8:4, 9). Either translation is possible here, but probably the construction with κατα suggests Luke is referring to a direction.

Philip is to head for Gaza. The question is — which one? The site which was destroyed in 96 B.C. by Alexander Jannaeus and left a ruin, or the new city built nearby? It is probably the former since v. 26 ends with the phrase "it is desert." This "it" (αυτη) could refer either to the road or to the site of old Gaza, probably the latter since there is some evidence that old Gaza was called η ερημος Γαζα.[58] In any event, these are strange directions, and that Philip follows them shows his faith and faithfulness.

Not only were the directions surprising, but what Philip finds on the road, according to *v. 27,* was equally surprising — an Ethiopian eunuch who was a court official. Each of these descriptions deserves careful attention. In

---

57. Notice, for example, how an angel announces the work of the Spirit as something distinctive from the angel's work in Luke 1:26ff. Notice also how an angel of the Lord in Luke 1:11 who appears to Zechariah is paralleled by the angel Gabriel who appears to Mary in 1:26. In Luke's theology angels are God's messengers, but the Spirit is the one who inspires and fills God's people so they may say and do what God wants them to say and do. Pentecost is not about an angelophany but rather about an encounter with God's presence directly in Luke's theology. In view of the various references to an angel of the Lord in both Luke and Acts, used in a fashion much as one finds in earlier Jewish literature, it is a reasonable inference that "Lord" in the phrase "angel of the Lord" does not refer to Jesus but rather to God. Certainly Luke does not see Jesus' postresurrection spiritual presence as the same thing as an encounter with an angel, nor is he interested in an angelomorphic Christology (see, e.g., Luke 2:9-11, where an angel of the Lord announces the birth of the distinct being Jesus). On Luke's Christology, see pp. 147ff. above.

58. See Barrett, *Acts,* vol. 1, p. 423.

the first place, it is quite wrong to ignore the fact that this man was an Ethiopian, which in all likelihood means he was a black man. Luke intends to highlight this fact because it suits his purposes of showing the gospel reaching different ethnic groups and sorts of people. As Snowden, C. J. Martin, and others have stressed, over and over again in the classical references "Blackness and the Ethiopian were . . . in many respects synonymous. . . . The Ethiopians' blackness became proverbial. . . . *Ethiopians were the yardstick by which antiquity measured colored peoples.*"[59] What is important to note is that, unlike the case in the West in the last three centuries, there is *no* evidence in antiquity of widespread prejudice against a particular group of people simply because of their color, or the combination of their color and distinctive ethnic features (hair, facial features, etc.).[60]

The geographical location Luke has in mind is the Nubian kingdom whose capital is Meroe, south of Egypt, which is today part of Sudan. This city was located well below Abu Simbel, between the fifth and sixth cataracts of the Nile, and was a capital of a major power as early as 540 B.C. and continuing to at least A.D. 339. In other words, this eunuch had traveled no small distance,[61] and was an official of no minor kingdom. Here, and after this passage in Acts (cf., e.g., Luke 10), Luke shows considerable interest in the conversion of people of relatively high social status, perhaps in part because of who Luke's audience is — Theophilus, probably a literate person of higher social status. Then, too, it "is no small part of apologetic literature to emphasize how one's special claims have met with approval from respectable people (see e.g. Josephus *Against Apion* 1.176-212)."[62] In fact, however, the eunuch for obvious reasons would have suffered from status inconsistency in Judaism (high in one regard, low in another) in a way that would not be true among

59. See Snowden, *Blacks in Antiquity,* pp. 5, 23; Martin, "A Chamberlain's Journey"; and Snowden, *Before Color Prejudice.*

60. This is not to say that there was no such thing as class, status, or ethnic prejudice in antiquity, but only that skin color, and in particular black or very dark brown skin color, was not to any significant degree the cause or basis of such prejudice so far as we can tell. The references making derogatory remarks about blacks are very rare in antiquity, and by contrast there are numerous comments that speak positively about black people, even going back to the time of Homer. The interest in and appreciation of blacks is also clear from the way they are often depicted in ancient art and sculpture (cf. Herodotus 3.114-15 on Ethiopians being the fairest and longest living among human beings). In art cf. the graceful statue of the black musician from 200 B.C. in Scarupa, "Blacks in the Classical World," p. 24; and for a handsome statue of a young black rhetorician, cf. Vermeule, "Greek, Etruscan, and Roman Bronzes," and figure 7, and also Snowden, *Blacks in Antiquity,* figure 64.

61. Ethiopia was widely viewed as on the southern edge of the earth, bordering the great sea Oceanus. See Martin, "A Chamberlain's Journey," pp. 112ff.

62. Johnson, *Acts,* p. 158.

the followers of Jesus, who not only valued singleness (cf. Acts 21:9; 1 Corinthians 7) but in fact spoke of it in terms of being a eunuch for the sake of God's dominion (Matt. 19:10-12).[63]

The man in question is called a εὐνοῦχος, which, while it can be used in a very general way to mean simply an official, normally refers to a man who has been castrated and often also dismembered.[64] In view of the fact that Luke uses not only this word but also the following term δυνάστης, it seems highly likely that the term εὐνοῦχος has its more literal sense here. For obvious reasons, it was a common practice in the ancient Near East to castrate those who were in charge of kings' harems or who had duties regularly involving close contact with the queen, such as a δυνάστης would have.

From the point of view of Judaism, this put this man permanently on the fringes of the religion in which he was showing great interest.[65] Deut. 23:1 was regularly interpreted to mean that eunuchs were to be excluded from God's assembly, though Isa. 56:3-5 held out promise of fuller participation in biblical religion in the future as a full member of God's people. In view of the focus on the Servant Songs in this very passage, it may be that Luke wishes us to see this story as a whole being about the fulfillment of that promise in Isaiah 56. The point would be that nothing hindered the eunuch from being a full-fledged follower of the one in whom Isaiah's promises were being fulfilled in the present, even though he could not be a full-fledged Jew.

Finally, the man is also described as a man of power, an official of Candace, queen of Ethiopia, in particular the queen's chief financial officer ("over all her treasure").[66] Actually, the term "Candace" is not a personal name but apparently a transliteration of an Ethiopic title (k[e]ut[e]ky),[67] applied to a royal line of queens over various generations ("the Candace").[68]

---

63. See my discussion of this passage in *Women in the Ministry of Jesus*, pp. 28-32.

64. During this period, eunuchs in the courts of this part of Africa were not only castrated but usually also partially dismembered, which means that this man in all likelihood could not have become a full proselyte to Judaism even if he had wanted to, for he could not be properly circumcised. Cf. on this Keener, *Bible Background Commentary*, p. 346. Marshall, *Acts*, p. 162, is quite right that such a person could not become a proselyte, pace Wilson, *Gentiles and the Gentile Mission*, p. 171 n. 5. He falls into that more fringe category of some sort of God-fearer. See pp. 341ff. below on this status.

65. Not just anyone who was not a full-fledged Jew would make the considerable pilgrimage this man made to worship in Jerusalem, especially when he would not be allowed to participate fully in such worship due to his being a eunuch. The great piety of Ethiopians is regularly remarked on in antiquity. Cf. Diodorus Siculus 3.2.2ff.; Philostratus, *Apollonius* 6.2; Pausanias 1.33.4-5.

66. Is there a play on words here between Gaza and the Greek word for treasure, γάζης?

67. See Barrett, *Acts*, vol. 1, p. 425.

68. See Cadbury, *Book of Acts in History*, p. 16.

We are told in *v. 27b* that the eunuch had come to Jerusalem to worship. Since it is unlikely he was a proselyte (cf. above), at the most he might have been permitted in the Court of the Gentiles,[69] or in some of the local synagogues (the synagogue of the Freedmen perhaps?).

V. 28 tells us he was returning home, seated in his αρμα and reading his Isaiah scroll.[70] The αρμα was not a military chariot but some sort of traveling carriage, perhaps even an ox-drawn wagon.[71] In any case it seems to have been a vehicle that could hold at least three persons — the eunuch, a driver, and also Philip. The fact that the eunuch was reading is another indication of his considerable status, and in all likelihood he was reading aloud, as was almost always the case in antiquity.[72] This is why Philip would know immediately what the eunuch was reading.

By the guidance of the Spirit Philip is directed to join the eunuch, according to *v. 29.* It was when he ran up to the carriage that Philip heard the eunuch reading and immediately asked him a leading question, "Do you understand what you are reading?" *(v. 30).*[73] The response of the eunuch in *v. 31* is elegant: "How could I be able unless someone will guide me?"[74] What was needed was the hermeneutical key to understand who the prophet was referring to when he spoke of the Servant, and this could come from the proper guide or teacher.[75]

---

69. This is perhaps not certain if it was known he was a eunuch, especially if he was a dismembered one.

70. It is an intriguing fact that one of the oldest fragments we have of Acts (p50) contains Acts 8:26-32 and 10:26-31 together, two texts which both deal with conversion and baptism and use the verb κολλαομαι (to join). Johnson, *Acts,* p. 160, plausibly suggests that this papyrus may have served as a sort of service manual or memory aid either for preaching or even for the occasion of a baptism, a conjecture which the addition of v. 37 at some point in the tradition would support.

71. Cf. Bruce, *The Acts of the Apostles,* p. 227; Marshall, *Acts,* p. 162.

72. See Achtemeier, *"Omne verbum sonat."* This was especially the case with lengthy scrolls where there was no separation between words, and it had to be read syllable by syllable to make sure where the word divisions came. Even as late as the early Middle Ages we hear remarks about Ambrose being unusual because he could read without moving his lips (Augustine, *Confessions* 6.3).

73. Notice the neat paronomasia — γινωσκεις α αναγινωσκεις. Luke is fully capable of such rhetorical devices that make the aural experience of hearing the text more pleasing. This is what makes it all the more likely, since we also find anacoluthons and other infelicities, that the text of Acts never received a final editing from Luke, for he was capable of very good Greek indeed.

74. Notice the very elegant Greek of the eunuch, using the optative with αν, a sign of education or at least conscious style. See Barrett, *Acts,* vol. 1, p. 428. Luke is quite capable of altering the style of the Greek to suit the speaker and occasion, and we find the optative at several points (cf. 17:18; 26:29).

75. Notice how at Qumran the ability to provide the proper interpretation *(pesher)* and application is ascribed to the Teacher of Righteousness (1QpHab 2:2).

The eagerness of the eunuch to understand is clear, for he implores Philip to come up and join him in the carriage in hopes of getting an explanation of this Isaianic material.

In *vv. 32-33* Luke reveals the passage in question that was puzzling the eunuch — Isaiah 53. The text in Acts is a direct quotation from the LXX of Isa. 53:7-8 with only small emendations.[76] Though this song is not directly cited all that frequently in the NT, it is clear from various texts that it had a considerable influence on early Christian thinking about Jesus (cf. John 12:38; Rom. 10:16; 1 Pet. 2:21-25). It is a mistake to make too much of what is *not* included in this quotation (i.e., the material immediately preceding and following this quote), as if Luke was deliberately avoiding a theology of the atonement.[77] Other texts show that he understands Christ's suffering as the means by which human beings are released from their sins (cf., e.g., Luke 24:44-47; Acts 2:36-38; 20:28 according to the most probable reading).[78]

The point at issue here is not the deeds of the Servant, but rather the identity of the Servant, as v. 34 shows. Nevertheless, the text speaks of one who was led away to slaughter and did not resist or protest.[79] The meaning of several phrases in *v. 33* is uncertain. As the Servant was being humiliated,[80] something he did not try to resist, his justice was denied.[81]

The rest of *v. 33* is even more difficult to decipher. Is it referring to the fact that the Servant by dying prematurely died without progeny? In its original Hebrew context this seems likely, for Isa. 53:10 speaks of a reversal of what seemed certain such that "he shall see his offspring."[82] In the Christian use of

76. For example, the aorist κειραντος is used in Acts instead of the LXX's present tense κειροντος, and αυτου seems to have been added after "lowliness." See Johnson, *Acts*, p. 156.

77. See Marshall, *Acts*, p. 164, who asks: "is this silence significant? To put the question in this way of course is to assume that Luke's choice of citation was his own and was not dictated by the actual facts of the story as he had revealed them from Philip or some intermediate source, and this is a dubious assumption. Since elsewhere Luke refers to Jesus' suffering for others (20:28; Lk. 22:19f.), it seems doubtful whether we are entitled to draw any conclusions from the silence."

78. On this whole matter see Moessner, "The Script of the Scriptures," pp. 218-50.

79. There is perhaps a deliberate contrast between the Servant, who "opened not his mouth" (v. 32), and Philip, who is said to open his mouth (v. 35), using the same sort of phraseology. Cf. Tannehill, *Narrative Unity of Luke-Acts*, 2:112.

80. The issue here is what was being done to the Servant, not his humble attitude.

81. It is just possible to read η κρισις αυτου ηρθη to mean "his condemnation/judgment was lifted or removed" (cf. Johnson, *Acts*, p. 156), but this makes less sense of the verse as a whole. From a Lukan perspective there is an emphasis in Acts on the injustice of Jesus' crucifixion in view of the intent and understanding of the human perpetrators of the act (cf., e.g., Acts 3:17; 5:30).

82. There are many problems in this passage both in deciphering the Hebrew and in the Greek. The Hebrew seems clearer than the Greek in referring to physical offspring.

this song, however, it is possible to read the last phrase to mean "his life is lifted up from the earth," alluding to the resurrection and/or ascension of Jesus. Then the preceding question could be seen as a matter of exultation and wonder (about the indescribable number of his spiritual offspring) rather than a lamentation. The text would be referring to Jesus' spiritual progeny as a result of the resurrection/ascension/sending of the Spirit.[83] This would be exceedingly apropos since the eunuch, who was a "dry tree" (cf. Isa. 56:3-4), could have no offspring and could not be a full participant in Judaism but was about to become one of the spiritual offspring of Christ and suddenly have a host of kinsmen and kinswomen.

V. *34* turns to the question of the identity of the Servant. It is understandable that the eunuch might think that the author of these songs might be speaking of himself when he spoke of the Servant, in view of the fact that various passages in these songs are in the first-person singular (cf. 49:5; 50:4). Furthermore, Jer. 11:18-20 shows that a prophet could describe his own experiences in terms much like these.[84] However, it would be equally natural to take the Servant to be a cipher for Israel as a nation since God clearly addresses the people of Israel as his servant in Isa. 44:1ff. Confusion is natural when one also sees in 49:5 a distinction between the Servant and Israel, and in 53:1-3 that the Servant is rejected by Israel. What is not clear is whether or not these passages were already being read as referring to the Jewish Messiah before and during the time of Jesus.[85]

More clearly, the general trend of referring ancient prophetic texts to contemporary persons and events is well known from the Qumran documents (cf., e.g., 1QpHab 2:1-15). With such a trend in the early first century there was nothing to prevent Jesus and his early followers from interpreting the Servant Songs in a contemporizing way, and certainly that is what is alluded to here in Acts 8. V. *35* leaves us in no doubt. Philip, as Luke portrayed Jesus before him (cf. Luke 24:27, 44-47), sees the Hebrew Scriptures as a prophetic book that speaks about Jesus. The good news about Jesus could be proclaimed starting with these very Isaianic texts.

The response of the eunuch is eager and almost instantaneous. V. *36* says that seeing a pool or stream of water, he immediately asked, "What is to prevent me from being baptized?" Well he might ask this question, for it appears that at this time a eunuch could not become a full proselyte to

83. See the helpful discussion in Spencer, *The Portrait of Philip,* pp. 178-80.
84. See Marshall, *Acts,* p. 163.
85. The older view of J. Jeremias, *TDNT,* 5:654-717, that there was such a messianic reading of these texts in early Judaism, is more often than not rejected these days. For one thing, the Qumran reading of the text is uncertain. Earlier claims that these Isaianic texts were used messianically at Qumran are no longer widely accepted. See, e.g., Barrett, *Acts,* vol. 1, pp. 430-31.

Judaism.[86] *V. 37* does not appear in our earliest and best manuscripts of Acts. It appears to be a later addition of Christian scribes who thought it unthinkable the eunuch would be baptized without the requirement of a confession of faith.[87] Luke shows no interest in clearly specifying the mode of baptism or the amount or sort of water that was used, though the use of εβαπτισεν coupled with v. 39a[88] may suggest immersion. In fact, Luke says nothing about whether this act was performed in a shallow or deep body of water, and whether the water was still or running.[89] He is concerned with the fact of conversion and the response to it.

V. 39 tells us that the Spirit snatched Philip away as soon as they had come up out of the water, and the eunuch departed in a very different direction, rejoicing in finally being a full member of a religion grounded in the Hebrew Scriptures.[90] *V. 40* tells us that Philip next found himself at Azotus (Ashdod), some twenty miles up the coast from Gaza.[91] Like the prophet Elijah, he was moved by God to his next point of ministry (1 Kings 18:12, 46; 2 Kings 2:16).

We are told he passed through this region proclaiming the good news in the various towns on or off the coastal road until he arrived at Caesarea. This may have included Jamnia, Antipatris (23:31), and Lydda and Joppa

---

86. This was especially so if he was dismembered, for circumcision along with baptism was a clear requirement to be a proselyte to Judaism (cf. the case of Izates in Josephus, *Ant.* 20.17-95). See Collins, "A Symbol of Otherness," p. 171, who shows that while there is no clear evidence of a requirement of baptism and sacrifice before the end of the first century A.D., circumcision was clearly required before then.

87. This verse is not found in p45, 74, ℵ, A, B, C, 33, and various other manuscripts and versions. See Metzger, *Textual Commentary,* pp. 359-60. It is included by E, a sixth-century text which is the earliest known manuscript including this verse, and also in various minuscules. That the tradition of this verse goes back well before the sixth century is shown by Irenaeus's quoting part of this material toward the end of the second century (*Against Heresies* 3.12.8). As Metzger says, there is no good reason why this material should have been omitted if it was originally in the text of Acts. It is interesting that this verse, though not in the Byzantine text, found its way into the Textus Receptus from the editions of Erasmus, who added it. On text criticism of the KJV text of Acts, cf. pp. 65ff. above in the introduction.

88. "When they came up out of (εχ) the water."

89. Notice by contrast Didache 7:1-3, where a preference for baptism in running water is stated, and pouring is allowed if running water isn't available. This is perhaps the earliest clear statement about the mode or manner of baptism in the early church, and probably dates to the first century A.D.

90. A few manuscripts (A correction by the first hand, 94, 103 et al.), in order to make clearer the conversion of the eunuch and conform the end of the story to its beginning (cf. v. 26), add here after "the Spirit" the following: "fell upon the eunuch, and an angel of the Lord caught up Philip." This is surely a later attempt to clarify and add consistency. Cf. Metzger, *Textual Commentary,* pp. 360-61.

91. Hengel, *History of Earliest Christianity,* p. 79, speculates that the evangelization of former Philistine territory could be seen as a reversal of the curse found in Zeph. 2:4f.

(9:32-43; 10:5-23). If so, Philip is again being portrayed as the forerunner of Peter, preparing the way for later ministry in that area.[92] In any case, Philip ends up at Caesarea, which is precisely where we find him much later in the narrative at 21:8-9. Clearly enough, Luke has concern about historical connections and matters of continuity. As Barrett says, "it is not unreasonable to consider the possibility that Philip provided a link at some point between the finished work and some of the stories in the first eight chapters."[93]

In conclusion it can be pointed out that while there is no first-century evidence of the church in Ethiopia, nevertheless several early church fathers attribute to the eunuch the evangelizing of the region (cf., e.g., Irenaeus, *Against Heresies* 3.12.8-10).[94] We can only say, it may be so, and in any case the eunuch can be seen as a fulfillment of the psalmist's words: "let Ethiopia hasten to stretch out its hand to God" (Ps. 68:31). For Luke's purposes, however, at least part of the point of this story is to show that with or without apostles, God was going to fulfill his plan to spread the good news to "all flesh" even unto the ends of the earth, even if it required using an evangelist rather than an apostle, and even if it required direct divine intervention in various forms. The human leaders of Christianity in Jerusalem could only try to catch up with the plan of God, which was operating often apart from and quite beyond their control.

It is no accident that in Acts 8–10 we see an ever increasing degree of direct evidence of the Spirit's involvement in the process,[95] for Luke wishes to stress God's direction of the events that affected and in fact changed the course in which the church would pursue its missionary work. We can see in Acts 8:26-40 that a deliberate mission to Gentiles cannot be far off,[96] and that also means one needs an account about those who were first called to set out on the path of a deliberate mission to Gentiles, which not coincidentally follows in Acts 9–11.

92. See Spencer, *The Portrait of Philip*, pp. 210-41.
93. Barrett, *Acts*, vol. 1, p. 436. Cf. p. 421: "Directly or indirectly Luke obtained information about the activities of Philip, one of the Seven." I would suggest it was directly, during his travels with Paul when he went to Caesarea and encountered Philip and/or his daughters. See pp. 165ff. above on Luke's use of sources.
94. The earliest clear traces of Christianity in the Nubian region date to the fourth century. See Metzger, "Christianization of Nubia."
95. See O'Toole, "Philip and Ethiopian Eunuch (Acts 8,25-40)."
96. So Haenchen, *Acts*, p. 314.

VII. Saul as the Salient Jewish Convert (Acts 9:1-31)

A. The Assaulting of Saul (9:1-19a)

As the ετι (still) indicates in *9:1*, we are meant to see the material in Acts 9 as a continuation of what has previously been said about Saul in 8:3 — that he was vehemently and violently opposed to the Jesus movement. Though only brief reference is made to Saul's pre-Christian period in Acts before Acts 22 (cf. 7:58; 8:1, 3; 9:1-3), there is enough here to raise important questions about his early life. The study of this period of his life has become something of a cottage industry of late,[1] with considerable debate not only about the nature and object of Saul's persecutions (Was he really involved in murdering Christians? Was his attack only on the Jerusalem church, or a part of it?), but also whether one can actually say that Saul was "converted," the persecutor of "the Way" becoming its strong advocate. What would it mean to speak about the conversion of a Jew from one form of Judaism to a messianic Jewish group that claimed to be the Way for Jews as well as for others, and saw itself as the continuation of true Israel? These questions are worth keeping in mind as we work through the material in this chapter.

In regard to the general subject of zeal for Torah and Torah piety, there can be little doubt, once one reads the Maccabean literature, that such zeal could and did from time to time lead to violent acts, even to violent acts perpetrated by zealous Jews against other Jews who were seen as apostate or

---

1. Cf., e.g., Jervell, *The Unknown Paul;* Hengel, *The Pre-Christian Paul;* Riesner, *Die Frühzeit des Apostels Paulus;* Segal, *Paul the Convert;* Legasse, "Paul's Pre-Christian Career."

violating the essence of the covenant with God.[2] We see this sort of behavior again in abundance during the Jewish War in A.D. 66ff. There is then nothing anomalous or impossible about Luke's portrayal of Saul in these matters. It will also be noted that nothing is said in Acts 9 about Saul being given permission to execute Christians, only that he received letters from the high priest (and his council? cf. Acts 26:12) to the synagogues at Damascus to extradite Christians, binding them and taking them back to Jerusalem, presumably for trial.

The extent of Saul's involvement in the *death* of Christians continues to be debated, and we will have occasion to say more on this subject when we deal with Acts 26.[3] For now it is sufficient to note that Paul's letters are as clear as Acts about Paul being involved in the persecution of Christians because of his zeal as a Pharisee for the keeping of Torah (cf. 1 Cor. 15:9: "I persecuted the church of God"; Gal. 1:13: "I was violently persecuting the Church of God and was trying to destroy it"; Phil. 3:6: "as to zeal, a persecutor of the church" [cf. Gal. 1:14]).[4] It should also be noticed that the terms Paul uses in these letters do not suggest the persecution of just one house church or even necessarily house churches in just one locale.

Without question, the story of Saul's "conversion" is one of the most important events, if not the most important event, that Luke records in Acts. It has contacts with what has gone before in that by the end of the account Saul is evangelizing in Damascus without the direction or permission of the Jerusalem church, as was also the case with Philip in Acts 8. Yet Acts 9 is even closer to Acts 10 in that both recount a crucial conversion narrative involving two visions and the overcoming of considerable obstacles, first in the case of the future primary missionary to the Gentiles, then in the case of a prominent Gentile, Cornelius.[5] The importance of Saul's conversion in Luke's mind is shown by the fact that Luke gives the story no less than three full treatments, from three slightly different angles, with the later narratives in Acts 22 and 26 supplementing the basic third-person account in Acts 9.[6] It is in order, before we look at Acts 9 in some detail, to compare and contrast the three accounts by means of a chart and

2. See the discussion in Hengel, *The Pre-Christian Paul,* pp. 63ff.
3. See pp. 668ff. below.
4. In the disputed Paulines see 1 Tim. 1:13.
5. See Tannehill, *Narrative Unity of Luke-Acts,* 2:113ff.
6. On the importance of the cumulative effect of the three accounts and their interdependence, cf. Hedrick, "Paul's Conversion/Call." It is clear enough that all three accounts are edited, Acts 26 perhaps more than the other two accounts. This may be because the only time Luke heard the full account in a language he knew (Acts 22 says Paul spoke in Hebrew or Aramaic, a language Luke shows no evidence of knowing) was on the occasion Paul spoke to Agrippa, and so more editing was required.

some analysis of it.[7] As a prelude to this exercise something should be said about how conversion was viewed in antiquity.[8]

As A. D. Nock demonstrated in his classic study,[9] there is a considerable body of evidence that "conversion" to various of the "newer" Eastern religions (including various of the mystery religions, Judaism, and then later Christianity) was not unusual during the Empire, and even before.[10] Conversion should be distinguished from "adhesion," which involves the acceptance of new worship as a useful supplement and not as a substitute and does not involve the taking of a new way of life in place of the old. By conversion we mean the reorientation of the soul of an individual, his deliberate turning from indifference or an earlier form of piety to another, a turning which implies a consciousness that a great change is involved, that the old was wrong and the new is right.[11]

On this showing, what happened to Saul on the Damascus road must surely be seen as more than a matter of mere adhesion. As Barrett puts it: "This was a radical change of religious direction, and it was accompanied by as radical a change of action: the active persecutor became an even more active preacher and evangelist. If such radical changes do not amount to conversion it is hard to know what would do so."[12] This has of late been recognized even by some Jewish NT scholars.[13] The point is that early Christianity, at least in some of its prominent forms, was such a radical departure from early Judaism in certain key ways (having to do with Torah, temple, territory, and even theology) that it is impossible not to speak of conversion.[14]

---

7. Some of the following material appears in different forms in my book *Paul's Narrative Thought World*, pp. 218ff., and in more detail in my article "Editing the Good News."

8. On salvation in general see the excursus, pp. 143ff. above, and Appendix 2 below, pp. 821ff.

9. Nock, *Conversion*.

10. The similarities between the story in Acts 9 and the story in the Jewish romance *Joseph and Aseneth* have often been mentioned. In particular, the address of the chief of the house of the Lord to Aseneth and her response is worth quoting (14.6-8): "The man called her a second time and said 'Aseneth, Aseneth.' And she said, 'Behold, here I am, Lord, Who are you, tell me.' And the man said 'I am the chief of the house of the Lord and commander of the whole host of the Most High. Rise and stand on your feet, and I will tell you what I have to say.'" As Barrett, *Acts*, vol. 1, p. 442, says, the similarities to our account are unmistakable but also superficial, and, one may add, both stories seem indebted somewhat to the story of the calling of Samuel in 1 Sam. 3:2-18, or other prophets (Isa. 6:1-13; Jer. 1:4-10; cf. Gal. 1:15). The story of Joseph and Aseneth involves romance and conversion that leads to marriage, and there is nothing comparable in Acts to Aseneth's prayer of penitence. Acts is not a romance, nor does it really contain much romancelike material. Its purposes and mode of operation are different from such accounts. See pp. 376ff. below.

11. Nock, *Conversion*, p. 7.

12. Barrett, *Acts*, vol. 1, p. 442.

13. See especially Segal, *Paul the Convert*, pp. 14ff.

14. Here both Qumran's and John the Baptist's approach provide certain parallels,

Acts 9:1ff. third person	*Acts 22:1ff.* first person	*Acts 26:1ff.* first person
Luke's summary from talking with Paul	in Hebrew/Aramaic Paul's Greek summary given to Luke?	spoken by Paul to Festus — Luke present
Saul to high priest letters to synagogues bring Christians back to Jerusalem (v. 1)	letters from high priest and council bring back Christians to Jerusalem for punishment (v. 5)	authorization from chief priests (v. 10)
light from heaven flashed about him (v. 3)	at noon, great light from heaven shone about me (v. 6)	midday, light from heaven shining around me and those with me (v. 13)
fell to ground, heard a voice (v. 4)	fell to ground, heard a voice (v. 7)	we all fell to ground, I heard voice saying *in Hebrew* (v. 14)
"Saul, Saul why do you persecute me?"	same as Acts 9	same as Acts 9 except "It hurts you to kick against the goads"
"Who are you, sir?"	same as Acts 9	—

---

though in the end inadequate ones. Both of these sects felt Judaism to be apostate enough that what was required was even for God's people, the Jews, to start over from scratch in their relationship with God — with repentance and some sort of entrance rite — lest they face God's coming wrath on sin and unfaithfulness. We may wish to call these radicalized forms of early Judaism, for they were basically calling people *back* to what they saw as the true Jewish faith. Early Christianity, however, especially in its Pauline and Johannine forms, seems to have been yet more radical, calling Jews and others *forward* to something new. Early Christianity was not a known form of Jewish messianism; on the contrary, it was an unrecognizable and unprecedented form of messianism. In calling Jews to worship a crucified Jewish manual worker named Jesus, and in speaking about the transcending of the ethnic and social distinctiveness of Judaism (in regard to circumcision, various of the purity and food laws, temple piety, and pilgrimages), this surely stretched all normal definitions of early Judaism past the breaking point. To be sure, early Christians like Paul and Luke saw their new faith as the true development or completion of the Jewish faith, but the majority of early Jews, including Saul of Tarsus before his Damascus road experience, saw this as not merely a *version* but rather a profound *perversion* of Judaism. It is with good reason that Segal subtitled his important work "The Apostolate and Apostasy of Saul the Pharisee."

Acts 9:1ff. *third person*	*Acts 22:1ff.* *first person*	*Acts 26:1ff.* *first person*
"I am Jesus, whom you are persecuting" (vv. 4-5)	"I am Jesus of Nazareth, whom . . ." (vv. 7-8)	The Lord said: "I am Jesus whom you are persecuting" (v. 15)
"Rise, enter city. You will be told what to do" (v. 6)	"What shall I do, sir?" "Rise, go into Damascus. You'll be told all that is appointed for you to do" (v. 10)	"Rise, stand on your feet. I have appeared to you for this purpose, to appoint you to serve and bear witness to the things in which you have seen me and to those in which I'll appear to you"
men stood speechless, hearing voice, seeing no one (v. 7)	men saw light, did not hear voice of one speaking to me (v. 9)	"Delivering you from the people and from Gentiles to whom I send you, to open their eyes, that they might turn from darkness to light (vv. 16-18)
Saul arises. Can see nothing. 3 days without sight and food. Led by hand into Damascus	Paul can't see due to brightness of light. Led by hand of companions into Damascus (v. 11)	—
vision of Ananias (vv. 10-16)	Ananias (no vision mentioned)	—
(vv. 8-9)	Brother Saul, receive your sight (v. 13)	—
Ananias lays hands on Saul. "Jesus sent me that you may regain sight and be filled with the Holy Spirit" (v. 17)	"God of our fathers appointed you to know his will, and see the just one, and hear a voice from his mouth. You'll be a witness to all people of what you've seen and heard" (v. 14)	—

Acts 9:1ff.	*Acts 22:1ff.*	*Acts 26:1ff.*
third person	*first person*	*first person*
something like scales fall from Saul's eyes, regains sight and is baptized (v. 19)	"rise and be baptized, and wash away your sins, calling on his name" (v. 16)	— (no mention of Ananias)
takes food and is strengthened (v. 19)	—	the above was a heavenly vision

A variety of scholars have argued that there are various contradictions between the Paul of the letters and the Paul of Acts,[15] and that this is most evident in the story of Saul/Paul's conversion and call to Christianity as told in the three places listed above in Acts and as referred to in Galatians 1–2 in particular. The issue of the Paul of Acts versus the Paul of the letters cannot be settled simply on the basis of an analysis of the conversion material in Acts and Paul's letters, because there are also other points of contact and contrasts between the two sources. As A. J. Mattill has stressed, points of comparison that call for discussion involve a wide range of issues, including: (1) Paul's curriculum vitae; (2) the working of miracles; (3) whether and in what way Paul continued to be an observant Jew; (4) the issue of the Apostolic decree; (5) doctrinal matters; and we would add (6) the portrayal of Paul's social status in the two sources; and (7) the treatment of Paul as a controversialist.[16] We will deal with these issues as they arise in the text of Acts.[17]

It is crucial to approach the matter of the Paul of Acts and the Paul of the letters with the proper methodology. The following are some caveats about how the methodological issue should be approached. (1) One must recognize that Paul's letters and Acts are different in genre, and thus simple comparisons that do not take into account this difference are not likely to prove satisfactory.

15. See, e.g., Vielhauer, "On the 'Paulinism' of Acts."

16. Cf. Mattill, "The Value of Acts." On Paul as a controversialist, cf. Barrett, *Paul*, pp. 22-54. Barrett is right that this dimension of Paul's ministry is underplayed in Acts, though it is not wholly absent (cf. also his *New Testament Essays*, pp. 70-100). I would suggest that this is largely because Luke is writing somewhat after A.D. 70, by which time the Judaizing controversy had passed, not least because of the demise of Jerusalem and the scattering of Jerusalem Christians. In an apologetic work like Acts, Luke wished to put early Christianity's best foot forward, and saw no purpose in dredging up old animosities that had been resolved or overcome with the passage of time. Luke's "idealization" of early Christianity comes not so much in what he says, for he strives and succeeds in recording much accurately and in an understandable order (see Luke 1:1-4), as in what he judiciously omits.

17. See the excursus below, pp. 430ff., on Paul's social status as represented in Acts and the Pauline corpus.

Historians do not approach matters in the same fashion as writers of ad hoc letters. It is well to listen to the advice of Hengel to take "seriously both the main sources, Paul *and* Luke, and weighing them up critically, in broad outline to arrive at something like an overall picture of the 'pre-Christian Paul.'" The apostle's own testimonies should have *some* priority over Luke, "but despite his contrary tendency Luke's accounts, some of which correspond with Paul in an amazing way, may not be swept away as being fictitious and utterly incredible."[18] (2) I would suggest that one must recognize that both Acts and Paul's letters are tendentious in character, and reflect rhetorical interests and purposes. Many of Paul's remarks about himself are apologetic in character (e.g., cf. 2 Corinthians 10–13) and must be judged accordingly. This means that Paul's letters cannot be taken as vastly superior to (or inferior to) Acts as sources for information about the historical Paul. (3) Though Paul's letters give us comments about the apostle's history from the apostle himself, these comments are almost always in passing, and are very selective, sometimes only arising because Paul is correcting a misunderstanding of his story. The letters are not by and large autobiographical. The epistles' silence about many issues (e.g., that Saul was from Tarsus) may have little or no significance since Paul did not set out to satisfy historical or biographical curiosity when he wrote these letters. (4) Though the accounts in Acts are not written by Paul, they are more direct in their treatment of the subject matter, and more complete on a host of subjects such as Paul's origins, education, citizenship, and the like. If, as we have suggested, Acts is written by a sometime companion of Paul, the comments may not be any less valuable in understanding the historical Paul than the comments in the epistles. As Mattill has rightly pointed out, "the evaluation of Acts as a source for the study of Paul is related to the estimation of the we-sections."[19] The more one is inclined to believe Luke was a sometime companion of Paul, the more one is inclined to believed in the veracity of his portrayal of the Apostle to the Gentiles.[20] As Legasse says, it is in any case necessary to use Acts to understand the life of Paul, especially because only Acts gives us any real quantity of usable data about the period before Paul's conversion and one cannot reconstruct the missionary travels of Paul solely on the basis of the letters. Both sources should have the same critical scrutiny applied to them.[21]

We must begin our discussion of Acts 9 and the portrayal of Saul's conversion by discussing the differences in the accounts of it. In the first place, some of the differences are likely due to the fact that these three

---

18. Hengel, *The Pre-Christian Paul,* p. 85.
19. Mattill, "The Value of Acts," p. 97.
20. On the "we" passages see the excursus, pp. 480ff. below.
21. See Legasse's conclusions in "Paul's Pre-Christian Career," p. 390.

accounts serve different purposes and may originally have been meant for different audiences, though now they are all part of Luke's account written for Theophilus. If Luke was indeed present at one of these recountings of the story (Acts 26) and was at least for a time the traveling companion of Paul, there is good reason to expect accurate summaries here of this dramatic turning point in Saul's life.

Yet it must always be kept in mind that all three narratives are now part of a literary account written up for the benefit of Theophilus, and perhaps others, and so their effect is meant to be collective, cumulative, and supplemental to each other. The argument that Acts 9 is the basic account and the other two are Lukan expansions does not work in view of the notable differences,[22] not least of which is the change of voice from third to first person.[23] Furthermore, Acts 26 is a compressed narrative which leaves Ananias altogether out of account, and it cannot be the basis of the other two. Taking at face value the "we" in Acts 21:17ff. and 27:1, I would suggest that Luke was present on the occasion of the testimony before Festus and Agrippa and had supplemental information from Paul as the basis for the other two accounts. Acts 9, as we have it, is Luke's own summary in his own words as he understood the conversion.

It cannot be stressed enough that these accounts are *summaries* and Luke has written them up in his own style and way. The accounts especially in Acts 22 and 26 appear to be condensations from speeches made by Paul himself. Paul would be presenting his story to two very different audiences here and wishing to convey some different aspects of the account to these two groups, but Luke is only summarizing these presentations at most.

A further complicating factor is that Luke tells us Paul spoke the speech we have in Acts 22 *not* in Greek but "in the Hebrew tongue," which likely means in Aramaic. We, however, have this speech in Luke's Greek translation and condensation. Furthermore, we are told in Acts 26:14 that Jesus spoke to Saul from heaven in Aramaic or Hebrew in the first place, but in all three accounts we only have a Greek version of his words.

Probably not based on any written source, Acts 22 should be seen as Luke's own composition based on Paul's summary report to him. We have no clear evidence that Luke could even understand Aramaic since he always seems to use the LXX or some Greek version of the OT in his two-volume work. Luke of course was not present on the Damascus road either, so the account in Acts 9 is likewise secondhand, perhaps based on Paul's relating of the account to Luke.

22. Cf. Stanley, "Paul's Conversion in Acts."
23. But see Hedrick, "Paul's Conversion/Call," pp. 415ff., and earlier Dibelius, *Studies in the Acts*, pp. 177ff.

Comparing Acts 22 and 26 one notices that in Acts 26 Paul presents himself as a prophet called of God and speaks in a way that will make this clear to Festus and Agrippa. In Acts 22 he is trying to present himself as a good Jew, a former Pharisee, to his fellow Jews and accordingly as one who is faithful to the God of Abraham. All three of these accounts go immediately back to Luke, who wrote them up, but in the case of Acts 9 and 22 ultimately they can go back to Paul, while Acts 26 is Luke's own firsthand account in all likelihood. One of the factors which must count in favor of seeing these as narratives of real events and real speeches is their obvious differences. If Luke were to set out to compose on his own multiple accounts of Saul's conversion, we would have expected the narratives to be somewhat more similar than they are.

Acts 9, 22, and 26 agree in essentials but differ in some details, some of which are inconsequential, others quite important. The essentials on which all three accounts agree are: (1) Saul was authorized by a or some priestly authorities in Jerusalem to do something against Christians, and as the story goes on it is implied that the authorization applied to Christians in Damascus; (2) while Saul was traveling to Damascus he saw a light and heard a voice; (3) the voice said, "Saul, Saul, why do you persecute me?" (4) Saul answered, "Who are you, sir/lord?" (5) the voice said, "I am Jesus, whom you are persecuting." Thus, all three accounts confirm that Saul had an encounter including a real communication from Jesus in the context of a bright light which turned Saul from an anti- to a pro-Christian person. This distilled summary comports with what one finds in Paul's letters when the apostle speaks of or alludes to his conversion, including the account in Galatians 1–2 and 2 Cor. 3:18 and 4:6. It is right to stress as well that both Luke's and Paul's portrayals of this seminal event indicate that conversion and call to ministry go together, and should not be radically distinguished.

There is also a stress in Luke that this encounter was not merely subjective, for it also affected those who were with Saul to some degree. Notice, too, that in Acts Saul's name does not change at the point of his conversion. Rather, when he first begins to be the missionary to the Gentiles he adopts the Greek (or Roman) name Παῦλος (cf. Acts 13:9).[24] It would appear, especially in view of the way Acts ends, that Luke's interest in Paul is not purely personal, but is

---

24. This story may suggest that Saul took the name in order to aid in the process of converting another Paul who was a Gentile and a proconsul on Cyprus, Sergius Paulus; see Acts 13:7. Possibly Παῦλος should be seen as a nickname, meaning "the small one." There was also reason for the apostle not to continue to use the name Σαῦλος, for in Greek this word was used of the wanton style of walking of prostitutes. Cf. Leary, "Paul's Improper Name"; Hemer, "The Name of Paul." Perhaps the most plausible suggestion is that Παῦλος was one of the three proper names a Roman citizen would have. Wilson, *Paul*, p. 30, conjectures that Paul's Roman name was Gaius Julius Caesar on the basis of his family being one of those enfranchised in Tarsus by Julius Caesar or Augustus.

chiefly because Paul is part of and a vital player in the growing early Christian movement. He is not trying to present an encomium or even simply an *apologia* for Paul in Acts, and thus there is no good reason to think he has significantly recast the telling of the story of Paul's conversion. Maddox is right to stress that in view of the fact that Luke does not sharply distinguish the essential Christian preaching of Paul from that of Peter in regard to the crucial matters of grace and the acceptance of Gentiles, the primary importance of Paul for Luke "does not consist in a distinctive theology, it must consist in his historical function."[25] This emphasis is only what we would expect in a historical monograph, whose primary aim is not to do theology.

The differences in the three Acts accounts must be examined very carefully. We must realize that ancient historians were not nearly so concerned as we are today about minute details.[26] Often they were satisfied with general rather than punctilious accuracy so long as they presented the key points, thrust, and significance of a speech or event. It is thus wrong to press Luke to be precise at points where he intended only to give a summarized and generalized account. Luke, like Paul, exercised a certain literary freedom with his material, arranging it so as to get the desired point across. This is only what one would expect from people who grew up in an environment saturated with and enamored of rhetoric.

An example of Luke's literary freedom may be found in the Acts 26 account, where we have the interesting sentence not found in the other two accounts — "It hurts you to kick against the goads."[27] A goad was a wooden stick with metal spikes against which it was fruitless to kick since one would only hurt oneself. This expression was a *Greek* not Jewish idiom, and it meant "It is fruitless to struggle against God, or against one's destiny."[28] This proverbial saying was one that Agrippa or Festus would likely have understood and perhaps even have heard before (see Acts 26 on its origins), but it is hardly something one would expect to originate on the lips of Jesus in Aramaic. Paul or Luke inserts this line into the discourse to make clear that Jesus had

25. Maddox, *The Purpose of Luke-Acts,* p. 68.

26. See the collection of essays dealing with such matters which I edited entitled *History, Literature, and Society in the Book of Acts* (Cambridge: Cambridge University Press, 1996).

27. Some Western copyists added this interesting proverb, in some cases at Acts 9:4 and in some cases at 9:5, to assimilate this account to Acts 26:14. See Metzger, *Textual Commentary,* pp. 361-62. Had the phrase been original here, there is no reason why our earliest and best manuscripts should omit it. One must recognize that Luke has deliberately reserved some details for the later two accounts, with the second account being longer than the first, and the third longer than the second. This is just good narrative technique. See Hedrick, "Paul's Conversion/Call," pp. 415ff.

28. Wilson, *Paul,* p. 76, presents an excellent example of the idiom from Euripides, *The Bacchae.* This shows at least Luke's, if not Paul's, familiarity with Greek idioms.

312						ACTS

indicated to Paul that he was struggling against God by persecuting Christians, and indeed against his own destiny. This phrase, which Jesus surely did not use when he spoke to Saul originally, indicated to the audience that Paul was pursuing his present mission because God had mandated for him to do so.

Another piece of evidence of literary license is that when one compares Acts 22 and Acts 26 one notices that the commission that comes to Saul from Ananias's lips in Acts 22 comes directly from Jesus in Acts 26, where there is no mention of the intermediary Ananias. Thus we must conclude that in Acts 26 either Luke or Paul has telescoped the account. This should not trouble us since the commission that came to Saul was ultimately from Jesus, even if it did actually come *through* Ananias. Ananias could be left out of the account in Acts 26 since the crucial point was that Paul was authorized by God to do what he was doing. The differences between the three accounts on this matter can be accounted for in terms of Luke's (or Paul's?) editing of the account to suit the purpose and audience currently being addressed.

Another point of difference in the accounts is that we are told in Acts 26:14 that "we fell to the ground," but in Acts 9 and 22 only Saul falls to the ground (the others stand; cf. Acts 9:7). Again, Paul or Luke is simply generalizing because Saul was not alone in this encounter. The others also saw and heard something. It is in any case unlikely that Saul knew the position of his companions at this juncture since we are told he was blinded by the light! The point, then, of saying "we" was to indicate that this experience involved more than one person and was not simply the product of Saul's imagination.[29]

The most difficult difference to account for in these three narratives is what seems to be a flat contradiction between Acts 9:7 and Acts 22:9. The former says, "the men stood speechless hearing the voice but seeing no one," while the latter says, "the men saw the light but did not hear the voice of one speaking to me." Scholars have argued that here is clear evidence that Luke was not a careful editor of his material. There are, however, two other possible explanations.

In classical Greek the verb ακουω ("to hear") with the genitive normally means that someone has heard the sound of something or someone, while this same verb with the accusative refers to both hearing and understanding something. At several points we have seen Luke's tendencies to archaize or follow older styles, and this could be another one, even if he does not pursue this agenda consistently throughout.[30] If Luke was following the classical

---

29. It will be noted that when Luke recounts the resurrection appearances in Luke 24 and Acts 1 he stresses their objective nature, as he does here.

30. See pp. 115ff. above. My own impression of Luke's technique is that from time to time he shows some literary and rhetorical flourish, but that either due to a lack of final editing or due to other concerns he does not pursue such agendas in a thoroughgoing fashion. See Cadbury, *The Making of Luke-Acts*, pp. 213ff., on Luke's style. A good example of my point is that the style of Luke 1:1-4 is not maintained throughout the work.

practice here, then the meaning of Acts 9:7 would be that Saul's companions, like Saul, heard the sound of the voice communicating to Saul, while in Acts 22:9 the point would be that unlike Saul, the companions did not hear intelligible words so as to understand what the voice was actually saying to Saul. In Acts 9:7 the text says the companions saw *no one* while in Acts 22:9 there is a stress that these men saw the light that accompanied Saul's personal encounter with Jesus.[31]

R. Bratcher has objected to the idea that Luke may be following classical style here on the basis that elsewhere Luke doesn't observe the distinction between having the object in the genitive as opposed to the accusative with verbs such as αχουω (cf., e.g., the accusative in v. 4).[32] The problem is that Luke is sporadic in his classicizing tendencies. Bruce in his early work, following the suggestion of Chrysostom, argued that the voice the men heard was Saul's voice.[33] The problem with this suggestion, as Bruce himself later said, is that the definite article before "voice" in v. 7 surely points back to the "voice" of v. 4. Perhaps Polhill is most cogent at this point in noting that the distinction is made between a voice "which was speaking" (22:9), as opposed to 9:7, which can mean the hearing of a sound or noise.[34]

Thus we can explain the differences in the two accounts as follows: (1) only Saul had a personal encounter with Jesus involving seeing someone and hearing distinct words; (2) his companions saw and heard the phenomena that accompanied this encounter but had no such encounter themselves. Notice that Acts 22:9 does not say they did not hear the sound of the voice at all, but only that they did not hear the voice of the one speaking *to me*.

One more difference is of note. Acts 9 says nothing about Saul as a missionary to the Gentiles, while Acts 22 and 26 stress this point. This is likely because Luke did not need to mention this matter in Acts 9 as it would be evident in what followed, while in Acts 22 and 26 Paul did have to mention this to his audiences to justify what he had been doing. Each of the narratives and speeches is shaped to serve a different purpose, and this is the major reason for the variables in the accounts.

Note that in Luke's telling of Saul's story the conversion experience was not instantaneous. He was blinded for three days and did not regain sight, receive the Holy Spirit, or receive baptism washing away his sins until the third day after the Damascus road experience. Conversion even in the case of Saul

31. See *MHT I*, p. 66, and *MHT III*, p. 233, and contrast Moule *IB*, p. 36.
32. See Bratcher, "Αχουω in Acts 9.7 and 22.9."
33. But later seems to have changed his mind; cf. Bruce, *The Acts of the Apostles*, p. 236; Chrysostom, *Hom. on Acts* 19 and 47.
34. In other words, the distinction is made by means of the added qualifying participial phrase, not on the basis of the mere case of the object of the verb "to hear." See Polhill, *Acts*, p. 235 and n. 15.

is seen as an event which precipitates a process, but the process of conversion is not completed till Saul receives sight, Spirit, and baptism. Something ought to be said at this point about Paul's own report about this event.

The clearest statement we have from Paul about his own conversion and its immediate consequences is found in Gal. 1:11-23. Paul is quite adamant in saying that he did not receive his gospel through human beings, nor is it human in origin or the result of some human instruction he received. To the contrary Paul claims he received his gospel by revelation directly. It must be stressed that in this passage Paul is defending the source and content of his gospel, *not* his conversion to Christ, and this goes a long way toward explaining the differences in this narrative from the three Acts accounts. Various scholars have seen a notable contradiction between what Paul says here and what is said in Acts 9 and 22. But is it so?

In the first place, both in Paul, and certainly in Acts 26, it is crystal clear that Paul does not see commission, mission, and message as deriving from a human source. There is no Christian instruction of Saul prior to the Damascus road, and, furthermore, Ananias is not the ultimate source of Saul's commission and mission as Acts 26 makes abundantly clear. This is equally clear in Acts 9:15, and to a lesser but real degree in Acts 22:14.

I take it, however, that the real issue in Galatians is not Paul's Christianity or his commission to be some sort of missionary or just the source of the Pauline gospel, but the *content* of that gospel. Much hinges on what we make of the key phrase in Gal. 1:7 — "the gospel of Christ." Does it mean the gospel that comes from Christ as a source, or the gospel of which Christ is the content? In this same context in Gal. 1:16 we likely have a clue to Paul's meaning, namely, that he is talking about a revelation *about* the Son of God. This is likely the meaning in Gal. 1:7 as well. If so, then note that in Acts 9 and 22 Ananias does not teach Saul at all *about* Jesus Christ. Rather, in Acts 9 he tells him to arise, receive his sight, and be baptized, while in Acts 22 he tells him something about his commission. In any event, in Acts 22 we are probably to think of Ananias speaking a prophetic word, not offering mere human instruction or opinion. I must then conclude that what Paul means by "the gospel of Christ" is the distinctive and essential insights he received directly from Christ either during or as a result of reflecting on the Damascus road experience. Paul, according to Gal. 1:16, saw as the purpose of his conversion that he might become the missionary to the Gentiles. This is not surprising since he saw his own conversion as purely a matter of grace to a persecutor, and thus there was no reason why grace could not be offered to all without Mosaic preconditions. It is very plausible that Paul deduced much of the heart of his gospel from his conversion experience.[35]

35. See Kim, *The Origins of Paul's Gospel*, passim.

A. Segal has rightly stressed that we must look at what happened to Paul on the Damascus road as a conversion, involving a major transvaluation of values, and not merely a calling, though that is also entailed in Paul's conversion.[36] One must delicately balance the elements of continuity and discontinuity between the belief systems of Saul the Pharisee and Paul the Christian. As Segal notes, Paul's conversion did not lead him to repudiate Torah, only to claim that he had badly misunderstood its meaning while a Pharisee.[37] This is why he is still able to draw on the stories in the Hebrew Scriptures to present his own and others' current narratives of faith.

The language Paul uses about his own and other Christian conversions suggests that more emphasis must be placed on the elements of discontinuity with the past. As G. Lyons says, the "stark contrast between Paul the persecutor and Paul the persecuted preacher, between his 'formerly' and 'now,' is well attested throughout the Pauline corpus" (cf. Phil. 3:6; 1 Cor. 15:9, and the whole of Gal. 1:10–2:21).[38] This especially includes the way Paul used to evaluate Jesus, and the way he did so after his conversion. He used to know or at least view Jesus from a fallen human point of view, but he does so no longer (2 Cor. 5:16-17). Herein lay the most drastic of the transvaluation of values, which carried in its wake a change in Paul's view of numerous other things such as the nature of the Godhead, the Law, the basis of salvation for Gentiles as well as Jews, and a host of other matters. Bearing these things in mind, we are prepared to turn to the exegetical details of Acts 9.

Acts *9:1* begins with a remark about Saul's attitude toward the "disciples of the Lord." The text literally speaks of "breathing out threat and slaughter," which may be an example of hendiadys and so mean "threats of slaughter."[39] That Saul was interested in more than just threatening or intimidating Christians is clear not only from his approaching the high priest and his journeying to Damascus, but also from Acts 22:4 and 26:10. It is probable that Saul's own references to persecuting Christians does not indicate anything less than what we find in Acts.[40]

V. 2 refers to letters granted to Saul by the high priest, probably Caiaphas. These letters were written to the synagogues in Damascus and requested permission to take, bind, and extradite any Christians back to Jerusalem. Probably too much ink has been spilled on whether the high priest actually had such a right of

---

36. See Segal, *Paul the Convert*, pp. 117ff.

37. Ibid., p. 119.

38. Lyons, *Pauline Autobiography*, p. 146, see pp. 146-52.

39. Ἐμπνεω is used in a very figurative way and seems to mean something like "fume" or breath vigorously. See *New Docs*, 3 (1979), no. 50, p. 147.

40. It is perhaps also possible to envision some of what Paul had in mind by what he says he himself experienced in the synagogue when he witnessed about Jesus — namely, the thirty-nine lashes, which he endured five times by the late 50s and which could sometimes cause death. Cf. 2 Cor. 11:24.

extradition during this period. In the first place our text says nothing about a *legal right;* the impression left is that the high priest was providing letters *requesting permission* for such actions by Saul. But even if a right is in view here, it is possible that the material found in Josephus, *Ant.* 14.192-95 is of relevance. There we are told that Julius Caesar confirmed such rights and privileges to the Jewish people and the high priest in particular, *even though they were no longer a sovereign or independent state.* This privilege may have still existed in Saul's day.[41]

The phrase "the Way" occurs six times in Acts (9:2; 19:9, 23; 22:4; 24:14, 22), and it is worthy of note that the Qumran community also referred to itself using this phrase (cf. CD 20:18; and for the use of the phrase in the absolute, 1QS 9:17, 18; 10:21; and CD 1:13; 2:6).[42] Acts 22:4 and 24:14 taken together suggest that the phrase in Acts refers not only to a type of behavior but also to those who exhibit it (cf. 22:4), for we hear of the Christian "sect" (αιρεσις) known as the Way.[43] It seems clear from texts like Acts 16:7 and 18:26 that Luke means "the way of salvation" when he uses this phrase, and these soteriological overtones appear to mean that Luke's usage goes beyond the "two ways" discussion we find in early Jewish and Christian literature, which has more of a paraenetic focus (cf. *1 Enoch* 91:18; *2 Enoch* 30:15; *Did.* 1-6; *Barn.* 18-21).[44]

Damascus was an important city 135 miles north-northeast of Jerusalem. Lying on the main route from Egypt to Mesopotamia, it became a commercial center. Part of the league of cities known as the Decapolis (Pliny, *Nat. Hist.* 5.74), it had a considerable Jewish population (cf. Josephus, *War* 2.561). This city formed part of the Roman province of Syria from 64 B.C. on, but retained its municipal independence as part of the Decapolis.[45] There is perhaps incidental confirmation of Saul's conversion near or in this city in the reference to a "return" to Damascus in Gal. 1:17.[46]

V. 3 suggests that it was near Damascus that Saul was suddenly accosted from above. Light or lightning is a regular feature of theophanies in the Bible (cf. Exod. 19:6; 2 Sam. 22:15), but here we are talking about a Christophany.[47]

---

41. This is of more relevance than the earlier material found in 1 Macc. 15:21, where a Roman ambassador requests extradition of Ptolemy VII in 138 B.C. with the person in question to be handed over to the high priest. See the discussion in Bruce, *The Acts of the Apostles,* p. 233, and Marshall, *Acts,* p. 168.

42. On these parallels cf. Fitzmyer, "Jewish Christianity in Acts."

43. See Barrett, *Acts,* vol. 1, p. 448.

44. It would seem that Luke reflects the old analysis that early Christianity was more focused on theology, early Judaism more on praxis.

45. See Bruce, *The Acts of the Apostles,* p. 233, and the discussion of Syria in general by Tracy, "Syria."

46. On Damascus's relationship to the Nabatean kingdom and Aretas IV, see pp. 321ff. below.

47. The similarities between this Christophany and theophanies surely suggest that Luke is comfortable using the language of divinity of the exalted Christ.

Saul's response to this assault is that he fell to the ground and heard a voice saying, according to *v. 4,* "Saul, Saul, why are you persecuting me?"[48] This suggests a connection between the exalted Christ and his followers on earth of a sort similar to that spoken of in the gospel (cf. Matt. 25:40). More to the point, this seems very similar to Paul's own description of sharing in or filling up the sufferings of Christ (cf. Rom. 8:17; Phil. 3:10).

Saul's response in *v. 5* can be read one of three ways: (1) κυριε could be the polite term of respect, equivalent to our "sir"; in favor of this is that Saul does not know whom he is addressing; (2) κυριε could have overtones of divinity or at least a supernatural being (whom Saul addresses as lord), but Saul simply does not know who it is; (3) κυριε could mean Lord, in the Christian sense, in which case it is anachronistic at this point since Saul doesn't yet really know the identity of the one who has accosted him. Against this last rendering is the fact that elsewhere Luke is quite careful in how he uses the term "Lord" in the dialogue portions of his two-volume work, avoiding anachronism.[49] Either (1) or (2) is possible, but since Saul knows he is involved in some sort of divine-human encounter (2) is perhaps most likely.[50]

Vv. 5b-6 provide the direct response, which indicates that the speaker is Jesus, who commands Saul to get up and continue on his journey into Damascus, where he will be told what to do. *V. 7* is added to make clear that this was an objective experience. Those traveling with Saul knew something significant was happening, for they remained speechless, hearing the sound of the voice but seeing no one. *Vv. 8-9* indicate Saul arose from the ground, and at this point he also saw no one, because he had been blinded by the light. He was led into Damascus by the hand, and for three days he neither ate nor drank.

At *v. 10* the second section of this narrative begins with the introduction of Ananias, a "disciple" who lived in Damascus. The term μαθητης is regularly used in Acts to refer to a Christian (cf. 5:1; 8:9; 9:1, 10; 16:1), but it seems likely that Luke also uses the term of the followers of John the Baptist in Acts as he had in the Gospel (19:1; cf. Luke 5:33; 7:18).[51] In this case it is clear

---

48. There is deliberate irony here. Saul has just been flattened by one who accuses the prone Pharisee of persecution. The form of the name here is the Hebraic Σαουλ, which is appropriate in view of the fact that Luke tells us that Jesus spoke in Aramaic or Hebrew (cf. 26:14). "This spelling is limited . . . to passages where he is directly addressed in the Semitic language" (Cadbury, *The Making of Luke-Acts,* p. 226). Luke is quite style conscious, and, as Cadbury notes (p. 224), as the narrative of Acts moves away from a Semitic environment and toward a more Greco-Roman one, the style becomes progressively more secular. Such style consciousness has as its aim an attempt to lend an air of authenticity to the historical narrative, and reflects Luke's rhetorical concerns.

49. See the excursus, pp. 147ff. above.

50. See Johnson, *Acts,* p. 163.

51. On this see pp. 569ff. below.

enough that Ananias is a Christian disciple, and apparently one who has always lived in Damascus, for he has only heard about Saul's persecuting of Christians in Jerusalem (v. 13). We do not know how Ananias first heard about Jesus Christ, but he is probably not one of those who fled from Jerusalem because of persecution.

Like Saul, Ananias has an encounter with the Lord Jesus through a vision (εν οραματι), in which Jesus calls him by name and, unlike Saul, he knows who is speaking so he responds like a true prophet of God — "Here I am, Lord" (v. 10). Like Saul, Ananias is told to get up and go somewhere, in this case to a street called Straight, which can still be seen today and is known as Darb el-Mostakim.[52] Ananias is directed to the house of a man named Judas. He is to look for "a man of Tarsus named Saul." This is the first mention in Acts about Saul's hometown, something that is not directly mentioned in Paul's letters. The narrative becomes intricate at *vv. 11-12* because we hear of a double vision. While Ananias is having a vision about Saul, Saul is having a vision about Ananias coming to him!

As Hedrick points out, the function of Ananias's coming and laying on of hands is that Saul may be cured of his blindness. In other words, a miracle narrative is part of this whole story. The point of all the visions and the miracle is to make clear that God is in control of and directing all these events so that Saul will undertake certain tasks God has in mind.[53]

The structure of the story here finds a counterpart in Acts 10, where Peter and Cornelius both have visions, and Peter objects. *V. 13* reflects Ananias's reluctance to do as the Lord instructs him, for he has heard about the evil Saul has done against the "saints" in Jerusalem. The term αγιος is only rarely used by Luke of Christians in Acts (cf. 9:32, 41 and 26:10), and it is possible that the term refers specifically to Jewish Christians, in particular Jewish Christians (originally) from Jerusalem, which is the way Paul uses the term in several of his letters (cf. Rom. 15:26; 1 Cor. 16:1; 2 Cor. 8:4, and possibly in Eph. 1:1; 2:19 of Jewish Christians in general).[54] Ananias's apprehensions are said in *v. 14* to be at least partially based on the fact that the chief priests[55] had authorized Saul to bind all who invoke Jesus' name.

---

52. Its line has been somewhat changed since Ananias's day.

53. Hedrick, "Paul's Conversion/Call," pp. 415ff. The theory, however, that the story began as a miracle story and later became an embellished Paul legend is unnecessary, and does not make sense of what precedes and follows the few verses about Saul's healing through the hands of Ananias.

54. See Barrett, *Acts,* vol. 1, p. 455.

55. The plural here may reflect the high priest and his council, or Luke may be thinking of the fact that Caiaphas was part of a family of priests that reigned throughout the period. Cf. a similar ambiguity in John 18:13, 14, 19, and 24. Was Annas still a force when Saul was a persecutor in the mid-30s?

V. 15 is of note, not least because Ananias is apparently told before Saul what Saul's future holds. He is to be God's instrument of election (σκευος εκλογης) "to bring my name before Gentiles and kings and before the people of Israel."[56] The order of this list is odd but no doubt intentional, and it anticipates what is said to Saul directly in Acts 22:15 and 26:16-18. By this remark, Luke indicates the comprehensive scope of Saul's commission, involving as it does both Gentiles and Jews, the fact that his especial focus will be on Gentiles, and that he will be testifying before authorities as well (cf. 25:23ff.; 27:24). As Tannehill points out, there are not only close parallels between this statement about Saul's commission and what is said in Acts 22 and 26, but also one must compare Paul's own statement about his mission in 13:46-47 and in 20:18-35. These five different texts include several repeated elements: (1) Paul was chosen by the Lord; (2) Paul is sent as a witness to both Jews and Gentiles; (3) Paul's mission will encounter rejection and require suffering; (4) Paul will bring light; (5) Paul will preach repentance; (6) Paul's witness will be based on his Damascus road experience — what he has seen and heard.[57] "Thus the one who is called to be a light of the nations and to open the eyes of Jews and Gentiles has encountered the Messiah in light and is himself a healed blind man, forced by the Messiah's light to recognize his own blindness and to receive his sight through him."[58]

V. 16 indicates that the Lord will reveal to Saul how much the one who caused Christian suffering will endure as a suffering Christian. Ananias does as he is told and even calls Saul "brother" (cf. 1:15) when he lays hands on him. Ananias says he has come so that Saul may both receive his sight and be filled with the Holy Spirit, hence receiving his second or spiritual sight. V. 18 says that immediately something like flakes or scales fell from his eyes,[59] and his sight was restored. We are not told that Saul received the Spirit,[60] but we are told in v. 19a that he was baptized,[61] presumably by Ananias, and that he regained his strength after he took some food. At this point the crucial initial

---

56. This language is used elsewhere of both vessels of wrath and vessels of mercy in Rom. 9:22f. and thus does not inherently convey the notion of the vessel's predestined salvation.

57. See Tannehill, *Narrative Unity of Luke-Acts*, 2:119-20.

58. Ibid., p. 121. Cf. Gaventa, *From Darkness to Light*, pp. 62, 85.

59. The term λεπις is used by medical writers (cf. Galen in *CMG* V,4,1,1, p. 77, 3), but Luke is using only an analogy here, "something like scales/flakes." The use of the term is, however, consistent with the view that Luke was a physician who knew the technical language.

60. This lack of presentation of visible or audible evidence of the reception of the Spirit by Saul is rather surprising in view of the importance of this story for Luke, and in view of the way the conversion of Cornelius is recounted in Acts 10.

61. Cf. 22:16, where the middle βαπτισαι is used, but it is hard to tell whether it is a true middle ("he baptized himself") or not. See Moule, *IB*, p. 26.

transformation of Saul from a persecuting Pharisaic Jew to a zealous missionary for Christ is complete.[62]

B. Saul's Early Efforts (9:19b-31)

Acts 9:19b-30 presents us with Luke's succinct remarks about the earliest stages
of Saul's missionary career, followed by another summary statement in 9:31.[63]
The latter is related to what precedes it by the fact that one of the contributing
causes of the "peace" that descended upon the church in various parts of the
Holy Land was first the conversion of Saul, who had spearheaded the persecution of the church, and secondly the removal of the always controversial Saul
from the premises of the Holy Land. As B. R. Gaventa points out, Saul is
portrayed as an overthrown enemy in the conversion accounts, a portrayal in
part based on the fact that even some of his newfound Christian friends appear
to have had certain suspicions about Saul, perhaps due to the suddenness of
his volte-face (cf. Galatians 1–2).[64]

It is also in order to note that there are similarities between Acts
9:20-35 and Luke 4:16-30: (1) both Jesus and Paul begin their ministries by
entering a synagogue and delivering a salvation message; (2) the audiences
react in shock or astonishment in view of the message delivered; (3) the
audiences ask in the one case if this is not Jesus the son of Joseph and in
the other case if this is not the same man who had opposed Christianity
violently; (4) both Jesus and Paul escape a rather violent response to their
messages.[65]

Vv. 23-30 provide us with one of the rare but helpful instances of a close
correspondence between Paul's own reflections on his career (found in 2 Cor.
11:32-33 and Galatians 1–2) and the book of Acts. One must recognize, however, that there are significant similarities as well as differences between the
Pauline and Lukan accounts of these events (see below), in part caused by the
different rhetorical purposes and functions of Paul's remarks as opposed to
those of Luke's account.[66] The differences in the accounts suggest that Luke is

---

62. Hengel, *Paul*, pp. 38-43, is right that we have no hint in Luke's narrative of any
psychological preparation for his conversion. Contrast Wilson, *Paul*, p. 60.

63. On the general function of these sorts of statements see the excursus above, pp.
167ff.

64. See Gaventa, "The Overthrown Enemy."

65. Here I am following Esler, *Community and Gospel*, p. 235.

66. Townsend, "Acts 9.1-29 and Early Church Tradition," is right to take the rhetorical
function of the material in Galatians into account, but unfortunately he seems to think
that Luke's account of Saul's conversion and its sequel is indebted to Paul's opponents

not slavishly copying material out of Paul's letters,[67] but rather is relying on a different source for this information, perhaps Paul himself.[68] Yet clearly Luke is also editing his Pauline source in order to focus on the fact that the Jews were the primary ongoing source of Paul's difficulties in ministry (cf., e.g., 20:19).

The narrative in *vv. 19-20* suggests that in a very short period of time, after a few days with the disciples in Damascus, Saul began to proclaim his new faith in Jesus in the synagogues of that city. There is nothing improbable about this, even though Paul does not mention such activities in Gal. 1:17.[69] There is the hint in Gal. 1:17 that Paul *had been* in Damascus before going to Arabia, for he speaks of "again returning (παλιν υπεστρεψα) unto Damascus." It is this sort of incidental correspondence that mostly characterizes the Lukan and Pauline accounts. One may also wonder about the fact that only in Acts 9:20 does Luke really speak about the proclamation of Jesus as the Son of God by Paul or other early Christian proclaimers,[70] and this is the very term or title Paul himself uses to describe his early encounter with and faith in Jesus (cf. Gal. 1:16; 2:20) and his call (cf. Rom. 1:1-4). This may suggest that Luke had heard Paul recount the story not only of his conversion but also of the events that immediately followed it, or at least he knew the form Paul's early proclamation took.[71] Another incidental correspondence comes in the fact

---

rather than Paul. This hardly explains why Luke's portrayal of Paul is so sympathetic here and elsewhere in Acts.

67. See Johnson, *Acts*, p. 172.

68. Particularly telling is the fact that Luke says nothing about Arabia or about a threat originating with King Aretas. Had Luke been composing at the very end of the first century or in the second century when various of Paul's letters, particularly the capital Paulines, seem to have been rather widely known in the church (cf. 2 Pet. 3:16), it seems likely his account would look rather different than it does. The difficulties of elaborate source theories, based on the assumption that Luke was not a companion of Paul but rather at least a third-generation Christian, are shown by the discussions of Lüdemann, *Early Christianity*, pp. 116-20, and Barrett, *Acts*, vol. 1, pp. 460-65. Perhaps the most telling criticism of all such long-chain theories is that there is nothing like a consensus among scholars about these matters, and even those who have devoted a good deal of their careers to deciphering Luke's sources end with very tentative conclusions. Cf., e.g., Dupont, *The Sources of Acts*, pp. 166-68.

69. The Greek of Gal. 1:17 does not require that we assume that Paul is saying that he went away into Arabia immediately after his conversion (despite the NRSV's insertion of "at once" here).

70. The possible example in Acts 8:37 is textually suspect. See Johnson, *Acts*, p. 171, but cf. 13:33 where Ps. 2:7 is quoted.

71. There was probably neither a need nor a purpose for Luke to speak about the time in Arabia since it does not seem to have involved successful missionary ventures. That this time did involve missionary ventures is perhaps suggested by the fact that Aretas's ethnarch was after Saul for some reason (see below).

that in *v. 21* Luke quotes Saul's hearers as describing his former persecuting activity as "causing havoc" (πορθησας) among the Christians in Jerusalem, the very term Paul himself uses to describe his persecuting activities there in Gal. 1:13 and 23. What makes this especially striking is that this term does not occur elsewhere in the New Testament.

The overall impression left by *vv. 21-22* is that the Jews of Damascus are dumbfounded by the transformation of the persecutor of Christians into the apologete for Christ who grows in power and persuasiveness, "proving that Jesus was the messiah." If first impressions are important, then the point of vv. 21-22 is to indicate that Paul was an effective rhetor or apologete. We already here see the pattern Luke uses throughout Acts — Paul, even as late as Acts 28:17-29, preaches first to the Jews and then turns to Gentiles when rejected by his ethnic kin.[72]

Luke does not tell us how much time elapsed between the time of Saul's preaching and his escape from Damascus in a basket. The point of the introductory phrase in *v. 23*, "when sufficient days were fulfilled," is to indicate that a specific span of time, apparently considerable, had been completed. More to the point it is an oblique way of indicating that Saul's life was in the control of God, who brings things to fruition or closure according to the divine plan.[73] There is nothing here that rules out a considerable period of time elapsing between when Saul was first in Damascus and when he escaped by means of a basket.[74] Indeed, if we are to believe *v. 25*, enough time had elapsed for Saul to have gained a following, for this verse speaks of "his disciples" taking him and helping him escape.[75] We are

72. See Barrett, *Acts*, vol. 1, pp. 464-65. It is worth noting that Paul himself suggests that the gospel is for the Jews first in Rom. 1:16. Johnson, *Acts*, p. 171, rightly notes that this is the first place that Luke really uses the term Ἰουδαῖος to indicate a group entirely separate from the Christians. This is perhaps a harbinger of things to come in Acts, based on the historical fact that it was probably Paul's missionary work more than that of any other one person that forced the issue of the relationship of the followers of Christ to non-Christian Jews. For Luke, writing in the 70s or early 80s, the "Jews" are distinguishable from the followers of "the Way."

73. On the importance of God's plan to Luke, see Squires, *Plan of God in Luke-Acts*, passim, and pp. 176ff. above.

74. Luke uses σπυρις, a larger wicker basket, while 2 Cor. 11:33 speaks of a σαργανη, which could refer to a woven bag but probably means a flexible basket. But see Polhill, *Acts*, p. 241 n. 38. On the comparison of this narrative with the material in 2 Corinthians 11 and the historical problems involved, see Harding, "On the Historicity of Acts." Harding believes Luke's ascription of hostility to the Jews reflects his anti-Jewish tendency. I would demur, not least because even in Acts 28 Luke is still concerned to show Jews responding positively to the gospel.

75. It is true enough that Luke does not usually speak of disciples of someone other than Jesus, but probably Acts 19:1 refers to some of the Baptist's disciples or followers. Clearly enough, "his disciples" is the more difficult reading here, and it should probably

told by Luke that this dramatic means of escape was necessary because of a plot of the Jews to kill Saul. This same language is used again in Acts 20:3, 19 and 23:30 to refer to similar plots by Jews elsewhere against Saul. Lest we accuse Luke of anti-Semitic polemics here, it is well to keep in mind that Paul himself suggests that he was at various times in danger from his own people and at least five times before he wrote 2 Corinthians he had been beaten by them (cf. 2 Cor. 11:24, 26).

Something needs to be said at this juncture about Paul's "Arabian nights" (and days) and the absence of any reference to this episode in Acts, even though Paul suggests it involved a considerable period of time. Strictly speaking, what the Greek of Gal. 1:17-18 suggests is that Paul's time in Damascus after his conversion *and* in Arabia took up at least portions of three years, after which time he finally went up to Jerusalem.[76] Luke, operating as a (salvation) historian whose major interest is in the events that caused the spread of the good news around the Mediterranean crescent from Jerusalem to Rome, was under no obligation to include episodes that did not contribute significantly to the growth of the church.[77] Both Luke and Paul omit any discussion of the some ten years during which Paul was in Cilicia (including Tarsus) and Syria. They both present very selective accounts.[78]

We learn something of the timing of the Damascus basket incident from the reference in 2 Corinthians 11 that this took place while Aretas (IV) was ruling the Nabatean kingdom, and had at least designs on Damascus if not clear control of it. The Arabia in question is surely Syrian Arabia, and in particular the Nabatean kingdom.[79] The Aretas in question died not later than A.D. 40 and probably in 39.[80] It is possible that either at the end of the reign

---

be accepted, though some minor witnesses have other readings trying to alleviate the perceived difficulty. But see Metzger, *Textual Commentary,* p. 366. Paul is perhaps being portrayed here as a teacher as well as a persuasive orator and apologete.

76. Notice that the reference to going up to Jerusalem once three years had elapsed comes *after* the reference to returning to Damascus. This could mean that Paul was in Damascus a considerable part of the three years.

77. Here as elsewhere Luke operates as a Hellenistic historian, not as a biographer. He is interested in significant deeds that affected the flow of history, not in biographical vignettes, however revealing of an important person's character, if they are not of historical import. Paul, on the other hand, is composing a rhetorical and polemical piece, a fool's discourse meant to shame his Corinthians into reevaluating what really amounted to power and weakness and being in touch with God. See my discussion in *Conflict and Community in Corinth,* pp. 442-64.

78. See Polhill, *Acts,* p. 244. Only the account in 2 Cor. 12:2-9 probably involves an event during this period of ten years about which Paul is otherwise totally silent.

79. The Roman province of Arabia doesn't come into existence until A.D. 106. On the whole subject of Roman Arabia, cf. Bowersock, *Roman Arabia.*

80. See ibid., p. 68.

of Tiberius or the beginning of the reign of Gaius Caligula, Aretas had re-claimed Damascus as part of the Nabatean kingdom.[81]

During the Empire, interregnums and times when power changed hands, or was about to, were also notorious for being times when lesser rulers espe-cially in the East took advantage of the lack of firm control from Rome. It is thus possible that during the period of about A.D. 37-39 Aretas was in control of Damascus by means of his viceroy. The problem with this theory is twofold: (1) the basic meaning of εθναρχης is one who is the head of a particular ethnic group, not a governor of a city,[82] (2) Paul may be suggesting that the ethnarch was keeping a watch on the city from the outside. It is probably correct to conclude from the account in 2 Corinthians 11 that Paul had raised the ire of Aretas because of his evangelizing activities in Arabia, perhaps even in its major city, Petra. More importantly, as J. Murphy-O'Connor has noted, Paul's time in Arabia probably reveals his prompt response to the commission to preach the gospel among the pagans (cf. Gal. 1:16).[83] We may date this occurrence no later than A.D. 39, and more likely about A.D. 37.[84] In any case, both Luke and Paul agree that Paul's life was in jeopardy and a quick escape was required.

Luke and Paul agree that the sequel to Paul's time in Damascus was a trip to Jerusalem. It must be admitted that the material in *vv. 26-30* is couched in rather different terms from what we find in Gal. 1:18-24. According to Luke, Barnabas is with Paul on both of his first two journeys to Jerusalem after conversion (cf. 9:27 to 11:30), and Luke indicates that both visits involved encounters with church leaders in Jerusalem (9:27 apostles, 11:30 elders). Paul also mentions meetings with Jerusalem leaders on the first two journeys, but Barnabas is said to be involved only during the second visit (cf. Gal. 1:18–2:1).[85]

---

81. The absence of any coins of Gaius in Damascus might point in this direction. See Barrett, *Acts*, vol. 1, p. 466.

82. See Lüdemann, *Early Christianity*, p. 119. See the inscription *IGRR* 3.1247 and its discussion by Hemer, *Book of Acts*, p. 215, who points out that the term in the inscription refers to an ethnic clan leader or chieftain.

83. Murphy-O'Connor, "Paul in Arabia." As Murphy-O'Connor suggests, Aretas would be quite suspicious of Jews preaching some form of biblical message in his territory, in view of his stormy relationship with Jews and their rulers (in particular the Herods) in the past.

84. See the discussion above, pp. 77ff.

85. It must be remembered, however, that Paul is using his best rhetorical skills to do damage control when he writes Galatians. In particular he is trying to establish that his authority as an apostle comes to him from Christ, not the Jerusalem authorities, and his authenticity is attested by his successful missionary work among the Galatians and others, an authenticity recognized but not bestowed by the Jerusalem authorities. It would not have been rhetorically helpful to mention a mediatorial role of Barnabas during the first visit to Jerusalem, for this would have suggested Paul was a lesser figure than either Barnabas or the Jerusalem apostles. In other words, there were good reasons for Paul to be silent at this point about this sort of thing if he wanted to establish his own credentials and independence. See Marshall, *Acts*, p. 175.

It must also be noted that Gal. 1:18 does not say that Paul stayed in Jerusalem for only fifteen days during his first visit as a Christian there, but that he visited with Peter for that period of time during his first visit, and that he did not see any other apostle except James, Jesus' brother.

No doubt Luke is generalizing somewhat when he says in *v. 27* that Barnabas took Paul to the apostles. Gal. 1:21 and Acts *9:30* appear to be two different ways of speaking of the same thing; the former refers to Paul going off to the regions of Syria and Cilicia once he left Jerusalem, while the latter says he was sent off by Christians from Caesarea Maritima to Tarsus, his birthplace and the chief city of Cilicia in the united Roman province of Syria and Cilicia.[86] Furthermore, the impression left by both Gal. 1:23 and Acts 9:26 is that the Jerusalem disciples were afraid of and amazed about Paul. It appears, then, that Luke and Paul are both discussing the same visit to Jerusalem — Paul's first Christian one.

This leaves us with the difficulties of *vv. 27-29* when we compare them with Gal. 1:22-23. The silence of Paul about Barnabas can be explained (see above). What about the fact that Paul says he was unknown by face to the churches of Judea, whereas Acts speaks of Paul going in and out among the churches in Jerusalem? On closer inspection, what Luke says is that Paul returned to Jerusalem and attempted to join the Christian disciples there, but they were afraid of him, doubting he was a Christian, *and* that Paul was speaking and arguing in the name of the Lord with the "Hellenists,"[87] presumably in the synagogue of the Freedmen mentioned in Acts 6:9, which involved Greek-speaking Jews from Paul's native region of Cilicia.

Acts says nothing about Paul being involved in the churches of Judea outside Jerusalem. It is possible that Paul uses the term "Judea" in Gal. 1:22 to mean the churches in the region outside of Jerusalem. Or, more broadly, he is using the term for the whole Roman province. Paul does not say he saw no other Christian in Jerusalem besides Peter and James; rather, he says he saw no other apostle. He could hardly deny he was known by face by some Jerusalem Christians. Luke himself seems to recognize a distinction between the churches in Jerusalem and disciples elsewhere in Judea, or at least between Jerusalem and Judea in general (see 8:1; 9:31; cf. 2:9 to 2:5).[88]

---

86. See Bruce, *The Acts of the Apostles,* p. 244.

87. On whom see the excursus, pp. 240ff. above.

88. J. B. Lightfoot, *Saint Paul's Epistle to the Galatians* (London: Macmillan, 1896), p. 92, long ago aptly summed up how the two accounts may be assessed: "To a majority therefore of Christians at Jerusalem he *might,* and to the churches of Judea at large he *must,* have been personally unknown. But though the two accounts are not contradictory, the impression left by St. Luke's narrative needs correcting by the more precise and authentic statement of St. Paul." This is only what one should expect since Luke, like Greek historians were wont to do, is summarizing and generalizing a great deal of data in a small space. It is worth adding, however, that Paul's rhetorical aims must also be taken into account.

In vv. 27-30 Barnabas begins to play the role of go-between or mediator between Paul and others, both Christian and non-Christian, that Luke suggests characterizes his ministry (cf. 11:25; 15:2). In short, he was living up to his nickname, Barnabas, given him by the Jerusalem apostles, which Luke says means "a son of encouragement" (4:36). V. 30 provides us with another example of a literary technique often noted in Acts. "Geographical locations are used to create links in the narrative lines that will be broken in by other material. One section of the story of Saul ends by placing him the location where the next section of his story will find him."[89] Luke leaves Paul in Tarsus in 9:30 only to pick up his story from that location again in 11:25, as he would also do with Philip (cf. 8:40 to 21:8). This however is more than just a literary technique. It reflects the modus operandi of a Hellenistic historian who is attempting to deal with his material κατα γενος, on the basis of regions and to some extent on the basis of ethnic groups who live in those regions or locales.[90]

V. 31 should be compared to the previous summary statement in 6:7. Such a comparison suggests that Luke is attempting to convey to Theophilus the sense of growth in numbers, the exemplary devotion of the disciples, the geographical spreading out of the church, and also the increase in danger as time went on. V. 31b speaks of living in the fear of the Lord and being encouraged or comforted by the Holy Spirit, two characteristics of a faithful church responding to a hostile environment (cf. 4:31; 5:13-14). The church is built up both internally and externally.[91]

Notice that Luke here uses the term εκκλησια in the singular to refer to the house churches in several regions (cf. also 20:28), though more often he uses the singular to refer to a congregation in one location. This also characterizes the way Paul uses the term εκκλησια, usually of a local assembly but occasionally of the church more broadly defined (cf. Gal. 1:22; 1 Thess. 2:14). Luke seems to know little of the church in Galilee beyond the fact of its existence.[92] I tend to agree with Barrett that it "seems more probable that there were few Christians in Galilee than that there were many and that the rest of Christendom engaged in a conspiracy of silence designed to conceal their existence. Christianity never became established in Galilee. . . . It is possible but not known that Christian missionaries had more success in the short period before A.D. 66."[93]

---

89. Tannehill, *Narrative Unity of Luke-Acts*, 2:124.

90. See pp. 32ff. on Ephorus and the κατα γενος approach.

91. See Barrett, *Acts*, vol. 1, p. 474, following Calvin.

92. See pp. 285ff. above.

93. Barrett, *Acts*, vol. 1, p. 473. Elaborate theories about Q communities or miracle and meal communities in Galilee that differed significantly from the Jerusalem church are largely based on ungrounded assumptions and silence. See my discussion of such theories in *JesusQuest*, chap. 2.

VIII. The Petrine Passages (Acts 9:32–11:18)

A. Peter the Healer (9:32-43)

The material in this subsection, while not an aside, is transitional, bringing the reader back to the subject of Peter's work in preparation for the major narrative in Acts about Peter and Cornelius. The emphasis here is not on *logos*, or evangelistic work, though the miracles have the effect of evangelism. Rather Luke is dwelling here on the rhetorically important matter of *pathos*, the deeper emotions. He seeks to arouse strong feelings in his listener not just for winsome characters like Tabitha but also for Peter himself. The miracle narratives themselves are for the most part told in traditional forms, already familiar to Theophilus from the first volume of this two-volume work. It is not accidental that the Aeneas story echoes Luke 5:17-26 and the Tabitha tale has an analogue in Luke 7:11-16, and like both those earlier narratives we find reminiscences of the stories about Elijah and Elisha (cf., e.g., 1 Kings 17:17-24; 2 Kings 4:32-37). Peter is being portrayed as standing in a long line of great prophetic healers from the northern part of the Holy Land.[1] It is to be noted, however, that both of these stories seem to focus on the benefits to believers of the miraculous work of a Christian leader (see below), unlike the earlier miracle tales in Acts, and thus they are not redundant.

It seems probable that these two stories should be treated as a pair in view of the following common features: (1) the persons being healed are both named, which is not generally characteristic of ancient (including Synoptic) miracle accounts; (2) the Christians in both stories are called saints (vv. 34,

---

1. On the Peter-Jesus parallels, see pp. 188ff. above and the discussions by Talbert in his *Literary Patterns*.

41), which is a rare designation for believers in Acts; (3) the command to rise is notable in both these narratives.[2] The first two of these features may also point to the use of a (Petrine) source here, as may the particular reference to Simon the tanner and his house in Joppa.[3]

Once it is recognized that these two narratives form a pair, then it is in order to note that Luke frequently deals in pairs, in particular in pairs of narratives one of which focuses on a man and the other on a woman.[4] H. Flender long ago rightly concluded that this deliberate literary pattern is Luke's way of suggesting that the good news and all the aspects of salvation, including healing, are intended equally for men and women. "They are equal in honor and grace; they are endowed with the same gifts and have the same responsibilities."[5] While it is true that Luke does not spend as much time on women in Acts as on men, he nonetheless provides us with a series of vignettes meant to show the various roles women assumed in the early church providing material aid, hosting the house church, teaching, and prophesying (cf. below). What is especially striking about Acts 9:32-43 is that more time, attention, and detail is given to the narrative about helping a woman disciple than is given to the story about Aeneas, suggesting that Luke wants to single this sort of thing out as especially noteworthy about early Christianity.

The story found in Acts 9:32-35 is succinct and capable of several interpretations, in particular, that Aeneas may or may not be a Christian, and that Peter may be telling him to get up and make his bed or to get up and prepare his couch (to recline for a meal). V. 32 may suggest that Peter is on some sort of inspection or visitation tour of the churches on the coastal plain, a tour of churches he apparently did not found.[6] If this is the correct interpretation of this verse, then it is in order to compare 8:14-15 where something similar is recounted about the Christian group started by Philip in Samaria. If we ask who did found these Christian groups in Lydda and Joppa, the most natural answer would seem to be Philip, since we have been told that he proceeded up the coastal plain from Azotus to Caesarea, passing through the region and proclaiming the good news in all the cities through which he passed (8:40).[7]

2. Here I follow Schneider, *Die Apostelgeschichte II*, p. 47, and Polhill, *Acts*, p. 246.

3. Even Lüdemann, *Early Christianity*, pp. 122-23, is not able to reduce these stories to pure Lukan creations, though he tries.

4. I have demonstrated this amply in *Women in the Earliest Churches*, pp. 129ff.

5. Flender, *St. Luke*, p. 10.

6. The Greek simply says that Peter was "passing through all (or the whole)," which could mean passing through all the cities in the region, or the whole region (see Bruce, *The Acts of the Apostles*, p. 246), or it could mean he was passing through all the congregations in the region (cf. the NRSV). See the discussion by Barrett, *Acts*, vol. 1, p. 479.

7. Cf. the use of similar language in 8:40 and 9:32, though the former verse is more explicit. Lydda and Joppa would have been just off the coastal road, east and west respectively, but not far off it.

An aqueduct built by Roman engineers and soldiers to bring water to Caesarea Maritima.

The construction of *v. 32b* is a bit odd — why does Luke speak of Peter *also* or *even* (και) going to the saints dwelling in Lydda? Perhaps he means to suggest that Peter did this in addition to evangelizing the non-Christians, or less likely the term αγιος could refer to non-Christian Jews. This last suggestion is unlikely in view of the fact that αγιος is used in 9:13 and 26:10 to refer to Christians.

V. 33 also has certain ambiguities — was Aeneas bedridden with paralysis for eight years or since he was eight years old? It could be read either way.[8] Aeneas is a familiar name, especially to anyone who knew something of Virgil's epic about those who survived the Trojan War (the *Aeneid*). While it could be argued that it was more likely than not to be the name of a Gentile, there is clear evidence that people in Palestine, perhaps even Hellenized Jews, bore this name.[9]

It is important to point out that these coastal towns such as Lydda and Joppa were much more open to Hellenistic and then Roman influence, being

8. These sorts of ambiguities could be taken as evidence not only that Luke was drawing on a source but that Acts did not undergo a final revision by Luke, hence the later efforts of the editors of the Western text, and of others. See pp. 66ff. above on this matter.

9. Cf. BAG, p. 23; and Barrett, *Acts,* vol. 1, p. 480.

near the coastal road, and in addition Lydda was one of the ten Toparchies or seats of local government.[10] Despite its close association with Judea, Joppa seems to have been in the main a Greek city during this era.[11] Caesarea Maritima, to which the narrative of Acts takes us next, was of course a thoroughly Hellenized (and Romanized) city, being the seat of Roman power and the site of the great construction projects of Herod the Great, including the famous theater on the sea for Greek drama and the great aqueduct. The point of mentioning all of this here is that Peter was traveling in increasingly more Hellenized territory, and so we should not be surprised that it was in this sort of locale that the question of Gentiles and the Christian faith seems to first have arisen in a significant way.

The narrative has been cut down to its bare bones. We are simply told in *v. 34* that Peter says, "Aeneas, Jesus Christ heals you. Get up and make your own bed (or prepare your table)." The verb in question literally means "spread for yourself,"[12] which may suggest preparation for a meal. In any case the point of the command and the explanation that Aeneas immediately got up are to indicate the completeness of the cure, just as the mention of the length of the illness is meant to create *pathos* in the audience. Notice that Peter makes quite clear that it is not he himself, but Jesus, who does the healing. This fact is indicated in another way in the following story, by mentioning Peter's prayer. This story involves a healing word being spoken, and apparently Peter took the initiative without any request from Aeneas, as is sometimes true of Jesus in the Gospels as well (cf. Luke 7:13-15; 13:12).

Like most Synoptic miracle stories, this narrative ends in *v. 35* with the response of the crowds — "All those who lived in Lydda and the (plain of) Sharon saw him and turned to the Lord." Here the use of πας, as elsewhere in Acts, should not be taken literally but is an example of rhetorical hyperbole, intended to indicate a large response and to impress the hearer.[13] Luke has no qualms about the idea that miracles can have an evangelistic value and effect.

The narrative in vv. 36-43 is considerably more substantial and impressive than the Aeneas story. As I have said elsewhere:

> In Acts 9.32-42 there is a clear crescendo in the miraculous — whereas Aeneas is healed of paralysis, Tabitha is raised from the dead (cf. v. 37 . . .). In other respects as well, the story and person of Tabitha are presented in a more positive light than the story and person of Aeneas. While it appears

10. See Pliny the Elder, *Natural History* 5.70; cf. Josephus, *Jewish Wars* 3.54-55.
11. So Schürer, *History of the Jewish People,* 2:114.
12. See Johnson, *Acts,* p. 177.
13. See pp. 105ff. above.

that Aeneas was a Christian (cf. 9.32), he is not specifically called a disciple as is Tabitha. Further, there is no real interest in Aeneas himself, only in the fact of his healing. By contrast, the story of Tabitha relates in a specific way what Tabitha did and why she was important to the community (cf. vv. 36, 39). There is an obvious interest in her person reflected in the mentioning of the details of the funeral preparations (vv. 37, 39). Finally, the story indicates that Peter recognized how important she was to the community, for he makes a point of presenting her to the disciples (v. 41), which did not happen in Aeneas' case. This story may be taken as an example of the Lukan interest in giving a woman more prominence than a man.[14]

Luke begins the narrative in *v. 36* by stressing that a woman in Joppa named Tabitha was a "female disciple."[15] The term μαθήτρια is found only here in the NT, but it is a good Hellenistic term used by Diogenes Laertius (*Lives of the Philos.* 4.2) of two students of Plato. In this case Luke is using the term to indicate not merely that Tabitha was a committed Christian but to suggest that she was a person of some status and importance in the Joppa Christian community. The name Tabitha is Aramaic, and because his audience does not know this language, Luke gives the Greek equivalent, Dorcas. In either language the term means "gazelle."[16] The text says literally that she was "full of good works and giving alms." Both of these descriptions suggest she was a woman of means, with the leisure and freedom to do good deeds for others. This comports with Luke's interest reflected elsewhere in Acts in showing that people of some means and status were becoming or were willing to become Christians (cf. 16:11-15; 17:4, 34), an understandable rhetorical tactic if Theophilus was also a person of some means and status.[17]

V. 37 makes clear that Peter would not be called upon merely to heal Tabitha. She became ill, died, and was washed and laid in an upper room. Several aspects of this verse are intriguing. Presumably Tabitha was laid out in her own home, and if so the mention of the upper room may be significant. First, it is reminiscent of the description of the meeting place of the early Jerusalem Christians described in Acts 1–3, but more to the point it may

14. Witherington, *Women in the Earliest Churches*, p. 150. It might be better to say that this reflects Luke's interest in highlighting the important roles various women played in early Christianity.

15. Joppa was a prosperous port city, controlled by the Romans since A.D. 6.

16. It was not uncommon in the Roman era to give women the names of female animals, especially slave women. It is possible that Tabitha was a freedwoman. Her ministry of charitable deeds suggests she was a person of some means and freedom. On the other hand, the name Dorcas is used in the LXX as a metaphor for the beloved in Song of Sol. 2:9; 8:14, and so the name may simply indicate Tabitha was of Jewish origins.

17. See pp. 64ff. above.

suggest not only that Tabitha had a house of some size but also perhaps that the church met in her house.[18] Washing the body was part of the normal Jewish process of preparing the body for burial (cf. *m. Shab.* 23:5), but it is striking that there is no mention of the anointing of the body. Is this because the task of preparing Tabitha for burial was left to poor widows who could afford no anointing oil? It was the normal procedure for women to prepare women's bodies for burial in Judaism.[19]

In *v. 38* we are told that the disciples in Joppa had heard Peter was in Lydda (we do not know how) and sent two messengers asking him to come without delay the ten miles to Joppa. It was a regular practice in early Judaism to send out emissaries in pairs, in part so that one could validate the testimony of the other (cf., e.g., Mark 6:7 and par. and Num. 35:30).[20] *V. 39* suggests that Peter was resting, but that he immediately got up and went with the messengers. Unlike the later incident involving Cornelius, Peter needed no persuading in this case because he was going to help someone who was already a Christian and presumably a Jewess. Peter arrived in the middle of the mourning period. It is not clear whether Luke means us to think that the widows were wearing the under and outer garments they showed to Peter or not, but in any case the point is that the clothing was part of Tabitha's ongoing ministry. It is thus quite possible that we are meant to see Tabitha as an important patroness or benefactor for the Christian community in Joppa.[21] If this is true, the loss of Tabitha, and perhaps her home and material support, could have been a serious blow not only to the widows but to the Joppa Christian community in general. The soliciting of Peter in regard to a dead woman suggests that the community knew about and believed in ongoing miracles of bringing the dead back to life continuing after the time of Jesus' ministry.

V. 40 indicates that Peter required privacy in order to pray and perhaps in order not to make a sensation out of bringing Tabitha back to life. First Peter knelt and prayed, and then he spoke to the corpse, saying, "Tabitha, arise." The close verbal resemblance between the first word of this command and that of Jesus to Jairus's daughter in its Markan and Aramaic form, "Talitha cumi" (Mark 5:41; contrast Luke 8:54), has caused various textual variants and errors at Mark 5:41 by scribes who confused Tabitha's name with the Aramaic word "talitha."[22] This is also no doubt due to the similarities between

---

18. The use of an upper room would likely provide a certain amount of privacy for early Christian meetings (cf. Acts 1:3, 13 and 20:8). See Barrett, *Acts,* vol. 1, p. 483.

19. See Keener, *Bible Background Commentary,* p. 349.

20. See the discussion in Jeremias, "Paarweise Sendung im NT."

21. See Keener, *Bible Background Commentary,* p. 349.

22. See Metzger, *Textual Commentary,* p. 87. It is worth noting that this confusion may have been caused at a very early stage in the tradition if Peter spoke to Tabitha in

the two stories. In fact both stories echo 2 Kings 4:33-36. Tabitha responds to the command by opening her eyes, sitting up, and seeing Peter, at which point Peter gives her a hand and helps her up. That Peter prayed before this miracle may distinguish Peter from Jesus, but in any case it indicates the source of the power. Lest there be any misunderstanding, *v. 41* indicates that Peter presented Tabitha alive to "the saints and the widows," which presumably means the Christians, even/especially including the widows.[23]

What may we say about this ministry and these widows? It seems clear that Tabitha had a rather specialized and ongoing ministry to these poor women. It is probably going too far, however, to suggest that Tabitha is part of or in charge of an *order* of widows. The widows are the recipients of aid in this story, not the bestowers of it, and we are not told Tabitha is a widow.[24] We will say more about Luke's views on women and ministry in the excursus below.

Despite Peter's best efforts to avoid sensationalism, the raising of Tabitha became known throughout Joppa, and many are said to have believed, according to *v. 42*. This verse would normally be the closure to a miracle story, but Luke has added *v. 43* to link the story with what follows in Acts 10. We are told that Peter remained for some days in Joppa with a certain Simon the tanner. This is interesting on several scores. Firstly, it may suggest the source of Luke's information about this story. Secondly, tanners, because of their contact with the hides of dead animals, were considered unclean by more scrupulous Jews. In fact the Mishnah and Talmud suggest they were despised because of their ongoing uncleanness caused by their trade, not to mention the bad smell associated with the tanning process (cf. *m. Ketub.* 7:10; *b. Pesaḥ* 65a; *Qidd.* 82b).[25] This is worth pointing out in view of the story that follows in Acts 10 about unclean human beings. Peter, not known for his consistency (cf. Galatians 2), had no problems of conscience (apparently) about staying with an unclean Jew, but balked at unclean Gentiles!

Aramaic, in which case the text of Acts 9:40 would have read "Tabitha cumi," which is even closer to Mark 5:41. It is also possible that Luke is deliberately intending to emphasize how Peter follows in the steps of his master.

23. The term αγιος here could mean the male believers, but probably has a more general significance. There is no implication that the widows are not Christians. See Barrett, *Acts*, vol. 1, p. 486.

24. But see my earlier discussion in *Women in the Earliest Churches*, p. 151 and the notes; and Barrett, *Acts*, vol. 1, pp. 484-85.

25. See on all of this Jeremias, *Jerusalem*, p. 310.

A Closer Look — Luke, Women, and Ministry

The discussion of Luke's views of women has developed considerably since the 1980s when I wrote my works on women in the NT. After early enthusiasm about Luke's enlightened view of women, more recent studies have been more negative. For example, J. Jervell has argued that Luke portrays women as living up to all the traditional expectations of withdrawn submission in the patriarchal structure of the culture, and that he has no particular interest in showing women as having more freedom or more prominent roles in early Christianity than in other religious settings.[26] Then, too, E. Schüssler Fiorenza has consistently maintained that Luke's presentation of women has contributed to a conspiracy of silence about prominent women in the early Christian movement, making them appear invisible or of little importance.[27] Most recently, I. Richter Reimer has argued that Luke has suppressed stories about women who were early Christian leaders, such as Mary Magdalene or Thecla.[28] There is, however, no evidence that Luke had any significant information about the existence of Galilean Christianity, and as for Thecla, she is not attested in any first-century sources, though she may have been a Christian within the Pauline circle.

In a somewhat more balanced and measured approach T. K. Seim has recently concluded that "Luke's version of the life of Jesus and of the first believers cannot be reduced either to a feminist treasure chamber or to a chamber of horrors for women's theology. It contains elements that bring joy to 'dignity studies' and other elements that give support to 'misery studies.' . . . The Lukan construction contains a double, mixed message."[29] Her basic contention is that while Luke leaves traces of evidence that women were important as followers of Jesus and in the early church, "Luke draws up quite strict boundaries for women's activity in relation to the Jewish and Greco-Roman public world. In this way he is in accord with the apologetic considerations that also colour the epistles." Luke's narrative in Acts is accused of "harboring an ironic dimension that reveals the reasons for the masculine preferences in Acts' presentation of the organization of the Christian group, of the public missionary activity and legal defence before the authorities."[30]

The problems with this analysis are several. (1) In the first place women are not restricted to domestic roles in Luke-Acts. Some, like Lydia or Priscilla, are businesswomen who are involved in the public sphere on a regular basis, and so the contention that Luke draws up strict boundaries between the two spheres will not work. (2) Seim admits that for Luke the "house" is a place of power and authority for the early Christian community, yet she fails adequately to take stock of the implications of this insight. In fact, for Luke the ultimate source of power, if we are talking about power that really matters in Luke's view, is the Holy Spirit, and Luke is quite clear in

26. See his collection of essays *The Unknown Paul,* pp. 146-57. This particular essay is entitled "The Daughters of Abraham: Women in Acts."
27. See, e.g., *In Memory of Her,* pp. 49f., 161, 167.
28. Reimer, *Women in the Acts,* p. 252.
29. Seim, *The Double Message,* p. 249.
30. Ibid., p. 259.

portraying women like Philip's daughters, and others, as being imbued with power and the authority that comes with it. (3) The public-private differentiation she makes also doesn't work because it does not adequately characterize the way the Greco-Roman world worked. There was a great deal more overlap than Seim allows, and this leads to our final point. (4) Seim's work is inadequately grounded in the sort of careful study of women and their roles in the Greco-Roman world which would have given a broader context for evaluating Luke's portrayal of women. Luke is judged by all-too-modern standards, with the assumption that modern assumptions about men and women are necessarily correct.

A good start has been made in evaluating the roles of Jewish women, especially in the Diaspora during the Empire, by B. J. Brooten and in some of the essays edited by A-J. Levine.[31] Some progress has also been made in evaluating the archaeological evidence of women playing important roles not only in the first century but up to A.D. 325 and beyond.[32] There is, however, a good deal more to be done.

Biblical scholars are, however, sorely in need of consulting the works of classicists and ancient historians on non-Jewish women in the Greco-Roman world if they wish to better understand Luke's approach.[33] For example, the extensive inscriptional evidence from the Empire of women as patronesses, benefactors, business owners, and the like is clear enough. This was not just true of Roman women either. The Hellenistic revolution had considerably changed the role of Greek women in various places, especially Macedonia and Asia Minor. A "number of inscriptions ranging in date from the first to the third centuries A.D. attest the prominent role played in the life of the cities of Asia Minor by wealthy Greek women, a number of whom held the Roman citizenship. These women held distinguished civic and federal magistracies and priesthoods, discharged liturgies which required lavish expenditure on various ceremonies, games, banquets and on civic buildings such as baths and colonnades. The offices which they held include federal positions such as Pontarch and Lyciarch, posts in the

31. Cf. Brooten, *Women Leaders*; A.-J. Levine, ed., *"Women like These": New Perspectives on Jewish Women in the Greco-Roman World* (Atlanta: Scholars Press, 1991). Probably the least helpful essay in this last volume is the one by Davies, "Women in the Third Gospel." Earlier Davies had been an advocate of Luke having an enlightened view of women, but now he has gone over to the negative side. Now he has been persuaded by R. Pervo (on whose theories, see pp. 376ff. below) that Acts is an historical novel akin to ancient romances, not an attempt to write history, and that it has close affinities with the later apocryphal Acts. As we shall see, there are at least three major problems with his approach. Unlike the later apocryphal Acts, Luke is not attempting to do hagiography; his interests are primarily historical, not biographical. His focus is on a movement, a historical development, not on a developing cult of human personalities. It is also anachronistic to try to read back into Luke some of the interests of the later apocryphal documents (such as extreme asceticism, the subordination of women, and the like; see my *Women in the Earliest Churches*, pp. 183-210 and the notes). Nor does Acts work as a romance — too many of the essential elements of ancient romances, such as male-female intrigues, are entirely absent from Acts.

32. Cf. Irvin, "Ministry of Women."

33. See the general bibliographic essay by Kraemer, "Women in the Religions," though this essay is somewhat dated now. More extensive is Cantarella's *Pandora's Daughters*.

imperial cult such as arch-priestess, and civic posts such as demiurge, agonothete, gymnasiarch, panegyriarch, archon . . . and even hipparchos, strategos, or dekaprotos. The extent of their services may be seen from the awards of statues, crowns, and titles such as 'patroness' or 'foundress' which they regularly received."[34] In such an environment it should not be a surprise to find a Priscilla or a Lydia, or "prominent women not a few," among early Christian converts who continued to exercise important roles both within and outside the church, especially as hostesses and patronesses but also as prophetesses, teachers, and the like.

One key to understanding how such roles for women were possible in an admittedly strongly patriarchal Mediterranean culture is understanding how status and *auctoritas* was achieved during the Empire. Increasingly money was able to create social status, standing, and civic positions for both women and men in the Roman world, as the older class distinctions and emphasis on inherited or birth rank and ethnic origins became less determinative.[35] Because the Roman world largely worked on the basis of the patronage system, anyone who had the money to be a patron and had not run afoul of the law could obtain considerable power and authority in the place where they lived.[36] It is by studying how the larger Roman world worked that one can better assess the roles of Christian women as portrayed by Luke. One final example on this score will have to suffice. As R. MacMullen long ago pointed out, women are rarely found in roles like that of a *grammateus,* which would require public speaking. They may be seen but are not to be heard.[37] Into this environment comes Christianity, which emphasizes the inspiration of the Spirit as determining who may speak and portrays both women and men as prophets and teachers.[38] This suggests that early Christianity was willing to swim against the current in these matters.

Another important area that has been inadequately explored by NT scholars is the structure of Roman and Greek families during the Empire, as a point of comparison for evaluating what Paul and Luke say about households, house churches, and household codes. For instance, I have discovered thus far no attempt in the NT community to take account of the essays edited by B. Rawson or the helpful study by K. R. Bradley

34. A. J. Marshall, "Roman Women in the Provinces," p. 123, citing the relevant inscriptions.

35. See the important discussions by Judge, *Rank and Status,* and by Garnsey, *Social Status and Legal Privilege.*

36. See Saller, *Personal Patronage under the Empire.*

37. Cf. MacMullen, "Women in Public," p. 216. Hortensia, who was known for her oratory, is the exception that proves the rule. Cf. also MacMullen's *Roman Social Relations.*

38. Another interesting piece of evidence that Christianity was at points going in the opposite direction from the larger culture is in regard to the mentioning of women by name. Schaps has shown ("The Women Least Mentioned") that women who were normally mentioned in public by name by orators in the Greco-Roman world were women of shady reputation, women connected with the speaker's opponent, and dead women. Reputable living women were left out of the conversation. By contrast Luke, Paul, and others proudly and willingly mention various women in positive ways in a variety of contexts, making known their important contributions to the movement. What some outsiders may have seen as shameful (a religion that gave "too much prominence" to women), early Christians were happy to speak of in public communications that were meant for oral proclamation.

A typical first-century windowless home in Judea. The home of the mother of John Mark was doubtless more substantial.

on the way the Greco-Roman family worked and was structured.[39] Roman homes, especially in their outermost rooms and shops, were largely open to the public, without a hard-and-fast distinction between the public and private sphere. Business was undertaken in the home (cf. the picture above of the home with a shop in the front). Furthermore, as Bradley points out, detailed social analysis of the lower classes of Roman families shows them to be "a social unit that was conceptually different from the pre-dominant modern form, one that could incorporate more extensive links to unrelated persons living in close physical proximity."[40] This sort of extended family structure, even involving nonrelated persons who are not household slaves raising children, is not unlike what we find in the early church communities where, for example, Tabitha is helping take care of unrelated widows. Perhaps there is something to be said for early Christianity adopting the lower-class family structure of the time for the family of faith, rather than following the upper-class patriarchal model where roles seem to have often been more rigidly defined and enforced. The above will have to suffice to indicate a few of the directions I think the study of women and their roles in the NT must go to have an adequate historical and social matrix out of which to evaluate what Luke, Paul, and others say about women.

My own view was and remains that Luke and Paul, like other early Christians, believed that their faith committed them to the reforming of some of the existing patriarchal structures so that women could play more vital and varied roles in the community of faith. The reform was to take place within the community. To this end, Luke presents five cameos of important Christian women and the variety of roles they assumed. In the mother of John Mark (Acts 12:12-17) and in Lydia (Acts 16:12-40) we see women assuming the role of "mother" or patroness and benefactor to the then fledgling Christian communities in Jerusalem and Philippi respectively. Like them, in the story of Tabitha (Acts 9), a notable female disciple with an ongoing ministry, we find someone providing material aid to a particularly needy group of early Christians — widows (cf. Acts 6). Luke's mention of Philip's daughters is brief (Acts 21:9), but when compared to Acts 2:17 it is sufficient to show that women played important roles of inspired proclaimers in the early church. Perhaps most important is Luke's reference to Priscilla as a teacher of a notable early Christian evangelist, Apollos, in Acts 18. Luke's portrayal of Priscilla is unreservedly positive, despite the later attempts of copyists to disguise her role (see below, pp. 562ff., on this text). We will examine these stories in more detail as the commentary goes on. Here it is sufficient to reiterate my earlier conclusions:

"By the very fact that Luke portrays women performing these various roles, he shows how the Gospel liberates and creates new possibilities for women. It is probably

---

39. See B. Rawson, ed., *The Family in Ancient Rome: New Perspectives* (London: Croom Helm, 1986). Especially the essays by Rawson and J. A. Crook on women's roles in the family are helpful, and a detailed, helpful bibliography on the Roman family is appended to this work. Cf. Bradley, *Discovering the Roman Family.* I am speaking of works on Acts at this point. The new study by Martin, *The Corinthian Body,* does interact with this sort of data to a significant degree, though I would disagree with various of his conclusions.

40. Bradley, *Discovering the Roman Family,* p. 95.

true that Luke is not interested in women and their roles for their own sake; rather
. . . [he stresses] how the Gospel manifested itself and progressed among the female
population in various parts of the Mediterranean world. In Jerusalem (1.14, 12.12-17),
in Joppa (9.36-42), in Philippi (16.11-15), in Corinth (18.1-3), in Ephesus (18.19-26),
in Thessalonica (17.4), in Beroea (17.12), and in Athens (17.34), we find women being
converted or serving the Christian community in roles that [in many cases] would not
have been available to them apart from that community. Thus Luke chronicles the
progress of women as part of the progress and effects of the Gospel. Though it is not
perhaps one of his major themes in Acts, nonetheless he takes care to reveal to his
audience that where the Gospel went, women, often prominent, were some of the first,
foremost, and most faithful converts to the Christian faith, and that their conversion
led to their assuming new roles in the service of the Gospel."[41] I still believe that the
reason Luke took the pains to portray women in these varieties of roles is because
when he wrote in the last quarter of the first century perhaps there was still much
resistance — perhaps increasing resistance — to such ideas, and so the case had to be
made in some detail.[42] In the end I quite agree with I. Richter Reimer that Luke's
portrait of early Christian women needs to be compared and supplemented by the
Pauline one to get a more full and accurate picture of the roles women assumed in
early Christianity.[43]

B. Peter's Vision and Missionary Ventures (10:1–11:18)

It is one of the purposes of Luke's historical writing in Acts to show how people
like Theophilus had and should come to be involved in a religious phenomenon which began as a Jewish messianic movement. This meant that some
considerable time had to be taken to show not only the geographical spread
of the movement but also its spread across ethnic barriers and social boundaries. We have seen that a κατα γενος approach to writing history was not
unprecedented in the realm of Hellenistic historiography (cf., e.g., Ephorus),
and Luke seems to a great extent to be following such an approach, dealing

41. Witherington, *Women in the Earliest Churches,* pp. 156-57.
42. Sometimes feminist analysis sheds a whole new light on a story. For example,
Reimer, *Women in the Acts,* pp. 23-24, argues that Sapphira's real sin is that she is complicit
in her husband's sin; she simply went along with the patriarchal authority structure, rather
than being an independent and self-determining person. The lying to the Holy Spirit is
a secondary sin caused by the larger one. In other words, Sapphira had a moral responsibility to resist or reject her husband's sinful suggestions, but instead she went along with
them. I think there is some truth in this analysis, but Luke's interpretation should not be
rejected. One also needs to ask whether the modern notion of being an independent,
self-determining person is an appropriate concept by which to evaluate either men or
women in antiquity.
43. Ibid., pp. 250-52.

with his subject matter both according to regions and according to ethnic types.[44]

Acts 10:1–11:18 must be seen, then, as another step along the way toward a more universal religion, universal both in its geographical and social scope. In this case Luke is presenting the all-important story of the transference of Gentile synagogue adherents into the Christian movement, and perhaps equally importantly those with some considerable social standing and status. Like the story of the Ethiopian eunuch, this narrative is about those at the fringes of Judaism who become Christians; also like that earlier story in Acts 8 it is about a person of some social status who made this change. T. M. Finn has stressed that early Christianity "spread in the packs of migrant Christians who traveled the great trade routes which laced the Empire. . . . [And] it spread upward in the Empire's system of social stratification on the backs of Christians who traveled the major avenues of social mobility, specifically, careers in the legions, in servile and liberal education, and in imperial civil service *(familia Caesaris)*."[45] Cornelius falls into the former of these sorts of careers which provided a certain upward social mobility.[46]

It is a measure of how important Luke thinks the Cornelius story is that he repeats various elements of it three and even four times between Acts 10 and Acts 15. Saul certainly could not be called your "typical" Jewish convert to Christianity, nor Cornelius your typical Gentile convert, yet Luke places especial stress on the changes that happen in their lives precisely because in Luke's view what happened to them served as the catalyst, humanly speaking, to change the character and general direction the early church would take thereafter. Saul's call to go to the Gentiles and Cornelius's response to the heavenly vision and reception of the Holy Spirit brought about a crisis, a crisis in some measure resolved at the "apostolic council" recorded in Acts 15. These events in Acts 9–10 are the harbingers of a turning point which is only fully reached when even the Jerusalem church endorses an outright mission to the Gentiles.

44. Plunkett, "Ethnocentricity," is right that this story is about Christianity's moving beyond the realm of ethnic Judaism, but wrong that Luke does not also understand and stress that this means moving beyond ethnocentric food laws which help reinforce the ethnic barriers. Unclean food and persons are related matters, and it is Luke's ultimate agenda to set the reader up for discovering that since God has declared all (ritually) clean (here in 10:15), that only moral purity is still an issue between Jews and Gentiles, as the decree in Acts 15 will make evident (see below).

45. Finn, "The God-Fearers Reconsidered," p. 75.

46. Luke is quite careful in the way he presents the progression of things. Cornelius is not a pagan, nor is this a story about a mission to those in Gentile lands. Cornelius is seen as significant in that his case raises the questions about preaching to pagans and going not only into their homes but into their lands. In other words, he is cast as a bridge figure standing at the boundary between Judaism and paganism, and living in a very Hellenized city full of Gentiles yet in the Holy Land.

It is of enormous importance to Luke to stress that the impetus to move in a Gentile direction comes directly from God, as is indicated by the visions and messengers divine and human who are employed to confront, convict, convince, and even convert the likes of Saul and Cornelius.[47] It may be of some relevance that we have evidence that claims were sometimes made in antiquity that certain associations or clubs were founded by means of a dream, vision, or oracle given by a god to a particular individual. The point of making such a claim is that the divine sanction for the association's founding would then be seen as beyond dispute. The vision has a similar initiatory and validating significance.[48] God's divine plan of universal salvation is being worked out, but it would be wrong to neglect the fact that humans must respond to it and carry out their part in the drama.[49] At this point it will be useful to address the vexed question of the historical likelihood of there even being God-fearers and of Luke's portrayal of them.

A Closer Look— Gentile God-fearers — The Case of Cornelius ———

Like so many other subjects that have to do with Acts, there has been no little amount of controversy about what Luke meant when he referred to people, such as Cornelius, as God-fearers or God-worshipers?[50] Is he using technical terminology or not? Was there really a special class of Gentile synagogue adherents separate from what we would call proselytes? Has Luke exaggerated the apparent prevalence of people like Cornelius and the importance of their involvement in the synagogues of the Diaspora and the Holy Land?[51] If we are to address any of these sorts of questions, we must take into account the larger semantic field in which the term "God-fearer" fits.

47. On the appropriateness of talking about conversion in these cases, see especially Segal, "Cost of Proselytism and Conversions," pp. 350ff.

48. See now Ascough, "Greco-Roman Associations."

49. On the divine plan see Squires, *Plan of God in Luke-Acts*, pp. 68ff. Tannehill, *Narrative Unity of Luke-Acts*, 2:128-32, is right to take Haenchen, *Acts*, pp. 362ff., to task for accusing Luke of virtually excluding human decision and response in the salvation drama. As Tannehill says, the visions and messages Peter and Cornelius receive are divine promptings — they are incomplete in themselves and require human reflection and action. The human action and response is not viewed as either automatic or coerced.

50. The literature on this subject is enormous. Still the best of the earlier discussions is Lake's "Proselytes and God-Fearers." Of recent discussions in commentaries one should especially consult Barrett, *Acts*, vol. 1, pp. 500-501; Bruce, *The Acts of the Apostles*, pp. 252-53. The flavor of the recent debate can be gotten by sampling the following articles: Krabel, "Disappearance of the 'God-Fearers'"; Wilcox, "The God-Fearers in Acts"; Finn, "The God-Fearers Reconsidered"; Overman, "The God-Fearers"; Williams, "Θεοσεβὴς γαρ ην."

51. Often overlooked is the fact that Luke suggests that there were such Gentiles as Cornelius not only in the Diaspora but in Israel as well.

It is necessary to start with the relevant data from the LXX. There are at least five important instances in the LXX where we hear about οι φοβουμενοι (2 Chron. 5:6; Pss. 115:9-11; 118:2-4; 135:19-20; Mal. 3:16). Even more striking is the fact that in the Psalms and Malachi references we have the phrase οι φοβουμενοι τον κυριον. In the Psalms texts it is possible but not probable that the reference is to non-Jews, while in the reference in Malachi the phrase seems to be used in a very general way to refer to those Jews who are pious, righteous, and loyal to the true God. Especially noteworthy is 2 Chron. 5:6, where the LXX differs from the Hebrew text in a crucial regard. The Hebrew text has no mention of "those fearing," but in the LXX not only are they mentioned but they seem to be distinguished from the Israelites, for the verse in question reads: πασα συναγωγη ᾽Ισραηλ και οι φοβουμενοι. As A. Overman says, these data alone are enough to show that Luke did not invent the phrase "those who fear the Lord" (or as in Acts, "God"). In fact a plausible explanation can be given for why he changed the term from "Lord" to "God" in the key phrase, namely, that for Luke Christ was the Lord.[52]

We must next consider the related term προσηλυτος. In the LXX the term is consistently used to render the Hebrew gēr, which means foreigner or alien. What is especially important is that in all the seventy-seven cases where the LXX renders gēr as προσηλυτος, always a non-Israelite is in view. When Israel is referred to as an alien in the Hebrew text, the LXX chooses the different term παροικος to render it. What all this means is that in the LXX προσηλυτος refers to the resident alien in the land, who might participate in Israelite worship (cf. Exod. 20:10; 23:12; Num. 15:13-16) but could not be called a "convert" in the later sense of one who wholeheartedly embraced Judaism and all its rituals, including circumcision. In Philo we find this same sort of use of προσηλυτος (Virt. 102-3; Quaestiones in Exod. 2.2). This warns us against reading back into the LXX or even the middle of the first century A.D. the later rabbinical definitions of a "proselyte."[53]

If we consider for a moment the two references to "proselytes" in Acts at 2:10 and 13:43 in light of the above evidence, it is worth pondering whether Luke really meant full-fledged "converts" in these two texts. Overman suggests that he did not since there would be a redundancy — a convert to Judaism is considered a full-fledged Jew and thus would not likely be distinguished from "Jews" as they are in these two texts. This in turn leads to the suggestion that the term may mean no more than "God-fearer" in these texts. There is room for hesitation on this matter, however, and if we were to find a threefold phrase "Jews, God-fearers, proselytes" in Acts, the hesitation might be fully justified. One could argue that Luke uses the term προσηλυτος in its later sense. There is not in Acts such a threefold phrase, and so we cannot rule out, especially in view of the obvious influence of the LXX on Luke, that he uses the term in the same way that the LXX does, to mean a non-Jew who is a sympathizer, even a participant in Jewish worship in various cases, but not someone bearing the full yoke of the Mosaic Law (but see below).

52. See Overman, "The God-Fearers," p. 21.
53. Lake, "Proselytes and God-Fearers," p. 83, warned against anachronism when one reads Acts, but he has often gone unheeded in the fifty years since he wrote his article.

Turning to the phrases σεβουμενοι τον θεον and φοβουμενοι τον θεον, Luke uses them five times each, but interestingly, as M. Wilcox stresses, he uses the latter exclusively prior to Acts 13:45-46 and the former thereafter.[54] This may well suggest the use of different sources,[55] but Wilcox's suggestion seems more plausible that the change is caused because in the earlier material the Jewish mission (and so more Jewish terminology) is uppermost, while after Acts 13:46 the mission is increasingly to Gentiles and so terminology more familiar to them appears.[56] Perhaps this is the place to stress that we do now have hard data in the form of an inscription from Aphrodisias which clearly distinguishes Jews (most of whom have Hebrew names) from οσοι Θεοσεβις (and those who are God-worshipers), none of whom have Hebrew names.[57] Equally important in the list on Face A of the stele, we have three people specifically listed as προσηλυτος (lines 13, 17, 22) and two more listed as Θεοσεβης (lines 19, 20). The problem of relating these data to Acts is that they appear to date from the third century A.D. — in short, from a time when the term προσηλυτος was clearly used by Jews and others of converts.[58] This evidence certainly shows that there were such people as "God-worshipers," surely referring to Gentile synagogue adherents. This is important because it provides independent corroboration that Luke was not making up the idea of such people, or of the terminology he chose to use of them. It should also be compared to the evidence in Juvenal (*Sat.* 14.96-106), where he satirizes "sabbath-fearing" *(metuens sabbata)* Romans who even keep the food laws (cf. also *CIL* 5.88 = *CIJ* 1.642). There is, furthermore, now the considerable evidence amassed by I. Levinskaya from the Bosphoran kingdom that shows the presence of not only numerous Jews there but also many Gentile God-fearers who participated in the Jewish communities.[59]

But what of Luke's actual use of the terminology — can we speak of technical terms? The answer to this must in all probability be no. For example, if we compare Acts 13:16 to 13:43 it would appear from this text that the term "proselyte" means the same things as the phrase "those who fear God." Both phrases refer to Gentiles who are Jewish sympathizers and synagogue attenders. "Proselyte" *may* be more specific (see Acts 6:5) in referring to a full-fledged convert, but we can't be sure Luke isn't simply equating proselytes with God-fearers. Indeed, on the face of it, it seems he is. Furthermore, it has even been suggested that in 13:26 Luke simply refers to Jews as "those who fear God,"[60]

54. Wilcox, "The God-Fearers in Acts," p. 118.

55. Something that would fit well with my suggestion that Luke relied on sources and information he gathered in Caesarea and Jerusalem on the third missionary journey for most of the material in Acts 1–13, but he relied on Paul for most of the material thereafter. See pp. 165ff. above.

56. This fits with the general trend in Acts which Cadbury long ago noted: that Acts moves from a more Semitic to a more Hellenized account, when one considers the vocabulary, syntax, and related matters.

57. See now Reynolds and Tannebaum, *Jews and Godfearers at Aphrodisias.*

58. See the discussion by Gempf in Appendix 2, "The God-Fearers," in Hemer, *Book of Acts,* pp. 444-47.

59. See Levinskaya, *Acts in Its Diaspora Setting,* especially the inscriptions in Appendix 3.

60. See, e.g., Cadbury, *Book of Acts in History,* p. 91.

but as Barrett points out, the whole phrase reads "those who fear God *among you*," which suggests converts, who are a full part of the Jewish community.[61]

How may we sum up these confusing data? Even though we should not talk about technical terminology, nonetheless Luke does on various occasions use the term "proselyte" and the phrases "God-fearers" and "God-worshipers" to *describe* Gentiles who worship the true God and are to some degree adherents of Judaism.[62] The terminology is certainly descriptive rather than technical in places like Acts 17:4, where we hear of σεβομενων Ἑλληνων. The term "proselyte" may on occasion be used by Luke in a more technical sense of a circumcised Gentile convert to Judaism, but we cannot be sure, especially in light of the LXX use of the term and the influence of the Greek OT on Luke. What is important about these people for Luke is that time and again they are seen as the bridge between Judaism and Christianity, and on various occasions they are seen as the most likely of those who are within or associated with the synagogue to be converted to Christianity (see, e.g., 18:7-8). Levinskaya is right to point out that the conversion of God-fearers would have been seen as a serious threat to the stability of various Jewish communities in the Diaspora, if these God-fearers were of some social status (see Acts 17:4) and had provided the key socially stabilizing link between Jews and Greco-Roman society.[63] Luke's obvious interest in folk like a Cornelius or a Titus might be because he himself, and/or Theophilus, had been a "God-fearer" before becoming a Christian.[64]

In regard to the source or sources Luke uses for the material in Acts 10:1–11:18, there has been no little debate. Most scholars are convinced that Luke is using sources here, not least because of some of the grammatical and syntactical problems in the material. In an influential essay M. Dibelius argued that there was originally a story of a Gentile conversion to which Luke added the speech of Peter, Peter's vision, and the clean/unclean discussion.[65] The conversion story as we have it, however, is triggered by and dependent upon the two visions. As Plunkett has rightly pointed out, Luke shows very little if any interest in the issue of clean and unclean as it involves Jewish food laws

---

61. Barrett, *Acts*, vol. 1, p. 26.

62. Notice that in Josephus the term θεοσεβης does usually mean a devout person who is an adherent of Judaism to some degree, but the nontechnical sense of the term is shown by the reference to priests in Egypt who are pagans but called devout (θεοσεβεις — *Contra Apionem* 2.140-41). See the discussion in Williams, "Θεοσεβης γαρ ην," pp. 100-109.

63. Levinskaya, *Acts in Its Diaspora Setting*, chap. 7.

64. Very possible is the idea that Theophilus had been a prominent Gentile who was a synagogue adherent before his recent conversion to Christianity (see, e.g., 17:4).

65. See Dibelius, *Studies in the Acts*, pp. 109-22. For a further elaboration of this sort of theory involving the combining of three originally separate traditions (two visions and a speech), cf. Bovon, "Tradition et redaction en Actes 10,1–11,18." Löning, "Die Korneliustradition," persuasively argues that the two visions at least were part of a unitary tradition from the beginning.

elsewhere in Luke-Acts.[66] He totally omits the material found in his Markan source in Mark 7 about this matter.[67]

It is hard to believe he would simply insert a vision about clean and unclean food into a story about the conversion of a Gentile, when the story could have been told expeditiously without such an insertion and Luke had no special interest in the subject. This means that Luke probably found the vision of Peter and the conversion story together in his source.[68] Lüdemann correctly argues that the historical nucleus of this story involves Peter in the conversion of a Gentile named Cornelius in Caesarea.[69] This means that we are not dealing with a colorless and nameless narrative that could have originally been about a Philip or a Paul but has been transferred to a Peter. The specifics of the story anchor it in Caesarea, a place where Luke seems to have spent a considerable amount of time. We may say that he drew this story from his Petrine or Caesarean source, material which he derived while there.[70]

Luke has used the device of repetition to emphasize the importance of the issues involved, as he does in the telling of Paul's conversion. Marshall then may well be right that Luke simply summarizes the tenor of what Peter would have said on the occasion in chapter 11:1-18. The original tradition may have simply involved the bulk of the material in Acts 10, including at least some of the speech of Peter in Acts 10:34-43, which has some unique features.[71]

Luke has carefully structured his source material in 10:1–11:18 into several separate scenes. The view with the longest pedigree is that there are seven scenes as follows:[72] (1) the vision of Cornelius (10:1-8); (2) the vision of Peter (10:9-16); (3) Peter's meeting with messengers and the journey to Cornelius's house (10:17-23a); (4) Peter's dialogue with Cornelius about the visions (10:23b-33); (5) Peter's sermon (10:34-43); (6) divine intervention and

---

66. Unless Acts 15 is an exception, but I do not think it is; see pp. 439ff. below. See Plunkett, "Ethnocentricity," pp. 465-77.

67. This may be yet a further example suggesting that Luke planned a two-volume work from the beginning, and so omitted some themes and stories from the first volume in order to focus on the topic later in the second volume. See pp. 4ff. above.

68. See the helpful discussion by Wilson in his *Gentiles and the Gentile Mission*, pp. 171-78. As Wilson says, it is often overlooked that visions frequently have a parabolic significance. They are ostensibly about one subject but have at the least intended implications for related subjects (i.e., what is said about eating unclean foods could have implications about receiving unclean persons).

69. *Early Christianity*, pp. 132-33.

70. See the discussion above on Luke and his use of sources, pp. 165ff.

71. See Marshall, *Acts*, pp. 181-82. Cf. the discussion in Barrett, *Acts*, vol. 1, pp. 491-98. On the unique features of the speech cf. below, pp. 355ff.; and Stanton, *Jesus of Nazareth*, pp. 67-85.

72. See the discussion in Polhill, *Acts*, p. 250, and Schneider, *Die Apostelgeschichte II*, ad loc.

Cornelius's baptism (10:44-48); (7) recapitulation by Peter of what happened in scenes 1-6 to the Jerusalem church (11:1-18).[73] We will deal with each of these subsections in turn.

1. Cornelius's Vivid Vision (10:1-8)

The narrative begins in *v. 1* by introducing one of the two main characters in the drama that is to follow — Cornelius. He is in all likelihood named after P. Cornelius Sulla, the famous Roman general who in 82 B.C. freed ten thousand slaves who subsequently attached themselves to his *gens* and took his name. Our Cornelius may well be the descendant of one of these freedmen. He is said to be a centurion from the cohort called "Italian." Various scholars have accused Luke of anachronism because the inscriptional evidence indicates the presence of this very cohort in Syria in A.D. 69 (*ILS* 9168), but nothing clearly points to a much earlier date. There is, however, another inscription about this cohort (*CIL* 11.6117) which may place it in Syria even earlier, but we cannot be certain as it is difficult to date.[74] The point to be made is that since we do not have specific evidence about what military units were in or near Palestine between about A.D. 38 and 44, we cannot rule *out* the Italian cohort being in the area well before A.D. 69.[75] It is *not* correct to argue that this cohort was not in existence and not in Syria before A.D. 69.[76]

What we do know is that cohorts such as this one were begun by the enrollment of freedmen in the auxiliary units,[77] and that it *was* auxiliary units which were used in Palestine both before, after, and perhaps even during the reign of Herod Agrippa I (A.D. 41-44). Here we are helped by the detailed work on the Roman presence in the East by F. Millar, who stresses that the situation in Palestine was anomalous in various ways, including the fact that it became a new kind of province, "a second-rank province with auxiliary units but no legions, and governed by a *praefectus* of equestrian rank, not by a senator."[78]

---

73. Note that 11:3-17 is basically a summary of chapter 10 with certain minor variations, a technique typical of Luke, and also characteristic of a proper rhetorical handling of material when one's source material is limited. See Cadbury, *The Making of Luke-Acts,* pp. 213ff.

74. See Hemer, *Book of Acts,* p. 164 and n. 9.

75. It is possible Luke is using a name given to this auxiliary unit sometime after this Cornelius episode transpired, a name with which Theophilus might be familiar, and in using the later name for the unit is being anachronistic.

76. See Broughton, "The Roman Army."

77. See ibid., p. 442, who suggests: "The Cohors II. Italica was probably a corps of freedmen . . . composed of local recruits of peregrine status."

78. Millar, *The Roman Near East,* p. 44.

Furthermore there was considerable fluidity not only in the changing from dynastic rule to Roman rule and back again briefly in A.D. 41-44, but also in the way the military functioned in Palestine. Millar shows that the auxiliary troops recruited by Archelaus from Sebaste and Caesarea probably passed into Roman service in A.D. 6, and more importantly the auxiliary units serving Herod Agrippa in A.D. 41-44 certainly passed into Roman service when Herod died.[79] Cornelius may well have been in one of the auxiliary units recruited in or around Caesarea which later passed into Roman service and was quite naturally attached to the Italian cohort in Syria, which was the Roman control center for the whole region.[80]

Much depends on when we date the Cornelius episode. It cannot be taken for granted that it happened during the reign of Herod Agrippa I, as it may have been somewhat earlier, perhaps in A.D. 39 or 40.[81] If this is the case, Cornelius may have been a centurion in the Roman provincial forces which were stationed in Caesarea, where the prefect resided. It is also possible that he was retired from the army and had chosen to live in Caesarea, though neither the grammar of 10:1 nor the reference to a military orderly in 10:7 favors this suggestion. More importantly for our purposes Cornelius is a person of some status and rank. If he was already retired he would have been awarded Roman citizenship at that point, but it is also possible that he was already one, since he may have enrolled in the army in Italy as a Roman citizen.[82]

Luke certainly intends by the description in 10:1 to make clear Cornelius was a person of some importance. Theophilus would perhaps be reminded of the somewhat similar story involving a centurion who sends messengers to Jesus to come heal his slave, and as the story unfolds we discover he also loves God's people and had built the local synagogue in Capernaum (cf. Luke 7:1-10). V. 2 indicates the piety of Cornelius — he is devout (ευσεβης), he along with his household all "feared" the God of the Jews, he prayed constantly, and he gave alms. In other words, he is depicted as performing most of the typical duties of a Jew (prayer, fasting, almsgiving). It may be said that Luke goes out of his way to make clear that neither Jesus nor his followers were antagonistic toward the Roman presence in the East or elsewhere, and that in fact even Roman soldiers found this new movement appealing and worth joining. This is part of the apologetic Luke is mounting so that Christianity

---

79. Ibid., p. 60.

80. See the discussion by Hengel, *Between Jesus and Paul,* pp. 203-4 n. 111.

81. See Bruce, *The Acts of the Apostles,* p. 252.

82. It was not uncommon for Roman soldiers to be transferred from service in a legion to help shape up an auxiliary unit in the provinces. That Cornelius is living with his kin in Caesarea may suggest, however, that he was a provincial. See Sherwin-White, *Roman Law and Roman Society,* p. 156.

will be more appreciated and accepted by the powers that be, and in general those of power and influence in the Empire.

V. 3 indicates that one afternoon at 3 P.M. Cornelius had a vision in which he clearly[83] saw an angel of God who came and spoke to him indicating that his prayers and alms "have ascended" to God — in short, that his prayers were about to be answered if he would but follow the angel's instructions. Three in the afternoon was a set time for Jewish sacrifice and prayer (cf. Acts 3:1), so we are meant to think of Cornelius encountering the angel at a time when as a devout God-fearer he would already be praying. Cornelius responds to the angel with some fear and trepidation, and also with respect, calling him κυριε (here a term of respect, like "sir" or the English use of "lord"). The angel in *v. 4* calls Cornelius's actions a "memorial offering" to God. The idea here is that spiritual sacrifices like prayer and almsgiving could be offered up to God in addition to regular sacrifices, or in their stead if one lived in the Diaspora and could not travel to Jerusalem, and God would accept them.[84] We find the notion of spiritual sacrifices elsewhere in early Jewish and Christian literature (cf. Tob. 12:12; 1QS 8:1-9; Rom. 12:1-2; and Phil. 4:18). It may be that Esler is right when he concludes about this verse, because of the close parallels between it and various texts in the LXX, that "Luke is suggesting that the prayers and the alms of this Gentile were accepted by God *in lieu of the sacrifices which he was not allowed to enter the Temple to offer himself. In other words, God had acted to break down barriers between Jew and Gentile by treating the prayers and alms of a Gentile as equivalent to the sacrifice of a Jew.*"[85]

According to *vv. 5-6* Cornelius was instructed to send men to find a certain Simon called Peter, staying at the seaside abode of Simon the tanner. Cornelius is immediately obedient to the heavenly vision and messenger and sends two slaves and a devout στρατιωτην, a military orderly who appears to have been part of his household. The first act of the drama is complete and the story has been set in motion. As Tannehill stresses, Cornelius

> is addressed like a Jew by the angel and portrayed like a Jew by the narrator. The narrator is not portraying a character as distant as possible from the Jews in order to display the potential of the Gospel to reach all. Rather the narrative uses a persuasive rhetoric that would be appropriate for Jewish Christians like Peter and those with him. They meet a character who has the central qualities that they recognize as true piety.[86]

---

83. Φανερως means distinctly or clearly, perhaps emphasizing that Cornelius certainly saw this; he was not dreaming or merely saw something which could not be clearly identified.

84. See the discussion in Johnson, *Acts,* p. 183.

85. Esler, *Community and Gospel,* p. 162, emphasis mine.

86. Tannehill, *Narrative Unity of Luke-Acts,* 2:133.

2. Peter's Food for Thought (10:9-16)

As Cornelius's messengers were approaching Joppa about noon on the follow-ing day,[87] Peter went up on the roof of the tanner's house to pray. The normal Palestinian home of this sort would have an outside staircase to the roof where one might go to be alone. It is possible there was an awning of some sort on the roof to protect a person from the relentless heat (see below).

V. 10 indicates that Peter became hungry while praying,[88] wanted some-thing to eat, and while it was being prepared a state of "ecstasy" came upon him,[89] leading to a vision about food.[90] V. 11 uses apocalyptic language to recount the vision of Peter (cf. Rev. 4:1) — Peter saw heaven open and a thing,[91] something like a large four-cornered οθονην, coming down. This word normally refers to fine linen, and so perhaps we are to imagine a sheet or something like a tablecloth. Notice that Luke is cautious when recording this vision, telling us only what it was like (ως), not intending a literal description.[92] This sheet was being lowered down onto the earth by its four corners.

V. 12 indicates that the sheet was full of creatures — all kinds of four-footed animals, reptiles "of the earth," and birds of the air. It seems reasonably clear in light of Rom. 1:23 and Gen. 1:20 and 24 that this list is meant to indicate all sorts of both land and sea creatures.[93] That is, it would include both clean and unclean animals. The laws distinguishing between clean and unclean animals may be found in Leviticus 11. After the vision Peter hears a voice telling him to get up, kill, and eat. Peter's refusal in v. 14 is emphatic — "by no means."[94] Yet the use of the respectful κυριε suggests that Peter knows

---

87. Though some manuscripts (‭א‬c, 225) read the ninth hour (3 P.M.) rather than the third, this is presumably because of scribal attempts to synchronize the two visions. See Metzger, *Textual Commentary*, p. 370.

88. Noon was not one of the regular hours for Jewish prayer, so it may be that Luke is suggesting that Peter is especially pious.

89. The Greek εκστασις means literally to be out of stasis, in other words, to be out of one's self, or, as we might say, to be beside oneself. Cf. Gen. 15:12 LXX.

90. The term προσπεινος used in this verse elsewhere only occurs in medical litera-ture; in particular it is used by Demosthenes, the medical writer. This is one more piece of evidence that may suggest, though it does not prove, that the author was a doctor. See Dillistone, "προσπεινος (Acts x.10)."

91. σκευος often means vessel in the NT; cf., e.g., Rom. 9:22-23. But it has a wider, more colorless sense of "thing," which is probably meant here. See Barrett, *Acts*, vol. 1, p. 506.

92. See similar caution in Acts 2:2-3.

93. The list here should be compared to the recapitulation in 11:6. Some copyists attempted to modify the text of 10:12 so it would match the later text. See Metzger, *Textual Commentary*, p. 371.

94. μηδαμως is found nowhere else in the NT except in the parallel account in 11:8, but in both the LXX and in secular texts it indicates a very strong negative reply. See Ezek. 21:5; Jon. 1:14; Gen. 18:25; Plato, *Protagoras* 334d.

he is speaking to either God or at least a heavenly messenger. What, then, are we to make of his refusal to obey this command? It is possible to argue that Peter thought he was being tested by God, and wished to pass the test. Commentators have sometimes pondered why Peter would think, with all the different sorts of creatures before him, that he was being commanded to eat an unclean animal. The answer may be that more attention needs to be paid to the exact response of Peter — he refers to both the common (κοινον) and the unclean (ακαθαρτον). The former probably refers to something that could be defiled by association with something unclean, the latter to something inherently unclean.[95]

In other words, Peter assumed that because of the considerable presence of unclean animals and the possible problem of contamination, there was nothing fit to eat in the sheet. The response of God in *v. 15* indicates that Peter must not call common or profane what God has made clean.[96] If indeed this vision is intended as a parable about people, rather than animals, then the verb here may refer to Christ's death and its effects.[97] In any case, *v. 16* indicates that "this" happened three times and then the "thing" was taken up into heaven. The τουτο (this) would seem to refer to the conversation, which means that once again we have Peter denying the Lord three times, only this time in regard to what he takes to be a discussion of food.[98] In later Jewish discussion there was a tradition that when Messiah came, all the animals in the world previously considered unclean would be declared clean (Midrash Ps. 146/4 [268]).

3. Peter's Puzzlement and Hospitality (10:17-23a)

The emissaries of Cornelius arrive right when Peter is trying to puzzle out his vision. The house he was staying in seems to have been substantial, for in *v. 17* we hear mention of a front gate, perhaps with a gatehouse, perhaps leading into

95. See House, "Defilement by Association." It may be true that no known ruling specified that clean animals were automatically made unclean by mere contact with unclean ones, but it stands to reason that this was often assumed to be the case in early Judaism. It was after all assumed in early Judaism that a person incurred uncleanness by mere contact with an unclean person, and it would be natural to assume the same with animals. It will be noted that the response of God in v. 15 suggests that the "common" animals in this case *did* require to be cleansed.

96. Note that the text does not say "declared clean" or "reckoned as clean" but rather "cleansed" (aorist).

97. On the close connection between humans and animals and the way they are evaluated in the holiness code such that it could be deduced that what made the one unclean also made the other unclean, cf. Wenham, "The Theology of Unclean Food."

98. See Barrett, *Acts*, vol. 1, p. 510.

a courtyard.[99] The men of Cornelius ask if Peter is staying at this house, but Peter does not overhear this, for he is still on the roof pondering the vision. Thus we are told in *v. 19* that the Spirit has to prompt Peter to look and notice that three men are seeking him. Peter is not being portrayed in any idealized way in this narrative; indeed, he is portrayed as one who is reluctant and resistant to the message of his vision. Peter is told in *v. 20* to go down without having any doubts (or possibly without making distinctions) because God has sent them.[100]

V. 22 reiterates what the hearer of the story already knows, except for three new additions: (1) Cornelius is said to be upright, (2) he is said to be well spoken of by the whole Jewish nation, (3) Peter is being summoned so Cornelius can hear what he has to say.[101] The conclusion of this encounter is intriguing. *V. 23* indicates that Peter invited the three of them into Simon the tanner's house and gave them lodging for the night. It was certainly less problematic for a Jew to invite a Gentile into his house, since there would not be the problem of nonkosher food, but nevertheless we may be meant to think that v. 23 indicates Peter is beginning to understand the message of the vision,[102] since truly scrupulous Jews tried to avoid all such contacts with Gentiles (cf. *Jub.* 22:16; Joseph 7:1).[103] There may also be some intended irony here, since Peter had earlier protested his scrupulousness about food, all the while staying in the house of a man whose trade made him unclean!

4. Journeying to the Gentiles (10:23b-33)

Luke in this section continues his usual technique of gradually revealing portions of a story as it unfolds in repeated tellings of the major events. Peter arises with his guests the next morning and departs with them to Caesarea, but he also takes with him some brothers from Joppa.[104] We learn at 11:12

99. Cf. Acts 12:13 and Barrett, *Acts*, vol. 1, p. 510: "If full weight is to be allowed to πυλων, a large building with a gatehouse is implied." In light of the parallel in Acts 12:13 this is probably the right way to read the data.

100. The use of διαχρινομενος is interesting especially in light of Acts 15:9, where it is used in the active tense to mean "make distinctions." It could mean this here as well, but the context seems closer to the sort of usage we find in Rom. 14:23; James 1:6.

101. It is not unlike Luke to hold back certain information in his telling of the story, so that when he repeats himself it will not involve mere redundancy. Cf., e.g., Acts 9 and 26, where new information and ideas are added to the story of Saul's conversion, for instance in 26:14. This is a rhetorically apt approach when one has limited source material and still wishes to be persuasive without losing one's audience.

102. It is also possible to read this story as another example of Peter's well-known tendency to vacillate about such matters (see Galatians 2).

103. See Johnson, *Acts*, p. 185, on the use of the verb χενιζω to mean "to lodge."

104. αδελφος in this case probably does refer to men.

that there were six of these Christians who accompanied Peter, and as it turned out it was a good thing, for they were to serve as witnesses to what Peter would later claim happened when he went to Cornelius's house. The traveling group must have spent the night along the way, for *v. 24* indicates that they arrived at Caesarea the day after they had left Joppa. This is not surprising since the distance of thirty miles was a bit more than a day's journey on foot. Cornelius was expecting this entourage, indeed v. 24b suggests that he was expecting someone or something momentous, for we are told that he had assembled in his house not only his relatives (and presumably other household members) but also his intimate friends. The Greek term αναγκαιος refers to persons who are related by natural (blood) or necessary ties, in this case surely the latter since relatives have already been mentioned.[105] These are likely to be Cornelius's retainers, those with whom he had various sorts of reciprocity relationships, through business or military connections or both (cf. the reference to the orderly in 10:7). As such, they could be considered part of Cornelius's extended household.

When Peter arrived, Cornelius greeted him by showing an extreme form of respect or reverence, falling at his feet. *V. 25* could be read in one of two ways. Προσκυνεω could actually mean worship here, in which case we are meant to think that Cornelius saw Peter as some sort of divine or angelic figure, perhaps even the man in his vision. This would make sense of Peter's response in *v. 26,* where he raises Cornelius up and stresses he is only a mortal. On the other hand, προσκυνεω could mean obeisance, a normal Middle Eastern form of greeting for an important person, in which case Peter's response would mean that he is only an ordinary man. V. 26 suggests the former conclusion, as does the same sort of response to such reverence in Rev. 19:10 and 22:9 (cf. Acts 14:14-15). This seems to be a stock feature of some early Jewish and Christian apocalyptic texts, but it is also a clue that Luke does not intend to present a romance or a novel here. He is not portraying Peter as some sort of divine man, worthy of extreme reverence or even worship. Indeed, he is portraying him as very mortal, thrice resisting the heavenly vision.

Peter briefly converses with Cornelius as he enters his house, and *v. 27* indicates that he was not forewarned that a crowd of non-Jews would be assembled when he arrived. This story, then, is not about a private audience that Cornelius, or even Cornelius and his immediate family, had. This was a story of great significance for the Caesarean church, for it was probably a major turning point in its life. We may suspect, since Philip had probably already evangelized at least some in this city (cf. 8:40), that the audience assembled were not totally unprepared or ignorant of what they were about to hear and see.

105. See Barrett, *Acts,* vol. 1, p. 513.

Peter, in *v. 28,* striking what seems to be a stern note, advises the assembled group that it was taboo for a Jew to associate with or visit a foreigner, that is, if he or she wished to remain a clean Jew in good standing. The word αθεμιτον here could be translated "unlawful," but it probably has its weaker sense of "taboo" or "strongly frowned upon." There was no formal law that strictly forbade Jews from associating with Gentiles, it was just that they had to be prepared to pay a price for doing so, the price being becoming ritually unclean. Texts written by Roman authors such as Juvenal (*Sat.* 14.104ff.) and Tacitus (*Hist.* 5.5) show that Jews did regularly refuse to associate with Gentiles, and were objects of suspicion because of their "antisocial" behavior. *Jubilees* 22:16 expresses the sentiment of many early Jews: "Keep yourself separate from the nations, and do not eat with them; and do not imitate their rituals, nor associate with them."[106]

Having reminded his audience that they themselves are aware that a Jew shouldn't be visiting or associating with Gentiles as he is now doing, Peter contrasts this approach with what God has now shown him. The second half of his opening remarks to the gathering in Cornelius's house begins with καμοι, and the και probably has some adversative force — "but to me, God has shown. . . ." Here it becomes evident that Peter has now concluded that his vision was not just about food but also or perhaps primarily about persons. No person should be called common or unclean.

V. 29 follows quite naturally from the second half of v. 28. Because Peter had deduced that he was to call no one unclean anymore, he put up no argument when he was asked to come to Cornelius's house.[107] But it is still not entirely clear to Peter why in particular he was summoned. He may, for instance, have thought he was being called upon to pray for, lay hands on, and help heal someone, as he had for Aeneas. Thus in *vv. 30-33* Cornelius is given an opportunity to explain why Peter was summoned.

V. 30 is another one of those grammatically convoluted verses in Acts that strongly hints at the fact that we are dealing with a rough draft or an unrevised manuscript of Acts.[108] Probably the meaning of the opening phrase is that at about the same hour four days previously Cornelius was praying when he received a vision.[109] Here the angel is said to be a man in dazzling clothes, a standard description of an angel, both within Luke-Acts and elsewhere (cf. Luke 24:4; Acts 1:10; Matt. 27:3; Mark 16:5; John 20:12). Here, too, instead of a reference to a memorial, we hear about the divine response to

---

106. A similar attitude was held toward Samaritans by many Jews (see John 4:9).

107. Αναντιρρητως means without contradiction or, as here, without argument.

108. See Barrett, *Acts,* vol. 1, pp. 516-17.

109. The problem with this translation is that μεχρι does not normally mean "about" but rather "to" or "up to," especially when coupled with απο.

Cornelius's actions — namely, God remembered him. Peter was immediately sent for, and was kind enough to come.

The crucial new element is the final part of Cornelius's response in *v. 33b:* "all of us are here in God's presence to listen to all the Lord has commanded you to say." In other words, God had told Cornelius, but not Peter, that Peter was to address him and his folk when he came. The language that Cornelius uses suggests a gathering prepared to worship God (see 1 Cor. 5:4), and possibly there is a deliberate echo of Acts 1:13-14 where the believers await Pentecost.[110] Luke may be suggesting that we are to see this story as the "Gentile Pentecost," the catalyst that would send forth a worldwide mission to Gentiles, just as Acts 2 indicated such a venture for Diaspora Jews and proselytes.[111] Perhaps more to the point, since Luke 24:47 and Acts 1:8 had already suggested a mission to the ends of the earth to all nations, and blessing for all the families of the earth in Christ (3:25-26), the issue here seems to be *how* such a mission could be carried out in view of the Jewish laws about clean and unclean. How could ethnocentric purity laws be overcome? The answer seems to be, by decree from God, in view of the new situation created by the Christ-event.[112]

Luke does not specifically say that the food laws have been abolished per se; what he focuses on is the fact that no *person* was to be treated as unclean any longer. This of course had implications for the keeping of the food laws if Jews and Gentiles were to share fellowship in Christ, but that was a secondary issue yet to be worked out, as Acts 11 and 15 show.[113] In any case, the stage is now set for Peter's first sermon to a specifically Gentile audience.

110. See Marshall, *Acts,* p. 189; Polhill, *Acts,* p. 259.

111. The whole discussion of clean and unclean in Acts 10–11 presupposes that Cornelius, while a God-fearing synagogue adherent, was not circumcised, and therefore not a full proselyte. In short he still falls into the category of a Gentile in Jewish eyes, though a righteous one. It is appropriate to call him a bridge figure, and thus a test case, which would force the issue of both the need for and basis of a Gentile mission. Wilson, *Gentiles and the Gentile Mission,* p. 177, is right that Luke sees Cornelius as the test case par excellence.

112. See Tannehill, *Narrative Unity of Luke-Acts,* 2:135. As he suggests, the story of Cornelius shows that though there were plenty of Gentiles in the Holy Land that could have had an intentional mission directed to them by the apostles, no such deliberate attempt had yet been made by the leaders of the early Christian movement.

113. Tyson, "The Gentile Mission," argues that Luke is taking a rather modern approach to the Scriptures, namely, that he thinks it is God's truth, but there are exceptions to this conclusion and thus to the authority of certain OT texts (e.g., the food laws). This probably doesn't accurately reflect Luke's view of Scripture. He is taking a historian's approach, and thus the issue is one of hermeneutics and timing. Like Paul (cf. Galatians 3–4), Luke seems to assume that the Mosaic covenant was true even in detail, but not *binding* on Christians, in view of the new covenant and the new situation brought about by the Christ-event. When the kingdom breaks into space and time, "new occasions teach new duties." The question for Luke was — for whom and when were the food laws applicable and/or binding?

5. By Word (10:34-43)

We have in vv. 34-43 a summary of a sermon which is broken off before its conclusion by an incursion of the Holy Spirit, something Peter had already experienced at Pentecost (see Acts 2). Because of its fragmentary character the sermon is difficult to analyze from a rhetorical point of view, and one must ask whether or not one is meant to include Peter's prior (vv. 28-29) and following remarks (v. 47) in the speech. On the whole, while vv. 28-29 could be taken as a preamble, it is better to see the speech as starting with v. 34 and see v. 47 as an afterword, a rhetorical question to Peter's companions, and thus not addressed to the same audience as the sermon.[114] Kennedy has argued that we have a piece of epideictic rhetoric here,[115] but this speech is not about praise or blame, it is an evangelistic speech meant to persuade the audience to come to a decision about Jesus Christ. As such it could be either forensic or deliberative rhetoric. If one takes vv. 36-42 as a *narratio* rehearsing the most recent and crucial installment of salvation history, and v. 43 as the intended transition to the proofs perhaps involving testimonies from the prophets that were to follow, it seems best on the whole to take this as an example of apologetic and therefore forensic or judicial rhetoric, which God interrupts. As such it should be compared to Peter's earlier sermons in Acts 2–4. Here of course the audience differs from that of earlier occasions, which helps to account for some of the differences in character in this speech from the earlier Petrine ones.

It is striking that there are no explicit quotations from the OT in this speech, unlike the speeches in Acts 2–3;[116] but there are a variety of allusions to the OT woven into the text. The detailed analysis of G. N. Stanton has shown, for instance, that behind Acts 10:38c lies the text of Ps. 107:20 and that Isa. 61:1, perhaps coupled with Isa. 52:7, lies behind Acts 10:38a. Inasmuch as some of the allusions to the OT in this sermon appear to be drawn from *testimonia* and reflect a common use of such texts in early Christian preaching (cf., e.g., Paul's use of a different part of Deut. 21:22 in Gal. 3:13 than that used in Acts 10:39), it is unlikely that this material is redactional. Luke is drawing on some kind of source, even if we cannot clearly delineate its extent.[117] The grammatical difficulties in vv. 36-38 probably point to a writer wrestling with the editing of a source.[118] If, as we have suggested, Luke is

114. But see the analysis of Soards, *The Speeches in Acts,* pp. 70-77.
115. Kennedy, *New Testament Interpretation,* pp. 122-23.
116. Cf. Lüdemann, *Early Christianity,* p. 128.
117. For the classic argument that what we have in these Petrine sermons is the apostolic kerygma in a nutshell, see Dodd, *Apostolic Preaching and Its Development.*
118. Cf. Stanton, *Jesus of Nazareth,* pp. 70-85, and Marshall, *Acts,* pp. 190-91; but cf. the critique by Schneider, *Die Apostelgeschichte II,* pp. 273-79.

following the practices of ancient Hellenistic historians, we may expect that he has reproduced the main outline of the sermon but written it up in his own words so that the material will appear rhetorically persuasive to his audience.

The formal introduction in *v. 34* signals the beginning of the speech (cf. Acts 8:35) — "Peter opened his mouth to speak." Here Peter makes clear what he has intimated before in v. 28 — namely, that God is no respecter of persons, if one is talking about ethnic or geographical or forensic matters. The impartiality Peter is speaking about refers specifically to God's justice or fairness in judging human beings in regard to what they have done. It is not the same as the modern notion that religious or theological differences are irrelevant in God's mind. Peter is not an early advocate of the view that all religions are one to God. Deut. 10:17 likely stands in the background here, where we are told specifically that God's impartiality is the basis not for considering all human beings automatically saved but rather for God's condemning human wickedness wherever God finds it, within or outside of Israel (cf. Ps. 81:2 LXX).

V. 35 follows naturally from v. 34. Anyone from any nation who fears God and does what is right is acceptable to God. Here clearly enough the reference to fearing God does not involve technical language, and Peter means that this statement applies equally to Jews or Gentiles. The question is — What does "acceptable" mean? It appears it refers to a person being in an acceptable state (of repentance) to hear and receive the message of salvation and release from sins. Luke is not advocating that Cornelius, because of his piety, is already saved, apart from having faith in Christ (cf. v. 43 to 4:12).

The "you know" which begins *v. 36* in the NRSV may simply be a *captatio benevolentiae,* but on the other hand it may be that Luke expected that his audience, living in the Holy Land, had heard something before about the life and works of Jesus. In fact, in the Greek it does not actually appear until the beginning of v. 37 (cf. below). The Greek syntax of vv. 36-38 is enormously convoluted, yet another hint of the unrevised state of this document, but the general sense and function of this review of Jesus' ministry are clear enough. On the whole I favor the view that suggests the following: (1) the ov in v. 36 which follows τον λογον should be retained;[119] (2) v. 36 continues the thought put forward in vv. 34-35; (3) τον λογον probably means "the message," and we are dealing in v. 36 with a statement in apposition to what has been said before. This leads to the translation "Truly I realize that God shows no partiality . . . [this is] the message which he sent to the children of Israel, proclaiming Good News of peace through Jesus Christ — this one is Lord of

---

119. Retaining it is clearly the more difficult reading; see Metzger, *Textual Commentary,* p. 379.

All!"[120] Thus the idea of impartiality and of being everyone's Lord frames this opening salvo.[121] The phrase πᾶντων κύριος was a familiar one in Greek literature (cf. Plutarch, *De Isis* 12 [355E]).[122]

It is at this point that the alert listener would hear echoes of the early material in Luke's Gospel; in fact, it echoes the angel's message to the unclean shepherds in Luke 2:10-14 in which he says he preaches good news for all the people concerning the birth of the Lord Messiah, which is followed by the angelic chorus proclaiming peace on earth on those upon whom God's favor rests. Our story is about to indicate dramatically that Cornelius is one of those upon whom that favor, in the form of the Spirit, rests, a piece of evidence even the most reluctant Jewish Christians cannot gainsay. It will also be remembered that that same chapter in Luke's Gospel goes on to speak not only of Christ as a light for revelation to the Gentiles and also for glory to Israel but of salvation prepared in the presence of all the peoples (2:30-32).[123] It can rightly be argued that Luke stresses in his two volumes the universal scope of the gospel. So Tannehill can speak of "the theological perspective that dominates Luke-Acts as a whole [is] the messianic Lordship of Jesus, which brings peace to the Jewish people in fulfillment of scriptural promises, applied to all peoples, for they are invited to share with Israel in this messianic peace."[124]

In terms of the summary itself, what this means is that Peter's précis stretches from the birth narrative to the final commissioning of witnesses at the end of Luke's Gospel, and especially recalls the angels' announcement in Luke 2, the paradigmatic quoting of Isaiah 42 in Luke 4 in Jesus' Nazareth sermon, and the risen Jesus' commissioning of witnesses.[125] This is the most comprehensive review of the career of Jesus found in any of the sermons in Acts, perhaps because the audience is Gentile. It may also be said that since this is the last of the Petrine sermons, Luke has edited it in such a way that it

---

120. Another viable alternative would be to follow Burchard's suggestion in "A Note," p. 293, that τὸν λόγον ὃν is an accusative of respect (the sentence would involve anacoluthon), which would lead to the translation "As to the word which God sent to the children of Israel bringing the good news of peace through Jesus Christ: This (Jesus Christ) is Lord of all (people)."

121. On this approach and translation one should cf. Riesenfeld, "The Text of Acts 10.36," and Neirynck, "Acts 10,36a τὸν λόγον ὃν."

122. Hengel's suggestion in *History of Earliest Christianity*, pp. 104ff., that one should compare the phrase to Rom. 10:12 is worthwhile, but his suggestion that Hellenist Christology is echoed here is suspect. The phrase is a common one in Greek, and Peter is no Hellenist, unless one means merely a Greek-speaking Jew. In any case we have precious little idea what a Hellenist's Christology would look like since Stephen's speech is no help. See pp. 240ff. above on the Hellenists.

123. On this echo see Tannehill, *Narrative Unity of Luke-Acts*, 2:138-39.

124. Ibid., p. 140.

125. So rightly ibid., p. 141.

sums up the early kerygma used by the apostles (especially Peter) in their preaching. The peace referred to in v. 36 is the peace that was hinted at in Luke 2, namely, one which involves the reconciliation not just of God and humankind but of Jew and Gentile.

V. 37 indicates that this good news spread throughout Judea but began in Galilee after the baptism announced by John. V. 38 follows naturally from this, referring to Jesus' baptism, not merely at the hands of John, but his anointing or "christening" with the Holy Spirit and power at that juncture.[126] Jesus' mighty works were performed by the power of the Holy Spirit, for we are told he was able to do good and heal those oppressed by the devil because God was with him.[127] This echoes the description of Joseph in Acts 7:9, and the point is that God's favor in the form of the Holy Spirit rested on Jesus, and on Peter, and now was about to rest on Cornelius and those with him.

V. 39 points out that Peter (and by implication the other apostles) was witness to what he accomplished in Judea and Jerusalem, and so could personally vouch for the truth of these remarks about Jesus. V. 39b echoes Deut. 21:23 — "cursed be everyone who hangs upon a tree." Even Jesus' death is seen as a fulfillment of Scripture, and thus as a part of God's divine plan for human salvation. This seemingly horrible conclusion to Jesus' life was reversed by God, for "this very one God raised on the third day" and permitted to be seen, not by everyone, but, as v. 41 puts it, by those who were his chosen witnesses. Peter here is emphasizing his and the Twelve's qualifications for proclaiming such a message (cf. Acts 1:21-22). To be one of the Twelve one must have witnessed Jesus' ministry from the baptism through the resurrection appearances; in other words, one must have comprehensively followed and seen Jesus' ministry. The proof that Jesus was really alive beyond death was that he even ate and drank with his followers after the resurrection.

V. 42 speaks of the commissioning of the inner circle to testify and preach about all the above, and about the fact that Jesus is the one ordained by God who will come to judge the living and the dead. It has been noted by scholars that this speech has some similarities to the Areopagus address of Paul found in Acts 17 (cf. v. 31), especially in the way it concludes. As Tannehill points out, we have an *inclusio* here — the reference to Jesus as Lord of all at the beginning of the speech is balanced by the reference to his exercising this role at the end of human history.

---

126. This is perhaps Luke's way of suggesting that Jesus was only fully equipped to take on the role of Messiah after this juncture, and this is why his ministry began after that occasion.

127. Luke uses the language of benefaction here — Jesus like a mighty ruler or emperor is described as ευεργετων, one who does good deeds. That this term was often applied to Hellenistic rulers (e.g., Ptolemy Euergetes) may have been suggestive to Cornelius and Theophilus. See Polhill, *Acts,* p. 262 and n. 103.

It is not clear whether the τουτο in *v. 43* should be taken as neuter or masculine ("this one" or "this message") — is it the message or the person of Christ to which all the prophets testify? As Barrett stresses, elsewhere in Acts the prophets are said to bear witness to the facts about the Christ, not to him or his existence (cf. 2:16, 30; 3:18, 21, 24; 13:27, 40; 15:15; 24:14; 26:22, 27; 28:23, 25). This is probably the sense here as well, and this comports with Luke's historiographical rather than biographical aims in this two-volume work. The Hellenistic historian's task was to focus on deeds and words, on the facts, and only in this indirect method on human character (cf. Luke 1:1-4; Acts 1:1).[128] The key to receiving forgiveness is believing the testimony of the prophets, and later prophetic figures like Peter, and so obtaining that release from sins through his name.[129]

6. And the Spirit (10:44-48)

One of the regular features of these narratives about conversions is that God takes charge of the situation, even interrupting an apostle, to bring someone new into the fold (cf. 17:32; 22:22; 23:7; 26:24). We have here at least the fourth outpouring of the Holy Spirit (cf. 2:1-4; 4:3; 8:17), and Peter will compare what happens here to the first one.[130] We are told in *v. 44* that the Spirit fell on *all* who heard the word on that occasion, including Cornelius's relatives and friends. Thus properly speaking it is not Cornelius alone, but Cornelius and his household, that becomes the test case of how Gentiles would be received by the Jerusalem church. The Ethiopian eunuch was an isolated individual and was not living in the Holy Land. What happened in Caesarea was too big an event, and too likely to have an ongoing impact in Israel, to be ignored.[131]

V. 45 relates the reaction of the circumcised believers who had accompanied Peter to Caesarea. They are astounded that the gift of the Holy Spirit

---

128. See the discussion on genre in the introduction, pp. 2ff. above.

129. Moessner, "The Script of the Scriptures," has rightly pointed out that Luke's theology of the cross has been somewhat underappreciated. Here in this speech we have at least implicitly the connection between the death on the tree and resurrection, and the forgiveness of, or release from, sins.

130. Scholars have often pondered what is said here and what is said in 11:15, where Peter says that he had *begun* to speak when the Spirit fell on Cornelius and company. There is, however, no great mystery. As Luke makes clear, Peter was interrupted by God's Spirit falling on the audience. From Peter's viewpoint he had only just begun to preach when this happened. See below on 11:15.

131. One should compare Acts 12:1-5, where James son of Zebedee and Peter can be roughly treated by the authorities and the former is even killed, presumably because the goodwill of most Jews was now lacking, unlike the case at the beginning recorded in Acts 2–4.

had been poured out even on the Gentiles. They were not expecting or prepared for this serendipitous event. As is often the case for Luke, it is the audible
phenomenon that accompanies the event that convinces these circumcised
believers that the Holy Spirit had fallen on the audience. They heard them
speaking in tongues and praising God. The question is whether Luke intends
us to see this as exactly the same experience as the one described in Acts 2.
Certainly the Western text, which appears to add the word ετεραις (other),
does what it can to make the two texts appear very similar.[132]

Too much, however, has been read into v. 47b, "as also we." Peter does
not say that Cornelius and company spoke in the same *manner* as at Pentecost,
he simply says they received the same Spirit as had happened to the audience
at Pentecost, which was made clear by some sort of audible phenomenon,
some kind of speech prompted by the Spirit. That there is no mention of
foreigners or foreign languages here, or of Peter and those accompanying him
speaking in a language the hearers did not recognize, suggests that we should
not try to press Acts 10 into the same mold as Acts 2, even if there is a certain
appropriateness about calling this the story of the Gentile Pentecost. Luke is
in all likelihood simply suggesting that inspired speech of a particular kind,
in this case speaking in tongues, ecstatic speech which is a form of praising
and magnifying God, is involved. The Spirit received was the same, but the
inspired speech differed somewhat in Acts 2 and Acts 10.

V. 47 recounts Peter's question to his fellow Jewish Christians: "What
hinders their being baptized. . . ?" The language is the same as in 8:36, and it
suggests that some Jewish Christians might have assumed that more evidence
would be required before they were proper candidates for baptism. Peter's
point seems to be that, having received the substance of what the sign of water
baptism points to, having received the change agent, the very Spirit of God, it
seemed inappropriate to withhold the sign that they were part of the body of
believers. *V. 48* tells us that Peter ordered Cornelius and his household to be
baptized, presumably because Peter's compatriots might have some hesitation
in doing this. This makes clear that the early church did not feel it necessary
to have an apostle perform this rite. They were baptized in the name of Christ,
and then Peter and his traveling companions were invited to stay for several
days. 11:3 indicates that the invitation was accepted, and food was shared, the
final proof that all reservations about these matters had been left behind by
Peter.

It must be stressed that what we have here is indeed a story of conversion;
indeed, it could be said to be a tale of two sorts of conversions — Peter was
converted to a new point of view about Gentiles as part of God's people, and

---

132. See Metzger, *Textual Commentary,* p. 381. One of the Vulgate manuscripts reads
quite clearly "linguis variis."

Cornelius and his household were converted to a new view of Jesus Christ. The former was an ecclesiological conversion, the latter a christological one. It is worth pointing out that here, as in the early narratives in Acts 2, the sharing of food in a home is taken as a sign of fellowship and presumably the existence of a house church.[133] That which makes this a story about conversion in the case of Cornelius is not just the christological factor, but also the fact that he will now not go on to be circumcised or keep the full ceremonial law. That is, he would not go on to be recognized as a full Jew by early Jews, or even as a proselyte to Judaism.

This story delineates how Luke views the issue of conversion — receiving the gift of the Holy Spirit is essential to being a Christian, as is belief in Jesus as the Christ and Lord of all. It also suggests a good deal about how Luke views ecclesiological matters. What Segal says about Paul applies equally to Peter: "From a legal perspective Paul may not have startled the Jewish Christian community so much by saying circumcision was unnecessary for gentile salvation *per se*, as claiming that the saved Jews and Gentiles could form a single new community and freely interact."[134] Peter must deal now with the fallout in Jerusalem for what has happened in Caesarea, and the way he responded to the situation.[135]

7. *Justification in Jerusalem (11:1-18)*

This long section completes the story of Peter and Cornelius, but the fallout from these events is not fully sorted out before the apostolic council spoken of in Acts 15. *11:1* is an important piece of Lukan narrative material linking what came before and what follows, and making quite clear that the story of Cornelius is not just an exceptional situation (as with the eunuch) but the acceptance by the Gentiles (τα εθνη) of God's word about Jesus. In other words, a whole new ethnic group, involving the multitude of pagan nations, has come into the picture. 11:1 should be compared with 8:14 for the similarity of language.[136] First it was the Samaritans, now it's the Gentiles, and the Jerusalem church is caught just as unprepared as they were with the results of the mission of Philip in Samaria. The comparison of 8:14 with 11:1 provides a rather clear clue that Luke is arranging his historical data κατα γενος, which

---

133. See the discussion in Witherup, *Conversion in the New Testament*, pp. 68-70.

134. See Segal, "Cost of Proselytism and Conversions," p. 363.

135. Hengel, *Paul*, p. 153, dates this event between Paul's first visit to Jerusalem (A.D. 36) and the reign of Herod Agrippa I, which began in A.D. 41. The importance of this event is of course that one of the pillars of the Jerusalem Church is involved.

136. As Lüdemann, *Early Christianity*, p. 129, rightly notes.

comports with the flow away from Jerusalem toward Rome. Henceforth the story in Acts will concentrate on the conversion of one or another sort of Gentile in various parts of the Mediterranean crescent. We are told in 11:1 that the apostles (other than Peter) and the believers in Judea got word of the momentous events in Caesarea before Peter ever went up to Jerusalem to report what had happened.

Thus according to v. 2 when Peter arrived in Jerusalem "those from the circumcision" (οι εκ περιτομης),[137] apparently a particularly vocal smaller group within the Jerusalem church, criticized Peter for his actions.[138] In Codex D a great deal more is added about Peter carrying on a ministry for a good while in Caesarea and that region before going up to Jerusalem.[139] Apparently this addition, which is written in the style of Acts 8:25 and 15:3, is either meant to avoid making it appear as if Peter was being suddenly called on the carpet by the Jerusalem church or to allow for time for the Jerusalem church to hear about and reflect on the events in Caesarea before Peter arrived.[140] It will be noted that we are not told that the apostles were the ones critical of Peter. Indeed, the distinction between them and the believers in v. 1 prepares for what is said in v. 2. Notice, too, that nothing is said here about James (unless the term "apostle" alludes to him) or about some sort of formal hearing.[141] Nevertheless, what follows in vv. 4-17 amounts to a defense speech, as we shall see. V. 3 suggests that the complaint of these Jewish Christians was not merely that Peter went and visited Gentiles, but that he ate with them, something only implied by 10:48.

---

137. The same phrase as is found at 10:45, where it simply refers to Jewish Christians from Joppa who accompanied Peter to Caesarea. Here, however, it would seem to refer to a particular subset of Jewish Christians who were very conservative in their handling of the Torah. If this is correct, then probably we are meant to learn more about this same group at 15:1 and 5. They were a group of Pharisaic Jewish Christians who were not surprisingly going to take great exception to the law-free gospel of another former Pharisee who now seemed to them to be more like a Gentile Christian — namely, Paul. Acts 15:1 should probably be coordinated with what Paul says about "the circumcision party" (using the very same phrase [οι εκ περιτομης] in Galatians [cf. especially 2:12]). See pp. 439ff. below.

138. Interestingly the same verb, διακρινομαι, is used here as at 10:20, where it probably meant "make distinctions" or "have doubts." See Johnson, Acts, p. 197. Here the sense is more strongly negative — to criticize. But this is precisely what God did not want anymore, the making of ethnic distinctions and the criticizing of those who refused to do so. Rather, Peter had come to understand that the plan was to unite Jew and Gentile in Christ as the people of God, with the two groups being on essentially equal footing in the new people of God.

139. See Metzger, Textual Commentary, pp. 382-84.

140. In other words, the Western text here is trying to ameliorate a perceived difficulty in the seeming abruptness of juxtaposing 11:1 and 2 and both with Acts 10.

141. It is unlikely the term αποστολος includes James the brother of Jesus, since he was not one of the Twelve and did not meet the criteria to be one of the twelve apostles on the showing of Acts 1.

Vv. 4-17 should be seen as a defense speech, a piece of forensic rhetoric which, as Johnson has recognized, follows the conventions properly, omitting the preamble or *prooemium* and going directly to a lengthy *narratio*. There is also the appeal to two different important forms of proof in the *probatio*, namely, the testimony of witnesses (v. 12) and the evidence of signs (v. 15). Finally, there is a brief *peroratio* which takes the form of a rhetorical question in v. 17, a question no one could gainsay or answer differently than Peter would.[142] As Soards says, the basic defense offered here involves a *metastasis*, namely, the transference of responsibility for what happened and even for Peter's own actions to God.[143]

Peter proceeds to explain what happened step by step. It is crucial to note that this account of the events is told from Peter's point of view, in the order he experienced the events, and with the benefit of hindsight.[144] Καθεξῆς here does not refer to a strict chronological account, but rather an orderly one that makes sense of the data.[145] Peter recounts in *v. 5* that he was in Joppa praying, minding his own business, when suddenly he went into a trance and had a vision (here ὅραμα) of a sheet and various animals. In *v. 6* for the first time we have mention of wild animals, beasts of prey (θηρία) which are mentioned in another of the OT lists of the varieties of animals (Gen. 1:24-25). *Vv. 7-11* add little new to the discussion.

V. 12 is more explicit than the account in Acts 10:19-20. The Spirit informed Peter not to make distinctions between the Gentile messengers who had come and "us" (i.e., Peter and his Jewish Christian companions). The Spirit was an authority with whom one should not argue, even though Peter three times had resisted the commands of the divine voice in the vision. Peter is careful to report that "these six brothers (from Joppa) went with me to 'the man's'" house. It is striking that Cornelius is not mentioned by name in this version of the narrative.

V. 13 presents the earlier event of Cornelius's vision, and *v. 14* presents the more detailed version that what the heavenly messenger had promised was

---

142. See Johnson, *Acts*, p. 200. Cf. also Kennedy, *New Testament Interpretation*, p. 123.

143. Soards, *The Speeches in Acts*, p. 77. It is saying too much, however, when Johnson, *Acts*, p. 199, wishes to insist this is a trial scene like those found in Hellenistic novels. Peter is defending his actions against ad hoc criticism in the Jerusalem church; he is not appearing before a judge, nor is there a ruling by a judge, as in Acts 15. The only "court" here is that of the public opinion of some in the church who have no authority over Peter, and are not bringing him to trial.

144. See rightly Tannehill, *Narrative Unity of Luke-Acts*, 2:143-44.

145. This is also the meaning in Luke 1:3. See pp. 12ff. above and Acts 18:26; 28:23. The basic meaning is "in sequence," which does often involve chronology in the broad sense but also has to do with a logical sequence. Thus Peter here recounts his own vision before dealing with what happened to Cornelius, for that is the order he learned of these things.

that Peter would give a message by which Cornelius and his whole household would be saved (πας ο οικος).[146]

Peter omits the sermon he gave, indicating that the Spirit fell upon them after he had begun the sermon (and before he had finished).[147] At *v. 16* we have new information. The falling of the Spirit on the household brought to Peter's mind the words of the risen Jesus in Acts 1:5, which in turn are an echo of John the Baptist's words (cf. Luke 3:16 and par.). The interesting thing about this quote is that when Jesus used it, it was addressed to his Jewish followers, but now Peter is applying it to Gentiles. For Peter, the decisive factor was that God gave the same gift to them, the Holy Spirit, as he gave those in the upper room when they believed in the Lord Jesus Christ. Thus he compares what happened in a Gentile house in Caesarea to what happened in the upper room in Jerusalem (Acts 2:1-4).[148] Peter ends his speech with an appropriate rhetorical question, "Who was I to be able to hinder God?" The language suggests obstacles to Gentiles becoming a full part of the body of believers, but these obstacles had been overcome directly by God.

V. 18 indicates that this speech silenced the criticism and then led to the praising of God, including the remark, "Even then to the Gentiles,[149] God has

146. On who was included in the definition of household, see pp. 210ff. above.

147. As Kilgallen, "Did Peter Actually," makes abundantly clear, Dibelius was wrong to accuse Luke of contradicting himself here in view of the account in Acts 10. Αρχομαι often has a pleonastic sense, and the phrase in question does not need to be taken to mean "as Peter just began to speak." Cf., e.g., Luke 7:24; 12:1 (212 words follow); 20:9 (120 words follow), where three rather lengthy speeches of Jesus are introduced by ερχατω plus the infinitive of speaking. Thus ερχατω λαλειν can suggest to Luke that a speech as long as, or longer than, the speech in Acts 10:34-43 (181 words) will follow. As Kilgallen goes on to point out, Luke does not want to convey the idea that Peter had finished his speech in Acts 10, but rather that it was a case of "Spiritus interruptus."

148. As Marshall, *Acts,* p. 197, points out, Luke compares the experience of the Gentiles, not to those of the first Jews' converts in the temple courts on Pentecost, but to the very experience of the original inner circle of Jesus' followers. Thus, their full equality is made evident.

149. As Barrett, *Acts,* vol. 1, p. 543, notes, the article τοις here indicates that the reference is to Gentiles as a class of people, not to Cornelius and his friends alone. This is perhaps why Cornelius's name is not included in the account in Acts 11 — Luke is stressing the broader implications of the events in Caesarea. This makes clear that in Luke's view it is this event which properly speaking involved the conversion of Gentiles, something at most foreshadowed in the Ethiopian eunuch story. See, however, Kelly, "The First Lukan Convert," who suggests this narrative is about Peter not being adequate to carry the message to Gentiles. More likely it is about how Peter, a pious Jew, overcame his reluctance and proved fully adequate to the task. Luke is not trying to discredit Peter in order to exalt Paul. Luke is concerned to show that the Gentile mission in fact was initiated by one of the pillar apostles and before Paul came on the scene, hence it had and deserved the support of the Jerusalem church. It could not be dismissed as an aberration caused by the radical missionary from Tarsus.

granted the radical change or turnaround (μετανοια) that leads to (eternal) life."[150] Thus ends what is in various ways the most crucial drama yet recorded in the book of Acts, involving events that would significantly change the direction of the mission and ministry of the early church from then on. "Sheer length and repetition are Luke's way of impressing upon his readers the immense significance which this event had for him. It is for Luke the test-case *par excellence* for the admission of Gentiles into the Church."[151] It has been said that there comes a tide in the affairs of human beings which if taken at the flood leads on to great things. The Gentile issue was not yet fully resolved, the debate had just been suspended, and the criticism temporarily silenced until Acts 15. Even Peter would later vacillate and withdraw from eating with Gentiles at Antioch under pressure from the Judaizers (see Galatians 2). Nevertheless, the door had been opened at Caesarea Maritima, and Luke is prepared to recount how an opportunistic and zealous evangelist (Paul), with another trustworthy brother (Barnabas), under the guidance and commissioning of a congregation that already involved Jews and Gentiles (Antioch), was going to seize the moment and begin the first efforts at overseas missions to the Gentile nations. Surprisingly, it would not be an initiative undertaken by the Jerusalem church itself, and thus "as a result it lost its importance in the course of time."[152]

150. One could of course translate it "repentance unto eternal life," but I think Johnson, *Acts*, p. 199, is on the right track here in suggesting the meaning "salvation that leads to life." Luke is not focusing on the action of the Gentiles in repenting; in fact he does not mention it at all. He is focusing on the change wrought by God by means of the Spirit in Cornelius and his kin.

151. Wilson, *Gentiles and the Gentile Mission*, p. 177.

152. Marshall, *Acts*, p. 198.

IX. The Antioch Chronicles
(Acts 11:19–15:35)

A. Christians and Collections (11:19-30)

Without question Antioch, called by Josephus "third among the cities of the Roman world" after Rome and Alexandria (*War* 3.29), was of great strategic importance to early Christianity. It was to be the first major cosmopolitan city outside Israel where Christianity clearly established itself as a force with which to be reckoned. Located on the Orontes, some eighteen miles upstream from its seaport on the Mediterranean (Seleucia Pieria), Antioch was a great commercial center and near an important religious center connected with Artemis and Apollo (Daphne). It was the Roman provincial capital for Syria, and by the middle of the first century had an estimated population of a half-million people. On its coins Antioch called itself "Antioch, metropolis, sacred, and inviolable, and autonomous, and sovereign, and capital of the East."[1] It had come a long way since its founding by Seleucus I about 300 B.C., who named it after his father Antiochus.[2] For our purposes it is crucial to note that Jews had played a part in this city from its earliest days, and there was a considerable and well-established Jewish community in Antioch in the middle of the first

1. See E. T. Newell, "The Pre-Imperial Coinage of Roman Antioch," *Num. Chron.* 19 (1919): 69-113.
2. There were numerous such cities bearing the family name, and this Antioch is not to be confused with Pisidian Antioch, which Paul was to visit on his first missionary journey. See pp. 405-6 below.
See now the extended discussion of Antioch's social milieu in Hengel, *Paul,* pp. 178-268.

century A.D. In a revealing remark Josephus tells us that proselytes to Judaism were especially abundant in this city (*War* 7.45; cf. Acts 6:5 above on Nicolaus). There were close ties between the Herodian family in Israel and this city, as is shown by the fact that Herod the Great paved Antioch's main street and placed colonnades along both sides of it.[3] This may in part explain how it was that Manean, a (former?) member of the court of Herod the tetrarch, came to be a notable teacher and/or prophet in the Christian community in Antioch (see Acts 13:1). Presumably he had been one of Herod's retainers in Antioch.

Of all the disputed sources of Acts, the one which continues to receive the most credence is that Luke had access to an Antiochene source.[4] Despite the historical questions this section raises (on which see below), most scholars believe the material in 11:19-30, which is at most a Lukan summary, is based on substantial historical traditions regarding who founded the Christian community in Antioch, the famine and famine relief, and the role Paul and Barnabas played in the community.[5] Matters are simplified considerably if, as I would suggest, *Paul* is Luke's source for his information on Antioch. This would explain why the material in Acts 11–14 focuses on the roles Paul and Barnabas play in, and as sent out by, the Antiochian church. I would not completely rule out the ancient suggestion (found in the anti-Marcionite prologue)[6] that Luke was from Antioch (but see below on 13:1),[7] but if this were the case we would expect the "we" sections of Acts to begin at this juncture and not in Acts 16. It is right to be suspicious of the "we" found in the Western text of Acts 11:28.[8] I thus must conclude that whether from Paul or whether Luke himself had direct access through personal contacts in Antioch, this material is solidly based in the tradition.

Luke, as a rhetorical historian, is interested in placing the story of salvation and early church history in the context of secular history. This is seen not only in this episode with its reference to the Emperor Claudius but also in the next (12:1-25) with its mention of Herod Agrippa's death. The

3. The city of the Roman period has been excavated. Among excellent resources for further study, cf. Downey, *A History of Antioch in Syria from Seleucus to the Arab Conquest*, which is abridged in his *Ancient Antioch*. On the religious communities in the city, cf. Meeks and Wilken, *Jews and Christians*; Brown and Meier, *Antioch and Rome*; Wallace-Hadrill, *Christian Antioch*; Tracy, "Syria," pp. 236-39.

4. See, e.g., Dupont, *The Sources of Acts*, pp. 62-72; Barrett, *Acts*, vol. 1, pp. 545-48.

5. Cf. Lüdemann, *Early Christianity*, pp. 136-39; Meeks and Wilken, *Jews and Christians*, pp. 14-18.

6. Cf. Kaye, "Acts' Protrait of Silas," p. 14 n. 2.

7. Note that Lucius is said to be from Cyrene and to be a teacher or prophet, not a physician.

8. The Western version (D [itp, and cop g67], and Augustine) of this verse begins, "When we were gathered together. . . ." See Metzger, *Textual Commentary* p. 391. See even the skepticism of so conservative a commentator as Polhill, *Acts*, p. 276 n. 137.

synchronisms are not numerous in Acts, but they are frequent enough to give the listener a sense of historical bearing as to when these events transpired. Luke, however, is not concerned to present a strictly chronological account, only an orderly one that makes sense of the relevant data, and thus the timing of various events recorded in Acts 10–12 is not given specificity. For example, *11:19* picks up the story where it was left at 8:1 in order to provide some background on the origins of the church at Antioch. The time reference in *11:27* is very vague, "in those days," as is the one at 12:1, "about that time. . . ." It is possible, indeed likely, that the proclamation of the Cypriots and Cyreneans in Antioch happened as soon as, if not before, the Cornelius episode.

What is relatively more clear is that the visit of Agabus to Antioch seems to have happened *during* the time Paul and Barnabas were teaching in Antioch and *before* the predicted famine, but perhaps only a few weeks or months before the famine hit Judea.[9] As we shall see, the famine should likely be dated to at least A.D. 45-46, and its effects a bit later, insofar as it hit Judea, which places it after the death of Herod Agrippa, in 44, an event recorded in Acts 12. Acts 12 then records some events which happened before those in Acts 11. In terms of Pauline chronology, it would appear from Galatians 2 when coordinated with Acts that Paul showed up in Jerusalem with the famine relief funds at least fourteen years after his conversion, or about 48 (or 47). This places him in Antioch about 46-47, after his "hidden years" in Syria and Cilicia (Gal. 1:21). There is almost a decade of Paul's Christian life (A.D. 37-46) about which we know next to nothing, and Luke gives us no clue about it other than that Paul was found by Barnabas in or around Tarsus (11:25), which comports with what Gal. 1:21 suggests. Luke's concern is to provide not a biography of Paul but rather a sketch of the birth and development of the early church.

We have spoken at various points about Luke's κατα γενος approach to the ordering of his narrative, arranging things by geographical region and ethnic grouping, an approach pioneered by Ephorus, and we see this continuing in Acts 11:19ff. As Tannehill rightly says, "The summary of the establishment of the church in Antioch presents an important new development, both geographically and ethnically. The gospel reaches a major city of the empire and finds a ready response from people of Greek culture, including Gentiles."[10] In other words, Luke's ordering principle is only secondarily chronology; it is primarily by region and ethnic or sociological group. Luke is presenting a historical narrative in a fashion that would seem orderly, familiar, and reasonable to his first-century audience.

---

9. The prediction could have come as early as A.D. 44 or during the reign of Herod Agrippa, but this is uncertain. See above, pp. 77ff., the chart on Acts chronology.

10. Tannehill, *Narrative Unity of Luke-Acts,* 2:146.

The persecuted Christians who had been in Jerusalem fled in various directions, up the coast to Phoenicia and as far as Antioch, but also to the island of Cyprus, which was in the northeastern corner of the Mediterranean, only about 90 to 100 miles off the Syrian coast.[11] *V. 20* tells us that some of these scattered Christians were men from Cyprus and Cyrene,[12] who spoke not only to Jews (cf. v. 19) but also to Hellenists, which surely suggests Greek-speaking Gentiles here, as the context implies.[13] It is these men who began what may be called the Gentile mission in Antioch. Taking Acts 8–11 together, one gains the rather clear impression that Luke is presenting a complex picture of the origins of the proclamation of the good news to Gentiles. It was not a mission originated by the leadership of either the Jerusalem or Antioch church but by God through a variety of means including Peter, Paul, these anonymous men from Cyprus and Cyrene, and perhaps even Philip. The message is here said to involve the proclamation of "the Lord Jesus," a message better suited to a Gentile audience than the proclamation of Jesus as the Christ or Son of Man.[14]

We are told in *v. 21* that this mission in Antioch prospered, for "the hand of the Lord" (cf. 4:30) was with them, which presumably means in this case that divine transforming power accompanied their proclamation (cf. 1 Sam. 5:3, 6, 9; 2 Sam. 3:12).[15] Luke says a great number who believed turned to the Lord, which suggests a two-stage process — belief followed by an adherence to the one in whom they have believed and to his teaching. The news of a significant number of Gentile converts reached Jerusalem, and *v. 22* seems to imply that the Jerusalem church sent Barnabas to check the matter out, much as Peter and John had been sent to Samaria earlier (cf. 8:14).

The choice of Barnabas was apt since he, too, was from Cyprus (cf. 4:36). Like Peter before him, when Barnabas saw the clear evidence of the grace of God in these Gentiles' lives, he did not censure the men from Cyprus and Cyrene or the new converts but rather rejoiced. He lived up to his nickname,

11. See the map on p. 875.
12. Presumably the country, rather than the city, since Cyprus is mentioned also. Cyrenaica was in northern Africa and, having been settled by the Greeks in the seventh century B.C., remained Greek-speaking during the Empire, and had a goodly number of Jewish inhabitants. It is possible that some of these Christians were of African descent (and so Gentiles), but it is also very possible they were Jews.
13. On the whole question of the Hellenists, see the excursus, pp. 240ff. above. The reading "Hellenist" is clearly more difficult here and should probably be preferred to the reading "Hellene."
14. It has often been noted that as the Acts narrative begins to focus more and more on Gentiles, the proclamation becomes progressively more Hellenistic, or at least less Jewish, with less emphasis on Jesus as Messiah, Son of Man, and the like.
15. See Johnson, *Acts,* p. 203.

"son of encouragement," not only rejoicing at the conversions but urging them to remain wholeheartedly faithful to the Lord.[16]

The editorial comment about Barnabas in *v. 24* is notable. He is the only man in Acts called good,[17] and he is said to be, like Stephen, full of the Holy Spirit and of faith (cf. Acts 6:5). V. 24a is connected to v. 23 by ὅτι, which may suggest that we should correlate the reference to him as a good person with his rejoicing in the previous verse and his being full of the Spirit with his exhorting the audience (cf. 2:18; 4:8; 6:10, 55). The phrase, then, about being full of the Spirit is not necessarily a statement about the level of Barnabas's sanctification, though in tandem with the word "good" it might be, but rather about the degree of inspiration — filled with the Spirit, he exhorted the new believers, and we are also told that through his preaching a great many more were brought to the Lord.

Barnabas, however, seeing an opportunity for even greater results, and perhaps already needing some help, goes off to Tarsus according to *v. 25* to seek out Paul.[18] Taken in combination with 9:27, this verse suggests that Barnabas had recognized Paul's ability when he observed him preaching in Damascus and was prepared to introduce him to the Antioch church, just as in a sense he had done earlier before the Jerusalem church. In this we see his bridge-building capacities, perhaps another reason the Jerusalem church wisely sent him to Antioch to deal with things.

The Western text has a somewhat different rendering of v. 25: "When [Barnabas] found him he exhorted him to come to Antioch. When they came, for a whole year a considerable crowd was stirred up. . . ." This version suggests a certain greater degree of independence of Paul from Barnabas (he had to be exhorted to come; he was not merely brought by Barnabas), and it may also suggest an image of Paul the controversialist,[19] always stirring things up wherever he went, an image not conveyed by the Alexandrian text. Especially in view of Luke's tendency to smooth over, or at least not highlight, the controversial side of things in the early church, the Alexandrian text is likely more original.[20]

Once in Antioch, we are told in *v. 26* that "it happened that for a whole year they met in the church and taught a great crowd."[21] The reference to a

---

16. The Greek phrase is literally "purpose of the heart." It seems to means something like with firm resolve (Johnson) or with determination; see Barrett, *Acts*, vol. 1, p. 553.

17. He only uses the term elsewhere to describe Joseph of Arimathea in Luke 23:50. He thus reserves the term for two Josephs (cf. Acts 4:36).

18. The city is mentioned only in passing here. We will say more about it at 22:3. See pp. 668ff. below, and see the still useful Ramsay, *Cities of Paul*, pp. 85-244.

19. On which see Barrett, *Paul*, pp. 22-54.

20. See Metzger, *Textual Commentary*, p. 390.

21. The verb συναχθῆναι could mean they were entertained or were the guests of the Antioch church for a year. In any case, we have here the first use of ἐκκλησία for a

crowd suggests a mixed group, certainly not just Jews, and thus the following remark is apt: "the disciples in Antioch transacted business (i.e. were known publicly)[22] for the first time [under the name of] Christians." The term Χρι-στιανοι is an important one, not least because it suggests a group distinguish-able from the Jews, presumably because of the large number of Gentiles involved in the church in Antioch. The analogies with terms such as "Herodi-ans" (Mark 3:6; 12:13) or Αυγυστιανοι (the partisans of Nero) are apt and suggest that the term means those belonging to, identified with, or adherents or followers of Christ. The term occurs in only two other places in the NT (Acts 26:28; 1 Pet. 4:16), and in both places it is a term found on the lips of others speaking about Christians, as seems to be the case here as well.[23]

When early Christians described themselves they spoke of being dis-ciples, believers, saints, brothers and sisters, or followers of "the Way," and they are elsewhere called also Nazarenes (24:5). It does not appear that Christians used the term Χριστιανοι of themselves before the second century, and inter-estingly it is Ignatius of Antioch who uses it, and does so frequently (cf. his letters *Eph.* 11:2; *Rom.* 3:2; *Magn.* 10:3; *Pol.* 7:3). It is, however, a term Romans, including Roman historians, certainly used of Christians (cf. Tacitus, *Ann.* 15.44). Of importance for our purposes is the fact that Luke is indicating that the followers of Jesus were first perceived to be a group clearly distinct from Jews in Antioch, a very significant fact for a historian presenting a κατα γενος account of early Christian history. Luke wants his audience to be able to distinguish Christians (both Jews and Gentiles) from Jews who are not fol-lowers of Christ. The means of distinction, however, is not ethnic, but as the -ιανοι ending suggests, on the basis of adherence or religious loyalties. Chris-tians make up a social but not an ethnic group. Of importance in another connection is the clear evidence that the term Χριστιανοι could also be spelled Χρεστιανοι,[24] which is of some importance in analyzing the reference to *chrestus* in Suetonius, *Claud.* 25.4, as to whether *christus*, that is, Jesus Christ, could be meant.[25]

Vv. 27-30 stand as a separate paragraph, probably a separate tradition, and deserve to be treated as a unit, perhaps coupled with Acts 12:25 (see below). We are told in *v. 27* that prophets (plural) came down from Jerusalem

---

group other than the Jerusalem church, and like the Jerusalem church it will undertake charitable activities and mission work. See Bruce, *The Acts of the Apostles,* p. 274.

22. The literal meaning of χρηματισαι; see ibid., p. 274.

23. On this whole matter cf. Mattingly, "Origin of the Name Christiani"; Bickerman, "The Name of Christians"; Cadbury, "Names for Christians." Hengel, *Paul,* pp. 228-29, rightly stresses the implications of this word for the Christology and content of the proc-lamation of the early Church.

24. Cf. *ND* 2 (1977), par. 102.3, and *ND* 3 (1978), par. 98.

25. On this see below on Acts 18:2.

to Antioch, including one Agabus. We shall meet him again in Acts 21:10 when he comes down from Judea to Caesarea to speak with Paul about his future. Traveling prophets were a regular feature of early Christianity well into the second century, and it is in order to bear in mind what is said about them in what may be the earliest extracanonical Christian book of the NT period, the Didache. At Did. 11:7-12 we find instructions about receiving and giving hospitality to such prophets, but not for an unlimited amount of time, and one should also compare *Herm. Man.* 11:1-21.

Clearly enough from the two Agabus episodes, Luke believed that prediction of the future was at least part of the function of early Christian prophets, in continuity with what we find in the OT. In this case we are told in *v. 28* that Agabus stood up (in the assembly) and through the Spirit predicted (indicated or signaled — εσημανεν) that there would be a severe famine in ολην την οικουμενην. While this could be translated "in the whole world" and taken as another Lukan example of rhetorical hyperbole used for the sake of emphasis,[26] it is also possible to translate the phrase, as Johnson has rightly suggested, "in the whole Empire."[27] Οικουμενη was a term that quite naturally referred to the inhabited world, but there is considerable evidence that during the Empire the phrase was used in a more political sense to refer to the inhabitants of the Empire (cf. Lucian, *The Octogenarians* 7; Josephus, *War* 3.29, where he speaks of the Roman οικουμενη), a sense the term seems to have in Acts 17:6 and 24:5 (cf. Luke 2:1 and 4:5). Clearly enough the frame of reference for Luke's history is the Roman Empire, as the reference to Claudius and other Roman rulers as well as the ending in Rome shows, and the political sense of οικουμενη comports with this approach. Thus Luke is talking about a famine that affected the Roman world. As K. S. Gapp pointed out long ago,[28] several factors need to be kept in mind. (1) Egypt was the breadbasket for the whole region. (2) During the Empire a famine in Egypt produced food shortages elsewhere, *whether or not those countries were then experiencing a drought.* (3) Obviously food shortages created by a famine in the region affected the poor the most. The well-to-do could stockpile grain and not experience a food shortage during a drought or famine. "In the ancient world . . . famine was always essentially a class famine."[29] (4) There is considerable evidence that poverty and food shortages were ongoing problems the early church in Jerusalem had to cope with, and did so by sharing resources in common and eventually appealing for aid from other churches (cf. 2:45; 4:32; 6:1 [need for a daily distribution of food]; Gal. 2:10). In short, from the point of view of

---

26. Cf. Luke's use of πας earlier in Acts, pp. 105ff. above.
27. Johnson, *Acts*, pp. 205-6.
28. Gapp, "Universal Famine under Claudius."
29. Ibid., p. 261.

the poor in Judea a drought or famine in Egypt meant trouble for them and many others all over the Empire, and thus in terms of its effects one could well talk about an Empire-wide famine if there was a severe one in Egypt.[30]

We have clear evidence that there was an unusually high Nile during the reign of Claudius,[31] indeed a hundred-year flood (eighteen cubits high) in A.D. 45, which in turn flooded the fields where the grain grew in Egypt, thus causing not only a severely late harvest but also one far below normal size.[32] By August-November of 45 the price of grain had already jumped to more than twice that of any other recorded price in the Roman period before the rule of Vespasian because it was known what sort of bad crop was in store by the end of that year. A.D. 46 was going to be a very bad year for those depending on buying grain to make bread. Indeed, the effects of the famine were likely to stretch well into 47 because of grain hoarding once the severe grain shortage in Egypt became widely known. Josephus speaks of the great Judean famine happening during the rule of the procurator Tiberius Alexander, which places it in 46-48.[33] "A universal famine, therefore, need not be explained by a general failure of the harvest. It is rather to be found in a general increase in the price of food, and in the universal inability of the poor to purchase food at the current price."[34]

There is a further possible aggravating factor in the case of Judea — the sabbatical year may have fallen in 47-48, but this may simply have aggravated the already bad condition of things which began to affect Judea in 46.[35] In any case the visit of Paul and Barnabas to Jerusalem should be dated about 48, or perhaps a little earlier depending on how quickly the congregation in Antioch responded to the looming crisis.

The food crisis became an early church crisis that required the strengthening of the networks of support between Antioch and Jerusalem. Agabus's dire warning reflects the view from below, the view of how a food shortage would affect the poor, not only in Jerusalem but throughout the Roman world. The prophecy then suggests that the social and economic level of many if not most early Christians was low, something we would have suspected anyway in view of texts like Acts 6:1ff., in view of the stress in Acts 2–4 on Christians sharing things in common, and in view of the mention in Acts 4:34-37 of the more well-off giving generously to meet the needs of other Christians.

---

30. See the general discussion of these sorts of recurring problems by Garnsey, *Famine and Food Supply*, pp. 37-39, 198-268.

31. On the interest of Claudius in Judaism and Christianity, and the question of Judaism as a *religio licita*, cf. below, pp. 539ff., and also Bruce, "Christianity under Claudius."

32. Gapp, "Universal Famine under Claudius," pp. 258-59.

33. Cf. *Antiquities.* 20.51-53; Orosius 7.6.17; Dio Cassius 60.11; Suetonius, *Claudius* 18.

34. Gapp, "Universal Famine under Claudius," p. 262.

35. See Jeremias, *Jerusalem*, p. 142, and Hemer, *Book of Acts*, p. 165.

The response to the crisis is recorded in *vv. 29-30*. Believers decided that each according to his or her ability would send relief to the believers in Judea, by means of Paul and Barnabas, who would turn it over to the "elders" in Jerusalem. Several points are notable. The text suggests not a taking of funds out of a general church fund in Antioch, but rather the raising of a collection through voluntary donations from individuals (cf. similarly 1 Cor. 16:2 and especially 2 Cor. 8:3). The relationship of this collection to the Pauline collection will be discussed later (see below on Acts 24:17), but it is sufficient to say at this juncture that the two should probably be distinguished. Antioch was not a church founded by Paul.

This is the first place in Acts where Christian elders are mentioned, apparently as officials who dealt with financial matters (cf. later 14:23; 15:2-23; 16:4; 20:17; 21:18). They were perhaps modeled on Jewish elders (cf. 2:17; 4:5, 8, 23; 6:12; 23:14; 24:1; 25:15). Possibly we are meant to see an allusion to the men mentioned in Acts 6:1-6. In any event, as we have argued earlier in this volume, it seems likely that Luke is here referring to the same meeting in Jerusalem as we find discussed in Galatians 2.[36] It will be in order, then, to comment briefly on Acts 12:25 at this juncture.

Acts 12:25 follows another of the typical Lukan summaries in v. 24. Thus, in effect it is a freestanding verse, unconnected with what immediately precedes it. The textual problem in 12:25 has puzzled many. Does the original text read εις or εκ (or possibly απο) before "Jerusalem"? Are we being told that Paul and Barnabas returned to or from Jerusalem? On the one hand, we have strong witnesses favoring the reading εις (א, B, and others), but there are also good and early manuscripts supporting εκ (p74, A, 33 et al.). The reading απο is supported by some Western manuscripts and lesser witnesses (D, E, 36 et al.).[37] Because of the divided witness suggesting Luke meant "from," and because εις is the more difficult reading, many, perhaps most, commentators have settled for the reading εις.[38] Yet there is clear evidence that Luke does on occasion use the verb υποστρεφειν plus a preposition to talk about the place from which a return is made (cf. Acts 1:12), so the readings απο and εκ cannot be ruled out. Barrett is right that the reading εις is simply too difficult if the sentence is read in the usual way (a "return" to Jerusalem), and makes little sense in view of the reference to John Mark, who lived in Jerusalem and did not need to be "returned" there (cf. 12:12).[39]

---

36. Cf. the discussion, pp. 86ff. above.

37. See the discussion in Funk, "Enigma of the Famine Visit," pp. 132-33.

38. See the discussion in Metzger, *Textual Commentary,* pp. 398-400.

39. Barrett, *Acts,* vol. 1, pp. 595-96; see the full discussion by Dupont, "La Mission de Paul a Jerusalem (Actes 12,25)."

The simplest solution is to accept that εις is original but that the difficulty can be resolved by a matter of punctuation: "Barnabas and Paul returned, having completed their mission unto (or in) Jerusalem, and brought with them John whose other name was Mark." The scholarly support for this conclusion is substantial,[40] and thus v. 25 can be nicely linked with what precedes in 11:30 and what follows in 13:1. It is worth asking, however, why Luke has set this one verse, 12:25, apart from the rest of the narrative in 11:27-30. Perhaps it is because he knew very well that the famine and the famine relief visit transpired *after* the death of Herod, and the placement of 12:25 reflects this knowledge. Perhaps there is also something in the suggestion of C. H. Talbert that in order to enhance the rhetorical effect of the narrative Luke deliberately transposed the Peter episode to after the famine visit so that he could have both halves of his document end with the imprisonment of an apostle followed by the declaration of the success of God's word (cf. 12:1ff. to 28:16ff.).[41]

Several final comments are in order that favor reading Acts 11:27-30 in light of Gal. 2:10 and vice versa. First, as Talbert pointed out a long time ago, since Luke is particularly interested in accenting the early Christian handling of issues of wealth and want, "it is no surprise to us to find the visit of Acts 11.27-30, 12.25 (Gal 2.1ff.) portrayed as an act of generosity on the part of the Antioch church"[42] rather than as a meeting between Paul and the pillar apostles. From Luke's point of view, whatever was privately agreed upon by the apostles during that visit did not publicly resolve the issues of circumcision, Jewish food laws, and what would be required of Gentiles. Secondly, as Bruce pointed out, the verb "remember" in Gal. 2:10 is in the present tense and can be readily taken as a continual present tense — "they wanted us to continue to remember the poor" (implying that they had already begun to do so by this visit to Jerusalem). The second half of the sentence with the aorist verb εσπουδασα could be taken as a pluperfect "which very thing I was eager to do."[43] The aorist then suggests an eagerness which had begun at some point in the past.[44] In short, the fewest problems both for reading Paul and for reading Acts come from the conclusions that: (1) Galatians is Paul's earliest letter,[45] and (2) Acts 11 = Galatians 2.[46]

---

40. Besides Dupont and Barrett, one may also point to Metzger, *Textual Commentary*, pp. 399-400, and Haenchen, *Acts*, pp. 379-91.

41. Talbert, "Again: Paul's Visits to Jerusalem," pp. 39-40.

42. Ibid., p. 39.

43. Or perhaps even translating it "had been eager."

44. Cf. Cadbury, "The Tradition," p. 279; Bruce, "Chronological Questions," p. 294 and n. 79; Barrett, *Acts*, vol. 1, p. 560.

45. Cf. De Lacey, "Paul in Jerusalem."

46. See the fuller discussion of the earliness of Galatians in Appendix 1 below.

B. Rescue and Retribution in Jerusalem (12:1-25)

This chapter contains a self-contained narrative that may be the end of Luke's Petrine source. He knows of Peter's participation at the apostolic council mentioned in Acts 15, presumably through Paul. The tradition in its present place serves as both a flashback and an interlude in the "Antioch Chronicles."[47] It is certainly one of the most colorful and entertaining narratives in all of Acts, including as it does both the humorous scene where Peter is prodded by an angel to put on his clothes and also the tale of how later he was left standing and locked out at the gate of the home of his Christian friends by an excited gatekeeper after having been led through numerous gates manned by his captors! These sorts of narratives have led to the suggestion that Acts should be seen as some sort of historical novel or romance, the main aim of which is to delight or entertain one's audience. This proposal deserves close scrutiny, even though it underestimates the degree to which serious ancient historians might have entertainment as one of their subordinate aims.

A Closer Look — A Novel Approach to Acts ────────────────

The recent work of R. I. Pervo has raised again the question of the genre of Acts, and whether or not Luke's two volumes need to be seen as the same kind of literature.[48] The basic thesis of Pervo is that Acts should be seen as one type of historical novel, involving some history but a great deal more fiction.[49] This theory has met with mixed reviews, to say the least,[50] but it should not be simply dismissed. Pervo's approach to the issue is to attempt to broaden the classification of what amounts to an ancient romance or novel on the one hand, and on the other to dispute the attempts to distinguish the canonical Acts from the apocryphal Acts. Both of these moves are problematic, and we shall deal with each in turn.

The study of the ancient novel has become again in the last couple of decades a topic of considerable interest to classicists,[51] and so it was only natural that the

---

47. As Barrett, *Acts,* vol. 1, p. 568, says, this tale is more easily detachable from the general flow of the text than any other in Acts. Plumacher, *Lukas als hellenistischer Schrift-steller,* p. 110, rightly remarks that the style of this story is that of a drama, in fact a drama in three acts: recapture, release, retribution.

48. Cf. especially Pervo's *Profit with Delight* and also Parsons and Pervo, *Rethinking the Unity.*

49. See, e.g., Pervo, *Profit with Delight,* p. 122.

50. See D. R. Edwards, *JBL* 108 (1989): 353-55; J. Jervell, *JTS,* n.s. 40 (1989): 569-71; M. Soards, *JAAR* 58 (1990): 307-10; M. C. Parsons, *Interp.* 43, no. 4 (1989): 407-10, and the discussion by Bauckham in "The *Acts of Paul,*" pp. 105-52, especially pp. 139-52.

51. Cf., e.g., Perry, *The Ancient Romances;* Reardon, *Form of the Greek Romance.*

insights gained from classical studies would eventually be brought to bear on NT studies. But what do we learn from such studies? In the first place the romance proper or erotic novel was a story about two lovers who remain faithful to each other, though separated through trials and adventures, and in the end are happily reunited. As R. Bauckham has properly remarked: "This is a genre which can be quite easily and strictly defined and in a field where genre definition is difficult we should be glad of that fact and not confuse issues by claiming that other works of imaginative prose narrative are much the same as those which indubitably belong to this genre."[52] If we look somewhat more broadly at ancient novels, we discover that the protagonist is always a private individual assailed by many troubles. In other words, the novel bore some resemblance to ancient biographies but much less to ancient historiography.[53] One major difficulty lies, as Bauckham says, in the fact that novels often posed as historiography, and thus verisimilitude was sometimes mistaken for actual history in such works, even though they were almost exclusively if not exclusively pure fiction.

But with Acts we do not find various of the essential components of such romances. (1) There is no romance in Acts properly defined, no interest in the sex lives or marital relations of Peter or Paul or other early Christian figures. (2) Acts is not a tale of two parties long separated and then reunited. (3) There is no happy ending or reunion at the end of Acts. Paul's fate is left untold, his case unresolved.[54] As William Brosend has put it, "if the purpose of Acts is to entertain and instruct, spellbinding and gruesome executions are the order of the day! Recall only the Acts of Peter, which recounts Peter's head-downward crucifixion (from which position he offers an extended sermon . . .). While our tastes may be repulsed rather than entertained by such grisly depictions, ancient audiences were apparently delighted."[55] In other words, the ending of Acts is seriously deficient if the major purpose is entertainment. It represents a missed opportunity if the purpose is delight. (4) We are not regaled with tales of encounters with colorful pirates or bandits. (5) To this one must add that the recounting of adventures or travels is not a feature found only in ancient novels. Indeed, from what one can tell ancient novels were indebted to ancient historiographical works for this feature. (6) Besides the lengthy speeches, which are also not characteristic of ancient romances,[56] there is the further problem that Acts shifts from one major human character to another, leaving the fate of the first "hero," Peter, completely unresolved, and Paul fares little better. Two things which do truly characterize ancient

52. Bauckham, "The *Acts of Paul,*" p. 144.

53. The ancients understood the distinction between "true" and "false" history, the latter constructed out of myths and genealogies, often dealing with pseudohistorical or legendary persons. The discussion of Gabba, "True History and False History," pp. 50-62 (on the novel and its relationship to history, p. 53), is instructive. The novel, if it is close to any history writing, is close to dramatic historiography, often called false history.

54. Contrast what Hägg, *Narrative Technique,* p. 310, says: Romance is characterized by "a beginning *ab ovo,* a linear succession of events, and a definite end."

55. Brosend, "The Means of Absent Ends," pp. 348-61.

56. Notice that Pervo can give almost no real examples of this phenomenon in romances. Cf. Pervo, *Profit with Delight,* p. 76, to Brosend, "The Means of Absent Ends," p. 354 n. 17.

novels are the biographic-like focus on a particular character and the tying up of loose ends as the novel concludes, neither of which can be said truly to characterize Acts.[57]

The essential problem for Pervo is that he must define the ancient novel much too widely in order to include Acts within its compass, and he must strain to show that Acts has features that are *distinctive* of, not merely characteristic of, ancient novels. Soards's conclusion bears repeating: "It will seem easier to many who weigh Pervo's case to conclude that Acts communicates with its readers using a different genre from the ancient novel rather than that genre minus most of its juicy parts. . . . Pervo's case that Acts is novelistic is made largely from Luke's own lively style and from the inclusion of accounts of miracles in the narrative. But any reader of Herodotus knows all ancient historians were not as skeptical about the miraculous as was Thucydides."[58]

On the other hand, Pervo is right to point out that the humor, wit, irony, and pathos in Acts have been underappreciated by scholars.[59] These features, however, are often found in historiographical works during the Empire *due to the influence of Greco-Roman rhetoric* on the genre, not due to the influence of the novel. It is problematic that Pervo nowhere adequately comes to grips with the influence of rhetoric on a variety of kinds of ancient literature.

Pervo seeks to make his case more plausible by pointing to works that were written either during the Hellenistic era in the East or after the period of early Roman imperialism, namely, during the period of the Second Sophistic. This is because novels are notable by their absence during the early Empire.[60] His theory as to why this is so is plausible: "Forms like the novel required the existence of a literate public with some leisure time and a moderate or better economic situation. . . . In short novels require a cosmopolitan society."[61] The question that then must be asked is whether Acts could have been written for such an audience. Jervell has no doubt this was *not* the audience of Acts. He argues: "The reader of the antique novels is surely not comparable to the reader of the Acts of Luke. He did not write at a safe distance from the history of the Church and the actual situation of his Church. He could not look back in a relaxed way on the success and victory of the Church in the world. His readers lived in the 'Mitte die Zeit,' with the prophecies and an uncertain future ahead. What had happened to the early church could happen to themselves any day. Luke had to meet more basic needs than leisure. They did not need diversion and entertainment through legal struggles, persecution, and cruelty, but consolation."[62]

---

57. In particular, the attempt to treat Acts as a story about the travels and travails of Paul requires that we treat almost all of Acts 1–8, and most of Acts 1–12, as a mere prologue, which does no justice to this material.

58. Soards, *JAAR*, p. 309.

59. See Pervo, *Profit with Delight*, pp. 58ff.

60. Ibid., p. 116, attempts to bridge the gap by tentatively suggesting that a work like *Ninus*, a fictionalized romantic portrait of a great Eastern leader, indicates that the novel continued to develop in the direction of the "historical" novel. The problem with this assessment is that most scholars who have examined the fragments are quite clear that the work is basically an erotic novel.

61. Ibid., p. 110.

62. Jervell, *JTS*, p. 570.

A further difficulty with Pervo's work, even when it has been further refined with more reflection and study, is that he continues to misread fundamental aspects of the way Luke handles his source material. For example, consider how Pervo continues to handle the issue of the characterization of Paul in Acts in *Rethinking the Unity of Luke and Acts*.[63] He argues that in essence Paul is presented as a "divine man," or at least a divinized one. This is failing to notice that it is the "barbarians" here, as in Acts 28:1-10, who make the mistake of thinking of Paul in these categories, and in both stories the narrator either directly or indirectly makes clear that their naive view is not accepted by the author nor is to be accepted by the audience. As Tannehill has shown, point of view is crucial in these two narratives, and Luke's viewpoint is not identical with that of the barbarians.[64] In other words, Luke's point of view of his main characters is not like the viewpoint the authors of ancient romances sometimes take of their heroes.[65]

My own view is that Luke is writing to a person of some social status, writing in an apologetic manner because he knows it will be an uphill battle for such a person to become and remain a Christian. While Theophilus apparently had the time to listen to a work of this kind, the basic function of this literature is *not* entertainment. It is not intended to be summer beach reading for those with time on their hands. Rather, it is intended to inform about the history of the movement, to enable Theophilus to take some pride in its course and leading figures, and to prepare him for the sort of difficulties he would face as a person of some station in an environment not very congenial to the Christian faith. As Jervell suggests, this is one thing which seems to distinguish the audience of Acts from the audiences of some of the apocryphal Acts written in the late second and third centuries.

Pervo's claim that the dangers and sufferings do not amount to much in Acts is frankly untrue, for they are always resolved or reversed in Acts. As Jervell points out, Acts 14:22 must be taken as a warning Luke wanted his own audience to hear, and Acts 8 and Acts 12:1 should not be ignored or dismissed. Furthermore, when one combines the Miletus speech with the ending of Acts, one has a profound sense of the impact of the (then impending) loss of the great apostle of the Gentiles. There is a real sense of *pathos* and tragedy not to be missed in Acts, both in the case of a figure like Stephen and in the case of Paul. This book is not just about happy endings for imperiled humans. Again, entertainment is not lacking in Acts (cf. Acts 20:7-12), but it is not the main purpose of the author to entertain. Luke is more interested in informing and

63. Parsons and Pervo, *Rethinking the Unity*, pp. 90-94.
64. See especially the discussion of Tannehill's view below, pp. 778ff.
65. Equally dubious is Pervo's misreading of Luke's Christology, or his characterization of Jesus in Luke and Acts, as if there were some great divide between these two volumes on this issue. Jesus is not merely presented as a prophet or man of the Spirit in the Gospel. Indeed, in a very obvious reflection of the author's own views, he calls Jesus "Lord" regularly in the narrative framework of his Gospel. See pp. 147ff. above, the excursus on Christology. At the end of the day, neither Peter nor Paul is seen by Luke as on the same plane as Jesus, though they can all be said to be prophetic and Spirit-filled persons. The imitation of Christ by the Christian protagonists in Acts does not amount to an indication of full similarity at the ontological or anthropological level.

persuading by a variety of means, and in any case ancient historians were also concerned about giving delight with profit, pleasure with censure.

There is also the problem that these romances, whether national or ethnic such as the Alexander romance or those of a more narrow scope, tend to be biographical in character centering on the life and deeds of one or more figures.[66] As Bauckham has pointed out, this is one of the features that to a real degree distinguishes the apocryphal Acts from the canonical Acts. In these later Acts of Paul or Peter or Thomas or John, there is an interest in a particular great apostolic figure for his own sake. This *is* much like an ancient novel which relates "the adventures or experiences of one or more individuals in their private capacities and from the viewpoint of their private interests and emotions."[67] The biographical interest in the apocryphal Acts is shown not only by the fact that we get a description of what someone like Paul may have looked like but also by the considerable interest invested in telling stories that have no other function than to reveal the noble character of the apostle (e.g., John and the bedbugs or Paul and the baptized lion). There is also considerable interest shown in the apocryphal Acts in how the lives of a Paul or a Peter ended. In short, the novel tended to be biographical in character, as do the apocryphal Acts, but the canonical Acts leaves us in the dark about the ends of Peter or Philip or James or Paul, gives us no description of them, and tells no purely anecdotal character-revealing tales. The canonical Acts is about salvation history, or about the saving acts of God in the person of the Holy Spirit through various human beings. It is not about human biography or hagiography, though it is clear how much Luke admired Peter, Paul, and other early Christian leaders.[68] R. Söder, in her definitive study on the ancient novel and the apocryphal Acts, was so struck by the *absence* of novelistic features in the canonical Acts that she insisted its genre differed from that of the apocryphal Acts.[69]

It is not an accident that the author of the Muratorian canon wondered why Luke did not go on to record Paul's final mission to Spain or Peter's martyrdom. He shared the same biographical (or hagiographical) interests that the authors and audiences of the apocryphal Acts had, interests characteristic of second-century Christians, but Luke's interests lay elsewhere.[70] It is a mistake to lump the canonical Acts together with the apocryphal ones in regard to genre, audience, and purpose. As Bauckham has shown, the later Acts which is most like the canonical one is the Acts of Paul, and yet its obvious focus on a single figure sets it apart from Acts. Furthermore, "the erotic themes of the story of Paul and Thecla are distinctive of the novel, whereas they have no parallel in the Lukan Acts. This relationship with the novel therefore enables us to understand one point at which the *Acts of Paul* departs from the model provided by Acts."[71] In short, there are serious flaws not

---

66. See Pervo, *Profit with Delight*, p. 116.
67. Perry, *The Ancient Romances*, p. 45.
68. See the discussion in the introduction, pp. 68ff. above.
69. Söder, *Die apokryphen Apostelgeschichten und die romanhafte Literatur der Antike*.
70. Bauckham, "The *Acts of Paul*," p. 142.
71. Ibid., p. 145.

only in the attempt to place Acts under the banner of ancient novel but also in the attempt to lump Luke's Acts together with the apocryphal Acts that focus on particular apostolic figures.

The preface found in Luke 1:1-4 needs to be taken seriously as a description that affects how we evaluate both Luke's Gospel and Acts.[72] That preface indicates that Luke intended for his work to be compared to other ancient works of Greco-Roman historiography. What Pervo's work does successfully show is that, among other things, one of Luke's minor aims is to instruct in an entertaining and persuasive manner. None of the features he singles out in Acts, however, is distinctive of ancient novels.

If there are several elements in this Petrine narrative that are the sort of thing one *also* finds in ancient novels (e.g., the ultramiraculous release from prison, the strong emotional response to meeting a lost friend unexpectedly, the capricious behavior of a tyrant whose clutches the hero eludes, or the horrible death of the villain),[73] it must also be said that there are clearly some indisputable historical traditions being used in this section involving the death of James and Agrippa, and few would dispute the likelihood that Peter may have been captured and then escaped from prison in Jerusalem or that Jerusalem Christians met in the household of the mother of John Mark.[74]

The story as we have it is of the same ilk as other stories of divine rescue both in Acts (cf. 5:18-20; 16:23-29; and Acts 27) and elsewhere in the NT (cf., e.g., Matt. 2:13-23), and often these sorts of stories focus on a rescue from tyrants. In the biblical tradition the paradigmatic story of this sort is found in the narratives about the Passover and exodus from Egypt, and so not surprisingly echoes of that story have been found here by scholars, particularly because of the reference to both the Festival of Unleavened Bread and of Passover (vv. 3-4).[75] Yet it is right to point out that Luke does not on the whole play up the Passover associations of these events,[76] and one should probably

72. On its application to both volumes see pp. 4ff. above.

73. Cf., e.g., the overwrought emotional displays in Longus, *Daphnis and Chloe* 2.30, or Achilles Tatius, *Clitophon and Leucippe* 1.3; 2.23, or the remarkable prison escape in Lucian of Samosata, *Toxaris* 28-33, even involving divine intervention in Ovid, *Metamorphoses* 3.690-700. It must be said, however, that all these elements can also be found in ancient historiography. Cf. on the death of the tyrant by maggots (or the like) Herodotus, *Persian Wars* 4.205; Josephus, *Ant.* 17.168-90 (Herod the Great); Eusebius, *Hist. Eccl.* 16.4.

74. Cf. the discussion in Lüdemann, *Early Christianity*, pp. 145-46.

75. Cf. Tannehill, *Narrative Unity of Luke-Acts*, 2:153-55; Dupont, "Pierre delivre de prison"; Radl, "Befreiung aus dem Gefängnis." That the use of seemingly innocuous phrases and words such as "the night before," "quick, get up," and "put on your sandals" suggests a strong echo of the exodus story seems to overpress the parallels.

76. The most striking parallel is Acts 12:11 and Exod. 18:4 (LXX), where the language is the same except for the name of the one from whom the person is being delivered.

look to the more proximate analogies with the story of Jesus,[77] and the role of the Herods in his story. It is surely no accident that Agrippa I here is not called Agrippa, but rather King Herod (12:1 cf. Luke 1:5), while his son later *is* called Agrippa (25:13–26:32). For a Christian hearer like Theophilus the associations with the Jesus story would likely be more obvious.[78] Luke seems to have had a special source on at least some of the Herod material,[79] and he uses some of this information at this point.

The parallels between the recounting of the death of Herod Agrippa in vv. 20-23 and Josephus's account of the same event (*Ant.* 19.343-52, cf. 18.200) are notable and suggest that Luke is well informed at this point.[80] Josephus gives us more specific information about the day in question (the day of a festival honoring Caesar, cf. Acts 12:21) and about what his royal robes were like (made of silver), but Luke gives us a somewhat more specific diagnosis as to what did Herod in — from the divine point of view God struck him down, but the material cause used to accomplish this was σκωληκοβρωτος, he was "eaten by worms."[81] The two accounts seem to be independent since they vary in their points of specificity.

Scholars have asked repeatedly what the point of this narrative is in Luke's narrative, since the story could have been left out without harm to the overall flow of the account of early Christianity. Is it only an entertaining

77. So rightly Garrett, "Exodus from Bondage," pp. 670ff. The imprisonment in darkness is seen as being like Jesus' death, the release of Peter is seen as being like Jesus' resurrection, the appearance to Rhoda whose witness is not believed about Peter is seen as comparable to Jesus' appearance to women whose witness is also not believed (cf. 12:13-15 to Luke 24:11), Peter's appearance to the gathered community inside a house is seen as like Jesus' comparable appearance (cf. Acts 12:16 to Luke 24:36), and finally Peter's departure to another place is seen as analogous to Jesus' ascension to heaven. Some of this is over-pressed, but Peter's encounter with Rhoda and its sequel seem intended to echo the story of Jesus.

78. The Passover allusions are especially overdone by A. Stobel, "Passa-Symbolic und passa-Wunder in Apg. 12.3ff.," *NTS* 4 (1958): 210-15, who argues that the early church believed on the basis of Jewish traditions that Jesus would return at Passover and that it was praying he would come on this one and rescue Peter. As Marshall, *Acts*, p. 208, says, this is not even hinted at in the text.

79. For the period of Jesus' lifetime the traditions might go back to Joanna of Chuza (cf. Luke 8:3), and for both this time and the later period to Manaen, a member of the entourage, at least during childhood, of Herod Antipas (13:1). See Barrett, *Acts*, vol. 1, pp. 570ff.

80. On the reliability of Luke in historical matters when compared to Josephus, see the excursus above, pp. 235ff.

81. Perhaps another small point suggesting Luke was, and had the interests of, a physician. Josephus simply says he had pain in his abdomen. The same word is used elsewhere of worm-eaten crops, but it is not possible from this word to be specific about the disease in question, the suggestions ranging from tapeworms to peritonitis; cf. Merrins, "The Death of Antiochus IV."

interlude? Is it told to indicate the shift of power in Jerusalem from Peter to James?[82] There is probably something to this last suggestion (see below), but it is also possible to see this story as a continuation of the persecution-in-Jerusalem theme, which for Luke helps explain why the mission to Gentiles took the course it did when it did. In other words, this story serves to help justify the shift in focus in the narrative from Jerusalem to Antioch and then even farther west. Jerusalem was not going to be the kind of place which, in the future, missionaries to the Gentiles, whether Peter or Paul or others, could call home base for long (see below on 21:27ff.).[83]

It is in order to ask what picture is painted of the social situation of the early church in this narrative. Four factors stand out. First, the early church in Jerusalem was not part of the Jewish power structure, nor was it well connected with either the Jewish kings or Roman governors that ruled in Judea between A.D. 30 and 60. Thus, the church was subject to persecutions and prosecutions of various sorts and degrees of severity. Secondly, in spite of this first social fact which suggests the marginalized status of the community of Jesus in Jerusalem, there is some evidence that there were some converts of social means, such as the mother of John Mark, who could provide a viable setting for the early church to meet, grow, and develop. As Fiensy points out, the social makeup of the early Jerusalem church seems to be a microcosm of the social makeup of Jerusalem as a whole.[84] Even in Jerusalem, where Acts suggests there was notable resistance to "the Way," the church still found a modus vivendi and a modus operandi by which it could not only endure but even grow.

Thirdly, the narrative suggests not only that there were multiple meeting places for the early church (cf. 8:3) but that the early church had not required everyone to sell or give up all property. Lastly, the example of Rhoda (cf. Luke 22:56) may suggest that the early church did not immediately require the abolition of slavery within the community, though there is a slim chance she may have been a hired freedwoman.[85]

Chapter 12 begins with a vague time reference (on which see above on 11:19, 27) and indicates that Herod Agrippa "laid violent hands" on some who belonged to the church. Since Herod ruled Judea only from A.D. 41 to 44, this event must have transpired during this period, probably sometime in 43-44, as we shall see.[86] This Herod was the grandson of Herod the Great, who as a child had been sent to Rome and received his education there. He was a friend of

82. On which cf. O. Cullmann, "Courants multiples dans la communauté primitive," and the analysis by Barrett, *Acts,* vol. 1, pp. 569-75. See also Wall, "Successors to the 'Twelve.'"
83. Cf. the discussion in Barrett, *Acts,* vol. 1, pp. 568-70; Polhill, *Acts,* pp. 276-77; Johnson, *Acts,* pp. 216-19.
84. Fiensy, "Composition of the Jerusalem Church."
85. Both her name and her function suggest otherwise; see below.
86. See Bruce, "Chronological Questions," pp. 276-78.

Caesarea Maritima: The Herodian theater in which Herod Agrippa I was stricken.

Caligula (who both established Herod as a ruler in the Transjordan and De-capolis in A.D. 37 and extended his territory to include Galilee and Perea in 39) and also of Claudius, helping the latter, who was his schoolmate, to obtain the emperorship. In return for supporting Claudius, Agrippa was given Judea and Samaria in A.D. 41. At the point at which we encounter him, Agrippa had the same-sized domain as his grandfather and was a ruler of considerable power.

Whether Herod went after James, the son of Zebedee,[87] to please the Jewish authorities or just to flex his muscles is unclear, probably the former. It should be noted that we are not talking about a persecution of wide scope. Perhaps the assumption was that if the leaders of the Jesus movement were eliminated, the movement would decline and/or die.[88] Thus, *v. 2* indicates that

87. There is no firm evidence that James's brother, John, was also martyred at this early date; indeed, Irenaeus, *Haer.* 2.22.5, suggests the opposite, that he lived to a ripe old age. The earliest we really hear of such an idea is in the writings of Philip of Side in the fifth century A.D. See *Beginnings*, 4:133-34. Probably the idea of an early martyrdom for both brothers arose because of a certain interpretation of Mark 10:39, but this latter text says nothing about the timing of these brothers' deaths.

88. Agrippa, perhaps in part for these actions as well as others, seems to have been regarded as a good Jew, even though when he was away from Israel he lived a Greco-Roman lifestyle. Cf. *m. Soṭa* 7:8; Josephus, *Ant.* 19.292-94, 331.

Agrippa had James killed with the sword. This may suggest that Christians were seen as a political threat, and the verse may also suggest that Agrippa followed a Roman form of execution — beheading with the sword.

V. 3 suggests that Herod was encouraged by the Jewish response to the execution of James, and so took action against Peter, during the Festival of Unleavened Bread.[89] This festival began on 14 Nisan on the eve of Passover and continued until 21 Nisan (cf. Exod. 12:18; Lev. 23:5f., cf. Acts 20:6). If Agrippa died after celebrating the emperor Claudius's birthday on August 1, then Peter may have been taken captive in A.D. 44, but if he died after celebrating the natal day of Caesarea's founding on March 5, then Peter must have been taken captive the previous year (A.D. 43), because Passover came *after* March that year. Either date suits Josephus's description (*Ant.* 19.343) that Agrippa was struck down on the occasion of spectacles in honor of the emperor, but *Ant.* 19.351 suggests that Agrippa died three years after his accession, hence in 44, as do the coins of latest date minted by Agrippa.[90]

V. 4 also suggests that Agrippa followed Roman procedures, procedures Luke appears to have understood quite well. Peter is put into prison, having been handed over to four squads of soldiers to guard him. The Roman procedure called for a change of guard at each of the four watches of the night (every three hours); hence four squads were required, composed of four soldiers each.[91] What this also suggests is that Herod relied on at least some Roman troops during his reign.[92] V. 4b seems to imply that out of respect for Jewish sensibilities Herod was going to resolve the case of Peter after the festival season was over. The phrase "bring him out to the people" suggests the Roman practice of public trial followed by execution if guilt was established.[93]

V. 5 indicates that the Jerusalem church prayed for Peter while he was in prison. The word εχτενως suggests fervency in prayer. Presumably we are to think they were praying for Peter's release, though the content of the prayer is not specified. V. 15, however, suggests that they did not expect Peter's release; indeed, the verse may suggest they thought he was dead!

The second major division of the story begins at *v. 6*, and here we learn that what is about to be recounted transpired at the most propitious moment possible — the very night before Herod was going to bring Peter out for trial

---

89. It may well tell us something about Luke's background that he dates various events by reference to the Jewish calendar (cf., e.g., the incidental reference in 27:9). Perhaps he had been a devout synagogue adherent before his conversion to Christianity.

90. See Hemer, *Book of Acts*, pp. 165-66; Meyshan, "Coinage of Agrippa the First."

91. See Conzelmann, *Acts*, p. 93.

92. See above on Cornelius, pp. 341ff.

93. On this and the following stories in Acts about imprisonment and the Roman procedures, cf. Rapske, *Paul in Roman Custody*.

and probable execution. Peter seems to have been shackled to two soldiers, one on either side, while the other two guarded the door from the outside. One gets the feeling Herod wanted to make very sure Peter didn't escape. Neither Herod nor the guards had reckoned on divine intervention, and presumably it would take nothing less than that to extricate Peter from this situation.

We are told at *v. 7* that an angel of the Lord appeared, illuminating the cell, and had to strike Peter with some force to rouse him, so soundly was he sleeping.[94] Like an army sergeant, the angel in *vv. 7-8* commands Peter to get up quickly (as the chains fell off his wrists) and put on his belt and sandals and cloak and follow him. The image conveyed is of a Peter who is still half asleep; indeed, *v. 9* indicates that Peter was in such a daze that he didn't even realize that what was happening was a reality, not just another vision or dream. After passing the two soldiers on guard outside the prison, Peter and the angel came to an iron gate leading into the city, which opened of its own accord, and once they were out in the city street we are told that the angel suddenly left Peter. It is very possible that Peter had been imprisoned at the Antonia Fortress, as Paul would later be (cf. picture above). *V. 11* indicates that it is only at this point that Peter comes to himself ("and when he happened upon himself") and realizes that the angel of the Lord had delivered him from the clutches of Herod, but also from "all that the Jewish people were expecting." The atmosphere in Jerusalem had changed dramatically after the Stephen episode. Luke suggests the Christians no longer had the admiration of the crowds in the Holy City; indeed, they seem to have turned against them. This episode seems to have transpired some ten or eleven years after the death of Stephen.

Once he came to his senses, *v. 12* indicates Peter went to the house of Mary, the mother of John Mark, "where many had gathered. . . ." Following his usual technique, Luke briefly introduces a new character in passing (Mark),[95] in preparation for a more extensive discussion of events he was involved in thereafter. The reference to "many" meeting in the household suggests a house of considerable size, as does the reference to a courtyard gate and a female gatekeeper. That a woman is the head of this house is noteworthy; presumably she was a widow. That Peter goes expecting to find Christians meeting at this location suggests this is a regular location of a house church,

94. παταξας suggests a strong, even violent blow. It is used elsewhere of God smiting his enemies (cf. Exod. 2:12; Judg. 1:5; Ps. 3:7; Luke 22:49-50; Acts 7:24); cf. Barrett, *Acts*, vol. 1, p. 580; Johnson, *Acts* p. 212. In fact it is the very same word used to refer to the angel smiting Herod in v. 23. Not surprisingly the Western text (D), seeking to modify the harshness connoted by this verb, changes the text in v. 7 to read νυξας, "nudged."

95. Cf. how he introduces Philip in 6:5, or Saul in 7:58.

and this is confirmed by the reference to ongoing gathering and praying at this location.

V. 13 refers to a παιδισκη named Rhoda. Though παιδισκη is the diminutive form of the word "girl," in the NT it is always used of someone who is a slave (cf. Matt. 26:69; Mark 14:66, 69; Luke 22:56; Acts 16:16, and especially John 18:17). The girl's name, Rhoda, which is actually a nickname meaning "rosebush," also points us in this direction. It is not impossible that this is an all-female prayer meeting, but the gender of ικανοι probably rules this out. If the reference to the "brethren" refers to the Twelve, then Peter's words certainly don't imply an all-female meeting. That Rhoda must come to the gate when Peter knocks may suggest she was taking part in the prayer meeting, thus implying that not just women but even slaves could participate in the early Christian meetings (cf. Acts 1:14). Yet this possibility is somewhat counterbalanced by the fact that this woman is apparently still a slave and her audience thinks she is mad (μαινη) when she reports seeing Peter. Nevertheless, Luke indicates her witness is true, and her testimony is finally vindicated at the end of this section of the story.[96]

Several other points in the story call for our attention. Besides the comical touch of Rhoda being so overjoyed she leaves Peter standing at the locked gate, *vv. 14-15* portray an interesting view of the early church. We are apparently meant to think that this house church no longer expected their prayers would help lead to Peter's release;[97] indeed, they seem to have thought he was dead.

The reference to Peter's angel[98] could allude to the Jewish belief in guardian angels in special relationship to humans (cf. Gen. 48:16 LXX; Tob. 5:22; Matt. 18:10). Though from a later period, there is some evidence that Jews believed that guardian angels had the same appearance as the one they protected (cf. *Gen. Rab.* 78 [50a], which interprets Gen. 33:10 to refer to the angelic prince of Esau who had Esau's appearance). To this it must be added that it was believed that one's spirit or angel often lingered on earth, appearing for several days after one's death, and that belief may be reflected here (cf. Luke 24:37).[99]

V. 17 indicates that after Peter had finally been admitted to the meeting and had conveyed his amazing story of rescue, he commanded his audience to inform James and the brethren about these things. Once again we see

96. On these matters see my *Women in the Earliest Churches*, pp. 146-47.

97. Were they praying for his faithful witness until the end, expecting him to face the same fate as James?

98. Notice how the Western text, by adding τυχον, nuances things, sparing the image of the house church a bit. In D and syr the church only says, "Perhaps it is his angel." See Metzger, *Textual Commentary*, p. 395.

99. See Polhill, *Acts*, p. 282.

---

another major character in the narrative introduced in passing, in this case James. Though Luke does not make his identification clear at this point, this is surely a reference to James the Lord's brother, in view of texts such as Gal. 1:19 and 1 Cor. 15:7. Notice how the latter text also expects the audience to know which James the author has in mind.

This verse is taken by R. Bauckham as the key clue to the function of this narrative, namely, that it intends to recount how the reins of power passed from Peter to James, and in view of 11:30, from the apostles to the elders.[100] Unfortunately for this view, Acts 15:2, 4, 6, 22 and 16:4 portray Peter and the apostles as still on the scene in Jerusalem and still having authority, though it is true that by the apostolic council James is now the leading figure. Furthermore, there is no reason to take 11:30 as a clue to the new form of Jerusalem leadership after the apostles. It may well refer to those who were in charge of practical aid, mentioned in Acts 6. James is not called an elder either in Acts. The most one can say is that this narrative intimates that Peter will no longer be the leading authority figure in Jerusalem, and that James is *already at this time* the one to whom this report must especially go.[101] In other words, he was already a leading figure in Jerusalem before Peter left, as Galatians 1–2 suggests, and did not need to be commissioned by Peter as he left. Bauckham is, however, right that Luke wishes in chapters 11–15 to show how the churches in Jerusalem and Antioch are intertwined, and both play a role in the developing Gentile mission (cf. 11:22, 27; 12:25; 13:5; 15:22, 40).[102]

The elliptical character of *v. 17b* has mystified many commentators, and numerous conjectures have been made as to where Peter went. The text simply says he went to another place.[103] It is quite unlikely that he went to Rome at this early date,[104] as Paul writing Romans in the late 50s knows of no apostle in Rome, much less one founding the church in Rome (see Rom. 15:20);

100. Bauckham, "James and the Jerusalem Church," pp. 432-39.
101. See, however, the discussion in Wall, "Successors to the 'Twelve,'" pp. 634-43. To say, however, that Peter, like Jesus, now commissions these disciples to take the word to James and others (Wall, p. 641; cf. Schneider, *Die Apostelgeschichte II*, p. 107) is overpressing the narrative.
102. Bauckham, "James and the Jerusalem Church," p. 434.
103. Gal. 2:11 does not tell us when Peter came to Antioch, but we must probably date this event no earlier than A.D. 46, in other words, several years after this episode in 44. His whereabouts in between these events is unknown, and in fact Luke never mentions his visit to Antioch. In view of how highly Luke regards Peter, as Acts 1–12 shows, this omission, it seems to me, is inexplicable, if Luke was in fact from Antioch, or knew of some tradition of Peter's visit to Antioch. It would further make his point that those involved with the Gentile mission, which went forth in earnest from Antioch, were connected with that city.
104. But cf. Wenham, "Did Peter Go to Rome?"

otherwise he would not have the same ambition and motivation to go and preach there that he reflects in Romans.[105] The point is simply that Peter is off the scene in Jerusalem at this point and beyond the clutches of Agrippa, presumably at least until the latter's death, which not coincidentally is narrated at the end of this subsection.

V. 18 indicates there was "no small commotion" in the prison the next morning when it was discovered that Peter was gone.[106] Herod himself is said to have searched for him, and when Peter was not found Herod first examined the guards and then we are told "they were led away," presumably for execution. This was normal Roman practice — a guard who permitted a prisoner to escape was to bear the same penalty as the escapee was to suffer.[107] *V. 19b* then indicates that Herod left Jerusalem and went down to his administrative capital, Caesarea Maritima.[108]

Vv. 20-23 should probably be seen as a separate tradition from Luke's Herodian source, referring to an event that transpired somewhat later, about five months later if the day in question was August 1 A.D. 44 when Agrippa was stricken. Luke records something Josephus does not mention, namely, that Herod was going to receive an embassy from the citizens of Tyre and Sidon, who had apparently fallen out of favor with him and were short of food supplies. Through the aid of Herod's chamberlain, Blastus, the embassy of these two cities approached Herod seeking reconciliation. The account that follows in *v. 21* suggests that Herod had donned his royal robes and had prepared to come and rule on this request on an appointed day. Luke does not tell us the content of his public address; he is only interested in the fact that the crowd who heard it responded by shouting, "the voice of a god and not a mortal" (cf. *Ant.* 19.344-45).[109] Luke and Josephus agree that it was just after this that Agrippa was stricken and that the cause was his failure to give

---

105. The *Acts of Peter* 7 and the *Clementine Recognitions* and *Homilies* place him there during the principate of Claudius to confront Simon Magus, but Lactantius (*De mort. persec.* 2.5) is surely right that he does not arrive there before the reign of Nero, something the canonical Petrine literature probably also suggests (see 1 Peter in general and 5:13 in particular). Cf. *1 Clem.* 5:4 and Bauckham, "James and the Jerusalem Church," pp. 432ff.

106. The ουχ ολιγος construction is an example of litotes, which is characteristic of Luke and another great Greek historian, Thucydides. Cf. Acts 14:28; 15:2; 17:4, 12; 19:23f.; 27:20. Cf. Cadbury, *The Making of Luke-Acts,* pp. 120-21; Metzger, *Textual Commentary,* p. 396.

107. Code of Justinian 9.4.4.

108. The NRSV inexplicably assumes that Peter is the one who goes down to Caesarea, even though Herod is the nearest antecedent of the verbs in v. 19b.

109. Josephus has "more than a mortal," and he says that Agrippa neither repudiated the acclamation nor rebuked the crowd's flattery. Was Agrippa here trying to portray himself as the sun god by wearing these light-reflecting robes? Cf. Morgenstern, "The Channukah Festival," pp. 89-90 and n. 167.

God the glory,[110] or as Josephus chooses to put it, because Agrippa failed to rebuke the impious remark (*Ant.* 19.346).[111] Josephus tells us Agrippa developed severe stomach pains and lasted for five days before he passed away.[112]

By contrast to Herod, who suffered a sudden end, the summary statement in *v. 24* indicates that the word of God continued to grow, to advance and gain adherents.[113] It is probably right to see this verse as the summary statement meant to round off Luke's account of the mother church in Jerusalem. Henceforth the focus shifts north and west, with only the apostolic council really returning Jerusalem back to the center of the discussion of church life and church growth.[114] The summary is followed somewhat anticlimactically by the indication that after delivery of the famine relief Barnabas and Saul returned to Antioch,[115] but this provides the necessary transition to what follows in Acts 13–14.

C. The Door for the Gentiles Opens — Part 1 (13:1–14:28)

Though there had already been clear contacts with and successes in converting Gentiles prior to the time of the events recounted in Acts 13–14,[116] it is Luke's intent to portray this missionary journey as being the inaugural efforts by a church at planned evangelism of Gentiles as well as Jews, indeed the first planned efforts at overseas missions.[117] Acts 13:1ff., then, must be seen as something of a turning point in the narrative.[118] The story clearly falls into

110. See Bruce, *The Acts of the Apostles,* p. 289, who contrasts the response of Paul and Barnabas in Acts 14:14-18.

111. Note that Josephus adds the mitigating remark that Herod neither affirmed nor denied the people's ascription to him of divinity.

112. Cf. *Ant.* 19.346-50, and Eusebius's remark about how Josephus provides independent confirmation for Luke's historical accuracy (*Eccl. Hist.* 2.10.10). It is interesting how Josephus describes the death of Herod the Great in terms very similar to Luke's account here (cf. *Ant.* 17.169; *War* 1.656), but then death by worms was often seen as the proper fate of tyrants. Cf. Jdt. 16:17; 2 Macc. 9:9, and pp. 228ff. above.

113. On Luke's summary statements and passages see pp. 157ff. above.

114. It will be noted that the discussions of Paul's last visit to and incarceration in Jerusalem do not really return to the issue of the Jerusalem church and its growth, but rather continue the theme that Jerusalem is where Christians find danger, persecution, and prosecution.

115. On Acts 12:25 see pp. 374ff. above and the discussion of 11:27-30.

116. On Cornelius see pp. 341ff. above.

117. The previous efforts by Philip or Peter or even Paul, while perhaps approved after the fact by the Jerusalem church, were not examples of efforts by a or the church to fulfill the mandate of Jesus given in Acts 1.

118. See Best, "Acts 13.1-3."

three major parts: (1) the commissioning of Barnabas and Paul and the mission to Cyprus (13:1-12); (2) the mission to Pisidian Antioch and Paul's synagogue speech (13:13-52); (3) the missionary visits to Iconium, Lystra, and Derbe and the return to Syrian Antioch (14:1-28). We will treat each subsection in turn, but some general remarks are in order about this section as a whole.

It will be remembered that at Acts 9:15-16 we were informed that Paul had specifically been chosen to bear the Lord's name before "Gentiles, kings, and the sons of Israel" and to suffer for his name. This prophetic word had yet to come to pass, and what it suggested was that Paul would at some point become the central human character in the narrative. From Acts 13 on, Paul assumes this role, always remembering that *the* major actor and catalyst of all that happens in this salvation historical drama is God in the person of the Holy Spirit.[119] That these three subsections should be taken together as a narrative unit is shown by comparing the summary in Acts 14:26-27 with 13:1-3.

1. The Commissioning and the Mission to Cyprus (13:1-12)

It was already clear from Acts 9 that Paul had been singled out by God as a special instrument to aid in the fulfilling of the divine salvation plan. Thus whatever is being described in these verses is not meant to suggest that only now had Paul been called or singled out for missionary work. Here the Holy Spirit is the one who indicates that Paul and Barnabas have been chosen for a particular role in the overall missionary work.

The narrative begins at *13:1* by providing us with a traditional list of prophets and teachers in the Antioch church,[120] and it is surely not accidental that Barnabas and Paul frame that list.[121] The three others in the list will be given further description at this point since they are unknown to the listener. Unfortunately it is impossible to be certain which were prophets and which teachers or if they were all meant to be seen as both. Paul and Barnabas, however, have already been portrayed as being teachers in Antioch (cf. 11:26), and Paul is about to be portrayed as a prophet in 13:9-11. Perhaps it is best to understand the list to refer to those who were both teachers and prophets, both informing and inspiring, being themselves informed and inspired.

119. See Tannehill, *Narrative Unity of Luke-Acts,* 2:159.
120. That the list is traditional is widely accepted by scholars. Certainly pointing in this direction is that Luke does not elsewhere refer to διδασκαλοι in Acts.
121. See Lüdemann, *Early Christianity,* p. 146. This arrangement might suggest that Barnabas was one of the first and most preeminent of these Antiochian conveyors of the word, and that Paul was one of the last to join this leadership circle, much as the traditional list of witnesses to the resurrection in 1 Corinthians 15 has a chronological arrangement.

The first new person mentioned is Simeon, who was also called Niger. The word Νιγερ is a Latinism, meaning black, and occurs nowhere else in the NT. In view of Luke's obvious interest in ethnography throughout this book,[122] the word probably does suggest that this Simeon was from northern Africa, which may explain why he is listed next to someone from Cyrene.[123] In regard to whether Simeon, too, might be from Cyrene, and so be identical with the man referred to in Luke 23:26, the answer is probably not. For one thing Luke spells the name differently here than in Luke 23:26 (Συμεων here, Σιμωνα there), for another the article before the word "called" indicates Luke is trying to distinguish this Simeon from another of the same or similar name in his narrative, namely, Simon Peter called Simeon at 15:14.[124] Since Simon of Cyrene is not mentioned elsewhere in Acts, Theophilus could not be expected to identify the man in this list with a man mentioned in passing in Luke 23 whose name is spelled somewhat differently.

Lucius of Cyrene is mentioned next in the list. He is in all likelihood not to be identified with the author of this volume. In fact, the use of the appositive here may mean he is to be distinguished from another Lucius, perhaps the one mentioned as greeting those in, and hence connected to, Rome (Rom. 16:21), or perhaps even the author, whose name in any case is spelled differently at Col. 4:14 (Λουκας as opposed to Λουκιας here). There is, furthermore, no church tradition that suggests that Luke the physician was ultimately from northern Africa.

We have already had occasion to speak about Manaen[125] as a possible source for Luke's information about the Herods. Here it is in order to point out that the word συντροπος if taken literally could mean that this man had the same wet nurse as Herod Antipas, here called the tetrarch,[126] but it was a common word to refer to an intimate friend, in this case a friend in the court.[127] Since he is not listed elsewhere we may assume that Luke mentions

122. On which see pp. 10ff. above.
123. On which location see pp. 240ff. above. Barrett, *Acts*, vol. 1, p. 603, points to the metaphorical use of the word for a Perean who was very brave (cf. Josephus, *War* 2.520), but this is surely not to the point here, in view of the fact that the next person's geographical location is specified.
124. Earlier in his narrative, Luke usually calls him simply Peter, but cf. Luke 22:31, where he is called Σιμων. This is why one can't be absolutely certain that the Simon in this list is not Simon of Cyrene. If he was, it is some seventeen or so years later and we find him in Antioch, not Jerusalem or its environs. For what it is worth, Mark (and his audience?) knows of Simon of Cyrene's children but apparently not any more about Simeon of Cyrene himself (cf. Mark 15:21b), which is perhaps strange if that Gospel was written by the same Mark who is connected with this venture that sets out from Antioch.
125. See pp. 165ff. above.
126. See Keener, *Bible Background Commentary*, p. 357.
127. Cf. 1 Macc. 1:6; 2 Macc. 9:29 on συντροπος.

him here to indicate that there were persons of some social standing in the Antioch church.

V. 2 indicates that it was while the disciples were worshiping in Antioch, which included fasting, that the Holy Spirit spoke (through a prophet presumably), saying, "Set apart for me Barnabas and Saul for the work to which I have called them." The word λειτουργειν occurs nowhere else in Luke-Acts (cf. the noun form in Luke 1:23) and refers to the doing of some sort of public service, which could include a religious service, as here.[128]

Fasting is rarely mentioned in Acts (cf. only 13:3 and 14:23),[129] and it is not possible to determine from this elliptical remark whether the leaders were simply given to fervency in their devotions or were seeking some specific guidance on a matter through intense worship and fasting. The αυτων (they) here would ordinarily have as its natural antecedent the previously listed prophets and teachers, and so probably we are to think of the leaders in Antioch being involved in this setting apart of Paul and Barnabas.[130] The wording here is important — Paul and Barnabas are called to this specific work by God, not by the Antioch church and its leaders, but they are "set apart" for the task by this church's leaders. The expression αφορισατε δη μοι is emphatic. Not only is the verb in the imperative,[131] but δη, an invitatory particle ("come now"), punctuates the matter, indicating the need for immediate action.[132] The Spirit is beckoning "set them apart for me now." The missionary task here is called an εργος, a work.

V. 3 indicates the prompt response of those who have received this command from the Spirit. After prayer and fasting the leaders laid their hands on Paul and Barnabas and let them go ("released them" literally). Luke does not portray this event as an ordination to some sort of church office, and certainly nothing is said here about the two being ordained as apostles at this juncture. Both men were already teachers and prophets in the congregation and so were already leading proclaimers.[133] They are simply being set aside for a specific missionary task, and the laying on of hands indicates the recog-

---

128. See the book of Hebrews for the more "liturgical" use of the term, and also *Did.* 15:1.

129. Acts 27:9 refers to a religious festival, the Day of Atonement. Paul apparently never uses the term νηστεια in a religious context, only in the more general sense of having to do without food (cf. 2 Cor. 6:5; 11:27).

130. See Barrett, *Acts,* vol. 1, p. 604, rightly; contrast Haenchen, *Acts,* pp. 395-96.

131. It is the same verb Paul uses himself to speak of his calling (cf. Rom. 1:1; Gal. 1:15).

132. See the similar use in Acts 15:26.

133. As Best, "Acts 13.1-3," p. 348, puts it: "if the distinction already existed Paul and Barnabas were, even prior to this ceremony, members of the 'clergy'; if the distinction did not exist this did not create it."

nition and endorsement by these church leaders of the call of God in this matter.[134] Bruce puts it well: "Not that they could by this act qualify Barnabas and Saul for the work to which God had called them; but by this means they acknowledged their recognition of the divine call and declared their fellowship with the two men, who were thus not only called by God but commissioned by the church (αποστολοι in the sense of 14.4, 14)."[135]

V. 4 makes abundantly clear that though the leaders in Antioch endorsed and prayed for these two men and their work, it was in fact the Holy Spirit who had both commanded the church to act and now sends these two men on their way. The journey begins with a trip to the city of Seleucia, which was some sixteen miles from Antioch and served as its port, though it was in fact some five miles from there to the mouth of the Orontes River. The Roman fleet for this region was stationed there, and one could obtain regular passage to many destinations from this port. They chose, not surprisingly, to sail to Cyprus, the home of Barnabas, which was only about sixty miles offshore.[136] What this destination may suggest is that Barnabas was, and was seen by the Antioch church as, the senior partner in this missionary venture. Marshall's assessment of Paul's missionary trips needs to be borne steadily in mind as we work through the next ten chapters.

> Paul's missionary work [during] this period has the best claim to being called a "missionary journey," as is customary on Bible maps. The later periods were much more devoted to extended activity in significant key cities of the ancient world, and we gain a false picture of Paul's strategy if we think of him as rushing rapidly on missionary *journeys* from one place to the next, leaving small groups of half-taught converts behind him; it was his general policy to remain in one place until he had established the firm foundation of a Christian community, or until he was forced to move by circumstances beyond his control.[137]

The account of the trip focuses on what was done in the two major cities on the island — Salamis and Paphos. A close reading of Paul's letters suggests that it was his primary strategy to focus on the major cities in the Empire, the capitals and the Roman colonies in particular. It may be that this was already

134. See Marshall, *Acts*, p. 216.
135. Bruce, *The Acts of the Apostles* p. 294. On "apostles" see below on 14:4.
136. Various sites on Cyprus have been well excavated, most recently the city of Kourion, which is between Salamis and Paphos. What these excavations show is that the Romans had made a considerable commitment to building projects and having a significant presence on the island, a commitment which was ongoing and resulted in the flourishing of Roman culture there by the second century. Cf. Soren and James, *Kourion*; Johnson, *Paul the Apostle*, pp. 59-61.
137. Marshall, *Acts*, p. 214. See the map at the end of the present volume.

a part of the thinking at this juncture, hence the focus on these two major cities. Salamis was of course famous even before the classical period of Greek history and had at one time been the capital of the island, but under the Romans, in 22 B.C., it had been made a senatorial province administered by a proconsul, a status it retained at the time of Paul and Barnabas's visit. The Romans had moved the capital to Paphos, or, more properly speaking, new Paphos. Luke is thoroughly familiar with the governmental arrangements of the Roman Empire, and in particular the differences between an imperial and a senatorial province, and time and again we find him giving the proper designations for the Roman officials he mentions.[138]

V. 5 informs us that the strategy in Salamis was to go first to the synagogues. Here we see inaugurated what is to be presented as a regular practice of Paul, offering the gospel message to the Jews first (cf. 13:14; 14:1; 17:1, 10, 17; 18:4, 19; 19:8). As Barrett says, this is Luke's version of Paul's "to the Jew first but also to the Greek" (Rom. 1:16).[139] The mention of synagogues (plural) suggests a considerable Jewish population, and in fact the Jewish community on this island dated to at least Ptolemaic times and was well established.[140] We are also told in v. 5 that John Mark (cf. 12:24) was with Paul and Barnabas and served as a ὑπηρετης. This term can have a variety of senses but its general sense is of a servant or helper, any subordinate assistant. Probably, in view of the use of the term in Luke 1:2 and Acts 26:16, it means more than just someone who helped with material aid or practical arrangements (though cf. Acts 5:22, 26; 20:34; 24:23). Presumably Mark helped in the preaching and teaching in some way, but Luke does not care to be more specific.[141] He is in any case not portrayed as a major figure in this venture.

In view of *v. 13* where we are told that John Mark leaves the other two and returns to Jerusalem when Paul and Barnabas decide to continue the evangelistic tour and sail from Paphos back to Asia Minor, a series of possibilities arise: (1) since Mark is not said to be commissioned for this venture in 13:1-3, it may be that he felt no compulsion to continue on the journey

---

138. That he is careful to get such details right suggests both a general concern for historical accuracy and perhaps a well-informed and well-traveled author.

139. It is, however, underestimating Luke somewhat to go on to suggest, as Barrett, *Acts,* vol. 1, p. 611, does, that what for Luke was little more than a missionary technique, was for Paul a theological principle. This is forgetting that Luke has portrayed this venture as directed by the Holy Spirit.

140. For Jews on Cyprus, cf. Philo, *Embassy to Gaius* 282, and Josephus, *Ant.* 13.284-87. Barnabas was of course one of their number before becoming a Christian, and we may assume he still had close contacts, perhaps family as well, in the Jewish community there. See Acts 4:36. On synagogue as a place and not just a gathering of people in Acts see the discussion, pp. 255ff. above.

141. See Barrett, *Acts,* vol. 1, p. 612.

once it left the territory where he had contacts and presumably relatives;[142] (2) the material in this chapter must, however, be compared to 15:37-39, where Luke indicates that Mark was guilty of deserting this particular missionary venture, though he does go with Barnabas on another mission to Cyprus, when Paul and Barnabas part ways; (3) the verb αποχωρεω, used in both 13:13 and in the form αποχωριζομαι at 15:39, can have the sense of betrayal or almost apostasy (cf. 3 Macc. 2:33) or at least a turning back in fear (Jer. 46:5 LXX). Epictetus uses it to refer to removing oneself from another's opinions (*Dis.* 4.1.53).[143] Thus the translation "deserted" is not too strong at 13:13. In view of Philem. 24; Col. 4:10; and 2 Tim. 4:11, fences were apparently later mended between Paul and Mark.

We are not told the outcome of the preaching in Salamis. Instead at *v. 6* we are told that Paul and Barnabas traversed the whole of the island until they came to Paphos, or more specifically new Paphos where the proconsul resided. While the verb διελθοντες could be taken to refer to a missionary tour of the island, it probably means no more than that they traveled along the main road on the southern coast between Salamis and Paphos, the former being on the eastern end of the island, the latter at the western end.[144] It was at Paphos that they happened to find a man named Bar-Jesus (or Bar-Joshua) who is characterized by three terms: (1) he is a μαγυς, (2) he is a false prophet, and (3) he is a Jew.

The term μαγυς could have the pejorative sense of quack magician, but it could also have the more neutral sense of an eastern priest, originally a Persian fire-priest. In view of the pejorative term "false prophet" with which it is coupled there is little doubt of its sense here.[145] A μαγυς was a diviner who through various rituals claimed to be able to evoke the dead, including the shades or spirits of one's ancestors; and coupled with the word "prophet" our text suggests that he claimed to be able to tell the future, perhaps through necromancy, perhaps through astrology or magical spells and rituals involving both.[146]

---

142. Remembering that Col. 4:10 tells us that Mark was Barnabas's cousin and so had at least Barnabas as a relative from Cyprus.

143. See Johnson, *Acts*, p. 229.

144. There is evidence that these two cities at each end of the island could be mentioned as representing the whole (cf. *Sib. Or.* 4:128-29), as we might say from New York to Los Angeles. Gill, "Paul's Travels through Cyprus (Acts 13.4-12)," argues for the southern route on the basis of the discovery of an Augustan milestone, and that the southern route between the cities was 115 days, the northern 142. Gill also suggests that Paul may have preached in some of the cities along the way (such as Tremithus or Amathus), especially since he had to stop various times on this long journey. Paul and Barnabas may have preached all along this road, but if so Luke makes nothing of it.

145. See, e.g., the pejorative use of the verbal form in *Did.* 2:2.

146. On all this cf. Nock, "Paul and the Magus," especially pp. 180-88.

For our purposes, what is important to note is that there is a pattern in Acts of confrontation between early Christian leaders and those who are characterized as magicians and the like, whether we are talking about Peter's confrontation with Simon Magus or this narrative or the conflict with the sons of Sceva in Acts 19:13-14. Note that in all three cases the opponents have some kind of association with Judaism or those on the fringes of Judaism.[147] The problems of syncretism were many, and on an island like Cyprus which had had contacts with and influence from a variety of cultures both in the past and the present,[148] it is not surprising to find a person of Bar-Jesus' sort playing an important role in the court (see below).

A Closer Look — "The Way" and Other Religions: Competition and Conflict

We may deduce from this and other narratives that Luke saw magicians as an ongoing threat, or at least a form of dangerous competition for Christianity.[149] He is at pains to distinguish legitimate miracles that happen through Christian leaders from magic, no doubt in part because he feels that Christianity must be portrayed as a legitimate religion, one that offers real help and healing to human beings and not just conjuring tricks.

It must also be added that Luke sees the non-Christian form of Judaism as competition as well, and much of the way he portrays the interchanges between the missionaries and the Jews reflects this. By contrast, he has much less to say about various traditional forms of pagan religion or philosophy (though see below on Acts 17). This must tell us something about the social location of early Christianity vis-à-vis other religions of the day.

Christianity is portrayed in Acts as a derivative or form of Judaism, and thus connected to an ancient Near Eastern religion that had some official recognition in and during the Empire.[150] Yet Christianity was a missionary and messianic form of that religion and as such was in direct competition both with other forms of Judaism and with magic and other forms of popular religion. Luke is not attempting to suggest what would be later suggested during the period of Constantine, that Christianity should be seen as the official religion of the Empire, nor on the whole does he suggest that there was any actual direct conflict with, for instance, the cult of the emperor or the traditional Roman cults in the earliest period of church history, though there

---

147. One may also wish to compare the reference in Acts 19:18-19, where pagan magic is probably also involved.

148. In the past the island had been colonized successively by Egyptians, Phoenicians, Greeks, Assyrians, Persians, the Ptolemies, Jews, and finally Romans.

149. See rightly Tannehill, *Narrative Unity of Luke-Acts,* 2:161.

150. On the issue of Judaism as a *religio licita,* however, see pp. 541ff. below.

are definite hints in the text that conflict with the emperor cult was probably inevitable.[151]

Interestingly, however, conflict with and superiority to the older Greek gods and goddesses (and Greek philosophy) are repeatedly maintained (cf. Acts 14:8-18; 17:16-33; 19:23-41). This suggests that Luke and other early Christians were more concerned with the indigenous and popular religions than they were with the Roman overlay and adaptation of Greek and other cultures.

It must be stressed that early on Christianity saw its main rivals as being other Near Eastern religions, especially other forms of Judaism; magic in various forms, especially in some combination with Jewish ideas; and traditional Greek deities and philosophies. The dominant Roman religious culture that was imposed to various degrees in all parts of the Empire is not engaged in any substantive way. There are no confrontations over Jupiter Optimus Maximus or the worship of the emperor in Acts, no discussions of the Roman religion of hearth and home.

Christianity arose during a time when there was already enormous religious curiosity on the part of Romans and other pagans about Eastern religions and divinities ranging from Isis to Jesus. It sought to take advantage of this curiosity, and it offered to pagans a religion that did not require certain rituals (such as circumcision or the keeping of food laws) that would have immediately alienated them in obvious observable ways from their fellow Gentiles.[152] It did not require temples, costly animal sacrifices, priests — the very essence of much of ancient religion. It could meet in homes, and its rituals were flexible. It is not surprising that in the course of the next two centuries it came to be seen by pagans as a much more appealing religious option than Judaism, ordinary magic, or various other forms of traditional and popular religion that existed in the Empire. The irony of course is that when Christianity was finally endorsed by the Roman emperor it was well on the way to taking on the very properties of other ancient religions with priests, temples, sacrifices, and the like. One must ask, then, whether in the end Christianity was more the bearer or the recipient of socialization in the Empire.

That Bar-Jesus is called a false prophet strongly suggests that he was being used as a consultant of sorts by the proconsul, part of his official *comitatus* or entourage. We should not be surprised that a Roman might use such a person with associations with Judaism. We know that Jews had a reputation in the Empire for depth of religious insight and understanding, and there is even a reference to a Jewish sorcerer from Cyprus who aided the Roman governor Felix in seducing Drusilla away from her husband Azizus (*Ant.* 20.236-37).[153] Equally revealing is the reaction of Vespasian to Josephus's

---

151. See pp. 539ff. below.

152. See below on Acts 15.

153. The conjecture that the sorcerer in question might be none other than Bar-Jesus is doubtful. (1) In the first place the event recorded in Josephus transpired some years later (between five and ten years at least). (2) The name or title Elymas has been conjectured to

famous prophecy that he would be emperor, or the trust a highborn Roman matron placed in the advice of a syncretistic Jewess (Juvenal 6.543-44). One may also point to Emperor Tiberius's reliance on the astrologer Thrasyllus, who was seen as a true prophet.[154] Finally, one may also refer to Nero's reliance on and initiation by one Tiridates.[155] These examples make Luke's association of Bar-Jesus with the Roman proconsul readily believable.[156]

V. 7 indicates that the name of the proconsul was Sergius Paulus.[157] The question is which member of the Pauli is referred to here. Of the three names a Roman normally bore, Luke gives us only his cognomen and his nomen but not his praenomen or first name, which would enable us to pinpoint him. We know for a fact that they had extensive property in the region of Pisidian Antioch.[158] There are in addition three other inscriptions which provide some information about the Pauli, two of which suggest a connection to Cyprus and the third being consistent with such a connection.[159] The first of these (*IGR* III.930), found on the north coast of Cyprus at Soloi, does indeed refer to a proconsul named Paulus, but the praenomen and cognomen aren't given, and of course it is possible that in this case Paulus *is* a praenomen. This particular Paulus held office in the tenth year of some emperor. If the emperor in question was Claudius, the inscription would date to about A.D. 50, but the very date line seems to be a later addition.[160] It thus remains possible that this refers to the same Sergius Paulus as mentioned in Acts, but it is also possible

---

be a garbled form of the Greek word ετοιμος (ready), which in fact the D text has instead of Elymas (as do with variants some Latin manuscripts and Lucifer). This conjecture is based on weak textual evidence — Elymas is clearly the more difficult reading. (3) In regard to the Josephus text there is considerable evidence for the reading ατομος instead of Simon, which *could* be a corruption of ετοιμος, but this is far from certain and based on an insecure reading anyway. In short, it is not wise to add conjectural reading to conjectural reading, both with less than immaculate textual pedigree in order to arrive at the identification of Elymas with this other Jewish μαγυς. Cf. Metzger, *Textual Commentary,* pp. 402-3; Barrett, *Acts,* vol. 1, p. 615; Polhill, *Acts,* p. 293 n. 13.

154. See on all this Nock, "Paul and the Magus," pp. 183-84.

155. Pliny, *Nat. Hist.* 30.17.

156. For the association of Jews and magic in pagan authors, cf. Strabo, *Geography* 16.2.39-43; Apuleius, *Apologia* 90; Pliny, *Nat. Hist.* 30.2.11.

157. On the suggestion that Paul was connected to Sergius Paulus as a freedman of the same gens, cf. Meeks, *The First Urban Christians,* p. 218 n. 68.

158. Though his broader conjectures about this family all becoming Christian may be doubted, the inscriptions unearthed by W. Ramsay, near Pisidian Antioch, of an L. Sergius Paulus, son of another L. Sergius Paulus, and of a daughter Sergia Paula found in Pisidian Antioch itself are firm evidence of a connection to this city. See Ramsay, *Bearing of Recent Discovery,* pp. 150-72. On the estate see Hemer, *Book of Acts,* p. 109 and n. 17.

159. It is instructive to compare and contrast the detailed discussion of these three inscriptions by Van Elderen, "Some Archaeological Observations," and Nobbs, "Cyprus."

160. See Van Elderen, "Some Archaeological Observations," p. 153.

on epigraphical grounds that the inscription comes from as late as the time of Hadrian in the second century. What this inscription does probably show is the connection of the Pauli to the island of Cyprus. The next inscription (*IGR* III.935), found in northern Greece at Kytharia, may be dated to the first century A.D. paleographically and refers to one Quintus Sergius, who was on Cyprus during the reign of one of the Julio-Claudian emperors, possibly Caligula, possibly Claudius, but the former would be too early to correspond with our proconsul.[161] The inscription can be read either way. The third inscription is in some ways the most clear and helpful and is in Latin rather than Greek (*CIL* VI.31545). Here we have a clear reference to one Lucius Sergius Paulus, who was one of the curators of the Tiber River under Claudius. There is nothing in this inscription that would rule out the possibility that this Sergius Paulus was either at an earlier or a later date a proconsul on Cyprus,[162] and in fact various classics scholars have been more ready than some NT scholars to identify the man mentioned in Acts 13 with the one in the Latin inscription.[163]

In sum, the inscriptional evidence clearly places the Sergii Pauli on the island of Cyprus, and the Latin inscription about Lucius of that family may point us to the man in question. Given what we know about the Roman career patterns of the time it is quite feasible that a curator of the Tiber might have before or after his curatorship served as proconsul on Cyprus. The fact that the Latin inscription datable to the 40s, like the text of Acts 13, mentions a prominent Sergius Paulus as a public official suggests a connection between the two since clearly Paul's visit to Cyprus must also be dated to the reign of Claudius in the later 40s. This would provide one more piece of evidence, though indirect, that Luke is dealing with historical data and situations, not just creating a narrative with historical verisimilitude.

Luke in *v. 7* evaluates Sergius Paulus as a proconsul (ανθυπατος) with συνετος (intelligence), presumably because he had the wisdom to summon Barnabas and Paul, wishing to listen to their proclamation and believe at least some of what they said. To a person such as the proconsul, Paul and Barnabas would have appeared to be traveling philosophers or rhetors, because they offered public teaching.[164] Luke will confirm this identification when he pre-

---

161. The insistence by Mitford that Caligula is the emperor in question may be disputed, as it is based on a reading of a fragmentary letter which could be either a Greek alpha or a delta. If it is the latter the emperor in question would be Claudius.

162. As Nobbs, "Cyprus," p. 286, points out, he may have held the curatorship after being proconsul, perhaps because he wished to return to Rome, or perhaps, as she conjectures, because he was awaiting a large appointment to a province, having finished his term in Cyprus.

163. Cf., e.g., Levick, *Roman Colonies*, p. 112; Mitchell, "Population and the Land."

164. See rightly Ramsay, *St. Paul the Traveller*, p. 75.

sents Paul's synagogue sermon in the form of deliberative rhetoric (see below). Luke is not interested in recounting any details about a stay at Paphos or any interaction with ordinary people but rather focuses on the encounter with the proconsul.

V. 8 seems to imply that Elymas interceded because he feared he might be out of work if the proconsul accepted the word from the two missionaries. We are told he opposed them and tried to turn Sergius Paulus away from "the faith."[165] Vv. 8-9 present us with two questions about names. First, Luke tells us that Elymas the μαγυς is the μεθερμηνευται of his name. This presumably means that Elymas etymologically means or is translated "magus." Clearly enough the former name is not a Greek name; indeed, it is not a Greek word at all. It may represent a transliteration of the Arabic *alim* (plus ending), which means "wise." It is understandable why it might be translated using the Greek term for a sage or wise man, just as modern translators have translated μαγυς as wise man in Matt. 2:1. Another possibility is that the Hebrew *ḥōlēm*, which means an interpreter of dreams, has been transliterated Elymas.[166] In any case, it seems clear that Luke is not telling us the translation or meaning of the name Bar-Jesus.[167]

The second name conundrum arises at *v. 9*, where for the first time we hear of Saul also being called Paul. As Barrett astutely puts it, this does not represent a change in name, but the identification of an alternative name.[168] Luke's way of putting it probably rules out the idea that Paul borrowed the name of the proconsul. It is probably right to say that Luke has introduced the name at this juncture because now Paul will be dealing with Gentiles and will accordingly want to use his Roman name in doing so. Presumably Paulus was the apostle's cognomen, though it may have been

---

165. It is often suggested that Luke's language here reflects the later period in which he wrote, a period in which της πιστεως would refer to a specific body of doctrine or beliefs. Yet we find this same sort of use of πιστις with the definite article in a letter Paul wrote in the 50s; cf. 1 Cor. 16:13. See my *Conflict and Community in Corinth*, p. 319. It is true, however, that here as elsewhere Luke writes as a Christian, using Christian jargon. If the proconsul summoned the missionaries, it was to hear their message; presumably he would not have yet called it the word of God, but Luke does.

166. See Hemer, *Book of Acts*, pp. 227-28.

167. Whatever Luke means, it seems clear from this that he assumes Theophilus wouldn't know the meaning of a Semitic name.

168. Cf. Ramsay, *St. Paul the Traveller*, p. 81; Barrett, *Acts*, vol. 1, p. 616. As Ramsay suggests, these alternative names would be used according to what audience Paul would be addressing, or, more to the point, according to what locale he was visiting. Part and parcel of a κατα γενος approach to history writing meant one was sensitive to the nuances involved in a change of ethnic or geographical setting. Luke is signaling that henceforth Paul would primarily be in regions where his Greek (or Roman) name would be apropos.

his praenomen or even a nickname or supernomen, for "paulus" in Latin means little.[169]

Paul, full of the Holy Spirit, cast a withering stare ("looked intently") at Elymas and then offers us a play on words — he calls him Bar-Satan (or in Greek υιε διαβολος) instead of Bar-Jesus.[170] Here in *v. 10* we have a contrast between Elymas, who is said to be full of deceit and fraud and an enemy of righteousness, and Paul, full of the Spirit and of truth and righteousness. Elymas is accused of doing the opposite of what the Scriptures call a person to do: "make straight the way of the Lord."[171] *V. 11* seems to involve a form of oath curse — "the hand of the Lord is against you and you will be blind." The αχρι καιρου suggests some mercy in this — it will only be for a time. Immediately darkness fell upon the man and he groped around for someone to lead him by the hand. The parallels with the experience of Saul himself are striking: (1) both strongly opposed God's word, (2) both were struck blind for a time, (3) both were said to need being led by the hand thereafter. What we have here is a punitive miracle story, and as such we should expect the reaction of the audience to be recorded last. This is what we find in v. 12.

V. 12 sums up the outcome of this encounter between two who claimed to have access to divine power and insight. We are told the proconsul believed, "being astonished (deeply impressed) at the teaching of the Lord." We might have expected Luke to say, astonished at the miracle performed in the Lord's name and power.

Are we to assume, then, that the proconsul became a Christian? This is possibly Luke's meaning, but in view of the lack of clear explication of *what* the proconsul believed,[172] the lack of any reference to the falling of the Spirit,

169. Acts 13:9 surely has the same intent as in 12:12, where an alternative name is in view. Cf. Leary, "Paul's Improper Name"; Hemer, "The Name of Paul"; and my *Conflict and Community in Corinth*, p. 5 and n. 12. Leary notes a reason why he would not have wanted to be called "saulos" in the Greco-Roman world, a word that refers to the wanton way of walking of prostitutes. Only Luke tells us Paul's Semitic name, but some possible confirmation that it is correct is that Paul says he was of the tribe of Benjamin (Phil. 3:5).

170. The reason for all these word and name plays in this passage is uncertain. Perhaps sociologically the point in regard to Elymas is that naming persons in antiquity was seen as a means of having control over them, or in this case revealing their true nature, unmasking them.

171. This could be an allusion to the process which began with John the Baptist and continued on into the era of the church. Cf. Luke 1:76, 3:4-5 quoting Isa. 40:3, and Acts 13:24-25. Elymas is thus seen as John's, Jesus', Peter's, and Paul's opposite, making crooked what these others were attempting to make straight. See Tannehill, *Narrative Unity of Luke-Acts*, 2:163.

172. Partly the issue turns on whether we are meant to see a subjective or objective genitive here at the end of the story. Are these the teachings Jesus offered or the teachings about the Lord? Presumably it is the latter here.

and the lack of any reference to baptism we cannot be certain. Astonishment was also the reaction of the crowds in Acts 3:10, but it did not mean they were all converted. Simon Magus in 8:13 is said to have believed,[173] but it is clear from the rest of the story that Luke does not see him as truly or fully converted. Certainly, the proconsul responded positively to the message, and apparently also to the miracle. Probably it is best to take the verb in question as an inceptive aorist — the proconsul "began to believe" at this juncture.[174] For Luke's audience it was important to point out that even those of high social status, even those who were governmental officials, could be favorably impressed with the gospel and not see it as a threat. Indeed, they might even be converted.

It is probably no accident that this subsection ends very similarly to what we find in Luke 4:32. In both conclusions we hear of amazement at the teaching of the Lord, and in both stories teaching and the first wonder recorded as being performed by the protagonist are clustered together.[175] Luke intends with Paul, as with Peter previously, to show how they follow closely in the footsteps of their Lord in their teachings and actions and lives, and receive a similar response. Paul, before his Damascus road experience, used to be like Elymas; now he is like Jesus.

2. The Mission to Pisidian Antioch and Paul's Synagogue Speech (13:13-52)

It is quite possible that the reason Paul and Barnabas went off to Pisidian Antioch, which is not necessarily the most obvious choice for the next place to evangelize, is that Sergius Paulus, who had family connections in that region, suggested it. Perhaps he even wrote a letter of recommendation for Paul and Barnabas to aid them along the way.[176] R. L. Fox puts it this way.

> The contact with Sergius Paulus is the key to the subsequent itinerary of the first missionary journey. From Cyprus Paul and Barnabas struck east to the newly founded colony of Pisidian Antioch, miles away from any Cypriot's normal route. Modern scholars have invoked Paul's wish to reach the uplands of Asia and recover from a passing sickness. . . . We know, however, that the family of the Sergii Pauli had a prominent connection with Pisidian Antioch . . . the Sergii Pauli's local influence was linked with their ownership of a great estate nearby in central Anatolia: it is an old and apt guess that

173. Έπίστευσεν is used in both cases without an object.
174. For proper cautions see Williams, *Acts*, p. 215.
175. See Tannehill, *Narrative Unity of Luke-Acts*, 2:162.
176. See Johnson, *Acts*, p. 227.

these connections go back to the time of Paul's governor. They explain very neatly why Paul and Barnabas left the governor's presence and headed straight for distant Pisidian Antioch. He directed them to the area where his family had land, power and influence. The author of Acts saw only the impulse of the Holy Spirit, but Christianity entered Roman Asia on advice from the highest society.[177]

The social significance of this conclusion must be emphasized. From the beginning of his missionary work Paul is presented by Luke as one who is comfortable in the circles of status and power, and finds at least a measure of acceptance in such venues. We will say more shortly about the implications of this portrait, especially as it relates to the Paul that is revealed by the letters.[178] V. 13 punctuates the impression of Paul's importance by speaking now not of Barnabas and Saul as before but of the Pauline circle or entourage (οι περι Παυλον).

We are told that this group came to Perga in Pamphylia in southern Asia Minor, and at this juncture Mark left the group and went back, not to Cyprus or Antioch, but to Jerusalem. Was he reporting on this new venture? Was he homesick? Luke does not tell us, but the impression left by reading this text together with 15:37-38 is that Paul (and Luke) saw this as a matter of desertion or abandonment. Nothing is said about any preaching in Perga at this juncture; rather, Paul and Barnabas set out on an arduous journey over the Taurus Mountains to Antioch near Pisidia.

The reading of p45, 74, ℵ, A, B, C, and others with the accusative construction in v. 14 ("Antioch, the [one near] Psidia"; cf. Strabo 12.6.4) is to be preferred to the genitive construction of D, E, Y, 33, 81, and others (Antioch of Pisidia) on textual grounds but also on historical grounds. Here we may, however, have a clue that the earliest form of the Western text postdates the changes that happened during the reign of Diocletian in A.D. 295 when Antioch was assigned to Pisidia.[179] Acts shows that the author had good knowledge of the provincial arrangements in Asia Minor during the first century A.D.[180] This Antioch was one of sixteen such cities of this name and was designated the one near to Pisidia to distinguish it from the others, especially from another city of the same name also in Phrygia but on the Maeander River. The Antioch presently under discussion was in the Roman province of Galatia (its political

177. Fox, *Pagans and Christians*, pp. 293-94. Fox is of course simply one of the latest to follow the suggestions of Ramsay, *St. Paul the Traveller*, pp. 71ff. See also Ramsay's *Cities of Paul*, pp. 245ff. See Wilson, *Paul*, p. 120, on Sergius Paulus as a convert.

178. See pp. 430ff. below on the Paul of Acts versus the Paul of the letters.

179. Cf. Metzger, *Textual Commentary*, pp. 404-5; Ramsay, *Cities of Paul*, pp. 245-314.

180. See Levick, *Roman Colonies*, pp. 34-35, 58-67, 130-44.

designation) and in the region of Phrygia (basically an ethnic designation), and thus was quite properly called "the Phrygian and Galatic region" or Phrygian Galatia (so Acts 16:6).[181] It is perfectly possible, and indeed likely, that those Paul addresses in Galatians are the converts he made in places like Antioch and Iconium on this first recorded missionary journey into Gentile territory.

Pisidian Antioch was some 3,600 feet above sea level and was the civil and administrative center of that part of the Galatian province. Augustus had made it a Roman colony in 25 B.C.[182] For our purposes what is crucial about this city is that besides its majority Gentile population it also had a sizable, well-established minority population of Jews, originally brought to the region during the Seleucid period.[183] There is still a limited measure of truth in Ramsay's summary of the social character of Jews in Antioch, though he considerably underestimates the degree to which Palestinian Jews were Hellenized.

> When Paul visited Antioch, the original Jewish Colony had been for three centuries and a half exposed to the influence [of Hellenism]. . . . It was inevitable that the Jews of Antioch should become very different in character from the narrow class of Palestinian Jews; they were hellenised Greek-speaking, able to move freely and win success in the free competition of the hellenic self-governing city. Yet . . . they were still Jews in feeling and religion, citizens of the Hellenic city of Pisidian Antioch, yet men of Judaea as the centuries passed. The religious teaching of the home and the synagogue held them firmly in the national character.[184]

Yet Ramsay is right to emphasize strongly the Roman superstructure and legal character of the city by the time Paul visited it. "It is in agreement with the strong Roman feeling and custom which characterized Antioch in the first century . . . that the population are not called by Luke Hellenes or Greeks

---

181. The older debate on this issue has died down in light of the ever mounting evidence that Phrygia could be used as an adjective to designate a particular region within the Roman province of Galatia. See the discussion in Hemer, *Book of Acts,* pp. 283ff., and in Hansen, "Galatia." The phrase Luke uses in Acts 16:6 is analogous to the well-attested phrase "Pontus Galaticus."

182. Of the various Roman colonies Paul visited, indeed seemed to gravitate to with regularity, Luke calls only Philippi a colony in 16:12, perhaps because of the events that transpired there, including the interaction with Roman authorities and Paul's use of the Roman citizen trump card.

183. See Josephus, *Ant.* 12.147-53, who speaks of some two thousand Jewish families being settled in Phrygia and Lydia somewhere around 210 B.C. Cf. now the discussion in Trebilco, *Jewish Communities in Asia Minor,* pp. 5ff.

184. Ramsay, *Cities of Paul,* p. 258.

[contrast 11:20], but only the Plebs or the Gentiles. The latter is a wider term, which included at once Greeks and Romans and Phrygians and other native races."[185]

V. 14b indicates that on the sabbath day Paul and Barnabas went into the synagogue in Antioch and sat down.[186] After the reading of the Law and the Prophets[187] a message was passed from the synagogue officials to Paul and Barnabas asking if they would address the congregation (cf. the order in 1 Tim. 4:13). The term used in *v. 15* for these officials is αρχισυναγωγοι, and some have been surprised by the use of the plural here, claiming Luke has made an error.[188] In fact, while it is true that there would normally be only one active ruler of the synagogue (but cf. Mark 5:22), sometimes the title could be honorary, sometimes former synagogue rulers were still addressed as such, sometimes husbands and wives could both be called by this term, and finally there may have been more than one synagogue in the town with the rulers all gathering in one place to hear these itinerant Jewish preachers. Thus the usage here is completely within the realm of possibilities. The synagogue ruler had as part of his or her function the direction of worship, apparently including assigning who would address the congregation.[189] Paul and Barnabas are recognized as brothers in the Jewish faith, and since Luke's account is elliptical we must assume some previous conversation with the synagogue rulers.

What they are asked to give is a λογος παρακλησεως, which must surely mean a word of exhortation to the people (cf. Heb. 13:22).[190] This phrase is

185. Ibid., p. 277.

186. For evidence of synagogues being built in the Diaspora even before the time of Christ, see *New Docs* (1978), pp. 121-22, with an inscription from Egypt dating from between 246 and 221 B.C. The term used in this inscription, however, is προσευχη, rather than Luke's preferred term, συναγωγος.

187. The regular procedure seems to have been that first the Shema would be recited, then the saying of the prayer (in later times the eighteen benedictions), then the reading of Torah often accompanied by a translation in the Diaspora, especially if the LXX was not used, then an exposition or homily would follow. Cf. *m. Ber.* 1:4; 4:3; 3:5; 1:2, on these different parts of the service.

188. Lüdemann, *Early Christianity,* p. 153.

189. See *New Docs* (1979), pp. 218-19. There is evidence also that in the Diaspora women could hold such an office, and not just as an honorary title. See *New Docs,* pp. 219-20 and also the extended helpful discussion in Brooten, *Women Leaders,* pp. 5-39. Further on this subject see A.-J. Levine, ed., *"Women Like These": New Perspectives on Jewish Women in the Greco-Roman World* (Atlanta: Scholars Press, 1991). See below on Acts 13:50 on prominent women connected to the synagogue. On the order of synagogue worship cf. Schürer, *History of the Jewish People,* 2:448.

190. Here λαος is used in the sense of the (Jewish) people of God, which is only appropriate on the lips of a synagogue ruler. Cf. 2:47; 3:9. It is possible that the phrase "word of exhortation" (or encouragement) had a somewhat technical meaning in the context of the synagogue to refer to a homily based on the interpretation of Scripture. This

important in understanding how Luke is characterizing this address — it is a piece of deliberative, not epideictic, rhetoric meant to urge a change not just in belief but also in behavior, as vv. 40-42 makes clear. While one can draw some analogies between *v. 16* and what one finds in Diaspora synagogues,[191] it is probable that Luke intends to portray Paul in his first major discourse in Acts as a great orator, as is suggested both by the reference to the hand gesture[192] and the deliberative and masterful form of the piece of rhetoric that follows, which may be divided as follows: (1) *exordium* or proem — v. 16;[193] (2) *narratio* — vv. 17-25; (3) *propositio* — v. 26; (4) the setting forth of the *probatio,* including using inartificial proofs (Scripture) of the *propositio* — vv. 27-37;[194] (5) a *peroratio* or final exhortation — vv. 38-41 — introduced by the direct address to the audience ("to you," v. 38).[195] This distinguishing form of address which separates speaker from audience in terms of their conditions should be compared with the emphatic use of "we" in v. 32 which has the same function,[196] not to be confused with the use of "our" in various places in the speech where Paul is trying to identify with the audience (cf. vv. 17, 26).[197]

Other forms of analysis of this significant speech are also helpful in getting at its structure. For instance, it is right that the three direct addresses

---

description would suit not only this speech quite well but also the homily we call Hebrews. Glombitza, "Akta XIII,15-41," is probably going too far, however, in suggesting that the phrase has the technical sense of a messianic interpretation of the OT. Cf. Dumais, *Le Langage de L'Evangelisation,* pp. 69-70. The translation of παρακλησεως is aided by asking the question, Does the speech seek to encourage, comfort, console, or exhort? — surely the latter, as vv. 38ff. indicate. See Kilgallen, "Acts 13,38-39," p. 482 n. 4.

191. See Philo, *De Spec. Leg.* 2.62, which speaks of scholars sitting while one with experience rises to speak.

192. See Barrett, *Acts,* vol. 1, p. 629.

193. See Bruce, *The Acts of the Apostles,* p. 302.

194. In fact a careful examination of this section of the address shows Paul drawing on all four types of a priori proofs (cf. Quintilian 5.10.12-13): (1) things perceived by the senses (appearance of the risen Jesus to credible witnesses, vv. 30-31); (2) things established by law or other recognized written authority (Scripture, vv. 27, 29, 33-35); (3) things about which there is general agreement (the providence and power of God, vv. 32-33, 37); (4) things pertaining to the issue that would be admitted by all parties (innocence of Jesus and his execution by Pilate, v. 28; the death and burial of Jesus and David, vv. 29, 36). So Black, "The Rhetorical Form," p. 9.

195. Cf. Kennedy, *New Testament Interpretation,* pp. 124-25; Bruce, *The Acts of the Apostles,* p. 311; Black, "The Rhetorical Form," especially pp. 9-10; and on the general conformity of the speeches in Acts to the requirements and form of ancient Greco-Roman rhetoric, cf. Satterthwaite, "Background of Classical Rhetoric," p. 359.

196. See Tannehill, *Narrative Unity of Luke-Acts,* 2:169.

197. The reading ημιν in v. 26 is to be preferred over υμιν here on the basis of strong and varied textual evidence (p74, ‭א‬, A, B, D), and because of the context as well. See Metzger, *Textual Commentary,* pp. 408-9.

signal new divisions in the speech: (1) men Israelites at v. 16, (2) men brothers at v. 26, and (3) men brothers at v. 38. But it will be seen that these signals correspond to some of the divisions already recognized from rhetorical analysis.[198] That these phrases do not, however, signal all the parts of the speech can be seen from the fact that the proem is not actually part of the narration of Israelite history, nor are the arguments based largely on Scripture, which begin in v. 27 introduced in this way.

Luke's approach will be to give three major representative speeches of Paul to three different sorts of audiences: (1) to Jews in a synagogue here, (2) to pagans in Athens (Acts 17:22ff.), and (3) to Christians at Miletus (Acts 20:17ff.). This reveals Paul to be an orator of some skill and flexibility, something his letters also suggest.[199] In addition to this, it has been shown that Paul, like Peter before him, is being portrayed as following in the footsteps of Christ — all three offer paradigmatic speeches about salvation at the beginning of their ministries and experience rejection thereafter (cf. Luke 4; Acts 2 and 4; Acts 13).[200] Paul is being portrayed here as one who sought to further the Christian cause by engaging in a persuasive campaign with both Jews and Gentiles as the target audience.[201] Such a campaign involved various stages including preparation, proclamation, penetration (of the target group), separation, and consolidation.

Since this speech is carefully crafted to be persuasive to a Diaspora Jewish audience, it not only has the form of deliberative rhetoric but it reflects the patterns of early Jewish argumentation. In particular it has been argued that Paul is following the Yelammedenu form with Deut. 4:25-46 as the seder text, 2 Sam. 7:6-16 as the haftorah, and 1 Sam. 13:14 as the bridging or proem text.[202] Other suggestions have been made, especially for the seder text, and

---

198. See Dumais, *Le Langage de L'Evangelisation*, pp. 47-66. Dumais, however, finally concludes that basically this speech in both structure and form has the traits of a midrash, or a pesher such as one finds at Qumran (p. 114). The problem with this conclusion is that this speech is not primarily a creative exegesis or homiletical handling of OT texts, or an attempt to contemporize the meaning of the OT text. It is a salvation-historical argument which also involves a creative presentation of the gospel. As such it is not really about exegesis or Jewish hermeneutics but about persuasion using OT and Gospel narrative.

199. Cf. the introductions to my two commentaries *Conflict and Community in Corinth*, pp. 1ff.; and *Friendship and Finances in Philippi* (Valley Forge, Pa.: Trinity, 1994), pp. 1ff.

200. As Tannehill, *Narrative Unity of Luke-Acts*, 2:160-61, shows, Paul's speech here resembles Jesus' in setting and reaction and Peter's in substance. All three speeches mention the inclusion of Gentiles in God's plan of salvation and contain or lead to Scripture citation, and all are followed by a scene in which a lame man is healed (cf. Luke 5:17-26; Acts 3:1-10; 14:8-10).

201. On this subject cf. Murphy, "Early Christianity."

202. Cf. Bowker, "Speeches in Acts." There is of course no certainty in this matter. Ramsay, *St. Paul the Traveller*, p. 100, suggested that the Torah reading was Deut. 1:1–3:22 and the prophetic text Isa. 1:1-22.

in fact it seems more apparent that the *gezerah shewa* technique is used where texts are chosen because they share a common word and it is assumed that the two texts in which the shared words occur can illuminate each other. At 13:34 the text referring to holy things and the further text referring to the holy one are allowed to interact.[203]

In *v. 16* Paul begins by distinguishing two groups in his audience — Israelites and others who fear God.[204] This address must be compared to v. 43, where Jews and devout proselytes are referred to.[205] It is possible that Luke is aware of the distinction between a mere synagogue adherent and a full proselyte, and that in v. 16 he is simply addressing two large groups in general, those who are ethnic Jews and those who are Gentile sympathizers, while perhaps v. 43 is more specific.[206] Thus this address, while perhaps primarily for Jews, is nonetheless targeting those on the fringes of the synagogue as well from the outset. A lengthy proem was unnecessary in a speech of this sort where Paul could already assume a degree of kinship with his audience and did not have to labor to establish rapport.[207]

V. 17 begins the review of salvation history at a somewhat different juncture than the speech of Stephen in Acts 7. Here the focus is on the Jews' election and the formative events of the exodus. Most striking is the omission of any real attention being paid to Moses, unlike the Stephen speech.[208] With uplifted arm[209] God led them out of Egypt, having "made them great" in number while there. *V. 18* presents us with a textual problem. Is Luke saying that God bore with the Israelites or that he cared for them in the wilderness? Both readings are well attested, and it is clear enough that our text is alluding

203. See Johnson, *Acts*, p. 238.

204. It would appear, especially in light of v. 50, that Luke uses the term "men" here and at vv. 26 and 38 in a more generic sense which would include female listeners, as would also be true of the use of the term "brothers" in the latter two texts. See pp. 120ff. above.

205. Notice how the latter group is not simply subsumed under the former.

206. On this entire subject see the excursus, pp. 341ff. above. Clearly the term "devout" in itself, being used here in v. 43 as an adjective of sorts, is not meant to be a technical term.

207. See rightly Black, "The Rhetorical Form," p. 7. Cf. Quintilian, *Inst.* 3.8.7; 4.1.5-6, 25-26.

208. The older argument (cf. Haenchen, *Acts*, p. 408) that Luke has tailored the various speeches in Acts so that they are not simply duplicates of one another, and intends for them to have an effect as a collective whole, has some merit. However, as Barrett, *Acts*, vol. 1, p. 632, points out, what seems to dictate the content of the speeches more than anything else is their purposes and differing audiences. The purpose of Paul's speech here is very different from Stephen's. Paul is not dealing with Israel's recalcitrance but with the blessings and promised benefits God has bestowed on Israel from time to time. This is a more theocentric speech; Acts 7 is more ecclesiocentric.

209. A phrase indicating God's power; cf. in the LXX Exod. 6:1, 6; 32:11; Deut. 3:24; 4:34 et al.

to Deut. 1:31 (LXX), where we find the same variants. The positive context favors the reading "cared for," and this is in fact the better-attested reading for Deut. 1:31.[210]

V. 19 continues the positive theme, indicating that God cleared the land of Canaan of seven nations (cf. Deut. 7:1) in order to give Israel its inheritance "for about 450 years." This would seem to be arrived at by adding 400 years in Egypt to 40 in the wilderness and another 10 for the conquest of the land.[211] V. 20 then refers to the period of the judges up to the time of Samuel. We are seeing in this speech a definite attempt at the periodization of history.

V. 21 continues with a mention of the beginning of the monarchy, when Saul, son of Kish of the tribe of Benjamin, is chosen and given by God but also removed by God in favor of David. V. 22 includes a partial quotation of three different texts: (1) "I have found David" (Ps. 89:20), (2) "a man after my own heart" (1 Sam. 13:14), (3) "who will do all I want him to do" (Isa. 44:28).[212] One could add to this 1 Sam. 16:1, which uses the phrase "son of Jesse." It is probably not coincidental that David is said to be raised up by God (εγειρω) for Israel, for this is the same language about to be used of Jesus in v. 30, with a different meaning.[213]

V. 23 comes to the crucial point in salvation history — of David's seed,[214] God brought to Israel a savior, Jesus, just as God had promised. It will be noted how strongly Luke stresses God's sovereign hand in this entire process — God is the primary actor in all these events. Vv. 24-25 backtrack briefly to refer to the ministry of John the Baptist. This reference may be thought to be apropos to this setting since it appears that there were disciples of the Baptist in Asia Minor well into the first century A.D.[215] The quote from the Baptist should be compared to Luke 3:16-17, and for the disclaimer John 1:19-27 should be consulted. The text in Acts is not simply a quotation of either of these traditions. The importance of this reference to John is at least in part that he proclaimed a baptism of repentance to all Israel. In short, he made clear that Israel was estranged from God and in need of reconciliation with Yahweh. The

210. Cf. Barrett, Acts, 1:632; Johnson, Acts, p. 231, and contrast Metzger, Textual Commentary, pp. 405-6.

211. The Western text is clearly inferior here, suggesting that there were judges for 450 years! See Beginnings, 4:150-51, but cf. Ropes's views in Beginnings, 3:121.

212. These texts are also cited in this sort of combination in 1 Clem 8.1, which may or may not indicate he knew Acts.

213. Johnson, Acts, p. 232.

214. Notice how "this man" is in the emphatic position in this sentence, stressing the connection between David and Jesus. See Johnson, Acts, p. 232.

215. Cf. Acts 19:3-4. This latter text is very close to vv. 24-25 of our text in its content. Thus Luke portrays Paul as having a rather clear knowledge of the Baptist's mission and his own messianic views about Jesus.

reference is also important in that it is meant to forestall any questions about the possible messianic character of Jesus' well-known contemporary.[216]

V. 26 indicates that the message of salvation was for both the descendants of Abraham and for those in Israel's midst who feared God, that is, for God-fearing Gentiles as well. Indeed, it is for the "we" that includes both the speaker and the listeners. *V. 27* sounds again the theme of the ignorance of the Jerusalem residents and leaders about who Jesus was.[217] It does not appear that Luke is emphasizing the guilt of those who were ignorant, only that they have missed the mark and the opportunity to recognize their savior, something the present audience is to be urged not to do. The ignorance is in part ascribed to a failure to understand what the prophets said in the Scriptures which were read every sabbath.[218] Yet ironically in behaving this way and by condemning Jesus these ignorant ones were fulfilling what the prophets said about these matters. *V. 28* stresses that Jesus' death happened in spite of the fact that the Jews could find no solid reason, no good cause to condemn him. For Luke it is important to make clear to his audience that Jesus was not a criminal deserving of Roman execution, even though he was in fact executed by Pontius Pilate, the legitimate procurator of the region.

V. 29 reiterates that all that was done to Jesus had been foretold in advance in the Scriptures, and thus was part of God's plan, in spite of the motives and plans of human beings. Luke knows the tradition that the cross was called the tree, but he makes little of this fact.[219] V. 29b emphasizes that Jesus was laid in a tomb, making clear that he was truly dead. God, however, raised him from the realm of the dead ones, after which he appeared for many days to a specific group — those who had traveled with him from Galilee to Jerusalem and who were now his witnesses. These are in Luke's view the primary witnesses about the Risen One, and it is striking that there is no mention of the appearance to Paul in this speech (cf. 2:32). This is perhaps because the subject here in *v. 31* is the witness to the people, that is, to Israel, whereas in *v. 32*, punctuated by an emphatic "we" beginning the verse, the witness of Paul and Barnabas is said to be to those in the Diaspora, both Jews and devout Gentiles. Tannehill is right, however, to reject the view that Paul is being denied here the status of an eyewitness of Christ (cf. 22:14-15; 26:16).

216. Dumais, *Le Langage de L'Evangelisation*, p. 279, is right that Paul is following the effective rhetorical technique of drawing on common traditions the audience would readily accept and also forestalling possible objections or questions by covering subjects such as the Baptist.

217. How this motif is handled is one of the clearest indicators of the tendentiousness of some of the editing found in Codex Bezae. On 13:27 see Epp, "The 'Ignorance Motif,'" pp. 57-59.

218. On this phrase cf. 15:21. Both the Law and the Prophets would normally be read each sabbath in the synagogue.

219. Cf. 5:30; 10:39; Gal. 3:13 and Deut. 21:22.

"These verses do not intend to contrast Paul with the Galilean witnesses but to make them companions in witness."[220]

V. 33 indicates that what was long promised to the Jewish ancestors God has now fulfilled for their descendants by raising Jesus from the dead. This point is verified by reference to Scripture.[221] Luke speaks of the citation being from the second psalm.[222] The psalm citation is about the coronation of the king, on which occasion he is designated or recognized to be God's son. Here this event is connected with Jesus' resurrection. This whole discussion is not far from what Paul says in Rom. 1:3-4, perhaps citing an earlier tradition.[223] The latter text speaks of Jesus as the Son who was descended from David according to the flesh (so Acts 13:22-23), but who was declared or designated Son of God in power by means of the resurrection from the dead.

V. 34 offers another citation from Scripture meant to support the notion of the risen Jesus never returning again to the corruption of human decay, a partial quote of Isa. 55:3 (LXX) followed quickly in *v. 35* by a citation of Ps. 16:10. The original psalm of course refers to God saving the psalmist from death, from going down into sheol, but here it is used to refer to being saved from the decay and corruption of death, because Jesus was God's holy one. The linkage between the two texts seems to be the term "holy" in variant forms (τα οσια in v. 34b and τον οσιον σου in v. 35).[224] There is ambiguity about what is referred to in v. 34 — are "the holy things" God's promises, or could it even be seen as an oblique reference to Jesus himself?[225] In view of Wisdom of Solomon 6:10 and Josephus, *Ant.* 8.115, it seems likely that the reference is to "the holy things said."[226]

---

220. Tannehill, *Narrative Unity of Luke-Acts,* 2:169.

221. For a detailed study of the use of Scripture in vv. 32-37, see Lövestam, *Son and Saviour,* especially pp. 84-87, and Evans and Sanders, *Luke and Scripture,* pp. 202-6.

222. The reading "second" as opposed to "first" psalm is very widely attested in the manuscript tradition, including all uncials except D. There are, however, various church fathers who call this psalm the first psalm, and there is some Jewish as well as Christian evidence that the first two psalms were connected together in some traditions. Origen, Tertullian, and Cyprian, as well as both Talmuds, reflect these traditions. It is not known when the Psalms were first numbered, but it may be that the tradition was flexible at the time the NT was being written. Probably D and the other witnesses that have the reading "first psalm" here are reflecting this alternate tradition which seems to have been current in certain parts of the church, perhaps the parts where D was put together. See Metzger, *Textual Commentary,* pp. 412-14, and Parker, *Codex Bezae,* pp. 261ff. The latter suggests the city of Berytus (Beirut) as the possible locale where this remarkable manuscript originated.

223. For other Paulinisms in this speech, see below on vv. 38-39.

224. For the use of Holy One as a title for Jesus, see 2:27.

225. Probably not the latter, in view of the "you" in this verse. Cf. Barrett, *Acts,* vol. 1, p. 647.

226. Johnson, *Acts,* p. 235. Cf. the whole discussion of J. Dupont, *Etudes sur les Actes des Apotres* (Paris: Cerf, 1967), pp. 337-59.

In v. 35 this speech is quite close also to that of Peter in 2:31-32, sharing a common citation. It raises again the question whether there might have been a primitive *testimonia* list, a list of scriptures regularly used to attest to various parts of the kerygma by various early Christian preachers. *V. 36* in our text is also quite close to Peter's speech (cf. 2:29), the point being that the promises in the psalms could not be about David since he not only died but his body experienced corruption. This was in contrast, says *v. 37*, with Jesus, who did not lie for generations with his ancestors as was the case with David, but rather was raised from the dead shortly after his death. The purpose of the entire argument up to this point was to make possible the final exhortation which follows in vv. 38ff. Since Jesus is the Messiah of Israel, and the savior for one and all, and since he is attested by the Scriptures and eyewitnesses as well as faithful preachers such as Paul, the audience must not make the same mistake the Jews of Jerusalem made. Just as Israel and David were God's chosen ones, so, too, is Jesus, and this must be recognized, for the promises of God are fulfilled in Him.

V. 38 begins the "word of exhortation" or *peroratio* proper, to which all that has come before is but a necessary prologue.[227] Probably v. 38 and v. 39 should be seen as two different ways to express the same truth — through this man forgiveness of sins is proclaimed to Paul's audience, which is to say that by Jesus everyone who believes in him is set free from sins. It is not impossible that *v. 39* means to make a comparison rather than a contrast between the Law of Moses and what is true in Christ. That is, it could mean that the Law of Moses was capable of setting things right in some matters, but that Jesus could provide justification in all cases. It must be remembered that sin offerings, according to the OT, were provided to expiate inadvertent sins, but no sin offering could expiate sins committed deliberately or with premeditation, those committed as the OT puts it "with a high hand."[228] It is also possible, however, that Luke simply means that Jesus sets one free from all sins, none

227. Kilgallen, "Acts 13,38-39," is quite right about what the climax of the speech is, but he does not understand the rhetorical significance of this conclusion. It shows that the exigency Paul or Luke must deal with is that while God had provided this salvation through Christ for his Jewish people, many had already rejected it, and so the speech must overcome this fact, and at the climax warn the audience against a similar rejection of Jesus and its consequence.

228. See Bruce, *The Acts of the Apostles*, p. 311. Bruce thinks that this interpretation must be rejected because nothing suggests the sacrificial law is in view — but this is surely precisely what the language of justification and forgiveness suggests. He also opposes it because it suggests that Jesus' death just atones for the hard cases — deliberate sins. The text, however, may be making a simple comparison and not a contrast, and if so the point would be that Jesus' death can atone for even those sins which the Mosaic Law wasn't able to deal with. If even such sins could be atoned for by this means, then, a fortiori, even lesser sins could be dealt with through Christ as well.

of which the Law of Moses could really deal with.[229] In any case the language of justification and faith in Christ certainly echoes the basic Pauline message and suggests at the least that Luke knew that message.[230] The judgment quoted by Ramsay that we have here not an un-Pauline but an incompletely Pauline way of putting things is perhaps fair. On the other hand, it may be that Luke is trying to portray here the early message of Paul, and thus this announcement might be seen as but preparatory or tending in the direction of the later, fuller Pauline gospel.[231]

V. 40 provides the concluding warning to the audience — they must beware lest they do not take the preaching to heart and so perish, as the prophets warned. The text cited in *v. 41* is Hab. 1:5, where Israel was warned about the rise of Nebuchadnezzar and the threat of invasion; in short, Paul doesn't want to see a similar disaster befall his audience.[232] *V. 42* indicates that the congregation urged Paul and Barnabas to speak again on this subject the following sabbath. Not only so but we are told in *v. 43* that many Jews and devout proselytes[233] followed the two Christian preachers as they walked away and urged them to continue in the grace of God, further evidence that Luke knows the basic themes of Paul's message.[234] It is not impossible that Luke means to suggest that God's prevenient grace is already working in Paul's audience, though they have not yet been fully converted.

With some rhetorical hyperbole Luke says in *v. 44* that almost the whole city came to hear the word of the Lord on the second sabbath.[235] *V. 45* indicates the first negative reaction, and it is on the part of some Jews. This reaction is said to involve jealousy, presumably because Paul and Barnabas were attracting

229. See Johnson, *Acts*, p. 236.

230. It is dangerous simply to assume that the way Paul addresses Christians in his letters would be exactly identical to the way he would address non-Christians in his missionary preaching. It is probably no accident that the one speech of Paul in Acts that sounds the most like the Paul of the letters is the Miletus speech in Acts 20, where Paul is said to be addressing Christians. Though even in that speech in Acts 20 there are Lukanisms, showing he has phrased the speech in his own language, this latter speech shows that Luke knows a good deal more about the basic message of Paul to Christians than one might otherwise suspect from the missionary speeches in Acts 13 and 17.

231. See Ramsay, *Cities of Paul*, p. 305.

232. See Moessner, "Paul in Acts," p. 101.

233. Marshall, *Acts*, p. 229, has the balance right in saying that the phrase means worshiping proselytes and as such is a description of these proselytes — σεβουμενων not being a technical term for a particular class of Gentiles here.

234. Barrett suggests that the message of salvation, which the audience has heard and at least in part received, is seen as grace, and thus the audience can be urged to continue in what they have already in some measure received. See Barrett, *Acts*, vol. 1, p. 654.

235. Ramsay, *Cities of Paul*, p. 311: "a certain degree of rhetorical stress and exaggeration may perhaps be felt in the expression; but one can not doubt that a large and impressive concourse of citizens to the Synagogue took place on the second Sabbath."

a large Gentile audience while apparently the local Jews themselves had been less successful in attracting Gentiles. There is some evidence for Jewish missionary activity during this era, though it is not plentiful, and it should not be assumed to indicate a widespread and regular effort on the part of the Jews. It may be that efforts were more strenuous in some parts of the Diaspora, particularly Rome.[236] It may be that in Antioch the Jews had simply relied on the curiosity of the Gentiles to attract them to the synagogue, but now Paul and Barnabas were setting out to direct the message to one and all. V. 45b indicates that some Jews were not only angry but they blasphemed and contradicted what was spoken by Paul. Presumably the word "blaspheme" means not that they took God's name in vain but that they denied the truth of Paul's message in strong terms, perhaps with oaths, or that they cursed Jesus (cf. 1 Cor. 12:3).

This response of the Jews in turn prompts a response involving boldness or free speech ($\pi\alpha\rho\rho\eta\sigma\iota\alpha$ — the characteristic of a good and honest orator). V. 46 indicates Paul's missionary principle but perhaps also a theological principle — God's word must be spoken to the Jews first, and then if they reject it Paul will turn to the Gentiles. With more than a little irony Paul says the rejection of the gospel means that the rejecters judge themselves to be unworthy of eternal life, which is to say unworthy of salvation and its ongoing benefits.[237]

In view of what follows immediately in 14:1ff. this "turning to the Gentiles" can only refer to what Paul will do while he remains in Antioch. "Turning to the Gentiles means the end of such preaching in the Antioch synagogue."[238] The mission is universal but salvation must be offered to the Jews first (so also Rom. 1:16) in place after place because God, as the previous speech has shown, has chosen them and the Messiah was promised by God to Israel. That Paul agreed with this conclusion and approach is probably shown by the fact that he mentions that he had been repeatedly punished in the Jewish manner, apparently for speaking in synagogues (cf. 2 Cor. 11:24). The clue that this turning is local and not permanent is shown by the end of this story, where Paul and Barnabas follow Jesus' dictum that if a *city* rejects the message the

236. See Matt. 23:15 and the very careful and persuasive study of McKnight, *A Light among the Gentiles*, pp. 74-77. See now Levinskaya, *Acts in Its Diaspora Setting*, chap. 2. On the whole I think she is right that even in the Diaspora it was more a matter of Gentile curiosity and attraction rather than of Jewish recruitment of Gentiles.

237. The phrase "eternal life" does not occur a lot in Luke's writings, in fact in Acts only here and in 13:48 below (but cf. 11:18 and 5:20). In view of Romans and Gal. 6:8 this language may have been thought by Luke to be typically Pauline. It is quite true, as Barrett, *Acts*, vol. 1, p. 656, says, that irony is not typical of Luke, but it was typical of rhetoricians, and this is part of how Paul is being portrayed in this narrative.

238. Tannehill, "Rejection by Jews," p. 133.

disciples were to shake the dust of that place off their feet as they left and go to another city (cf. Luke 9:5; 10:11 to Acts 13:51).[239]

In other words, it is incorrect to say that this announcement about turning to the Gentiles means either that the Jews will not be preached to (or respond) again or that the Gentiles are offered God's word only because of the rejection by the Jews, as a sort of afterthought or second choice. Luke's view is made clear enough at the beginning of his Gospel — God intends to work salvation for all peoples (Luke 2:30-32),[240] but the Jews must be allowed to hear and respond first.

V. 47 presents a scriptural rationale for turning to the Gentiles. Here part of Isa. 49:6b (cf. Isa. 42:6 and 9:2) is used, a saying also drawn on in the Jesus saying in Acts 1:8b (cf. also Luke 2:32). Interestingly this saying is said to be a command of the Lord for Paul and Barnabas. They are assuming the role and tasks of the Servant in the Servant Songs, which is to say the tasks of Israel.[241] According to v. 48 the reaction of the Gentiles to this last remark is the opposite of that of the Jews — they were glad to hear about the mission to the Gentiles, praised the Lord, and "as many as were destined for eternal life became believers."

Throughout Acts we have seen Luke's emphasis on God's plan and sovereign hand guiding the circumstances in the life of Jesus and then in the life of the church, and here we are told that the Gentiles who came to faith were already within God's predetermined plan. This is certainly as strong a statement about predestination as one finds in Luke-Acts.[242] The upshot of all this activity is that, as v. 49 says, the word of God spread throughout the region.[243] This merely further incited those who were opposed to the gospel,

---

239. Here I am in full agreement with and am following Tannehill, "Rejection by Jews." On the further references to turning to the Gentiles in 18:5-6; 28:29, cf. pp. 548ff. and pp. 811ff. below.

240. Here I am simply agreeing with and paraphrasing the powerful arguments of Tannehill, "Rejection by Jews," p. 130.

241. These concluding verses of speech material (vv. 46-47) are dealt with at length and their importance shown by Buss, *Die Missionspredigt des Apostels Paulus im Psidian Antiochen.* I am not persuaded that these verses should be seen as part of the earlier speech. They serve rather as a sequel or epilogue-like comment meant to give the rationale for a change in audience. But see Soards, *The Speeches in Acts,* pp. 79-88.

242. In fact Barrett, *Acts,* vol. 1, p. 658, says, "The present verse is as unqualified a statement of absolute predestination . . . as is found anywhere in the NT." This verse involves a Jewish way of putting the matter; cf. Exod. 33:32-33; Ps. 69:28; Dan. 12:1; *1 Enoch* 47:3; 104:1; 108:3; *Jub.* 30:20, 22; *b. Ber.* 61b; and from Qumran CD 3:20.

243. This verse shows that it is not possible always to take such summary statements as markers in the text of new sections in the book. It is also unlikely that Luke is using the term χωρας here in a technical sense of a subdivision of a Roman province. See Bruce, *The Acts of the Apostles,* p. 315, correcting Ramsay.

and they in turn incited the devout women of high standing[244] in the city and the leading men, who may have been Roman magistrates,[245] so that Paul and Barnabas were persecuted and driven out of the region. This reaction may in part be explained by Levinskaya's suggestion that the high-status God-fearers (in this case apparently mainly women) provided the vital link with the Greco-Roman majority in the city, which if lost to conversion to Christianity might threaten the stability of the Jewish community in this city.[246]

It is clear that Luke is quite concerned about how those of high social standing, such as Theophilus probably was, react to the gospel. Though he often records a favorable response to the gospel of people of considerable social status (cf. below on 17:4), it is to Luke's credit that as a historian he also records the negative reaction to the gospel of such people, as he does here.[247] His apologetic tendencies do not lead him totally to ignore or leave out the opposition to the gospel, or the problems within the Christian community (cf. below on Acts 15).

Undaunted, Paul and Barnabas, after shaking the dust off their feet, went on to Iconium. Nevertheless they had made their mark on the city, for we are told that the disciples there were filled with joy and the Holy Spirit, the clear and regular signs in Acts that they had been truly converted (cf., e.g., Acts 8:38; 10:44-46).

3. The Mission to Iconium, Lystra, and Derbe and Return to Syrian Antioch (14:1-28)

Iconium was a good ninety miles southeast of Antioch and was the easternmost city in Phrygia. Under Emperor Claudius the city was given the privilege of calling itself Claudiconium, and it may be that at this juncture, or perhaps later during the reign of Hadrian (A.D. 117-38), it became a Roman colony.[248]

244. These seem to have been at least synagogue adherents in Antioch; otherwise the reason for calling them devout is unclear (cf. v. 43 and 17:12). Josephus, *War* 2.561, speaks of the majority of women in Damascus becoming Jewish converts, and Juvenal in Satire 6 (542) complains of the addiction of Roman women to Judaism. On the use of the term θεοσεβης in Jewish inscriptions in Asia Minor, see Trebilco, *Jewish Communities in Asia Minor*, pp. 152ff. Clearly enough the term is used of non-Jews who nonetheless worship the Jewish God.

245. See *New Docs*, 3:30-31. Also some of the leading families of Antioch were associated with the traditional cult of the god Men, and so the preaching may have been seen as a threat to this institution in Antioch.

246. See Levinskaya, *Acts in Its Diaspora Setting*, chap. 7.

247. On this whole matter see now Neyrey, "Luke's Social Location of Paul," pp. 260-68.

248. See now Mitchell, "Iconium and Ninica."

It is important to notice that the route Paul and Barnabas are following and their persecutions may be independently attested in 2 Tim. 3:11 and also in the Acts of Paul.[249] This route involved following, among other roads, the Via Sebaste, the main Roman road connecting the Roman colonies in the region. The road was broad and well paved, built to accommodate wheeled vehicles traveling to Iconium and Lystra, both cities in the region of Lycaonia. However, in order to reach Derbe Paul and Barnabas would have had to take an unpaved road about one hundred kilometers in a southeasterly direction from Lystra.[250]

Luke tells us immediately in *14:1* that things happened in the same way in Iconium as they had in Antioch, by which he means that Paul and Barnabas once again started by entering the synagogue, speaking in a similar fashion to what they had done in Antioch,[251] and experienced the same results. A great many[252] responded in faith, but others did not. It was not only Jews who believed but also "Hellenes" (i.e., Greeks). Ramsay has suggested, and he may be right, that the use of Ελληνων here, and not of the other Galatian city residents, reflects Luke's precise knowledge that Iconium was not yet a colony city, but rather a Greco-Asiatic one and proud of its Greek heritage.[253]

---

249. I say may be, for it is possible that the Pastorals were written by Luke himself, perhaps at the behest of Paul, or some would suggest later as a sort of sequel to Acts making clear what happened to Paul. Cf. Wilson, *Luke and the Pastoral Epistles*. The latter half of the previous sentence is more debatable than the former since in fact the Pastorals *don't* make perfectly clear what happened to Paul. On the Acts of Paul, cf. Lüdemann, *Early Christianity*, p. 157, and the apocryphal book itself (conveniently found in Hennecke-Schneemelcher, *New Testament Apocrypha II* [Philadelphia: Westminster, 1965], pp. 353-57, 360-64).

250. See Hansen, "Galatia," pp. 384-85. The precise locale of Derbe is still disputed. Van Elderen, "Some Archaeological Observations," pp. 156-61, suggests it is found at Kerti Hüyük, rather than at Gudelisin, the site Ramsay thought was likely. Whether Van Elderen is right or not (cf., e.g., Johnson, *Paul the Apostle*, p. 64, who says the site of Devri Shehri in the same region has been identified as the site in question by means of an inscription), it is very likely that Derbe is in the region of Kerti Hüyük, for inscriptions and tombstones mentioning Derbe have been found in the region. It is not absolutely certain that this last city was in the Roman province of Galatia during Paul's life, but it appears to have been, in view of the fact that the governor of Galatia from A.D. 49-54, Annius Afrinus, renamed the city Claudioderbe in view of the progress and achievements (i.e., the Romanization) of the city (see Hansen, p. 389). Notice that in 20:4 one person from Derbe and Timothy from Lystra accompany Paul to Jerusalem, presumably with the collection. This may be coordinated with 1 Cor. 16:1, where Paul speaks of the directions he gave to the Galatian church about the collection. It will be noted that no cities listed in 20:4 would support a northern Galatian hypothesis, but the two aforementioned probably support a southern one.

251. This is possibly the force of ουτως, if it does not just mean "so"; see Barrett, *Acts*, vol. 1, p. 667.

252. πολυ πληθος.

253. Ramsay, *Cities of Paul*, p. 359.

Scholars have often thought that *vv. 2-3* are actually in reverse order,[254] but there is no reason why μεν ουν cannot have an adversative force here,[255] as it does at Acts 25:4 and 28:5 (possibly also 17:7). The unpersuaded Jews incited and embittered the minds[256] of some Gentiles against the brothers (presumably meaning the new converts), and this is precisely why Paul and Barnabas spent considerable time in the city speaking freely and boldly for the Lord. *V. 3* also stresses that upon this word of God's grace,[257] God added the blessing or confirmation of signs and wonders through the hands of Paul and Barnabas. Here as elsewhere in Acts, Luke is concerned about the evidential value of miracles, that they confirm and certify the truthfulness of the spoken word (cf. 2:19, 22, 43; 4:16, 22, 30; 5:12; 6:8; 7:36; 8:6, 13; and especially 13:22; 15:8; 20:23). He is not interested in miracles in the abstract. Not surprisingly, the city as well as the synagogue community heard about these things and were divided about them, some siding with the Jews, the others with the apostles.

It will be well to discuss the use of αποστολοι in *v. 4* and in *v. 14* together. In v. 14 there is a textual problem. Some Western manuscripts (D, syr-p, it-gig) omit the words "the apostles," but this is not likely what Luke originally wrote.[258] There is in any case no doubt that this is the proper reading in v. 4. The question then becomes, why is it only here in all of Acts that Luke calls Paul (and Barnabas) an apostle? On the one hand, one could argue that Luke is simply using an (Antiochene?) source and has not fully conformed it to his usage elsewhere in this volume.[259] The problem with this suggestion is that this passage certainly reflects Luke's hand in various ways, indicating that whatever source he may have been using, he had made it his own.[260] A second suggestion which makes considerably better sense of the text is that Luke is not using the term "apostle" in this chapter in the usual sense that he does (to mean someone who not only had seen the risen Lord but had traveled with him during his ministry — cf. Acts 1:21-26), but rather in the sense one finds in 2 Cor. 8:23 (cf. Phil. 2:25 and Did. 11:3-6) to refer to those commissioned and sent out by a particular local church to perform some sort of Christian service or work. This suggestion takes into

254. See *Beginnings,* 4:161-62.

255. See Sharp, "The Meaning of μεν ουν," for the suggestion that μεν ουν here should be translated "rather," not "therefore."

256. Literally "they made evil the spirits/souls of the Gentiles against the brothers."

257. This could mean God's gracious word or the word about God's grace, probably the latter. See Johnson, *Acts,* p. 246.

258. Cf. Metzger, *Textual Commentary,* pp. 423-24, and Barrett, *Acts,* vol. 1, pp. 679-80.

259. See Brown and Meier, *Antioch and Rome,* p. 36 n. 85.

260. See Lüdemann, *Early Christianty,* pp. 159-63.

account the fact that everywhere else Luke uses the term "apostle," it always refers to a member of the Twelve (in Acts 1 the original eleven plus Matthias).[261] This view is perhaps the correct one, and it means that "apostle" here is not used as a sort of technical and theologically loaded term as it is elsewhere in Acts (and in Paul). Perhaps, as Barrett suggests, we should think of Paul's subsequent missionary work, which we are not told in Acts he was commissioned to do by the church of Antioch or any other church, as a more independent work, done purely under the Lord's authority and commission.[262]

The possibility cannot be ruled out, however, that Luke does mean to call Paul an apostle with a capital A here, being familiar with Paul's own usage; and perhaps the use of αποστελλω in 22:21 and 26:16-17 reflects this fact.[263] The sporadic usage of the term in the Pauline chapters of Acts would perhaps reflect the fact that Luke as a historian is not concerned about Paul's personal authority or power in these narratives but about the power and authority of the word and the Spirit.[264] This may also be why Luke largely refrains from dealing with Paul's personal controversies in his churches, unlike what we find in some of the letters.

V. 5 indicates that the opposition became so substantial that an attempt was made by both Gentiles and Jews, along with their rulers,[265] to abuse and even to stone Paul and Barnabas. Before this could transpire, however, v. 6 says the two missionaries got wind of the plan and fled to Lystra first and then Derbe, two Lycaonian cities, and, Luke adds, to the surrounding countryside. In other words, they went beyond the jurisdiction of Phrygian officials. Lystra was some eighteen miles away, but Derbe was at least a further fifty-five miles away. They were undaunted by the opposition in the two cities they had just visited. V. 7 makes clear they continued to preach the good news.[266]

The account of what transpired in Iconium is considerably less colorful

261. See Barrett, *Acts*, vol. 1, pp. 671-72.

262. Ibid..

263. See Marshall, *Acts*, pp. 233-34.

264. This makes good sense if Luke is trying to write history of a sort here, but it does not make sense if one sees Acts as biography, especially since almost half of Acts is devoted to Paul's travels and work.

265. We are presumably to think of Gentile magistrates and Jewish synagogue rulers.

266. There are various grammatical and syntactical difficulties in vv. 2-7 that the Western text seeks to smooth out. For example, the phrase "but the Lord gave peace" is added after the reference to the minds of the Gentiles being poisoned in order to make the transition to the next verse less abrupt. See Metzger, *Textual Commentary*, pp. 419-20. It is difficult to believe that the process could have gone in the other direction, with the Western readings being more original.

than what follows in *vv. 8-20.*[267] This narrative, or at least vv. 8-18, seems almost to be a self-contained one, a separate tradition that can be lifted out of the narrative without being missed.[268] The story transpires in an important Roman colony city established by Augustus in 26 B.C., the full name of which was Julia Felix Gemina Lustra (cf. *CIL* 3.6786).[269] It is difficult not to read this story in light of a famous myth recorded in Ovid, *Metamorphoses* 8.626ff., which is set in the Phrygian (or Lycaonian?) hill country:

> Here came Jupiter [Zeus] in the guise of a mortal, and with his father came Atlas' grandson [Mercury or Hermes], he that bears the caduceus, his wings laid aside. To a thousand homes they came, seeking a place for rest; a thousand homes were barred against them. Still one house received them humble indeed, thatched with straw and reeds from the marsh; but pious old Baucis and Philemon of equal age, were wed in that cottage in their youth, and in that cottage had grown old together; there they made their poverty light by . . . bearing it in a contented spirit. It was of no use to ask for masters or servants in that household, the couple was the whole household, together they served and ruled. And so when the heavenly ones came to this humble home and stooping entered by the lowly door, the old man set out a bench and urged them to rest their limbs, while over this bench Baucis threw a rough covering. Then she raked aside the warm ashes on the hearth and fanned yesterday's coals to life. . . . Then she took down from the roof some fine-split wood and dry twigs, broke them up and placed them under the little copper kettle. [The tale proceeds to explain how they prepared the best meal they possibly could for their guests, even attempting to set up couches on which the gods could recline and dine in comfort.] Besides all this, pleasant faces and lively and abounding good will were found at the table.
>
> Meanwhile they saw that the mixing bowl, as often as it was drained, kept

---

267. It is certainly less colorful and circumstantial than the later fictional biographical accounts found in the *Acts of Paul and Thecla,* which regales us with the further exploits of Paul in Iconium and includes various of the elements of a historical romance novel or pseudobiography, complete with enhanced opposition from Gentiles and ascetical tendencies. For example, consider the detailed description of Paul in *Acts of Paul and Thecla* 3.3: "a man small of stature, with a bald head and crooked legs, in a good state of body, with eyebrows meeting and nose somewhat hooked, full of friendliness; for now he appeared like a man, and now he has the face on an angel." The second-century deacon who produced this work is said to have been removed from office for producing it. Its goals were entertainment and edification rather than education about the early church. This is precisely the sort of material R. Pervo's study helps to shed light on, containing just the right sort of juicy biographical anecdotes, told for their entertainment or purely edificatory value, that Luke does *not* give us. On Pervo's study of ancient romances see pp. 376ff. above, and on the proper evaluation of the *Acts of Paul and Thecla* as a romance, unlike the canonical Acts, see Johnson, *Paul the Apostle,* p. 63.

268. See Plümacher, *Lukas als hellenistischer Schriftsteller,* pp. 92-93.

269. See the discussion by Blaiklock, "Lystra."

filling of its own accord, and that the wine welled up of itself. The two old people saw this strange sight with amazement and fear, and with upturned hands they both uttered a prayer, Baucis and the trembling old Philemon, and they craved indulgence for their poor food and meager entertainment. [They then seek to kill their only goose to feed the gods, but he eludes them.] Then the gods told them not to kill the goose. "We are gods," they said, "and this wicked neighborhood shall be punished as it deserves, but to you shall be given exemption from this punishment." [The gods lead them out of their house up the hill to witness the flooding of the whole region and the destruction of their neighbors, and meanwhile their own house is transformed into a temple.] Then calmly the son of Saturn spoke: "Now ask of us, good old man and wife, worthy of your good husband, any blessing you will." When he had spoken a word with Baucis, Philemon announced their joint decision to the gods: "We ask that we may be your priests, and guard your temple; and since we have spent our lives in constant company we pray that the same hour may bring death to both of us — that I may never see my wife's tomb nor be buried by her." Their request was granted.

Several further bits of information are important at this point to understand vv. 8ff. An inscription has been found near Lystra with a dedication to Zeus of a statue of Hermes, another inscription speaks of priests of Zeus, and even more telling is a stone altar found near Lystra dedicated to the Hearer of prayer (i.e., surely Zeus) and to Hermes.[270] The local Zeus, Zeus Ampelites, was portrayed on reliefs as an elderly man with a beard, and his companion (Hermes) as a young male assistant. The identification of Barnabas and Paul in these roles has led to the suggestion that the audience may have even thought these two *resembled* the familiar local reliefs of Zeus and Hermes. D. S. Potter thus concludes, "The passage is therefore of considerable importance as evidence for the physical appearance of Paul at this stage of his career."[271] At the least it probably suggests Barnabas was the elder of the two men and Paul was perhaps in his forties at most (cf. Acts 7:58).

The narrative begins with a miracle story. This story has rightly been seen as close in several respects to the miracle narrative found in Acts 3. For one thing the man in each story is introduced with the same description — "and a certain man lame from his mother's womb" (3:2 and 14:8). Furthermore each man is said to leap up and walk once healed. The verbs used here (περιπατεω and αλλομαι) are found at Acts 3:8 and 14:10 and nowhere else in Acts. Also in both accounts the healer (Peter or Paul) is said to look intently at the lame man in question, and in each case ατενισας is used (3:4 and 14:9).

270. See Bruce, *The Acts of the Apostles*, pp. 321-33; Calder, "A Cult of the Homonades"; and Hansen, "Galatia," p. 393.
271. Potter, "Lystra," p. 427.

Of course the settings of the two healings are very different, and in one case we are dealing with a Jew and in another a Gentile. Nevertheless the parallels are such that one must ask why Luke has cast these two narratives in such similar language at key points.[272] In fact they are part of a larger sequence of parallels between the actions of Peter and Paul involving first the giving of a paradigmatic sermon followed by the healing of a lame man and then a strongly negative, even violent reaction to each man (cf. Acts 2–4 to Acts 13–14).

Since Luke has obviously carefully edited this material, it may be surmised that there is some reason for this schematization. Besides the rather straightforward suggestion that Luke is attempting to show that God works out the divine plan in regular and orderly patterns, it must be remembered that ancient historians looked for and believed in the existence of repeated cycles or patterns in history, such that one could learn from what has gone before and to a certain degree know what to expect from the future.[273] This sort of thinking was characteristic of various of the Hellenistic historians, especially Polybius, to whom we have had occasion to compare Luke already.[274] G. W. Trompf's conclusions bear repeating at this juncture:

> Like the Polybian *Historiae* Luke's work is important for reflecting a large variety of recurrence notions and models. . . . Like Polybius, too, Luke has eclectic tendencies. . . . Although many of his historiographical presuppositions and methods derived from the Hebraic tradition, Luke went out of his way to accommodate Gentile tastes, like many writers in that tradition before him. . . . Luke was concerned to bridge the conceptual boundaries between two quite different cultures. . . . There are, however, significant differences between the approaches of Polybius and Luke. . . . Luke made known his ideas of recurrence through allusion, and particularly through the special organization of his material. . . . Luke's reenactments are either events which could happen at any time, or stages within sequences which reflect a divine plan. . . . In both Polybius and Luke, moreover, the workings of the moral order reveal divine or suprahuman causation. For monotheistic Luke, of course God lay behind all patterns of recurrence; the different levels of causality do not make their appearance in Luke. That is not to say that Luke cannot be regarded as "a genuinely classical historian," for the way he elicited paradigmatic incidents, the way he did not reproduce everything

272. Cf. Praeder, "Miracle Worker and Missionary"; and her further study, "Jesus-Paul."

273. See the discussion by Trompf, *Idea of Historical Recurrence*, of Polybius, pp. 78ff., and of Luke, pp. 170ff.

274. See in the introduction, pp. 10ff.

with "photographic fidelity" but displayed "only what is typical and significant," indicates otherwise.[275]

V. 8 speaks of a certain man disabled in his feet since birth. According to v. 9 the man was listening to Paul speaking when Paul looked intently at him and "saw" that he had the faith to be healed.[276] Thus Paul calls out, "Stand up on your feet," at which command the man jumped up and began to walk. The story is brief and to the point without further elaboration, only containing the basic elements characteristic of an ancient miracle story (description of illness, interaction with healer, proof of healing, reaction of the crowd or audience), with the reaction coming in v. 11 in dramatic fashion.[277]

Though apparently the crowd had been able to discern what was happening between Paul and the man because Paul was speaking in Greek, nevertheless the Lycaonian language was the native tongue, a language Paul himself did not know.[278] The crowds, apparently familiar with the myth that Ovid recorded (cf. above),[279] assumed that once again "the gods have come down to us in human form!" They called Barnabas Zeus[280] and Paul Hermes, because Paul was the one who had been addressing the man and Hermes was the messenger of the gods.[281] In the minds of the crowd, they must make a great sacrifice to honor the gods, who appeared again incognito, lest judgment fall on the region once more. It must also be borne in mind that Zeus and Hermes were the guarantors of emissaries and missions. They were the gods thought to protect ambassadors when they traveled in foreign lands so long

---

275. Trompf, *Idea of Historical Recurrence*, pp. 177-78.

276. This is what "saved" means here, though it may have additional nuances. Cf. my discussion "Salvation and Health in Christian Antiquity," Appendix 2, pp. 821ff. below.

277. Praeder, "Jesus-Paul," p. 35, is surely right that the striking similarities in language between this account of the healing of a lame man and the one in Acts 3 lie more in the similarities of the condition and reaction of the recipient of the miracle than in the similarities between Peter and Paul. This points away from the sort of conclusions drawn by Talbert and others who think that the parallels help demonstrate the book's biographical character and interest in Peter and Paul as interesting individuals. See Tannehill, *Narrative Unity of Luke-Acts*, 2:178-79.

278. If, as I would suggest, this story has a historical basis, then we must think of Paul later learning what the crowd had said, perhaps from someone present whom he later converted, someone such as Timothy, his future coworker (cf. Acts 16:1).

279. Ovid of course wrote at a later time, but the local myth was apparently ancient.

280. Διά is the usual accusative of Ζεύς.

281. On this point cf. Horace, *Odes* 1.10.1-6; Iamblicus, *De Myst. Aeg.* 1.1. Presumably Luke has chosen to use the familiar Greek names for these gods (just as Ovid used the Latin ones), but the locals may have used local divine names such as Pappas and Men. See Barrett, *Acts*, vol. 1, p. 676. It is very possible that Paul is alluding to this incident in Gal. 4:14. Cf. Cadbury, *Book of Acts in History*, p. 21.

*The Cn. Ahenobarbus altar relief: a sacrificial procession
with major offerings of a bull, a sheep, and a pig for the god Mars.*
(Louvre; © Photo RMN, photo by Chuzeville)

as the ambassadors faithfully delivered the messages they were sent to pass on (see Plato, *Leg.* 941A).[282]

V. 13 suggests that things moved rapidly. The priest of Zeus, whose temple stood just outside the city, brought bulls with garlands on their necks to the city gates, because both the priest and the crowd wanted to sacrifice to the apostles immediately. Though they had not understood the language spoken, Paul and Barnabas clearly understood what was happening, having surely seen a pagan sacrificial procession with bulls before. *V. 14* indicates that Paul and Barnabas immediately tore their clothes, a gesture suggesting they thought blasphemy was about to be committed (cf. Mark 14:63 and par., and *m. Sanh.* 7:5), and ran into the midst of the crowd to prevent this travesty.

There follows in *vv. 15-17* a very brief but significant speech summary, the first of its kind, addressed by Paul to a purely Gentile audience.[283] It is right to note that in many ways these verses foreshadow the longer Areopagus speech found in Acts 17, only there the audience includes more sophisticated pagans and so the speech there is pitched at a higher intellectual level.[284] In both, the subjects treated included creation or natural theology, the endured

282. See the discussion by Martin, "Gods or Ambassadors of God?" His argument that the Lystrans merely saw Paul and Barnabas as ambassadors invited to participate in Lystran ceremonies and receive their hospitality is not, however, fully convincing, not least because this does not seem to be how Luke evaluates the Lystrans (see v. 11).

283. For parallels to the general approach to pagans in this speech from Josephus, see Downing, "Common Ground."

284. Cf. Gärtner, "Paulus und Barnabus in Lystra," and Lerle, "Die Predigt in Lystra."

ignorance of pagans, and the first broaching by Paul of the subject of good news for Gentiles.

The speech has been characterized as a combination of epideictic rhetoric, attempting to cause the audience to hold a particular belief in the present, and forensic rhetoric.[285] The problem with this analysis is v. 15, where the goal of the speech is said to be the changing of not just belief but of behavior in the near future, as a result of hearing this speech. It is more convincing to see this as an example of a speech summary that includes only the introductory matter of a deliberative speech and a brief *narratio,* explaining what God has done for the pagans in the past (vv. 15c-17). Like the speech in Acts 17, it does not reach its proper conclusion because of the reaction of the audience.[286]

The speech begins with a question — why are you doing this? It continues with an affirmation, "we are only human like you." This last remark should be compared to Peter's in Acts 10:26, where we also find the rejection of excessive reverence for a human being.[287] On the positive side, Gentiles were a natural audience for those who wished to preach about God appearing to human beings in the form of the man Jesus and offering help or salvation.[288] *V. 15c* should be compared to 1 Thess. 1:9 — "they tell how you turned to God from idols, to serve the living and true God." The significance of this Pauline verse lies not only in its similarity in content to v. 15c, d, but that here Paul is probably summarizing what was preached to Gentiles in Thessalonica. Luke knows more about Paul's evangelistic preaching and thought than is often recognized. The message the apostles brought was to be seen as good news, delivering the audience from vain or worthless things (cf. Rom. 1:21; 8:20) and into the hands of a living God.[289] This theme is also found in the major speech in Acts 13.

This living God is said to have made heaven and earth and the sea and all things.[290] In short there was only one creator God, the one of whom Paul and Barnabas speak. If this pronouncement foreshadows Acts 17:24, then *v. 16* presages Acts 17:30 (and cf. 3:17). Here it simply states that in the past God

---

285. Soards, *The Speeches in Acts,* pp. 88-89.

286. Interrupted speeches is a characteristic of Luke's approach in Acts; cf. pp. 339ff. above.

287. See Soards, *The Speeches in Acts,* p. 89. One should compare the very similar reaction of Alexander, who says such reverence would endanger his soul. See Pseudo-Calisthenes, *Life of Alexander* 12.22.

288. See Johnson, *Acts,* p. 251.

289. Zeus was seen as the god who gave life (his very name derived from the Greek ζωη). The similarities between this passage and Romans 1 should also not be overlooked, both involving the familiar Jewish critique of pagan religion as vain, worthless, and empty.

290. Breytenbach, "Zeus und der lebendige Gott," suggests we have polemics here against the beliefs in southern Asia that Zeus was the heavenly creator God who gave life to the plants and other living things. This is possible in view of the context.

let the pagan nations go their own ways. God did not give them special or direct revelation, but they were not without a witness altogether for the kindness or blessing of rain from heaven and the granting of crops in due season.[291] "The reference to God's doing good and supplying human needs is similar to the declaration of 17.25, and the focus on natural order, especially the 'seasons' (καιρους), is comparable to 17.26. Indeed, the implication here that humans could discern God because of the 'witnesses' is similar to the notion expressed in 17.27."[292] God had provided plenty to feed both their mouths and hearts.[293] Rather than dampening the audience's enthusiasm, this speech seems if anything to have fanned the flames.[294] The result according to *v. 18* is that they were barely able to prevent the crowd from sacrificing to them.

At *v. 19* an unexpected conclusion is recorded. Jews from both Antioch and Iconium showed up and won the crowd over,[295] which led to the stoning of Paul,[296] after which they dragged him outside the city and left him, "thinking him dead." Luke is very careful at this juncture not to say Paul died, only that the angry crowd made this assumption, which must at least suggest a beaten and unconscious or semiconscious Paul. *V. 20* is elliptical. Are we to think that the new converts (here called disciples) prayed and/or laid hands on Paul and his wounds were healed, or only that they surrounded and protected his body from further abuse? In any case, we are told he got up and remarkably went

291. Lerle, "Die Predigt in Lystra," pp. 55ff., thinks that the teaching here on God's providence ultimately goes back to Jesus' teaching about God's mercy.

292. Soards, *The Speeches in Acts*, p. 90.

293. The Greek here is a bit elliptical — literally God "fills your hearts with food and rejoicing."

294. Marshall, *Acts*, p. 238, may be right that Luke is only trying to show here what more, beyond the usual Christian kerygma, missionaries were apt to say to pagans. He adds (p. 239) that the end of the speech suggests there would have been a continuation in terms of the distinctly Christian gospel, as perhaps Acts 17:31 also suggests, but that speech was interrupted just as this one was.

295. It is sometimes thought incredible that Jews from Antioch (almost one hundred miles away) and Iconium would go to such great lengths to oppose the work of Paul, but this is overlooking at least two considerations: (1) Acts has already recorded that Saul had gone to such lengths to deal with Christians in Damascus; (2) as pointed out in *Beginnings*, 4:162, there was a statue of Concord in Antioch put up by the Roman colony city of Lystra. This suggests some sort of close relationship (sister cities of a sort?) between the two cities. At the very least it implies a considerable social network between the two Roman colonies with a regular flow of information and perhaps support of various sorts going from one to the other. Consider also the actions of the circumcision party in Galatia.

296. Presumably not Barnabas because he had not initially spoken or healed the lame man. Barrett, *Acts*, vol. 1, p. 684, points out that there is no historical problem with this presentation. "Paul's was the face the crowd knew, for he had performed a public and well-publicized act in healing a lame man; he would be a natural target."

back into the city.[297] This course of action is not surprising on two counts:
(1) undoubtedly Paul would need at least some rest and attention before he
could travel again; (2) as we have already seen at 14:3, Paul and Barnabas were
courageous men who did not wilt under pressure but showed great loyalty to
their new converts. Thus we are told at *v. 20b* that Paul and Barnabas left Lystra
in an orderly fashion the next day. The verb ἐξῆλθεν here does not suggest
that they made the entire trip to Derbe the day they left, which was certainly
more than a day's journey away (fifty to sixty miles), but only that they set
out for Derbe the next day. Throughout this account Luke's interests are other
than biographical or novelistic. As Johnson says, "Luke draws our attention
here not so much to the personality or power of Paul as to the process by
which early Christian communities came into being and were nurtured."[298]
Christianity as an important historical development is his subject, or to put
it another way, God's saving acts in history that produced the Christian movement and community are his theme.

V. 21 tells us nothing of the details of what happened in Derbe, only that
the good news was preached and a large number of converts were won. Derbe,
as Strabo points out (*Geog.* 12.6.3), appears to have belonged to the province
of Galatia even in the 50s, and would have been a frontier post at the border
with Antiochus IV's kingdom of Commagene.[299] It has often been pointed out
that it would have been much easier for the two missionaries to continue on
in the direction they were going and return to Antioch by way of Paul's own
city of Tarsus. This is true enough, but the goal of these two men was not to
get home in as expeditious a fashion as possible, but rather to complete their
initial pastoral tasks, making sure all their hard work was not for nothing.[300]
Returning the way they had come was necessary to "strengthen" the fledgling
disciples in each of these cities in the Galatian province. *V. 22* indicates that
this work of strengthening and exhorting the new converts went on in each
of these cities they had already visited.

The basic message to the new converts is summarized in *v. 22b:* "We
must go through many hardships to enter the kingdom of God." The word
θλίψις refers to difficulties or sufferings, in this case sufferings that come from
persecution for loyalty to one's faith. This may in fact allude to the early Jewish
notion that believers must suffer the messianic woes at the outset of the
eschatological age before the kingdom will come. The mention of a βασιλεία
that one will enter at some future time, but only after suffering, is not charac-

297. The Western text adds that Paul got up with difficulty.
298. Johnson, *Acts,* p. 256.
299. There is some uncertainty about this matter, in part because of the uncertainty
of Derbe's precise locale. Cf. pp. 418ff. above and Ogg, "Derbe."
300. See Barrett, *Acts,* vol. 1, pp. 685-86.

teristic of the way Luke normally talks about God's coming dominion. It was, however, a feature of Paul's preaching and teaching (cf. 1 Cor. 6:9-10; 15:10), and Luke faithfully represents this aspect of his thought.[301] We are told in *v. 23* that Paul and Barnabas, no doubt in order to give the local Christian community some stability through having recognized leaders, appointed[302] some elders (πρεσβυτεροι) for each congregation. Some have found this problematic since in the undisputed Paulines there is no mention of elders. The term is not unusual, however, and was probably originally borrowed from the Jewish usage of the term, during a time when the Christian church was still in close contact with the synagogue (cf., e.g., Acts 4:5; 11:30; 15:6; 1 Tim. 5:17; 1 Pet. 5:1-2; 2 John 1; 3 John 1; and especially compare our text to Titus 1:5).[303]

There may be something to Ramsay's suggestion that επισκοπος is Paul's equivalent term for elder (see Phil. 1:1).[304] Perhaps Paul deliberately chose a different term to distinguish Christian leaders from Jewish ones in the cities where he had planted churches. This act of appointing was accompanied by prayer and fasting, and thus they were committed to the Lord, the one in whom they had so recently put their trust.

Vv. 24-25 refer to the return journey going through Pisidia and then Pamphylia, and after having preached the word in the city of Perga (the results of which Luke does not tell us), Paul and Barnabas went down to Attalia, from which point they sailed back to Antioch. *V. 26* shows that Luke is rounding off this part of his narrative by means of an *inclusio*.[305] He speaks of them returning to the place where they had been committed to God's grace for the work now completed, and so quite naturally on returning they gathered the congregation[306] and gave a report. The report spoke of all God had done through the two missionaries, and especially how the door of faith had been opened to the Gentiles. This sort of terminology (θυρα used metaphorically) is also found in Paul (cf. 1 Cor. 16:9; 2 Cor. 2:12; Col. 4:3). The function of

301. See my discussion in *End of the World*, pp. 51-58.

302. Despite its root meaning of stretch out the hand, χειροτονησαντες probably does not mean lay hands on here. In fact it had come to have the meaning of appointment by an authority, which seems to be the sense here. See Lucian, *De Morte Peregrini* 41.

303. It is possible that Luke is using the terminology only later applied in his own era to describe these appointed leaders, though there is no reason why the term couldn't have been used in Paul's own day. The use of it here is perhaps one more piece of evidence that may suggest Luke's being responsible for writing the Pastoral Epistles. Cf. pp. 430ff. above.

304. Ramsay, *St. Paul the Traveller,* p. 121.

305. See Polhill, *Acts,* p. 320.

306. Here εκκλησια has its basic sense of an assembled group, in this case a group of Christians, though the term is not an ecclesiological one. It was often used in an earlier era and even in the NT era to refer to a Greek city assembly. See my discussion in *Conflict and Community in Corinth,* pp. 90-93.

v. 27 is to prepare the hearer for what is to follow in Acts 15.[307] Now that planned missionary work to Gentiles had been undertaken, the Jerusalem church, always playing catch-up with God's plan, had need of some major rethinking about what the church would be like and how it would go about its missionary work. *V. 28* informs us that Paul and Barnabas did not immediately set off on another missionary endeavor; they stayed in Antioch for a considerable, but undefined, amount of time. Toward the end of this period, perhaps in A.D. 49, Paul probably wrote Galatians from Antioch, shortly before going up to Jerusalem for the council on the Gentiles.

The summary of Tannehill on Acts 13–14 is worth quoting:

> Acts 13–14 presents a representative picture of Paul's mission and includes many themes that we will encounter again. He preaches first in the Jewish synagogue but turns to Gentiles when the synagogue preaching is no longer possible. He announces the one God to Gentiles who have no contact with Jewish monotheism. He repeatedly encounters persecution and moves on when necessary, but he does not abandon his mission. He works signs and wonders. He strengthens the new churches. In this mission Paul is fulfilling the Lord's prophecy that he would "bear my name before Gentiles, and kings and sons of Israel" and "must suffer for my name" (9.15-16).[308]

A Closer Look — The Paul of Acts and the Paul of the Letters

The narrative in Acts 13–14 already raises a number of salient questions about the portrayal of Paul by Luke as compared to what we find in Paul's letters, for instance in regard to his apostleship. In Acts we hear precious little about Paul being an apostle or being concerned with a collection, but these are clearly very important matters in the epistles. Furthermore in Acts we hear a great deal about Paul being a preacher and miracle worker but nothing whatsoever about his being a letter writer, while the Paul of the letters only rarely mentions his working of miracles but often refers to his letters. Furthermore, the Paul of Acts preaches some sermons that sound very little like the Paul of the letters (e.g., what we find in Acts 14 or 17). It is because of the above factors and some I have not mentioned that R. Brawley complains, "The problem with the Lucan Paul in its briefest form is that the Paul of the Epistles is a different Paul."[309] Barrett gives this complaint a bit more precision when describing the Paul of Acts: "This is the legendary Paul, if the adjective may be used to describe a picture by no means wholly fictitious but one made, in good faith, by omissions, arrangements, and emphases, so as to present to later generations the Paul that Luke, and no doubt some

---

307. Marshall, *Acts*, p. 240.
308. Tannehill, *Narrative Unity of Luke-Acts*, 2:182.
309. Brawley, "Paul in Acts," p. 129.

of his contemporaries, wished them to see. It is not quite the Paul of the letters, and it is not quite the Paul of the Pastoral Epistles, but it is fairly closely related to both."[310] It is perhaps fair to say that the major reason why many scholars feel Luke did not know Paul, but rather was himself an admirer of Paul in a later generation, is precisely because of the portrait of Paul found in Acts.

There are many problems involved in comparing the Paul of the letters to the Paul of Acts, which we can only begin to canvass and address here. There is first of all the issue of methodology in getting at the historical Paul. It is almost always assumed that Paul's letters must be considered a vastly superior source of information about Paul than any "secondary" sources such as Acts.[311] I doubt this is a safe assumption, especially if Luke was even a sometime associate and traveling companion of Paul and especially for the very good reason that one must take into account the rhetorical and ad hoc character of Paul's letters. Furthermore, often a person is more objectively and correctly evaluated by others than by himself.

If Luke's account is tendentious and apologetic in character, Paul's letters, especially in the biographical remarks, are equally so.[312] Furthermore, *all* of Paul's autobiographical remarks in his letters are ad hoc, tendentious, partial, and often given in passing. The same may be said about the mention of Paul's deeds and mission itinerary in the letters. When W. G. Kümmel praises T. H. Campbell[313] for finally coming up with a Pauline itinerary from the letters, and then remarks that "Campbell has proved convincingly that the sequence of Paul's missionary activities that can be inferred from his letters is so remarkably compatible with the information from Acts that we have good grounds for deriving the relative chronology of Paul's activity from a critical combination of the information from Paul's letters with the account in Acts,"[314] he is in effect admitting that both sources must be read critically and consulted carefully, and treated as virtual equals, to come up with such information.

Finally, there is the genre problem. Paul is writing directly, if rhetorically, but his letters are not primarily about himself. Rather, they are ad hoc documents addressing his churches and their problems and progress. Luke, on the other hand, does have as his subject matter history, and he writes directly about Paul's conversion/call (three

310. Barrett, *Paul,* p. 161.

311. See, however, the proper cautionary remarks about too straightforward a reading of Galatians by Townsend, "Acts 9.1-29 and Early Church Tradition," pp. 124-25.

312. See especially Lyons, *Pauline Autobiography.* Sometimes his remarks are apologetic and defensive, part of a forensic rhetorical tour de force (e.g., 2 Corinthians 10–12; Galatians 1–2); at other times his remarks are part of a larger deliberative argument and he is deliberately playing down the importance of his past, even while being proud of it from a human point of view (e.g., Philippians 3). The same can be said about his remarks about being and suffering as a Christian apostle — they always have a rhetorical edge and angle to them.

313. In a much neglected article, "Paul's Missionary Journeys as Reflected in His Letters."

314. Kümmel, *Introduction to the New Testament,* rev. ed. (Nashville: Abingdon, 1975), p. 254.

times!), his missionary travels, and his trials.[315] If Luke was a sometime companion of Paul and had reliable sources of information, the type of document he has produced may provide more direct access to the historical Paul in various ways.[316] All this is by way of saying that one cannot afford to *assume* that one only has the real Paul in the letters while one has a faint echo (or overblown distortion) of him in Acts. Such a conclusion must be demonstrated.

Broadly speaking, the complaints about the portrait of Paul in Acts can be placed into two categories: (1) distortion of the social status and abilities of Paul; (2) distortion of Paul's theology. The former complaints are more recent, and the latter go back a very long way, but the modern discussion of the theological issues was sparked by P. Vielhauer's programmatic essay, "On the Paulinism of Acts."[317] We will deal with each of these matters in turn and then conclude with some discussion of Luke's omissions, deliberate or otherwise, which affects the overall picture.

When we think of the social portrait of Paul in Acts, we think of Paul the man of the world equally at home with Jews and Gentiles, with those of low and high social status, with men and women. We think of an educated Paul capable of considerable rhetorical skill as reflected in his speeches, and a Paul who knows at least basic Greek philosophy and Jewish belief and practice in detail. He is at once a loyal Jew, a loyal Christian, a good Roman citizen, and apparently a citizen of Tarsus ("no mean city"). We think of a Paul who works miracles and works with his hands, and a Paul who itinerates throughout the eastern half of the Mediterranean. He is at once evangelist and teacher, pastor and preacher, deeply loved and greatly hated. If we ask what is wrong with this picture, J. C. Lentz is ready to give an answer: "By the end of Acts, the Paul who has been described is, frankly, too good to be true."[318] J. H. Neyrey prescinds from such a value judgment on the historical accuracy of Luke's portrayal, but he is in fundamental agreement that Luke presents Paul as a person of considerable social status.[319]

On these issues the following can be said on the basis of Paul's letters. (1) The letters *also* suggest a man of considerable education and knowledge, and not just of Jewish matters. For instance, they suggest a man who has some knowledge of Greek philosophy (in particular Stoicism)[320] and a good deal of knowledge of Greco-Roman

315. See pp. 302ff. and 430ff. above for more on this subject.

316. See Bruce, "Paul in Acts and Letters," p. 680: "If the author of Acts was, as seems most probable, an acquaintance and occasional companion of Paul, then Acts has claims to be recognized as a *primary source of information about Paul*" (emphasis mine). Bruce also makes the point about Luke being a more objective observer of Paul than Paul himself.

317. This article originally appeared in *Evangelische Theologie* 10 in the 1950-51 issue and was translated into English for the *Perkins School of Theology Journal* 17 in 1963. It then received wider attention when it was included in the volume *Studies in Luke-Acts,* pp. 33-50, in 1966, some fifteen years after it originally appeared in print. It is still regularly referred to as a starting point for the discussion.

318. Lentz, *Luke's Portrait of Paul,* p. 171.

319. Neyrey, "Luke's Social Location of Paul."

320. Malherbe, *Paul and the Popular Philosophers,* and various of the essays in *Greeks, Romans, and Christians,* ed. D. Balch et al. (Minneapolis: Fortress, 1990).

rhetoric.[321] (2) In general the letters suggest, as E. A. Judge has demonstrated at some length, that the Paul of the letters is a person of considerable social status deliberately stepping down in order to serve and identify with all sorts of converts, including the weak, by, among other things, working with his hands. Paul in general doesn't insist on his rights, and this presupposes that he believes he has such rights (see 1 Corinthians 9). He portrays himself as a socially flexible person who can be the Jew to the Jew and the Greek to the Greek.[322] (3) There is absolutely no *direct* evidence about Paul's citizenship(s) in the letters, and this also means there is nothing in the letters that casts doubt on the evidence of Acts on this matter. What one can say is that it was not historically impossible or improbable for a Diaspora Jew to hold these sorts of citizenships, even concurrently, and there are some hints in the letters that Paul might have done so.[323]

In short, while it appears that Lentz and Neyrey have correctly evaluated the social portrait of Paul in Acts as a man of virtue, a rhetor, a man of consequence and social status, there is nothing in the letters that would lead us to think this portrait does not represent the historical Paul, and in fact what positive hints we do have in the letters also point us in this direction. The social portrait of Paul in Acts as a man who has divine approval and access to divine power, a man of virtue with a high level of culture who adheres to an ancient sacred tradition, would have commended Paul to many in the Greco-Roman world, Gentiles as well as Jews.[324] We know from his letters that Paul was in fact well received by many, both Jews and Gentiles, in the various cities he visited, including various people of considerable social status. The most reasonable explanation for this phenomenon is that Paul was indeed the sort of socially impressive person Luke says he was.

In various ways the theological issues are considerably more thorny and difficult to assess. For one thing, all of Paul's letters are addressed to those who are already Christians. There is not a single "missionary" letter that we have from Paul's hand. What we do have in these letters is what Paul feels he needs to say to exhort or commend those who are *already* believing Christians. It is, I think, a rather large assumption to take it for granted that Paul's missionary preaching would be identical or nearly identical to what we find in the letters, and then to conclude that the speeches of Paul in Acts necessarily couldn't be summaries of Paul's preaching since they don't match the letters. This sort of approach is especially problematic when we actually evaluate the sorts of traditions Paul tells us he had already passed on to his converts (e.g., in 1 Corinthians 7; 11; and 15), and the few hints in the letters that suggest something about his initial preaching.

---

321. On these points see my *Conflict and Community in Corinth,* pp. 19ff.

322. Cf. the following from Judge: "Paul's Boasting"; "St. Paul and Classical Society"; "Radical Social Critic"; "The Social Identity"; *Rank and Status;* "Cultural Conformity."

323. On the legal issues cf. Sherwin-White, *Roman Law and Roman Society,* and now Rapske, *Paul in Roman Custody,* pp. 71-112. Hengel, *Paul,* pp. 160-61, cites two epitaphs found in Jaffa of Jews who were citizens but lived in Israel like Paul. One was even in textiles like Paul. Wilson, *Paul,* p. 52, notes what a good place Jerusalem would be for one who works with animal hides because it was a place of sacrifices and of many pilgrims needing tents while visiting.

324. On this portrayal see Brawley, "Paul in Acts," pp. 134-40.

For example, in one of his earliest letters Paul offers a revealing assessment of how he evaluates the change in the lives of his mostly Gentile converts in the region — they turned from idols to serve a living and true God (1 Thess. 1:9). I would suggest that this remark tells us something not only about Paul's aims when preaching to pagans but also what he exhorted them to do in that initial preaching. I would also suggest that it is not an accident that this is precisely the gist and aim of the famous Areopagus speech we find in Acts 17.[325]

Based on their importance and prominence in Paul's letters, grace and justification by faith can be reasonably surmised to be two themes Paul used in his missionary preaching, especially in view of the way the argument proceeds in Galatians. I would suggest it is no accident that these two themes come up in the first two presentations of Pauline speech material in Acts 13–14. Luke knows very well these were important Pauline themes, and he doesn't hesitate to emphasize them near the beginning of his portrait of Paul as a missionary. It must always be kept steadily in view that we really have only *one* Pauline speech to Christians recorded by Luke in Acts, the Miletus speech, and we should not be surprised that this is the one speech that sounds most like the Paul of the letters. Indeed, the speech is a veritable mosaic of major Pauline themes.[326] There are of course differences in diction and in ways of phrasing things. Luke makes all his source material his own, but the suggestion of serious distortion simply does not ring true.

Let us consider one of Vielhauer's and Barrett's more detailed complaints. This falls under the heading of the complaint that Paul in Acts is too Jewish, too Law observant. The view of the Law expressed by Paul in his life and teachings in Acts is said not to be Paul's own. Barrett puts the matter succinctly: the "picture of Paul the good Jew is not what one finds in the epistles."[327] He has in mind the picture in Acts of a Paul who takes part in the apostolic council and agrees to implement the decrees, the Paul who has Timothy circumcised (Acts 16:3), the Paul who acquiesces to go through the rite of purification in the temple (Acts 21:23-24), perhaps also the Paul who always visits the synagogue first wherever he goes, the Paul who protests before Jewish and Roman authorities from Acts 21 on that he is a good Jew.

These matters must be taken individually and can be addressed only briefly here. First it must be admitted that Paul is portrayed as some sort of good Jew in Acts.[328] It must also be said that if Acts 15 is about Jewish food laws Noahic or otherwise, it appears unlikely Paul did comply with or implement the decree. But in fact it may be disputed that this is the subject matter of the decrees. The decrees are about Gentiles abstaining from going to pagan temples and attending pagan feasts, where food offered to idols was both sacrificed to pagan gods and eaten, and where sexual immorality was also known to transpire. In short the decrees are about avoiding active participation in idolatry and immorality. To this stipulation Paul would and did readily agree, and we may see his attempt to implement the decree in 1 Corinthians 8–10.

325. On which see below.
326. See the comparative chart on this speech in Acts 20 and its echoes of the letters, pp. 610ff. below.
327. Barrett, *Paul*, p. 164.
328. See the useful discussion in Jervell, "Paul in the Acts."

In regard to Paul engaging in Jewish practices for pragmatic reasons having to do with his missionary work, there is no reason to doubt that he might have done so — indeed, 1 Cor. 9:20 suggests as much.[329] There is no problem with the idea that he might have undertaken an act of purification on one occasion in the temple as a gesture of peace. It will be noted that Acts 21 does not suggest that Paul came up with this idea but that it was strongly put to him by others as something he must do. In regard to Paul going to synagogues to preach to a variety of people, not only does Rom. 1:16 say the gospel is for Jews first, but 2 Cor. 11:24 suggests Paul repeatedly went to synagogues, and on some occasions paid a stiff price for his witness there. That he submitted to the Jewish punishment for the wrong sort of teaching is surely because he wanted to return to the synagogue again and have further chances to witness. As for the circumcision of Timothy, this, too, is not unthinkable as a missionary tactic. It would only be unthinkable if Luke portrayed Paul as believing this was some sort of necessity or if Timothy was simply a Gentile. Timothy was in fact partly Jewish through his mother, and Paul wanted him to be in a position to do as he himself was doing, approaching Jews as a Jew and Gentiles as a Gentile. An uncircumcised Jew sent all the wrong signals to the Jews in the area.

Perhaps one reason Paul himself touts his Jewish heritage as something he *could* boast of (cf. Phil. 3:5-6; 2 Cor. 11:22-23) is that as a missionary it was useful to him when he spoke in a synagogue. It would have been necessary to indicate his heritage and credentials as a Jew in order to be permitted to speak, even if he would go on to say these were things he had left behind. In any case, leaving Timothy as he was in a theological no-man's-land, neither truly Greek nor truly Jewish, was not making the most of a promising convert who had a mixed heritage.

The issue here is whether Luke portrays Paul as one who was still necessarily under the yoke of the Law, and therefore not merely free to choose to keep aspects of the Law but also avoiding violating those aspects of the Law that most marked out Jews (e.g., the food laws). In fact, Luke does *not* portray Paul as a consistently observant Jew *after his conversion*. Rather, Paul the Christian is revealed to be one who regularly associated with, had fellowship with, and even on occasion stayed in the houses of Gentiles (including Gentile synagogue adherents — cf. Acts 11:20, 26; 16:15, 34, 40; 17:4, 5, 7). There is also nothing in the important speech in Acts 22 to suggest that Paul as a Christian was claiming to keep all of the Law, or was consistently submitting to all the Mosaic requirements. Nor is there anything in Acts 26. The two speeches speak of Paul's course of life as a zealous and faithful Pharisee *before* his conversion, and Acts 26 indicates that he continued to hold the Pharisaic belief in the resurrection, but this is as far as the matter goes. I thus conclude that it is a mistake to suggest that Luke portrays Paul as one who continued to submit to the yoke of the Law as a necessary part of his faith in God, even after his conversion to Christianity. Vielhauer and others have been taken in by the rhetorical form and persuasive character of the speeches in Acts 22 and 26,[330] and have failed to note that Luke's Paul (in these speeches) does not claim that he was *continuing* to act like a zealous Pharisee in every respect. We will

---

329. See my discussion in *Conflict and Community in Corinth*, pp. 212-13.
330. See Long, "The Paulusbild."

say more about these speeches and their import at the appropriate points in the commentary.

The question then becomes what Luke would have meant by insisting that Paul was a good Jew. It seems clear that he understands this to mean one who believes what the Scriptures say, especially in regard to the promises about Messiah and his people and the salvation promised therein. It would also be one who believes that God's promises are first for Jews and that they include the promise of resurrection. In addition, being a good Jew would mean avoiding idolatry and immorality, and from time to time willingly and freely demonstrating one's solidarity with one's Jewish kin with a vow of one sort or another (cf. Acts 18:8 and 21:23-24, 26).[331] The Paul of the letters would likely have said something similar if he had been asked.[332] Jervell's thesis, while not fully cogent, is convincing in stressing the Jewishness of Paul: "I think we can trace the Lukan Paul, the material connected with that of Paul, back to Paul himself. . . . The Lukan Paul, the picture of Paul in Acts, is a completion, a filling up of the Pauline one, so that in order to get at the historical Paul, we can not do without Acts and Luke. . . . we have in Luke of course not the whole Paul. But the practicing Jew Paul the missionary of Israel and to Israel. . . ."[333] Both Acts and the letters portray Paul as some sort of good Jew.

Before we conclude this somewhat lengthy discussion it is necessary to discuss Luke's prominent omissions and see if they can be explained. It is Barrett's contention that Luke fails to present us with Paul the controversialist, always debating with other Christians and Christian leaders, staking out his own turf, fighting for the viability and recognition of his mission to Gentiles. There is some truth in this complaint. Luke is writing at a later time, at least a decade or so after the latest event recorded in Acts, when some of these controversies with the Jerusalem church (for instance, over the circumcising of Gentile converts) had either become defunct (due to what happened in A.D. 70 to Jerusalem) or had been resolved. Luke is striving to put early Christianity's best foot forward in this work, emphasizing harmony over discord, and presumably he saw no point in recounting battles that were long over and *that did not change the course of early Christian history.* Luke writes chiefly as a historian and with an apologetic

---

331. We will postpone the discussion of whether the Areopagus speech in Acts 17 is a plausible speech on the lips of a Paul who says what he does in Romans 1 until the exegesis of that speech. It should suffice to say here that B. Gartner changed the character of the discussion of Acts 17 after Vielhauer wrote, and showed this speech to be very Jewish in various respects, reflecting Jewish apologetics in a largely non-Jewish world. A very significant part of Vielhauer's case, as also Barrett's, rests on a certain interpretation of the Areopagus speech as being un-Pauline in certain key ways. There is, however, a difference between seeing the speech as possibly uncharacteristic of Paul's preaching and seeing it as un-Pauline. See pp. 511ff. below.

332. The apologetic character of Luke's portrayal of Paul is rightly stressed by Carroll, "Literary and Social Dimensions." We will say more about the image of Paul on trial at the appropriate junctures, but the main point is to indicate that Paul was a person of virtue, a good citizen of the Empire, and blameless of all charges whether by Jews or others. Brawley, "Paul in Acts," p. 144, also stresses that Luke's portrayal is both apologetic and irenic.

333. Jervell, "Paul in the Acts," p. 70.

and rhetorical historian's sensibilities. Those difficulties which had *historical* importance or significance he does not neglect, as is quite clear from the central place in Acts and the amount of attention he gives to the apostolic council (Acts 15). Equally clearly he is prepared to provide some samples of other in-house difficulties — such as the problems caused by Ananias and Sapphira (Acts 5), or the problems that arose due to the inequitable distribution to the widows in the Jerusalem church (Acts 6), or the dispute and split between Paul and Barnabas because of Mark's behavior (Acts 13–14; 15). That he does not dwell on the heated debates between Paul and the Jerusalem church is because he believed that the two parties came to a meeting of the minds, as Acts 15 is meant to demonstrate.[334] Luke then should not be accused of gilding the lily. He is simply placing the emphasis where he thinks it ought to lie.

Of course a second notable omission involves Paul's apostolicity. We have already concluded from the texts in Acts 14 that probably, but not certainly, the term "apostle" in that chapter means a missionary agent or emissary of the Antioch church.[335] Why, then, has Luke failed to portray Paul as an apostle with a capital *A*? A close examination of Acts will show that it is a missionary document about the planting of churches across the eastern Mediterranean part of the Roman Empire. It is not by and large about the ongoing dilemmas or internal struggles of already established churches, although some attention is paid in Acts 1–8 to the internal life of the chief non-Pauline church, the mother church in Jerusalem. The most we hear about already established Pauline churches is brief suggestions by Luke that Paul went around visiting and strengthening the churches he had already founded.

A close reading of Paul's letters will also show that Paul's apostolicity is mentioned when questions of *internal authority and control* come up. For example, in Philippians Paul does not present himself as an apostle, but rather as a servant of Christ, like Christ himself (cf. 1:1 to 2:7). Why not? Because there was no need to do so with the Philippians. His authority was not in question or being challenged in that congregation, unlike the case in Galatia or in Corinth. First Thessalonians would be another good example of a letter where Paul doesn't make anything of his apostolic status or power because it is not disputed or challenged. What then about Romans (cf. 1:1)? Here Paul is writing to a congregation not his own which is already established, but with which he must establish rapport and display his credentials at the outset as he hopes through this letter to influence them through the art of persuasion. In other words, Paul's apostolic status had to be claimed. It could not be taken for granted that the Roman Christians knew or recognized that status. In every case, however, when Paul's apostolic status is referred to, it has to do with internal matters in which he is seeking to exercise authority or influence.

Paul is not an apostle to the Gentiles, he is an apostle to the churches which are largely made up of Gentiles, if by apostle one means a person who exercises authority over a particular group of people. In relationship to outsiders he has no inherent authority or control, other than the power of the word and the Spirit. In other words,

---

334. On the issue of whether Paul actually tried to implement the decree of James, cf. pp. 411ff. below.

335. See pp. 419ff. above.

to an outsider he is a missionary and evangelist, armed with the weapons of a missionary and evangelist, the word and the Spirit. This is precisely how he is portrayed in Acts. We probably should not fault Luke for not telling us more about the internal life of the early church since the focus is on missions and the growth of the movement. Had he done so he might have told us a great deal or at least some more about Paul the Apostle.

What about Luke's omission of Paul as letter writer? The same logic applies here as in the last paragraph. Acts is about beginnings and missionary endeavors. Paul's letters, so far as we know, were written to congregations that were already established. This falls outside the purview of what Luke seeks to describe. Such an omission was only natural since Luke chose not to record the further developments of church life within the congregations Paul founded.

This brings us to the matter of the collection. Why would Luke mention the collection of funds for the Jerusalem church only briefly at most, in view of how much importance Paul places on the matter?[336] It is clear enough from a text like Rom. 15:25-28 how much Paul hoped the collection would be seen as a sign of recognition on the part of the Gentiles of their indebtedness to the Jerusalem church, and perhaps as a means of reconciliation between two groups in the church that Paul saw as growing further and further apart (see Romans 11). Perhaps there is, however, an answer to this conundrum. Perhaps the collection was accepted but did not produce the recognition of the Gentiles or the reconciliation Paul had hoped it would. Perhaps it only provided physical sustenance to the poor in Jerusalem, far less than Paul had hoped for. If this is so, it is not surprising that Luke mentions such matters only in passing. It did not have the historical or theological significance Paul had envisioned. It will be noted that Paul himself does not mention the matter in his later letters (Philippians, Philemon).

At the end of the day it must be admitted that Luke does not give us, and probably did not intend to give us, a full-orbed portrait of Paul. His interests are not biographical but rather historical, and so he chronicles the part Paul plays in the advance of the gospel from Jerusalem to Rome, his roles as evangelist, teacher, preacher, rhetorician, and missionary, giving only brief mention to his pastoral roles (e.g., in Acts 20). If we see a portrait of the Paul of Acts as a supplement to what we can learn from the letters, and in some cases a confirmation of what we find there, we will not impose undue expectations on Luke's historical account. The author knew Paul but probably not many (if any) of his letters, being only a sometime traveling companion of Paul in Asia, Macedonia, Greece, and Israel.[337] Most of his omissions are understandable under such circumstances, and taking into account the factors mentioned above. The Paul we see in Acts is not un-Pauline, much less anti-Pauline, but in some cases a Paul we do not hear about in the epistles, and in some cases a familiar Paul, though from a different and fresh perspective. It is a Paul interpreted through the eyes of admiration and respect.[338]

---

336. See pp. 374ff. above on Acts 11:29-30 and below, pp. 602ff., on 20:4.

337. See Bruce, "Paul in Acts and Letters," pp. 680-81.

338. The older and now dated study by Mattill, "The Value of Acts," is still useful in making clear that whatever view of Luke's portrait of Paul one takes, the judgment on this matter is closely related to one's estimation of the "we" passages in Acts. On the latter see pp. 480ff. below.

D. Settlement in Jerusalem (15:1-35)

It is no exaggeration to say that Acts 15 is the most crucial chapter in the whole book. Marshall is right to note that this chapter is positioned both structurally and theologically at the very heart of the book.[339] It raises all the key questions of what Luke's relationship to Paul was, what the relationship is between Acts 15 and Galatians 2, and therefore what sort of history Luke is writing.[340] A measure of the importance of this meeting for Luke is shown in that after it the Jerusalem church virtually disappears from sight in Acts (but see below on Acts 21) and Peter does not appear again. In any case, after recording the council, Luke's focus is clearly on the missionary work in points west of Jerusalem from Antioch to Rome.

Throughout this commentary we have noted the signs that Luke was following ancient historiographical conventions in the way he presents his material, in particular his penchant for dealing with matters from an ethnographic and region-by-region perspective. With these concerns the extended treatment in Acts 15 comes as no surprise. Here the matter must be resolved as to what constitutes the people of God, and how the major ethnic division in the church (Jew/Gentile) shall be dealt with so that both groups may be included in God's people *on equal footing*, fellowship may continue, and the church remain one. Luke is eager to demonstrate that ethnic divisions could be and were overcome, despite the objection of very conservative Pharisaic Christians.

Luke's universalism has often been remarked on, but to my knowledge no one has noted the connection of this theme to ancient ethnography. At least a significant part of Luke's purpose is not merely to display or explore ethnic diversity in the Empire, as might be the case if he merely intended to entertain or inform the curious, but show how out of the many could come one, a united people in a saved and saving relationship to the one true God. His social premise is not the pagan one of one emperor and so one Empire,[341] but rather one God, and one redeemed people gathered out of the many.

---

339. Marshall, *Acts*, p. 242. See Conzelmann, *Acts*, p. 121, who argues that Acts 15 is the real center of the book because it makes possible and official the Gentile mission. "From now on the whole history of the church is compressed into the story of Paul's work. He represents the connection between the early days of the church and the present."

340. Our earlier conclusions that Luke was only a sometime companion of Paul after the time of the apostolic council needs to be borne in mind, and also that Luke is a rhetorical historian.

341. It will be seen that one of the main reasons for the rise and flourishing of the cult of the emperor as the Empire grew was to provide a religious foundation for the unity of the Empire. Since it could not be centered on one particular pagan deity, not even Jupiter Optimus Maximus, the divinizing of the emperor, who had to be universally recognized as ruler, was necessary.

We have spoken of how Luke, in part due to his apologetic concerns, has omitted discussing some of the controversies that bedeviled the early church, in particular some of those which set Paul at odds with other early Christians (e.g., the Judaizers).[342] However, it was, according to the principle of τάχος, appropriate to do this so that one could leave more space for the truly momentous controversies that changed the shape of the early church.[343] Such a controversy is presented at some length in Acts 15, and Luke lets his reader know that it was a heated one — there was "no little dissension and debate" (v. 2) involved.

We have addressed the issue of the dating of Galatians elsewhere in this study,[344] and here we will only sum up the reasons for evaluating the relationships between Acts 11, 15, and Galatians 1–2 as we do.[345] First, according to Acts, Paul had made three visits to Jerusalem by the time of the apostolic council. There is little dispute that the first visit referred to in Acts can be correlated with the first one spoken of in Galatians (Acts 9:26-29 = Gal. 1:18-20). Reading the text of Gal. 2:1 straightforwardly suggests that Paul is now referring to his second visit to Jerusalem; the text reads literally, "after fourteen years I went up again. . . ." Now if, as perhaps the majority of scholars think, this visit is the same as that referred to in Acts 15, then either Paul has left out any reference to the visit spoken of in Acts 11:27-30 or Luke has invented a further visit, or perhaps bifurcated one visit into two parts (such that Acts 11 + Acts 15 = Galatians 2).[346]

The reasons for identifying Acts 15 with Galatians 2 may be summed up as follows: (1) both events happened in Jerusalem; (2) both events have the same people involved in them; (3) both events deal with the same issue; (4) the chronological fit is good — even if Paul meant it was seventeen years after his conversion that he went up again to Jerusalem, this might still fit before Paul's visit to Corinth in A.D. 50-51, probably in 49;[347] (5) both Acts 15 and Galatians 2 have the same outcome — no circumcision required of Gentile converts to Christianity; (6) the problem in both cases is "in-house."

342. See pp. 235ff. and 430ff. above. Notice how Luke says nothing about Paul being challenged or scrutinized closely on his second visit to Jerusalem in Acts 11, and even in Acts 15:1-4 it is not just Paul but Paul and Barnabas who enter into controversy with the Judaizers. Luke is to some extent trying to avoid overemphasizing the controversial nature of Paul's particular ministry to the Gentiles.

343. See the helpful discussion in van Unnik, "Luke's Second Book," p. 53. See Lucian, *De arte* 56.

344. See Appendix 2, pp. 821ff.

345. Cf. the detailed discussion along the same lines by R. N. Longenecker, *Galatians* (Waco: Word, 1990), pp. lxx-lxxxviii; and Wenham, "Acts and the Pauline Corpus," pp. 226-43.

346. See Haenchen, *Acts*, pp. 400-404, 438-39.

347. This of course requires that Paul be converted about A.D. 32, which I would suggest is a bit too early in view of all the various events and time lapses referred to in Acts 1–8. Cf. above, pp. 86ff., on Pauline chronology.

There are, however, substantial problems with this identification. (1) There is the second visit or third visit problem, which raises substantial questions about Luke as a serious ancient historian. (2) In Acts Paul is sent up by the church, while in Galatians Paul is emphatic that he went up by revelation. (3) In Galatians it appears that the circumcision issue is raised after he arrives, whereas in Acts it is going on beforehand. (4) Paul says in Galatians he met privately with the pillar apostles, while clearly Acts 15 is portrayed as a larger public meeting. (5) Paul calls Judaizers false brothers, while Luke speaks only of Pharisaic brothers. (6) Paul does not mention the decree in Galatians at all, which would have been tremendously advantageous for him to do, as it would have provided support for his view that the Galatians didn't need to be circumcised and so should ignore the Judaizers on this point. (7) In Galatians 2 Paul plays a significant role in the discussions, but in Acts 15 he is clearly overshadowed by Peter and James and only *one verse* is devoted to his report. This is passing strange in view of Luke's view of the importance of Paul and his ministry for the future direction and character of the church. (8) One must ask quite seriously whether the events recorded in Gal. 2:11ff. are more likely to have transpired before or after the decree. We can understand Paul's extreme defensiveness and Peter's vacillation about eating with Gentiles before the council, but they are much less explicable afterward. As Longenecker says, the situation described here "could only have arisen where there were no clear guidelines to govern table fellowship between Jewish and Gentile Christians."[348] (9) Acts 15 discusses not only the matter of circumcision, about which it is concluded the Gentiles shouldn't be troubled, but also food. This reads very differently than Galatians 2, where the topic of conversation was Paul and his gospel, which Paul laid before the Jerusalem pillars. Paul's legitimacy seems to be the main issue according to vv. 2, 7-9.[349] (10) Finally, it is assumed by some that Paul visited Galatia *between* his first and second visits to Jerusalem, but in fact Paul tells us quite clearly that he was in Syria and Cilicia only at this time, presumably principally at Antioch and Tarsus (Gal. 1:21). This straightforward reading of the data leads to the conclusion that Paul visited the province of Galatia only *after* the second visit to Jerusalem described in Gal. 2:1-10.[350] This comports nicely with the thesis I will put forward in the next paragraph.[351]

---

348. Longenecker, *Galatians*, p. lxxxi.

349. See Wenham, "Acts and the Pauline Corpus," p. 232.

350. See on this Longenecker, *Galatians*, p. lxxxi.

351. It is interesting that in his detailed and critical evaluation of both Galatians and Acts, P. Achtemeier concludes that Gal. 2:1-10 is much closer in substance to the material found in Acts 11:1-18 (not 11:27-30) than to what we find in Acts 15. He is right about this, but what his work shows is that not just Paul but Peter also had to wrestle with these same issues of the basis of table fellowship between Jews and Gentiles in Christ. See his *The Quest for Unity*, pp. 49-51.

The factors that favor identifying the meeting referred to briefly in Acts 11:30 and 12:25 with the one recorded in Gal. 2:1ff. may be stated as follows. (1) Both visits were made on the basis of a revelation (cf. Acts 11:28-29 to Gal. 2:2 — Paul does not say he went in response to a revelation he himself personally had).[352] (2) This view solves the thorny second-visit, third-visit problem and also the silence in Galatians about the decree. Galatians was written before the decree was ever given. (3) Acts 11:30/12:25 is about famine relief given to the church in Jerusalem, and Paul mentions this at Gal. 2:10 as the one matter James and the other pillars wanted him to remember. "Continue to remember the poor" (Gal. 2:10) is a present subjunctive implying a hoped-for continuing of an activity Paul had already begun to undertake[353] when he delivered the first funds from Antioch to the Jerusalem church.

The problems suggested with the Acts 11/12 = Galatians 2 view are far less severe than those associated with the Acts 15 = Galatians 2 view. For example, it is pointed out that Luke doesn't mention circumcision at Acts 11/12, but it is often his way to gather up a subject and discuss it in one place, in this case at Acts 15. There is no hint of any public or official resolution of the circumcision matter, in any case at the meeting recorded in Galatians 2. At most that text shows us the direction the pillars themselves were in favor of taking (Gal. 2:3).[354] It is also pointed out that Luke refers to elders receiving the funds at 11:29b, while Paul speaks of visiting with the pillar apostles. But Luke also closely associates the elders with the apostles elsewhere (Acts 15:6), and earlier in Acts 6 we have already seen that the apostles had delegated such practical matters having to do with funds to others. Furthermore, it seems very probable that Luke viewed James the brother of Jesus as an elder, not as an apostle, in view of the criteria for apostleship specified in Acts 1:21-22. If this is the case, then James may indeed be alluded to in Acts 11:30, and this may also explain the double reference to apostles and elders in 15:4, 6.[355] There is nothing in Galatians 2 that contradicts this presentation; Paul's focus in

352. See the discussion by Hemer, "Acts and Galatians Reconsidered."
353. See Hall, "St. Paul and Famine Relief."
354. The text speaks of not being compelled to circumcise Titus, who was with Paul. It is one thing to speak of not being compelled, it is another to speak of an official verdict that the Gentile converts in general should not be troubled in this matter. One refers to a not insisting on this activity by the Jerusalem authorities, the other to a policy that suggests it is not necessary to impose this covenantal sign and therefore should not be insisted on by anyone.
355. While some have suggested that Paul saw James as an apostle on the basis of 1 Cor. 15:7, this is not what that text says. It says James saw the risen Lord, as did "all the apostles." If anything, the text distinguishes James from "all the apostles." Furthermore, if Paul is citing an earlier list of appearances, then this tradition of distinguishing James from all the apostles has an older pedigree, and Luke may also be reflecting it. For another view see Barrett, *Freedom and Obligation*, pp. 91-108.

Galatians is simply on what is of paramount importance to him to report about that occasion to his Galatian converts. Finally, it is sometimes pointed out that the same persons are mentioned in Acts 15 and Galatians 2 (Paul, Barnabas, James, and Peter), but of course Paul and Barnabas are also mentioned in Acts 11. Thus their presence in Acts 15 no more favors the equation Acts 15 = Galatians 2 than it does the equation Acts 11/12 = Galatians 2.

It seems probable, then, that in a private meeting during the Acts 11/12 visit, a meeting Luke does not fully record,[356] Paul had gotten the endorsement of the pillar apostles for his mission to the Gentiles, a mission he then took the first major planned part of thereafter, as is recorded in Acts 13–14. There were clearly many in the Jerusalem church who opposed this activity, especially if it was undertaken on the basis that Paul did undertake it, for Paul was not going to require Gentiles to become Jews and submit to the Mosaic Law in order to be Christians.[357]

356. If James is seen by Luke as an elder (cf. above), then at least the meeting can be said to be mentioned in passing.

357. Barrett, *Freedom and Obligation*, pp. 92ff. (and see his "Things Sacrificed to Idols"), finds it hard to fathom that if Paul's basic approach to the gospel had been accepted in an earlier visit (i.e., if Acts 11 = Galatians 2), the matter would have to be settled all over again later (Acts 15). He is, however, probably reading too much into Paul's defensive rhetoric in Galatians 2. The following points are crucial to a true reading between the lines of Gal. 2:1-10. (1) Notice the qualification in v. 2 — κατ' ἰδίαν δὲ τοῖς δοκοῦσιν, literally "separately (or apart) to the well thought of." (2) Titus is said not to be *compelled* (aorist passive of ἀναγκάζω) to be circumcised. This, however, probably suggests there was still a strong sentiment, even among the pillars, that circumcision was an important factor, even if compulsion shouldn't be used. (3) V. 5 probably suggests that the "false brothers" slipped into this private meeting and caused debate and trouble, with Paul vigorously defending his gospel and approach to Gentiles. (4) V. 7 only says that it was recognized that God's grace was working through Paul and that he had been entrusted by God with the gospel for the uncircumcised. This recognition came from the three pillars; it does not say it came from all that were there present (cf. vv. 4-5). (5) Paul stresses that this whole episode was not a matter of his being authorized by the Jerusalem officials (v. 6), only that the legitimacy of his work was recognized. (6) Finally, the only real request made by the pillars was in regard to the poor (v. 10).

There is nothing here to suggest that any ruling was made on whether Gentiles should be circumcised, perhaps on a voluntary basis, nor is there anything to suggest that a compromise was worked out on a means by which Gentile and Jewish Christians could eat together. What was settled was that a mission by Paul to the uncircumcised was seen to be of God and should be continued. The specifics of how Gentiles would be fully integrated into the community were not settled. This is precisely why Paul is so defensive about his approach to proselytizing Gentiles in this letter. He knows that no compulsory circumcision is a far cry from an agreement that circumcision should not be expected at all of Gentiles. He is fearful that he may still be working in vain, and he has only one small piece of evidence, the case of Titus, to suggest that the pillars agreed more with him than with the Judaizers on the circumcision matter. While Paul cannot be said to be grasping at straws here, he is, to use another metaphor, paddling hard and upstream in this letter. He wants

Until there was a public resolution of the matter, the time was ripe for a Judaizing controversy, which did indeed transpire and is recorded in Galatians.[358] The Judaizers seem to have left Jerusalem, gone to Antioch, and then continued on following in Paul and Barnabas's footsteps to the newly founded churches in Galatia sometime in A.D. 49.[359] Acts mentions their presence in several places. First, at 11:2 we are told that Peter gets criticism from the circumcised believers.[360] Then they appear again at Acts 15:2, 5 (perhaps two different contingents of the same Pharisaic Christian group; cf. below).[361] It will be noted that Luke is careful not to identify James with this group, at least at the juncture when the apostolic council transpires. Though no view is without its problems, the one which causes least difficulties and makes best sense of what both Acts and Galatians suggest is the view that Acts 11:30/12:25

---

concord and unity between himself and the leadership of the Jerusalem church on the important details of these matters. It is clear he has not yet fully obtained it.

358. It appears there may have also been an ongoing rearguard action even after the matter was publicly and officially settled, as a text like Phil. 3:2-6 may suggest. It is a mistake to lump all of Paul's Jewish Christian interlocutors together. Especially those in 2 Corinthians seem to have other agendas than circumcision. See my discussion in *Conflict and Community in Corinth*, pp. 343-50.

359. See the chart, pp. 77ff. above.

360. It is not clear whether the men who came from James are identical with the Judaizers or circumcision group, but Gal. 2:12 probably suggests they were. Perhaps at this point, before he issues the decree, James had not resolved in his mind the food issue which is what is under debate at Gal. 2:11-13.

361. I would suggest that one of the main reasons for the confusion about the relationship between Galatians 2 and Acts 15 is that it is likely that 15:1-2 *does* record the same event as that spoken of in Gal. 2:11-13. *Neither* Luke nor Paul dates this event which transpires in Antioch, and it is understandable why some would lump together what is recorded in Gal. 2:11ff. closely with what precedes in Galatians 2 (even though 2:1-10 is about what happened in Jerusalem), and at the same time assume that what is recorded in Acts 15:1-2 is the events immediately preceding the apostolic council. The order of events seems to have been as follows: (1) Paul and Barnabas evangelize Galatia; (2) they return to Antioch; (3) the Jerusalem church hears of their recent work, perhaps in part from John Mark; (4) James sends some of the more conservative Jewish Christians to Antioch to investigate this matter *and* what is happening in the Antioch church which had sent Paul and Barnabas on this missionary undertaking; (5) the Judaizers have some effect on the Jews in Antioch, and even on Peter when he came to town and on Barnabas who was already there; (6) this led to a confrontation between Paul and Peter in Antioch; this transpired after the Judaizers already left for Galatia (and Cyprus?); (7) Paul in Antioch receives an oral report of the effect of the Judaizers on his new converts in Galatia; (8) Paul writes Galatians; (9) shortly thereafter, Paul and Barnabas are appointed by the Antioch church to help resolve *both* the matter of circumcision *and* of food laws, to resolve how Gentiles will be treated at the point of conversion and the basis of table fellowship between Jews and Gentiles in the church thereafter. They go up to Jerusalem to accomplish this mandate. Events 2-9 transpired in A.D. 49 (or late 48 and early 49), prior to the Jerusalem council later that year.

= Gal. 2:1-10, and thus that Galatians was written *prior* to the apostolic council, which Luke rightly places at the center of his historical account. In fact, if this view is accepted, a rather remarkable degree of correspondence can be seen between Luke's ordering of events in Acts and what we find in Paul's letters, taken basically in chronological order.

Chronological Comparison — Paul's Letters and Acts[362]

LETTERS	ACTS
Paul the Persecutor	
Gal. 1:13-14	Acts 7:58; 8:1-3
Paul's Call/Conversion near Damascus	
Gal. 1:15-17	Acts 9:1-22 (etc.)
To Arabia	
Gal. 1:17b	
Return to Damascus	
Gal. 1:17c (three years)	
Flight from Damascus	
2 Cor. 11:32-33	Acts 9:23-25
First Visit to Jerusalem as a Christian	
Gal. 1:18-20	Acts 9:26-29
To the Regions of Syria and Cilicia	
Gal. 1:21-22	Acts 9:30 (Tarsus from Caesarea)
(visionary experience — 2 Cor. 12:1-10)	
To Antioch	
(see Gal. 2:11-14)	Acts 11:25-26

362. This chart represents my own reaction to and adaptation of some of the elements in the charts found in Campbell, "Paul's Missionary Journeys," and Fitzmyer, "The Pauline Letters." My basic disagreement has to do with the placement and date of Galatians and the parts of the province of Galatia likely addressed in that letter.

LETTERS	*ACTS*

Antioch Famine Fund/Second Visit to Jerusalem

Gal. 2:1-10	Acts 11:29-30/12:25

First Missionary Journey

Gal. 4:13-15	Acts 13–14

Return to Antioch

(see Gal. 2:11-14)	Acts 14:26-28

Judaizers to Antioch/Antioch Incident

Gal. 2:11-14	Acts 15:1-2

Judaizers to Galatia

(Cf. Gal. 1:6-9; 3:1;
4:17–5:12; 6:12-13)

Paul Writes Galatians (from Antioch)

Gal. 6:11

Paul and Barnabas Go Up to Jerusalem/Third Visit

Acts 15:2-29

Return to Antioch/Reading of Decree

Acts 15:30-35

Second Missionary Journey with Silas, Timothy

Acts 15:36–18:18

Return to South Galatia
(picking up Timothy),
passing through Galactic
Phrygia, Mysia, Troas
(picking up Luke — 16:10)

1 Thess. 2:2	Philippi (Luke left here), Amphipolis, Apollonia,
Phil. 4:15-16	Thessalonica, Acts 17:1-9; Beroea, 17:10-14
1 Thess. 2:17–3:1	Athens (17:15-34, Timothy and Silas to Thessalonica)

LETTERS	ACTS
	Paul in Corinth for eighteen months (18:1-18)
1 Thess. 3:6	Acts 18:5
Timothy arrives in Corinth, probably with Silas (see 1 Thess. 1:1)	

Paul, Timothy, and Silas Evangelize Corinth at Length

2 Cor. 1:19

1 and 2 Thessalonians Written from Corinth by Paul and Silas

	Paul leaves from Cenchreae (18:18b)
	Paul leaves Priscilla and Aquila in Ephesus (18:19-21)
	Apollos sent to Achaia by Ephesian Church and Priscilla and Aquila (18:17)
	Paul to Caesarea Maritima (18:22a), and to Jerusalem? (18:22b)
	Return to Antioch for a while (18:22c)

Return to Antioch by Way of Jerusalem

Acts 22:22-23a

Third Missionary Journey

Galatians instructed about collection (1 Cor. 16:1)	Travels through Galatia and Phrygia (18:23)
Paul in Ephesus (1 Cor. 16:2-8)	Paul in Ephesus for two to three years (19:1–20:1, 31)
Apollos also in Ephesus urged to go to Corinth (1 Cor. 16:12)	

Letters	*Acts*
Visit of Chloe, Stephanas et al. to Paul in Ephesus bringing a letter (1 Cor. 1:11; 7:1; 16:17)	

1 Corinthians Written from Ephesus

Timothy sent to Corinth (1 Cor. 4:17; 16:10-11)	
Paul in debacle in Ephesus, dragged into theater by rioting mob (1 Cor. 15:32; 2 Cor. 1:8-11)	Acts 19:21-41
Paul plans to visit Macedonia, Achaia, Jerusalem (1 Cor. 16:3-8; cf. 2 Cor. 1:15-16)	19:21
Paul's second painful visit to Corinth (2 Cor. 13:2)	
Titus sent to Corinth with letter written in tears (2 Cor. 2:13)	
Ministry in Troas (2 Cor 2:12)	
Ministry in Macedonia (2 Cor. 2:13; 7:5; 9:2-4)	Acts 20:1b
Arrival of Titus in Macedonia (2 Cor. 7:6)	

2 Corinthians Written from Macedonia

Titus sent ahead to Corinth with 2 Corinthians (2 Cor. 7:16-17)	
Paul in Illyricum? (Rom. 15:19)	
Paul in Achaia (third visit to Corinth) (Rom. 15:26; 16:1)	three months in Achaia (20:2-3)

LETTERS	ACTS
Romans Written from Corinth (Plans to Visit Rome and Spain)	
	Paul begins return to Syria via Macedonia (20:3-6)
	and Troas (20:6-12)
	and Miletus (20:15-38)
	and Tyre, Ptolemais, Caesarea (21:7-14),
	and Jerusalem (21:15–23:30)
	Two-year imprisonment in Caesarea (23:31–26:32)
	Journey to Rome (27:1–28:14)
	Rome (28:15-31)

I would suggest it is probably not a coincidence that the earliest events in the chart are spoken of in Galatians almost without exception, and the next earliest in 1 Thessalonians. Paul's letters are topical and tend to refer to events of the recent past. All other things being equal, this points rather strongly to the earliness of Galatians as well as the earliness of 1 Thessalonians.

The narrative in Acts 15 in fact records not one event but a series of events, in chronological order, and Luke does not make clear the time intervals between the events (for example, between the dispute in Antioch and the meeting in Jerusalem). In terms of sources for this material, while Luke may be relying on material from Paul, at least in part, it seems more likely that he is relying on either a Jerusalem (perhaps Petrine)[363] or possibly an Antiochian source. This would explain why we once again find Barnabas placed first when mentioned together with Paul in 15:12 and 25.[364] In other words Luke in his own writing up of the narrative in 15:1-5 reflects the order he prefers, but at vv. 6ff. he begins to follow a source up through v. 21. V. 22 is Lukan editorial

---

363. On Luke and sources see pp. 165ff. above.

364. In the eyes of both the church in Jerusalem and Antioch, Barnabas was recognized as the senior partner, so to speak, in this missionary team.

introduction, and then in vv. 23-29 he cites a Jerusalem document, followed by Luke's own summing up of the aftermath in vv. 30-35. This view of the material accounts for why Paul's contribution to the meeting is barely mentioned (v. 12).[365]

At *15:1* Luke begins to record the chain of events that led to the so-called apostolic council. It is interesting to compare and contrast this summit to the ones before the Sanhedrin that occur prior to it in Acts 4 and Acts 5 and the one that follows it in 22:30–23:11. Luke portrays the church as good at conflict resolution,[366] but the Sanhedrin comes off less well in this regard. In addition, Gamaliel, though probably not portrayed negatively, comes off less well than James as a mediator and resolver of problems (cf. 5:34ff. to 15:13-21).[367] Luke does not immediately identify who came down from Judea to Antioch and were teaching that "unless you are circumcised according to the custom of Moses, you cannot be saved." This extreme view, which not merely requires circumcision but sees it as necessary for salvation, is precisely what we find Paul combating in Galatians (cf. 2:15ff. to 5:2ff. and 6:15-16), and thus there is good reason to think it is this same very conservative Jewish Christian faction that not only came to Antioch but proceeded on to Paul's newly founded churches in Galatia to spread their own message. Presumably they are also the same as the false brothers who debated this issue in Jerusalem according to Gal. 2:4, although it is very possible that Paul is already in Gal. 2:4 referring to the same debate in Antioch recorded in Acts 15:2. We are told that Paul and Barnabas had "no small debate with them," a phrase which reflects good classical understatement meaning there was a lot of debate. But there was not just debate, there was στασις, conflict, requiring conflict resolution.[368]

The main way to resolve such conflict in antiquity was to call a meeting of the εκκλησια, the assembly of the people (cf. vv. 12, 22), and listen to and consider speeches following the conventions of deliberative rhetoric, the aim of which speeches was to overcome στασις and produce concord or unity.[369] It is no accident, then, that Luke portrays both Peter and Paul as presenting

365. Contrast the discussion in Lüdemann, *Early Christianity,* pp. 166-73, who suggests a substantial use of sources here, to Dibelius, *Studies in the Acts,* pp. 93-108, who thinks that Luke only knows there was a conflict, but not its substance. This is a remarkable conclusion since Dibelius entertains the notion that Luke was a sometime companion of Paul.

366. And it is right to note that only a group within the church was causing disputes and difficulties. See Marshall, *Acts,* p. 243.

367. Here I disagree with Johnson's conclusion that Gamaliel is portrayed unfavorably. See his *Acts,* p. 99 and pp. 260-61.

368. The word implies disorder; cf. Luke 23:19, 25; Acts 19:40; 23:7, 10.

369. See my discussion of the function of 1 Corinthians in *Conflict and Community in Corinth,* pp. 39ff., 73-77, and also the discussion of the relationship of deliberative rhetoric to dealing with stasis in Mitchell, *Rhetoric of Reconciliation,* pp. 60ff.

deliberative speeches to resolve this conflict. Theophilus would have recognized the appropriateness of this procedure, and the need for calling a large assembly to settle the matter, regardless of who and how many spoke.

We are told at *v. 2* that Paul and Barnabas are appointed to go up to Jerusalem as representatives of the Antioch church to discuss the problem with both the apostles and the elders — in short, the Jerusalem leadership. Luke is tacitly acknowledging that the Jerusalem church was still seen as the mother church at this time, and that any agreement produced could not leave the Jerusalem church out of the discussion. As Johnson has ably pointed out, the "attention Luke gives to *how* the Church makes the decision required of it is an intrinsic part of his narrative message."[370] The procedure followed in decision making as portrayed here involved: (1) a process of discernment and recognition of God's activity; (2) the interpretation of Scripture in such a way as to make sense of what has happened; (3) a view that debate and dispute are a part, a necessary part, of the process of discernment — "such disagreement serves to reveal the true bases for fellowship, and elicit the fundamental principles of community identity";[371] and (4) finally, the consent or agreement of the εκκλησια to the ruling offered by the church leader, in this case James.

On this last point I would demur. V. 22 is about the decision to send representatives of the Jerusalem church with Paul and Barnabas with the decree. It is not about a confirming of the decree by the assembly's consent.[372] Though a secular assembly in the Greco-Roman world would not refer to Scripture to resolve matters, it would, however, call upon important witnesses to testify and refer to authoritative documents to resolve a crisis. There would also often be a formal document drawn up at the end of such an assembly indicating the decision arrived at and addressed to those upon whom it would be incumbent to carry it out. Just as with documents from the emperor or the Roman Senate, it would be sent to those requesting the ruling in the first place. This is why it is that we are told that the so-called decree was sent to the churches in Antioch and in the region of which it was the major city (15:23). They were the ones who had asked the questions and sent the delegation, though of course they were not the only ones for whom the response was relevant or binding (cf. 16:4).[373] Theophilus is being presented here with a picture of the church as a self-governing entity, a subculture in the Roman Empire, a people living in orderly fashion by their own rules, but nonetheless following procedures not unlike those recognized in the larger culture to be proper.

370. Johnson, *Acts,* p. 271.
371. Ibid.
372. Nevertheless, v. 22 shows that *some* decisions were made by leaders with the consent of the assembly of believers.
373. On this whole procedure cf. Garnsey and Saller, *The Roman Empire,* pp. 20-40.

The Western text, whose author(s) recognized the importance of this chapter and made numerous alterations in vv. 1-35 to make the text more useful in its time and setting,[374] specifies that the "certain men" who came to Antioch were those who had believed from the party of the Pharisees, and the dispute is enhanced by adding "for Paul spoke maintaining firmly that they should stay as they were when converted; but those who had come from Jerusalem ordered them . . . to go up to Jerusalem to the apostles and elders so that they might be judged before them" in vv. 1-2.[375] This last alteration also introduces into the text the idea that the Judaizers thought they (or at least the Jerusalem church) had authority over converts in other locales.

V. 3 indicates that Paul and Barnabas were "sent on their way" by the Antioch church. This language refers not just to the idea that Paul and Barnabas were accompanied on their journey by other delegates to the meeting; rather, it is a semitechnical phrase referring to the giving of provisions and financial aid so that one can reach the intended destination in good order (cf. 1 Cor. 16:6).[376] The delegation would certainly have needed some resources, for the journey was a good 250 miles long.

V. 3b states that the delegation passed through Phoenicia and Samaria,[377] and shared the news of the conversion of the Gentiles, which we are told brought great joy to *all* the believers who heard about it.[378] Presumably we are to think that the delegation visited some of those previously converted by Philip or Peter (cf. Acts 8; 10). The reception of the news has been seen as a harbinger of the decision in Jerusalem,[379] but Luke does not tell us the joy is a reaction to a Law-free offer of salvation to Gentiles, only to the conversion of Gentiles.

V. 4 indicates that the Jerusalem leadership, both apostles and elders, as well as the Jerusalem εχχλησια, welcomed this group, which promptly reported "all that God had done with them."[380] This way of putting it makes clear how Luke views the matter — namely, that the Gentile mission had divine

---

374. See Ellis, "Codex Bezae at Acts 15."

375. In D, cf. itgig, syrhmg, copG67. Cf. Metzger, *Textual Commentary,* pp. 426-27. Clearly the D text is more sympathetic to the idea that the Jerusalem church had, and should have, authority over such matters.

376. See the discussion in Peterman, "Giving and Receiving," pp. 104ff. The verb προπεμπειν frequently has the meaning of giving material aid. See White, "Social Authority."

377. A detail which shows that Luke knows very well where Samaria is and that one must pass through it to reach Judea and Jerusalem. On Luke's knowledge of Palestinian geography, cf. Hengel, "Geography of Palestine in Acts."

378. On Luke's rhetorical use of πας for emphasis see pp. 105ff. above.

379. See Johnson, *Acts,* p. 260.

380. Here Luke uses οσα for stylistic variation, having just used πας.

sanction. *V. 5* says, however, that the Christians from the "sect"[381] of the Pharisees stood up and said that Gentiles must be circumcised and ordered to keep the Law of Moses. In other words, they were to be treated as proselytes to Judaism.[382]

V. 6 has often been taken to suggest there was a private meeting first in which the Jerusalem leaders considered the matter, which may be so, but in view of v. 4 Luke probably doesn't think so. After "much debate" which Luke does not record, Peter stands up and offers a speech. This summary of the speech is clearly presented as an example of deliberative rhetoric[383] in which Peter expects, after a brief *exordium*, that his *narratio* followed by two brief arguments (one in the form of a question) will be sufficient to silence the objectors to the Gentile mission. The appeal to divine approval shown by the falling of the Spirit on Gentiles is thought to be a sufficient argument, almost by itself, to determine the issue of whether or not the Law should be imposed on the Gentile converts. Thus after the *narratio* Peter simply offers a rhetorical question as an indirect argument (v. 10), followed by a further and final argument against imposing the Law — Jews as well as Gentiles are saved through faith (v. 11). The outcome of this speech (the silencing of debate) is perhaps recorded in v. 12a.

The speech of Peter begins with the by now familiar form of address, *men, brothers* (cf. 1:16). Peter will appeal to what his audience already knows due to his previous report, recorded in Acts 11:4-18, and probably Luke chooses not to include many of the repetitive elements involved in this reminder. It is telling that it was Peter who answered the circumcised believers before (11:2-3), and chooses to do so again here. Here in *v. 7* Peter indicates that considerable time had passed since the events recorded in Acts 10, and thus a reminder was in order.[384] Cornelius's conversion happened in "the early days" of the church. Peter indicates that in those days, now long gone by, God had chosen him to be the one through whom the Gentiles would hear the good news and become believers. This stands in rather striking contrast to what Paul says in Gal. 2:7-8, but perhaps, since Luke knows very well that Paul was called to be a light to the Gentiles (9:15), we are meant to think that Peter is claiming to have been chosen to *first deliberately* approach the Gentiles with the gospel.[385]

---

381. αιρεσις does not have the pejorative sense of "heresy" as it often does later (cf. 2 Pet. 2:1) but means a party or identifiable sect. It is used of the Sadducees in 5:17, the Pharisees here and in 26:5, and the Nazarenes in 24:5 (cf. 24:14; 28:22). In a Greek context it can refer to a philosophical school. See M. Simon, "From Greek Hairesis to Christian Heresy," *Theologique Historique* 53 (1979): 101-16.

382. On God-fearers and proselytes see pp. 341ff. above.

383. See the discussions of Soards, *The Speeches in Acts*, pp. 90-91; Bruce, *Speeches in the Acts*, p. 19; and Kennedy, *New Testament Interpretation*, pp. 125-26.

384. Perhaps as many as ten years had gone by.

385. See pp. 290ff. above on the Ethiopian eunuch story. Philip was not notified in

Not only did his mission to Cornelius come as a result of the electing and prodding of Peter by God, but *v. 8* adds that God testified directly on this matter by giving them the Holy Spirit before they had kept all the Law or for that matter before they had received water baptism.[386] God knew the hearts of these converts and that they were and would respond in genuine faith to the gospel. There was not a difference between the Spirit they received and one received earlier by the Jewish Christians at Pentecost.

It is thus Peter's conclusion from his own previous experience that God accepted the Gentiles apart from observance of the Law, and so in *v. 10* Peter accuses his interlocutors of putting God to the test by attempting to place a yoke on the neck of the disciples that "neither our ancestors nor we have been able to bear." It has been argued that this is a surprising remark for a devout Jew to make, since there is plenty of evidence that many early Jews saw the bearing of the yoke of the Law as a privilege and a joy.[387] This view, however, does not take into account a variety of factors. (1) Peter as a Galilean, and a Galilean fisherman at that, may well have seen at least parts of the Law as a considerable burden, especially in regard to keeping the feasts which required pilgrimage up to Jerusalem and the abandoning of work necessary to provide for one's family. (2) The various attempts in Peter's day to extend various of the priestly requirements of the Law to all Jews, by the Pharisees and the Qumranites, may have led to this sort of view on the part of ordinary work-ing-class Jews as well. (3) Jesus seems to have suggested that the yoke of the Law was heavy (cf. Matt. 11:30; Sir. 51:26).[388]

The Peter we hear in this speech sounds something like Paul in his emphasis on grace and faith as the means of salvation for all, but there is no reason why Peter could not have also believed this to be true.[389] As Bruce says, Paul himself suggests that various matters at the heart of his gospel were part of a shared early Christian tradition (cf. 1 Cor. 15:11).[390] We have no evidence that Peter at this point in his life shared the views of the Judaizers. Indeed,

---

advance that he would be approaching a Gentile and so had no conscious choice to make about the matter. There is also the remote possibility that the eunuch was a Diaspora Jew.

386. This verse and the next make clear the allusion to the Cornelius story. Peter now understands more clearly that his vision was about the purification of the human heart.

387. See Haenchen, *Acts*, p. 446. On the Law as a yoke see *m. 'Abot* 3:5. On the Law as a gift of God's mercy and a joy, cf. *Pirqe 'Abot* 1:19 and Nolland, "Fresh Look at Acts 15.10." On the Law as not too great a burden, see Philo, *De praem. et poen.* 80.

388. See Barrett, *Freedom and Obligation*, p. 95, on the reaction of the ordinary people of the land in Galilee to the Law.

389. Ramsay, *St. Paul the Traveller*, p. 162, makes the interesting point that Peter may have used at the council the argument for freedom which Paul had impressed upon him so recently in the Antioch dispute recorded in Galatians 2.

390. Bruce, *The Acts of the Apostles*, p. 337.

not only Acts but also Gal. 2:11-14 suggests that Peter both lived like and ate with Gentiles, and only withdrew from the latter under severe pressure from the Judaizers. K. Lake's judgment was right: "The figure of a Judaizing St. Peter is a figment of the Tübingen critics with no basis in history."[391]

The speech raises the question of whether or not Luke, in lieu of using sources, resorted to the rhetorical art of προσωποποιια, a word which means impersonation and in this case refers to the composing of a speech appropriate to the person speaking, the audience being addressed, and its place in the narrative in which it occurs.[392] This is not impossible, but it needs to be made absolutely clear that the idea that there was a historical *convention* of composing speeches for historical narratives is a modern myth. That "appropriate" speeches were sometimes created out of thin air and put on characters' lips in ancient works is certainly true; that there was a historical convention encouraging such a practice, much less that Thucydides encouraged such a practice, is untrue. The student of ancient history C. W. Fornara deserves to be quoted at this point:

> conventions set the parameters of conduct; we are not entitled to proceed on the assumption that the historians considered themselves at liberty to write up speeches out of their own heads. That some or many or most actually did so is perhaps hypothetically conceivable. We must recognize, however, that such a procedure would have been contrary to convention and not, as all too many moderns seem to suppose, a convention in its own right.[393]

This leads to the question as to whether Luke may have been composing *this* speech without the benefit of sources. I think the answer to this must be no, if by this one means that Luke was not relying on source material here. If one merely means that Luke has written up whatever sources he had in his own way, especially since he is only presenting a summary here, then the answer is likely to be yes. As Soards has shown at length, the speeches in Acts share many common Lukan words and phrases, and this speech is no different.[394] This leaves us with the question about "impersonation." The speech as

---

391. K. Lake, *The Earlier Epistles of Paul* (London: Hodder, 1930), p. 116. Cf. Dunn, *Unity and Diversity*, p. 385: "Peter was probably in fact and effect the bridgeman who did more than any other to hold together the diversity of first-century Christianity."

392. Training in this sort of composing was part of the elementary exercises students of rhetoric had to undergo. Cf. Clark, *Rhetoric in Greco-Roman Education*, p. 199, and on this passage see, e.g., Tannehill, *Narrative Unity of Luke-Acts*, 2:186.

393. Fornara, *History in Ancient Greece and Rome*, pp. 154-55. See my extended discussion of this whole matter in *History, Literature, and Society*, pp. 23-32, and also pp. 10ff. above in the introduction on Thucydides.

394. See Soards, *The Speeches in Acts*, passim.

it stands is appropriate to its setting and in some regards to Peter's former experiences recorded in the narrative. If, however, Luke had really been trying to compose a distinctively Petrine speech, we would have expected this speech to sound a bit more like what we find in the speeches in Acts 2–4, and a bit less like Paul. Luke probably had some brief notes or oral testimony about what Peter said on this occasion, which he wrote up in his own way.[395]

V. 12 gives in very brief fashion an indication of Barnabas and Paul's contribution to this meeting. The assembly is said to be hushed as these two reported the signs and wonders God had done through them while they were among the Gentiles. Luke clearly believes in the evidential quality of miracles and refers to the tandem of signs and wonders regularly (cf. 2:22, 43). We are told nothing about the content of their preaching, which strongly suggests that Luke is not following a Pauline source about this counsel. Otherwise he would likely have given more space to the one whom he will portray as the main human protagonist in the rest of his narrative.[396]

It also becomes clear that this report that Luke gives of this counsel relies to an overwhelming degree on the two speeches of Peter and James and the document that records the final decisions of the meeting. There is very little narrative or editorial material in this whole section of the book, and Luke does not really report the give-and-take of whatever debates or disputes were involved. In particular, he gives no space to recording the arguments or rebuttals of the Judaizing party, only to speeches of the figures whom he portrays in a positive light. Accordingly, we move directly to the crucial speech of James in v. 13.

This speech is another clear example of deliberative rhetoric,[397] with James offering only a brief *exordium* (men, brothers) to listen to him in *v. 13*. *V. 14* provides the briefest of *narratios*, and it becomes clear that Luke has edited his material so that James's speech picks up where Peter left off. In the main James will provide an inartificial proof, citing a previous written source, namely, Scripture, in *vv. 16-17* as a further argument in favor of the case Peter had already begun to make about how the Gentiles could be a part of God's people.[398] The issue to be decided is what will be required of Gentiles so they can be full participants in the fellowship, fully accepted by Jewish Christians.

395. On the use of notes by historians see pp. 165ff. above.

396. Unless of course in actual fact Paul did not play a bigger role at this meeting, and Luke felt obliged not to overstate things.

397. See Soards, *The Speeches in Acts*, pp. 92-95; Bruce, *Speeches in the Acts*, pp. 19-20; Kennedy, *New Testament Interpretation*, p. 126, offers very little at this point.

398. V. 18 is thus elliptical, and serves only as James's brief addition to the Scripture quotation, that various scribes attempted to fill out the verse by adding various phrases. For instance, after the word "known" some added "to God" and after "from of old" is added "are all his works." See Metzger, *Textual Commentary*, p. 429.

The "proof" or argument from Scripture is seen to be so conclusive and final that on its basis James is able to draw a conclusion and reach a decision that resolves the matter. In other words, James is portrayed as more than just another rhetor; he is portrayed as a judge or authority figure who can give a ruling that settles a matter. Unlike a rhetorician who merely proposes a certain course of action, James is portrayed as one who can take action.

It has been objected to the authenticity of this speech not only that it is in Greek, but that it relies on the LXX version of Amos 9:11-12, something it has been thought James wouldn't have done. On the former point it is appropriate to point out not only the degree to which first-century Palestinian Jews had been affected by Hellenization,[399] perhaps especially those who had grown up in Galilee where bilingualness was not uncommon,[400] but also the fact that at least a part of the audience that came to this meeting from Antioch likely required that the discussion be in Greek. On the matter of whether James might cite the LXX, R. Bauckham's remarks are apt:

> When Lake and Cadbury remark that the LXX here is "apparently based on a misreading of the original Hebrew," and conclude that, "It is incredible that a Jewish Christian could thus have used the LXX in defiance of the Hebrew," they entirely misunderstand the way in which Jewish exegesis of this period treated the biblical text, as the Dead Sea Scrolls in particular have now made clear to us. A Jewish Christian familiar with both the Hebrew and LXX of this verse would not regard the latter as a misreading of the Hebrew. He may have known a Hebrew text like that translated by the LXX, but, even if not, would have recognized that the LXX represents, not a misreading, but either a variant text or a deliberate alternative reading of the text. Jewish exegetes were accustomed to choosing among variants the reading which suited their interpretation, or to exploiting more than one. . . . The "misreading" of the Hebrew text presupposed by the LXX of Amos 9.12 is quite comparable with many examples of deliberate "alternate readings" (*'al tiqre*) in the Qumran pesharim. Thus there is not the slightest difficulty in supposing that a Jewish Christian exegete, familiar with the Hebrew text of the Bible but writing in Greek, should have welcomed the exegetical potential of the LXX text of Amos 9.12 as a legitimate way of reading the Hebrew text of that verse.[401]

In addition to all the above, more attention should be paid to the various verbal similarities between what we find in this speech (and in the letter of vv.

---

399. See Hengel, *The Hellenization of Judaea.*
400. See Williams, *Acts*, p. 249.
401. Bauckham, "James and the Gentiles (Acts 15.13-21)," pp. 160-61. This entire article should be consulted on what follows.

23-29) and the Epistle of James.[402] None of this proves the historical substance of this speech, but it does show that the usual objections to its authenticity are without much merit. It may be that Luke had access to the letter which was sent to the churches and had a report that James had cited Amos 9:12 in its LXX form as an argument and put together what we find here on the basis of that material.[403]

The speech, after the *exordium,* begins in *v. 14* with a reference to Simeon, using the literal Semitic form of the name (Συμεων) for the only time in Luke-Acts (cf. 2 Pet. 1:1).[404] It is part and parcel of Luke's approach, reflecting his interests as a historian in ethnographic and linguistic differences between peoples, that he portrays James as using this Semitic form when speaking of a fellow Palestinian (and Galilean) Jew.[405] *V. 14b* offers a further striking, or even startling, usage. Instead of the usual term for Gentiles (εθνη), λαος is used not of Israel here, as usual elsewhere in Acts (cf. 2:47; 3:23; 4:10; 5:12; 7:17, 34; 13:17), but to refer to Gentiles as a group from among whom God chooses a "people" (cf. 18:10). V. 14 makes clear that it was the Cornelius episode that was viewed as the first time God looked favorably on the Gentiles. The phrase "for his name" means for himself.[406] It seems likely that Zech. 2:11 stands behind some of this verse, for it reads "many nations shall join themselves to the Lord on that day and shall be my [LXX his] people."[407]

402. Long ago noted by J. B. Mayor, *The Epistles of James* (London: Macmillan, 1897), pp. iii-iv. For example, the form of address in v. 13 should be compared to Jas. 2:5. One should also compare the letter in vv. 23-29 to the letter of James.

403. Various scholars think that the letter version of the four stipulations is the earlier and more authentic form. See Lüdemann, *Early Christianity,* pp. 169-71. Few are convinced that Luke invented the Decree.

404. See Cadbury, *The Making of Luke-Acts,* p. 227. While it is interesting that John Chrysostom in Homily 33 thought Luke was referring to the Simeon of Luke 2, the narrative logic here makes this very unlikely. James's audience in the text could never have understood him to mean this. S. Fowl, however, suggests that the use of this term only here reflects polyvalence — the reference is to both Peter and Simeon of Luke 2. See his paper delivered at the 1995 SBL meeting in Philadelphia and abstracted as "The Simeons of Acts 15.14" (see bibliography). He is dependent on the arguments of Riesner, "James Speech," who is no more convincing. Even at the level of Luke's relationship to his own audience, it is asking a lot for Theophilus to be expected to remember this name from Luke 2, when it appears the two volumes of Luke's work were sent separately and so read separately as well. Chrysostom reflects early canonical thinking that Luke's audience likely had not yet cultivated.

405. Clearly he is not referring to some other Simon such as Simon Niger mentioned in Acts 13:1. The narrative allows no other conclusion. See Johnson, *Acts,* p. 264.

406. See Dahl, "A People for His Name."

407. See the discussion of Bauckham, "James and the Gentiles," p. 169: "It is not implied that they become Jews, but that precisely as 'all the nations' they are included in the covenant relationship. It is doubtful whether any other OT text could have been used to make this point so clearly." Bauckham shows the closeness of this text to Amos 9:12 especially in the LXX. We see here, then, that James is already alluding to the Scriptures in preparation for properly citing them.

The events that happened when Peter visited Cornelius are said in *v. 15* to agree with the words of the prophets, indicating that what follows will be a composite citation. It is rightly noted about *vv. 16-18* that "all the variations of the text of Acts 15.16-18 from that of Amos 9.11-12 LXX belong to a consistent interpretation of the text with the help of related texts which refer to the building of the eschatological Temple (Hos. 3.4-5; Jer. 12.15-16) and the conversion of the nations (Jer. 12.15-16; Zech. 8.22; Isa. 45.20-23) in the messianic age."[408] The Lord returns to rebuild the fallen tent of David, *so that* (οπως) all other peoples may seek the Lord. In other words, the eschatological restoration of God's people was always intended to attract Gentiles to seek God. The Hebrew and LXX versions of the text of Amos at this point of course differ significantly, the former speaking of Israel not only regaining all its own land but also "possessing the remnants of *Edom* and all the nations which are called by my name," while the Greek version speaks of the remnant of humankind *(Adam)* seeking God.[409] These two very different renderings come chiefly through two different vocalizations of two key words: (1) instead of *yārēsh* (will possess) as in the MT, the LXX presupposes the reading *dārāsh* (will seek); and (2) instead of *edom, adam* (the radical is the same in either case) is assumed. There is the further difference that in the MT "remnant" is seen clearly as the object of the verb "possess." It is not impossible that the LXX here is offering a more accurate reading of the original Hebrew than the Masoretes offered, but probably not in view of Amos's interest elsewhere in the nations surrounding Israel and their fate, including Edom (cf. Amos 1:11; 2:1).

The phrase "all other peoples" (οι καταλοιποι των ανθρωπων) is important for Luke, for it is part of his main argument that there is one savior for all of humanity, and that it is God's intent to make out of the many diverse ethnic groups one people by means of the spreading of the word throughout the Roman Empire, indeed "unto the ends of the earth." In other words, there is a considerable social program implied in this gospel, a program not dissimilar to Alexander's Hellenizing agenda, or the emperor's Romanizing one (through setting up colonies and the emperor cult in many places). The difference comes in the means of accomplishing this Christian program — through proclamation and signs and wonders and religious conversions, not through armies marching throughout the earth. Nevertheless, this social program is rightly seen as an attempt to turn the world upside down (Acts 17:6), and in this text the Pharisaic Jewish Christians are the ones who feel threatened. If Gentiles are acceptable to God by grace through faith without circumcision or keeping of the Mosaic Law, if they are becoming part of the people of God without such things, then where

---

408. Ibid., p. 165.
409. See Evans and Sanders, *Luke and Scripture,* pp. 207-8.

does that leave the ethnic exclusiveness of various aspects of Judaism? V. 18 makes evident that no one should be surprised that these things are happening, namely, that the Gentiles are joining God's people in numbers, because God had made it clear long ago that this would happen.

This brings us to the so-called decree, which in fact we find the essence of in three places in Acts — 15:20; 15:29; and 21:25. There are textual problems in all three mentions of the "decree," and we must deal with them before discussing the meaning of the decree.[410] Basically there are three forms that the decree takes:

1. p74, ℵ, B, and various Byzantine texts have ειδωλοθυτον, blood, things strangled, and πορνεια
2. p45 has only ειδωλοθυτον and things strangled
3. D and various Western texts have ειδωλοθυτον, blood, πορνεια, and the negative Golden Rule "Do not do unto others. . . ."

The vast majority of NT scholars are convinced that (1) above is the earliest form of the decree.[411] The Western version seems a rather transparent attempt to turn a decree apparently about ritual requirements into a decree of purely ethical requirements (e.g., blood in [3] would mean murder rather than the drinking of blood, or eating meat with blood in it).[412] Clearly enough, both (1) and (2) have something to do with food. P45 is surely not original, for we can account for why πορνεια might be omitted (it doesn't appear to have anything to do with food), while we cannot account for why someone would later add πορνεια to a decree about food. Thus we are left with the task of making sense of text type (1) as above, and here is where too many scholars have simply assumed they knew what the two key and ambiguous words, ειδωλοθυτον and πορνεια, mean without adequate linguistic research.

Having examined all the examples of the word ειδωλοθυτον that the TLG can produce, some 112 examples, I have shown elsewhere that all but two of the references are found in Christian literature, and that the other two examples

410. The literature on this subject is enormous. Some of the more helpful treatments outside the commentaries include Bammel, "Der Text von Apostelgeschichte 15"; Barrett, "Things Sacrificed to Idols"; Bauckham, "James and the Gentiles" and "James and the Jerusalem Church"; Boman, "Das Textkritsche Problem des Sogennanten Aposteldekrets"; Catchpole, "Paul, James"; Lake, "The Apostolic Council"; Simon, "The Apostolic Decree"; and Wilson, *Gentiles and the Gentile Mission*, pp. 178-95. I have dealt at some length with the meaning of ειδωλοθυτον in my article "Not So Idle Thoughts," which I will be drawing on and adding to here.

411. See the earlier list in Haenchen, *Acts*, pp. 450ff. On the various text types of the decree see Bammel, "Der Text von Apostelgeschichte 15," pp. 439-46.

412. See the careful discussion in Metzger, *Textual Commentary*, pp. 429-34.

(4 Macc. 5:2 and *Sib. Or.* 2:96) are very likely to be Christian interpolations. *Sibylline Oracles* 2:96 is very close to the decree with its reference to ειδωλοθυτον and the command not to eat αιμα; in fact, this verse in the Oracles is found in only one manuscript, which is based on Pseudo-Phocylides, *Sententiae* 31, which in turn surely derives from Acts 15.[413] The example in 4 Maccabees 5:2 also very possibly involves an interpolation, for ειδωλοθυτον is coupled here with swine's flesh, but the following discussion focuses only on the compelled eating of the latter (cf. v. 6 — "I would advise you to eat of the swine's flesh" — to v. 8).[414] In short, it appears that this term is a Christian and not an early Jewish term, and that its meaning should be determined by the context in which it is used. No one doubts that the term originated on the lips of those of Jewish extraction, for pagans would not call their gods idols, nor does anyone doubt this word is therefore a polemical term. My suggestion is that the term comes from Jewish Christians such as James, and the word is perhaps the negative counterpart to the term "corban." Corban refers to something dedicated or given to the true God in the temple, while ειδωλοθυτον refers to something given, dedicated, even sacrificed to idols. Its parallels in the Greek realm are θεοθυτον, which means something offered/dedicated to a god, and ιεροθυτον, which means something offered/dedicated in a temple. With all of these terms, including "corban," the question of venue and not just of menu is important. All refer or allude to activities that take place in temples. That is, the social context conjured up by the decree needs to be taken into account.

Furthermore, the issue is not just where one might find one or another of the four elements of the decree in isolation, but in what social setting one might find them together. Here the answer is again likely to be in a temple, not in a home, and in particular at a temple feast.[415] That Jews regularly thought such a combination of activities was likely by pagans in a temple can be seen from a text like 2 Maccabees 6:4-5, which in recording the suppression of Judaism and the defiling of the Jerusalem temple by the forces of Antiochus tells us the following

413. See P. van der Horst, *The Sentences of Pseudo-Phocylides* (Leiden: Brill, 1978), pp. 135-36.

414. Fourth Maccabees is usually thought to date from the last third of the first century A.D., which would clearly place it after the material in 1 Corinthians 15, and probably after Luke's source material used here as well.

415. I have dealt with the issue of the frequency of the eating of meat by ordinary people in the first century A.D. in *Conflict and Community in Corinth*, pp. 188ff. Garnsey, "Mass Diet and Nutrition," p. 100, is right to stress that "meat was relatively expensive and could have only been available on a regular basis to those with money to buy." The poor or working-class Gentile would ordinarily only have meat at a public celebration, and in particular at a feast in a temple. The decree, if it is historical, as most scholars still believe, and was indeed addressed to Gentiles, and in particular Gentiles in Syria and Cilicia, will have been issued in a social context where the most natural way to read it would be to see it as a prohibition of attending such feasts and all that they entailed.

transpired: "For the temple was filled with debauchery and reveling by the Gentiles, who dallied with prostitutes and had intercourse with women within the sacred precincts, and besides brought in things for sacrifice that were unfit. The altar was covered with abominable offerings that were forbidden by the laws." Here we see the very same sort of combination of idol meat and sexual activity in the temple venue as in Acts 15 with an emphasis that it is Gentiles who undertake such abominations. It is not accidental that the decree is directed specifically to Gentiles, not to Jewish Christians, or a mixed audience of Jewish and Gentile Christians. It is also in order to stress, as G. Alon did some time ago, that the evidence from Jewish sources shows that during the NT era Jews believed that the chief source of Gentile impurity was their contact with "the defilement of idols," not their contact with nonkosher food.[416]

There are a variety of hints in the text of Acts 15 that what is being prohibited is the attending of temple feasts and all that they entail. (1) The first occurrence of the decree in 15:20 is crucial, for it sets the tone for how the other two examples should be read. James says quite clearly that what should be avoided is *"the pollution of idols."* The term αλισγηματα refers as Bruce says to "pollutions resulting from contact with idol worship,"[417] not merely to some kind of uncleanness incurred from eating meat bought in the marketplace but originally sacrificed in the temple.[418] Especially instructive at this point is Mal. 1:7 (LXX) where the term refers to polluted food *offered on altars.* Gregory of Nyssa understood quite well what was being referred to here — "the pollution around the idols, the disgusting smell and smoke of sacrifices, the defiling gore about the altars, and the taint of blood from the offerings" (*Vita. Greg. Thaumaturg.,* PG 46.944).[419] In fact the term ειδωλοθυτον does not even arise in this first giving of the decree, but only at 15:29 for the first time. Clearly Luke's audience

416. See the extensive survey of the evidence in Alon, *Jews,* pp. 146-89, here p. 187. This chapter is entitled "The Levitical Uncleanness of Gentiles."

417. Bruce, *The Acts of the Apostles,* p. 342, though he does not draw the proper conclusion from this observation.

418. It is interesting that Wilson, *Luke and the Law,* pp. 99ff., thinks that an ethical interpretation of the decree much better suits Luke's view of what portions of the Law are incumbent on Gentile Christians, and he even toys with equating ειδωλοθυτα with ειδωλολατρια (p. 100). These suggestions are on the right track, but they do not fully recognize the proper social matrix for which all this advice is very relevant.

419. The Twentieth Homily of Chrysostom on 1 Corinthians 8.1ff. is equally telling. At the beginning of the homily he says that if the issue had merely been meat eaten outside the temple context the words of Jesus about nothing being unclean would apply (citing Matt. 15:11). No, says Chrysostom, the issue in 1 Corinthians 8–10 is partaking of the table of demons. This is what Chrysostom understands ειδωλοθυτον to be about, a conclusion only confirmed by examining his treatment of Acts 15, which is perhaps the earliest real extended commentary on the text. In fact, Chrysostom seems to have been the first in the early church to comment on Acts at considerable length.

would interpret the meaning of the key leading term in 15:29 by what has already been said in 15:20. One must then ask where one would find "the pollutions of idols," by which is surely meant more than just meat but includes the meat eaten in the presence of the idol.[420] (2) The term πορνεια in its most basic meaning refers to prostitution, including so-called sacred prostitution. While it is of course true that one could from time to time find sexual infidelity happening at symposiums in pagan homes, as Greco-Roman literature attests, we would have expected the term μοιχεια, not πορνεια, to be used to prohibit marital infidelity, especially in one's own or a neighbor's home (cf., e.g., Matt. 5:27-30). Πορνεια is, however, precisely the right term to be used if James is thinking of the sort of thing that sometimes accompanied, or at least was believed to accompany, the pagan rites and feasts in pagan temples.[421] (3) James says he is not troubling the Gentiles in what he is about to announce.[422] Clearly, however, if he imposed food laws on Gentiles, in particular food laws meant originally to apply to Gentiles dwelling in the Holy Land in the midst of God's people (e.g., Leviticus 17–18), he would indeed be troubling or burdening them. (4) It is natural to see a simple contrast between v. 19 and vv. 20-21. The Gentiles have turned to the living and true God; what they are being asked to turn from is idolatry and the accompanying acts of immorality. Abstaining from idolatry and immorality were after all the most basic things required by the Mosaic Law, and the cryptic *v. 21* need no longer be seen as cryptic. The point is that the Mosaic Law, and not least the Ten Commandments, is already proclaimed throughout the Empire in synagogues. The witness of Gentile Christians was important to James. They must not give Jews in the Diaspora the opportunity to complain that Gentile Christians were still practicing idolatry and immorality by going to pagan feasts even after beginning to follow Christ.

420. One rather clear pointer in this direction is the D text. As is widely recognized, this text understands ειδωλοθυτον to mean idolatry, not simply idol meat whenever and wherever it might be found. This may be said to be one of our earliest clear indications (probably ultimately from the second century) that the term doesn't mean what scholars have often thought it meant. It may also be added that the Western text was not entirely on the wrong track in avoiding the conclusion that James was imposing ritual requirements. What was overlooked was that all four items in the decree were shorthand for things that took place in pagan temples, and thus a prohibition of certain pagan social activities was being offered by James.

421. It is frankly irrelevant how frequently such things actually did transpire in pagan temples. As long as they happened at all, and were believed by Jewish Christians to be continuing to happen from time to time, the decree is quite understandable. No devout Jewish Christian such as James would likely even have been at such a feast in a pagan temple, or taken a survey of the frequency of various activities that went on at such feasts.

422. Grant, *Saint Peter,* p. 141, concludes from the Acts 15 account that it is wrong to paint James as radically conservative, for he is not of the opinion that Gentiles should have to keep the whole of Jewish Law.

Also relevant to our discussion is the evidence that the choking of the sacrifice, strangling it, and drinking or tasting of blood transpired in pagan temples. In regard to the former, we have evidence from the magical papyri of the attempt to choke the sacrifice and in essence transfer its life breath or spiritual vitality into the idol,[423] and in regard to the latter R. M. Oglivie points to the practice, mentioned occasionally in the literature, of the priest tasting the blood of the sacrifice.[424] The singular reference to blood at the end of the decree would be superfluous after the reference to abstaining from things strangled or choked if the meaning was to avoid meat with the blood still in it.[425] It is more likely that each item in the decree should be taken separately and all be seen as referring to four different activities that were known or believed to transpire in pagan temples.[426]

At this point something must be said about the inadequacies of the usual interpretations, namely, that James is alluding either to the so-called Noahic commandments or certain Levitical laws. Gen. 9:3-4 is about abstaining from meat that has blood in it but not from meat in general, and nothing is said about meat with associations with pagan worship. The term εἰδωλόθυτον does not occur here at all, and furthermore the Noahic commandments were regarded as incumbent on "the stranger within the gates," that is, Gentiles living in the land of Israel.[427] The decree we are examining is particularly for Gentiles in the Diaspora, a very different social setting. In addition, nothing is said in this Genesis text about πορνεία. It would be anachronistic to bring the latter rabbinic concept of *seven* Noahic commandments, binding on all descendants of Noah, into our discussion.[428]

This brings us to Leviticus 17–18. It may be said that if the interpretation of the decree offered above is not correct, then these texts may provide the background for the decree. There are serious problems with this assumption however. First, there is the problem that the relevant Levitical material was for

423. See the discussion of Ciraolo, "Warmth and Breath of Life." Especially telling are the instructions in PGM XII.14-95: "Take also on the first day seven living creatures and strangle them; one cock, a partridge, a wren. . . . Do not make a burnt offering of any of these; instead, taking them in your hand strangle them, while holding them up to your Eros, until each of the creatures is suffocated and their breath enters him. After that place the strangled creatures on the altar together with aromatic plants of every variety."

424. See Oglivie, *Romans and their Gods*, pp. 49ff.

425. See Boman, "Das Textkritsche Problem des Sogennanten Aposteldekrets," p. 28, on what the later rabbis required of Gentiles (cf. *b. Sanh.* 74a; *Yoma* 88a).

426. A second possibility is indeed that blood here refers to murder, since in early Judaism the three cardinal sins of pagans were seen to be idolatry, sexual immorality, and murder.

427. See the discussion in Hunkin, "Prohibitions of the Council."

428. See rightly Bauckham, "James and the Gentiles," p. 174. There is no real evidence that these seven were already viewed in NT times as implied by the text of Genesis.

the Gentile dwelling *within* Israel, which once again is the wrong social context. All of Leviticus 17–18 is addressed to Israel and to the strangers who live within the Holy Land. The decree is for Gentiles in the Diaspora. Secondly, the key term ειδωλοθυτον does not occur anywhere in Leviticus 17–18 (LXX). Thirdly, Lev. 17:10-14 prohibits the eating of blood, but nothing more. Nothing is said here about things strangled or πορνεια, and more importantly the text is not about food partaken of during an act of idolatry. Leviticus 18 does indeed prohibit sexual relationships with one's own flesh (relatives or kin), members of one's own sex or animals, or menstruating women, but the term πορνεια is not used to describe these sexual sins, and in any case the focus in this chapter is primarily on sexual relationships that occur between people who are too closely related by blood. Whether James could have this in mind or could be understood to mean this by merely mentioning πορνεια in the decree may be doubted. Above all, it is crucial to note that "There is, in fact, no known Jewish parallel to the selection of precisely these four commandments from the Law of Moses as those which are binding on Gentiles or a category of Gentiles."[429] Perhaps it is time to stop looking for such a precise scriptural background.[430] The rules that James offers, if interpreted as references to the ritual law, are much too limited to regulate matters of table fellowship, for, as Wilson says, "they do not even guarantee that no forbidden meat or wine (for example, pork or wine from libations) is used."[431]

It may be asked, if this is indeed the meaning of the decree in Acts 15: Are there traces of this decree in the letters Paul wrote soon after the apostolic council, showing he complied with and agreed with the decree? The answer to this question is, yes, I believe. We find these hints in the very next letter Paul wrote (1 Thessalonians), and in another he wrote not long thereafter (1 Corinthians). Notice the emphatic statement of what the Gentiles in Thessalonica gave up when they became, and in order to become, Christians — they turned to God from idols, they turned to serving a living and true God (1 Thess. 1:9).[432] This is the theological component of the decree, but there

---

429. Ibid. The survey of Callan, "Background of the Apostolic Decree," was an attempt to demonstrate some such background, but his review of all the relevant Jewish sources shows that there is no real parallel to the enumerating of these four items together.

430. It may be added in conclusion that if James had been prone to insist on a few basic Mosaic ritual requirements of Gentiles, it is very surprising that nothing is said about the sabbath requirement. The sabbath after all would be the context in which Gentiles would hear the Mosaic Law in the Diaspora synagogue, and sabbath keeping was expected of synagogue adherents or God-fearers. That James is silent on this point suggests that his interests were not in ritual matters.

431. Wilson, *Gentiles and the Gentile Mission*, p. 189.

432. It is also, I think, not accidental that this letter was written shortly after the Areopagus speech was given by Paul (after he left Athens and went to Corinth). See below, pp. 511ff., on this important speech in Acts 17.

was of course also an ethical component — that πορνεια should be avoided. This subject is addressed in 1 Thess. 4:1-9. The fuller discussion of Paul's understanding of the decree comes, however, in 1 Corinthians, especially chapters 5–10, where, as here, ειδολωθυτον refers to meat sacrificed and eaten in the presence of idols. We may see the prohibition of πορνεια already in 1 Cor. 5:1-8, but Paul deals more specifically with the connection of sexual sin with dining in a pagan temple feast in 1 Cor. 10:7-8. For Paul, the issue is clearly one of venue rather than menu, as the advice in 1 Cor. 10:23-28 shows. It was okay to eat food sacrificed in a pagan temple at home. Paul specifically chooses a different term to refer to food that comes from the temple and is eaten elsewhere — ιεροθυτον (1 Cor. 10:28). In short, Paul, like James, insists that pagans flee idolatry and immorality and the temple context where such things are thought to be prevalent.[433] Moses after all primarily required, in the Ten Commandments and elsewhere, this sort of fidelity.[434] Finally, I would suggest that Luke himself portrays Paul, in a narrative that follows shortly after this one (Acts 17), as preaching in accord with the essential requirements of the decree.[435] Here Paul offers his own essential critique of idols.[436]

One must also take into account such texts as Rev. 2:14, 22, where ειδωλοθυτον and πορνεια are associated. These texts likely reflect a knowledge of the decree, and Rev. 2:13 probably alludes to the notable pagan temple in Pergamum built in 29 B.C. to Augustus. In other words, here as in Acts and Paul it was understood that the prohibitions involved staying away from pagan temples, and perhaps especially away from emperor worship in this case. In the Didache as well (6:2) the matter is made more explicit — "in matters of food do what you can; but abstain at any cost from ειδωλοθυτον, which is the worship of dead gods." In other words, mere food is not the issue and can be

---

433. See my arguments in "Not So Idle Thoughts."

434. It is easy to see how this may have been an adaptation of Jewish synagogue requirements for those pagans who wanted to be synagogue adherents or God-fearers but were not prepared to become proselytes. Basic biblical monotheism and morality would have been the minimum obedience to the Mosaic Law expected for such people — "for in every city Moses has those who proclaim him, for he has been read aloud every sabbath in the synagogue" (Acts 15:21). For a different sort of argument that the decrees were primarily ethical from the outset, see Wilson, *Luke and the Law*, pp. 73-102.

435. Soards, *The Speeches in Acts*, p. 95, notes how the prohibition of idolatry anticipates 17:24-27. It is striking to me at least that this speech, if it is Pauline, precedes only by a little the probable time of the writing of 1 Thessalonians from Corinth. See pp. 445ff. above on Acts and Paul synchronisms.

436. The connection between the decree and Acts 17 has to my knowledge not previously been recognized, not least because the implications of the use of the term ειδολωθυτον weren't understood. Yet James is clear enough in Acts 15:20 — he is concerned about things polluted by idols, which after all are found in pagan temples, and the pollution of sexual immorality.

contrasted with ειδωλοθυτον, which must be abstained from at all costs since it entails or involves pagan worship.

As we turn to *v. 22* it is important to note that this verse is not about the assembly ratifying the decree of James. James had the authority to issue such a ruling or judgment, as the verb κρινω in *v. 19* suggests. In fact the addition of εγω prior to κρινω makes the ruling more emphatically one of James's in particular — "I myself judge/rule."[437] V. 22 describes what the apostles and elders, with the consent of the whole assembly, decided to do as a result of James's ruling. They would send a delegation back to Antioch with Paul and Barnabas, consisting of two Christian leaders who were prophets (v. 32). These leaders were Judas called bar Sabbas and Silas. Of the former we know nothing, but the latter is surely the Silas that Paul later traveled with (cf. v. 40) and wrote the Thessalonian correspondence with (1 Thess. 1:1; 2 Thess. 1:1; 2 Cor. 1:19).[438] It is perhaps probable, in view of Acts 16:37-38, that Luke intends us to see him as a person of significant social status, like Paul (i.e., a Roman citizen).[439] In any case, the practice of sending four persons (two from the people and two from the council) on a legation with an official document is attested.[440]

The letter, recorded in *vv. 23-29*, has the proper form of an official document, and E. A. Judge may well be right that the author of Acts meant for "his readers to take them [i.e., the letters found here and at 23:26-30] as the direct citation of transcripts available to him."[441] It was the job of ancient historians to seek out documents and use them in their narratives, and since this document is said to have circulated on the second missionary journey,[442] there were a

437. This way of putting it is equivalent to the familiar Latin phrase *ego censeo* used by Roman rulers and judges. See Bruce, *The Acts of the Apostles*, p. 341. Bruce is quite wrong that James is putting forward a "motion" to the assembly. Various parties have spoken and conferred, and now James will conclude the matter. We are indeed dealing with a decree or ruling from a recognized authority.

438. Silvanus is simply the Latin form of the name. The man's name may suggest that he shared the same tribal heritage as Paul, for the name Silas seems to mean "little Saul." See ibid., p. 344. This may partly explain Paul's affinity for him, but no doubt also Paul wanted a representative of the Jerusalem church with him, whether Barnabas or Silas, making clear that his ministry to the Gentiles was endorsed by the mother church and its leaders.

439. If this is so it would have helped Paul considerably on the second missionary journey, especially when he was in colony cities like Philippi and Corinth.

440. See Chariton, *Chaereas and Callirhoe* 3.4.17, and the discussion of Johnson, *Acts*, p. 276.

441. E. A. Judge, in *New Docs*, 1 (1976), no. 26, p. 78. On legal proceedings and documents resulting from speeches see Winter, "Official Proceedings." See Dibelius, *Studies in the Acts*, p. 99, for Luke's incorporation here of a preexisting document.

442. At least as far as Galatia (see 16:4), but surely even farther since Silas continues on to Corinth with Paul.

variety of places he may have found a copy or rescript of it, including in Philippi where Luke seems to have spent some time.[443] Kennedy has rightly remarked that the "letter of Acts 25.23-29 resembles the rescript of a Roman magistrate to a query from a subordinate and has the rhetorical characteristic of a public letter of the Roman period. . . . The letter well expresses the ethos of the senders and their concern for their brethren at Antioch."[444]

The letter is very specifically addressed from the leadership in Jerusalem, both the apostles and the elders, to Gentile believers in Antioch and Syria and Cilicia.[445] After the standard addresser/addressee tandem the letter begins with the customary Greek greeting — χαιρειν.[446] The word επειδη in *v. 24* ("inasmuch," cf. Luke 1:1) introducing the letter is solemn, indicating the beginning of an important document. In fact the combination of this word with the following εδοξεν in v. 25 finds a close parallel in Diogenes Laertius, *Lives* 2.142, showing the rhetorical effect of such ethos-establishing openings. The leadership in Jerusalem is informing the addressees that they have made a decision that affected them.

Vv. 24-26 form one long, tightly woven and periodic sentence indicating the formality and importance of the document.[447] V. 24 provides a disclaimer — the certain persons who went out from the Jerusalem church and disturbed the addressees had no authorized instructions from the Jerusalem church to do so.[448] Thus this letter now provides such instructions on the disputed matters about which the Antioch church had sent a delegation to Jerusalem. There is a rather close parallel to the use of the verb εταραξαν here in Gal. 1:7. In both cases the authors are referring to the disturbing effect the Judaizers have had on Gentile converts with whom Paul (and Barnabas) have already been involved.[449]

---

443. See pp. 480ff. below.

444. Kennedy, *New Testament Interpretation*, p. 127.

445. As Ramsay, *St. Paul the Traveller*, p. 173, says, the letter is addressed to those who had asked for questions to be answered by the Jerusalem authorities. There is a textual problem here. Should a και be added after "elders" and before "brothers"? See Metzger, *Textual Commentary*, p. 436: probably it is a later addition. This means that brothers should be taken in apposition to the two leadership groups such that the letter is being sent as an official document by the leadership, not by the leadership plus the assembly of believers.

446. The only other places in the NT we find this greeting are in the letter at 23:26 and in the Epistle of James.

447. See Polhill, *Acts*, p. 334.

448. This suggests that the reference in Gal. 2:12 means that while James may have endorsed a fact-finding visit by Pharisaic Jewish Christians to Antioch, they had exceeded their commission by disturbing the Gentiles in Antioch and making unauthorized demands.

449. To clarify what it was that unsettled the Gentiles, some manuscripts add "saying, You must be circumcised and keep the law," on the basis of 15:1 and 5 no doubt. See Metzger, *Textual Commentary*, p. 436.

V. 25 indicates that the decision to send delegates to accompany Paul and Barnabas with this letter was unanimous. The feelings about Paul and Barnabas are made very clear — they are called our beloved ones. The intent is to indicate that the Jerusalem church and leadership are not at odds with them or their ministry to Gentiles. Indeed, these men are admired, according to *v. 26*, for risking their lives for the name of our Lord Jesus. Παραδιδωμι could simply mean "devoted" their lives (see 14:26; literally it means "handed over"), but the Western text's addition, "to every trial," is probably a clue that "risked" is the proper translation. Thus this verse would be alluding to the suffering these men underwent on the first missionary journey.[450] We learn in *v. 27* that the function of Silas and Judas on this trip will be to confirm orally the written report, since documents could be forged, and in many places in the first century an oral testimony was valued more highly than a written one.[451]

V. 28 indicates that the decree ultimately comes from God (here the Holy Spirit) as well as the Jerusalem authorities. The language here is that of a formal decree — "it seemed good to us . . ."[452] — and should not be taken as the expression of a mere opinion. Indeed, the invoking of the Holy Spirit means that the words have divine sanction and so should be readily obeyed. The verse also makes clear that no burden would be imposed except the essentials, reiterated in *v. 29*, only now with ειδωλοθυτον. Those essentials involved avoiding idolatry and immorality, in particular in the context of pagan temple worship and/or feasts. *V. 29b* involves the language of reciprocity.[453] If the Gentiles will keep from idolatry and immorality, they will do well in the church. The letter concludes with the formal Greco-Roman closing greeting "farewell" (in Latin, "valete"). The overall impression left by the letter is that the Jerusalem leaders are making every effort to communicate in an authoritative form and fashion that would be well received by the Greekspeaking Christians in Antioch.[454] From the Lukan point of view, the issue of food and fellowship between Jewish and Gentile Christians was discussed in Acts 10–11 and its proper means of settlement was intimated there. Here in Acts 15 another social matter is under discussion, namely, what

450. See pp. 420ff. above.
451. Luke is also introducing, as is his style, a character who will play a significant role in what follows.
452. See the Decree of Domitian cited by Deissmann, *Ancient Near East*, p. 444: "uisum est mihi edicto signifare", or even closer we find in Josephus, *Ant.* 16.6.20, the quoting of a letter of Augustus: "It seemed good to me and to my council. . . ." Williams, *Acts*, p. 260, notes the resemblances between this letter and 1 and 2 Thessalonians and suggests that this may be because Silas was involved in the composition of each of them.
453. See Danker, "Reciprocity in the Ancient World."
454. See Polhill, *Acts*, p. 334.

to do about Gentiles' associations with pagan temples, both before and even after their conversion to Christianity (see 1 Corinthians 8–10), a rather different matter.[455]

V. 30 records the trip by the delegation to Antioch, the gathering of the Christian assembly there, and the first delivery of the letter. The result of the reading of the letter was rejoicing at the exhortation, which reaction may suggest that the decree was not understood to impose additional ritual requirements on the Gentiles in regard to food laws. *V. 32* indicates that in addition Silas and Judas said a great deal to exhort and strengthen the believers there. They spent considerable time in Antioch, and then the Jerusalem delegation was sent back in peace to the Holy City.[456] This section closes with a reference in v. 35 to Paul and Barnabas remaining in Antioch and with many others there teaching and preaching God's word to Gentiles and Jews alike unhindered. Lüdemann puts it this way: "Acts 15 is the junction at which the transition from the mission undertaken under the auspices of Antioch to Paul's independent mission takes place. It is legitimated by the Jerusalem church before it has really begun — for reasons of salvation history."[457]

---

455. Esler, *Community and Gospel*, p. 95, like many others, misreads Acts 15, and it skews his reading of Acts 10–11 as well. It is strange, then, that on p. 85 he admits that in fact there is nothing in Mosaic Law that forbids table fellowship between Jews and Gentiles. He concludes that observant Jews in the period we are concerned with did not eat with Gentiles, but one cannot make universal statements on this sort of matter (see, e.g., Tob. 1:11). Even good Jews may have been willing to do so from time to time, precisely because there was always a proper remedy for ritual defilement if it was incurred, and in the end this was primarily what was at stake if a Jew dined in a Gentile's house.

456. The later Greek text followed by the Textus Receptus adds v. 34 — "but it seemed good to Silas to remain there." Codex Bezae has an even more expansive addition to the same effect. See Metzger, *Textual Commentary*, p. 439. None of these additions is likely original. They are meant to account for v. 40. The addition was unnecessary since v. 35 indicates a considerable period of time during which Paul and Barnabas remained in Antioch, plenty enough time for Silas to make a later return trip to Antioch.

457. *Early Christianity*, p. 169.

X. Making a Second Effort — The Second Missionary Journey (Acts 15:36–18:23)

A. Back to Galatia and Beyond (15:36–16:10)

In the second half of his work, Luke often marks the major divisions in his narrative by using μετα plus an expression of time in accusative case (cf. 15:36; 18:1; 21:15; 24:1; 25:1; 28:11, 17),[1] but the connective μεν ουν, which is generally left untranslated (16:5; 17:12, 17, 30; 19:32, 38; 23:18, 22, 31; 25:4, 11; 26:4, 9; 28:5), also continues to be used (cf., e.g., 1:6; 13:4; 14:3; 15:3), indicating minor divisions or breaks in the narrative. Longenecker is perhaps correct in saying that in the first half of his work where he is following written sources by and large, Luke uses μεν ουν in his redactional introductions and conclusions to tie units of material together, but in the second half of the work, based more on verbal reports and personal reminiscences, he uses μεν ουν *within* the narrative to connect the various parts of a larger unit.[2] It follows from this that we should probably see 15:36 as the beginning of a new division, with 16:5 providing a minor break. In terms of its content 15:36–16:5 should be seen as transitional, connecting the previous material in Acts 15 about the council and its fallout with what follows. The new mission to Gentiles in previously unevangelized territory does not begin until after the summary statement in 16:5.[3] There is a sense in which Luke

---

1. See Bruce, *The Acts of the Apostles,* p. 349.
2. Longenecker, *Acts,* pp. 257, 453.
3. What this discussion shows is that the summary statements, while marking some sort of break in the narrative, do not necessarily indicate a major break. 16:5 comes where

471

for the rest of Acts will compress the whole of the church's missionary work into the story of the Pauline mission, for Peter and the apostles basically disappear after this point, except when they intersect with the story of Paul's work (see, e.g., Acts 21).[4]

As he has just done earlier in chapter 15, Luke once again indicates that the early church was not without its heated disputes and divisions. The term παροξυσμος found in 15:39 (cf. Deut. 29:28; Jer. 32:37 LXX) indicates a sharp disagreement. "Luke does not portray his heroes as free from human passions; he uses a strong term to describe this quarrel."[5] V. 36 indicates that after some time,[6] Paul proposed to Barnabas that they return to visit the brothers and sisters in "every city" where they had previously proclaimed God's word. This would presumably include the places they visited on Cyprus. Barnabas was not averse to this suggestion, and the very fact that Paul suggested it intimates that he had no qualms about working with Barnabas again.[7] The idea behind this trip is said to be to see how the new converts are doing. V. 37 indicates that Barnabas wanted to take John Mark with them. Paul, however, was strongly opposed to this notion, and it appears from v. 38 that Luke sides with Paul in this matter because he describes the action of Mark in Pamphylia as a form of apostasy or desertion of the ministerial work (αποσταντα, cf. 5:37-38), or at least a failure to accompany them in the ministerial work that was beginning in Galatia.[8] The dispute over this matter became so heated that Paul and Barnabas parted company, and we hear no more about Barnabas in Acts after v. 39.

Barnabas sailed off to Cyprus with Mark to continue the work there, while Paul chose Silas, presumably summoning him from Jerusalem, to ac-

---

it does summing up what has gone before, and in effect indicating the completing of the missionary work begun during the first missionary journey. On the summary statements and their function, see pp. 157ff. above. They not only divide, they also link together a variety of material as here.

4. See rightly Conzelmann, *Acts,* p. 121.

5. Bruce, *The Acts of the Apostles,* p. 249.

6. The term "days" is used in a very general manner here in v. 36, as 15:33-35 show. Paul and Barnabas returned to Antioch with Silas and Judas. The latter two stayed for a while, and then returned to Jerusalem. After this Paul and Barnabas remained and taught in Antioch for a while. Then the events recorded in 15:36ff. transpired.

7. Even though the dispute recorded in Gal. 2:11-14 had probably transpired before this time, and before the council recorded in Acts 15.

8. The Western text enhances Mark's blameworthiness in v. 38 by adding after "the work" the phrase "for which *they* had been sent, should not be with them." This suggests that Mark was also supposed to be evangelizing, not merely accompanying Paul and Barnabas. See Metzger, *Textual Commentary,* p. 440, and Delebecque, "Silas, Paul et Barnabé à Antioche selon le text 'Occidental' d'Actes 15,34 et 38."

company him to Galatia (and beyond).[9] This was a wise choice in many regards: (1) Silas could speak for the Jerusalem church and make clear that Paul was not at odds with the mother church regardless of what the Judaizers may have said when they visited Galatia; (2) he could interpret the decree (cf. 16:4 below), a matter of no small importance for the viability of the ongoing Pauline mission; (3) as 1 and 2 Thessalonians and 2 Corinthians (1:19) were to show, Silas was a capable coworker, and probably also a coauthor of, or at least the secretary for, two of Paul's earlier letters; (4) it appears from 16:37-38 that he was also a Roman citizen, which would be especially useful in colony cities like Troas, Philippi, or Corinth.[10] *V. 40* says the believers dedicated Paul "to the gift or grace of the Lord," after which he and Silas set out.[11] The first task, according to *v. 41*, was to go through Syria and Cilicia strengthening the existing churches there, and presumably conveying the decree to those who had not yet heard of it (see the map at the end of this commentary).[12]

Paul chose the overland route in returning to Galatia, presumably for several reasons: (1) he could pass through his own home territory and strengthen the churches there; (2) perhaps also he took into account that traveling west in the Mediterranean could involve delays due to prevailing or contrary winds blowing in an easterly direction.[13] This meant he passed through the Cilician gates and traversed some rugged territory in order to reach Derbe.

Nothing is said at *16:1* about what transpired when Paul visited Derbe, but an important event is recorded in vv. 1-3, the recruiting by Paul of Timothy, who appears to have been a resident of Lystra. He is said in v. 1 to be already a disciple, which likely means we are meant to think that he was converted on

---

9. That Paul was eventually reconciled with Mark is shown by Philem. 24; Col. 4:10; and 2 Tim. 4:11. Probably he was also reconciled with Barnabas as well, for 1 Cor. 9:6, written perhaps four or more years after this dispute, suggests no animus still existed, but rather that Barnabas was recognized by Paul as an important fellow missionary and evangelist. For the odd view that Silas only joined Paul at Corinth, see Dockx, "Silas à-t-il ete le compagnon de voyage de Paul d'Antioche à Corinthe."

10. Kaye, "Acts' Portrait of Silas," argues that Silas's presence denotes the Jewish character of this Pauline mission, which works through Jewish institutions, and that only at Corinth is there a change to a Gentile mission. This hardly explains Acts 17 with Paul in Athens. He is right, however, that Paul did make it a practice to start with the synagogue, and the point of this was that it was the best place to reach both Gentiles and Jews who knew something about the Hebrew Scriptures and presumably also Jewish messianic hopes.

11. The language is in part a repetition of what we find in 14:26, indicating the ongoing support of the Antioch church for Paul's ministry.

12. The Western text makes this explicit, referring to the handing over in these regions of the commands of the apostles and elders, or just the elders in Codex Bezae. Cf. Metzger, *Textual Commentary* p. 440; Tissot, "Les Prescriptions des Presbytres (Actes xv,41,d)."

13. See Murphy-O'Connor, "On the Road," p. 46.

one of the two visits Paul paid to the city on his first missionary journey.[14] In fact, 1 Cor. 4:7 seems to suggest that Paul did convert Timothy, since he calls both him and the Corinthians his (spiritual) children.[15] Luke wishes to make clear that Timothy was a good choice as a coworker and so we are told at *v. 2* that both the Lystran and the Iconium Christians bore witness about him. More controversial are Luke's remarks about his background. Timothy is said to be the son of a Jewish woman who was also a believer,[16] but his father was Greek. The Jewish part of his ethnic background is mentioned first, presumably to help explain what follows in *v. 3*. It has often been thought unbelievable that the real Paul, the Paul of the letters, would have Timothy circumcised. This position overlooks a variety of factors: (1) Timothy was at least part Jewish. Had he simply been a Gentile, then indeed it would have been historically unbelievable that Paul would have circumcised him, even for prudential reasons, especially after the Acts 15 council. (2) There is no evidence that Paul objected to Jewish Christians practicing their ancestral religion so long as it was understood that doing so was not *necessary* for salvation, either for them or for Gentiles. The problem with the Judaizers was aptly stated at 15:1 — they believed that unless one was circumcised and kept the Mosaic Law, one could not be saved.[17]

S. Cohen has argued at some length that Acts 16:3 implies that Timothy

---

14. Lüdemann, *Early Christianity*, pp. 175-76, inexplicably seems to think that Luke and/or the tradition he follows suggests that Timothy was converted by someone other than Paul or his coworkers. Acts says nothing of the kind. If anything, Acts implies he was converted through the previous efforts of Paul and Barnabas in Lystra.

15. The material in 2 Tim. 1:5 suggests several members of the family had been converted. That his grandmother came to faith first, then his mother, and finally Timothy suggests an order of events, but nothing about the length of time in between these conversions. It does not suggest that these family members converted Timothy. Indeed, 2 Tim. 1:6 may suggest, as the data in 1 Corinthians does, that Paul did.

16. Πιστός here could mean trustworthy/faithful, but probably means believing, and after the comment about Timothy being a disciple, πιστός probably suggests a Christian believer, not merely a person of Jewish faith. Had she been a strict Jewess she probably would not have married someone who was simply a pagan, and she likely would have insisted on Timothy's circumcision while he was an infant. Marshall, *Acts*, p. 258, is right to object to Haenchen's calling the material about Timothy's family in 2 Timothy simply a legend (cf. his *Acts*, p. 478 n. 3). Acts confirms that his mother at least was also a Christian.

17. The first real statement of what was at issue in Galatia between Paul and the Judaizers comes at Gal. 2:15 — on what basis is one, whether Jew or Gentile, justified or set right with God, by works of the Law or by faith? The issue in Galatians is not whether or not it is all right for Jewish Christians to practice their ancestral religion. Paul has no objection to this so long as it is not made a matter of salvation or justification. The argument throughout the letter, but especially in Galatians 3–5, presupposes that Paul's opponents were indeed arguing that circumcision and Law keeping were necessary for salvation, even if one was a Gentile.

was a Gentile, and that even if he had a Jewish mother he would still have been viewed by Paul (and Luke) as a Gentile, because the matrilineal principle that the son of a Jewish mother and a non-Jewish father did not come into Judaism before the second century A.D.[18]

Neither of these arguments is compelling. The very reason for mentioning *first* in v. 2 that Timothy was the son of a Jewish woman is to prepare for what is said in v. 3 — Paul has him circumcised. Had this information been omitted in v. 2, v. 3 would have been inexplicable. There is obviously some connection between the two facts in the author's mind. Furthermore, we are told that Timothy was circumcised because of the Jews in Lystra and Iconium (v. 3). The assumption is surely that they would assume he should have been circumcised.[19] Whether they would have or not, in Luke's narrative outline this story prepares for the remarks in 21:21 and makes clear to Theophilus in advance that there was no basis for the complaint that Paul was insisting that *Jews* forsake Moses, in particular that they not circumcise their children.

Secondly, the key anonymous ruling found in *m. Qidd.* 3:12 is admitted by Cohen to be Yahvnean or even earlier. It reads in part: "Wherever there is potential for a valid marriage but the marriage would be sinful, the offspring *follows the parent of the lower status.* And what is this? This is . . . an Israelite woman with a *mamzer* or a *natin.*" The *latest* this principle became

---

18. His argument should be consulted in full. See Cohen, "Was Timothy Jewish?" It is very interesting that both Jerome and Augustine saw Timothy as a Gentile, but unfortunately part of the reason seems to be because of their own anti-Semitism, not because they had any independent historical evidence for such a conclusion. Their older contemporary "Ambrosiaster," however, saw Timothy as a Jew by birth (see pp. 258-59).

19. See Lüdemann, *Early Christianity,* p. 175, and Neh. 13:23; cf. Ezra 9:2; 10:2, 10. For some reason Cohen, "Was Timothy Jewish?" p. 254, focuses entirely on the clause that refers to his father being Greek as proof that Luke (and the Jews in Lystra and Iconium) thought of Timothy as being a Gentile. This makes Paul's actions, which Luke clearly records, quite inexplicable. Probably the γαρ clause should be seen as an explanation of why Timothy had not *yet* been circumcised, as his fellow Jews were well aware. The circumcision was a witness to the Jews that whatever missionary work Paul and Timothy would do in this area, it would not be without respect for Jewish sensibilities. Christianity was not to be seen as an anti-Jewish religion that led even half-Jews into a further apostate state. It may be that we should also take into consideration the fact that Paul had been stoned in Lystra by Jews (14:19), and Paul did not want to provoke them against the Christians who would continue to dwell in Lystra and Iconium long after Paul and his coworkers left. It must be also remembered that Timothy had a family in Lystra, indeed a family which included some believers. If, as Luke says, Timothy was widely known in Iconium and Lystra to be a Christian, what Paul did with him would likely be seen by Christians and Jews alike in these cities as something of a test case. Was Paul trying to lead Jews away from Judaism? The example of Timothy was meant to suggest otherwise.

a rule was in the first quarter of the second century A.D., as Cohen admits, and surely it is reasonable to assume it was already widely recognized as a valid idea by early Jews in the first century.[20] Cohen is not convincing when he dismisses the reforms of Ezra as setting a precedent for the matrilineal principle.[21]

Thirdly, Cohen's reading of Acts 16:1-3 makes no sense in light of Acts 15. The decree made clear that circumcision was not expected or required of Gentiles. As C. Bryan has put it, "Is it likely that Luke would show Paul choosing to do this while accompanied by a companion who was a walking contradiction of the very thing the decree said?"[22] One must also not dismiss the evidence of 1 Cor. 7:14, for there Paul himself enunciates the principle that the believing partner in a mixed marriage not only "sanctifies" or makes clean the marital partner, but makes the child of such a union αγιος as well. This does not prove a matrilineal principle, but it is based on the reasoning that as is the ritual state of the mother (or father), so is the ritual state of the child. Finally, something should be said about Gal. 5:11. This may imply that Paul is still willing to make positive remarks about circumcision in the right context and for prudential reasons, and thus his currently being persecuted by Jewish Christians is inexplicable.

In any case, Lüdemann is right to conclude: "the polemical statements of Galatians are not timeless dogmatic statements, and Paul's concept of freedom allowed him 'to become a Jew to the Jews' (1 Cor. 9.19). In other words, for utilitarian reasons, Paul could very well have circumcised a colleague who came from a mixed marriage, all the more since his mother was Jewish and thus Timothy was a Jew by rabbinic law. . . . Paul's intrinsic attitude to the act of circumcising a Jewish Christian is expressed in 1 Cor. 7.19; 'Circumcision is nothing and the foreskin is nothing.'"[23] Since circumcision was nothing in itself, it could be used in the service of the gospel, so long as no one made it necessary for salvation.[24]

Lastly, it should not be thought that the real Paul would never perform such an act. He says clearly enough that in order to win Jews to the Christian faith he was willing to be a Jew, indeed to become as one under the Law to do so (1 Cor. 9:20). There is no reason to assume he wouldn't encourage

---

20. See Cohen, "Was Timothy Jewish?" pp. 265-66.

21. The argument (see ibid., pp. 266-67) that various early Jewish authors such as Philo or Josephus do not know the principle because they do not mention it, is an argument from silence.

22. Bryan, "A Further Look," p. 293.

23. *Early Christianity,* p. 176.

24. See rightly Johnson, *Acts,* p. 289: "everything appropriate to that [Jewish] tradition could still be practiced so long as it was understood to have cultural rather than soteriological significance."

other Christians with some Jewish heritage to do the same, as a missionary tactic.[25]

16:4 tells us that Paul and his cohorts went from Galatian town to town delivering the decree for observance by the Christians in these places.[26] It would appear from 1 Corinthians and perhaps also 1 Thessalonians that Paul continued to implement the decree in his congregations even in Macedonia and Greece. In Luke's view this action of visiting and encouraging the congregations and implementing the decree was a good thing, for he concludes this subsection of his narrative with another summary statement — so the Christian assemblies were strengthened in the faith and increased in numbers daily. The decree, far from dividing the church, helped unite it, for it made clear that idolatry and immorality were all that Gentiles *must* avoid to have fellowship with Jewish Christians.[27]

Vv. 6-10 provide a brief summary of Paul's travels that eventually lead him to Troas, an important port on the coast of Asia. What this passage suggests is that while Paul seems to have planned to head directly across Galatia and into the province of Asia, and perhaps on to Ephesus, not once but twice God had to correct his course.[28] V. 6 is controversial, especially when coupled with 18:23. Do we read the latter in terms of the former, or vice versa? It is surely more natural to assume that Luke would most clearly or specifically indicate his meaning in the first of these two regional designations so that his audience would know how to interpret 18:23 when they came to it. There is, however, something of a textual problem at 16:6. The Textus Receptus, following E, H, L, P, and most minuscules, reads "the Phrygian and the Galatian region," which in view of the double use of

---

25. On the Paul of Acts and the Paul of the letters, see pp. 430ff. above. It is of a piece with this reasoning that we discover in 2 Cor. 11:24 that Paul had received the disciplinary thirty-nine lashes five times from his fellow Jews. That Paul submitted to this painful and possibly even life-threatening Jewish custom repeatedly, presumably so that he could go on attending Jewish synagogue service and bearing witness to Christ in that setting, shows the lengths to which he would go in a Jewish direction to win some to Christ. Once the full weight of 2 Cor. 11:24 is appreciated, having a half-Jew circumcised on one occasion or observing a Jewish rite of purification on another (cf. Acts 21:23-26) seems perfectly possible for Paul.

26. On the meaning of the decree see pp. 460ff. above. The word δογμα here does not have its later theological sense of dogma, but rather refers to an official decision and declaration made by qualified authorities (see Plato, *Laws* 926D). The use of this term reminds us that not the Jerusalem assembly but rather James, speaking for the apostles and elders, made this decision. This is why Acts 16:4 speaks of the "dogma" reached by the apostles and elders.

27. See pp. 157ff. above on the summary statements as opposed to the summary passages.

28. Ramsay notes (*St. Paul the Traveller*, p. 195) that there was only a prohibition against preaching in Ephesus at this juncture, but there was a prohibition against entering Bithynia at all.

the definite article may suggest two regions rather than one. Yet the testimony of various of our earliest and best manuscripts, including p74, ℵ, A, B, C, and D, should not be regarded lightly, indeed it should be preferred.[29] This is all the more so because there is now clear evidence produced by C. J. Hemer for the adjectival use of Φρυγια.[30]

It is thus right to see "the Phrygian and Galatian region" here as referring to one region and not two, namely, Phrygian Galatia, which can be distinguished from Asian Galatia and is analogous to the phrase Pontus Galaticus (*CIL* 3.6818) or Phrygian Asiana (Galen, *De aliment facult.* 1.13.10). The construction here is the same as we find in Luke 3:1, which refers to "the Ituraean and Trachonitian region." The objection that a resident of Phrygia would not see or call himself a Galatian can also be dismissed. An inscription of A.D. 57 tells of a man of Apollonia in Phrygia Galatica who thanks Zeus for bringing him safely to his home "in the land of the Galatians."[31] Thus it is much more likely that Luke means here that Paul finished traveling through the region he had been through before including going through Iconium and Pisidian Antioch with the intent to go straight on into Asia, rather than that he now took a visit to north Galatia.[32]

It is unclear what Luke means by saying that the Holy Spirit forbade Paul from going into Asia. Was there a prophetic word given to Paul or one of his companions as they approached the border with the Asian province? Did Paul simply have an internal leading from the Holy Spirit that made him change his course? We cannot be sure, but probably Luke doesn't mean anything different here than he means in *v. 7*, when he refers to the Spirit of Jesus not allowing entry into Bithynia. This is the only reference to the "Spirit of Jesus" in the NT and presumably is simply another way of referring to the Holy Spirit which Jesus sent (cf. Luke 24:49; Acts 1:8). What these verses show is that Paul was not clear in advance of the beginning of this journey what direction God had in mind for him to go once he completed the circuit of the already founded churches in Syria,

29. See Metzger, *Textual Commentary,* p. 441.

30. See the following: Hemer, "The Adjective Phrygia," and his "Phrygia: A Further Note," and finally the discussion in Hemer, *Book of Acts,* pp. 280-99. Hemer finds clear evidence of "Phrygia" as a feminine adjective or ethnic designation in a very wide variety of sources including Dio Chrysostom, Diogenes Laertius, Strabo, and a variety of inscriptions from Athens, Delphi, Ephesus, Rhodes, the Crimea, and elsewhere. It will be seen that the evidence is not only plentiful but is found in a variety of regions and authors. See also *New Docs,* 3 (1987), no. 90, p. 174.

31. See the discussion in Bruce, *The Acts of the Apostles,* p. 354.

32. This is especially likely to be Luke's meaning in view of his record of Paul's intentions in 15:36 which refers to returning to *every city* where they had been before. Presumably Paul felt that since Barnabas was going to Cyprus, he did not need to go to Paphos as well. See E. D. Burton, *A Critical and Exegetical Commentary on the Epistle to the Galatians* (Edinburgh: T & T Clark, 1921), pp. xxxi-xxxii.

Cilicia, and southern Galatia. Paul would thus try various possibilities until divine guidance opened a door and showed him the way. That guidance was to come eventually in the form of a vision (v. 9).

According to *v. 8* Paul passed by Mysia and eventually went down to Troas.[33] But why? W. P. Bowers plausibly suggests that the only real reason to head for Troas is if one wanted to book passage for Macedonia, for Troas was the major port if one wanted to head in that direction.[34] In other words, the vision confirmed an intention already formed in the mind of Paul. This reasoning is not wholly convincing, for we know that Paul tended to head for colony cities such as Philippi or Corinth, and Troas was one such city. The city's proper name was Alexandria Troas, and it was made a colony city long before this time by Augustus.[35] It was an important center of commerce, trade, and travel, and very important in the Roman network of communications. In fact, Julius Caesar had seriously considered making Troas the governmental center for the entire region (cf. Suetonius, *Divus Iulius* 79; Horace, *Odes* 3.3). There are thus other reasons why Paul might have gone on minor roads and across rugged terrain to reach Troas.[36] We learn from 2 Cor. 2:12-13, 2 Tim. 4:13, and probably Acts 20:7-12 that a Christian community was founded in this city; 2 Cor. 2:12-13 may suggest that Paul founded that community in Troas.

V. 9 has been endlessly debated, in regard to the vision. The portrait here of Paul as one who had visions or revelations comports with what we find in 2 Cor. 12:7. Divine guidance was regularly believed to come in antiquity by means of dreams or visions. Here it is possible that Luke means that Paul had a vision in the form of a dream, since we are told this vision comes to him during the night.[37] The vision involved a "certain man of Macedonia" standing and exhorting Paul, saying, "Come over to Macedonia and help us."

The speculation of who this certain man of Macedonia was and how Paul knew he was a Macedonian has ranged from the sublime to the curious. Some have thought that the Macedonian was Luke himself because the "we" passages begin in the next verse.[38] The problem with this conclusion is that the person referred to by "we" in v. 10 is in Troas, not in Macedonia. Another more interesting if speculative suggestion is that since Luke refers to a *certain* Mace-

---

33. The Western text (D et al) attempts to simplify matters by offering the easier reading "passing through Mysia." Metzger, *Textual Commentary,* p. 442.

34. W. P. Bowers, "Paul's Route through Mysia: A Note on Acts XVI.8," *JTS,* n.s. 30 (1979): 507-11.

35. See the discussion of Hemer, "Alexandria Troas."

36. The language of v. 8 suggests he skirted by Mysia, or passed only through the edge of it, presumably without evangelizing the area.

37. Codex Bezae makes this explicit, adding *"When therefore he had risen up,* he related to us the vision. . . ."

38. See Ramsay, *St. Paul the Traveller,* p. 202.

donian, this could be taken to mean a particular one, and certainly there was no more famous or familiar Macedonian than Alexander the Great.[39] There is a certain logic to this suggestion. Alexander was the Greek who desired to make the world one by a shared common culture, and Luke is indeed interested in suggesting that the gospel could cross a variety of ethnic lines and make of the many peoples one true people of God. Nevertheless, Luke does not make clear that this is his intent here, and so it is best not to base anything on this sort of speculation. It is also right to point out that the nationality of the man in the vision is surely indicated by what he says — "come to Macedonia and help *us.*" This verse is important because it makes clear the divine commissioning for what is to follow, and should be compared to 13:4 in this regard.[40]

V. 10 concludes this section by indicating that Paul and those who were with him were not disobedient to the heavenly vision. They immediately sought to cross over to Macedonia convinced God had called them to proclaim the good news in Macedonia, in a way that God had not called them to do so in Asia or Bithynia at this time. Luke wishes to make quite clear that this action was taken on the basis of divine guidance. It was not based on mere human desires or interests.[41] The question to be asked is who is included in this "we" — Paul certainly, and Silas and Timothy would seem also to be included, but was there also another? The least problematic answer to this question is to assume that the author is also included, but this requires a more detailed discussion of the problems raised by the "we" passages in general.

A Closer Look— Of "We" Passages and Sea Passages

Certainly one of the most controverted and controversial topics in all of Acts studies is what to make of the so-called "we" passages found in Acts 16:10-17; 20:5-15; 21:1-18; and 27:1–28:16.[42] Among the major issues raised by these passages are: (1) whether or

39. W. Barclay, *The Acts of the Apostles* (Philadelphia: Westminster, 1955), pp. 131-32.

40. See Tannehill, *Narrative Unity of Luke-Acts,* 2:195.

41. On God's guidance of, empowering of, and control of the Gentile mission, compare this passage to 13:47 discussed on pp. 400ff. above on Paul's role in this part of salvation history.

42. As with most such topics in Acts, the literature on this subject is voluminous. Some of the more helpful treatments of the matter are: Cadbury, " 'We' and 'I' Passages"; Dockx, "Luc, a-t-il ete le compagnon d'apostolat de Paul?"; Fusco, "Le sezione-noi degli Atti nella discussione recente"; E. Haenchen, " 'We' in Acts and the Itinerary," *JTC* 1 (1965): 65-99; Hemer, "First Person Narrative"; Plümacher, *Lukas als hellenistischen Schriftsteller;* Plümacher, "Wirklichkeitserfahrung und Geschichtsschreibung bei Lukas"; Praeder, "The Problem"; Robbins, "The We-Passages in Acts" and "By Land and by Sea," the latter of which should be compared to Hanson, "The Journey of Paul"; Ropes, "St. Luke's Preface"; Wehnert, *Der Wir-Passagen der Apostelgeschichte;* Fitzmyer, *Luke the Theologian,* pp. 16-22.

not there is any relationship between the "we" in these passages and the "I" in Luke 1:3 and Acts 1:1, and the "to us" in Luke 1:2; (2) whether or not it was a historical convention to indicate the author's presence by the first person in his historical work; (3) whether or not it was a literary convention to use the first person in accounts of sea voyages in antiquity; (4) why the "we" passages occur only in the places they do; (5) why they begin to appear without introduction;[43] (6) whether or not these references could be accounted for by the suggestion that our author used an eyewitness source or diary account from someone else.[44]

Our discussion must begin with the frank admission that if one takes Luke-Acts as a whole, or even just Acts, it seems clear enough that the author seldom intrudes himself directly into the text. There are only a few parenthetical remarks, for example, where the author interrupts the narrative to make an explanatory comment (Acts 17:18), and even fewer places where he offers what is obviously a personal opinion (see, however, Acts 17:21). If one were evaluating these documents on the basis of Lukan "tendencies," one would be forced to conclude that it was unlikely that the author would unnecessarily conjure up "we" passages simply for effect, or to suggest (for the sake of verisimilitude?) that he was present on some occasion when in fact he was not. Were he of such a mind we would have expected many more "we" passages, and "we" passages well before — and in more strategic spots than the places we find them. Why, for example, would the author in his very first "we" passage suggest the notion of eyewitness presence for a voyage between Troas and Philippi, when this actual trip is one of the least consequential matters he could validate in this way?

A definitive discussion of the complex questions raised above cannot be offered here, but certain important points can be made that will point us in the right direction. The first issue raised above can be dealt with somewhat quickly. The "us" of Luke 1:1-2 would seem to comprise Luke and his audience, Theophilus, or even the larger Christian community of which author and audience were both a part. Thus it is of no relevance to settling the "we" passages controversy.[45] The "I" found in Luke 1:3 and Acts 1:1 is another matter, however. It is clearly an authorial "I," indicating responsibility for the composition of these documents. It appears that this "I" is distinguishing himself, at least in the main, from the eyewitnesses and servants of the word mentioned in Luke 1:2. It could be argued that he has in mind here the events recorded in the Gospel, rather than those of Acts, depending on whether or not one thinks this preface is for both volumes. I believe the

43. We have already had occasion to comment on the "we" reading found in D (itp) (copG67), and Augustine at Acts 11:28. It is not likely original, but rather a later attempt to place Luke in Antioch in conformity with second-century church tradition. Cf. pp. 373ff. above.

44. In an important lecture entitled "The Pauline Itinerary and the Archive of Theophanes," at the 1996 meeting of the SNTS at Strasbourg, L. C. A. Alexander provides evidence of: (1) how an itinerary and a diary may have been preserved of Paul's journey since there are precedents for both; (2) personal pronouns are used in such itineraries; (3) by contrast, in literary sources such as novels or romances there are characteristically few details about travel, unlike Acts; and (4) the "we" in Theophanes' travel account is *not* artificial.

45. See pp. 12ff. above in the introduction on the prologue.

preface is for both volumes, since the one in Acts 1:1 is only resumptive, so the aforementioned argument does not help at this juncture. I would suggest, however, that our author in Luke 1:2-3 is thinking of the main or major witnesses to the events in Luke-Acts, the ones who were mainly responsible for handing on the eyewitness testimony. He did not place himself in the category of one of these primary witnesses, such as the apostles or Paul, who passed on the key traditions. This does not rule out that he may have played a secondary role as an eyewitness of a minority of the events he records in the second half of Acts, especially since the author also says in Luke 1:1-4 that he has been following the things accomplished "among us" closely for a long time.[46]

The "we" passages do not suggest a major eyewitness role, if they refer to an eyewitness. In other words, Luke 1:2-3 does not rule out that the author might have been an eyewitness of a few of the later events he records. It comports with this that the author is not more intrusive into his accounts than what we find in Luke-Acts. He is, the great majority of the time, passing on the testimony of others, using sources.

Was there a convention in antiquity that those who wanted to present a history-like narrative, one with verisimilitude, would be bound to include some "we" passages in their accounts especially in conjunction with recording a sea travel account, even though such a person was not in fact an eyewitness? Plümacher argues that Luke reserves first-person narration for Paul's sea voyages because they are the only sea voyages in his account and he is trying to show he is a good Hellenistic historian, which required that he show he had traveled and was personally acquainted with some of his major figures in the narrative.[47] It is, however, incorrect to say that the sea voyages which involved Paul (and the author) are the only ones recorded in Acts. Furthermore, A. D. Nock could find only one plausible case for "the emphatic use of a questionable 'we' in consecutive narrative outside literature which is palpable fiction."[48] Praeder has also critiqued Plümacher for doing a very selective survey of ancient historiographical works in regard to the "we" passage matter. After her own extensive survey of the matter she is right to conclude that "ancient historians sometimes refer to their travels, but it is not their practice to relate sea voyages to prove they are experienced travelers or personally acquainted with peoples and places"[49] (cf. Dio Cassius 76.13.3-5 to Ammianus Marcellinus 27.4). In the end Plümacher has to concede that there are no parallels to a person using sea voyages in particular to prove his historical credentials.[50] Furthermore, what is said to be the hallmark of a Hellenistic historian is his veracity (Polybius, *Hist.* 12.1-3; Lucian, *Hist.* 40–41). Had Polybius reviewed Acts and known that the author did not participate in the events recorded

---

46. As Nock, *Essays on Religion*, vol. 2, p. 828, says, this assertion in the prologue goes beyond what is implicit in the "we" passages. He claims to participate in a few of the later events recorded, and to have followed matters closely for a much longer time than that. In other words, he is claiming some sort of contact with the eyewitnesses and servants of the word.

47. Plümacher, "Wirklichkeitserfahrung und Geschichtsschreibung bei Lukas," pp. 14, 16-22.

48. Nock, *Essays on Religion*, vol. 2, pp. 827-88.

49. Praeder, "The Problem," p. 207.

50. See Plümacher, "Wirklichkeitserfahrung und Geschichtsschreibung bei Lukas," p. 22.

in the "we" passages, his reaction would have been about the same as his reaction to Timaeus's methods — calling for detailed and sometimes scathing critique. He would not have seen Luke as following a historical convention.

In regard to (3) above it can now be said with a high degree of certainty that there was no *convention* in antiquity for sea voyages to be recorded in the first person. As S. Praeder has shown, sometimes they are in the first person because they are part of first-person works (e.g., in Achilles Tatius's *Clitophon and Leucippe* 2.31–3.5 the person of narration in the voyages comports with what one finds in the larger work of which the voyages are a part). Acts, however, is not a first-person work, but rather one told in the third person with the very rare exception of the "we" passages and the prologue. In ancient fictional accounts offered in direct discourse the sea voyages are also told in the first person (e.g., Virgil's *Aeneid* 3). "First person narration is required by the direct discourse form and because the reporters participated in the sea voyages."[51] Even more importantly, there are as many or more third-person sea voyage accounts as there are first-person ones (e.g., Seneca, *Agamemnon* 392a–578), indicating no first-person convention existed. Finally, Praeder has shown that Robbins has simply misread those texts (e.g., the fragmentary report on the Third Syrian War or *Hannonis Periplus*) where there appear to be shifts from third-person narrative into first person at the juncture where a sea voyage is recorded. In the Syrian War text the shift from third to first person is a sign of authorial participation after the recording of events in which the author didn't participate. In *Hannonis Periplus* the introduction is in the third person, but the rest is a first-person report. The shift occurs not because of the beginning of a sea voyage report but because the introduction is over.[52] Finally, as Polhill has pointed out, the "we" passages extend into the narrative of Acts far beyond the sea voyages (cf. 16:17), and furthermore the "we" occurs only in three of the ten or twelve voyages recorded in Acts.[53] Acts 13:4-5; 14:20-28; and 18:18-23 all refer to sea voyages in the third person, and some of the "we" material focuses on land travel.[54]

The suggestion that the author of Acts may have used a diary or some other sort of source in the "we" passages deserves careful consideration.[55] Lucian states that the

---

51. Praeder, "The Problem," pp. 211-12.

52. See rightly Praeder, "The Problem," p. 212, and also the telling critique of Robbins by Fitzmyer, *Luke the Theologian,* pp. 16-23. See also below, pp. 480ff., on the sea voyage and shipwreck and Barrett's critique of Robbins.

53. Polhill, *Acts,* p. 346 n. 17.

54. Notice that Barrett, "Paul Shipwrecked," p. 55, concludes: "In fact, the occurrence of the first person plural in such narratives means, in almost every case, that the writer was claiming to be present — and that not only on the sea. Just as the 'we' of Acts is not confined to the water so neither is it in, for example, the voyage of Hanno. Of course, any of the authors concerned may be lying. . . . And he may perhaps quote someone else's first person narrative, though I do not find that this happened. There is therefore . . . a fair measure of probability in what may seem an old-fashioned, and was to me an unexpected, conclusion, namely that the narrative of Acts 27 was written by one who actually made the voyage."

55. See Dibelius, *Studies in the Acts,* pp. 198-206; also Fitzmyer, *Luke the Theologian,* pp. 2ff.

use of such diaries is appropriate for a serious historian (*Hist.* 16). There is a problem with this suggestion in regard to Acts, however, if the author is not using his *own* diary or notes — in other words, if the "we" does not include the author. Praeder puts it this way: "Source critical solutions involve an unlikely set of compositional circumstances. Luke was interested in retaining first person narration from one or more of his source authorities but uninterested in identifying these one or more eyewitnesses and, what is more, saw to it that none of the named companions of Paul could be identified as the first person narrator!"[56] Praeder is right. A close reading of the "we" passages shows that the author can be distinguished from Silas or Timothy or the other possible candidates who are named in the narrative, because they can be referred to in these very narratives in the third person as well. One may also wish to ask what kind of source it would have been that recorded such scanty material from the second missionary journey but a great deal more from the third, or why Luke would not turn at least the skimpy material on the second journey into third-person narrative.

The close analysis of the grammar, syntax, and vocabulary found in the "we" passages in comparison to those factors in the rest of Acts shows that even in regard to some peculiar constructions found in the "we" passages, they can be paralleled in the rest of Acts.[57] Furthermore, the general style and vocabulary found in the "we" passages is consistent with and indeed reminiscent of the style and vocabulary in the rest of Acts.[58] "This also suggests that there is not sufficient evidence to argue either that 'we' is an addition to a source or that it is retained from a source. . . . Thus we have not discovered any basis in the syntactic style of the text for isolating this material from the rest of Acts."[59]

Surely the most reasonable explanation for the why here? or why this? questions is still that Luke was present for a very limited amount of time with Paul during the second missionary journey and more extensively during the third. The author does not wish to make a great deal of his own personal participation in these events, especially since he seems only to have been an observer and recorder of the actions and words of others, and so he quietly and subtly includes the "we" material, without fanfare, and thus without introduction.[60]

56. Praeder, "The Problem," p. 215.

57. See pp. 53ff. above in the introduction on the evidence introduced by Hawkins.

58. Wehnert, *Der Wir-Passagen der Apostelgeschichte,* pp. 202-3, argues that Luke is following a Jewish redactional practice in adding the "we" to the narrative, but in view of the homogeneity in grammar, vocabulary, and style of the "we" passages and the passages that surround them, Wehnert has failed to prove his point. The argument for the redactional character of the "we" and "we" passages must be based on more than just possible Jewish parallels.

59. Schmidt, "Syntactical Style." Cf. the comments on style by Schneider, *Die Apostelgeschichte I,* p. 89. Some scholars remain confident, however, that they can isolate fragments of a journal that someone, presumably Luke, kept. See Boismard and Lamouille, *Les Actes des deux Apôtres,* pp. 321-23.

60. See Nock, *Essays on Religion,* p. 828. Ropes, "St. Luke's Preface," p. 67ff., is right to note that since other new characters are introduced by name, by a process of elimination one is led to the conclusion that the author comes into the story only when the "we" passages begin.

Perhaps the "we" passages are the way they are because Luke primarily played a role other than that of "minister of the word," that is, of coworker in the gospel in the usual sense of fellow evangelizer or helper in church planting. Perhaps he was the team's sometime doctor. More attention should be paid to the fact that Paul sometimes practiced his trade as he traveled from city to city, and perhaps some of his traveling companions did as well. There is inscriptional evidence of doctors, both men and women, operating during this period and in this region, and some were clearly itinerant.[61] It is quite possible that Luke lived in Troas or perhaps Philippi and traveled back and forth between these locations. This would account for the brief "we" passages during the second missionary journey and why they occur just where they do. We would then have to assume that by the time of the third missionary journey Luke had agreed to travel with the group for a more extended period of time.

It is, however, right to say that, even with the above discussion, there are some anomalous features to the "we" passages in Acts. They are not completely like what we find in first-person narration in other ancient historiographical works. Numerous historians (e.g., Josephus, Caesar, Thucydides) used the third person to refer to their participation in key events. Various others, such as Cassius Dio, refer to themselves in the first-person singular as participants in events or use the first-person plural along with the first singular to indicate they and others participated in something.[62] Acts appears to be unique in referring only to the author's participation by using the first-person plural, but then this may be dictated by the author's desire to be unobtrusive and by his view that he played a minor role as part of a team of Paul's coworkers.

It is important to note at this juncture that the earliest evidence of how the "we" passages were understood by second-century Christians comes from Irenaeus (*Adv. haer.* 3.14.1), who takes these passages to mean that Luke was Paul's "inseparable" companion. This is going much too far. What they do suggest is that beginning in the middle of the second missionary journey Luke was Paul's sometime companion. Here Fitzmyer's conclusion seems on target:

> [I]f one takes the We-sections at face value — and does not overinterpret them, as Irenaeus did — one could still admit that Luke was a companion or fellow worker of Paul for a time, without having been with him inseparably. . . . Luke was not with Paul during the major part of his missionary activity, or during the period when Paul's most important letters were being written. . . . Luke was not on the scene when Paul was facing the major crises in his evangelization of the eastern Mediterranean world, e.g. the Judaizing problem, the struggle with the factions in Corinth or the questions that arose in Thessalonica. Luke would not have been with Paul when he was formulating the essence of his theology or wrestling with the meaning of the gospel. This would explain why there is such a difference between the Paul of Acts and the Paul of the letters. . . . If one takes more seriously the indications furnished by the We-sections of Acts and admits that Luke did not write his two

61. See the discussion in *New Docs*, 2, sec. 2.
62. See Praeder, "The Problem," pp. 208-9.

volumes until a decade or two after Paul's house-arrest . . . is there not a reason to expect differences between Paul's theology and Lucan "Paulinism"?[63]

In concluding the discussion of this subsection it is worth pointing out that incorrect remarks have often been made about Paul crossing over into "Europe" at this point. This is an entirely anachronistic point of view. "A broad distinction between the opposite sides of the Hellespont as belonging to two different Continents had no existence in the thought of those who lived in the Aegean lands . . . and the distinction had no more existence in a political point of view, for Macedonia and Asia were merely two provinces of the Roman Empire, closely united by common language and character, and divided from the Latin-speaking provinces further west."[64] It is, however, right to note that the crossing of ethnic and geographical boundaries is important to Luke, because he is offering a κατα γενος, or one geographical region (i.e., one mission field) at a time approach.[65] His view is that the gospel transcends such distinctions and so crosses such boundaries without difficulty in the quest to create one people of God out of the many (cf. Acts 2).

B. Macedonian Call and Response (16:11–17:15)

Once the "we" sections of Acts begin, the narratives of particular happenings tend to become much more circumstantial and vivid with less dependency on set speeches and more description and dialogue. This trend can be seen immediately in 16:11-40. If the "we" sections are what they appear to be, we may suspect that here we are seeing pure Lukan style and composition, without the constraints of editing non-Lukan sources. It is intriguing that in all the sea voyage portions of the "we" passages (cf. 16:11-12; 20:5, 13-15; 21:1-8; 27:1–28:16) we have a specific port-to-port description of the voyage complete with specific mention of the time it took and usually a description of the weather conditions and the like.[66] When we contrast this with the description of land travel (for example, between Caesarea and Jerusalem, or Puteoli and Rome), the latter comes off much more matter-of-factly. Perhaps there is something in Ramsay's old conjecture that this keen interest in the sea springs from Luke's "natural and

63. Fitzmyer, *Luke I–IX*, pp. 48, 51. He reaffirms this conclusion in *Luke the Theologian*, p. 22. The mature reflections of Cadbury ("'We' and 'I' Passages") led him to the conclusion that Luke is claiming personal participation by his use of "we."
64. Ramsay, *St. Paul the Traveller*, p. 199.
65. See Johnson, *Acts*, p. 290.
66. See Longenecker, *Acts*, p. 459. See now Alexander, "The Pauline Itinerary."

national character [i.e., that he is a Greek, or more specifically a Macedonian], and not from his occupation."[67] Perhaps supporting this conclusion is the observation that there certainly does seem to be some pride involved in Luke's description of the "honor rating" of the city of Philippi (cf. below).

I have argued elsewhere that Luke chooses representative and notable examples of conversions in each area or geographical region of his region-by-region account of the advance of Christianity. It is no accident that he focuses in 16:11-40 on the conversion of one woman and one man in Philippi in order to stress the equality of women and men in God's plan of salvation and their equal importance in the new community. This importance is seen immediately by the way the narrative in 16:11-40 is told, climaxing as it does with the final Christian meeting in the household of Lydia. It was vital for Paul to find a venue where Christians could meet in this Roman colony, for he was promulgating a foreign religion, and one not clearly licit, especially if it was distinguished from Judaism. Lydia's providing of a meeting place was thus crucial to the existence and growth of Christianity in this place.[68] Furthermore, the "Gospel is seen to triumph in the midst of the Jewish meeting place (16.14-15), and in the midst of the Roman stronghold (in the city cf. 16.18-19, and in their prison cf. 16.25-26). It is seen to triumph over natural and supernatural powers, whether it be magistrates and their jails, or demons. Luke is at pains to show that the Gospel and its followers can exist within the confines of the place of Roman authority by creating its own space 'in house.' . . . Thus he shows that the faith, while not subservient to Rome, is not fundamentally at odds with the Roman empire or its authorities."[69]

The voyage from Troas set a straight course for the mountainous and very visible island of Samothrace, which lay between Troas and Philippi.[70] It

---

67. Ramsay, *St. Paul the Traveller,* p. 206.

68. It is hard to express the importance of the welcoming into a home for Christians in such a city. Roman anti-Semitism was widespread; indeed, Roman antipathy to any Oriental religion that seemed to threaten the traditional gods and customs was considerable. If Jews were forced to meet outside the city gate in Philippi, Christians would not have fared much better, without a sponsor of some social status and means, in particular means of providing a meeting place. Clubs and societies of various sorts met in large homes, and if Christianity had such a venue it would likely be viewed in this light, and not be seen as a dangerous foreign cult. It must be remembered that early Christianity had no temples, priests, or sacrifices, the very heart of almost all ancient religions, and so it would be more likely to be seen as a philosophy or society, the sort of thing that met in homes. On the importance of the home as a place for early Christian preaching and teaching, cf. Stowers, "Social Status."

69. Witherington, *Women in the Earliest Churches,* p. 148. On the structure see Redalie, "Conversion ou liberation?" and Torrance, "St. Paul at Philippi."

70. Mount Fengari on this island is 5,577 feet high. Poseidon, the Greek god of the sea, is said to have surveyed Troy from this mountain's summit (Homer, *Iliad* 13.12).

was a well-known stopover for ships in the northern Aegean (see Pliny, *Nat. Hist.* 4.23). Luke tells us in *v. 11* that they managed to sail on the very next day all the way to Neapolis, presumably because of favorable winds.[71] Neapolis was the port for Philippi, which was some ten miles farther inland.

Philippi was an important Roman colony city, in fact the only such colony city that Luke actually describes as such *(v. 12)*. It lay on the Via Egnatia, the main east-west route across Macedonia, connecting Rome with its eastern provinces. While the city was originally built and fortified by Philip of Macedonia in about 358 B.C. and named after him, the Philippi that Luke and Paul knew was a metropolis run on Roman principles and Roman law, a not-unimportant fact as this story develops. Roman citizenship was highly prized in such a place. The city prospered not only because it was in a very fertile region but because there were still active mines in the area, in particular gold mines. It also prospered and outstripped other cities in this district of Macedonia, including the city that had been named in 167 B.C. the capital of the district, Amphipolis.

Perhaps the main reason in Paul's era why it had surpassed other cities in the district is that when Antony had been defeated by Octavian in 31 B.C. near this city, he not only made Philippi a Roman colony and populated it with retiring Roman soldiers but he even gave the city the *ius italicum,* the legal character of a part of Italy, even though it was outside Italy. This was the highest honor that could be bestowed on a provincial city, for it meant exemption from poll and land taxes, and it meant that colonists could purchase or sell land and engage in civil lawsuits. It was, in short, Rome in microcosm. The city was in a senatorial province after A.D. 44, and was governed by a proconsul whose administrative seat was in Thessalonica rather than Philippi.[72] Among other things, this meant that the supreme authority to which Philippian Roman citizens could appeal was in another city, a fact that is probably not unimportant to Luke's narrative. The cultural orientation of the city would have been Greco-Roman, and there is no reason to think there was any significant Jewish presence in this city at this time.[73] The thoroughly Romanized character of the city in Paul's day is shown by the fact that over 80 percent of the extant inscriptions from the period from Philippi are in Latin, compared to only 40 percent in another Roman colony Paul had visited — Pisidian Antioch.[74]

---

71. The total distance from Troas to Neapolis was some 156 miles, and while this trip took only two days, the return trip mentioned in 20:5 took five.

72. Thessalonica was the capital of the whole province of Macedonia, which was made up of four districts.

73. See my discussion in *Friendship and Finances in Philippi* (Valley Forge, Pa.: Trinity, 1994), pp. 21-22.

74. See Keener, *Bible Background Commentary,* p. 369.

V. 12 has been the subject of much debate in regard to Luke's historical credibility. Part of the difficulty is tied up with a text-critical problem. ℵ, A, C, and p74 have the reading πρωτη της μεριδος, and B has πρωτη μεριδος της. D and syrpesh have κεφαλη της, while E copsa.codd have πρωτη μερις, and finally 614, 1241, 1739, 2495 pc syrhcl have πρωτη της. In short we have a significant number of variants at this point, indicating considerable uncertainty about the original text's reading. It is a step of desperation to start offering conjectural emendations based on no textual witnesses.[75] We can also rule out the reading of D because Thessalonica and not Philippi was the capital of the Macedonian province at this point, a fact the scribe who produced D obviously did not know. Of the remaining readings the combined witnesses of ℵ, A, C, and p74 deserve to be followed. The question then turns on the meaning of the word πρωτη, and something also should be said about the meaning of the word μεριδος. The latter literally means portion or share and probably should not be taken as a technical term meaning district.[76] Macedonia had four districts; it was not a district itself, but rather a province. The phrase in question then can mean "a first (or leading) city of (that) portion of Macedonia."[77] In short, this is not a statement about Philippi's political role in the province, but rather Luke's view of its honor rating in that portion of Macedonia.[78] What Luke has done here is praised the city in accordance with the rhetorical rules for the praise of a city (cf. Menander Rhetor, *Treatises* II 369.17–370.10 to Dio Chrysostom's treatment of Tarsus in *Or.* 33.17-18, 21).[79] Since Luke rarely does this with other cities (except Tarsus, 21:39, the hometown of Luke's hero), we may ask why. Here the conjecture of Ramsay is plausible — Luke is proud of his hometown.[80]

75. Yet this is what we find even in so conservative and cautious a commentator as Bruce, *The Acts of the Apostles*, p. 357, who, following F. Blass and C. H. Turner, proposes the adding of a final sigma to πρωτη.

76. Johnson, *Acts*, p. 292, argues that the word was not recognized as a term meaning "district," but *SEG*, xvi, n. 391, provides a Flavian-era piece of evidence that μερις could be used of a district. Whether or not it is a technical term here is the issue.

77. See Metzger, *Textual Commentary*, p. 446; Longenecker, *Acts*, p. 460. The conjecturally added sigma to πρωτη would make the text speak of a city of the first district of Macedonia, but as we have already pointed out the other key term means portion — it is not a technical term for a district. The suggestion that Luke may have meant that this was simply the first city Paul visited in Macedonia does not explain the way the Greek is phrased here, but see Wikgren, "The Problem of Acts 16.12," on this matter and on the textual problem in general.

78. See now the discussion by Neyrey, "Luke's Social Location of Paul," pp. 268-69.

79. On the rhetorical rules for praising a city see Menander Rhetor's list in *Menander Rhetor*, trans. D. A. Russell and N. Wilson (Oxford: Oxford University Press, 1981), pp. 33-75.

80. Ramsay, *St. Paul the Traveller*, pp. 206-9. As Ramsay points out, this honor rating comports with what can be known of how the *Philippians* viewed the importance of their own city. Sherwin-White, *Roman Law and Roman Society*, p. 93, says that the use of the phrase here portrays local knowledge.

A. N. Sherwin-White has a further suggestion: "The Roman colonies were well aware of their superiority to any provincial Greek city [such as Amphipolis], however large. They did not need to print the title First City on their coins and inscriptions. They *were* the First People of the province . . . why did the author go out of his way to introduce Philippi thus, when he never formally describes the technical status of any other city? The reasonable answer could be that it was because Paul had an adventure at Philippi of which the significance depended upon the special status of the place" (see below on v. 37).[81]

It is appropriate here to mention another two pieces in this puzzle: (1) Philippi was famous for its school of medicine, with graduates throughout the Roman world, and as Col. 4:14 informs us, the Luke who was a companion of Paul was a beloved doctor;[82] (2) if this was indeed Luke's town, as the "we" passages may suggest, then it is a reasonable conjecture that the "true yokefellow" or, better, "loyal companion" (NRSV masculine form of the noun) referred to in Phil. 4:3 was Luke, who was still based in Philippi at the later time when that epistle was written (somewhere between A.D. 60 and 62), though like many another ancient doctor he was itinerant.[83]

Luke tells us in *v. 12b* that "we" stayed in this city for some days, and so a series of events that occurred in this city is recorded in the remainder of Acts 16. By the way things are phrased in vv. 12-13, it appears they were in the city for several days before the sabbath came around and they looked for a group of worshiping Jews. *V. 13* mentions specifically going out of a particular city gate down to the river.[84] The significance of this is twofold. In various Roman colony cities, as in Rome, foreign cults, especially small ones that were not well established in a particular locale, were often not allowed within the city walls, which may explain in part why Paul and his coworkers looked outside the city gates. The location of the assembly Paul finally finds probably suggests its lack of social recognition in Philippi. Secondly, it may be, as has often been suggested, that the Jewish meeting was held by a river, in this case probably the Gangites, because Jewish water rituals could easily be practiced here. In particular, this group seems to involve various women, who had to do ritual ablutions after their monthly period in order to be considered clean and able to attend Jewish worship. The locale was especially appropriate from their point of view.

81. Ibid., pp. 94-95.
82. See Longenecker, *Acts*, p. 460.
83. His primary circuit being between Philippi and Troas. On the loyal companion see my other conjecture in *Friendship and Finances in Philippi*, pp. 106-7.
84. There are still the ruins of an arched gateway at Philippi which may be the one referred to here. See McDonald, "Archaeology and St. Paul's Journeys."

Luke says they went down to the river because they thought there was a place of Jewish worship there.[85] Luke calls the meeting place a προσευχη (here and at v. 16). While it is possible that this refers to a building,[86] previously in his narrative Luke has used the term συναγωγος (cf. Acts 6:9; 9:2), and also in what follows in 17:1, 10, 17.[87] This suggests Luke simply means a place of prayer.[88] When they arrived at the place of prayer, Paul sat down, assuming the posture of a Jewish teacher, and addressed the women who had gathered there. Presumably these women had assembled to recite the Shema, to pray the Shemoneh Esreh, and to read from the Law and Prophets and perhaps discuss its meaning, to hear from a teacher, and to receive a final blessing.[89] In this case, Paul was the guest teacher.

V. 14 introduces us to Lydia, a seller of purple cloth from the city of Thyatira, which was originally in the region called Lydia before the Roman province of Asia was constituted. While it is possible that the Greek means "the Lydian woman," there is now clear evidence for Lydia as a proper name (e.g., Julia Lydia from Sardis),[90] and this is the most natural way to read the Greek here — she was named Lydia. That she is mentioned by name may be quite significant. Roman women were normally called by their family's cognomen, not by a personal name or nickname. That Lydia is called by her personal name suggests she is of Greek extraction, and it probably also indi-

---

85. Lüdemann, *Early Christianity*, p. 182, suggests that the phrase may reflect an eyewitness report. Cf. Cadbury, *Book of Acts in History*, p. 87.

86. See the discussion of Brooten, *Women Leaders*, pp. 139-40.

87. There is, however, evidence for synagogues being built near bodies of water. See Josephus, *Ant.* 14.258. Johnson, *Acts*, p. 292, makes the novel suggestion that this meeting was not at a synagogue but on the way to the synagogue, just as the later encounter with the Pythoness was (cf. 16:16).

88. This conclusion is probable without trying to answer the vexed question of whether women in the Diaspora, especially in an "enlightened" city like Philippi, might have been able to make up the quorum for an official synagogue. This is perhaps possible, as Brooten suggests, especially in view of the prominent role various women played in Diaspora synagogues, but we cannot be sure, especially in light of the contrary evidence in *m. Sanh.* 1:6; *m. Pirqe 'Abot* 3:6, and one would still have to provide an adequate explanation for the change of terminology here. The argument that προσευχη indicates Luke used a source here is not convincing in view of what we know about how Luke made his sources his own. But see Brooten, *Women Leaders*, pp. 5ff., on women's roles in Diaspora synagogues. If there was not a significant Jewish presence in Philippi, the only real precedents for Philippian women to learn what their roles might be in Christianity would be to consider what their roles were in Greco-Roman cults in Philippi, such as the cult of Diana, and in other non-Christian foreign cults. On this basis, they would have expected to play significant roles. Cf. MacMullen, "Women in Public." We should not be surprised to find Philippian women playing such roles as coworkers of the apostle in Phil. 4:2-3.

89. See Longenecker, *Acts*, p. 460.

90. See *New Docs* (1987), p. 54.

cates she is a person of some status, since it was normal in such a Greco-Roman setting *not* to mention women by personal name in public unless they were either notable or notorious.[91]

The term πορφυρόπωλις refers to someone who is a seller of purple cloth (see *CIG* 2, 2519).[92] It is clear enough from the reference to Lydia's house and household that she should not be seen as someone of servile status, and the term πορφυρόπωλις also suggests the opposite.[93] There is evidence that dealing in this color was an imperial monopoly, though it may date from later than this period,[94] in fact that those involved in this trade were members of "Caesar's household."[95] This would not be patricians but the elite among the freedmen and freedwomen (and some slaves) who were in the imperial service. It is then possible, but far from certain, that the greeting found in Phil. 4:22 could be from Lydia, away in Rome on business, to her fellow Christians in Philippi.[96] In any case, she is clearly being portrayed here as a person of some social importance and means, and as we have already seen Luke has an interest in recording the conversion of this kind of folk, perhaps because they were of a similar station to Luke's audience.

Such women of means were not unusual in Macedonia, which since at least the Hellenistic era had allowed women important social, political, and religious roles.[97] More relevant for our purposes, however, since Philippi was a Roman colony, is the survey of A. J. Marshall on the roles of Roman women in the provinces.[98] He demonstrates that various women owned provincial estates and were well-off, and furthermore the wives of Roman provincial officials are often honored in inscriptions and took on important religious roles in various local cults. In addition J. Wiseman provides clear evidence that there were prominent Macedonian families that continued to play important roles in society in Philippi and elsewhere, and this included female members of these families.[99] It was money and social status that procured women or men important roles in such religious settings, and it is no accident

91. See the discussion in Schaps, "The Women Least Mentioned."
92. The Vulgate has *purpuraria*, a much less specific word which could refer to a purple dyer as well as a purple seller. This may reflect the tendency to minimize the social importance of women in various texts of Acts.
93. Haenchen, *Acts*, p. 494, cites an inscription referring to a Thyatiran purple dyer who was being honored by his fellow members of the trade.
94. See *New Docs*, 2:26.
95. See the discussion in *New Docs*, 2:28.
96. See my discussion in *Friendship and Finances in Philippi*, pp. 135-37.
97. See Tarn and Griffith, *Hellenistic Civilisation*, p. 98, and compare the discussion in W. D. Thomas, "The Place of Women in the Church at Philippi," *ET* 83 (1971-72): 117-20; Redalie, "Conversion ou liberation?"
98. Marshall, "Roman Women and the Provinces."
99. Wiseman, "A Distinguished Macedonian Family."

that higher-status women played important roles in early Christianity as well, in this case providing a venue for the church to meet and be nurtured (see below, v. 40). Lydia is also said in *v. 14b* to be a σεβομενη. As we have noted earlier, this term is not found in Acts prior to Acts 13:45-46, and is the only term he uses thereafter, instead of φοβουμενοι τον Θεον, to refer to this sort of person. This seems to be because as the account deals more and more with Gentiles and Gentile territory, Luke carefully uses terminology that reflects the direction the mission is going, terminology more familiar to Gentiles.[100] The term σεβομενη is perhaps not a technical one, but it does connote here not merely a devout person of any sort but a Gentile who worships the biblical God and so is devout in that way. We see here again Paul's modus operandi — to Jews first in every locale, if they can be found.

V. 14c indicates that it was the Lord who opened her heart to listen eagerly to the gospel taught by Paul and so be converted.[101] *V. 15* refers immediately to her and her household being baptized, which presumably would include her household servants and children if there were any.[102] She is perhaps to be seen as a widow, or less probably a single woman of means. The proof of her conversion is shown in her imploring Paul and his colleagues to come and stay at her home, "if you have judged me to be faithful to the Lord." This was a powerful rhetorical approach. To refuse hospitality was always a serious breach of etiquette in antiquity, but to do so in this case would in addition suggest that Paul and Luke and Silas and Timothy thought Lydia's conversion and faithfulness were less than genuine. Thus Luke concludes by saying, "and she prevailed upon us." Here as elsewhere "Luke connects spiritual dispositions to the disposition of possessions."[103] Lydia's generosity of spirit suggested the genuineness of her faith.

V. 16 indicates that Paul and his coworkers stayed in Philippi for a considerable period of time; presumably a week at least had passed and the group was going to the place of prayer again (on the sabbath) when they met a slave girl.[104] This girl is said to have a πνευμα πυθονα, a Python spirit, by which is meant that, like the oracle at Delphi, she was inspired by Apollo, the Pythian deity. It was believed that Apollo was embodied at Delphi in a

---

100. See the discussion, pp. 441ff. above.

101. On the phrase cf. 2 Macc. 1:4 to Luke 24:45.

102. On household baptisms see pp. 339ff. above. They may or may not have included the baptism of infants. Household inclusion in the church may not always have involved the faith commitment of every household member. In the Greco-Roman world the head of the household usually determined the household's religion, and servants may have followed suit out of loyalty to their master.

103. Rightly Johnson, *Acts*, p. 297.

104. Here as in 12:13 παιδισκη means more than just a young girl; it means a slave girl.

snake, the Python. It seems that Luke sees this as a case of possession by an evil spirit, which requires exorcism, especially in view of the behavior of the girl both before and then after Paul confronts her, which is quite similar to what we find in Luke 4:33-35 and especially Luke 8:28-35. Here, as in the story of Simon Magus in Acts 8 and in Acts 19:11-41, Luke sees a close connection between magic, pagan or false religion, and the profit motive of humans. We are told that the prophecies of the girl had brought her owners a considerable amount of money.[105] The girl had been in essence a fortune-teller, offering prophetic answers to questions individuals asked about their future.[106] Plutarch, who had been a priest at Delphi, speaks of such soothsayers as ventriloquists who uttered words beyond their own control (*De defectu oraculorum* 9.414E). There was considerable suspicion even by many pagans about charlatanism, especially with a profit motive (cf. the satire by Lucian, *Alexander the False Prophet*, and Apuleius, *The Golden Ass* 8.26-30), though this does not mean that they considered all "prophets" as false prophets.

V. 17 records one of her utterances — she followed Paul and Silas crying out, "These men are slaves of the Most High God, who proclaim to you a way of salvation." This utterance, especially in view of Luke 8:28, has often been taken to be a true utterance by a demonic spirit. This conclusion has been argued by P. R. Trebilco to be very questionable, or at least in need of some nuancing, in view of the setting of this story. The Jewish influence on this city is not seen to be great, and the pagan use of υψιστος Θεος of various pagan deities is documented (see *SIG* no. 1181).[107] "In Philippi the term 'Highest God' must have been misleading. In view of the pagan usage of Hypsistos, the term would not have suggested the referent was the Jewish God, unless that person was a Jew or Judaizer. There were many 'highest gods' and a pagan hearer would understand the referent of the term to be that deity he or she considered to be supreme. Hearers would not think of Yahweh. Thus the primary effect of the term on pagans must have been to

---

105. Johnson, *Acts*, p. 294, assumes that the use of μαντευομενη indicates that the girl was engaging in "ecstatic" prophecy. This is far from certain, if by this one means she was uttering unintelligible sounds. In a detailed study, the classics scholar Fontenrose, *The Delphic Oracle*, p. 10, has argued at length that a "close study of all reliable evidence for Delphic mantic procedures reveals no chasm of vapors, no frenzy of the Pythia, no incoherent cries interpreted by priests. The Pythia spoke clearly, coherently, and directly to the consultant in response to his question." One must be able to distinguish between an ecstatic process and the coherent product that resulted from it.

106. Notice that nothing is said about her requiring an interpreter. Her utterances were intelligible.

107. In fact, as Bruce, *The Acts of the Apostles*, p. 361, says, "Among Gentiles σωτηρια was the object of many vows and prayers to Θεος υψιστος and other divinities."

mislead them."[108] Furthermore, the text does not clearly say that the Pytho-ness was suggesting that Paul and Silas were proclaiming *the* way of salva-tion.[109] Her utterance should be seen in its proper polytheistic and pluralistic context. *V. 18* indicates that this behavior continued for many days, and no doubt Paul found it annoying, but the verb διαπονηθεις surely means being deeply troubled. In other words, Paul is not merely annoyed. The story is not about a true proclamation come from a dubious source, which is how most commentators have understood this scene.[110]

Paul is disturbed because the message being proclaimed was at the very least misleading. He was troubled about the content of her proclamation. The very word "salvation" without further explanation would often connote health or healing or rescue to a pagan, just as the phrase "Most High God" would not suggest monotheism to a pagan, but rather would suggest the deity one saw as being at the top of the pantheon of all gods. Thus *v. 18b* indicates that Paul turned and spoke to the spirit (τω πνευματι), which was actually speaking through the girl, and ordered it to come out of the girl in the name of Jesus.[111]

In a neat wordplay or pun Luke says in *v. 18c* that the spirit "left her" (εξηλθεν) that same hour, and at the same time her "lords'" or owners' hope of making money left them (εξηλθεν, *v. 19*). The mention of lords (plural) suggests that this was some sort of ongoing business partnership, now without a source of revenue. "Luke connects spiritual dispositions to the disposition of possessions."[112] Naturally enough they were incensed and so dragged Silas and Paul into the agora before the local magistrates, wanting if not compen-sation then revenge through the courts.[113] The second-century agora has been

---

108. Trebilco, "Paul and Silas," p. 60. One must be cautious at this point, however, because as Levinskaya, *Acts in Its Diaspora Setting*, chap. 5, points out, the use of the "most high God" terminology is abundant in Jewish sources and inscriptions, and quite rare in pagan ones. Nevertheless, the lack of a significant Jewish presence in Philippi perhaps tips the scales in favor of a pagan use of the term here.

109. The absence of the definite article from the noun and the dependent genitive (οδον σωτηριας) means that the context must determine whether to translate "a way" or "the way."

110. See Pesch, *Die Apostelgeschichte (Apg. 13–28)*, p. 113.

111. The difference between this exorcism and those in Luke 4 or 8 by Christ is the use of "the name of Jesus," by which is meant by the authority and power of Jesus. This indicates the lesser status of a Paul, or a Peter (cf. Acts 3:6; 9:34). Jesus is the source of the power and authority for such actions. Bruce, *The Acts of the Apostles*, p. 360, rightly notes that toward the end of the various "we" passages, Paul is distinguished from "us," while he had been identified as one of "us" in the body of the passage (cf. 16:17; 21:18; 28:16).

112. Johnson, *Acts*, p. 297.

113. It will be noted that Paul and Silas, not Timothy and Luke, are the subjects of the attack. This is presumably because these two were the proclaimers, exorcists, and leaders of the group. There may also be the additional factor that these two were Jews, while Timothy and Luke could at least pass for Gentiles.

uncovered, and on its northwest side there was a raised podium or *bema* (judgment seat) with stairs on two sides, before which civil cases would be tried, with the city prison apparently immediately adjacent thereto and perhaps even beneath this locale.[114] The owners of this slave girl should probably be seen as persons of considerable social status in the community, for it was normally only people of considerable financial wherewithal who would take the risk of going to court with expectation of winning.[115]

The magistrates are called ἄρχοντες in v. 19, a more general Greek term for the chief rulers or authorities in a city, while in *v. 20* they are called στρατηγοῖς, the Greek equivalent of *praetores*. Because there were two of these, they were called *duoviri* (see Cicero, *De leg. agr.* 2.93).[116] As was often the case, the complaint offered to the officials was couched in polemical forensic rhetoric and masked the real cause of the action. Paul and Silas are described as rabble-rousers, Jews, and advocates of customs unlawful for "us Romans" to adopt or observe. In other words, the speakers have established their own ethos (Roman citizens), and have attempted to destroy the ethos or character of Paul and Silas by making an emotional appeal to the basic fear of foreigners, and suspicion about Jews and their customs. The appeal appears to have been as much an astute playing to the prejudices of the crowd of observers as an appeal to the feelings of the officials, for we are told in *v. 22* that the crowds joined in attacking Paul and Silas, and the officials, presumably operating on the where-there-is-smoke-there-is-fire theory, and sensing trouble, perhaps in the form of a riot, if they did not act very quickly, immediately had the two missionaries stripped[117] and beaten with rods. This was the task of the *lictores*,[118] those who carried the bundle of rods which was not merely the symbol of Roman justice and authority but also the means

114. See McDonald, "Archaeology and St. Paul's Journeys," pp. 20-21. It appears probable (see Polhill, *Acts*, p. 352) that the second-century structures were built on the same site as the first-century ones.

115. See the discussion in Garnsey, *Social Status and Legal Privilege*, p. 279: "The principal criterion of legal privilege in the eyes of the Romans was *dignitas* or *honor derived from power, style of life, and wealth.*" The Roman judicial system was subject to a variety of improper influences which made equality under the law virtually unattainable in practice (see Garnsey, p. 207).

116. For the Latin titles of Philippian officials cf. *CIL* 3.633, 3.654, 7339, and especially 3.650 on *duoviri*. Here and elsewhere Luke shows an accurate knowledge of the appropriate terms for officials in this part of the Roman Empire, both in colony cities and elsewhere (cf. pp. 503ff. below on Thessalonica). See Hemer, *Book of Acts*, p. 115.

117. The Greek would allow the interpretation that the officials had rent their garments, but since stripping was the normal preliminary to beating in a Roman setting, this is probably what is in view here.

118. Luke uses the term ῥαβδίζειν in v. 22. Acts 16:15 should be compared for the noun form of the word, which refers to the wooden rods or *fasces* used for the beating.

used to inflict "lighter" punishments or inducements to confession (cf. Acts 16:15).

V. 23 says they were given a severe flogging and then thrown into prison, with strict orders to the jailor to keep them securely.[119] The jailor followed orders and placed them in the innermost cell in his jail and for good measure fastened their feet into stocks (cf. Acts 12:4; Herodotus, *Persian Wars* 9.37), which could be very painful. Nothing in vv. 19-24 strongly suggests that Paul and Silas had been given opportunity to defend themselves before the magistrates. The magistrates had simply taken the word of their fellow Romans and acted accordingly and summarily. They did not know Paul and Silas were Roman citizens, and so they treated them like *peregrinoi*, mere foreigners without local rights or privileges, and Jewish ones at that. "In a Roman colony it appears that arrest, beating, and imprisonment were normal for aliens, but that it was potentially dangerous to give citizens the same treatment."[120] It remains to be seen whether we may see Paul's failure to announce his Roman citizenship at this point as simply involving the absence of opportunity or a missionary strategy (see below).

Whatever the exigencies of their confinement, Paul and Silas did not allow them to dictate how they would respond to the circumstances. *V. 25* indicates that Paul and Silas were singing and praying, even as late as midnight, and the other inmates were listening. *V. 26* indicates that suddenly there was a rather violent earthquake, strong enough to shake the foundations of the jail, open doors, and shake loose the wall brackets of the chains, but not strong enough to bring the roof of the jail down on their heads. There is evidence of earthquakes shaking this region; indeed, it was not uncommon throughout Greece and Macedonia.[121] According to *v. 27*, when the jailor woke up and saw the prison doors open, he assumed the worst and drew his sword, preparing to commit suicide. This was not a surprising reaction, because the jailor was considered responsible for the safekeeping of his inmates, and rather than suffer the public shame and humiliation of being publicly beaten (much less being executed) for dereliction of duty he chose what he saw as an honorable way out.[122] This story, though often compared to the stories in Acts 5:18-19

---

119. This appears not to be an example of *coercitio*, which was a flogging which preceded a trial, as a means of extracting the truth. It is much more likely, as Keener, *Bible Background Commentary*, p. 369, suggests, that we have an example of a public beating meant to humiliate those involved and perhaps also to discourage their followers.

120. Garnsey, *Social Status and Legal Privilege*, p. 268.

121. And these earthquakes were often seen as the work of a god or even the sign of a visitation of a god to an area. Cf. Ovid, *Metamorph.* 9.782-83; 15.669-78; and Lucian, *Lover of Lies* 22.

122. See Code of Justinian 9.4.4 — a guard who allows a prisoner to escape is liable to the punishment the prisoner would have received. See the discussion in Johnson, *Acts,*

and 12:1-11, is different from both in two essential respects: in this story there are no angel deliverers and no escape by the Christian inmates.

V. 28 says Paul shouted to the jailor not to harm himself. Whether this was some sort of prophetic insight on Paul's part or whether he was close enough and there was light enough to be able to see the jailor, Luke does not tell us. Paul speaks for all in saying "we are all here."[123] The jailor, apparently seeing this as nothing less than a miracle, or at least a divine sign, called for lights and ran in and fell down at Paul and Silas's feet trembling. Gathering himself, he then took these two prisoners outside, perhaps assuming the earthquake had been an indicator the Divine was not pleased with the incarceration of these two men.[124] He asks them, "Sirs, what must I do to be rescued/saved?" It is very possible that he meant no more than rescued from the coming and apparent judgment signaled by the earthquake. There is no indication that he had heard Paul's or Silas's earlier preaching.

Whatever he may have meant, Paul and Silas saw this as an opportunity to share the word of the Lord. According to v. 31 they offered the basic message: "Believe in the Lord Jesus, and you will be saved, you and your household." V. 32 suggests that the jailor's house must have been adjacent to the jail itself because it says they spoke God's word not only to the jailor but also to those in his house. Out of gratitude the jailor immediately took the two evangelists and washed their wounds, and in turn was washed by them, the jailor and his whole family being baptized on the spot. V. 34 indicates that the jailor also brought the two into his own house and set food before them.[125] It was a

---

p. 303, who points out that the jailor now sees Paul and Silas as his benefactors, who deliver him from shame by not escaping or encouraging others to do so. He is also right to note that Paul then has an honor/shame showdown with the officials who placed them in jail, and the officials come away shamed, a not-so-subtle message to Roman authorities that it was not wise to oppose the gospel or its messengers.

123. Luke also does not bother to explain why the other prisoners had not tried to escape, but perhaps this had all transpired within the first few minutes after the earthquake. But Ramsay, St. Paul the Traveller, p. 221, suggests the time span was short and the earthquake had badly frightened the pagan inmates.

124. Seeing an earthquake as divine displeasure or judgment was not uncommon in antiquity.

125. De Vos, "Significance," suggests that οιχος in vv. 31, 34 refers to the jailor's family unit/household in the narrower sense, but that οιχια in v. 32 refers to the wider *familia* of the jailor, which would include the public slaves under his charge, including the other guards. The upshot of this distinction is that "salvation is promised to a different group of people from that which hears the preaching and is baptised"; the *familia* hears the preaching, but the promise of salvation is given to the jailor for the family unit without their yet hearing the message. This would suggest that the Greco-Roman practice of household inclusion in the religion of the head of the household is being alluded to. This is a possible conclusion, but elsewhere certainly Luke stresses that faith, not just family association, is necessary for salvation.

joyous feast, the whole household celebrating the jailor becoming a believer in the true God.

All of the previous events apparently transpired in, or in the vicinity of, the jail, because according to *v. 35* when the morning came the magistrates sent the lictors, or police (ραβδουχοι), to the jail to tell the jailor to let Paul and Silas go. Apparently they thought the crimes of these two were not so serious that they required more than the punishment they had already received for being a public nuisance.[126] The jailor conveyed the message that they could go in peace, but at this juncture, and not before, Paul replied that he would not accept a secret discharge because he and Silas were beaten, unconvicted, uncondemned *Roman citizens*.[127] In fact he insisted that the authorities come and publicly escort them out of the jail. It was a very serious matter when a local magistrate in a Roman colony took action against a Roman citizen, especially when he did so without proper cause or reason. The magistrates could lose their posts or be recalled and disgraced for such actions. Thus *v. 38* is understandable — the magistrates were frightened by Paul's report that he and Silas were Roman citizens. According to Julian law binding or beating a Roman citizen without trial was forbidden (see Cicero, *Pro Rabirio* 12).[128]

Thus *v. 39* indicates that the magistrates came and apologized to the men, but then asked them to leave the city, hoping to avoid a trial where their mistake would come to light. Instead of leaving immediately, *v. 40* indicates Paul and Silas went to Lydia's house, saw and encouraged the brothers and sisters who met there, and only then departed the city. "Lydia's significance was not confined to her being a disciple or hostess to traveling disciples. Luke wishes us to understand that what began as a lodging for missionaries, became home of the embryonic church in Philippi."[129] This narrative is an important one for Luke because it shows the mission's encounter with the Roman world.

Luke is not one-sidedly interested in Jewish resistance or hostility to Christianity; here we see the clash between pagan religion and customs and the Christian faith, and we will see it again even more vividly in Acts 19:23-40. Luke seeks to show that the Roman authorities do not necessarily oppose or at least ought not to oppose the Christian faith, but "both Jews and Gentiles

---

126. The Western text, through various changes in vv. 35-40, suggests that the officials made a connection between the earthquake and these men, and so released them. See Metzger, *Textual Commentary*, pp. 450-51. See the discussion in Tannehill, *Narrative Unity of Luke-Acts*, 2:199.

127. The penalty for falsely claiming Roman citizenship was severe, and could even involve execution by means of the ax. See Suetonius, *Claudius* 25.3.

128. Cicero, however, also is well aware that sometimes a magistrate simply ignored a claim of Roman citizenship; see *Verr.* 2.5.161f. See the discussion in Sherwin-White, *Roman Law and Roman Society*, pp. 72-76.

129. Witherington, *Women in the Earliest Churches*, p. 149.

view the mission as a threat to the customs that provide social cohesion, to the religious basis of their cultures and to political stability through Caesar's rule."[130] They were right to do so — Paul and his coworkers are those who turn the religious world upside down, offering one God and savior instead of many (and also instead of the emperor), one way of salvation instead of many, one people of God that is not ethnically defined.

The above experiences are referred to in two places in the Pauline corpus. First Thessalonians 2:2, part of the next letter Paul wrote, probably in this same year from Corinth,[131] speaks of the suffering and the shameful mistreatment he received in Philippi, which apparently he had reported to the Thessalonian Christians when he was first there. In addition, 2 Cor. 11:25 speaks of three times when Paul was beaten by the Roman rods, and surely this would be one of those occasions. We thus have independent confirmation for the truth of several aspects of this story. In addition, for the exorcism or miracle performed one may point to Rom. 15:18-19 and 2 Cor. 12:12 as indications that Paul did such things. Thus most scholars are inclined to view these stories as having some real historical substance.[132] What they find doubtful is the idea that if Paul was a Roman citizen he would undergo such indignities without indicating his status instantly. Indeed, many take Paul's long litanies of sufferings all over the Roman world as a clear indication he was not a Roman citizen (cf. 1 Cor. 4:9-13; 2 Cor. 11:24-29). Can these difficulties be explained as being consistent with Paul's being a Roman citizen?[133]

In regard to the story in Acts 16, it is possible to argue that Paul simply had no opportunity in the frenzy of the mob shouting and the hasty reaction of the magistrates to present his claims. This, however, would not explain the other incidents where Paul's citizenship comes into play in Acts, and at the least this story in Acts 16 would have raised questions in the mind of Luke's audience.[134]

It may first be said that there is historical evidence from before the middle of the first century A.D. of Jews being Roman citizens.[135] Paul's behavior could be construed as unusual here only if he had opportunity to present his citizenship claims, but it is not at all clear he had such an opportunity. Even if, however, he did have such an opportunity, some consideration

---

130. Tannehill, *Narrative Unity of Luke-Acts*, 2:203.

131. See the chart on Pauline chronology, pp. 82ff. above.

132. See the discussion of Lüdemann, *Early Christianity*, pp. 183-84.

133. Lentz, *Luke's Portrait of Paul*, pp. 131-33, e.g., thinks that Paul's Roman citizenship is a Lukan creation. Stegmann, "War der Apostel Paulus ein römanischer Bürger?" also sees as unhistorical the suggestion of Paul's Roman citizenship.

134. See Cassidy, *Society and Politics*, pp. 100-101 and 150.

135. Cf. *New Docs*, 4, no. 111; Schürer, *History of the Jewish People*, vol. 3.1, pp. 133, 161; and Rapske, *Paul in Roman Custody*, pp. 89-90.

must be given to Rapske's suggestions that Paul experienced considerable status inconsistency, and that sometimes his commitments to the gospel or his fellow Jews took precedent over any claiming of his citizenship rights.[136]

Presumably Paul would not have wanted the reception of the claims of the gospel to rest on his claims to Roman citizenship. Furthermore, Paul did not recognize the emperor and his decrees as the ultimate authority over his life; rather, Christ the Lord was. Also, his prior commitments to Judaism would likely have led to a certain detached approach to his Roman status already. That Paul took this sort of attitude of detachment about his Jewishness is suggested in 1 Cor. 9:20, and there is good reason to think he would have taken a similar approach to his Roman citizenship. He believed the form and institutions of this world were not of ultimate value because they were passing away (1 Cor. 7:29-31), and therefore they should be used or taken advantage of insofar as they furthered the cause of Christ. Paul also believed there was an eternal commonwealth or *politeuma* which Christians were already a part of, a point he makes with some force when he later writes to the Christians in Philippi (Phil. 3:20). When all this is put together, it suggests that Paul could well have chosen to use his Roman citizenship in an opportunistic way when it furthered his Christian purposes and not merely when it was personally advantageous. Paul's sense of identity came first from his Christian faith, secondly from his Jewish heritage, and only thirdly from his Greco-Roman heritage.

How would one be able to demonstrate that he or she was a Roman citizen? Though Acts does not mention it, it is possible that Paul carried a *testatio,* a certified private copy of evidence of his birth and citizenship inscribed on the waxed surface of a wooden diptych, in a stereotypical five-part form — part of which in abbreviated form read "c(iuem) r(omanam/um) e(xscripsit)."[137] This would provide evidence when presented to authorities, though not conclusive proof since such documents could be forged, and officials were in general wary of this in an age when more and more people were being granted Roman citizenship and more and more wanted it.[138]

Thus Rapske's conclusion is believable as an explanation of why Paul reacted as he did in Philippi and elsewhere:

> the self-defense of an early citizenship claim would probably have been construed by the magistrates and populace as an assertion of commitment to the primacy of Roman, over against Jewish (i.e. Christian), customs. The

---

136. See the discussion in Rapske, *Paul in Roman Custody,* pp. 129-34.

137. See the discussion in Sanders, "Birth Certificate," and cf. Schulz, "Roman Registers," parts 1 and 2.

138. See the discussion in Rapske, *Paul in Roman Custody,* pp. 131-32, and Cadbury, *Book of Acts in History,* p. 71.

signals sent would also have put the church at risk of dissolution if the new Philippian converts did not possess the Roman franchise. At the least there would have been uncertainty surrounding Paul's commitment to his message. Converts might wonder whether only those suitably protected (i.e. by Roman citizenship) should become believers in Christ and they might think it disingenuous for Paul and Silas to ask others to suffer what they themselves were able to avoid.[139]

No, Paul would much rather suffer than cause trouble for his converts, and by the same token he did not want to present false inducements for conversion, namely, having an opportunity to follow a teacher of high social status — a Roman citizen who in addition was well trained in rhetoric, among other things. He wanted to present no offense or inducement to anyone other than the inherent appeal or "offensiveness" of the good news of salvation through the crucified Christ available to all races, classes, and genders of humankind.

The material in Acts 17:1-15 is noticeably less circumstantial than the previous material on Philippi, and here we see the return of the familiar theme of preaching in the synagogue followed by acceptance by some Jews and rejection by many.[140] Success with Gentiles leads to jealousy among the rejecting Jews, which in turn leads to persecution of Paul and his coworkers and finally precipitates their moving on to another city.[141] The evidence on the whole suggests that the missionaries moved on when circumstances dictated that they do so. Tannehill is right, however, to point out that the differences in the response in Beroea as opposed to Thessalonica show that "the author has not completely stereotyped Diaspora Jews. Despite repeated emphasis on Jewish opposition, the narrator here inserts a contrasting picture, preserving a sense of local variety of response."[142]

There is in fact an effort to maintain some balance in the description of the second missionary journey. Paul is said to be twice accused by Jews (17:5-7; 18:12-13) and twice by Gentiles (16:19-21; 19:24-27) in the presentation of four scenes in which Paul is accused of something. On two occasions the charges against him are at least partially believed by the adjudicating authori-

---

139. Rapske, *Paul in Roman Custody*, p. 134.

140. Pesch, *Die Apostelgeschichte (Apg. 13–28)*, p. 120, suggests Luke only had an itinerary and brief anecdotal notes about this part of Paul's journey. This is possible, but the notes would have had to have been substantial enough to catch the nuances of the situation in Thessalonica, and the differences between the responses of the Jews in that city and in Beroea.

141. There is a pattern of Jewish pursuit of Paul to the next city that we saw in the first journey in the case of Iconium and Lystra and here in the case of Thessalonica and Beroea.

142. Tannehill, *Narrative Unity of Luke-Acts*, 2:207.

ties (16:22-24; 17:8-9), but on two other occasions the charges are dismissed as insubstantial (18:14-17; 19:35-40).[143] Though these narratives are brief, as we shall see they are in fact full of social and rhetorical signals and presuppose an audience that would be adept at reading such signals.

17:1 narrates a considerable journey along the main Roman road, the Via Egnatia, which eventually turned west and went across Macedonia. The journey from Philippi to Thessalonica was some one hundred miles, and we are told that Paul and his coworkers passed through Amphipolis and Apollonia on the way. That no other locations are mentioned may suggest they were traveling by mule or horse, if, that is, they made Amphipolis after a day's journey, Apollonia after another day, and Thessalonica after three days of travel. The reading in Codex Bezae (D) implies that the party stopped at Apollonia, which is likely in any case on such a long journey. When they arrived in Thessalonica, we are told the group went to the synagogue, which means Paul had not changed his basic mode of operating.

Thessalonica was an important city in many respects. It was capital of the Roman province of Macedonia. For its support of Octavian it had become a free city in 42 B.C. and was not turned into a Roman colony. It minted its own coins (both imperial and autonomous), had its own form of government (with politarchs, see below), but nevertheless had close ties with Rome, and there is evidence of the imperial cult existing in this city.[144] One may point especially to the coins with the head of Julius Caesar, minted even before the time of Christ, which involved the recognition of Julius as a god, and the fact that Augustus replaces Zeus on the coins of the city.[145] These coins reflect the ongoing benefactions that Rome bestowed on Thessalonica, which the city had apparently come to depend upon, and the growing imperial theology and eschatology that was part of the rhetoric of response in such a city.[146] The essence of this theology was that the emperor was the universal savior whose benefactions and aid should be proclaimed as good news throughout the region.[147]

143. Here I follow ibid., p. 209.

144. A statue of Augustus was found in the western part of the city, among other pieces of evidence that suggest the existence of the cult. See Gill, "Macedonia," p. 415.

145. See the discussion by Donfried, "The Cults of Thessalonica," p. 346.

146. On imperial eschatology in Corinth see my *Conflict and Community in Corinth,* pp. 295-98.

147. As numerous inscriptions make clear. See the discussion in Fears, "Rome," p. 103. Cf., e.g., the famous *Res Gestae* of Augustus indicating the benefactions of the emperor to the Roman people, including the subjugating of the whole world. Sherk, *The Roman Empire,* pp. 41-52. In the provinces the language of subjection changes to the good news of liberation and the bringing of civilization and order. For Claudius as a benefactor of religious cults in the East, see Sherk, pp. 96-97, mentioning a benefaction to the Dionysiac performers in Miletus.

Though officially free, Thessalonica was yet another city caught in the emperor's social network involving patronage and the response of homage and loyalty. Local officials would be expected to enforce loyalty to Caesar in order to maintain the peace and help the city stay in the good graces of the emperor. Here we have another story indicating Luke's understanding in detail of both the de facto and de jure situation of the municipal institutions and officials governing in this area.[148]

V. 2 indicates that Paul followed his regular custom (εἰωθός) by going to the synagogue. There is inscriptional evidence for a synagogue in Thessalonica, but the evidence dates to at least the late second century A.D. (CIJ 693). We are not told that he went immediately to the synagogue. In fact it appears likely that Paul and his coworkers would first have had to establish themselves by finding a place to stay and providing a means of support. This support came at least in part in Thessalonica from Paul's and apparently Silas's practicing of the trade of tentmaker/leatherworker (see 1 Thess. 2:9). Setting up shop in the agora, or perhaps working out of the home of a fellow Jew who practiced the same trade (Jason? see 17:6), these Christians were able to avoid the entanglements of a patron-client relationship and the burdening of those who were new converts. Through this business enterprise there would have been ongoing contact with numerous Gentiles in the city.[149] Support also came to Paul while in Thessalonica from the Philippians (Phil. 4:16).[150] All the above suggests a stay of some weeks, probably more than a month, in Thessalonica. We are told in v. 2 that Paul was in the synagogue for three sabbath days, presumably in succession, but we are not told that these were the only sabbaths Paul was present in town.

The language we find in vv. 2-4 describing what happened when Paul visited the synagogue is thoroughly rhetorical. We are told, for instance, in v. 2 that Paul διελέξατο with those in the synagogue using the Hebrew Scriptures.[151] This word does not mean preach but refers rather to the presenting of arguments using Scripture as a basis or the engaging in dialogue and debate over the meaning of scriptural texts.[152] V. 3 reveals what Paul sought to prove

---

148. See Cadbury, Book of Acts in History, p. 41.

149. See the discussion in Haenchen, Acts, pp. 509-12. He suggests that perhaps Jason had first housed Paul and Silas and then through the contact in his home was converted. This housing may have been provided because of a shared trade, and presumably a shared Jewish faith.

150. The meaning of this verse is debated. See my Friendship and Finances in Philippi, p. 128. If the καί is a true connective, then the meaning would be that aid reached Paul and his coworkers once while in Thessalonica, and more than once elsewhere (perhaps Corinth?). See P. T. O'Brien, Philippians (Waco: Word, 1991), p. 563, and Morris, "Kai hapax kai Dis."

151. Presumably texts like Psalms 2; 110; and Isaiah 53 would be discussed.

152. See the full-length discussion of these verses by Kemmler, Faith and Human Reason, pp. 35ff.

by his arguments. The form of the argument is that of the *enthymeme,* the rhetorical form of a syllogism, usually in three parts, but sometimes as here two parts are mentioned with the third implied.[153] Luke intends to show that Paul did not just appeal to the emotions but presented reasonable arguments for his claims about Christ.[154] The argument is as follows: (1) the Messiah must suffer and rise again as the proper interpretation of the Scriptures prove, (2) Jesus died on the cross and rose again (as Paul and various eyewitnesses would attest), (3) therefore, this Jesus Paul is proclaiming must be the Messiah.[155] The middle member of the proof is omitted here, but the reader is supposed to fill out this summary of Paul's message and method by remembering what he (and Peter) had been said to preach or teach earlier in Acts.

Paul, then, is said to be engaging in an act of persuasion or rhetoric in the synagogue. The verbs διανοιγων and παρατιθεμενος in *v. 3* indicate the process of opening the mind and understanding of the hearers[156] followed by the putting forward of proper proofs in good rhetorical form (see Lucian, *Professor of Public Speaking* 9; Dio Chrysostom, *Or.* 17.10).[157] Taken together these two verbs explain what was meant or entailed by "argue" or "dialogue" referred to in the previous verse. The argument about the death and resurrection of the Christ is one from necessity (εδει), by which is meant divine necessity, the event being planned by God and foreshadowed in Scripture. Paul did not resort to sophistic rhetoric but rhetoric of a more sophisticated and substantial sort, involving proofs and not mere flattery or emotional appeal.

It is then not surprising that we are told in *v. 4* that some in the audience were persuaded (επεισθησαν), which is the hoped-for outcome of any good rhetorical discourse. As Kurz puts it, the "proof is clearly aimed at persuasion and conversion: in rhetorical terms it is protreptic."[158] The art of persuasion

---

153. This rhetorical form of arguing goes back to at least Aristotle, *Rhetoric* 1.1.3-6 (1356A-1358A). Aristotle understood the *enthymeme* as a rhetorical application of a logical syllogism.

154. On Paul's use of such rhetorical forms of syllogism see 1 Cor. 15:12-28 and my discussion in *Conflict and Community in Corinth,* pp. 301-4.

155. See the discussion by Kurz, "Hellenistic Rhetoric."

156. See Kemmler, *Faith and Human Reason,* pp. 38-39.

157. First Thessalonians 2:3-5 should not be taken to mean that Paul avoided using rhetoric. As it says there, Paul made an appeal, but it was grounded in solid evidence, and its motive was not to impress or flatter or use verbal trickery on the audience or to take advantage of them for the sake of financial gain, which was often the case with visiting rhetors. Rather, the motive was to please God and to help the Thessalonians by sharing the good news about how they might be saved.

158. Kurz, "Hellenistic Rhetoric," p. 180. Such rhetoric usually took the form either of forensic rhetoric or deliberative rhetoric, or some mixture of both, as seems likely here. On the one hand, Paul is trying to defend the heart of the gospel by putting forth proofs

had worked not least because Paul had based his (inartificial) proof on a source that both he and the audience recognized as authoritative — the Scriptures — but also because he appealed to them as people of intelligence who could discern the truth if the case was laid before them in good logical fashion.[159]

Those persuaded and joining with Paul and Silas were not only some Jews but also a "great many" (πληθος πολυ) devout Greeks, which surely refers to synagogue adherents, as well as γυναικων τε των πρωτων, which likely means prominent women (see 17:12).[160] There is a decidedly antifeminist tendency in the Western text which is especially noticeable in Acts 17–18, where prominent women are turned into mere wives of prominent men and Priscilla's role of teaching Apollos is omitted.[161] We had already noticed this tendency in Acts 1:14. The producers of the Western text, among their other agendas, were seeking to cover up evidence of women playing important roles in the early church, an agenda which clashes rather sharply with Luke's own attempt to highlight the roles women played throughout Luke-Acts.[162]

According to *v. 5* the unpersuaded Jews were jealous of the success that Paul had had, apparently especially with the Gentiles, and so they stirred up the "agora men." These were the frequenters of the agora or marketplace, and may have been unemployed day laborers (cf. Plato, *Protagoras* 347C; Xeno-

---

from Scripture that the Christ must suffer (on which subject see now Moessner, "The Script of the Scriptures"); on the other hand, he is arguing to convince the audience to change their behavior (as 1 Thess. 1:9 puts it, to turn to God from idols), to see what will be beneficial for them in the future.

159. One of the significances of this sort of presentation of Paul's approach is that it suggests that it was believed that the gospel could be substantiated and be shown to be reasonable to both Jews and Gentiles (cf. below on Acts 17:1ff.); at the same time it was assumed that the gospel should be responded to freely on the basis of the appeal to the mind in addition to the pull of the *pathos* inherent in the message. Proclaiming the gospel was not to be seen as an attempt to dupe an unsuspecting public and suck them in by mere eloquence without rational substance. See Kemmler, *Faith and Human Reason,* pp. 72-75.

160. It is possible that it means wives of leading men, and the Western text makes this translation a certainty by omitting the τε and adding και. See Metzger, *Textual Commentary,* p. 453. The D text in fact creates four categories at 17:4, inserting a και between devout and Greeks, thus indicating there were some pagans (Greeks), in addition to God-fearers who were converted along with the Jews and prominent women (or wives of prominent men). It is probably of some relevance to point out that the rhetorically adept orators and writers of the age had been instructed to try to avoid mentioning the names of living, honorable, socially prominent women, unless there was some particular need to do so. Women who were connected to one's opponents, or dead women, or women of shady reputation were much more likely to be mentioned by name. See Schaps, "The Women Least Mentioned." *New Docs,* 1 (1981), no. 25, p. 72, suggests some evidence that "first of women" is an honorific title.

161. See the variants at 17:12 and 18:26 and my discussion in "Anti-Feminist Tendencies."

162. See my discussion in *Women in the Earliest Churches,* pp. 128-52.

phon, *Hellenica* 6.2.23). There is an overtone in the word αγοραιων suggesting it means something like malcontents, agitators (see Plutarch, *Aemilius Paullus* 38), which is not surprising if we are talking about people who have been marginalized by the highly stratified society of the ancient world and reduced to catch-as-catch-can work when someone needed temporary help. The word also had the sense of loafer or ne'er-do-well or even lowlife (cf. Aristophanes, *Ranae* 1015; Theophrastus, *Char.* 4.2; Herodotus, *Persian Wars* 2.141).

Luke's social worldview is reflected in these last two verses. He is concerned to show that Christianity was seen as appealing by various people of some social status, and on the other hand was opposed by those generally recognized to be malcontents or rabble. It is easy to see how Theophilus, probably a person of considerable status, would likely react to this sort of portrayal.

An uproar was created by the combination of the angry Jews and the "agora men." We are told that they searched for Paul and Silas to bring them before the δημον. The city assembly of its citizens had juridical functions in a free city and it would have been competent to deal with charges brought against Paul and Silas, but the offending party needed to be produced, which the mob and the Jews for some reason could not do. They thus resorted to attacking Jason's house, presumably under the assumption they were staying there, and dragged Jason and some believers before the city authorities. While action could not be taken directly against Paul and Silas, it could be taken indirectly by laying a legal restriction upon Jason.

The authorities mentioned in *v.* 6 are quite properly called politarchs, a designation appropriate to this city and region, as is attested by inscriptions.[163] There were five of these officials, and their rulings were valid as long as they were in office. There are basically two accusations made: (1) Paul and his coworkers are itinerant troublemakers who were upsetting things here and elsewhere in the Empire;[164] (2) they have acted contrary to the decrees (δογ-ματων) of the emperor by saying there was another King, named Jesus. The latter was the more serious charge.

163. See Horsley, "Politarchs," especially the chart on p. 387. For first century A.D. politarchs in this region see *IG* 10/2 1.848. On the unlikely possibility that the Aristarchus mentioned in Acts 19:9 and 20:4 was the politarch of the same name, see Horsley, "The Politarchs," but contrast Winter, *Seek the Welfare,* pp. 46-47. When would Paul have had opportunity to convert one of the politarchs, especially once banished from the city?

164. The word αναστατωσαντες refers to those upsetting the *stasis* or stable conditions of the city (see the usage in Gal. 5:12). The translation of Johnson, *Acts,* p. 307 — "subverting the Empire" — is probably on target in view of the second charge. Claudius had written a stern letter in A.D. 41 to the Jews of Alexandria about Jews who were "fomenters of what is a general plague infecting the whole world" (P. Lond. 1912). One may suspect that officials were on the lookout for such people, especially in the wake of the expulsion of Jews from Rome in A.D. 49 (see below on Acts 18).

Could there have been any plausibility to such charges? Consider the following: (1) Paul comes to Thessalonica urging Gentiles to turn from idols, presumably including statues of emperors past or present, to the one true God (1 Thess. 1:9) and urging Jews to recognize that Jesus was God's anointed one. (2) He also preaches about the parousia (1 Thess. 4:15) of the Lord Jesus, also said to be God's Son (1:10). (3) Jesus is said to be the one who brings the Thessalonians into God's own kingdom and glory (2:12). (4) While the emperor had offered the world "peace and security," Paul had attacked such an idea as an illusion since Christ would coming bringing God's judgment on unprepared human beings (1 Thess. 5:3). The politically charged language in 1 Thessalonians is evident and becomes even more apparent in 2 Thess. 1:5–2:12, where the discussion is again couched in the language of the coming King and the coming kingdom.[165]

At this juncture in the middle of the first century A.D. it is right to point out that the crime of treason (*maiestas*) was a matter of public law, not Caesarean decree.[166] What decrees, then, could be alluded to here? E. A. Judge has plausibly suggested the reference is to a ban on certain kinds of predictions, particularly predictions that have to do with the change of rulers or that suggest the demise of the current one due to ill health or the like. Tiberius had already issued in A.D. 16 a decree (*dogma*) prohibiting the practicing of such an art in the cities of the Empire (see Dio Chrysostom 57.15.8).[167] In other words, from a careful analysis of the Thessalonian correspondence one can deduce that Paul could plausibly be charged with violating the decree against predictions of the coming of a new king or kingdom, especially one that might be said to supplant or judge the existing emperor (see 2 Thessalonians 2 and cf. Dio Cassius, *Hist.* 56.25.5f.; 57.15.8). These charges would be serious if Jews and others could substantiate that Paul's discourse could be seen as potentially politically subversive.

Thus *vv. 8-9* indicate that the officials took this as a serious matter, as did the people listening to these proceedings. The benefactions of the emperor might stop, indeed a city might be censured, if it was known that it harbored "enemies of the Roman order."[168] Thus the politarchs took immediate action,

---

165. See Cassidy, *Society and Politics*, pp. 89-91.

166. See Sherwin-White, *Roman Law and Roman Society*, p. 103. This is overlooked by many commentators, and also by Tajara, *The Trial of Paul*, pp. 35-36.

167. See the helpful discussion in Judge, "Decrees of Caesar at Thessalonica," and also Donfried, "The Cults of Thessalonica," pp. 343-44.

168. To borrow R. MacMullen's appropriately titled book, which has as its subtitle *Treason, Unrest, and Alienation in the Empire* (Cambridge: Harvard University Press, 1966). Traveling philosophers, prophets, and other sorts of orators were often seen as dangerous and potentially subversive. See MacMullen's discussion, pp. 144ff. On the cult of the emperor and its developing influence, see Tajara, *The Trial of Paul*, pp. 36-42.

in effect banishing Paul and Silas from returning to Thessalonica during their rule, a fact probably alluded to in 1 Thessalonians, where on the one hand Paul tells us Jews were ultimately responsible for persecuting the likes of Jason and other Christians (2:14), driving Paul and his coworkers out of the city (2:15), and on the other hand he tells us that Satan blocked their return (2:18).

The particular form that the legal action took was that security was taken from Jason. Λαβουντες το ιχανον is the Greek equivalent of the Latin phrase *satis accipio* and refers to Jason providing guarantee of the good behavior of his friends, in this case that Paul and Silas would leave the city quietly and would not return so long as this ruling was in force.[169] This ruling apparently did not list Timothy, since he was apparently not accused by the Jews. Thus we should not be entirely surprised to learn of his return to the city after a short interval.

Jason and the other believers were let go once the security had been paid, and *v. 10* indicates that that very night Paul and Silas were sent off to Beroea. This city, lying in the foothills of the Olympian range, was not on the Via Egnatia but rather some fifty miles south and west of Thessalonica by means of a lesser road. Cicero tells us it was off the beaten track (*In Pisonem* 36.89), and one may well wonder whether it was somewhere Paul had intended to go. Yet such an intention is possible, for this was the most significant city in the area, being capital of one of the divisions of Mace doniafrom 167 to 148B.C. It is, however, also possible that Paul's plan had been to continue along the Via Egnatia and thence on to Rome (cf. Rom. 1:13; 15:22-24). Like Thessalonica, Beroea was administered by politarchs, but the rulings of those in Thessalonica had no force in another city like Beroea.

Once again Paul and Silas go to the synagogue, but here, according to *v. 11*, the Jews were more noble (ευγενεστεροι)[170] than those in Thessalonica, by which Luke means they were more receptive to the gospel. It is noticeable that here and at 17:21 Luke openly offers value judgments about the peoples in these regions. Is this due to the personal knowledge of one who had grown up in Macedonia and knew the characteristics of the peoples in his region? These Jews welcomed the message "with all eagerness," daily examining the Scriptures to see whether Paul's message was true. Here again, as in Thessalonica, the emphasis is placed on the intellectual component of conversion. The result, according to *v. 12*, was that many believed, including not a few Greek women and men of high standing.[171]

---

169. See Sherwin-White, *Roman Law and Roman Society*, pp. 95-96.

170. The word comes from the root indicating noble birth (see 1 Cor. 1:26), but by extension it refers to those who act nobly and graciously, as here. Cf. 4 Macc. 6:5; 9:13; 10:3.

171. Ευσχημονων means proper or decent and indicates social status. It follows the word "women," but it probably also refers to the men mentioned last in the sentence. That the high-status women are mentioned first probably suggests that there were more of them

As had happened to Paul before in Lystra (14:19), when Jews in the city Paul had just visited (in this case Thessalonica) got wind of what was happening in Beroea they came to Beroea to stir up a crowd against Paul. Thus we are told at *v. 14* that the new believers took quick action and sent Paul off toward the coast, but Silas and Timothy stayed behind, presumably to strengthen the church and make sure it endured this crisis. The Greek is such in v. 14 that one could assume that Paul took passage on a boat and sailed on to Athens; however, *v. 15* seems to suggest, he was guided by a land route to Athens.[172] Those who conducted him were given instructions to take back and to tell Timothy and Silas to join him as soon as possible. This, when coupled with 18:5 and a closing reading of 1 Thessalonians, has led to a series of questions and conjecture.

Lüdemann, for instance, assumes that 1 Thess. 3:2 implies that Timothy had traveled with Paul to Athens, from which point Paul sent him back to Thessalonica, and after that he met Paul again in Corinth.[173] In other words, Luke has gotten some of the details wrong at this point.[174] This is of course possible, but it is equally possible, since both the accounts in Acts 17 and 1 Thessalonians are partial and elliptical, that Bruce, Marshall, and Polhill are right that Timothy and Silas did rejoin Paul in Athens briefly, from which point, after hearing their reports, Paul sent them to Thessalonica and Philippi respectively,[175] after which they met Paul again in Corinth.[176] First Thessalonians 3:6, written from Corinth, matches up with Acts 18:5. There is perhaps some confirmation for our narrative in that in Acts 20:4 we hear of one Sopater son of Pyrrhus from Beroea as accompanying Paul, and at an earlier time Paul himself, while writing from Corinth, mentions having with him Timothy, Lucius (Luke?), Jason, and Sosipater (Rom. 16:21). The conjunction of the last two names may suggest that representatives of the congregations in Thessalonica and Bereoa had perhaps accompanied Timothy and Silas to Corinth to

---

that converted than men. The antifeminist tendency in D is seen here as well: "and of the Greeks and the high status men and women many believed . . . ," thus placing the status description closest to the men rather than the women mentioned in the sentence. See below on 17:34.

172. The B text does indeed seem to assume Paul went to sea, but Luke mentions no port of embarkation.

173. Lüdemann, *Early Christianity,* p. 188.

174. Against this conclusion is the rather detailed correspondence between 1 Thessalonians 1–3 and what is described in Acts 16–17. See Johnson, *Acts,* pp. 308-9.

175. Phil. 4:15 (and 16) may suggest that Silas delivered a gift of money to Paul while he was in Corinth, since it speaks of a reciprocity relationship that existed *after* Paul left Macedonia. See Longenecker, *Acts,* p. 471.

176. See Bruce, *The Acts of the Apostles,* pp. 374-75; Marshall, *Acts,* p. 281; Polhill, *Acts,* p. 364. They are in fact following the older reconstruction suggested by K. Lake, *The Earlier Epistles of Paul* (London: Hodder, 1930), p. 74.

visit with Paul.[177] In any case, Paul at this stage of his missionary work is spending time with both Jews and Gentiles, and not just with Gentiles connected to the synagogue, as we shall see in what follows in Acts 17:16-34.

C. Proclaiming the Unknown at Athens (17:16-34)

This passage is in many regards one of the most important in all of Acts, as is shown by the enormous attention scholars have given it.[178] It is not merely the famous setting of this brief passage which has rightly attracted attention, but especially the content of Paul's speech, which takes up most of the passage. The message delivered has frequently been thought to be in conflict with what the Paul of the letters has said about such subjects as natural theology (see, e.g., Romans 1–3).[179] Whether this is so or not, Luke has presented us here with the fullest example of Paul's missionary preaching to a certain kind of Gentile audience (namely, an educated and rather philosophical pagan one without contacts with the synagogue), which should be compared to the shorter but similar speech in Acts 14:15-17.[180]

For our purposes the passage is extremely significant because of what it reveals about Luke's purposes and approach as a historian. We have noted repeatedly how Luke has arranged his material on the basis of geographical regions and ethnic groups, following the example of Ephorus and other ethnographically oriented historians. We have also repeatedly noted Luke's univer-

177. Perhaps they had come with or at least about the collection (see 2 Cor. 8:1), which seems to be what Acts 20:4 is about; see pp. 603ff. below. See Lüdemann, *Early Christianity*, p. 188.

178. In fact it has attracted more scholarly attention than any other passage in Acts. Besides the commentaries, some of the more important treatments of these verses are: Balch, "The Areopagus Speech"; Barrett, "Paul's Speech on the Areopagus"; Conzelmann, "The Address of Paul"; Dibelius, "Paul on the Areopagus" and "Paul in Athens"; Gärtner, *Areopagus Speech and Natural Revelation*; Hemer, "Paul at Athens" and "The Speeches of Acts II"; Nauck, "Die Tradition und Komposition der Areopagrede"; Neyrey, "Acts 17, Epicureans, and Theodicy"; Stonehouse, *Paul before the Areopagus*; Wilson, *Gentiles and the Gentile Mission*, pp. 196-218; Zweck, "The *Exordium.*"

179. See Vielhauer, "On the 'Paulinism' of Acts," who sees the natural theology of this speech as post-Pauline.

180. As Tannehill, *Narrative Unity of Luke-Acts*, 2:210, points out, "Careful planning is indicated by the fact that we have three different types of speeches addressed to three different audiences; a mission speech to Jews (13.16-41), a mission speech to Gentiles (17.22-33), and a farewell speech to the elders of the Ephesian church (20.18-35)." Whether the Areopagus speech should be seen as a model or exemplary speech will be discussed below.

salism — salvation is for all, for every sort of person. In this speech we finally see the connection between these two things.

It was God's plan to make from one human being the various groups or nations and to establish their boundaries, but it was also God's plan to unite all these different peoples into one people of God through Christ (hence the recounting of salvation history). Nevertheless, those who reject this good news must face the one final coming judgment also brought about by the same Christ. Paul Schubert put it this way: "the Areopagus speech is not only a hellenized but also a universalized version of Luke's βουλη-theology." Thus he concluded, "Luke regarded the Areopagus speech as the final climactic part of his exposition of the whole plan of God."[181] To gain a proper perspective on the passage it is crucial to note the interplay and interdependency of the narrative and the speech. The speech reflects and presupposes the experiences of Paul in Athens and his encounters with Stoics and Epicureans. Then, too, there are signals in the narrative which are meant as clues as to how the speech should be understood. For example, in v. 16 we are told that while Paul was alone in Athens he became very upset at the veritable forest of idols, or statues of the gods and heroes. Παρωξυνετο is a strong verb (cf. the cognate in Acts 15:39), from which we get our English word "paroxysm." At the least it means that Paul was very irritated by what he saw.[182] In the LXX this term is used to refer to God's extreme anger at the idolatry of the chosen people (cf. Deut. 9:18; Ps. 106:29; Isa. 65:3; Hos. 8:5).[183] It is unlikely that Luke intended the following speech to suggest Paul had a change of heart. Bearing these things in mind, let us consider the text itself.

Paul is portrayed in v. 16 as taking something of a tour of the city, while he is waiting for his coworkers in Athens. This idea is especially conveyed by the word κατειδωλος, which means full of idols.[184] Presumably we are meant to think not merely of what could be seen on the Acropolis, which even included statues of Augustus Tiberius, Germanicus, and Drusus, but of the numerous pillars that could be found in various places in the city displaying the head of Hermes and also an erect phallus (cf. Livy, *Hist.* 45.27; Pausanias, *Descrip.* 1.14.1 to 1.15.7).[185] These statues would only have confirmed Paul in

181. Schubert, "Place of the Areopagus Speech," pp. 260-61. The second part of this quote pushes things a bit far, since there are subsequent speeches and narrative that also have something to tell us about Luke's theology of God's plan.

182. See Polhill, *Acts,* p. 366; Cadbury and Lake, *The Beginnings of Christianity,* 4:209.

183. See the discussion in Stonehouse, *Paul before the Areopagus,* p. 6.

184. Wycherley, "St. Paul in Athens," offers the translation "a veritable forest of idols."

185. There was apparently a notable collection of these statues in the northwest corner of the agora near the Stoa Basileios where Paul debated with the philosophers. See Gill, "Achaia," p. 444. A useful full survey of Athenian statues and temples can be found in Broneer, "Athens 'City of Idol Worship' "; and Montague, "Paul and Athens."

The Parthenon, one of the many temples Paul saw in Athens.

the early Jewish Christian impression that idolatry and immorality went together, as the reaction to both in the Acts 15 decree suggests.[186]

Athens at the time of Paul's visit was a free and allied city within the Empire, for the Romans respected Athens because of its illustrious past. As a city of political import Athens had passed its prime, but it continued to be a leading center of learning. Its size seems also to have dwindled some, down to perhaps as few as five thousand to ten thousand voting citizens in Paul's day. Nevertheless, as Pliny the Elder put it, her "celebrity is more than ample" (*Nat. Hist.* 4.24); she had become something of a museum for the world of the grandeur of Greek culture.[187]

V. 17 has the construction μεν ουν, marking a new division in the narrative, which suggests that we must see v. 16 as a general introduction or heading for what follows, with v. 17 being transitional, linking Luke's redactional introduction to his source material which follows, perhaps beginning in 17bff.[188] As was his wont, Paul went first to the synagogue and reasoned there (διελεγετο) with both Jews and devout Gentile synagogue adherents. This verb continues the emphasis already seen earlier in this chapter (see

186. See pp. 439ff. above.
187. So Conzelmann, "The Address of Paul," p. 218.
188. See the discussion of Longenecker, *Acts,* p. 473.

17:2ff.) on Paul's use of logic and rhetoric to persuade his audience. The text goes on to stress that he also argued or dialogued in the agora with whoever happened to be there. In what follows, Luke is building up a portrait of Paul as being able to stand on equal footing with the intellectuals of his day, even in Athens. Indeed, he seems to be presenting Paul as a new Socrates, as we shall see.

V. 18 tells us that both some Epicurean and some Stoic philosophers engaged in argument (συνεβαλλον) with Paul. Both of these groups, along with the Platonists and Peripatetics, had subsidized teaching chairs in Athens at this time (see Lucian, The Eunuch 3). The Epicureans took their name from Epicurus (341-270 B.C.), whose philosophical and ethical worldview was based on the materialistic atomic theory of Democritus. Even the gods were viewed as in essence material in this system. Pleasure was seen as the chief end in life, and the highest pleasures were seen not as the sensual ones but as the pleasures of the mind, in particular αταραξια or tranquillity — being free from both passions and superstitious fears. The gods were seen as modeling this quality, being far removed from the lives of human beings and taking no real interest in them. A motto, written by Diogenes, an Epicurean, in about A.D. 200, sums up this belief system: "Nothing to fear in God; Nothing to feel in death; Good [pleasure] can be attained; Evil [pain] can be endured."[189]

The Stoics, who seem to have been somewhat more popular at this time, recognized Zeno of Cyprus (ca. 340-265 B.C.) as their founder, but they got their name from their meeting place, the Stoa Poikile, or painted portico on the northwest side of the Athenian agora. The Stoics were basically panentheists, believing there was a divine rational ordering principle that was in all things and beings. God's relationship to the world was seen as analogous to that between the soul and the body. Like the Epicureans, the Stoics were essentially materialists, for even the essence of God and of soul was seen as made up of highly refined matter. The goal of the Stoic system was to live in accord with the rational principle that indwelt all things, and so to live according to nature. Like the Epicureans, the Stoics emphasized the preeminence of the rational over the emotions, believing in self-sufficiency or autonomy (αυταρχεια) as the highest good. They were also highly principled in regard to ethical and civic duties.[190]

The reaction to Paul in the "marketplace of ideas," however, was not notably positive. V. 18 tells us that some asked what this σπερμαλογος wished to say, while others suggested that he seemed to be a purveyor of foreign δαιμονιων. Both of these complaints are significant. The former term is based

189. See Murray, Five Stages of Greek Religion, pp. 204-5.
190. For a very useful summary of the belief systems of these two "schools" of thought, see Ferguson, Backgrounds of Early Christianity, pp. 333-56.

on the image of a bird which picks up and drops seeds, and therefore a gossip of sorts (see Philo, *Embassy* 203), but more to the point it came to connote someone who was a conveyor of snippets of knowledge or philosophy or religious ideas (see Philostratus, *Life of Apollonius* 5.20; cf. Plutarch, *Moral.* 516C), in short a dilettante. The term definitely has a derogatory sense. The second complaint, however, could be said to be more than derogatory; it was dangerous. The word δαιμονιων has its original Greek sense of divinities or gods, and the charge of being a herald[191] of foreign or strange divinities is the very one which led to the demise of Socrates (see Plato, *Apol.* 24B-C; cf. Xenophon, *Mem.* 1.1.1).[192]

The word "divinities" (plural) is explained by Luke in a parenthetical remark indicating that this conclusion was drawn because Paul was telling the good news about Jesus and the resurrection. Presumably, some in the audience had concluded that Paul's arguments about αναστασις referred to a second god, perhaps even a divine male/female pair (Jesus and Anastasia). The idea of the dead rising was a novel one to Greeks, and it is possible it was assumed Paul was using a name, not referring to a concept or event.

V. 19 must be allowed to have its full force after the Socratic allusion to foreign divinities. While the verb επιλαμβανω can simply mean to lead (cf. Acts 9:27; 23:19), it also can have the much stronger force of "to take by force" or "to arrest" (cf. Acts 16:19; 18:17). Both the immediate narrative context with its allusion to Socrates and then the reference to the Areopagus, and the usage of the verb in the immediately surrounding chapters where Paul is regularly being hauled before officials to answer charges, suggest the latter rendering. The Αρειον παγον could refer either to a location or to a council or to both, a council which met at Mars Hill and so was named after it. Again the context must decide, and here the clues point to an appearance before a council: (1) the reference to Paul standing in the midst (v. 22) is odd if the reference is to a hill, but not if the primary referent is to a council who is hearing Paul out;[193] (2) more decisive is the reference to Dionysius the Areopagite (v. 34), where the latter term clearly refers to a member of the council. As to the location of Paul's meeting before the council, the evidence suggests that in Paul's time the council met in the Stoa Basileios, just off the agora, rather than on the hill, where they may originally have met.[194] In a free

---

191. Καταγγελευς, cf. *OGIS* 456.10. See now the discussion of Winter, "On Introducing Gods to Athens."

192. Notice how later the reference is to "new teaching" in v. 19, another probable allusion to the Socrates story, as Pesch, *Die Apostelgeschichte (Apg 13–28)*, p. 135, notes.

193. Cf. Acts 1:15; 2:22; 4:7; 27:21; Luke 2:46; 22:27; 24:36. Luke frequently uses this phrase to refer to persons being in the midst of other persons. See Stonehouse, *Paul before the Areopagus*, p. 9.

194. See the discussion in Hemer, "The Speeches of Acts II," pp. 239-40.

The Acropolis in Athens, seen from "Mars Hill."

city like Athens the appropriate place to prompt an official hearing of some new teaching or ideas was before the Areopagus. Among other things the council would have had the responsibility for maintaining religious customs and order in the city, and to act as a court dispensing verdicts and justice when necessary.[195] That Paul was probably led here forcibly suggests that Luke is painting a picture of an adversarial situation.[196]

V. 20 suggests that Paul's dialogue partners wanted to know more about this new teaching, which seemed strange to them, so they wanted further explication. The word ξενίζοντα is perhaps yet another allusion to the situation of Socrates — he who was accused of proclaiming *strange or new divini-*

195. See Barnes, "An Apostle on Trial." Even during the Empire this council had the authority to have criminals executed. Cf. Tacitus, *Ann.* 2.55, and the case of one Theophilus who was executed for forgery in A.D. 18. Geagan, "Ordo Areopagitarum Atheniensium," p. 50, stresses that the account in Acts 17 illustrates this council's surveillance over the introduction of foreign gods.

196. See Haenchen, *Acts,* p. 527, who says the description here sounds unpleasantly like an arrest.

ties. V. 21 furthers the negative ethos and portrayal leading up to the speech. In one of his rare overt remarks Luke characterizes Athenians and those foreigners resident there as themselves being the busybodies or dilettantes, spending all of their time in telling or hearing something new.[197] We are not, then, to see those who take Paul to the council as mere inquiring minds, or noble truth seekers. Ramsay has suggested that "they certainly did not act as his friends and sponsors in taking him before the Council, therefore we must understand that they took him there from dislike and malice."[198] This is perhaps somewhat too strong, but clearly the scene is not portrayed as a friendly one.[199] Luke's evaluation of the Athenians should not be seen as mere personal animus; in fact, it seems to have been a typical way outsiders viewed the Athenians (cf. Thucydides, *Hist.* 3.38.5; Demosthenes, *Phil.* 1.10).

In a recent detailed study B. W. Winter has argued that Paul is not on trial before the Areopagus in any formal sense, but rather is appearing before an initial hearing, because the word was out that he was a herald of foreign gods seeking to introduce these new deities into the Athenian pantheon. The Areopagus was the very council before which such an effort needed to be made, and there is evidence that this council functioned this way in the first century A.D. Winter goes on to argue that Acts 17:19 should be read to mean "we have the power/authority to judge what this new teaching [is] being spoken by you."[200]

V. 22 informs us that Paul assumed the position of an orator, "standing in the midst" (of the council) and delivering his discourse. At this point a rhetorical analysis of the speech is in order. This sort of analysis of this speech has been undertaken in some detail by Kennedy, Soards, and Zweck.[201] Kennedy is surely right that Paul's anger establishes a basically judicial situation when it comes to his speech, though Paul also has the deliberative aim of changing his audience's behavior. The means, however, that he uses to reach that aim is forensic — he presents arguments of defense and attack for his vision of God, humankind, salvation, resurrection, and judgment, drawing on

197. Whether or not this is a reflection of Luke as a Macedonian looking down his nose at an Athenian crowd or not (see Ramsay, *St. Paul the Traveller,* p. 248), it is a negative assessment. It is not a novel view; cf. Chariton, *Chaereas and Callirhoe* 1.11.6-7.

198. Ramsay, *St. Paul the Traveller,* p. 246.

199. That we are not to think of a formal trial here is suggested by the fact that in Athens trials on religious matters were ultimately tried in the popular courts, but this does not prevent seeing here a serious (pretrial?) hearing of some sort.

200. Certainly δυναμεθα can mean "we have the power," see P. Oxy. 899, and the historian Herodotus knows the use of γνωσαι to mean "form or give a judgment" (cf. 1.74; 6.85; Isocrates 17.6). See Winter, "On Introducing Gods to Athens," pp. 81-82.

201. See Kennedy, *New Testament Interpretation,* pp. 129-32; Soards, *The Speeches in Acts,* pp. 96-97; Zweck, "The *Exordium,*" pp. 94-103.

both Hellenistic Jewish and Greek philosophical sources. It is not surprising that Paul must resort to forensic rhetoric, for, while he may not be on trial per se, the scene does suggest that he must present an argument for his teaching at a hearing before the officials of the Areoapagus, officials charged with maintaining the religious order of Athenian society.

The speech can be divided up as follows: (1) *exordium*, including *captatio benevolentiae*, vv. 22-23; (2) *propositio*, v. 23b; (3) *probatio*, vv. 24-29; (4) *peroratio*, vv. 30-31.[202] The absence of a *narratio* in this speech can be variously explained, and does not necessarily suggest the speech is wholly deliberative. I would suggest that since Luke is only presenting a précis of the speech in any case, and since what the *narratio* would contain would simply be a reduplication of what we find in vv. 18-19 (namely, the charges that Paul was a dilettante, guilty of sound-byting Greek philosophy, and that he was guilty of offering new teaching, proclaiming foreign deities, and his statement of the facts about his speaking about Jesus and the resurrection), he has omitted it here. Perhaps the major exigence that Paul must overcome in this speech is the fact that he is a preacher of an idea that Greeks basically did not accept — namely, resurrection of the dead, coupled with the idea of a final judgment by the one true God. These notions were so difficult for Greeks to accept that Luke or Paul resolved to refer to them only at the very end of the speech once some rapport and more or less convincing arguments had already been presented. He is following the proper rhetorical procedures when defending a difficult matter, namely, using the delaying tactics characteristic of an *insinuatio* sort of approach.[203] The major bone of contention arises only at the end of the speech and is dealt with with much *pathos* — all people everywhere need to repent, for the world will be judged in righteousness on a day fixed by God, judged by a man suited to the task as was shown by God's raising of him. The speech in general follows the basic rhetorical pattern of first establishing *ethos*, then offering *logos*, finally concluding with *pathos*, and in this case an indirect appeal.[204]

Throughout the speech, Luke or Paul is using various somewhat familiar notions to pass judgment on and attack idols and the idolatry involved in polytheism. In other words, what we see here is not an attempt to meet pagans halfway, but rather a use of points of contact, familiar ideas and terms, in order to make a proclamation of monotheism in its Christian form (cf. v. 23 to 30-31).

202. Here the basic outline of Zweck is convincing.

203. On this approach when dealing with a difficult subject or case, see Bower, "*Ephodos* and *Insinuatio*." This is precisely the same sort of approach we find Paul using in 2 Corinthians, where he delays until the very end (chaps. 10–13) dealing with the false teachers; see my *Conflict and Community in Corinth*, pp. 429ff.

204. It is not direct, probably because this is not a piece of deliberative rhetoric, but rather forensic in character.

This subtle but unwavering approach comports with Paul's commitment to the decree, the essence of which was to make sure Gentiles are led away from idolatry and immorality. This speech should be compared to what we find in the letters Paul wrote not long after his visit to Athens, the Thessalonian correspondence, especially 1 Thess. 1:9-10 — converts must turn from idols to serve the one living and true God and await God's Son from heaven whom God raised from the dead, who rescues the righteous from the wrath to come.[205]

It is quite possible also that Winter is right that Paul's speech is meant to deny the suggestion that he was introducing new deities into Athens. To the contrary, says Paul, he is simply proclaiming a deity that Athens had unawares already been honoring and recognizing, in a sense. Furthermore, Paul would be denying that there was any need to follow the usual procedures when introducing a new deity into Athens of buying a piece of land and erecting an altar and temple, and setting up sacrifices because the God Paul proclaims doesn't dwell in such structures and doesn't need such sacrifices. Paul's deity is self-sufficient.[206]

---

205. About the historical fact of Paul's visiting Athens at about this time in his missionary career, there can be little doubt in view of 1 Thess. 3:1. On the content of the narrative Cadbury and Lake are right to conclude: "Taken as a whole, it commends itself as a genuinely historical narrative" (*The Beginnings of Christianity,* 4:208). The narrative is a very accurate portrayal of the milieu of Athens at the time, and there is no good reason to doubt that Paul may have had some public debates with Athenian philosophers and as a result be taken before some local authorities. Hemer, "The Speeches of Acts II," pp. 244-45, is right to point to the interlocking nature of narrative and speech here, with the one depending on and building on the other, but perhaps more telling are the intimations in the speech itself that it is authentic. (1) The citation of Aratus is appropriate on the lips of Paul, not least because he was Paul's fellow Cilician. Is it an accident that another portion of this same quote shows up elsewhere in the Pauline corpus (Titus 1:12)? (2) Though Luke shows no apparent knowledge of this tradition, it appears that the speaker knew about the story of how the Athenians consulted Epimenides during a plague and he advised them to set up altars in various places (Βωμοι ανωνυμι) in the city and sacrifice to the "appropriate" God (see Diogenes Laertius 1.110). (3) There also seems to be knowledge of other important Athenian traditions. Aeschylus's *Oresteia,* which climaxes with a homicide trial, records the event which according to tradition provided for the original occasion for the setting up of the Areopagus as a place where cases could be tried. In addition in the final play of the cycle, *Eumenides,* we find the very rare use (in classical Greek literature) of the term αναστασις to mean resurrection in a declaration that educated Athenians would know well: ανδρος δ'επειδαν αιμ' αναςπαςη κονις απαξ θαναντος, ουτις εστ' αναςταςις (*Eumen.* 647-48). (4) Lüdemann, *Early Christianity,* p. 194, though he sees problems with ascribing the speech summary as it stands to Paul, nevertheless finds it plausible that in view of material like 1 Thess. 1:9-10, "in Athens Paul gave one speech (or more . . .) to the Gentiles, the basis of which has perhaps been preserved in the tradition of Acts 17." There is nothing in the narrative portion of the text that is historically implausible, and as for the problems the speech raises, we will deal with them as they arise.

206. See Winter, "On Introducing Gods to Athens," pp. 84-87.

The speech is very carefully crafted with considerable alliteration, assonance, and paronomasia.[207] Some of its distinctive traits can be understood, once one recognizes the rhetorical form and nature of the speech. For example, the opening address in *v. 22*, "men, Athenians," has been thought peculiar if Paul was addressing the Areopagus; however, it was a rhetorical convention to begin speeches in Athens in this fashion (cf., e.g., Aristotle, *Pan. Or.* 1 — ω ανδρες Αθηναιοι).[208] The narrative in any case suggests that more than just the council was present to hear this speech (e.g., the philosophers, and perhaps other curious parties — see v. 33).

The *captatio benevolentiae* in v. 22 is subtle because on the one hand the piety or religiosity of the Athenians was proverbial (cf. Pausanias, *Descript.* 1.17.1; Sophocles, *Oedipus at Colonnus* 260), but on the other the word δεισιδαιμονεστερους is ambiguous, capable of being taken in either a positive or a negative sense — in other words, meaning either religious or superstitious. However it may have been heard, it seems very likely in view of v. 16 that Luke intends for us to see Paul using it in the negative sense. This is confirmed by the usage in Acts 25:19, where it clearly has a negative sense. This interpretation of the word for the verse presently under discussion is further confirmed by the reference to the Athenians' ignorance in such matters — they were truly too superstitious, even building altars to gods whose names they did not even know, just to protect themselves! It is worth pointing out that this opening, which was capable of several interpretations, also probably allowed the speaker to avoid overtly doing what Lucian says one must not do when speaking to the Areopagus — offer complimentary exordia to secure the goodwill of this court (*De gymn.* 19).

V. 23 tells us that Paul had taken an inspection tour of the σεβασματα. Here the background of the use of this term in earlier Jewish sources, which refers to objects of worship, is important. In Wisdom of Solomon 14:20 and 15:17 it is clearly used for the worship of idols (see also Josephus, *Ant.* 18.344). In other words, this term on the lips of a Jewish Christian like Paul would likely be intended to have negative overtones as well.

Paul claims that among these "objects of worship" he found an altar with an inscription "to an unknown God." Endless debate has been offered as to whether historically there were such inscriptions to individual gods in the singular. The evidence can be interpreted in various ways, but one thing is clear

207. Notice the way the initial letter π sets up an alliterative pattern, with Luke's favorite πας playing a significant role. Cf., e.g., v. 26, επι παντος προσωπου, or in v. 30, παντας πανταχου.

208. See the discussion in Zweck, "The *Exordium*," p. 101. Especially worth comparing is Demosthenes, *Exordia* 54, which begins, "It is just and right and important, men of Athens, that we should exercise care . . . that our relations with the gods be piously maintained. . . ."

— flat dismissal of the historical possibility of such inscriptions is out of the question, since it is based largely on an argument from silence.[209] At this juncture a more detailed discussion of this much controverted issue is in order.

A Closer Look — Altars to Unknown Gods

The debate over whether or not there was any such thing as an altar to an unknown god in Athens in Paul's day has largely proved sterile, due to a lack of hard evidence one way or another. It has been suspected that Luke or Paul altered the plural into a singular for apologetic purposes. Some scholars, such as H. Conzelmann, have been willing to be dogmatic about the matter.[210] It is certainly true that thus far *clear* evidence of such an altar has not been forthcoming, though there is considerable evidence for altars to uncertain or unnamed gods (plural) in antiquity. This evidence should be reviewed briefly as it still may have some bearing on the matter.

First, we must note that all the relevant evidence of any kind postdates the first century. For example, Pausanias's *Descriptions of Greece*, written in the third quarter of the second century A.D., speaks of altars of gods called unknown (βωμοι δε θεων τε ονομαζομενων Αγνωστων, 1.1.4). The especial relevance of this is that Pausanias the inveterate traveler says he saw these altars in Athens. It is worth asking what exactly Pausanias means. Does he mean various altars each dedicated to *an* unknown god, or altars each of which is dedicated to more than one unknown god?

P. W. van der Horst has rightly pointed out, after surveying all the relevant material in detail, "[w]hen Greek and Latin authors speak of βωμοι θεων or *arae deorum* they usually mean a number of altars dedicated to a number of individual gods (e.g. Homer *Iliad* XI,808; Juvenal *Satur.* III,145), not altars dedicated to a plurality of gods."[211] As van der Horst says, it is thus logically and grammatically possible that Pausanias might be referring to altars each one of which was dedicated to an unknown god. Here the parallel texts in Pausanias that speak about altars for unknown heroes (6.20.15-19; 6.24.4; 10.33.6) may be relevant since there are certainly altar inscriptions which read "altar for a hero" of unknown name (*IG* 2.2.1546, 1547).[212] This may

209. For such dogmatic dismissals cf., e.g., Lüdemann, *Early Christianity,* pp. 190-94; Conzelmann, "The Address of Paul," p. 220.

210. Cf. Conzelmann, *Acts,* p. 140: "Paul's use of the altar inscription as a point of contact with the Athenians is a purely literary motif, since there was no inscription in this form. Luke has taken up a type of inscription well known in Athens, and has altered it to suit his purposes."

211. The emphasis is mine; cf. van der Horst, "Altar of the 'Unknown God,'" p. 167. This essay is by far the most helpful one written on our subject in the last fifty or so years and eclipses the older ones by Deissmann, *Paul,* pp. 287-91, and by Lake, "The Unknown God."

212. Not unlike the tombs of an unknown soldier or soldiers that can be found even today in Washington, D.C., and elsewhere in the world.

suggest that what Paul (or Luke) actually saw was an inscription which simply read "altar to a god," since the god's name or identity was unknown, and he added the explicatory term "unknown." One factor which may be thought to count against this reasoning is another text in Pausanias's work (5.14.8) which clearly refers to "*an* altar of unknown gods" (αγνωστων θεων βωμος), and the wording here suggests that this is exactly what the inscription on the altar read, whereas in the previously quoted text it could be thought to be Pausanias's way of describing the altar in view of the term "called." The evidence from Diogenes Laertius (*Lives* 1.110) and from Philostratus's *Life of Apollonius of Tyana* (4.3), both from the early third century, confirms that in Athens there were altars for unknown gods, with both altars and gods being in the plural.

The one relevant piece of archaeological data comes from an altar from the second century A.D. found in the precincts of the temple of Demeter in Pergamum in Asia Minor. Unfortunately, the inscription is broken off at the crucial point, but it appears probable in view of the number of letters per line and the fragment of a word we do have that it should be restored to read "to gods unknown (ΘΕΟΙΣ ΑΓ[ΝΩ-ΣΤΟΙΣ]) Capito the torch-bearer [dedicated this altar]." The discussion by van der Horst shows that this reconstruction is very possible and was favored by three of the great experts in this century on Greco-Roman religion, A. D. Nock, M. Nilsson, and O. Weinrich.[213] Jerome (*Commentary on Titus* 1.12; *Epist. 70 ad Magnum*) suggests that Paul rephrased an inscription which originally read "To the gods of Asia, Europe, and Africa, to the unknown and foreign gods."

What the above evidence does seem to establish is that there were altars to unknown gods (plural) in antiquity, and that they were especially known to have existed in Athens. What this evidence does not rule out is that there were also altars that read "to a god" or even "to an unknown god" which archaeologists have simply not discovered yet.

There are at least several possible scenarios which could have led to the erection of an altar to an unknown god. First, as F. F. Bruce points out, altars were frequently reused and rededicated, especially after a natural disaster or a war. If an altar was found partially destroyed, and the name of the god it was originally dedicated to was missing, it is very possible that such an altar would be rededicated either in the form "to a god" or even "to an unknown or unnamed god."[214]

Secondly, there is now some evidence discussed by van der Horst[215] that God-fearers living in places like Athens or elsewhere outside of Palestine could have erected an altar to the god of the Jews with the inscription "to the unknown (or unnamed?) god" of the Jews. It must be remembered that to "many Greeks the god of the Jewish religion was definitely an unknown god *par excellence* because he could not be called by name and he had no image."[216] If a God-fearing Gentile dedicated such an altar, then of course the inscription would have referred to *a god*, namely, the only one Jews

213. Van der Horst, "Altar of the 'Unknown God,'" p. 173.
214. See the discussion in Bruce, *The Acts of the Apostles*, pp. 380-81.
215. "New Altar of a Godfearer?"
216. Van der Horst, "Altar of the 'Unknown God,'" p. 187.

and their Gentile adherents recognized. There is some evidence, admittedly late, that quotes Livy's now-lost 102d book of his *Roman History* as saying about the god worshiped in Judea, "the god worshipped there is unknown."[217]

The word "unknown" could of course be a term used by a foreigner of a god that simply had a name unknown to him or her, or it could be an expression of doubt about the true name of a god, or it could be a word used to avoid misnaming a god, since it was believed that to misname could bring the wrath of a god. In any of these circumstances, it is conceivable that there could have been a dedication to a particular unknown or unnamed god. Thus, van der Horst's conclusion is fully warranted: "It is not improbable that there were altars with dedications in the singular, though it is likely that they were an exception to the rule, most dedications being in the plural."[218]

Even if Paul did not see an inscription that read exactly as the relevant phrase in the Areopagus speech reads, he may well have seen an inscription "to a god" or less probably a God-fearer's altar "to the unknown/unnamed god," which he then refers to as "the unknown god" in order apologetically to find a point of entry to discuss the one true God who has now revealed the divine nature in Jesus, the man whom he has raised and appointed for judgment.

V. 23b strikes a balance notable throughout this speech, between making contact with the audience and condemning their idolatry. On the one hand, Paul says that the Athenians, in a fashion, worship this unknown God. On the other hand, they do not really know this God and need to repent and receive instruction on who this God is and what this God has done. In short, Paul is suggesting here that the Athenians have an inkling that such a God exists, as is shown by their actions, but they do not either really know or properly acknowledge this God. This way of putting it is not much different from what we find in Rom. 1:20-23. Rom. 1:23 shows that instead of proper worship pagans have chosen to honor images or idols resembling humans or animals, just as Paul saw in his tour of Athens. Rom. 1:22 says their thinking was futile because they rejected what they could know of the true God from creation and so their minds were darkened. As we shall see, this comports with what is said in Acts 17:27 about pagans groping around in the dark for the true God. In both texts there is an affirmation of natural revelation but not of anything that amounts to an adequate natural theology as a response to that revelation. This is why in Acts 17:23 Paul insists he must proclaim the truth about this God's nature and activities to his audience. Without such proclamation they would not really know it.[219]

217. See van der Horst, "New Altar of a Godfearer?" p. 70.
218. Van der Horst, "Altar of the Unknown God," p. 196.
219. Nothing in Romans 1 should be taken to contradict what Paul plainly says elsewhere in Romans, namely, that the true nature of God can only be truly known in a saving way by fallen human beings if it is proclaimed to them as the gospel about Christ (see Rom. 10:14-17). One cannot properly call upon or name a God whose name one has never yet heard.

Two different approaches have been taken to what follows in vv. 24-31. On the one hand, Dibelius and others who have followed him have argued that there is nothing particularly Christian about the speech before v. 31, that essentially it reflects Greco-Roman thought with something of a monotheistic slant. By contrast, Nauck, Gärtner, and others have argued that the speech reflects the sort of thinking that one finds in Hellenistic Jewish apologetics, with the addition of the idea of God appointing the man Jesus, raised from the dead, as judge at the final judgment.[220] The former view tends to suggest that Luke or Paul assumes some true knowledge of God on the part of pagans which must be built upon or further expanded to lead to an adequate knowledge of God, while the latter view tends to suggest that the speech critiques idolatry, suggesting that the audience does not really know the true God but rather is groping around in the dark, needing revelation and proclamation to enlighten them. On the whole, the latter view seems much nearer to the truth, but the use of elements of Greek thought, philosophical and popular, in this speech is not to be denied.

What has happened is that Greek notions have been taken up and given new meaning by placing them in a Jewish-Christian monotheistic context. Apologetics by means of defense and attack is being done, using Greek thought to make monotheistic points. The call for repentance at the end shows where the argument has been going all along — it is not an exercise in diplomacy or compromise but ultimately a call for conversion, after a demonstration of what the Athenians obviously do not truly know about God. Familiar ideas are used to make contact with the audience, but they are used for evangelistic purposes to bolster arguments that are essentially Jewish and Christian in character.

One of the key threads that binds the whole together is the various forms of words referring to the audience's ignorance (v. 23a, "unknown"; v. 23b, αγνοουντες;[221] times of ignorance, v. 30). The second of these terms clearly characterizes the worshipers as without knowledge; the translation "ignorantly" is somewhat misleading.[222] As Polhill rightly points out, v. 23b refers to *what* (o), not who, the audience worships. "Their worship object was a thing, a 'what', and not a personal God at all."[223]

---

220. Cf. Dibelius, "Paul on the Areopagus," pp. 26ff.: "we see that it is a monotheistic sermon and only the conclusion makes it a Christian one" (here p. 27), and p. 56: "What we have before us is a *hellenistic* speech about the true knowledge of God." See Vielhauer, "On the 'Paulinism' of Acts," pp. 34-35. Contrast Nauck, "Die Tradition und Komposition der Areopagrede," pp. 11ff., and Gärtner, *Areopagus Speech and Natural Revelation*, pp. 248-52.

221. This participle has been translated "unknowingly" (Johnson, *Acts*, p. 315); "as unknown" (NRSV); or "in ignorance" (Polhill, *Acts*, p. 372).

222. See Stonehouse, *Paul before the Areopagus*, p. 19.

223. Polhill, *Acts*, p. 372.

V. 24 discusses two topics: that there is one Creator God of all the universe and its contents, and that this God does not dwell in shrines made by human hands. The former argument sets the tone for all that follows. There is one particular God who made the κοσμος and everything in it, and this same God is the one who is Lord of both heaven and earth.[224] The familiar Greek term "cosmos" is used here, but it is immediately explicated by the way the Hebrew Scriptures would put things, speaking of heaven and earth. This argument lays the groundwork for the assertion that follows. Precisely because this God made everything and rules over all, it should be obvious that such a God could not be confined to shrines made by human hands.

The similarity of terminology to what we find in Acts 7:48 has often been noted, but it must not be missed that this idea of God not being confined to human-made buildings can be found in both biblical and pagan sources (cf. 1 Kings 8:27; 2 Chron. 6:18; Euripides frag. 968). Overall, the thought of both vv. 24-25 should be compared to Isa. 42:5 (LXX).[225] "The description of God as the source of breath is drawn from Is. 42.5 (cf Gn. 2.7) but Paul has utilized the triad of life and breath and everything from current terminology. Since the word for life (ζωη) was popularly associated with 'Zeus' the name of the supreme Greek god, it is possible that Paul was saying 'Not Zeus but Yahweh is the source of life.' "[226] There is also certain common ground between Paul's attack on superstitious popular religion here and the attacks of the Epicureans on the same religious phenomenon, as Barrett has rightly noted.[227]

V. 25 asserts that God is not served by human hands, as if God had needs that human beings could meet by sacrifices and other religious activities. To the contrary, God is the one who provides for all the needs of human beings, giving them the gift of life and all things that they need. Here there may be an echo of the Epicurean idea that God needs nothing from human beings, and the Stoic notion that God is the source of all life (see below on v. 28). Plato records that Socrates had discussed whether human service to the gods was possible or not (*Euthyphro* 12E-15E), and here we see Luke portraying

224. As Johnson, *Acts*, p. 315, points out, the demonstrative pronoun ουτος which introduces the second clause is emphatic. It is *this same creator God* who is Lord, now ruling over heaven and earth.

225. See, e.g., Haenchen, *Acts*, p. 522; Schneider, *Die Apostelgeschichte II*, p. 239.

226. Marshall, *Acts*, p. 287. The thought here is not unfamiliar to Greek-speaking Jews; cf. 2 Macc. 14:35; 3 Macc. 2:9; and Ps. 50:7-15. As Marshall points out, Dibelius ("Paul on the Areopagus," pp. 42-46) and Haenchen (*Acts*, p. 522) were wrong to insist we have purely Hellenistic expression here, as if these ideas had no basis in early Jewish thought.

227. Barrett, "Paul's Speech on the Areopagus," pp. 72-75. Barrett also suggests that the speech strikes a middle course between flattery and telling the audience off. I would agree that the speaker seeks to make contact by using some familiar terms and ideas, but whether even the recognition that Athenians are "very religious" could be called flattery is another matter — I think not.

Paul doing the same. The discussion of this topic would be familiar to Athenians, as would the idea of God's providential provision for humankind and all
creatures.[228]

V. 26 introduces a further development of the idea that God is creator,
but the text has been much debated. Of some relevance may be the fact that
Athenians believed that they originated from the soil of their own land of
Attica.[229] By contrast Paul asserts that all human beings came "from one." The
question is, one what? Typically the Western text, and various early versions
and patristic witnesses, add the word αἱματος (blood) to make the reference
clearer.[230] Clearly the shorter text is the more difficult, because more ambiguous, reading. Elsewhere Luke traces the genealogy of Jesus all the way back to
Adam (Luke 3:38).

On this issue Paul would have agreed with the Stoics that the human
race is one, but unlike them he sees what is ahead as involving not a confla-
gration and then a new beginning of an age-old cycle, but rather a definitive
judgment of the world by Jesus. Clearly enough Paul is closer to the Stoics
than the Epicureans in this speech, but the point to note is that he differs in
crucial ways from and critiques both.[231]

Having announced the theme of creation, it seems very likely that the
author has such texts as Gen. 1:27-28 and 2:7 in mind, and thus the reference
is to the creation of the whole human race from Adam, a fundamental idea
for Pauline thought (cf. Rom. 5:12-29; 1 Cor. 15:45-49). In reaction to
Athenian beliefs, Paul is countering notions of ethnic exclusivity with a statement about the human race being one in its origins. This idea was not a Greek
one, as Nock recognized.[232]

The text then becomes complex and highly debated. On the first issue
of whether we have two parallel purpose infinitives in vv. 26-27 (God created
humans for two purposes — to dwell and to seek), it seems likely we do, in
view of the Genesis allusions. The Genesis story emphasizes that humankind
was created so as to fill the earth with creatures made in God's image.[233] Even
more controversial is how we should translate καιρους and οροθεσιας. Is the
speaker referring to seasons of the year and inhabitable zones of the earth (or
even boundaries between the sea and dry land), or is he talking about periods
of history and national boundaries? In favor of the translation "seasons" is

228. See Neyrey, "Acts 17, Epicureans, and Theodicy," pp. 122-24.
229. See Bruce, The Acts of the Apostles, p. 382.
230. See Metzger, Textual Commentary, p. 456.
231. See the discussion by Barrett, "Paul's Speech on the Areopagus," pp. 74-75.
232. See Nock, Essays on Religion, vol. 2, p. 831.
233. As Wilson, Gentiles and the Gentile Mission, pp. 200-201, points out, ποιησας
in v. 24 means "create" and so is likely to mean the same here in v. 26, and the allusion to
Adam provides yet a further link with Genesis.

Acts 14:17, where in a somewhat similar speech to Gentiles καιροι refers to seasons of the year (cf. Cicero, *Tusc.* 1.28.68). In Acts 14, however, the references to rain and the fruit of harvest make this meaning clear, whereas here there are no such contextual signals in that direction.[234] Without such additional clues, the term would naturally be understood to refer to time, and so periods of history. Among other things, this comports with Luke's overall approach in this book (see above). The second term, οροθεσια, is a rare word, but what little evidence we do have suggests it normally means the boundaries that divide nations (see Eusebius, *Demonstr. Evan.* 4.9).[235]

This comports nicely with and probably draws upon Deut. 32:8, which reads: "When the Most High apportioned the nations, when he divided humankind, he fixed the boundaries of the people according to the number of the gods."[236] This has an immediate relevance to the argument in our speech. The speech is monotheistic and opposes polytheism. On the basis of the Deuteronomic text multiple gods and multiple nations go together, and by the same token if God is working to unite all peoples in Christ, crossing national boundaries, then God is also working against polytheism. There would be no more concessions to human fallenness or "times of ignorance" (see below).

Paul thus is contending that the one true God who created all humankind from one person is now reuniting all throughout the earth in one people of God. More remotely in the background may also stand the Genesis story of the Tower of Babel. God divided the nations into speech groups and gave them separate territories lest they be united in their fallenness and seek to build a tower to the heavens and make a name for themselves (cf. Genesis 10–11).

To interpret the term οροθεσια to mean inhabitable zones on the earth flies in the face of v. 26, which says quite specifically that God created human beings to dwell on *all* the face of the earth. The qualifying phrase "their habitations" probably also points us to the translation "boundaries." Finally, then, we must ask about the term εθνος. Does it mean nations, or does it mean

---

234. Ibid., p. 203, rightly notes that either a qualifying adjective or the general context signals when καιροι means seasons, neither of which we have in Acts 17.

235. See ibid., pp. 204-5.

236. There is a significant textual problem here. The earliest Hebrew text we have of this verse comes from Qumran and reads as we have translated it above (see 4QDtq), and furthermore the LXX and the Greek targums seem to be compatible with this reading. The NRSV follows this reading of the Qumran text as well. The MT, on the other hand, has "the sons of Israel." Clearly, the reading in the Qumran text is the more difficult one and is probably to be preferred. The text goes on to speak of God's own portion, Israel, which should be distinguished from the other nations and their gods whose boundaries God had fixed. The text presupposes the fallenness of humankind, including God's own people, who are called in 32:5 a perverse and wicked generation.

races? Either is possible, but if Deuteronomy 32 stands in the background it is probably the former, and in either case the point is the same — from the one human being came all other human beings whatever their race or national group. The etiological legend about the origins of the Athenians could not be affirmed.

Since we probably have two parallel purpose clauses, we should not see *v. 27* as explaining why God created the various nations to inhabit the various parts of the earth. To begin the translation of *v. 27* with "so that they would seek" (so NRSV) suggests that the divisions into various national groupings living in various places was done to foster a seeking after God. This is the opposite of what the speaker wishes to assert. Humankind was not created to inhabit various places *and so* to seek God since they were scattered across the face of the earth, as if looking for some sort of divine unifying factor.

To the contrary, by nature, not by locale or placement, human beings were made to be in fellowship with God from the beginning of creation. The verb ζητειν here has been variously explained. Does it have its Greek pagan sense, as Dibelius suggested, of seeking after and examining what is true,[237] or with Gärtner should we see it as having its OT sense of trusting and obeying God, and thus referring largely to a response of the will, not an act of the intellect?[238] The latter seems to be meant, in view of how the speech ends — with an exhortation to repent and so turn to or cleave to God.

This interpretation is supported by a proper understanding of the rest of v. 27. The ει αρα γε plus a verb in the optative indicates uncertainty about the end result of the "seeking," and this sets this sentence off from Stoic thought since Stoics believed that God's existence could readily be inferred and known from examining nature.[239] Secondly the verb ψηλαφω occurs only four times in the NT (here; Luke 24:39; 1 John 1:1; Heb. 12:18). In Luke 24:39 and 1 John 1:1 it seems to have the sense of making physical contact with something with the intent of proving its reality or existence. This concrete sense of "touching with hands" does not really fit our text. More helpful is the evidence found in both classical and biblical texts that the word refers to the groping of a blind person or the fumbling of a person in the darkness of night (see Aristophanes, *Ec.* 315; *Pax* 691; Plato, *Phaedo* 99b; Isa. 59:10; Judg. 16:26; Deut. 28:29; Job 5:13-14; 12:25 [all from the LXX]).[240] The image is not an encouraging one,

---

237. Dibelius, "Paul on the Areopagus," pp. 32ff.; cf. Plato, *Apol.* 19b, 23b; *Rep.* 449a.

238. Gärtner, *Areopagus Speech and Natural Revelation,* pp. 155ff. See Deut. 4:29; 2 Sam. 21:1; Hos. 5:15. In the LXX ζητειν τον θεον means normally to turn to or to cleave to. See Wilson, *Gentiles and the Gentile Mission,* p. 206.

239. See rightly Wilson, *Gentiles and the Gentile Mission,* p. 206.

240. See the discussion in Gärtner, *Areopagus Speech and Natural Revelation,* pp. 160-61.

even when coupled with what follows it — "and yet God is not far from each one of us." As in Acts 21:17, the καὶ γε should be seen as concessive.[241]

The overall effect of this verse is to highlight the dilemma and irony of the human situation. Though God is omnipresent, and so not far from any person, ironically human beings are stumbling around in the dark trying to find God. When one is blind, even an object right in front of one's face can be missed. The sentence does not encourage us to think the speaker believes that the finding of the true God is actually going on, apart from divine revelation. To the contrary, the true God remains unknown apart from such revelation. The history of the pagan search for God can be characterized under the banner "the times of ignorance" (see below).

Our speech has often been compared to Dio Chrysostom's *Olympic Oration* 12.28, which speaks of God not being far off. Chrysostom, however, is building on Stoic notions that all persons have innate conceptions of God by nature, for God indwells all things and persons, and that humans are inherently one with or kin to God, the individual soul connected to the world soul. By contrast our orator is building on the notion of the creator/creature distinction that then requires a relationship of adherence to create fellowship. Dio does not attack idolaters in his speech; he sees in the manufacture of idols a noble attempt to make an adequate image or representation of Deity,[242] but our orator is very distressed by idols and calls for repentance from pagan religion.

In *v. 28* we see some effort made by the speaker to relate what he has just asserted to familiar ideas. First we hear "in him we live and move and are," which idea is supported by a quote from "one of your poets"[243] to the effect that "even we are his family/offspring." It is in order to point out that the speaker does not say God lives and moves and has being in us, a pantheistic assertion, but rather the converse, and it is even possible that εν here, especially on the lips of a Jewish Christian, would mean "by."[244] The point is that God is the source of life and of power for activities, and so humans are radically dependent on this one God for their very being and all that they do. It may be that the first assertion goes back to words originally addressed to Zeus in a poem attributed to the Cretan poet Epimenides, another part of which is quoted at Titus 1:12.[245] We do not have the original poem, however, and there are similar assertions by pagans (see Dio, *Or.*

---

241. See Bruce, *The Acts of the Apostles,* p. 383.

242. See Gärtner, *Areopagus Speech and Natural Revelation,* pp. 163-64.

243. Some manuscripts (p74, b, 33, 326, 614, and a few others) have "our" instead of "your" at this point. This change was likely made in view of the fact that Paul is about to quote his fellow Cilician, Aratus. See Bruce, *The Acts of the Apostles,* p. 385.

244. See Cadbury and Lake, *The Beginnings of Christianity,* 4:217.

245. Here is yet another connection between Luke's presentation of Paul in Acts and the presentation in the Pastorals. See pp. 430ff. above.

12.43). As Lake and Cadbury long ago noted, Epimenides was no Stoic, being earlier than Zeno, and in any case an address to Zeus would not be seen as an address to the pantheistic deity of Stoicism.[246]

As for the quote from Aratus (*Phaenomena* 5), as Wilson rightly stresses, it is not used primarily, if at all, to affirm Aratus's notions on the kinship[247] of God and human beings, but rather "to attack idolatry and the false conception of God which underlies it."[248] The ουν in *v. 29* links what has been said before with this verse. V. 29 makes plain that what is being attacked here is not merely the practice of making idols, but the underlying assumptions behind such activities, in particular the assumption that the deity is like a thing, an "image formed by the art and imagination of human beings." The converse is the case, says the speaker — we are God's offspring or kin; God created us, not the other way around. Whatever the notion of kinship meant in the original quote, the idea has been taken up and transfigured into a support for the notion that human beings are created by God and in God's image; God is not created in ours. As Soards points out, "the condemnation of idolatry forms an implicit parallel to the denunciation of eating meat offered to idols in 15.2; 21.25."[249]

From a rhetorical point of view the function of the quotation or quotations here is to cite an authority recognized by one's audience to support one's point. It would have done Paul no good to simply quote the Scriptures, a book the audience did not know and one that had no authority in the minds of these hearers. Arguments are only persuasive if they work within the plausibility structure existing in the minds of the hearers.

In forensic speeches there is a building toward the decision of the judges (see Quintilian, *Inst. Or.* 3.11.5-6), and Neyrey has pointed out that in the forensic speeches in the latter half of Acts it is always the resurrection that brings us to the "point of judgment."[250] We are dealing, however, with deliberate irony here, for while this council is brought to decision by the raising of the issue of resurrection, Paul says that resurrection proves that his audience themselves will one day face judgment. There is some question of whether we should see the end of this speech as interrupted.[251] The answer in this case is probably not. As Kennedy suggests, "The abrupt end of the speech as we have

246. Ibid., 1:217.
247. Γενος is not used in Luke-Acts to mean merely a "kind" or "species" but refers to "a human group with a common origin and social life" (Tannehill, *Narrative Unity of Luke-Acts,* 2:219). The point here is that all humans come from God and are members of God's family.
248. Wilson, *Gentiles and the Gentile Mission,* p. 208.
249. Soards, *The Speeches in Acts,* p. 99.
250. See Neyrey, "Acts 17, Epicureans, and Theodicy," p. 121 n. 16. Besides this one, he is particularly referring to the speeches in Acts 22–26.
251. See, e.g., Shields, "The Areopagus Sermon," p. 25.

it seems to be part of the rhetoric of the author of Acts, who throughout the passage seeks to polarize. He clearly holds philosophers in some contempt and wishes to leave a picture of Paul the radical Christian amid mocking and ignorant philosophers."[252] It is also true to say that the orator here is seeking to force his audience to a point of decision and judgment, and it is the mention of resurrection that pushes them over the edge.

The conclusion of the speech in *vv. 30-31* should not be seen as anomalous, or a mere tacking on of a Christian addendum to an otherwise Hellenistic piece of rhetoric.[253] All along the speaker believed that the Greco-Roman world needed "to break decisively with its religious past in response to one God who now invites all to be part of the renewed world. The culture that Athens represents is called to repent because it makes God dependent on human temples, rites and images (vv. 24-25, 29)."[254] The argument, while drawing on some Greek ideas, has been thoroughly biblical from the start, and is not unlike other early Jewish examples of apologetics for monotheism. The conclusion follows naturally from the argument. God in mercy previously overlooked the times of ignorance, the times when pagans were groping in the dark for God and making idolatrous images, but now, as a result of what has happened through Christ's death and resurrection, such ignorance will no longer be endured. The other passages about the ignorance of both Jews and Gentiles (Acts 3:17; 13:27; 14:16) should be compared at this juncture.[255] Both Jews and Gentiles find themselves in the same position, in need of repenting and being reconciled to God through Christ.

Luke's analysis of history, including the times of ignorance, owes little or nothing to Stoicism. As Conzelmann pointed out, Luke "does not say that man formerly possessed a knowledge of God and later lost it, as Stoic theory would have had it. Rather Luke asserts that such knowledge was always possible but was never realized."[256] In short, he does not believe that a Jewish or Christian knowledge can simply be added to what pagans already know about God, with salvific results. Conversion to a new worldview, not merely additional knowledge, is required.

Thus, God commands everyone everywhere to repent, because the day of judgment for the whole world has been fixed, the world will be judged in

---

252. Kennedy, *New Testament Interpretation*, p. 131.

253. This was rightly recognized by Conzelmann, "The Address of Paul," pp. 226ff., who also rightly associates this speech with 1 Thess. 1:9-10.

254. Tannehill, *Narrative Unity of Luke-Acts*, 2:218.

255. Notice once again the anti-Semitism of the Western text, which in D at v. 30 reads "*this* ignorance" to distinguish it from the culpable ignorance of the Jews referred to in Acts 3:17 (see above, pp. 182ff., on this text and the Western text's version of it). See rightly Epp, "The 'Ignorance Motif,'" p. 60.

256. Conzelmann, "The Address of Paul," p. 228.

righteousness by one particular man, and the proof[257] of this coming event God has given to all by raising this same man from the dead. The reaction which follows in *v. 32* is said to be that some mocked when they heard about the resurrection. This is not surprising for Athenians who had been taught by Apollo at the founding of the Areopagus that "When the dust has soaked up a person's blood, once he is dead, there is no resurrection" (Aeschylus, *Eumenides* 647-48). On the other hand, there is a contrast between the some who mocked and the some who said, "We will hear you again about this."[258] Presumably it means that some were immediately unconvinced by the argument when resurrection was mentioned, but others were prepared to hear more. It is possible, however, to see v. 32b as dismissive — in effect, "enough for now, perhaps another time."

Luke, however, does not want to suggest that this speech produced no positive results. Though Paul left from the midst of the council (*v. 33*, presumably once and for all), he was not left without a witness in Athens. It is important to the setting of this speech to realize that besides the council, there were others listening to this speech of Paul's. As Ramsay long ago said, in "the rhetorical displays of that period, the general audience *(corona)* was an important feature,"[259] and Luke wants to make clear that a larger audience heard this than the Areopagus.

Some persons,[260] according to *v. 34,* joined Paul and became believers, and notable among them was one particular man, Dionysius the Areopagite,[261] a member of the council before which Paul had spoken, and one woman named Damaris.[262] This name seems to be a variant of the common female

257. Within a rhetorical argument such as this one, πιστις here refers to a proof; cf. Aristotle, *Nic. Eth.* 1173A; Josephus, *Ant.* 15.69. For the precise phrase "provide proof," see Vettius Valens 277.29f. In this argument Paul has used both artificial and inartificial proofs. The reference to an altar to an unknown god is not really a point of contact with the audience, since it is unlikely that the god in question was Yahweh, and so this amounts to a manufactured argument on Paul's part, but recent events, such as the resurrection, or recognized authorities such as Greek writers, fall into the category of inartificial proofs.

258. The μεν . . . δε construction suggests a contrast here. The question is, how much of one?

259. Ramsay, *St. Paul the Traveller,* p. 248.

260. ανδρες clearly means persons here in view of the reference to Damaris.

261. Who according to later tradition became the first bishop of Athens. This is probably pure legend, but see Eusebius, *Hist. Eccl.* 3.4.11; 4.23.3.

262. Characteristic of the antifeminist tendencies of the Western text, D omits any reference to Damaris as a convert. See pp. 65ff. above and Metzger, *Textual Commentary,* pp. 459-60. Winter, "On Introducing Gods to Athens," plausibly suggests that the phrase "and others with them" could refer to the members of the households of Dionysius and Damaris, possibly including clients. Winter is able to explain their presence by the fact that the people of Athens traditionally had played a role in sanctioning any new deities to be introduced to the pantheon and so would be present at this hearing if Paul's preaching had piqued their interest and sense of responsibility for such new teaching.

name Δαμαλις, which means heifer. This may suggest she was a foreign woman (see v. 21), or even a εταιρα, an educated woman who would serve as a companion of a citizen of Athens at public occasions where the presence of highborn Athenian women was frowned upon (such as at a meeting of the Areopagus).[263] In any case Luke wants to suggest that there were some converts, at least two of note, and at least Dionysius would have been of some social standing in Athens. All had not been for naught in Athens.[264] Nevertheless, there is no evidence of an ongoing vital Christian community being founded in Athens at this time, as is shown by 1 Cor. 16:15, which refers to the household of Stephanas of Corinth as being the first converts in Achaia. Perhaps this means that his house, through the conversion of the family, became the first Christian household and locus for a house church in Achaia.

While some have suggested that 1 Cor. 2:1-4 indicates that Paul renounced his approach in Athens when he arrived in Corinth, and instead resolved to stick with the heart of the kerygma, this is probably reading too much into this text. In fact it would appear that Paul adjusted his missionary strategy due to the situation he found in Corinth, not as a reaction to supposed previous failures.[265] It is hard to doubt that Luke sees this speech in Acts 17 as something of a model for how to approach educated pagan Greeks, and means it to reflect positively on his hero Paul, especially since he records only three major speech summaries from Paul's travels, and this is the only major one specifically directed at Gentiles (see above).[266] It is surely not seen as merely a record of a unique occasion, or of something tried, which failed and was later discarded. Athens is one of the few places on this journey where Paul is not in fact run out of town!

A few concluding remarks are in order about whether this speech comports with what we know of Paul's thought from his letters. It must be said that the matter is difficult to judge since we do not have any pure samples of Paul's evangelistic preaching to Gentiles in these letters, only a few hints here and there, such as we have noted in 1 Thess. 1:9-10. Some scholars are of the opinion that this speech definitely doesn't comport with the thought of the Pauline letters, especially with Romans 1. Wilson, for example, puts the matter this way:

> There is no castigation of Gentile immorality in Acts 17 [as in Romans 1] and the interpretation of the Gentile response to the natural revelation is different

---

263. In general, Athenian society was more restrictive of the roles of citizen women or wives of citizens than in Macedonia and some other places in the Empire. On this matter and on εταιραε see my discussion in *Women in the Earliest Churches*, pp. 5-16 and the notes and articles cited there.

264. Εν οις indicates that these two were only among the converts; there were more who are unnamed.

265. See my *Conflict and Community in Corinth*, pp. 121-29.

266. See Dibelius, *Studies in the Acts*, p. 82.

from Paul's. For whereas Paul claims that the Gentiles knew God but did not honor him, Luke claims that they worship God but do not know him. The one view emphasises the Gentiles' culpability, while the other interprets their basic response as correct but misguided. Paul's is a passionate condemnation, while Luke's is a combination of magnanimity and admonition.[267]

This conclusion, which is not uncommon, in my judgment involves a significant misreading of the tone and thrust of the Areopagus address, and a less serious misunderstanding of Romans 1. In the first place, this speech, like Romans 1, emphasizes the culpability of the Gentiles. The times of ignorance are over and done with; now is the time when repentance is required lest one face the judgment. In the second place, Paul does not say that Gentiles have any inherent saving knowledge of God, nor that they could deduce any from nature. What nature reveals is the existence of a Creator God and this God's eternal power (Rom. 1:20). It is thus misleading to suggest that Paul says that pagans know God apart from the gospel in any further sense than is suggested in Acts 17. Acts 17 suggests that pagans have some inkling that God exists, as is shown by their erecting of altars and creating of objects of worship for this God. They simply do not know his name or true nature. This is made very clear by the repeated stress that pagans are groping around in the dark, and their efforts at worship of the true God are distortions, inadequate, shots fired in the dark.

Furthermore, this speech no more suggests that pagans' basic response to God is correct but misguided than does Paul. The forensic character of this speech, driving forward as it does toward vv. 30-31 and pressing a particular monotheistic agenda all along the way against pagan idolatry, must not be overlooked. The Areopagus speech is no example of magnanimity, or even of a damning with faint praise. Nor is it correct to say that Acts 17 suggests that pagans were already groping in the right direction toward the biblical God. Paul must proclaim to his audience what they do not truly know. Then, too, the critique in v. 29 of idols and idolatry and the basic notions behind both is strong. The response at the end of the speech of the majority shows that they are not viewed as being on the right track, but just inadequately informed.

The critique in Acts 17 of popular pagan religious notions, such as that God dwells in temples, is most severe, but the critique of Stoicism and Epicureanism is no less notable. Against the latter, God is said to be near and caring a good deal about human beliefs and behavior. Against the former God is distinguishable from his creation and true knowledge of God is not simply gained by evaluating nature. There must be proclamation of what God has revealed and is now doing. Against both of these philosophies the speech

267. Wilson, *Gentiles and the Gentile Mission*, p. 214.

affirms resurrection, future judgment, and a teleological character to human history.

Paul in Romans 1 is speaking about willful ignorance of God, caused by a deliberate choosing of darkness over what little light was available through creation. Luke does not clearly say whether the ignorance Paul is referring to in this speech is willful or not, but the condemnation of the building of idols, and of the belief that God dwells in temples, and that God has needs humans can meet, suggests that he thinks it is. Indeed, the editorial comment in v. 21 suggests strongly that they are dilettantes — seekers after the new rather than the true; seekers after the curious rather than the Κύριος. In the end they are the ones seen as serving strange gods. Both the Paul of the Areopagus and the Paul of Romans 1 see pagans groping in the dark. That their thinking is futile and that their senseless minds have become darkened is precisely what the reaction of Paul both in the narrative introduction and in the speech in Acts 17:16ff. suggests.

It is true enough that Paul speaks about the passing over of previous sins in Romans (3:25-26) while in Acts we hear about the passing over of previous ignorance, but the two ideas are not unrelated. The call for repentance and the warning about future judgment imply as much. Both the Paul of the letters (see Rom. 1:4) and the Paul of this speech (17:31) see the resurrection as a decisive divine demonstration or proof of God's intentions in regard to humankind, and the decisive shift in the ages which turns times of ignorance or sin into the age of accountability. In sum, there are differences of emphasis in the two texts, but they are far from irreconcilable.[268]

It is even possible to suggest that the speech in Acts 17 was a sort of trial balloon by Paul, later abandoned, but I think this is unnecessary. There is nothing here that requires the conclusion that Luke was not Paul's sometime companion, or on the other hand that he knew Paul's letters. The correspondences between the two sources are all the more remarkable in view of this latter likelihood.[269]

D. Congregating at Corinth (18:1-23)

Paul journeyed on alone to Corinth,[270] pursuing his policy of sharing the gospel in major cities in the Empire, including especially Roman colony cities.

268. See Hemer, "The Speeches of Acts II," pp. 251-52.
269. See the discussion in ibid., pp. 244ff.
270. Μετα ταυτα, meaning "after these things," is another general way, along with μεν ουν, that Luke introduces a new narrative unit in the latter half of Acts, without indicating the precise amount of time that had passed since the previously recorded events. See Longenecker, *Acts,* p. 482.

*Typical Roman male public attire,
such as Gallio would have worn.*

It is fair to say that "Corinth and Ephesus were the two most important cities visited by Paul in the course of his missionary work, and he stayed in each for a considerable period in order to establish churches which would then evangelize the surrounding areas."[271]

Polhill has suggested we may learn something significant about Luke's approach to his source material from this narrative. His coverage of Paul's stay in Corinth is briefer than his coverage of Paul's time in either Philippi or Athens, even though he tells us that Paul's stay in Corinth was much longer. Luke's concern was not to give any sort of full-scale history of the Pauline mission but to present salient or typical episodes, and to abbreviate the rest of the data.[272] There is some truth in this assessment, and yet in the case of Corinth it may simply be that Luke did not have extensive sources.

It is hard to doubt, for example, that had Luke known the Corinthian correspondence he would have failed to mention Stephanas and his household, Fortunatus, Achaicus, Gaius (but see below), or Phoebe, or at least some of the aforementioned persons. As Johnson rightly points out, when one compares this Acts account with what we find in the Corinthian correspondence, "the points of agreement tend to confirm the basic reliability of the Acts account, while the points of omission . . . tend to suggest Acts did not use 1 Corinthians as one of its sources."[273] The points of convergence are substantial, including the mention of Aquila and Priscilla, Paul's earning a living by practicing a trade in Corinth, the conversion and baptism of Crispus (Acts 18:8; 1 Cor. 1:14), the experience of fear and trembling (Acts 18:9; 1 Cor. 1:3), the participation of Timothy in the ministry in Corinth (Acts 18:5; 1 Cor. 4:17; 16:10-11), and possibly the reference to Sosthenes (Acts 18:17; 1 Cor. 1:1).[274]

The narrative as we have it in 18:1-17 is structured around three significant pronouncements: by Paul (v. 6), by the Lord (vv. 9-10), and by Gallio (vv. 14-15).[275] Here as elsewhere Luke gives significant space to the recording of speech material, not least because he is chronicling the spread of the word, and the word's effect, and it is the word which gives and changes the direction of the narrative.

271. Marshall, *Acts*, p. 291.
272. Polhill, *Acts*, pp. 379-80.
273. Johnson, *Acts*, p. 324.
274. See ibid., pp. 324-35. These sorts of convergences of course favor the suggestion that Luke was a sometime companion of Paul, and it is also worth noting that if Luke is reliable in a narrative like this, where his sources seem to have been scanty, this gives us even more reason to trust him in longer narratives when his sources seem to have been more extensive, even if we can no longer clearly identify those sources, or independently confirm Luke's conclusions.
275. See Tannehill, *Narrative Unity of Luke-Acts*, 2:221.

Roman Corinth, when Paul visited it in the early 50s A.D., was well on the way to becoming the largest, most prosperous city in Greece. Julius Caesar himself, shortly before his death in 44 B.C., had ordered that Corinth be rebuilt as a Roman colony, for the Romans had destroyed the classical city in 146 B.C. Like Philippi, Roman Corinth was never simply a Hellenistic city during this period; its architecture, law, and official language (Latin) all reflect the Roman dominance and control of the city during Paul's era.

The city was in many regards the best place possible in Greece for making contacts with all sorts of people and for founding a new religious group. Corinth was at the crossroads between the eastern and western portions of the Mediterranean, having ports on either side of the Isthmus of Corinth, and between the northern and southern regions of Greece. It was also the chief sponsoring city of the Isthmian Games, which brought a host of travelers to the city on a biennial basis, a not insignificant portion of whom would be needing tents while they stayed for the games.

Religiously, the city was pluralistic and included temples or shrines to traditional Greek gods and goddesses (including Aphrodite on the Acro-Corinth), recently founded Roman cults that included the practice of emperor worship, and a considerable and long-established Jewish colony. Here Paul was likely to meet people of varying social statuses and religious orientations who if converted could help establish a significant congregation in this place, not to mention many itinerant businessmen and businesswomen who if converted could help spread the word elsewhere in the Empire. It was in most regards an ideal place for Paul to spend at least eighteen months sharing the gospel.[276]

V. 2 tells us that when Paul arrived in Corinth he met a Jew from Pontus,[277] which was in northern Asia Minor, bordering the Black Sea, whose name was Aquila and whose wife's name was Priscilla (the diminutive of the more formal name Prisca; cf., e.g., Rom. 16:3).[278] Aquila is a Latin name meaning "eagle," and the fact that he had recently lived in Rome suggested to Ramsay that he was a Roman from the Roman province of Pontus.[279] Priscilla's

276. On all this in much more detail see my *Conflict and Community in Corinth*, pp. 5-35.

277. Luke does not tell us whether he means the region of Pontus or the Roman province of Bithynia-Pontus, presumably the latter.

278. Luke tends to use the less formal form of those he names, while Paul uses the more formal style of identification. Thus, e.g., Paul uses Prisca and Silvanus, Luke Priscilla and Silas. See Polhill, *Acts*, p. 382. Perhaps this is a literary technique on Luke's part, possibly suggesting that Theophilus should know about some of these familiar early Christian figures already, but it is also possible and perhaps more likely that it simply suggests that Luke himself knew various of these people. See Johnson's suggestion (*Acts*, p. 325) that Priscilla and Aquila supplied some of the information for this portion of the narrative.

279. Ramsay, *St. Paul the Traveller*, pp. 253-54.

name may suggest that she was a freedwoman of a famous Roman matron of the same name. This couple is always mentioned together in the NT, and in most of the instances Priscilla's name comes first (Acts 18:18, 26; Rom. 16:3; 2 Tim. 4:19). This is somewhat surprising and may well reflect her having higher social status than her husband, or greater prominence in the church (see below on 18:26), or both.

These two had not come to Corinth from Pontus, but rather from Italy, because, we are told, "Claudius had ordered all Jews to leave Rome."[280] Both the fact and the date of this expulsion have been much debated, and a more detailed comment is in order at this juncture.

A Closer Look — Claudius, Jews, and a *Religio Licita*

In order to understand Claudius's dealings with Jews and Jewish Christians it is necessary first to say something about the history of the relationship between Roman rulers and their Jewish subjects. In the first place there was a long history of expelling adherents of "foreign" religions, including Jews, from Rome. In 139 B.C. city authorities expelled Jews for "attempting to corrupt Roman morals" (Valerius Maximus, *Facta et dicta memorabilia* 1.3.3). Again during the Empire under the reign of Tiberius they were expelled in A.D. 19 because they "had flocked to Rome in great numbers and were converting many of the natives to their ways" (Dio Cassius 57.18.5). Tiberius in fact had sent several thousand to Sardinia and executed a few of the leaders.

Thus when we come to the statement in Acts 18:2, there is nothing very surprising about an edict of expulsion of Jews by a Roman ruler. There was more than sufficient precedent for such an action. Dio tells us that Claudius in A.D. 41 took action against the Jews in the following fashion: "As for the Jews, who had again increased so greatly that by reason of their multitude it would have been hard without raising a tumult to bar them from the city, *he did not drive them out*, but ordered them, while continuing their traditional mode of life, not to hold [open?] meetings" (60.6.6).

It must be remembered that Claudius in 41 also had to deal with a problem between Jewish and non-Jewish residents of Alexandria caused by the growing influence and status of Jews in that city. Two deputations went before Gaius Caligula in Rome in the winter of 39-40, one led by Philo and the other by the philosopher Apion, but no decision was rendered before Gaius was assassinated. This left the matter to Claudius, who received a further, new set of delegations from both parties and issued a famous edict (see below) in the summer of 41. Claudius refused to rule on past actions but warned both sides about future conduct, which could arouse the anger of the emperor. More importantly, he ruled that (1) Jewish customs were to be respected,

---

280. No doubt this sentence involves yet another example of Luke's rhetorical use of πας, on which see pp. 105ff. above. The point is to indicate that a very large number were involved.

(2) Jews were not to be confined to one quarter of the city, and (3) Jews were not to infiltrate (or break up?) the local Greek games.[281]

We can see from this policy an attempt not to try to snuff out Jewish religious practices, but at the same time to insist that Jews should not try to be Hellenes nor bring into Alexandria their coreligionists when disputes broke out. It must be remembered that Claudius was a philhellene himself and did not like to see its cultural traditions diluted or polluted. In short, the Claudian policy in regard to Jews involved some respect but also some attempt to keep Jews within bounds.[282]

In A.D. 44 Claudius raised new fears among Jews by abolishing the Jewish state and thus in effect annexing it and putting it under direct Roman control after a brief hiatus during the rule of Herod Agrippa. On the other hand, in A.D. 46, perhaps as an act of appeasement, Claudius wrote to then Procurator Cuspius Fadus and granted the Jews the right to regain control of the sacred robes of the high priest.

Finally, we come to the much-controverted evidence found in Suetonius that Claudius made an edict expelling Jews from Rome due to disturbances or riots caused at the instigation of Chrestus (*impulsore Chrestus* — *Life of Claudius* 25). It is doubtful this records the same event we have quoted above as found in Dio, and notably classics scholars and ancient historians do not tend to identify the two texts.[283] Orosius, a fifth-century writer, does mention this last incident and dates it to the ninth year of Claudius's reign (Jan. 25, A.D. 49 to Jan. 24, A.D. 50), information he says he obtained from Josephus (see Orosius, *Historia contra Paganos* 7.6.15). Because Orosius also used other sources, including apparently Julius Africanus, he may have derived this information from another source, since it does not exist in the extant form of the corpus of Josephus's works.[284]

In regard to the name Chrestus, it can be taken as a colloquial Latin spelling of Christus,[285] since Justin Martyr attests to the fact that the name "Christianus" was occasionally spelled *Chrestianus* in Latin, and a wordplay with the Greek word χρεστος (good) is also mentioned (*Apol.* 1.3-4).[286] I quite agree with the ancient historian B. Levick that it is unconvincing that a *second*-century historian like Suetonius would have *misunderstood* a reference in his sources to Christians.[287] He may have been referring to a person who lived in the 40s in Rome, named Chrestus, but since Chrestus and Christus were two spellings of the same name, it is more probable that this is a

---

281. On the attempt to conflate what happened in A.D. 41 and 49, see J. Murphy-O'Connor, *Paul: A Critical Life*, pp. 8-13. See my forthcoming critique in *PaulQuest: The Search for the Jew from Tarsus* (Downers Grove: InterVarsity, 1998).

282. It is possible that the prohibition in regard to the games had to do with the general uproar that might have been created if circumcised Jews participated in the games. On all this cf. P. Oxy. 3021, and P. Berl. 8877.

283. See, e.g., Benko, *Pagan Rome*, p. 18; Levick, *Claudius*, p. 121.

284. On this matter see the essay by K. Lake, "The Chronology of Acts," in *Beginnings*, 5:459ff. and the discussion there.

285. See Benko, *Pagan Rome*, p. 18.

286. See ibid., pp. 2ff. Tertullian also knows the wordplay and the use of χρεστος; see his *Apol.* 1 and *Ad nationes* 6.

287. Levick, *Claudius*, p. 121.

reference to "Christ" or debate about him being what instigated the turmoil. If this is correct, it is apposite to note that it appears that Priscilla and Aquila were *already* Christians when they left Rome and came to Corinth.

Tacitus indicates that Claudius, like various other Roman emperors, had a pro-Greco-Roman and thus also anti-Oriental general orientation in his policy making. This would have included anti-Semitism to some degree, but obviously not in as virulent a form as could be found in Caligula and other Roman rulers. Tacitus says (*Ann.* 11-12) that Claudius tried long and hard during the second half of his reign to preserve and even perpetuate the old Roman religion and for that reason attempted also to suppress foreign "superstitions."[288]

What needs to be said about the above data is the following: (1) Despite the predilections of some NT scholars,[289] there is no good reason to identify the actions of Claudius in 41 in regard to Jews with the actions reported by Suetonius and Orosius. Indeed, there are good reasons to distinguish them. Dio says the action in 41 did *not* include driving out Jews (or presumably Jewish Christians) (60.6.6), while Suetonius and Orosius agree that the opposite happened, probably on another occasion. (2) The case for two or more edicts by Claudius about Jews during his reign, even about Jews in Rome, is a strong one in view of the history recounted above of expelling Jews from Rome, and in view of Claudius's record of restricting or regulating Jews on a variety of occasions during his reign.[290] (3) The correspondence between Suetonius and Acts 18 must be taken seriously, as these are surely independent witnesses to the same event. (4) What must be taken equally seriously is the synchronism between Acts 18 and what is said in Orosius about the date of the expulsion, since Orosius says he is relying on an earlier source, and *what* he says suggests Acts 18 is not that source. (5) As Tajara has noted, the accession of Claudius to the throne witnessed a number of measures taken in favor of Jews in A.D. 41 (e.g., the establishment of Herod Agrippa I in Palestine). It is not likely that at the same time he was taking such actions he would have also expelled any large number of Jews from Rome.[291] The date of 49 fits nicely with the fact that Paul seems to have arrived in Corinth in 50 or 51, shortly after Priscilla and Aquila will have arrived.

This leads us to the matter of whether or not Judaism was seen as a *religio licita* during the Roman Empire. It must be said that this is certainly a widespread assumption by many scholars,[292] and for justification of this view the decree of Claudius in 41 is usually mentioned. In an important and influential study, E. M. Smallwood has concluded that "[t]hroughout the history of Rome's dealings with the Jews runs the thread of the toleration and protection of Judaism as a religion. . . . Judaism as a cult fulfilled the Roman criteria for permitted survival: it was morally unobjectionable and, at least among the Diaspora . . . politically innocuous. Rome therefore made the

---

288. See Lake, "The Chronology of Acts," p. 460.

289. See, e.g., Lüdemann, *Early Christianity,* pp. 10-12.

290. See the recent defense of the edict of expulsion as originating in A.D. 49 by Lampe, *Die stadrömischen Christen in den ersten beiden Jahrhunderten,* pp. 7ff. See also Tajara, *The Trial of Paul,* pp. 53-54.

291. See Tajara, *The Trial of Paul,* pp. 52-53.

292. See, e.g., Winter, *Seek the Welfare,* p. 133.

sensible and generous choice of a policy of toleration, and pursued it with almost complete consistency during the period of the pagan empire, despite the vicissitudes of her political relations with the Jews both in Palestine and elsewhere. . . . The charter of Jewish religious liberty formulated by Julius Caesar and confirmed, with extensions, by Augustus, gave Judaism the status of a *religio licita* throughout the empire, a status which it retained basically unaltered for three centuries, except during the last few years of Hadrian's reign."[293]

There are, however, some reasons to doubt that this was the case before Claudius and that Claudius's decree made it or reaffirmed it to be the case. In the first place, it was general Roman policy to allow local tribes and people to maintain a good deal of their own culture and religious customs. For example, Claudius himself says that "Augustus . . . desir[ed] that the several subject nations should abide by their own customs and not be compelled to violate the religion of their fathers."[294] This was *not* a policy applied uniquely to Jews.

Secondly, had there been something like a universal Roman policy or universally recognized law or edict involving a Jewish exemption in particular *before* Claudius's time, it is hard to see how Caligula could have thought he could insist on having a statue of himself placed in the temple in Jerusalem, or for that matter how Pontius Pilate could have thought, he could get away with bringing the Imperial Eagles into the Holy City and into close proximity with the temple precincts. Then, too, the growing cult of emperor worship, as a practice increasingly expected throughout the Empire especially of Roman citizens, would have put very severe strains on such a special Jewish exemption, if it existed.

Thirdly, the phrase *religio licita* is not found in any of the extant literature before Tertullian, and T. Rajak has argued that Tertullian originated it.[295] Whatever policies may have existed in the first century, Jewish religion was not spoken of using this sort of terminology. Indeed, Judaism, as later Christianity, was often popularly viewed as the very opposite of a *religio licita*, namely, a *superstitio*. This is clearly what Cicero calls Judaism (*Pro Flacco* 66), and other later Romans seem to have agreed (cf. Tacitus, *Hist.* 5.5).[296]

It is often supposed, on the basis of a certain sort of reading of key passages in Josephus, that Julius Caesar conferred on Jews the status of a *religio licita*. This conclusion has been challenged by Rajak. In the first place, the material in *Ant.* 12.138ff. and *War* 12.147-53 involves a citing of documents of Antiochus III about a Jewish colony in Phrygia and Syria. This material is *not* about an Empire-wide edict.

The material found in Philo, *Leg.* 152-56, suggests that Caesar was tolerant of Jews and their distinctive religious practices, especially in Rome, which is mainly what Philo is talking about, but he says nothing about an edict by Caesar declaring Judaism to be a *religio licita*. Rather, Judaism is treated like other religions that could claim

293. Smallwood, *The Jews under Roman Rule*, p. 539.

294. Josephus himself quotes this very relevant edict in *Ant.* 19, here at 283.

295. Rajak, "Roman Charter."

296. In Tacitus's view the only saving grace for Judaism was that its form of worship could claim antiquity, unlike other *superstitions* such as Christianity.

antiquity and involved nothing inherently morally or politically offensive to Rome; it was treated with a measure of toleration, not with an endorsement of validity.

The material found in Josephus, *Ant.* 14.211-28, constitutes the heart of the case for the idea that there was an Empire-wide edict making Judaism a *religio licita* first established by Caesar. Notice first that the decree sent to Parium (213-16) simply says Caesar was displeased about statutes there that prevented Jews from following their ancestral customs and sacred rites, including religious society meetings and meals. He tells the officials in Parium that they would do well to revoke any such statutes against Jewish practices. The decree to the people of Sidon (190-95) confirms that the high priest had the right to follow the ancestral practices and rule over the Jewish nation, but this is another local decree and its aim is not to establish that Judaism is a licit religion. The grants of privileges made by Dolabella, the governor of Asia, to the Jews simply exempt Jews who are Roman citizens from military service and allow them to continue to maintain their ancestral customs (16.223-25). There is nothing in any of this that amounts to a granting of Judaism the status of a *religio licita*. In several cases we do have a recognition that Jews should be allowed to *continue* to practice their religion, or that there should not be statutes interfering with such practice, but none of this warrants Smallwood's conclusion quoted above.

The quotation of the edict of Augustus in Josephus, *Ant.* 16.162-66, which was to be set up in the temple of the imperial cult in Ancyra, is an edict reaffirming what Caesar had said before — namely, that Jews were *allowed* to follow their own customs, "according to their forefathers," in regard to matters of the priesthood, the temple tax, and sabbath observance, and that anyone caught stealing their sacred books (of the Law) would be guilty of sacrilege and would have his property confiscated. Again, in general this policy is the sort of thing applied widely to ancestral religions and the sanctity of their shrines by the Romans and does not amount to a declaration that Judaism was a *religio licita*. It was more of a protective edict to prevent efforts both to coerce Jews into doing something that violated their religious scruples and to interfere in or desecrate their cultic centers. In all of these cases we are talking about decrees made to address some specific situation in the Empire, and none of them amounts to an Empire-wide edict about the legality of Judaism.

Furthermore, even the edict of Claudius in A.D. 41 is directed to a particular situation in Alexandria and is also not an Empire-wide edict about a *religio licita*. Nevertheless, while the edict cited in *Ant.* 19.299-307 was not a Magna Carta for the Jews, it was soon taken to have Empire-wide ramifications in part because it was based on the long-standing practice of allowing indigenous peoples to follow their own customs (within limits). For example, Petronius shortly after this time invoked Claudius's ruling in rebuking the people of Phoenician Dora for their mistreatment of the Jews.[297]

Claudius's edict in A.D. 41 allowed Jews to redress grievances, more than it granted them certain kinds of inalienable rights. It did not change the basic anti-Semitism of many Romans, even including Claudius, nor did it change the widespread view that Judaism was a *superstitio*. Rather, it simply provided Jews with a certain

---

297. See the discussion in Rajak, "Roman Charter," pp. 115-17.

umbrella of protection from attack, or at least of redress after the fact. It allowed them to be left alone and in peace so long as they did not intrude in other people's religion.

For a good part of the first century, Christianity was safe under this Jewish umbrella mainly because Judaism was a known *ancient* religion with ancient rites, not because it was a *Jewish* religion deemed "licit." In short, once Christianity was recognized as a *novelty* and not a long-standing religion of a particular people, it was in trouble. It was not its lack of Jewishness that was the main factor endangering emerging Christianity. Jewishness was seen as a liability by most Romans. It was its lack of antiquity. In these circumstances it is not surprising that part of Luke's apologetics involves demonstrating that Christianity is an ancient religion, being the true development of the long-existing religion of Judaism. In Luke's view, Jew and Gentile united in Christ constitute true Israel, true Judaism.[298]

P. Esler has made much the same point in considerable detail, showing how Luke stresses the connection of Christianity and its leading figures with the ancestral traditions and "fathers" of Israel (cf. 3:13; 5:30; 15:10; 22:3, 14; 24:14; 26:6; 28:17). He concludes that the "last thing in Luke's mind was to recommend Jewish customs *per se* to his readers, his energies were devoted to attracting existing Roman respect for Jewish customs to such Christian beliefs and practices as could be shown to possess a lineage deriving from Jewish tradition."[299] Even more to the point, he is right to stress that there could have been little or no benefit under Roman law to demonstrating Christianity was a form of Judaism, especially because the Christian community in Luke's day likely had many Gentile converts, and thus many who did not keep the various Jewish customs that distinguished Israel. "Many of his fellow-Christians did not observe the sabbath or the Jewish dietary laws, did not celebrate Jewish festivals, did not circumcise their children, and no longer attended synagogue. Why would such an author wish to attract Roman protection for a set of practices, in which a large part of his community did not engage?"[300] Why indeed? But all the relevant data in Acts make very good sense if Luke's aim is to legitimate Christianity to its own adherents as a religion with an ancient pedigree.[301]

298. The conclusions of Polhill, *Acts,* p. 444 n. 1, is warranted: "There is no question that Judaism was granted certain privileges by various emperors, such as the banning of the military standards from Jerusalem and exemption from paying homage to the emperor. But the concept that there was an imperial list of officially recognized religions, which the *religio licita* concept maintains, has never been adequately documented."

299. Esler, *Community and Gospel,* p. 216. He is right, I think, in maintaining that the function of demonstrating Christianity had strong links with the past is not apologetics per se, but legitimization of an existing phenomenon to a Christian audience that needed some reassuring. See Esler, p. 218.

300. Ibid., p. 213.

301. It must be remembered that the Jews were allowed to practice their ancestral religion, which was known to include monotheism, long before the rise of the Emperor cult: Therefore, Jews were not, at the inception of the Emperor cult, given a special exemption from participating in it. Rather, the practice of Julius Caesar was simply continued, which implied that they would not worship the Emperor. That Jews were not forced to worship the Emperor does not demonstrate that they had the legal status of a recognized alternative, or *licit religion.*

Thus we may fix this expulsion in all probability in A.D. 49,[302] and the evidence probably, though not certainly, also suggests that Aquila and Priscilla were already Christians before they arrived in Corinth. Were this not the case, we would expect their conversions to be mentioned either in Acts or in Paul's letters, and we find no such mention in either source. As Haenchen puts it, that "a Jewish couple expelled because of the conflict with Christians in Rome deliberately gave a Christian missionary work and shelter is far more improbable than that Paul found lodgings with Christians who had fled from Rome."[303] V. 2 then alludes to earlier events, since Paul meets Aquila and Priscilla in Corinth and he did not likely arrive there before the fall of A.D. 50 at the earliest.[304] If we ask how it was that there were already Christians in Rome, apparently well before Paul or Peter ever got there, it is in order to point to the fact that Luke notes that at Pentecost, among Peter's listeners were "visitors from Rome, both Jews and proselytes" (2:10).[305] That Luke tells us that Aquila and Priscilla had *recently* (προσφατως) come from Rome comports with the data we have that suggest that Paul arrived probably within a year of the arrival of this couple.

That Paul practiced the same trade and shared the same religious background as Aquila and Priscilla would have made them a natural contact as well. V. 3 tells us that by trade they were σκηνοποιοι, which in its most basic sense means tentmakers, but the term could have the wider sense of leather-workers. It is possible that *cilicium* is what Paul made, a cloth made of goats' hair, for this was one of the chief products made in Paul's native region of Cilicia,[306] but this is far from certain. It is probably safer to take the Greek term in its generic sense of tentmaker.[307]

---

302. It should be recognized that any such edict would only likely remain in force during the reign of the emperor who issued it, in this case until A.D. 54. If in fact it was directed at the leaders involved in the disputes in the Jewish community in Rome, other Jews and Christians are likely to have remained in the city but kept a low profile, while still others left but returned quietly not long thereafter. Luke is only interested in the big picture of "secular history" insofar as it impinged on and explained events involving or affecting Christians, such as Aquila and Priscilla. See Bruce, "Christianity under Claudius," pp. 315ff.

303. Haenchen, *Acts*, p. 533 n. 4. See my discussion of this couple in *Women in the Earliest Churches*, pp. 153-54.

304. See the discussion in Bruce, "Chronological Questions," pp. 282-83; and on Christianity during this period see his "Christianity under Claudius," pp. 316-18.

305. These are especially singled out by this way of putting things for some reason. See pp. 130ff. above on this verse.

306. See Bruce, *The Acts of the Apostles*, p. 392.

307. It may be that v. 3 suggests that they practiced their trade in the home of Aquila and Priscilla. This practice was not uncommon in the Roman world; one might have a shop in the front of one's house. It is also possible that they shared a shop in the market.

A shop in Roman Corinth.
Paul, Priscilla, and Aquila may have practiced their trade in a shop like this.

This is the first mention in Acts of Paul's working at a trade, and it is in order to say something about its social significance at this point. First, the Jewish view of working with one's hands differed from the view held by various Gentiles of higher social status in the Greco-Roman world. Only some of the latter tended to look down on such "menial" and manual tasks (cf. Plutarch, *Pericles* 2.1). Furthermore, both Greeks and Romans who practiced the various trades themselves were proud enough of their work to pay for inscriptions touting what they had made. Thirdly, the trade guilds were alive and well in Paul's time, providing much natural fellowship, mutual support, and even hospitality for travelers.[308]

Recently R. F. Hock, in an intriguing study, has suggested that

far from being at the periphery of his life, tentmaking was actually central to it. More than any of us has supposed, Paul was *Paul the tentmaker*. His trade occupied much of his time — from the years of his apprenticeship through the years of his life as a missionary for Christ, from before daylight through most of the day. Consequently, his trade in large measure determined his daily experiences and his social status. His life was very much

308. On all this see MacMullen, *Roman Social Relations*, pp. 73ff.

that of the workshop, of artisan-friends like Aquila, Barnabas, and perhaps Jason; of leather knives, and awls; of wearying toil; of being bent over a workbench like a slave and working side by side with slaves; of thereby being perceived by others and by himself as slavish and humiliated; of suffering the artisan's lack of status and so being reviled and abused.[309]

There is something to this assessment, but not as much as Hock wants to make of the matter.[310] From what we can tell, in many of the cities Paul visited his stays were brief (a matter of weeks in some cases), and he probably had neither the time nor the opportunity to set up shop and practice a trade. Neither Paul's letters nor Acts suggests he practiced his trade in all or most of the places he visited. The evidence as we have it only clearly suggests that Paul practiced his trade in two or perhaps three places — Thessalonica (1 Thess. 2:9), Corinth (cf. Acts 18:3 and 1 Cor. 9:12), and probably Ephesus (Acts 20:33-34).[311] The evidence also suggests that the reason he did so was either so as not to place an obstacle in the way of his proclamation of the gospel free of charge, or so as not to be a burden to his new converts. It is a key indicator of Paul's perception of his own social status that he sees such manual labor as a sacrifice made for the sake of the gospel, part of being a servant of Christ, and as demeaning to himself (cf. 2 Cor. 11:7; 1 Cor. 4:9, 12; 9:19). Paul was not just continuing to act as he had always acted, he was stepping down the social ladder for the sake of Christ.[312]

Luke deliberately notes that Paul was in Corinth for a year and a half,[313] which gave him time to set up shop, and one may suspect that he practiced his trade again when he was in Ephesus with Priscilla and Aquila. He was there for an extended period of time as well, perhaps as much as three years.[314] It is then probably an exaggeration to suggest that practicing a trade was Paul's continual modus operandi as he traveled around the Greco-Roman world.

There are probably several additional reasons, however, for why he did practice his trade in a place like Corinth. For one thing, he did not want to give the impression of being a huckster, a traveling philosopher, peddling God's word and then disappearing with people's money or at least having abused privileges of hospitality (see 2 Cor. 2:17). Corinth, being the crossroads town it was, had more than its share of such people, including Sophists who came

---

309. Hock, *Social Context of Paul's Ministry,* p. 67.

310. On Paul's practicing his trade in Jerusalem while growing up there, see Wilson, *Paul,* p. 52. It would have been a good locale for tentmaking.

311. See my discussion in *Conflict and Community in Corinth,* pp. 208-9.

312. See the discussion in Hock, "Paul's Tent-Making"; on Paul's actual social status and its portrayal in Acts, see pp. 430ff. above.

313. It is possible that he was there a bit longer. See below on vv. 11 and 18.

314. See pp. 562ff. below.

and offered impressive rhetorical discourses in the city for a fee. Paul also did not wish to get caught up in the social web of patronage, wherein he would be beholden to a person of high social status and obligated to locate in a specific place and teach in the house of his patron. A good degree of the anger of the high-status Corinthians with Paul seems to have come from his refusal of patronage because of the strings that would be attached to it.[315] To accept patronage would place an obstacle in the way of the gospel of free grace, for it would mean he was not offering it free of charge. Finally, Paul, being the opportunist he was, knew that the Isthmian Games happened nearby, and he knew that if he did practice his trade in Corinth he would have enormous opportunities through his work, providing tents for visitors to the games, to meet a wide variety of people of varying social strata, with whom he could share the gospel. Paul wanted to be free to identify with people up and down the social ladder, and working with his hands was one way to identify with those considered by the upper echelon of society to be "less honorable" or "weak" (cf. 1 Cor. 12:23; 9:22).[316]

V. 4 indicates that Paul continued his regular practice of going first to the synagogues, and that in Corinth he did this sabbath after sabbath (cf. 17:2).[317] In an interesting addition the Western text (D) adds, "and he inserted the name of the Lord Jesus" after "he reasoned." Presumably, the idea here is that Paul would indicate that various references to the Lord in the OT actually referred to Jesus Christ (cf. 1 Cor. 10:4 on Paul's insertion of Christ in the OT narrative).[318] Once again the language of logic and rhetoric is used to characterize Paul's presentation of the gospel. Paul was presenting arguments to persuade or convince both Jews and Greeks.[319] V. 5 must be handled carefully. The verb συνείχετο is imperfect and reflexive and refers to Paul's devoting himself exclusively to the sharing of the word once Silas and Timothy came to town.[320] We may deduce from 2 Cor. 11:9 and Phil. 4:14-15 that Timothy and Silas brought not merely good news with them from Macedonia but also funds, which allowed Paul to forgo working with his hands, at least for a while, and concentrate on ministry in the synagogue

---

315. See my discussion in *Conflict and Community in Corinth*, pp. 208ff.

316. Notice that in 1 Cor. 9:22 Paul does not say he became the strong to those who were strong. He was deliberately stepping down the social ladder to identify with those of lower status, for he himself had several high-status attributes (education, knowledge of rhetoric, Roman citizenship; see pp. 430ff. above).

317. On the synagogue of the Hebrews in Corinth, and the lintel which has been found, see my *Conflict and Community in Corinth*, pp. 24-28. The lintel probably dates to the second century A.D.

318. See Metzger, *Textual Commentary*, p. 461.

319. See above, pp. 390ff.

320. See Longenecker, *Acts*, p. 482.

and elsewhere.[321] The testimony of Paul in the synagogue was inevitably different from what it would have been elsewhere. In the synagogue the message was "the Messiah is Jesus." This message inevitably prompted opposition, and we are told those opposed "blasphemed" (βλασφημουντων) or spoke harshly (cf. Acts 13:45) to Paul.

Paul's reaction to this response was to perform a gesture familiar to Jews (cf. Neh. 5:13) — he shook out his clothes, a symbolic way of indicating he would have no more to do with them. Perhaps he saw it as following the instructions of Jesus (cf. Luke 9:5; 10:11; Acts 13:51), but the gesture here is a little different (shaking out of clothes rather than shaking of dust from one's feet), and this may be because Paul does not perform this gesture as he is leaving town, unlike what we find in 13:51 and in Jesus' instructions in Luke 9:5.

V. 6 should not be overinterpreted, as Tannehill has properly warned.[322] It does not signal a new direction in ministry henceforth, but rather an announcement of plan B, which is implemented when Paul has been rejected in his attempt to carry the gospel to the Jews first *in a particular location*. This incident should be carefully compared to the one in Acts 13:44-47. The response "Your blood be on your own heads. I am innocent" indicates that those Jews who have rejected Paul's message are responsible for their own fate. Paul has performed the task of watchman over Israel, warning them of what was coming, like Ezekiel (cf. Ezek. 33:1-7; 3:18).[323] It is possible to take καθαρος, which is in an emphatic position in v. 6b, in its ritual sense of "unpolluted," in which case Paul is not merely affirming that he has a clear conscience or is innocent, but that he will not be defiled by going into or staying in a Gentile house.[324]

V. 7 tells us that Paul did not go far once he left the synagogue — in fact he only went next door, to the house of one Titius Justus, who had been a devout Gentile synagogue adherent but apparently now was a convert to Christianity. Besides showing Paul's boldness, this move may also reflect Paul's desire to continue to try and convert Jews, even though he would be outside the synagogue and would be concentrating his efforts on Gentiles.[325] Titius

321. See Marshall, *Acts*, pp. 293-94.
322. Tannehill, *Narrative Unity of Luke-Acts*, 2:222.
323. As Polhill, *Acts*, p. 384, rightly points out, it was the task of the watchman to blow the trumpet when he saw trouble coming, and if some chose not to respond, then the watchman was not responsible for what happened to those who ignored the warning.
324. So Esler, *Community and Gospel*, p. 100.
325. The Western text (D, ith) confuses the issue here by emending the text to suggest that Paul moved his residence from Aquila and Priscilla's house to the house of Titius Justus. This would have been both unnecessary and unlikely. This verse is about Paul moving his venue for preaching. See Metzger, *Textual Commentary*, p. 462. Ramsay, *St. Paul the Traveller*, p. 256, sees Paul's actions as, if not provocative, at least more than ordinary Jews would be able to stand, going next door and continuing to proselytize.

Justus's name in all likelihood indicates he is of Roman extraction. There is no evidence to suggest that we should identify him with the Gaius of Rom. 16:23 who hosted Paul in Corinth on a later occasion, though we cannot completely rule out the possibility, nor does it seem plausible to suggest Titius is an error for Titus, who was an apostolic coworker. We have no evidence Titus was originally a resident of Corinth (cf. 2 Cor. 8:23).[326]

V. 8 informs us that the ἀρχισυνάγωγος, Crispus by name, became a Christian, as did his whole household. It was a notable accomplishment to convert a ruler of a synagogue, and 1 Cor. 1:14-16 confirms his baptism. This verse in addition suggests that once Crispus converted many other Corinthians followed (one would presume Jews and synagogue adherents). One may suspect this precipitated something of a crisis in the synagogue, and what follows in vv. 12ff. is not entirely surprising under such circumstances.

In this sort of volatile atmosphere where danger loomed for Paul, the experience recorded in vv. 9-10 is also not surprising. Paul has a vision of reassurance, intending to steel Paul to stay the course until the work is finished in Corinth, in spite of the opposition and persecution he may face. We may perhaps coordinate v. 9 with 1 Cor. 2:3, which reveals the human face of Paul. It suggests an apostle who was somewhat shell-shocked from the strong opposition he had faced from both his fellow Jews and some Gentiles in various places on this missionary trip, doubtless including Philippi, Thessalonica, and Beroea. Paul had entered into his task at Corinth with some fear and trepidation, but had taken it up nevertheless. Now as trouble loomed large on the horizon, would he leave town under pressure as before, or would he stay the course? This vision strengthens Paul and prompts the correct decision, as will also be the case on other occasions in the apostle's career (see 23:11; 27:23-24). There is a good deal of similarity between what the voice in the heavenly vision says here and what we find in various commissioning scenes in the OT, though here "the Lord" seems likely to refer to Jesus.[327] The usual pattern is that God or God's representative confronts and commissions (or in this case recommis-

---

326. See Goodspeed, "Gaius Titius Justus." One of the problems with Goodspeed's argument is that while Gaius is to be sure a *praenomen* and Titius is in all likelihood a *nomen,* Paul usually identifies his coworkers more formally than Luke identifies them. But here we have an example of the reverse procedure. There is also no good reason to identify this Titius with Titus, as a few manuscripts (including surprisingly ℵ) do. In all likelihood this correction reflects a scribal tendency to substitute a more familiar Christian name. See Metzger, *Textual Commentary,* pp. 462-63. Here as elsewhere Luke tends to mention by name those of relatively high status that are converts.

327. Marshall, *Acts,* p. 296, is right to point out how Christ in Acts (and elsewhere in the NT) fulfills the functions God undertook in the OT. In other words, this scene is no less a theophany than the ones recorded in the OT, which strongly suggests something about Luke's own Christology.

sions) someone for a task, reassuring that person of aid or protection or both, after which it is recorded that the task is carried out (which is the function of v. 11, see below). Our narrative, then, may be profitably compared to Exod. 3:2-12; Josh. 1:1-9; Isa. 41:10-14, and perhaps especially Jer. 1:5-10, as well as to such earlier texts in Acts as 5:17-21; 9:10-18; 16:6-10.[328] The Greek should probably be translated here "Stop being afraid (present imperative) . . . go on speaking; don't be silent."[329] The reassurance in v. 10 would be particularly welcome and timely. Notice that the text does not say that no one would lay hands on Paul, only that no one would do so with harm resulting.[330] V. 10 is also important for indicating that God has many in this city who are "my people." Λαος here as in 15:14 is used of God's new or, better said, true people, which includes Gentiles as well as Jews.[331] A great work remained to be done in Corinth, and so *v. 11* indicates that Paul stayed in the city a total of eighteen months, probably between the fall of A.D. 50 and the spring of A.D. 52.[332]

V. 12 indicates that when Gallio was proconsul of the province of Achaia various non-Christian Jews banded together and brought Paul before this official. Gallio was the son of Marcus Annaeus Seneca, a notable Spanish rhetorician, and more importantly was the younger brother of the famous Stoic philosopher and politician Lucius Annaeus Seneca (4 B.C.–A.D. 65). Both these brothers were born in Cordova around the time of the inception of the Christian era. Our Gallio obtained the name Lucius Junius Gallio because during the reign of Claudius he came to Rome with his father and was adopted by the famous rhetorician of this name. Thereafter he had a somewhat notable political career. Gallio's brother Seneca speaks highly of him ("No human is so pleasant to any person as Gallio is to everyone" — *Nat. Quaest.* 4a, Preface 11) and Dio Cassius remarks about his wit (*Hist. of Rome* 61.35), but neither of these friendly sources should cause us to ignore that like his brother, who spoke of Jews as a *gens sceleratissima,* and for that matter like many Romans of higher status, he was anti-Semitic.[333]

328. See the discussion in Hubbard, "Commissioning Accounts in Acts."

329. See Bruce, *The Acts of the Apostles*, p. 394.

330. Johnson, *Acts*, p. 324, is right that we should see a result rather than a purpose clause, for those who later lay hands on Paul do indeed intend to harm him.

331. We may perhaps contrast the usage of the term in Acts 2:47; 3:9; 4:10; 5:13. See Longenecker, *Acts*, p. 484.

332. It is true that one could read v. 11 as referring to the time which elapsed up to the appearance before Gallio, after which Paul stayed a while longer (v. 18). In light of vv. 9-10, it is, however, probably better to see v. 11 as a statement of the entire length of the stay, indicating the extent of Paul's obedience to the vision. In this case, v. 18 is simply referring to the same period of time as v. 11, and indicates that this period of a year and a half included some time after the appearance before Gallio. On the chronological issues see pp. 537ff. above, and Haacker, "Die Gallio-Episode und die paulinische Chronologie."

333. See the discussion in Pesch, *Die Apostelgeschichte (Apg. 13–28)*, pp. 150-51.

We know that Gallio's time as proconsul in Corinth was brief, for we are told by his brother that he had to leave the province due to a fever (*Ep. Mor.* 104.1), and in any case the length of tenure of a proconsul in such an office was only about two years. Fortunately, the rescript of Claudius to the citizens at Delphi (*SIG* 3 no. 801) helps us fix a date for Gallio's appearance in Corinth. The rescript mentions the twenty-sixth acclamation of Claudius as emperor, which occurred during the first seven months of A.D. 52.[334] The rescript probably dates to May or June of A.D. 52 and implies Gallio is no longer in office. It was Claudius's policy (cf. Dio Cassius, *Hist.* 60.17.3) to send out his proconsuls from Rome no later than mid-April, which means Gallio probably arrived in Corinth not later than May A.D. 51.[335]

Luke does not tell us when Paul appeared before Gallio, whether it was at the beginning of his tenure or not, but it is clear enough it is after Paul has been in town for some time. Probably we should think of this event as having occurred in the fall of A.D. 51. The word βῆμα in v. 12 probably refers to the judgment seat (cf. 2 Cor. 5:10) which has been found at the center of the lower terrace of the Corinthian forum.[336]

The accusation made against Paul is recorded in *v. 13*, and is in itself somewhat ambiguous. Does it refer to the Roman law or the Jewish law that Paul is persuading people to violate by the sort of worship he is advocating? Three factors point to the Jewish law being in view: (1) the reference to the worship of God (singular); (2) the reaction of Gallio that this is an internal matter about "your own law" (v. 15); (3) the emphasis on Paul's work in the synagogue and his teaching Jews that the Messiah was Jesus (v. 5).

It is possible that the Jews deliberately made the charge ambiguous, hoping that Gallio would think Paul had offended against Roman religion.[337] It may also be the case that they were suggesting that Paul was preaching a new religion that was illicit, not a form of Judaism, and thus upsetting the Jewish community whom Claudius had said had a right to be allowed to practice their own religious customs in peace. In either of the latter two cases, they could hope Gallio would intervene to preserve order by punishing or expelling Paul.

---

334. See the discussion of Bruce, *The Acts of the Apostles*, p. 395.

335. See Oliver, "The Epistle of Claudius." There is no good reason to follow Lüdemann's suggestion (*Paul, Apostle to the Gentiles*, pp. 158-73) that the Gallio incident came on Paul's later visit to Corinth. He wishes to date the first visit to A.D. 41, based on a dubious coordination of Suetonius's word about the riots in Rome and Acts 18:1-2. This puts Paul in Corinth at an impossibly early date on Paul's own showing (cf. Galatians 1–2).

336. On the archaeology of Corinth, see my *Conflict and Community in Corinth*, pp. 48-52.

337. Notice the ambiguous use of "people" in v. 13, which could mean Jews or Gentiles or both.

The bema in Corinth where Paul was judged by Gallio.

Neither of these wished-for outcomes happened. Gallio sees the charges as not being about a matter of real crime or serious fraud or deception (ῥαδιούργημα, see Acts 13:10),[338] but a dispute about "words and names and law as observed by you" *(v. 15)*. Nor was any possible allusion to Claudius's

338. V. 14 is in the form of a contrary to fact conditional sentence. See Johnson, *Acts*, p. 328.

earlier rulings about Jews and their right to worship appropriate since Paul was a Jew, as even his opponents couldn't dispute, and not an outsider trying to prevent Jews from worshiping their God. In other words, this complaint is seen by Gallio as not being about actions, but about Jewish religious or philosophical debate.

Gallio says he would have been justified to accept and act on this complaint if it had to do with criminal behavior. Instead he returns the matter to the plaintiffs with the dismissive "see to it yourselves," and with the formal phrase, correctly recorded here, "I do not wish to be the judge of this matter." As Sherwin-White noted, this is "the precise answer of a Roman magistrate refusing to exercise his *arbitrium iudicantis* within a matter *extra ordinem*."[339] It was well within Gallio's competence to decide whether or not to accept an unusual (or suspicious) charge that fell outside the normal system of judgments and punishments, and in this case he refuses to do so.[340] In doing this Gallio has implicitly recognized that the Jewish community had a right to settle internal matters themselves. It has also been suggested that by refusing to rule, Gallio refused to recognize that Christianity was an "illicit" religion or a "superstition." This is true, but, as Polhill says, we "should not see Gallio's action as taking Paul's side, however. Paul would have been ejected along with the Jews."[341]

As Cassidy has pointed out, there are several clues in the narrative to suggest that we should not see Gallio as any friend of the Jews. Besides his refusal to hear their case, which apparently included not even allowing Paul to testify, the way he addresses them as an ethnic group ("O Jews") probably reflects disdain, and his having the Jews "driven" from the judgment seat and especially his turning a blind eye when Sosthenes is beaten both point to his dislike of Jews and Jewish disputes.[342] In other words, we do not see here a positive portrayal of a Roman official. He may have disregarded the charge out of sheer prejudice, as his not hearing from Paul at all suggests. Since the case was simply dismissed without the defendant even having to or being allowed to defend himself, it is inappropriate to say that Paul was either acquitted or exonerated by Roman justice. Humanly speaking, Paul escapes because of the bias or prejudice of this official, not because the message of the gospel wasn't really upsetting things in the Jewish community in Corinth.

---

339. Sherwin-White, *Roman Law and Roman Society,* p. 102.

340. Proconsuls had considerable latitude in such extralegal or extraordinary matters (matters falling under the heading of *cognitio extra ordinem*). Gallio could dispense justice according to local customs or on the basis of his own considered judgment in such affairs. See ibid., pp. 99-101.

341. Polhill, *Acts,* p. 388.

342. Cassidy, *Society and Politics,* pp. 92-93.

However, from a larger perspective, Paul escapes because God was with him and promised no harm would come to him in Corinth.[343]

Several of the details of this account deserve closer scrutiny. *V. 14* indicates that it was just as Paul was about to open his mouth that Gallio said what he did, dismissing the case. In other words, this verse makes clear that Gallio was not interested in hearing from Paul and ruling on the legitimacy of his actions at all. Equally, he was not interested in ruling against Paul, and this was perhaps politically more important for the ongoing well-being of the Christian movement. It is going too far to say that "Gallio's refusal to act in the matter was tantamount to the recognition of Christianity as a *religio licita*";[344] rather, only the converse of such a conclusion was ruled out or at least not demonstrated on this occasion. As Conzelmann rightly notes, there is no evidence that Romans kept a list of officially recognized religions, from which Christianity could be excluded by failing to include it on the list.[345] In Gallio's eyes, Paul was a Jew and the dispute was a Jewish one, not an intramural debate between two religions. Gallio says nothing, however, about the legitimacy of Paul's arguments or claim to represent true Judaism. Secondly, *v. 16* includes the verb απηλασεν, which as in Ezek. 34:12 (LXX) probably refers to physical expulsion;[346] presumably the lictors would have been called upon to expel the crowd. Thirdly, it is not at all clear who the "all" in *v. 17* is who seized Sosthenes. The Western text, followed by the AV, adds the clarifying words "the Greeks," while several minuscules (307 and 431) read "all the Jews." These clarifying additions bear witness to the ambiguity of the original text, and it is unlikely that either of these readings is original.[347] As to the sense of the text, it could be read either way. On the one hand, it could be argued that what we see here is an anti-Semitic outburst perpetrated by Greeks on the Jewish leader, to which Gallio turns a blind eye. On the other hand, it is also quite possible in an honor/shame situation as this was that Jews might beat their own synagogue leader either because

---

343. This episode, while it may be said to suggest that Roman authorities were right not to oppose Christianity since it was a movement that had divine sanction, does not in fact warrant the assumption that Luke is presenting an *apologia* for Christianity to Roman officials, much less an *apologia* for Roman due process of law. The most one can say is that Luke is concerned to show Theophilus how the Romans were right not to oppose the Christian movement, since it was of God. Luke is not arguing that Christianity is politically innocuous, but he may be arguing that it has the proper claims to antiquity, being the legitimate development of Judaism, and so deserves official tolerance. See ibid. Johnson, *Acts,* p. 334, aptly remarks: "Luke's *apologia* is ultimately not for Paul or for the Christian movement or for the Roman Empire, but for the power of God at work in human lives."

344. Longenecker, *Acts,* p. 486.

345. Conzelmann, *Acts,* p. 153.

346. See Johnson, *Acts,* p. 329.

347. See Metzger, *Textual Commentary,* pp. 463-64.

he had shamed them by not successfully prosecuting Paul, and so made them look bad in the eyes of the proconsul, or because Sosthenes was believed to be a Christian sympathizer. This last possibility has led to the conjecture that Sosthenes was later converted to the faith, and left town with Paul, being the man of the same name mentioned in 1 Cor. 1:1 as later writing to the Corinthians. This may well be so. In any case, the text suggests that Paul converted at least one synagogue ruler, and he may have converted another.[348] The narrative concludes by saying that Gallio paid no attention to what happened to Sosthenes. As Tannehill remarks in closing, "Paul is released by Gallio, and this is the result of the Lord's promised protection. Nevertheless, the human instrument of this protection is no model of just and enlightened policy."[349]

V. 18 indicates that Paul stayed on in Corinth after the Gallio episode for an undefined but apparently considerable number of days.[350] We may suspect that Paul stayed until the sailing season began in the early spring, though he may have left in the late fall, if his meeting with Gallio transpired in the summer.[351] We are told in this same verse that, having said farewell to the believers in Corinth, Paul sailed for Syria, accompanied by Priscilla and Aquila. It is quite possible, as Haenchen has pointed out, that Luke is here using a provincial designation as he seems to do elsewhere, in which case the fact that the sea voyage ends in Caesarea would not necessarily indicate a failure to arrive at the intended destination.[352] Palestine, including Caesarea, was politically a part of the province of Syria, and Luke seems to be well aware of this fact (see Luke 2:2-3). It is nevertheless also possible that Luke intended that the term "Syria" allude to Syria proper, for Paul is said to visit Antioch in v. 22.

Before departing on this sea voyage, Paul, we are told, had his hair cut

---

348. Some scholars, such as Lüdemann, *Early Christianity,* p. 200, have been adamant that a synagogue had only one ruler at a time, despite texts like Acts 13:15, and the fact that the title could in some cases be carried for life as honorific or hereditary. This dogmatism is unjustified. For instance, *CII* 587 mentions an infant head of a synagogue, who could not have actually functioned in that capacity. Two inscriptions (*CII* 584, 1404) mention synagogue heads who were sons of synagogue heads. Notice how in *CII* 766 we have listed together both a synagogue head for life, a synagogue head, and an archon, suggesting these could be distinguished. On all this see Brooten, *Women Leaders,* pp. 5-33.

349. Tannehill, *Narrative Unity of Luke-Acts,* 2:229.

350. Ἱκανος literally means "enough" but often has the sense of "many," as is likely the case here.

351. This is quite possible. It may be that the Jewish leaders wished to take advantage of Gallio while he was new at this post, and before he heard anything adverse about their community. If this was their aim, Gallio disappointed them.

352. See Haenchen, *Acts,* p. 542.

off at the eastern Corinthian port of Cenchreae.[353] Luke does not explain either the timing or purpose of this action, and though there were pagan rituals involving the dedication of hair which had remain uncut for the duration of a vow,[354] it is most unlikely that this is alluded to here. In all likelihood we are to think of this as Paul fulfilling a Nazaritic vow which he had earlier made. Though some have suggested that Paul cut off his hair to begin a vow, the evidence as it stands suggests that the hair cutting was to transpire at the end of the period of the vow (see Num. 6:1-21; *m. Nazir* 1.1–9.5; Josephus, *War* 15.1). Strictly speaking, such a vow had to be fulfilled at Jerusalem, where the hair would be presented as a burnt offering and a sacrifice would be offered as well. This may explain Paul's desire to go on to Jerusalem, rather than stay in Ephesus. Jews tended to make vows to thank God for past blessings or as petitions for future ones. Probably we should relate the vow here to Paul's thankfulness for being kept from harm in Corinth, and perhaps we should think of Paul taking the vow to remain unshorn in response to the vision he had.[355]

Various scholars have objected to this incident on either historical or theological grounds. The historical grounds are that one could not fulfill such a vow outside of Jerusalem. While it is true that the final sacrifice connected with the vow had to be made in Jerusalem, the cutting off of the hair could in fact transpire elsewhere, as is the case here (see *m. Nazir* 3.6; 5.4), and in any event Paul appears to have gone up to Jerusalem, presumably, along with other purposes, to complete the vow (see below).[356] Haenchen argues that the historical Paul would not have undertaken such a vow because it violated his notions of grace.[357] This might be the case if Paul had undertaken a vow in order to obtain certain blessings from God, but the evidence suggests that the vow was an act of response, in gratitude for the safety God had guaranteed Paul during his time in Corinth. One may make the further point that 1 Cor. 9:20 must have some concrete meaning, and the taking of a Nazaritic vow would not have violated Paul's

353. There was a local Christian community in this port city. See Rom. 16:1. The verb κείρω here means to cut with scissors, whereas in 21:24 ξυρέω is used, which means to shave. See Bruce, *The Acts of the Apostles*, p. 398.

354. See *New Docs*, 1 (1976) no. 4, p. 24; and *New Docs*, 3 (1978), no. 46.

355. See Marshall, *Acts*, p. 300.

356. This apparently, to judge from later Mishnaic rules (which is always precarious for our period), would have required him to stay in Jerusalem for thirty days.

357. Haenchen, *Acts*, p. 546. Interestingly, trying to be more specific since the Greek is somewhat ambiguous about the antecedent, the Latin Cod. h has Aquila cutting off his hair, while the Vulgate has both Aquila and Priscilla doing it. But as Longenecker, *Acts*, p. 490, says, Luke is economical and usually does not provide such details about minor characters in the story. What would be the point of mentioning such a thing in passing here?

commitment to a gospel that rejected a requirement of circumcision and keeping kosher. In fact this vow is a purely voluntary act in any case, and it simply shows that Paul did not completely cease being a Jew when he became a Christian. The historical Paul could well have submitted to this rite, just as we know in fact that he voluntarily submitted to other Jewish rites and customs (see, e.g., 2 Cor. 11:22-24).[358]

Vv. 19-21 are elliptical, and this section of the text probably provides another piece of evidence that the book did not receive the sort of final editing that Luke's Gospel did. The phrase "he left them [i.e., Aquila and Priscilla] there" in Ephesus presumably should have come in v. 21, before "Then he set sail from Ephesus."[359] It is not implausible, especially if Paul had to wait for his boat to depart for "Syria" from Ephesus, that he briefly visited the synagogue in Ephesus and dialogued there, laying the groundwork for a planned return visit in the not too distant future. One may also suspect that while Priscilla and Aquila no doubt carried out business in Ephesus, Paul had primarily left them there to adequately lay the groundwork for his missionary efforts when he returned.

V. 20 indicates that the initial response was not unfavorable, for Paul was asked by the Jews to stay longer but could not, especially since the time between the beginning of sailing season and the start of Passover was short. In A.D. 52 it fell in early April, and the seas only opened for navigation March 5-10.[360] In A.D. 53 Passover fell on March 22.[361] He told them, however, using a phrase familiar to both Jews and Gentiles in the ancient world, that "if God wills" (see Epictetus, *Diss.* 1.1.17; Josephus, *Ant.* 7.373; 1 Cor. 4:19; 16:7; Heb. 6:3; Jas. 4:15) he would return to them.

---

358. Johnson, *Acts,* p. 330, conjectures that what is meant is that Paul was cutting his hair *prior* to beginning the Nazaritic vow period. This is possible, especially if one takes the verb as a strict imperfect ("he was making").

359. Various texts, chiefly Western ones, saw the problem here and placed the reference to Paul leaving Aquila in Ephesus at this later spot in the text. Unfortunately some of these texts failed to delete the phrase from v. 19 and make a straight transfer, thus creating a redundancy. It is also telling that some of these Western texts deliberately leave Priscilla out when making this transfer — probably another piece of evidence of the antifeminist bias of the Western text. See Metzger, *Textual Commentary,* p. 465.

360. Here again note the emphasis on dialogue or debate in the synagogue. See pp. 480ff. above. The Western text offers a clarification that may well be the right one, suggesting that Paul was eager to get to Jerusalem in time for one of the Jewish feasts. See Metzger, *Textual Commentary,* p. 465. On the opening of the seas on March 10 see Vegetius, *On Military Affairs* 4.39.

361. This fact may favor the conclusion that Paul made this journey in A.D. 52, if he intended to make the feast, for March 5-22 plus the foot journey of some sixty-five miles from Caesarea to Jerusalem is surely too short a period of time to make such a trip from Ephesus.

V. 22 tells us that the sea voyage which set out from Ephesus landed at Caesarea. While it is possible that this was not the intended destination but had to be accepted because of prevailing northeastern winds,[362] Luke gives no hint of a detour. Ramsay was surely right that the language of going up and going down found in v. 22 surely refers to Paul's going up to Jerusalem, especially when coupled with the reference to *the church* (cf. 3:1; 8:5; 11:27). One does not go "down" from a seaside city like Caesarea to an inland city like Antioch, but this is an apt description of the journey from Mount Zion to Antioch.[363] Presumably Paul stayed long enough to finish his vow and report to the church in Jerusalem, as well as "greet" them.

We are told in *v. 23* that Paul, after spending some time in Antioch, departed and went overland from Antioch into Asia Minor through regions he had visited before, "strengthening all the disciples." This last phrase strongly favors the conclusion that we are basically not talking about Paul going to north Galatia on this journey, but revisiting previously evangelized areas. The phrase Γαλατικην χωραν και Φρυγιαν has been much debated, and it may well mean nothing other than what the phrase in Acts 16:6 means, especially since Luke is famous for his "stylistic variations" of phrases that essentially have the same meaning.[364] There are, however, three notable differences in the way of putting the matter here: (1) here Phrygia is used substantively rather than adjectivally; (2) here the term "region" is coupled only with "Galatian," whereas in 16:6 it follows the mention of both regional terms, which may suggest a distinction is meant here; (3) the term καθεξης rightly is said to point to the author, meaning the visiting of two distinct districts (see Luke 1:3, where it means "in order").[365] Hemer's conjecture may well be right: "I am now inclined to think that 'the Galatian country' is resumptive of 16.6, and refers generally to Paul's sphere of work in ('South') Galatia and that 'Phrygia' (here, but not there, a noun) is appended loosely *in the awareness that Phrygia extended into the province of Asia, beyond Galatia in any sense, and on Paul's present route towards Ephesus.* Possibly Luke knew of Paul's preaching on this journey in Asian Phrygia in e.g. Apamea Cibotus or Eumenea, major cities on or near the route implied by a likely geographical interpretation of 19.1."[366]

In any case, this trip through the Cilician gates and on to Ephesus will have had to transpire during the spring and summer when the passage through

362. See Haenchen, *Acts*, p. 547; Pesch, *Die Apostelgeschichte (Apg. 13–28)*, p. 156. There is nothing in the text to suggest a detour, nor anything to suggest this journey transpired during the summer when such winds were strong, but see *Beginnings*, 4:231.

363. See Ramsay, *St. Paul the Traveller*, p. 264.

364. See pp. 477ff. above.

365. See Haenchen, *Acts*, p. 545.

366. Hemer, *Book of Acts*, p. 120, emphasis mine. On 19:1 see below.

the gates was possible, apparently the summer of A.D. 53.[367] It was a long and arduous journey of some fifteen hundred miles, undertaken on foot. This strongly suggests that whatever other calculations we make, it is unlikely Paul *arrived* in Ephesus before the fall of A.D. 53.

It is well to ask at this juncture what the function of vv. 18-23 is. Luke could easily have simply omitted the reference to the journey to Jerusalem and Antioch and simply said that sometime later Paul returned to Ephesus, and then continued the account of missionary work in Ephesus begun in vv. 19-20. Here we are helped by Tannehill, who, rightly in my judgment, points out that Luke wants to make clear that Paul was accountable and kept contact with the church's old centers. "Paul is not a loner, founding a separate, Pauline church, but a major figure in the one mission which began in Jerusalem and was effectively continued from Antioch. . . . [While in] Jerusalem he simply greets the church, . . . in Antioch he spends some time (18.22-23). The stay in Antioch appropriately rounds off a missionary journey that had begun there (15.35-41)." Tannehill goes on to make the valuable point that Paul's work included not only conversion of new disciples but also strengthening of those already converted. "Once churches have been established in an area, Paul will visit them again in order to strengthen them. Only then is Paul's work in an area relatively complete."[368]

Thus the motif of disciples being strengthened is a boundary marker, indicating the completing of one missionary task and the transition to a further work. What this means is that, while Paul could view his work in Galatia (and Cilicia) as complete after this journey through these regions, there was still unfinished work, more "strengthening" to be completed in Macedonia and Greece. This latter task Paul undertakes by taking the circuitous route from Ephesus to Jerusalem by way of these Greek regions near the end of his third missionary journey (see 19:21; 20:1-3).[369] Finally, we should note the recurrent pattern of Paul's three missionary journeys.[370] Each journey began in Antioch and can be said to end either in Jerusalem or in Antioch. Luke gives us one major speech during the course of recounting each journey — in Pisidian Antioch to Jews during the first journey, in Athens to Gentiles during the

---

367. The summer of A.D. 52 is not impossible, but seems unlikely because Paul stayed beyond the time of his judgment in Corinth, and he also spent some time in Antioch, to which we must add the time of the journey to get back to Jerusalem and Antioch. Much depends on when Gallio judged Paul — was it in A.D. 51 near the beginning of his tenure in Corinth, or in A.D. 52? When he arrived in Ephesus also depends on how long he spent strengthening his previously established churches in Derbe, Lystra, Iconium, and Pisidian Antioch.

368. Tannehill, *Narrative Unity of Luke-Acts*, 2:230.

369. Here I am following ibid., p. 231.

370. See Polhill, *Acts*, p. 391 n. 130.

second, at Miletus to Christians during the third. This reflects careful structuring by Luke of his source material.

Thus the narrative turns to Ephesus, an extremely important city that Paul had wanted to reach on his second missionary journey, but he had initially been thwarted and then had been able to visit only briefly. As we shall see, the importance of this city for Paul's missionary work should not be underestimated. "Ephesus is not just another stop in a series. It is Paul's last major place of new mission noted in the last stage of Paul's work as a free man."[371] Here Paul was to stay for some three years to establish the Christian faith in this region. It is no wonder that Luke pays considerable attention to what happened there in 18:24ff.

371. Ibid.

XI. The Third Wave — The Last Missionary Efforts (Acts 18:24–21:26)

A. The Ephesus Chronicles — Part 1: Apollos (18:24-28)

It becomes apparent, on a close reading of Acts 18:24–20:38, that it is in various ways not all that useful to speak of a third missionary *journey*. For one thing we are told at 19:10 that Paul was in Ephesus for at least two additional years after already spending three months teaching in the synagogue there (Acts 19:8; cf. 1 Cor. 15:32; 16:8). The material we find in this section of Acts focuses almost entirely on Ephesus and its immediate environs. Even when Paul leaves Ephesus to strengthen churches in Macedonia, Greece, and elsewhere in Asia, the section draws to a close by recording a speech to the Ephesian elders in nearby Miletus (20:17-38). As Tannehill has rightly stressed, "Ephesus is not just another stop in a series. It is Paul's last major place of new mission work as a frcc man. . . . The fact that Paul's farewell speech will be addressed to the Ephesian elders is a further indication of the special importance of Ephesus."[1] One must assume that Luke is reliant on Ephesian traditions for what he records in these chapters. It may well be that he received not only these materials but also his information about what transpired in Corinth from Priscilla and Aquila.[2] This would explain his knowledge of the story that begins this "Ephesian" chronicle, which does not involve Paul. Even so, this story in

---

1. Tannehill, *Narrative Unity of Luke-Acts*, 2:231. See the map at the end of the present volume.
2. See Lüdemann, *Early Christianity*, pp. 206-7, on the use of traditions here, and Johnson, *Acts*, p. 335, for Priscilla and Aquila as a possible source here.

18:24-28 when compared with 1 Corinthians 1–4 sheds considerable light on the latter text, and the latter text sheds some light on what we find here, without suggesting that Luke knew 1 Corinthians.[3]

Ephesus, after Corinth, is undoubtedly the most important city Paul sought to evangelize, for it was the hub of all culture and commerce in western Asia, and from Ephesus the church could and did spread out into the interior, following the Roman roads (see the listing of the seven churches in Revelation 2–3 in the order one would reach them following the main road from Ephesus, and Colossians and Philemon).[4]

Ephesus is also, after Corinth, the city about which we are best informed on the basis of literary and archaeological data.[5] Ephesus was not a Roman colony, but had rather retained its status as a "free" city, even though it had come under Roman control in 133 B.C. when Attalus III bequeathed his kingdom to Rome. In addition, since Asia was a senatorial province, emperors generally stayed out of its administrative affairs while at the same time promoting the welfare of the province, not least because it was an enormous source of wealth and other resources. This was true from the time of Augustus through the time of Claudius, the period which concerns us. Since it was the seat of provincial government, the proconsul lived here, along with some 200,000 to 250,000 other residents, making this the largest city of Asia Minor and the third-largest city in the Empire after Rome and Alexandria.

It is important to stress the strategic location of the city, both in terms of the land routes that led to the interior of Asia and the sea routes from Asia west. It is no accident that a Roman "college" of messengers was based in this city, since it was a major connecting link for the Empire's communications network. Lying near the mouth of the Cayster River, Ephesus had been a major commercial port, but the harbor required constant dredging due to the alluvium, and in Paul's day its importance as a port was beginning to wane. Economically, this made the religious tourist trade all the more important, and such tourists continued to come in great numbers to see the Temple of

---

3. Contra Ramsay, *St. Paul the Traveller,* p. 267, who thinks this episode is included to make intelligible the opening of 1 Corinthians! This would require that Theophilus already had 1 Corinthians in front of him, which seems more than a little unlikely.

4. The main Roman road to the East, connecting the eastern and western portions of the Empire, went forth from Ephesus.

5. For a helpful introduction on this subject insofar as it is relevant to NT study see Trebilco, "Asia," 302-57, and also his *Jewish Communities in Asia Minor.* See further Oster, *A Bibliography of Ancient Ephesus,* "Ephesus as a Religious Center," and "Ephesus"; Horsley, "The Inscriptions of Ephesos," who condenses an enormous amount of information found in eight volumes edited by Wankel et al., *Die Inschriften von Ephesos;* Magie, *Roman Rule;* Filson, "Ephesus and the New Testament"; Elliger, *Ephesos;* Arnold, *Ephesians;* Schnackeburg, "Ephesus."

Artemis, one of the great wonders of the ancient world.[6] Of major importance for our purposes is the fact that there was a large Jewish colony in this city (cf. Josephus, *Ant.* 14.225-27; 16.162-68, 172-73).

In *v. 24* Apollos is first mentioned, and mentioned as a Jew. Apollonius is the full form of the name.[7] The evidence suggests Apollos was a rather common name in Egypt, while being virtually unattested elsewhere.[8] That Luke stresses he is a Jew who comes from Alexandria reflects again Luke's ethnographic interests, but it also indicates he came from the large Hellenized Jewish community in that city. In view of the way he is described in this verse (see below) he seems to reflect the general character of well-educated Jews from that city. In particular, Horsley suggests that he may have been a onetime pupil of Philo, which is certainly chronologically possible.[9] That Apollos is identified as a Jew by Luke has fueled the speculation that he is not here presented as a Christian, which is unlikely in light of what else Luke says. The term "Jew" here then would primarily be an ethnic, not a religious term. We do not know when Christianity first came to Alexandria, but perhaps, as Pesch intimates, he may have become a Christian on an occasion when he was visiting other Alexandrian Jews in Jerusalem at the synagogue of the Freedmen (Acts 6:9).[10]

We are told that Apollos was an ανηρ λογιος, which could mean either that he was a learned man (which would comport with classical usage) or an eloquent man, which is more likely in view of Luke's interest in rhetoric and in view of the highly rhetorical age in which he wrote.[11] His learning is referred to in the next phrase used to describe him and later in vv. 25 and 28 — he is "powerful in the writings" (of Scripture, see v. 28).

What are we to make of *v. 25?* Is this a description of someone who knows some things about Jesus but is not yet a full-fledged Christian, or is Apollos described as a Christian who simply did not know about the practice of Christian baptism? J. Munck thought he was a disciple of John the Baptist;[12] E. Schweizer argued he was simply a Jewish missionary;[13] E. Käsemann sug-

---

6. Unfortunately, though the ruins in general of Ephesus are spectacular, there is nothing left of this temple but one column standing in a rather swampy area.

7. See the text of D, which uses the full form.

8. See *New Docs,* 1 (1976), no. 50, p. 88.

9. Ibid. This might provide further fuel for the popular and plausible conjecture that Apollos was the author of Hebrews, writing to other Hellenized Jewish Christians in a rhetorically, philosophically, and religiously familiar manner.

10. See Pesch, *Die Apostelgeschichte (Apg. 13–28),* p. 160.

11. The meaning "eloquent" is certainly attested for this period; see Demetrius, *De elocutione* 38 (ca. A.D. 50-100); Lucian, *The Cock* 2. This is the way the term was understood by lat syr and the translators of the KJV. Keener, *Bible Background Commentary,* p. 377, suggests it means formally skilled in rhetoric, "the more practical form of advanced learning."

12. Munck, *Acts,* p. 183.

13. Schweizer, "Die Bekehrung des Apollos."

gested he was an unorthodox Alexandrian Christian;[14] and finally various scholars have seen him as a pneumatic or charismatic Christian.[15] Käsemann was right to note that we should compare this story to the one that follows in 19:1-7, where we have various disciples who were baptized into John's baptism, but when we do so, what stands out more is the dissimilarity between Apollos and these other disciples. They have not even heard of the Holy Spirit, whereas Apollos was ζεων τω πνευματι. While this phrase might mean "boiling over in (his own) spirit" and thus indicate he was zealous about his task of religious instructing, this is unlikely on several accounts: (1) the phrase in question should surely be compared to the very similar one in Rom. 12:11 (τω πνευματι ζεοντες), where the reference seems clearly to be to the Holy Spirit; (2) the position of this phrase, between two others which are accurate descriptions of what would be true about a Christian, not merely a Jew, favors the conclusion that the Holy Spirit is meant; (3) Acts 6:10 and 1 Cor 14:2 should also be considered, where the reference is clearly to the Holy Spirit;[16] (4) the failure to mention Apollos's Christian baptism would be a problem if he were not already a Christian, but it is much less of a problem if he is, since for Luke reception of the Spirit and not water baptism is the crucial factor which identifies a person as a Christian (see Acts 10). Furthermore, nowhere else in Acts do we find a Jew who is said to have been instructed in the things of the Lord and teaching accurately the things about Jesus who is *not* also a Christian.

One suspects that various scholars are hesitant to see Apollos as a Christian because of assumptions about Christian baptism and its relationship to the reception of the Holy Spirit, but these assumptions are questionable. In Acts itself we find disciples receiving the Spirit prior to receiving water baptism (Acts 10), and receiving the Spirit after they receive water baptism (Acts 8). Later beliefs about a necessary correlation between "water and Spirit" should not be imposed on Luke or early Christianity. What this text and others in Acts remind us of is that early Christianity did not immediately have a universally recognized and set approach to discipling people.[17] History, even early Christian history, is full of incongruities.

---

14. Käsemann, "The Disciples."

15. See Dunn, *Baptism in the Holy Spirit,* pp. 88-89; M. Wolter, "Apollos und die ephesinischen Johannesjünger (Acts 18.24–19.7)," *ZNW* 78 (1987): 51-73.

16. See Käsemann, "The Disciples," p. 143, on the first two points, and Tannehill, *Narrative Unity of Luke-Acts,* 2:233. Tannehill is also right that Apollos is not being portrayed here as a troublemaker in the church (contra Wolter), but rather a positive contributor to the ongoing missionary work. This is Paul's basic view as well, as 1 Corinthians 3 shows.

17. It is worth pointing out that Christian baptism is not mentioned in the Synoptic Gospels at all apart from the post-Easter example in Matthew 28, and what John 3–4 suggest is not clear. Were Jesus' disciples, who had formerly been John's disciples, simply continuing

The phrase "having been instructed in the way of the Lord" indicates that Apollos had received formal Christian instruction, for the term "Lord" here, as often elsewhere in Acts, probably refers to Jesus. This phrase then explains the one which follows it indicating how he could teach "accurately the things about Jesus." V. 28 likely makes clear at least part of what is meant by this latter phrase, namely, that he was able to show from the Hebrew Scriptures that the Messiah was Jesus. This is perhaps confirmed by the fact that already in v. 24, before he ever met Priscilla and Aquila, Apollos is said to be "powerful in the writings of Scripture," which from Luke's Christian point of view means precisely that he is able to use them christologically in an effective manner (cf. Luke 24:44-49).

Luke then indicates that Apollos has only one deficiency in his knowledge when he comes to Ephesus — he knows only the baptism of John. It seems most likely that this was noticed by Priscilla and Aquila when they heard Apollos teach in the local synagogue, and so they took him aside and explained the "way of God" more accurately to him.[18] The phrase "the way of God" is probably to be contrasted somewhat with the phrase "the things concerning Jesus." The latter refers to the story of Jesus and what was true about him as God's Messiah, while the former would seem primarily to have to do with Christian praxis. That Luke does not tell us explicitly what the content was of the instruction of Apollos suggests that Luke's concern is with the fact that he was taught by this couple. That Apollos's knowledge seems to be an odd combination of Christian and Baptist ideas must count in favor of the earliness and accuracy of Luke's narrative, for in "the transition from Judaism to Christianity it must have been quite possible to find such surprising combinations."[19]

V. 26 indicates that Apollos taught boldly, though not entirely accurately,

---

John's practice during Jesus' ministry, or beginning a rival but identical process? If the Fourth Gospel was written to Christians in the vicinity of Ephesus, it may be that there was considerable confusion about the relationship of the Baptist and Jesus, and the baptisms they endorsed. Is it mere coincidence that Acts 18:24–19:7 suggests such confusion among some in Ephesus and only the Fourth Gospel presents the relationship of Jesus and John and baptism in this fuller manner?

18. Ἀκριβέστερον is probably a true comparison here (but see my *Women in the Earliest Churches*, p. 154), and alludes back to the earlier use of the phrase "way of the Lord" (notice that 323, 945, 1739, 1891, and other witnesses in fact have "way of the Lord" here, though "way of God" is probably the correct reading). The Western text in fact simply has "the way" here, but this is probably an attempt to conform the usage to what we find in 9:2; 19:9, 23; 22:4; 24:14, 22. See Metzger, *Textual Commentary*, p. 467. The use of the term "the way" strongly suggests that matters of practice and not just belief were what was being taught by Apollos and other early Christians. This being so, it was all the more urgent for Apollos to be instructed more accurately.

19. Munck, *Acts*, p. 183.

in the synagogue.[20] That both Priscilla and Aquila instructed Apollos is significant, for Luke wishes to show the variety of roles women played in early Christianity (cf. below on Acts 21:9).[21] The significance of this episode was not lost on that first great commentator on the book of Acts, John Chrysostom, who says when discussing Acts 18:18-19: "He sailed to Syria . . . and with him Priscilla — Lo, a woman also — and Aquila. But these he left at Ephesus with good reason, namely that they should teach."[22] This couple is portrayed as Paul's coworkers.[23] The obvious question to ask about this text is why Priscilla and Aquila had not baptized Apollos, or at least why Luke did not care to record the event if they had and he knew of it.

It is possible, as Bruce points out, that they might have thought it unnecessary, since he already had the Holy Spirit.[24] It may also be that they thought that John's baptism was valid as a foreshadowing of Christian baptism, and perhaps Apollos had undergone that baptism. It is interesting that we have no evidence that the Twelve ever received Christian baptism, and it is even more interesting that Paul not only seems to imply that not all of his converts were baptized but also that he was glad, under the circumstances in Corinth, that this was the case (see 1 Cor. 1:14-17). All of this cautions us against assuming that later beliefs about the necessity of Christian baptism, even its necessity for salvation, were shared by all or perhaps even most early Christians.

---

20. The use of the verb ηρξατο here should be compared to the usage in several other places in Luke-Acts, in particular Luke 4:21 and Acts 1:1. It seems unlikely in any of these cases that the verb means that the person in question started to do something but was then interrupted or did not complete it. Accordingly this should be seen as an example of Lukan stylistic variation that simply means he taught in the synagogue, not that he merely began to teach. See above on Acts 1:1, pp. 105ff. Ακριβεστερον is probably an elative comparative, which means that Apollos was not so much corrected by Priscilla and Aquila, as more adequately informed by them.

21. See also my *Women in the Earliest Churches*, pp. 153-54, and the excursus above, pp. 334ff.

22. See G. B. Stevens's translation in the *Nicene and Post-Nicene Fathers*, vol. 11 (Grand Rapids: Eerdmans, 1975), p. 145. The conjecture that only Priscilla taught Apollos is based on a reconstruction of Chrysostom's text of Acts 18:26, and is probably incorrect in view of the manuscript evidence of Acts itself, but see Blass, "Priscilla und Aquila"; cf. Schumacher, "Aquila und Priscilla." What is true is that the Western text (here D, itgig, syr, copsa arm, and others) once again has tried to diminish the significance of the role of a woman, in this case Priscilla, by inserting the name Aquila without including Priscilla at vv. 3, 18, 21, and here in v. 26 by placing Aquila's name first, intimating that he took the lead in this teaching activity. See Metzger, *Textual Commentary*, pp. 466-67.

23. It is clear that the identity of Apollos and of his Christian teachers is of importance to Luke. That Luke presents Priscilla as involved in a positive way in teaching this important early Christian figure implies he approves of such activities by a Christian woman.

24. See Bruce, *The Acts of the Apostles*, p. 403.

V. 27 indicates that Apollos desired to evangelize elsewhere, in the province of Achaia. There was, however, already a Christian community there, a community which would not know Apollos. For this reason the believers in Ephesus, which surely must include Priscilla and Aquila, perhaps especially them,[25] wrote Apollos a letter of introduction. These letters took a remarkably regular form during this era (see, e.g., P. Oxy. 787 from A.D. 16, or P. Oxy. 292 from A.D. 25), and we probably have at least a part of one in Rom. 16:1-2 (cf. 3 John 12).[26] This was at least in part because there were manuals indicating how such letters should be written if they were to be considered proper and valid.[27] What these letters did was secure entry of someone unknown to the recipients into their household or group (cf. Acts 15:22-29, and possibly 2 Corinthians 8). Often the letter would include a request for hospitality or whatever other forms of aid the bearer of the letter might need (usually in the form "help him in whatever he needs from you," see Rom. 16:2). In v. 27 we are told that the Ephesian believers wished to encourage Apollos in his efforts and so wrote the Christians in Achaia to welcome him.

In *v. 27b* we find an interesting phrase that seems to reflect Luke's knowledge of the Pauline message. We are told that on his arrival, Apollos was a great help to those who had come to believe through God's grace.[28] The help he rendered was apparently not just in teaching those who were already Christians but in doing apologetics. As *v. 28* puts it, he thoroughly refuted the arguments of the Jews in Achaia in public, proving (ἐπιδεικνύς) from the Scriptures that Jesus was the Messiah.[29] This last verse reflects the language of public debate used of a contest in which rhetoric is used, which involves arguments (or "proofs") and refutations offered back and forth to convince the audience.

This portrayal of Apollos, when coupled with v. 24, aids in the understanding of 1 Corinthians 1–4 to a great degree. As I have shown elsewhere,[30] baptism, rhetorical superiority, and pneumaticism were all factors involved in the divisions in Corinth, and it appears that Apollos, unwittingly, had followed

---

25. Nevertheless, Pesch, *Die Apostelgeschichte (Apg. 13–28)*, p. 162, is right that the word "believers" surely means more than just this couple; it suggests that they and Apollos, and perhaps also earlier Paul in his brief stay in Ephesus, had already had some success in making converts in Ephesus.

26. See the helpful discussion in Keyes, "The Greek Letter of Introduction."

27. Ibid., pp. 40-42, discusses these.

28. The position of the phrase δια της χαριτος surely favors this rendering, rather than the suggestion that the meaning is "he greatly helped through grace (which *he* had) the believers." But see Bruce, *The Acts of the Apostles*, p. 404; Marshall, *Acts*, p. 304; and contrast Polhill, *Acts*, p. 398.

29. As often is the case, the Western text expands this to "reasoning and proving."

30. See *Conflict and Community in Corinth*, pp. 82-86.

Paul in Corinth, had been his usual eloquent self, and had furthered comparisons between his *ethos* and oral presentation of the gospel and Paul's, to the latter's disadvantage. This is why Paul takes pains to stress he and Apollos work together and are not in a rhetorical contest to see who can win more converts or personal adherents through speaking and baptizing (see 1 Cor. 1:12; 3:4). This unintended outcome of Apollos's visit to Corinth is also supported by the brief mention in 1 Cor. 16:12 that Apollos was apparently reluctant to return to Corinth. The problem lay primarily with the Corinthians and their expectations in regard to rhetorical performance and spiritual dynamics.

B. The Ephesus Chronicles — Part 2: The Baptist's Disciples (19:1-7)

There is no doubt that Luke grouped 18:24-28 and 19:1-7 together for a reason, intending a comparison. The point of similarity between the stories is of course the connection of both Apollos and "the disciples" with John the Baptist's baptism. The question is whether there is an even greater similarity between the two tales. Are both stories about Christians whose understanding is in some ways defective, or do the two stories diverge at this point? We will say more on this shortly, but for now it is in order to note with Tannehill that the larger issue which primarily prompted the inclusion of these two stories is the issue of the ongoing Baptist movement and its relationship to or with Christianity.[31] The Baptist movement seems to have continued well into the fourth century A.D. and certainly would still have been an issue when Luke wrote Acts.[32] Furthermore, these two stories in Acts speak of Baptist influence in as diverse places as Alexandria and Ephesus. It is then wrong to underestimate the importance for Luke of clarifying this issue. As Johnson points out, this is now the fifth occasion when John's role as precursor to Jesus has been clarified in Acts, indicating the matter's ongoing importance (see 1:5; 11:16; 13:25; 18:25).[33] What the relationship of Christianity to a sectarian Jewish baptizing movement was, was a critical matter not just because of the relationship between Jesus and John, and the Jewish origins of Christianity, but because of the ongoing similarity in the rituals of the two groups, especially since in the

31. Tannehill, *Narrative Unity of Luke-Acts*, 2:233-34.
32. On the relationship of Jesus and John see my *The Christology of Jesus*, pp. 34-56, and Meier, *A Marginal Jew*, 2:1ff. On the ongoing Baptist movement see Scobie, *John the Baptist*, pp. 187-202, and on the possible polemics of Christianity against the Baptist movement see Lichtenberger, "Taufergemeinden und frühchristliche Tauferpolemik im letzen Drittel des I. Jahrhunderts."
33. Johnson, *Acts*, p. 338.

Greco-Roman world rituals were widely seen as the essence or definitive aspect of religion.

The passage begins by picking up the narrative thread from 18:23 with a further reference to Paul's journeying to Ephesus. *19:1* tells us that while Apollos was away from Ephesus in Corinth, Paul passed through the interior regions or districts in order to reach Ephesus. While this could mean that Paul passed through the Lycus and Maeander valleys on the main road to Ephesus, Col. 1:7 and 2:1 suggest Paul was not the founder of the Christian community in Colossae, but rather it was founded by one of his coworkers, Epaphras. Instead Paul may have taken a higher road farther north, leaving the main road at Apamea.[34]

We are told that when Paul arrived in Ephesus he found some disciples. The question is — whose disciples? E. Käsemann argued strongly that these disciples were in fact disciples of John, not Christians, but that Luke has portrayed them as rather strange Christians, or on the fringes of the Christian movement.[35] It has been objected to the view that they were non-Christians that Luke could hardly have meant John's disciples without further qualifying the word "disciples" in view of its widespread use of Christians in Acts. This last argument is not cogent for several reasons. In the first place, this is the only place in Luke-Acts where the word μαθητας is used without the definite article.[36] Elsewhere Luke does use this very term for disciples of John the Baptist (see Luke 5:33; 7:18-19).[37] To the complaint that further qualification of what sort of disciples they were is needed to conclude they were non-Christians, we may note that Luke proceeds to indicate this by referring to the fact that they had experienced only John's baptism (v. 3). Finally, from Luke's own point of view, having received the Holy Spirit was the *sine qua non* of being a Christian (see Acts 11:17), and these disciples have not even heard of the Spirit's coming![38] One must conclude that Luke believed they were not Christians, and there is no sound reason to think he was wrong.[39] There is no

34. See Bruce, *The Acts of the Apostles*, p. 405.

35. Käsemann, "The Disciples."

36. See Dunn, *Baptism in the Holy Spirit*, pp. 83-88.

37. Luke is not much given to using technical terms, or vocabulary, in an exclusively Christian sense. Note, for example, how he speaks of Simon as having believed something (8:13) but not becoming a Christian (see pp. 285ff. above), or how the sons of Sceva are seen as exorcising demons in Jesus' name. The point is that the terminology alone does not tell the tale.

38. See Marshall, *Acts*, p. 305.

39. Käsemann's logic fails precisely because Luke is interested in portraying the *conversion* of various sorts of groups on the fringes of Judaism to Christianity (as is shown by his interest in the Samaritans and the Ethiopian eunuch in Acts 8). There was no reason for him to hide the fact that these disciples were *not* Christians. See rightly Haenchen, *Acts*, p. 557, who notes Luke's desire to portray Paul as converting members of the sects.

reason to resort to the suggestion that the story is told from Paul's point of view and they *appeared* to be disciples to him, at least at first.[40]

Paul's question, found in *v. 2*, gets right to the heart of the matter — "Did you receive the Holy Spirit when you became believers?" The answer to this question would determine whether they were Christians or not. The reply should probably be translated literally, "But we have not heard if the Spirit is."[41] The reply then could mean they had not heard that the Spirit is now manifest, present, given, or poured out (see the similar phrase in John 7:39). This would be understandable if they had had little or no contact with Christians prior to meeting Paul. The more difficult reading is that they are claiming not even to have heard there *was* a Holy Spirit. This is hardly likely if they were Jews, much less if they were disciples of the Baptist, who likely spoke of the Spirit (see Luke 3:16).[42]

The disciples' response led to a further question from Paul *(v. 3)* — "Into what then were you baptized?"[43] This way of putting matters is interesting and seems to have been common in early Christianity (see Rom. 6:3; 1 Cor. 1:13, 15; 10:2; 12:13; Gal. 3:27).[44] The image is of being immersed in the Spirit, surrounded by the Spirit's presence as if it were the very air the Christian breathed. The disciples, however, had only been baptized into John's baptism. This was in Paul's mind inadequate, but he does not suggest that John's baptism was of no value at all. Rather, *v. 4* explains that John's baptism was preparatory, it was a baptism of repentance which itself was a form of preparation for what was to come thereafter. He reminds the disciples that John had told people to believe in the one who was to come after him, and Paul now identifies this one as Jesus (see Luke 3:16; 7:19).

The response of the disciples to this preaching was immediate. *V. 5* says they were baptized in the name of the Lord Jesus. The sequence of v. 5 followed by *v. 6* makes quite clear that the disciples did not receive the Holy Spirit by means of water baptism. Rather, the Spirit came when Paul laid hands on these

40. But see Haacker, "Einige Fälle von 'Erlebter Rede' im Neuen Testament."

41. The Western reviser, in order to make the text easier to understand, has instead: "We have not even heard whether people are receiving the Holy Spirit." See Metzger, *Textual Commentary,* p. 469.

42. Notice that the disciples refer to the Spirit as if they understand the concept, and Paul does not bother to explain the meaning of the term "Spirit."

43. It is right to note the connection here between the Holy Spirit and baptism, not as synonymous but as being closely associated with one another when one is dealing with persons entering the Christian community for the first time. See pp. 279ff. above on the relationship of water and Spirit. It is clear enough that Luke does not wish to suggest either that the Spirit always came with the water, or that there was a uniform order of events since we see the order "water, then Spirit" in Acts 8 and its converse in Acts 10.

44. See Johnson, *Acts,* p. 337.

disciples,[45] and the evidence that this in fact had happened was that the disciples spoke in tongues and prophesied.[46] This is much like what we find in Acts 8 with the Samaritans (see Acts 8:17). The narrative concludes by informing us that there were about twelve persons involved in this baptizing and laying on of hands.[47] This is the only example in all of the NT where rebaptism is mentioned,[48] and the text makes quite clear that we are not talking about one form or act of Christian baptism being supplemented by another. John's baptism, while valid and valuable as a baptism of repentance, was not Christian baptism. The conjecture by Longenecker, that John's baptism was seen as sufficient in the case of Apollos when it was understood as pointing forward to Jesus but not sufficient if it was seen as a rival practice to Christian baptism, is interesting, but Luke does not make this clear.[49]

C. The Ephesus Chronicles — Part 3: Proclamation to Jews and Gentiles (19:8-10)

The further one proceeds in Acts 19, the clearer it becomes that Luke intends the material in this chapter and the next to depict the climax of Paul's ministry and missionary work as a free man.[50] It is here in Ephesus that he has the longest stable period of ministry without trial or expulsion, here that he most fully carries out his commission to be a witness to all persons, both Jew and Gentile (see 22:15). Viewing this material retrospectively on the basis of the content of the Miletus speech in 20:18-35 reinforces the notion that here Luke

45. The laying on of hands is also only sporadically associated in Acts with the receiving of the Spirit; for example, it is not mentioned in Acts 2 or 10. There is no evidence of a regular or formal association of the two being assumed by Christians before about A.D. 200. See Hanson, *Acts*, pp. 190-91.

46. It is clearly the fact (and evidential value) of these manifestations, not the content of the prophesying, that Luke is concerned about, because he does not tell us the content. It is interesting that here we have in the Western text (itp, vgmss, and Ephraem) yet another clarifying addition — they spoke in "*other* tongues and they themselves *knew them, which they also interpreted for themselves; and certain* also prophesied." See Metzger, *Textual Commentary*, p. 470.

47. Luke often uses ὡσεί or ὡς with numbers; see Acts 1:15; 2.4; 4:4; 5:7, 36; 10:3; 13:18, 20; 19:34. Since Luke says "about," it is doubtful there is any symbolic significance in the number twelve despite Johnson's insistence (*Acts*, p. 338).

48. See Parratt, "Rebaptism of the Ephesian Disciples."

49. See Longenecker, *Acts*, p. 494. This entire subsection reflects Luke's style, and it appears clear his sources were not extensive at this point. On his redactional work here see Lüdemann, *Early Christianity*, p. 210, and Wolter, "Apollos und die ephesinischen Johannesjürger," pp. 71-73.

50. See Pereira, *Ephesus*, pp. 138-76.

is intending to present a lasting model of what a universalistic Christian mission ought to look like.[51] The crucial nature of this material is also shown later when it is Jews from Asia who incite the riot in Jerusalem, and they do so because they believed Paul brought an Ephesian Gentile Christian into the temple (21:27-29, see 24:19).[52]

Both from the material in Acts and from 1 Corinthians we learn of the opportunities and opposition to Paul's ministry in Ephesus (cf. Acts 19–20 to 1 Cor. 15:32; 16:9). The letter we call 1 Corinthians was written from Ephesus, apparently toward the end of his time there. Though there is clear enough evidence of opposition to Paul's Ephesian work in both sources, there is no indication that Paul was imprisoned in Ephesus.[53]

The opposition to Paul does not, however, manifest itself immediately. *19:8* tells of Paul's return to the Ephesian synagogue, where he had been previously well received (see 18:19) and of his taking up of the tasks of a rhetorician, the tasks of persuasion in that place. Like Apollos, Paul spoke boldly there (see 18:26), and spoke persuasively (cf. 18:4) about the kingdom of God. This is of course a brief summary of the content of the message which surely also spoke of Jesus as Messiah (18:5, see 28:23).

Though Paul had some success in the synagogue, there were some who grew hardened and disbelieved, like some of the ancient Israelites (Deut. 2:30; 10:16; Ps. 94:8; Isa. 63:17; Jer. 7:26; 17:23; 19:15; cf. Acts 14:2; Rom. 2:5; 9:18). But the opposition was not merely in refusing to respond, it was also active — some spoke ill of "the Way" (see on 9:1-2; 19:23; 22:4; 24:14, 22). Here as elsewhere the active opposition to the gospel causes Paul to move elsewhere,

51. See rightly Tannehill, *Narrative Unity of Luke-Acts,* 2:236.

52. Ibid.

53. First Corinthians 15:32 has sometimes been taken literally, but it is in order to point out that: (1) κατα ανθρωπον probably means "as they say," introducing a familiar proverbial statement; (2) the statement is in the form of a simple conditional remark with ει and not εαν, and there is nothing to require we take it as a contrary to fact condition. When Paul writes 1 Corinthians he is clearly not in prison, and if taken literally the meaning would likely be that at some point in the past he had been taken captive and imprisoned in Ephesus and then thrown to the wild beasts, but had survived and been freed! As Malherbe, *Paul and the Popular Philosophers,* pp. 79-89, has shown, however, the metaphorical sense is much more likely (see Ignatius, *Rom.* 5.1; Appian, *Civil Wars* 2.61; Philo, *Moses* 1.43-44; Plutarch, *Can Virtue Be Taught?* 439), especially as a description of the sage's struggles with opposition (of opponents as beasts see Phil. 3:2; Acts 20:29; Titus 2:12; Ignatius, *Eph.* 7:1; *Smyrn.* 4:1; on Paul's portrayal of himself as an embattled sage see my *Conflict and Community in Corinth,* pp. 388-89), opposition which Paul refers to in 1 Cor. 16:9. This being the case, there is no real historical evidence, direct or indirect, that Paul was imprisoned in Ephesus, and thus no reason to think that he wrote the Captivity Epistles (Philippians, Philemon, and the disputed ones — Colossians, Ephesians) from this locale at this juncture in his ministry. This being the case, Luke's not mentioning an Ephesian imprisonment is no oversight — there probably wasn't one.

though nothing is said here about Paul making a pronouncement about turning to the Gentiles. In fact, in what follows it appears that we are meant to think of Paul continuing to appeal to both Jews and Gentiles. This is in no way surprising, for in Ephesus Paul was about as likely to meet Jews outside the synagogue as inside it. The Jewish community in Ephesus was a large one, the largest in the area, and had been there since the third century B.C. (see Josephus, *Ant.* 12.3.2; lamps with menorahs have also been found there).[54] More to the point the syncretism that characterized much religion in the region had affected Judaism in that locale, with the result that both Jews and then Christians dabbled in the magical arts while still practicing their traditional religions (see below). Wandering Jewish exorcists were also not uncommon, not least in an area where the practice of magic was prevalent and was seen as the chief but not the only means of warding off evil spirits and demons.[55] Exorcisms were in some respects the Jewish counterpart and answer to the felt need for magical help.

When Paul left the synagogue, he did not leave alone, but rather took his converts with him to a new venue — the "hall of Tyrannus." In antiquity an orator or philosopher, in order to get a real hearing, needed to speak or teach in an appropriate place for such activities, whether it be in the home of a patron or in a public lecture hall.[56] The term σχολη could refer to a group of people meeting under the aegis of Tyrannus,[57] but more likely it refers to a guild or lecture hall (see Plutarch, *Mor.* 42A; P. Giss. 1 [1912] 85.14; Aristotle, *Pol.* 1313B; Epictetus, *Diss.* 3.21.11). Though our term "school" derives from σχολη, translating the word this way gives the wrong impression — it was a public auditorium or lecture hall. The Western text seems to understand the reference to be to a place and adds that Paul spoke there from the fifth to the tenth hour, or from about 11 A.M. to 4 P.M.[58] Whatever the source of this information or conjecture, it is a plausible one, for we know that in the Greco-Roman world the business day or the period of public affairs ended at 11 A.M., having started at dawn (see Martial, *Epig.* 4.8.3). In other words, the hall would likely have been free beginning at 11 A.M., the time when most would have a meal and then a siesta time. As Lake aptly puts it, at "1 p.m. there were probably more people sound asleep than at 1 a.m."[59]

Formal lectures for a clientele who could afford to attend in the mornings would be over by eleven. Paul's clientele, however, would not in the main be

---

54. See Arnold, *Ephesians,* pp. 29-32; Trebilco, *Jewish Communities in Asia Minor,* pp. 24-27.

55. On itinerant Jewish exorcists see *b. Shab.* 67a, and Arnold, *Ephesians,* p. 185.

56. See the helpful discussion of Stowers, "Social Status."

57. See Horsley, *New Docs,* 1 (1976), pp. 129-30.

58. See Metzger, *Textual Commentary,* p. 470.

59. Lake, *Beginnings,* 4:239.

high-status persons with the leisure to attend morning lectures. Paul, especially if he was going to speak on anything like a daily basis, would have to speak at a time when most of his clientele could attend — either in the afternoons or in the later part of the evening (see below on 20:7-8), outside normal working hours. Part of the importance of the reference to the hall of Tyrannus for our purposes is that it reflects Luke's attempt to portray Paul as being like a popular rhetor or philosopher seeking to persuade an audience on some subject. This is how he would have been perceived by much of his audience if he lectured in such a hall, rather than just in a synagogue.[60] This impression that he was a rhetor or philosopher would only have been compounded when it was discovered that he was not talking about what in the Greco-Roman world would have been seen as an organized religion — one with temples, priests, and sacrifices.[61]

There are several imponderables about the hall of Tyrannus. In the first place it is not entirely clear whether this is a hall of which Tyrannus was a landlord, or in which he was a regular orator (or both if he was a rich rhetorician like Herodes Atticus). The name Tyrannus (meaning Tyrant and thus presumably a nickname, perhaps of students for their teacher?) is attested in Ephesus in the first century A.D. (see *I. Ephes.* 1001.5; and for our exact period 20b.40).[62] It does not appear that this Ephesian site has yet been found or excavated, for though an αυδειτωριον has been found near the second-century Library of Celsus, it appears to have been used as a courtroom by the proconsul, not as a lecture hall.[63]

If Paul rented the hall, this would have become expensive if he argued daily there for two years (see *vv. 9-10*).[64] The expenses may have been defrayed by a convert of some means, or in part by the work of Paul, Aquila, and Priscilla, which they could have undertaken in the mornings or late afternoons. It is also not impossible that Tyrannus had become a convert, or that he let the hall very cheaply due to the odd hours Paul wanted it.[65] In any case, Paul "dialogued" or argued in this hall with regularity for about two years, seeking to persuade both Jews and Gentiles about the Christian faith.

---

60. See rightly Ramsay, *St. Paul the Traveller,* p. 271.

61. On Christianity being viewed as a religious association or club see Keener, *Bible Background Commentary,* p. 378.

62. See also *New Docs,* 3 (1987), no. 101, p. 186. The name is found in both these cases in a list of χουρετες from the late first and early second century.

63. See Trebilco, "Asia," pp. 311-12, against Hemer, *Book of Acts,* p. 121 n. 53.

64. Like Luke's use of "all" in Acts (on which see pp. 105ff. above), the use of "daily" could be another example of Lukan rhetorical hyperbole or intensification for the sake of emphasizing that this was a very regular ongoing activity (cf., e.g., Luke 9:23).

65. On the renting of a hall see *New Docs,* 1 (1976), pp. 126-28. On Tyrannus as possibly a Christian see Marshall, *Acts,* p. 309.

If we add the two years in the lecture hall to the three months in the synagogue plus the "some time longer" of v. 22, we arrive at approximately the three-year period Acts 20:31 later says was Paul's tenure in Ephesus.[66] It was apparently one of the most fruitful periods of Paul's ministry (see 1 Cor. 16:9 — "a wide door for effective work has opened"). V. 10 says somewhat hyperbolically that "all" the residents of Asia, both Jew and Greek, heard the word during this period of time (cf. 20:21).[67] No doubt what Luke means is that the word spread from Ephesus to Jews and Gentiles in various other nearby locales, including the Lycus Valley no doubt (see Col. 1:7; 2:1, 4:16; Revelation 2–3), the carrying of the word to nearby places being undertaken by Paul's coworkers while he remained and worked in Ephesus itself.[68]

D. The Ephesus Chronicles —
Part 4: Miracles and Magic in Ephesus (19:11-20)

We have just seen Paul the man of powerful words, but now Luke wishes to portray Paul, like Peter and Jesus before him, as also a man of mighty deeds, and thus offer a full-orbed picture as he brings to an end his portrait of Paul's missionary work as a free man. It is, however, right to add that this does not reflect a biographical interest on Luke's part. The "narrator is not simply glorifying Paul. It is finally the power of the word of the Lord, or the name of the Lord (19.17), that stands behind these events."[69] The narrative we find in these verses is full of local color and reflects a clear knowledge that Ephesus was indeed the magic capital of Asia Minor. If Christianity could triumph there, its God would clearly be seen to be great. This subunit is clearly set off by the references to the word of the Lord in v. 10 and v. 20 which frame the passage.[70] Indeed, v. 20 must be seen as in effect an attempt to indicate that

---

66. On the historical plausibility of this period of time in Ephesus see Lüdemann, *Early Christianity*, p. 214.

67. See Pesch, *Die Apostelgeschichte (Apg. 13–28)*, pp. 168-69.

68. There was plenty of time during the Ephesian ministry for Paul to write a lost letter to Corinth (1 Cor. 5:9-10) and 1 Corinthians, to be visited by Chloe's people and Stephanas and others from Corinth, and even to make a quick, painful visit to Corinth and then come back to Ephesus (2 Cor. 2:1; 12:14; 13:1), though Acts does not record it. Luke is by and large interested in recording what succeeded or worked, not what failed among Paul's many activities.

69. Tannehill, *Narrative Unity of Luke-Acts*, 2:238.

70. See ibid., p. 239: "The ring composition noted above reinforces this sense of closure, as endings are commonly indicated by a return to themes of the beginning. Paul's missionary journeys come to a climax and a point of relative closure through the narrator's description of his powerful ministry in Ephesus."

Paul's ministry of the word had come to a climax in this place. Henceforth it would be troubles, travels, and trials for Paul. The narrative is also not without an intended element of humor as Luke attempts to mix the light with the dark in what follows (see also 20:7-12).[71] Thus this section requires close scrutiny. In view of the interesting mix of miracle and magic in this passage (and possibly magic used to produce miracles), it will be useful at this juncture to say something on these related matters in more detail.

A Closer Look — Miracles and Magic in Antiquity and in Acts

The detailed study of ancient attitudes about sicknesses and their sources, and cures and their means, whether miraculous or magical, has been undertaken for some time, and the benefits of such studies for the understanding of the New Testament have been made clear and need no rehearsing here.[72] It is, however, in order to dispel a myth before discussing miracles and magic in more depth. It is certainly not true that all ancients were incapable of distinguishing between natural and supernatural causes and cures. E. Yamauchi has shown that in various civilizations both before and during the New Testament era various people could distinguish between illnesses that were naturally or supernaturally caused or cured.[73] Furthermore, authors such as Luke who record stories of signs and wonders and couple them with other sorts of stories show that they were capable of distinguishing the mundane from the miraculous. The more important question is whether they distinguished miracle from magic or not. The answer seems to be that there was perceived to be something of a sliding scale with pure miracle at one end and pure magic at the other, with some cases seeming to involve both.[74] Luke certainly focuses on miracle, but a case can be made that he believes in the idea of *mana* or sympathetic influence, the conveying of the power of cure through the medium of a piece of clothing (or even the shadow) from the healer (see below).

What characterizes magic is the attempt through various sorts of rituals and words of power to manipulate some deity or supernatural power into doing the will of the supplicant. "The overriding characteristic of the practice of magic throughout the Hellenistic world was the cognizance of a spirit world exercising influence over virtually every aspect of life. The goal of the magician was to discern the helpful spirits from the harmful ones and learn the distinct operations and the relative strengths and authority of the spirits. Through this knowledge, means could be constructed (with spoken or written formulas, amulets, etc.) for the manipulation of the spirits in the interest of the individual person."[75]

71. On entertainment, and the secondary but real role it plays in Luke's purposes in Acts, see pp. 376ff. above on Acts as a novel.
72. See, e.g., Hull, *Hellenistic Magic*; Kee, *Miracle*.
73. Yamauchi, "Magic or Miracle?"
74. See the helpful work of Meier, *A Marginal Jew*, 2:212-13, on what follows.
75. Arnold, *Ephesians*, p. 18.

There are in fact a variety of regular features in ancient magic: (1) complicated rituals, (2) magic spells and recipes, (3) the reciting of various names for various gods or even nonsense syllables in hopes of landing on a combination of sounds or names that will force a god to do one's bidding, (4) the reliance on a professional technician who demands payment and relies on secrecy, (5) syncretism, (6) coercion and manipulation as opposed to personal relating and supplication. None of these features appears in our text, insofar as the activities of Paul are concerned, but 19:12 does appear to be an example of *mana* (cf., e.g., Mark 5:28-30 and Luke 8:44), and perhaps the same can be said about Peter's shadow in Acts 5:15. Even in the case of Acts 19:12 Luke makes emphatically clear that it was God who caused these miracles to happen (v. 11). It is important to add that Luke does not say Paul traded in healing handkerchiefs or the like, or that he initiated such practices. It appears not to be Paul who takes these clothing items and lays them on the ill, but others who apparently did believe in the magical properties of the clothing of a healer. Furthermore, one must pay close attention to the flow of the narrative here, which concludes with the repudiation of magical recipes and books. The function of this narrative would seem, at least in part, to be to get Luke's audience to reject magic and trust in the power of God and God's word.[76] In this regard Luke was on the side of religion rather than magic, if with Arnold one agrees that "in religion one prays and requests from the gods; in magic one commands and therefore expects guaranteed results."[77]

The social significance of what we see in Acts in the miracle and magic narratives deserves comment. Especially in a text like Acts 19 it becomes clear that Christianity is being portrayed as an alternative to "popular" religion, the religion of magic and mysteries, the religion of astrology and fate. Magic "appears to have been far more popular among the lower classes in the Greco-Roman world than among the upper classes"[78] (cf. Philostratus, *Vit. Soph.* 523, 590). Christianity is also being portrayed in Acts 19 as a religion which one cannot manipulate for one's own ends, or dabble in without harm. The Jewish exorcists who try to use Jesus' name come to grief. Luke is exercised to show that Christianity reveals the impotence of such popular religion and leads to its renunciation. The same message comes across in Acts 8 in the story of Simon Magus. The real power lies not in magic or μάγοι but in God and God's emissaries, such as Peter and Paul. In other words, Christianity is being portrayed as the real source of human and world transformation and redemption, in contradistinction to both popular panaceas (such as magic) and to "official" saviors such as the emperor. If Christianity is true and the Christian faith really changes lives, then the emperor has no divine clothes. The power of the word and its effects lead to charges along the way of subversive activity as we have already seen in Acts 16, and as we will see in more detail when we deal with the arrest and trials of Paul. Such power in the hands (or, better said, operating through the hands) of a Peter or a Paul is a threat to the existing structures of power, whether Jewish or Roman. Yet Luke labors mightily to show that Christianity is not a form of revolution against the state. It is seen as more of a religious reform movement changing things from within, one individual at a time.

76. On this whole subject see Aune, "Magic in Early Christianity."
77. Arnold, *Ephesians*, p. 19.
78. Ibid., p. 19.

Yet this conversionist sect also has a thaumaturgic dimension, as Acts 19 shows.[79] Luke shares the common belief in the influence of evil spirits, as well as in ordinary illnesses, and believes the gospel is the answer to both concerns. His world has only a limited spiritual dualism, with the power of good much greater than the power of evil, and greater than the effects of human fallenness. Chiefly, in the Lukan view of things, miracles serve conversionist ends, either by attracting people to the faith or by validating that the faith is powerful once believed. Inasmuch as spiritual gifts fall under the category of the miraculous, they, too, have an evidentialist function in Acts, bearing witness to the authenticity of a conversion (see Acts 10). What this means is that Luke is not interested in miracles for their own sake, or even for their entertainment value in a narrative, but he is interested in them insofar as they punctuate the central message about the spread of the word and the conversion of the various sorts of people that make up the Greco-Roman world. This also means that miracles in Acts are not seen as means of mere benevolence, making a person whole but without changing his or her own worldview, but rather they tend toward the transvaluation of the healed one's values. In Luke's hierarchy of values conversion is the primary value, and others, such as health, are subservient to it. Nevertheless, wholeness, involving the entire person, is a real concern for Luke, and both body and spirit are seen as a part of salvation.[80]

V. 11 informs us that Paul did "no ordinary powerful deeds," a pleasant redundancy that highlights Luke's rhetorical skills of understatement (*litotes*, cf. the use of ουκ ολιγος in v. 23).[81] This verse serves as something of a heading for what follows. *V. 12* illustrates specifically what Luke has in mind — σουδαρια and σιμικινθια which had touched Paul's skin were brought to the sick and possessed with the result that their diseases and demons left them. Both of these terms are Latin loanwords (originally *sudaria* and *semicinctia*), the former of which seems to refer to sweat rags or kerchiefs worn on the head (cf. Luke 19:20; John 11:44; 20:7), while the latter refers to aprons or less probably a belt.[82] The image conjured up is that when Paul's reputation as a miracle worker got around, people came to see him while he was at work, and

79. For this reason early Christianity does not fit neatly into either a conversionist or a reformational social model as a movement, but see Wilson, *Magic and Millennium*, pp. 9-30.

80. See above on salvation, pp. 143ff.; and see my essay "Salvation and Health in Christian Antiquity," pp. 821ff. below in Appendix 2. See also Pilch, "Sickness and Healing in Luke-Acts." I would suggest that Pilch is right that the heart-eyes zone is an important emphasis in the discussion in Luke-Acts of health and salvation, and the reason for this is that salvation is the subject matter of Luke's work — involving especially a change in the human heart and the way people see the world.

81. His use of πας of course shows he is capable of using overstatement as well. See pp. 105ff. above.

82. See Bruce, *The Acts of the Apostles*, p. 410; Trebilco, "Asia," pp. 313-14.

upon their request he gave them items of his clothing, used in his trade apparently (leather working or tentmaking).[83]

Clearly the belief that the bodies of particular persons and whatever touched them had healing powers was widespread in antiquity (Plutarch, *Pyrr.* 3.4-5; Eusebius, *PE* 9.27). The verb ἀπαλλασσεσθαι, used only here in the NT of the removal of sickness, is a word used very frequently in the medical writings of Luke's day. Though this does not prove Luke was such a person, it, along with other evidence, is consistent with such a view and may be a small pointer in that direction.[84]

Success encourages imitation, and this seems to be what we are meant to understand is the subject of *v. 13*. We hear of itinerant Jewish exorcists[85] trying to use the name of the Lord Jesus to exorcise evil spirits from some who were possessed by them. Their incantation or conjuring phrase addressed to the demons was, "I adjure you by the Jesus whom Paul proclaims." This in no way compels us to think of these people as Christians (as the sequel makes quite clear), but rather bears witness to the syncretistic environment that existed in Ephesus,[86] and also is reminiscent of the curse formulas found in the magical papyri, in which various gods Jewish, pagan, and even Christian would be invoked in the hopes that one of the divine names would be powerful enough to produce the desired effect.[87] As H. D. Betz has said, "Jewish magic was famous in antiquity," and so a wide variety of people would invoke Jewish divine names to try to heal or exorcise or curse someone (on Jewish exorcists, see Josephus, *Ant.* 8.42-49).[88]

V. 14 further identifies these exorcists as the seven sons of a certain Sceva, a chief priest of the Jews. Scholars have often pondered what to make of this identification, not least because, if one is to believe the list in Josephus, there was certainly no *high priest* named Sceva before the fall of Jerusalem in A.D. 70 (see

83. See above on Acts 18:3, pp. 547ff.

84. Of the same order as the scientific character of Luke's preface language in Luke 1:1-4. See pp. 14ff. above.

85. Here we have the only use in the NT of the noun εξορχιστης, but it is found elsewhere in Greek literature in Lucian and Ptolemy as well as in the Greek church fathers. On the later order of exorcists in the church see *New Docs*, 1 (1976), no. 79.

86. See Metzger, "St. Paul and the Magicians," p. 27: "Of all the ancient Graeco-Roman cities, Ephesus the third largest city in the Empire was by far the most hospitable to magicians, sorcerers, and charlatans of all sorts."

87. For example, the famous Paris papyrus 574, which includes the following spell, "I adjure you by Jesus the God of the Hebrews," and also, "Hail God of Abraham, hail God of Isaac, hail God of Jacob, Jesus Chrestus, Holy Spirit, Son of the Father." See the discussion in Arnold, *Ephesians*, pp. 13-31.

88. H. D. Betz, "Introduction to the Greek Magical Papyri," in *The Greek Magical Papyri in Translation* (Chicago: University of Chicago Press, 1986), p. xlv. Betz, p. xli, upholds the general reliability of our account here, indicating how typical this episode is. The original edition of the magical papyri is Preisendanz, *Papyri graecae magicae*.

Ant. 18.34–20.179). The Western text (D and others) seems to have felt the difficulty, for it simply has the word ιερεως here.[89] This looks like an effort to simplify a problematic text, and so the attempt by W. A. Strange to argue for the originality of the Western text is unconvincing, not least because no adequate explanation can then be given for why the reading αρχιερεως arose.[90] The debate, however, is probably pointless, especially if, as is likely, Luke is not using the term αρχιερεως in some technical sense for "the high priest" in Jerusalem. The term here probably is used in a general way and means no more than "a chief priest" (noting the absence of the definite article).[91] The real point, however, in mentioning Sceva's priestly status or suggesting that he comes from a priestly family[92] is probably that it was priests who were most especially believed to know the divine names, names used in exorcism, hence the sons are pursuing an activity that reflects a knowledge that was part of their family heritage.

Vv. 15-16 may be described as the comic relief in an otherwise serious narrative. The evil spirit responded to these exorcists as follows: "Jesus I know and Paul I recognize (or respect), but who are you?"[93] This demon saw that these exorcists had no power or authority and so turns the tables on them, driving them out! *V. 16* says that the possessed man leaped on the exorcists and "mastered" them all.[94] They were so overpowered that they fled from the house naked and wounded![95]

89. See the discussion in Metzger, *Textual Commentary,* pp. 470-71.

90. Strange, "The Sons of Sceva."

91. I agree with Polhill, *Acts,* p. 404, that it is quite unnecessary to suggest Luke meant Sceva was a pagan high priest, since he is clearly identified as a Jewish one, and the chances of a Jew being a high priest in a pagan cult are extremely remote.

92. See the discussion in Mastin, "Scaeva the Chief Priest," and also his "A Note on Acts 19.14." Several of the points he makes are worth repeating: (1) the term αρχιερευς both in the NT and in Josephus does not always refer to a reigning high priest and in fact in the plural especially can have a wider meaning; (2) there are various passages in Josephus where this term refers to someone who was never a ruling high priest (*War* 2.566; 4.574; 5.527); (3) though the term is in fact used of a high priest in the imperial cult, or even the Pontifex Maximus (see *Ant.* 14.190; 16.162), if Luke had seen this man as a renegade Jew or as one who merely claimed to be high priest, there are ways he could have conveyed such a view (see Hemer, *Book of Acts,* p. 121 n. 54).

93. Ephesus was widely known as a place of demonic activity; see Philostratus, *Life of Apollonius* 4.10. This question of the demon is a clever reversal of the normal procedure where the demon is asked to name itself before it is driven out (see, e.g., Mark 5:9). These exorcists are not known by name and so are themselves exorcised.

94. There is no good reason to insist that αμφοτερων must mean "both" here since it can also mean "all," and in fact it does so at least one other time in Acts at 23:8. See also P. Lond. 336.13, where the word refers to five men.

95. There is clearly enough a roughness to this narrative showing a lack of revision. The house is not previously mentioned, and there are other infelicities in the account as well. See Johnson, *Acts,* p. 341. On Acts as an unrevised first edition see pp. 65ff. above.

V. 17 informs us that when this incident became known to *all* the Jews and Greeks of Ephesus (i.e., became very widely known), fear fell upon all of them and they praised the name of the Lord Jesus. This is not to be seen as an indication of mass conversion, but rather as an act of self-preservation or something like what we find in Acts 3:10 and 4:21, where a general respect or thanksgiving is indicated for a good deed, or like what we find in 2:43 and 5:11, where fear of great supernatural power is meant.

V. 18 speaks of many of those who had already been believers (noting the force of the perfect tense of πεπιστευκοτων) making confession and divulging the spells they had been using (πραξις here is a technical term for magical practices).[96] As Bruce says, the power of spells lies in their secrecy, and thus to divulge them is to render them powerless and useless.[97] What we are dealing with here is very much like what Paul was dealing with in Corinth, as 1 Corinthians makes amply clear — partially socialized Christians who did not immediately give up all their old religious practices when they converted.[98]

V. 19 continues the report of the sort of repenting and renouncing some believers did as a result of the incident with the sons of Sceva. Those who practiced magic collected their books and burned them publicly. The practice of burning books that were seen as dangerous or subversive is well known in this era.[99] Suetonius tells us that in 13 B.C. Augustus collected whatever Greek or Latin prophetic writings were in circulation that were anonymous or written by those of low repute and burned them (*Augustus* 31; cf. Livy 39.16). Livy speaks of the burning of books in the sight of the people that were subversive of true and authorized religion (40.29.3-14). Diogenes Laertius refers to the burning of the books of Protagoras in the marketplace in Athens (9.52). The trickster Alexander burned the maxims of Epicurus (Lucian, *Alexander* 47). There are also Jewish examples of such burnings (see Jer. 36:20-27; 1 Macc. 1:56). The great difference in our account is that the owners here are voluntarily burning their own books — these books were not seized. Inasmuch as books were very expensive, and in view of the stress Luke places on the worth of these books, fifty thousand pieces of silver (presumably drachmas, and thus fifty thousand days' pay for a day laborer), we are presumably meant to think that those undertaking this act were of some social means. Perhaps v. 18 refers to the actions of the lower-status and poorer Christians, and v. 19 to the actions of the higher-status and more wealthy Christians. Because Ephesus was in any case the home of all sorts of magic, the phrase "Ephesian writings" (εφεσια

---

96. See Haenchen, *Acts*, p. 567.
97. Bruce, *The Acts of the Apostles*, p. 412.
98. See my *Conflict and Community in Corinth*, pp. 186ff.
99. See Trebilco, "Asia," pp. 314-15, and for the account of such an instance by Tacitus, see pp. 68-69 in the introduction.

γραμματα)[100] came to be used for documents that contained spells and magical formulas (see Athenaeus, *Deipnosophistae* 12.548; Clement of Alexandria, *Stromata* 5.242), and there is some reason to think that some of the magical words or phrases meant to ward off demons or curses and found in such writings were engraved on the crown, girdle, and feet of statues of Artemis.

These actions of public renunciation are seen as clearing a path for the gospel, or can be said to be the proper negative response to pagan religion by those who had turned to the Christian faith. As such they may be seen to be a further fulfillment of the basic thing expected in the Acts 15 decree.[101] *V. 20* is connected with what has gone before by ουτως, indicating that this purgation of magic led to the word of God spreading and prevailing mightily. Here is the climax of the account of Paul's ministry as a free man; after this it is largely troubles, travels, and trials. It is no surprise that Luke, who does not give a great deal of attention to the demonic world, does so in Acts 19, for Ephesus and its environs had the reputation of being a center or haven of demonic activity. Thus, as v. 20 indicates, the word of God is shown to have superior power to them.[102]

E. The Ephesus Chronicles — Part 5: Riot in Ephesus (19:21-41)

In the remainder of Acts 19, we find an excellent example of what can be called Luke's capacity and flair for "the dramatic episode."[103] The positioning of this episode here is important in several regards. In the first place, from a rhetorical point of view, it prepares the reader or hearer for the troubles Paul is to encounter in the following chapters (cf. the riot in Jerusalem in Acts 21) by already arousing and appealing to the deeper emotions *(pathos)*. In the second place, this narrative provides us with the final confrontation between Paul as a free man and pagan religion and shows how God continues to work his plan, even in the face of stiff opposition from one of the most powerful and widespread of pagan cults. Though the message Paul preaches is correctly seen as a threat to the cult of Artemis, yet because of the divine hand involved in the matter Paul is not tried or punished. Such things will not transpire out of due season.

---

100. In Plutarch, *Moral.* 706E, the "Ephesian letters" are seen as a magical formula against demons.
101. See the discussion, pp. 439ff. above.
102. See Arnold, *Ephesians,* p. 30. Notice, however, that Luke does not think that demons have no power, as the fate of the would-be exorcists shows.
103. Plümacher, *Lukas als hellenistischer Schriftsteller,* pp. 98-100.

Paul is in fact not a major actor in this subsection, appearing only in vv. 30-31,[104] a fact which again reminds us that even after Acts 16 the story is not primarily about Paul and his exploits but about the progress of a social movement ("the Way") and of the unstoppable word of God as it transforms lives and thereby threatens established religious and social ways. It may also be said that this narrative presents a certain political apologetic for the Way. The story makes clear that those who oppose this social movement are wrong to do so, and that right-thinking officials recognize that Christians should be left alone, or perhaps even given the same privileges and status given to Jews, since the Way is a derivative of Judaism.[105]

Cassidy has rightly pointed out that the use of the phrase "the Way" "identifies the disciples as constituting a socially cohesive movement, a movement arising out of and grounded in their shared faith in Jesus."[106] What is interesting about Luke's use of this terminology is that we find it chiefly in connection with the church in Jerusalem and its environs (see 9:2; 22:4) and with the church in Ephesus and its environs (see 19:9, 23). This emphasizes that the movement is heading west, is translocal, and can incarnate itself both at the heart of Jewish culture and at the heart of the somewhat Romanized Hellenistic culture found in Ephesus. As the phrase itself suggests, the Christian movement involves a new way of living as well as a new set of religious beliefs. The latter was something rather distinctive about Christianity because by and large Jewish religion was chiefly a matter of orthopraxy and Greco-Roman religion was largely, though not exclusively, a matter of the performance of right rituals.[107] The heavy theological content coupled with the absence of priests, sacrifices, and temples set the Way apart from both Judaism and paganism.

Considerable local knowledge about Ephesus, and in particular about the political and religious situation there (especially in regard to the Ephesian Artemis), is reflected in the verses now under scrutiny, and it appears to have led H. Koester[108] to the suggestion that Acts was written from Ephesus by

---

104. See Tannehill, *Narrative Unity of Luke-Acts*, 2:241.

105. See the helpful discussion by Stoops, "Riot and Assembly." Stoops ably shows that this story is not an incoherent jumble of traditions, but that in fact almost all of its elements can also be found in accounts of riots against Jews during this period (see Josephus, *War* 7.3.2-4 and 7.5.2). He is also right to object to Haenchen's analysis of the narrative. It is certainly not the account of a rescue miracle, and in the end physical violence does not happen due to the powerful city clerk's interceding (see Stoops, pp. 76-77).

106. Cassidy, *Society and Politics*, p. 95.

107. This can especially be seen in the theodicy of Roman pagans, who when calamity struck, such as an earthquake, invariably placed the blame on themselves for a failure sometime in the past to sacrifice properly or read the omens correctly. See the helpful discussion by Phillips, "On Ritual and Theodicy."

108. See his "Ephesos in Early Christian Literature," pp. 130-31. The conjecture of Koester on the provenance of Acts can be found on p. xviii.

someone who knew such things as: (1) the use of the phrase "temple keeper" (19:35) with respect to the cult of Artemis;[109] (2) the production of the small silver shrines of Artemis for sale in Ephesus; (3) the existence of the Asiarchs as local political figures (19:31);[110] (4) the mention of the "scribe of the Demos" as perhaps the most powerful Ephesian official (19:35).[111] Koester's suggestion about the provenance of Acts need not follow from the above data, but what does follow is that Luke has a good source of information about this locale.

The story itself is compelling, accurately portraying the sort of reaction one would expect if there was a perceived threat to the cult of the local deity and especially if that threat bore economic implications.[112] That there was

109. On this see Friesen, *Twice Neokoros,* pp. 55-56.

110. They are widely attested in Ephesian inscriptions. See Hemer, *Book of Acts,* passim.

111. See Koester, "Ephesos in Early Christian Literature," p. 130 n. 42.

112. Haenchen, *Acts,* pp. 576-79, finds this narrative a mass of historical improbabilities. He finds the action of Demetrius incomprehensible; the lack of involvement of the priests of Artemis, if Paul's preaching really was a threat, unlikely; the attitude of the Asiarchs toward Paul improbable; the Jewish "intermezzo" with Alexander contrived; the response of the scribe or clerk amazing (how could Paul, who denies the divinity of Artemis, not be seen as a threat); and the lack of focus on Paul and lack of correspondence with what Paul says about his Ephesian experience in 1 Corinthians 15 and 2 Corinthians 1 inexplicable. As Marshall, *Acts,* pp. 315-16, says, most of these complaints disappear under close scrutiny. In the first place one must reckon with the fact that Demetrius is exaggerating the immediate threat of Paul's preaching to rally his supporters. The inactivity of the priests of Artemis is understandable in a pluralistic environment if they were not feeling the pinch and did not see this tiny minority sect as a real threat as of yet. As for the action of the Asiarchs, it must be remembered that they were connected to the imperial cult and the worship of Roma, not the worship of Artemis. In view of their imperial connections they may well have viewed anything that might diminish the influence of this powerful non-Roman deity as good news for their own cause of advancing the imperial cult. They may also have seen the riot as serving their own purposes, for it threatened the free-city status of Ephesus and could be used as an excuse to encourage more Roman control of the city and its cultic activities in the name of "peace and order." The fears of the scribe were not unjustified. Demetrius emerges as an artisan who is no rhetor and therefore does not understand how to persuade the audience forcefully when he is standing in front of a large crowd. This portrait of such a person is quite believable, as he would not be a person likely to have had the educational training in oratory required to make the most of the occasion. If Paul indeed was a Roman citizen, there is no reason why during his almost three years in Asia he could not have cultivated some friends of high social status who had Roman connections, as he did in Corinth in the case of Erastus (see my *Conflict and Community in Corinth,* pp. 32-34, and Rom. 16:23). The Jewish "intermezzo" which leads nowhere is not the sort of episode Luke would likely invent, and the not-so-latent anti-Semitism of the crowd and their inability to distinguish Judaism and Christianity is very believable. Finally, as Marshall points out, Luke is summarizing here, and thus various elements of the tale are deliberately left out. Luke does not tell us

some serious conflict near the end of Paul's time in Ephesus seems to be clearly suggested by 2 Cor. 1:8-10, which speaks of a rescue from a deadly peril, and this episode may well be alluded to in 1 Cor. 15:32 (see also Rom. 16:4, which may refer to Priscilla and Aquila's involvement in the matter as well). There is no sound historical reason why Acts 19:21-43 could not be an accurate account of this perilous situation.[113]

Because of the extensive work of Austrian archaeologists and various American scholars, we now know quite a lot about the cult of Artemis. D. Knibbe sums up matters as follows:

> [Artemis] worship was not very different from that of other deities in pagan cults. Not every goddess had processions, however. . . . processions from the Artemision around Panayirdag occurred on certain days . . . probably during the ιερομηνια, the holy month of Artemis, which was called "Artemision." The wooden statue of Artemis, carved by Endios, was probably carried on a four-wheel carriage. . . . The statue would have been dressed and adorned with the necessary care that was given to her in the imperial period by women of the high society in that city who served as . . . "adorners of the goddess." The procession presumably stopped at the altars along the road, where worshippers sang, prayed, and made offerings. All who participated were then invited to a common meal that took place after the procession, when Artemis had returned to her temple. . . . in processions to the Artemision, the goddess represented by the most beautiful woman returned from hunting accompanied by hunters, dogs, and a crowd of people.[114]

This last point brings to light the fact that Ephesian Artemis, even before Paul's day, had taken on various of the attributes of the Greek Artemis while retaining some of her local traits as the Anatolian "Great Mother."[115] There continues to be much controversy about what the numerous orbed objects on the front of the Artemis statue are, with the usual guesses being either breasts

---

all we would like to know about motives and the like. Had he been inventing this scene, however, we would have expected him to make the role played by Paul more central and important. On the relationship of what is referred to here and the material in the Corinthian correspondence see above, pp. 584ff.

113. But see Lüdemann, *Early Christianity*, pp. 216-21, who wants to argue that Paul has been added to a secular narrative about a riot in Ephesus. This fails to explain why Luke or other early Christians would have remembered or passed down such a story in the first place. On 1 Cor. 15:32 as a metaphorical reference to strong human opposition. see pp. 583ff. above, and cf. Ignatius, *Rom.* 5:1.

114. Knibbe, "Via Sacra Ephesiaca," pp. 153-54. Some of this description is based on Xenophon's *Ephesiaka* 2.2–3.3.

115. See Thomas, "At Home," p. 95. As she points out, in fact the earliest coins we have of Ephesian Artemis, dating to the third century b.c., have the Greek huntress image.

or bull's testicles or some sort of eggs.[116] In any of these cases, the image would connect the goddess with fertility. One of the reasons for debate on this issue is that Greek Artemis was also known as a major supporter of chastity, being a virgin goddess.

Another matter of considerable importance is that the temple of Artemis was widely recognized as a place of asylum and sanctuary, and part of this involved its being a safe place to deposit one's money. In such circumstances, there was always an economic significance to the temple, not limited to the religious tourist trade. The temple of Artemis and its precincts was some four times the size of the Parthenon (425 feet by 225 feet with 127 sixty-foot columns) and was considered one of the seven great wonders of the ancient world.[117] Its religious significance and power were widely recognized. Pausanias, writing in the middle of the second century A.D., states: "All cities worship Artemis of Ephesus and individuals hold her honor above all the gods. The reason, in my view, is the renown of the Amazons who traditionally dedicated the image, also the extreme antiquity of this sanctuary. Three other points as well have contributed to her renown, the size of the temple, surpassing all other buildings among humans, the eminence of the city of the Ephesians and the renown of the goddess who dwells there" (4.31.8).[118]

One of the major points of our narrative is to show that Christianity could even challenge and be seen as a threat to one the greatest and most potent of the pagan cults. In fact Pausanias informs us that this cult was the most widely followed in the ancient world (*Descript.* 4.31.8), with some thirty-three worship sites from Spain to Syria in the Empire (Strabo, *Geog.* 4.1.5). Finally, the inscriptional evidence shows us the degree to which Paul's proclamation would be seen to be challenging the claims about the benefits of Artemis worship. For example I. Eph. 504 portrays Artemis as one who answers prayer. In other inscriptions she is acclaimed as savior (Σώτειρα — I. Eph. 26.4, 18) and seen as having lordship over the supernatural powers, including demons.[119]

The temple statue of Artemis also wore a zodiac necklace indicating her power over fate and the control of the stars.[120] Of course the salvation being asked of Artemis has to do with rescue from danger or the restoration of health or sanity, but, as we have seen, this is part of the salvation package from a

116. See the discussion in Oster, "The Ephesian Artemis," pp. 28-29.

117. See Ekschmitt, *Die Seben Weltwunder,* pp. 3ff.

118. See the discussion of Artemis and Ephesus in *New Docs,* 6 (1992), no. 30, pp. 202ff.

119. See the discussion in Trebilco, "Asia," pp. 317-18, and in Oster, "Ephesus as a Religious Center," p. 1724.

120. LiDonnici, "The Image of Artemis."

Lukan point of view as well.[121] We might have a tendency to think that what was at issue was two rival forms of private devotion and belief, but this would be a mistake. Religious activity in the Empire's cities was in the main a very public affair intertwined with politics and beliefs about the well-being of the city as a whole.[122]

V. 21 should be seen as transitional, bringing to a close the account of the positive ministry of Paul and setting the agenda for what will follow in the rest of the book by providing some insight into the mind of Paul and his future intentions.[123] Paul believed that he had accomplished what he had set out to do in this region, and his plan is to go west to the very heart of the Empire in Rome, but by way of Jerusalem. While the phrase εν τω πνευματι could refer to Paul's human spirit in view especially of Acts 21:24 (but see also 18:25 and 20:22), in view of the sense of divine compulsion driving Paul (see v. 21b) it probably refers to the Holy Spirit. His remark here should be compared to what he wrote not long after this occasion when he was in Corinth, and indeed vv. 21-22 as a whole should be closely compared to Rom. 15:23-25: "But now, with no further place for me in these regions, I desire, as I have for many years, to come to you when I go to Spain. . . . At present, however, I am going to Jerusalem in a ministry to the saints; for Macedonia and Achaia have been pleased to share their resources with the poor among the saints in Jerusalem."[124]

Luke does not tell us the motivation for the trip, as Paul does in the quoted passage. It cannot be urged that Luke is unaware of the collection, for Acts 24:17 shows this is not the case (see also on 20:4 below). Why then does he not make more of it? The most reasonable explanation is that Luke writes with the benefit of hindsight and so with the knowledge that the collection did not accomplish the sort of things Paul had hoped it would (see Rom. 15:16, 27, 31), and thus he writes without the enthusiasm and hope Paul expresses for the project in his earlier letters, particularly in the Corinthian correspondence and Romans, before the collection was delivered.[125]

---

121. See the excursus, pp. 143ff. above, on salvation in Acts, and especially Appendix 2.

122. See the discussion by Mitchell, *Anatolia,* p. 113.

123. It has often been noticed that in what follows in Acts 19:21–Acts 28 there are a variety of parallels between Jesus' last journey to Jerusalem and Paul's journey to Jerusalem and beyond. See Moessner, "The Christ Must Suffer," pp. 249-56.

124. Polhill, *Acts,* pp. 406-7, is quite right that Romans 15 is the best commentary on this verse.

125. If it is allowed that at least some of the Captivity Epistles are Pauline, then it is striking that Paul makes absolutely no reference to the collection in these letters, not even in Philippians, when the Philippians made a substantial contribution to the collection. This silence is telling, and like its counterpart in Acts it bespeaks a project that did not accomplish all Paul hoped. It also speaks for the fact that the Captivity Epistles were not written prior to Paul's period of Roman house arrest.

A comment on the use of δεῖ in v. 21b is in order. When Paul says he must see Rome, he is not speaking as an eager tourist who longed to tour the Eternal City, but as one under the compulsion of God to keep heading west with the gospel. Luke frequently uses this verb to express such an idea.[126] It is worth noting that the verb of compulsion is related to going to Rome, but also by implication (noting the καί, "I must *also* see . . .") to his going first to Jerusalem. One must compare this passage to Acts 20:22-23. The Spirit compelled him to go to Jerusalem. Scholars have rightly compared this idea with the similar notion we find in the Gospels in regard to Jesus' being under the same divine necessity to go to Jerusalem, the place where prophets and sages often suffered (cf. Luke 9:51).[127] The parallels are of course not perfect, since Paul does not die in Jerusalem, but they are sufficient to suggest a pattern — rejection and suffering come for Jesus and his followers in Jerusalem. Paul had not abandoned Jerusalem, any more than he had abandoned Jews despite rejection time and again, but it did not take great foresight for him to wisely urge the Roman Christians to pray for him as he undertook this final trip to Jerusalem "that I may be rescued from the unbelievers in Judea, and that my διακονία [i.e., the collection, see below] may be acceptable to the saints" (Rom. 15:31). On neither score did things turn out as Paul had hoped.

Thus, Paul was going to go through Macedonia and Achaia first, prior to going to Jerusalem, and in fact, as *v. 22* makes clear, he would send two of his coworkers before him to Macedonia while he remained in Ephesus a while longer. The reason for sending the two ahead was perhaps so that the collection could be gathered before Paul arrived, and thus he would not have to make an issue of it when he arrived and so shame these congregations (see 2 Corinthians 8–9). It is probably not accidental that the two are called διακονούντων αὐτῷ, for they were to render to Paul the practical service of collecting funds. Luke elsewhere uses the term διακονία for the collection taken up by the Antiochian church for the church in Jerusalem (11:29; 12:25). Notice, too, how Paul himself uses the term διακονία in reference to the collection for the saints in Jerusalem (Rom. 15:31; 2 Cor. 8:4; 9:1).[128]

The two persons Paul sends are Timothy (who has not been mentioned since 18:5, but we know from 1 Cor. 4:17 and 16:10-11 that he served with Paul in Ephesus) and Erastus. It is not impossible that this is the same Erastus mentioned in Rom. 16:23, but if he held his Corinthian aedileship during this period it is unlikely that he would be traveling around collecting funds for

126. See Cosgrove, "The Divine Δεῖ in Luke-Acts"; cf. Acts 23:1; 27:24.
127. See Tannehill, *Narrative Unity of Luke-Acts,* 2:239-40; Radl, *Paulus und Jesus im lukanischen Doppelwerk,* pp. 103-26.
128. See Johnson, *Acts,* p. 346.

Paul in other cities,[129] even though there would be a certain fitness to having a treasurer do so. The name Erastus was in any case a very common one, and so this may well be another Erastus than the Corinthian convert.

As is often the case with Luke, a general time reference introduces *v. 23* — it was about that time that no little disturbance broke out concerning the Way. Once again we see Luke's characteristic use of *litotes* (ουκ ολιγος), here indicating that a large disturbance broke out (cf. 12:18; 17:8 on the construction). As 16:17 made clear, the social movement called the Way had at the heart of its message the way of salvation which could also be called the way of God or the Lord (18:25-26), meaning God's way of dealing with us. Luke clearly believes in the power of the word, as is shown not only by his emphasis that the movement was proclamation centered but also by the way he presents his narrative here. One man's speech begins the riot, another's ends it. Words not merely interpret the action in Acts, they prompt it or are even the active cause of things happening.

V. 24 introduces us to a certain man by the name of Demetrius, a silversmith by trade.[130] There has been some controversy over what exactly Demetrius made. The most probable text says he made replica silver temples (ναους) of Artemis, not silver statues of Artemis as many commentators have assumed. Terra-cotta and marble examples of such miniature temples have been found,[131] and it is not surprising that silver objects of this sort have not been found, as they would have been readily melted down and used for other purposes over the centuries. In fact, however, in the Metropolitan Museum of Art in New York there is a bronze matrix of Artemis in her temple dating to the second or first century B.C. This was the mold into which the silver would be poured or pressed to make such objects as are described in our verse.[132] These objects would not primarily be bought as souvenirs, but would be used as votive offerings dedicated to the goddess when one visited the temple,[133] or occasionally as amulets or even in family worship in the home. We are told that the making of these shrines brought no little profit to artisans such as Demetrius.[134]

It is one of Luke's major themes that greed or acquisitiveness is regularly seen as an obstacle to fully accepting God's salvation or wholeheartedly serving

---

129. See Marshall, *Acts*, p. 314.

130. Various inscriptions from Ephesus attest to the existence of silversmiths, for example I. Eph. 425.10, and I Eph. 2212.a.6-7.

131. See Trebilco, "Asia," pp. 336-37.

132. See Reeder, "The Mother of the Gods," especially pp. 424-28. See the discussion in Larkin, *Acts*, pp. 280-81.

133. See *IGR* 1.467: "To Artemis, he gave a ναισκον as a vow."

134. The term εργασιαν found here and in the next verse can mean either business or the gain from doing business, i.e., profit.

God (see Luke 16:1-14; Acts 1:17-20; 5:1-11; 8:20-22; 16:16-18). As Johnson has aptly put it, Luke believes that one's attitude toward material possessions reveals one's attitude about God.[135] The wholehearted acceptance of God and God's salvation leads to free sharing of possessions (Acts 4:32-37), and the converse is also true (cf., e.g., the less than wholehearted devotion and giving of Ananias and Sapphira in Acts 5). Luke is no purveyor of bourgeois ethics, though he does seem to believe that those who have more should voluntarily, not by compulsion, share with the have-nots.[136]

Demetrius seems to have been the head of the local guild of silver-smiths,[137] and he called these artisans together along with workmen in related trades, for example workers in lead, marble, and semiprecious stones.[138] His brief speech begins in *v. 25* with what is uppermost on his mind — "Men, you know we get our prosperity/high standard of living (ευπορια) from the profits from these things."[139] The speech is blunt, direct, emotional, and without rhetorical merit.[140] Demetrius appeals to his audience's weak spot — fears about the continuance of their business and its ongoing profitability. In other words, this speech has no subtlety and simply appeals to one of the deeper emotions. *V. 26* should be seen as a classic example of fear-mongering by means of exaggeration. Demetrius claims that "not only in Ephesus but in nearly (σχεδον) the whole of the provenance of Asia this Paul has persuaded and drawn away a number of people saying that gods made with hands are not gods." Two aspects of this claim are significant. First, even allowing for dramatic hyperbole, the point is that the influence of Christianity had spread well beyond Ephesus during Paul's almost three years in Asia. Secondly, the summary of Paul's evangelistic preaching echoes the content of his preaching to pagans in Athens (see especially 17:24-25). From the Lukan point of view, what this means is that Luke does not view the speech in Athens as a failed experiment, after which Paul did not attempt to preach in that fashion.[141]

Demetrius's implied point is that if gods made with hands are no gods, then the artisans who make such things are in danger of being put out of

135. See Johnson, *Acts,* p. 353.

136. See the excursus, pp. 210ff. above, on Luke's social ethics.

137. On which see I Ephes. 636.9-10 — το ιερον συνεδριον των αργυροκοπων. See the discussion in Hemer, *Book of Acts,* p. 235.

138. Religious objects have been discovered made of these materials in Ephesus for the cult of Artemis. See Crocker, "Ephesus." Crocker (p. 76) rightly notes the independent testimony to the existence of a guild of silversmiths in the Ephesian inscriptions and to the mention of one by name — a certain M. Antonias Hermeias.

139. Tannehill, *Narrative Unity of Luke-Acts,* 2:243, is right that "the narrative undermines the validity of the protest from the beginning by having Demetrius reveal his self-interested motives."

140. But see Soards, *The Speeches in Acts,* p. 103.

141. See the discussion, pp. 533ff. above.

business, or, as *v. 27* puts it, in danger of being seen as people practicing a discredited, perhaps even a disreputable or sacrilegious trade.[142] The point is that they were in danger of being publicly shamed, and of being seen as dishonorable men practicing a discredited trade. In an honor-shame culture such as this one, public humiliation, or being seen as merely mercenary individuals, could ruin reputations and so one's livelihood. Once again in v. 27b we see exaggeration — there will be disastrous effects on the cult of Artemis as well because of Paul's persuasive preaching. It is true enough that in the second century Pliny the Younger reports that sacrifices were down, as was the buying of sacrificial meat in the nearby area of Pontus and Bithynia, because of the increasing success of Christian evangelism (see *Ep.* 10.96), but that has no relevance here. Demetrius is not being portrayed as a credible speaker.[143] The phrase "the great god(dess) Artemis" is well attested in the inscriptions from a period slightly later than the NT era (see I. Eph. 27, lines 224-25, 407 and 27.535-36, and cf. Xenophon, *Ephesiaka* 1.11.5).

Even if Demetrius was exaggerating things considerably, there is clear evidence that Ephesians would take any threat to the cult of Artemis very seriously. Even well before the turn of the era forty-five persons from Sardis who mistreated an embassy from the temple of Artemis were condemned to death, and the event was inscribed in the records in Ephesus.[144] The very idea that Artemis might be scorned or deprived of the majesty that had attracted "all Asia and the Empire (οικουμενη, though it may mean world here) to worship her"[145] was enough to get many Ephesians up in arms.

V. 28 expresses the outrage of the artisans.[146] They set about chanting, "Great is Artemis of the Ephesians." If her greatness was threatened, so was

142. Απελεγμος is found only here in the NT, and has as its basic meaning "refuted," and so "discredited." See Kilpatrick, "Acts xix.27 απελεγμον." The terminology is rhetorical and follows upon the claim that Paul had used powerful rhetoric and so had persuaded many about the Christian faith.

143. Oster, "Acts 19.23-41 and an Ephesian Inscription," is right in critiquing the article in *Beginnings,* 5:251-56, by L. R. Taylor, who suggested that Paul's preaching had actually caused a significant decline in temple trade in Ephesus, and that this was paralleled a century later in the inscription (cf. *CIG* no. 2954) which Taylor thought spoke of Artemis being dishonored in her own city. Oster shows this interpretation of the inscription is flawed, and it is doubtful that we should see the cult of Artemis in eclipse on the basis of Demetrius's say-so. One must consider the source of this speech.

144. See the discussion in Sokolowski, "A New Testimony."

145. Again obvious hyperbole is involved here, but there is no doubting that Artemis was worshiped by many throughout the Empire; see Pausanias, *Descrip.* 2.2.5 and 4.31.8.

146. It was a regular feature of Hellenistic historiography to record such dramatic scenes filled with violent emotions. See Josephus, *War* 2.402; 5.420; 7.42, 57. Note that as usual the Western text tries to fill in the gaps by adding the detail that the artisans "ran out into the street" and began to shout.

their own, for as Oster says, "the quintessence of Artemis was forever related to the well-being of Ephesus. . . . the principal force of her cult was upon the interrelated components of the city's urban life, e.g., the civic, the economic, educational, patriotic, administrative, and commercial facets. . . . There was no other Graeco-Roman metropolis in the Empire whose 'body, soul, and spirit' could so belong to a particular deity as did Ephesus to her patron goddess Artemis."[147] It is worth noting that guilds or associations of artisans are recorded as having started or are warned against starting disturbances in this eastern part of the Empire we now call Turkey.[148]

The social situation of artisans was tenuous. They might make a good deal of money, but money was the only basis for their status claims. Their lack of education or a proper family background meant they were looked down upon by the elite of society, especially for working with their hands. Anything that threatened their income also threatened the status and standard of living they had worked so hard to obtain in a highly stratified society.[149] They were some of the more easily marginalized members of society, trying to be upwardly mobile, and their volatile reaction to an inflammatory speech such as Demetrius gave is quite believable.

Such shouting got the attention of many, which is not surprising in view of the overcrowded *insulae* that characterized ancient cities like Ephesus,[150] but as is often the case with a disturbance involving shouting, there were many who wanted to know what was happening but were confused. Luke says the city was filled with confusion, and the normal way such matters were dealt with was by gathering in the place where a meeting of the local assembly (the εκκλησια, see v. 32) would normally be held.[151] In this case, the largest and

147. Oster, "Ephesus as a Religious Center," p. 1728.

148. For example, Dio Chrysostom, addressing the assembly at Tarsus apparently at the end of the first century A.D. about a riot or "stasis" caused by linen workers in Tarsus (see *Or.* 34.21-22). Notice also the warning in a second-century-A.D. inscription to the bakers' guild, apparently in Magnesia on the Maeander though some have argued for its Ephesian provenance, not to hold meetings as a faction or be leaders in recklessness or start a riot (*SEG* 28.863).

149. On the upper echelon's view of working with one's hands see Plutarch, *Pericl.* 2.1. This of course was not the view of the artisans, or the general view from below; see MacMullen, *Roman Social Relations,* p. 76, and my discussion of associations in *Conflict and Community in Corinth,* pp. 241-45.

150. The population of the city has traditionally been estimated at about 200,000 in the mid–first century A.D., though it may have been closer to 180,000. Even so, the evidence suggests that there was a very high density of population which dwelt in the *insulae* of such cities, perhaps as many as 200 persons per acre in Rome, and somewhat fewer in Ephesus, since there were various outlying villages (see the discussion of White, "Urban Development and Social Change," pp. 40-48).

151. See I. Eph. 29.19-20 and *OGIS* 480.9.

The theater in Ephesus where Paul faced the mob.

most natural venue would be the great theater in Ephesus which was carved out of the side of Mount Pion, was 495 feet in diameter, and could hold close to twenty-five thousand people. Both the setting and the acoustics were quite excellent here.

The artisans and their partisans were acting in haste, not on the basis of a well-thought-out plan, and so they grabbed whomever of Paul's entourage was ready to hand, in this case Gaius and Aristarchus. Demetrius apparently wanted quick action while the crowd's ire was still aroused, and so there was no time for a systematic search for Paul. *V. 29* may refer to the Gaius whom Paul had baptized in Corinth (1 Cor. 1:14) and who at one point hosted Paul and a house church meeting (Rom. 16:23). Whether this Gaius is the same as the Corinthian Gaius we cannot be sure, since it is a very common name, but it is less likely that we may identify him with the Gaius Luke mentions in Acts 20:4, since that Gaius is from Derbe and is one of the delegates who would gather the collection and deliver it to Jerusalem with Paul. Aristarchus may be the same as the Aristarchus mentioned in Col. 4:10 and Philem. 24, but he is surely the one Luke mentions in 20:4 and 27:2. There is some difficulty with the word Μακεδονας in this verse. Some minuscules read the singular Μακεδονα here, probably because the B text of 20:4 tells us Gaius was from Derbe. Aristarchus, as 20:4 and 27:2 indicate, was from Thessalonica, but if the plural is original, and it is certainly the more difficult reading, one would have to conclude that this is a different Gaius than Gaius from Derbe. This would not prevent an equation of this Gaius with the one from Corinth, since he may have moved there from Macedonia.

V. 30 informs us that Paul desired to go into the δημον, but the disciples would not let him. Undoubtedly they feared for his life. The δημος was in fact one of the proper terms for a local assembly of citizens in a free Greek city such as Ephesus. Since this was an irregular meeting, one could translate δημος here simply as "crowd," but Luke may intentionally be subtle here. The people may have thought they were holding a proper assembly, but really they were just a crowd, and the "scribe" would soon make them aware of the improper nature of their behavior.

More remarkable is *v. 31,* which says that even[152] some of the Asiarchs who were friends with Paul sent him a message not to go to the theater. The use of friendship language here may have a somewhat technical sense. The Asiarchs were the leading men of the province (see Strabo, *Geog.* 14.1.42), members of the noblest and wealthiest local families who among other things were current or former holders of important offices in the league of Asian cities, and more importantly it appears that from their ranks was annually elected the high priest of the imperial cult.[153] Their main task was to promote the cult of the emperor and of Roma, and secure allegiance to Rome. They would have a natural relationship with all local Roman citizens, which in a free Greek city may not have been a very large number, and in any case would be assumed by the Asiarchs to be their core constituency. If Paul was indeed a Roman citizen, and one who deliberately assumed a public face by means of public orations, he may have been well known to the Asiarchs.[154] The friendship language here could mean that Paul had one or more of the Asiarchs as a patron or at least an advocate in Ephesus (could this be how he obtained the hall of Tyrannus?).[155]

As for what Luke is trying to tell us here, we see a possible distinction being implied. While the Way might well be a threat to this or that local cult, or to a basically ethnic religious group like Jews, time and again Rome's authorities do not see Christianity as being a threat to their primary interests. Is it Luke's apologetic tack to suggest that Christianity challenged society at

152. Another example of an ascensive και.

153. There is now evidence of their existence in the early first century A.D.; see Hemer, *Book of Acts,* pp. 121-22 and n. 58, and especially Kearsley, "The Asiarchs."

154. On Paul's Roman citizenship see pp. 445ff. above. On the Asiarchs as a group spoken of together see Strabo, *Geog.* 14.1.42, writing a generation before this Ephesian riot.

155. On Asiarchs as patrons and benefactors in Ephesus see Kearsley, "The Asiarchs," p. 369. Kearsley, however, disputes the idea that the Asiarchs were also high priests in the imperial cult (see pp. 366-67).

the social levels below the imposed Roman superstructure but need not disturb Rome's basic legal and military authority? This is possible. Haenchen puts it this way: "A sect whose leader had Asiarchs for friends cannot be dangerous to the state."[156]

V. 32 suggests that the δεμος was in disarray — some were shouting one thing, some another, and most didn't know why they had come together. Luke is perhaps being somewhat sarcastic here. He certainly has no high opinion of this meeting.

Vv. 33-34 are not at all clear. What was Alexander trying to accomplish? First, we should note the use of οχλος here and in v. 35. Though the Ephesians may have thought they were holding a popular assembly, Luke emphasizes that it was just a crowd in vv. 33 and 35.[157] Second, a clear sign of confusion about the meaning of this text on the part of some early Christians is the fact that the Western text has κατεβιβασαν instead of the probably more primitive reading συνεβιβασαν. The former means "they pulled him down," the latter "they instructed or shouted instructions to him." In other words, the Western text suggests that while the Jews put Alexander up to speak, the crowd pulled him down, perhaps because they knew he was a Jew.[158] It is a plausible conjecture that the Jews put Alexander forward as a spokesman to make clear to the crowd that true Jews had nothing to do with Paul's activities and did not endorse them.[159] Can sense be made out of the more difficult reading συνεβιβασαν? Yes, if we note that the δε may be contrastive and thus v. 33 may be contrasted with v. 32 in some respect. Alexander may have been one of those who did not know why the crowd had come together, *but* when some of the crowd instructed him on what this was all about he then was prepared to stand up before the crowd, representing the Jewish constituency there, and speak to it.

V. 33b indicates that once put forward by the Jews, Alexander made the common gesture for silence and prepared to make an oration, in particular, an απολογια to the popular assembly. The use of the verb means to make a

156. Haenchen, *Acts*, p. 578.

157. It may be, too, that especially in v. 41 εκκλησια has its formal sense of a regularly summoned political assembly when the proconsul came around (on which see below). See Larkin, *Acts*, pp. 284-85.

158. This Alexander might well be the same Alexander mentioned in 2 Tim. 4:14 (the one mentioned in 1 Tim. 1:20 seems to have been a former Christian and so a different person. Alexander was after all a very common name among both Greeks and Jews). There would be a certain appropriateness to putting forward a person who may well have been part of the guild of metalworkers in Ephesus, and may have been well known to people such as Demetrius. Such a person would be a good liaison between the Jewish community and the artisans of the city.

159. See Bruce, *The Acts of the Apostles*, p. 419; Haenchen, *Acts*, pp. 574-75.

defense and suggests that the conjecture is accurate that Alexander was going to defend his community and disassociate them from Paul's activity. He was not, however, given the opportunity, for at least many in the crowd recognized Alexander as a well-known Jew and began to chant their slogan about Artemis for about two hours! To the crowd, at this point in time, there was no major difference between an Alexander the Jew and a Paul the Jewish Christian. Both were monotheists who did not endorse the worship of Artemis, and thereby would be seen as suspect by local pagans, not least because of the always latent and widespread anti-Semitism in Greco-Roman culture.[160]

After the period of chanting a new figure appears in the story — the γραμματευς.[161] This person was a city official charged with keeping records, being present when money was deposited in the temple, serving as a registrar, and the like (see Apollonius of Tyana, *Letters* 32).[162] He was the very sort of person one would expect to step forward and object if some sort of irregular or illegal assembly was occurring. He would know what the records would say about when assemblies should and should not meet and how they should be carried out. Furthermore, as the scribe of this very assembly, he was its chief executive officer. He was not appointed by Rome but rather came from within the local assembly itself. In order to appreciate his argument one needs to bear in mind that this was a free assembly, and subject to careful scrutiny by the Roman officials, especially the proconsul of the province. Any irregularities might give the Romans an excuse to take away the city's freedoms, including the right to their popular assembly. As the Empire continued to expand and the imperial cult grew, some Roman officials became less and less patient with elements of local autonomy, especially those elements with any political power.[163]

The speech of the clerk, unlike that of Demetrius, is in proper rhetorical

---

160. It is probable that there was resentment by many pagans that past proconsuls of this province had granted Jews special privileges and exemptions from the cultic activities of the dominant religion in the city. See Josephus, *Ant.* 14.227, 263-64, who speaks of the large Jewish community in Ephesus and their exemptions.

161. See Sherwin-White, *Roman Law and Roman Society,* p. 86: "The prominence accorded to the town clerk in Acts fits the fairly copious evidence about this office at Ephesus and other cities of Asia Minor."

162. See the discussion of Keinath, "Contacts of the Book," p. 196.

163. See Dio Chrysostom's *Or.* 38.33-37 in dealing with the fear of losing freedoms and the respect of Roman authorities. Note Plutarch's famous advice to local officials (*Praec. ger. reip.* 813E-F): "You must say to yourself: You who rule are a subject, ruling a State controlled by proconsuls, the agents of Caesar; these are not *the spearmen of the plain* nor is this ancient Sardis. . . . You should arrange your cloak more carefully and from the office of the generals *keep your eyes upon the orators' platform,* and not have great pride or confidence in your crown, since you see shoes of the proconsul just above your head." See the discussion by Trebilco, "Asia," pp. 346-47.

form and is deliberative, attempting to persuade the audience not to do anything precipitous and instead do what is useful and beneficial to all in Ephesus
by using the normal legal remedies available for resolving problems. As Kennedy says, the clerk relies heavily on his *ethos* (and authority) to persuade the
mob. There was no need here for a *captatio* since the clerk was well known to
the audience, and so the summary of this speech begins with a rhetorical
question, followed by the basic proposition (that the audience not do anything
rash), which in turn is followed in vv. 37-39 by the arguments used to persuade,
and then finally we have a *peroratio* in v. 40 appealing to civic pride.[164]

V. 35 begins with the address "men of Ephesus," which may in fact be
intended literally here, though elsewhere Luke uses ανδρες inclusively. The
city of Ephesus is said to be the νεωκορον of Artemis. The term means temple
keeper, and there is evidence from a Neronian coin that the term was used
during this era not just of the "temple keeping" of the imperial cult but also
of the temple of Artemis.[165] There is probably no basis here to charge Luke
with anachronism. V. 35b refers to the διοπετους. The word is a combination
of the genitive for Zeus and the verb "to fall." Thus the clerk refers to that
which fell from Zeus or heaven. There was at Taurus a meteorite worshiped
as an image of Artemis (see Euripides, *Iphigenia in Taurica* 87-88, 1384), and
though we have no record of it, this may also have been the case in Ephesus,
for in fact it was not an unusual practice in this era to treat meteorites as cult
objects (cf. Cicero, *Verr.* 2.5.187 for the same practice at Enna but in connection
with the god Ceres, or at Emesa of El Gabal as mentioned in Herodian, *Hist.*
5.3, 5).[166] Could the mention of the meteorite be a response to the criticism
about gods made with hands?[167]

---

164. See the discussion in Kennedy, *New Testament Interpretation*, p. 132, and Soards,
The Speeches in Acts, p. 104.

165. See *New Docs*, 6 (1992), no. 30, p. 205; Oster, "The Ephesian Artemis," p. 30.
The attempt by White, "Urban Development and Social Change," p. 37, to suggest that the
phrase "neokoros of Artemis" was a new label and may even have dated from later in Nero's
reign than the time of this riot (and thus Luke is guilty of anachronism), is largely an
argument from silence. The Neronian coin may well be from the 50s, and in any case it
surely reflects a *practice* that antedates the minting of the coin. It may be nothing more
than an accident that we have not found still earlier evidence of this designation used with
temples other than those serving the imperial cult. In any case, as Sherwin-White, *Roman
Law and Roman Society*, p. 89, points out, the title Warden of Artemis for actual civic temple
keepers in Ephesus dates back to 333 B.C. (see *SEG* 1,282).

166. Nock, *St. Paul*, p. 133, argued that Ephesian Artemis had as her "most sacred
idol a meteorite." He is right that officials would not likely pay much attention to philosophical debates about whether gods lived in temples made with hands or not, but anything
that touched the honor or prestige of the city and of Artemis, anything that might lower
the city's honor rating in the eyes of the world, was another matter.

167. See Trebilco, "Asia," p. 353.

The intent of the rhetorical question is to silence unwarranted fears by mentioning undeniable facts. The question then serves as something of a *narratio* on the basis of which the clerk is able to go on and argue that since these things cannot be denied the crowd should be quiet and do nothing rash.

V. 37 makes a bold assertion. While the clerk might well know that no one had violated or robbed the temple of Artemis lately, we do not know how he could have known that Gaius and Aristarchus were not blasphemers of Artemis. Perhaps the point is that no one was claiming they heard *these two men* speak *against Artemis,* whatever they may have been speaking for (i.e., Christ), though the case may have been different with Paul himself (see v. 26 above). The clerk hereby indicates the sort of activities that the local law was bound to take seriously and act against. That the Ephesian officials would likely take any real threats against the temple very seriously is shown by the continued passing on of stories about the attempt to burn the temple of Artemis down (see Lucian, *Peregrin.* 22).

V. 38 suggests that instead of precipitous action, Demetrius used the normal legal channels to air his complaints or charges. These remedies were twofold: (1) the court system, which could handle financial disputes, and (2) the regular meeting of the citizen legislature, which dealt with any attack on the city's honor or prestige.[168] The plurals "courts" and "proconsuls" used here are probably examples of generalizing plurals (the clerk would be saying, "there are such things as courts and proconsuls"; see the NEB), and thus the latter is probably not an allusion to the fact that shortly after Nero gained the throne in October A.D. 54 the proconsul of Asia, M. Junius Silanus, was poisoned and died and two local officials (Helius and Celer) were put in charge of the emperor's affairs until the successor arrived. These two men, however, were not really proconsuls even *pro tempore* (see Tacitus, *Ann.* 13.1-3; Dio Cassius, *Hist.* 61.5.4-5). If they were alluded to here, it might provide another clue about a more precise date of these happenings. Luke knew quite well that a province would not have two proconsuls (cf. Acts 13:7; 18:12).

According to John Chrysostom (see *Hom.* 42.2) the Ephesian εχχλησια met three times a month, and there is also clear evidence of the holding of a *conventus* in each of various cities in the province of Asia including Ephesus (see Pliny, *Nat. Hist.* 5.105-26 and Cicero, *Ad fam.* 3.8.6), as the proconsul traveled through the region.[169] On these occasions and in these settings the bringing of charges would be appropriate. The implication is that the present time and place is not appropriate for dealing with such matters.

The inappropriateness of the present ad hoc assembly is made evident in *v. 39* when the clerk says that if there is anything further the crowd wants

---

168. See Larkin, *Acts,* p. 286.
169. See the helpful discussion by Burton, "Proconsuls, Assizes," especially pp. 97ff.

to know, it must be settled in the *legal* assembly (εννομω εκκλησια).[170] Rome was not likely to pass a blind eye over an unlawful assembly, and so now the clerk turns the tables on the crowd. If there was an unlawful assembly the city could be charged with "stasis," that is, with acting seditiously, creating factions in the Empire, rioting. The terminology the clerk uses here at the end of his speech is legal and correct. His point is that if questioned, the Ephesians could give no legal justification for this particular meeting, and so would be suspected of, and, as *v. 40* puts it, in danger of being charged with, subversive activities. This might well be used as leverage to take away Ephesus's freedoms.[171] The clerk is clearly in charge here, even though this is an illegal assembly, and so after his masterful speech *v. 41* tells us that having silenced the crowds, having argued them out of any vigilante sort of actions, and having in fact accused them of potentially bringing down the law on their own heads, he dismissed the assembly, and we hear no more about it. That Paul later bypasses Ephesus (20:16) strongly suggests that he realized there would be ongoing danger for him in this locale, once the riot had transpired, for of course Demetrius had not been able to act against Paul in the way he wanted on this occasion.

F. Final Tour of Duty (20:1-16)

The material in this subsection provides yet further evidence that Acts,[172] as we have it, is probably not in a state of final revision, a fact which helps explain the expansions and alterations of the later Western text in this passage and elsewhere. This particular passage is elliptical in the extreme until we get to the tale about Eutychus in vv. 7-12. What appears to be the case with Acts 20:1-5 is that we have a very minimal expansion upon certain notes about Paul's travel and travel companions, something which can also be said about vv. 13-16.

---

170. Luke uses here the appropriate terminology for such a meeting in Ephesus, as the Salutaris inscription shows. See the discussion in Sherwin-White, *Roman Law and Roman Society,* p. 87. According to this inscription there was one special monthly meeting called ιερα και νομιμος εκκλησια. Chrysostom may reflect a later practice, or as Sherwin-White conjectures, there may have been one regular and two extra monthly meetings.

171. Pace Ramsay, *St. Paul the Traveller,* p. 282, this speech is not an *apologia* for the Christians, but rather a prudential speech trying to protect Ephesus's freedoms against the ongoing encroachments of Roman power. It does, however, foreshadow the themes of some of the apologetic speeches that follow in Acts. For evidence that the Romans were eager to get rid of such popular democratic assemblies, perhaps especially in Asia Minor, see Sherwin-White, *Roman Law and Roman Society,* pp. 83-85.

172. For earlier evidence see pp. 65ff. above.

The passage opens with *20:1,* a transitional verse which indicates that Paul was not driven from Ephesus but left of his own free will, after the uproar had died down. Nevertheless the verse suggests he maintained a low profile, summoning the disciples to himself, rather than returning to a public venue like the hall of Tyrannus. Here we are told that Paul παρακαλεσας, which may mean he exhorted them, but it could also mean that he encouraged or comforted them. The verb recurs again at v. 12, where it seems more clearly to mean comforted (cf. Acts 11:23; 14:22; 15:32; 16:40). The verb appears again in v. 2, where it seems to mean exhort, since it is added that "much words," or perhaps we might translate "many speeches," were involved.

It was Paul's practice to reinforce and strengthen churches he had already founded, and this we see him doing in 20:1-5 as he travels back through Macedonia and Achaia. If we compare this material to what we find in Paul's letter, especially 2 Corinthians 1–7, v. 2 would seem to cover a considerable amount of time. Before leaving Ephesus for good, at some point Paul had made a quick visit to Corinth, been rebuffed, and wrote a painful letter as a result, a letter which is mentioned in 2 Cor. 2:3-9 but now appears to be lost.[173] He was anxious about how the Corinthians would respond to such a letter, and in his anxiety, though a door for ministry had been opened to him in Troas, he passed on to Macedonia, where he met again his coworker Titus, who brought good news about how the Corinthians had reacted to the letter. In response, while in Macedonia Paul wrote 2 Corinthians, probably sometime in A.D. 56.

One of the great imponderables about Acts is that nowhere is Titus mentioned. One may suspect that Luke does not know about his work, or does not know enough to mention him.[174] This fact again suggests that Luke was only a companion of Paul briefly during the second missionary tour, and on a more extended basis during the third. Bruce has plausibly suggested that the period of time covered in 20:2 was considerable, and that it was probably at this juncture that Paul traveled as far as Illyricum (Rom. 15:19). V. 2 also refers to Paul's coming to Ελλαδα. This is not the provincial designation of course, but rather the more popular term, and shows that Luke is capable of using either sort of designation (cf. 18:12; 19:21).[175] The term here probably designates the same area as the earlier references to Achaia, especially since Paul once again ends up in Corinth.

---

173. See my discussion in *Conflict and Community in Corinth,* pp. 328-33.

174. Is the lack of mention of Titus connected with the lack of mention of the collection in Acts, since Titus is closely connected with the latter in 2 Corinthians 8?

175. See Bruce, *The Acts of the Apostles,* p. 423. In other words, this is another example of Luke's concern for variation for stylistic or rhetorical reasons, not because of a change of meaning.

V. 3 refers to the fact that Paul stayed for three months in Corinth, perhaps the winter months of A.D. 56-57, during which he wrote Romans. Claudius died in A.D. 54, and so it is quite possible that the peripatetic couple, Priscilla and Aquila, could by this juncture be back in Rome, especially since special decrees of Emperor Claudius would have almost certainly expired or fallen into abeyance with the accession of Nero.[176] There is thus no necessary reason why Romans 16 could not have been directed to the church in Rome, even if originally it had been part of a separate letter of introduction for Phoebe.

The rest of v. 3 is unclear in regard to the timing of events. Were the Jews plotting to do something against Paul while he was traveling? Why would they not simply deal with him while he was in Corinth? Perhaps the social and legal situation was not favorable for a frontal assault on Paul in Corinth, especially since he appears to have had by now some friends in the city of considerable social status, for example Erastus. Thus the Jews may have plotted in a more secretive fashion to do away with Paul while he was on board the boat to Syria, for he would have nowhere to flee and no legal protection there. It has been suggested that Paul may have been planning to sail on a ship with Jewish pilgrims going from Corinth to the Holy Land, but the text in fact says he was planning to set sail for Syria. Perhaps Paul was planning to go there first on the way to Jerusalem, and then on to Rome (see 19:21).

Another conjecture worth pondering is that Paul may have decided to avoid going by boat at this point because the considerable sum of money he would be carrying would be in more danger — from pirates — on the high seas.[177] This conjecture, however, ignores the fact that the danger mentioned in the text has to do with a Jewish plot against Paul and not against the collection, which isn't mentioned here, and more to the point, Paul was prepared to sail from Macedonia shortly after this time.[178]

---

176. See above on Acts 18:1ff.

177. See Polhill, *Acts,* p. 416. The problem with this suggestion is that Claudius had pretty well rid the seas of pirates, but of course this would not protect Paul from extortionists onboard ship.

178. It is also an open question how serious a problem piracy was at this point in the eastern Mediterranean. With all the sea voyages referred to in Acts, Luke never once mentions this problem, and while Paul mentions danger from bandits in 2 Cor. 11:26, he does not connect this with the dangers he faced at sea mentioned in v. 25 as including shipwreck and being adrift in the sea (see also the general reference in v. 26b — danger at sea). Rather, the reference to bandits is sandwiched between dangers from rivers and dangers from Paul's own people, both of which are surely problems that happened while on land. Most of the literature on this subject suggests that banditry was less of a problem during the early Empire than during either the Republic or the late Empire. See the fine essay by Shaw, "The Bandit." Most of the discussion in the literature of the period has to do with bandits (on land) as opposed to pirates. Plutarch speaks of the period before the Empire, before there were guardians on the sea, as a time of piracy; see *Life of Pompey* 24.1-4; 25.1.

Paul then decides to go overland through Macedonia, and v. 4 gives us a list of those who accompanied Paul on this sojourn. The list is interesting in several respects. First, it appears to be arranged geographically by region, perhaps another small piece of evidence that Luke thinks in terms of a κατα γενος pattern for arranging his material. The first two locales mentioned are Beroea and Thessalonica, places Paul visited in succession (in the reverse order, cf. 17:1-15); the next two are either Derbe or Douberios, from which Gaius hailed, and Lystra, which Luke informed us in Acts 16:1-3 was the home of Timothy; and then Asia, where Tychicus and Trophimus were from. In view of the coupling of Gaius with Timothy, it is much more probable that the original reading here was Derbe, with Douberios (a city in Macedonia) being a later correction, in view of 19:29.[179] If we ask why the listing of place-names in connection with all these persons (except Timothy), the most plausible answer is that these persons were converts in these places and thus represented the churches Paul founded in these places. The place-names are not random, nor do they reflect an abstract interest in these men's places of origin. It is curious that no representative is mentioned from Corinth (see 1 Cor. 16:1-3; 2 Cor. 8:16-23), but perhaps in the end the Corinthians allowed Paul to represent them.[180] It is also odd that no representative from Philippi is mentioned, but perhaps Luke was that representative (2 Cor. 8:18-19?), and he joined the entourage when Paul reached Philippi again. That Luke is not more directly forthcoming about the collection may well be because "the failure of the Jerusalem Church to rally to Paul's aid when he was arrested was an embarrassment and a sign that Paul's intended gesture of reconciliation had failed."[181]

V. 5 indicates that a group went ahead to Troas and were waiting for "us" there. "We," however, are said to have sailed only *after* the days of Un-

---

179. It is Codex Bezae, supported in part by syr(har.mg) and Ephraem, that has the reading Douberios, but this is by no means the only change. Tychicus is changed to Eutychus(!), and he and Trophimus are identified more specifically as Ephesians in the Western version, and furthermore the Western text says Paul wished to sail to Syria as a result of a Jewish plot in Corinth, which is not the impression the general received text gives. Then the Western text adds that the Holy Spirit, not the plot, was the reason for Paul's deciding to set off on the journey over land rather than by sea. See the discussion in Metzger, *Textual Commentary*, pp. 474-76, and in Delebecque, "Les Deux Versions du voyage de saint Paul de Corinthe a Troas (Ac 20,3-6)." What the reviser ultimately responsible for this text did not realize is that the names are grouped by geographical region, and that they are only mentioned at all because they represent churches in these areas, presumably accompanying the collection to Jerusalem.

180. It is not impossible that in the end the Corinthians failed to make a contribution to the collection due to some problem.

181. Johnson, *Acts*, p. 357. See the discussion in Ollrog, *Paulus und die seine Mitarbeiter*, pp. 52-58.

leavened Bread.[182] This reference may suggest that Paul was celebrating the Passover, or perhaps a Christianized version of the Passover.[183] This time reference is of some importance because it lets us know that Paul had fifty days from this point to get to Jerusalem in time for Pentecost.[184] The narrative returns to the "we" material again, and in this instance this verse makes clear that none of the aforementioned delegates or congregational representatives are part of this "we," unless the ουτοι mentioned at the beginning of v. 5 refers only to some of the listed persons in v. 4, in particular the last two names grouped together — Trophimus and Tychicus.[185] The "we" here clearly involves Paul plus someone else. In view of the fact that the "we" left off in Philippi at 16:16 and now picks up from the same location, we must assume that the first-person narrator is the one involved, especially in view of Luke's carefulness elsewhere to pick up a person in the narrative where he or she was left earlier (see, e.g., the case of Philip in Caesarea; cf. 8:40 to 21:8). Still the most plausible explanation for this phenomenon in view of (1) the practice of Greek historians to place themselves in the story only where and when they were actually present,[186] and (2) the fact that the "we" passages do not appear at places where one would readily suspect pure redaction or invention since they do not generally involve crucial junctures in the narrative (especially in the first two "we"

182. As Tannehill, *Narrative Unity of Luke-Acts,* 2:247, points out, here we see part of Luke's attempt to stress in the latter part of his narrative that Paul was a loyal Jew. Luke clearly and rightly associates the Feast of Unleavened Bread with Passover (see Luke 22:1; cf. for the conjunction of the two festivals in the first century Josephus, *Ant.* 14.21; *War* 6.421-27). These days *began* on Passover eve and continued on for a week (Nisan 14 to Nisan 21; see Acts 12:3; and cf. Exod. 12:18; Lev. 23:5-6). It is noteworthy that Luke occasionally marks time by the use of the Jewish festivals, for instance, especially at 20:16, or by the sabbath, as at 16:13. This is perhaps primarily because the main character in the narrative here, Paul, followed such a calendar (cf. 20:6 and 16; cf. 1 Cor. 16:6), but it may also imply something about the author's own background. He may have been a Gentile God-fearer before becoming a Christian.

183. See Marshall, *Acts,* p. 325. It may be that Lydia and others continued to celebrate the Jewish festivals, and Paul and his companions, at least the Jewish ones, joined them.

184. The timing of the delivery of the collection at Pentecost may not be accidental, for it was, according to Acts 2, then that Peter proclaimed the good news that the Spirit would be poured out on all flesh and that all who called on the Lord's name would be saved. The coming of these Gentiles with the collection to Zion on this occasion would have considerable symbolic significance, especially in light of prophecies like that found in Zech. 8:20-23.

185. See the discussion of Praeder, "The Problem," p. 97, and Schneider, *Die Apostelgeschichte II,* p. 282. It is a bare possibility but unlikely that Luke means that all of the delegates but the last two mentioned stopped in Macedonia as Paul had, and then either did or did not travel on with Paul (and Luke) after the festival time.

186. See the introduction, pp. 24ff. above.

passages),[187] is that the author, Luke, the sometime companion of Paul, is among those called "we" in these various passages. He does not claim to be a major actor in these events; he only claims to be a sometime personal observer of some of the happenings from the second missionary journey onward, and the chronicler of all he recounts.[188] This claim to be an eyewitness was considered vital in Greek historiography, unlike Roman historiography where being an armchair historian was much more acceptable.

As Longenecker says, from "20.5 through the end of Acts (28.31), Luke's narrative gives considerable attention to ports of call, stopovers, and time spent on Paul's travel, and includes various anecdotes. It contains the kind of details found in a travel journal."[189] The journey to Troas this time took five days, no doubt due to the direction of the head winds (cf. 16:11), after which the group stayed at Troas for seven days.[190] Troas was another strategically placed city, which had been turned into a Roman colony by Augustus (Colonia Augusta Troadensium). The congregation there seems to have been founded by Paul

187. See the discussion of the "we" passages above, pp. 480ff.

188. The explanation of Tannehill, *Narrative Unity of Luke-Acts,* 2:247, that the "we" is a device meant to encourage the listener to enter the narrative as a participant is entirely too modern, and Praeder, "The Problem," p. 199, is right to object: "There is little in this portrayal of Paul's first person traveling companions to invite readers to involve themselves with them and their travels." Tannehill responds that he meant participation only as a silent observer like the narrator himself (p. 247 n. 5). The problem with this explanation is that the reader has all along been that sort of silent partner in the tale, and there is no good reason why the author should have so sporadically interjected the "we" in places like Acts 16 and here if that was the function of the "we." We would have expected it much earlier in the narrative, and especially in association with major events like Pentecost. Furthermore, it is underestimating Luke's role here to call him nothing more than a silent observer, for he is also at least a recorder of these events, *unlike Theophilus or whoever else this narrative was first written for.* Thus he is not really just another observer like the audience; the "we" suggests more than the silent observer role.

189. Longenecker, *Acts,* p. 508. Greek historians believed that geographical and ethnographical material should be included in one's history. Polybius, for example (12.25e.1), whom Luke seems to be most like as a historian (other than perhaps Ephorus), says the three necessary preparations for writing history are: (1) the study of sources (see Luke 1:1-4); (2) knowledge of cities, rivers, lakes, peculiar features of land and sea and distances; (3) knowledge of political affairs. It follows from this that in Acts 21–28 Luke is trying to end his work by making clear his serious historical intentions in the whole work, for it is here especially that we have the "we" material, the attention to geographical detail, times and distances and the character of travel, the interaction with political authorities, and the like. Up to Acts 21 Luke's focus has been on the crossing of ethnic and geographical boundaries. This means of finishing his work would surely have signaled to someone familiar with Greek historiography the genre of Luke's work.

190. The more precise time references at this juncture, immediately after the introduction of the "we," are probably no accident. The author, being now a participant, has more precise information from the notes he himself took.

on his way to Macedonia, even though he did not stay as long as he would have liked (see 2 Cor. 2:12-13; cf. 2 Tim. 4:13).[191] Here we have another example of the Pauline urban missionary strategy, establishing congregations in major cities in the Empire, particularly in Roman colonies such as Troas, Philippi, or Corinth.[192]

The material in Acts 20:7-12 is much more substantial in detail than the previous subsection. In *v. 7* we have perhaps the first reference to the fact that it was on the first day of the week (i.e., Sunday) that Christians met to have fellowship and hear preaching. Did Luke follow the Jewish way of reckoning time in which days were reckoned from sundown to sundown, or the Roman way in which midnight to midnight was seen as the way of dividing days? If the former, then this meeting would apparently have been held on what we would call Saturday night; if the latter, on Sunday night. Pointing in the direction of the former way of reckoning days is Luke's use of the Jewish phrase here, "the first of the sabbath," which originally meant the first day after the sabbath, then the first day of the week (cf. Mark 16:2; 1 Cor. 16:2; Rev. 1:10; *Did.* 14:1; *Barn* 15:9).[193] Against Luke's following the Jewish way of reckoning days are texts like Acts 2:15 and 3:1, where, like the Romans, Luke reckons the hours of daytime beginning at dawn (6 A.M.). In short, Luke seems to follow the Jewish religious calendar but the Roman means of reckoning time (cf. Luke 24:1), another clue that our author had one foot in the Jewish and another in the Greco-Roman world.[194]

It is not clear from the reference to the breaking of bread whether this includes the celebration of the Lord's Supper or not, but if 1 Corinthians 11 is any guide, probably the Lord's Supper was shared in the context of a Greco-Roman meal.[195] It may be more than coincidence that we have in this narrative the combined mention of the first day of the week, an upper room, and the breaking of bread (cf. Luke 22:12; 24:30-35; Acts 1:13). Luke is drawing on the paradigmatic images of the primitive fellowship of the followers of Jesus.[196]

---

191. Luke does not mention this occurrence. Cf. Acts 20:1.

192. On Troas see the discussion by Trebilco, "Asia," pp. 357-59, and Hemer, "Alexandria Troas."

193. But see Polhill, *Acts*, p. 418.

194. See Marshall, *Acts*, p. 326.

195. On the practice in the Jerusalem church see pp. 156ff. above. In any case, Luke places no great emphasis here or elsewhere on the interior life and rituals of the early Christian community, especially once one gets beyond Jerusalem. His primary concern is with recording the spreading of the word and thus the chronicling of the evangelistic activity. This is shown in this very narrative. The meal is mentioned in passing, but the focus is on Paul's speaking and dialoguing.

196. See Johnson, *Acts*, p. 358.

V. 7 also tells us that because Paul intended to leave the next day, he dialogued until midnight with the Christians of Troas.[197] In *v. 8* Luke paints a vivid picture of the many lamps in the room upstairs where the meeting was held, apparently in someone's home. That we are told in v. 9 that the meeting was held two floors above ground level (which in most countries would be called the third floor, as it is in the Greek [τριστεγον], but in America is called the second floor) may suggest something about the social status of these Christians. If this is an *insula,* or apartment building, then the hosts of this meeting were not among the social elite.[198] In a more wealthy person's home, meetings normally took place on what Americans would call the first floor, especially if it involved using the dining room, or *triclinium.*

V. 9 refers to a boy or young man named Eutychus. His name means "good fortune" or "lucky," but he was about to be distinctly unlucky.[199] This verse calls him a νεανιας, which could mean he was a young man, but if παις in v. 12 means a "boy," it refers to someone between nine and fourteen years of age (see Philo, *Opif. Mundi* 105). Παις, however, could mean a slave, as this youth's name suggests, in which case Eutychus may even have been in his thirties. Whether the atmosphere in the room was too warm or Eutychus was simply worn out from a long day's work (which may well have been the case if he was a slave), in any case he fell asleep while Paul preached on well into the night, and unfortunately he was sitting in a window when he did so, and so he fell to the ground level "two" floors below. Though there has been considerable debate, v. 9b does say he was picked up dead; the text does not say it appeared as if he was dead (contrast 14:19).[200] In short, in what follows we have a miracle tale about the raising of the dead, following the usual form of such a tale with the confirmation of the cure and the reaction of the observers at the very end of the narrative.[201]

V. 10 suggests that Paul responded immediately, going down to the street, bending over the corpse, taking him up in his arms, perhaps even breathing into him, and then declaring, "Do not be alarmed, for his life (ψυχη) is in

197. As is the case throughout the account of Paul's third missionary venture, we find again in vv. 7 and 9 the emphasis on Paul's using persuasion or rhetoric to convince his (mainly?) Gentile audiences. See Longenecker, *Acts,* p. 509 n. 7.

198. See rightly here Marshall, *Acts,* p. 326.

199. This narrative only has humor, with Paul droning on and the young man falling asleep, because its ending was not tragic. Yet Luke does not play up the entertaining aspect even of this story; but see Pervo, *Profit with Delight,* pp. 65-66.

200. See Polhill, *Acts,* p. 419 n. 64. Had Luke wanted to say he was taken up *as if* dead, he certainly could have done so (cf. Matt. 28:4; Mark 9:26; Rev. 1:17).

201. This is perhaps why we find the material now found in v. 12 where we do, rather than immediately after v. 10. Ramsay, *St. Paul the Traveller,* p. 291, makes the suggestion that Luke tells the tale from an eyewitness point of view — he saw the boy fall, and then the next thing he saw was Paul reappearing in the room saying he was okay. Afterward he learned what had become of the boy.

him." This is not a declaration that he had not died, but rather that now that Paul had ministered to him he was alive.[202] The story may reflect the early Jewish notion that the spirit of a dead person did not depart from the body until after the third day he or she had been dead, in which case though someone might die, he or she might be raised from death (cf. Gen. Rab. 100 [64a]). This is precisely what makes the story in John 11 so spectacular. It is possible that Paul is being portrayed here as being like the great OT prophets such as Elijah or Elisha, who also raised the dead (see 1 Kings 17:17-24; 2 Kings 4:33-36, especially the latter), but more to the point he would be seen by those who heard Acts read as being like Peter in Acts 9:36-43.[203] Both men are portrayed as great and powerful early Christian leaders, and in the case of Paul this is the last miracle he is said to perform as a free man (but see below on Acts 28:5-6). Yet our author does not make the miracle the centerpiece of this tale. The proclamation is deliberately indicated to be more crucial, as the return to it in *v. 11* makes evident.

V. 11 tells us that Paul, after reviving "Lucky," went back upstairs, broke bread and ate, and then having received nourishment continued to talk with the gathered assembly until dawn, at which time he left them. This prepares us for what follows in *v. 13*. In *v. 12* we are told that some (presumably members of the congregation) had taken the slave or boy away alive, and that they were not a little encouraged by this fact.[204]

The next subsection (vv. 13-16) leads us up to the Miletus speech. We are told that "we," in this case *not* including Paul, went ahead to the ship and sailed away without Paul for Assos. Here "we" presumably means Luke and the traveling companions carrying the collection.[205] The intent was to take Paul on board at Assos, which Paul would reach by traveling overland from Troas. This was an easy day's journey of twenty miles, and perhaps Paul wished to stay in Troas until the last moment to make sure all was well with Eutychus and/or to complete his final exhortation to this congregation. Paul had informed his traveling companions of his intention to meet them at Assos.[206]

202. This is probably not a "magical" performative utterance but rather a declarative one on the basis of what Paul had already done, but cf. Philostratus, *Apollonius* 4.45, and Johnson, *Acts,* p. 356.

203. See the discussion, pp. 328ff. above.

204. Here again we see Luke's use of litotes, except that on this occasion, for stylistic variation, he uses μετριως rather than ολιγον.

205. The Aremenian catena, resting upon the Old Syriac text, has, instead of "we" at v. 13, "I, Luke, and those with me went on board" (see Metzger, *Textual Commentary,* p. 477). Whatever else one can say about this reading which may ultimately go back to the third century A.D., while it is not original, it certainly provides one of the earliest Christian interpretations of the "we" passage here, and for that reason it is significant.

206. The sail from Troas around Cape Lectum was longer and more difficult than the trip over land, and gave Paul the extra time to complete his work at Troas.

V. 14 tells us this plan worked well, Paul was taken on board, and they sailed on to Mitylene, the chief city on the island of Lesbos. Luke's description here seems to be an account of what was accomplished on each day's sail. The normal method of sailing a small craft in this era was to hug the coast and put into a port at night when the winds died down. *V. 15* indicates that on the next day the boat arrived opposite of Kios, the island which was famous as the birthplace of the great Greek poet Homer. This verse tells us also that on the following day they either passed by, or perhaps touched land briefly at, Samos (the birthplace of Pythagoras, the great mathematician),[207] and the following day they finally arrived at Miletus. This was at least sixteen or seventeen days after Paul had left Philippi's port (Neapolis) at the end of the Feast of Unleavened Bread.

V. 16 informs us that Paul had decided to sail past Ephesus so he would not have to spend time in Asia. He was eager to be in Jerusalem, if possible in time for Pentecost. Luke could only have known the latter if he had heard Paul say so or if it had been reported to him. While it may be that there were additional reasons for not stopping at Ephesus — for example, to avoid trouble or entangling commitments to the many Christians there — Paul's haste to get to Jerusalem is given as the primary reason. It has been objected to this that Miletus was some thirty miles from Ephesus, and in v. 17 Paul will summon the Ephesian elders to meet him in Miletus. The time taken to go and summon the elders and then lead them back would be at least five days. Wouldn't it have been quicker just to meet them in Ephesus and then continue the journey? Various other factors may have been involved, including the possibility that the ship's schedule called for a stop at Miletus rather than at Ephesus.[208]

More probably, Paul's view was that though he would lose five days by meeting the elders at Miletus, he would lose even more if he went to Ephesus, in view of all the friends, supporters, acquaintances, and enemies he made there during his almost three years in that city.[209] Paul had already lost five days crossing from Philippi to Troas, then a week in Troas, then a day of travel to Assos, then at least another three or four days to get to Miletus. He needed about another twenty-five or so days' sailing to arrive in Israel in time to make it to the festival of Pentecost, which in A.D. 57 began on May 29. As Acts 21:27-29 will show, this meeting in Miletus was probably a wise move as Paul still had various enemies in Asia who would have recognized him immediately.

---

207. The verb παρεβαλομεν could mean either stopped at, or passed by. The Western text interprets it in the latter sense. See Polhill, *Acts,* p. 421 n. 70.

208. Marshall, *Acts,* p. 328, suggests that Paul wished to avoid a long period of time in the ship at Ephesus while it was unloading and reloading.

209. See Trebilco, "Asia," p. 362.

G. Paul's Farewell Address (20:17-38)

If there is a case to be made that Luke knew Paul's letters, or at least the Pauline message found in those letters, it must be made in the main on the basis of the Miletus speech. This is the only extended piece of speech material found on Paul's lips that is addressed to Christians. It is not an accident that this speech sounds more like the Paul of the letters than any other of his speeches in Acts. The following chart will show the similarities in content:

Term/Concept	Acts	Paul's Letters
reminder of how he lived when with his converts	20:17-18	1 Thess. 2:1-2; 5:10-11; Phil. 4:15
Paul's work called serving the Lord	20:19	Rom. 1:1; 12:11; Phil. 2:22
on humility (refusing to claim anything for himself)	20:19	2 Cor. 10:1; 11:7; 1 Thess. 2:6
on his fears/showing personal concern		Rom. 9:2; 2 Cor. 2:4; Phil. 3:18
Jewish persecution	20:19	2 Cor. 11:24, 26; 1 Thess. 2:14-16
taught from house to house	20:20	Rom. 16:5; Col. 4:15; Phm. 21
helpful/profitable teaching	20:20	Gal. 4:16; 2 Cor. 4:2
preaching to both Jew and Greek	20:21	Rom. 1:16; 1 Cor. 9:20
faith in our Lord Jesus	20:21	Rom. 10:9-13
Paul's uncertainty about his future	20:22	Rom. 15:30-32
lack of attempt to preserve his own life	20:24	2 Cor. 4:7–5:10; 6:4-10; Phil. 1:19-26; 2:17; 3:8
his job — to preach the gospel of God's grace	20:24	Gal. 1:15-16; 2 Cor. 6:1
being innocent of his converts' blood	20:26	1 Thess. 2:10

The above chart does not tell the whole tale, for there are also various Lukanisms in the speech. For example, Paul says little about repentance in his letters, though we do have indication that in his preaching he insisted that Gentiles must turn from idols (1 Thess. 1:9; Rom. 10:9). Or again the language about preaching the kingdom is sometimes thought to be more Lukan than Pauline (cf. v. 25 to Acts 28:31), but Paul does use the phrase "kingdom of God" at various places in his letters, and though his letters are not records of his preaching he may well have done so in his preaching also (cf. Gal. 5:21; 1 Thess. 2:10-11; 2 Thess. 1:8; 1 Cor. 4:20-21; 6:9-10; 15:50; Rom. 14:17).[210] Or again, the image of God's people as a flock which needs shepherding or guarding is not particularly Pauline (but cf. 1 Cor. 9:7), but it is certainly found in the OT (Ps. 100:3; Isa. 40:11, etc.) and thus is within the range of Paul's own discourse. The reference to the "church of God"[211] in v. 28 is certainly Pauline (cf. 1 Cor. 1:2), especially as it is probably used here of the local church. The probable reference to Christ's blood as the purchase price for the redemption of a people (v. 28) can basically be paralleled with Rom. 8:31. The discussion in vv. 29-30 about predators who invade the church from without and disturb it can be paralleled in 2 Corinthians 10–13 or Phil. 3:2-6 or Rom. 16:17-20 or Galatians. There is nothing un-Pauline about this speech in its content, though in some of its choice of terms it seems more Lukan than Pauline. What is of especial note, as the above chart and discussion have suggested, is that the bulk of this speech is parallel to terms and ideas found in the undisputed Paulines, *not* the later, more controverted Pastorals.

The case for labeling this a Paulinist but not a Pauline speech is weak, even in regard to the more disputable material in vv. 28-30. One should not even quibble too much about the use of the term "elders" of the leaders of the Ephesian church, for while the term itself might be anachronistic (reflecting usage during the time when Luke wrote Acts), it was used in early Judaism, and it is clear enough that Paul did indeed help establish local church leadership during his own lifetime in various places. The time of this speech is already A.D. 56, and only a short time later Paul would write his letter to the Philippians and especially address an already existing, distinguishable group of leaders there as "overseers" and deacons. The former term (επισκοπος) is precisely what Paul calls the Ephesian "elders" in the Miletus speech (v. 28), and it is to be noted that this term is used interchangeably with the term πρεσβυτερος elsewhere in the Pauline corpus (cf. Titus 1:5-7).[212]

---

210. Paul's kingdom teaching has been consistently overlooked in Pauline studies. See my discussion in *End of the World*, pp. 51-58.

211. See below on the textual problems, pp. 623ff.

212. The attempt to make this speech the linchpin of an argument to prove Luke

This speech has often been compared to other "farewell" speeches such as that of Jacob in Genesis 49, of Joshua in Joshua 23–24, and especially of Samuel in 1 Samuel 12. The later Jewish material in *Assumption of Moses* and the *Testaments of the Twelve Patriarchs* should also be considered. In terms of the form, and some of the content, it is also in order to compare John 13–17; 1 Tim. 4:1-16; and 2 Tim. 3:1–4:8. More importantly, we have already noticed the way Luke has deliberately placed echoes in Paul's final journey to Jerusalem of Jesus' journey to the same city, and therefore it is not surprising that there are certain correspondences between the farewell speech in Luke 22:14-38 and the Miletus speech. It has been shown by J. Munck, among others, that such speeches generally have the following common elements: (1) the assembling of family, friends, and/or followers; (2) the note that the speaker will be leaving or dying soon; (3) exhortations to keep the faith or behave in a certain way, especially in view of; (4) warnings about upcoming trials and tribulations.[213] There is, however, a difference between Paul's speech here and some of the above-mentioned material in that this is a true farewell speech that does not have the same "last will and testament" character that some of the above speeches by one right at death's door have.

What has not usually been noticed is the rhetorical form of this speech. Dibelius, it is true, saw this speech as a sort of encomium (i.e., a piece of epideictic rhetoric) praising the deceased apostle Paul.[214] He cites only one parallel (Lucian, *De peregrini morte* 32), and, as Hemer has pointed out, the analogy is doubtful: "Peregrinus is a tasteless self-exhibitionist, whose practice is anything but a norm, who delivers a funeral oration upon himself before self-immolation."[215]

D. F. Watson has made a more substantial case for seeing this speech as epideictic rhetoric, but there are some real problems with his arguments. (1) The basic issue that must be determined is *how* the example of Paul functions in this speech. Is the speech an effort in the main to praise Paul or to guide the future conduct of the elders? Surely it is the latter. (2) Watson's analysis argues for a lengthy *exordium,* no *narratio,* and a considerable *peroratio.* The first and last of these are not characteristic of epideictic rhetoric. It is much easier to see little or no *exordium* followed by a substantial *narratio* in

---

knew Paul's letters places far too many eggs into one basket, but cf. Aejamelaeus, *Die Rezeption der Paulusbriefe in der Miletrede, Apg. 20,18-35.* If Luke knew Paul's letters, many of Luke's omissions and observations in Acts become virtually inexplicable, especially in regard to the way he treats Paul's apostleship, his coworkers, and most importantly Paul's letter writing itself, *which Luke never mentions.*

213. See Munck, "Discours d'adieu dans le Nouveau Testament et dans la litterature biblique."

214. See Dibelius, *Studies in the Acts,* pp. 155-58.

215. Hemer, "The Speeches of Acts I," p. 78.

this speech (cf. below). (3) Epideictic rhetoric is mainly about emotion, not substantive arguments, but this speech not only has arguments, it even has an enthymeme or partial syllogism (vv. 26-27), as Watson admits. (4) Warnings such as we find in this speech and in various farewell speeches were indeed a standard element in Greco-Roman rhetoric (called *comminatio*), but they were certainly better suited to and more frequently found in the rhetoric of advice and consent, deliberative rhetoric, than in epideictic rhetoric (cf. Cicero, *Or.* 40.138; Aristotle, *Poetics* 19.1456b); (5) Watson's case to a large extent hinges on the assumption that this is a "farewell" speech of the traditional sort anticipating Paul's death.[216] As we shall see as the exegesis of the text proceeds, this speech is not given with Paul's death in view, but rather with his permanent departure from Asia in view. It is given in light of Acts 19:21, which stressed that Paul had accomplished what he needed to accomplish in this area and needed after the collection visit to Jerusalem to head west to Rome (and possibly beyond, see Rom. 15:23-24). In short, this speech *is* a sort of farewell address, but not a funeral oration — it involves not the rhetoric of praise or blame of the great man, but rather the rhetoric of advice and consent, of what is useful and imitable, that one was supposed to deliver to an εκκλησια.

It is quite true that the partial apologetic tone of the speech gives it a forensic cast, even though the overall function or aim of the speech is deliberative.[217] This fact is indirectly attested to by Lambrecht, who concludes that the "image of Paul which emerges from the apologetical passages is meant by Luke more as an example for others than as a personal apology."[218] Just so, and it is mainly the warnings about *future* attacks and need for guardianship that give it an apologetic flavor, but it is advice about the apologetics the elders will need to undertake.

The audience is a well-known one, not one with which Paul really has to establish his ethos,[219] and there is no need here for a *captatio* or any significant *exordium* to make the audience favorably disposed to what he intended to say. In effect, the speech begins with a *narratio* reminding the audience of Paul's way of life while he was in Ephesus (vv. 18-21), a topic which is revisited later in the speech when the final appeal is made. The *narratio* is most appropriate in a forensic speech that has some apologetic purposes, where a substantial *narratio* is essential to establishing the facts of the case, but it is also appropriate in a deliberative speech if it is part of the essential

216. Watson, "Paul's Speech."

217. But see the discussion in Kennedy, *New Testament Interpretation*, pp. 132-33; Soards, *The Speeches in Acts*, pp. 104-8.

218. Lambrecht, "Paul's Farewell," p. 318.

219. I find it most strange that Kennedy, *New Testament Interpretation*, p. 133, reads the first half of this speech as an attempt to establish ethos. In view of the audience this was quite unnecessary.

argument to demonstrate what conduct would be useful, as is the case here. In v. 22 we have a transitional statement about what is true in the present, which then leads in vv. 22b-25 to a discussion about Paul's future.[220]

The key transition in the speech comes, however, at v. 26, where the διοτι indicates that all that has been said up to this point, especially what has been said in v. 25 about the audience not seeing Paul again (appealing to the stronger emotions at this juncture), is the basis for the arguments that come in vv. 26-30. In essence Paul is arguing that he has successfully discharged his duties in Ephesus, and that therefore they are now responsible for heeding his example and teachings on their own.[221] This in turn is followed by a dramatic *peroratio* in vv. 31-35, which appropriately revisits in vv. 33-34 Paul's behavior while in Ephesus in order to urge *imitatio* of his way of life, backed by the ultimate sort of sanction — an appeal to the commonly recognized authority on such matters, Jesus.[222]

The speech achieves its desired end, and Luke records a scene full of pathos in vv. 36-38. If one examines the rhetorical form of Paul's argument in 1 Corinthians 9–10, involving as it does in chapter 9 the discussion about Paul's way of life while among his converts followed by the citation of a word of Jesus (9:14) and at the end of the argument an exhortation to imitate Paul (11:1), all of which elements also feature in the *peroratio* of the Miletus speech (which is after all only the summary of a speech), it seems clear that Luke knows the sort of pattern of deliberative rhetoric Paul used when addressing Christians facing some problems while the apostle was (or would be) absent. One of the most telltale signs that we are primarily dealing with deliberative rhetoric is Paul's clear insistence that he did (and was doing through this speech) what was συμφεροντων, useful or helpful or beneficial.[223]

---

220. This progression through the past, present, and future of Paul's life ultimately serves the hortatory purpose of urging imitation of Paul's pattern of life, hence my point about the deliberative function of the speech, meant to urge the audience to prepare for the future and behave in ways that will help them.

221. The judicial and apologetic tone of v. 26 should not be missed. Paul is defending his record and behavior, but since he is preaching to an audience already disposed to receive what he is saying, the material functions as a memory aid and guide for the audience's future deliberations and course of action.

222. It is especially this appeal to "imitate" that signals the overall deliberative aim of the speech. On imitation in Paul's rhetoric see my *Conflict and Community in Corinth*, pp. 144-46. Dibelius, *Studies in the Acts*, p. 157, noted that every major subdivision of the speech seemed to end with a reference to the apostle's example. This is correct, and it shows the essentially deliberative character of the speech.

223. It is no accident that in Luke's other use of this verb in Acts 19:19 it does not bear this same sense of what is useful or helpful. This is because the former usage is not in the context of a piece of deliberative rhetoric which has as its essential goal conveying what is useful. The usage is common in the deliberative rhetoric found in some of the

As for the setting of this speech, it is hard to believe that Luke would have conjured up out of thin air the idea of a grandstand finish and a farewell speech for Paul in Miletus, which was not even one of the three most prestigious cities in this portion of Asia, nor was it apparently a place that Paul had even visited or evangelized before this occasion![224] It is much easier to believe that Luke knew about this speech because this was the one speech given while Paul was a free man that Luke himself was both present to hear and took considerable notes on, due to the importance of the occasion.[225] The argument of Barrett, that the setting of the speech is authentic but the speech is post-Pauline, depends on a certain kind of reading of some of the key terms in the speech (e.g., εκκλησια), which is doubtful, as we shall see.[226]

Barrett, however, is right that if ever Luke was going to show interest in things like apostolic succession, or the passing on of ecclesial "offices" from Paul to the leaders of his converts, this speech would be the ideal place to reveal such interests. The fact that the speech shows no interest whatsoever in how the elders became elders in Ephesus, other than perhaps the vague intimation that the Holy Spirit had something to do with the raising up of such people (20:28), shows that Luke is no proponent of *Frühkatholizismus*.[227]

Rather than calling this a post-Pauline speech, it is much nearer the mark to say that we have here a Lukan summary of the Pauline message to Christians, and it meets the rhetorical requirements for προσωποπιια or the delivery of

---

undisputed Paulines; cf., e.g., 1 Cor. 6:12; 7:35; 10:23, 33; 12:7. See Johnson, *Acts,* p. 360. There are numerous proposals about the structure of this speech, no two of which are alike, and none of which notes the rhetorical character and shape of the address; thus they misread its structure, imposing instead chiasm and the like on the address; see C. Exum and C. H. Talbert, "The Structure of Paul's Speech to the Ephesian Elders (Acts 20.18-35)," *CBQ* 29 (1967): 233-36. They are right on one point — the statement "you will see me no more" is crucial, but as the presupposition of the advice here given, not as the central message of the speech. See also Dupont, who offers several structural analyses in *Le discours de Milet,* pp. 21-26. See the critique by Soards, *The Speeches in Acts,* p. 105 n. 285. Nearer the mark is Lambrecht, "Paul's Farewell," p. 318, who offers the following two-part breakdown: (1) self-defense and announcement (vv. 18b-27); (2) exhortations and farewell (vv. 18-35).

224. Certainly in terms of its honor rating, as determined by where games were held and the like, Miletus falls behind Ephesus, Pergamum, and Smyrna. See the discussion in Trebilco, "Asia," pp. 360-62.

225. Notice Kennedy's conclusion in *New Testament Interpretation,* p. 133. He takes the "we" to indicate that this speech "could be quite close to what was actually said. That this is so is further confirmed by similarities of style and content to Paul's writing in the epistles especially the epistle to the Philippians. Philippians is one of the last letters, written in Rome shortly after the events described in Acts."

226. But see Barrett, "Paul's Address."

227. See Barrett, "Apollos."

a speech that is appropriate to the speaker, audience, and occasion.[228] As Johnson says, "Luke accurately represents not only a number of distinctively Pauline themes, but does so in a language which is specifically and verifiably Paul's."[229] It is perhaps worth pointing out that the reference to Paul not seeing the Ephesians anymore may count in favor of the authenticity of this speech, for Luke may have known that Paul, or traditions about him (the Pastoral Epistles), later claimed that after being released from house arrest in Rome he returned east because of problems.[230]

As the beginning of the speech indicates in *v. 18,* this is a speech grounded in and presupposing the memory of the audience. They already know at least most of what Paul will say about the past, and so the speech serves in part as a reminder (cf. v. 18, "you yourselves know"; v. 31, "remembering that for three years . . ."; v. 34, "you yourselves know")[231] and in part as a revelation of what Paul knows but they do not yet know (v. 25, "I know"; v. 29, "I know"), and finally as a statement about what neither Paul nor his audience knows (v. 22). What Paul wishes to remind them of is not merely his message but his manner of life, for he is instructing fellow leaders who must themselves take up the mantle of setting examples for others. Paul insists on the consistency of his behavior — it was the same from the very first day he set foot in the province of Asia until now when he is leaving it.

V. 19 indicates that Paul's aim was to serve the Lord, manifesting the appropriate attitude of a servant,[232] even though it involved many tears and

228. This of course does not settle the issue of whether the speech has an historical basis and thus is appropriate and suitable for that very reason, or whether it is just an example of Luke's literary cleverness. What is clear is that since this is a summary, a précis at best, it cannot help but be telegraphic in the use of the Pauline idiom, and should not for this reason be labeled as "superficially Pauline," as Barrett does.

229. It is interesting that Cadbury, *The Making of Luke-Acts,* pp. 189-90, argued that the supposition of some authentic written or oral source material behind this speech "is most attractive." This contrasts with the dominant view in German scholarship, which views the speech as a Lukan creation; according to it, even if sources were used, they are not thought to go directly back to Paul. See the discussion of Lüdemann, *Early Christianity,* pp. 226-30. Lüdemann's case is a hard sell since there are so many Pauline words, phrases, and ideas in this speech, and equally to the point non-Lukan ones, and even a variety of terms that do not occur elsewhere on Paul's lips in Acts.

230. See Polhill, *Acts,* p. 426 n. 81.

231. For this as an authentic Pauline move see 1 Thess. 2:1-11; 3:3-4; 4:2; 2 Thess. 2:5; 3:7; Gal. 3:2-5; 4:13; 1 Cor. 6:11; Phil. 2:22.

232. "Humility" was not seen as a virtue in the Greco-Roman world, especially by those of higher status. The term ταπεινοφροσυνης in fact was often used in a pejorative sense to mean "base-minded" or "slavish." This concept is thoroughly Pauline and shows the way he tries to re-envision models of leadership in light of his servant position in relationship to the real Lord, Christ. Cf. Rom. 12:16; 2 Cor. 7:6; 10:1; 11:7; 12:21; Phil. 2:3, 8; 3:21; 4:12. See my discussion in *Conflict and Community in Corinth,* p. 407 and the notes.

trials, and plots by his fellow Jews against him. Paul in the course of almost three years in Ephesus had surely related to his Ephesian converts various of his experiences that took place elsewhere; thus even if the Jews had not plotted against him in Ephesus, this audience might well know about the plots in Pisidian Antioch, Iconium, Lystra, Thessalonica, Beroea, and Corinth. The subject was likely to be fresh in Paul's mind in view of the fact that his very presence in Miletus, instead of being on a boat heading for Syria, was due to such a plot (cf. 20:3).[233]

V. 20 refers in a negative way to Paul's boldness of speech — he held nothing back that would be helpful or useful to those he addressed.[234] He both proclaimed the message and taught, in both public and private locales. Doubtless the Ephesians would think of Paul's public teaching in the hall of Tyrannus as well as his "in-house" discourses.[235] Paul's testimony was not, according to *v. 21,* just to Gentiles but to both Jews and Greeks. This comports not only with Paul's beliefs of how things ought to be (Rom. 1:16) but also with his actual practice (see 1 Cor. 9:20-23; 10:32-33).

V. 21b has often been seen as Lukan in character because of its reference to "repentance toward God and faith toward our Lord Jesus," but it is in order to point out that though it is not his favorite terminology Paul does indeed speak of the need to be led to repentance (Rom. 2:4), and even of the need for Christians who sin to repent (2 Cor. 7:9, 10). Furthermore, the formulation in this verse is close in thought to 1 Thess. 1:9-10,[236] which speaks of what converts have turned from and what they have turned to, the living and true God (and cf. Rom. 10:9). In short there is nothing here that is un-Pauline or anti-Pauline, and only if this speech is seen as "the characteristic Pauline message or legacy to the church universal" is there any reason to argue for the Lukan character of v. 21b at all.

V. 22 speaks of Paul's being "bound in spirit" or "bound by the Spirit" to go to Jerusalem, probably the latter in view of v. 23. Paul avers that he does not know what will happen to him there, except that imprisonments and persecutions are to be involved. Clearly from v. 24 Paul is prepared to die, as

---

233. See Polhill, *Acts,* p. 424.

234. See Johnson, *Acts,* p. 360.

235. It is noteworthy how proclaiming and teaching are distinguished here, and it may be that these two verbs largely correspond to the public and private spheres respectively; that is, Paul in the main preached in public, but he instructed disciples in private. Johnson, *Acts,* p. 361, points to the contrast between Paul's behavior and that of various sophists and false philosophers whose private activities contradicted their public discourse (see Lucian, *Timon* 54). There is no need at all to see an allusion here to third-generation problems with Gnostics and their secret teachings here, pace Barrett, "Paul's Address," p. 111.

236. See Johnson, *Acts,* p. 361.

is clear also from 21:12, which speaks of his being prepared to die in Jerusalem, but nothing is said here that predicts Paul's death either in Jerusalem or in Rome. Indeed, nothing in all of Acts clearly refers to Paul's death after house arrest in Rome, but this conclusion requires further discussion in some detail.

A Closer Look — Paul's "Departure" — Intimations of Immortality or Recognition of a Problematic Absence?

The prophecy of Agabus in 21:11 affirms that Paul will be bound and handed over to the Gentiles. It says nothing about death but certainly alludes to loss of freedom, confinement, even trials. The warning not to go to Jerusalem in 21:4 says nothing about death or Rome. The reassurance in 23:11 from the Lord makes clear that Paul would not die in Jerusalem, but rather would testify in Rome just as he testified in Jerusalem.

It is clear enough that Luke in what follows in Acts 21–28 wants to demonstrate that though serious charges were made against Paul, none of them were proved (see, e.g., 25:6-12), and Paul by a strategic move avoided being handed over to the Jewish authorities, who may well have done away with him if given the chance. The Roman authorities in their own conferrals make clear that he was not charged with any treasonable offenses (25:18), and Festus even says to Agrippa that he had not found that Paul had done anything deserving death (25:25), indeed he had nothing definite to write against Paul to the emperor (25:26). Furthermore, the conclusion of the matter is that if he had not appealed to the emperor he could have been set free, for he had done nothing deserving either imprisonment or death (26:31). Even in Rome it is clearly affirmed by Paul himself (28:18) that the Romans had examined him and found no reason for the death penalty.

In the light of what we know on the basis of both the above evidence and the widely acknowledged observation that Luke does not generally portray Roman jurisprudence in an unfavorable light, is it really plausible to argue that Luke intends his audience to think that Paul, after two profitable and rather unhindered years of house arrest, ultimately fell victim to a Roman miscarriage of justice? Would they not rather conclude, especially in view of the portrayal of Paul's appearance before Festus and Agrippa and the lack of any evidence of real enemies or litigious Jews in Rome (see below on Acts 28), that Roman justice was finally done? This would mean that following his two-year house arrest, Paul, the Roman citizen, testified before the emperor and was released. To simply assume that Luke's audience would already know for a fact that Paul's life did end in A.D. 62 is to assume too much.

It must be kept steadily in view that we have no clear evidence in the NT about the precise timing of Paul's death, and the value of the much later extrabiblical testimony may be debated. For what that later testimony is worth, it does not suggest Paul's demise in the early 60s A.D. More importantly in Philippians, in my view the last letter written during house arrest and the resolution of his case, Paul expresses real optimism about being released (see Phil. 1:24-26).

This brings us to the important matter of how to interpret αφιξις in Acts 20:29. Does the word simply refer to Paul's leaving Asia, no more to return (see v. 25), or does it refer to Paul's death? Elsewhere, when Luke wants to use a euphemism for death he uses the term εξοδος, not αφιξις (Luke 9:31). In fact this latter term is not found elsewhere in the NT. Αφιξις comes from the verb αφικνεομαι, which has as its basic meaning to "arrive" or to "reach" but can also mean to go or depart. It has been argued that in Josephus, *Ant.* 2.18, it seems to have this latter meaning of departure (see also *Ant.* 4.315), but this is not completely clear. In both cases in Josephus the term *is* used in reference to a destination.[237] Clearer perhaps is the usage in Demosthenes, *Ep.* 1.2; 3.39, where the meaning seems to be departure. The most important thing that can be said about all such references is that there is no known evidence of the term being used metaphorically to refer to someone's impending death. Surely the natural inference that Luke's audience would have drawn, in view of the discussion of Paul's upcoming trip to Jerusalem, is that Luke is referring to Paul's intent to leave the area of Ephesus for good.[238]

There is also nothing surprising or particularly prophetic about Paul warning his converts about "wolves" within or intruding from outside the Christian community when he was absent and could not deal with such troublemakers.[239] We find from reading Galatians, 1-2 Corinthians, and Philippians that such problems did indeed arise in Paul's absence, and Paul's discussion of the matter in Acts 20 in no way necessarily implies Paul's impending death, only his impending absence.

Now if Luke's audience did not know or did not know clearly how Paul's life ended, it is evident that upon reading Acts they would not have been led to assume it ended with death by execution in Rome at the hands of the emperor. There is nothing in the narrative that clearly prepares for or anticipates such a conclusion. There is nothing necessarily ominous about the promise made by an angel that Paul would

237. See Hemer, "The Speeches of Acts I," p. 81 n. 17.

238. See Larkin, *Acts,* pp. 294-95. It is important to note that whether one argues that Luke does or doesn't allude to Paul's impending death in Acts, in either case the argument is based on inference, not clear evidence. Much also depends on how one understands the ending of Acts, which is of course silent about the outcome of the legal proceedings. Does silence mean that Luke doesn't want to portray the untimely demise of his hero, though he knows he died right after the end of house arrest, or does silence rather mean that the reader should have pondered the clues that exist in Acts 20–28, which suggest Paul was not guilty of any serious offense and that no Roman authority had convicted him of anything? If Luke's aims were not biographical (on which see pp. 15ff. above), the ending of Acts is understandable — the goal was to record the successful spread of the word and the Christian movement from Jerusalem to Rome, not to write an apologetic brief for Paul. As a subsidiary point, Luke was happy to state that Paul was guilty of no chargeable offense, and perhaps to imply his release, in view of the tenor and official opinions expressed in Roman proceedings against Paul thus far.

239. Like the pejorative term "dogs" (see Phil. 3:2), this language comes from a Jewish environment when discussing those who are seen as predators who water down, corrupt, or destroy one's faith (cf. Ezek. 22:27; Matt. 7:15; 10:16; Luke 10:3; John 10:22). There is certainly nothing in this very general reference that need suggest late first or early second century problems with Gnostics are in view.

stand before the emperor in 27:24. One must remember that Paul's appearance before Nero, if it came after the two years of house arrest, will have occurred before the fire of Rome and before Nero degenerated into tyranny as he looked for a scapegoat to bear responsibility for the fire. The point of 27:24 is that Paul has nothing to worry about in the interim, for he will indeed stand and testify before Caesar. Luke throughout has been striving to show how the proclamation of the word went from Jerusalem to Rome, and this event of the word being shared with the emperor would climax such progress.

The reasonable inference a reader or hearer familiar with Roman jurisprudence would draw from the Roman legal proceedings, and the failure of Roman Jews to act against Paul (28:17-29), is that Paul was released after his two years under house arrest, not that he was executed.[240] Luke's narrative has too often been the victim of too much reading between or behind the lines on the basis of certain undemonstrated assumptions about the timing of Paul's death. Paul's farewell address at Miletus is probably not to be seen as a premature last will and testament. Even if it was the case that Paul died after two years of house arrest in Rome, that was over four years after this speech was ostensibly given (cf. 21:27; 28:30). The placing of a last will and testament speech here, instead of in Rome, seems an unlikely literary move on Luke's part, especially since he will record Paul's further preaching and discussions in Rome.[241]

V. 23 is interesting in several respects. Despite translations like the NRSV, the word πασαν is only found in a few manuscripts and patristic sources, with the earliest being from the Western text (D gig [vg], sy: Lcf). It is probably not an original reading but rather yet another example of Western expansion and hyperbole.[242] Thus v. 23 simply reads that the Holy Spirit testifies to Paul in cities (unspecified) that imprisonments and persecutions await Paul. This verse is both retrospective and prospective. Paul is heading to Jerusalem. We are probably meant to think of the reception he expects at the hands of his fellow Jews. If this is a correct inference, then it is germane to point out that the cities Paul may have in mind are those where he previously experienced persecution and plots and imprisonments at the hands of his fellow Jews (e.g., Pisidian Antioch, Iconium, Lystra, Thessalonica, Beroea, Corinth). In these cities the Holy Spirit showed or taught Paul what to expect in the future. Thus, this verse is probably not a premature and displaced reference to what Paul had yet to experience when he was warned at Tyre and Caesarea about going to Jerusalem (21:4, 11, 12).[243]

240. See the detailed discussion below, pp. 755ff.

241. See Ramsay, *St. Paul the Traveller*, p. 297, who stresses that this is Paul's farewell before he enters upon his enterprises farther west.

242. Note that the twenty-seventh edition of Nestle-Aland does not have the word in the text.

243. Against Lambrecht, "Paul's Farewell," p. 307 n. 1.

Nero.

V. 24 is typically Pauline. Paul is not interested in clinging to his own life; what he really cares about is accomplishing the διαχονια given him by the Lord Jesus (cf. 2 Cor. 5:18). As Johnson points out, this could indeed be a reference to the collection (cf. 2 Cor. 9:13 and 8:9; Acts 19:22).[244] The phrase "finish my course" is of course an athletic metaphor that Paul uses at 1 Cor.

244. Johnson, *Acts,* p. 362.

9:24 and Phil. 3:14, and an even closer parallel is found in 2 Tim. 4:7.[245] The phrase "the good news of God's grace" is an excellent summary of the Pauline gospel, even if this precise formulation is not found in Paul's letters.[246]

V. 25 indicates that Paul knows that none (presumably in this area) will ever see his face again. He says he has gone about preaching the kingdom among them. We have seen above that "kingdom" is a term that Paul uses in various contexts, and it cannot be ruled out that it was part of his preaching to non-Christians. This verse is important as it provides the rationale for and helps explain the character of the speech. It is indeed a farewell message to a church he had spent more time with than any other so far as we can tell, but it is not a last will and testament to the church, for Paul does not know whether he is facing death or not.

V. 26 says something about how Paul envisions his role in relationship to his converts. In this case he sees himself as like the watchman in Ezek. 33:1-6 (cf. also *T. Sim.* 6:1; *T. Lev.* 10:1) who, once he has fully warned the people he looks out for, has discharged his duty and cannot be held responsible for what happens to them if they ignore his warnings. The language here is rather like what we found at Acts 18:6, only there Paul's fellow Jews in that locale are those for whom he sees himself as no longer morally responsible (in regard to their fate). There is an interesting point and counterpoint between this verse and v. 28. Paul is innocent of his converts' blood, but the blood of God (or Christ) is that which really placed them in the position of being redeemed and belonging to God and so not facing God's condemnation.

V. 27 further indicates how Paul has discharged his duty to his converts — he declared to them the whole salvific plan or will (βουλη) of God. This is of course one of the major ideas in Acts,[247] stressing as it does what God had planned and had in mind for both Jews and Gentiles. The language here is Lukan (cf. Acts 2:23; 4:28; 5:38; 13:36), but the thought is not un-Pauline.

---

245. It is my view that Luke wrote the Pastorals (cf. Wilson, *Luke and the Pastoral Epistles*), but I would differ from Wilson in concluding that Luke did it at the behest of Paul, near the end of Paul's life. Linguistic and vocabulary parallels between Acts and the Pastorals do not need to lead to the conclusion that Acts represents a post-Pauline viewpoint. It may merely mean that both books reflect a late Pauline viewpoint about the organization of the church and the like.

246. Here Barrett, "Paul's Address," p. 112, is simply quibbling, and is wrong to conclude that "Luke uses words that are superficially Pauline, but improbably represents words that Paul actually used." No one is disputing that we have a summary statement here or that Luke has phrased things in his own way at points. This speech is not intended to function as anything like a full exposition of the Pauline message, and any summary when compared to Paul's extended discussions in his letters will appear superficial by comparison. The fact that this phrase is non-Pauline (i.e., without precedent in Paul's letters) does not make it un-Pauline in substance.

247. See pp. 176ff. above and Squires, *Plan of God in Luke-Acts,* passim.

Paul expresses a similar idea using θελημα του θεου (1 Thess. 4:3; 1 Cor. 1:1; Gal. 1:4).

That this is an address meant specifically for Christian leaders and not a generic address to all the church is shown from verses like *v. 28*, where the leaders are specifically exhorted to keep watch over themselves and the flock. The language is similar to what we find in 1 Pet. 5:2-3, but of course both this passage and the Petrine one reflect the biblical tradition of the people of God being called a flock (cf. Mic. 5:4; Isa. 40:11; Jer. 13:17; Ezek. 34:12). There is nothing in this speech about Paul's passing the torch of leadership to these elders by some sort of ceremony or bequeathal. To the contrary we are told it was the Holy Spirit, not Paul, that has made them shepherds. The discussion does not reflect the later postapostolic concerns of people like Ignatius of Antioch, and the term επισκοπος is surely used in its functional, not titular sense of "overseer." As such it is an alternative metaphorical way of speaking about the same role described by the verb ποιμαινειν (to shepherd).

There is considerable debate about the meaning of the phrase εκκλησια του θεου. There is first of all the textual problem of whether we should read it as I have just rendered it or whether it read originally "church of the Lord." The latter phrase occurs seven times in the Septuagint but nowhere in the NT. This might lead one to think this is the earlier reading, except clearly "church of God" is the more difficult reading in view of what follows in this verse, and is supported by ℵ and B. It is also a phrase found regularly in Paul's letters (1 Cor. 1:2; 10:32; 11:16, 22; 15:9; 2 Cor. 1:1; Gal. 1:13; 1 Thess. 2:14; 2 Thess. 1:4), and as Johnson says, "Luke's usage throughout this discourse is remarkably faithful to Paul's own."[248] God "obtained" or "acquired" (cf. Isa. 43:21) the εκκλησια by means of αιματος του ιδιου. Here again we have a problem. Does this mean with his own blood, or possibly with the blood of his Own? Does God have blood, or is this a reference to Christ as God?[249] In the papyri there is a use of ο ιδιος as a noun as a term of endearment for near relatives, so the translation "blood of his Own" is quite possible.[250] The phrasing is not specifically Pauline, but one should compare Rom. 8:32. On the blood of Christ as the means of redemption one should compare Rom. 3:25 and 5:9.

It is often complained that Luke evidences no theology of the cross, but this verse is an obvious exception to such a conclusion. Inasmuch as Luke was not attempting to represent his own thought directly, it is hard to know what

---

248. Johnson, *Acts*, p. 363. See the discussion of this textual problem in Metzger, *Textual Commentary*, pp. 480-81.

249. This is one of the conclusions of DeVine, "The 'Blood of God.'" This study is especially helpful in reviewing how this verse was interpreted in the patristic literature and in reviewing the textual data.

250. See Metzger, *Textual Commentary*, p. 481.

Luke himself did or did not believe about Christ's death. This verse, however, conveys the notion of redemption, the buying out of bondage of a people by means of Christ's blood. If one adds to this the various places where we hear about the release of sins in Acts,[251] there is in fact more to Luke's theology of the cross than is usually allowed.[252]

It is also urged that εκκλησια here refers to the church universal. This is doubtful because the term comes in the very same verse where the Ephesian elders have been specifically urged to watch over *their* flock and themselves. The Ephesian elders are not being called to shepherd the church universal, but to oversee all the flock of which the Spirit has made them leaders. Even if, however, the phrase were used in a nonlocal sense here, this would not make it un-Pauline, for occasionally Paul uses the term εκκλησια in such a sense (see Gal. 1:13; cf. 1 Cor. 11:22; in 1 Cor. 1:2 and 2 Cor. 1:1 the universal church and the local expression of it are both referred to).[253] Furthermore, Paul himself speaks in terms similar to what we find here when he refers to a particular individual for whom Christ died (1 Cor. 8:11). There is no problem with the idea of Paul speaking about God obtaining this particular church by the blood of his Own,[254] and Luke is thoroughly familiar with the idea as well, as the parallel in Luke 22:20 also suggests.[255]

In this verse as in v. 19 Paul refers to his tears, something we also hear of in 2 Cor. 2:4. Paul is being portrayed here as one who cares deeply about his converts, a man of pathos. This comports very well with the picture that one can derive from the capital Paulines.

Vv. 29-30 refer to predators that attack from without and from within after Paul has left the area. The latter are accused of distorting the truth or speaking deceptive things for the purpose of getting persons to follow them. This is similar to what is said about Bar Elymas (Acts 13:10). Here it would seem Ezekiel 34 lies in the background, which discusses negligent shepherds and ravaging predators.[256]

V. 31 is important, for it not only urges the audience to be alert but it reminds them that Paul had already warned them, night and day for three years, about the sort of things he has just spoken of. This verse makes clear that this speech is addressed to an audience that Paul had instructed previously, and that it builds on that earlier instruction. It is a speech grounded in memory and recall.

---

251. See the discussion of Moessner, "The Script of the Scriptures," pp. 218ff.

252. See the discussion of Moule, "The Christology of Acts," pp. 170-71.

253. See the discussion in Giles, "Luke's Use," p. 137: "The only thing we can confidently assert is that the ecclesiology and soteriology of Acts 20.28 closely resembles that of Paul. If it is not a record of what Paul actually said, then it is the sort of thing that he would have said."

254. See ibid., p. 141 n. 11.

255. See Lambrecht, "Paul's Farewell," p. 326.

256. See the discussion in Lovestam, "Paul's Address at Miletus."

V. 32 indicates that though the flock has been entrusted to the shepherds, they in turn have been commended to God. The message of God's grace is said to be able to build up these leaders and give them an inheritance among all those who have been sanct:fied (i.e., the saints). On the latter phrase we should compare Acts 26:18; Rom. 15:16; 1 Cor. 1:2; 6:11; 7:14, and on the idea of an inheritance that comes from God on the basis of grace we may compare Gal. 3:18, 29.

V. 33 provides the disclaimer that Paul coveted no one's possessions. As Johnson points out, the use of the verb "covet" here is interesting because the one commandment of the ten that Paul singles out for special attention is the commandment to avoid coveting (see Rom. 7:7; 1 Cor. 10:6; Gal. 5:17).[257] The content of this verse is close to what we find in 1 Cor. 9:12; 2 Cor. 7:2; 11:7-11, and it is somewhat similar to what we find in the farewell discourse in 1 Sam. 12:3-5. If greed is seen as a sign in Acts of one's spiritual poverty,[258] then Paul's attitude here is seen as a sign of his largeness of soul. According to *v. 34* Paul supported himself using "these hands." The way this is phrased indicates more than just a verbal reference. Paul resorts at the end of the speech to a dramatic gesture, not uncommon and an effective rhetorical device. That Paul supported himself from time to time is clearly recorded in 1 Cor. 9:12; 2 Cor. 7:2; and 11:7-11, and one should especially compare 2 Thess. 3:6-10. What is new here is the idea that Paul also supported some of his companions. This is not inherently improbable. There may be something to Hemer's suggestion that this part of the exhortation was especially necessary and pointed because Paul was now carrying or accompanying the collection and needed to scotch any rumors or slander that he might ultimately have done all he did to acquire these funds for himself.[259]

V. 35 is intriguing, suggesting not only that Paul has given this speech in order to provide these leaders with an example to follow[260] but also that Paul's work was done so as to aid the "weak." Perhaps we should think of those who are the opposite of the "strong" in Rom. 14:1-2, 21 or 1 Cor. 8:11-12; 9:22; 12:22. In view of the rest of Acts, Luke would seem to have in mind those of low social status who tended to be marginalized in the Greco-Roman world, a condition found even in the church (see Acts 6:1-6). Luke has also at various points suggested that it was those of somewhat higher social status, those with houses large enough for the community to meet in, who tended to assume leadership positions in the church. If this was the case in Ephesus, then Paul would be appealing to others of about the same social status as himself to be

257. Johnson, *Acts,* p. 365.
258. See pp. 213ff. above.
259. Hemer, "The Speeches of Acts I," p. 84.
260. On "imitation" and deliberative rhetoric, cf. pp. 39ff. above.

willing to "become more vile" and deliberately step down the social ladder by working with their hands and so serve the weak, rather than have them serve the leadership (see 2 Cor. 9:8-12).

The sanction or "proof" that such activities should be undertaken is a quotation from "the Lord Jesus" which is not found in the Gospels: "It is more blessed to give than to receive." This is a wisdom saying in the form of a beatitude. There is an early variant form of it found in *1 Clem.* 2:1, which may suggest by the criteria of multiple attestation that this goes back to the earliest period of the Jesus movement, perhaps even to Jesus.[261] The sapiential form of the saying and the fact that the idea here echoes what we find in a text like Sir. 4:31 may also point to its origins in the teaching of Jesus, for Jesus' teaching often took such a form and was indebted to early Jewish sapiential traditions.[262] The essence of what we find here is also found in Luke 6:35-38 and other Christian sources such as *Did.* 1:5 and *Herm. Man.* 2:4-6. There are some more remote parallels in Greek literature (Plutarch, *Moral.* 173D, 181F), and one from Greek historiography that is much closer except that it is addressed to Persian kings (Thucydides, *Hist.* 2.97.4). It is the character of gnomic wisdom that one often finds parallels because of the generic and transcultural nature of the advice it gives, for it is grounded in widely held cultural assumptions.[263]

One of the most interesting aspects of this quotation is its social implications. The Greco-Roman world was honeycombed by social networks grounded in the principle of reciprocity, of "giving and receiving." Paul's exhortation here is to break that cycle and serve and help those who can give nothing in return. This is the practical expression of what being gracious means — freely they had received the good news, and they should freely give with no thought of return. While this speech should not be seen as addressed to or as Paul's legacy to the whole church, it can be argued that it distills Paul's advice to *leaders* in such a way that it would be equally valuable and valid for leaders in Luke's day as for these Ephesian elders.[264]

---

261. See Jeremias, *Unknown Sayings of Jesus,* pp. 77-81. What this saying shows is that there were likely many sayings, even free-floating sayings of Jesus, that were never collected into a Q-like document or a Gospel.

262. See my demonstration of this point in *Jesus the Sage,* pp. 147-208.

263. See Hemer, "The Speeches of Acts I," pp. 82-83.

264. For the argument that this speech is of a universal nature meant to give a summary of the Pauline legacy for the postapostolic church, see Lambrecht, "Paul's Farewell," pp. 334-37. The assumption that this speech is a Lukan creation directed (only) to Luke's own day assumes we know a good deal more about what the situation was in Luke's day with his audience than we do. For one thing, there is no agreement among scholars about when Luke was writing, with guesses ranging from the 60s to the second century. For another thing, there is no agreement as to whether just an individual named Theophilus was in fact the audience of this book, or some larger constituency was being addressed.

Kennedy was right that this speech does not follow the rhetorical requirements to be an encomium or piece of epideictic rhetoric.[265] It does, however, meet the requirements of deliberative rhetoric that seeks to give advice, exhortation, and examples for the audience to imitate.[266] As Tannehill says, this speech makes clear that Paul's legacy to these leaders was not just his sacrificial example but also his universalistic message about grace and salvation for all.[267] Paul concludes his speech with two of the best things he could possibly leave them with, a word of Jesus about giving and a prayer.

The speech now ended, according to *v. 36* Paul knelt down and prayed with all there. It was an emotional time with much hugging and kissing and weeping, showing that at least in some quarters Paul was greatly loved. The grieving involved is said to have a specific cause in *v. 38,* namely, that they would not see Paul again. This gut-wrenching scene was followed by the elders accompanying Paul back to his ship.[268] The verb προπεμπω refers to the accompanying or escorting of someone to his or her point of departure, but, as Polhill points out, the term can also imply the sending of someone on his or her way by giving food and other provisions.[269] In other words, these leaders were already demonstrating that they had learned the lesson that "it is more blessed to give. . . ." In conclusion it is worth quoting Moule, who says that in this speech we do not merely have various Pauline snippets "introduced by the author to give the speech a Pauline stamp"; rather, "this is Paul, not some other speaker; and he is not evangelizing but recalling an already evangelized community to its deepest insights. In other words, the situation, like the theology, is precisely that of a Pauline epistle, not preliminary evangelism."[270]

H. Journey to Jerusalem (21:1-16)

Properly speaking, Paul's third missionary tour comes to a conclusion in this section of Acts. The parallels with Jesus' final journey to Jerusalem have often

---

265. Kennedy, *New Testament Interpretation,* pp. 132-33, thinking of the rules set down by Menander Rhetor, but representing a long tradition.

266. That this speech was a word on target for the Ephesian or Asian church would seem to be shown by Rev. 2:1-7; 1 Tim. 1:3; and 2 Tim. 1:15.

267. Tannehill, *Narrative Unity of Luke-Acts,* 2:257.

268. These sorts of scenes full of pathos were not uncommon in ancient historiographical works (cf. Philo, *Embassy* 243; Josephus, *War* 2.402).

269. Polhill, *Acts,* p. 430.

270. Moule, "The Christology of Acts," p. 171. Cf. the more limited claims of Barrett, "Paul's Address," pp. 116-17, who argues that the general picture of Paul here is in harmony with the Paul of the letters.

been noted and are considerable: (1) the final journey in each case involves or is precipitated by a Jewish plot; (2) there is a handing over to or a falling into the hands of the Gentiles in Jerusalem; (3) there is a triple prediction of coming suffering (cf. Luke 9:22, 44; 18:31-34 to Acts 20:22-24; 21:4; 21:10-11); (4) there is in the end a resignation to God's will in both cases (cf. Luke 22:42; Acts 21:14).[271]

Yet it is possible to overdo these parallels, for Paul does not meet his demise in Jerusalem and in fact is not handed over to Gentile authorities. It is nearer the mark to say they rescue him from the mob. If Jerusalem may be said to be the religious center of the Empire for Jews and Christians, Rome is certainly the Empire's political center. Tannehill stresses that Jerusalem and Rome are the centers of the two powers that Paul has disturbed and to whom he must give a reckoning. He heads for the centers of power, where he will defend his ministry and carry his witness to the high authorities who embody that power. The narrator avoids suggesting that Paul goes to Jerusalem for ordinary human purposes.[272] Paul is controlled by a larger purpose. Thus the completion of Paul's ministry apparently requires the extensive defense of his work against religious and political accusations that actually follow in the narrative.[273] In other words, the narrative is part of a larger apologetic that is not just religious in character but also social and political.

Lüdemann stresses that there is considerable and substantial source material behind this section in Acts, as is shown by its circumstantial details.[274] The section also involves a return to the "we," which is neatly integrated into the narrative itself. As Bruce points out, Philip, last seen in Caesarea in 8:40, is found in the same place here as part of a "we" section (v. 8),[275] or again Agabus shows up in this "we" section and previously he was in the third-person narrative in 11:27-28. In both places he is introduced in similar fashion. This suggests that the author of the "we" section is the one who composed the whole.[276] It is also to be noted that the "we" here has two other significant features: (1) "we" is distinguished from Paul and tries to dissuade him from going to Jerusalem (v. 12);[277] (2) "we" involves travel not just by sea but also

271. See Longenecker, *Acts*, p. 515.
272. It may also be said that he does not avoid going to Jerusalem for human reasons.
273. Tannehill, *Narrative Unity of Luke-Acts*, 2:266-67.
274. Lüdemann, *Early Christianity*, pp. 233-36.
275. Bruce, *The Acts of the Apostles*, p. 440.
276. Ibid., p. 44.
277. Thus the "we" does not partake of the quality often remarked about in modern literary criticism, the so-called omniscience of the narrator. At the time he did not share the divine insight into the situation Paul had. See Tannehill, *Narrative Unity of Luke-Acts*, 2:264 n. 5. This suggests that Luke does not claim to know more than he actually knew by narrating things about which he had no source of information.

on land (vv. 8-11). In short, a travel diary may have been used, but the author is not following some sort of supposed convention about the use of first-person plural in narratives about sea travel.[278]

V. 1 refers to the fact that Paul and his companions had to "tear them-selves away"[279] from the Ephesians in order to set sail, so great was their affection for Paul and his companions. The first leg of the journey involved a trip to the island of Cos, followed the next day by a trip to Rhodes. Its major city, bearing the same name, was the capital of the Dodecanese island chain upon which were located the first two stops on this journey. It was conventional for small ships in antiquity to hug the coastline as much as possible and put into port each night when the winds died down. The next port of call was actually a Lycian city on the southwest coast of Asia Minor — Patara.[280] It had a large harbor and was a major commercial city, thus making it a regular stopping point for major trade ships traveling in the eastern Mediterranean. It was surely here that Paul and his companions boarded a large merchant vessel that would travel nonstop the some four hundred miles to Tyre,[281] even though the Western text suggests a further stop at Myra.[282]

Luke calls their destination Phoenicia in *v. 2,* though he had previously said at 20:3 it was Syria (and ultimately Jerusalem, 20:16, though not by ship, which is the point in these other two cases). The Roman province of Syria included old Phoenicia, the capital city and chief port of which was Tyre. *V. 3*

---

278. As Praeder, "The Problem," pp. 208-12, convincingly demonstrates, in ancient sea voyage accounts the use of the first person is either because there was factual partici-pation by the author or authors, or, in a fictional account, because the author wanted to claim that certain characters participated in such voyages. In other words, it is not merely a literary convention, especially since there are sea voyage accounts both in Acts and elsewhere where "we" is not used (cf. Praeder and Acts 13:4-15)!

279. This is the literal meaning of αποσπασθεντες. See Bruce, *The Acts of the Apostles,* p. 438.

280. Hemer, *Book of Acts,* p. 125, rightly notes that Luke here gives the neuter plural form of the city's name, which is the form also found in local epigraphy and literature.

281. There were few if any major vessels in antiquity that were simply passenger boats, where human cargo was the main thing aboard, except of course in the case of slave ships. Those wanting to travel speedily would book passage on a large merchant ship. In the eastern Mediterranean these usually traveled from the granary of the Empire (Egypt) north and west to Greece and Rome, and of course vice versa. There was also significant travel to and from Tyre, dating back to the days when Phoenicia had its own Mediterranean empire of sorts, or at least its own colonies, built on sea travel and trade.

282. This was probably added in view of Acts 27:5, but it may also reflect a knowledge of the later document the *Acts of Paul and Thecla,* which recounts Paul's residence in Myra. See Metzger, *Textual Commentary,* p. 482. As Haenchen, *Acts,* p. 53, points out, the redactor who added this may have known Myra was the main transshipping point, but unfortunately the distance is too far from Rhodes for a single day's sailing. Just from Patara to Myra is fifty miles.

seems to reflect an eyewitness touch, for it speaks of "having made Cyprus visible," that is, making it arise out of the ocean on the port side, a phenomenological description of what a person sailing would have seen.[283]

Cyprus was of course the site of Paul's first overseas missionary work,[284] and also the only land one would see on the journey from Patara to Tyre. John Chrysostom states that the journey took five days with prevailing winds (*Hom.* 45.2), and apparently this expeditious journey left Paul with extra time before he had to go to Jerusalem. The boat landed at Tyre because that is where it unloaded its cargo, not because that is the destination on the eastern Mediterranean coast Paul hoped to reach.

V. 4 states that Paul and his companions "located" the Christians in Tyre and stayed with them for a week.[285] The verb ανευρισκω here is used in much the same sense as in Luke 2:16 (see 4 Macc. 3:14). The meaning of v. 4b has been much debated. Did the Holy Spirit, speaking through the Tyrian Christians, really tell Paul and his companions not to go up to Jerusalem? It was the Spirit who had compelled Paul to go up in the first place (see 19:21; 20:22). It is possible that δια is not used in a causal sense here, but rather in an occasional sense. On the occasion when the Spirit was inspiring some to speak, some urged Paul not to go up to Jerusalem.[286] On this scenario the Spirit had once again predicted what awaited Paul in Jerusalem (see 20:23), and this resulted in the Tyrians urging Paul not to go.[287] There is, however, another possibility.

Early Christian prophecy seems to have been in some ways like OT prophecy, but also in some ways unlike it. Like OT prophecy, it could be conditional in nature (if one did *x* . . . then *y* would happen). Unlike the OT, where discerning between a true and false prophet was urged, in the NT Christians are urged to weigh or sift the prophecies of true prophets. In view of 1 Corinthians 14, NT prophecy would seem to have had an authority of

---

283. Bruce, *The Acts of the Apostles,* p. 439, says αναφαναντες is apparently a nautical term.

284. See pp. 390ff. above.

285. While ανευρισκω could mean "discover," in view of Acts 15:3 it is likely that Paul already knew about the disciples in Tyre. See Johnson, *Acts,* p. 369. Acts 11:19 suggests that missionaries had passed through the region much earlier.

286. Tannehill, *Narrative Unity of Luke-Acts,* 2:263, points out that the use of indirect discourse here makes the message one step removed from an example of the Spirit's direct expression.

287. See Longenecker, *Acts,* p. 516. Conzelmann, *Acts,* p. 178, seems to hold the view that the Tyrians had mixed in their own conclusions with the Spirit's message. See further the discussion by Bovon, "Le Saint-Esprit, L'Église et les relations humaine selon Actes 20,36–21,16," p. 350. Whatever view one finally accepts, this is not Luke's usual way of speaking about the Holy Spirit speaking through someone; see Keener, *Bible Background Commentary,* p. 385.

general content and was not taken as a literal transcript of God's words, but rather was something that needed to be weighed or sifted (see 1 Cor. 14:29).[288] This makes sense out of the prophecy of Agabus which follows in v. 11, for in fact Paul is not bound by the Jews and handed over to the Gentiles (as Jesus was), but he does end up in bonds in the hands of the Gentiles. For the most part OT prophecy seems to have had a "thus saith the Lord" quality, the quality of God speaking directly through the prophet.[289] A further possibility is that suggested by Tannehill and others. He argues that Acts 21:11 reflects Luke's desire to conform the predictions about Paul to the pattern of the predictions about Jesus.[290] This is not impossible, but it does nothing to explain 21:4. On the whole the second explanation seems to make best sense of this and other texts.[291]

In *v. 5* we have another farewell scene with Paul resolved to travel on despite the exhortation of the Tyrians. In this scene full of pathos, but somewhat less emotional than the one at Miletus, not only the men but also the wives and children[292] escort Paul and his companions outside the city, kneel together on the soft sand of the Tyrian beach,[293] pray, and say farewell. *V. 6* tells us that Paul's entourage boards the boat, and the Tyrians go back to their homes.[294] The overall impression left by these scenes is the strong support and admiration for Paul and his work in these Christian communities. This is not surprising since there were likely a goodly number of Gentile Christians in the Tyrian community and also at Ptolemais and Caesarea. This

288. See the helpful discussion in Grudem, *The Gift of Prophecy,* pp. 29-30.

289. But cf. 2 Kings 19:7, 28, 33, 35.

290. Tannehill, *Narrative Unity of Luke-Acts,* 2:265. Larkin, *Acts,* p. 302, suggests that the Spirit's words were intended to stiffen the resolve of Paul, but Luke does not indicate this is the case.

291. What is striking about the entire section is that Luke is perfectly willing to portray a deep difference of opinion between equally sincere Christian groups (even between "we" and Paul or more notably between "we" and God's will) on an important matter. This must count against the view that Luke is portraying the early church in a totally idealistic fashion.

292. This is one of the rare direct mentions of children in Acts. See Polhill, *Acts,* p. 434. It goes without saying that children are not likely part of Luke's target audience in this work. Marshall, *Acts,* p. 339, sees this as historical reminiscence, as there is no point in mentioning the wives and children. One could reply that it shows Paul had won the affections of whole families, and so shows the extent of his impact.

293. The word αιγιαλον refers to a smooth beach. This was probably near the Alexandrian causeway where there was a harbor. See Bruce, *The Acts of the Apostles,* p. 439.

294. τα ιδια has as its literal sense "one's own things/private property," as opposed to common or public property (see Acts 4:32). This text then suggests that communal property, or living in community together in one locale, was not the norm in this Christian community (see pp. 156ff. above on the Jerusalem church). Cf. Johnson, *Acts,* p. 369, who also compares Luke 18:28; John 1:11; 19:27.

contrasts with the mixed reception Paul gets in the Jerusalem church (cf. below).

V. 7 begins with reference to the completion of the voyage from Tyre to Ptolemais.[295] The latter city was called Acco in antiquity (Judg. 1:31), and it was made a Roman colony during the reign of Claudius. Somewhere around the same period of time Christianity must have come to this city, probably brought by those referred to in Acts 11:19. Here Paul and his companions greeted the believers and stayed with them for one day.

While the entourage may have returned to a boat and sailed down the coast, Caesarea was only thirty-two miles away, one long day's journey. In v. 8 Luke mentioned a specific and famous person as providing the venue where Paul and his companions stayed. Philip the evangelist opened his home to them. He was last mentioned in Acts 8:40 as coming to Caesarea, which is where we find him much later. Here we have the only use of the noun εὐαγγελιστής in Acts (cf. Eph. 4:11; 2 Tim. 4:5), though the verbal form was used of Philip in 8:12, 35, 40. Presumably Philip is called this to distinguish him from Philip the apostle, as does the indication that he was one of the Seven. It is entirely possible that this was the occasion when Luke got his information about the earlier events in Caesarea involving Peter and Cornelius.[296]

According to v. 10 Paul stayed at this location for a number of days, which may suggest that his plan was to arrive in Jerusalem on the Day of Pentecost and not before (see 20:16).[297] This may be because the crowds would be at their peak then and Paul could blend in, or more likely Paul saw symbolic or prophetic value to appearing in the city with the collection and these Gentiles on this occasion, perhaps fulfilling the old prophecies (see Rom. 15:25-27 and Zech. 8:20-23).

While Philip was an evangelist, his four daughters are all said in v. 9 to be prophetesses. Luke makes a point of indicating that his exemplary and most important characters in his two-volume work are prophets or prophetesses (e.g., John the Baptist, Jesus, Peter, Paul, Agabus, Elizabeth, Mary, Anna, Philip's daughters). More importantly, Luke appears to use this terminology to refer to a select group, that is, some of the church leaders (cf. Acts 15:22, 32).[298] Prophecy is seen as a gift of the Holy Spirit which may or may not be accompanied by glossolalia and is not simply identical with the latter. NT prophets and prophetesses seem to have a twofold function, either discerning by means

---

295. The verb διανύσαντες could refer to the continuing of the voyage (see the discussion of Xenophon, *Ephes.* in Haenchen, *Acts,* p. 601), but here the voyage terminates at Ptolemais and so completed or finished seems more apt.
296. See pp. 346ff. above and the introduction on Luke's use of sources, pp. 165ff.
297. See Longenecker, *Acts,* p. 517.
298. See the discussion in Ellis, "Role of the Christian Prophet."

of the Spirit's insight the fulfillment of OT prophecies (cf. Acts 2) or on occasion giving new predictive prophecies (cf. Acts 11:28; 21:11; 27:10, 23-24, 31, 34). Luke of course also refers to false prophets, but they are not seen as being as powerful as the Christian ones (Acts 13:46; cf. Luke 6:26).[299]

These four daughters are mentioned as παρθένοι, but it is not clear whether this is meant to be a comment on the fact that they were young and single or whether Luke thinks there is some connection between this condition and prophesying. Luke 1:39-56 surely suggests that Luke does not think women needed to be unmarried to prophesy, nor that they needed to be virgins, since Elizabeth was not (but see Anna in Luke 2:36-38). There is then likely no necessary ascetical connection being made by Luke between women, virginity, and prophecy. According to the later comments of Eusebius, at least one of these daughters married (*Hist. Eccl.* 3.30.1).[300] In view of the material in Luke 1–2, it is unlikely that Luke is trying to upstage these women by having Agabus do the prophesying in this passage. More likely, as I. R. Reimer suggests, Agabus prophesied because he had just come from Jerusalem and could give prophetic insight into what awaited Paul there.[301] The term used to describe these women, προφητεύουσαι, is a participle indicating an ongoing activity rather than some sort of office, but perhaps we should not make a rigid distinction between gift/function on the one hand and status/office on the other.[302] It is very unlikely Luke is trying to avoid calling them prophetesses (using a noun — see Luke 2:36).[303] Since neither they nor Philip does anything in this account, they may have been mentioned, as Harnack long ago thought, because they served as Luke's source of information about the Caesarean church.[304] They also may be said to show that the prophecy of Joel reiterated and reinterpreted by Peter in Acts 2 had come true.[305]

In *v. 10* we hear about the coming of Agabus, after Paul and his companions had been with Philip for a few days. He is introduced almost as if he were a new character in the story, but presumably this is because he is a minor figure who was previously only mentioned briefly in Acts 11:27-28, and Theophilus might not remember him. He is said here to have come from Judea, whereas in 11:27 Jerusalem is mentioned. Luke appears to use the terms

299. See my discussion of all this in *Women in the Earliest Churches*, pp. 151-52.
300. The later tradition has Philip and at least three of these daughters ending up in Asia Minor in Hierapolis and Ephesus (*Eccles.* 3.31.3-5).
301. See Reimer, *Women in the Acts*, p. 249.
302. Longenecker, *Acts*, p. 517, rightly points out that had Luke been in the business of making up speeches, here was a golden opportunity once he introduced these women as prophetesses.
303. See my *Women in the Earliest Churches*, p. 152.
304. See Harnack, *Luke the Physician*, pp. 155-57.
305. See Pesch, *Die Apostelgeschichte (Apg. 13–28)*, p. 215.

interchangeably, or at least by "Judea" he usually means Jerusalem if he is thinking of a particular place.[306]

V. 11 says he took Paul's girdle or belt (ζωνη), a long strip of cloth Paul wrapped around his waist and in which he could keep money and other items. With this belt he physically and symbolically demonstrated the meaning of his words (not unlike various OT prophets — see Jer. 19:1-13; Ezek. 4:1-17). This is the only clear example of this prophetic phenomenon in the NT. The symbolic action was accompanied by words introduced by "thus says the Holy Spirit," a unique and apparently unprecedented formula.[307] "This is the way the Jews of Jerusalem will bind the one who owns this belt and will hand him over to Gentiles" (cf. Acts 28:17).[308] Paul will indeed be put in a bind by Jews in Jerusalem, and he will indeed be actually bound by Gentile authorities (see 21:33), but he is not literally bound by the Jews nor is he handed over by them to the Gentiles. It may well be, at the price of precision, that Luke is deliberately conforming these words to the Passion predictions found in Luke 9:44 and 18:32, but they mention nothing about being bound, nor are Jews mentioned specifically in these predictions. It is better, then, not to press the parallels with the Jesus story, for in any case Paul is not executed in Jerusalem. Agabus's words have authority and accuracy in a general way, and serve as a further warning of trouble awaiting in Jerusalem.

V. 12 indicates that the words certainly had their effect on Paul's friends, for both the locals and "we" urged Paul not to go up to Jerusalem. Agabus, however, offered no such exhortation; he merely foretold, by way of warning, something of what would happen if he did. *V. 13* is interesting. Paul with much pathos asks why they are weeping and pounding on (or breaking) his heart.[309] Paul's resolve is firm, and he does not wish to be caused to waver. He is prepared to be bound or even die in Jerusalem, but clearly enough from what follows he does not yet know the specific form of suffering he will endure there. Paul is not looking for martyrdom, but he is prepared for it if it comes, for he considered it an honor to die for the name of the Lord Jesus.

V. 14 indicates that the pleaders relented, for Paul would not be persuaded not to go to Jerusalem. No amount of rhetorical skill or pathos would

---

306. See Hemer, *Book of Acts*, p. 126.

307. See Johnson, *Acts*, p. 370.

308. This brief message has no real rhetorical form, despite the claim of Soards, *The Speeches in Acts*, p. 109, that it is epideictic. It is certainly not the rhetoric of praise or blame; rather, it is a warning by way of prediction. It is being overly dramatic to suggest that Agabus's prophecy sets the binding of Paul in motion or at least makes it certain, but see Patsch, "Die Prophetie des Agabus."

309. The verb συνθρυπτω was used of washing clothes and seems to allude especially to the beating of the clothes with stones to get the dirt out of them. See Polhill, *Acts*, p. 436. The verb can also mean to crush to pieces, shatter, or break.

change his mind, and so it was that the one who is portrayed as the great persuader on this third missionary tour[310] cannot himself be swayed even by personal and heartfelt appeals. Those present fell silent and quietly affirmed that "the Lord's will be done," which is what all Christians should and must do in the face of the manifestation of God's plan.

V. 15 indicates preparation for the journey up to Jerusalem. While the verb here may refer to the preparing of supplies for the trip, it can also refer to the equipping of a horse for a journey (cf. Xenophon, *Hell.* 5.3.1), in which case Paul may have ridden to Jerusalem and traveled much faster the final sixty-four miles.[311] The Western text, as usual, expands on the narrative to make things clearer. In its version of *v. 16* (and 17) it makes clear that the journey to Jerusalem took two days, and it adds the idea that Mnason lived in a village along the way, not in Jerusalem.[312]

Interestingly, some of the Caesarean disciples traveled with Paul and his companions to Jerusalem, perhaps providing a protective escort and making sure he had a safe place to stay when he arrived in Jerusalem. Mnason of Cyprus is the disciple with whom Paul and company lodged, and he is called an "early disciple," perhaps one of those converted during Paul's first missionary journey to Cyprus, or even earlier by Barnabas (see Acts 4:36). He may have been one of the missionaries from Cyprus who had preached early on in Phoenicia (11:20) and was known by the Christians who lived north of Jerusalem up the coastal road from Caesarea to Tyre. Luke may well mention him by name, not merely because he was a good host but because he provided Luke with considerable information about the Jerusalem church, since he had been a believer for a long time, presumably in that locale.[313]

It is well to remember at this juncture that Christ had told Paul on the Damascus road that he would suffer for him (9:16), but he had not said anything about dying. Luke is faithful to record the evidence that this revelation came true. Paul and his companions were now safely ensconced in the Holy City, for the time being, and perhaps this is a good juncture to discuss the nature and problems of traveling in antiquity.

---

310. See pp. 430ff. above.

311. Cf. Ramsay, *St. Paul the Traveller,* p. 302, and Polhill, *Acts,* p. 436 n. 118, who point out that the classical usage of επισκευαζω had the sense of saddling a horse or pack animal.

312. See Metzger, *Textual Commentary,* p. 483, commenting on D syr-hmg. On the textual variants here, in particular the longer Bezan text, see Delebecque, "La derniere etape du troisieme voyage missionairie de saint Paul selon les deux versions des Actes des Apotres (21,16-17)." For an argument urging seeing B and D as separate developments of the original Lukan texts both of which have some readings which probably go back to Luke, see Wilcox, "Luke and the Bezan Text."

313. See pp. 165ff. above on hospitality and Luke's sources.

A Closer Look — The Pauline Perils: Travels and Travails in Antiquity —

There could hardly be a better description of the perils of travel in antiquity than one finds in the tribulations catalog in 2 Cor. 11:23-29. Paul speaks of danger from bandits, from rivers; of being shipwrecked three times, being adrift in the sea for a night and a day; of having sleepless nights, going hungry and thirsty, being cold and even on occasion almost naked; of experiencing anxiety, and this doesn't even include the difficulties Paul faced because of determined opposition to his ministry by both Jews and Gentiles.[314]

From Paul's list of perils one might come to the conclusion that it was a very dark time to be on the road. In fact, another, more optimistic view is possible. L. Casson has argued that "the first two centuries of the Christian Era were halcyon days for a traveller. He could make his way from the shores of the Euphrates to the border between England and Scotland without crossing a foreign frontier, always within the bounds of one government's jurisdiction. A purseful of Roman coins was the only kind of cash he had to carry; they were accepted or could be changed everywhere. He could sail through any waters without fear of pirates, thanks to the Emperor's patrol squadrons. A planned network of good roads gave him access to all major centres, and the through routes were policed well enough for him to ride them with relatively little fear of bandits. He needed only two languages: Greek would take him from Mesopotamia to Yugoslavia, Latin from Yugoslavia to Britain. Wherever he went, he was under the protective umbrella of a well-organized, efficient legal system. If he was a Roman citizen and he got into trouble, he could, as St. Paul did, insist upon trial at Rome."[315] This is somewhat too optimistic, but it is near enough to the truth to explain why so many both within and outside the Christian movement did so much traveling in the first century A.D.

Paul was by no means what one would call a professional traveler in the sense of a Pausanias who set out to travel for its own sake and to record his observations, such as his "Descriptions of Greece." Nevertheless, one can certainly call Paul a veteran traveler, and not merely a fair-weather one.[316] In some respects Paul was like a traveling merchant hawking his wears in foreign parts, and covering the same territory on more than one occasion. As the Pauline catalog referred to above shows, he was somewhat like the merchant Flavius Zeuxis from Hierapolis who bragged on his tombstone that he had rounded Cape Malea (in Greece) seventy-two times on sea voyages to Italy (i.e., about two or three trips per summer). Paul after all did practice a trade in various of the places he visited, including Corinth and apparently Thessalonica, and it is worth noting that his extensive travels provide a hint about the nature of his trade. "If Paul's overland journeys were generally undertaken on foot, the recently popular explanation of Acts 18.3 that Paul was a weaver of tentcloth made from goats hair or linen . . . is

---

314. We do not mention these things because they are not inherent dangers in travel.
315. Casson, *Travel in the Ancient World*, p. 122.
316. On the basis of 1 Cor. 16:5-6, Jewett, *A Chronology of Paul's Life*, p. 55, posited he was a fair-weather traveler, but the catalog in 2 Corinthians 11 suggests otherwise, as Rapske, "Acts, Travel, and Shipwreck," has pointed out.

rendered even less probable. Such an occupation, requiring tools and equipment inconvenient in size, weight and shape, is hardly in keeping with the impression in Acts of a highly mobile Paul — even less so a pedestrian Paul. The maker/repairer of tents and other leather products, carrying his bag of cutting tools, awls, sharpening stone and such, presents a more consistent and more credible picture."[317]

In other respects Paul was more like the wandering sophists, rhetors, and philosophers who went from place to place offering their teachings or acts of persuasion. Like them all, he took advantage of the Pax Romana, the network of Roman roads and Roman colonies, to spread the gospel. Not only were the roads often quite good, but there were in addition mile markers in Latin on the major Roman roads.

It is well to bear in mind that many of the Roman roads Paul traveled had been there for some time. For example, the Via Egnatia that went through Macedonia was built already in 148 B.C., and by the turn of the era there were already good roads across Asia Minor through Syria and down to Alexandria.[318] Plutarch had witnessed the building of these Roman roads and the procedures followed and described the earlier work of Gaius Gracchus in about 123 B.C. as follows: "The roads were carried straight across the countryside without deviation, were paved with hewn stones and bolstered underneath with masses of tight-packed sand; hollows were filled in, torrents of ravines that cut across the route were bridged; the sides were kept parallel and on the same level — all in all the work presented a vision of smoothness and beauty" (*Gaius Gracchus* 7). The major concern of Rome was to provide very straight all-weather roads, suitable for their armies to travel under any conditions. These roads also provided all-weather means of travel for merchants and for teachers and rhetors like Paul. The gospel of peace and world reconciliation spread so quickly in the first century in part because of the network of good roads built for quite the opposite sort of purposes. These Roman roads were not equaled or surpassed before the nineteenth century when the innovations of W. L. McAdam revolutionized the road-making trade and "paved the way" for modern roads. In terms of durability and reliability and straightness, however, modern roads pale in comparison to ancient Roman roads. They are only much smoother to ride upon.

It is in order to say something about the *cursus publicus,* the governmental mail system, at this juncture, since it largely was carried over land. The system was essentially put together by Augustus so his dispatches could be forwarded to where they needed to go, and so the emperor could receive reports back from the various battlefronts and parts of the Empire. Basically only persons carrying mail for the emperor or the Empire's purposes were given permission and the privileges of using the *cursus publicus.* One had to have a *diploma,* the authorizing warrant signed by the emperor or his agent (such as governors of provinces). The privileges involved getting to use government-maintained hostels and inns throughout the Empire while one traveled. There was the ancient equivalent of AAA Trip-Tics, guides called *itineraria* telling the exact distances between locations, in particular between hostels, and the location of these hostels and the facilities available at each one. Government couriers were able to travel up to fifty

---

317. Rapske, "Acts, Travel, and Shipwreck," p. 7.
318. See Casson, *Travel in the Ancient World,* pp. 164-65.

The Via Appia.

miles a day, and more in an emergency. Needless to say, the private citizen like Paul
had no access to the *cursus publicus,* nor to free use of public facilities.

No doubt he sometimes stayed at the same facilities at a cost, when he was
beyond the network of friends and acquaintances, but the general impression one gets
is that Paul stayed in homes most of the time, or even camped out when not near a
town. His letters he sent by his own couriers, his trusted coworkers and converts.
Doubtless his letters were written on papyrus using a reed pen and ink made of

lampblack which was mixed when it was about to be used. There were no envelopes; the scroll would just be rolled up with the writing inside, a seal affixed. Obviously the time it took for a letter to reach its destination depended on the time the travel took for the one carrying the letter. A letter from Corinth to Rome or from Rome to Philippi might take a considerable period of time to deliver, especially because it went over water. A letter from Macedonia to Corinth, or even from Ephesus to Corinth, might get there more quickly. On a very small scale Paul set up his own *cursus publicus,* and relied largely on the system of standing hospitality that existed in early Judaism and Christianity. It is interesting to note, as Casson points out, that the running of inns in the Greco-Roman world was largely a task undertaken by women.[319] It may be that this social convention made it easier for Paul to accept the offer of accommodations by a Lydia (Acts 16), or for the mother of John Mark to house and host the church in Jerusalem (Acts 12).

In some parts of the Empire travel on land could be undertaken year-round, or almost so, but travel on sea was limited to the sailing season. The prime time was between May 27 and September 14, but troops and others who had a necessity or were adventurous might sail in March, April, October, or even November. The sea was very changeable from March 10 to May 26 and from September 14 to November 11, but still sailable. The winter storms made the seas extremely dangerous for sailing in December, January, or February.[320]

There were no passenger ships as we know them in antiquity. One had to pay an exit tax to leave a country and book passage on a merchant ship, and while the big ones would venture out into the sea, such as the one Paul sailed on from Patara to Tyre, the smaller ones tended to hug the coastline and pull into port each night. On a big vessel, and with prevailing winds, passage from Rome to Corinth took about five days at least, and Alexandria was ten days from Rome. Most travelers on large ships simply booked passage as deck passengers, sleeping in the open or under a small tent. They would travel with bags *(viduli,* or *manticae)* which would contain not only clothes but also cooking ware, food, bathing items, and sometimes bedding as well. Sometimes a very large vessel might hold up to six hundred passengers or slaves, but this was exceptional.

In general, ships never left on a fixed schedule, but according to the winds and weather, which meant that if one wished to go on such a ship, one needed to stay near the port, where one could hear the herald signal departure. Also sailors, like many others in the Roman world, were a superstitious lot, and there were certain days (e.g., August 24, October 5, November 8, religious holidays, and in general the end of the month) when it was thought unwise to sail. Most ship captains or owners would make a sacrifice before sailing, and if the omens were ill, sailing would be delayed. Some of the above explains why it was that on the one hand Paul was so anxious to sail from Troas and bypass Ephesus and on the other hand he had spare time in Tyre and Caesarea. One had to go while the going was good, and one could never be sure of making a passage by a certain date unless one made allowance for some of the delaying factors mentioned above.

319. Ibid., p. 208.
320. See Rapske, "Acts, Travel, and Shipwreck," p. 22.

The most expeditious, large, and reliable of all the ships were the grain ships that made the run from Alexandria to Rome with as few stops as possible. One of the biggest, the *Isis*, was 180 feet long and 45 feet wide with a hold 44 feet deep, holding close to one thousand tons of grain and nearly that many passengers as well. By comparison, Paul sailed on a medium-sized craft that carried close to three hundred passengers (see below on Acts 27:37).[321]

Before we conclude this brief study, something must be said here about arguments about the genre of sea travel accounts. In the world of Greek literature such accounts were already made popular by Homer in the *Odyssey*. In other words, there was a long-standing tradition of such accounts. The accounts could be factual, legendary, fictional, or some admixture of all three, but almost all of them sought to paint a vivid portrait of what was happening during the journey. The not infrequent surprises and crises involved in sea travel were the stock-in-trade of such accounts. If one could throw in a mythical monster like a Scylla, or even an ordinary poisonous snake and a shipwreck along the way, so much the better. While the vividness of Luke's final sea voyage account may not point to the historical authenticity of the account, its accuracy about places and distances, and even small details, probably does point in that direction, for many of the fictional and legendary accounts either deliberately exaggerate or make up things, or are careless about the details.

In regard to the claim of V. K. Robbins that one of the conventional features of the genre of accounts of sea voyages was first-person-plural narration,[322] Praeder has shown that this was not a convention. There are a multitude of third-person sea voyage accounts, both historical and fictional, just as there are many in the first person as well.[323] The "we" in Acts 27–28 or elsewhere cannot be explained on the basis of Luke's following some supposed sea voyage convention.[324] In the second place, as S. E. Porter has shown, some of the major examples of sea voyage literature, such as the *Odyssey*, do not reflect any sort of systematic use of "we" during the sea voyage parts of the narrative. In fact, the majority of the account of the *Odyssey* is not told in the first person at all, and in the case of the *Periplus* the first person plural is used interchangeably with "one" at various points.[325] In the third place, it is probably saying too much, as Robbins does, that by the first century the sea voyage threatened by shipwreck had established itself as a distinctive genre.[326] What is nearer the mark is that the legendary accounts found in the *Odyssey* and the *Aeneid* affected how even historical accounts

321. It is instructive to compare the somewhat serious, somewhat exaggerated account of a sea voyage by the Greek intellectual Synesius, who later became a Christian bishop of Ptolemais, who sailed in A.D. 404 from Alexandria to Cyrene, conveniently found in Casson, *Travel in the Ancient World*, pp. 160-61. Such travel, especially late in the fall or early in the spring, could be filled with frights and delights.

322. See his "By Land and by Sea."

323. See the detailed lists in her "The Problem," pp. 210-11.

324. Even if one didn't reflect on the Greek parallels, one could be rightly suspicious since there are accounts in Acts of sea voyages in the third person in Acts 13 and some of the "we" accounts involve more than a little travel on land.

325. See Porter, "The 'We' Passages," p. 553.

326. Robbins, "The We-Passages in Acts," p. 221.

of sea voyages were told in this era. In the fourth place, one should not use the apocryphal Acts accounts, which were influenced by the canonical Acts as Robbins admits, to discern what the features of this genre might be, for these works are probably not independent witnesses to such features and they are certainly later. Fifthly, in citing Josephus's *Life* 3.14-16 Robbins also fails to make his case about the fictional nature of such accounts, for here we have the alternation between first person singular and plural within the context of an historical account.[327] If this example proves anything, it favors the suggestion that the account in Acts is likewise historical and involved the personal experience of the author. Sixthly, as Barrett has pointed out, various of these accounts, including *Odyssey* 9.39-41, do not use "we" in a conventional way but rather in an occasional way. "It is simply that in any vehicle larger than a bicycle there may well be a number of passengers who become, for a time, a community. 'I left Durham on the 14.55, and we reached London on time. So *we* did.' "[328] Seventhly, for what it is worth, the earliest opinion about the "we" passages in Acts including the sea voyages suggested to Irenaeus not a literary convention but the presence of Luke with Paul on these journeys (*Adv. haer.* 3.14.1). Finally, Dibelius's old theory about Luke's using a (fictional) secular sea voyage narrative, which he then tailored to fit what he wanted to say about Paul, has at least two problems with it. (1) Using the same criteria that Dibelius applied to the data, R. P. C. Hanson, with tongue firmly in cheek, argued that the journey of one Nikias was also fictional, though he knew it was an historical account. In other words, there was something wrong with Dibelius's methodology. The form of the narrative does not reveal whether it was historical in substance or not.[329] (2) Haenchen showed other flaws in Dibelius's case and argued that the account in Acts 27 must be based on an actual sea voyage.[330]

What we have sought to show here is not just the perils of Pauline travel, but also the perils of analyzing and making historical judgments about that travel with the use of very partial analogies. A good case can still be made for the historical substance of the "we" passages, including the final travel accounts about journeys on land and sea.

327. See the discussion by Fitzmyer, *Luke the Theologian*, pp. 16-22 and the notes, in which he offers a helpful detailed critique of Robbins's whole proposal. As he says, various of the examples do not come from Hellenistic literature, and many that do are not true parallels to Acts after one gives them close scrutiny. For example, in *Odyssey* 9.41-53 we also find the use of the first-person plural, not just in the sea voyage material, and here it has to do with the looting of a town. Fitzmyer (p. 21) also rightly notes that in Josephus's *Life* 3.14-16, while the narrative does shift into the first plural from the first singular, yet later in the same narrative it shifts back to first singular and continues that way to the end. The point is not that there was not a type of storytelling involving sea voyages and shipwrecks. There appears to have been such a subgenre, but the fact remains that this does not explain why the "we" is used as we find it in Acts, where it involves both land and sea ventures.
328. Barrett, "Paul Shipwrecked," pp. 53-54.
329. See Hanson, "The Journey of Paul."
330. Haenchen, "Acts 27."

XII. The Trials of Paul (Acts 21:17–26:32)

A. In Church and Temple (21:17-26)

Once Paul has arrived in Jerusalem, the narrative slows down tremendously. Less than twelve days are covered in 21:17–23:35 (cf. 24:11), while 24:1–26:32 covers two years (cf. 24:27).[1] This expansiveness of coverage suggests that Luke deems these events extremely important.[2] The legal proceedings against Paul in Palestine then appear to cover a two-year period (plus or minus a bit), from about Pentecost A.D. 57 until sometime in A.D. 59, including the time when Felix ceased to be and Festus began to be the procurator.

On any showing, Paul had arrived in Jerusalem during very turbulent times (on the fifteen years leading up to the Jewish War, cf. Josephus, *War* 2.254-65; *Ant.* 20.160-72).[3] There had been a string of mediocre to poor governors in Judea who had merely exacerbated the problems that were already festering. Felix was certainly no better than his predecessors, though he lasted

---

1. See Polhill, *Acts,* p. 445.

2. See Ramsay, *St. Paul the Traveller,* pp. 303-7. It probably also shows that he had more evidence about these events than many others he recorded. I would suggest this is because he was present with Paul during these events.

3. See Keener, *Bible Background Commentary,* p. 386: "Jerusalem was not what it had been in Acts 2; tensions are rising, and the temple *sicarii,* or assassins, are murdering aristocrats suspected of collaborating with the Gentiles. Jewish nationalism is on the rise, and nationalism's exclusivity makes it intolerant of supposedly faithful members of its people who have fellowship with members of other peoples. Thus it is incumbent on Paul to prove the integrity of his Jewishness; he can not compromise the Gentile mission, but he will intentionally affirm his Jewish heritage at any cost short of unbiblical exclusivism." On Luke's hand in this apologetic portrayal of Paul see Jervell, *Luke and the People,* pp. 197-99.

longer than most in Judea, probably ruling from A.D. 52 to 59.[4] There is no good reason to doubt Tacitus's judgment that Felix "wielded royal power with the instincts of a slave" (*Hist.* 5.9). Felix had often killed innocent citizens, but perhaps the most egregious example of abuse of power was how he dealt with an Egyptian Jew (cf. below on Acts 21:38) who had prophesied a takeover of Jerusalem by his followers. In an attempt to nip the Egyptian's movement in the bud Felix massacred many, which appears to have galvanized the political and religious zealots in the land into joining forces and planning a general rebellion, which among other things involved the looting and burning of the homes of Romans and Roman sympathizers.

Things became so chaotic that in the end Nero was forced to recall Felix sometime between A.D. 58 and 60 and send a much more able and honest man, Porcius Festus, who unfortunately after only two years in office died. His successors were of the ilk of Felix, not Festus, and thus E. Schürer's judgment on the Judean procurators is on the whole quite accurate. "It might be thought, from the record of the Roman procurators . . . that they all, as if by secret arrangement, systematically and deliberately set out to drive the people to revolt. Even the best of them had no idea that a nation like the Jews required above all consideration for their religious customs. Instead of showing moderation and indulgence, they severely clamped down on any manifestation of the people's national character."[5] The end result of this severe policy was the full-scale rebellion which began at least as early as A.D. 66.

As for the Jerusalem Jews themselves during this period, things were preparing to boil over. If one cannot say things were already quite violent by A.D. 57, they were certainly quite volatile, and anything that was perceived to threaten the purity of the national shrine, such as bringing a Gentile into a forbidden area of the temple precincts, would be reacted to with great emotion and possibly with violence. Polhill sums up the situation and its import for the Jerusalem church aptly:

> Josephus described the period of the mid-50s as a time of intense Jewish nationalism and political unrest. One insurrection after another rose to

---

4. There is considerable debate over when Felix left the area. The earliest evidence we have, however, is from Josephus, which suggests that Festus stepped down from office in A.D. 59 or 60. According to *Ant.* 20.137 he was sent by Claudius in A.D. 52, and *War* 2.271 suggests he was replaced in 59 or 60. Notice that Paul speaks of Felix's "many years" of involvement with Judea in Acts 24:27. Josephus seems to know more about Felix than even Tacitus, probably because he has paid closer attention to the happenings in his home province. Josephus tells us that Felix's first name was Claudius, while Tacitus says it was Antonius. The inscriptional evidence supports Josephus at this point. See the discussion in Bruce, "The Full Name."

5. Schürer, *History of the Jewish People,* vol. 1, p. 455.

challenge the Roman overlords, and Felix brutally suppressed them all. This only increased the Jewish hatred for Rome and inflamed anti-Gentile sentiments. It was a time when pro-Jewish sentiment was at its height, and friendliness with outsiders was viewed askance. Considering public relations, Paul's mission to the Gentiles would not have been well received. The Jerusalem elders were in somewhat of a bind. On the one hand, they had supported Paul's witness to the Gentiles at the Jerusalem Conference. Now they found Paul a *persona non grata* and his mission discredited not only among the Jewish populace, which they were seeking to reach, but also among their more recent converts. They did not want to reject Paul. Indeed, they praised God for his successes. Still they had their own mission to the Jews to consider, and for that Paul was a distinct liability.[6]

Under such circumstances, it is very believable that the collection will have failed to accomplish what Paul intended. Marching into Jerusalem with Gentiles from various parts of the Empire at this xenophobic moment would hardly have produced a positive response from Jews in general, or from ardent Pharisaic Jewish Christians in Jerusalem. Zech. 8:20-23 would not be fulfilled on this occasion, nor would Jews be made jealous to follow the Christ. Rather, they would be made more zealous to stamp out any movement that seemed to threaten their survival as a distinct ethnic and religious group. The picture Luke paints in Acts 21 is quite believable, and equally understandable is Luke's choice to pass over in silence the failure of the collection to accomplish the ends intended by Paul, even though Luke in good conscience has to mention the matter (though only in passing at Acts 24:17).

For our purposes, what needs to be stressed about the facts mentioned above is that Acts does not suggest a different evaluation of Felix or of Festus, or of the Jews during this period of time, than our other sources, both Roman and Jewish. The portrayal of the mixed reception of Paul in Jerusalem is also very believable.

In this section of material we find the introduction of a theme which will continue on until the very end of the book — Paul will be arguing to various audiences that he is a loyal Jew and his mission to Gentiles was not an anti-Jewish one: he opposed neither his people nor their keeping of the Law. We find the accusation against Paul already in 21:28, and it and Paul's defense are reiterated before the Sanhedrin, before Agrippa, and even before the Jews in Rome (see 28:17-20). What this likely reflects, as Tannehill rightly urges, is that the relationship of Christianity to Judaism was still very much problematic and was a live issue in Luke's own day. The problem became an acute one for someone like Luke who recognized God's promises to the Jewish

6. Polhill, *Acts*, p. 447.

people but also knew that the majority of Jews had rejected the notion that these promises were fulfilled in Jesus.[7]

The majority of our passage is composed of speech material (vv. 20b-25), and here we find the interesting phenomenon, also found in Greek historians like Thucydides (see his *Hist.* 1.68), of attributing a speech to more than one person. The function of such a speech is to indicate that a community decision was involved, or perhaps that more than one person spoke (but that the author has compressed the various comments into one speech). This speech is deliberative, and Kennedy suggests that vv. 20-22 should be seen as the proem with vv. 23-24 giving the specific exhortation backed up with a rationale.[8]

The "we" material comes to a halt, not surprisingly, before this speech begins (in v. 18), and, more to the point, it comes to an end when the narrative begins to focus on the events surrounding one particular person and his plight, namely, Paul.[9] In other words, the "we" ceases until Acts 27 because the author is not directly involved in the actions he recounts. Notice also how Paul is distinguished from the "we" in v. 18 to prepare for the absence of the "we" thereafter. It does not follow from this that Luke did not remain in Palestine for the next two years, for the "we" resumes from this locale in Acts 27, only that he played no part of any historical significance during this time.[10] It is quite possible that it was during this time that he managed to investigate and gather source material about the churches in Jerusalem, Caesarea, and the surrounding area, especially in conjunction with the former activities of Peter, Philip, James, and John.[11]

V. 17 should probably be seen as transitional and taken with what preceded it, in which case the "brothers" who warmly welcome and receive Paul and his companions are those connected with Mnason, which may in the main refer to other Hellenized or Diaspora Jewish Christians like Mnason.[12]

---

7. See Tannehill, *Narrative Unity of Luke-Acts*, 2:269-70.

8. Kennedy, *New Testament Interpretation*, p. 134; cf. Soards, *The Speeches in Acts*, pp. 109-10.

9. On the use of source material in this section, leaving out of account the "we" source theory, see Lüdemann, *Early Christianity*, pp. 233-37. Perhaps the greatest historical mystery of this narrative is why James and the Christian community in Jerusalem did not come to Paul's aid when he was taken captive. Was it just that they tried, but it was of no avail, and so Luke omitted reference to it? Or were there more sinister goings-on involved? See below, pp. 670ff.

10. See the discussion in Longenecker, *Acts*, pp. 518-19.

11. See the discussion, pp. 165ff. above, on Luke's use of sources.

12. Larkin, *Acts*, p. 307, says that since Luke does not specify he must mean a delegation from the whole church greeted Paul. This is possible but by no means a necessary conclusion, in view of what follows. Some in the Jerusalem church were not so thrilled to see Paul (see below). There is probably not an allusion to the collection in this verse. See Polhill, *Acts*, p. 446.

If this is the case, then we should not connect this warm reception with the meeting that follows and is referred to beginning in the next verse.

V. 18 provides the last mention of "us," and it is perhaps part of the reason why the "we" drops out of the narrative — Paul's companions, once they had given the collection to the Jerusalem church, had fulfilled their responsibilities and no longer played an active part in the story. Some of them may have immediately or very soon after this occasion returned home. There are several possible reasons why Luke may have chosen not to record the giving and receiving of the collection at this point. (1) These gifts were not received, but rather rejected, because it might make the Jerusalem church look like a less than truly Jewish entity.[13] This suggestion would be believable if in A.D. 57 there were none but Judaizers in charge of the Jerusalem church and if James, a mediating figure, was dead.[14] The evidence we have suggests otherwise, and it is important to remember that according to Gal. 2:9-10 it was the "pillars," including James, who had solicited such support from Paul and Barnabas in the first place. (2) The collection was not delivered. This solution seems ruled out by Acts 24:17 and even a minimal allowance of historical substance to this narrative. Very few scholars dispute that Paul actually made it to Jerusalem and was taken captive there, and there is really nothing substantive to commend the suggestion that the collection visit came earlier than this. It must have come after Paul had had occasion to evangelize Macedonia and Achaia and subsequently got them to contribute to the fund (see Rom. 15:25-29). (3) The collection was delivered but did not have the effect Paul had hoped and desired. The Jerusalem church was too divided within itself and the timing was all wrong (cf. above) for it to have such an effect. This third possibility is far more likely than the other two. Paul himself had feared the collection would not be seen as totally acceptable to all in Jerusalem (Rom. 15:31), and his fears were justified.[15]

One reason why such fears would be justified is that apparently by this time the apostles were no longer in Jerusalem, for v. 18 does not mention them. This would mean that two out of the three original leaders (Peter and John) who had originally requested the funds were no longer present. In other words, James was left in a somewhat tenuous position in view of the radicalizing of Jewish sentiments at this point in time, a radicalizing that had affected the church. We have heard about these Jerusalem elders before (15:6), and it may be that the leadership structure of the Jerusalem church was set up like

---

13. Cf. Lüdemann, *Early Christianity*, p. 2347; Pesch, *Die Apostelgeschichte (Apg. 13–28)*, p. 222.

14. On James as a mediating figure see pp. 439ff. above.

15. See Longenecker, *Acts*, p. 519.

the Sanhedrin, especially after the apostles left.[16] Their mention here reminds us that early Christianity saw itself as an expression of Judaism, and the mention of elders here, but also probably in texts like Acts 20:17, reflects this fact rather than reflecting "early Catholic" church structure.

V. 19 should be compared to v. 17. There we have Paul and his companions being warmly greeted. Here we have Paul doing the greeting, but not being said to receive any. He related one by one what God had done among the Gentiles through his διαχονια. Could this be a reference to the collection? Paul does refer to the collection using this very sort of terminology in Rom. 15:31, and so this may be the meaning here. If so, then *v. 20* indicates that the Jerusalem church, accepted the collection, because they praised God for what Paul just spoke of. On the other hand, Johnson may be correct that we have here a deliberate echo of the earlier report of Paul and Barnabas to the Jerusalem church where we hear of "what God had done among the Gentiles" (15:12).[17] This is even more likely when one couples this with the fact that in the immediately preceding chapter διαχονια refers to Paul's ministry in general, not to the collection (20:24). On the whole the latter interpretation is more probable here, not least because of the way things are put in v. 19 — Paul is relating the things *God* has done among the Gentiles through Paul's ministry. Is Paul really reading a detailed ledger of the money God collected through him from his Gentile churches? Probably not, especially in view of what follows.

Having recounted the great work God had done among the Gentiles, saving many, the Jerusalem church praised God, but then they responded that God had also done great things in Jerusalem among the Jews. The text of v. 20b refers literally to "how many thousands" of believers there were among the Jews, and that they are all zealous for the Law. The reference is to local Jewish Christians, and if this statement is not mere rhetorical hyperbole it suggests that the evangelism in Jerusalem had gone on apace since the 30s and had had good results, growing well beyond the five thousand male converts mentioned in Acts 4:4 (cf. 6:7 and 9:31). In other words, the Jerusalem church was not so much worried about the impact of Paul's coming on non-Christian Jews, but about the impact on these Torah-observant Jewish Christians. It may be that we are meant to think that it was the Pharisaic Jewish Christians (15:1-2, 5) who had been the most successful at proselytizing, but Acts 21 does not speak of Judaizers (that is,

---

16. Hengel, *Between Jesus and Paul,* p. 108, speaks of James receiving Paul like a prince of the church a court of elders. The historicity of James having had a dominant position in the Jerusalem church is ably demonstrated by Hengel, "Jakobus der Herren-bruder — der erste Papst?" Hengel also argues that Luke is an eyewitness at this point, accompanying Paul on his last journey.

17. Johnson, *Acts,* p. 374.

those who wanted Gentile Christians to be Torah observant) but merely of those who were themselves observant and were concerned that Paul might be teaching *Jews* in the Diaspora not to be observant.

V. 21 speaks of what these Torah-observant Jewish Christians had heard (from whom it is not said) about Paul. The complaint is threefold: (1) Paul had taught *all* the Jews who live among the Gentiles to forsake Moses,[18] (2) he had taught them not to circumcise their children, and (3) he had taught them not to observe the customs. The first complaint is the most general and in fact encompasses the next two. It is understandable how this impression of Paul's preaching might have arisen.

In the first place it was likely true that some of Paul's Jewish converts, when joining communities that were largely made up of Gentile believers, had perhaps ceased to be Torah observant as they had been in the past. Teachings like one finds in Gal. 4:9; 5:6; and Rom. 2:25-30 may well have been seen as encouragement in this direction. Doubtless, too, Paul had not *insisted* that they had to be Torah observant, especially since he himself was on some occasions Gentile to the Gentile and on other occasions Jew to the Jew (cf. 1 Corinthians 9). There is, however, as Marshall points out, no evidence that Paul went around actively trying to persuade Jewish Christians to be nonobservant Jews.[19] The ritual law was a matter of adiaphora in Paul's mind, and so he himself could either observe it or not so long as it was understood that either way it had no soteriological significance. Luke seems to have agreed with this assessment, seeing Law observance as a good means for a Jew to express her or his piety but not as a means of salvation for either Jew or Gentile.[20]

A small, telltale sign that Luke has cast this speech in rhetorical form is found in *v. 22,* where we have the stock rhetorical question, "What therefore is it?" (τι ουν εστιν), widely found in the rhetorical literature and especially in the diatribes (see Epictetus, *Diss.* 1.6.12; 1.7.7; 2.4.8).[21] The question means, "What therefore is to be done?" and should follow the *narratio* once one gets to the point in the deliberative discourse of argument, exhortation, or the stating of what will be beneficial or profitable.

Vv. 23-24 provide what was seen as a solution to this dilemma. Paul was to undertake an action that would make clear that he supported those who were Torah observant, and that he himself not only did not object to keeping

18. The word αποστασια refers to either political and/or spiritual rebellion (cf. 2 Chron. 29:19; 1 Macc. 21:5; Acts 5:31, 39; 2 Thess. 2:3). Here it is unlikely to have a solely spiritual sense, and while it contains the idea, it is not synonymous with the later transliterated English term "apostasy." Here the social component is important: Jews are changing their way of life, not merely, perhaps not even primarily their beliefs.

19. Marshall, *Acts,* p. 344.

20. See the discussion in Wilson, *Luke and the Law,* pp. 101-2.

21. See Johnson, *Acts,* p. 375.

the Law but was prepared to be seen doing so himself at the very heart of Judaism — in the temple. This, it was thought, would squelch the rumor.

There has been considerable debate over what ritual is envisioned in these two verses. There are four men under a vow, and in view of the reference in v. 24 to the shaving of their heads, it must be seen as a temporary Nazaritic vow (see Num. 6:2-21). Paul is to join with these men in some fashion, go through a rite of purification, and pay for the fulfillment of these men's vows, which involved costly sacrifices. Does Luke envision Paul undertaking a Nazaritic vow here?[22] Probably not, not least because one could not undertake such a temporary vow for less than thirty days (*m. Nazir* 6:3; cf. Josephus, *War* 2.313).

Haenchen is likely correct that Paul is undertaking a different sort of ritual of purification, the sort required of those who come from foreign, unclean lands (*m. Oholot* 2:3; 17:5; 18:6). This sort of rite could be completed in seven days (cf. Num. 19:12), and thus Paul would have been in position to accompany the four to the temple at the end of their vow, pay the expenses for the closing sacrifices of these men (Num. 6:13-20), as well as conclude his own rite. As Larkin says, both the LXX and Luke use purification terminology (αγνισθητι here) to refer to both the process of removing ritual impurity (Num. 19:12) and undergoing a Nazaritic vow (Num. 6:3, 5).[23] Thus Paul can be said to join them in a purification rite.[24]

It has been suggested that this proposal of the Jerusalem leaders had a sinister side to it. There were those who knew that the prescribed ritual would give a golden opportunity to Paul's enemies to attack him, for it required Paul not merely to appear in the temple but to state in advance when he would complete his vow in the temple, thus giving his enemies a timetable to plan an attack (see Rom. 15:31).[25] Thus, those who suggested this plan saw a way

---

22. It is not probable that Luke thought Paul was here fulfilling a vow he undertook much, much earlier (see 18:18), for surely he fulfilled that vow on his previous trip to Jerusalem, mentioned in 18:22 (see pp. 558ff. above).

23. Larkin, *Acts*, p. 309 and the notes on these verses.

24. See Haenchen, *Acts*, p. 612. Once Paul had been sprinkled with the water of atonement on the third and seventh day, then and then only would he be deemed Levitically clean and only then could he be allowed to be present at the final ceremony for the four, which took place in the temple. That Paul has money to pay for these rather expensive sacrifices may say something about his social condition and position at this point, unless of course the money came out of the collection. This is perhaps not impossible, and perhaps the Jerusalem church suggested Paul use some of the money this way, thus making clear that their receiving of the rest was not some sort of bribe or inducement to overlook the Jewish violation of the Law supposedly encouraged by Paul.

25. While the church probably did not plot against Paul, it is not unbelievable that others who found out about Paul's arrangements in the temple might do so. For instance, that members of the priesthood would not be above such an attack on early Christians, even the most conservative Jewish ones among them, is shown by Ananias's successful attempt to get rid of James himself during the interregnum after Festus died in A.D. 62, only a few short years after Paul encountered trouble in Jerusalem (see *Ant.* 20.197-203).

to get rid of the problem of Paul once and for all.[26] The problem with this suggestion is that James would never have consented to it, and 21:18 makes clear that he, if anyone, is the main speaker here. It may be nearer the mark to suggest that if Paul performed this act, then these Jerusalem Christians would feel they could accept the collection from Paul in good faith.[27]

V. 24b states the hoped-for outcome of Paul's fulfilling the above-requested activities — that all will know the rumors are not true, for Paul both personally observes and guards the Mosaic Law. This must be seen at least in part as an exercise to change public perception rather than regulate Pauline practice. In any event, v. 25 makes clear that this request was not to be understood as an attempt to go back on the agreement reached earlier at the apostolic council discussed in Acts 15. Paul of course knows very well that such a letter has been sent with the decree in it, for he helped disseminate it (see Acts 15:30), but the point here is to reiterate the commitment to that arrangement.[28] The point of the reiteration is to make clear that while more may now be required of Paul in a Jewish ritual direction, this did not imply that more would be required of Gentile converts in that direction.[29]

As we have argued earlier in our discussion of the decree in Acts 15,[30] what is essentially being required of the Gentiles here is to avoid idolatry and immorality by staying away from the place where such things could be found together — idol feasts in pagan temples. The order of items here corresponds with what we find in 15:29, with the significance and venue being signaled by the first term, ειδωλοθυτον, which refers to meat sacrificed and eaten in the presence of idols. In the first mention of this topic in Acts this is made clear by referring to "something polluted by an idol." The issue is not just one of menu but of venue where this meat has been offered and eaten. To avoid that venue would clearly signal to Jews and Jewish Christians that Gentile Christians were serious about severing their ties with their pagan past as Paul himself had insisted they must do (cf. 1 Thess. 1:9-10; 1 Corinthians 8–10).

It is interesting that in the Western text of v. 25 we find something a bit different from the readings that text offered at Acts 15:20, 29. Here the order is different and the negative Golden Rule is omitted, which suggests that the

---

26. See Mattill, "The Purpose of Acts," pp. 115ff.
27. So Dunn, *Unity and Diversity,* pp. 257-58.
28. As a secondary point, Talbert, "Again: Paul's Visits to Jerusalem," pp. 37-38, is surely right that Luke wanted this material reiterated as well to make clear to his own audience that there was no going back on the decree. Talbert is also helpful in showing there is no good reason to suppose that Paul didn't hear about the decree until his last visit to Jerusalem.
29. See the discussion in Longenecker, *Acts,* p. 520.
30. See pp. 439ff. above.

latter was an addition to the earlier texts, as we have argued.[31] There is also in Codex D a further explanatory addition after the phrase "believing Gentiles": "they [i.e., the Jewish Christians] have nothing to say against you, for we have sent the decision. . . ."[32] As Johnson says, the point of this addition is to make clear that the charge to Paul does not have to do with the validity of the Gentile mission, which would not be gone back on, but with the behavior of Jewish Christians only, in this case Paul in particular.[33]

V. 26 indicates that Paul complied with their request or stipulations. The next day Paul went into the temple, purified himself, and with the four men made public the terms of the completion of their "days of purification" when the sacrifice would be made for each of them. Some commentators have thought it unlikely that Paul would submit to such a request, but this is overlooking three important things. (1) Both in the case of the Nazaritic vows (cf. 18:18) and in the case of the purification from the uncleanness caused by being in pagan lands, we are talking about onetime actions that conclude *temporary* states. (2) Paul freely chose to submit to this request. There is nothing to suggest he was compelled to do it, though he may have felt it was necessary to maintain the bond of peace between the mother church and his converts. There was not, for instance, any threat by the Jerusalem authorities that if he did not comply he and his mission would be rejected by the Jerusalem church. (3) Paul himself says he was willing to be the Jew to the Jew, which would include observing at least parts of the Mosaic Law, especially while among Jews (1 Corinthians 9), in order to win more to Christ, so long as the means of one's salvation was not in question and this Law was not imposed on his Gentile converts. The Jerusalem authorities had just reiterated that the latter was not the case, except of course for the requirement to stay away from idolatry and immorality. If a matter of principle had been raised about the nature of salvation by faith or the means by which Gentiles could become full Christians, Paul would not have submitted to these requests (see Gal. 2:3), but the Jerusalem authorities made quite clear that the issue was about Paul as a Jew and what he was believed to be causing Jewish converts in the Diaspora to do, not what he was saying or preaching to Gentiles.[34] Paul's willingness to pay for the completion of these men's vows would be seen as an especially pious act, not unlike when King Herod Agrippa I (A.D. 41-44)[35] apparently underwrote the expenses for various poor Nazarites (Josephus, *Ant.* 19.294).

31. See Bartsch, "Traditions-geschichtliches zur 'goldenen Regel' und zum Aposteldekret," especially p. 130.
32. See Metzger, *Textual Commentary,* p. 485.
33. Johnson, *Acts,* p. 376.
34. See Bruce, "The Church of Jerusalem," p. 658.
35. See above, pp. 235ff.

B. Purity and Profanity in the Temple (21:27-36)

The subsection which follows the meeting with the authorities of the Jerusalem church is full of deliberate irony. Paul is falsely accused of profaning the temple while he is in the process of a Jewish purification ritual(!), and in fact it is his character which is being desecrated and defamed. The temple is sacred, the crowd is profane, and Paul is purified and remains true to his character. This will be the last scene we have in Acts that is set in the temple in Jerusalem, and it is probably not accidental that this scene involves the final shutting out of Paul and his message from the temple precincts — the temple doors are closed against him.

As for the historical substance of this account, Johnson is right to stress that anyone who has read Josephus's accounts of these turbulent times, and of the sort of riots that could happen so quickly in this temple during this period if Jews felt their heritage was being seriously threatened, will realize that Luke knows the character of both this place and this time (cf. Josephus, *War* 2.315-20).

> Luke puts things in their proper place. He knows why Paul's supposed transgression of the Temple limits with a Gentile was a grievous offense, and why the mob could assume to get away with murdering him for it. He knows the way the Temple is connected to the fortress area by stairs, and how rapidly a military contingent could get from one place to another. He knows the sorts of officers and soldiers involved in the Jerusalem garrison. He is aware of the revolutionary movements that stirred the mobs in the Temple precincts at the time of the great pilgrimage feasts. And like our other major source for the events of this period, he is not altogether clear on the distinctions between the various revolutionary forces. To any reader of Josephus' *Jewish War* for this period, this riot scene in the Temple rings absolutely true. There is nothing, in other words, intrinsically unlikely about a figure like Paul creating just such a scene as Luke describes.[36]

V. 27 speaks of the seven days being about to be brought to an end, or to fulfillment, which probably means that on the seventh day (Num. 19:12) Paul was sighted in the temple as he was going to receive the water of atonement and complete the purification period and ritual. This ritual had to be completed before Paul would be ritually clean and could participate in the completion of the four men's Nazaritic vow.[37] He was sighted by Jews from Asia. Here Asia is probably used as a provincial designation, and the meaning is likely Ephesus. There have been hints of ill will of Jews from this locale

---

36. Johnson, *Acts*, p. 384.
37. See Larkin, *Acts*, p. 311.

earlier in the narrative (19:9; 20:19), even though Luke had not given a full account of their opposition to Paul before now. It was perhaps these Jews who had been spreading the story in Jerusalem that Paul was teaching Diaspora Jews to stop observing the Mosaic Law and customs (cf. v. 21 above).

These Jews stirred up the large crowd already in the temple precincts and took direct action, seizing Paul and, according to *v. 28,* shouting, "Fellow Israelites, help! This is the man who is teaching everyone everywhere against our people, our law, and this place; more than that, he has actually brought Greeks into the temple and has defiled (made common) this holy place."

The former charge is reminiscent of the charge against Stephen (Acts 7:13-14), and indeed this whole scene is reminiscent of the Stephen scene, only with a slightly different outcome — Paul does not become a martyr at this point. Then, too, Stephen can be argued to have been the victim of a lynch mob,[38] but in Paul's case this is probably not so, as we shall see. Tannehill points out the following parallels between Paul and Stephen: (1) the charges about what they teach are essentially the same; (2) both make speeches before their accusers; (3) both speeches begin with the same address, "brothers and fathers" (7:2; 22:1); (4) both speeches produce a violent response (7:54-58; 22:22-23); (5) both are accused by Diaspora Jews (6:9-12; 21:27); (6) Paul in his speech makes a connection with Stephen, by referring to his death (22:20).[39] Luke was well aware of the value of parallel accounts for teaching lessons, and of course he wrote during the age of Plutarch (ca. A.D. 46-120?), the author of the famous biographical and moralistic *Parallel Lives,* likely written somewhat later than Acts. Such an approach was a popular and rhetorically effective literary device used by Hellenistic historians and biographers of the time. It is noteworthy that though Luke has suggested and continues to suggest various parallels between the story of Jesus' last trip to Jerusalem and Paul's (cf. below), this account is more notable for a contrast with the end of the Jesus story — Paul not only doesn't die in Jerusalem, he does something the Lukan Jesus does not do: he gives a defense speech to his accusers. Johnson is right to note: "Here is the sharpest difference between the philosopher/prophet Jesus, who went to his death without self-defense, and his philosopher/prophet successor. Luke's Paul is much more a character of late antiquity, at home in the *paideia* of Hellenism and the *politeia* of the Roman world."[40] Paul of Tarsus is portrayed as a great rhetor in the Greco-Roman mold; Jesus of Nazareth is, for obvious reasons, not.

There are then two charges, with the latter, because it involved an action, being much more serious than the former. The perfect tense of the verb "has

38. See pp. 255ff. above.
39. See Tannehill, *Narrative Unity of Luke-Acts,* 2:273ff.
40. Johnson, *Acts,* p. 385.

defiled" suggests that the accusers see the profanation of the temple as ongoing, and only to be eliminated if its cause is wiped out.[41] In fact the charge is very specific — Paul has defiled the ιερον, which must mean here the inner courts (cf. Josephus, *War* 5.193-94). Non-Jews were permitted into the outermost court, the so-called Court of the Gentiles, but not into any of the three inner courts, the Court of the Women, the Court of the (Israelite) Men, the Court of the Priests, and of course not into the Holy of Holies, which only the high priest could enter.

Josephus describes the wall which separated the Court of the Gentiles from the inner courts as a stone barricade about four and a half feet high reflecting excellent workmanship (*War* 5.193). He adds that at regular intervals there stood stone slabs giving warning, some in Greek, some in Latin, that no foreigner was permitted to enter the Holy Place (*Ant.* 15.417; cf. *War* 5.194; Philo, *Legatus* 212). Two of these notices have now been found. One, in Greek, was found by C. S. Clermont-Gennau in Jerusalem in 1871, though it now is in a museum in Istanbul. The second was found in 1935 outside Saint Stephen's gate and resides in a museum in Jerusalem. The message read: "No foreigner may enter within the barricade which surrounds the temple and enclosure. Anyone who is caught doing so will have himself to blame for what follows — death."

As Polhill points out, it is not completely clear whether this inscription was of a common ancient taboo sort (i.e., God will strike you dead if you pass this barrier), or whether the inscription meant that Jews would enforce this warning by summary execution.[42] From Josephus, *War* 6.124-26, one would gather that the Romans understood it to mean the latter, for Titus speaks in this text of allowing Jews to execute violators, even if they were Roman citizens. There is no clear evidence of anyone being executed for this offense in Jerusalem, but it was apparently a live possibility. This policy comports with what we know of Roman practice elsewhere. For example, the power of execution was granted, even against Roman citizens, to those protecting the Greek temple at Eleusis.[43] In general, Romans saw it as their job to help protect the sanctity and good order of the great temples in their Empire, and one of the ways they accomplished this was by in certain cases relinquishing the otherwise closely guarded privilege of capital punishment. Thus, we are probably not meant to see this scene as merely an example of mob "justice." The accusers were well within their rights to execute Paul, if in fact he had committed the very serious crime with which he was charged.

Luke, however, in *v. 29* makes clear that a bad mistake was being made.

---

41. See Tajara, *The Trial of Paul*, pp. 64-65.
42. See Polhill, *Acts*, p. 452.
43. See Keener, *Bible Background Commentary*, p. 387.

The Asian Jews had seen Trophimus with Paul in the city and had simply assumed Paul brought him into the temple's inner courts.[44] It is interesting that Luke does not say that they simply concocted this charge. Perhaps they had seen Paul entering the temple area with others (the four Jerusalem Jewish Christian Nazarites?), and having previously seen Trophimus with Paul, supposed or thought (ενομιζον) he was with Paul on this occasion. They had recognized Trophimus as a convert from Asia (i.e., probably Ephesus, cf. 20:4).

The response to the alarm raised by these Asian Jews was immediate and impressive. Even allowing for a certain amount of rhetorical hyperbole,[45] if we bear in mind that the Court of the Gentiles was something of the marketplace of the city where most people gathered for various purposes, it is not too much of a stretch when Luke says that "all the city was aroused, and the people rushed together." The point is to emphasize the massive and unified response of the large Jewish crowd which was present, a not unprecedented phenomenon when a slight was perceived against Jewish customs (cf. Josephus, *War* 1.88-89; 2.8-13; 2.42-48; 2.169-74; 2.223-27; 2.229-31; 2.315-20; 2.406-7; 2.449-56).[46]

V. 30 indicates that Paul was seized and dragged out of the temple proper, into the Court of the Gentiles, and immediately the doors into the inner court were shut behind them, perhaps by the *sagan* or chief of the temple guard, presumably to prevent any human blood being spilled in the Holy Place.[47] Various commentators have noted the symbolism of the shutting out of Paul from the cultic center of Judaism. Is Luke also suggesting that this event is symbolic of the final refusal of the good news that leads to the downfall of the temple? This is probably overallegorizing the story, for Luke does not give any clear clues that this is his intent here.[48]

The crucial point to reiterate, however, is that this charge of desecration of the Holy Place, echoing as it did earlier "abominations that made desolate" the Holy Place, from a Jewish viewpoint warranted such an enormous and immediate response if the charge was true. No trial need be held; rather, the

44. Marshall, *Acts*, p. 348, argues that "the possibility that Trophimus might have wandered of his own freewill into the forbidden area is about as likely as that somebody should wander into private rooms in the Kremlin for the purpose of sightseeing." This was an apt analogy before the fall of Communism, not so apt today with tours of the Kremlin going on apace. The point is well taken, however, that it is very unlikely Trophimus wandered beyond the barricade either on his own or with Paul.

45. On Luke's rhetorical use of πας and related words such as ολη here, see pp. 105ff. above.

46. See Johnson, *Acts*, p. 381, who first pointed to these references.

47. This action was presumably taken by the temple police. Cf. Jeremias, *Jerusalem*, pp. 209-10.

48. See, however, the discussion in Bruce, "The Church of Jerusalem," p. 659, and Tannehill, *Narrative Unity of Luke-Acts*, 2:273; Larkin, *Acts*, p. 313.

The Antonia fortress as represented in the Holy Land Hotel model
of Herodian Jerusalem.

accused could simply be dragged outside and beaten to death (for example, with clubs, having one's skull split open, cf. *m. Sanh.* 9:6; Philo, *Legatio ad Gaium* 212). As Larkin stresses, the "Jews believed the temple remained profaned until the trespasser had been executed."[49]

It is at this juncture, according to *v. 31*, while the crowd was trying to kill Paul, that word came to the "chiliarch of the spieres," in other words, to the military tribune in charge of the cohort, whose name we later learn is Claudius Lysias (23:26), that "all" Jerusalem was in an uproar.[50] Josephus refers to the permanent stationing of a Roman cohort at the Antonia Fortress with the specified duty of suppressing any disturbance during the festivals (*War* 5.244).[51] A cohort had a strength, on paper, of 1,000 men (hence the Greek term "chiliarch" used of their commander), including some 760 infantry and 240 cavalry. Undoubtedly we must identify this commander and his troops as the Roman troops stationed at the adjoining Antonia Fortress (cf. Josephus, *War* 5.244), not as the temple police. Josephus also tells us of the two flights

49. Larkin, *Acts*, p. 314.
50. It is interesting that the Harclean Syriac adds with asterisks at this point "See therefore that they do not make an uprising." See Metzger, *Textual Commentary*, p. 485.
51. See the discussion in Hemer, *Book of Acts*, p. 126.

of stairs that went straight from the towerlike structure of the fortress directly down into the outer court of the temple precincts (5.243).[52] We are told of this unit that two of its centurions went with Claudius to investigate the row (v. 32), and that some 470 soldiers escorted Paul to Caesarea (23:23), which suggests that the unit was at full strength.[53] This is especially likely to have been the case during festivals, when there was the greatest potential for violence and riots.

It is often said that Lysias came and rescued Paul from the mob, and this indeed proved to be the effect of his actions, but what he no doubt intended was to try to prevent a full-scale riot and restore order in the temple precincts.[54] He shows no especial concern about Paul's life, at least before he finds out he is a Roman citizen; indeed, he assumed that Paul was some sort of rebel leader. V. 32 indicates that Lysias acted very quickly, running with his troops and centurions to the spot of the trouble, and when the crowd saw them coming they stopped beating Paul. V. 33 indicates that Lysias, acting on the where-there's-smoke-there's-bound-to-be-fire theory, immediately arrested Paul. His suspicions about Paul will be expressed in v. 38 (cf. below). Paul is bound with two chains, and if Luke is using terms properly, two hand chains (ἁλύσεσι), which means he is bound between two soldiers (cf. Acts 12:6), not bound hand and foot.[55] We see here the general fulfillment of what Agabus had predicted if Paul went to Jerusalem.[56]

It is important to stress that at the beginning of this legal process Paul was arrested by the Romans, not by the temple police. Had the latter happened, he would have been tried and sentenced by the Sanhedrin. "Now the supreme Jewish body would have to obtain his extradition in order to try him. Paul had no intention of leaving Roman jurisdiction; he would fight any attempt by the Sanhedrin to have him extradited."[57] Even if he had to appeal to Caesar, he would not accept "justice" at the hands of his fellow Jews. He knew very well what had happened to Jesus, and even more to the point he knew what had more recently happened to Stephen, and probably about the killing of James the brother of John as well (cf. Acts 12:2). It was not mere rhetoric when he stated that he was prepared to go to Jerusalem and face death in the Holy City (21:13).

It is not completely clear whom Lysias asked about what Paul had

---

52. One of the towers of this fortress is said to have been about one hundred feet high.

53. See Johnson, *Acts*, p. 382.

54. See rightly Cassidy, *Society and Politics*, p. 97.

55. See Tajara, *The Trial of Paul*, p. 68; Bruce, *The Acts of the Apostles*, p. 451. Fetters or foot chains were called πέδαι.

56. See pp. 634ff. above on Acts 21:11.

57. Tajara, *The Trial of Paul*, p. 68.

done, but *vv. 33-34* suggest that he asked members of the crowd, not Paul. The crowd, however, was still volatile, and, as is often the case, one person shouted one accusation and another a different one. Here we see a sort of makeshift *cognitio* period, but because the witnesses did not agree and Lysias could not discern the facts of the case because of the uproar, he ordered Paul to be taken back to the barracks.[58] *V. 35* indicates that the crowd resumed their attack on Paul, perhaps fearing they were about to lose their opportunity to do away with him. Paul and the troops came to the steps leading up to the fortress, but the violence against Paul was so great that the soldiers had to carry Paul up the stairs. Haenchen thinks this historically unlikely because it would further expose Paul to abuse by lifting him above the crowd. This would only be true if Paul were in some open area where the crowd could take up stones, but he was in the Court of the Gentiles and was being beaten, not stoned. There is nothing improbable about this action by the soldiers.[59]

V. 36 indicates that the crowd followed Paul and the soldiers, shouting, "Away with him!" The reader or hearer familiar with Luke's Gospel would detect an echo here of the cry against Jesus in Luke 23:18 (cf. Acts 22:22 and John 19:15). The cry means more than send him away, it means do away with him. Paul is clearly in dire straits. From now on in Acts he would be Paul in chains, and here most assuredly we see how Acts parts company with ancient novels and romances. There would be no more miraculous releases from prison or custody for Paul; rather, there would be real experiences of weakness and suffering, with no final resolution of the matter by the end of the book. The irony of all this is that Paul sees his whole experience of legal bondage as a result of and as an act of loyalty to Israel.[60] He says at the end of the book: "For the sake of the hope of Israel I wear this chain" (28:20). He is a prisoner not only because of his fellow Jews but also for their sake. Thus Paul's ritual action in the temple leads to the opposite of its intended effect. "Rather than clearing Paul of a charge before Jewish Christians, it leads to a lengthy imprisonment with repeated accusations and trials."[61] To these trials and defense we must now turn.

---

58. The phrase γνωναι το ασφαλες (cf. Acts 22:30; 25:26) means literally to know something certain, and reflects the fact-finding stage of Roman justice. See Johnson, *Acts*, p. 382.

59. See Haenchen, *Acts*, p. 618. Some have suggested that Paul was so beaten he needed to be carried, but Luke apparently does not think so since Paul will immediately turn and give a speech at the end of this episode.

60. See Tannehill, *Narrative Unity of Luke-Acts*, 2:271.

61. Ibid. Different scholars will read the long accounts of the trials differently, but I think there is some merit in Ramsay's old argument (*St. Paul the Traveller*, p. 308) that

C. The First Defense (21:37–22:29)

Vv. 37-40 must be seen as transitional, preparing for the speech which follows (the chapter division being very infelicitous). It is important to understand clearly the narrative logic or rhetorical shaping of what will follow in the section in Acts 21:37–26:32 that deals with trials and defense. As Tannehill says, it is important to study this material not as a loosely connected series, or as isolated passages, for there are major themes and ideas Luke is trying to make clear throughout the section.[62]

The first thing that needs to be stressed is the Jewishness of the material. The charge made against Paul in 21:28, already intimated in 21:21, is the essential charge being answered in the defense speeches that follow right to the end of chapter 26. Political charges do not dominate the defense scenes here; they play only a secondary role. The main attack being rebutted with the use of forensic rhetoric is "the charge that Paul is anti-Jewish, that his mission is a fundamental attack on the Jewish people and its faith. Charges punishable by Rome are mentioned, and at points Paul responds to them, but the overriding issue is one between Paul and his Jewish attackers."[63] Even when we get to the very end of Acts, we still have in Acts 28 what can only be called an in-house debate between two forms of Judaism, involving again a defense to the local Jewish leaders of Paul's conduct in which Paul claims he is bound due to "the hope of Israel." This is followed by Paul's trying to convince Roman Jews from the Law and the Prophets about Jesus. The overwhelming impression left by the speech material in the last quarter of Acts is that "the Way's" relationship to non-Christian Judaism is still very

---

"the importance of the trial for Luke is intelligible only if Paul was acquitted. That he was acquitted follows from the Pastoral Epistles with certainty for all who admit their genuineness; while even those who deny their Pauline origin must allow they imply an early belief in historical details which are not consistent with Paul's journeys before his trial, and must either be pure inventions or events that occurred on later journeys. . . . But if he was acquitted, the issue of the trial was a formal decision by the supreme court of the Empire that it was permissible to preach Christianity: the trial therefore was really a charter of religious liberty, and therein lies its immense importance." If, as I think, Luke wrote the Pastorals at the behest of Paul, he not only knows the sequel to his Acts volume but has recorded it as well. It seems to me very inadequate to argue that because Theophilus (perhaps living in Rome) knows the unfavorable outcome of the trial, Luke need not record it. If the trial did not, in the end, turn out favorably for Paul, more explanation would certainly be necessary, in view of Luke's stated purposes in Luke 1:1-4. Theophilus would not be assured, made firm, or given certainty in his faith by an account that failed to explain such a known end to such an important figure as Paul.

62. See the helpful essay of Tannehill's, "The Narrator's Strategy."
63. Ibid., p. 256.

much a live issue for the author, requiring repeated instruction to his audience on this subject.[64]

The second major thing to note is the way the two autobiographical defense speeches frame the trials section of Acts, and how they are both addressed to Jewish audiences — the former in 22:1-22 to the Jewish crowd and the latter to King Herod Agrippa II in 26:2-29. We will examine the differences in the speeches as the exegesis proceeds, but one is struck at the outset by their obvious Jewishness and similarities. It becomes clear that not just Paul's personal behavior or teaching is at issue but the larger issue of whether Paul's evangelism, and the church's evangelism in general, can be said to indicate that the Way is an anti-Jewish movement.[65]

The third quite extraordinary thing about Acts 22–26 is that Paul's defense speeches are given to Jews, but he appears on trial before Gentile authorities. There are only two proper trial scenes in this section, the trial before Felix in 24:1-23 and the trial before Governor Festus in 25:6-12, but Paul does not direct major defense speeches primarily to *either* of these officials. Though Festus is present at the second speech, the speech is directed to Agrippa and is thoroughly Jewish in character.

Scholars have rightly thought that the last quarter of Acts gives clear clues about the author's interests and purposes. What these chapters show is that Luke is not mainly interested in doing apologetics either to or for Roman officials. Were that his interest we would surely have at least one speech where Paul addresses the relationship of the Way to Roman interests and the Empire's concerns. Were that his real concern we might expect a grandstand finish with an apologetic speech before the emperor in Rome. His concern with Rome is in fact basically a negative one — that Roman officials not oppose or ban the Way, making it some kind of proscribed *superstitio*. The Way must be seen as not a proper target for Roman judicial investigations and litigation. It is no accident that from Gallio to Festus the stress is placed on the judgment that there is nothing about Paul and his preaching that should concern Roman jurisprudence, much less cause a guilty verdict to be rendered against Paul. By contrast, the issues of debate with Judaism are positive and substantive — who is the Messiah, what is God's plan for his people, who is included in that people, by what means are they included?

An important fact about the speeches in Acts needs to be kept steadily in view as we investigate the speeches and defense scenes in Acts 22–26. It is true to say that the speeches prior to Acts 20 are in the main deliberative in

---

64. All things considered, this must surely favor a first-century date for Acts. On this subject cf. pp. 55ff.

65. See Tannehill, "The Narrator's Strategy," p. 257.

character, while those which come after Acts 20 are forensic.[66] This corresponds with the change in character of the narrative itself. Prior to Acts 20 we have chronicles about evangelism and missionary work, in other words attempts to make people change their minds and lives in preparation for, and in ways that will be profitable or beneficial for, the future. This is the essential aim of deliberative rhetoric. By contrast, from Acts 20 on we have not missionary chronicles but apologetics in various forms, and so the rhetoric of defense and attack, forensic rhetoric, is apropos. The speeches and narrative work together to achieve the rhetorical aims of the author in regard to persuading his audience about matters he deems important. With this background we are prepared to look at the defense speeches and trials in Acts 22–26.

V. 37 does not say so explicitly, but in view of what we know about Roman procedure it seems likely the tribune was taking Paul back to his barracks to complete the fact-finding portion of his investigation, using torture if necessary. Just before Paul is brought into the barracks, Paul takes the initiative and speaks to the tribune in formal and polite Greek — "Is it permitted to me to say something to you?"[67] This line of approach not only shows politeness but also implicitly recognizes the tribune's authority in this situation. The tribune is taken by surprise. He responds, "Do you know Greek?"

Probably the sentence that follows in *v. 38* should also be seen as a question and be read "Then are you not the Egyptian who recently stirred up a revolt and led the four thousand daggermen out into the wilderness?"[68] The tribune knows very well that Greek was spoken widely in Egypt as a result of the long-standing Hellenistic influence there, and since he assumes Paul is a rebel of some sort, the fluency of Greek suggests to him that Paul is no mere local Jewish troublemaker, whose Greek would not likely be this good. We have here another of the incidents which Acts and Josephus both recount, and as we have shown elsewhere in this study, there is good reason to prefer Luke's account of the matter.[69] Luke's numbers are certainly more believable (four thousand as opposed to Josephus's thirty thousand), as also is the Lukan version that the Egyptian led his followers out into the desert, like a new Moses figure. There were various such messianic pretenders during this era seeking to perform signs to gather a great following and perhaps to rally them against their Roman overlords.[70] Here we have a chronological marker in the text. The evidence of both Josephus and Acts dates the Egyptian's activities to the

66. See Watson, "Paul's Speech," p. 184.

67. The ει introduces a direct question here, as in Acts 1:6; 7:1; 19:2; and 22:25.

68. As *MHT* III, p. 283, rightly point out, this second question expects an affirmative answer. The particle αρα is inferential, based on hearing this good Greek.

69. See the excursus, pp. 235ff. above.

70. See my discussion in *The Christology of Jesus*, pp. 90-96, and also Barnett, "The Jewish Sign Prophets."

reign of Felix, from what we can tell, about A.D. 54 (cf. *War* 2.261-63 and *Ant.* 20.168-72).[71] When they got wind of what the Egyptian was about to attempt — not only to cause the city's walls to fall miraculously but to have himself installed as the people's new ruler — Felix and his troops took preemptive action, killing four hundred and capturing another two hundred, but the Egyptian himself escaped. The question then of the tribune here is quite plausible, and suggests the incident was still fresh in his mind. It would be a considerable coup for his career if he had managed to capture the Egyptian.[72]

The tribune refers to the σιχαριων, the daggermen, of whom Josephus has a good deal to say. These were violent Jewish revolutionaries who gained their name from their practice of carrying daggers under their cloaks and stabbing to death various Jewish aristocrats and others who collaborated with the Romans right in the temple precincts, then slipping away untouched (cf. *War* 2.254-57; *Ant.* 20.162-65, 185-87). Considering the setting in which Paul is apprehended, this question of the tribune is both apt and understandable. He naturally associates various groups with revolutionary potential, even if they were actually separate movements.

According to *v. 39* Paul responds immediately to this last question, in order to disassociate himself from such dangerous company. In fact, as Lentz has pointed out, Paul's response may suggest that he takes the suggestion that he is an Egyptian as a racial slur.[73] In other words, Paul's response is not just a legal self-description but also a rebuttal of a twofold sort meant to restore his *dignitas:* (1) the suggestion that he, a Jew, was an Egyptian would be taken as a slur; (2) the suggestion that he, a faithful Jew, was a revolutionary false prophet was adding injury to insult.[74] First of all, Paul proudly states that he is a Jew, and not one from Egypt. Rather, he is from Tarsus, "no mean city,"[75] and secondly he is a citizen of that city.

Tarsus was indeed widely recognized as an important city in various regards, not least as a center of Hellenistic culture, including the teaching of rhetoric and of Stoic philosophy (cf. Strabo, *Geog.* 14.5.13-15; Dio Chrysos-

---

71. As Polhill, *Acts*, p. 455 n. 19, points out, there are discrepancies between the two accounts of Josephus. For example, *Antiquities* mentions collapsing walls of the Holy City as the sign the Egyptian planned to perform, but the parallel account in the earlier *War* suggests a more normal seizure of the city.

72. This dates our story to after A.D. 54, and certainly A.D. 57 is not too late for this encounter between Paul and Lysias to have occurred. Felix was still in power.

73. See Lentz, *Luke's Portrait of Paul*, pp. 28-30. Jews in Alexandria resented being identified as Egyptians.

74. See the discussion in Rapske, *Paul in Roman Custody*, pp. 136-37.

75. Note again Luke's fondness for litotes. This phrase is in fact a stock one applied to cities that one wants to boast about; cf. Euripides, *Ion* 8; Strabo, *Geog.* 8.6.15; Achilles Tatius, *Clitophon* 8.3.1.

tom, *Or.* 33.48; 44.3). At the height of its importance Tarsus had approximately five hundred thousand residents, only a minority of whom were citizens. It had been proclaimed a free city (like Ephesus) by Antony in 42 B.C. It is important to note that Paul mentions his legal citizenship to the tribune, but not to the crowd (cf. 22:2), for the crowd, unlike the tribune, would not have responded well to a boast about being a citizen of one of the centers of Hellenization in the Empire.[76]

It is important to recognize that to a great extent in antiquity people were judged by the importance of the place where they were born. Their own personal honor and dignity was in part derived from the honor rating of the place from which they came.[77] Paul is making a claim here to be a person of considerable social status, indeed probably higher status than the tribune himself, which can explain why the tribune allows him to address the crowd.

As for the older complaint that Jews could not hold citizenship in such cities as Tarsus because of the religious requirements involved, this complaint may be laid to rest. As Hemer shows, the synagogue in Sardis provides inscriptional evidence to the contrary, where a Jew is called a prominent citizen of Sardis.[78] Nock also produces an example from Antioch.[79] The chief prerequisite for being a citizen of a prominent city such as Tarsus is that one had to meet a property requirement. Since the requirement of Jews performing various pagan rites was waived as a matter of course in the Empire in other circumstances because of the Roman policy of allowing people to practice their indigenous religion, this waiver must also have been allowed, from time to time and place to place, when the issue was citizenship in a local *polis*.[80] One can also point to Philostratus, *Life of Apollonius* 6.34, where some Jews seem to be included in a discussion about citizens of Tarsus.[81] We will discuss the question of dual citizenship for Paul (Tarsian and Roman) when the

---

76. See Rapske, *Paul in Roman Custody,* p. 76. The argument of Tajara, *The Trial of Paul,* pp. 79-80, that πολίτης is used in some sort of loose and not legal sense is predicated on the assumption that Paul grew up in Tarsus and would have had to have worshiped pagan gods. Both assumptions may be doubted, as the discussion by Rapske cited above shows. The former assumption will be addressed below, pp. 668ff., when we discuss 22:3 (cf. 26:4). See now Hengel, *Paul,* pp. 158-61; Murphy-O'Connor, *Paul,* pp. 32-36.

77. On the honor rating of cities in the Empire, see the important essay by Neyrey, "Luke's Social Location of Paul," pp. 268-74.

78. See Hemer, *Book of Acts,* p. 127.

79. A. D. Nock, *Essays on Religion and the Ancient World* (Oxford: Harvard University Press, 1972), p. 961; cf. Rapske, *Paul in Roman Custody,* pp. 79-83.

80. The suggestion that the Jew from Sardis was a thoroughly Hellenized and non-observant one surely won't work, since his name is on the honor role of the synagogue! See the helpful discussion on Paul's Tarsian citizenship in Rapske, *Paul in Roman Custody,* pp. 75-79.

81. See Johnson, *Acts,* p. 383.

Roman citizenship issue arises in the text,[82] but here it is sufficient to point out that holding Roman citizenship and that of another city was not deemed incompatible during the Empire, especially from the time of Claudius onward. The strictures against this had been relaxed at the end of the Republic period and in early days of the Principate.[83]

Haenchen has objected to the historical plausibility of this account because the tribune would not likely allow Paul to speak to the crowd, because Paul was incapacitated after the beating, and because the crowd becoming quiet was unlikely after just trying to beat Paul to death.[84] One may respond to this by saying that the text says nothing about Paul being knocked out or made incapable of speaking. It also says nothing about his being inherently incapable of standing — it is the violence of the crowd, not Paul's collapse, that causes him to be carried in v. 35.

The objection to the idea of Paul being allowed to speak is a result of a serious misunderstanding of the social situation and how honor claims affected ancients. Paul had shown respect for the tribune's authority, spoken an educated man's Greek, and made considerable honor and status claims. On these grounds the tribune's action is quite believable. He had no evidence that Paul was not who he claimed to be, and it was always very unwise to refuse or offend someone of equal or higher social status than oneself. He may have seen this as making up for the perceived social slight and slur of calling a high-status person an Egyptian revolutionary! Finally, the quieting of the crowd is believable if the tribune supported Paul or stood by him, while he made the well-known gesture of a rhetor who is about to speak (cf. Acts 13:16; 19:33; 26:1). It does not say they immediately became silent, as 22:2 will show, only that they quieted down.[85] We are told that Paul spoke to them in the "Hebrew dialect." This may indeed mean Hebrew, in view of the evidence from Qumran that Hebrew seems still to have been a well-known language, but it is more likely that Aramaic is meant (cf. 22:6; 26:14, in this case western Aramaic), the lingua franca of the most eastern portion of the Empire. Paul is here portrayed as a cultured man, fluent in the two major spoken languages of the western and eastern portions of the Empire.[86] It is improbable that the

82. See pp. 668ff. below.

83. Cf. Sherwin-White, *Roman Law and Roman Society*, pp. 182-83; Lüdemann, *Early Christianity*, p. 241. Conzelmann, *Acts*, pp. 124ff., argues that it was possible to have dual citizenship from the time Claudius became emperor, but in fact it was earlier than this.

84. Haenchen, *Acts*, pp. 620-21.

85. Johnson, *Acts*, p. 384, rightly suggests the translation "substantial silence."

86. See the discussion by G. H. R. Horsley in *New Docs*, 5 (1989), pp. 23ff. This ability to speak Hebrew or Aramaic does not come as a surprise, if in fact Paul was raised in Jerusalem. That Paul himself seems to make such a claim is probably suggested by a text like 2 Cor. 11:22 where a distinction is made between Hebrews and Israelites.

tribune knew either Hebrew or Aramaic, and thus he likely did not understand the discourse which followed.

It is understandable that various commentators have often looked at the last third of Acts as biographical in character, due to its singular focus on Paul. Especially in the speeches in Acts 22–26 a biographical interest is reflected. On the basis of this and other considerations Talbert and others have made a plausible case for reading Acts as a whole as a sample of biographical literature in the form of a sequel about a great person's successors or followers.[87] This sort of analysis, however, fails to take into account Luke's rhetorical interests, and especially the rhetorical shaping of the defense speeches in Acts 22–26, which we will discuss at length shortly. Here it is sufficient to stress that the issue of *ethos,* or the character of a person, is paramount in forensic rhetoric. As Lentz says, "according to the forensic handbook it was of utmost importance to portray the defendant as a person of moral integrity and high social standing."[88] Quintilian stresses that if the one being defended "is believed to be a good man, this consideration will exercise the strongest influence at every point in the case" (*Inst. Or.* 4.1.7). In other words, the interest in Paul's life story and character in the last third of Acts has to do with Luke's apologetic and rhetorical purposes to defend the gospel and its major exponents, not with a desire to write a biography about Jesus' successors.

There are several major points that need to be taken into account before we can examine the speech itself. (1) We have already dealt in detail with the similarities and differences in content in the three versions of Paul's conversion found in Acts 9, 22, and 26, and so we will not repeat those data here.[89] (2) The speeches in Acts function as an essential part of the story, not merely commentary on the story. They often precipitate or cause the action, because as P. Schubert pointed out some time ago, Acts is the story of the proclamation and progress of the word. Schubert estimates that up to 74 percent of Acts is devoted to either speeches or their immediate settings.[90] This is an overestimate, but the larger proportion of speech material in Acts, compared to other ancient Greek historiographical works (e.g., in Thucydides speeches amount to 25 percent of the whole), is to be explained by Acts's subject matter; the story he is trying to tell is about the word and the Way that spread it. (3) Attention must be given to the fact that these speeches occur in a literary work, and so their effect is intended to be cumulative. That is, Luke

---

87. See the discussion on this matter in the introduction, pp. 20ff. above, and especially Talbert's fine essay, "The Acts of the Apostle."

88. Lentz, *Luke's Portrait of Paul,* p. 106.

89. See pp. 305ff. above.

90. Schubert, "The Final Cycle," p. 16. He is following Haenchen in this conclusion.

does not include all the details he wishes to convey in any one telling of the story, but adds fresh details in the accounts subsequent to Acts 9, not merely for the sake of stylistic variation but so that there is a cumulative effect on the hearer. The full picture is not gained until one has heard Acts 26. This has to do with the rhetorical shaping of the narrative and speech material so it will be serviceable in a literary work.[91] (4) It cannot be stressed too much that while the account in Acts 9 is third-person narrative, both accounts in Acts 22 and 26 are in direct speech and therefore not surprisingly follow the rhetorical conventions for speeches rather closely. This explains some of the significant differences between Acts 22 and 26 on the one hand and Acts 9 on the other. (5) Even more of the differences between Acts 22 and 26 may be attributed to the differences in audience. As Tannehill points out, the "audiences of the two major speeches differ. The first speech is delivered to determined opponents who have just tried to kill Paul. . . . King Agrippa differs from this audience not only in rank but in attitude . . . he is not identified with Paul's Jewish opponents and is open to Paul's message. Indeed, before Agrippa Paul boldly moves from a defense speech into a missionary appeal."[92] (6) Some of the differences in the account must be put down to a difference in speaker. It is Paul who speaks in these speeches, whereas Luke speaks in Acts 9. For example, Ananias's part in the story is considerably shortened in Acts 22 because the story is told from Paul's vantage point.[93] (7) As Hedrick notes, Acts 9 is more of a miracle story with a commissioning conclusion than Acts 22 or 26 is, and the formal features associated with miracle stories explain some of the differences between Acts 9 and the two speech accounts in Acts 22 and 26.[94]

The speech in Acts 22 has been analyzed rhetorically in several ways. Kennedy, for example, sees it as essentially *narratio* without the following formal proofs and *peroratio*.[95] F. Veltman also points out that the speech is mainly

---

91. Hedrick, "Paul's Conversion/Call," saw this point already (see p. 432). There are, however, two very different explanations of this phenomenon: (1) Luke has shaped his source material so that it will have a cumulative effect; (2) Luke has created these speeches. It must be remembered that at most we have summaries of speeches in Acts, and no one denies that Luke has edited and shaped these summaries. In the case of multiple speeches on one subject, such as Paul's conversion, it was not necessary to include all the details in any one presentation, even though when the speeches recorded in Acts 22 and 26 were actually given they likely included much more than we find here. Judicious editing is as good an explanation of what we find in Acts 22 and 26 as free invention when we bear the above considerations in mind.

92. Tannehill, "The Narrator's Strategy," p. 257.

93. See Marshall, *Acts*, p. 356.

94. Hedrick, "Paul's Conversion/Call," p. 417. On healing as a part of salvation in Luke-Acts see Appendix 2 below, pp. 821ff., on "Salvation and Health in Christian Antiquity."

95. Kennedy, *New Testament Interpretation*, p. 134.

biographical and does not specifically refer to charges.[96] W. Long has argued that the speech should be divided as follows: (1) 22:1-2, *exordium;* (2) 22:3, *narratio;* (3) 22:4-21, proofs.[97] This analysis, however, will not stand close scrutiny. There are no formal proofs, artificial or inartificial, in vv. 4-21, rather there are hints or elements of what could be later used as proofs in the *narratio* which extends to v. 21. Some of these elements include the mention of signs, witnesses, and probabilities, but no formal proofs are made on the basis of these allusions. J. Neyrey appears to make the same mistake as Long, referring to items in the *narratio* as already proofs.[98] The interpretation of this speech must be guided by two facts — the very hostile audience and the fact that the speech is interrupted before it is finished. Not only do we not have a *peroratio* in this speech, we do not even reach the formal *probatio* — the crowd interrupts before formal proofs are given. Had such a stage in the speech been reached, we could have expected not only a reply to the charges against Paul's teaching but also an explanation about his actions in the temple and those of Trophimus. Veltman is right that the interruption here is not a mere literary device, when actually the speech is over, nor should we see the point of interruption as signaling the main point of the speech.[99] Here, as in Acts 17 at the Areopagus, the speech is interrupted at the most contentious point. The main point that the speech in Acts 22 seeks to prove is that Paul is a loyal Jew, thus rebutting the charges against his teaching. What has been overlooked is that the hostile audience requires that Paul spend a considerable amount of time on the *narratio*, establishing just what the facts of the case were, and how they should be viewed. Whenever one has a hostile audience one must be very careful to lay the groundwork properly before advancing to the proofs. In fact, Paul may well be using the technique of *insinuatio* here. He cannot directly attack his audience, and so he more subtly seeks to identify with them as a fellow zealot for God and the Law, indeed a fellow persecutor, as a means of explaining his actions.[100] The "speech from the steps of the Fortress of Antonia deals eloquently with the major charge against him — that of being a Jewish apostate (cf. 21.28a)."[101]

---

96. Veltman, "Defense Speeches of St. Paul," p. 253. His study is mainly of use in showing how such defense speeches were used in various kinds of ancient literature. Perhaps his most interesting conclusion is about the differences between the defense speeches in Acts 22–26 and what we find in the speeches in the later Christian *Acts* of the martyrs. In the latter the "Christian had no desire to plead innocence of the charges and no wish to please Rome, hence . . . the omission of the *captatio benevolentiae* and the claim of innocence." This is the opposite of what we find in Paul's speeches, as we shall see.

97. Long, "Paulusbild," p. 98.

98. See Neyrey, "Forensic Defense Speech," p. 221.

99. See Veltman, "Defense Speeches of St. Paul," p. 254 n. 44.

100. See Tannehill, "The Narrator's Strategy," pp. 257-58.

101. Longenecker, *Acts*, p. 524.

I would suggest the structure of the speech is simply: (1) *exordium*, vv. 1-2 (cf. Quintilian, *Inst. Or.* 4.1.1-79); (2) *narratio*, vv. 3-21 (*Inst. Or.* 4.2.1-132; Cicero, *De Invent.* 1.19.27), in which Paul will insinuate what the following proofs will involve, but they are never developed.[102] The *exordium* is brief; the audience is made receptive to hearing what would be said in two ways: (1) Paul appeals to the ethnic and religious heritage he shares with his audience by addressing them as "fathers and brothers." Implied in this form of address also is Paul's obedience to the teachings of Judaism, including respect for the "fathers" who passed these traditions down.[103] This form of address is found elsewhere in Acts only at 7:24 at the beginning of the Stephen speech, under similar circumstances — in both cases the audience is quite hostile. (2) The form of the *exordium*, and indeed of the whole speech, likewise involves a patriotic move, for Paul chooses to speak not in Greek but in Hebrew, or perhaps more likely Aramaic. In either case one of the two sacred languages of the Hebrew Scriptures is used.[104] The *exordium* ends with a clear declaration as *v. 1* closes that this is an ἀπολογια, that is, a forensic defense speech. The term was a technical one used in rhetorical literature to signal that judicial rhetoric was to follow (cf. on the form of such speeches, Quintilian, *Inst. Or.* 3.9.1; Cicero, *De Invent.* 1.14.9; and on the use of the term, Wis. 6:10; Josephus, *Against Apion* 2.147). Paul calls his audience to "hear my present defense."[105] As Aristotle suggested, one should state up front the kind and aim of the speech (*Rhetoric* 3.14), and Paul does so.

Vv. 3-5 state clearly and succinctly Paul's pedigree, in a fashion meant to impress a Jewish audience zealous for the Law. The most remarkable aspect of this recital is that Paul not only seeks to identify with his audience in speaking of his own zeal for the Law but he also even identifies with them as persecutors! The description of Paul here is similar to what we find in Gal. 1:14. The threefold formula "born, raised,[106] educated," as van Unnik demonstrated some time ago, is a stock item (cf. Plato, *Crito* 50E, 51C; Philo, *Vita Mos.* 2.1; *Flaccus* 158).[107] It is used at Acts 7:20-22 to speak about Moses' early life. If we compare what we find here and the parallel account in Acts 26, we

---

102. Cf. Keener, *Bible Background Commentary*, p. 390.

103. See Long, "Paulusbild," p. 99.

104. See ibid., p. 98. The significance of Paul's speaking one of the sacred languages should not be underestimated. This may in part be what Paul is alluding to in Phil. 3:5 when he says he is a Hebrew from Hebrews. Marshall, *Acts*, p. 353, notes the infrequency of (Western) Diaspora Jews knowing Hebrew or Aramaic. As he points out, even Philo did not know Hebrew.

105. See Long, "Paulusbild," p. 99 and n. 73.

106. The key term ἀνατεθραμμενος refers to childhood upbringing, much as our term "reared" does. See the details in van Unnik's *Sparsa Collecta I* (Leiden: Brill, 1973), pp. 259-327, where his two main articles on the subject can be found.

107. See the full-length study, van Unnik, *Tarsus or Jerusalem.*

learn that Paul was in fact raised from an early age in Jerusalem, *not* in Tarsus.[108] His Tarsian citizenship, then, was purely hereditary, and there was no question of his having been of such an age while in Tarsus that he might have been confronted with the problem of involvement in pagan religion, though we cannot even be sure that such a question would have arisen for a Jew in Tarsus (cf. above). Perhaps some small corroborating evidence for the conclusion that Paul was raised in Jerusalem is the mention of his sister's son at 23:16, indicating he still had family in Jerusalem.[109] Lüdemann also rightly notes that since there is no real evidence of Pharisees being trained outside of Jerusalem, or at least outside the Holy Land, this favors Paul's being raised in Jerusalem (cf. Phil. 3:5 to Acts 26:5).[110] The phrase "at the feet of Gamaliel" goes with the following verb, πεπαιδευμενος, which indicates that Paul was a disciple of Gamaliel and was educated accurately in the ancestral law by him.[111] Johnson points out that elsewhere in Luke-Acts where this phrase "at the feet of" occurs, it always symbolizes submission (cf. Luke 7:38; 8:35, 41; 10:39; 17:16; 20:43; Acts 2:35; 4:35, 37; 5:2, 10; 7:58; 10:25).[112] This is indeed the same Gamaliel (later called Gamaliel the Elder) mentioned in Acts 5:34, who appears as a somewhat more level-headed orthodox Jew than his zealous pupil Saul.[113] The point of the reference to Paul's education is to make clear that he was brought up in a very orthodox manner. He was given a precise knowledge of the Law, and trained to follow it strictly. Paul, however, was not just zealous for the Law, he was zealous for God,[114] and in this, Paul stresses, he was just like his audience was "today." A fair and probable summary of Paul's pre-Christian life is given by Keener: "As a son in an educated and perhaps aristocratic home (his father being a citizen; cf. also 9.1), Paul probably began to learn the Law around his fifth year and other Pharisaic traditions around his tenth year, and was sent to pursue training to be able to teach the Law sometime after turning thirteen. . . . Paul's model for zeal may have been Phinehas, who killed for God (Num. 25.13), and his successors in the Maccabees."[115]

---

108. Contra Pesch, *Die Apostelgeschichte (Apg. 13–28)*, p. 238, who on the one hand doubts Paul being raised in Jerusalem, but on the other doesn't doubt he was a pupil of Gamaliel.

109. The use of the term "youth" of Paul at Acts 7:58 probably also points in this direction. Cf. pp. 276ff. above.

110. Lüdemann, *Early Christianity*, p. 240.

111. κατα ακριβειαν could mean "according to exactness" or "according to strictness"; cf. Acts 26:5.

112. Johnson, *Acts*, p. 388.

113. See pp. 233ff. above.

114. Some later variants (e.g., the Vulgate) have zealous for the Law. Cf. Metzger, *Textual Commentary*, p. 485.

115. Keener, *Bible Background Commentary*, p. 389.

Does *v. 4* suggest that Paul persecuted the Way until various Christians died, or does the Greek mean up to the point of death? In view of 26:10 most commentators have thought the former is meant. But even in the case of Stephen, Paul does not seem to have actually been involved in the stoning. Perhaps the more general point is being made — Paul took actions and cooperated with efforts that led to the death of various Christians (cf. 9:1). *V. 5* indicates that both the person who was then high priest in the mid-30s A.D. (Caiaphas) and the council of elders could testify that Paul had acted as a persecutor of Christians, indeed he was involved in binding not only men but also women and putting them in prison. Furthermore, his zeal was so great he got letters of reference from these Jewish authorities to Jews in Damascus and was prepared to extradite Jewish Christians to Jerusalem for punishment. The net effect of this recital is to make clear Paul's extreme zealousness for Torah and Torah's God, as the highest authorities in Judaism could testify. He had unimpeachable witnesses of what he had been like. He had been like his present audience, and therefore his autobiography was especially relevant to precisely this audience. "Paul is testifying to the power of the Lord to change persecutors. His story of the radical change that took place in his own life is an invitation to present persecutors to reevaluate Paul and Jesus, and thereby be changed themselves."[116]

Vv. 6-11 provide the description of the encounter between Paul and Christ, followed by a commissioning. There are several major differences between this account and the one found in Acts 9: (1) the reaction of astonishment of Paul's companions is omitted; instead we have in v. 9 Paul's own description of what they did and did not encounter (cf. 9:7); (2) as (1) suggests, the story in Acts 22 is told from Paul's point of view, not from the viewpoint of some omniscient narrator, and this is why he will omit Ananias's vision in vv. 12ff.;[117] (3) it is possible, as Hedrick suggests, that κυριος in v. 10a means more than "sir" and the question here means "What is my commission, Lord?";[118] (4) there is no clear statement of where the commission comes from in Acts 22 (cf. Acts 9), nor is it explained why Ananias sought out Paul, nor

116. Tannehill, "The Narrator's Strategy," p. 258. Cf. also Loening, *Die Saulustradition in der Apostelgeschichte*, pp. 175-76.

117. See the discussion in Tannehill, *Narrative Unity of Luke-Acts*, 2:275. Hedrick, "Paul's Conversion/Call," p. 430, is, however, wrong that Paul's companions do understand the Christophany in Acts 9 but do not understand or participate in it in Acts 22. They are outsiders in Acts 9 as well. His analogy (p. 429) with John 12:27-29 is helpful, however, where God speaks to Jesus but the crowd only hears sound or noise. Luke does not wish to exclude Paul's companions from the experience on the Damascus road altogether. Indeed, they provide corroborating witness that something happened. It is just that he wants to stress that only Paul received a revelation and a commission as a result of this encounter.

118. Hedrick, "Paul's Conversion/Call," p. 424.

is it stated that Paul arose from the ground, but all this is information already given in Acts 9, which Luke does not choose to repeat here. He intends the effect of the three accounts to be cumulative.

Paul says he was approaching Damascus about noon when a light from heaven shone about him. The emphasis is on the fact that the revelation is objective, for it came in broad daylight and is not said to be a vision or dream. In this regard we may both compare and contrast what happened to Paul with the description of Peter's midday vision in Acts 10:9-16. Paul is more immediately responsive and obedient to the revelation than Peter. As in Acts 9, Paul is persecuting Jesus, not merely his followers, as is indicated in *v. 7*.[119] Thus he has the horrible realization that he has been persecuting the risen and exalted Messiah, and in fact doing the opposite of what God would want him to do.[120] In *v. 8* Jesus indicates he is from Nazareth, something not mentioned in Acts 9:5. This is perhaps part of the strategy of this speech to emphasize the Jewishness of Paul, and of his Lord. In *v. 10* the question of what Paul is to *do* as a result of this encounter is both asked and answered. He must go into Damascus and there be told what he has been assigned to do.[121] The activity of the companions is mentioned briefly only at *v. 11* (nothing is said about their standing or falling during the revelation) because they aid the blinded Paul to enter the city of Damascus, leading him by the hand. Johnson suggests a literal translation of this verse — Paul could not see "because of the glory of that light."[122] This translation suggests that God's self-manifestation, not merely a natural phenomenon, has blinded Paul, and one should compare Paul's similar language in 2 Cor. 4:6.[123] Again, the story is told from Paul's point of view.

In *v. 12* Ananias is introduced in a different fashion than was the case in Acts 9. There he is described as a Christian disciple (9:10), here as "a devout man according to the Law and well spoken of by all the Jews living there" (in Damascus). The reason for this difference is that the audience Paul addresses in Acts 22 is a hostile orthodox Jewish one, while Luke in Acts 9 is addressing a convert, Theophilus. Ananias, then, is here presented as another unimpeachable Jewish witness who can testify to claims about

---

119. Several Western texts (E and various Latin, Syriac, and Georgian versions) add to v. 7 the idiom found at 26:14 about kicking against the goads.

120. See Larkin, *Acts*, p. 321.

121. Contra Larkin, *Acts*, p. 320, there is no clear evidence here that Paul is anxious about being under judgment, as the crowd in Acts 2:37 was; rather, it would seem that Paul's commission is being alluded to.

122. Johnson, *Acts*, p. 389.

123. Acts 9:3 comports with this conclusion, since the light is said to be from heaven.

another phase of Paul's life. *V. 13* has Ananias simply proclaim the words "Brother Saul, regain your sight." Actually αναβλεπω can have a double meaning here, "look up" and/or "recover sight again," depending on how one takes the prefix ανα.[124] Two aspects of this are worth noticing. In the context of Acts 22, "brother" here would normally be understood to mean fellow Jew, but in Acts 9, since Ananias has been introduced as a Christian and goes on to speak of the Lord Jesus, who sent Ananias to Paul (9:17), it would mean "fellow Christian." Once again we see the rhetorical shaping of the account in view of Paul's present audience. The second aspect of this verse worth noting is the absence of any reference to laying on of hands, perhaps because there was a concern that the hostile audience might construe this as some sort of unorthodox magical act. Here it is quite clear that God healed Paul — within that very hour he regained his sight and saw Ananias.

Vv. 14-16 continue the very Jewish presentation of this call/conversion/commissioning story. The name Jesus does not occur here on Ananias's lips; rather, he speaks of the "God of our ancestors" (cf. Acts 3:13; 5:30; 7:32; 13:23) and the Righteous One. The latter is a title for Jesus which has occurred before in Luke-Acts only in very Jewish contexts (Luke 23:47; Acts 3:14; 7:52). Paul has been chosen to see this Righteous One and hear his very voice. *V. 15* announces that Paul will be a witness to "all persons" of what he has heard and seen. This more general reference should be contrasted to the Lord's more direct words in Acts 9:15: "you will bring my name before Gentiles, kings, and before the people of Israel." The more general reference here comports with Paul's attempt to avoid offending his hostile audience. *V. 16* adds a note not found in Acts 9. Here Ananias asks why Paul delays,[125] and then commands him to get up, be baptized, and "have your sins washed away, calling on his name." There is perhaps a deliberate ambiguity here as to whether "his name" refers to the God of our ancestors or to the Righteous One. The verb "baptized" here is in the middle voice, and could be construed to mean "baptize yourself," which might comport with the Jewish practice of ablutions such as one finds at Qumran, and with the usual reflexive force of Greek verbs of washing in the middle voice.[126] Probably we once again see the deliberate ambiguity of the narrative here. Since, however, "baptized" is coupled with "have your sins washed away," we should probably construe the former verb in the passive.

124. See Bruce, *The Acts of the Apostles*, p. 457.

125. The Greek phrase τι μελλεις is a common one meaning "What are you waiting for?" Marshall, *Acts*, p. 357, however, suggests the meaning "What are you going to do about it?" In either case the point is that it is now time for Paul to act, to respond to what has happened. Cf. Polhill, *Acts*, p. 461.

126. See Bruce, *The Acts of the Apostles*, pp. 457-58.

*The Court of the Jews and the Holy of Holies as represented
in the Holy Land Hotel model of Herodian Jerusalem.*

Vv. 17-18 introduce new information, which is especially apropos in view
of Paul's audience.[127] Paul explains that on his first visit to Jerusalem after his

127. V. 17 is awkward, involving a lack of concord in the use of pronouns and in the
use of the genitive absolute, which has some sort of noun or pronoun antecedent in the
sentence, but there is no attempt to make the cases of the words agree. Also γινομαι is used

conversion he was in the temple, was praying, and fell into a trance (εχστασις) in which he saw Jesus telling him to leave Jerusalem quickly "because they will not accept your testimony about me." We may perhaps connect this incident with the conflict in which Paul was involved in the synagogue of the Hellenists mentioned at Acts 9:29-30, and/or with Gal. 1:18-21.[128] "Paul's visit to the Temple signifies, as an implicit rebuttal of the charge against him, his long-standing devotion to the *ethos* of Judaism and in particular to the Temple . . . the fact that he prayed there also proves his piety, and his recognition of the Temple as a place of prayer."[129] Many scholars have heard allusions here to the call narrative of Isaiah, who likewise has a vision in the temple and learns that God's people would resist his message (cf. Isa. 6:1-10), but of course there was a long tradition of God giving revelations to prophets and other messengers in the Holy Place (cf. 1 Sam. 3:3-10; 1 Kings 3:4-5).[130] In any case, this introduces the first negative note in Paul's speech, and prepares for what follows. From the perspective of the presentation in Luke-Acts, the temple is the site where previously it was announced that salvation was prepared for all peoples (Luke 2:30-32) and where Peter reminded those whom he addressed in Solomon's portico of the Abrahamic promise of blessing for all the families of the earth (Acts 3:25).[131] One may also note that Paul totally leaves out the fact that he had to leave Damascus because of his conflict with the Jews there (9:23-25).[132]

Vv. 19-20 speak of Paul's role in persecuting Christians. The Jerusalem crowd already knows that Paul was involved in imprisoning and beating various of the earliest Jewish Christians, going from synagogue to synagogue to find them.[133] Here Paul is appealing to another unimpeachable Jewish witness on his behalf — the audience themselves. The final witness he appeals to in this speech is Stephen — Paul stood by approving of the stoning and keeping the coats of the stoners (cf. Acts 7:58-60). Stephen is here called a μαρτυρος, and though the word simply means witness, at this point it seems well on the way to having its later meaning of martyr (cf. Rev. 2:13; 17:6).[134]

---

in two different ways in this sentence. See Bruce, *The Acts of the Apostles,* p. 458. Here we have yet another piece of data which points to Acts not receiving a proper final revision. See pp. 65ff. above.

128. See Polhill, *Acts,* p. 462.

129. Johnson, *Acts,* p. 390.

130. See Keener, *Bible Background Commentary,* p. 390.

131. See Tannehill, *Acts,* p. 283.

132. Rightly noted by Johnson, *Acts,* p. 390.

133. One may make allowance for a certain amount of rhetorical hyperbole here, but the Greek in all probability means not "every synagogue" but "one synagogue after another." See Marshall, *Acts,* p. 357.

134. See Bruce, *The Acts of the Apostles,* p. 459.

The mention of "shed blood" using εξεχυννετο suggests the pouring out of blood in a sacrifice (cf. Exod. 24:6; Num. 35:33).[135]

V. 21 records the ending of the speech: Jesus commanded Paul, "Go, for I will send you far away to the εθνη." This is close to the same message we find in 9:15 in Ananias's vision. As Acts 13:47 already hinted, Paul must follow the Isaianic vision of being a light to the Gentiles (Isa. 49:6). While εθνη could mean nations in a very general sense, which would include Diaspora Jews, with the hint already given in v. 15, the crowd rightly takes this to be a reference that primarily means "to the Gentiles," hence the reaction that follows.[136]

Despite Paul's eloquence, this speech does not accomplish what Paul had hoped it would. As a defense speech it is a failure, for the verdict from the crowd, which is the judge here, is very negative.[137] "The violent reaction at the end is a dramatic indication of a persistent problem. Paul will keep trying to remove the deep suspicion against him and his mission, and the later narrative will suggest the possibility of a better result among some Jews. However, the problem will not be solved even at the end of Acts."[138] *Vv. 22-23* indicate that the crowd reacted by both word and deed to Paul's speech. They shouted, "Away with such a fellow from the earth," and at the same time they performed certain gestures, the overall import of which signaled their displeasure and rejection of what Paul had said. In particular, it is not clear what they did with their cloaks. Did they (1) shake them out, (2) take them off, (3) tear them, or (4) wave them wildly? The question largely turns on the meaning of the word ριπτεω. The earliest commentary on this verse comes in Chrysostom's *Hom.* 48.2, which suggests that the meaning is shaking out. The gesture then seems to be similar to "shaking the dust off one's feet" gesture (cf. Acts 13:51), and when combined with the throwing of dust in the air (presumably because there were no stones in the temple precincts to use, cf. 2 Macc. 4:41), suggests that they consider Paul's words wicked, blasphemous, and thus totally repugnant. One must bear in mind the volatile climate in Jerusalem at this point in time (cf. above), when there was no great love for Gentiles there, much less for a mission to Gentiles, especially if Paul was suggesting some Gentiles might be taking some Jews' (who rejected Paul's message) places in the kingdom. Johnson aptly describes these gestures as apotropaic — attempting to repel

---

135. See Johnson, *Acts*, p. 391.

136. Tannehill, *Narrative Unity of Luke-Acts*, 2:277, suggests that we may have to understand εθνη geographically rather than ethnically here, but the crowd certainly understands the reference in the latter sense.

137. As Long, "Paulusbild," p. 100, says, under normal circumstances the result of a speech will be determined by the strength of the proofs, but in this case the audience is intransigent, and furthermore Paul does not even get to the formal proofs here.

138. Ibid.

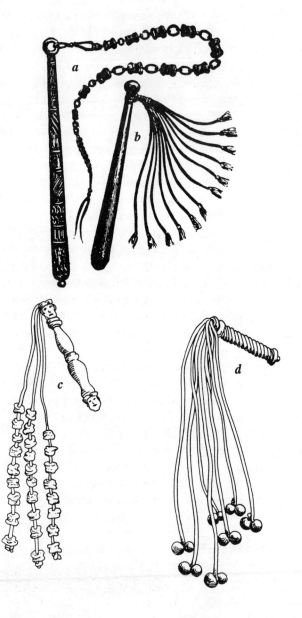

Variations of the Roman Scourge: a. Chain and Knuckle-Bones; b. Leather
Thongs; c. Leather and Knuckle-Bones; d. Leather and Lead Shot.

the wickedness and perceived defilement from the temple that these words suggested to them.[139]

Though the tribune probably did not understand Paul's speech, given in Hebrew or Aramaic, he knew hostile and violent reactions when he saw them, and was prepared to take drastic action to restore order. His assumption was that Paul was the obvious cause of these problems, and he deemed it wise to get to the bottom of the matter quickly. Thus, *v. 24* indicates that the tribune ordered that Paul be taken into the barracks and interrogated by flogging, to find out the reason for the outcry against Paul and his words. This was a regular and legal, though brutal, Roman means of extracting testimony from someone, often used against either slaves or aliens. The μαστιξ or *flagrum* was a much more dangerous instrument than the lictor's rods, or the lashes Paul was given by the Jewish authorities. It had various designs; it was often constructed with a wooden handle and leather thongs strung with lead pellets or knucklebones but could also be made with wires with ends bristled.[140] The instrument would be used on the subject's back and could tear flesh, and so maim a person for life, or even kill him if used repeatedly. According to Roman law (cf. *Digest* 48.18 prol. 1) this procedure was recommended only when all noncoercive means had failed to resolve the matter, or perhaps when the situation was so extreme it was deemed necessary. The tribune may have felt that he had exhausted the earlier methods (see 21:33-34, 39-40), but in any case he felt the gravity of the situation warranted such action.[141]

V. 25 indicates that when they had stretched Paul out for the beating with the thongs,[142] he asked the centurion standing by (centurions being regularly those left in charge of extracting confessions or supervising executions, cf. Luke 23:47), "Is it legal for you to scourge a Roman citizen who is uncondemned?"[143] The question is a legally precise one, for a Roman citizen was not subject to this means of inquisition.[144] Cicero reacted strongly to such a procedure against a Roman citizen: "To bind a Roman citizen is a crime, *to flog him an abomination*, to slay him almost an act of murder" (*Verrine Ora-*

---

139. Johnson, *Acts*, p. 391.

140. See Rapske, *Paul in Roman Custody*, p. 139.

141. Rapske, ibid., is right here and elsewhere to criticize Lentz, *Luke's Portrait of Paul*, p. 30, who misinterprets the import of various of these scenes in Acts. Lentz reads too much into various scenes, on the basis of too little understanding of Roman law and procedures.

142. The Greek here probably should be understood to mean "they stretched him out for the thongs," not "they stretched him out with the thongs" (i.e., "they tied him up," as the NRSV inteprets it). Cf. Johnson, *Acts*, p. 391; Bruce, *The Acts of the Apostles*, p. 460.

143. ακατακριτον could mean either without condemnation or without a charge.

144. Torture as a means of inquisition must be distinguished from a beating as a means of punishment.

tions 2.5.66). Notice that Paul does not blurt out a claim to citizenship; rather, he insinuates such a claim.[145] As to why he waits until this point to do so, Keener plausibly suggests: "Paul waits until he has been chained for the same reason as in 16.37; he now has legal room to maneuver against *them*."[146] It may also be, however, that Paul did not know or knew only a little spoken Latin, and the gist of the conversation around him may not have been clear.

The centurion reacted immediately, going to the tribune and asking him what he was about to do. The centurion accepts at face value Paul's claim to be a Roman citizen, and with good reason. The penalty for a false claim of Roman citizenship was severe; indeed, it could lead to death (cf. Epictetus, *Diss.* 3.24, 41; Suetonius, *Vita Claud.* 25). A centurion could certainly not afford to be wrong about such a serious matter as scourging a Roman citizen, and for that matter neither could the tribune.

V. 27 suggests that the tribune reacted immediately to this situation. When he heard the report of the centurion he went to Paul immediately and asked him point-blank: "Are you a Roman citizen?" to which Paul answered simply, "Yes."[147] It is possible to read *v. 28* as a straightforward remark, but some commentators have seen it as a sarcastic one — "It cost me a large sum of money[148] to get my citizenship," with the implication that perhaps Paul had gotten his in similar fashion, or that such citizenships were too easy to obtain by the late 50s. There is a more likely explanation, as we shall see. The tribune is engaging in damage control by comparison (see below). The tribune, however, was in for a shock. Paul obtained his citizenship honestly; he inherited the right from his father, and so he states, "But I was born a citizen." In a challenge to honor, Paul had just gotten a leg up on his inquisitor. According to *v. 29* this bold assertion caused those who were going to "examine" him (by torture) to draw back in fear, and indeed even the tribune was afraid, for the reasons already mentioned. Luke comments editorially in v. 29 that the tribune was afraid not merely because of what he was about to do, treat a Roman citizen as if he were a slave or an alien by subjecting him to torture before there had even been a trial, but because of what he had already done, bound a Roman citizen before he had even been formally accused, much less condemned (cf. the quote above from Cicero).

What may we say about this dramatic and remarkable turn of affairs in

145. The hypothetical question with ει and the verb tense as we have it suggests a true condition. Cf. Rapske, *Paul in Roman Custody*, p. 143.

146. Keener, *Bible Background Commentary*, p. 390.

147. Interestingly the Western text alters this to "ειπεν ειμι," "I am, he said," instead of "Yes, he answered." Is this Western "improvement" in imitation of Jesus' words (cf. Luke 22:70)?

148. On κεφαλιον meaning a sum of money, cf. *P. Sakaon* nos. 64-66, and 96. Cited in *New Docs*, 4 (1983), no. 43, p. 70.

this account? Is it historically plausible? Haenchen for one thinks the account has various historical improbabilities.[149] These reservations, however, seem to be largely based on an inadequate understanding of how Roman law worked, coupled with a failure to take into account the situation in the late 50s in Jerusalem. Let us consider briefly, in the form of an excursus, three of the major questions usually raised about this narrative: (1) Why does Paul only reveal his citizenship, if he had such citizenship, when and where he does in this narrative? (2) Why should the tribune be afraid if he acted in ignorance of Paul's citizenship status? (3) Is the claim that Paul was born a Roman citizen, while the tribune bought his citizenship, really believable, especially since Paul never mentions such a citizenship in any of his letters?

A Closer Look — Paul and Lysias, Roman Citizens ─────────────

In the first place, in regard to the general plausibility of this account, it is striking to me that those who know the most about Roman law and Roman citizenship, ancient Roman historians and classics scholars, seem to have far fewer difficulties with this and other narratives in Acts 21–28 than do various NT scholars who do not have the same level of expertise in the relevant areas.[150] It may be true that these scholars in other disciplines are not well attuned to the redactional and form-critical studies done by NT scholars on these texts in Acts, but such studies do not in the end settle issues of historical plausibility, and often they do not even raise such questions. So let us briefly reconsider the above three questions.

The first question is in some ways the easiest to answer. As Cassidy has noted, in only two places does Paul's Roman citizenship really become an issue, in Acts 16 and 22, and in *both* cases "Paul only draws his citizenship to the attention of Roman officials and those working under them" and "in both cases Paul's announcement of his citizenship is made for the purpose of influencing the conduct of his fellow Roman citizens. He brings it to the fore only as a means of forcing his fellow citizens into altering their plans for treating him improperly."[151] In other words, in general Luke makes very little more of Paul's Roman citizenship than Paul himself does, and Paul makes nothing of it. It is only brought up as a defense (and perhaps secondarily as an

---

149. See Haenchen, *Acts*, p. 639.

150. I am thinking here of the work of Sherwin-White, not only his *Roman Law and Roman Society*, pp. 48-75, but also his more detailed work, *The Roman Citizenship*; the work of A. H. M. Jones, *Studies in Roman Government and Law*, his *The Criminal Courts of the Roman Republic and Empire*, and his important article, "Imperial and Senatorial Jurisdiction in the Early Principate"; Balsdon, *Romans and Aliens*, pp. 82-98; Burton, "Proconsuls, Assizes, and the Administration of Justice under the Empire"; Garnsey, *Social Status and Legal Privilege in the Roman Empire*. One should see now the updating of the whole discussion in Rapske, *Paul in Roman Custody*, pp. 72-149.

151. Cassidy, *Society and Politics*, p. 102.

honor) device in Acts. When Paul in Acts is addressing either a Jewish or a pagan Gentile audience, or a Christian audience in a non-Roman nonlegal setting, he *never* mentions the matter. In the vast majority of material in Acts that involves Paul the matter does not come up at all. In view of this, it might be better to ask why the matter comes up just where it does in Acts 16 and 22–23, rather than asking why it doesn't come up elsewhere and earlier in Acts.

Nevertheless, in regard to the latter question, we have already addressed the matter as it involves Acts 16,[152] and there is a ready answer in regard to Acts 22 as well. Paul does not mention his Roman citizenship while still within earshot of the volatile Jewish crowd, even when he is addressing the tribune, for the very good reason that this would not have helped his cause with the Jewish audience. Before or during his speech to the crowd, mentioning his Roman citizenship would simply have amounted to pouring gas on an already raging fire. These Jews were precisely the ones who did not want to hear anything about the possibility of compromise or rapprochement between the dominant Roman culture and Jewish culture, and Paul knew this quite well. To reveal or allude to himself as a Roman citizen would only have confirmed the worst suspicions of this crowd. It would have encouraged them even more strongly to believe Paul was likely to have brought a Gentile into the forbidden area of the temple.

As to why the revelation comes just at the point it does in Acts 22, the remarks of Cassidy and Keener cited above are appropriate. To them one may add that Paul's Roman identity was at least third, if not fourth, in order of importance for him, ahead of which came his identity as a Christian, as a Jew (in particular a Pharisaic one), and probably as a citizen of Tarsus. There are no situations in Paul's letters where he either addresses or answers Roman charges against himself, and therefore no comparable situations where there was need or occasion for Paul to mention the matter in his letters. Neither Acts nor Paul's letters suggest it was a matter Paul boasted about or regularly spoke of.

In regard to the second question, there are two plausible answers. In the first place, during the period of *cognitio,* it was indeed the responsibility of the Roman interrogator, whoever he might be, to find out the status of the person being investigated. As Garnsey rightly concludes, in "law as in other aspects of Roman society, the principal benefits and rewards were available to those groups most advantageously placed in the stratification system by reason of their greater property, power and prestige."[153] Because the principal criterion of legal privilege in the eyes of the Romans was based on one's *dignitas* or honor, and these qualities were most often associated in the early Empire with Roman citizens,[154] it was indeed crucial for the tribune to ask a few questions before proceeding with torture. "The Tribune is drawing Paul into disclosing more personal information for the purpose of comparison . . . as an [exercise] in social/juridical damage assessment. . . . Lysias may have hoped that Paul was even more recently granted citizenship under less auspicious circumstances than his own, rightly thinking that one might only lightly punish or even forgive the treatment

---

152. See pp. 413ff. above.
153. Garnsey, *Social Status and Legal Privilege,* p. 280.
154. Ibid., p. 279.

by a superior of his social inferior. That Paul was a citizen by birth, however, threatened great damage to Claudius Lysias' person and career."[155] In the second place, even if, however, there was not an absolute *legal* obligation for the tribune to find this out, as Lentz says, a severe breach of social convention would have been involved if a more "honorable" Roman citizen had been mistreated by one who had merely bought his citizenship. In either case, the fear of the tribune is understandable.[156] On a straight-forward reading of the Valerian and Porcian laws, amplified by edicts of Augustus, Roman citizens were clearly exempt from torture as a means of examination.[157] They could only be scourged after conviction on capital crimes and before execution. The case of Paul, precisely because he was a Roman citizen, was very different from the case of Jesus.

This leads us to the third question. Let us consider first the question of the tribune's buying of his citizenship. This of course was not actually the case, because it was not legal to do so. What is meant is that through the paying of a bribe, citizenship had illegally been obtained. This was certainly possible, and in fact during the reign of Claudius there seems to have been considerable trafficking in citizenships.[158] Dio Cassius, in a famous passage, speaks of citizenship being not only obtainable by the payment of a bribe, but even obtainable cheaply through Messalina, or other members of Emperor Claudius's household or court (60.17.5-7). That the tribune has the name Claudius (see 23:26) points to his having obtained his citizenship during the reign of Claudius, for it was customary to take the name of one's sponsor or patron.[159] Probably Lysias had worked his way up through the military ranks but would have been barred from the rank of tribune because he was not already a citizen of equestrian rank. He solved this problem through a bribe. There is, then, nothing improbable about Lysias's side of the comparison, but what about Paul's claim to be born a citizen?

Various scholars have thought it improbable that Paul could have had dual citizenships (Tarsian and Roman), much less have been born a Roman citizen, because he was a Jew. We have already spoken of the matter of Paul's Tarsian citizenship, and that there are no insuperable difficulties to his having had such a citizenship as a Jew during the early Empire.[160] It can now be added that there is no reason why during this same period he could not have had dual citizenships. As Tajara has ably demonstrated,

---

155. Rapske, *Paul in Roman Custody,* pp. 144-45.

156. See Lentz, *Luke's Portrait of Paul,* p. 138.

157. See the careful discussion in Rapske, *Paul in Roman Custody,* pp. 51-52.

158. See the discussion in Sherwin-White, *The Roman Citizenship,* pp. 237-50.

159. See Balsdon, *Romans and Aliens,* p. 89, and on p. 91: "In the Empire the first names taken by auxiliary soldiers who had completed their military service were more often than not those of the ruling emperor who authorized their citizenship-grant."

160. See pp. 430ff. above. Possible, but less likely, is the suggestion of Tajara, *The Trial of Paul,* p. 80, that Luke in Acts 21:39 is using the term πολιτης loosely and in a nonjuridical sense to mean a Jew who was a member of the Jewish community of Tarsus (part of its *politeuma*). The problem with this conclusion is that Paul is not addressing Jews at this point, who might be impressed or happy to hear Paul was a practicing Jew in Tarsus. He is addressing Claudius Lysias, for whom a different and more generic sort of honor and citizenship claim would likely be necessary to stifle his suspicions.

it "was not at all uncommon for a man coming from a higher social class to enjoy dual citizenship especially in the Eastern part of the Empire."[161] Even as early as Cicero's day, Cicero was able to write of one Cato who was a Tuscan by birth but also a Roman citizen (*De Leg.* 2.2.5). Sherwin-White points out that the laws against holding dual citizenship had already been relaxed by the end of the Republic and the beginning of the Empire.[162] As for the general plausibility of Jews being Roman citizens, Josephus of course refers to various Jews who had such a status (cf. *Ant.* 14.10.13-19; *Ag. Apion* 2.40-41), and one may point to the example of Publius Tyrronius Klados, who was both a citizen and head of a synagogue in the late first century A.D. in Acmonia.[163] But could Paul have been *born* a Roman citizen? The answer to this is yes.[164]

There were a variety of legal means by which one could become a Roman citizen: (1) by slave manumission which led to citizenship; (2) by serving in the Roman military, after which when one retired one would be granted citizenship; (3) by the establishment of a Roman colony in a particular place, which led to the instant enfranchisement of goodly numbers of persons in various places in the Empire; (4) by the granting of citizenships to individuals or groups or communities which had distinguished themselves by some sort of service or loyalty to Rome. This last is by far the most probable means by which Paul's family could have obtained citizenship.[165] Though it is only conjecture, it is a plausible one to suggest that Paul's family may have provided tents to the Roman army, for which service Paul's father or both parents, or even his grandparents, may have received a grant of citizenship.

One last question needs to be addressed. How could Paul have proved his Roman citizenship? It is quite possible, because he traveled a great deal and the issue would be raised, that he carried a *diploma civitatis Romanae.* This small document or certificate was in effect a birth and citizenship certificate inscribed on a small wooden diptych.[166] Another possibility is that Paul had a *libellus,* which recorded

161. Tajara, *The Trial of Paul,* p. 76.

162. Sherwin-White, *Roman Law and Roman Society,* p. 182.

163. See Rapske, *Paul in Roman Custody,* p. 89.

164. It is perhaps significant that the ancient historian M. Grant, who is otherwise very skeptical about the historical substance of Acts, is convinced it is correct to conclude that Paul is a Roman citzen, though it is directly mentioned only in Acts. See most recently his *Saint Peter,* pp. 133-34.

165. See Bruce, *The Acts of the Apostles,* p. 461. Tajara, *The Trial of Paul,* p. 83, however, considers it more probable for Paul's ancestors to have served in the Roman army. This seems less likely to me in view of the fact that Paul's parents were devout Jews, which meant not only that they could not pray to pagan gods for victory, nor eat the usual army rations, nor share table with unclean Gentiles, but perhaps most importantly they could not fight on the sabbath (a day only Jews recognized as a day of rest). More probable than this suggestion is the suggestion that Paul's father was a freedman of a Roman citizen, but the suggestion offered in the text is the most probable one.

166. See Sherwin-White, *Roman Law and Roman Society,* pp. 146-49. One may point to the famous story of Nero handing certificates of citizenship *(diplomata)* to some young Greek dancers, so pleased was he with their performance (Suetonius, *Nero* 12). This also illustrates the climate which Lysias's case also attests, where citizenship could be had for a song, so to speak.

that the person concerned had this or that sort of citizenship or status, with the original remaining in the municipal registers of the person's hometown.[167] Of course all such documents could be cleverly forged, and a traveling man such as Paul could not be expected to produce hometown witnesses to his status on the spot, and so documents, even if not absolute proof, could have been Paul's means of substantiating his claim. As we have already said, however, the penalty for a false claim of citizenship was such that the tribune could not afford to ignore such a claim. The claim of Roman citizenship by Paul at this juncture in the narrative is crucial, and this claim will partially dictate how the rest of the narrative will be played out, including whether Paul would be turned over to the Jews, and whether in the end he would go to Rome. Lüdemann, who is generally skeptical about the historical value of much of Acts, nonetheless concludes that Paul probably was a Roman citizen precisely because of his Roman imprisonment in Palestine and his being transported to Rome by the Roman authorities.[168]

We may conclude by adding several other telltale signs from Paul's letters that suggest he was a Roman citizen. (1) Paul bears a Roman name; whether it is his *cognomen* or one of the other two requisite names of a citizen may be debated, but not the fact of the name.[169] The name itself is rare in the East and suggests high birth.[170] (2) Paul's strategy of evangelizing Roman colonies (Pisidian Antioch, Philippi, Corinth), which were not necessarily the best places for Jewish religions to be nurtured due to Roman anti-Semitism, and especially in view of the competition from the growing emperor cult, suggests that Paul wished to take advantage of some status or standing he would have in such colonies for the sake of the gospel. (3) Paul's desire to go to Spain (Rom. 15:28), the center of a considerable amount of Romanization, may be in part precisely because of Paul's own Roman status, and the instant foot in the door he would have among all sorts of people who lived in the Roman colonies there.[171] (4) Paul's claim, and apparent ability, to be a Gentile to Gentiles as well as a Jew to Jews (1 Corinthians 9) requires that he was a multicultural person. It suggests a cosmopolitan person, and certainly the sort of person best able to be cosmopolitan in the Empire was a Roman citizen. (5) Since Roman names occur very frequently in some of Paul's greetings and among his converts (cf. 1 Corinthians 16; Romans 16), including even Romans of high status such as an Erastus the aedile, we should probably assume that Paul was even able to be a Roman to the Romans.[172]

---

167. On all this cf. Schulz, "Roman Registers," parts 1 and 2.

168. See Lüdemann, *Early Christianity,* pp. 240-41.

169. On the name and why it begins to occur where it does in Acts, cf. pp. 430ff. above.

170. See rightly Lüdemann, *Early Christianity,* p. 241, following Mommsen.

171. Ibid.

172. For a more negative assessment of the possibility of Paul's Roman citizenship, but one that does not take into consideration various of the points made above, cf. Stegmann, "War der Apostel Paulus ein römischer Bürger?"

From henceforth, Paul's Roman citizenship and Roman law will dictate how the narrative will proceed, determining not only who will try Paul's case but ultimately where it will be tried. It will also affect how Paul is treated while in Roman custody. The narrative from now on not only moves inexorably forward toward its geographical destination of Rome, but it turns on things Roman.

D. The Hearing before the Sanhedrin (22:30–23:11)

Though Dibelius has conditioned us to speak of five trial scenes in Acts 22–26,[173] this is in fact not correct. We do not have any trial scenes, properly speaking, before Acts 24. What transpires before this point in time falls into the category of pretrial hearings, and that includes the particular episode with which we are now concerned. It must be kept in mind that because of the custody issue and because Claudius Lysias is taking the initiative, Roman procedures, not Jewish ones, were being followed. The scene before the Sanhedrin must be understood, as 22:30 makes very clear, as still part of the *cognitio* process. No one from the Sanhedrin actually assumes the legal role of plaintiff before Acts 24. The tribune is still trying to discern the facts of the case and whether Paul is guilty of an offense that is chargeable under Roman law.

It is right, then, to speak of a legal or forensic process beginning already in Acts 22, and certainly, as has often been noted, there is plenty of legal and even technical forensic language to be found in Acts 22–26.[174] We are not, however, yet at the point where Paul is on trial. What is perhaps most crucial about the scene before the Sanhedrin is the way Paul, in a very adroit and effective rhetorical move, sets the terms for all the following discussion by defining what *the real issue* or main question or bone of contention is.[175] Quintilian stresses how important the *narratio* or statement of facts is to a case — "a statement of facts is not made merely that the judge may comprehend the case, but rather *that he may look upon it in the same light as ourselves*" (*Inst. Or.* 4.2.21). Paul is presented here as an effective rhetor, for he successfully defines the terms of the following discussion.

The person he must impress or affect in this matter, since he is in Roman hands, is Lysias, not the Sanhedrin, and Lysias's subsequent letter (see especially 23:29; cf. 24:21) makes clear that he has been successful in accomplishing the

---

173. See his *Studies in the Acts*, pp. 11-13.
174. See the sampling in Trites, "The Importance."
175. See the helpful discussion by Tannehill, *Narrative Unity of Luke-Acts*, 2:286-89, and Neyrey, "Forensic Defense Speech," p. 215.

considerable feat of getting the Roman authorities to see *the real issue of dispute* as Paul presents it. This means that one must not view the Sanhedrin scene as nothing more than an example of Paul's being clever by using a divide-and-conquer approach, setting his opponents at each other's throats. Paul does not merely wish *not* to be judged by the Sanhedrin or the Jewish authorities, though that is also true (cf. 25:9, 10); he *does* wish to be judged by the Roman authorities. This is so because he knows that if they can be convinced that the dispute is over matters of Jewish law and belief and not over some offense deemed serious or treasonable under Roman law, that barring a miscarriage of justice, as a Roman citizen he should be in a good position legally.

There is a further factor involved that needs to be mentioned at this point. From Paul's (and Luke's) point of view, the crucial thing is not so much for Paul to defend himself, but rather for him to bear witness about the gospel to the authorities, both Jewish and Gentile.[176] In Paul's defining of the "main question" he gives a presentation of the gospel, so that in effect it is the gospel that is really on trial. Luke has carefully edited his source material so that the "witness" of Paul moves from the general to the more specific, as Acts 22–26 develops. Paul begins by speaking generally about the hope and the resurrection of the dead (plural — 23:6). This discussion is continued at 24:15 and 21 and again at 26:8, but only at the end of this judicial process at 26:23 do we hear about the resurrection of Jesus in particular. Paul's full Christian witness does not occur until the climax in Acts 26, and after this we have the missionary appeal to Agrippa and Festus in 26:27-29. The effect of the scenes and the witness in Acts 22–26 is intended to be cumulative, and the discussion progresses to a climax.[177] Paul's apologetic approach in this entire section, leaving the more specific and objectionable material until last, is very much the same as we find in the Areopagus speech in Acts 17, which, as we said before, should not be viewed as a failed experiment.[178] Paul presents Christians with an example of how to bear witness before hostile or neutral audiences.

Luke has all along shown great interest in displaying how the gospel is for everyone, including the social elite and even the politically high and mighty.[179] He will end his masterful presentation in Acts by showing how the gospel reaches the elite and powerful in the Greco-Roman world through the courageous witness of Paul, and will allude to the fact that beyond the end of his account Paul will go on to greater heights still, testifying about the gospel not only in Rome but before Caesar (cf. 23:11 to 27:24). In the end the gospel must not merely cross geographical boundaries and unite various geographical

---

176. See Marshall, *Acts*, p. 367.
177. See rightly Tannehill, *Narrative Unity of Luke-Acts*, 2:289-91.
178. See pp. 533ff. above.
179. See pp. 68ff.

regions, it must cross social boundaries and unite the well-to-do with even the ne'er-do-well. It must also unite Jew and Gentile, and Luke's presentation, especially in Acts 28, suggests he has not given up on the witness to either of these groups, even though the majority of people on both sides of this ethnic divide had not accepted the gospel in his day.[180]

Acts 22:30 introduces what follows in 23:1-11 and helps us to understand how the narrative should be understood. Claudius Lysias is still in the dark about what the Jews are accusing Paul of.[181] Being conscientious and diligent, he wishes to know *with certainty* (γνωναι το ασφαλες) about this matter. It is quite possible that ελυσεν αυτον here means that Paul was released from the chains that bound him to the Roman soldiers (cf. 21:33),[182] but it may have the broader sense of his being released from custody.[183] In either case, this was a temporary expedient so that Paul could appear before the Sanhedrin. There has been much debate about whether historically the tribune had the authority to order the chief priest and the Sanhedrin to meet.[184] Josephus appears to confirm that the procurator had the right to convene the Sanhedrin, indeed to confirm that the Sanhedrin could not meet without the procurator's permission (*Ant.* 20.202), and the tribune as the chief representative of the procurator in Jerusalem may also have had the right to convene such a meeting. Sherwin-White is perhaps right to doubt that the Sanhedrin prior to the Jewish War had to have Roman permission to meet,[185] but this does not settle whether the procurator or his tribune could order such a meeting or not. As Marshall rightly points out, in any case we are probably not dealing with a formal meeting or trial of the Sanhedrin but rather with a hearing so that the tribune would know what to report to the procurator about Paul's case.[186] The letter which the tribune writes afterward suggests he did not view the meeting of the Sanhedrin as a trial (23:28).[187] The tribune did not have the *imperium*, once order was restored, to decide a judicial matter, especially when a Roman

---

180. See Haenchen, *Acts*, p. 643.

181. The word κατηγορειται can of course refer to a formal accusation, but so far there have only been the complaints of the crowd, and since we are not yet at the point of a trial, the term here should be understood in its broader sense — a formal complaint has not yet been lodged with the Roman authorities.

182. See Longenecker, *Acts*, p. 530.

183. See Bruce, *The Acts of the Apostles*, p. 462.

184. Lüdemann, *Early Christianity*, p. 242, thinks the summoning historically unlikely.

185. Sherwin-White, *Roman Law and Roman Society*, p. 54.

186. Marshall, *Acts*, pp. 361-62. Cf. Pesch, *Die Apostelgeschichte (Apg. 13–28)*, pp. 240-42. This may in part explain why Paul does not recognize the high priest for who he is. The meeting was hastily called, and he was not wearing whatever formal attire he would need to wear for a trial or court session.

187. Rightly noted by Rapske, *Paul in Roman Custody*, p. 147.

citizen was involved, but we need not doubt that he was authorized to use all necessary means, including calling on the Sanhedrin to meet, to decide the facts and main issues of a case, and not trouble the procurator until the disposition of the matter, including complaints or charges, was actually known. It would appear, in view of the fact that the tribune does not intervene in Paul's hearing when Paul is slapped, that he may not have been directly present *in* the meeting, or at least he did not wish to interfere unless a matter of order required it. His exact physical location is indeterminable, but presumably he was close by, within earshot, such that when the row broke out, he could summon some soldiers to restore order.[188]

Acts 23:1 begins with the interesting reference to Paul looking intently at the council (cf. the use of ατενιας at 1:10; 3:4; 6:15; 7:55; 10:4; 11:6; 13:9; 14:9). While this may refer to a rhetorical gesture of making good eye contact with one's audience, more probably we should view this in light of texts like 13:9 and 14:9, which indicate that Paul had the ability to discern a person's spiritual condition by this sort of intent gazing, especially in light of the comment at 23:3 about the hypocrisy of the high priest. In other words, Paul discerns the character of his audience before he speaks, a wise thing to do, especially when one is confronting a hostile audience. This no doubt affects how he addresses them.

The speech fragment, such as it is, is an example of judicial rhetoric. Paul begins with a defense of his conduct up to the present. That he addresses them with the familiar "men brothers" is perhaps an attempt to make the audience favorable to his speech, but it also suggests that Paul sees himself as their equals, for he does not address them as his superiors, much less his judges.[189] Paul says that in all good conscience he has lived as a good citizen unto God until this very day. The verb πεπολιτευμαι (cf. 2 Macc. 6:1; Josephus, *Life* 12) should be allowed to have its natural sense here, especially in light of the mention of Paul's Roman citizenship in the previous chapter. Paul is first and foremost a citizen of the kingdom of God, and this dictates how he will live his life. Other citizenships are of lesser importance to him. This remark has rightly been compared to Paul's advice given at Phil. 1:27 to "live as citizens worthy of the good news of Christ," and Paul also mentions that their πολιτευμα is in heaven (Phil. 3:20). Here, as there, Paul is concerned not merely about his civic duty but more properly about doing his Christian duty. In Philippians he is calling his converts to be good citizens of a greater commonwealth than a Roman colony or Empire; here Paul is stating that he himself

---

188. The issue of having an unclean Gentile present in a meeting involving scrupulous Jews and the high priest may explain why the soldiers had to be summoned (23:10), and why the tribune, while nearby, would not be an active part of the meeting itself. Contrast ibid. with Tajara, *The Trial of Paul*, p. 97.

189. See rightly Tajara, *The Trial of Paul*, p. 92.

has done so.[190] The appeal to conscience is also more characteristic of Paul than of any other NT figure or writer (cf. Rom. 2:15; 9:1; 13:5; 1 Cor. 8:7, 10, 12; 10:25, 27, 28, 29; 2 Cor. 1:12; 4:2; 5:11). Paul is probably referring to his recent behavior that has caused him to stand before the Sanhedrin, about which he feels no guilt or shame.[191]

V. 2 indicates that Ananias is the high priest. Everything we learn from Josephus about this chief priest suggests that the action he is said to take here is quite believable and in character. The son of Nedebaeus, Ananias was appointed by the brother of Herod Agrippa I (Herod of Chalcis) in A.D. 47 and remained in power until A.D. 58 or 59 (cf. *Ant.* 20.103). That he was far from priestly in character is shown both by his acts of bribery and by his allowing his servants to steal the tithes intended for the priests (*Ant.* 20.205-13). That he was prone to violence is shown by the fact that he was summoned to Rome because of his part in the ambush of various Samaritan pilgrims (*Ant.* 20.131). Ananias was also known for his pro-Roman sentiments, and this in the end got him killed by Jewish zealots when the Jewish war with Rome started in A.D. 66 (*War* 2.441-43; cf. 2.426-29). As a collaborator with Rome, it is quite believable that he would work closely with Claudius Lysias, and would have been willing to call a council meeting or at least an informal hearing if the tribune required it. In assessing what follows, it is in order to point out that Paul had probably had no occasion to meet this man, and certainly not during the period of his high priesthood. Paul had been away from Jerusalem itself for about five years, but more importantly away from the corridors of Jewish power in Jerusalem for over two decades by the time this meeting occurred.[192] Much had transpired since the days of Saul's Damascus road conversion.[193]

Ananias ordered those standing near Paul to strike him in the mouth, a gesture which suggests a strong rejection of what Paul had just claimed.[194]

---

190. See my *Friendship and Finances in Philippi* (Valley Forge, Pa.: Trinity, 1994), p. 51. This is another example of correspondence between the Paul of the letters and the Paul of Acts that should not be overlooked.

191. See Marshall, *Acts,* p. 362, against Haenchen, *Acts,* p. 637, who wrongly complains that the real Paul couldn't say this in view of his persecuting of Stephen and others. Johnson, *Acts,* p. 396, perhaps in response to the latter, points out that at that time, so far as we know, Paul believed he was acting in good conscience when he was persecuting (cf. 22:3-4).

192. See Hemer, *Book of Acts,* pp. 192-93.

193. Tajara, *The Trial of Paul,* pp. 92-93, is right that Paul's attitude here is not typical of most defendants in the midst of a legal process. It shows something of Paul's attitude that he is really accountable only to God (cf. 1 Cor. 4:2-4).

194. Marshall, *Acts,* p. 362, suggests a possible echo from the trial of Jesus (cf. John 18:22-23), but if so, it is one that Luke doesn't include in his Gospel, and so he is not suggesting a strong parallel to his own audience. Is this, however, another instance of Luke deliberately omitting an idea from his first volume because he knew he would include it in the second? Cf. pp. 264ff. above on the Stephen speech.

Paul was not without a response to this violence, saying, according to *v. 3*, "God will strike you, you whitewashed wall! Are you sitting there to judge me according to the law, and yet flouting that law you order me to be struck!" Some have seen this as a predictive curse, which would in fact be fulfilled in A.D. 66 when followers of the Zealot leader Menaham did away with Ananias.[195] The figure of a whitewashed wall may draw on the same image found in Ezek. 13:10-16, and was apparently popular in Paul's own day (cf. Zadokite Document 8:12). The wall would appear clean and sturdy but in fact would be crumbling beneath the thin veneer of the paint. In short, it is an image of hypocrisy, of appearance contradicting inner reality. That Paul goes on to speak of Ananias sitting in judgment of him strongly suggests that he knows very well whom he is addressing, indeed knows his identity as well as his character. The particular law Paul has in mind here is probably the prohibition of rendering an unjust judgment, of punishing before guilt is established and a verdict rendered (cf. Lev. 19:15; *m. Sanh.* 3:6-8). It is in order to point out, however, that Ananias, as a puppet of Rome, may be mimicking Roman procedures, where violence or torture to extract a true confession was not uncommon. The response of Paul here shows he is human, and capable of an angry retort.[196]

According to *v. 4* those standing by replied to Paul, asking if he dared to insult God's high priest. It is possible and plausible that Paul did not know the high priest by face. It is also very possible that Paul's words are a fine example of irony: "I did not realize, brothers, that *he* was high priest," the point being that Ananias's action made him unrecognizable as high priest.[197] Paul knows how he should have behaved and quotes Exod. 22:27 (LXX) against himself — "Do not speak evil about the ruler of your people." The reply of those standing by had shifted the discussion from the individual to the role — the man was God's high priest, and Paul to make amends now quotes Scripture indicating he, as a Torah-abiding Jew, respects God's representative.[198]

V. 6 is interesting because it suggests there would be some visible, noticeable difference in appearance between Sadducees and Pharisees, presumably a difference in apparel. As a result of this on-the-spot observation Paul blurts out in the assembly: "I am a Pharisee, a son of Pharisees. I am

---

195. See Bruce, *The Acts of the Apostles*, p. 464.

196. In other words, his words fired off in anger here are not an example of turning the other cheek, or even heaping coals of fire on the head of one's enemies. Paul was a sinner like other mortals, and capable of an unchristian response. See Longenecker, *Acts*, pp. 530-31.

197. Marshall, *Acts*, p. 327. On the priest not being recognizable because of his not wearing his formal attire at this informal hearing, cf. Keener, *Bible Background Commentary*, p. 391.

198. See Polhill, *Acts*, p. 469.

*The Jewish cemetery on the summit of the Mount of Olives. Orthodox Jews,
like Rabbi Menahem whose grave inscription we see here, seek to be buried
here so that at the resurrection they may be first to rise and greet the Messiah.*

on trial concerning the hope[199] of the resurrection of dead[200] persons."
Schubert calls this the "shortest but centrally important speech of Paul"
because it so aptly sums up the real issue on which the rest of the book
turns.[201]

Paul knew very well that both the high priest and probably still the
majority of the Sanhedrin were Sadducees, who did not believe in the resurrection for the very good reason that they could not find it in the Pentateuch,
which is all they accepted as their canon.[202] Paul here is speaking in the sort
of general terms to which the Pharisees in the audience could assent. They,

199. On the importance of this theme of the hope of Israel for assessing the Paul of
the letters and the Paul of Acts, cf. Haacker, "Das Bekenntnis des Paulus zur Hoffnung
Israels nach der Apostelgeschichte des Lukas," especially p. 447. Haacker points especially
to Rom. 1:3ff.; 4:17; and 11:15.

200. The Greek here is probably an example of hendiadys; literally it reads "concerning the hope and the resurrection of the dead ones." In view of the further clarification of
the "main question" in what follows in Acts 23–26, resurrection must be seen as the essence
of the hope, not something separate from it.

201. Schubert, "The Final Cycle," p. 6.

202. On Sadducees and Pharisees and their beliefs, cf. pp. 220ff. above.

too, believed in the hope of the resurrection, at least of the righteous. What may we say about this rhetorical move of Paul's? It should be noted that Paul takes this step only after he realizes the character of the high priest and his supporters here, in short after he realizes he has no chance for an impartial hearing before this judge. Thus he must hope to divide the assembly by causing a debate, which will lead some to come to his support, at least in a general way.[203]

Paul's claim to be a son of Pharisees might mean that he was a product of Pharisaic instruction, for it was not uncommon for disciples to call their teachers things like "father" or rabbi.[204] This might make sense of the use of the term "Pharisees" (plural). On the other hand, it is perfectly possible, especially if Paul was raised in Jerusalem,[205] that his parents had embraced Pharisaic practices and ways when they came to the Holy City.[206] Paul mentions his Pharisaic background only once in his letters (Phil. 3:5-6), and it simply reiterates what we hear in this text.[207] It is not, however, adequate to speak only of Pharisaic background, for Luke is stressing his Pharisaic foreground as well. Paul is not being disingenuous, as texts like 1 Corinthians 15 show, when he stresses that resurrection is at the heart of the matter for himself and for other Pharisees.[208] Rather, "Paul is seeking a shared starting point that will lead beyond controversy to effective witness."[209]

V. 7 indicates that as a result of Paul's adroit move a στασις or dissension broke out which divided the assembly. In *v. 8* we have one of the rare Lukan asides, which suggests that Luke's audience would not have known

---

203. This sort of diversionary tactic is known in Greek oratory, a good example being the case where Aeschines, when speaking to the Amphictionic Council at Delphi, turned their attention from the actual issue at hand to the Amphissians' illegal occupation of sacred land (see *Against Ctesphion* 107). See the discussion of Kennedy, *New Testament Interpretation*, p. 135.

204. See the discussion of the use of *abba* language in my *Christology of Jesus*, pp. 216-21, and cf. Dibelius, *Studies in the Acts*, p. 212.

205. On which see pp. 659ff. above.

206. It need not mean, contra Johnson, *Acts*, p. 397, that Pharisaism had spread to the Diaspora, though I would not rule this out. Once again Lentz, *Luke's Portrait of Paul*, p. 54, jumps to conclusions, based on insisting on a particular reading of this text. He argues that Luke assumes there were Pharisees in the Diaspora, and not only so, but Pharisees who were Greek citizens. The text need not be read this way. Contrast the more careful discussion of Rapske, *Paul in Roman Custody*, pp. 95-96.

207. On Paul as part of the Pharisaic movement, including the way he viewed matters of righteousness, the Law, and the like, see Lührmann, "Paul and the Pharisaic Tradition."

208. See rightly Rapske, *Paul in Roman Custody*, pp. 96-98, and Jervell, *Luke and the People*, pp. 153-83. Jervell, pp. 169-70, suggests that Acts 23:1ff. portrays Paul to be a Jew more faithful to the Law than the high priest, but in fact they both violate it here. Jervell on p. 174, I think, is also wrong in suggesting that Luke thinks the time for mission to Israel is now past.

209. Tannehill, *Narrative Unity of Luke-Acts*, 2:288.

about the differing beliefs of Sadducees and Pharisees. This is quite believable if Theophilus is a person living somewhere in the Diaspora, and especially if he was a Gentile. This aside has puzzled many a commentator, not for its statement that the Sadducees don't believe in the resurrection but because it adds "nor angel, nor spirit." It is very doubtful that the Sadducees denied the existence of angels altogether, since they do appear in the Pentateuch, and it may also be doubted that Luke, who is otherwise quite well informed about early Judaism, would have made such a major mistake about Sadducean beliefs.

Here the study of D. Daube helps us.[210] He points out that it was believed in some circles in early Judaism that the good Jew spent "the span between death and resurrection . . . in the realm of angel or spirit."[211] This belief stood in contrast to Sadducean belief which suggested either that the person perished at death, or that at most she or he had some sort of shadowy existence in Sheol, not in the dwelling place of God or angels. One may compare the critique of the Sadducees (*1 Enoch* 39:5; 54:1-2) that they deny "the dwelling of the holy ones and the Lord of the spirits" as well as the resurrection, and so shall not experience it. Notice how in Luke 24:36-43, when Jesus appears to his disciples, he is mistaken for "a spirit." Notice further how in Acts 12:15 the Christians at the mother of John Mark's house conclude that it is only Peter's angel at the gate (the Greek reads literally "it is the angel of him"). Finally, notice how in what immediately follows in our text in 23:9 the Pharisaic scribes speak of the appearance of Jesus to Paul as the case of an angel or a spirit speaking to Paul. If we put all this together, it is reasonable to conclude that the term "angel" (cf. *1 Enoch* 22:3, 7; 103:3-4) or "spirit" was sometimes used to refer to a deceased person, perhaps especially in circles affected by Pharisaic speculations about angels and the like. The point, then, of the explanation in v. 8 is that the Sadducees believe in no positive form of afterlife, either in the interim before the resurrection or at the resurrection. Possibly a small confirmation that we are on the right track with the above interpretation is that in the statement "the Pharisees confess τα αμφοτερα" the latter literally and normally means "both of these" (see Luke 1:6-7; 5:7; 6:39; Acts 8:38). This would suggest that "angel or spirit" is seen as two different ways to refer to the same thing, and the second item making up the "both" is of course the resurrection.[212]

V. 9 indicates that some of the Pharisaic scribes stood up and asserted that they found nothing wrong with Paul — what if a spirit or an angel spoke

210. See Daube, "On Acts 23."
211. Ibid., p. 493.
212. See Johnson, *Acts*, p. 398.

to him?[213] This rhetorical question is interesting in several regards. It suggests they know something about Paul's past. Though they would not accept the claim that Jesus was the Lord or Messiah, they might accept that Paul had communicated with the dead Jesus, or, as they put it, with his spirit or angel.[214] Secondly, it reveals what we know otherwise in any case, that the Pharisees believed in ongoing revelation from God and otherworldly beings to receptive humans. Paul would not be seen as unique in this regard. Finally, it cannot be stressed enough that their verdict is "we find nothing wrong with this man." This will be a recurring theme from now on, found on the lips of both Jews and Gentiles (cf. 23:29; 25:18-20, 25; 26:31, 32).[215] Far from writing off all Jews, even at this late point in the narrative, Luke continues to suggest that some of them, in particular the Pharisaic ones, may be receptive to the claims of the gospel.

V. 10 indicates that the dissension grew greater and that the tribune feared that Paul would be pulled to pieces in an ideological but also physical game of tug-of-war. He thus ordered soldiers to go down to the Sanhedrin, located on the southwestern slope of the temple hill (*War* 5.144) from the Antonia Fortress, take Paul by force, and bring him to the barracks. In this instance, we might properly speak of the tribune rescuing Paul, unlike the case in 21:37.

After this tumultuous day of events, we are told at *v. 11* that the Lord appeared to and stood near Paul that night and said, "Keep up your courage," indicating that just as he had testified for Christ in Jerusalem, so he would also do in Rome. Here again we see an instance of the belief that the ascended and exalted Lord continued to communicate directly with his followers long after his death and resurrection. Certainly after a day like he had had, Paul could use such divine reassurance that what he had hoped to do would come to pass after all (cf. 19:21). It is noteworthy that such dramatic visions or reassurances come at crisis or turning points in the story for Paul (cf. 9:4; 16:9; 18:9; 22:17; 27:23-24).[216] It is also important that there are no more miraculous releases or escapes for Paul. "The Lord's reassurance must take the place of miraculously opening doors. The divine power that rescues from

---

213. In the Greek we have in fact, apparently, a protasis without an accompanying apodosis, or so it is taken by the Western text, which adds at this point after "spoken to him," "let us not contend with God," drawing on the words of an earlier Pharisee in Acts 5:39. See Metzger, *Textual Commentary*, p. 487, and Delebecque, "Paul entre les Juifs et Romains selon les deux Versions de Act. xxiii." I would suggest rather that we have a shortened rhetorical question, as the NRSV suggests.

214. Whether this is a reference to his conversion or to his vision in the temple is unclear, but the former seems more likely.

215. Soards, *The Speeches in Acts*, p. 116.

216. See Bruce, *The Acts of the Apostles*, p. 467.

prison has become a powerful presence that enables the witness to endure an imprisonment that lasts for years."[217]

E. The Plot and the Plan (23:12-35)

Following the melee at the end of the Sanhedrin meeting, tempers were apparently still running hot, for we are told in *v. 12* that the next morning "the Jews" joined together in a συστροφην in order to do away with Paul.[218] We are told who Luke has in mind by "the Jews" in the next verse.[219] They are clearly not the chief priest and elders of the Sanhedrin themselves, but presumably some of the Jewish crowd that had previously tried to do away with Paul in the temple precincts.[220] The term συστροφην must surely be seen here as a virtual equivalent to συνωμοσιαν in v. 13,[221] meaning something like a conspiracy. The former term literally refers to a gathering for seditious purposes (cf. Polybius, *History* 4.34.6; Herodotus, *Persian Wars* 7.9), the latter to a league bound by an oath (Plato, *Apology* 36B).[222] The latter term is especially appropriate since we are told that this group of plotters put themselves under an anathema or curse, swearing an oath that they would neither eat nor drink until they had killed Paul. Jewish law, however, specified that if one was unable to fulfill an oath due to circumstances beyond one's control, one could be let off the hook (*m. Ned.* 3:3). *V. 13* mentions that more than forty had taken this oath, indicating the degree of opposition Paul and his preaching had aroused. They went to the chief priests and elders and told them of their oath and their intent. Their plan involved subterfuge. According to *v. 15*, the chief priests and elders must notify or make

---

217. Tannehill, *Narrative Unity of Luke-Acts*, 2:292.

218. Notice how various Western and Byzantine texts at this point again attempt to clarify matters by saying "some of the Jews." See Metzger, *Textual Commentary*, p. 488.

219. It is a caricature of the evidence to suggest that Luke has set up his narrative to portray "the Jews" as the real villains who reject Christ and his emissaries, and so are finally rejected by God in favor of the Gentiles, but cf. Sanders, "Salvation of the Jews." Cf. the fairer assessment of Johnson, *Acts*, p. 408: "Luke's readers are not likely to miss Luke's point by concluding either that all Jews are closed to the good news (much of his narrative has been constructed to show exactly the opposite), or that the Roman state is an unequivocally just and benign force. Luke will show us the inconsistency and moral inadequacy of Roman leaders (24.25-26) and the continuing openness of some Jewish leaders to dialogue (28.17-22)."

220. As Larkin, *Acts*, p. 331, says, Luke from now on in Acts highlights the hostility and responsibility of "the Jews" for Paul's troubles, but in each case the context makes clear that Luke does not mean all the Jews.

221. See Bruce, *The Acts of the Apostles*, p. 467.

222. See the discussion of Johnson, *Acts*, p. 403.

clear to the tribune to bring Paul down from the Antonia Fortress to the Sanhedrin, on the pretext that they wanted to make a more thorough examination of his case. Somewhere between the two locales Paul would be waylaid and done away with before he ever arrived at the Sanhedrin. It should be noted that Luke does not explicitly tell us that the Sanhedrin consented to this demand, and a demand it was (notice the aorist imperative εμφανισατε — to make clear to, to convey or notify; cf. v. 22 and Josephus, *Ant.* 4.43), but this consent is presumably implied in view of what follows.

V. *16* refers, for the only time in the NT, to a relative of Paul, his sister's son. The term νεανιαν is used of this young man in v. 17, and νεανισκος in v. 18 and v. 22. The latter form is a diminutive, and because of this and the reference to the tribune taking him by the hand, some have thought that this young man was a boy or a teenager.[223] This may be so; however, the basic meaning of the term νεανιαν is a young man between the ages of twenty and forty, and Philo says a νεανισκος is one who is between twenty-two and twenty-eight (*De Opificio Mundi* 105, following Hippocrates). The presence of this relative of Paul's in Jerusalem supports the suggestion that not just Paul, but his family, had moved to Jerusalem some time ago.[224] V. 16 rightly calls what the plotters are about to attempt an ambush (ενεδραν). Some scholars have objected to the idea that this young man could gain access to the barracks and visit with Paul, but this fails to take at least four factors into account. (1) Paul had not yet been convicted of any crime. Confinement in this case was not a punishment but a matter of Roman custody until the legal matter could be resolved, and protective custody at that. There was no reason not to admit the young man. (2) Because Paul was a Roman citizen and thus a person of status, it was common Roman practice to allow such persons in custody to be visited by friends and relatives, not least because they were responsible for taking care of the person's physical needs. (3) Examples of these practices can be readily cited (cf. Lucian, *De Morte Peregrini* 12-13; Phil. 2:25; 2 Tim. 1:16-17; and the various references in the later Christian Acts — *Acts of Andrew* 14; *Acts of Paul and Thecla* 18-19; *Passion of Perpetua and Felicity* 3).[225] (4) We are talking about a case of military custody in a barracks, not in a prison, and such a confinement was certainly less severe than being in a prison.[226]

Once the young man told Paul of the plot, Paul immediately called one of the centurions and told him to take the young man to the tribune. This was probably one of the centurions that had been present when Paul was about to be

223. See Bruce, *The Acts of the Apostles*, p. 469.
224. See pp. 659ff. above.
225. Johnson, *Acts*, p. 404, points us to these texts.
226. Rapske, *Paul in Roman Custody*, pp. 28-35. It was not unknown for higher-status persons in custody to have rather spacious and comfortable quarters and be allowed to be attended by one or more of their slaves. Paul is being treated as a Roman citizen, and this determines the degree of respect and the number of privileges he receives.

flogged. He was a person of lower social status and class rank than Paul, not being a Roman citizen, and there is nothing improbable in his doing what Paul told him to do. He was not going to make the mistake almost made before by centurions in this barracks of mistreating someone of higher status and incurring enmity, to the probable detriment of his career (cf. 22:25-26). According to *v. 17* Paul does not tell the centurion what the young man had to report — he wanted as few persons as possible to know of the plot. *V. 18* indicates that the centurion saw what Paul said as a request. Paul is called here for the first time "the prisoner Paul," a term Paul himself sees as something of a badge of honor reflecting his service and suffering for Christ (cf. Phil. 1:3; Philem. 1, 9; Eph. 3:1; 4:1).[227]

The tribune, perhaps sensing this was a delicate matter, takes the young man aside so he can speak privately to him. *V. 20* indicates that "the Jews" had agreed to ask the tribune to bring Paul down to the council so they could inquire "more thoroughly" concerning him. *V. 21* urges the tribune not to be persuaded by their rhetoric, because it was a ruse so they might ambush and kill Paul. V. 21b adds a new piece of information — the high priest and the elders are ready and waiting for the tribune's consent to their request. The tribune is obviously a man capable of acting with dispatch. He dismisses Paul's nephew, telling him to inform no one that he has reported this matter to the tribune. He then devises his own plan.

V. 23 says two of the centurions are summoned and told to be ready to leave for Caesarea by the third hour of the night, or somewhere between nine and nine-thirty, depending on what time of year we are talking about. The tribune is concerned to act with speed but also with safety in mind. He therefore commits some two hundred soldiers, seventy horsemen, and two hundred δεξιολαβους. There is considerable debate about what this last term means since it is a *hapax legomenon* not only in the NT but for all of Greek literature up to the sixth century A.D., where it is said to be a technical military term by Joannes Lydus.[228] In terms of etymology the term means to grip with the right hand, which has led to the speculation that it refers to spearmen (so the Vulgate), or javelin throwers (so syr-pesh).[229] It is possible, however, that it refers to those who led horses (with the right hand).[230] It has been complained that Luke has engaged in rhetorical hyperbole in regard to the numbers here, perhaps in the service of demonstrating the importance of Paul. This is possible in view of Luke's use of πας elsewhere in this book,[231] but in view of the tenseness of the

227. See Williams, *Acts,* p. 387.
228. Kilpatrick, "Acts xiii,23. δεχιολαβοι," suggests these are local Jerusalem militia, reducing the size actually taken from the Roman contingent. This speculation is based on an obscure scholion, and nothing in the text itself supports this conjecture.
229. See Bruce, *The Acts of the Apostles,* p. 470.
230. See Williams, *Acts,* pp. 389-90.
231. See pp. 105ff.

times, with various people of high social status being assassinated by the *sicarii* (cf. 21:38), it is not impossible that Claudius Lysias might commit this size of a force for a short mission such as this, if he felt Paul's safe conduct to Caesarea was very important and the situation very dangerous.

Actually the situation is doubly dangerous not only because of the plot but also because of the route that had to be traveled to Caesarea. Even somewhat before the time of Felix, Josephus tells us of Cumanus, an imperial slave carrying a considerable amount of money, who was attacked and robbed while on the main road from Jerusalem (*War* 2.228; *Ant.* 20.113), and somewhat later in A.D. 66 we hear of the governor of Syria with thirty-three thousand men only narrowly escaping annihilation from ill-equipped Jewish rebels at the pass that leads down to Lydda (*War* 2.540-55).[232]

Luke is also thought to have exaggerated how far a group like this could travel in one day on a forced march — Antipatris is some thirty-five miles away (by the Roman road),[233] leaving about another twenty-five miles to Caesarea for the next day. Three things may be said in response to this: (1) the first day's journey is mostly downhill; (2) we have clear evidence of Roman troops traveling these kinds of distances in this amount of time (e.g., Caesar, *Gallic Wars* 7.40-41 — forty-five miles covered with full baggage train in twenty-eight hours, with three hours rest; in very adverse conditions twenty-seven miles was covered in one night; see Plutarch, *Mark Antony* 47.2); (3) Josephus says Sebaste in Samaria could be reached from Jerusalem in a day, and it was forty-two miles away (*Ant.* 15.293). Armchair scholars are ill equipped to make pronouncements about the historical likelihood of such ancient journeys in such periods of time.[234] It does not pay to underestimate what Roman troops were capable of when a crisis situation was involved, especially when the only person in this entourage perhaps not capable of such a strenuous effort due to recent abuse was riding on a horse!

V. 24 informs us that mounts (κτηνη — plural) were to be provided Paul. This may mean a horse for Paul and a pack animal for his baggage, or both mounts may be simply for Paul, the one spelling the other in a rapid journey.[235] Williams may be right, in view of 24:23, that Paul's traveling

---

232. See the discussion in Hengel, "Geography of Palestine in Acts," pp. 65-66.

233. See Hemer, *Book of Acts*, p. 128 n. 79.

234. Haenchen, *Acts*, p. 650, and Lüdemann, *Early Christianity*, pp. 245-46, are repeatedly guilty of this sort of error. In general it is a good rule to be skeptical about modern scholars who think they know more about ancient roads, distances, travel times, and what a Roman commander might do in handling a crisis than Luke did. Hengel has demonstrated at some length that Luke knows a good deal about the geography and distances involved between Caesarea and Jerusalem, but less about the interior. See the original form of his essay in *Between Jesus and Paul*, pp. 97-132.

235. See Longenecker, *Acts*, p. 535.

companions are also being provided for, which would probably include Luke
in view of the fact that the "we" picks up again in Caesarea (27:1).[236] It is
interesting that the Western text adds that Lysias "was afraid the Jews would
seize him [Paul] and kill him, and afterwards he would incur the accusation
of having taken money" to allow Paul to be killed.[237] Paul is to be taken to
Felix the ηγεμονα, which is a general term meaning ruler, or in this case
governor. In Luke 2:2 the cognate term is used of the imperial legate of Syria,
and there is other evidence of the term being used of a prefect.[238] While under
normal circumstances Lysias might have waited for the procurator to make
his usual visit to Jerusalem on his judicial tour of duty to various spots in the
region, he had no such luxury at this point. He must opt for a change of venue
but not a change of jurisdiction, which would be beyond his authority.[239]

According to *v. 25* Paul was to be accompanied by a letter "having this
pattern" (τυπος). This phrase is sometimes taken to mean "to this effect" (cf.
NRSV), indicating that Luke is summarizing the gist or general purport of
what was *likely* said in the document, since he is unlikely to have had access
to it.[240] This conclusion may be correct, but there are reasons not to leap to
it. (1) This letter surely would have been read out loud upon Paul's arrival at
the initial meeting between the prefect and Paul, in which case Paul heard
what it said and could have conveyed its contents to Luke, if Luke himself did
not accompany Paul on this journey. (2) E. A. Judge rightly points out that by
rights τυπος ought to refer to a replication copy or verbatim, or perhaps more
likely the whole phrase means "according to (the following) set pattern." We
are talking about a certain type of letter — an *elogium*, an official report
explaining a legal matter.[241] (3) Precisely because it was an official report, it
was the sort of document that would be preserved for the trial of Paul as an
important reference work for Felix (and others?) to use. That Felix did indeed

236. Williams, *Acts*, p. 390.
237. See Metzger, *Textual Commentary*, p. 489.
238. Cf. *New Docs*, 1 (1976), pp. 47-51, of an Egyptian prefect.
239. See the discussion of Cadbury, "Roman Law," p. 306.
240. See Longenecker, *Acts*, p. 536; Marshall, *Acts*, p. 370.
241. See the discussion in *New Docs*, 1 (1976), pp. 77-78. See similar use of τυπος
in 3 Macc. 3:12-29, where we find a similar letter. Cf. also 1 Macc. 11:29; 2 Macc. 1:24;
3 Macc. 3:30. An official copy of this report may have been given to Paul or his Roman
custodian as a portion of the documentation of things when he was transferred to Rome.
The original may have been in Greek, but it is more likely it was in the official and legal
language of the Empire, Latin; see Williams, *Acts*, p. 390. This raises the question of
whether Paul or Luke or both knew some Latin. It seems likely, as well traveled as they
were and as much time as they seem to have spent in Roman colonies in the Empire, that
they had at least a rudimentary knowledge of Latin. This also is probable in view of the
fact that both of these men were interested in the conversion of all sorts of Gentiles to
the Christian faith.

think the evaluation of Claudius Lysias was important is shown by 24:22 (cf. below on this). Judge's conclusion is possible and worth pondering: "We must ask both with regard to the letter of Lysias and the . . . decision of the Jerusalem council (Acts 15.23-29) whether the author of Acts did not mean his readers to take them as the direct citation of transcripts available to him."[242]

The letter takes the typical ancient form — addresser, addressee, greeting, body of letter. Knowing this typical form, various scribes added the appropriate closing greeting ερρωσο ("farewell") at v. 30.[243] Felix is addressed as κρατιστω, "Excellency," which, if the term is used properly (but cf. Luke 1:3 for its general use), is perhaps a bit of flattery in view of the fact that it was normally reserved for some official of equestrian rank, but Felix, being a freedman, was not of such a station.

A brief statement about Felix is in order at this point. Felix, like his brother Pallas (perhaps the most famous and influential of all freedmen under Claudius), was a freedman. The cynical Roman historian Tacitus, who always believed that one's true character or origin would eventually show itself no matter how high up the social ladder one rose, says of Felix as a procurator that he "practiced every kind of cruelty and lust, wielding the power of a king with all the instincts of a slave" (*Ann.* 12.54; cf. *Hist.* 5.9). Apparently through his brother's connections in Rome, Felix, whose first name may have been either Antonius (so Tacitus) or Claudius (so Josephus),[244] became governor of Judea about A.D. 52 and ruled until either 59 or 60. There is some uncertainty in these matters in regard to the earlier date, because it appears that Felix may have held some sort of office in Palestine at an earlier date, perhaps under Cumanus in A.D. 48-52 (see Tacitus, *Annals* 12.54).[245] Despite Tacitus's social snobbishness, his comment about the cruelty and brutality of Felix as procurator is not wide of the mark. Like many another Roman he was anti-Semitic, and the brutal way he dealt with zealots alienated many Jews. The coup de grace came for him when he was recalled in either A.D. 59 or 60 (cf. below on 24:27), probably the former, because of the violent and unsuccessful way he dealt with riots between Jews and Gentiles in Caesarea. Despite all of this, he somehow managed to marry three women of royal birth (cf. Suetonius, *Claud.* 28), the first being the granddaughter of Antony and Cleopatra and the last being Drusilla the

---

242. *New Docs,* 1:78.

243. The Textus Receptus, followed by ℵ, E, Ψ, 056, 0142, and various minuscules. See Metzger, *Textual Commentary,* pp. 489-90, who is right to say that it is hard to imagine the omission of this standard epistolary element if it was originally present in the text.

244. Depending on whether he was manumitted by Claudius or Claudius's mother, Antonia — probably the latter. On the name cf. Bruce, "The Full Name," and the rejoinder by Hemer, "The Name of Felix Again."

245. See Aberbach, "The Conflicting Accounts."

daughter of Herod Agrippa I (cf. Tacitus, *Hist.* 5.9; Josephus, *War* 2.247-70; *Ant.* 20.137-82).[246]

Lysias's letter must of course be read critically, for the tribune has done his best to put the matter so that his own conduct will be seen in a favorable light by the governor. Hence, in *v. 27* we hear of Lysias's heroic intervention to save Paul's life when he had been seized and was about to be killed by the Jews. This is said to happen once he had heard Paul was a Roman citizen. Unless this is a reference to the rescue of Paul from the clutches of the members of the Sanhedrin, which possibility must be ruled out in view of the general chronological order of the report with v. 28 following v. 27, Lysias has deliberately altered both the order of things in the former verse and the interpretation of his intent. As Theophilus would already know, Lysias had not intervened to rescue Paul in the temple, but to restore order, and he had not found out about Paul's Roman citizenship until later. V. 28, however, correctly represents his intent in bringing Paul before the Sanhedrin — to know the αιτιαν, the legal charge, the Jews were bringing against Paul. As we have already noted, *v. 29* reveals that Lysias accepted Paul's interpretation about what the real bone of contention or chargeable offense was. The accusations[247] had to do with questions of the Jewish law, and from a Roman point of view Paul was charged with nothing deserving death or even imprisonment. As Marshall says, this "is the Roman attitude all along (26.31); from Luke's stress on the point it is hard to believe that he knew that in the end Paul was executed as a result of these proceedings,"[248] unless of course there was a total miscarriage of justice.

V. 30 indicates that Lysias, learning of the plot against Paul, quickly sent Paul to Felix and also ordered his accusers to "state before you [Felix] what they have against him." This is new information for Luke's audience, and it prepares us for what follows in Acts 24. On the whole, and in light of both the previous narrative and the speech of Tertullus which follows, it would appear that Luke intends for us to get something of a chuckle from Lysias's face-saving, self-serving report. It seems an all too typical example of the ability of those in power to bend the truth to suit their ends and stay in power.[249] The report is important, for it reveals for the first time that the tribune thinks no substantive charges (from a Roman point of view) have been proffered against Paul. Cassidy aptly puts matters this way: "Luke understands Lysias to have 'covered' himself with Paul at the same time he sought to 'cover' himself

246. Cf. Bruce, *The Acts of the Apostles,* p. 471; D. W. J. Gill, "Acts and Roman Policy in Judaea," in AIIFCS, 4:15-26, here pp. 21-25.
247. το εγκλημα (cf. 24:16) is the accusation or crime with which a person is charged. See Tajara, *The Trial of Paul,* p. 108.
248. Marshall, *Acts,* pp. 371-72.
249. Hemer, *Book of Acts,* p. 348.

with Felix. In this reading Luke understands Lysias' letter to be an adroitly political move: Lysias is sending the governor a prisoner who is not only a Roman citizen, but a highly articulate one; and, to the degree possible, he wishes the 'prisoner' as well as the governor to have a positive estimation of the way he handled the matter."[250]

When Lysias committed himself to transfer Paul to Caesarea even though he was convinced that Paul was guilty of nothing that Roman law should take cognizance of, he is clearly acting to protect a Roman citizen, not merely to restore law and order in Jerusalem.[251] *V. 31* recounts the transport of Paul to Antipatris, a small military station *(mutatio)* on the border between Judea and Samaria (probably modern Kulat Ras el Ain).[252] From there one moved down to the coastal plains and increasingly Gentile territory. Once Antipatris was reached, the two major dangers of the trip — contact with the plotters or being waylaid in treacherous terrain — were behind this party, and thus there was no need for the whole contingent of soldiers to go all the way to Caesarea. According to *v. 32*, most, except the horsemen, returned to the barracks in Jerusalem. *V. 33* indicates that the letter and then Paul were delivered to Felix, as was proper Roman procedure.

Felix is a literate person and so he himself reads the letter, but probably does so out loud, as was the almost universal practice in antiquity.[253] Felix then asks what province Paul belonged to, to which Paul replies he is from Cilicia. Some commentators have found it surprising that Felix then immediately says, "I will give you a hearing when your accusers arrive." One might have expected him to say, as Pilate does in Jesus' case (cf. Luke 23:6-7), that the case is beyond his jurisdiction, but this would be a mistake for several reasons. Perhaps most importantly, as Sherwin-White has pointed out, the Roman law or custom of *forum domicilii*, that is, of referring an accused person back to the jurisdiction of his native region, was only optional in the early Principate, not required, and the practice was not widespread before the second century.[254] Even so, one may wonder why Felix did not avail himself of this option and save himself some trouble.

The answer in part probably lies in the fact that eastern Cilicia, where

---

250. Cassidy, *Society and Politics*, p. 100.

251. See rightly Tannehill, *Narrative Unity of Luke-Acts*, 2:294-95.

252. Even Lüdemann, *Early Christianity*, p. 246, who is generally skeptical about the historical substance of the narrative, thinks this transfer of Paul to Caesarea by Lysias is historical.

253. On the aural dimension of reading in antiquity see Achtemeir, "*Omne verbum sonat.*"

254. See Sherwin-White, *Roman Law and Roman Society*, pp. 55-56. As Sherwin-White also says, this accurate knowledge of the first-century practice probably points in the direction of Luke's having composed this document *before* the second century.

Tarsus was, was in all probability at this point in A.D. 57 still part of the combined province Syria-Cilicia. The legate of Syria was in charge of both this region and Judea. Had Felix transferred Paul to another Roman official in the region, it would have had to have been to the legate of Syria. But this would be problematic on two accounts: (1) the legate would probably not want to be bothered with a minor matter of this sort and would wonder why Felix, who had the *imperium* to do so, since he was not *required* to send Paul back to Tarsus, had not settled the matter; (2) it would make it much more difficult for Paul to face his accusers, for they would have to travel a much greater distance, and Roman law placed a premium on the accusers appearing in person and making formal charges that the defendant would then be expected to answer in his απολογια.[255] Had Felix sent Paul on to Syria he would likely have only created more troubles for himself with both Roman and Jewish officials with whom he had to have ongoing dealings.[256] Thus it was that Paul was placed under guard at the Praetorium, or governor's residence, which was originally built by Herod the Great[257] and appears to have recently been excavated, and has many rooms.[258] Paul then does not seem to have been treated initially in any harsh way by Felix. The real trial would begin shortly.

F. Paul's Trial before Felix (24:1-27)

The trial proper is recorded in Acts 24, and is presented to us as an oratorical duel between two accomplished rhetoricians, Tertullus and Paul, offering us (in précis form) samplings of forensic rhetoric. The chapter may be divided into three parts: (1) the prosecution (vv. 1-9), (2) the defense (vv. 10-22), and (3) the aftermath (vv. 22-27). B. Winter has pointed out that it is not beyond the realm of possibility that Luke, if he wasn't present on the occasion, had access to the records of the proceedings of the trial, which included the taking down in shorthand of the speeches given during the trial.[259] Though some

---

255. See Sherwin-White, *Roman Law and Roman Society*, pp. 56-57; Tajara, *The Trial of Paul;* and especially J. Dupont, *Etudes sur les Actes des Apotres* (Paris: Cerf, 1967), pp. 527-52, here p. 535.

256. See Rapske, *Paul in Roman Custody*, p. 155.

257. See Josephus, *Ant.* 15.331.

258. See Burrell, Gleason, and Netzer, "Uncovering Herod's Seaside Palace."

259. See Winter, "Official Proceedings." These documents had to be forwarded to Rome with Paul, and Luke may have had access to them during the journey to Rome or thereafter. Notice the reference to *litterae dimissoriae* that Festus must produce in Acts 25:26 (cf. Winter, pp. 307-9). On samples of official proceedings in rhetorical form, cf. Coles, *Reports of Proceedings in Papyri*, pp. 13-19.

scholars have complained about the vagueness of the charges against Paul, "they are perfectly clear when related to the system *extra ordinem*."[260] The essence of this system, which worked outside the usual *ordo* of Roman trials, is that the accuser simply alleges "facts" against the accused, without necessarily producing any hard evidence, or even eyewitnesses, and then invites the Roman provincial official to evaluate and deal with the matter. The charge did not have to be dealt with exactly as formulated in the looser *extra ordinem* procedure — the official had more latitude.[261] Furthermore, in this procedure "the governor could render justice directly in virtue of his personal *cognitio*."[262]

Luke correctly reports the proper order of these legal affairs following Roman procedure: (1) the prosecution comes before the governor and reports its case, (2) the accused is then summoned, (3) the prosecution makes its accusations, (4) the defendant must respond, (5) the judge must decide the issue. In *extra ordinem* cases, the case was heard by the governor in person, while seated on the tribunal, assisted by his advisory council and a scribe or *notarius* who wrote up the minutes of the proceedings. The trial was open to the public and followed the accusatorial, not inquisitial, method of proceeding. This involved the defendant being confronted by his accusers face-to-face, after which he made his *apologia* or defense. The burden of proof lay on the *accuser* in such trials. The judge had flexibility in both establishing what the "crime" or real bone of contention was and in determining punishment. He could reach an immediate decision, but if he chose to postpone rendering a verdict neither party involved in the litigation could readily speed matters up.[263] The governor could postpone matters indefinitely.[264] Postponements either before or after trials could happen even in the case of notable defendants, as is shown by the case of the famous historian Polybius, who was under arrest for an amazing fifteen years "under suspicion" without trial (cf. below on v. 27).[265]

Acts 24:1 begins by referring to a period "five days later," which presumably means five days after Paul had arrived and been placed into Felix's custody in Caesarea. This brief interval shows how very much the Jewish officials wanted to eliminate the "Paul problem," as does the fact that they took the trouble of bringing a professional rhetor[266] with them to argue their

---

260. Sherwin-White, *Roman Law and Roman Society*, p. 49.

261. See ibid., p. 18, and the parallel case in Pliny, *Ep.* 10.81.2ff. and cf. *Ep.* 82.

262. Tajara, *The Trial of Paul*, p. 114.

263. Cf. Mommsen's judgment that the trial scene of 24:1-23 is in detailed agreement with what we know of Roman legal proceedings in "Die Rechtverhältnisse des Apostels Paulus."

264. See Tajara, *The Trial of Paul*, pp. 115-16.

265. See the discussion of Balsdon, *Romans and Aliens*, pp. 193ff.

266. The term ῥήτωρ here in all likelihood has its more narrow sense of a legal advocate (cf. Dio Chrysostom, *Or.* 76.4; Josephus, *Ant.* 17.226), not merely an orator who was rhetorically adept (Lucian, *Professor of Public Speaking* 1).

side of the case (which may also reflect their knowledge that their case was weak). The fact that no less than the high priest himself and various elders come down from Jerusalem also reflects the importance of this matter in their eyes. They were hoping their high social status in Israel would help determine the outcome of the case, since this was often the case in Roman trials.[267] Unfortunately for these high-status Jews, Felix was no great lover of Jews in general.

The name Tertullus (cf. the longer form Tertullianus) is a Latin name, probably a diminutive of Tertius.[268] This does not mean Tertullus was a Roman, but this is possible. Some have taken the "we" in Tertullus's speech (vv. 2-8) to indicate that he was a Jew, but on the other hand he seems to distinguish himself from "the Jews" in v. 5, and in v. 9 Luke distinguishes him from "the Jews." All that was really required was that he had a good knowledge of Roman law and legal procedure and was informed about the case he was prosecuting.[269] He was likely simply a hired advocate.

Before the trial proper began, the Jewish delegation came before the governor and made a formal charge against Paul which set the trial in motion.[270] Paul would not be present at this pretrial hearing. Then Paul was called forth from custody. Luke is probably giving us the equivalent of the Latin *vocare*, where a crier summons the accused to the courtroom.[271]

Once in the courtroom, Tertullus immediately began the accusations by offering a formal rhetorical speech. Without a doubt, Luke has only presented a summary of the speech and the charges leveled, as is shown by the fact that the *exordium* takes up all of vv. 2-4, with the charges in the form of a *narratio* mentioned only briefly in vv. 5-6, and the *peroratio*, appealing for the governor to act by investigating Paul himself, concluding the matter in v. 8. What is entirely missing here is the formal proofs or arguments that would have been developed out of the "facts" mentioned in

---

267. See Garnsey, *Social Status and Legal Privilege*, pp. 279-80, here p. 280: "In law, as in other aspects of Roman society, the principal benefits and rewards were available to those groups most advantageously placed in the stratification system by reason of their greater property, power, and prestige."

268. See Polhill, *Acts*, p. 479 n. 97.

269. Normally one would expect the trial to be undertaken in Latin, which might militate against Tertullus being a Jew, unless he was from the Diaspora. It is not impossible, however, that the trial, or at least the speeches, was in Greek, the lingua franca of the provinces. This would explain perhaps how the Jews were able to support and agree with what Tertullus said (cf. v. 9).

270. As Johnson, *Acts*, p. 410, points out, εμφανιζω (cf. 23:15) has its legal sense here of make a charge. Cf. Tajara, *The Trial of Paul*, p. 119: "The beginning of a judicial action consisted of a formal declaration on the accuser's part that he wished to pursue such and such a person as being guilty of a crime."

271. See Polhill, *Acts*, p. 479.

the *narratio*.[272] Winter is correct to stress the great importance of the *captatio benevolentiae* in the *exordium,* and its greater length here is partly explained by this fact.[273] It is comparable to what one finds in forensic petitions that also summarize charges and arguments.[274] As we shall see, it is carefully linked to the charges which follow and is not an example of mere flattery.

Tertullus begins his address to Felix with the same complimentary high-status term as Lysias used in his letter (23:26), calling Felix "Your Excellency." Especially in a trial it was crucial to establish rapport with the judge and to relate to him in terms he would appreciate and understand. There are then two main things Tertullus was relying on to make his case: considerations of *ethos,* that is, relying on the establishing of goodwill and so a willingness to act on the part of Felix; and the making of the sort of political charges that a Roman governor had to take seriously. The *captatio benevolentiae* is seeking to establish the proper rapport so that the political charges would be considered viable. It is probable that Tertullus was unaware of the content of the report of Lysias that suggested another conclusion, a report that Tertullus clearly takes very seriously (cf. v. 22).

The *captatio* in essence states that because of Felix, the country has had conditions that are quite the opposite of what Paul was stirring up. Felix had brought the Pax Romana to Israel "for a long time" and made important "reforms"; Paul by contrast will be charged with bringing a plague, agitation, trouble, sedition, and indeed even riot and revolution by attempting to profane the temple.[275] It was of course not true that Felix had brought peace to Israel. Quite the contrary, he is usually credited with being most responsible of all the governors leading up to the Jewish War for stirring up ill will and trouble by his brutal suppression of various Jewish and Samaritan groups, some messianic, some more revolutionary.[276] What needs to be

272. See the discussions in Kennedy, *New Testament Interpretation,* p. 135; Soards, *The Speeches in Acts,* pp. 117-18; Neyrey, "Forensic Defense Speech," pp. 216-17 (note the lack of discussion of a *probatio* in the case of this speech); Veltman, "Defense Speeches of St. Paul," pp. 253-54; Winter, "Importance of the *Captatio Benevolentiae,*" pp. 505-31; and Lösch, "Die Dankesrede de Tertullus: Apg. 24.1-4," pp. 295-319.

273. Against Dibelius, *Studies in the Acts,* p. 171, who thinks it unimportant and merely art for art's sake. He is also wrong that Luke has neglected to present the nature of the dispute.

274. Winter, "Official Proceedings," pp. 320-21.

275. See the discussion in Winter, "Importance of the *Captatio Benevolentiae,*" pp. 510ff.

276. Tacitus tells us that because of his influential brother Pallas in Rome, Felix felt he had carte blanche, thinking "he could do any evil act with impunity" (*Ann.* 12.54). On his brutal suppression of various groups including robber bands, cf. Josephus, *Ant.* 20.8.5; *War* 2.13.2. Josephus is quite clear that the net effect of Felix's rule was to add more fuel to the fire (cf. *War* 2.13.6; so also Tacitus, *Ann.* 12.54).

recognized is that Tertullus is using stock phrases here used to describe the wise and judicious ruler who brings "much peace."[277] Felix is being praised as one who is carrying out his essential Roman mandate to bring peace and order to his province. It might be better to say that he made forceful efforts to bring "pacification" to the land, but they did not tend toward peace in the long run. We may remember from Acts 21:38 the mention of an incident in which the Jews of Jerusalem had cooperated with Felix in the suppression of the Egyptian's messianic plans.

The next item praised is Felix's "foresight" (προνοια; cf. 2 Macc. 4:6). This word might be better translated "providence," a theme also common in the *captatios* in the forensic papyri used to praise a Roman ruler.[278] In other words, the two common themes of peace and providence used in forensic rhetoric, the two great virtues or actions looked for in a Roman ruler, are attributed to Felix here. Providence in "reforms" in this case refers to the revision of the law, or perhaps a flexible use of it.[279] This of course is precisely what those Tertullus represented wanted from Felix, that he would quiet or silence Paul once and for all by a flexible use of the law and his *imperium* or *auctoritas*. Just as he had done against the Egyptian, so it was hoped he would do against Paul, and Paul was about to be made out to be the same sort of fellow as the Egyptian. In other words, this is a masterful *exordium* playing just the right notes that should have sounded like music to Felix's ears.

V. 3 indicates that the Jewish authorities, for whom Tertullus speaks, welcome everywhere and in every way with all gratitude these actions of Felix.[280] This is actually not just flattery, for the Sadducean rulers of Israel and their aristocratic supporters knew quite well that they depended to a large degree on Roman support and, where necessary, military intervention suppressing Jewish rebel groups to maintain the status quo and remain in power.

A further common rhetorical topos is used in *v. 4*, where Tertullus prom-

---

277. On the idea of the ruler bringing "much peace" (πολλης ειρηνης, v. 2) cf. Plutarch, *Alcibiades* 14.2; Josephus, *Ant.* 7.20.

278. See Winter, "Official Proceedings," p. 319, citing P. Fouad. 26, P. Ryl. 114, l. 5.

279. See Lösch, "Die Dankesrede de Tertullus: Apg. 24.1-4," pp. 307-10, who suggests that διορθωμα points to the reestablishment of law and order, but it can also refer to the revision or reform of the law itself. The term προνοια is used in the introductory formulae of Egyptian prefects to describe their work, especially in the revision or flexible use of the law. See Winter, "Official Proceedings," p. 319.

280. This sentence involves rhetorical alliteration (παντη τε και πανταχου . . . πασης) and a topos of secular speech when praise was the aim. Cf. Philo, *Flacc.* 98f.; *Leg. ad Gai.* 284. The word ευχαριστιας in these contexts means "gratitude," the appropriate submissive response to the ruler. See the use of the term in honorific decrees praising a ruler in *New Docs*, 1, no. 37, p. 83.

ises to delay the judge no further and get to the point of the accusations.[281] Felix is urged to give ear to the charges "with your usual graciousness," presumably referring to the fact that he had been ready and willing to believe the worst about various Jewish troublemakers in the past. Johnson also rightly points out that επιεικεια was a quality that involved one's willingness to go beyond the strict bounds of the law because of one's mercifulness or reasonableness.[282] This suggests that Tertullus and his clients realized that it would be hard to prove Paul guilty within the strict bounds of the law, and therefore they were relying on Felix's "willingness" to bend a few rules to accomplish certain desired ends in the service of "peace and order."

Vv. 5-6 provide us with the charges, and there has been debate as to whether there are two or three of them. It would appear that there are only two charges: (1) that Paul, as a pestilence, is guilty of fomenting a στασις in Jerusalem, being the ringleader of a dangerous sect; and (2) that he attempted to profane the temple. These were very serious political charges indeed, either of which could lead to Paul's death. According to the rhetorical handbooks στασις was precisely the right charge to bring against someone in criminal proceedings (cf. Cicero, *De Inventione* 2.516–8.28; *Ad Herrennium* 2.3.3–3.4).[283] The especial appropriateness of this first charge, in view of the volatility of things not only in Israel at this time but also during the reign of Claudius and during the early years of his successor Nero, is rightly stressed by Sherwin-White.[284] Claudius in a famous letter of warning to Alexandrian Jews stressed his objection to certain political activities they were engaging in and said they were "stirring up a universal plague throughout the world" (κοινην τινα της οικουμενης νοσον εξεγειροντας).[285] The striking similarity of this to what we find in v. 5 should be noted. Paul is being classed with these sorts of troublemakers. The word λοιμος as a noun means pestilence or plague, and as Cassidy says, this means more than what we mean by pest or someone who is merely eccentric. It means that Paul is analogous to a contagious disease or plague transmitting the sickness of disruption, dissension, even revolution wherever he goes throughout the civilized world

---

281. As Johnson, *Acts,* p. 410, rightly points out, though the verb εγκοπτω usually means "to hinder," when applied to time, as here, it means "to delay." Advocates were indeed expected to be succinct and to the point with their forensic rhetoric (cf. Quintilian, *Inst. Or.* 8.3.82; Lucian, *Dis Indict.* 20-21 and 26: "But in order not to make a long speech, since much time has elapsed already, I will begin with the accusation . . ."), though they often were not. Lucian also tells us that a water clock was used to time the judicial speeches (*Dis* 15, 19).

282. See Johnson, *Acts,* p. 410.

283. See the discussion in Neyrey, "Forensic Defense Speech," pp. 215-16.

284. Sherwin-White, *Roman Law and Roman Society,* p. 51.

285. See Smallwood, *Documents,* pp. 99ff., no. 370, lines 99-100.

(οικουμενην).[286] There must be a vigorous response to stop the spread of this disease. This charge was dangerous especially because if the high priest could have produced some of the Asian Jews or other Diaspora Jews whom Paul had addressed in various synagogues who could personally attest to the melee that ensued when Paul spoke in synagogues, it was very possible that this charge could be made to stick. Fortunately for Paul, the case had been prepared in haste, and the high priest did not have even any of the Asian Jews with him who had made charges against Paul when he was in Jerusalem who could attest to his activities elsewhere in the Empire (cf. 21:27). It will be noted that Paul, in his defense, making a rhetorically effective move, confines his response to what he had done during the some twelve days he was in Jerusalem prior to his being taken into custody (see below).

The charge that Paul was a ringleader (πρωτοστατην)[287] of the Nazarenes[288] who is described as a αιρεσεως is not a separate charge, but further explains the first one. He is not merely a fomenter of dissension, he is the leader of such activities. The term αιρεσεως here could be translated as sect or party (cf. 28:22), but it seems to begin to have its later pejorative sense of a "heresy" (but cf. the apparently more neutral use of Pharisees and Sadducees in 5:17; 15:5; 26:5).[289]

V. 6 is interesting in the way it varies from what he heard in 21:28. Here the milder form of the accusation is found — "he attempted to profane the temple, and so we seized him." Of course Luke's audience will know that neither half of this statement was true. In fact, as Paul will show in his rhetorically effective response, he was doing just the opposite, seeking to purify himself! This charge was actually somewhat lame, because technically speaking it would have been Trophimus and not Paul who had been the defiler of the temple if he had gone beyond the zone permitted to Gentiles.[290] The final part of this charge is, however, a bald-faced lie if it means that the temple police or Jewish authorities had seized Paul, and not merely ordinary Jews in the temple precincts. The purpose of this bold statement was to claim juris-dictional rights to judge Paul under Jewish law by Jewish authorities.

286. Cassidy, *Society and Politics*, p. 104.

287. This word, which means a person who stands in the first place, a leader, appears only here in the NT. As Johnson, *Acts*, p. 411, says: "The Jewish leaders assign to Paul the same importance as standard bearer of the messianic movement that Luke himself does."

288. Only here in the plural in the NT. Probably the term was first applied to Christians in a pejorative way, suggesting their illegitimacy, because a messiah from Nazareth was not anticipated (cf. John 1:46; Luke 18:37; Acts 2:22). Later the term was used of Jewish Christian sects (cf. Jerome, *De Viris Illustribus* 2-3; *Epistles* 20.2), and in the Talmud Christians came to be called *nozrim*, e.g., *b. Ta'anit* 27b. See Polhill, *Acts*, p. 480.

289. See Williams, *Acts*, p. 396. The word literally means a choice, or that which one has chosen, or finally those who made such a choice.

290. See pp. 653-54 above on Trophimus.

Felix, however, already had Lysias's report to the contrary, indicating Paul was a Roman citizen taken into custody by a Roman tribune. There is a noteworthy addition in some manuscripts to v. 6 as follows: "and we would have judged him according to our Law (v. 7), but the chief captain Lysias came and with great violence took him out of our hands." It is very difficult to explain the omission of these words in various of our earliest and best Greek manuscripts (p74, ℵ, A, B, H, L, P) if they were original, and so they should probably be omitted from the text (cf. Nestle-Aland and the NRSV).[291] While it is certainly believable that the Jewish authorities resented Roman "interference" in their affairs, it is not wholly plausible that their advocate would show this sort of animus toward a Roman official in a trial where they were trying to get the Roman authority to judge Paul. For this reason as well the addition is likely secondary.

V. 8 provides us with the *peroratio*, which may seem surprising, but it makes sense because this trial was an example of the *extra ordinem* procedure. Tertullus implores Felix to "examine" Paul himself to learn from him everything of which he was being accused. Ἀνακρίνας (cf. Luke 23:14; Acts 4:9; 12:19) here has the legal sense of interrogate.[292] Felix could have done this, but he declines to do so at least at this juncture (cf. vv. 24-25), even though v. 9 indicates that the Jewish authorities present all joined in stressing that all that Tertullus said was true.

Instead Felix, in a regal manner, simply gestured to Paul to make his defense.[293] V. 10 indicates that Paul with cheer or gladness (εὐθύμως)[294] makes his defense[295] before Felix, knowing that he has been a judge over Israel for "many years." Luke evidently agrees with Josephus (*Ant.* 20.317f.; cf. *War* 2.247) that Felix succeeded Cumanus as procurator in about A.D. 52, just before Agrippa II was given the tetrarchies formerly ruled by Philip and Lysanias.[296] This speech would have been given in A.D. 57, and so with a little rhetorical liberty perhaps, he speaks of Felix's many years as judge over the nation.[297] This *exordium* is both briefer and more factual than Tertullus's. Paul

291. So Metzger, *Textual Commentary,* p. 490.

292. See Trites, "The Importance," p. 280.

293. Interestingly, the Harclean margin of the Syriac adds that Paul assumed a godlike bearing as he began to speak. Metzger, *Textual Commentary,* pp. 490-91. It was customary for a rhetor to strike an impressive pose before speaking.

294. If this speech was originally given in Latin, which is unlikely, one might suspect Paul of making a play on the governor's name (Felix — happy).

295. Haenchen, *Acts,* p. 654, rightly calls the term ἀπολογία and its cognates the catchwords of these chapters. Cf. 22:1; 24:10; 25:8; 26:1, 2, 24.

296. The latter event occurred in the twelfth year of Claudius's principate, i.e., A.D. 53. See the discussion in Bruce, "Chronological Questions," pp. 285-86.

297. Perhaps he also had in mind some time he may have spent under Cumanus working in the region prior to his procuratorship. Cf. pp. 702ff. above.

seems to exude confidence in this speech. His appeal to the governor's knowledge and experience is especially appropriate in proceedings *extra ordinem*. It
appears that he is relying on what Felix already knows about the source of
disruptions in the region, and that "the Nazarenes" were not involved.

In *v. 11* we have a brief *narratio*, while in *vv. 12-20* we have Paul's actual
response to the charges, with a brief *peroratio* in v. 21.[298] A *narratio* was
necessary because the facts of the case were in dispute (cf. Quintilian, *Inst. Or.*
4.2.5). Paul states clearly that Felix would be able to verify for himself[299] that
it had been only twelve days since he went up to Jerusalem to worship, hardly
time to cause all the trouble alleged against him. The form of this statement
makes quite clear it is intended as a rebuttal to the charges.[300] Investigation
would certainly not lead Felix to the conclusions Tertullus urged, quite the
contrary. Scholars have debated which particular twelve days Paul has in mind.
Are we to add the seven days of purification (21:27) to the five days of 24:1?
But this neglects the three days before Paul began his week of purification (cf.
21:18, 26). Haenchen's explanation seems best — that what is meant is the
time between Paul's arrival in Jerusalem and his transfer to Caesarea, as follows: (1) day one, arrival in Jerusalem (21:18); (2) day two, negotiations with
James and the elders (21:18); (3) days three through nine, the seven days of
purification (21:27); (4) day ten, Paul before the Sanhedrin (22:30); (5) day
eleven, discovery of the plot against Paul (23:12); (6) day twelve, transfer to
Caesarea.[301] The point is that there were only twelve days total that Paul was
in Jerusalem and could make any trouble, and in fact three of these must be
subtracted because during his last three days there he was in Roman custody,
as Lysias could attest!

Beginning in *v. 12* he refutes the charges point by point. "They" had not
found Paul disputing with anyone in the temple or stirring up any crowds in
the synagogues or throughout the city.[302] The emphasis here in v. 12 and in
the following ones is on what "they," Paul's accusers, could attest to. Notice
that in *v. 13* Paul stresses that "they" could not *prove* either that he was a plague
throughout the world or that he had profaned the temple, their essential

298. Cf. the rhetorical analysis of Long, "The Trial of Paul," pp. 230-31, to Winter,
"Official Proceedings," pp. 322-23.

299. Here as in v. 8 we are talking about the ability to accomplish something, not
the actual undertaking of the activity. Both the Jewish authorities and Paul appeal to the
governor's ability to verify or examine something for himself, as is appropriate in the *extra
ordinem* procedure where things hinged to a great degree on the *cognitio* of the judge
himself. Cf. Polhill, *Acts*, p. 482 n. 110.

300. See Soards, *The Speeches in Acts*, p. 118.

301. Haenchen, *Acts*, p. 654 n. 2. He is following the older suggestion of A. Schlatter.

302. The reference to synagogues (plural) is intriguing and should be compared to
Acts 6:9, which surely implies there were several synagogues in Jerusalem.

charges.[303] The issue here is what they could prove — Paul could see that they had not brought any Asian Jewish witnesses with them (cf. above). It was then his word against theirs in these matters. In a striking and effective move Paul makes a confession in *v. 14*.[304] "Confessing what was not a crime was a typical masterful rhetorical move, it would heighten one's credibility while doing nothing for the opponents' charge that the defendant had broken the law."[305] Paul freely admits that he worships the God of his Jewish ancestors "according to the Way." This is of course a designation for the Christian movement he is a part of, a designation which suggests it involves a particular manner of approach to the ancestral religion, but certainly not a different religion. He stresses that "they" call it a "sect" or "heresy" (cf. above); those are not his preferred terms. The use of the designation "the Way" may in fact go back to or at least parallel the sort of usage we find at Qumran, which also saw itself as "the Way," based in part on their understanding of the key text in Isa. 40:3 about preparing in the wilderness a way for the Lord (cf. 1QS 9:16-21; 8:13-16).[306] Paul stresses his complete orthodoxy: he believes everything laid down according to the Law or written in the Prophets.[307]

As *v. 15* stresses, Paul, like his accusers, has a hope in God, but when he goes on to define that hope he says they share a hope of the resurrection of both the righteous and the unrighteous. This would only be the case if some of the elders present were Pharisees, but perhaps Paul means he shares with the majority of the Jews (and some of their leaders) this form of hope. Paul characteristically does not speak of the resurrection of the unrighteous in his letters because he sees resurrection as a matter of conformity of believers to the image of Christ (1 Cor. 15:20-23; Phil. 3:20-21; but cf. John 5:28-29; Rev. 20:12-15; Dan. 12:2).[308] It is, however, likely he believed in some sort of raising of the unjust because he says all must appear before the judgment seat of Christ (2 Cor. 5:10), and this probably means more than just all believers. *V. 16* begins with the statement that, in view of this reality, Paul seeks always to have a "conscience void of offense," whether one is referring to offending God or human beings. The resurrection (and ensuing judgment, see v. 25

---

303. On Paul's narrowing of the field of focus away from the more dangerous charges to those he could easily refute, see Tannehill, *Narrative Unity of Luke-Acts*, 2:299.

304. Johnson, *Acts*, p. 412, rightly notes that the "this" is emphatic here: "But *this* I do confess. . . ." Here again Paul is turning the argument away from political charges to personal confession of his faith, and so he testifies before this official, as Jesus said he would.

305. Keener, *Bible Background Commentary*, p. 395.

306. See the discussion in Pathrapankal, "Christianity as a 'Way,'" pp. 535-36.

307. This says something about his (and/or Luke's) view of the inspiration and authority of all the Hebrew Scriptures, though he does not specifically mention the Writings here.

308. On the resurrection of the just in Luke-Acts, cf. Luke 14:14; 20:35-36.

below) are strong motivators to behave properly in this lifetime. Thus far, Paul's defense against the charges that he was a troublemaker and "heretic." It will be seen that here, as at the Sanhedrin hearing, Paul seeks to shift "the main issue" from a discussion of political charges to a discussion of differences in theology, which would not involve a chargeable offense under Roman law.

Beginning with *v. 17* Paul begins to answer the second charge of profaning the temple. After some years away, Paul had returned to Jerusalem. At least five seem to have elapsed since his last visit mentioned in 18:22, but Paul may even be thinking of his last lengthy visit some seven or eight years previous (15:4-29).[309] Paul says he came to bring "alms" to his nation, and προσφοράς. In an important discussion Tannehill has argued that this does not refer to the collection at all, but to the acts of piety of a pilgrim, involving the temple treasury.[310] This is a possible conclusion,[311] but it does not make very good sense of why Luke refers to a delegation accompanying Paul to Jerusalem in Acts 20:1-4. It also overlooks that Paul himself says that the collection is funds designated "for the poor among the saints of Jerusalem" (Rom. 15:26) — in other words, alms for his people. It also overlooks that the initial mandate for the collection was precisely for the poor (Gal. 2:10). Paul's longer exposition in 2 Cor. 8:1–9:15 indicates clearly enough that this gift was given in thanksgiving to God as well as in aid of "the saints."[312] It may well be, as Williams suggests, that we should take alms as referring to the collection but προσφοράς as a reference to Paul's offering sacrifices in the temple precincts, perhaps those referred to in 21:26 in which Paul was involved.[313] This makes sense of what follows in *v. 18*, where εν αις would refer back to the sacrifices just mentioned, and to Paul's completing the rite of purification.[314] There was no crowd or disturbance while Paul was engaged in these acts. This mention of money becomes important later on, for it seems to have suggested to Felix that Paul had resources (cf. below on v. 26).

V. 19 presents us with perhaps the most powerful of Paul's arguments — namely, that some Jews from Asia stirred up the crowd against him, but they are not present to charge him with anything. The sentence here involves anacoluthon, as if on the spot it dawned on Paul that they ought to be present to make their accusations. Roman law took very seriously those who were guilty of *destitutio*, the abandonment of their charges against someone (see

309. See Bruce, *The Acts of the Apostles*, p. 480.
310. See Tannehill, *Narrative Unity of Luke-Acts*, 2:300.
311. See Polhill, *Acts*, p. 484 n. 117.
312. See the discussion in Bruce, *The Acts of the Apostles*, p. 480.
313. See Williams, *Acts*, p. 400, and also Marshall, *Acts*, p. 379.
314. An additional possibility is that Paul made his own thank offering in the temple, quite apart from the ritual of purification, perhaps for the safe delivery of the collection. See Williams, *Acts*, p. 400.

Appian, *Rom. Hist.: Civ. Wars* 3.54). Claudius had himself worked on legislation to prevent this from happening, and shortly after this time in A.D. 61 the legislation was completed and passed.[315] Paul had now struck a note, whether in a moment of inspiration or not, that could provide the basis for the dismissal of the case outright.

As for the accusers who actually stood before Paul, *vv. 20-21* make evident that the only thing they could testify to was the one claim Paul had made to them — that he was on trial over a theological matter, "the resurrection of the dead." In other words, *v. 21* narrows the field of focus. V. 20 might allow them to restate what crime they found Paul guilty of when he stood before the Sanhedrin, but of course they never found him guilty of anything, and there was only this one thing that Paul would concede he had really confessed. In a master stroke, Paul has made his accusers witness on his behalf that he had spoken only of theological matters!

Without doubt, we are meant to think that Paul was the more persuasive rhetor and had the better of the argument, but Felix simply adjourned[316] the hearing without deciding the case.[317] We are told he did this, according to *v. 22*, having a "more accurate" knowledge of the things concerning the Way.[318] It is probable that we should take ἀκριβεστερον as a true comparative, in which case we must ask, "More accurate" than whom? and the answer must be the accusers. This may suggest that Felix knew very well that the charges against Paul were basically bogus. He had been in Israel long enough to know that the Nazarenes were not rabble-rousers. Furthermore, he would rather not do an injustice to a Roman citizen. Yet at the same time his brutal policies had placed him in a tenuous position. He had to placate the authorities in some way, and simply dismissing the case would not accomplish this end. We know of the tenuousness of his position from the fact that during the two years of Paul's stay in Caesarea, probably in A.D. 58, violence broke out between Gentiles and Jews, and Felix entered the fray on the side of the Gentiles, which led to a strong Jewish protest going to Rome against Felix's policies. This led to

---

315. See the discussion in Sherwin-White, *Roman Law and Roman Society,* p. 52. This principle was also recognized in *extra ordinem* procedures; see Pliny, *Ep.* 6.31.9-12.

316. Ἀνεβαλετο is technical language. Cf. P. Tebtunis 1.22.9. In this case the specified reason for adjournment is the hearing of new evidence. The Latin here would likely be *pronuntiavit amplius,* a phrase which in Cicero, *Verr.* 2.1.29.74, means further trial is required. A temporary adjournment is in view. See Tajara, *The Trial of Paul,* p. 129.

317. See rightly Winter, "Official Proceedings," p. 327: "The author of Acts intended his readers to see Paul handling his defence with great dexterity, and refuting these charges. He had done this by prescribing the limits of the evidence based on Roman law proscribing the charges of absent accusers, using forensic terminology, and not least of all, presenting a well argued defence, even if preserved in summary form."

318. See the use of ἀκριβεστερον in 18:26.

his removal from office but not to his punishment (Josephus, *War* 2.13.7; *Ant.* 20.182).[319] As a favor to the Jewish leadership, whom he could not afford to alienate any further, he left Paul in custody because his own fate was undecided, and the Jewish leaders could still make trouble for him at his hearing in Rome. V. 22 indicates that as a public "reason" for the adjournment without decision, Felix said he would decide the case when Lysias came down to speak to him about it. On the one hand, this made good sense, for he was the one independent witness to these affairs. Yet of course he already knew Lysias's judgment on the matter, he had it in writing, and therefore we must see this as either a ruse or a delaying tactic.

V. 23 is also of considerable importance, for it may be meant to hint at something of Felix's attitude toward the case. Felix ordered the centurion to keep Paul in custody, but it was not to be a harsh one. He was to be allowed to have some liberty or relief,[320] and the centurion was not "to prevent *any* of his friends from taking care of his needs." Various scholars have seen this as an example of *custodia libera* or open custody, and analogies have been drawn with other examples of this sort of captivity, such as the story in Lucian's *De morte peregrini* 12 telling of the luxurious meals and treatment given to Peregrinus while he was in prison. Much depends on whether Paul was kept in chains while in Caesarea after the trial, and in view of the fact that Paul is placed in the care of a centurion we must speak of some form of military custody. Rapske, largely on the basis of the mention of chains in 26:29, argues that we are not dealing with an example of *custodia libera* but rather with some form of lenient military custody. Certainly, Paul was not transferred to a private residence or to the safekeeping of a local magistrate. He remained in the governor's palace. This, too, speaks against *custodia libera* at this point in Paul's captivity.[321] Paul is allowed to have some freedom of movement and to be attended by friends. A useful parallel is found in the case of Agrippa, also a Jew and a Roman citizen who was also under military custody, which meant he was still guarded and watched but some leniency was shown in regard to his daily activities (*Ant.* 18.235). That Paul was guarded by no less than a centurion may suggest that Felix thought it important that Paul not escape.

Ramsay long ago rightly raised the question of Paul's financial situation while in captivity.[322] The length of the trial and imprisonment without the ability to work could be expensive, since the Romans did not provide sustenance or clothing and the like for captives, not even higher-status ones. This

---

319. Cf. Brunt, "Charges of Provincial Maladministration."
320. See Josephus, *Ant.* 18.235, where ανεσις has the sense of leniency or relief.
321. See Rapske, *Paul in Roman Custody,* pp. 171-72. Contra Williams, *Acts,* p. 402.
322. Ramsay, *St. Paul the Traveller,* pp. 310-12.

led Ramsay to suggest that Paul had independent resources, perhaps from the selling of some family property in the area. He supported this with the reminder that Paul rented lodgings in Rome when he arrived (cf. below on 28:16). This conclusion may be correct, and may be supported by Felix's request for a bribe and also by Paul's funding of the fulfillment of the Nazaritic vows, which would have involved expensive sacrifices (21:24-26), but three things can be said against this supposition:[323] (1) Felix also supposes that Paul will be taken care of by his friends; (2) Phil. 4:10-20 suggests that Paul received, even though he probably did not solicit, support from friends in Philippi while in Rome, and he was also attended by local Christians while there; (3) Felix is probably approaching Paul for a bribe because of his status as a Roman citizen, and his reference to the collection and sacrifices in the temple. Paul may have had considerable personal assets, but we cannot be sure.

V. 24 tells us that some days later Felix came with his Jewish wife Druscilla (cf. above) and sent for Paul, who came and spoke to them about faith in Christ Jesus.[324] V. 25 says he also spoke pointedly to them about justice or righteousness,[325] self-control,[326] and the coming judgment. These remarks were apparently sufficiently on target to unsettle Felix, for he had not been practicing justice, and the very presence of Drusilla, whom he had lusted after while she was still the teenage bride of Azizus the king of Emesa,[327] and the message about future judgment for bad behavior while on earth would probably have been disturbing and not very familiar to Felix, unless he had heard of it through his Jewish wife.[328] The message of Paul terrified Felix,[329] but apparently not enough to lead him to repent. Nevertheless, though he abruptly

323. Rapske, *Paul in Roman Custody,* pp. 166-67, rightly points out that since Paul did not mention that the funds he brought to Jerusalem were communal funds, Felix might well deduce Paul had personal wealth.

324. The Harclean margin of the Syriac adds that it was Drusilla, the Jewess, who asked to hear Paul, and that Felix went only to satisfy her. See Metzger, *Textual Commentary,* p. 491. This is not the impression Luke leaves, especially in view of Felix's seeking of a bribe.

325. δικαιοσυνη is of course a forensic term, but here the term would surely have ethical overtones. The similarity between the summary of the message here before a judge and the message given before the Areopagus in Acts 17 is noteworthy. In both cases judgment (and resurrection) is part of the evangelistic message; see Polhill, *Acts,* p. 486 n. 120.

326. εγκρατεια is a very broad term for self-control.

327. On εγκρατεια meaning chastity, cf. 1 Cor. 7:9; *T. Naphtali* 8:8; *Acts of Paul and Thecla* 4-6. See Schneider, *Die Apostelgeschichte II,* pp. 351-52.

328. Larkin, *Acts,* p. 343, rightly points out the vagueness of Roman beliefs about the afterlife. Felix may have had a vague notion that souls went down into the underworld, where they received rewards or punishments, but it was probably not a significant part of his belief system.

329. εμφοβος is a strengthened or intensified form of φοβος suggesting considerable fright or fear. See Longenecker, *Acts,* p. 542.

dismissed him, he told Paul he would send for him again, and in fact Luke says he sent for him often and conversed with him, but for the wrong sort of reasons — he was hoping for a bribe. The *Lex Repetundarum* (or *Lex Iulia de repetundis*) prohibited anyone holding a position such as Felix's from either soliciting or accepting a bribe either to free or take someone into custody.[330] This law, however, was not infrequently violated by provincial governors, and for an example in Judea we can point to one of Felix's successors, Albinus (A.D. 61-65), whom Josephus tells us explicitly accepted money for these very purposes (*War* 2.14.1).

V. *27* refers to a period of two years, and in view of Acts 24:10 (many years), even allowing for some rhetorical hyperbole, Luke surely does not mean us to see this as the total period of Felix's reign. Rather, it must surely refer to the period of time Paul was in custody under Felix in Caesarea prior to the coming of Porcius Festus. At this point we are helped by Roman coins to date the reigns of Felix and Festus and better identify the time of the handing over of power. I have in my own possession a coin minted during the governorship of Felix in Judea which clearly reads in part on the obverse side KLAY.KAIC, which makes abundantly clear that he was already governor *before* Nero took the throne in about A.D. 54.[331] In addition, there was a change in the Judean provincial coinage attested for Nero's fifth year (A.D. 58/59). As Smallwood says, it is most unlikely that this would be the work of an outgoing procurator, especially since Felix had already minted a large issue of coins previously. It is much more likely to be that of an incoming one.[332] Thus we should likely place the time of the departure of Felix to Rome in A.D. 58, and the arrival of Festus in A.D. 59 (probably during the summer), announced by a new minting of coins.[333] Only the intercession of Pallas, his brother, with Nero spared Felix punishment (*Ant.* 20.182), and nothing is known of his fate after this time. As for Paul, it was not unusual for a governor to leave cases unresolved when he left office.[334]

The overall portrait one is left with of Felix is not positive, and Felix certainly does not pronounce Paul innocent of charges, nor does he really attest to his innocence, though the leniency of custody may be thought to point this way.[335] This, however, may just be Felix covering his bases because

---

330. See Tajara, *The Trial of Paul*, pp. 131-32.

331. See also Reinach, *Jewish Coins*, pp. 40ff.

332. See Smallwood, *The Jews under Roman Rule*, p. 269 n. 40; Cadbury, *Book of Acts in History*, p. 10; Bruce, "Chronological Questions," p. 286.

333. Lüdemann, *Early Christianity*, p. 250 (cf. pp. 248, 251), mistakenly suggests that the two years refers to the length of Felix's term. Cf. Hemer, *Book of Acts*, p. 173.

334. Sherwin-White, *Roman Law and Roman Society*, p. 53, rightly points to Josephus, *Ant.* 20.9.5, which suggests it was unusual for a governor (in this case Albinus) to deal with all pending charges before leaving office.

335. Contra Haenchen, *Acts*, p. 658.

Paul is a Roman citizen. As Cassidy points out, three negative things are said about Felix toward the end of this section: (1) Felix is terrified by Paul's message and dismisses Paul without responding positively to the gospel; (2) Felix seeks a bribe; and (3) Felix seeks to protect himself rather than do justice, and so leaves Paul in jail as a favor to the Jewish authorities.[336] "Such a report clearly does not portray an impartial Roman governor."[337] Luke, then, is not interested in these chapters in suggesting that Roman officials were all fair-minded or attested to Paul's innocence. The response is of a mixed quality, as is the character of various of these officials.[338]

It may be in order to ask in passing what Luke might have been doing during this two-year span, other than perhaps attending to Paul. Longenecker's suggestion that he used this time to investigate "everything closely from the beginning" commends itself. Here in Israel he would have access both to traditions about the time of Jesus and also to what happened in the Jerusalem church between about A.D. 35 and 57, the time about which Paul could inform him very little. Perhaps also "he had begun to sketch out during this time the structure and scope of his two-volume work we know as Luke-Acts."[339]

G. An Appealing Time with Festus (25:1-12)

About Felix's successor, Porcius Festus, very little can be said, for our sources are limited to what we find in Acts 25–26 and in Josephus, *Ant.* 20.182-97 and *War* 2.271. We know that he was the member of the famous *gens Porcia*, and that his tenure in office in Judea was very brief. He seems to have died in office in A.D. 61 or 62, after only about two or three years of service. This is unfortunate, for if the impression Josephus leaves is correct, he was much more honest and able than either his predecessor or his successor as procurator.[340] Josephus says he acted with dispatch to get rid of the "daggermen"[341] and bandits in the land. *Ant.* 20.8.10 says he attacked and killed yet another messianic imposter who had led a multitude into the wilderness.[342] This in fact is the view "from above" as reported by Josephus, and it suggests that the Jewish authorities, wishing for the preservation of the status quo, would have found

336. Cassidy, *Society and Politics,* p. 106.
337. Ibid.
338. See Tannehill, *Narrative Unity of Luke-Acts,* 2:302.
339. Longenecker, *Acts,* pp. 542-43.
340. Ehrhardt, *The Acts of the Apostles,* p. 117, calls him "the one honourable governor Rome ever sent to Judea."
341. On which cf. pp. 235ff. above.
342. Cf. pp. 235ff. above on the Egyptian.

in Festus an ally, if not a friend. They, too, wanted to do away with the troublemakers, among whom they numbered Paul. It is, then, wholly believable that Festus might be willing to "do the Jewish authorities a favor" (cf. below on v. 9) and accept a change of venue for this trial, if not also a change of jurisdiction (cf. below). A possible synchronism which helps us date various events can be derived from comparing Eusebius and Josephus on Festus. Eusebius refers to Festus in his chronological tables and places his coming to Judea in the tenth year of Agrippa II. Josephus (*War* 2.14.4, 284) says the beginning of Agrippa's reign was in A.D. 50. His tenth year would have been 59-60. This comports with what we have concluded about the terminus of Felix's reign and when Festus became procurator.

Porcius Festus seems to have been a person who acted with some dispatch. *Acts 25:1* says that only three days after arriving in Israel he went up to Jerusalem to meet with the Jewish authorities.[343] This was wise because, as J. R. Fears has put it, "crucial . . . in securing continuity and stability was the network of personal alliances with the ruling classes throughout the empire. These were the practical material sinews of imperial rule."[344] The interests of peace, security, and justice had to be worked for in concert with the local elite. Festus surely knew of the volatile situation in the land he was about to rule, and this made the securing of these social networks of support and power all the more crucial. What he could not have known is that this elite did not speak for a very large segment of Jewish society, as it did not have their trust, nor could he have known the extent of corruption among the elite and the lengths they would go to stay in power and rid themselves of troublemakers.[345]

Josephus tells us, for example, that during the reign of Ishmael b. Phiabi as high priest, who was appointed by Herod Agrippa II near the end of Felix's reign (*Ant.* 20.179, 194-96), some of the "influential" or "powers," by which is meant the ruling class, tried to beat some of their political rivals by using gangs to hurl stones and seize the tithes due to the poorer priests (*Ant.* 20.179-81). He also tells us of the power struggle that existed between some of the elite and members of Herod's family who continued to be influential, such as Herod Agrippa II. "The leading figures in the factional fray were thus certain incumbent and retired High Priests and junior members of the

343. It is possible that because this portion of Acts 25, like Acts 24, is riddled with legal and technical terminology (on which see Dupont, *Études sur les Actes des Apôtres*, pp. 529-41), scholars have been bewitched into thinking that these procurators were and would necessarily act strictly according to Roman law. This is a dubious assumption, especially in view of the general track record of procurators in this far-flung province of the Empire.

344. Fears, "Rome."

345. On this whole matter, see the helpful work of Goodman, *The Ruling Class of Judaea*, especially chap. 6 on why the ruling class failed.

Herodian house."[346] Ishmael, for example, fell out with Agrippa II over the building of a tower which would allow him to see into the temple (*Ant.* 20.189-96). "Ishmael was, then, deliberately and provocatively opposed to Agrippa."[347] But Ishmael did not act alone. He acted in concert with former high priests who were still influential such as Ananias, who seems to have remained influential until about A.D. 66 (cf. *Ant.* 20.205, 209).

The above tells us some significant things about our narrative. (1) It is not surprising that *v. 2* tells us that Festus met with high priests (plural) and "the first of Judea" (i.e., members of the ruling elite). He was seeking as wide a base of support as possible, and his interest was not just in those who were actually in power but also in those who wielded power whether officially or behind the scenes. (2) In view of what Josephus tells us about the way Ishmael and the elites dealt with their rivals, it is totally believable that they might be party to an ambush of Paul. (3) That Festus wanted stable alliances with all the local elite is also shown by his consulting of Agrippa and Bernice. This consultation and Paul's appearance before them are quite believable since the Jewish elites were not all united, but rather were factionalized. The regiving of Paul's defense speech is also believable since Agrippa had not personally had the matter presented to him.

In fact Festus may have turned to Agrippa for help in the Paul case, precisely because the other rival elite had been no real help in resolving the Paul matter legally. Agrippa had close ties with Rome — indeed, what power and wealth he had was because of Rome — and Festus was more likely to have known and trusted Agrippa. That he did trust Agrippa more is shown by his favoring Agrippa over Ishmael in the matter of the tower (*Ant.* 20.193). Furthermore, Agrippa may have been very willing to agree with the transfer of Paul to Rome, just to spite Ishmael and his circle of power.

What is often overlooked in the discussions of these chapters by biblical scholars is the difference between Roman law and Roman officials, between what was legally the case and what was actually the case. In other words, what is overlooked is the social networks and channels of influence. As we shall see, Roman law was indeed on Paul's side — he was not guilty of a chargeable offense. This does not mean that local Roman officials would necessarily be on Paul's side just because he was a Roman citizen. While Festus appears to have been more honest and less venal than either Felix or Albinus, this does not mean in the end he was not subject to "influence" by means of the elite in the land, even if at first he resisted such influence. Since throughout the Empire provincial governors depended on the support of the local elites to secure peace, order, and justice, this inevitably made these governors subject to the influence of the elites.

346. Ibid., p. 141.
347. Ibid., p. 142.

The reciprocity conventions also made this almost inevitable. If the Jewish elites cooperated with the procurator, they would expect "favors" in return.

The situation was much more complex than Haenchen knew.[348] Luke is not portraying Festus as taking Paul's part in this matter, any more than he really portrayed Felix doing so. Neither exonerated Paul, and neither is truly a witness for the defense except by implication and unofficially, though Paul has the law on his side. Their actions were more governed by the social than the legal situation. As Cassidy says:

> Haenchen . . . encounters great difficulty in trying to explain why Luke does not present Paul insisting on continuation [or resolution] of his trial at Caesarea instead of appealing to have it shifted to Rome. . . . However, once one drops the false premise that Luke wanted to portray Roman officials taking Paul's part in various situations, the difficulties concerning the appeal passage vanish. For, read without presuppositions about political apologetic, the passage clearly shows Festus colluding with Paul's enemies. It thus comes as no surprise that Paul acts to remove his case from Festus' jurisdiction.[349]

V. 2 tells us that the high priests and their elite supporters[350] gave a report to Festus against Paul and that "they kept on begging him"[351] and, according to v. 3, requested a "favor" (χαρις; in Latin, gratia), namely, that Festus transfer Paul to Jerusalem. The language of "favor" is a significant theme, which we have already seen raised in 24:27. It occurs here and in v. 9 and will recur significantly in the form of a verb in vv. 11 and 16. As Tannehill rightly points out, at least from v. 9 on, one must take the narrator's word that Festus's primary motive for suggesting a change of venue was to do the Jewish authorities a "favor," not merely that he was at a loss as to how to investigate theological questions (v. 20).[352] Bias enters the picture, and justice ceases to be blind when Festus succumbs to the desire to placate the Jewish elite and do them a favor in the Paul matter.[353] Luke tells us in v. 3b that the intent was not even to allow Paul to get to Jerusalem. He was to be ambushed along the way. It is a measure of the importance the Jewish officials placed on this matter that they not only confronted Festus with this matter as soon as he came to town but also were willing to go to such lengths to eliminate the Paul problem.

---

348. Haenchen, *Acts*, pp. 668-70.
349. Cassidy, *Society and Politics*, p. 202 n. 35.
350. Josephus speaks on various occasions of the δυνατοι, the men of power, cf. *War* 1.242; *Ant.* 14.324.
351. The imperfect tense verb παρεκαλουν.
352. Tannehill, *Narrative Unity of Luke-Acts*, 2:306.
353. Ibid.: "Festus' desire to grant a favor to the Jewish leaders shows sensitivity to power relations in his province."

Vv. 4-5 tell us that at least initially Festus resisted being importuned in this way. Paul was being kept at Caesarea, Festus planned to go there shortly, and so those who had authority could come down with Festus, "and if there is anything amiss or out of place (ατοπος)[354] about the man, let them [the authorities] accuse him." It is as if Festus is reopening the case all over again, starting from the beginning.[355] This being the case, what follows in Caesarea could and probably should be seen as another official preliminary hearing, part of the investigating by Festus of what the real issues under debate were (see especially v. 20).[356] Festus, having *imperium,* would hold his own trial and not rely purely on the documents and judgments left by his predecessor, whatever they may have been. V. 5, then, would be about the sort of formal accusatorial report that had already been given before Felix at 24:1.[357] What Festus has done is to assert his authority, making clear that he is in charge of the matter and will settle the case in his own time and way. It may be, however, that Tannehill is also right that "his first response in Jerusalem was the response of a political novice not yet aware of who hold the power and what their interests are."[358]

V. 6 indicates that after a brief stay of from eight to ten days in Jerusalem, Festus went to Caesarea and on the very next day sat down on the rostrum[359] and ordered Paul to be brought forth, just as Felix had (24:2). *V. 7* describes a very adversarial situation. Paul is surrounded by his foes, who make many and serious charges against him which, Luke reminds us, they could not prove. In view of Paul's response, we must assume that the charges were both theological and political, with the latter obviously being the more serious ones in a Roman setting. Taking a straightforward approach, *v. 8* tells us that Paul asserted in his *apologia* that he had committed no offense against Jewish law or the temple or Caesar.[360] This last adds a new note to the defense. The term

354. Here the term surely has the overtones of wrongdoing; cf. Luke 23:41; 2 Thess. 3:2.

355. See Johnson, *Acts,* p. 420.

356. See Keener, *Bible Background Commentary,* p. 396.

357. Lüdemann, *Early Christianity,* pp. 252-54, sees the Felix and Festus scenes as a case of Luke manufacturing a doublet. In his view, there was no trial before Felix, only before Festus, but Luke, having used up his speeches in Acts 24, resorts to summarizing briefly in Acts 25. There are, however, too many differences between the two chapters for this to be a wholly convincing conclusion. Paul's appeal to Rome comes only here, with no hint of it in Acts 24, and Roman provincial justice often involved the carrying over of cases from one procurator to the next, with duplication of various parts of the legal process.

358. *Narrative Unity of Luke-Acts,* 2:306.

359. βημα (cf. Acts 12:21; 18:21, 16-17; 2 Cor. 5:10) has no obvious English equivalent, but it refers to a judgment seat on a raised platform where a judge would hear cases and render a decision. See Josephus, *War* 2.172.

360. Paul's remarks are undoubtedly forensic, but they are too brief for any sort of significant rhetorical analysis. But cf. Soards, *Speeches in Acts,* pp. 119-20.

"Caesar" was of course a family name before it was ever a title, but it was especially properly used of all the early emperors from Augustus through Nero since they were all from the Julian gens. This mention of Caesar prepares us for Paul's appeal.

V. 9 indicates that Festus's response was, since he wished to do the Jewish authorities a favor,[361] to ask Paul, "Do you wish to go up to Jerusalem and there be judged concerning these things before me?"[362] It is not at all clear what Festus is actually proposing. Is he suggesting a mere change of venue with a Roman trial in Jerusalem?[363] Is he also suggesting a change of jurisdiction? Is he suggesting Paul go appear before the Sanhedrin, and that Festus would merely ratify or implement whatever they decided?[364] On the surface of things, it would appear that Festus was reassuring Paul that he was not relinquishing jurisdiction — Paul would still be judged "before me," said Festus. Paul, however, appears to have read something else between the lines.

The response of Paul in vv. 10-11 should be seen as vigorous and something of a rebuke to Festus. Paul says he is standing before the judgment seat of Caesar already, "where it is necessary for me to be judged." Paul says emphatically that he has done no wrong to the Jews, "as you know very well." In v. 11 Paul shows his good character and that he is not trying to escape death. He is perfectly willing to be judged by Roman law and to die if he has committed some crime worthy of death. Paul's overall strategy is clearly to remain under Roman jurisdiction, even if he had to go over Festus's head.[365] Paul then says in a pointed way that if there is nothing to the Jewish charges against him, no one can give him, as a favor, over to them (χαρισασθαι).[366] Then, finally, Paul plays his trump card with the simple "I appeal to Caesar" (cf. Tacitus, Ann. 6.5.2). We will speak in detail about this appeal and its ramifications in the excursus below, but here it is sufficient to point out, as Cassidy does, that "Paul does not lightly or cavalierly exercise his right of appealing to Caesar. Similar to the earlier two instances in which he claimed his rights of citizenship, Luke again depicts Paul asserting his right to appeal

---

361. Perhaps his discussions with the Jewish authorities before Paul appeared, and perhaps even discussions he had while traveling to Caesarea, had led him to conclude that in the interests of "peace" and winning friends and influencing people, he ought to try to cooperate with the Jewish authorities in this matter. He would have to work with them again over a period of years, while the Paul situation was simply a temporary problem.

362. Note Haenchen's remark, Acts, p. 670, that a procurator's question is basically the same as his decision.

363. See Longenecker, Acts, p. 545; Marshall, Acts, p. 384; Polhill, Acts, p. 490.

364. See Larkin, Acts, p. 347. Williams, Acts, p. 408, suggests that this change would imply Paul's exoneration of Roman charges. Cf. Tajara, The Trial of Paul, pp. 140-41.

365. See Tajara, The Trial of Paul, p. 142.

366. On this translation see Tannehill, Narrative Unity of Luke-Acts, 2:307.

before a small, predominantly Roman, group and only at the point in the proceedings when he could no longer tolerate a course of action being proposed by a Roman official. . . . Paul exercised his right of appeal only under considerable pressure."[367] Indeed, in view of Acts 28:19, one must say he felt compelled to do so, and did not bring up the matter *before* he felt so compelled.[368]

This sudden appeal to Caesar stopped the judicial hearing[369] and caused Festus to consult with his own judicial council normally made up of Roman citizens who lived in that area, military personnel and officials who attended the governor, among whom would likely be at least one expert in Roman (and Jewish?) law. This council was only an advisory body.[370] The discussion may have been about whether the appeal should be granted, if one agrees with Garnsey that Festus was not obligated to grant such an appeal.[371] Sherwin-White and A. H. M. Jones, however, argue that the procurator was obliged to honor such an appeal in an *extra ordinem* case.[372] If this is so, then the council will have been consulted to determine whether this was in fact an *extra ordinem* sort of case.[373]

Even if Paul's case could have been subsumed under the ordinary sort of crimes, it would apparently have fallen into the category of treason (acting against the emperor), and this matter was beyond the authority of the provincial matter since it involved the *dignitas* and final "authority" of the emperor directly.[374] Whatever the nature of this consultation, we are told the result was that Festus came forth and proclaimed that, having appealed to Caesar, to Caesar he would go. It is important at this juncture to bear in mind that Paul is not making an appeal of a verdict already rendered. What we are dealing with here is a case of *provocatio*, not *appellatio*. The disposition of Paul's case had not yet been determined. These matters must be discussed in some detail at this point.

367. Cassidy, *Society and Politics*, p. 109.
368. On the general import of this see Hemer, *Book of Acts*, p. 131 n. 92.
369. This cessation was required by law; see Ulpian, *Digest* 48.6.7.
370. Tajara, *The Trial of Paul*, pp. 148-49.
371. See Garnsey, "The *Lex Iulia*," pp. 184-85.
372. Sherwin-White, *Roman Law and Roman Society*, pp. 57-70; Jones, *Studies in Roman Government*, pp. 53-65.
373. There seem to have been a few cases under the *ordo* in which a governor could try to execute a Roman citizen in the provinces, without acting contrary to the laws which spoke of *provocatio* (cf. pp. 727ff. below), for example in cases where kidnapping, violence, or counterfeiting were involved. See Tajara, *The Trial of Paul*, pp. 150-51.
374. Sherwin-White, *Roman Law and Roman Society*, p. 65.

A Closer Look — Justice, Citizenship, and Appeals in the Provinces —

There was during the Empire a steady widening of the franchise of who might be a Roman citizen.[375] By the mid-50s A.D. the situation had not yet become even close to what it would be in the late Empire when everyone but slaves was considered a Roman citizen of some sort (after A.D. 212 when Caracalla granted wholesale citizenship), but Claudius's reign had extended the rights and privileges considerably. This in turn affected the way justice was administered not only in Rome but also, and perhaps especially, in the provinces. Justice in the provinces was not something one could get just any time, for the proconsul had to make assize tours through various cities under his charge, and one had to appear before the procurator when he was in one's area.[376] As Burton says, "vast though the powers of the proconsul were in theory, there were severe physical restraints upon the manner in which he could exercise them; his interventions were bound to be unevenly spread geographically, and sporadic in their frequency."[377] This is of relevance for our discussion because it meant that (1) there could be long delays in rendering justice in particular cases, especially if they were carried over from one administration to another; (2) circumstances would often prevent the procurator from thoroughly investigating a matter. The temptation to render summary justice and get on with the next case or to the next town would be great, as would the temptation to pass cases on to other authorities, whether inferior or superior, if one could legally do so;[378] (3) as the Empire developed, the rule of the emperor through his emissaries became more intrusive in local affairs, and this was often greatly resented. No doubt it galled the Jewish authorities that Caesarea was the provincial seat of power and that they had to go there to try to obtain justice about some matter. For them the temptation was great to take matters or even stones into their own hands and settle things. Notice, for example, that during the interregnum between the time of Festus and the coming of Albinus the Jewish authorities (e.g., Ananus), recognizing a power vacuum and thus a window of opportunity, willfully took matters into their own hands and had James, the brother of Jesus, killed (*Ant.* 20.200).

Roman citizens cannot have been plentiful in Judea in the mid-50s, and Jewish ones even more rare. Thus, there were probably few precedents in dealing with a case like Paul's, a person apparently caught between Jewish and Roman law. The question of jurisdiction must have been very puzzling for the procurators in view of the fact that the accusers stressed political charges but really wanted to judge Paul themselves, while Paul stressed theological matters but insisted on Roman justice.

The sort of appeal which is called *provocatio* was originally a matter of appealing to the people, but during the Empire Caesar took the people's place as the court of last resort. In the early Empire, before all the ramifications of Empire were worked

---

375. See the discussion, pp. 679ff. above, on citizenship.

376. See the helpful discussion in Burton, "Proconsuls, Assizes."

377. Ibid., p. 106.

378. One must also bear in mind that justice in antiquity was often a matter of which advocate or witness was the most persuasive in court, for thorough investigation of a crime and what we would call forensics were unknown in the ancient world.

out, for example before appellate jurisdictions were all made clear and became regular and systematic, emperors apparently were more willing to take appeals from provincial citizens than was the case in the second century and later.[379] "The *imperium* of the magistrates was inhibited by the right of *provocatio*,"[380] which in turn meant that the actual power of the emperor was increased as judicial power became more centralized. In fact, Augustus had encouraged appeal in general as he established the Empire.[381] In regard to the issue of whether *provocatio* functioned outside Rome as well as within its boundaries, there can be little doubt (cf. Cicero, *Verr.* 2.5.63).[382] The *Lex Julia* had affirmed or reaffirmed such a right of appeal in strong terms, and had made clear the penalties for a magistrate's interfering with the process: "Anyone invested with authority who puts to death or orders to be put to death, tortures, scourges, condemns, or directs a Roman citizen who first appealed to the people, and now has appealed to the Emperor, to be placed in chains, shall be condemned under the *Lex Julia* relating to public violence. The punishment of this crime is death, where the parties are of inferior station; deportation to an island where they are of superior station" (Paulus, *Sent.* 5.26.1; *Digest* 48.6-7). This law, then, protected the citizen both from coercion by a procurator and also from his exercising his right of capital punishment.[383] As Balsdon says, on paper the most valuable element in the citizenship package, especially if one lived in the provinces, was the right of appeal to the emperor.[384] There might be little need for such appeal if one was faced with a good governor, but Festus was new, and his judgments an unknown quantity. Clearly, Paul does not trust him; indeed, he accuses him of bias. Furthermore, precisely because Festus couldn't determine what the crime or issue really was between Paul and his accusers, he had to treat the matter as *extra ordinem* or assume a worst-case scenario among the *ordo* sort of crimes and treat the matter as treason.[385] In either case, the resolution of the matter was beyond his *imperium*.

While Festus appears to have had little knowledge of Jewish law and thought, Paul must have known that he had such a right of appeal, and also that he would get no justice before the Sanhedrin. His appeal is both legal and logical in view of the above discussion, and as Rapske says, it had its "appealing" aspects: "The advantages of appealing to the Emperor . . . [included that] . . . it could interrupt what might otherwise be an inexorable progress to personal disaster, remove one from a biased or hostile court, and, finally, perhaps put the defendant before a more favorably inclined tribunal."[386] The downside of an appeal is that it could prove costly, but this would surely have seemed the lesser of the two evils to Paul. There is, finally, one other reason why Paul appealed, a theological one. He had been promised by Christ that he would testify before the emperor. He may have felt led to take part in the process of making

379. See Jones, "Imperial and Senatorial Jurisdiction," p. 476.
380. Ibid., p. 478.
381. Ibid., p. 475.
382. See the discussion in Rapske, *Paul in Roman Custody*, pp. 50-51.
383. Tajara, *The Trial of Paul*, p. 146.
384. Balsdon, *Romans and Aliens*, p. 93.
385. Ibid., p. 94, defines it as involving a crime of "indeterminate" nature.
386. Rapske, *Paul in Roman Custody*, p. 55.

this opportunity possible.[387] In fact in v. 10 Paul specifies that it is a must (δεῖ) that he be judged before the tribunal of Caesar.[388]

Finally, it may be asked why Paul would appeal to Caesar, when this Caesar was none other than Nero. This question overlooks the fact that the early years of Nero's reign, especially the period from A.D. 54 to about 61 or 62,[389] bore few adumbrations of Nero's later injustices (Suetonius, *Nero* 9ff.). Nero during this period was under the tutelage of one of the great Roman philosophers, the Stoic Seneca, and he was also greatly helped along in this period by the prefect of the Praetorian Guard, Afranius Burrus. Some even saw this period as something of a golden age for Rome, though that is stretching things a bit.[390] The point is that Paul in A.D. 59 might well hope for better things in Rome than he could get at the hands of a Felix or a Festus. As the above discussion suggests, and Johnson says about 24:24–25:12 in general, "the better our knowledge of the social and historical context, the more plausible Luke's account becomes."[391]

H. A Royal Visit (25:13-27)

Paul's appeal to the emperor placed Festus in a difficult spot.[392] He would have to write an official report (see below on v. 26) specifying the charges that stood against Paul, and the reason for the appeal. On the one hand, if the charges were insubstantial or not sufficient under Roman law, the emperor would surely wonder about Festus's competence. Why had he not resolved the matter in Judea, one way or another, even if it meant dismissing the matter and setting Paul free? On the other hand, if Paul, a Roman citizen, had appealed to Rome, there must have been something about the situation that was grave enough to warrant this action. What was Festus not telling the emperor that he ought to know about the situation in Judea involving the Jewish authorities?

387. See the discussion of Cosgrove, "The Divine Δεῖ in Luke-Acts," p. 183.
388. See Soards, *The Speeches in Acts*, p. 120.
389. That is, well before the famous fire in Rome.
390. This should not be overdone, but Tacitus is clear enough that beginning in A.D. 62 things took a turn for the worse during the first of the *maiestas* trials, because of the death of Burrus and the withdrawal of Seneca. See the helpful discussion in Griffin, *Nero*, pp. 83-103.
391. Johnson, *Acts*, p. 424.
392. On the verb επικαλουμαι used of an appeal, see Acts 25:11, 12, 25; 26:39; 28:19, and *New Docs*, 3 (1979), sec. 20, p. 85.

These are the sorts of thoughts that were likely running through Festus's mind as he sought a way to write his report so that he himself would not fall under suspicion. As *fortuna* would have it, he was about to receive help from an unexpected quarter — Jewish nobility.

V. *13* tells us that several days after the hearing had come to an abrupt conclusion, King Agrippa and Bernice arrived at Caesarea to officially welcome Festus to the land. The Agrippa in question is Herod Agrippa II (A.D. 27-100), whose Roman name was Marcus Julius Agrippa and who was the very last ruler in the famous or infamous Herodian line. He was the son of Agrippa I[393] and the great-grandson of Herod the Great. He was raised in Rome at the court of Emperor Claudius and was a personal favorite of that ruler. Though Claudius would have liked to make him the ruler of Israel in A.D. 44 when his father died, he was still only a teenager of seventeen and was deemed too young to handle the difficult situation in the Holy Land. This is why Palestine became a Roman province in 44. In 50, however, Claudius found a safe way to make Agrippa II a monarch in his native region, giving him the small kingdom of Chalcis, which was north and east of Judea. In 53 Claudius gave him a better situation, exchanging the kingdom of Chalcis for Herod Philip's tetrarchy and also Abilene, Trachonitis, and Acra. In 56 Nero added to Agrippa's realm the Galilean cities of Tarichea and Tiberias and the surrounding territory along with the city of Julias in Perea and fourteen small villages in the same area (cf. Josephus, *War* 2.220-33, 247, 252; *Ant.* 20.104, 138, 159). In honor of Nero he changed the name of his capital from Caesarea Philippi to Neronias. It was quite natural for Agrippa as ruler of the neighboring territory to come to pay his respects to the new Judean governor, especially since Agrippa was a supporter of Rome and interested in Roman affairs.[394] Agrippa's importance was not limited to the territory over which he ruled, because he also had been appointed by Claudius curator of the temple in Jerusalem, giving him the power to appoint the high priest, possession of the priestly vestments worn on Yom Kippur, and the task of looking after the temple treasury. It would be natural for Festus, for a variety of reasons, including Agrippa's power over the temple and priestly apparatus and his ties with Rome, to view Agrippa as a *higher* Jewish authority than the ones he had previously been dealing with, indeed to regard Agrippa as the king of the Jews.[395] A further reason why Festus might lay Paul's case before Agrippa is

393. On which see pp. 228ff. above.

394. Notice how later Agrippa tried hard but in vain to prevent the Jews from revolting against Rome (*War* 2.343-407), and when the war was in progress he was clearly on Rome's side in the matter.

395. According to the inscriptions his title was Βασιλευς μεγας φιλοκισαρ ευσεβης και φιλορωμαιος (*OGIS* 419; 420). Notice the emphasis on his love of the emperor and things Roman.

that in his report to the emperor he would be able to assert that Agrippa, someone respected by Nero, had concurred in the way he handled matters. For these reasons, it is historically very believable that Festus might have consulted Agrippa on the Paul matter.

With Agrippa was his younger (by one year) sister Bernice, who had married her uncle the former king of Chalcis, but when he died in A.D. 48 she returned to live with her brother. This in due course led to rumors that she was having an incestuous relationship with her brother (on the Eastern pattern of the sister/consort/wife, cf. *Ant.* 20.145-47; Juvenal, *Sat.* 6.156-60), which in turn forced her to make a marriage of convenience with Polemon, the king of Cilicia, in 63. This lasted but three years, after which she returned to her brother's house. At the very end of the Jewish War she became the Roman general Titus's mistress and returned to Rome and lived with him. Though Titus wanted to marry her, Roman anti-Semitism was such that the very relationship, never mind a marriage, caused a major scandal (Tacitus, *Hist.* 2.81; Suetonius, *Titus* 7; Juvenal, *Sat.* 6.156ff.). In the end Titus, because of his political ambitions (he became emperor in 79), had to dismiss Bernice.[396]

V. 14 informs us that since Agrippa and Bernice were staying for several days, Festus laid Paul's case before the king. In what follows in vv. 14-22 we find a rehearsal of material that, for the most part, we have already heard about earlier in this chapter. It may be, since it seems unlikely that Luke would have access to the private discussions of Festus and Agrippa and Bernice, that here Luke followed the historical convention of making the persons say what they were likely to have said on the occasion.[397] What is of interest for our purposes is noting the differences from what we have already learned in 25:1-12 as a revelation of Festus's attempt to put himself in the best possible light before this Jewish ruler.

First, he implicitly blames Felix for not resolving the matter — Paul is left in prison by Felix (v. 14). Secondly, he portrays himself as the great upholder of Roman law against the importuning of the Jewish authorities that

---

396. She returned once more to Rome in A.D. 79 when Titus began to rule, but Titus would not see her, and in the end she returned again to Palestine (see Dio Cassius, *Hist. of Rome* 56.18). It is interesting that inscriptions call her a queen (Βασιλισσα — an inscription in Athens, *CIG* 361) and *regina* in Latin; see Hemer, *Book of Acts*, p. 174 n. 27. The terms were usually reserved for reigning queens, but perhaps she was viewed this way at various points in her career.

397. See pp. 116ff. above on προσωποποιια, in this case the creating of a speech that is nonetheless in character and appropriate. Cf. even so conservative a commentator as Marshall, *Acts*, p. 386, and also Williams, *Acts*, p. 411. Longenecker is right to point out that Luke may have deduced what was said from the hearing that followed and the resultant actions. Longenecker, *Acts*, p. 547. I would not rule out a court informant; see Larkin, *Acts*, p. 349 and the note on 25:13-22.

Paul be sentenced (vv. 15-16). Thirdly, he portrays himself as a person who acts with dispatch, who will dispense justice in good time and order (v. 17). Fourthly, he cites the incompetence of the accusers. They did not accuse Paul of any of the crimes he was expecting them to charge him with (v. 18); rather, it appeared to be a purely internal Jewish matter about certain points of religion (v. 19). Next, he suggests that this matter left him at a loss as to how to investigate or examine such charges (since they were not Roman charges),[398] and so quite naturally he asked Paul if he wished to go up to Jerusalem and be tried there on such (religious) charges (v. 20). Nothing whatsoever is said here about Festus's desire to do the Jewish authorities a favor. Festus is too busy portraying himself as an able governor doing what seemed right and fair in a difficult situation. Then, says Festus, Paul had appealed to be kept in custody for the decision of the emperor, an action Festus will later suggest is illogical (v. 27) since there were no substantive charges against him. In fact, as Cassidy says, Paul had not appealed to stay in custody; he had simply appealed to the emperor.[399]

As Tannehill has warned us, too many commentators have been beguiled into taking Festus's report at face value, rather than as a self-serving report. But the voice of Festus is not the voice of Luke, and his words should be evaluated critically.[400] The overall net effect of this portrayal of Festus is that he is revealed to be not only self-serving but also a novice. Indeed, to judge from the way he refers to "a certain Jesus" (25:19), he seems not even to have heard of Jesus.

This sort of self-serving rhetoric is continued in what follows in the hearing scene as well.[401] In v. 24 he may be referring to the whole Jewish people clamoring for his action against Paul (but see below), but more clearly in v. 25 he places the blame for the outcome of the judicial hearing on Paul and his appeal (note the contrast between "I" and "but this fellow himself . . .").[402] Festus paints a favorable picture of himself, but neither he nor Felix was willing to bite the bullet and do the brave thing — dismiss the charges against Paul

---

398. Cassidy, *Society and Politics*, p. 11, is probably right that Festus's words about being at a loss are not a confession of incompetence but a plea for sympathy (or help) from his listeners.

399. See ibid., p. 111.

400. See Tannehill, *Narrative Unity of Luke-Acts*, 2:309-10. He advised that we "should be inclined to trust statements that go beyond the narrator's account in 25.6-12 if they do not conflict with anything there and show a perspective that harmonizes with the dominant perspective of Acts. When there is tension between the narrator's and Festus' accounts and Festus' interests are being served, however, we should suspect bias."

401. The speech of Festus to Agrippa reflects more polished Greek, including in v. 16 the use of two optatives (εχοι and λαβοι). As Tajara, *The Trial of Paul*, p. 156, suggests, Luke shows that the rhetoric fit the occasion.

402. See Tannehill, *Narrative Unity of Luke-Acts*, 2:313.

as frivolous (or at least not such as Roman law required action upon) and set him free. With this in mind we must attend to some of the details in vv. 14-22.

Festus's presentation of things is dramatic and progressive, with a series of imperfects used to indicate the action (was bringing, was suspecting, was claiming, was asking).[403] In *v. 15* the noun καταδικην probably has its juridical sense of condemnation (cf. Plutarch, *Coriol.* 20.4; Josephus, *War* 4.5.2). The Jewish authorities were not asking for just any sort of judgment but rather specifically a negative one against Paul. In v. 16 εθος refers to what was the legal custom among the Romans. Festus is citing the well-known principle here of a defendant having the right to be accused and to defend himself in the presence of his accusers (see Ulpian, *Digest* 48.17.1; Appian, *Roman Hist.: Civil War* 3.54; Josephus, *Ant.* 16.258).[404] *V. 18* refers to when Paul's accusers stood around him and brought charges, but not of the sort of evils Festus was expecting to hear about.[405] Rather, as *v. 19* says, it had to do with "their own δεσιδαιμονιας." This last word can be taken in a positive sense (religion), or a negative sense (superstition; cf. Acts 17:22). On the one hand, Festus might have been sensitive in view of the Jewishness of Agrippa and Bernice not to call Jewish religion a *superstitio.* On the other hand, as Johnson suggests, he may have seen Agrippa as a Hellenized Jew and an outsider to such religious disputes and so spoke in a negative way.[406] In fact the word *superstitio* was almost always pejorative,[407] and δεισιδαιμονια frequently was (e.g., Theophrastus, *Characters* 16.1); thus the negative sense is more probable. V. 19b also refers to "a certain man Jesus who had died, but whom Paul asserted to be alive." It is believable that this would be how an outsider would put the matter, but what is of especial note is that Paul had not specifically mentioned Jesus in the previous proceedings, unless of course we are meant to think that Luke had deliberately edited the reference out of his source material for the earlier occurrences so that he could gradually develop the resurrection theme in Acts 22–26 from more general to more specific in character.[408]

V. 20 indicates that Festus was puzzled, or at a loss about how to investigate[409] the questions under dispute. *V. 21* reflects Festus's interpreta-

---

403. See Larkin, *Acts,* pp. 350-51.

404. See the discussion in Dupont, *Etudes sur les Actes des Apotres,* pp. 527-52. It was indeed one of the major points of Roman jurisprudence that an accuser must face the accused and make his or her charges in person in court.

405. There may be here a reflection of the legal phrase "of which I could take cognizance" *(de quibus cognoscere volebam).* See Hemer, *Book of Acts,* p. 131.

406. See Johnson, *Acts,* p. 426.

407. See Ross, "Superstitio."

408. As I think is likely. See Soards, *The Speeches in Acts,* p. 121, and pp. 4ff. above.

409. Ζητησιν could refer to investigation here (see Johnson, *Acts,* p. 426), but it could also refer to a matter of dispute or debate, equivalent to the Latin *quaestio* (Tajara, *The Trial of Paul,* p. 158).

tion of Paul's appeal (see above).⁴¹⁰ It may be a correct interpretation, but Cassidy is more likely right that Paul would have preferred release and freedom (and going to Rome on his own terms as a free man).⁴¹¹ He appealed to Caesar; he did not appeal to be kept under guard until he could appear before the emperor. Caesar in v. 21 is called Σεβαστός, the Greek equivalent of *augustus*, a word which in itself meant something like venerable (deserving veneration, if used of a person)⁴¹² or sacred (of a thing).⁴¹³ The title was first conferred on Octavian by the Senate in 27 B.C. (*Res gestae divi Augusti* 34), but later it was bestowed on subsequent emperors, becoming, like Caesar, a title for the emperor. We seem in fact to have a Greek equivalent of a technical Latin phrase *a cognitionibus Augusti* (*IG* 14.1072). The meaning would be for the full judicial investigation of and trial by the emperor.⁴¹⁴ Festus thus orders Paul to be held until he could be sent to the emperor. "Luke shows neither shock nor surprise at such creative shaping of the story. Politicians do such things."⁴¹⁵

V. 22 tells us that Agrippa's response to all this was that he should like to hear the man himself.⁴¹⁶ Many have noted the parallels between this narrative and the appearance of Jesus before Herod Antipas and its sequel (cf. Luke 23:6-12). Both Herods expressed a desire to meet or hear the person in question (cf. Luke 23:8). Both do indeed meet the party in question, but they do not determine the issue. Both also appear before a Roman governor. Both have Roman officials say they could find nothing chargeable against them under Roman law. Neither should have been on trial in the first place.⁴¹⁷ These parallels can of course be overdone, since Jesus goes on to be unjustly crucified, but Luke neither says nor implies any such outcome for Paul.⁴¹⁸ In any case, Festus informs Agrippa he will hear Paul on the next day.

V. 23 describes a state occasion, complete with full regalia and much

---

410. Itgig adds here "and since I was not able to judge him, I commanded . . ." after the reference to the request to be kept in custody for the emperor. See Metzger, *Textual Commentary*, p. 493.

411. Cassidy, *Society and Politics*, p. 203, is probably right that the proper translation is "appealed to be kept under guard," but this Luke clearly never suggests Paul did, and so Festus is distorting things here.

412. Literally the term meant someone who was augmented or lifted up above ordinary mortals (e.g., in the case of an *apotheosis*). See Longenecker, *Acts*, p. 551.

413. See Tajara, *The Trial of Paul*, pp. 158-59.

414. See ibid., p. 159. A διάγνωσις is in this case a judicial examination.

415. Johnson, *Acts*, p. 429.

416. Εβουλομην here probably means "I should like," not "I was wishing," though the latter is not impossible and would imply that Agrippa had heard about Paul in the past and had wished to hear him in person. See Bruce, *The Acts of the Apostles*, p. 493.

417. See Longenecker, *Acts*, p. 548.

418. See above, pp. 618ff., on Paul's departure.

pomp and circumstance. A judicial hearing has been turned into royal entertainment and theater. The term φαντασια when coupled with the preposition μετα means "with pomp" (cf. Polybius, *Hist.* 16.21.1) and refers in part
to the grand entrance Agrippa and Bernice made into the audience chamber.[419] After them, various other guests of honor came in, including military
tribunes[420] (indicating more than one cohort in the region)[421] and leading
men from the city of Caesarea, who would probably be almost exclusively,
if not exclusively, Gentiles.[422] Then Festus ordered that Paul be brought in.
He would surely have presented a striking contrast to those who had come
before, wearing simple clothes and appearing in chains (see 26:29). Looks,
however, are deceiving, for Luke portrays Paul as delivering a powerful testimony about his life and witness to his audience, which climaxes the great
speeches in Acts.

In *v. 24* Festus introduces his audience to Paul in terms somewhat
similar to what another procurator used to introduce Jesus to the Jewish
crowd (cf. John 19:6).[423] Notice how in this verse Luke uses ανδρες once
again, even though there is also a prominent woman present.[424] Festus says
that "all the πληθος" of the Jews petitioned him about "this fellow." While
the term πληθος could refer to the whole multitude of the Jews, in which
case Festus is guilty of considerable hyperbole,[425] it is more likely, in view of
the way this word is used elsewhere in similar settings in Acts, that it means
the whole *assembly* of the Jews, referring to a specific gathered group of them,
in this case the legal representatives of the nation (cf. the use of the term
especially in Luke 23:1, and in Acts 4:32; 6:2, 5; 14:1; 15:12, 30).[426] The point
is not a minor one in terms of Luke's own perspective, for, as Johnson says,
Luke has consistently portrayed in Acts a particular group of Jews as being
opposed to the Christian movement, namely, the bulk of the leadership, not

419. This was surely a room in the palace meant for hearings, receptions, and state
occasions.

420. Could this have included Claudius Lysias?

421. Josephus, *Ant.* 19.365, says there were in fact five auxiliary cohorts at Caesarea,
each of which would have had a tribune.

422. See Bruce, *The Acts of the Apostles*, p. 493.

423. In John 19:6 it is "behold the human being" (ιδου ο ανθρωπος, for *ecce homo*
in Latin). Here it is θεωρειτε τουτον, which probably should be rendered "you see this one,"
though it might be taken in the imperative: "behold this one."

424. On Luke's use of not just ανθρωπος but also ανηρ to refer to both men and
women, see pp. 120ff. above.

425. See Tannehill, *Narrative Unity of Luke-Acts*, 2:313; Cassidy, *Society and Politics*,
p. 112.

426. The most important of these parallels is the one in Luke 23:1, which speaks of
the same Jerusalem group of leaders. This dovetails nicely with the other parallels between
Luke 23 and this scene. See rightly Johnson, *Acts*, p. 427.

the nation as a whole.[427] Also favoring this conclusion is what Festus had just said to Agrippa in 25:15, namely, that he was petitioned by the chief priests and elders in regard to Paul, not by the whole people.[428]

Festus's conclusion, however, was that he had found Paul had done nothing deserving death. This judgment is an important one, for it means that Paul, in Festus's view, whatever he might be guilty of, was not guilty of a capital crime that violated Roman law.[429] In other words, he had concluded that the political charges that might lead to Paul's death had not been proved. Just as there had been a threefold declaration of no litigable wrongdoing under Roman law in the case of Jesus (see Luke 23:4, 15, 22), so also with Paul (Acts 23:29; 25:25; 26:31), and so Paul would be given a third time to speak and defend himself. Paul, however, had appealed to "His Imperial Majesty" (Σε-βαστος), and Festus had resolved to send him. The problem was, Festus had nothing ασφαλες, nothing certain or definite, to report to the Lord.[430] Here, as in 21:34 and 22:30, the phrase τι ασφαλες has the sense of "definite facts."[431] Paul, then, has been brought to speak before this body of dignitaries so they might help Festus know what to write in his letter of report. Paul has especially been brought before Agrippa, so that after Paul has been examined by the entire body, Festus will be better prepared to make his report, called *litterae dimissoriae siue apostoli* (in *Digest* 49.6.1).[432]

---

427. See Johnson, *Acts*, p. 427, in contrast to Sanders, *The Jews in Luke-Acts*, p. 294, who is rightly critiqued by Tannehill, *Narrative Unity of Luke-Acts*, 2:313 n. 13.

428. The Harclean margin of the Syriac adds a good deal to vv. 24-26, including in v. 24: "that I should hand him over to them for punishment *without any defense.*" And then in v. 25: "But I could not hand him over because of the orders that we have from the Emperor," and later in the same verse: "But when I had heard both sides of the case, I found that he was in no respect guilty of death. . . ." The net effect of these remarks is to make Festus appear even more the efficient and able Roman administrator, and even more self-serving. The point, however, of these later expansions was surely to enhance the picture of the injustice being done to Paul. See Metzger, *Textual Commentary*, p. 494.

429. Notice that Festus does *not* say he had concluded that Paul had done nothing wrong at all. See Tajara, *The Trial of Paul*, p. 162.

430. The use of κυριος as a title used of the emperor really came to prominence during the time of Nero, and so is appropriate here. Its usage increased until it became very common by the end of the century during the reign of Trajan (A.D. 98-117). See the discussion in Deissmann, *Ancient Near East*, pp. 353-57 and the examples cited there.

431. See Johnson, *Acts*, p. 427.

432. He could not simply send along the report of Lysias or Felix; rather, he had to make his own report, with definite charges in it (see *Digest* 49.5-6), since *he* was sending Paul to Caesar. The idea that Paul had merely appealed to Caesar's tribunal, which he already stood before in the person of Caesar's representative (whether Felix or Festus), but that Festus took the liberty of interpreting this as an appeal to Caesar himself to get Paul off his hands, is very unlikely. Cadbury, "Roman Law," pp. 318-19, says it would be difficult to appeal from the emperor (in the person of his representative) to the emperor himself, but

V. 27 indicates that Festus thought it αλογος, which here likely means senseless, illogical, or unreasonable, to write to the emperor without specifying the charges against Paul.[433] There is strong irony in this remark.[434] Not only was it unreasonable, it could prove fatal to one's career to send a person to the emperor on appeal with few or no charges to report.[435] Festus here is indirectly blaming Paul for this absurd situation because he appealed to Caesar, but in fact it was his own fault. Paul only appealed when he saw he was about to be packed off to Jerusalem and granted as a favor to the Jewish authorities! As Longenecker says, this last remark of Festus's "is typical of the face-saving language used among officials when what is really meant is that the failure to specify charges would be dereliction of duty."[436] The stage has now been set for Paul to fulfill what Jesus had long ago promised — that his witnesses, and Paul in particular, would testify before kings and governors (cf. Luke 21:12-13; Acts 9:15).[437] The scene which follows involves once again a judicial hearing or inquiry, but it is not a trial.[438] "But above all, perhaps, it was an entertainment — 'a gala performance of Roman justice.'"[439] Especially in view of Festus's admission that he had no chargeable offenses to report, it must have appeared to Paul like the theater of the absurd, for he had to go through yet another hearing that resolved nothing. Yet Paul saw in it an opportunity to share the good news. From Luke's vantage point the repetitions in Acts 22–26 served the purpose of emphasizing the importance of what was done and said on these occasions. "Festus' introduction provides a useful summary for understanding Paul's whole experience."[440]

---

this is precisely what happened in the *extra ordinem* cases that ended with *provocatio* in the provinces. He is, however, right that Paul is primarily appealing against the jurisdiction of the Jewish court in the first place.

433. The report was mandatory if one was sending a prisoner on to the higher official on appeal. See Conzelmann, *Acts*, p. 207.

434. Which Haenchen, *Acts*, p. 678, misses and so deems this statement impossible of Festus's lips.

435. See Polhill, *Acts*, p. 496.

436. Longenecker, *Acts*, p. 551.

437. Marshall, *Acts*, p. 389.

438. The term used in v. 26, αναχρισεως, technically means "preliminary investigation" or, in a looser sense, inquiry (see Bruce, *The Acts of the Apostles*, p. 495). It may have its more technical sense here, and in any case it indicates that we are not here dealing with another trial.

439. Williams, *Acts*, p. 414.

440. Polhill, *Acts*, p. 496.

I. Hearing the Last Witness (26:1-32)

The series of judicial hearings in Caesarea come to a climax and a conclusion in Acts 26, but there is also a larger sense in which Paul's speech, which takes up the vast majority of this chapter, is the climax of all of Paul's speeches in Acts.[441] This speech has also been seen as something of a summary of the christological message that is being conveyed in Acts.[442] It thus behooves us to give this material closer and more detailed attention than some of the earlier material.

This speech is the longest and most detailed of the Pauline speeches in Acts 22–26, indeed the longest apologetic Pauline speech in all of Acts. It presents us with almost a full rhetorical outline of a speech, as we shall see. It is important to recognize from the start the character of this speech. Commentators have repeatedly and rightly drawn attention to the references that indicate that this is some sort of contribution to the overall case Paul is making for his defense, as is signaled by the term απολογια in v. 2 and v. 24. As Bruce says, however, Paul in this "defense" speech is not operating in the usual forensic mode (offering attacks on opponents or extended rebuttals of charges). It is a broader appeal, more of an *apologia pro vita sua*.[443] Tajara was right to note that here Luke "does not have Paul defend himself at length and in detail against specific political charges. From the strictly judicial point of view, Paul's *apologia* was irrelevant in a Roman court of law."[444]

This is correct and leads to three important observations. (1) Paul is not now on trial, he is in a judicial hearing meant to aid the procurator in knowing what to write to the emperor about Paul's case, through consulting the opinion of Agrippa (and others) on this unique case. (2) The primary audience for this speech is not Festus, though there are nods in his direction, but rather Agrippa, as the references to the latter in vv. 2, 19, and 27 show. (3) It is therefore primarily a Jewish speech in which Paul presents his testimony or witness to Agrippa and indeed to both "small and great" (see v. 22).

It is the argument of Haenchen that "Luke no longer hoped for the conversion of the Jews . . . [a]lthough Paul speaks in Chapter 22 to the Jewish people, in 23 to the Sanhedrin and in 26 to King Agrippa. Luke with all this is not canvassing for a last-minute conversion."[445] I quite agree with Tannehill

---

441. See Schubert, "The Final Cycle," p. 8, who sees the speech as rounding out the main aims of all of Luke-Acts, part of which is to "clinch the significance of Paul."

442. See the full-length study by O'Toole, *Christological Climax of Paul's Defense;* cf. Tannehill, *Narrative Unity of Luke-Acts,* 2:315-29.

443. Bruce, *The Acts of the Apostles,* p. 496.

444. Tajara, *The Trial of Paul,* p. 163. This means that this speech should not be seen as an example of a speech created as an appropriate utterance of the defendant in a Roman trial.

445. Haenchen, *Acts,* p. 328.

that this is a serious misreading of Luke's purposes. As Tannehill argues, Paul is being portrayed in Acts 22–26 as the model evangelist, and this includes evangelism to Jews.[446] This interest in the salvation of the Jews continues right to the end of the book in Acts 28 (see 28:24), and is not terminated by the reminder at the very end that the salvation of God has been sent to the Gentiles because some Roman Jews, but only some, have rejected the message about Jesus.[447]

This speech is an example of forensic or judicial rhetoric, but the question remains, What kind of example?[448] Is it really a defense speech? This does not seem to be the case except in the broadest sense that Paul is doing apologetics. It appears instead to be the testimony of a witness rather than a re-presentation of the defense. This is not a trivial point. Paul is playing the part of witness in his own defense rather than defendant fending off charges. The latter are only briefly mentioned in this speech.[449] The whole speech leads forward toward the *peroratio* in which we not only have emotion but also an appeal to Agrippa and others to become as Paul is, except for the chains. Paul is bearing witness to a Jewish king by means of a rehearsal of his own life, in the context of a judicial hearing. The form of the speech is determined by the social context, but the content is largely determined by the primary audience and what the orator Paul wants to accomplish by his testimony. In the end, Festus gets frustrated, and it is Agrippa who is backpedaling and on the defensive! At a secondary level, this speech serves Luke's literary aims to show the fulfillment of Acts 1:8 — the witness of the gospel not only to the ends of the earth but also to the great and to the small.[450]

This speech is perhaps the most elegant of all the speeches in Acts, reflecting careful preparation and attention to elements of style. We are

---

446. Tannehill, *Narrative Unity of Luke-Acts,* 2:328ff.

447. As earlier in the story, when Paul is rejected by some Jews he then turns to and concentrates on the Gentiles. This is a missionary strategy, or is seen as divine direction of the mission, not a theological renunciation of the Jews or the possibility of their salvation.

448. Though O'Toole's analysis of the content of the speech in *Christological Climax of Paul's Defense,* pp. 156-60, is helpful in focusing on the christological issues, his analysis of the structure is flawed and fails to take into account the rhetorical dimensions of the text.

449. See rightly Cassidy, *Society and Politics,* p. 113: "in a speech twenty two verses long (26.2-23) only the last five constitute anything close to an explicit defense and even these latter verses stand more as a general statement concerning Paul's uprightness than they do as a specific refutation of the charges that have previously been made against him." See Hedrick, "Paul's Conversion/Call," p. 432, on how facts in this speech are necessary to complete the hearer's understanding of the other two accounts of Paul's conversion in Acts 9 and 22, and vice versa.

450. See the discussion of Kilgallen, "Paul before Agrippa (Acts 26,2-23)," on this speech as a testimony or witness speech and on its fulfilling of Luke's aims in Acts.

perhaps meant to think that, unlike the case when he spoke to the Jews in the temple precincts, here Paul has had time to reflect and prepare a rhetorically persuasive piece.[451] "Paul is here an orator of some distinction," as is shown by his "excellence in rhetoric."[452] W. R. Long points to the following elements of style: (1) the classical use of the perfect ηγημαι as a present in v. 2, (2) the literary elegance of the *exordium* (cf. below), (3) the use of the classical ισασι (v. 4) and ακριβεστατην (v. 5), (4) the addition of the Greek proverb (v. 14), (5) genitive of the articular infinitive (v. 18), (6) litotes (v. 19), (7) Attic use of πειρασθαι (v. 21), (8) use of the classical phrasing ουδεν . . . λεγων (v. 22), and (9) the classical παθητος meaning "must suffer" (v. 23).[453]

The rhetorical structure of the speech is as follows: (1) *exordium* (vv. 2-3),[454] (2) *narratio* (vv. 4-21), (3) *propositio* (vv. 22-23); (4) the formal proofs are omitted here, in part perhaps because they have been offered previously in Acts 22–25, in part because they are briefly but sufficiently alluded to at various points in the *narratio*[455] and the *propositio*.[456] There is, however, a brief (5) *refutatio* (vv. 25-26), followed by the (6) *peroratio* (vv.

451. So Kennedy, *New Testament Interpretation,* p. 137: "Paul has clearly had an opportunity to prepare his address in advance, something which was not possible when he spoke in Jerusalem."

452. C. J. A. Hickling, "The Portrait of Paul in Acts 26," in *Les Actes des Apotres,* pp. 499-503, here pp. 500-501.

453. Long, "The Trial of Paul," pp. 237-39.

454. Soards, *The Speeches in Acts,* p. 123 n. 329, rightly notes that the *captatio* ends with v. 3.

455. Among the proofs, evidences, or signs alluded to are: (1) the objective witness of Paul's companions on the way to Damascus; (2) the testimony of the Jews in Jerusalem; (3) Agrippa's own knowledge; (4) the Scriptures; (5) a heavenly revelation; (6) Paul's own testimony; (7) Paul's very presence before these dignitaries as a sign that God is with him. Much of the above is marshaled not merely to support the general credibility of Paul's case but specifically to support the main proposition, namely, that Christ died and rose from the dead and is the hope of Israel. See Neyrey, "Forensic Defense Speech," pp. 216-21.

456. As we have said before, pp. 659ff. above, Luke means the effect of these Pauline speeches in Acts 22–26 to be cumulative, and so a certain amount of "judicious" editing has been applied to the forensic speech material to avoid mere redundancy. Some elements which could have (and may have historically) appeared in the earlier speech material, Luke has reserved to present here, for various rhetorical and theological reasons. On the other hand, some material which was perhaps originally part of the proofs of this later speech has already been summarized in the earlier material, and so is omitted here, as part of a larger literary work that has a cumulative effect. The clearest evidence of the dependency of this speech on what the reader already knows from the previous ones is the total omission of the blinding, healing, Ananias part of the story. The focus here is on commission and witness, and so the aforementioned material could be deleted. On the differences between the three accounts of Paul's conversion see above, pp. 305ff., and my article "Editing the Good News," and cf. Hedrick, "Paul's Conversion/Call."

27, 29).[457] The speech is interrupted twice (vv. 24, 28) but continues on until v. 29.

The analysis above draws attention to the fact that the bulk of this speech is a simple *narratio* or chronicling of the events right up to the point where Paul becomes a captive (v. 21). It omits the chronicling of what happened to Paul when he appeared before Felix and the other events during the two years in captivity in Caesarea. The reason for the lengthy *narratio* is that Paul is establishing that he is and has been a sincere Jew who became and remains a witness for Christ.

As Kennedy says, the *stasis* in this case is *metastasis*. Paul cannot deny the salient facts of his life as a zealot for his religious convictions, indeed he rehearses them again, but Paul explains that in regard to his witness for Christ, which some Jews find offensive, he could do no other. God changed his life by divine intervention, and therefore ultimately Paul is suggesting "transference of responsibility to God"[458] for what he has been and even at this moment is doing — witnessing.

Acts 26:1 begins on a rather surprising note. It is Agrippa, and not Festus, who gives Paul permission to speak about himself. This signals to Luke's audience the person to whom Paul will in the main direct his remarks, but it also signals the essential content of what follows. It will be autobiographical, and in fact the periodic direct address to Agrippa (cf. vv. 2, 7, 13, 19) makes clear that the speech is something of a personal appeal to him. It will be noted that, unlike Agrippa I (see above, pp. 376ff. on Acts 12), this Agrippa is not called Herod, and is presented in a rather favorable light. The tenor of this whole encounter is different from when Paul gave the speech to the Jews in Acts 22, even though there is similarity in content. Paul is not in Acts 26 addressing an audience full of hostility toward him and his work, and this makes it possible for this speech to be more of a testimony or witness rather than a defense.

Before beginning his speech Paul stretches out his hand in the traditional rhetorical gesture indicating he is assuming the pose of an orator (cf. Apuleius, *Meta.* 2.21).[459] The text of the Western reviser found in the Harclean margin

---

457. It is a mistake to see the end of this speech as deliberative rhetoric. Paul is not giving advice about what is useful or beneficial for Agrippa's or Festus's future, he is making a direct appeal to his audience, which was approriate in the *peroratio* of a piece of forensic rhetoric. But see Soards, *The Speeches in Acts*, pp. 122-26. More helpful in the rhetorical analysis of the speech are in a general way Veltman, "Defense Speeches of St. Paul," pp. 255-56; Larkin *Acts*, pp. 355-65; Neyrey, "Forensic Defense Speech," p. 221; Kennedy, *New Testament Interpretation*, pp. 137-38. Note Cassidy's (*Society and Politics*, p. 113) astute observation that the speech is primarily oriented to the conversion of King Agrippa.

458. Kennedy, *New Testament Interpretation*, p. 137.

459. See rightly Haenchen, *Acts*, p. 682; Soards, *The Speeches in Acts*, p. 122; Bruce, *The Acts of the Apostles*, p. 496, misses this, but he is right that this is not an appeal for quiet, like the gesture in 13:16 or 21:40.

of the Syriac adds the charming and pious remark before mentioning the gesture that Paul was "confident, and encouraged by the Holy Spirit,"[460] which was likely true but not in the earliest text of Acts. We are told at the close of v. 1 that Paul began to give an *apologia* for himself.

Vv. 2-3 present us with an elegant *captatio benevolentiae*. The speech begins by suggesting the subject matter will be all of the things of which the Jews have accused him. As the speech proceeds, it will be seen that this is only partially the case, for nothing is said at all about Paul's defiling the temple by bringing a Gentile into it, nor about his upsetting Jews in the Diaspora. In fact Paul once again will insist that the main bone of contention has to do with the essence of the gospel, which he also identifies as the hope of Israel, namely, the resurrection (cf. below on v. 23). This is another good example of the rhetorical tactic of redefining what the real issue or bone of contention is.[461]

Paul says he considers[462] himself blessed (μακαριον)[463] to be speaking with a fellow Jew such as Agrippa.[464] Throughout this speech, part of Paul's approach is to use language conveying to Agrippa that he is a pious Jew. But as Paul says in *v. 3*, Agrippa is not just any Jew, but one who could be called an expert[465] in the εθος and disputes of the Jews.[466] The former term refers to the customs of the Jews (cf. Josephus, *Ant.* 15.286). The point of this flattering remark is that Agrippa will be conversant, in a way Festus was not, with the various religious practices and parties, and the theological and social disputes between these parties. Paul then appeals to Agrippa to listen patiently, which is one of the chief desirable traits Luke associates with a good judge (cf. Luke 18:7). This also suggests that Paul does not plan on speaking briefly here.[467]

In a bit of rhetorical hyperbole,[468] Paul says at the beginning of his

---

460. See Metzger, *Textual Commentary*, p. 498.

461. See pp. 39ff. above.

462. The verb is in the perfect but has a present sense; cf. 2 Cor. 9:5; Phil. 2:3, 6.

463. Paul is speaking to a Jew, and there is no reason why the term here should not have the same force as elsewhere throughout Luke-Acts (cf. Luke 1:45; 6:20-22; 7:23; 10:23; Acts 20:35). Contra Johnson, *Acts*, p. 431.

464. Bruce, *The Acts of the Apostles*, p. 497, suggests the translation "I congratulate myself," but this neglects to note that Paul is trying already to establish his *rapport* with his audience and his general *ethos*.

465. Γνωστης has this sense of one so knowledgeable that he or she should be called an expert in some particular matter. Cf. the LXX of 1 Sam. 18:3, 9; 2 Kings 21:6; Isa. 19:3. See Johnson, *Acts*, p. 432.

466. On ζητημα cf. 18:15; 23:29; 25:19.

467. See Bruce, *The Acts of the Apostles*, p. 497.

468. On Luke's penchant for rhetorical hyperbole with πας, as a way of stressing the great magnitude or extent of something, see pp. 105ff. above.

narration of his life[469] that *all* the Jews know his life story, or, more likely, here βιωσιν means the character or way of his life (cf. the preface to Sirach) from his youth. He says that from the beginning he spent that youth "among my people" (cf. 10:22; 24:2, 10, 17), and more particularly in Jerusalem. Here is further confirmation of what was already suggested in 22:3, that Paul was brought up a Jew in Jerusalem.[470] The reference to Jerusalem may narrow the scope of "all Jews" to those dwelling in Jerusalem. About these Jerusalem Jews, Paul says in *v.* 5 that they have known all along, if they were willing to testify (on Paul's behalf!), that Paul lived as a Pharisee, which he characterizes as the strictest sect "of our religion."[471] The tense of the verb "live" here is aorist, making it clear that Paul is speaking about his past at this point, though in 23:6 he speaks in the present tense on this subject. There is a difference, however. There in Acts 23 Paul is talking about his belief in the resurrection. In this regard he could still say he was affirming something distinctively and essentially Pharisaic. Here, however, Paul is talking about his religious way of life, orthopraxy, and on this score, though he had once done so, he no longer *lived* as a Pharisee.[472]

As *v.* 6 suggests, the important part of that Pharisaic system that Paul still affirmed is what he stood on trial for — "on account of my hope in the promise made by God to our ancestors,"[473] a promise the twelve tribes hope to attain as they eagerly worship day and night.[474] Paul is apparently alluding here to the gathering of the twelve tribes at the eschaton which is being associated with the resurrection.[475] The irony and tragedy are that it was for

469. The μεν ουν sets off v. 4 from v. 3, and thus properly speaking the narration begins here. It is, however, rightly seen as a transitional verse because it speaks in a general way about Paul's *ethos* or character, and so closes off the *exordium* as well.

470. Pace Tajara, *The Trial of Paul,* p. 164, εθνος here certainly does not refer to "my own nation" of Cilicia, in view not only of the way Luke elsewhere uses the term εθνος in similar contexts, but especially in view of 22:3.

471. Θρησκειας here in all likelihood refers to religious practice, and not just religion in general; cf. Col. 2:18; Jas. 1:26-27.

472. Here Jervell, *Luke and the People,* pp. 153ff., is unconvincing. Acts suggests that Paul continued to be a Jew even after his conversion; it does not suggest he continued to be a practicing Pharisee, especially in regard to whom he stayed and ate with and the like (cf., e.g., Acts 11:19-26 — in-house fellowship with both Jewish and Gentile converts; and Paul is party to the apostolic decree, Acts 15:22-35; staying with Lydia in Acts 16, who did not likely follow the strict Pharisaic interpretation of clean and unclean).

473. The similar phrase in Acts 13:32 is to be noted. Some of the major themes of the first great Pauline speech in Acts are recapitulated here. See Tannehill, *Narrative Unity of Luke-Acts,* 2:320.

474. The language here of striving and hoping to attain to the resurrection is very similar to what we find in Phil. 2:11-14. There are various distinctly Pauline notes in this speech. See below, pp. 745ff.

475. Tannehill, *Narrative Unity of Luke-Acts,* 2:320, has helpfully pointed out how

proclaiming this very Jewish hope that Paul had been accused and seized by the Jews. Here again Paul is very respectful toward Agrippa, calling him βασιλευ, in contrast to the way he earlier spoke to the high priest in Acts 23:3-5. *V. 8* is a rhetorical question which specifies quite clearly what Paul is referring to by this hope, namely, the resurrection from the dead. The point is that a Jew, such as Agrippa, who knows Jewish customs and beliefs and the Scriptures, should not find resurrection incredible or even a novel idea. The verse, however, probably makes the broader point as well that once one admits there is an all-powerful God, why should anyone find the idea of resurrection incredible. From a rhetorical point of view vv. 6-8 should be seen as something of a *digressio* which foreshadows, even down to its way of putting things, the *propositio* in vv. 22-23.[476]

V. 9 signals the return to the *narratio* by μεν ουν.[477] In a candid moment, Paul admits that before his conversion he had been convinced he ought to do many things against "the name of Jesus of Nazareth." Paul saw it as a religious duty to try to snuff out the Christian movement. While "the name" could be said to represent the presence and power of Christ among his people,[478] more likely is the suggestion that it refers to the Christian movement itself, which is so closely identified with Jesus that to do something against it is to do something against Jesus himself, as v. 14 will make clear (cf. 2:38; 3:16; 4:7, 12, 17-18; 9:14-16).[479] Another possibility would be to take the phrase "to do many things against the name" to mean to make many Christians blaspheme or renounce the name of Christ (see v. 11 below).

Paul states in *v. 10* that he performed such activities in Jerusalem with the authority of the high priests (cf. 9:2).[480] Paul says he locked up many of the "saints" in prison. It is interesting that here Paul speaks as a Christian about those he persecuted, as Ananias had before (9:14, cf. 9:2). The next clause of this verse has been heavily debated. Should we take Paul literally when he says "I cast my pebble against them when they were condemned to

---

this speech draws together some of the major Lukan themes going even as far back as Luke 1–2. Anna, for example, was a Jew who worshiped day and night in the temple and expected the fulfillment of this hope (Luke 2:37). This is the first known occurrence of this compound adjective δωδεκαφυλον. It expresses the totality of Israel, or at least Israel as a collective group. See Bruce, *The Acts of the Apostles,* p. 498.

476. Notice the "And now I stand here on trial on account of my hope" in v. 6 and the "to this day . . . and so I stand here" in v. 22. In both cases the verb is εστηκα.

477. On Luke's use of this phrase as a division marker, see pp. 68ff. above.

478. So Polhill, *Acts,* p. 500.

479. See Johnson, *Acts,* p. 433.

480. On the use of the plural here and earlier in Acts, see pp. 663ff. above. The idea is that more than one high priest had influence or actual power at the same time, though only one officially held the office.

death,"[481] in which case Paul would be claiming to be a member of the Sanhedrin at the time? This is not impossible, but it seems very unlikely. Paul was a young man at the time of the stoning of Stephen (cf. 7:58), and the Sanhedrin in Jerusalem seems to have been made up almost exclusively of the older leaders (the "elders") of Judaism, and, furthermore, largely of Sadducees. It is perhaps just possible that Paul might have been one of the young Pharisaic scribes in the Sanhedrin who helped in the interpretation of the Law. The alternative is to take this half of the verse as metaphorical, in which case Paul would mean that he approved of their condemnation. A final suggestion is that Paul is punning here on the idea of stoning, but it seems an unlikely bit of gallows humor that does not suit the tenor of this speech.[482] The point would be that he contributed to the cause of their death, as 7:58 suggests, even if he didn't actually stone them. Paul, on the other hand, himself says in Gal. 1:13 that he violently persecuted Christians (cf. Gal. 1:23; 1 Cor. 15:9).

Another issue raised by v. 10 is whether we should see "many" being condemned as a generalizing plural, or whether we are actually to think that the Sanhedrin (or their supporters) took matters and stones into their own hands on several occasions against Christians. This raises an interesting political point. Is Paul indirectly trying to incriminate the Sanhedrin for acting illegally (exercising capital punishment) in the presence not only of Agrippa but more importantly of Festus? This is not impossible.[483]

V. 11 indicates that Paul punished Christians who were in the synagogue,[484] presumably using the thirty-nine lashes and attempting to force them to say "anathema Jesus" (cf. m. Mak. 3.10-15; Pliny, Ep. 10.96).[485] Paul says he was so angry with the Christians, beyond all measure or reason, that he pursued them to foreign cities. Presumably he has Damascus particularly in view. The net rhetorical effect of vv. 9-11 is to enhance the portrait of Paul the zealous persecutor of Christians beyond what has been said before in Acts 9 and 22. Ironically, this information is used as part of a larger argument meant to make clear Paul's strong commitment and loyalty to Judaism.

Vv. 12-18 rehearse the by-now-familiar tale of Paul's conversion on the road to Damascus. Paul had been authorized and commissioned by the high

---

481. This idiom comes from the ancient practice of voting by means of small stones, white for yes, black for no. See Philo, The Unchangeableness 75; Josephus, Ant. 2.163; 10.60.

482. See Johnson, Acts, p. 434.

483. See Keener, Bible Background Commentary, p. 399.

484. Presumably we should see the use of πας as rhetorical here, indicating extensive efforts. Perhaps, however, he means all the synagogues in Jerusalem.

485. The Jewish whip did not contain the studs or bits of metal or glass that the Roman whip did. Paul himself experienced this punishment more than once; cf. 2 Cor. 11:24. See also Matt. 10:17; 23:34; and Williams, Acts, p. 418.

priests to go to Damascus to persecute more Christians. In *v. 13* Paul again directly addresses Agrippa (again βασιλευ), wanting him to pay especially close attention to what he is about to say. We are told that the event happened at midday, and the light Paul saw from heaven was even brighter than the sun at noon. The light was shining not only around Paul but also around his companions. The point of this remark and the following one about all falling to the ground is to stress the objective nature of what happened.

Paul says in *v. 14* that he heard a voice, speaking in Hebrew (presumably Aramaic),[486] call, "Saul, Saul." It is not clear whether or not, since this is the only occasion that it is mentioned that the voice spoke in a Semitic tongue, we are meant to think that Paul then spoke the message in Aramaic, which presumably Agrippa would have known. If that is the case, then this part of the speech is directed very particularly to the king (cf. v. 12), and perhaps Bernice as well. The much-debated aphorism "it hurts you to kick against the goads" is a Greek proverb (cf. especially Euripides, *Bacchae* 794-95; Aeschylus, *Agamemnon* 1624; Terence, *Phormio* 1.2.27). The proposed parallels from Jewish literature are far less convincing (cf. *Pss. Sol.* 16:4; Philo, *De Decalogo* 87),[487] and, as Bruce says, the proverb has never been found in an Aramaic source.[488] As Longenecker says, this is an explanation for the benefit of the audience to explain the implication of the question, "Saul, Saul, why do you persecute me?" The point is that it is fruitless for Paul to resist God and what God has planned for him.[489] This proverb is not about Paul's uneasy conscience over his persecuting activity.[490]

There is no account here of Paul being blinded, or of the role of Ananias, and here it is the Lord who commissions Paul. We have offered one explanation for this telescoping of the narrative in our discussions of Acts 9 and 22.[491] Historically, to judge from Paul's own account of things in Gal. 1:1 and 1:15-16, it was on the Damascus road that Paul was commissioned by the Lord. If we examine Acts 9 and 22 a bit more closely, we discover that Ananias does not in fact commission Paul in these earlier accounts. Acts 22:14-15 probably alludes back to the commission on the Damascus road,[492] and what Ananias seems to be doing is confirming Paul in what he is called to do and completing

---

486. See pp. 302ff. above.

487. The proposed parallel from the *Psalms of Solomon* is an analogy between God pricking the author and a horse being goaded, not a proverb. The arguments of Larkin, *Acts*, pp. 358-59, for the historical likelihood of Jesus having used such a proverb in this vision are not convincing.

488. Bruce, *The Acts of the Apostles*, p. 501.

489. See Williams, *Acts*, p. 420.

490. See Bruce, *The Acts of the Apostles*, p. 501.

491. See pp. 305ff. above and pp. 659ff. above.

492. See Larkin, *Acts*, p. 360 and the note there.

the conversion and healing process. Hedrick is right to note that Luke has reserved this important part of the story for this account for maximum dramatic effect, and because he wants to concentrate on the commissioning of Paul in this retelling.[493]

V. 16 is of some importance for its use of the tandem of υπηρετην και μαρτυρα. A very similar tandem is found in Luke 1:2. In the case of Acts 26:16 it is quite clear that they both refer to the same person, Paul. What this latter text suggests is that we should see both as referring to the same persons in Luke 1:2 as well — "they are eyewitnesses who became ministers," just as Paul was.[494] This in turn means that Luke is indeed claiming contact with the eyewitnesses in his prologue to this two-volume work.[495] The second half of this verse is also intriguing. There seems to be an echo of Acts 22:15, which speaks about witnessing to the things seen and heard. In our case, however, the Greek is somewhat convoluted, with a direct object με disrupting the syntax. The textual evidence is very equally balanced for retaining or omitting this word,[496] and probably it should be retained, in which case we have an anacoluthon here. For our purposes the gist of the sentence is that it is referring to things in which Paul has seen Jesus (i.e., his conversion), but it also refers to those things in which Christ will appear to him. In other words, the latter refers to ongoing revelations in the form of visions to Paul, a promise which is recorded as being fulfilled at 16:7; 18:9; 22:17; and 23:11 (cf. 2 Cor. 12:1-10).[497]

V. 17 promises rescue from both "your people" and from Gentiles, a clear reminder that Paul witnessed to both, in synagogues and elsewhere. Indeed, the text goes on to suggest Paul was *sent* to both, not just to Gentiles. The εις ους (to whom) probably does not refer just to the Gentiles, but it may indicate that Paul is to go especially or particularly to them. It is important to note, as Tannehill does, that the images of turning to God and of opening blind eyes (v. 18) are also used of Jews in Luke-Acts (1:16, 78-79; 4:18),[498] to which one must add the various callings of Jews to repentance in Acts (cf., e.g., 2:38; 5:31; and note the case of the Jewish false prophet Bar-Jesus in 13:4-12, where we see the reverse process of the blinding of an opponent).[499]

---

493. See Hedrick, "Paul's Conversion/Call," p. 427.

494. See rightly Johnson, *Acts*, p. 437.

495. See the discussion, pp. 12ff. above.

496. See Metzger, *Textual Commentary*, p. 495. ℵ, p74, A, E, and others omit the word, while B, C*, and others include it. This gives a slight edge to the former reading, except that the latter is clearly the more difficult reading.

497. Notice how in general these occurrences happen at times of crisis for Paul.

498. *Narrative Unity of Luke-Acts*, 2:324.

499. The fact that Paul appeals to Agrippa in this very story shows that he believes he is called to witness to Jews as well as Gentiles.

V. 18 indicates that Paul is to do for others what in fact happened to him — to open their eyes so they may turn from darkness to light, from the power of Satan to God (cf. 1 Thess. 1:9-10).[500] The result of this turning is that people will receive forgiveness of sins and a portion[501] among God's people, here called "those made holy[502] through faith in me." This language is yet another indication that Luke knows the essential Pauline message (cf. 1 Cor. 6:11; Eph. 5:26).

Throughout Luke-Acts the movement from darkness to light is used as a metaphor for salvation in dependence on the Isaianic ideas (cf. Luke 1:77-79; 2:30-32; Acts 13:47). The Isaianic passage especially in view is Isa. 42:6-7. God says there, "I called you" as "a light of the nation, to open the eyes of the blind" (cf. Isa. 49:6). The point of importance to us is that these ideas and scriptures that originally applied to the Servant in Isaiah and were later used by and referred to Jesus himself in the paradigmatic speech in Luke 4 (cf. Luke 4:18 to Isa. 61:1) are being applied to Paul here and elsewhere in Acts (cf. the use of Isa. 49:6 of Paul in 13:47).[503] Paul is being seen as the further fulfillment of the Servant role, in continuity with his Lord. Furthermore, in dependence on these same notions earlier in Luke 24:47, the apostles were also called as witnesses to preach repentance and release of sins. Paul then stands in a long line of proclaimers with a salvific mission that includes Jesus and the apostles. The reference to rescuing Paul probably alludes to another prophecy made to a persecuted prophet found in Jer. 1:7-8, and the reference to standing on his feet probably alludes to Ezek. 2:1-3.[504] The reader of Acts has already seen the numerous times Paul has been rescued from prison (16:9-40) and other calamities, and is about to see further instances of such rescues in Acts 27–28. The net effect of all this is that the reader understands that God's hand continues to be on Paul, and God's plan for his life will be worked out. It may also be suggesting that since the officials can find no wrongdoing on Paul's part, there is good prospect of Paul's eventual release from this prolonged legal process.

Vv. 19-21 continue the *narratio* relating what happened after the encounter on the Damascus road. Paul was not disobedient to the heavenly

---

500. As Johnson, *Acts,* p. 437, points out, in Luke-Acts there is a presentation of an ongoing battle between the kingdom of God and that of Satan (cf. Luke 4:6-11; 11:14-23), and in Acts this especially involves the association of the satanic with magic (8:11, 20-23; 13:10; 19:13-19).

501. On the meaning of κλῆρον in Acts cf. pp. 122ff. above on Acts 1:17, 25.

502. The verb is a perfect passive participle indicating a condition that began in the past and had continuing effect into the present.

503. See the discussion of Tannehill, *Narrative Unity of Luke-Acts,* 2:322-23.

504. Ibid.

vision. The word οπτασια here should not be seen as a reference to a purely subjective and internal experience, as is shown by the stress in vv. 13-14 on the objectivity of the occurrence, but rather one that originated from heaven but penetrated the inner being of Paul in a way that was not true of his companions. Indeed, it can be argued that this term (cf. Luke 1:22; 24:23) must be somewhat distinguished from the word οραμα, with the latter being more subjective and meaning vision, but the former meaning heavenly appearance.[505] V. 19 is another example of Luke's fondness for litotes, but of course Paul also used the device (Rom. 1:16). Again Paul speaks directly to Agrippa, this time mentioning his name. The reference to obedience to a heavenly vision would have struck a responsive chord not merely in Agrippa but perhaps also in Festus and others present, for the Romans certainly believed in paying very close attention to and heeding signs, omens, and prophecies.[506]

V. 20 recounts how Paul, as a response to the vision, proclaimed in Damascus, in Jerusalem, and πασαν τε την χωραν της 'Ιουδαιος. This is difficult, on both grammatical and historical accounts. This last phrase is in the accusative, while the others are in the dative. Furthermore, Acts offers no word about Paul's ministry in all the region of Judea, and Gal. 1:22 would seem to exclude it. This has led to various conjectural emendations of the text, the simplest of which suggests the omission at a very early date of an εις at the beginning of the phrase, in which case it reads "in every country, to Jews and to Gentiles."[507] Another possible suggestion is that we take this accusative clause as an accusative of extent referring to all Paul's subsequent witnessing activity throughout the Judean region (cf. 15:3; 18:22; 21:7-16; and perhaps also the witnessing during the two-year period in A.D. 57-59 while in chains is in view).[508]

V. 20b indicates that the content of Paul's preaching was that Jews and Gentiles must both repent, turn to God, and "do deeds worthy of or consistent with repentance." These deeds would be subsequent to or a manifestation of repentance, and we are meant to hear an echo of the Baptist's call to the Jews to do likewise as they repented and received baptism (cf. Luke 3:8-14 and Matt. 3:8). Here again we see Paul being portrayed as standing in the line of the great prophets and apostles. The *narratio* ends with v. 21, where Paul says that because of this sort of preaching and these sorts of activities with both Jews

---

505. Cf. Acts 9:10-11; 10:3, 17, 19; 11:5; 12:9; 16:9-10; 18:9. See Larkin, *Acts,* p. 361 and the note.

506. See my discussion, pp. 659ff. above.

507. See Bruce, *The Acts of the Apostles,* p. 503.

508. See Williams, *Acts,* p. 423. The point would be that the remarks in Galatians refer to what was the case very early on after Paul's conversion, not what was the case later in the 40s and 50s.

and Gentiles Paul was seized in the temple and murder was attempted. The subsequent events are not recounted perhaps because it is presumed that Agrippa has been informed about them by Festus.

In *vv. 22-23* we find Paul's statement of the essential proposition that he claims has been at issue all along in these legal proceedings. We have seen the references to Israel's hope and the resurrection gradually revealed as the real bone of contention in Acts 22–26 (cf. 22:14, 18; 23:6, 29; 24:15, 21, 25; 25:19; 26:6-7). Paul in a successful rhetorical strategy has convinced his inquisitors that the real issue between himself and the Jewish authorities is religious and theological, not social and political. He will in v. 23 give a full explanation of what it is that he preaches that so inflames some Jews, and here we have one of the more compact and helpful summaries of the essential apostolic kerygma, proclaimed by Peter, Paul, Philip, and others, as the first fourteen chapters of Acts have revealed. Paul introduces the proposition with the crucial statement that God has been with and helped Paul to this very day, indeed aided him to be able to stand here and testify before small and great at this very moment. In other words, this very hearing was within the providence of God, and was an intended part of Paul's fulfilling of his mission to bear witness even unto kings and other dignitaries, both Jew and Gentile (cf. Acts 9:15). Paul emphasizes the inclusiveness of his mission here, involving all social ranks of society.[509] The note of fulfillment, a frequent theme in Luke-Acts, is struck by the second half of v. 22. Paul has said nothing but what the prophets and Moses said would take place.

There are considerable parallels between the climax of this speech in vv. 22-23 and what is said by Jesus in his last speech in Luke 24:44-48. In both cases there is talk of the Scripture being fulfilled and in both cases the essential message that is said to be fulfilled in Jesus is that the Messiah must suffer and rise from the dead.[510] It is possible to take the two examples of ει as conditional in *v. 23*, in which case there are two conditions Jesus had to fulfill in order to complete his mission of salvation, namely, that if he would suffer and if he would be the first of the resurrection of the dead, then salvation would be available.[511] It is also possible to take the ει as a virtual equivalent to οτι, in which case we would take vv. 22-23 together and read "saying nothing but what the prophets and Moses said would come to pass, *namely that* the messiah must suffer. . . ."[512] The similar use of ει in v. 8 must be taken into account.

---

509. See Tannehill, *Narrative Unity of Luke-Acts,* 2:326.

510. See O'Toole, *Christological Climax of Paul's Defense,* p. 159, who says the theme of the resurrected Christ unifies this material.

511. See Tannehill, *Narrative Unity of Luke-Acts,* 2:326 and n. 40. Larkin, *Acts,* pp. 362-63, argues that the ει indicates the essential propositions to be argued out, which are in dispute.

512. See Longenecker, *Acts,* p. 554.

From a rhetorical standpoint the major function of the ει is to signal what the essential proposition or propositions under dispute are. In other words, as we said when discussing the rhetorical analysis, we must see vv. 22-23 as the *propositio* of this speech, as foreshadowed in the digression vv. 6-8. The translation "if" better conveys the sense that these are the points to be proved, though "that" is possible if we take it in the sense Lake and Cadbury do.[513] "Paul is proposing a topic or proposition that can be debated on the basis of Moses and the Prophets concerning the future Messiah."[514]

The summary statement in v. 23 speaks of the divine necessity (δει) of Christ suffering as part of God's salvation plan,[515] a theme already heard earlier in Acts at various points (cf. especially Acts 17:3 and 13:29; 2:23).[516] The theme of Christ being the first raised out from among the dead strikes a familiar Pauline note (cf. 1 Cor. 15:20) which indicates that Christ's resurrection not merely signals but also inaugurates the resurrection of other human beings. By these two events Christ proclaims light both to "our people" and to the Gentiles. Luke here uses λαος of the Jewish people as elsewhere in Luke-Acts. The prophecy of Simeon in Luke 2:32 is echoed here, and both of these texts depend on the Isaianic word about a light to humankind (Isa. 49:6). Paul (cf. Acts 13:47) is a witness to this light — indeed, he personally experienced it on the Damascus road.[517] It is the light that comes through and is seen in the glorified Christ. Second Corinthians 3:6 may perhaps be seen as Paul's own commentary on his Damascus road experience: "For it is God who said, 'Let light shine out of darkness,' who has shone in our hearts to give the light of the knowledge of the glory of God in the face of Jesus Christ."[518]

It is at this juncture, according to *v. 24*, that the first interruption comes in Paul's speech, from Festus.[519] The procurator bursts in, in a loud voice, saying, "You are out of your mind,[520] Paul, your many writings (or letters or

---

513. Cadbury and Lake, *The Beginnings of Christianity*, 4:321, argue for the translation "that" and add "but there is in ει a stronger implication that the proposition which follows is denied and must be argued out, than would be made by the simple οτι."

514. Johnson, *Acts*, p. 438.

515. In fact, παθητος properly means "is able to suffer." See Williams, *Acts*, p. 426.

516. As Moessner, "The Script of the Scriptures," has shown. The claim that Luke has no theology of the cross neglects the considerable data to be mined from the kerygmatic summaries in the speeches in Acts.

517. The Acts 26 account wishes to make very clear that Paul was not a victim of sunstroke or that his experience was merely a matter of staring at the sun. It was a light far greater than the sun that shone on him.

518. See my *Conflict and Community in Corinth*, pp. 382-83.

519. Kennedy, *New Testament Interpretation*, p. 137, is right to note that the interruption comes at basically the same spot as in Acts 22 (cf. vv. 21-22).

520. In this verse μανια surely refers not to Paul's divine inspiration which has made him εκ-στασις, out of a steady and normal state of mind; rather, it has the sense we find

much learning) have turned you unto madness." It is possible to take πολλα γραμματα to mean "much advanced learning" (cf. John 7:5; Letter of Aristeas 121; Plato, *Apology* 26D), in which case what we have here is a portrait of a down-to-earth Roman not willing to believe anything esoteric that goes beyond his view of common sense. Paul is in a sense complimented for his great learning, but, on the other hand, too much learning has driven Paul beyond the realm of "common sense."[521] What is not meant is that Paul is incoherent or has taken total leave of his senses, but rather that he is given to outlandish ideas because of his "much learning." It is also just possible to take πολλα γραμματα to refer to the many sacred writings of the Hebrew Scriptures, in which case what would be meant is that Paul had been studying God's word too much and it had led him to conclusions that go beyond common sense.[522]

Paul must refute this charge, and he does so directly in *v. 25* by stating that he is not a "maniac" and has not taken leave of his senses, but in fact his message is the very opposite of any wild and crazy ideas, it is truth and soberness that he is speaking. Notice that Paul addresses Festus politely as "most excellent Festus" (cf. Luke 1:3). Probably we should see αληθεια και σωφροσυνης as an example of hendiadys, in which case we should translate "I am speaking the sober truth." The contrast between "mania" and sobriety was a well-known one in Greek literature (cf. Xenophon, *Mem.* 1.1.16; 3.9.6-7). Sobriety or sanity was seen as an ideal in Greek philosophy (see Plato, *Protag.* 323B; *Republic* 430E-431B; Diogenes Laertius, *Lives* 3.91; Justin, *Dial.* 39.4).

Perhaps sensing that Festus was out of his depth and not going to be persuaded, Paul directs the argument once again to Agrippa, and in a masterful rhetorical move attempts to bring him in as a witness on his side. He says that the king knows about these things,[523] and so he feels he can use "free speech" (παρρησια)[524] with him about these matters. He says he is certain that Agrippa, being an astute observer of the events going on in Israel, had not failed to notice all these things, for this "was not done in a corner." This idiomatic expression has a considerable history (cf. Plato, *Gorg.* 485D; Epictetus, *Diss.* 2.12.17; Terence, *Adelphoe* 5.2.10) and stresses that the events about which Paul preached, the message itself, and the movement spawned by the

---

in Dio Chrysostom 12.8 and in Acts 12:8, where it refers to someone who has lost or is out of his or her mind.

521. See Ramsay, *St. Paul the Traveller,* p. 313.

522. See O'Toole, *Christological Climax of Paul's Defense,* p. 159; Williams, *Acts,* p. 426. In Roman law (cf. *Digest* 48.4.7) the defendant's mental state when he committed the supposed crime was supposed to be taken into account. See Tajara, *The Trial of Paul,* p. 169.

523. Actually we have another example of litotes here — "none of these things has escaped his attention."

524. On this as an attribute of a noble orator or philosopher, cf. pp. 39ff. above.

events and message were all public phenomena, not something done in secret. As A. Malherbe has shown, all through this final portion of Paul's speech he has been presenting himself as a responsible philosopher, one who speaks freely or boldly, but also one who speaks sober truth. The reference to "not in a corner" draws on the larger discussion about the propriety of a philosopher who withdraws from public life and does his dialectic or syllogisms in a corner as opposed to the one who takes part in public life and human affairs.[525] Paul is claiming to be like the latter, and furthermore he is asserting that Christianity is a public phenomenon subject to public scrutiny.

In *v. 27* Paul asks Agrippa directly, "Do you believe in the prophets?" This bold, direct approach puts Agrippa on the horns of a dilemma. If he says yes, then Paul will no doubt claim that he must go on to believe what they say about the Messiah. If he says no, he disqualifies himself from being a good Jew, much less a good Jewish ruler.[526] But in fact, Paul answers for the king, saying that he knows he believes. Before he can then drive home his point Agrippa interrupts. The force of *v. 28* has often been debated. In particular the question turns on both an interpretive and a textual matter. The Byzantine text (E, P, Ψ, 049, most minuscules), followed by the Textus Receptus, has the reading γενεσθαι. Stronger is the evidence for πειθεις, which is supported by p74, ℵ, B, 33, 81. This reading certainly explains the reading of Codex Alexandrinus (πειθη), and probably best accounts for the other readings as attempts to clarify the text.[527] The rhetorical nature of the speech also favors a response that speaks about persuasion. The phrase εν ολιγω could be taken temporally to mean "in a short while," or perhaps quantitatively, "in small measure" (cf. the KJV's "almost"), or even "with so few words (or arguments)."[528] The context must condition how we interpret the phrase because Paul responds in v. 29 with the contrast between εν μεγαλω and εν ολιγω. P. Harle thinks we must read v. 29 in light of v. 22 and so translate the former "Whether small or great (in social stature) I would wish. . . ."[529]

Two further difficulties with this complex v. 29 are: (1) interpretive decisions have in part to be based on what one thinks is the tone of Agrippa's response. Is this a jest? Is it sarcasm? Is it anger? Is it an expression of partial conviction?[530] (2) Do we take the verb ποιησαι in the straightforward sense of "to make" or does it have a more idiomatic sense, such as Haenchen and Bruce suggest, meaning "to play" (cf. 1 Kings 21:7 MT = 3 Kgdms. 20:7

---

525. See the whole discussion. Malherbe, " 'Not in a Corner,' " pp. 147-63, here pp. 154-57.

526. See Bruce, *The Acts of the Apostles,* p. 506.

527. See rightly Metzger, *Textual Commentary,* p. 496.

528. On the latter see Longenecker, *Acts,* p. 554, who goes on to reject this option.

529. See Harle, "Un 'private-joke' de Paul dans le livre des Actes (xxvi.28-29)."

530. See Larkin, *Acts,* pp. 364-65 and the note, and also Williams, *Acts,* p. 426.

LXX)?[531] As for this last suggestion, Harle is right to ask why we should expect a theater idiom here when the proselyte one better suits the character of this speech and how Paul hopes Agrippa will respond. A better comparison would be with the phrase "to make (ποιησαι) a proselyte" in Matt. 23:15.[532]

Probably most commentators think the meaning of this difficult verse is "In so brief a time,[533] do you persuade me to become a Christian?" to which Paul responds, "Whether short or long. . . ." This may well be so, but all of the proposals mentioned so far have not really taken into account the rhetorical nature of this speech. The rhetorical context suggests that what is meant is "With so few (or brief) arguments, do you persuade me to become a Christian?" The complaint has to do with the fact that Paul has not really offered fully developed proofs, but only mentioned some of the elements of proof in his *narratio* and what follows it. Paul's response, then, would mean that whether his arguments were brief (or few) or great in size (or number). . . . The tone here is not bitter, nor sarcastic, but more incredulous. Paul has not properly completed the acts of persuasion, and so there is perhaps a bit of a jest or touch of humor in the response. The king is not hostile to Paul or his case (cf. v. 31). "The tone is sophisticated avoidance by a slightly embarrassed king."[534] Finally, it should be noted that the term Χριστιανοι here appears on the lips of one who is not a Christian (cf. 11:26). While perhaps not always a term of contempt (it simply means one who belongs to Christ), it is also not a term Christians used of themselves. It is, however, a term that Roman and Jewish writers often used of them (cf. Tacitus, *Ann.* 15.44; Pliny, *Ep.* 10.96-97; Lucian, *Alex.* 25.38; cf. Josephus, *Ant.* 18.64).[535]

V. 29 indicates Paul's sincere desire to convert Agrippa, and indeed all his listeners. The speech closes in very polite and elegant style with an optative form of the verb "to pray": "I could pray . . . ," or as in old English, "I would (or wish) to God that. . . ." It also ends with the sort of *pathos* that one would expect in the *peroratio* of such a speech. His wish prayer is that all listening might become as he is, "except of course for these chains." At this juncture it would appear that he held up his chains, evoking perhaps some sympathy from the crowd.[536]

531. Haenchen, *Acts,* p. 689; Bruce, *The Acts of the Apostles,* p. 506.

532. Harle, "Un 'private-joke' de Paul dans le livre des Actes (xxvi.28-29)," p. 528.

533. See the use of εν ολιγω in Eph. 3:3.

534. Larkin, *Acts,* p. 365, note.

535. The only NT example where it seems clearly to be used by a Christian is 1 Pet. 4:16, but even here the author seems to be thinking of how those who are persecuting Christians will identify them.

536. Kennedy, *New Testament Interpretation,* p. 138, notes how the speech as a whole relies on *ethos,* which creates sympathy. Here is a well-educated but lonely figure who has had a transcending religious experience and seeks to relate it straightforwardly. Such ap-

But the hoped-for conversion of some of the audience does not happen, even though they are not hostile to Paul. Agrippa's case then falls into the category of tragedy, like that of other Jews who stand in danger of losing what God had promised to them by rejecting the fulfillment of Jewish hope in Christ.[537] Luke does not see this as a universal tragedy, for some Jews continue to respond, and he seems to believe Christians should continue to approach them. Nevertheless, that the majority does not respond positively is a theme found throughout Luke-Acts and it is full of irony and pathos.

The aftermath of the speech is recorded briefly in *vv. 30-32.* Just as there was a formal procession following a certain order in terms of social and political rank, so the recession. The king rises, indicating the hearing is over, and the governor, and Bernice. After this, those who had been seated with them (the advisors and centurions) are mentioned.[538] We are perhaps meant to think that the consensus of all these dignitaries was that "The man is doing nothing to deserve death or imprisonment," for the most natural antecedent of "they" in v. 31b is all of those just mentioned, especially since it says "they said to one another." This means that it was not just one person's conclusion, such as Agrippa's, though it surely must have been his among others, since Agrippa was the one being consulted.

In fact *v. 32* tells us that Agrippa alone said to Festus, "This man could have been set free if he had not appealed to the emperor."[539] Attempts have been made to explain this in light of Roman law. Sherwin-White, for instance, says that while the procurator could not scourge or rule negatively against Roman citizens once they had appealed to the emperor, legally they could still acquit them, dismissing the case. Thus Paul's being sent to Rome "is not a question of law, but of the relations between the emperor and his subordinates, and of that element of non-constitutional power which the Romans call *auctoritas,* 'prestige', on which the supremacy of the Princeps so largely depended. No sensible man with hopes of promotion would dream of short-circuiting the appeal to Caesar."[540]

Lentz, in a significant misreading of Sherwin-White, assumes he is re-

---

parently guileless testimony was often effective when coupled with an appeal to the deeper emotions at the end of the speech, as we find here.

537. See Tannehill, "The Narrator's Strategy," p. 265.

538. The term συγκαθημενοι is sometimes a technical term for an advisory council; cf. Haenchen, *Acts,* p. 690 n. 1.

539. It is not at all clear how Luke could have known about this remark, unless Paul overheard it as the dignitaries were leaving the room. Perhaps it was his deduction based on what "everyone" was saying to each other as they left. But cf. Marshall, *Acts,* p. 400. Tajara, *The Trial of Paul,* p. 170, rightly notes that the verb "appealed" is in the pluperfect, speaking of an action taken in the past that had ongoing status and effects.

540. Sherwin-White, *Roman Law and Roman Society,* p. 65.

ferring to King Agrippa's hope for promotion(!), but this is not the case.[541] It is Festus's report, and the emperor's view of Festus as a result, that is at issue here. Lentz is also likely wrong that the story paints the picture that Paul's status and authority placed the case out of Festus's jurisdiction.[542] What placed this case out of Festus's jurisdiction was probably a variety of factors: (1) Festus's desire to be rid of a troublesome case; (2) his desire not to alienate the Jewish authorities he would have to continue to deal with, especially in light of what had just recently happened to Felix; (3) his desire not to appear to usurp any of the emperor's *auctoritas* in a complex case that he had had great trouble figuring out and to form a list of chargeable offenses. In the slight chance that Paul had offended against the emperor, since the charges were so murky, it would be better not to dismiss the case than to make a mistake and make Jews and the emperor angry. Finally, bear in mind that it is Agrippa's stated judgment only that Paul could have been set free. This is not said to be the legal conclusion of Festus himself, based on his knowledge of Roman law, though he may have agreed with Agrippa.[543] Perhaps "Agrippa's opinion of the case . . . [was] . . . noted in the report to Rome and may in some part account for the treatment accorded Paul on his arrival (28.16)."[544] So it was that Festus undertook to make arrangements to send Paul to Rome.

541. See Hemer, *Book of Acts*, p. 132.
542. See Lentz, *Luke's Portrait of Paul*, p. 152.
543. The caution of Cassidy, *Society and Politics*, p. 113, is salutary here. He notes that Agrippa is not depicted as helping Festus formulate any charges, and furthermore the opinion that Agrippa does express at least implicitly criticizes Festus's conduct, for Festus had not come to the conclusion that Paul could be released.
544. Ibid., p. 113.

XIII. The Journey to Rome
(Acts 27:1–28:12)

According to Haenchen's reckoning, there are some eleven or twelve accounts in Acts of Paul traveling to some destination by sea, beginning with the account in 9:30 and finishing with the account we find in 27:1–28:10, some involving "we" passages and some not. Taken together, these accounts suggest that Paul covered some three thousand miles on the sea during the nearly three decades of his ministry recorded in Acts 9–28.[1] Though Luke does not record an occasion prior to that depicted in Acts 27 when Paul had misadventures on the water, we can well believe, with all the traveling by both sea and land, the report from the middle to late 50s A.D. in 2 Cor. 11:25 that "three times I was shipwrecked; for a night and a day I was adrift at sea." By the time we get to Paul's journey to Rome, he is a well-seasoned sea traveler and knows the dangers of sailing during the middle to late part of the fall. He even knows how to cope with a crisis at sea.

Since we have already had occasion to speak about Paul as a more than occasional traveler in the Mediterranean world as well as about sea travel in particular,[2] we will not rehearse that material again here. It is in order, however, before we look at the details of Acts 27–28, to answer Pervo's query as to why so much space is devoted to the trip to Rome (some sixty verses)

> when nothing was said about the beginnings of Christianity in Galilee, Rome, Alexandria, Illyricum . . . and other places? . . . Why not edit this

---

1. See Haenchen, *Acts,* pp. 702-3.
2. See pp. 480ff. above.

sequence a bit to permit describing what Peter did after converting Cornelius, how Paul died, what heresies arose, what came of the Collection, and kindred subjects. . . . Even if Acts is classified as a biography of Paul, this lack of balance is not very defensible.

Pervo goes on to answer his own question by suggesting: "One answer is that storm and shipwreck were a staple of ancient adventure writings. Historians had no need to liven up their material with a shipwreck, but composers of fiction did."[3]

That Luke's account of the journey to Rome is a lively one, no one would dispute. That such accounts, having been influenced by the *Odyssey* (5.291-332; 9.62-81; 12.201-303) and the later ones by the *Aeneid* (1.44-153), were staple items in ancient Hellenistic novels or romances is also beyond question (cf., e.g., the novels of Chariton, Achilles Tatius, Petronius, Heliodorus, and Xenophon, among others). But as Johnson rightly points out, such tales were also not uncommon in historical works in Greek (cf., e.g., Thucydides, *Pelop.* 2.6.26; 6.20.104; 8.24.31; 8.24.34; Herodotus, *Pers. Wars* 3.138; 7.188).[4] The presence of such material in Acts then gives us no sure clue to the genre of this work and to whether it is largely history or fiction.[5]

This still does not answer the question of why Luke offers such a detailed account of this voyage when other important items are summarized or omitted.[6] I would offer the following suggestion. First and foremost, if, as we have argued throughout, Luke was following the conventions of Greek historiography, *autopsia* was a crucial element of such works. As we discussed in the introduction to this work, the Greek historical tradition emphasized the importance of travel, investigation, and eyewitness participation and testimony. For the sake of the credibility of his work as a piece of Greek history writing, at some point Luke needed to be able not merely to claim but demonstrate that he had participated in at least some of the events he chronicled.

Luke lived at a time when he could still speak of "the things fulfilled among us" and he had "investigated everything closely from the beginning," even though his introduction in Luke 1:1-4 suggests that he was only in touch

3. Pervo, *Profit with Delight*, p. 51.

4. See Johnson, *Acts*, pp. 451-52.

5. See Praeder, "Acts 27.1–28.16," p. 705: "The literary relation of the sea voyage, storm, and shipwreck to sea voyages in ancient literature is not the sort of relation that would allow for conclusions about the literary genre of 27.1–28.16 or the literary genre of Acts or of Luke-Acts. Travelogues, forecasts, and concerns for safety are not limited to any one literary genre. Storm scenes and speeches in storm scenes are characteristic of Greek and Latin epics but not confined to them."

6. On this see Johnson, *Acts*, pp. 456-57. He is right especially that the many mundane details in this account discourage us from seeing the account as some sort of allegory about salvation, or Paul as a Christ figure, or about the Eucharist (cf. below).

with the earliest eyewitnesses and ministers of the word, not that he himself was one of the first group of converts in the Holy Land. Thus it is only toward the close of his two-volume work, beginning in Acts 16 and then much more fully in Acts 27–28, that he is actually able to claim that he fulfilled the requirements in order to be a good Greek historian. Indeed, it is precisely in this part of his work that he demonstrates most clearly that he is much more indebted to Greek traditions of historiography than to Roman or even to Jewish ones. Here he probably also reveals himself to be a Gentile, with a Greek (and decidedly non-Jewish) love of sea travel and tales about such travel, and an audience who would appreciate such an account.[7]

As for the issue of balance, I would suggest that this comes down ultimately to a matter of sources. If Luke was a serious historian and did not have access to any significant traditions about the origins of Christianity in Galilee or what happened to Peter during the period between the 40s A.D. and 62 or other such matters, he would not have felt free to make up such traditions. He had to use the sources he had, and the most detailed source he had was surely his own account of this interesting journey to Rome. Any ancient historical work on a large subject such as the origins of Christianity that limits itself to its sources is bound to both appear and be unbalanced, from a modern perspective.

Pervo is, however, right, I think, that Luke as a rhetorical historian had some interest in giving his audience pleasure as well as information. I would say this was a secondary interest and not the one that determined the genre or historical substance of the work; nonetheless, it should not be ignored.[8] It is quite likely that he has deliberately written up and edited this account in Acts 27–28 in a way that was meant to keep his listener on the edge of his seat. After all, Luke's two-volume work was a lengthy work by ancient standards, and the inclusion of some real adventures near the end of the work would help bring not merely Paul but also the reader into port in Rome, without nodding off. To this end, Luke offers us some of his most elegant Greek. "Within Acts 27 are nearly thirty instances of literary allusion and elegant usage, as well as two oblique optatives, twelve genitive absolutes, and ten occurrences of the particle τε. This is the most sustained passage of good

---

7. See Plümacher, *Lukas als hellenistischer Schriftsteller*, pp. 4ff., who sees Luke here catering to the interests of Hellenistic readers. This is not to deny that there are a few echoes of the story of Jonah (cf. particularly the language of Jon. 1:4-16 and the storm narrative in Acts 27) to be found in this account, but Paul is not being portrayed here as the reluctant prophet that Jonah was. To the contrary, he seeks to rescue his pagan fellow travelers by, among other things, good advice, and prophecy. But cf. Krantz, *Des Schiffes Weg mitten im Meer.*

8. See my critique of Pervo, pp. 376ff. above, and also Brosend's "The Means of Absent Ends."

writing in Luke-Acts."[9] With Paul in a situation familiar to the readers of classical literature, Luke resorts to more classical Greek.

It is a measure of Luke's consummate skill that he has not integrated into his narrative a superfluous but entertaining journey, but rather one germane to the plot and plan of his work — chronicling the spread of the unstoppable good news from Jerusalem to Rome. Furthermore, it is a journey that at point after point has been shown to be historically accurate or at least plausible even in detail by both ancient and modern experts on these sorts of sea accounts.[10] Even very critical scholars tend to believe that Acts 27–28 is based on an actual journal account of a voyage, though they often add that it is considerably embellished.[11] Much depends on how one estimates the portrait and role of Paul in these chapters, a matter we will address as the occasion arises.

Here, however, we must address the claim that the references to Paul in this material (vv. 9-11, 21-26, 31, 33-36, 43) are detachable and therefore were inserted to a preexisting narrative.[12] This claim is doubtful on several counts. First, these are not the only verses in this context which mention Paul (see also vv. 1, 3). Secondly, the mention of Paul's companions must also be taken into account (v. 2). Thirdly, some of the verses in question are part of sentences involving other verses as well, and these other verses will not stand on their own (cf., e.g., vv. 43-44). Fourthly, passengers on a ship, and especially those like Paul who are prisoners, are not the major actors when a boat is being sailed. It is hardly surprising that the action goes forward without extensive reference to Paul or his companions. This is no clear evidence that the verses about Paul are later insertions. Fifthly, if one accepts Haenchen's theory that the account is based on a real sea voyage, one must ask which is easier to believe — that by remarkable coincidence Luke found a true account of a journey from Sidon to Rome that so suited his purposes and so paralleled the

9. Pervo, *Profit with Delight,* p. 52.

10. See especially Smith, *Voyage and Shipwreck of St. Paul;* Ramsay, *St. Paul the Traveller,* pp. 314-43; Casson, *Ships and Seamanship;* Hemer, *Book of Acts,* pp. 132ff.; Rapske, "Acts, Travel, and Shipwreck."

11. See Haenchen, *Acts,* pp. 86ff. Dibelius, *Studies in the Acts,* offers two suggestions. On pp. 7-8 he assumes that the account ultimately goes back to an actual stormy journey Paul took to Rome, though in its present form it has been considerably elaborated following literary conventions. On pp. 204-6 he sees Acts 27–28 as largely based on a secular account of a voyage and shipwreck, into which the author has integrated a few Pauline snippets here and there. What these theories have in common is the acceptance that a source, perhaps even a source with considerable historical detail, is being used. What Haenchen especially objects to is the Lukan portrait of Paul in this material (see pp. 710-11 of his commentary).

12. This suggestion ultimately goes back to Dibelius, *Studies in the Acts,* pp. 213-14, but he is largely followed by Haenchen, Conzelmann, and more recently Lüdemann, *Early Christianity,* pp. 257-58.

little he knew about Paul's journey to Rome, that all he basically had to do was add a few verses here and there about Paul; or that the narrative which in *all of its verses reflects Lukan style* was written up in the first place by Luke?[13] Sixthly, the account of this voyage is not a foreign body in Acts but admirably suits the purposes and aims of Luke to chronicle how the gospel reached Rome, to relate how the message was conveyed to pagans, to recount how God's plan and providence were such that even severe obstacles were overcome in getting Paul to Rome and his appearance before the emperor.[14]

A. Faring Well until Fair Havens (27:1-12)

Acts 27:1 begins with the statement that when it was decided[15] to send Paul to Italy, "they"[16] transferred Paul and some other prisoners[17] to a centurion named Julius of the σπειρης Σεβαστης. There are two possible interpretations of this reference to a particular cohort: (1) it refers to one of the cohorts of "Sebasteni" mentioned in Josephus as forming a large part of Agrippa I's garrison in Caesarea Maritima (cf. Josephus, *Ant.* 19.9.2.365-66; *War* 2.3.4.52); (2) it refers to a cohort in the army of Syria and Judea with this very name attested in *ILS* 2683 = *CIL* 3.6687, and more importantly in *OGIS* 421, which locates this cohort in Batanea (Bashan) in the Transjordan under Herod Agrippa II.[18] The latter suggestion is more probable, not least because "Augusta/Sebaste" is first and foremost an attested title and the cohorts Sebasteni were not imperial units likely to be involved in transporting prisoners

---

13. Hanson, "The Journey of Paul and the Journey of Nikias," pp. 22-26, ridicules the idea of Luke happening upon such a perfect account for his purposes. He is more helpful when he points out that, following Dibelius's criteria, one would have to judge Nikias's journey recorded by Thucydides, *Pelop. War* 6.1-61, as fictitious, but in fact it wasn't.

14. See Tannehill, *Narrative Unity of Luke-Acts,* 2:330-39; Marshall, *Acts,* p. 402; Praeder, "Acts 27.1–28.16," pp. 704-6, who points out that no one ancient travelogue parallels what we find in 27:1-8; 28:11-16; Miles and Trompf, "Luke and Antiphon." See now also Talbert and Hayes, "A Theology of Sea Storms," on how these narratives show that Paul is deemed not guilty by God.

15. The Western text (including the Harclean margin of the Syriac and by 97 and 421), as it often does, specifies matters more clearly: "So then the governor decided to send him to Caesar. . . ." See Metzger, *Textual Commentary,* p. 496.

16. Unspecified, presumably the centurion and his assistants in charge of watching over Paul; cf. 24:23.

17. As Keener, *Bible Background Commentary,* p. 400, suggests, they may well have been going to Rome not for trial but to serve in the arena as part of the entertainment of the emperor and the citizens.

18. See Hemer, *Book of Acts,* pp. 132-33 and n. 96.

to Rome.[19] Rather, they were auxiliary units, associated with the city of Sebaste.[20]

The centurion is called only by his first name, Julius, a name which may suggest that one of his forebears acquired his freedom (and citizenship) during the reign of either Julius Caesar or Augustus.[21] In the Julio-Claudian period the use of the simple *nomen* would be really appropriate only for an older man, and in particular one who already possessed Roman citizenship, for Claudius had prohibited the use of the *nomen gentile* if one was not a Roman citizen.[22] Perhaps we see here a clue as to why Julius treats Paul kindly (cf. below). It was the sort of courtesy one Roman citizen would extend to another, especially since Paul was not yet a condemned man, which may have distinguished him from the other prisoners on this trip.

It would appear that Paul is being transported with some who have already been convicted of crimes, but by what means would they all get to Rome? Bearing in mind that there were no passenger boats at this period,[23] it would have been necessary for the centurion to book passage on a commercial boat. We are told at *v. 2* that Paul and the others embarked on a boat of Adramyttium, ready to sail for the ports along the southern coast of Asia. Adramyttium was a city north of Pergamum in the region of Mysia in Asia. In short this boat was a long way from home. The normal and safe way for this boat to proceed home would be to go north from Caesarea hugging the coast and then west, working its way along the southern coast of Asia.[24] Only the largest grain boats set out into the open sea of the Mediterranean.

The "we" reappears at this point and will continue until 28:16. As Praeder says, we have here an example of the "first person peripheral narrator,"[25] for the speaker is neither Paul nor Aristarchus nor the captain nor one of the crew nor Julius, but rather an observer of what happens, and so apparently not a major actor in the drama. Aristarchus, who also makes this journey, is identified here as a Macedonian from Thessalonica.[26] He has been previously mentioned as one of the emissaries traveling with Paul to Jerusalem at 20:4. In Col. 4:10 he is identified as Paul's fellow prisoner, apparently in Rome,

19. See Tajara, *The Trial of Paul*, p. 173.

20. See Hemer, *Book of Acts*, p. 133; Bruce, *The Acts of the Apostles*, p. 511.

21. See Larkin, *Acts*, p. 366.

22. See Rapske, *Paul in Roman Custody*, p. 269.

23. See the discussion, pp. 480ff. above.

24. The phrase εις τους κατα την Ασιαν τοπους, "unto the places along the Asian (coast)," surely refers to the southern coast of Asia. Cf. Smith, *Voyage and Shipwreck of St. Paul*, p. 62.

25. See her discussion in "Acts 27.1–28.16," pp. 683ff.

26. A few Western manuscripts (614pc, syH) also mention Secundus at this point, doubtless on the basis of Acts 20:4.

which has led to the speculation that Aristarchus was already one of the prisoners on this voyage to Rome from Caesarea. In Philem. 24 he is identified as Paul's fellow worker. What both of these Pauline texts have in common is that Luke is mentioned in the same context as Aristarchus in Col. 4:14 and in the same verse in Philemon. This provides some slight further evidence in favor of identifying our narrator as Luke, and also for the suggestion that Aristarchus and Luke traveled all the way to Rome with Paul.[27]

It is unlikely that the centurion Julius was, as Ramsay speculated, one of the couriers of the emperor *(frumentarii)* who only in the second century came to be responsible for prisoners and matters of policing.[28] It is also unlikely that this task would have been assigned to a centurion in a Samaritan unit.[29] Probably Julius had booked passage not on an imperial boat but rather on a privately owned one, on which others such as Luke or Aristarchus could also book passage.[30] There was no state fleet assigned to taking prisoners to Rome, nor was there really a state merchant fleet taking grain to Rome. Rather, as Garnsey and Saller say, this "function was performed by private shipowners paid by the government" (cf. below on v. 6 and on 28:11 on the "Twin Brothers" ship).[31] There was the possibility of a Roman soldier impressing or requisitioning a ship for a state purpose, but perhaps this is not the case here.[32]

As far as Myra, Paul and the others were on a coaster that moved slowly north and west. We are told in *v. 3* that the next day the ship put in at the port of Sidon, north of Tyre. This was some sixty-nine nautical miles from Caesarea.[33] Here we are told that Julius treated Paul with φιλανθρώπως (on the cognate φιλανθρωπια, cf. 28:2). This term and its closest cognate are rare in the NT, occurring only in Acts and Titus 3:4, but they are exceedingly common in Hellenistic literature, and are used to describe what it means to be truly human, or humane, or civilized (cf. Plutarch, *Moralia* 402A).[34] The term literally means love for one's fellow human beings. This behavior is especially understandable between equals such as two Roman citizens. It was also prudent to allow Paul to go and visit the Christians in Sidon so that he

---

27. See Longenecker, *Acts,* p. 558.

28. But see Ramsay, *St. Paul the Traveller,* pp. 315, 348; and contrast Sherwin-White, *Roman Law and Roman Society,* p. 109, who points out that nothing associates these couriers with policing functions in the first century.

29. See Rapske, *Paul in Roman Custody,* pp. 267-70; Marshall, *Acts,* p. 403.

30. Notice how Aristarchus is associated with the "we," not with the prisoners at this point in the narrative.

31. Garnsey and Saller, *The Roman Empire,* p. 88.

32. See Rapske, "Acts, Travel, and Shipwreck," pp. 14-19.

33. See Marshall, *Acts,* p. 404.

34. See the discussion in Johnson, *Acts,* p. 445.

could be cared for and fed and not be a burden to the centurion. Presumably, the centurion sent a guard with Paul into the city.

We do not know exactly when Sidon was evangelized, but presumably it was reached by some of the Hellenists on their way to Antioch (cf. 11:19). Paul probably visited the city on one or more of his trips to and from Jerusalem (cf. 11:30; 12:25; 15:3). This will explain why we are told here in v. 3 that Paul visited with his "friends" (φίλους). Some have suggested that this is something of a technical term for Christians (cf. 3 John 15). This is possible, but Luke does not use this language in this way elsewhere to describe Christians.[35] We know from Paul's letters that he had no problem with accepting hospitality or even with allowing Christians to provide him with occasional traveling funds and supplies, which was different from placing himself in an ongoing relationship with a patron.[36]

V. 4 says that once they put out from Sidon contrary winds forced the boat to sail under the lee of Cyprus. This is not exactly the reverse of the route Paul followed when he had sailed from Patara to Tyre (21:1-3), for then he had sailed the more direct route on the west side of Cyprus. On this occasion the ship had had to sail on the east or leeward side of Cyprus because they were sailing late in the season when winds from the west and northwest prevailed.[37] *V. 5* says they sailed across or through the sea off the coast of Cilicia and Pamphylia and into the port of Myra. This was called Andriace; it lay about three miles west and south of the city.[38] Myra was in Lycia, which was the southernmost part of Asia.[39] It was nearly due north of Alexandria and was a regular stopping-off spot for the grain ships that sailed from Alexandria to Rome. It is then no surprise that we are told in *v. 6* that it was an Alexandrian ship bound for Italy that the centurion got his charges passage on in Myra.

V. 7 suggests that the journey from Myra to near Cnidus, across from the island of Rhodes, was slow and arduous, even though the craft likely hugged the coast and relied on the land breezes. Cnidus was a seaport frequented by ships from Alexandria according to Thucydides (*Pelop. War* 8.24.35). Once out into open water, the boat headed for the next-nearest substantial landmass farther west, namely Crete, but the winds were such that they had to sail under the lee of this island off Salmone. This led them with

---

35. See Bruce, *The Acts of the Apostles*, p. 512.

36. Called being "sent on my way by you"; cf. 1 Cor. 16:6; Rom. 15:24. See my discussion in *Friendship and Finances in Philippi* (Valley Forge, Pa.: Trinity, 1994), pp. 123-24.

37. See the discussion in Smith, *Voyage and Shipwreck of St. Paul*, pp. 67-68.

38. See Polhill, *Acts*, p. 517.

39. The Western text (614, 1518, 2138 ith, and others) plausibly suggests the journey from Cyprus to Myra took fifteen days. Cf. Metzger, *Textual Commentary*, p. 497.

difficulty, according to *v. 8*, to a harbor called ironically Fair Havens, on the southern side of Crete, near the city of Lasea. The problem with Fair Havens was that it was not enough of a haven for a good-sized boat to be able to weather the winter storms there. It is probably to be identified with modern Limeonas Kalous about five miles east of Cape Matala.[40]

V. 9 illuminates why this journey had already been too arduous with much time lost — it was very late in the sailing season, in fact it was a period of time in which the sailing was quite dangerous. Luke tells us that *even* (καὶ) the Fast had already gone by. This is a reference to the fall Day of Atonement, which according to the Jewish calendar fell on the tenth day of the month called Tishri.[41] The Jewish calendar being a lunar one, the date on which this day fell differed from year to year, though the general time frame of this month was always September-October (cf. Josephus, *Ant.* 14.66; 18.94; *m. Menaḥ* 11:9). If Luke is following the most widely known Jewish calendar, this day fell on October 5 in the year A.D. 59, but not nearly that late in the years immediately before and after 59 in the period from 57 to 62.[42] Conzelmann, however, has suggested that Luke was following a Syrian Jewish calendar, which would place the Fast as late as October 28 in 59.[43] It seems likely, however, that Luke would use the more widely known calendar. In either case the date is significant, for the Roman writer Vegetius, *De re militari* 4.39, states plainly that the dangerous season for sailing in the fall was from September 14–November 11, after which all sailing basically ceased for the remainder of the winter.[44]

Luke does not tell us how much time had passed since the Fast, but he does inform us that Paul took the liberty to advise those in charge as follows: "Sirs, I can see the voyage will be with danger and much heavy loss, not only of the cargo and the ship, but also of our lives."[45] In other words, Paul was advising battening down the hatches and staying in Fair Havens throughout

40. See Longenecker, *Acts*, p. 559.
41. Williams, *Acts*, p. 432, rightly notes that Luke's use of Jewish means of reckoning time suggests he is writing at a time when the Christian ethos was still largely Jewish, or in touch with Judaism.
42. See Bruce, *The Acts of the Apostles*, p. 515; and more fully in his "Chronological Questions," p. 289. This argument was worked out in detail, based on this verse, by Workman, "A New Date-Indication in Acts."
43. Conzelmann, *Acts*, p. 141.
44. Kratz, *Rettungswunder*, pp. 336-37, insightfully suggests that the reason for so much focus on the nautical terms and features of the journey in Acts 27 is that this journey took place during the season when unusual nautical measures might and would be necessary.
45. Ψυχή, here as elsewhere on Paul's lips in Acts, refers to human life, not the Greek notion of the immortal soul (cf. 20:24; 27:10, 22). See Schneider, *Die Apostelgeschichte II*, p. 388.

the winter. It is a measure of Luke's honesty and accuracy that he reports this advice in full, for in fact when the craft does sail on there is no loss of life, and Paul himself says God had informed him this would be the case (cf. vv. 21-24). We should then probably take v. 10 not as an example of prophetic insight but simply as the sort of commonsense advice a seasoned traveler on the seas would offer at this time of year.[46]

V. 11 suggests that Paul had primarily offered this advice to the centurion, but that he paid more attention to the κυβερνητη και τω ναυκληρω. There has been some debate as to who these two persons were. The latter term seems to refer to the owner of the vessel, while the former refers either to the captain or pilot of the ship, probably the latter since an owner who traveled with the boat was likely to be the captain of it as well, and in any case κυβερνητη literally means a pilot or one who steers (see Plutarch, *Mor.* 807B).[47] It is not certain whether Paul had been consulted on the matter of further travel, being a Roman citizen and one who had traveled in this vicinity before, or whether he simply overheard the conversation and offered his advice.[48]

It is understandable that a Roman might not take the advice of a Jew about the future, for Romans trusted divination more than Eastern prophecies or the advice of Eastern sages.[49] In any case, the centurion paid more attention to the owner and pilot, who apparently were in favor of traveling on since *v. 12* says that "the majority" were in favor of putting to sea. The rationale given was that the harbor was not suitable for wintering there. There may have also been another reason, namely, the profit motive.

Claudius had given extra incentives to shipbuilders and shipowners willing to take risks by sailing in the dangerous season to get extra grain to Rome. He had stated that he would not only give a bounty to successful ventures but also would recompense the shipowners' losses, and these incentives and promises remained in effect under Nero (cf. Suetonius, *Claud.* 18.2).[50] The reason why Claudius had made such statements and why he developed a considerable freighter service for grain portage from Alexandria

---

46. See rightly Bruce, *The Acts of the Apostles*, p. 516, and Barrett, "Paul Shipwrecked," pp. 58-59 (the first is Paul's human opinion, the last a supernatural message).

47. See the discussion in Hemer, *Book of Acts*, pp. 138-39 n. 110; and further his "First Person Narrative," p. 97.

48. As Aelius Aristides, *Or.* 50.32-37, and Cicero, *Ep. ad Fam.* 16.9.4, suggest, decisions whether to sail or not were not usually left up to the sailing professionals. Thus, as Praeder, "Acts 27.1–28.16," p. 691 n. 18, suggests, it is not implausible that Paul could have taken part in the discussions about whether to sail or not, based on his knowledge and social status.

49. See Keener, *Bible Background Commentary*, p. 401.

50. See the discussion by Rapske, "Acts, Travel, and Shipwreck," pp. 22-43.

to Rome was that famines happened during and threatened his reign.[51] We
are told by Tacitus that in one case the famine led to an insurrection which
personally endangered Claudius (*Ann.* 12.43).[52] There is an account by Lucian
of Samosata of the voyage of a grain ship from Sidon to Rome that is quite
similar to the account in Acts (*Ship* 1-9).

The hope of "the majority" was that they would be able to reach a better
harbor of Crete called Phoenix. This harbor is said in *v. 12* to face southwest
and northwest. We have reference to the city of Phoenix in Crete by Strabo
(*Geog.* 10.4.3), though its location is debated. It is probably to be identified
with modern Phineka, though not much is at stake in determining this issue
since the boat never reaches this point.[53] Paul's unheeded advice was about to
be proved sound.

B. Storm and Shipwreck (27:13-44)

For those familiar with the works of Homer, certain echoes of those works,
in particular the *Odyssey,* will be apparent in Acts 27:13-44. For example, in
Acts 27:41 we hear about the beaching of the ship using the words επεκειλαν
την ναυν. This verb and noun are used several times in the *Odyssey* to describe
this activity (cf. 9.148, 546; 13.113-14), but there are no other occurrences of
this verb or noun anywhere in Luke-Acts or the rest of the NT. Elsewhere in
this very passage Luke uses πλοιον to refer to the ship in question (cf. 27:2, 6,
10, 15, 17, 19, 22, 30, 31, 37, 38, 39, 44; 28:11).[54] Again, the idea of praying
for the day to come in v. 29 echoes what we find in *Odyssey* 9.151, 306, 436.[55]
It would be a mistake to under- or overestimate these sorts of echoes. A
balanced approach to this matter is necessary. As S. M. Praeder puts it, the
"onslaught of the storm, the sailing operations, and the sentiments of the

51. See pp. 539ff. above on Claudius and famines, and Hemer, "First Person Narrative," p. 90 n. 19, and *New Docs,* 3 (1978), no. 26, pp. 116-17.
52. It is also true that Claudius and later emperors had pretty well cleaned the seas of pirates and brigands, which made sailing easier and safer in this regard as well. See Arrian, *Epict.* 3.13.50ff.
53. See Hemer, "First Person Narrative," pp. 97-98, and contrast Smith, *Voyage and Shipwreck of St. Paul,* pp. 87-92. What Smith failed to take into account was that there was seismic activity in the region after the first century, which changed the landscape and made Pineka an unsuitable place. Also against his view is the natural meaning of the phrase κατα λιβα και κατα χωρον, which surely means southwest and northwest.
54. See the discussion in Praeder, "Acts 27.1–28.16," p. 701.
55. See Bruce, *The Acts of the Apostles,* p. 523, who rightly also stresses that many of the concepts and some of the wording of the *Odyssey* became part of a literary tradition in accounts involving nautical matters.

sailors and the passengers in vv. 13-20 show first-hand or second-hand familiarity with the storm scenes in Greek and Latin literature. *As a whole, however, the passage falls short of the formulas for literary or rhetorical storm scenes.*"[56] These conclusions are the very opposite of those of Lüdemann, who sees vv. 6-44 as almost entirely a result of Luke's reading and literary art.[57] Even Dibelius saw in these verses either Luke's eyewitness report or a reliable tradition about Paul's misadventures on his journey to Rome, though he thought the report was written up on the basis of literary models.[58] There appears to be some truth to this latter claim.

According to *v. 13* things began well. There was a moderate south wind, which led to the belief that they could rather easily sail the four to six miles past the point of Crete (Cape Matala) and then around to the bay where Phoenix lay, another thirty-six miles or so farther. They sailed very close to shore just to be on the safe side. What they had not counted on is a northeaster rushing down from eight-thousand-foot-high Mount Ida. Luke says two important things about this wind. (1) He calls it τυφωνικος, from which we get the word "typhoon." This word refers to swirling clouds and sea caused by the meeting of opposing air currents. Whether it was a full-fledged funnel cloud or not, Luke is describing a very volatile and dangerous weather condition for any ancient ship. (2) Luke says the condition was produced by a Ευρακυλων.[59] This hybrid word is produced by the combination of the Greek word for the east wind (Ευρος) and the Latin *Aquilo*, the word for the north wind. Though there is no evidence elsewhere in Greek literature for this word, its Latin equivalent, *euroaquilo*, has in fact been found at Thugga in the province of Africa on a piece of pavement with the twelve points of the compass. From its position it surely refers to the direction north-northeast (cf. *CIL* 8.26652).[60] This particular wind, which today we call a northeaster, was the most feared of all winds, and is called in the Mediterranean world the *gregale* or *grigal*. Luke is not using technical language but rather the common language used in his world for such phenomena (cf. below on v. 17 on Syrtis).

V. 15 indicates that the ship was caught by this wind and was unable to look the wind eye to eye (αντοφθαλμειν; cf. Polybius, *Hist.* 1.17.3). This last expression likely comes from the practice of painting eyes on each side of the bow of a ship.[61] In fact, ancient ships were not made so that they could tack

---

56. Praeder, "Acts 27.1–28.16," p. 689, emphasis added.
57. Lüdemann, *Early Christianity*, p. 260.
58. See Dibelius, *Studies in the Acts*, pp. 7-8.
59. The Textus Receptus has ευροκλυδων, which may mean either rough water or a southeaster, but this is surely a later mistake. Cf. Larkin, *Acts*, p. 370 and the note.
60. See the discussion in Hemer, *Book of Acts*, pp. 141-42.
61. See Smith, *Voyage and Shipwreck of St. Paul*, p. 98 n. 2.

and sail directly into such a violent wind, so the only other choice was to give way to the wind and be carried along by it, trying to maintain some control. Thus *v. 16* indicates that they sailed under the lee of the small island of Cauda (modern Guzzo, some twenty-three miles southwest from where they were struck by the wind), which no doubt they hoped would block some of the wind so they could regain control of the boat. *V. 17* refers to at least two operations: (1) they hoisted the dinghy up onto the deck of the boat; (2) they did something to strengthen the boat. The verb ὑποζωννύντες literally refers to undergirding the ship with ropes. What is not so clear is whether the technique called "frapping" was used, in which case the ropes were passed under the ship, or whether some method of bracing the ship by tying ropes around the hull or transversely across the deck was used.[62] Though they were a long way from the Syrtis (here likely a reference to the greater Syrtis, which is shoals and sandbars located at the Gulf of Sidra off the Libyan coast), indeed some four hundred miles from Cauda, the wind was such that they feared being driven that far and so they lowered "the gear" and continued to be driven along. What exactly "the gear" was is not clear. The word in question, σκεῦος, could refer to a sail (cf. Jon. 1:5 LXX; Acts 10:11) that was lowered, or perhaps an anchor of some sort, or, as Smith has suggested, it refers to gear connected with fair-weather sails.[63] None of these activities stopped the boat from being driven.

The storm stirred up by the wind continued to be very violent into the next day, and the ship was taking a pounding. A clear indication of the growing desperation on board the ship is that *v. 18* indicates that the cargo began to be jettisoned. *V. 38* makes clear that not all the cargo was thrown overboard at this time, and presumably what is meant is that some of the grain or perhaps some expendable personal effects were tossed out. *V. 19* indicates that this process continued the next day, with the σκεους, perhaps some sails and their gear (cf. above on v. 17), being thrown overboard. It is not clear why here the word αὐτόχειρες appears, unless the point is to indicate the intentionality of the sailors in getting rid of this gear with their own hands. The storm did not sweep it off the deck. Luke is painting a picture of growing desperation on the part of the crew. *V. 20* recounts the further decline into despair and hopelessness. A ship in a storm without its full gear, and without either sun or stars or landmarks to guide it for many days, was clearly lost at sea. Luke indicates that at this point the general mood was that all hope of being "saved" was finally abandoned. The "we" must surely include not merely the crew and other passengers but also presumably the author as well, but not Paul (see

---

62. See the helpful discussion in Polhill, *Acts*, p. 521 n. 23, and *Beginnings*, 5:345-54.
63. Cf. Smith, *Voyage and Shipwreck of St. Paul*, p. 111, to Bruce, *The Acts of the Apostles*, p. 520.

below).[64] The verb σωζω and its cognates begin to appear here and recur throughout the rest of the chapter, and much has been made of the suggestion that this terminology has spiritual overtones.[65] The tendency to overallegorize the account should be resisted. Luke's focus is on the rescue of the passengers from danger, including especially Paul. There is no proclamation of the gospel message by Paul, and the pagans on board remain pagans after they arrive on the shore of Malta. At most, there may be a vague allusion to the Lukan notion that in regard to *God's part* or action in this narrative, God's desire is for the salvation of all humankind (cf., e.g., Luke 3:6).[66]

In *vv. 21-25* Paul makes a brief speech to counter the despair that had set in. This speech summary is too brief for detailed rhetorical analysis, but its general character seems to be deliberative — exhorting the audience to take action that will be useful or beneficial to them in the near future.[67] After the opening address (ω ανδρες), there is a brief *narratio*, where Paul reminds his audience of what he had previously advised, advice which had gone unheeded. The function of the mention of the earlier advice is to strengthen the force or authority of the advice to eat that was about to follow. The speech has some nice rhetorical touches such as the irony in referring to the "*gaining* of this injury and *loss.*" Various commentators have questioned the credibility of this speech, which they think would be unlikely to be given during a raging storm.[68] Praeder also points out, however, that such speeches were commonplaces of the accounts of storm scenes (cf. Homer, *Ody.* 5.299-312; Lucian, *Bel. Civ.* 5.653-71; Seneca, *Ag.* 510-27; Virgil, *Aen.* 1.92-101).[69] It seems unlikely to me that this widespread convention was based on pure human imagination. Furthermore, this speech is, in character and rhetorical function, quite the opposite to what we find in the literary speeches in some of the sources cited above. In those speeches the message is about the danger of the situation and preparation for impending doom.[70] Here the message is one of hope in the midst of despair.

There must surely have been historical incidents in antiquity in which people attempted to exhort and rally crew and passengers in such situations,

---

64. The note of hopelessness is common in these sorts of storm-at-sea accounts; cf. *Odyssey* 5.297-304; 12.277-79; Aelius Aristides, *Sacred Tales* 2.12. The important point to note is that it is not confined to legendary or fictional accounts of this sort but is also found in historical works; cf. Thucydides, *Pelop.* 1.2.65.

65. See Tannehill, *Narrative Unity of Luke-Acts*, 2:336-39, and Praeder, "Acts 27.1–28.16," pp. 692-95.

66. See my discussion of the salvation language in Luke-Acts: "Salvation and Health in Christian Antiquity," Appendix 2, pp. 821ff. below.

67. Contra Kennedy, *New Testament Interpretation*, p. 138, who sees it as epideictic, as does Soards, *The Speeches in Acts*, p. 127.

68. See, e.g., Roloff, *Die Apostelgeschichte*, pp. 361ff.

69. Praeder, "Acts 27.1–28.16," p. 695.

70. See rightly Polhill, *Acts*, p. 523.

as there have been in the modern era (e.g., during the sinking of the *Titanic*). Notice we are not told the location of this Pauline speech, which may have been given below deck (where the food was kept) to all but a skeleton crew who were above trying to control the boat. Notice also that v. 21 suggests they had all been sitting down, and Paul rose up in their midst to speak. I conclude that while this speech may be a literary creation, its lack of conformity in function and message to such literary speeches suggests otherwise. Luke was likely present to hear these stirring words, and in view of the "we" in v. 20, he himself apparently needed and would have remembered this exhortation in a desperate situation.

V. 21 refers to ασιτια, which has to do with voluntarily going without food, and πολλης suggests this had been going on for a long time. This may have been caused by seasickness, or anxiety, or because the food had been spoiled, but presumably not the latter since they go on to eat after this exhortation. As Bruce says, Paul is clearly not being portrayed here as a "divine man" or perfect person. He was not above a bit of "I told you so" at the beginning of this speech.[71] He does not perform nature miracles, reversing the storm's effects or the like. He is portrayed as a passionate person who cares deeply about the lives of his fellow travelers, and this pastoral portrait comports with what we know of Paul from his letters. He is also seen as a prophet, one who receives revelations and visions from God.[72] Paul begins by speaking of how it was *necessary* (εδει) for them to have listened to him when he urged not sailing on from Fair Havens. They could have avoided "gaining this loss." But Paul was not going to dwell on the mistakes of the past, especially since his audience was already at the point of despair.

V. 22 provides us with Paul's exhortation for all to keep their courage up, and he offers the reassurance that they will all be kept safe, only the ship and cargo will be lost. The difference between this message and that found in v. 10 is presumably that now Paul has had the benefit of a divine revelation about what would happen, whereas before he was simply giving the opinion of a seasoned traveler. V. 23 indicates that "an angel of the God to whom I belong and whom I worship" appeared to him and reassured him. What this verse makes quite clear is that Paul is addressing a largely pagan audience, and so he refers to the God that he worships. This is the only place where we are told an angel of God, as opposed to Jesus (e.g., cf. 18:9-10; 23:11), appeared to Paul,[73] but he has appeared before in Acts (cf. 5:19; 7:26; 10:3; 12:7, 23).

---

71. See Bruce, *The Acts of the Apostles*, p. 521.

72. See Johnson, *Acts*, p. 459.

73. Bruce, *The Acts of the Apostles*, p. 521, suggests that Paul was evidently able to distinguish the angel from Christ because he didn't have the same appearance as Christ had on the Damascus road!

The message given to Paul by the angel, as recorded in *v. 24*, is both on the one hand generic and on the other more specific than the previous divine messages Paul had received. The exhortation not to be afraid is common in such scenes (cf., e.g., Luke 1:13, 30), but here for the first time we are told that Paul must stand before the emperor. Before in 23:11 Paul had simply been reassured he must bear witness in Rome. We are also told that God had granted safety to all those who were traveling with Paul. The focus here is clearly on Paul's safety, but there is benefit to the others who are traveling with him.

This account has led to comparisons not only with the story of Jonah but also with other stories about sea journeys and rescues in pagan literature. In the former case, however, Jonah was the cause of the storm and trouble being endured by those with him on the ship, while the opposite is the case in this story. The implication of our story is that all would have been lost if Paul had not been on board.

There is something, however, to be said for the work of G. B. Miles, G. Trompf, and separately D. Ladouceur, who try to analyze how Luke's audience would have understood this account.[74] The former two scholars have suggested that in view of other accounts in Greek literature of sea travel and being rescued from storms, or being given safe passage through them, a Gentile reader would have read Acts 27–28 as indicating not merely that God was on Paul's side, but that he was innocent of any crimes; otherwise the miraculous rescue of Paul and all the passengers would never have transpired. This is based on the widespread belief that the gods punished the wicked, and that misfortunes at sea were no accident. Entailed in this belief was also the notion that the innocent also sometimes got hurt, by being associated with the guilty, for instance on a sea voyage. This latter notion seems to be evident not only in Greek literature but also in Jon. 1:1–2:1. Miles and Trompf point to the parallels in Antiphon (περι του Ηεροδου φονου 82-83) with our account. They go on to suggest that the trial at the end of Paul's journey is omitted because a Gentile audience would see it as superfluous — Paul's rescue at sea had already demonstrated his innocence.[75]

Ladouceur attempts to refine the argument of Miles and Trompf by pointing out a far closer parallel to our account, namely, that recorded in Andocides, *De myst.* 137-39. Here we have a speech which indicates not only that sea travel was seen as the most perilous situation of all, and the most likely time for a god to exercise justice on a wicked person, but also the clear affirmation that "the dangers of the sea [are] the work of God" (139). Conversely as well, the account suggests that rescue from such perils at sea is also the work of God.

---

74. See Miles and Trompf, "Luke and Antiphon"; Ladouceur, "Hellenistic Preconceptions."

75. See Miles and Trompf, "Luke and Antiphon," p. 265.

There is, as Ladouceur says, further indication that Luke wishes us to read this story in light of the Greek literature on the subject. The only time in all of Acts that Luke mentions a ship's sign is in 28:11, where we hear that the craft is named the *Dioskouroi,* a reference to Castor and Pollux, the deities sailors prayed to for protection while on the seas. Perhaps more importantly these gods were related to the imperial cult, and there was a frequent comparison between these gods and the emperor, or even the identification of the emperor with one of these gods during the reigns we are most interested in (the Claudian and Neronian periods).[76] This makes plausible the suggestion that the "fact that Paul sailed from Malta not only under the Dioskouroi's protection but also with their favor may be, then, an indirect reference to an implicit rendering of the imperial verdict that awaited him before the last representative of that same house."[77] In other words, Acts 27–28 may be intending to send signals to a Gentile audience familiar with the above not only about Paul's innocence in God's eyes but also ultimately his vindication and release when he appeared before the Flavian "Castor" in person. These signals or allusions work only if the audience was in fact Gentile, and to some degree literate, as is likely.[78]

Vv. 25-26 present us with the end of the speech, which is much like the beginning in its exhortation to courage, but the stress that Paul has faith in God (πιστευω τω Θεω, here meaning trust in God) is a new note. The trust in this case is in the fact that God is as good as his word — "it will be exactly a I have been told." V. 26, almost an addendum, leaves the bad news for last and indicates that unfortunately safety is only going to come by or after the ship by necessity (δει) runs aground on some island. Here again, as in v. 10, Paul is less than exact in his remarks, as in fact the ship seems to have run aground on a shoal or reef and not an island (cf. below on v. 41). Paul is clearly being portrayed as the spiritual leader and pastor, and he was about to lead by example.

V. 27 indicates that when the fourteenth night had come, the ship was drifting across the Sea of Adria. This should not be confused with the modern body of water called the Adriatic Sea, which lies between the west coast of Italy and the former Yugoslavia. The references in ancient authors (cf. Strabo, *Geog.* 2.5.20; Pausanias, *Periegesis* 5.25.3; Ptolemy, *Geog.* 3.4.1; 15.1) indicate that the body of water Luke is referring to included the Ionian Sea and the northern part of the Mediterranean between Greece and Italy and extending down to Crete and Malta.[79]

---

76. See Scott, *Imperial Cult under the Flavians,* pp. 114, 141-43.
77. Ladouceur, "Hellenistic Preconceptions," p. 447.
78. See pp. 62ff. above.
79. See Hemer, *Book of Acts,* p. 146 and n. 129; Polhill, *Acts,* pp. 524-25.

One of the most convincing portions of Smith's detailed study of Paul's journey is the calculation of how long it would take a ship of the sort Paul was on, in the face of a northeaster, to drift from Cauda to near the mouth of Saint Paul's Bay at Malta at the point called Koura. The distance is some 475 miles, and Smith's detailed comparison of nautical accounts from this region showed that it was likely to take right at fourteen days to drift this far.[80] This is a rather striking confirmation of the accuracy of Luke's account.

About midnight of the fourteenth day after the storm began, the sailors began to suspect "that some land was approaching."[81] This is of course the way it would appear to someone on board a ship.[82] This sense of land led, according to *v. 28*, to the taking of soundings. Βολιζω is in fact the correct technical term for sounding. This process involved the casting of lead weights tied to long cords into the water. The weights would have hollow spots on their undersides that were filled with grease or tallow so that when they were pulled up, if they had touched bottom there would be debris from the bottom adhering to the tallow (Herodotus, *Hist.* 2.5).[83] At first they were in twenty fathoms of water, or about 120 feet, but soon thereafter they were in only fifteen fathoms.

V. 29 indicates the sailors feared running onto rocks in the dark, so they lowered four anchors from the stern and prayed for day to come. This might seem an odd procedure since modern ships almost always anchor from the bow, but as Smith points out, it would not be so if the object was to run the boat aground on a safe piece of shore in the morning.[84] Furthermore, ancient ships were very much the same shape in the bow and stern, and so nothing in their form made one end or the other more advantageous for anchoring (see the picture on p. 782 below).

V. 30 suggests that the sailors also had their own skins primarily in view. We are told here that they lowered the dinghy into the sea and tried to escape, P on the pretext of putting out anchors from the bow.[85] Paul, according to

---

80. Smith, *Voyage and Shipwreck of St. Paul*, pp. 124-27. He reckoned the time beginning with when the storm hit and calculated the drift of the ship at about one and a half miles an hour.

81. B* has προσαχειν, "to resound," surely a secondary emendation. See Metzger, *Textual Commentary*, p. 498; cf. Marshall, *Acts*, p. 411 n. 1.

82. Smith, *Voyage and Shipwreck of St. Paul*, p. 120 n. 1, calls this the vivid language of sailors, "to whom the ship is the principal object, whilst the land rises and sinks, nears and recedes. . . ."

83. See Hemer, *Book of Acts*, p. 147.

84. Smith, *Voyage and Shipwreck of St. Paul*, p. 135.

85. This was no doubt an act of desperation, but as ibid., p. 137, points out, using examples, even in the modern era such risks have been taken by sailors when the alternatives seemed worse. We may also note Achilles Tatius, *Leucippe and Clitophon* 3.3, and Petronius, *Satyricon* 102, where the sailors fight off the passengers to get possession of the dinghy and

v. 31, immediately reported this activity to the centurion and the soldiers, stating emphatically, "Unless these men stay in the ship, you cannot be saved." This presumably is not a prophetic word but a sagacious observation. If the boat is to be run aground, the skilled hands on board — the sailors — would be needed to do this properly.[86] The centurion on this occasion acted promptly on Paul's advice and the soldiers cut away the dinghy, so no one could use it to escape.

V. 33 indicates that just before dawn Paul urged all on board to take nourishment, urging that this was critical since they had eaten nothing for some fourteen days.[87] Paul's calm demeanor here may suggest that we are meant to see him as a true philosopher (cf. Diogenes Laertius, *Lives* 2.71; Lucian, *Peregrin.* 43-44). "Ancient people evaluated the sincerity of philosophers (e.g. Aristippus) according to how calm they stayed under pressure."[88] This may perhaps mean that there had been no formally prepared meals during the storm.[89] *V. 34* states that eating was necessary for their survival (cf. NRSV). In fact, echoing a well-known Jewish maxim, Paul says that not one hair on their heads will be harmed (cf. Luke 12:7; 21:18; and the background in the LXX versions of 1 Sam. 14:45; 2 Sam. 14:11; 1 Kings 1:52). The term σωτηρια here in all likelihood means survival in the mundane sense, not salvation. As with the σωζω language, commentators have been much too eager to see Paul as serving some sort of eucharistic or symbolic meal at this point. The only point really in favor of this conclusion is the similarity in language between 27:35 and Luke 22:19 (cf. 1 Cor. 11:23f.).[90]

Against this conclusion are weighty considerations. (1) There is nothing anywhere in Luke-Acts that suggests that Luke believed that salvation came by

---

escape from a ship (in the former account), and simply abandon ship in the latter by means of a boat. Though these are fictitious stories, they are likely based on known examples of human behavior.

86. As Keener points out (*Bible Background Commentary*, p. 402), pagans felt that if they died at sea they would never enter the realm of the dead, but rather their souls would wander aimlessly at sea. When a pagan feared for his life, the last place he wanted to be was on a foundering boat.

87. Praeder, "Acts 27.1–28.16," pp. 696-97, rightly notes that vv. 33-38 are unique, and show that this account is not simply a literary composition based on other storm scenes in Greek literature.

88. Keener, *Bible Background Commentary*, p. 402.

89. See Marshall, *Acts*, p. 413; Polhill, *Acts*, p. 526. Paul is probably speaking somewhat hyperbolically here to get his point across, as a good rhetor was likely to do to be sure the response was proper. V. 33 surely builds on v. 21, as Polhill notes.

90. One might also mention the listing of how many were on the ship at the end of this account (cf. Mark 6:46), but notice that in Luke's account of the feeding of the five thousand (Luke 9:10-17), Luke doesn't mention the size of the crowd at the end of the account, unlike Mark, but rather in the middle. In any case, the feeding miracle was also not a Lord's Supper story.

means of taking part in the Lord's Supper. In fact we have noted earlier in the commentary how little attention Luke pays to the Lord's Supper in general. Some would say he may not even mention it in Acts![91] (2) The language of taking bread, breaking it, and giving thanks ultimately comes not from the Lord's Supper but from Jewish thanksgiving meals. The Lord's Supper was indebted to this earlier Jewish practice, not the other way around.[92] (3) There is no mention here of wine at all, nor any interpretive discussion of the elements.[93] (4) Paul does not distribute anything to anyone; rather, he sets the example of eating and others follow him. (5) This meal is said to satisfy the hunger of the passengers (v. 38), and so is more like the account of the feeding of the five thousand than the Lord's Supper. (6) This meal, unlike the Lord's Supper, is not a community-forming or community-building meal. The pagans remain pagans after eating, and are not being treated as potential Christians here.[94] (7) The focus of this narrative is on Paul's heroic actions to rescue his fellow travelers, not on ecclesiology. The Lukan portrait of Paul is what we are meant to notice here, and here he is portrayed as a good Jewish Christian pastor, drawing on his Jewish heritage and caring for his fellow passengers.[95]

At *v. 37* Luke mentions parenthetically that there were 276 persons on board, and here the "we" is all-inclusive of the passengers on the boat.[96] This means that Paul was on a fairly substantial-sized boat, though not as large as the one in which Josephus traveled on a similar route in about A.D. 63. He, too, experienced shipwreck in the Sea of Adria with some 600 persons on board, but only 80 survived (*Vita* 15).[97] *V. 38* indicates that once everyone had eaten, they then assisted in lightening the boat by throwing the wheat into the sea. Thus we learn at this point that Paul is clearly sailing on an Alexandrian wheat vessel.

V. 39 indicates that when morning came, no one recognized the land

91. See pp. 156ff. above.

92. See rightly Polhill, *Acts*, p. 527: "The breaking of bread and giving of thanks was the customary Jewish form of blessing a meal, and Jesus was observing that custom in the Lord's Supper. Paul was also observing that custom and in the presence of a predominantly pagan group."

93. See Praeder, "Acts 27.1–28.16," p. 699: "It is true that the historical meal, if there was such a meal, could not have been a eucharistic meal. It is also true that the narrative meal is not a celebration of Christian community. Paul and the passengers are not pictured as sharing bread and wine; rather they take separate meals from whatever stores of food are at hand."

94. See Marshall, *Acts*, p. 413.

95. Especially unconvincing are the arguments of Pokorny, "Die Romfahrt des Paulus und der antike Roman," that Luke means us to think all 276 received eternal salvation.

96. You might say that here the "we" indicates everyone was in the same boat.

97. Is this another example of Josephus's inflated numbers, compared to Luke's? See pp. 235ff. above.

they saw, but a bay was noticed with a beach where they could run the boat
ashore. This was in fact their battle plan. The first step in realizing the plan
was the casting away of the anchors, leaving them in the sea, the loosening of
the ropes that tied the oars (and the lowering of the oars into the water), and
the raising of the foresail[98] to make for the beach. Unfortunately they never
got there, for *v. 41* indicates that they ran aground by striking the place of two
waters. There has been debate as to where this was located, with some arguing
that it refers to a shoal or sandbar and others that it refers to the channel
between Salmonetta Island and the mainland of Malta. In favor of the latter
is that this narrow channel, not more than one hundred yards wide, was a
place where the bay water and the sea met. This latter was Smith's view, but
he did not take into account that in ancient times the shoal, now called Saint
Paul's Bank, was much more substantial than it is today.[99] Saint Paul's Bank
is a more probable location, for the sailors were unlikely to try to squeeze their
boat through so narrow a passage in order to reach the beach, when they were
having trouble controlling it anyway. This conclusion is also supported by the
use of the key word in Dio Chrysostom which suggests that it refers to a feature
of land that creates "two seas," that is, a sandbar (Dio Chrysostom, *Dis.* 5.9;
cf. Strabo, *Geog.* 1.1.8; 2.5.22).

What in fact happened was that the bow of the ship got stuck,[100] and
the stern was beaten into pieces by the waves. According to *v. 42* the soldiers
resolved to kill the prisoners, so they wouldn't swim off and escape. This action
would likely only be taken against those who were already condemned criminals.[101] The other reason for acting in this fashion was the severe actions taken
against a soldier who let a criminal slip from his grasp, sometimes even
involving capital punishment for the soldier (cf. on 16:25-28).[102] The centurion, however, intervened, because we are told in *v. 43* that he wished to save
Paul. Instead he ordered those who could swim to jump overboard and do so.
V. 44 indicates the rest followed, clinging to planks of wood or holding on to
the backs of some of the swimmers.[103] "And so it was that all were brought
safely to land."[104] The overall impression left by this narrative is of God's

98. This is apparently what αρτεμων means. The foresail was the one used for guiding.
99. See Smith, *Voyage and Shipwreck of St. Paul*, pp. 143-47; Bruce, *The Acts of the Apostles*, p. 527.
100. Ramsay, *St. Paul the Traveller*, p. 341, says the ship struck a bottom of mud which became clay, holding the ship's bow fast.
101. See pp. 679ff. above.
102. See pp. 652ff. above.
103. επι τινων των απο του πλοιου could either mean "on some of the things from the ship" or less likely, "on some of the people from the ship." See Haenchen, *Acts*, p. 708.
104. On the general plausibility of Luke's account of this voyage shipwreck see Rapske, "Acts, Travel, and Shipwreck," pp. 29-46.

providence overruling all the natural circumstances which could have led to death and total disaster, and that Paul's presence on the ship, on whom God had placed his protective hand, saved the rest of those traveling as well. While it is probably too much to call this a ministry to Gentiles, especially since there are no converts, nevertheless what happened was a testimony to the pagans of the power of Paul's God.[105]

C. Hospitality and Healing on Malta (28:1-11)

According to *Acts 28:1* it was not until after they reached land that Paul and his fellow travelers learned that they were on the island called Μελιτη.[106] There has been some debate as to whether this is the island of Malta (Sicula Melita) or Mljet (Melita Illyrica).[107] The evidence points strongly to the former location. The first writer to suggest Mljet was apparently Emperor Constantine VII in the tenth century A.D., and the suggestion seems to be based on a more narrow and later understanding of the meaning of the Sea of Adria (cf. 27:27). Furthermore, a northeaster would not blow a boat from Cauda to Mljet, which is far to the north of the island of Malta. Finally, the grain transport network between Alexandria and Rome did not have Mljet as an intermediate stopping-off point, but Malta was such a stop, which explains the presence of the *Dioskouroi* there.[108]

Malta,[109] a small island only 18 miles long and 8 miles wide, lies about

105. See Cassidy, *Society and Politics*, p. 126. Not an allegory about Paul reliving or mirroring the end of the life of Christ, pace Jacobson, "Paul in Luke-Acts." The shipwreck is hardly a symbol of death, especially when Paul promises beforehand that not one hair on anyone's head would be harmed, and in fact all survived, not just Paul. Are we to think of 276 Christ figures here?

106. B* and other manuscripts have the reading Μελιτηνη here, but this is probably an example of the scribal error known as dittography. Some Latin manuscripts presuppose the reading Μυτιληνη, but this is likely an error through a mental combining of 20:14's Mitylene with what we find here in 28:1. See Metzger, *Textual Commentary*, p. 500.

107. Cf. Hemer, "Euraquilo and Melita," to Acworth, "Where Was St. Paul Shipwrecked?"

108. Lüdemann, *Early Christianity*, pp. 262-63, considers a stay by Paul on Malta likely historical, though he thinks the substance of the account here is highly legendary if not a pure Lukan creation, perhaps especially because it seems superfluous to the ongoing story line, being in his eyes a piece of hagiography. I would suggest that Longenecker, *Acts*, p. 564, is nearer the mark to see this narrative not as hagiography but as an important part of the case Luke is mounting that "Paul was not only a heaven-directed man with a God-given message but also a heaven-protected man." On the historical character of this narrative see Rapske, "Acts, Travel, and Shipwreck," pp. 44-45.

109. It is perhaps fitting that Melita in fact means a place of refuge, for so it became for Paul and those with him.

58 miles south of Sicily and 180 miles northeast of the coast of Africa. The latter is important because it was colonized by the Phoenicians about 1000 B.C., apparently from their base in Africa. Even in Paul's day the vernacular language was still a Punic or Carthaginian dialect, though clearly some Greek and Latin were spoken there as well, primarily by Rome's representatives and the various Greek and Roman settlers who had come to live there over the generations. In fact, most of the inscriptions that have been found on the island are in Greek or Latin, though the first-century ones are mostly bilingual with Greek and Punic.[110] This suggests that the islanders would have been perfectly capable of speaking to these shipwrecked travelers in Greek, though they likely spoke in Punic among themselves.

Augustus had set up a Roman magistrate over the island whose title appears to have been *municipi Melitesium primus omnium,* or the chief man over all in the municipality of Malta (cf. *CIL* 10.7495; *CIG* 5754).[111] It is not impossible, however, that these inscriptions refer to the chief benefactor on the island, rather than the chief official, which might better comport with the character of our story about Publius the estate owner.[112] Luke is well aware of the title of this man, whether an official or simply the island's most prominent benefactor, and calls him τω πρωτω της νησου ("the first of the island" — v. 7).

The language of benefaction pervades this entire story, and what we see is a reciprocity relationship set up between Publius and the islanders on one hand and Paul and his fellow travelers on the other. The natives of Malta provide warmth and hospitality at the beginning of the story, and Paul (and Luke?) provides healing on his part. Then at the end of the story the Maltese reciprocate by providing provisions and funds for these sojourners to travel on. One subliminal message of this narrative is that such reciprocity or "friendship" relationships can and should exist between Christians and pagans.

Luke reveals something of his own character in *v. 2* when he calls the natives of this island βαρβαροι. The basic meaning of this word is a person who does not speak Greek,[113] and it usually also implies a person lacking Greek culture. It does not mean a "barbarian" here, though this English word is a transliteration from the Greek term. The use of this term strongly suggests that Luke, if not from Greece, is at least the gentile child of Greek culture,

---

110. See Cadbury, *Book of Acts in History,* p. 24.

111. This local magistrate is not to be confused with the proconsul who was over both Malta and Gozo. See Larkin, *Acts,* p. 381 n.

112. See Hemer, "First Person Narrative," p. 100.

113. The term is onomatopoetic and seems to have originated from the sound that Greeks thought they heard when non-Greeks (those who lived beyond or mostly untouched by the influence of Greco-Roman culture) spoke to them, namely, "bar, bar, bar." See Longenecker, *Acts,* p. 564.

sharing something of its worldview.[114] In fact, the whole of the first portion of Acts 28 breathes the air of Greco-Roman antiquity, a world where it was widely believed that all people eventually faced their fate, and especially the wicked in due course met their Nemesis in the form of divine justice.[115] With a classical subject it is no surprise that this narrative also reflects a certain amount of classical style (two examples of litotes, two genitive absolutes). The narrative is about one of the most highly regarded virtues of antiquity, hospitality, being a tale of "the kindness of strangers," but it is also about the providence of God that places Paul and his companions in a place where they could receive such hospitality, after such a rough journey.

V. 2 says the "natives" showed "no ordinary love (Lukan litotes) of their fellow human beings" (φιλανθρωπιαν), or as we would say, no little philanthropy or kindness.[116] This kindness initially took the form of building a bonfire on the beach, not only because these travelers had just come out of the sea but also because it had already begun to rain,[117] even though the temperature at this time of year on Malta was probably about fifty degrees Fahrenheit.[118] Once the fire was built they welcomed all of the weary travelers around it.

Paul himself took part in helping build the fire, for v. 3 tells us that he had gathered some brushwood and put it on the fire when a snake, aroused by the fire, fastened itself on Paul's hand. Luke uses the word εχιδνα for this creature, which suggests some sort of poisonous viper. It has been complained that Malta does not have any poisonous snakes, and it has also been noted that poisonous snakes such as vipers strike and withdraw rather than fastening themselves on their victims. On the basis of these two facts Conzelmann and Haenchen have suspected that this is not an eyewitness account.[119] It should be noted, however, that nineteen hundred years of civilization and the gradual extinction of various species of creatures on that island caused by human expansion can easily account for the absence of poisonous snakes on Malta today.[120]

---

114. See Ramsay, *St. Paul the Traveller*, p. 343: "The term 'barbarians,' v. 2, is characteristic of the nationality of the writer. It does not indicate rudeness or uncivilised habits, but merely non-Greek birth; and it is difficult to imagine that a Syrian or a Jew or any one but a Greek would have applied the name to the people of Malta, who had been in contact with Phoenicians and Romans for many centuries."

115. On the character of this entire narrative, see Cadbury, *The Making of Luke-Acts*, pp. 341-42.

116. The phrase τας τυχουσας φιλανθρωπιας seems to have been a common one. Cf. Dionysius of Halicarnassus 14. frag. 6.1.

117. The perfect tense of the verb here indicates a condition which began in the past and continued to have effects into the present.

118. See Haenchen, *Acts*, p. 713 n. 3.

119. See Conzelmann, *Acts*, p. 223; Haenchen, *Acts*, pp. 713, 716.

120. Hemer, *Book of Acts*, p. 153.

It may also be the case that Luke has not used the term εχιδνα with precision (but see Lucian, *Alex.* 10). There is a snake, which has long been found on Malta, belonging to the species *Coronella austriaca*,[121] which is a type of constrictor. This is thought to better fit the description of a snake fastening itself on Paul's hand.[122] A belief that this snake was poisonous does not necessarily distinguish the Maltans from other ancients, for Pliny the Elder indicates it was a common belief, even among the educated, that all snakes were poisonous and that they were often agents of divine vengeance (see *Nat. Hist.* 8.85-86).[123] This comports with what follows, where they are indeed depicted as "religious" in a primitive sense and see the snake as an agent of Justice. Perhaps the Maltans were familiar with some of the stories we now find in the *Greek Anthology*, for example, about a shipwrecked sailor who escapes storm at sea only to be bitten by a viper and die (see *Grk. Anth.* 7.290 and 9.269).

One of the more important things to note about this entire tale is the matter of point of view. Luke focuses on the reaction of the Maltese to what happens to Paul. It is a mistake to assume that their point of view is that of the author's, either in regard to their first or final estimation of Paul.[124] Luke certainly does not think of Paul as a murderer, and, equally, earlier texts make clear that he has no desire to portray him as a divine man either (cf. especially 14:11-19). Paul is, however, portrayed as one through whom God works and speaks, doing miracles and offering prophecies.[125] It is God and God's providence that is ultimately being glorified here.[126]

V. 4 tells us that the natives deduce that Paul must be a murderer whom Justice had finally punished by not allowing him to go on living. Η Δικη was the Greek goddess of justice, the virgin daughter of Zeus. She kept watch over

---

121. Another similar species, *Cornella leopardinus*, was also known on this island. See Bruce, *The Acts of the Apostles*, p. 531.

122. Cf. Pesch, *Die Apostelgeschichte (Apg. 13–28)*, p. 298; Polhill, *Acts*, p. 532.

123. Larkin, *Acts*, p. 380 n., thinks we should trust the Maltans' knowledge of snakes on their island, but this disregards that the Maltans are also depicted as first thinking Paul is a murderer and then that he is a god. This does not speak well for their powers of discernment. In short, they are portrayed here as friendly but superstitious, and snakes were often part of such primitive religious thinking. Notice, for example, Mark 16:18, which may in fact be based on this story in Acts (see Bruce, *The Acts of the Apostles*, p. 532).

124. See rightly Tannehill, *Narrative Unity of Luke-Acts*, 2:340-41, and Praeder, "Acts 27.1–28.16," p. 702, and also her "Miracle Worker and Missionary," critiquing Dibelius, Conzelmann, and others.

125. See Barrett, "Paul Shipwrecked," pp. 56-59, rightly critiquing the divine man theories of H. Koester and others.

126. Dibelius, *Studies in the Acts*, p. 204 n. 27, misses the point, for this story does indeed sound like a Christian tradition about Paul as a prophet and healer protected by God. It is not a merely secular story.

injustices on the earth and reported them to her father, who dispensed final justice (cf. Hesiod, *Work and Days* 239, 256; Plutarch, *Moral.* 161F). The Phoenicians also had a god or demigod Justice (Sydyk), and presumably Luke is simply using the equivalent Greek term.[127]

When Paul suffered no real harm and in fact shook the snake off his hand and into the fire according to *v. 5*, the natives changed their tune altogether.[128] Luke tells us in *v. 6* that they waited a long time to see what would happen, and he speaks of their expectation that Paul would swell up[129] or die.[130] When they saw nothing unusual happening to Paul, they began to say he was a god.[131] There is no worship of Paul or attempt to worship recorded here, and so there is no rebuke for doing so as in Acts 14. From a Jewish context the most interesting parallel to this story is the tale told about Hanina ben Dosa, who was once bitten by a poisonous snake, but he was such a holy man that the snake died instead of the man (*y. Ber.* 5:1; cf. *t. Sanh.* 8:3)! More proximately it is in order perhaps to see this story as an example of the fulfillment of the word in Luke 10:18-19 about Jesus' followers having the power or authority to walk over snakes and scorpions.

V. 7 shifts gears a bit and refers to the "first man of the island," one Publius. Ποπλιος is the Greek equivalent of the Roman *praenomen* Publius, and it is probably right to suggest that he had received a grant of Roman citizenship as the top official (or most notable citizen?) on the island.[132] This was presumably the governor, though it is not impossible that Luke is referring to the most wealthy and leading citizen of the island.[133] Luke does not use the full Roman name of this person, which may suggest that he was a man who

---

127. See Larkin, *Acts*, p. 380 and note on 28:4 and the reference there to Philo of Byblos's *Phoenician History*, which refers to this deity.

128. As is often the case in the second half of Acts, μεν ουν is used in v. 5 to connect two parts of a particular narrative, not two sources or narratives as was the case in the first half of Acts. See Longenecker, *Acts*, p. 565.

129. The term πιπρασθαι, found only in Luke-Acts in the NT, is the ancient medical one for an inflammation. Its use here does not prove the author is a doctor, but it is suggestive, and certainly consistent with such a view. As Harnack, *Luke the Physician*, p. 179, long ago noted, this whole section of vv. 3-10 is "tinged with medical coloring." The argument for revisiting the suggestion that narratives like this suggest the author was a doctor can be found in *New Docs*, 2 (1977), no. 2, pp. 20ff.

130. Luke here is not reading minds but reflecting the common knowledge that poisonous snakebites did often lead to the victim swelling, in particular at the point of the bite.

131. This total change of evaluation is perhaps meant as a touch of ironic humor that Luke's cultivated audience would appreciate. See Marshall, *Acts*, p. 417.

132. If Publius was in fact simply a citizen it is possible he was not a Roman, but rather one who had obtained a Roman name with his citizenship. See Keener, *Bible Background Commentary*, p. 404.

133. See Johnson, *Acts*, p. 462.

was mature in years (though see below on his father)[134] and also that Luke was not likely a Roman himself.[135] Perhaps looking for some fresh company and an interesting diversion, Publius "received and entertained us hospitably for three days." It is not clear who is included among the "we" here. All 276? All except the soldiers and criminals? Just the centurion and Paul and his companions? Just the private citizens on the boat? Whoever else may have been involved, it certainly included Paul and the author.

V. 8 indicates that the father of Publius was lying in a bed suffering from dysentery and fevers. This may in fact be a case of Malta fever, which in the nineteenth century was discovered to be transmitted by drinking goat's milk. Paul visited him, laid hands on him, and prayed, and the man was cured. This is the only time in Acts where we find the combination of prayer and the laying on of hands in a miracle story. The story and what follows it is reminiscent of the story in Luke 4:38-44 where Peter's mother-in-law is healed of a fever and this in turn brings the crowds to Jesus for healing. The differences between the two stories are also instructive, for they show Paul is not being portrayed here as a god or divine man. In the Gospel story Jesus does not pray to a higher power for the cure but rather rebukes the fever on the basis of his own power. Afterward he is proclaimed the Son of God by the demons, and Luke stresses that he was in fact known by them to be the Messiah. Nothing similar is said of Paul after this healing.

Somewhat hyperbolically no doubt, v. 9 says the rest of the sick on the island came to Paul after this first miracle and were cured. Instead of bestowing on Paul great divine titles, they offer instead τιμαις, which may mean honors (cf. 2 Macc. 9:21; John 4:44; Rom. 13:7; 1 Cor. 12:24; 1 Tim. 5:7), but Luke regularly uses the term in a monetary sense (cf. Acts 4:34; 5:2-3; 7:16; 19:19). In view of the connection in v. 10 of these gifts with provisions that were put on board the ship when Paul and the others were leaving, it is probable that we should see this as traveling funds, something that elsewhere Paul was willing to receive from grateful supporters (cf. 1 Cor. 16:6).[136] As Johnson says, the sharing of possessions is a sign in Acts of sharing in the good news, and so perhaps we are to think that Paul did indeed share the gospel in Malta, though the text does not say so.[137] While the focus of this entire narrative is on Paul, it is not impossible, in view of

134. See pp. 775ff. above.

135. Notice that another Greek historian that Luke seems to be indebted to, Polybius, also uses Roman nomenclature in this way. Bruce, *The Acts of the Apostles*, p. 533, citing the example of Polybius, refers to P. Cornelius Scipio Aemilianus simply as Ποπλιος.

136. See my discussion of this matter in *Friendship and Finances in Philippi*, pp. 125-33. Given the healing context, texts like Sir. 38:1 and 1 Tim. 5:17 suggest that honoraria or money is meant by τιμαις here.

137. Johnson, *Acts*, p. 463.

the "we" in v. 10, that Luke aided in the curing of various people, practicing his profession.

V. 11 informs us that it was some three months before Paul and his companions were able to sail on toward their destination. If the ship wrecked in early November or less likely late October (remembering that it was after the Fast that they had left Fair Havens), they would not be leaving before about the beginning of February.[138] In view of the fact that we do not know how long after the Fast Fair Havens was left, nor do we know if the three-month figure is a round number, it seems likely that the ship that Paul and the others boarded was following the rule of thumb we find in Pliny, *Nat. Hist.* 2.47, that the beginning of the sailing season was when the west winds began to blow, on or about February 8. Vegetius (*De re mil.* 4.39), however, says that March 10 was the beginning of the sailing season. In fact, ships would sail whenever the prevailing winds from the west began to blow, and with the extra incentives offered by Claudius and Nero, a ship such as the *Dioskouroi* might well leave in the first week or two of February, weather allowing. No doubt the boat was found in the major port on Malta, Valletta.

We have already spoken of the possible overtones of the mention of the name of the sign on this grain vessel from Alexandria.[139] The twin brothers Castor and Pollux were represented by the astral sign called Gemini. They were indeed the protectors and patron "saints," or in this case deities, of both sailors and innocent travelers (see Epictetus, *Discourses* 2.18.29). Horace says Gemini was seen as a sign of good fortune in a storm.[140] We know their cult had followers in both Italy and Egypt.[141] Furthermore, Euripides (*Electra* 1342-55) regards them as guardians of truth and punishers of those who committed perjury. What better sign for the innocent Paul, the carrier of the good news of God's truth, to sail under to Rome?

On the whole, the account of the sea journey and the stay on Malta seem intended to display "images of cooperative relationships between Christians and non-Christians, to the benefit of all . . . the narrative undermines any

138. My calculations would be as follows: (1) the Fast (Acts 27:9) in question was on October 5 A.D. 59, but Luke says even it had passed when the plan was hatched to sail on from Fair Havens. We must, then, allow a few additional days, perhaps four or five. This would put departure on October 10; (2) fourteen days (Acts 27:27) later the boat is off the coast of Malta; this puts us up to about October 25; (3) on the fifteenth day Paul and the others come ashore; (4) the stay on Malta lasted about three months (perhaps plus or minus a few days). This puts us up to January 25 at the earliest, and perhaps closer to February 1.

139. See pp. 754ff. above.

140. Horace, *Od.* 1.3.2; 3.29.64.

141. See Larkin, *Acts,* p. 383.

A typical small first-century sailing vessel of the sort Paul, Barnabas, and
Mark would likely have sailed in to Cyprus or Paul and Luke to Mitylene.
Mausoleum of C. Munatius Faustus, Rome.
Erich Lessing/Art Resource, NY

tendency for Christians to regard the world in general as hostile and evil."[142]
The focus is not on missionary preaching but on the generally positive way
Paul was being received in the pagan world, perhaps as a signal to Luke's
audience that such cooperation and kindness were still possible when this
document was written.[143]

142. Tannchill, *Narrative Unity of Luke-Acts*, 2:340. This generally positive assessment
of the possible relationships between Christians and the larger Greco-Roman world differs
markedly from the tone of Revelation, or even second- and third-century Christian apologetic literature. This in itself may suggest a first-century provenance for this book, and
probably one before the last decade of the century when things seem to have begun to go
wrong.

143. See Barrett's proper stress ("Paul Shipwrecked," p. 59) that the response of the
Maltans is not depicted as the response of Christians, but rather of friendly pagans.

XIV. All Roads Lead to . . . (Acts 28:12-31)

A. Journey's End (28:12-16)

The journey from Malta to Rome, probably undertaken in the early part of
A.D. 60, appears to have gone quite smoothly, especially compared to what
preceded it. Luke has chosen to begin and end the discussion of Paul's journey
to Rome with a straightforward travelogue (cf. 27:1-8; 28:11-16). As Praeder
says, the ones in 27:1-8 and 28:11-16 are shorter than many such travelogues
that are found in Greco-Roman literature, but one can not discern the genre
or purpose of Acts, or this section of it, purely on the basis of the presence of
a travelogue in Acts 27 and 28. They do, however, suggest the author's interest
in personal reports and reminiscences.[1]

V. 12 tells us that the first port of call for the *Dioskouroi* once Malta was
left was Syracuse, some ninety miles away. This was the capital city of Sicily
during the Roman era and was located on the eastern end of the south side
of this island. It was blessed with two harbors and was a regular stopping place
for ships going to and from Italy's ports. In fact, the city was famous for
shipbuilding, as well as for fishing and making various objects out of bronze.
From the Roman point of view it was known as the storehouse of Rome,
because of its very fertile land producing fruit, vegetables, and impressive herds
of cattle (see Strabo, *Geog.* 6.2.7). The *Dioskouroi* only paused here for three

---

1. Praeder, "Acts 27.1–28.16," p. 688. She is right that it is not necessarily the case
that these travelogues suggest the travel notes of a companion of Paul, but when one
evaluates their character and takes into account the use of "we," these travelogues favor
such a conclusion. Vv. 12-13 could have been entirely omitted without any loss in the flow
of the story and without any damage to Luke's larger aims. The unnecessary circumstan-
tiality of the account suggests a firsthand report.

days, perhaps just long enough to take on a few supplies and drop off any passengers and freight appointed for this destination.[2]

Both the form and the meaning of the main verb in *v. 13* are in dispute. א, B, and various other manuscripts have περιελοντες, while the Byzantine text type has περιελθοντες. It is easy to see how a copying error could have been made since the two words differ only by the letter Θ. Probably the former verb is the original reading in view of the terms used in 27:40, though here we do not have the full phrase.[3] The term is a nautical one and here is likely to mean something like "casting off" or weighing anchor as they pressed on to Italy.[4] Luke's style in this travelogue is notably less expansive than the material that has preceded it.

Rhegium was a city some seventy miles from Syracuse, situated on the southwest coast of Italy. The major reason for its existence was to protect the Strait of Messina between Italy and Sicily.[5] It was the habit of ships to wait in Rhegium's harbor until a favorable southern wind arose, especially because of the famous rock of Scylla and the swirling water of Charybdis.[6]

After only one day in Rhegium, a proper and powerful wind arose, so powerful that by the second day of sailing the boat had covered some 175 nautical miles and was already at Puteoli. *V. 14* indicates that this is where the sea travels of Paul and those with him came to an end. This port city was located in the Bay of Naples. It was Rome's main port of entry from the east, and this made it the major port for the grain trade from Alexandria. Strabo speaks of Puteoli (modern Pozzuoli) as a great emporium (*Geog.* 5.4.6; cf. Seneca, *Ep.* 77.1-2, who speaks of watching the Alexandrian ships come in).

We have no independent evidence of any house churches in this city this early in the first century, but it is not improbable if we recall that at Pentecost there were already visitors from Rome who heard the gospel message preached by Peter (2:10), and more importantly Acts 18:2-3 probably suggests there were already Christians in Rome in A.D. 48-49.[7] Christianity certainly came to Rome from the east, and probably the first place in Italy Christians came to and through was Puteoli, if they came by sea.[8] We know for a fact that there

---

2. See Clarke, "Rome and Italy," pp. 478-79.

3. See Metzger, *Textual Commentary,* pp. 500-501.

4. The alternative is to accept the other verb, which would apparently suggest the ship circling around until it could come into port. See Ramsay, *St. Paul the Traveller,* p. 345.

5. See Clarke, "Rome and Italy," p. 479.

6. See Williams, *Acts,* p. 448.

7. See pp. 544ff. above on this text.

8. Notice Juvenal's satirical remark that the "Syrian Orontes first disgorged its crowds [here] on the way to the Roman Tiber" (*Sat.* 3.62). Williams, *Acts,* p. 448, suggests that the first Christians may have come to Puteoli from Alexandria, in view of the many grain ships that went back and forth between these cities.

was a considerable presence of Jews in this city (cf. Josephus, *War* 2.104; *Ant.* 17.328).

Luke tells us that "we" found "brothers" in Puteoli. While the term "brothers" could conceivably refer to Jews as in Acts 2:29 and 13:26, three things count against this conclusion: (1) this reference to brothers comes in a "we" passage and it is doubtful Luke would have spoken of Jews as "brothers," being a Gentile; (2) vv. 14-15 are most naturally read as being about Paul's reception by Christians in Italy, especially in view of Paul's reaction to their welcome in v. 15b; (3) the two references to Jews as brothers come in speeches by Jewish Christians (Peter and Paul), but here we are in indirect speech, and elsewhere in Acts in indirect speech "brothers" means Christians (cf. 1:15; 6:3; 9:30; 10:23; 11:1; 15:1, 32; 16:40). In view of this, there is nothing to commend the thesis of Conzelmann and Haenchen that Luke intends to portray Paul as the founder of Christianity in Rome or Italy.[9] Of course Paul's letter to the Christians in Rome makes very clear that he was not the founder of Roman Christianity (cf. Rom. 1:8, 15; 16:3-16), and makes equally clear Paul's great desire to visit the Christians in Rome (Rom. 1:10-13; 15:22-24).

There may, however, be something to be said for Paul's being the pioneer in Rome of the gospel of universal salvation in Christ for Jew and Gentile on equal terms (by grace through faith). Heretofore, it is likely that the vast majority of Christians who were in Italy were either Jews or Gentiles who had (former) connections with the Jewish community (see 18:2-3), and their form of Christianity *may* have been more like that found in the Jerusalem church.[10] This may be why Acts 28 so emphasizes Paul's contact with the Jewish community in Rome.[11]

The remark that "we" were invited to stay for a week in Puteoli with the

9. See Haenchen, *Acts,* p. 720; Conzelmann, *Acts,* p. 224, and the critique by Tannehill, *Narrative Unity of Luke-Acts,* 2:342.

10. See now Brändle and Stegemann, "Die Entstehung der ersten 'christlichen Gemeinde' Roms im Kontext der jüdischen Gemeinden." Their thesis is: "Im Rom sind Nichtjuden anfänglich mit dem Christusglauben nur dann Kontakt gekommen waren und also entweder als ProselytInnen oder als Gottesfürchtige in einer mehr oder weniger engen Kommunikation mit den jüdischen Gemeinden lebten." They are perhaps right that we need to distinguish between when there were Christian believers in Rome and when there was an actual Christian community there. Acts 18 may suggest that there was the former, and that they were part of the Jewish community, but that there was not already the latter in A.D. 49.

11. Romans, written in the mid to late 50s, probably suggests a Christian community that has more Gentiles than Jews, but the question is — what sort of Gentiles? The elaborate scriptural argument in Romans 9–11, directed primarily to Gentiles (cf. 11:13), nonetheless presumes a considerable understanding of the OT by these Gentiles. This best suits an audience largely made up of former God-fearers and proselytes, not those who were simply pagans.

Christians there has surprised most and been thought unlikely by many. There are several comments that need to be made. First, it is probable that "we" here has its narrower sense of Paul and his companions, although it is not impossible that there was a well-to-do Christian who entertained the Roman centurion (and soldiers?) as well. Secondly, the main way for a Roman centurion to deal with the expenses of transporting prisoners was by requisition. Thus, the suggestion of Rapske makes good sense:

> The evident material pressures and the hostility that was often felt toward officials who had to be billeted at cost to proprietors and private individuals would have made the centurion's responsibility for seeing to his party's needs along the way a generally tension-filled and unhappy one. Might not then the sincere offer of hospitality (Acts 28.14) to the entire party from a Christian community (perhaps staying in the home of a wealthy Christian patron?) have been a quite welcome alternative?[12]

A further consideration makes this suggestion even more plausible. The general quality of lodging at wayside inns and *taberna* was poor, often very poor, and a centurion not on a tight schedule to get to Rome may well have appreciated some good hospitality and rest before making the last leg of the trip, which according to the *Acts of Peter* 2.6 involved a demanding walk up a rough and flinty road to Rome. The centurion may also have expected little room and even less welcome for soldiers and prisoners in such inns, especially in a crowded town full of visitors like Puteoli. The entire journey to Rome from Puteoli was some 130 miles, and would be undertaken on foot, taking probably five days of hard walking through some hill country and passing through the Pontine Marshes. It is not surprising if rest and refreshment were seen as necessary before this trip.

The second half of v. 14 has puzzled many scholars, especially in view of the fact that v. 16 seems to repeat the same information. One suggestion is that Luke's travelogue source ended with v. 14.[13] Another is that Luke was referring to the *ager Romanus* in v. 14, the whole territory belonging to the city and its original tribes or Rome's administrative district, while in v. 16 the reference is to passing within the walls of the city proper.[14] Against this last suggestion is v. 15's reference to "from there," which surely means from the Rome of v. 14.[15] The former suggestion is more plausible, and yet it would appear that in fact the travelogue continues in v. 15.

Perhaps the least objectionable suggestion is that the καὶ οὕτως at the

---

12. Rapske, *Paul in Roman Custody*, pp. 274-75.
13. Cf. Haenchen, *Acts*, p. 719, to Lüdemann, *Early Christianity*, p. 263.
14. See Ramsay, *St. Paul the Traveller*, p. 347.
15. See Bruce, *The Acts of the Apostles*, p. 536.

beginning of v. 14b is used not in a resumptive or a concluding manner (and so) but rather in an anticipatory sense, perhaps describing the manner in which Rome was reached. In this case we would either translate "Here is how we came to Rome" (cf. the use of ουτως in Acts 13:47; 27:25)[16] or "in this way we came to Rome."[17] Acts 1:11 and 13:34 especially show that the translation "in this manner" is possible, and 1:11 provides a clear example referring to a future event preceded by ουτως.

V. 15 indicates that believers from Rome came out as far as the Appian Forum and the Three Taverns to meet "us." Paul and his companions will have trekked up the Via Compania from Puteoli until it met the Via Appia.[18] Unlike the Via Compania, the Via Appia was a smooth road which Statius calls "the worn and well-known track of Appia, the queen of the long roads" (*Silvae* 2.2.12). The Appian Forum was a marketplace about forty-three miles south of Rome proper that had not received the most appealing press. Horace says it was filled with boatmen and very stingy tavern owners (*Sat.* 1.5.3). The town was at the northern end of the Pontine marsh where the canal which had been built to help drain the marsh stopped. The group of travelers was also met by Christians at the town called the "Three Taverns," which was about thirty-three miles from Rome, or about a single day's journey away from the Eternal City. Cicero mentions both these places as stations or resting places along the Via Appia (*Att.* 2.10).

The word απαντησιν suggests some sort of official welcome or greeting, in this case extended by Roman Christians who went out to meet Paul and walk with him into the city.[19] Its use in 1 Thess. 4:17 and Matt. 25:6 of Christ suggests this connotation. The news must have traveled to Rome while Paul and the others spent time in Puteoli. Paul is then depicted here as some sort of dignitary, whose "epiphany" was seen as an important event, with a reception committee meeting him outside the city and returning with him into it. Though it is probably going too far to see an allusion to the Roman triumph here, this verse does suggest the importance of Paul to early Christianity, and that he was seen as something of a celebrity by this time, one who had overcome many obstacles to bring his gospel to Rome.

Paul's response to this warm welcome was both to thank God and to take courage. Paul is not portrayed here as a divine man, but as one who is truly human and quite naturally might become anxious or even depressed as his date with Roman justice drew nearer.[20] The welcome by these Christians

---

16. See Johnson, *Acts*, p. 464.

17. Marshall, *Acts*, p. 419.

18. Longenecker, *Acts*, p. 567, disagrees. He argues that the Via Domitiana would have been taken to meet the Via Appia at Neapolis. But did this road even exist in the early 60s A.D.?

19. See Bruce, *The Acts of the Apostles*, p. 536.

20. See Johnson, *Acts*, p. 465.

refreshed his heart and renewed his courage. Paul had for a long time wished to come to Rome, and this show of affection reassured him he had friends in Rome.

V. 16 concludes this brief travelogue and the "we" sections of Acts.[21] We are informed that Paul was allowed to live basically by himself, but with his constant companion, the soldier, guarding him. Nothing whatsoever is said here or later in the chapter about Paul's meeting with Roman officials or his trial, if it ever transpired. The question becomes whether Luke gives us any clues as to how things turned out.

Before dealing with the particulars of the meaning of this verse we must sort out a textual matter. The Western text is much more expansive, adding that the centurion gave the prisoners over to the στρατοπεδαρχω and that Paul was allowed to stay outside the barracks. While this statement is not likely an original part of the text of Acts, nevertheless it may reflect accurate information, as there is no plausible reason why a scribe would invent such an idea.[22]

If this is an authentic tradition the following remarks are in order. The term "stratopedarch," which seems to mean something like captain of the guard, is in the singular here, referring to a particular individual. He has been identified with one of three people: (1) the Praetorian prefect himself, Afranius Burrus, who was the sole prefect from A.D. 51 to 62, (2) the *princeps peregrinorum*, (3) the *princeps castrorum*. It is very doubtful that the *castra peregrinorum* already existed in the time of Nero, in which case the office of the one in charge of it did not exist.[23] Sherwin-White argues that the person meant is the *princeps castrorum*, the head administrator of the *officium* of the Praetorian Guard and the subordinate of Afranius Burrus the prefect. This is possible, but we have no record of this office before the time of Trajan.[24] This being the case, Burrus may in fact be in view in this Western expansion.

Now if Burrus himself, or even his immediate subordinate with his approval, had treated Paul with this sort of leniency, it strongly suggests that Paul was not thought to be any serious threat to Rome or the committer of any heinous crime punishable by Roman law. Burrus was in fact officially responsible for all prisoners coming from the provinces to be tried by Caesar, and certainly could have been the official the Western text had in mind (cf.

---

21. The remarks about Luke in Col. 4:10-14 and Philem. 23-24 suggest that Luke remained in Rome for at least a part of these two years, and presumably knew personally how matters turned out for Paul.

22. See Metzger, *Textual Commentary*, p. 501.

23. See the discussion in Tajara, *The Martyrdom of St. Paul*, pp. 42-43; Sherwin-White, *Roman Law and Roman Society*, pp. 109ff.

24. But see the arguments of Sherwin-White, *Roman Law and Roman Society*, pp. 110-12.

Pliny, *Ep.* 10.57.2).[25] Bearing this in mind, we return to the better-attested text of 28:16.

First, we must note that Paul appears to have been under the most lenient form of military custody, with only a soldier guarding him. V. 16 indicates Paul was not in prison, and probably not kept in a military camp either.[26] The most likely conclusion, in light of v. 30, is that Paul lived at his own expense in his own rented dwelling, being under a relaxed form of house arrest.[27] This conclusion is probably supported by the last word found in Acts, that Paul's preaching and teaching went on "unhindered."

A στρατιωτη was certainly not a centurion, but rather an ordinary soldier. The significance of this fact has been underappreciated because it probably tells us something about the estimation of Paul's case, as it was conveyed in the official documents that would have been transported with him to Rome. It must be remembered that up until his arrival in Rome, Paul has continually been under the supervision of a centurion, beginning at least as early as his custody in Caesarea (see 24:23) and continuing with his journey to Rome (see 27:1ff.). This is not the case once Julius relinquishes Paul.

It is not feasible to see the ordinary soldier as an indication that Paul was no longer seen as a prisoner of some social status and importance, since the narrative has stressed this fact up to this point and Paul's treatment while in custody in Rome would be based on his Roman citizenship and the estimate of him and the seriousness of his case conveyed in the official documents from Palestine. Generally "the more important the prisoner was, the higher ranking and more experienced the soldier assigned to him and the great number of co-watchers."[28] Here we have one ordinary soldier guarding Paul, not even the two that was the customary Roman practice (cf. Acts 12:6), though presumably the duty was rotated among the many soldiers in the nine or more cohorts of Caesar's elite guard. Josephus suggests the rotation was every four hours (*Ant.* 18.169). Knowing Paul, he would have seen this as opportunity for witness to a "captive" audience, as Philippians in fact suggests.

The above comports with the evidence we find in Phil. 1:13, which suggests that Paul was guarded on a rotation basis by various members of the

25. See Keener, *Bible Background Commentary,* p. 405.

26. Whether or not it was near a military camp, in particular near where the Praetorian Guard was stationed, is a good question. If Paul was living at his own expense, as v. 30 suggests, this likely means he was practicing his trade, in which case he may have lived in the region of Rome where tanners and leatherworkers lived. The Praetorian Guard of course could assume duties in various places in the city. For what it is worth, various manuscripts of the Western text (614, 1611, 2147 et al.) add that Paul lived "outside the camp (or barracks)." See Metzger, *Textual Commentary,* p. 501.

27. See below, pp. 810ff., on v. 30.

28. Rapske, *Paul in Roman Custody,* p. 181.

Praetorian Guard but was in no way prevented from having ongoing dealings with his coworkers (Phil. 2:19-30) and various Roman Christians (4:19), not to mention lesser members of Caesar's own household, presumably slaves.[29] One may also compare the evidence in Colossians and Philemon of Paul's ongoing dealings with people in Rome, which also does not suggest a different conclusion from what Acts indicates.

Now if Paul was considered a dangerous malefactor, but one of considerable social standing, one might expect light custody but restricted access to the outside world. As Rapske says, Paul is granted considerable leniency in both regards. The remainder of Acts 28 suggests that all and sundry had access to Paul and his lodgings, and that he could summon people to come to his house. He is portrayed as master of his own quarters with a regular flow of visitors.[30]

What we see here is that Paul's custody in Rome is the least restrictive of all the forms he had endured since being taken captive by the Romans in Jerusalem. What conclusions should we draw from this fact? Here I can only agree with Rapske that since social status cannot entirely account for this phenomenon, "the only other rationale for such a light custody must be found in the weakness of the case against Paul as indicated in the documentation sent with him to Rome."[31] The *litterae dimissoriae* of Festus would have included not only Paul's appeal to the emperor but also the rehearsal of what Felix, Festus, and for that matter Agrippa had concluded about the matter — namely, that Paul was not guilty of any significant crime *(crimen maiestatis)* under Roman law.[32]

There are three other significant clues in Acts 28, the legal importance of which has often been overlooked. First, Acts 28:19 has been neglected. Paul here reassures the Roman Jews that he had and has no charge to bring against his nation, and this is said to be the reason he called the Jews to come visit him. Now there was very little reason for Paul to speak about this matter unless there was some fear in Rome that Paul might pursue a countersuit. What

> seems to be present is the real prospect of Paul's doing serious damage to his countrymen in a Roman court of law. Paul is implying that he could launch a successful countersuit, perhaps charging that his opponents were guilty of malicious prosecution. Whatever the specific charge, the statement must surely presuppose the general strength of Paul's own case and the weakness of his opponents' case, but also more specifically that Pauline

---

29. See the discussions of all these texts in my commentary *Friendship and Finances in Philippi* (Valley Forge, Pa.: Trinity, 1994), ad loc.

30. Rapske, *Paul in Roman Custody,* p. 181.

31. Ibid., p. 183; cf. Winter, "Importance of the *Captatio Benevolentiae,*" p. 528.

32. Rapske, *Paul in Roman Custody,* p. 185.

countercharges were capable of proof on the strength of the facts and the witness of available Roman documents.[33]

Secondly, Acts 28:30 tells us that Paul lived in Rome for two whole years at his own rented dwelling. While our narrative does not go beyond this point, it is clear that our author knows that after two years something else happened. The custody didn't go on indefinitely. It is a wiser way to proceed to argue on the basis of evidence rather than on the basis of silence. The evidence of Acts 21–28 suggests that the Roman authorities (and Agrippa) thought Paul was not guilty of any significant crime under Roman law, that the charges against him had to do with Jewish law and theology, and that he could have been released if he had not appealed to Rome.

In the face of this evidence and the clues in Acts 28 we are now examining, the natural way to read this evidence, especially if Theophilus was not someone fully informed about what happened after A.D. 62 to Paul, is that Paul was acquitted or his case was dismissed. The alternative is to conclude that Luke and his audience knew that Paul was martyred at or near the end of the two-year period and Luke did not feel it necessary to explain why this happened, *in spite of* all the hints in and the flow of the narrative, which suggested a different outcome.[34] This is hard to believe, especially if there is any merit in the suggestion that Luke is arguing for the legitimization of the early Christian movement, much less if he is defending Paul against later suspicions.

Thirdly, Acts 28:21 states flatly that the Jews in Rome had received no letters about Paul from Judea, and more importantly that none of the Jews who came visiting from Jerusalem had anything evil to say against Paul. Tajara suggests plausibly that this may indicate that the Sanhedrin had decided to avoid the expense of sending a delegation to Rome, and thus they had withdrawn from the case. "It would have been unthinkable for the Sanhedrin to have pursued the case against Paul without soliciting the active help of the Roman Jewish community which enjoyed marked influence in the imperial court."[35] Yet if there was one thing Roman law was adamant about, it was that accusers must follow through on their accusations, pursuing due process of Roman law to its proper conclusion.[36]

Nevertheless, this did not always happen, and though there was no formal statute of limitations after which time a charge would automatically be dismissed,[37] nonetheless Roman law stated that if a person did not pursue

33. Ibid., p. 189.
34. Lüdemann, *Early Christianity*, p. 265; Schneider, *Die Apostelgeschichte II*, p. 412.
35. Tajara, *The Martyrdom of St. Paul*, p. 73.
36. See Sherwin-White, *Roman Law and Roman Society*, pp. 108ff.
37. Ibid., pp. 112ff., has shown that Cadbury, in *Beginnings*, 5:319-26, was wrong on this point.

his accusations to the point of getting a verdict in a case, then "if he has stopped at an earlier stage, *he has not made an accusation,* and we observe this rule. But if he has given up *when an appeal has been lodged, he will be indulgently regarded as not having carried through his accusation*" (*Digest* 38.14.8). The *imperium* of the emperor was such that he could choose to show clemency and dismiss various cases, especially when the charges were not being actively pursued.[38]

We know that Nero, during the early years of his reign, followed closely the advice of both Seneca and the head of the Praetorian Guard, Afranius Burrus, whom Paul may well have been handed over to by the centurion Julius. Seneca had preached clemency as a major virtue of someone who had aspirations of being a great emperor. Suetonius tells us that Nero severely disliked signing warrants of execution (*Nero* 16.2-17). We also know that, unlike Claudius, until after the black days in A.D. 62 when Nero lost both Burrus and Seneca as advisers, Nero showed no real interest in holding lengthy court sessions and personally sorting out the backlog of appeal cases. There are thus good reasons to think, then, that after a pro forma appearance in court and a statement of his case and appeal, Paul's case was dismissed due to lack of evidence of any serious crime. Perhaps also it was due to a lack of accusers present to pursue the matter.

The words of Eusebius, though from a much later era, should not be ignored or dismissed since they are based on earlier tradition. He states: "tradition has it that after defending himself the Apostle was again sent on the ministry of preaching, and coming a second time to the same city suffered martyrdom under Nero. . . . We have said this to show that Paul's martyrdom was not accomplished during the sojourn in Rome which Luke describes" (*Hist. Eccl.* 2.22.1-7). This is also what the much earlier testimony of Clement of Rome (see *1 Clem.* 5.5-7) suggests, and one would think he was in a perfect position to know what transpired. This text may in fact suggest Paul was exiled, perhaps in the "West" in A.D. 62, but that in any case he preached at the furthermost reaches of the West, which would likely mean Spain, a place Paul stated in Rom. 15:24 he wished to reach.

What we should probably deduce from the account as it stands in Acts 28 is that Luke made clear statements about Paul's innocence, and hinted about his acquittal in various ways in Acts 21–28, but that these issues were not his primary concern in writing this material.[39] He was not writing a biography of Paul, he was writing a historical work about the spread of the good news

---

38. See Sherwin-White, *Roman Law and Roman Society,* pp. 112ff.

39. See Tajara, *The Martyrdom of St. Paul,* p. 44: "Luke's account clearly implies that there had been a favorable legal conclusion to Paul's appeal to Caesar or at the very least that the worst had been avoided."

from Jerusalem to Rome, and doing some apologetics for or trying to legitimize the Christian movement and message. Nor was he trying to defend the Roman legal establishment to Christians who doubted it should be respected. The mixed portrayal of Festus and Felix and the absence of a clear account of how the trial turned out must count against this suggestion,[40] but on the other hand P. W. Walaskay is likely right that Luke was surely writing at a time when positive relationships between Christians and Rome were assumed to be possible, in other words probably between A.D. 70 and 90.[41]

The focus in Acts 28:17-31 is on Paul's dealings with Jews and in particular his preaching and teaching in Rome. Luke's emphasis and real interests lay primarily in the message Paul preached, and the growth of the social movement of which he was a part. That it reached the heart and capital of the Empire (Horace, *Odes* 3.29.12) and was having success there was a fitting climax in view of the larger purposes of his historical work.

B. Paul and the Roman Jewish Leaders: The First Encounter (28:17-22)

In antiquity, as well as today, people appreciated a surprise ending to a good story. Luke provides us with one in Acts 28:17-31. All along the narrative has led the hearer or reader to expect one of two things — either there would be a Roman trial at which Paul would be vindicated or exonerated, or Acts would close with a picture of Paul finally getting to spend time with the Christians in Rome, as he had long wished to do. What we did not expect was to see the resumption of Paul's ministry to Jews, or a defense given to Jews in Rome, or a resumption of the earlier pattern "to the Jew first, and then also to the Gentile" (cf. 13:42-48; 18:5-7; 19:8-10),[42] all three of which we have here. This can only mean that clarifying Paul's relationship with Judaism was extremely important to Luke.[43] It was crucial to make clear that Paul's missionary work (and that of those who followed in his footsteps?) was not anti-Jewish in character; in fact, in a tour de force argument Paul is going to argue that he is in chains for the sake of Israel's hope and people, not because he opposed them.[44]

40. But see Walaskay, *"And So We Came to Rome,"* especially pp. 64-67.

41. Ibid., p. 64.

42. See Conzelmann, *Acts*, p. 227.

43. Cassidy, *Society and Politics*, p. 128, rightly stresses that Paul is portrayed in Acts as placing his Jewish and Christian identity ahead of his Roman one. The latter is the least mentioned and apparently the least important to him.

44. See the discussion by Tannehill, *Narrative Unity of Luke-Acts*, 2:344-46.

The basic structure of the concluding portion of Acts has been helpfully delineated by H. J. Hauser.[45] Acts opened by raising the question of the relationship between Israel and the kingdom of God (1:6), and it will close on this note as well.[46] The matter is brought to closure by two scenes in which Paul interacts with Roman Jews, the second building on the first, and the two scenes are framed by a brief mention of Paul's living situation while in Rome (vv. 16, 30-31). The pattern of the two encounters with the Jews follows what we have already seen of the reaction of the Jews to Paul at various places in the Empire — initial interest in Paul's message is followed in due course by a rejection of the message by the majority of the Jewish audience.

Only a very short time after he arrived in Rome, namely, three days according to v. 17, Paul summoned the local Jewish leaders to come visit him where he was staying. What we know about Jewish communities in Rome at this point in the first century suggests that they were substantial in number but no central organization oversaw the various synagogues. They apparently had not formed a *politeuma* as they had in other cities in the Empire, such as Alexandria and Tarsus. There is probably a good reason for this less visible approach in Rome at this time. We have already chronicled the difficulties Jews faced during the reign of Claudius, including the expulsion of at least some Jewish leaders in A.D. 49.[47] Roman anti-Semitism had by no means died out after the reign of Claudius. It is probable that after Claudius died in A.D. 54 Jews, including Jewish leaders and even Jewish Christians like Aquila and Priscilla, quietly filtered back into Rome, and at least in the case of the non-Christian Jews resolved to maintain a rather low profile.

There was a further problem creating considerable tension. Jews had various Roman sympathizers, and some Romans had even converted to Judaism and abandoned their ancestral pagan gods, which most Romans regarded as scandalous behavior. In fact, Jews even had an advocate in the imperial household, Nero's second wife, the beautiful Poppaea Sabina, who most scholars think was at least a sympathizer with Jewish interests if not a Jewess.[48] Nero's relationship with her began at least as early as A.D. 58 and continued until about 64 or 65 when he killed her by kicking her when she was pregnant.[49]

---

45. See Hauser, *Strukturen der Abschlusserzählung der Apostelgeschichte (Apg. 28,16-31)*; cf. Dupont, "La conclusion des Actes et son rapport a l'ensemble de l'ouvrage de Luc," pp. 360-404.

46. See Polhill, *Acts*, p. 538.

47. See pp. 539ff. above.

48. But see Smallwood, "Alleged Jewish Tendencies."

49. See the discussion in Griffin, *Nero*, pp. 75ff. One factor which might count in favor of the conclusion that Roman Jews may have entered the legal proceedings involving Paul on one side or the other is that Poppaea Sabina definitely intervened on behalf of the

The inscriptional evidence suggests that there were at least four or five synagogues in Rome by A.D. 60, but there may well have been more. There was a particular region in Rome where Jews tended to live, for Philo speaks of "the great [Jewish] section of Rome on the other side of the Tiber" (*Legatio ad Gaium* 155-57), that is, the area known as Trastevere. It is estimated that there were between forty thousand and fifty thousand Jews in Rome in the early first century, but Penna estimates only twenty thousand by the time of Nero, perhaps because many had been expelled in the 40s.[50] Apparently Judaism first took root in Rome when Jews were brought there as slaves in the second century B.C., and though many of them remained slaves, many also became freedmen and freedwomen, and in fact were Roman citizens.[51] It is important to note that our Roman sources, such as Juvenal and Tacitus, suggest that the Roman Jews were not on the whole a particularly rich group of people, and the catacomb inscriptions do not suggest a particularly literate group.[52]

These factors are important in evaluating why Roman Jews were unlikely to enter the lists against Paul. Prosecution required money, not the least of which went to a rhetor or lawyer to prosecute one's case. The Roman judicial system was heavily weighted in favor of those who were of high social status and/or had considerable money with which to hire a good advocate.[53] The Jews of Rome, in light of their recent history in Rome during Claudius's reign and their general socioeconomic status, were unlikely to go after Paul even if privately many may have hoped he would be found guilty.

The leaders are here called "the first of the Jews," just as Publius on Malta was called "the first" (v. 7). This is a generic way of putting things. The inscriptional evidence from Rome informs us that the ruling elders were called gerousiarchs.[54] It appears from the balance of this chapter that Paul was not

---

Jews twice with Nero during the period A.D. 62-65 when she was imperial consort (see *Ant.* 20.189ff.), and one might suspect she had done so before then in Paul's case (if it took place before she was officially consort). The problem with this theory is that if she did not have an officially recognized position as consort before A.D. 62, she probably would have been reluctant to try to jeopardize her more unofficial position before then. See Williams, "Θεοσεβὴς γὰρ ἠν."

50. Penna, "Les Juifs à Rome au Temps de l-Apôtre Paul," p. 328.

51. See Larkin, *Acts*, p. 386.

52. See the discussion in Tajara, *The Trial of Paul*, pp. 182-83. Cf. Juvenal, *Sat.* 3.296, and J. B. Frey, *Corpus Inscriptionum Iudaicarum*, vol. 1 (Vatican City: Institute of Christian Archaeology, 1936), and vol. 2 (Vatican City, 1952), and see his summary article, "Le judaisme à Rom aux premiers temps de l'Église." The Roman sources must be used with great caution, for most Roman writers, including Juvenal and Tacitus, were notably anti-Semitic.

53. See Garnsey, *Social Status and Legal Privilege*, pp. 234ff.

54. See Penna, "Les Juifs a Rome au Temps de l-Apotre Paul," pp. 327ff.

free to go out into the city and visit others, but he could receive guests (cf. Josephus, *Ant.* 18.6.5). That not only some leaders but also Jews "in even larger numbers" (v. 23) could visit Paul suggests that Paul had fairly substantial quarters in Rome. The word ξενια in v. 23 seems to refer to Paul's lodgings, not to his hospitality.[55] When these Jewish leaders had assembled in Paul's lodgings, he proceeded to give them an *apologia* on his behalf.

In *vv. 17b-20* we have the penultimate Pauline speech summary, and it is an example of forensic rhetoric.[56] The speech is a defense speech being made to Jews, and should be compared to the speech Paul made in Acts 22 to a more hostile Jewish audience. These two speeches frame the whole "legal" section of Acts and show that Luke is as concerned with a defense of Christianity to Jews as he is to other audiences. The tone of this speech is generally conciliatory, defending Paul rather than attacking either Jews or Romans. The speech begins first with the word εγω before the salutation, indicating a personal *apologia* was to follow.[57] Then comes a brief address ("brothers") followed by a *narratio*, showing how Paul came to be arrested and how he ended up in Rome. It will be seen that this sets the stage for the *propositio* given in v. 20, which is essentially the same as we were presented with in Acts 26:6-8 in the speech before the Jewish ruler Agrippa II. The main issue was also stated to be the same before Felix in 24:14-15, 21, and before the high priest in 23:6. Paul had previously used rhetoric to successfully convince at least his Roman judges and Agrippa that the main bone of contention between himself and other Jews was theological and not political — it was a matter of the hope of Israel, the resurrection of the dead, in particular the resurrection of Jesus. This is his approach in Rome as well.

Here, as often before, the detailed arguments for Paul's essential proposition ("I am on trial because of the resurrection, the hope of Israel") are not presented, but Luke does go on to speak indirectly about the arguments and persuasion that took place at the second meeting. This particular speech summary ends with the same appeal to Paul's chains in v. 20, meant to arouse *pathos* in the audience, as we found in 26:29. A brief reply by Paul's audience follows in vv. 21-22.

V. 17b boldly affirms Paul's innocence. Paul claims he has done nothing against either the Jewish people or the ancestral customs. The term λαος is used here of the Jewish people, which throughout Luke-Acts designates them

---

55. See Rapske, *Paul in Roman Custody,* pp. 179-80.

56. Not epideictic, as suggested by Soards, *The Speeches in Acts,* pp. 130-31; Kennedy, *New Testament Interpretation,* p. 139, is right in saying that this "is a short speech explaining why Paul has come to Rome, anticipating charges against him, and exonerating the Roman officials and the Jewish nation as a whole (28.19)." As such, its judicial character should be evident.

57. See rightly Longenecker, *Acts,* pp. 569-70.

as God's people (cf. Luke 1:68; 2:32; 7:29; 18:43; 20:1; Acts 2:47; 3:23; 4:10).[58] The conciliatory tone is signaled by the choice of this term at the outset, and it serves as something of a *captatio benevolentiae,* meant to make the audience favorable to what Paul would say thereafter. The verse also states rather surprisingly that Paul was arrested in Jerusalem and "handed over to the Romans." It is possible that this language, which is not strictly accurate about what happened to Paul *in* Jerusalem, is meant to echo the Passion predictions about Jesus (Luke 9:44; 18:32; cf. 24:7),[59] but it is also possible that we should translate more literally here "from Jerusalem I was delivered into the hands of the Romans," in which case Paul does not state who handed him over and is thinking of his transfer from Jerusalem to Caesarea, at which point he was placed into the hands of the ultimate Roman authority in the region.

V. 18 brings a second possibly surprising statement. When "they" (presumably the Romans) had legally examined Paul and his case, "they wanted to release me." Here again, the narrative earlier in Acts did not say that either Festus or Felix *wanted* to release Paul, but it is said in Luke 23:15-18 that Pilate wanted and intended to release Jesus. There may again be a deliberate echoing of the language of Jesus' trial.[60] It is not implausible for either Paul or Luke to have spoken of Paul's own experience in the language used in earlier tradition about the experience of Christ. The narrative, however, is ambiguous here as in v. 17b. The "they" who examined Paul could include Agrippa, who had made the comment that Paul could have been released if he had not appealed (26:32). This allusion back to that occasion is perhaps made more plausible when one compares 26:31 to v. 18b. In both places it is stated that there was no reason for the death penalty, but of course Pilate said the same of Jesus (Luke 23:15), so an allusion to the Jesus story cannot be ruled out.[61]

V. 19 says "the Jews" objected to Paul's release. Now it was true that the Jewish authorities in Jerusalem objected to the release of Jesus (Luke 23:18), but this is never explicitly said to be the case with "the Jews" at the trial of Paul, though no doubt they did not want Paul to be exonerated and released. The opposition to release may be implied by 25:2, 7, which show Jews still hoping to get a verdict against Paul two years after his being taken captive.[62] Here as elsewhere in Acts, Luke does not mean all Jews by the phrase "the Jews" but merely those Jewish authorities who opposed Jesus and his fol-

---

58. See the discussion of Johnson, *Acts,* p. 469.
59. Tannehill, *Narrative Unity of Luke-Acts,* 2:345.
60. See ibid., p. 346.
61. Marshall, *Acts,* p. 422, plausibly suggests that Festus may have thought that two years' detention was enough of a punishment for whatever Paul had done, and would have been prepared to release him.
62. See Williams, *Acts,* pp. 452-53.

lowers.[63] Paul says he was compelled to appeal to the emperor because of the opposition of the Jews to his release, and this may indeed have been the ultimate cause, but the more proximate cause, as we were informed by Luke himself at 25:9, was that Festus wished to do the Jewish authorities a favor and was prepared to change the venue of the trial back to Jerusalem. The speech thus far is seeking to give a rather different perspective or interpretation of the proceedings against Paul, placing ultimate blame for Paul's predicament on the Jerusalem Jewish authorities.[64] Historically this is likely to be correct, even if the details in this version of the speech are compressed and could be misleading if not read in light of what has come before in Acts 21–26. It must be remembered, however, that this is a speech summary in a literary work, and Luke is counting on his audience to remember what has been said before in the previous few chapters. As such, he did not need to present a full speech here.

V. 19b brings us to an interesting new twist or turn in the argument. Paul says he appealed to the emperor, *even though he had no charge to bring against his nation*. We have already spoken of the likely reason and significance of why Paul would speak like this.[65] It was the ultimate defense strategy, the threat of a countersuit. No doubt Roman Jews did not want to get embroiled in any such matter and risk incurring the animus of the emperor, who knew very well about the expulsions of "pestilent Jews" from Rome only about a decade before this time.

Notice how *v. 20* follows on the not-so-veiled allusion to possible charges against the Jewish nation. The διά clause in v. 20 should probably be seen as going primarily with what precedes it. In fact, one could translate it "Because of *this* charge then, I have asked to see you . . . ," which would make clear that the αιτια, when modified by "this," having as its most natural antecedent the κατηγορειν, refers back to the charge against the nation.[66] Paul had wished to see and speak to the Roman Jewish leaders to make his defense to them, and especially to reassure them that he had no charges to bring against his nation. Indeed, as v. 20b makes clear, just the reverse was the case — "for the sake of the hope of Israel, I am bound with

63. See pp. 200ff. above. Cassidy, *Society and Politics*, p. 128, says "the Jews" refers to that portion of the larger Jewish community which adamantly refused to believe in Jesus.

64. The Western text, reflecting a frequent tendency to enhance the negative portrayal of Jews, adds at v. 19, after mentioning the Jews objected, "and crying out 'Away with our enemy.'" See Metzger, *Textual Commentary*, p. 502.

65. See pp. 783ff. above.

66. There is no good reason to take αιτια in v. 20 in any different sense than the legal sense it has in v. 18. This is a forensic speech, where such legal language is to be expected.

this chain."[67] Beyond the *pathos* of this last remark, Marshall suggests a possible ominous overtone. Judaism was a religion that was not proscribed by the Romans. If Paul was indeed chained because of his Jewish beliefs, this ought to concern Roman Jews greatly.[68]

This tour de force argument, then, is meant to indicate the true Jewishness of Paul (vv. 17, 20), make clear his innocence, and place the ultimate blame for his predicament on the Jewish authorities in Jerusalem, not on the Roman Jewish leaders, against whom Paul had nothing. The Temple Scroll (11QT 64:6-8) calls treasonable any attempt of a Jew to present information against his own people before foreigners. Paul's disavowal here should then probably be seen as another attempt by Paul to show he is a good Jew.

The reply of the Jewish leaders in *v. 21* has sometimes been seen to be unlikely, but two things must be remembered: (1) Paul had been in Rome only three days, hardly enough time for Jewish authorities to have heard other oral reports about Paul's case from visiting Jews;[69] (2) Paul in all likelihood arrived in Rome in February of A.D. 60, *before* most ships would have been expected to arrive at Puteoli, for it was the very beginning of the navigable season. Furthermore, we noted that all along the ship Paul was on was trying to rush to get to its destination before winter truly set in. It is hardly very plausible that another ship had gotten to Italy before Paul's in view of when both would have set out from Caesarea.[70]

Perhaps more significant is the fact that the Jewish community had received no letters from Jerusalem about Paul's case. Since correspondence may well have been carried by land most of the way, it might well have reached Rome prior to Paul's arrival. This lack of correspondence may well suggest that the authorities in Jerusalem had decided not to incur the costs of pursuing a case further which they appeared not to have a good chance of winning, in view of the stated views of both procurators during Paul's trial in Caesarea. Paul was out of sight, not likely to come back to Jerusalem, and therefore out of the minds of the Jewish authorities. Then, too, Paul was a Roman citizen appearing before the Roman emperor. Noncitizen Jews from Jerusalem would understandably not stand a good chance of proving a case against Paul, especially in view of the recorded views of the procurators of Palestine on this subject. Understandably, Roman Jews would not want to be entangled in such a weak case.[71]

---

67. Though we know what Paul means by "the hope of Israel," if Paul said no more than this on his first visit with Roman Jews it may well have been taken to refer to Yahweh, who is called the hope of Israel in Jer. 14:8; 17:13 (MT).

68. Marshall, *Acts*, p. 423.

69. See Hemer, *Book of Acts*, p. 157.

70. See Bruce, *The Acts of the Apostles*, p. 539.

71. See Longenecker, *Acts*, p. 570. Williams, *Acts*, p. 453: "their own position was a precarious one and they would hardly have wished to draw attention to themselves by prosecuting Paul."

V. 22 and v. 21b make for an interesting point and counterpoint. The Roman Jewish leaders had heard nothing evil spoken against Paul by the Jews coming to Rome, but on the other hand, about this "sect" (cf. 5:17; 15:5; 24:5, 14; 26:5)[72] of the Nazarenes they had heard nothing good — it was everywhere spoken against (see Acts 13:45; 17:30). They therefore solicited Paul's opinion about this controversial sect of Judaism. This discussion is said to have been reserved for another day, and, as we shall see, v. 23 intimates that the Jewish leaders wanted a wider audience to hear Paul's arguments on this matter, and so a larger crowd gathered for the second meeting.

C. Paul and the Roman Jewish Leaders: The Second Encounter (28:23-28)[73]

To appreciate the scene that follows in vv. 23-28 properly, one must compare it to the other major encounter with the Jews, the second from the beginning of the Pauline ministry, found in 13:44-47 as part of the narrative about Paul's witness in Pisidian Antioch. In both of these accounts there seems to be an initial positive or neutral response (13:42; 28:22), followed by a second encounter on a subsequent day (13:44; 28:23). It is during the second meeting that strong Jewish resistance to and rejection of Paul's message surface (13:45; 28:24). This in turn is followed by a quotation from Isaiah in both narratives (13:47; 28:26-27). Here there is a difference because the text in Acts 13 is Isa. 49:6, which stresses the divine mandate to witness to the Gentiles, while the text in Acts 28 is Isa. 6:9-10, which stresses the rejection by the Jews of God's message (and messenger).[74] The question becomes how much and what sort of weight to place on the latter quote from Isaiah and what follows it in 28:28.

V. 23 indicates that the second meeting with Paul did not happen by chance or haphazardly, but that a day was designated in advance to gather together again with Paul. While it is possible to take the phrase εις την ξενιαν to refer to hospitality rather than housing, with Paul providing a sort of reception for the Jewish leaders,[75] this conclusion seems unlikely in view of

---

72. Αιρεσις does not have the later sense of heresy here.

73. V. 29 does not appear in our earliest and best manuscripts of Acts. It is an attempt by the scribes who produced various Western manuscripts (383, 614, vg.mss, and others) to soften what appeared to be an abrupt ending with v. 28, or an abrupt transition from v. 28 to v. 30. The expansion, which reads "And when he had said these words, the Jews departed, and had much reasoning among themselves" really adds nothing to the story and seems to be based on vv. 24-25. See Metzger, *Textual Commentary*, p. 502.

74. I am indebted to Polhill, *Acts*, p. 541, for these insights.

75. See Cadbury, "Lexical Notes on Luke-Acts," p. 320.

what precedes and follows the reference to ξενια. One must attend to both 28:16 and 28:30 in assessing v. 23, and the overall impression left is that "by himself," "paying his own rent" (or more likely "in his own rented lodgings"; see below on v. 30), and "in his ξενιαν" are three different ways to refer to Paul's lodgings, which were separate from the military camp and paid for by Paul himself.[76] Furthermore, in the only other NT occurrence of ξενια at Philem. 22 it likely connotes a place of residence, not just hospitality (cf. also Philo, *Life of Moses* 2.33; Josephus, *Ant.* 1.200; 5.147). The suggestion, then, that Paul is inviting the Jews to a meal or a reception does not really fit the purpose of the occasion, which is a debate and detailed discussion of the gospel, though since the discussion lasted from morning until night one may assume that food was consumed at some point. This is simply not what Luke wishes to focus on here. Πλειονες should probably be seen as a comparative here meaning the Jewish leaders came in greater numbers than on the first visit.

V. 23b indicates a marathon session from morning to evening, with Paul both bearing witness and trying to persuade his audience about the kingdom of God and about Jesus using the Law of Moses and the Prophets as the shared sacred texts providing authority and insight for these acts of persuasion. The use of the verb πειθω both here and in v. 24 is meant to convey the impression that, as with the first encounter with the Jews, Paul used various forms of persuasion, that is, rhetoric, to try to convince his audience.[77] The first occurrence of the verb in v. 23 is probably to be taken as a conative imperfect, "was trying to persuade," while the second is an imperfect passive meaning some "were persuaded."

This later usage in *v. 24* is quite important, for elsewhere in Acts the verb unambiguously points to heartfelt conviction and conversion (cf. 13:43; 14:1-2; 17:4; 19:8-9).[78] Especially the intended parallels between Acts 13 and our text (see above) would point us in this direction here as well. Two things have been taken to count against this conclusion: (1) the quotation of Isaiah 6 which follows, and (2) the fact that our account here speaks of even the persuaded Jews leaving without any mention of repentance or baptism.[79]

In regard to the second, Paul was confined to his quarters, and so there was presumably no possibility for a baptismal event here. Note that vv. 24-25 indicate a division of opinion among the Jewish leaders and that they leave debating and disagreeing with each other. This division of Jews into the believ-

76. See the helpful discussion by Rapske, *Paul in Roman Custody*, pp. 177-80.

77. On the use of this verb signaling rhetoric in the "Pauline" portion of Acts, see pp. 39ff. above.

78. See Polhill, *Acts*, p. 542; Larkin, *Acts*, pp. 388-89.

79. See Haenchen, *Acts*, p. 723; Marshall, *Acts*, p. 424.

ing and those who refuse to believe is the same pattern we have seen all along in the Pauline portion of Acts, and even before. More importantly, note how Luke puts the matter in v. 24. The contrast is between those who were persuaded and those who refused to *believe* (ηπιστουν — imperfect). In other words, this must be seen as a contrast between those who do believe and those who refuse to believe what Paul said. We will deal with the quotation of Isaiah 6 in a moment.

V. 25 indicates that the positive and negative responses to Paul's message in turn led to disagreements[80] between the Jewish leaders, who responded in these varying fashions.[81] Paul's testimony and acts of persuasion had set up a division within Roman Jewry. V. 25b indicates that it was as both groups (those persuaded and those refusing to believe) were leaving Paul's lodgings that Paul offered a "parting shot." The introduction to the scriptural citation is in some ways as important as the scriptural text itself.

Paul first of all affirms that what is said in the Scriptures represents the voice and mind of the Holy Spirit, not merely a human opinion. The Spirit speaks through the Scriptures. "In every instance in Acts where a scriptural quote is introduced by a reference to the Spirit, the Spirit is described as having spoken (cf. 1.16; 4.25). In this manner the written Word is shown to be a dynamic, 'living' Word."[82] It is also a way of making clear that the scriptural word is still applicable to God's people.

Paul or Luke (or both) recognizes a kinship between the current behavior of these Jewish leaders and that of the people Isaiah faced long ago. The Holy Spirit was right in speaking in this fashion about those hard-hearted Jews long ago, and by analogy Paul is suggesting that scripture is apropos again in the immediate situation because the response is in part similar. Notice the shift to "your" ancestors in v. 25b, and the notable change from "our" people and customs in v. 17. Paul refuses to identify with those Jews who turned and continue to turn a deaf ear to the prophet's warnings. What is important to note about the citation of this scripture here is that it did not signal a total rejection of the Jews in Isaiah's day, nor does it do so in this context for Paul's day. Isaiah asked how long this judgment against Israel would last, and the

---

80. Ασυμφωνοι indicates a lack of harmony between them. As Jesus had warned, his message would cause division even within a household if it was not accepted by all (cf. Matt. 10:34-39 and par.).

81. See rightly Cassidy, *Society and Politics*, p. 130: "there would seem to be solid grounds for holding that Luke understands those present as having divided into two camps with respect to Paul's proclamation. Proceeding along this line, it would seem that Paul's indictment actually falls only upon those who steadfastly 'refuse to believe' his proclamation. They and only they are the ones to have Isaiah's words directed against them."

82. Polhill, *Acts*, p. 543. Cf. Bovon, " 'Schön hat der heilige Geist durchen den Propheten Jesaja zu euren Vatern gesprochen.' "

answer was until the Lord sends everyone far away and the cities lie in waste; but he adds at the very end of the prophecy that a stump will remain — "the holy seed is its stump."

This is a remnant concept, and its appropriateness to the situation in Acts should be apparent. From Acts 13–28 we have seen a minority but not insignificant number of Jews persuaded and converted by the Pauline gospel message, but the majority has rejected it. Both Luke and Paul (cf. Romans 9–11) shared a remnant view about Israel. The righteous remnant was those who responded to the gospel, but to the rest this word of Isaiah was appropriate. "The reference to some being persuaded indicates there is still hope of convincing some Jews in spite of what Paul is about to say about the Jewish community of Rome. Although the Jewish community, operating as a social entity controlled by its leadership, is deaf and blind, there are still those within it who are open to the Christian message."[83] God's plan, announced in Luke 3:6, was that all flesh see God's salvation, which of course first and foremost included Jews. Paul himself was sent as a light to both Jews and Gentiles to open their eyes so that they might accept Jesus as Messiah (Acts 26:17-18, 23).

Notice that, according to vv. 30-31, Paul continues to preach the same message about the kingdom and Jesus after this encounter with the Jewish leaders as he had shared with them. Furthermore, v. 30 indicates that Paul welcomes all comers, whether Jews or Gentiles, to his lodging, where he continues to share the same gospel message.[84] In other words, v. 24 and v. 30 frame the quotation and suggest that even in Rome some, including some Jews, continue to be persuaded and believe the gospel.[85] What, then, do we make of the citation of Isaiah itself?

First, it is right to note that it is cited as a parting shot, as v. 28 is as well. It is a polemical but appropriate response to the *rejection* of the gospel by some, probably the majority, of the audience. We have already seen that the first encounter with the Jewish leaders involved forensic rhetoric (see above), and this continues here in the scripture citation and the concluding remark in v. 28. The citation must be interpreted in light of the forensic context, which involves the rhetoric not only of defense but here also of attack due to the rejection of the gospel. It does not indicate that the rejection was God's desire, but that it was the foreseen result of the preaching. This conclusion is supported by the form of the citation itself, which follows the LXX, not the Hebrew form of the text (cf. below).

Secondly, Tannehill is correct that the citation of this scripture is quite

---

83. Tannehill, *Narrative Unity of Luke-Acts,* 2:347.
84. See ibid., p. 351.
85. Ibid., p. 352.

appropriate because there is throughout Acts a dark theme of rejection of the gospel by many Jews, especially by Jewish leaders, starting in Jerusalem.[86] Luke does not seek to gild the lily here. He presents what I would call a mixed conclusion to Acts, one part triumph, with the gospel being proclaimed unhindered in the capital, but also one part great tragedy, with many Jews, indeed the majority of the Jewish people and its leadership, rejecting the gospel which was intended for them first and foremost. This tragedy was no doubt an ongoing one in Luke's own day, and Luke provides a partial explanation for it here. Yet he holds out hope for a minority of Jews responding positively, as v. 24 shows.

In short, whatever else we make of vv. 26-28, they do not signal either that the Jews were all along rejected by God[87] or that now in A.D. 60 they were totally rejected after the extensive efforts by Paul to reach them.[88] V. 28 must be seen in the light of the similar statements to this effect in Acts, which are a reaction to rejection of the gospel, not a program for all future missionary efforts (cf. below).

Vv. 26-27 do not contain a verbatim quote of the LXX of Isa. 6:9-10,[89] but rather a very slightly altered version of the LXX. The phrase "to this people" is pushed forward in the Acts citation to follow the first verb.[90] More importantly, the LXX and the Acts citation differ from the Hebrew in that the Hebrew has imperatives ("make the heart of this people fat/heavy") whereas the LXX version Acts is following has the aorist indicative (the heart "was made heavy" or "has become fat/dull"). As Longenecker says, the result of the switch to finite verbs in the LXX is "that the entire blame for Israel's estrangement from God is placed on the stubbornness of the people themselves."[91] Also, at the end of the quotation the Hebrew has the third person, "I heal him," whereas the LXX has the future, "I will heal him," which is perhaps a replacement for the subjunctive, a not uncommon switch in Hellenistic Greek. One further important question is how the conjunction μήποτε should be translated. It is usually rendered "lest" (in order that not), but it certainly could be rendered

86. Ibid., pp. 347-49.
87. Sanders, *The Jews in Luke-Acts*, p. 80, offering the most extreme view, reads the final scene in Acts as clear evidence that the Jews were never the intended recipients of God's salvation. This makes no sense of the numerous scenes in Acts where Jews are converted.
88. See Conzelmann, *Acts*, p. 227. Haenchen, *Acts*, pp. 128-29, speaks of a failure of the Jewish mission and a replacement of it with the Gentile one. See also Tyson, "Problem of Jewish Rejection," p. 137.
89. See rightly Soards, *The Speeches in Acts*, p. 132 n. 354, against Bruce, *The Acts of the Apostles*, p. 540.
90. See Larkin, *Acts*, p. 389.
91. Longenecker, *Acts*, p. 571.

"perhaps."[92] The difference between the two is that the second rendering is more hopeful and suggests that if perhaps they would see and hear and understand and so turn, then God will heal them. This rendering makes better sense in our context here, and is probably how Luke understood the quotation.[93]

It is clear that Isa. 6:9-10 was a very crucial text for the Jesus movement, and perhaps for Jesus himself, in explaining and coping with the rejection of the gospel message by the majority of Jews both within and outside the Holy Land. It is not only a text we find used repeatedly in the Gospels (cf. Mark 4:12; Matt. 13:14-15 cited in full; Luke 8:10; John 12:39-40) but it is also specifically used by Paul in his detailed reflections in Romans 9–11 on the subject of Jewish rejection of the gospel (Rom. 11:8).[94] Paul's use of this text in the face of the rejection his message experienced in Rome is believable in the light of the parallel in Rom. 11:8, where he was of course dealing with this very subject in an address to Roman Christians.[95]

This brings us to *v. 28*, which is addressed to the departing Jewish leaders and is part of the response to the rejection of the gospel by various of these leaders. This text has often and rightly been compared to Acts 13:46 and 18:6, where the same subject of Jewish rejection and Gentile reception of the gospel is broached. In neither of the two previous texts was this pronouncement meant to be seen as a final, fateful turning away from sharing the gospel with Jews and a turning to Gentiles only. It rather stated the next step which would be followed when the Jews by and large rejected the gospel in a particular place. The mission would focus on evangelizing the Gentiles.

It is perfectly possible to read this third example in the same light. The mission in Rome would henceforth concentrate on Gentiles, but v. 30 is quickly added to make clear that all would be welcome to come and hear and accept the message. It is interesting that this third statement is the only one

92. Cf. the similar subject matter in 2 Tim. 2:25, though the verb is in the aorist there. See the discussion in N. Turner, *Grammatical Insights into the New Testament* (Edinburgh: T & T Clark, 1965), pp. 46-50.

93. The alternative is to suggest a causal connection between the hard-heartedness and the resultant not understanding — i.e., the purpose of their hearts growing hard or dull was so they would not understand. But this makes less sense of the text.

94. If any text could make a case for the existence of an early Christian *testimonia* collection, this text is a prime candidate. See Dodd, *According to the Scriptures,* pp. 38ff.

95. It is also instructive to reflect on the quotation of Isa. 6:9-10 here and the experience of Paul and his Jewish companions on Damascus road. The companions had heard and seen but not understood or perceived, unlike the case with Paul and the light that shone from heaven in the person of the exalted Christ. The light to the Gentiles became possible only because of the light first shining on Jews such as Paul and Peter, after which the truth dawned on them.

of the three where in fact Paul does *not* say explicitly that he is *turning* from the Jews to the Gentiles.[96] He simply makes known to the departing Jewish leaders that "this salvation" (the one involving Jesus and the kingdom),[97] the same one offered to them, has already been sent to the Gentiles. The verb here is in the past, not in the future tense, and so refers to an activity of God that has been announced since the beginning of Luke-Acts and has been underway at least since Acts 13. It does not refer to a course of action that will be begun for the first time only after the Roman Jews have rejected the gospel (or during the time of Luke).

"What is contrasted is not the missions [to Jews or Gentiles] but the different audiences' *responses* to the one mission."[98] The one mission, as outlined clearly at the beginning of Luke-Acts (cf. Luke 2:29-32; 3:6; cf. Acts 1:6), was the spreading of the universal gospel universally to the Jew first and also to the Gentile throughout the Empire. This mission neither Paul nor Luke ever gave up on, though the final remark of Paul, "they will listen," would no doubt ring true in the ears of Luke's listeners. It was overwhelmingly Gentiles who would henceforth respond positively to the gospel. The great tragedy was that the majority of Jews continued to respond negatively to and even reject the message about Jesus and the kingdom.[99] Luke does not compound this tragedy by suggesting at the end of his work that God had rejected them as well, or that the gospel should no longer be offered to all.[100]

96. So rightly Larkin, *Acts*, p. 391.

97. It is crucial to note that σωτηριον is found in the neuter form only here and in Luke 2:30 and 3:6. The salvation message does not change at the end of Acts as if henceforth it would only be for Gentiles. Rather, Acts 28 reiterates the salvation message announced already in Luke 2:30 and 3:6. It is "this same salvation" now as then. See Polhill, *Acts*, p. 545 n. 93.

98. Larkin, *Acts*, p. 391, emphasis added.

99. See rightly Johnson, *Acts*, p. 476: "The message itself does not deafen, or blind, or stun. It is because the people have grown obtuse that they do not perceive in the message about Jesus the realization of their own most authentic 'hope.'"

100. See rightly Soards, *The Speeches in Acts*, p. 132 n. 352, and Moessner, "Paul in Acts." Polhill, *Acts*, p. 545, is right that this passage is not about those whom God excludes but about the unexpected inclusion of the Gentiles by faith within God's people along with believing Jews. This of course is the new message that the church had not merely to come to grips with but come to embrace at the apostolic council recorded in Acts 15; see pp. 439ff. above. It is a modern tragedy that some see the book of Acts as an anti-Semitic book, following perhaps the example of some of the scribes who edited the Western text.

D. The Beginnings of Christianity (28:30-31)

It is a commonplace in the discussion of Acts to assert that the way the book ends provides us with significant clues about Luke's purpose or purposes in writing this book. Yet there is by no means any agreement about what this particular ending signifies. In particular, there is no agreement among scholars as to why the book ends when it does, without recounting the trial of Paul and its outcome. While there is no possibility of coming to a definitive answer on this question, since we have no independent historical sources covering the period and subject matter of our interest, nevertheless some theories are much weaker than others, and so we must address this subject.

One popular older theory, which is still espoused by some scholars today, is that the book had finally caught up with the events being chronicled.[101] The problem with this view is severalfold: (1) Acts 28:30 indicates that our author knows that *something* happened to Paul after the two-year house arrest in Rome, otherwise he would not have specified this definite period of time as he does; (2) there is 27:24, which strongly suggests our author knew that Paul would and did appear before the emperor; (3) there is the matter of the perspective of the whole of Luke-Acts, which especially in the two prefaces in Luke 1:1-4 and Acts 1:1 suggests some time and distance separating our author from these events; (4) there is the matter of the clear dependence of Luke's Gospel on Mark's. If Acts is a sequel to Luke's Gospel, this would probably mean that both were written after Mark's Gospel, unless one opts for some form of proto-Luke hypothesis, and perhaps also for the theory that we have an unrevised version of Acts in the canon but a second edition of Luke's Gospel.[102] Taken cumulatively, these arguments rather strongly suggest that our author did not write this work around A.D. 62.[103] The theory that Luke died before he could finish the work has problems because of the same factors mentioned above, to which we may add that the Pastoral Epistles likely reflect a tradition that Luke was still alive probably at least several years after the last event chronicled in Acts (see 2 Tim. 4:11).[104]

---

101. Following the older suggestion of Harnack and Bruce, *Acts* (NICNT), p. 536 n. 49, but also Munck, *Acts*, p. 260.

102. I would not rule this suggestion out, especially since it can be shown that Luke, unlike Matthew, tends to use his source material in blocks. See pp. 165ff. above, the discussion on Luke and his use of sources.

103. To this one could also add the evidence that most scholars think that Luke 21:20-24, especially when compared to Mark's version in Mark 13, seems to have been edited with a knowledge of how things actually turned out in Jerusalem in A.D. 68-70.

104. It is my view that Luke may have, at the behest of Paul, written the Pastoral Epistles, which would explain the oft-noted similarities in grammar and vocabulary between these works. It does not follow from this that the Pastorals should be seen as the third volume of a work by Luke.

It will be seen that most theories about this conundrum are arguments from silence. Take, for instance, the view of Ramsay that Luke intended to write a third volume,[105] a view more recently revised and revived in the form of the argument that that third volume is the Pastoral Epistles, despite the difference in genre between those letters and Luke-Acts. Now it must be said that this theory in either form arises because of the sense of incompletion (and dissatisfaction) that the modern reader often has after reading Acts 28:30-31. But would an ancient reader or hearer such as Theophilus have felt the same way?

I think this last question depends in part on what genre Acts was understood to be. Clearly enough, if with Talbert and others we see Acts as an attempt at a biographical work about Jesus' successors or followers, then something is definitely missing here, especially when one takes into account all the earlier parallels in Acts between the story of Jesus and the story of Paul, parallels which seem to continue almost to the very end of the work (cf. above on Paul's speech in vv. 17-22).[106] In antiquity it was widely believed that how a person died revealed something essential about that person's character, and it is clear enough from a close reading of Luke 23:44-48 and Acts 7 that Luke not only knew of such beliefs but subscribed to them. If Acts is biography, it would seem clearly to be an unfinished work, for the audience is left suspended in midair, waiting to hear about the fate of the hero of the last half of the book. Arguments that the author and audience shared a common knowledge of how things turned out are arguments from silence, and furthermore Luke lets us know quite clearly in Luke 1:1-4 that he believes his audience needs to be better and more accurately informed about the "things accomplished among us." Would not this likely include the nature and timing and locale of Paul's death, especially since Paul in Acts speaks on this very subject (cf. Acts 21:13)? It is better to argue on the basis of the evidence we have than on the basis of assumptions about and arguments from silence.

The recent suggestion of Pervo that we should see Acts as some form of romance or Hellenistic novel intending to entertain the audience also fails to provide an adequate explanation for why Acts ends as it does.[107] W. F. Brosend rightly points out:

> if the purpose of Acts is to entertain and instruct, spellbinding and gruesome executions are the order of the day! Recall only the *Acts of Peter,* which recounts Peter's head-downward crucifixion (from which position he offers an extended sermon), or the *Acts of Paul,* which recounts his beheading

---

105. Ramsay, *St. Paul the Traveller,* pp. 345ff.
106. See Talbert, "The Acts of the Apostle," and pp. 20ff. above.
107. See his *Profit with Delight,* and my discussion, pp. 376ff. above.

(complete with spurting milk instead of blood)[108] and his appearance, res-urrected, before Caesar. While our tastes may be repulsed rather than en-tertained by such grisly depictions, ancient audiences were apparently delighted. For Luke to skip an opportunity to delight his audience is prob-lematic for Pervo's reading.[109]

In regard to the genre question, the book's ending makes much better sense if Acts is some sort of historical work, meant to chronicle not the life and death of Paul but the rise and spread of the gospel and of the social and religious movement to which that gospel gave birth. In particular, it is meant to chronicle the spread of the good news from Jerusalem to Rome, from the edge of the Empire to its very heart. Rome was not seen in Luke's day as the ends of the earth, so the reader would know very well that the mission and task of spreading the gospel to the ends of the earth (Acts 1:8) were still ongoing in his own day, but it was critical for that further spread of the gospel that the message reach the heart and hub of the Empire, from which it could indeed spread to the ends of the earth.

The open-endedness that the modern reader senses in the ending of Acts is intentional. Luke is chronicling not the life and times of Paul (or any other early Christian leader), which would have a definite terminus, but rather a phenomenon and movement that was continuing and alive and well in his own day. He was chronicling what God had planned and accomplished and was continuing to accomplish in regard to the salvation of the world by means of the sharing of the good news.

It is appropriate to ask if there are endings to other familiar books that are analogous to what we find in Acts 28 that may help us understand the latter. The answer to this seems in part to be yes, if we compare the ending of 2 Kings (25:28-30).[110] Here we find King Jehoiachin of Judah in exile and furthermore in prison (cf. 24:8-12). When a new Babylonian king begins to rule, Jehoiachin is released from prison in Babylon after having been there for some thirty-seven years, and is spoken kindly to by Evil-merodach but placed under a sort of house arrest. Jehoiachin is allowed to put aside his prison clothes and along with other royalty attend the new king. He dined regularly in the Babylonian king's presence and was given an allowance as long as he continued to live. This ending is indeed surprising as a conclusion to a chron-icle of the kings of God's people. What this story has in common with ours

---

108. Cf. Eusebius, *Hist. Eccl.* 2.25.5.

109. Brosend, "The Means of Absent Ends," p. 352. Brosend is also quite right that Acts is more than a little bit short on sex and romance and happy endings to fall into the classification of romance or Hellenistic novel.

110. See the discussion by Davies, "The Ending of Acts," and Trompf, "Why Luke Declined."

is that not only do both endings surprise and seem rather abrupt but in both cases we have captives far from home who, though under house arrest, are permitted room to maneuver and are treated with some kindness. Also in both cases the economic aspects of the house arrest are discussed. Paul wishes to appear before the sovereign and testify; Jehoiachin is already in the king's presence and since he dines with him presumably converses with him. Finally, Paul's message is about Jesus, the messianic son of David, and a new kingdom, while Jehoiachin represented the old kingdom and Davidic line.

These parallels are far from exact, but they are sufficient to suggest that Luke may have wanted to present an ending not unlike those of earlier biblical historical books. They are sufficient to intimate that Luke saw himself as writing a historical work in some respects not unlike that which he found in the historical books of his Bible.[111]

One major clue to understanding the ending of Acts comes from recognizing that v. 31 is not just a continuation of v. 30, though that is of course true, but it is the final summary statement in Acts and should be compared to the other summary statements about the unstoppable word of God — 6:7; 9:31; 12:24; 16:5; 19:20. This last verse can be seen as the summary statement for the final "panel" of Acts, which may be said to begin at 19:21 when Paul makes the fateful decision to go to Jerusalem one more time.[112] Thereafter the narrative chronicles the series of events that brings Paul to Rome.

Is Acts an apologetic work? The answer to this must be yes, but not in the sense that it defends the faith to outsiders. Rather, it seeks to legitimate the faith to new insiders. Luke is no neutral observer, but a strong advocate for the gospel and the Christian cause, as is especially shown in the many acts of persuasion he includes in his work, namely, the speeches. But what sort of *apologia* is Luke offering? Consistent with his historical purposes, Luke is not content merely to defend one or another particular Christian leader. It is most unlikely that Acts should be seen as a brief for a trial, or even as written for some other purely secular audience. Theophilus is someone already in part

111. I do not agree, however, with Trompf's conclusions ("Why Luke Declined," pp. 232-34) as to why Luke chose not to recount Paul's death. He argues that it would have led to the wrong moral conclusions about Paul's character and life (especially since it was not followed by Paul's resurrection), and it would have placed Roman response to the gospel in an awkward light (the Paul who was said by Roman officials to be not guilty of any significant crimes is later inexplicably executed by Rome). In regard to the former point, the case of Stephen shows that Luke had no problems with presenting martyrs as positive examples, and as for the latter it is a mistake to think that Luke was greatly concerned about presenting Roman officials in a positive light (cf. below). It is altogether better and simpler to ask why Luke did do something, than why he failed to do something, for there are many possible and plausible explanations for the latter, and there is no adequate historical measuring rod by which to measure such theories.

112. See Longenecker, *Acts*, p. 572.

informed about the things that have happened "among us," and in view of how scanty was the information even the greatest of Roman and Jewish historians of the period had about Christianity (including Josephus and Tacitus), we must assume he had gotten this information through contact with Christians directly. Luke intends to instruct him further, perhaps setting the record straight.[113] The "us" is surely likely to include Theophilus himself, presumably a recent convert to the Christian faith, but one who needed instruction and convincing on various of the matters he had heard about.

Were Jesus and his followers propagating a subversive message? Was the Christian movement for everyone up and down the social ladder and of various races and nationalities, or only for a particular group of persons, in particular for Jews? Luke's apologetic is nuanced in various ways. It is too sweeping a claim to suggest he is defending the Empire and its representatives to Christians. This explanation makes little sense of the actual portrayal of Romans when Paul finally goes on trial in Caesarea.[114] Felix and Festus are not portrayed in the most favorable light.[115] Julius the centurion does not at first listen to Paul, to his cost. Luke's aim is not to present a flattering portrait of Roman authorities.

Does Luke really want to suggest that there is nothing subversive about Christianity? Even Tajara, who does think this is one of the apologetic aims of Luke, is forced in the end to admit:

> Yet Luke's lenitive writing does not always succeed in obscuring how conflictual Paul's relationship to the Roman State really was. The Apostle's preaching of the Kingship of Jesus, of His exclusive sovereignty, of salvation in His name alone, ran counter to the very tenets of Emperor-worship which formed one of the most important ideological bases of the Principate. Paul's evangelism induced men to cease worship of the old gods and drew them away from the cult of *Roma* and of the divine-like rulers; and this was a direct challenge to the majesty of the Emperor and the authority of the State.[116]

It would be better to say that Luke respects Roman law and citizenship and perhaps some of the old Roman values and virtues (which would not include emperor worship), not necessarily particular Roman officials, who could be venal. He sees them as useful tools to call upon when necessary in the service of spreading the gospel.

113. See the introduction, pp. 12ff.
114. And even before. Note the portrayal of Claudius Lysias at the outset of the debacle in the temple precincts.
115. See pp. 702ff. above.
116. Tajara, *The Martyrdom of St. Paul,* p. 36.

Luke is not interested in defending the Empire to Christians or Christianity to Roman officials. He is interested in defending or legitimizing the viability of being a Christian in the Greco-Roman world, regardless of one's sex, race, social status, or place of residence. He wishes to speak about the whole gospel for the whole person in the whole world. His is a message of universalism that rivals the claims of the emperor, not endorses or builds upon the latter's claims. The kingdom of Jesus is not seen as a subset of the Roman Empire that fits nicely and quietly into that Empire without requiring any fundamental transvaluation of values.

Luke recognizes that Christianity was indeed changing, and was intending to change, the social landscape of the Empire by revising some of its most basic religious and social commitments. He understands that there is more than a little justice to the claim that Christians are at least attempting to turn the world upside down (17:6),[117] by changing some of that world's fundamental values. He does not disguise these facts because he is writing to and for insiders, albeit new ones, not to outsiders. His is a historical manifesto about missions and the unstoppable word of God, following the historical and rhetorical conventions of his day. Part of the apologetics Luke must do for his audience is explain how it is that this apparently unstoppable word had not in fact been accepted by the majority of the one group one would most likely expect to embrace it — Jews. He cannot chronicle the triumph of the word without also chronicling its tragic rejection by many Jews to whom the word first did come and in Luke's view should still come. It is in the light of these observations that the ending of Luke, which is an intended ending, makes very good sense.[118]

V. 30 stresses the duration of Paul's living under house arrest in Rome — "two whole years," from about A.D. 60 to 62.[119] The phrase εν ιδιω μισθωματι has been much debated, but D. Mealand has carefully demonstrated that the term had long been used to designate rent (cf., e.g., Ditt. Syll. 1024, 1200).[120] What he is not able to show is the meaning of the term in a phrase such as the

---

117. In particular it is the Jewish world that is especially seen as being turned upside down by the proclamation of the good news, and only to a lesser extent the larger Greco-Roman world.

118. On this whole issue, and on how Luke returns to the themes announced at the beginning of his Gospel (salvation to all) and at the beginning of Acts (Jesus and the kingdom), as well as bringing to closure the matter of the rejection of the majority of Jews, see Dupont, "La conclusion des Actes et son rapport à l'ensemble de l'ouvrage de Luc."

119. There was no statute of limitations on the length of a Roman case in Paul's days so far as we can discover. BGU 2.628, which Cadbury used to suggest an eighteen-month limitation during which the prosecution had to gather its witnesses and act (cf. Beginnings, 5:322-27), is in fact a third-century-A.D. papyrus. See Bruce, The Acts of the Apostles, p. 541.

120. See Mealand, "Acts 28.30-31," pp. 584-85.

one cited above. It cannot be translated "in his own rent," but it is equally doubtful that εν should be taken to mean "at," with the translation "at his own expense." Μισθωματι does not likely refer to just any sort of expense.

Here we are helped by Rapske, who shows why this phrase would be used to convey the notion of "in his own rented dwelling." The usual term for dwelling in Greek, οικια/οικος, would have indicated the wrong *sort* of accommodation, as the English rendering "in his own house" would equally do. One's own οικος would not connote a rented dwelling to Luke's audience, hence Luke uses the phrase he does to indicate accommodation in a rented dwelling.[121] This dwelling was presumably rented at Paul's own expense, but that is not really what Luke is stressing here. It was a temporary dwelling place, the sort one would take up if one did not expect to be there indefinitely.

The word διετια is the normal Greek word used to refer to a two-year period (not an eighteen-month one), and we are reminded of Acts 24:27, where Paul is also incarcerated for a two-year period. Paul spent some four years of his life waiting for his case to be resolved. This is hardly a ringing testimony on behalf of swift and sure Roman justice. It is perhaps noteworthy that Mealand has also found evidence that lease or rental contracts were often set up for a two-year period (cf., e.g., *P.Mich.* 9.563.19).[122] The close proximity of the time reference and the reference to the rented dwelling may suggest that Paul entered into a two-year rental agreement.

More importantly for our purposes is the last half of the verse, which indicates that Paul welcomed all who came to visit him. Here Western revisers surely drew the right conclusion when they added at the close of v. 30 the explanatory addition "(both) Jews and Greeks."[123] The quotation of Isa. 6:9-10 and v. 28 should not be taken to indicate that henceforth Paul would have nothing to do with Jews or with sharing the gospel with them if they came to his dwelling. The word πας is a very important one for Luke, and it is no accident he ends Acts by using it.[124] He wished to stress that the good news continued to be for everyone.

The final verse of Acts, *v. 31,* should be seen as something of a summary statement about Paul's activities not only during house arrest but throughout his missionary work. This work had two main facets — preaching and teaching. Larkin suggests that preaching appeals largely to the will, calling for a decision, but teaching to the mind, urging growth in knowledge and under-

---

121. See Rapske, *Paul in Roman Custody,* pp. 178-79. That there is no clear precedent for this precise usage of a place is rightly pointed out by Lüdemann, *Early Christianity,* p. 265.

122. See the discussion in Mealand, "Acts 28.30-31," pp. 588-89.

123. Added by 614, 1518, itgig,h Ephraem, and others. See Metzger, *Textual Commentary,* p. 502.

124. See pp. 105ff. above.

standing.[125] There is some measure of truth in this, but probably here there is not that much distinction between κηρυσσων and διδασκων since we are told that Paul proclaimed the kingdom and taught about Jesus, and it is doubtful Luke is trying to convey the notion that Paul didn't preach Jesus and didn't also teach about the kingdom.[126]

The phrase μετα πασης παρρησια is an important one and is found in other contemporary sources as well (see Josephus, *Ant.* 16.379; Dionysius of Halicarnassus, *Ant. Rom.* 9.53.7). It refers to the virtue one would expect from a good philosopher — boldness of speech. In short, from the internal point of view, Paul held nothing back.

This phrase, then, is complemented by the elegant adverb ακωλυτως, the very last word of the book. This in all likelihood refers to the fact that there were no external restraints or hindrances placed on Paul in regard to his proclamation (cf. the usage in Strabo, *Geog.* 17.1; 25.18; Dio Chrysostom 5.8).[127] Perhaps most striking is the use of the word in Josephus, *Ant.* 16.166, where the right of Jews to perform their ancestral customs without hindrance or interference from Caesar is referred to (cf. also *Ant.* 16.41 and 12.104).[128] One is tempted to cite 2 Tim. 2:9 at this point — "being chained like a criminal, but the word of God is not chained." The legal associations and overtones of the term ακωλυτως have rightly been stressed by Tajara and Mealand.[129] These overtones would not likely be missed by Luke's audience when he was describing a legal situation of house arrest.

Perhaps more relevant for the whole discussion of this entire verse is the fact that Paul himself speaks in these kinds of terms toward the close of the period of house arrest in Phil. 1:12-14. Paul continued to spread the word while being chained to a member of the Praetorian Guard, and he did so with greater boldness (περισσοτερως) and without fear. The lack of external con-

---

125. Larkin, *Acts,* p. 392.

126. Or are we to think of the preaching as more generic and apologetic in character, having to do with the broader issue of the coming of God's divine saving activity on earth, God's dominion, and then this was followed up with the more specific teaching about Jesus as the agent who brought in and was bringing in that kingdom? This is a possible conclusion, but Luke does not expand on the matter, unlike the Western text (here itp, vg.mss, and syrhtxt), which seems never satisfied with Luke's telegraphic style and adds at the end of v. 31, "[saying] that this is Jesus the Son of God, through whom the whole world is to be judged." See Metzger, *Textual Commentary,* p. 503.

127. Larkin, *Acts,* p. 392, is probably right that part of the thrust of this last word is to indicate Rome's attitude toward Paul's message.

128. Marshall, *Acts,* p. 427, rightly suggests that the picture of Paul preaching with boldness and without hindrance is the image Luke wishes to leave with his audience, with the probable implications not only that God is with Paul but also that the charges against him are false.

129. Tajara, *The Martyrdom of St. Paul,* p. 51; Mealand, "Acts 28.30-31," pp. 589-91.

The Colosseum in Rome, built after the time of Nero and so after the deaths of Peter and Paul.

straints, then, has probably rightly been seen as a comment on how the Roman authorities viewed Paul's case. Paul is being treated with the respect a Roman citizen under house arrest and not thought to be guilty of any serious crime would expect to be treated.[130] In such a case it is understandable why he might write to his converts in Philippi that he continued to have good hopes of soon being delivered from his detention (Phil. 1:19).[131]

However things ultimately turned out with Paul (and it is my view that he was released from house arrest but was later taken captive again and executed during the reign of Nero, probably during the Neronian crackdown following the fire in A.D. 64),[132] Luke's main concern is to leave the reader a

130. See Cassidy, *Society and Politics*, p. 131.

131. The parallels between Acts 28:31 and Phil. 1:12-14 are striking enough to at least raise the question of whether Luke was writing the conclusion of Acts with these words of Paul ringing in his ears. He may have known about the document in Rome, if he stayed there the whole two-year period with Paul. On the other hand, he may have heard Philippians read in a congregational meeting in Philippi as may be suggested by Phil. 4:3, but this is only at best a reasonable guess. See my *Friendship and Finances in Philippi*, ad loc. on all these Philippian texts.

132. Tannehill, *Narrative Unity of Luke-Acts*, 2:356, argues that if Luke knew Paul was found innocent and released, he would surely have recorded this as a sign of the

reminder about the unstoppable word of God, which no obstacle — not ship-wreck, not poisonous snakes, not Roman authorities — could hinder from reaching the heart of the Empire, and the hearts of those who dwelled there.[133] It was a universal message that was proclaimed, and yet it was from the start of Acts to its conclusion the same story over and over again about the coming of the kingdom and of Jesus (cf. Acts 1:6-8 and 28:31). It was a message that asserted that God in the end was sovereign, and that God was faithful to both his word and his people.[134] It is this same message and mission that galvanizes the church today, giving it its marching orders and calling us to emulate the behavior of those like Paul who spoke boldly and freely, believing no external obstacle was too great for the God who raised Jesus to overcome in saving the world.[135]

---

vindication of both Paul and the gospel. This argument at first appears to be telling, until one bears in mind that according to Christian tradition, while Paul was released, only a few years, perhaps three, thereafter he was once again taken prisoner and executed in Rome. If indeed, as is likely, Luke wrote after *both* these events, it is doubtful he would have thought he could make very much out of what turned out to be a temporary reprieve, since Rome in the end found him guilty and executed him.

133. See Mealand, "Acts 28.30-31," p. 595.

134. See rightly Johnson, *Acts*, p. 476.

135. See Larkin, *Acts*, p. 391: "If Luke's purpose was primarily evangelistic and secondarily to encourage the church in its mission, then Acts ends at a very appropriate point in Paul's life and in a very appropriate way."

Appendix 1
Internal Clues of the Earliness of Galatians

We have already had occasion to discuss the relationship of Acts 11 and 15 to Galatians 1–2,[1] but because how one evaluates the dating of Galatians affects the way one evaluates the portrait of Paul in Acts, as compared to the way he appears in the letters, it is in order to discuss some hints in Galatians itself of its early provenance. There is first of all the fact that Paul accuses the Galatians of "so *quickly* (ταχεως) deserting the one who called you" (1:6). This suggests that the conversion of the Galatians was recent, which means that Paul had visited the region in the not too distant past. Unless one is prepared to disregard totally the itineraries of Paul's journeys in Acts as having any basis in fact, this surely favors a dating for Galatians shortly after the first missionary journey, unless one is also prepared to reject the considerable evidence produced by Hemer and others for a south Galatian locale for Paul's Galatian converts.[2] Acts gives little if any hint of any significant Pauline activity in north Galatia (Acts 16:6 probably does not suggest such activity).[3]

It is also notable that nowhere in Galatians is there any reminder to the Galatians that they should *already* have been involved in collecting funds for the collection, unlike what we find in 2 Corinthians 8–9 (cf. 1 Corinthians 16) in the instructions to the Corinthians. There is instead the first-time mention that Paul himself was already eager to remember the poor and would continue

1. Cf. pp. 366ff. above. See now my *Grace in Galatia.*
2. Cf. Hemer, *Book of Acts,* pp. 277ff.
3. Cf. the exegesis of this verse, pp. 477ff. above. Notice that the list of those accompanying Paul in 20:4 includes one representative from Derbe (Gaius) and one from Lystra (Timothy), but none from "north" Galatia.

to do so (Gal. 2:10 — cf. the NIV translation). This sounds like a first broaching of the subject with the Galatian audience, but Paul does not solicit the Galatians at this point, perhaps because other, more major problems had to be sorted out first. Yet we know from 1 Cor. 16:1 that Paul had *already* given instructions to the Galatians prior to the writing of 1 Corinthians in A.D. 53 or 54. Unfortunately, 1 Cor. 16:1 has been much neglected in the discussion of the dating of Galatians. It makes quite clear that Paul had been in Galatia prior to A.D. 53-54 and probably had written to the Galatians prior to that date as well.

There is thirdly the fact of Paul's defensive posture in Galatians in relationship to the Jerusalem church and its authorities. Nowhere else in Paul's letters do we find this defensive posture in relationship to *this* particular group of Christians.[4] It is of course true that both in Galatians and in 2 Corinthians the question of Paul's authority and apostleship is raised. The crucial question to be asked is, Raised by whom and under what circumstances? Careful scrutiny will show that there is no evidence that the ultimate source of the problem when Paul wrote 2 Corinthians or, even later, Philippians was the Jerusalem leadership. It is a mistake to lump all of Paul's antagonists from the whole of the Pauline corpus together.

In Galatians we have, for the only time in the Pauline corpus, Paul closely associated with Barnabas and with Christians in Antioch, something Acts suggests was the case before and after the first missionary journey. According to Acts 15:36-41 they had a falling out before the second missionary journey and Barnabas went off to Cyprus, not to be heard from again in Acts. Paul mentions Barnabas only in passing in 1 Cor. 9:6, and the reference there does not suggest either that he was currently working with Barnabas or even necessarily that Barnabas had visited Corinth at some point. At most the reference suggests that Paul expects his audience to be familiar with who Barnabas was, and perhaps that they both handled the patronage issue similarly.

While we are discussing the issue of personalia in Galatians, one may also wish to ask at what point Peter might have been in Antioch at the same time as Paul and Barnabas and at what point James may have sent some men to Antioch, apparently to deal with a controversy. If Acts suggests anything, it is that this conjunction of persons and events likely transpired *after* Peter left

---

4. Neither the material in 2 Corinthians nor Philippians suggests that the problems Paul is dealing with in those letters ultimately go back to the pillar apostles. In 2 Corinthians the problem is itinerant Jewish-Christian missionaries who offered some sort of ecstatic and sapiential message to the Corinthians, slickly packaged in the form of Greco-Roman sophistic rhetoric. In Philippians there is a bare warning about Judaizers in general and no suggestion they had anything to do with Peter, James, or the Jerusalem church leadership. Cf. my discussions in *Conflict and Community in Corinth*, pp. 343-50, and *Friendship and Finances in Philippi* (Valley Forge, Pa.: Trinity, 1994), pp. 27-29.

Jerusalem (Acts 12:17) and *after* the initial period when Antioch had been evangelized by those from Jerusalem and elsewhere (cf. Acts 11:19-29; 13:1-3), but *before* the Acts 15 council. First Corinthians may suggest that Peter is already considerably farther west than Galatia, having apparently visited Corinth.

One further note about personalia is also in order. It is usually Paul's practice to send greetings to and from various people, particularly at the end of his letters. This he does not do in Galatians. The only persons referred to by name in Galatians are church leaders and Pauline coworkers — James, Peter, John, Barnabas, Titus, and of course Paul. Furthermore, these are all mentioned at the beginning of the letter in regard to the controversies Paul is having over circumcision and table fellowship. Nothing is even said about and no appeal is made to local Galatian church leadership, something one would expect if there were problems (cf., e.g., 1 Cor. 16:15-16). All other things being equal, the names mentioned and the way they are mentioned suggest a very young congregation with whom Paul only has recent contacts, not long-term friendships, and also a congregation which has not yet developed a leadership structure.[5]

In regard to the issue of the Judaizers, it must be stressed that Paul seems to be in the dark about who precisely had bewitched the Galatians (cf. 1:8; 3:1; 5:7; and especially 5:10). This also suggests a point in time before Paul has the sort of social network set up in Galatia that we find, for instance, in 1 Corinthians, by which Paul received regular letters and oral reports. It suggests a time before he has coworkers already on the site or nearby upon whom he can call.

One may also wish to ask why it is only in Galatians that we have any detailed reflections by Paul about his pre-Christian days, his conversion/call, and his persecution of the church. These things are of course mentioned because Paul's authority and gospel have been called into question, but it is telling that on other occasions when Paul's authority is at issue, such as when Paul writes 2 Corinthians, he does not choose to rehearse his conversion story as he does here. One may also wish to compare and contrast Paul's remarks in Philippians about himself to those in Galatians. He seems decidedly more self-assured in both 2 Corinthians and Philippians than here. On the whole the material in Galatians 1–2 and the way it is discussed suggest a time earlier in Paul's ministry than when he wrote the Corinthian or Philippian correspondences.

It seems that often the subject matter of the letter to Galatians and its similarity to some of Romans is the chief reason why many scholars want to date the letter later in the 50s. This sort of logic could also be used to date

---

5. And thus is all the more vulnerable to the Judaizers' overtures.

Galatians earlier. For example, only in Galatians and 1 Corinthians does the idea of the law of Christ really come up (cf. Gal. 6:2; 1 Cor. 9:21). I do not personally put much stock in these sorts of arguments one way or another because Paul could easily address the same subject with different audiences at different points in his ministry. Furthermore, Galatians and Romans are very different sorts of letters and discuss similar topics in different sorts of ways. This is true even of the subject of justification by grace through faith.

Perhaps, however, more stock should be put in surprising correspondences between Galatians and Acts. For instance, in Acts 14 Luke informs us that while Paul was in Galatia he was mistaken for Hermes/Mercury, the messenger of the gods. Is it pure coincidence that only in Galatians Paul says he was received as an αγγελος of God when he first arrived there (Gal. 4:15; cf. 1:8)? Paul also more than once refers to his own injuries, which were on display when he was in Galatia (cf. Gal. 3:1 to 6:17), and the fact that he was and is persecuted (cf. Gal. 4:13-14; 5:11). Now no account in Acts so well comports with this data as the account of Paul's time in Pisidian Antioch, Iconium, Lystra, and Derbe.

Taken separately, none of these arguments requires the conclusion that Galatians was a very early letter of Paul's, but taken together they do surely suggest such a conclusion, indeed favor such a conclusion. If also taken together with the analysis we have offered of Acts 11, 15, and Galatians 1–2, one has a rather compelling case for seeing Galatians as Paul's earliest extant letter, written prior to the council of Acts 15. If this is a correct conclusion, it requires a different assessment of a series of things: (1) Luke as a historian; (2) the portrait of Paul in Acts as pitted against the portrait in Paul's letters; and (3) the degree of *ongoing* controversy between Paul and the Jerusalem church, to mention but three important matters.

Appendix 2
Salvation and Health in Christian Antiquity: The Soteriology of Luke-Acts in Its First-Century Setting

Though it undoubtedly will seem strange to anyone not familiar with pagan antiquity, it is nonetheless true that much of ancient pagan religion had little or nothing to do with attempts to obtain eternal life or be "saved" in the Christian sense of the term. The "salvation" most ancients looked for was salvation from disease, disaster, or death in this life, and the "redemption" many pagans cried out for was redemption from the social bondage of slavery, not the personal bondage of sin. When a slave went to a temple looking for redemption, he was looking for having his manumission formalized; when a petitioner went to Delphi to ask the Pythia about important matters involving "being saved," the questions were always about whether a person would be kept safe from some danger or be released from some disease or be protected from death.[1] Pagan religion, even when the subject of salvation did come up, was decidedly this-worldly in its focus, aims, and perceived benefits.[2] " 'Savior' . . . or 'salvation' had to do with health or other matters of this earth, not of the soul for life eternal."[3]

1. This discussion appears in a somewhat different form in vol. 6 of AIIFCS. See on the questions to the oracle at Delphi, Fontenrose, *The Delphic Oracle*, pp. 10ff.; cf. my discussion of pagan views of salvation in *Conflict and Community in Corinth*.
2. MacMullen, *Paganism in the Roman Empire*, p. 49: "The chief business of religion, it might then be said, was to make the sick well."
3. Ibid., p. 57. This is well illustrated by the famous Greek epitaph carried over into

Thus we must not be misled by statements like those Tacitus made about his father-in-law Agricola: "Great souls do not perish with the body; your spirit will live forever," for he goes on immediately to add, *"what we loved and admired will never die" (Agricola* 46). Tacitus clearly means that Agricola will not be forgotten, not least because of his endearing and enduring qualities, which live on in those like Tacitus, whom the man influenced. This was the primary form of immortality most noble pagans hoped for, perhaps also coupled with a wish to be immortalized in someone's poetical, biographical, or historical writings. In addition, if Tacitus is thinking simply of Agricola's influence on his family *(gens)* and not of the influence of the great man on all and sundry, then he may well be alluding to the Roman concept that members of a family are closely linked throughout the generations by a spirit *(genius)* which is the guardian and embodiment of the values and achievements of the previous generations of the family.[4] It will pay us before examining soteriology in Luke-Acts to provide some evidence for the conclusion that pagan religion looked for this-worldly salvation.[5]

I. Salvation in a Greco-Roman Mode — Spared, Healed, Blessed

As R. MacMullen has reminded us, when examining the traditional pagan cults "assurances of immortality prove unexpectedly hard to find in the evidence. Even the longing for it is not much attested."[6] Among the inhabitants of Mount Olympus there was "no easily recognizable, universal, or at least very familiar deity to name, whose followers all trusted in his power to save them from extinction."[7] Nor is it entirely accurate to characterize the early Empire as an "age of anxiety" in which paganism was on the decline and becoming less vital.[8] To the contrary, there was generally speaking much quiet on the Western front as the Pax Romana took hold. One should not draw general conclusions from the local, partly religiously motivated turmoil in Judea and Galilee in the first two-thirds of the first century A.D.

Latin as *non fui, non sum, non curo* — "I was not, I am not, I care not" — and then abbreviated "n.f., n.s., n.c." See ibid., p. 173 n. 30.

4. See Mellor, *Tacitus,* p. 51.

5. In general one should consult the data amassed by W. Foerster and G. Fohrer in their lengthy contributions on the σωζω/σωτηρια word group in *TDNT,* vol. 7 (1971), pp. 965-1024; cf. also Schneider and Brown, "Redemption."

6. MacMullen, *Paganism in the Roman Empire,* p. 53.

7. Ibid., p. 56.

8. I am thinking of the work of Dodds, *Pagan and Christian,* and see the critique in ibid., pp. 64ff.

Yet while Greco-Roman paganism was by no means in turmoil or on its last legs in the first century A.D., it was nonetheless vulnerable to, and in some cases looking for, a new infusion of lifeblood by way of participation in new cults and religions. One sees this in the enthusiasm for Mithra or Isis in the first century A.D., though we know only a little of what their secret rites involved and what benefits they were thought to convey.[9] Apuleius's somewhat tongue-in-cheek and allusive account of an "initiation" which may be said to entail a "conversion experience" is not as revealing as we might like it to be (cf. Apuleius, *Metamorphoses* 11.28.1–11.30.4).[10] Furthermore, this same material suggests that whatever benefits there were from participating in such rites were temporary, for when new problems and anxieties arise the initiation must be repeated again by the same person.

Many of the "new" religions that gained popularity in the first century A.D. in the Roman Empire originated in the Near East, in particular in Egypt, Israel, and in areas even farther east which had formerly been part of the Babylonian and Persian empires.[11] The cult of emperor worship, which was to become an increasingly major factor affecting the Mediterranean crescent in the first century A.D., may be thought to be an exception to this rule but in fact is not totally so. The emperor was earliest and most eagerly acclaimed *Deus et Dominus Noster* in the eastern part of the Empire, in particular in Asia and Egypt.[12]

To judge from the official response of Rome to the mystery religions, to Judaism, and then increasingly in the second half of the first century to Christianity, all were viewed as leading too many good pagans away or astray from the traditional gods and goddesses.[13] This concern seems to have focused

9. The cult of Isis and Serapis was already becoming popular during the time of the Ptolemies in Egypt; cf. Gill, "Behind the Classical Facade," p. 86. Cf. also Fox, *Pagans and Christians,* pp. 64ff. Cf. especially MacMullen, *Paganism in the Roman Empire,* pp. 53ff.

10. Notice that *salus*/σωτηρια refers to the freeing of Lucius from his animal form, and thereby freeing him from the power of fate (cf. bk. 11 in general).

11. Some of these, of course, were only new to most Romans and other dwellers in the western part of the Empire.

12. I use the term "new" loosely here, thinking from the point of view of Greco-Roman pagans, because of course Judaism, like some other Oriental religions such as the cult of Isis, was by no means a "new" religion in the first century A.D. Nevertheless, Judaism was receiving new, and perhaps unprecedented, attention from pagans who were looking for something more or different in their religion.

13. See, e.g., my discussion of the effects of Isis worship on women in the first century, and the official Roman response, in *Women in the Earliest Churches,* pp. 5ff. The reaction of Tacitus is rather typical. He is suspicious of "Eastern" religions in general, inclined to lump them together as superstitions, and surprisingly ill informed about the origins and natures of even such a long-established religion as Judaism. Cf. his *Hist.* 5.2-10 on Judaism (he thinks Jews are natives of Crete!), and *Hist.* 4.83 on Isis and Serapis. Cf. now Mellor, *Tacitus,* p. 21: "Tacitus's bias against Eastern religions got the better of his judgment." This explains what he says in his few remarks on Christianity (cf. below).

especially on women, slaves, minors, and others on the margins of society who had the least to gain from traditional patriarchal Greco-Roman forms of religion and therefore also the least to lose by trying something else.[14] That there was cause for alarm is shown by the fact that over one-third of the known funerary reliefs at Athens from the Roman period show women in the dress of the goddess Isis![15] The alarmed response of the silversmith in Ephesus in Acts 19:27 about the possible effects of Christian preaching on traditional pagan cults was surely not an isolated one. He is depicted as realizing what the social and economic consequences of successful Christian preaching might be: "There is danger not only that our trade will lose its good name, but also that the temple of the great goddess Artemis will be discredited, and the goddess herself. . . ."

In such circumstances the likelihood of Christianity being branded a *superstitio* was a serious one, especially once it became clear that Christians, as least Gentile ones, were not simply another sort of Jew, nor would they assimilate to the dominant polytheistic or imperialistic religious culture (cf. Tacitus, *Annals* 15.44). Conversion to Christianity without question could and would have significant social as well as religious repercussions for the individual involved and his or her family as well. As H. Flender reminds us, as the cult of the emperor grew in the first century and it was increasingly seen as the emperor's responsibility to provide "salvation" for the Empire, by which was meant a stable social order, any religious group or sect seen as upsetting the social order on the one hand and offering a different source and sort of salvation on the other would fall under significant suspicion.[16] Luke seems to be writing his two-volume work with one eye on the larger concerns of the powers that be, and goes out of his way to show that Christianity and the salvation it offers is no threat to the existing social order — indeed, it benefits it in various ways by producing good citizens, like Paul.

Before we explore Luke's use of the language of salvation, it will be instructive to consider briefly some of the inscriptional and literary evidence that shows how the terms σωζω, σωτηρ, σωτηριον, and σωτηρια or their Latin equivalents were used in the newer Eastern cults, such as the cult of Isis or of Mithra. This will give us some degree of insight into what pagans were looking for as they embraced these so-called Oriental cults.

It is said of Isis that she has the authority to *forestall* impending death and to grant a new life *novae salutis curricula* (Apuleius, *Metamorphoses* 11.21.6). As W. Burkett says, while this does entail "new life," it is life in this world and "not of a different order but rather a replacement to keep things

14. Cf. the essay by Gill and Winter, "Acts and Roman Religion."
15. Cf. Walters, *Attic Grave Reliefs,* to Gill, "Behind the Classical Facade," p. 88.
16. Flender, *St. Luke,* p. 58.

going, prolongation instead of a 'substitute.'"[17] Isis was also recognized to work cures, and in such circumstances σωτηρια amounted to good health, with Isis seen as Hygeia, health deified. Elsewhere devotees to Isis credit her with "salvation from many dangers" (cf. *SIRIS* 198, 406, 538).[18] Followers of Meter refer to her as *matri deum salutari* (*CCCA* 3, 201),[19] or as the one who saved them from captivity.[20] Mithra is lauded in the inscriptions for providing σωτηρια from water (*CIMRM* 568).[21] The designation σωτηρ was also common for the god of healing, Asklepius (I Cretiae i, 171 no. 24).[22] In some ways, the stiffest competition Christianity had in the ancient world was the ever expanding cult of the emperor, with its realized eschatology, proclaiming the emperor as the one who brought peace, safety, and prosperity to the Empire.[23] In the sanctuaries of Meter, Isis, and Mithras we often also find vows *pro salute Imperatoris* (*SIRIS* 404, 405, 535; *CIMRM* 53, 54; *CCCA* 4, 172). More importantly Caesar, by his patronage distributing grain, money, land, work, and because of his military exploits, is seen as a savior (cf. *IG* 12.5.1.557).

It is true that people like Cicero do from time to time suggest that the mysteries, in particular the Eleusinian mysteries, have a benefit in the afterlife, for at Eleusis it is shown "how to live in joy, and how to die with better hopes" (*De legibus* 2.36). Yet even in such cases the focus is clearly on the first half of this statement, and the afterlife, if spoken of at all, is seen as an extension of, not a compensation or alternative to, this life. Pagan religion knows little or nothing of the idea of mortification or sorrow here and now in order to have bliss in the hereafter.[24] One can hardly imagine a pagan using the formula of

17. Burkett, *Ancient Mystery Cults*, p. 18.

18. S*IRIS* is the abbreviation for *Sylloge inscriptionum religionis Isiacae et Sarapiacae*, ed. L. Vidman (Berlin, 1969).

19. *CCCA* is the abbreviation for M. J. Vermaseren's collection, *Corpus Cultus Cybelae Attidisque* (Leiden, vol. 2, 1982; vol. 3, 1977; vol. 4, 1978; vol. 5, 1986; vol. 7, 1977).

20. Burkett, *Ancient Mystery Cults*, p. 139 n. 12. Notice how earlier in Xenophon, *Hist. graec.* 5.4.26, σωζω is used to mean deliverance from judicial condemnation.

21. *CIMRM* is the abbreviation for M. J. Vermaseren's collection, *Corpus inscriptionum et monumentorum religionis Mithriacae*, 2 vols. (The Hague, 1959-60). Already in Homer frequently σωζω has the sense of saving someone *from death or destruction* (cf. *Iliad* 8.500; 9.78; 14.259), and in particular on the sea (cf. *Iliad* 9.424; 10.44). It can also be used to refer to the safe and happy return home from a voyage (cf. *Iliad* 9.393; Epictetus, *Diss.* 2.17.37-38).

22. The inscription on a stone pedestal can be seen in Cambridge at the Fitzwilliam Museum. Even minor deities like Opaon Melanthios, who was worshiped on Cyprus, received inscriptions of gratitude, expressions of thanks for the rescue ("saving") of family members (*SEG* 13, no. 588). Cf. Mitford, "Religious Documents from Roman Cyprus," pp. 36-39.

23. See my discussion in *Conflict and Community in Corinth* on 1 Corinthians 15 and its relationship to imperial eschatology.

24. See Burkett, *Ancient Mystery Cults*, pp. 25ff.

Paul about "living in the world but not being of it." Pagans sought out the help of the gods and goddesses in order to be able to better live *this life* to the full in safety and hopefully in good health and with some wealth.

As it turns out, even that most spectacular of mystery rituals, the *taurobolium* (being bathed in bull's blood), was seen as providing not a guarantee of passage to some sort of afterlife but rather potency, virility, full life in this world, and equally importantly a shield against all evil that may befall one. This benefit, however, was apparently only good for a period of twenty years. The initiate only "takes up his vows for the circle of twenty years, '*bis deni vota suscipit orbis*'" (*CIL* 6.504 = *CIMRM* 514).[25] Even in the Dionysiac mysteries, as we find them spoken of in the Orphic hymns, the aims of the rites and that for which prayers are offered in the ceremonies is the provision of σωτηρια in the mundane forms of health and wealth, or for safe travel at sea, a good year or good crops, and in general a happy and pleasant life here and now.[26]

While some of these rites mentioned above seem to be aimed at overcoming the fear of death (and its obscure sequel; cf. Plutarch, *Non posse* 1105b) and fear of the gradual decline of physical life and health, even this overcoming of such normal human fears amounts to a this-worldly benefit. The most the majority of pagans looked for in the afterlife was peace, the absence of suffering, sorrow, worry, and turmoil, for their shade or spirit (cf. *SIRIS* 464; Apuleius, *Metamorphoses* 11.6.5). At least one major function of the mystery rituals of Isis seems to have been to reassure a person of such an outcome.[27] Pagans were also not above resorting to various forms of magic or charms to assure the quiet and peace of their own ancestors (cf. perhaps 1 Cor. 15:29).[28] "Thus mysteries were meeting practical needs even in their promises for an afterlife. . . . The initiate finally proclaimed: 'I escaped from evil, I found the better.' This, then, must have been the immediate experience of successful mysteries: '*feeling better now*'" (cf. Aristotle, *Politics* 1342a, 14f.).[29] These factors must be borne in mind as we begin to consider what the author of Acts says about the means, nature, and benefits of salvation.

25. It is probably right to see the late inscription (from A.D. 376) in CIL 6.510 which does speak of *renatus in aeternum* through *taurobolium* as reflecting Christian influence, or as a late pagan attempt to co-opt the perceived benefits of Christianity while maintaining the "traditional" pagan religions. Cf. MacMullen, *Paganism in the Roman Empire*, p. 172 n. 24, and ibid., p. 25.

26. Cf. the listing of the inscriptions by R. Keydell in *Pauly's Realencyclopädie der classichen Altertumswissenschaft*, ed. G. Wissowa et al., 17:1330-32.

27. Cf. Burkett, *Ancient Mystery Cults*, p. 26.

28. See my *Conflict and Community in Corinth*, ad loc.

29. The quotes are from Burkett, *Ancient Mystery Cults*, pp. 23 and 19, to whom, along with Prof. MacMullen, I am indebted throughout this section of the appendix.

II. Helped, Cured, Delivered in Luke-Acts

Luke is by no means unfamiliar with Greco-Roman uses or earlier Jewish uses of the σωτηρια word group. For example, at Acts 27:34 σωτηρια is used in its mundane sense of health, well-being, safety.[30] Paul urges the storm-tossed travelers to eat, for it is necessary for their well-being; or if he is referring to the fact that they will need strength to accomplish what is necessary to survive, eating is necessary for their safety.

There are also a variety of examples in both Luke and Acts where the verb σωζω is used to refer to healing, not eternal salvation. For example, we may point to Acts 4:9, where very clearly the verb means "healed," as the reference to sickness shows. Perhaps healing in this text is seen as an indicator that eschatological salvation is now available through Christ (cf. 4:12), but "healing" is not seen as either a necessary or a sufficient description of what "salvation" in Christ entails.[31] Or again, at several points in the Gospel we find the phrase η πιστις σου σεσωκεν σε. In Luke 8:48 it occurs as a final pronouncement of Jesus to the woman with the flow of blood and surely means "your faith has made you well" (cf. NRSV). The same is the case at Luke 17:19, where Jesus speaks to the Samaritan leper who has just been healed of his disease. At Luke 18:42 as well, when Jesus gives sight to the blind beggar near Jericho the sense surely is "your faith has healed you." More debatable is the use of the phrase in Luke 7:50, for here no physical healing is involved. Rather, a woman's sins are forgiven and pronouncement is made: "your faith has saved you." Even here one could argue for a medicinal sense, if one is thinking of the healing of the emotions by means of the cleansing of the conscience, but in view of the association of salvation with the forgiveness of sins elsewhere in Luke-Acts it is perhaps better to see the more pregnant sense of σωζω here, which would *include* but not be limited to the concept of emotional healing. More clearly, in Luke 6:9 Jesus is asking if it is lawful to do material good, in this case to heal or cure a person (ψυχην σωσαι) on the sabbath.[32] All these passages demonstrate very clearly that Luke knows the way σωζω/σωτηρια and the cognate terms were frequently used in the pagan world. The much more difficult question to answer is whether any of these passages demonstrate that for Luke healing is seen as an *essential* part of "Christian salvation," or

---

30. Cf. Bruce, *The Acts of the Apostles*, pp. 524-25. Cf. Thucydides, *Hist.* 3.59.1, and Heb. 11:7, NRSV: "it will help you to survive."

31. By this I mean that while healing may be involved, according to Luke, true salvation after Pentecost never involves physical healing alone, and it may not involve physical healing at all. Cf. Bruce, *The Acts of the Apostles*, pp. 151-52.

32. Ψυχη here, as often elsewhere in the NT, refers not to the Greek idea of the soul but to the Hebrew idea of physical life, the life principle, or in this case more generally to a human life or a living human being (cf. 1 Cor. 15:45).

whether Luke is simply using the σωτηρια language in these passages in its secular sense.

In view of the speech of Jesus in Luke 4:18-27 where Isa. 61:1-2 and 58:6 are quoted as being fulfilled, a speech which has rightly been seen as programmatic for what follows in Luke-Acts, it appears to me that Luke does believe that healings, such as recovery of sight to the blind, are an important part of what the salvation that comes from Jesus entails.[33] One must hasten to add, however, that Luke has a more full-orbed view of salvation than these few healing passages might suggest, and clearly his main emphasis and interest lie elsewhere (see below). Perhaps one may conclude that healing is seen by Luke as a viable *aspect* but not always a necessary *consequence* of the "salvation" Jesus brings. Some who are healed are not necessarily "saved" *thereby* in the fuller Christian sense of the term,[34] and some who were "saved" were not necessarily healed *thereby* (cf., e.g., Cornelius in Acts 10:34-48, where sickness and healing do not enter the picture). This at the very least means that we cannot assume that Luke's Christian use of the σωτηρια language always *includes* the more mundane sense of physical healing, material wealth, or preservation from danger, and on the other hand we cannot assume his more ordinary use of the σωτηρια language always *includes* the Christian notion of eternal salvation.

There does, however, seem to be a larger eschatological matrix out of which Luke interprets these events of healing/salvation. Jesus was sent by God as the "mightier one who can join the battle with Satan and return those under his sway to the camp of the saved. That is to say, Jesus' healing activity is a central feature of his messianic vocation to restore God's people and usher them into the era of salvation."[35]

It is also easy to demonstrate that Luke's view of "salvation" is considerably broader and often different from the usual pagan sense of the term. For example, Paul is definitely viewed as a saved person, yet he is not spared from imprisonment (cf. Acts 16:16ff.) or excruciating suffering (Acts 14:19), though one may argue that he was delivered through or given the

---

33. See also especially Luke 7:22 and 11:20. In the latter text exorcism is certainly seen as a manifestation of the in-breaking reign of God.

34. Cf., e.g., Tabitha, who was already a believer (Acts 9:36-43). One may also properly wonder about examples like Luke 8:48; 17:19; 18:42. The fact that we are told in the latter two passages that these healed persons praised or glorified God for their healing does not necessarily imply that we are meant to think that they were led then and there to believe in or confess Jesus as their Lord or Savior (in the fuller Christian sense of that latter term). The point I would make about both sorts of texts is that healing doesn't amount to saving in the Christian sense, for in the Gospel stories Christ is not confessed or followed as a result and in the Acts story Tabitha was already a Christian.

35. Carroll, *End of History*, p. 284.

ability to overcome such events, even miraculously so in both of these incidents.

Luke is familiar with the concept of "salvation" as rescue or deliverance or even protection from harm. Using the term in a sense familiar to both Jews and Greeks alike at Acts 7:25, Luke speaks of God giving deliverance to or rescuing (σωτηρια) someone. Acts 27:20 also falls into this category where the hope seems to be that other human beings will come along and "rescue" Paul and his companions as they flounder in the deep. This is a sense of the term that pagans would readily understand, and as we have already seen, they used it in this sense when they prayed for safe passage upon the sea or deliverance from stormy seas (cf. above).[36]

At least the first half of Luke 9:24 surely falls into the same category. Jesus is talking about those who attempt to preserve their physical lives from harm and those who by contrast even give up their lives for his name's sake and paradoxically find themselves in the end "saved."[37] Finally, in the crucifixion scene in Luke 23:32-43 we find on the lips of *others* the use of σωζω to mean rescue. The Jewish leaders stand by and scoff, saying that Jesus rescued others (from demon possession?), so now "let him rescue himself" (from this death on a cross). Likewise the Gentile(?) soldiers exhort Jesus to rescue himself (v. 37), and one of the thieves on a cross pleads with Jesus to rescue himself and the two thieves (v. 39). Particularly notable in this passage is the connection between Jesus being Messiah and his ability to rescue self or others from harm.[38] Acts 2:40, where Peter says, "Rescue (σωθητε) yourselves from this corrupt generation,"[39] might be thought to fall into this category of usage of the salvation language, but on closer inspection (cf. v. 21) it appears likely that

36. It will be seen that here in Acts 7:25, as often in the LXX, the term σωτηρια is not referring to some spiritual deliverance from one's own sins or their effects, but rather is speaking of actual physical rescue, in this case rescue of the Israelites from their actual bondage and state of slavery in Egypt.

37. The second use of σωζω, unlike the first in this verse, probably does have the more pregnant sense of "save."

38. Clearly enough from the use of σωζω to mean heal or deliver (see above) Luke does believe Jesus can do such things, but equally clear since these statements are coming from Jesus' detractors it would appear that Luke is suggesting here that such a view of Messiah's role is inadequate, indeed woefully inadequate since part of what being Messiah means is dying a shameful death on a cross (cf. Luke 24:26). Thus the detractors seem to envision a Messiah who comes and resolves all earthly dilemmas of illness, potential harm, poverty, danger, or oppression either human or supernatural. Jesus' view is portrayed by Luke as being much more complex than that, though it certainly includes some acts of healing, help, rescue.

39. Though Peter is indeed appealing to the audience to repent and be baptized in Acts 2:37-42, in view of the way he stresses elsewhere that "salvation" is of God, not something humans do for themselves (cf. below), it is best to translate σωζω here as rescue.

Luke has in mind the more profound notion of rescue from coming divine judgment by means of disassociation from "this generation's" moral and spiritual darkness.

There is in addition one important text, Acts 16:30-31, which is usually thought to suggest that there must be a certain content to a person's faith response to the good news if he or she is to be "saved." The usual way of reading this text is that when the jailor asks Paul and Silas what he must do to be "saved,"[40] he is told, "Believe on the Lord Jesus, and you will be saved, you and your household." Notice, however, that the response of the apostles involves not just the jailor, who is present and has experienced the earthquake, but also his family, who appear not to be present. One must ask if Luke is really suggesting that the jailor's faith will be sufficient to "save" in the Christian sense his whole household. If the answer to this is no, then it is very believable that what is meant is that the jailor and his house will be spared from calamity if he believes on Jesus. In this case we might translate the crucial verses: " 'Sirs, what must I do to be rescued (from this calamity)?' They answered, 'Believe on the Lord Jesus Christ and you will be kept safe — you and your whole household' " (cf. 1 Tim. 2:15). The one thing that may argue against this interpretation of Acts 16 is that the promise of "salvation" here is similar to what one finds in Acts 11:14, where we also hear about a person and his whole household being saved. The differences, however, in the two stories are important: (1) in the Cornelius story there is no earthquake or calamity to be delivered from; (2) not only Cornelius but also his entire household hear the word and respond to it.[41]

---

40. Σωζω can surely not mean "be healed" here, but in view of the earthquake mentioned in v. 26 one can plausibly argue that the proper translation here is "rescued" or "delivered" (from calamity).

41. It can be argued that the larger sense of "salvation" is implied in the passage, since v. 32 in fact says the word of God was spoken not only to the jailor but to his household, and v. 33 adds that they all were baptized. Surely, however, the jailor's family is not envisioned as being present in the jail, especially in view of the separation of the jail and the jailor's home (cf. v. 34). Thus, Luke has telescoped the narrative in v. 32 to include the later outcome of witnessing to the entire family.

My point is that the jailor is not a potential disciple in training, and thus his response in vv. 27-29 must be seen as the natural reaction of a pagan to a perceived calamity and the terror of the manifestation of the supernatural (cf. Euripides, *Bacc.*, lines 443ff., 586ff.). That all the prisoners were still present and none had escaped would have brought some relief no doubt, but it surely would not entirely erase the unsettling emotional effects of an earthquake, which was often seen as a sign of God's anger in pagan thought. Of course, the apostles respond by offering the man salvation in the larger and more Christian sense of the term, which could nevertheless include rescue from potential immediate traumas and calamities such as losing one's job or even one's life because the jailor *thought* he had lost the inmates in his charge. Notice how in v. 23 the jailor is charged with "keeping them safely." Cf. Marshall, *Acts*, pp. 270-73, for a different reading of this text.

B. Rapske has recently drawn a similar conclusion to the one suggested above: "The jailer's cry, 'Sirs, what must I do to be saved?' . . . may . . . be the expression of Gentile religious sensitivity to the numinous. Such religious terror reflects his perception that his abuses [of Paul and Silas] had aroused the ire of the apostles' god."[42] In short, he was looking for rescue or deliverance, not necessarily Christian salvation, but with Paul's response he got more than he bargained for.

It would be wrong to give the impression that "rescue" or "spare" is the main way in which Luke uses the σωτηρια/σωζω word group. To the contrary, his interests primarily lie elsewhere. For example, of the some seventeen uses of the noun forms of this word group in Luke-Acts, only Acts 27:34 clearly and Acts 7:25 possibly do not have some sort of "spiritual" overtones. Furthermore, it is very striking that Luke never uses the terms σωτηρ, σωτηρια, or σωτηριον when he relates stories about the healing of the sick or the raising of the dead, though obviously the verbal form σωζω, with the meaning "heal," does appear from time to time, as we have shown. It is as though Luke has basically reserved these nouns to refer to something of more enduring and eternal significance.

This last observation leads to another one. Luke above all the other Evangelists has a sense of and concern about historical development, about growth and change of human beings and movements (cf., e.g., Luke 2:40). This affects not only his Christology but also his soteriology. As C. F. D. Moule showed some time ago, the Christology of Acts is not simply identical with the Christology found in Luke, but is rather a further development of it, drawing especially on the crucial events at the close of Jesus' earthly life. The ascension of Jesus leads to what has been called an "absentee" Christology, but it is also true that it leads to an exaltation Christology which stresses the new roles Christ assumes as a result of the resurrection and ascension.[43] It is not accidental, I would suggest, that we find in the Gospels much more use of the mundane sense of the words for salvation than we do in Acts. This is because in Luke's way of thinking salvation in the fuller and more spiritual sense comes about because of Christ's death and resurrection, and the means of receiving the benefits of these climactic events is the Holy Spirit, who is not sent before Pentecost to be and convey God's soteriological blessing.

---

42. Rapske, *Paul in Roman Custody,* p. 264.

43. See Moule, "The Christology of Acts." Moule especially points to the "absentee" Christology found in Acts.

III. The Means of Salvation in Luke-Acts

Luke has often been viewed as one who places the Christ-event in the "middle of time"[44] and so enunciates a theology of salvation history, making the history of the rise of Christianity but a part of a larger drama in which God enacts his plan for humankind. I would suggest that this is not a fully adequate way of viewing the matter, though there is no getting away from the fact that Luke is interested in the concept of salvation and does indeed wish to make clear that salvation ultimately is "of the Jews."[45] It will not do, however, to argue that Luke's concept of salvation is simply an extension of the concepts found in the Hebrew Scriptures, or that the salvation found in Christ is seen as simply an extension of the salvation referred to in the OT. The term "salvation history" suggests a continuum with what God did in earlier times for Israel, but it would be better to speak not of a continuum but of the final fulfillment in Christ of God's promises, particularly those found in the late prophetic literature. It is not historical development but divine eschatological intervention in and through Jesus and his followers that dictates how Luke will speak about these matters.[46] Luke's language of salvation in the Christian sense differs with rare exception from all the earlier or contemporary Jewish literature.

For example, Luke's Christian usage of σωτηρια is significantly different from what we find in the writings of his contemporary Josephus, where σωζω/σωτηρια and cognates "are not theologically freighted terms."[47] Or again, all the surveys of the salvation language in the Hebrew Scriptures and also the LXX fully justify S. R. Driver's conclusion that salvation and deliverance in the OT "Seldom, if ever, express a spiritual state exclusively: their common theological sense in Hebrew is that of a *material deliverance attended by spiritual blessings* (e.g. Is. 12.2; 45.17)."[48]

Luke's language seems, however, to have some precedent in the late prophetic literature and in the Qumran material. The clearest examples seem

---

44. Cf. Conzelmann, *The Theology of St. Luke.*

45. I have some strong reservations about the way Conzelmann set up the equation. There is, however, no getting away from the fact that Luke is trying to place the ministry of Jesus and the Christian movement in the framework of the larger work and plan of God. Cf. Squires, *Plan of God in Luke-Acts.* Basically, he seems to see the coming of Jesus and what ensues thereafter as the fulfillment of promises God made long ago to his people in the Hebrew Scriptures. In other words, he believes that Jesus inaugurated the coming of God's eschatological dominion on earth, a fact which must be proclaimed to all as "good news."

46. See now Jervell, "The Future of the Past."

47. Foerster, "σωζω," *TDNT,* vol. 7 (1971), p. 987.

48. S. R. Driver, *Notes on the Hebrew Text and Topography of the Books of Samuel,* 2d ed. (1913), p. 119.

to be those from Qumran. 1QH 15:15-16 surely speaks of eternal salvation, not merely temporal and temporary deliverance, and in 1QM 1:12; 18:11 redemption is eternal. God saves his people from temporal difficulties with a view to eternal salvation (1QH frag. 18:5), which can be contrasted to the eternal destruction of the wicked (cf. 1QM 15:2).[49]

In the late prophetic material the issue is not always as clear-cut. Texts like Jer. 46:27 or Zech. 8:7 do speak of a future eschatological deliverance by God of God's people from foreign lands and foreigners, but here the subject is a final temporal deliverance into the Holy Land, not forgiveness of sins, not conversion, not a heavenly reward, not a final resurrection. A text like Isa. 45:21-23 clearly enough speaks about not only Jews but all the ends of the earth *turning* to the Lord and being saved, but even here "saved" seems primarily to mean being spared or rescued from God's final judgment on idolatry (cf. v. 20). Isa. 49:6 speaks of God's servant whose task it is to raise up the tribes of Jacob, restore the survivors of Israel, and be a light to the nations "so that my salvation may reach to the end of the earth." These Isaianic texts come the closest of any texts in the Hebrew Scriptures to what we find in the Lukan corpus, for example in Luke 2:29-32, which alludes to this last Isaianic text, or to some of the material in Peter's speech in Acts 2. What is lacking even in the most pregnant of these earlier Jewish texts is any clear association of "salvation" with the idea of conversion, though Isa. 45:21-23 may begin to point in such a direction.[50]

One must speak, then, of both continuity and discontinuity of Luke's use of the language of salvation with what we find in both earlier and contemporary pagan sources and earlier and contemporary Jewish sources. It is especially the frequent, almost purely "spiritual" use of this language to refer to conversion, forgiveness of sins, cleansing of the heart, and its eternal personal benefits that makes Luke's work stand out from the non-Christian sources. Also, the christocentric focus and preoccupation of Luke's salvation language make it stand apart. Among the Synoptic writers, only Luke gives Jesus the title Savior (e.g., Luke 2:11), and it is his view that the purpose of the ministry of Jesus and his followers is to bring to fulfillment the promises of God (cf. Isa. 25:9; 26:18; 45:17; 61:1), proclaiming salvation to all peoples, but especially to Israel (cf. Luke 4:18-21; 7:22; 19:9; Acts 4:12; 13:46-47).[51]

Salvation in the Lukan sense of the term is something that comes from and properly belongs to God. From the early Semitic chapters of the Gospel

49. Cf. on these passages Foerster, "σωζω," *TDNT*, vol. 7, pp. 982-83.
50. On this whole subject one should consult J. F. A. Sawyer, *Semantics in Biblical Research: New Methods of Defining Hebrew Words for Salvation*, SBT, 2d ser., vol. 24 (Naperville, Ill.: Allenson, 1972).
51. See Johnson, *Acts*, pp. 16-18.

where Simeon claims to have seen "your σωτηρια" (Luke 2:30) to the very
end of Acts where we hear that God's salvation (το σωτηριον του θεου) has
been sent to the Gentiles (Acts 28:28), it is clear what the ultimate source of
salvation is.[52] Salvation is something humans can only receive, not achieve. It
must be sent to them by God. It would appear from Luke 3:6 that Luke's use
of the term σωτηριον with the possessive qualifier was suggested to him from
his reading of the LXX of Isa. 40:3-5 (which he quotes at Luke 3:4-6). There
we are told that "all flesh" shall see God's salvation (σωτηριον). But what
exactly does this mean? Clearly it implies a this-worldly and not an otherworldly manifestation of God's salvation, though equally clearly in light of the
larger context of Luke 3:1-3 it would appear to have to do with something
other than the immediate, literal deliverance of Israel from her oppressors.
John comes proclaiming "a baptism of repentance for the forgiveness of sins"
(v. 3), and it is this latter concept that Luke seems to mean primarily by the
term σωτηριον, at least as it is manifest in the present.

There are only four passages in Luke-Acts where the term σωτηρ is used.
In Luke 1:47 the term is clearly used by Mary to refer to God as "my savior,"
not to Jesus. The larger context lets us know that savior here means one who
scatters the proud, brings down the powerful, lifts up the oppressed, feeds the
hungry, and takes away the reproach or shame of being a mother without a
son in a patriarchal culture. As is consonant with the whole Semitic flavor of
Luke 1–2, savior here has its basic OT sense of the God who delivers the lowly
and puts the high and mighty in their place. Yet in the very next chapter at
2:11 we hear the announcement of the birth of a savior — who is Messiah
and Lord. This announcement in the form in which Luke presents it, and
especially in light of the reference to Emperor Augustus at 2:1, is in all likelihood meant to be seen as a counterclaim to those made about Augustus.
Augustus's birthday was publicly celebrated as the birthday "of the god [which]
has marked the beginning of the good news through him for the world"
(Priene inscription, 40-42, see OGIS 2 no. 458).[53] Furthermore, in the eastern
part of the Mediterranean Augustus was hailed as σωτηρ του συμπαντος
κοσμου (savior of the whole world).[54] In the official propaganda Augustus's
reign and public benevolences were seen as a manifestation of the favor of the
gods, indeed even as a bringing in of an eschatological golden age. Tacitus by
contrast, writing about a century later, had a very different opinion: "After

52. It is interesting that only at the very beginning of Luke-Acts and at the very end
does Luke speak of salvation using the term σωτηριον.

53. OGIS is the abbreviation for the collection of W. Dittenberger, Orientis graeci
inscriptiones selectae (Leipzig: Hirzel, 1903-5).

54. This is conveniently found in Jones, Documents, no. 72. This particular inscription
comes from Myra.

Augustus dropped the title of triumvir and made himself consul . . . he seduced the soldiers with bonuses, the people with cheap food, and all with the sweetness of peace. Gradually growing stronger, he took over the functions of the Senate, the magistrates, and the law" (*Annals* 1.2). Luke, while not openly criticizing Augustus as his near contemporary Tacitus did, nevertheless clearly has another opinion of who the universal savior really is. While Luke is happy to speak of Jesus' appearance on earth as God's bringing to Israel a savior (Acts 13:23), his view of the scope of Jesus' rulership is not limited to Israel.

Especially interesting is the fourth of the uses of the term σωτηρ in Luke-Acts, found at Acts 5:31. Here Luke's sense of the historical narrative of faith takes hold in the way he expresses his soteriology.[55] Properly speaking, Jesus does not assume the full role of savior and leader prior to God's having raised him from the dead and installing him at his right hand. It is only after his death on the cross that he can offer repentance to Israel (especially for her role in what happened on Golgotha) and forgiveness of sins. It is also only then that Jesus can send the Holy Spirit, which in Lukan theology is seen as Christ's agent bringing salvation to the world (cf. Acts 2:33-38, 47; 10:15-18). After the initial Jewish reference to God as savior in Luke 1, the rest of Luke-Acts concentrates on Jesus as the one who fulfills that role, indeed exclusively so.

The prophecy of Joel 2:28-32 cited in Acts 2:16-21 ends with the promise that whoever calls on the name of the Lord will be saved.[56] But who this Lord is, is explicated in what immediately follows in vv. 22ff. — Jesus of Nazareth. It is thus not a surprise, since the author is a monotheist, that we hear the exclusive statement in Acts 4:12 — "There is salvation in no one else, for there is no other name under heaven given among mortals by which we must be saved." Luke clearly enough believes in a universal gospel about universal salvation for all peoples (cf. Luke 2:32), but the sole means of obtaining this salvation is through Jesus. He is the horn of salvation alluded to in Luke 1:69.[57] The *means* by which Jesus will convey knowledge of salvation to his people is said in this same canticle to be by the forgiveness of sins, a crucial association, as we shall see when we turn to the issue of the *meaning* of salvation for Luke.[58]

---

55. On the narrative and historical framework in which Luke views salvation, see my forthcoming article on "Lord" in the InterVarsity Press dictionary on Acts and the rest of the NT canon not covered in their first two NT dictionaries.

56. The sense of σωζω here would seem to be "rescued," for the context speaks of the coming of the *Yom Yahweh*, the day of judgment, the negative consequences of which those who call on the Lord will be spared.

57. Here again in Luke 1 this canticle focuses on the OT idea of one who delivers from one's enemies. Cf. vv. 71 and 74, where it becomes clear that "saved" means rescued or delivered in this text.

58. Foerster, "σωζω," *TDNT*, vol. 7, p. 997, is absolutely right that again "and again in Ac. the content of σωτηρια is the forgiveness of sins 3.19, 26; 5.31; 10.43; 13.38; 22.16; 26.18."

If we seek to identify the subjective means by which someone appropriates this salvation that comes through Jesus (the objective means), several texts help us. First, Acts 11:14 indicates that salvation comes about by hearing the proclamation of "a message from God." This pattern is in fact repeated over and over again in Acts and perhaps explains the unusual language used in texts like Acts 6:7, where we hear about the word of God "growing" or "increasing," which is explained to mean that the number of disciples increased. This "hearing the word" approach is to be contrasted with a text like Acts 15:1 where some Jews who seem also to have been Christians go to Antioch and proclaim that "unless you are circumcised according to the custom of Moses, you cannot be saved." As Acts 15 progresses, it becomes clear that the Jerusalem leadership rejects this ritual requirement for salvation.[59]

While baptism is certainly seen as important in Acts, it is not seen as a means of salvation. Not only do we have stories where "salvation" happens through hearing the preached word and baptism only follows (Acts 10:44-48), but we also have stories where faith and receiving the Holy Spirit precede water baptism (Acts 8:15-16). Notice the important contrast that while John baptized with water, the crucial baptismal event in the NT era is baptism with the Holy Spirit (Acts 11:16). Furthermore, we have Apollos, who only hears about Christian baptism long after his conversion (Acts 18:24-28), and on the other hand disciples of the Baptist who had not even "heard there is a Holy Spirit" (19:2). The latter group receive Christian baptism but then apparently only receive the Holy Spirit when Paul lays hands on them in addition to baptizing them (19:6-7). It is fair to conclude from all this that while baptism may be seen as a sign or symbol of conversion or salvation for Luke,[60] it surely is not seen as the means of salvation. Even in the case of Saul/Paul, his conversion, which included at the end of the process regaining his sight and receiving the Holy Spirit, is only followed by water baptism.[61] One must also not underestimate the role of faith for Luke in a person's being saved. This is clear as early as the explanation of the parable of the sower in Luke 8:11-12, where we have the sequence proclaiming and hearing the word, the word lodging in the heart, believing, and so being saved (cf. Acts 11:16).

There is one text where Luke makes a bit clearer what the objective means

59. On the meaning of the decree in Acts 15, see now my essay, "Not So Idle Thoughts."

60. That is, a sign of cleansing and the forgiveness of sins in the present.

61. It will be noted that not only in his theology of baptism but also in his lack of real attention to any sort of clear theology of the Lord's Supper (it may even be debated whether the references to disciples breaking bread in Acts point to the Lord's Supper), Luke can hardly be classed as one who manifests the approach of so-called early Catholicism or other second-century trends. This must count against the idea that this work was written after the first century was over.

of salvation is — the grace of the Lord Jesus (Acts 15:11). While it is proper to talk about Christ as savior as the objective means of salvation, or of his death making possible the forgiveness of sins, or of the Holy Spirit conveying the benefits of salvation, including the cleansing of the heart through faith (cf. vv. 8-9), yet the reason that salvation is made available in the first place is because of the character of God in Christ — that he is gracious. Acts 15:11 is also important for a second reason, namely, that it reminds us that Luke, while stressing the present and processive dimensions of salvation (cf., e.g., Acts 2:47 — "the Lord added to their number those who *were being saved* [σωζο-μενους]"), knows about and affirms the future dimensions of σωτηρια as well. This leads us to examine more carefully how Luke views the meaning and benefits of the salvation that comes in and through Jesus.

IV. The Meaning and Benefits of Salvation in Luke-Acts

We have already seen the interesting connection of forgiveness and salvation in several contexts in Luke-Acts, and also the argument in Acts 5:31 that Jesus is able to be savior and offer forgiveness of sins to Israel and others because of his death on the cross and the subsequent resurrection and exaltation of Jesus by God the Father. In other words, it is not accurate to say that Luke has no or at least no adequate theology of the cross, and that he does not connect it with salvation. This point has recently been made forcefully by D. Moessner.[62] For Luke, Christ's death and resurrection are at the very heart of God's saving plan for humankind which is revealed in the Scriptures, as is made evident in a text like Luke 24:45-49. This text clearly links forgiveness of sins/salvation and its proclamation with the death and resurrection of Jesus, and should not be ignored.[63]

For Luke salvation at its very core has to do with God's gracious act of forgiving sins through Jesus which causes the moral, mental, emotional, spiritual, and sometimes even physical transformation of an individual. We can see this already in a text like Luke 19:1-10, the story of Zacchaeus. Here we are not talking about Jesus healing the man physically, or exorcising a demon, or delivering him from his foes or from danger. Rather, the story climaxes at vv. 9-10, and we are told that "today salvation (σωτηρια) has come to this

---

62. Moessner, "The Script of the Scriptures."
63. That Luke does not *fully* explain all the *other* benefits or implications of Christ's death on the cross besides forgiveness of sins is a moot point. One could very well point to a text like Acts 20:28 to make clear that Luke knows of and affirms the idea of Christ's shed blood as the means by which God creates and assembles a people, an εχχλησια.

house." What is meant is the recovery of a spiritually lost individual by means of Jesus' gracious behavior toward the man. Salvation is something which can happen in the present, and involves the character transformation of a human being. That such a change or conversion has happened to Zacchaeus is shown by his sudden willingness to give to the poor and pay back fourfold to those he had defrauded. Certainly "salvation" for Luke has social consequences, but equally clearly it is a spiritual transformation of human personality that leads a person to see the logical social consequences of receiving Jesus.

The two texts in Acts which indicate that salvation has a future dimension are Acts 2:21 as part of the quote of Joel 2, and Acts 15:11. The former text is interesting, drawing as it does on the OT concept of the Day of the Lord (*Yom Yahweh*). Notice that this day is called a great and terrible day in Joel 2:32, and more importantly, what "saved" means in that text is "those who escape" the judgment and attendant calamity that comes on that day. This could also be what is meant in Acts 2:21, in which case it might be best to translate the crucial phrase "shall be delivered/kept safe/spared." There is, however, one noteworthy change in the Acts quotation of the text from Joel. Peter calls the day the great and "glorious" (ἐπιφανη, v. 20) day. This may suggest that the emphasis in Peter's sermon is not on the coming judgment but on the coming redemption, the positive side of the equation, in which case the translation "saved" may after all be preferable. In any event, we are *not* told in any full way what this future "salvation" amounts to. For instance, it is not here associated with resurrection. The same may be said about the other future-oriented salvation text in Acts 15:11. Salvation there is referred to as future, but what it entails or what its benefits will be is not stated. This drives us back to the Gospel texts once more.

Besides Luke 19:10, Luke 18:26-27 is an important text. Here being saved (in the future) is equated with entering the dominion of God (also in the future — v. 24). The question about the number of the saved in Luke 13:22 leads to a discussion about entering the dominion and finally about who will be in the dominion — Abraham, Isaac, Jacob, the prophets, and people coming from all four major points of the compass to eat in the dominion of God. This shows that Luke knows about the messianic banquet traditions, and that he associates future salvation with such traditions. Luke 9:24b in light of this in the second reference to "save" likely alludes to such ideas. Those who lose their lives for Jesus' name's sake will be saved, that is, will participate in the coming dominion of God on earth, an event triggered by the coming of the great and glorious Day of the Lord (Acts 2:20).

What we have learned from this discussion is that for Luke salvation, in the present, means the forgiveness of sins, the cleansing of the heart by the Holy Spirit and through faith. As Paul says in Acts 13:38-39, the good news is that through the crucified and risen Jesus forgiveness of sins and indeed being set free even from sins that were not forgivable under Mosaic Law is possible.

In the future, salvation means entering God's dominion and being a participant in the messianic banquet when the Lord returns. If we may legitimately look briefly at other future-oriented texts which do not mention salvation explicitly, we may expand on these conclusions. For example, one can argue that the parable of the rich person and Lazarus shows that Luke affirms that the pious will go to heaven when they die, into intimate fellowship with the OT saints, in particular Abraham (Luke 16:19-31). Or again in the sayings material in Luke 20:35-36 a place in "that age" is associated with a place in "the resurrection of the dead" and being like the angels. Or again, redemption (ἀπολυτρωσις) as a future event is explicitly associated with the future coming of the Son of Man at Luke 21:27. Paul in Acts 17:31 proclaims the Day of Judgment and that Christ will be the Judge on that day, and he indicates that Christ's resurrection is the past event that assures that this other future event will transpire. When one broadens one's search it turns out to be incorrect to say either that Luke fails to affirm or has no clear concept of what salvation in the future amounts to, or to say that Luke has no clear theology of the cross or understanding of its connection with salvation. It is certainly correct to say, however, that when σωτηρια/σωζω occurs and is used in a theologically loaded sense in Luke-Acts, the large majority of the time he focuses on the present reality and benefits of salvation.

Before we conclude this appendix, something must be said about the suggestion that Luke's portrayal of who may and will be saved reflects anti-Semitism, or at least anti-Judaism. For instance, J. T. Sanders in an important essay has argued that Luke, especially in Acts, portrays God's salvation as coming to the "nations" (i.e., Gentiles) rather than to the Jews, in view of the Jewish rejection of Jesus as savior.[64] He believes that "Luke's entire theology about the Jews may be seen in the Stephen episode," and his whole view of salvation is seen in the programmatic speech in Luke 4. The rejection of a mission to the Jews at the end of Acts is seen as final and what the two volumes have been pointing toward all along.[65] There are a variety of problems with these suggestions.

First, there is a consistent overplaying and overvaluing of the polemics found in the Stephen speech.[66] This speech reflects forensic rhetoric and

---

64. Sanders, "Salvation of the Jews."

65. Ibid., p. 116.

66. See now the careful discussion of this speech and its significance for Luke's work by Hill, *Hellenists and Hebrews*, pp. 41-101. He concludes that Stephen was not a radical critic of either the temple or the Law, and insofar as his speech represents Luke's own views, neither was Luke.

involves defense and attack, but even so it does not negate the "dominant tone of good will" in Acts 1–5, where the Jews are addressed and many respond to the gospel.[67] Nor does the Stephen speech prevent Luke from presenting a variety of Jews, synagogue adherents, and God-fearers as responding positively to the good news throughout Acts right to its very end. Paul starts by preaching in the synagogue in almost every place he goes precisely because salvation is for the Jew first.

It is only when many in the synagogue reject the message that we hear the repeated statement about turning to the Gentiles (cf. 13:46; 18:6).[68] Furthermore, Acts 28 portrays Paul calling the leaders of the Jews in Rome together and explaining about Jesus and the kingdom of God to them, and we are told that "some were convinced by what he said, but others would not believe" (v. 24); in other words, the response was mixed, even here at the end of Acts.[69] In short, Sanders's view represents a serious distortion of Luke's view of salvation. Even in Luke 4, what the programmatic speech sets in motion is a series of mixed responses to Jesus, sometimes involving rejection by Jews, as in his hometown, sometimes involving acceptance and discipleship, as is clear beginning in the very next chapter, Luke 5.

The point of the remarks about salvation having come to the Gentiles in Acts (cf., e.g., Acts 10:45; 15:7) is not to deny that salvation is still for the Jews (cf. 15:16-17; 28:24) but to justify the new and surprisingly successful saving action of God among non-Jews. Luke writes as a Gentile for Gentiles, and their salvation is a matter of crucial import for him and his audience. He must verify the *new* thing that God is doing, namely, that the Gentiles are and have been in the divine plan of salvation as the Scriptures foretold (cf. Acts 15:17).[70]

Luke's vision of salvation is truly universal, and that means it must include both Jews and Gentiles — all humankind must see the salvation of God (Luke 3:6). Human beings are called to be like Simeon and recognize in Jesus God's "salvation, which you have prepared in the sight of all people, *a light for revelation to the Gentiles and for glory to your people Israel.*" If we are going to talk about programmatic remarks we would do well to begin not just in Luke 4 but already in Luke 2:29-32.[71]

---

67. Tyson, *Images of Judaism in Luke-Acts,* p. 125.

68. Notice how even after 18:6, where the remark about turning to the Gentiles is clearest, Paul returns to the synagogue again in Ephesus in 19:8-9 and we find the same mixed response as in the latter part of Acts, including Acts 28.

69. See rightly Johnson, *Acts,* p. 18.

70. On the "plan of God" cf. Squires, *Plan of God in Luke-Acts.*

71. It is also important to set the whole of Luke-Acts in the larger context of Jewish interaction with Gentiles during the second temple period. See McKnight, *A Light among the Gentiles.* The first Jewish followers of Jesus in their approach to Gentiles were simply

Note that the polemics against Jews who reject Jesus are tempered by recognition that even the most heinous acts committed by Jews which led to the crucifixion of Jesus were committed out of ignorance (Acts 3:17). In short, the polemics in Acts, including in Stephen's speech, are a reaction to and have to do with the *rejection* of Jesus and of God's salvation plan which involves both Jews and Gentiles *by some Jews;* they do not have to do with any sort of total or final rejection or disenfranchising of the Jews by God. They are antirejection remarks, not anti-Jewish remarks.

V. Conclusions

While modern Christianity has never been quite sure what the precise relationship of health to eternal well-being might be, it is undeniable that the author of Luke-Acts sees the curing of diseases, the healing of the lame, and even the raising of the dead as possible benefits of being in touch with the power available from Jesus Christ. Even contact with an apostle's garments is seen to have this sort of effect on some (Acts 19:11-12). Yet it is equally clear that Luke sees this as a general benefit which can be bestowed on either Christian or pagan or Jew, and this benefit in and of itself does not amount to nor necessarily produce conversion to the Christian faith. As was the case in the Gospels with Jesus, healing is something early Christians do in passing, on the way to accomplishing other tasks of more enduring value. It is not seen as an absolutely necessary part or benefit of sharing the gospel in the ancient world. It is surely no accident that the noun forms σωτηρια/σωτηριον/σωτηρ do not appear in texts where the primary subject is healing, but by contrast such language features prominently in texts like Luke 19:1-10 where the subject is the transformation of human character.

It is also clear, especially from the final voyage of Paul recorded in the last chapters of Acts, but from a variety of other texts as well, that Christian salvation is not something that is viewed as preventing one from suffering or experiencing disaster, though it may be said to entail being providentially preserved through disaster if God's plan involves the using of a particular

---

in a more aggressive and systematic and outgoing fashion following in the footsteps of some Pharisees and a few others who were already either seeking proselytes and synagogue adherents among the Gentiles, or, more frequently, responding positively to inquiries from interested Gentiles. I quite agree with McKnight that early Judaism was not in general a missionary religion in the way that early Christianity was, nor apparently was it a widely shared goal of early Jews to see the Gentile world converted, but this should not cause us to overlook that there were some precedents set in early Judaism that involved some forms of evangelistic activity. See McKnight, pp. 116-17.

person for some further work of ministry thereafter. There are, then, some immediate, temporal, and even physical benefits envisioned for those who come in contact with the living exalted Christ, including especially Christians, but clearly enough the emphasis lies elsewhere. Luke knows and frequently uses the terms σωτηρια/σωζω and their cognates in senses very familiar to pagans in the Greco-Roman world to refer to healing, delivering, rescuing, keeping safe, and preserving someone. These are some of the purely temporal benefits of God's eschatological saving activity. Being "saved," however, in the pregnant sense does not seem for Luke to carry with it any *guarantees* of long life, being kept safe through trials, wealth, or perpetually good health either. Luke believes in God's temporal providence, but he does not see such intervention as the be-all and end-all of the salvation that one receives by calling on the name of Christ.

The use of σωτηρια/σωζω which stands out from the vast majority of uses in pagan writers, from the inscriptions from the mystery religions, and from the large majority of Jewish writings is the purely religious or "spiritual" uses of these terms, and especially the *eternal benefits* that σωτηρια carries with it in such contexts. We do not see anything like this in the large corpus of writings of Luke's contemporary — Josephus. Normally in the OT and in other Jewish writings as well what salvation amounts to is the this-worldly events of rescue, deliverance from enemies, being kept safe, being kept well or being healed, and perhaps occasionally resurrection of the dead could be seen as a means of preserving someone and her or his family (cf. 1 Kings 17:17-24). Forgiveness of sins is of course a familiar concept in the OT, but one is hard-pressed to find texts where it is called salvation. The closest one gets is in the Psalms, for instance Psalm 32, where forgiveness and preservation from trouble and deliverance from danger are closely connected.

One may say that if a person with a Jewish background read Luke-Acts there would be enough overlap in the use of the σωτηρια/σωζω language with what one finds in the Hebrew Scriptures that some comprehension would surely be possible. The same could be said for someone of pagan background who read this work. Where Luke's language may have caused some puzzlement is when he uses terms like σωτηρια in a more exclusively spiritual or eternal sense. Luke 1:1-4, however, suggests that the person to whom this document was written was already a Christian, one who had had such things explained to him but needed assurance and clarification about a variety of matters.

It is striking that if one analyzes the salvation language of Luke-Acts carefully, one finds the more mundane sense of rescue, heal, deliver, and keep safe much more frequently in the Gospel (cf., e.g., Luke 1:47, 71; 6:9; 8:36, 48, 50; 9:24a; 17:19; 18:42; 23:35, 37, 39) than in Acts (e.g., 4:9; 7:25; 14:9; 27:20, 31, 34), and on the other hand one finds the more specifically Christian use of the salvation language more often in Acts than in the Gospel. This last fact may be put down to Luke's historical sense that the full-orbed good news about salvation could not be proclaimed until after the death and resurrection of Jesus, since it was only when he was exalted to Jesus' right hand that it was really or fully possible to offer forgiveness in his name and on the basis of the completed Christ-event (Acts 5:30-31).

Luke knew well about salvation and health and its various and variegated forms in antiquity, and he relates his discussion to such understandings. At the heart of his salvation message, however, is the new thing that God has done in Christ through Christ's life, death, and resurrection, which in Luke's view makes possible a sort of salvation not previously available at all and only occasionally hinted at in some of the later Jewish prophets.[72] The summary of J. A. Fitzmyer is apt when he says that salvation history in Luke-Acts

> is not an identification of history as salvation, but rather the entrance of salvation into history. Luke focuses on the inbreaking of divine salvific activity into human history with the appearance of Jesus of Nazareth among [hu]mankind. Jesus did not come as the end of history, or of historical development. He is rather seen as the end of one historical period and the beginning of another, and all of this is a manifestation of a plan of God to bring about the salvation of human beings who recognize and accept the plan.[73]

I would add in conclusion that Luke sees the coming of Christ as not just another epoch of history but the beginning of the eschatological age when the dominion of God breaks into human history, and the coming of the Spirit at Pentecost as the means by which this age can be properly proclaimed and inaugurated as the age of salvation for all peoples, as "a light for revelation to the Gentiles and for the glory to your people Israel" (Luke 2:32). Not the emperor but Christ is depicted as the means and catalyst of this greatest of all blessings, and the benefits are seen as both temporal and eternal, unlike the largesse of Caesar.

72. It is more than a little surprising to me that H. C. Kee can write an entire and very helpful book on the theology of Acts and say so very little about salvation in its more full-orbed Christian sense and how important that concept is to our author, but cf. his *Good News*.

73. Fitzmyer, *Luke I–IX*, p. 179. See his careful discussion of Conzelmann's proposal on pp. 180-92.

Index of Modern Authors

Aberbach, M., 699n.245

Achtemeier, P. J., 297n.72, 441n.351, 701n.253

Aejamalaeus, L., 612n.212

Alexander, L. C. A., 6n.20, 14, 15, 54, 79n.256, 79n.257, 105n.2, 172n.29, 481n.44, 486n.66

Alon, G., 462

Arnold, B. T., 123n.32

Arnold, C. E., 563n.5, 574n.54, 577n.75, 578, 581n.87, 583n.102

Ascough, R. S., 341n.48

Aune, D. E., 6n.19, 7n.21, 7n.22, 9, 10n.38, 11n.45, 34n.118, 44n.158, 46n.171, 46n.172, 50n.182, 76, 578n.76

Balsdon, J. P. V. D., 681n.159, 703n.265, 725n.384

Bammel, E., 460n.410, 460n.411

Barclay, W., 480n.39

Barnes, T. D., 516n.195

Barrett, C. K., 4n.9, 7, 9n.34, 25n.94, 80, 80n.260, 80n.265, 81n.267, 105n.1, 106n.7, 114n.41, 120n.24, 123n.32, 126n.39, 131n.7, 132n.12, 135n.19, 136n.25, 137n.33, 157n.99, 158n.102, 160n.113, 162n.118, 163n.124, 165n.2, 175n.40, 175n.43, 175n.44, 182n.67, 182n.70, 182n.73, 187n.92, 190, 193n.119, 194n.126, 195n.128, 195n.131, 201n.6, 207n.40, 209, 214n.73, 216n.79, 225n.119, 229n.140, 230n.143, 238n.180, 241, 252, 253n.239, 254n.241, 265n.282, 269n.298, 275n.316, 281n.10, 283n.17, 284n.19, 287n.31, 287n.34, 288n.36, 294n.58, 296n.67, 297n.74, 299n.85, 301, 304, 307n.16, 316n.43, 318n.54, 321n.68, 322n.72, 324n.81, 324n.91, 324n.93, 328n.6, 329n.9, 332n.18, 333n.23, 333n.24, 341n.50, 344, 345n.71, 349n.91, 350n.98, 351n.99, 352n.105, 353n.108, 359, 364n.149, 367n.4, 370n.16, 370n.19, 374, 375n.40, 375n.44, 376n.47, 382n.79, 383n.82, 383n.83, 386n.94, 392n.123, 393n.130, 395n.139n., 399n.153, 401, 401n.165, 407n.192, 409n.208, 410n.210, 412n.225, 414n.234, 415n.237, 416n.242, 418n.251, 419n.258, 420, 424n.281, 427n.296, 428n.300, 431n.310, 434, 436, 442n.355 443n.357, 454n.388, 460n.410, 483n.52, 483n.54, 511n.178, 525, 615, 616n.228, 622n.246, 641, 661n.70 778n.125, 782n.143

Bartsch, H. W., 651n.31

Bauckham, R., 173n.32, 376n.50,

844

Index of Scripture and Other Ancient Literature

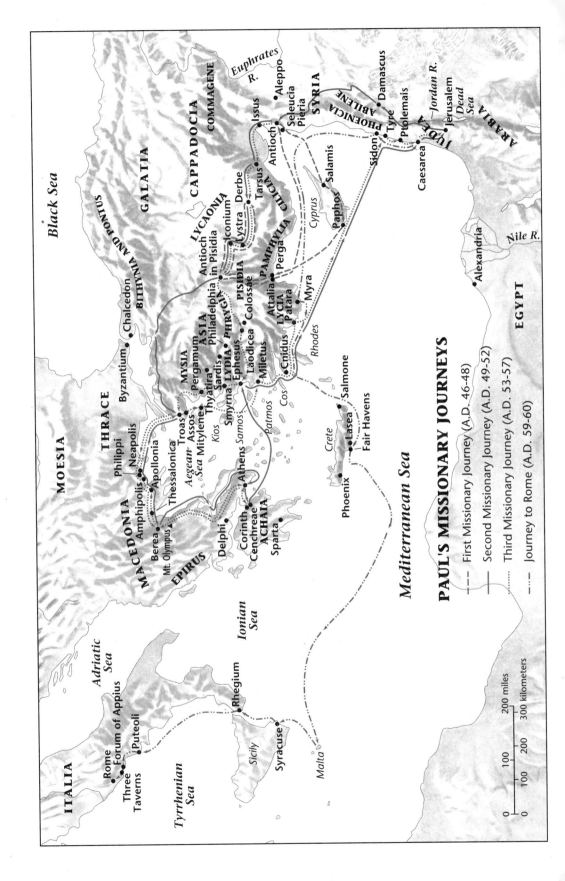

PAUL'S MISSIONARY JOURNEYS

- - - First Missionary Journey (A.D. 46-48)
——— Second Missionary Journey (A.D. 49-52)
········· Third Missionary Journey (A.D. 53-57)
-·-·-· Journey to Rome (A.D. 59-60)